Java Programming

Java Programming
A COMPREHENSIVE INTRODUCTION

HERBERT SCHILDT

DALE SKRIEN
Colby College

Mc Graw Hill

Connect
Learn
Succeed™

The McGraw-Hill Companies

Mc Graw Hill

Connect
Learn
Succeed™

JAVA PROGRAMMING: A COMPREHENSIVE INTRODUCTION

1 2 3 4 5 6 7 8 9 0 DOC/DOC 1 0 9 8 7 6 5 4 3 2

ISBN: 978-0-07-802207-4

MHID 0-07-802207-X

Vice President & Editor-in-Chief: *Marty Lange*
Vice President & Director Specialized Publishing: *Janice M. Roerig-Blong*
Editorial Director: *Michael Lange*
Global Publisher: *Raghothaman Srinivasan*
Senior Marketing Manager: *Curt Reynolds*
Developmental Editor: *Robin A. Reed*
Senior Project Manager: *Lisa A. Bruflodt*
Buyer: *Sandy Ludovissy*
Design Coordinator: *Brenda A. Rolwes*
Media Project Manager: *Prashanthi Nadipalli*
Cover Design by *Studio Montage, St. Louis, Missouri*
Cover Image: *© Iconotec/Alamy*
Compositor: *RPK Editorial Services*
Typeface: *10.5/12 Times Roman*
Printer: *R. R. Donnelley Crawfordsville, IN*

Library of Congress Cataloging-in-Publication Data

Schildt, Herbert.
  Java programming : a comprehensive introduction / Herbert Schildt, Dale Skrien. -- 1st ed.
    p. cm.
  Includes bibliographical references and index.
  ISBN 978-0-07-802207-4
1. Java (Computer program language) I. Skrien, Dale John. II. Title.
  QA76.73.J38S332 2013
  005.13'3–dc23
                            2011047187

www.mhhe.com

BRIEF CONTENTS

CONTENTS

PREFACE

This book teaches the fundamentals of programming by way of the Java language. It assumes no prior programming experience and begins with the basics, such as how to compile and run a Java program. Next, it discusses the keywords, operators, and constructs that form the Java language. The book also covers several parts of the Java Application Programming Interface (API) library, including Swing, which is the framework used to create programs that have a graphical user interface (GUI), and the Collections Framework, which is used to store collections of objects. In short, this book is intended as a comprehensive introduction to Java. Like most computer languages, Java has evolved over time. At the time of this writing, the latest version is Java 7 (JDK 7), and this is the version of Java covered by this book. However, most of the material is also applicable to other recent versions of Java, such as version 6.

A STRAIGHT AHEAD APPROACH

This book uses what we characterize as a "straight ahead" approach. By this, we mean that topics are introduced in a cohesive sequence that is intended to keep the focus of each discussion on the topic at hand. This approach simplifies and streamlines the presentation. On occasions when a departure from the main presentation flow is necessary, we attempt to do so in a way that minimizes the disruption. The goal of our approach is to present the Java language in a way that clearly shows the interrelationship of its parts, rather than as a jumble of disconnected features.

To help manage the material, this book is organized into three parts. Part One describes the elements that define the Java language and the core elements of programming. It begins with an overview of Java followed by the basic concepts of data types, operators, and control statements. It then progressively introduces the more sophisticated features of the language, such as classes, methods, inheritance, interfaces, packages, exceptions, multithreading, and generics. Part One also describes I/O, because it is integral to many Java programs, and applet fundamentals, because the applet is a quintessential Java application. Part One ends with a chapter on object-oriented design.

As it relates directly to Part One, our "straight ahead" approach keeps the focus on the elements of the Java language and the fundamentals of programming, with each new section building on the foundation of what comes before. Where possible, we avoid digressions that distract from the main topic. For example, discussions of GUI programming via Swing are handled in Part Two, rather than being intermixed with discussions of basic concepts. This way, the presentation in Part One remains firmly rooted in the core issues of Java and of programming.

Part Two introduces Swing. It begins with an overview of GUI programming with Swing, including the basic concepts of components, events, and layout managers. Subsequent chapters advance in an orderly fashion, presenting an overview of several Swing components, followed by menus, dialogs, painting, and so on. This "straight ahead" approach is intended to help students more easily integrate each new feature into the overall picture they are forming of the Swing framework.

Part Three explores portions of the Java API library. Because the API library is very large, it is not possible to discuss it in its entirety in this book. Instead, we focus on what we consider to be those parts of the library with which every Java programmer should be familiar. In addition to covering large portions of **java.lang** and **java.util** (with special emphasis on the Collections Framework), we also present an overview of networking, and introduce the concurrency API, including the Fork/Join Framework. The material is presented in a straightforward manner that is designed to give the student a solid overview of several core library elements.

OBJECTS SOON...BUT NOT TOO SOON

One of the first commonly-asked questions about a programming book is whether it uses an "objects early" or an "objects late" approach to teaching the key tenets of object-oriented programming. Of course, what constitutes "early" or "late" can be somewhat subjective, and neither term precisely describes the organization of this book. The phrase we use to characterize our approach is "objects soon, but not too soon." Our goal is to introduce objects at the appropriate time for the student. We believe that this is not until key features of the language have been learned.

Towards this end, the focus of the first three chapters is on the fundamentals of the Java language, such as its syntax, data types, operators, and control statements. We believe that mastery of these elements is a necessary first step because they form the foundation of the language, and the foundation of programming in general. (In other words, it is difficult to write meaningful programs without understanding these elements.) In our view, only after the basic elements of a program have been learned, is the student ready to move forward to objects.

After the book has covered the fundamentals, objects are introduced in Chapter 4, and from that point on, object-oriented features, techniques, and concepts are integrated into the remaining chapters. Additionally, objects are introduced in a carefully paced, step-by-step fashion. This is intended to help the student grasp each new feature in context, and without being overwhelmed.

PEDAGOGICAL FEATURES

This book includes several pedagogical elements to facilitate and reinforce learning. Each feature helps ensure that students are fully aware of key skills, can gauge their advancement, and can verify that all concepts are learned.

- Key Skills & Concepts: Each chapter begins with a list that identifies the key skills and concepts presented in the chapter.
- Ask the Expert: At various points throughout the book are Ask the Expert boxes. These contain additional information or interesting commentary about

a topic, and use a Question/Answer format. They provide supplemental information without disrupting the main presentation flow.

- Try This Elements: Each chapter contains one or more Try This elements. These are step-by-step examples that walk through the development of a program that demonstrates an aspect of Java related to the chapter's topic. Typically, these are longer examples that show a feature in a more practical setting.

- Progress Checks: Throughout each chapter, Progress Checks are presented to test the student's understanding of the preceding section. The answers to these questions are at the bottom of the same page.

- Exercises: Each chapter concludes with exercises that include short answer, fill-in-the-blank, and true/false questions, and coding exercises. The answers to selected exercises are in Appendix C.

ACM RECOMMENDATIONS

The 2008 update to the ACM Curricula Recommendations (http://www.acm.org/education/curricula/ComputerScience2008.pdf) recommends that all computer science students be fluent in at least one programming language and have some understanding of object-oriented and event-driven programming. We believe that students who learn the material covered by this book will have the desired knowledge and skills. We have included in the book not just an introduction to programming using the Java language, but broader coverage that includes advanced Java features, the Swing framework, and large parts of several important API packages.

The first part of the book covers a significant portion of the topics in the Programming Fundamentals (PF) knowledge area of the ACM Recommendations (the main exceptions being the knowledge units FoundationsInformationSecurity and SecureProgramming). The first part also includes a chapter on object-oriented design, which covers a number of the topics in the PL/ObjectOrientedProgramming and SE/SoftwareDesign knowledge units. The second part of the book, which introduces GUI programming with Swing, addresses some of the topics in the knowledge unit HC/GUIProgramming. The third part includes, among others, topics that relate to concurrency. In fact, we devote Chapters 12 and 27 to multithreading and concurrency because we feel, as the ACM Curricular Recommendations discuss, that concurrency is becoming increasingly relevant to the discipline of computer science.

ONLINE RESOURCES

Students can access all of the source code for the programs in the text at the website that accompanies *Java Programming: A Comprehensive Approach*: www.mhhe.com/schildt1e. This site also offers a number of useful resources for the Java instructor.

- A Solutions manual for end-of-chapter exercises.

- Instructor Notes, including suggested curricula and suggestions for teaching particular topics.
- Supplemental Exercises that can be used to create quizzes and tests.
- PowerPoint Slides that serve as an outline for in-class instruction.

Please contact your McGraw-Hill representative for access information.

Additional instructor resources include:

CourseSmart
Learn Smart. Choose Smart.

This text is available as an eBook at www.CourseSmart.com. At CourseSmart your students can take advantage of significant savings off the cost of a print textbook, reduce their impact on the environment, and gain access to powerful web tools for learning. CourseSmart eBooks can be viewed online or downloaded to a computer. The eBooks allow students to do full text searches, add highlighting and notes, and share notes with classmates. CourseSmart has the largest selection of eBooks available anywhere. Visit www.CourseSmart.com to learn more and to try a sample chapter.

create

Craft your teaching resources to match the way you teach! With McGraw-Hill Create™, www.mcgrawhillcreate.com, you can easily rearrange chapters, combine material from other content sources, and quickly upload content you have written, such as your course syllabus or teaching notes. Find the content you need in Create by searching through thousands of leading McGraw-Hill textbooks. Arrange your book to fit your teaching style. Create even allows you to personalize your book's appearance by selecting the cover and adding your name, school, and course information. Order a Create book and you'll receive a complimentary print review copy in 3–5 business days or a complimentary electronic review copy (eComp) via email in minutes. Go to www.mcgrawhillcreate.com today and register to experience how McGraw-Hill Create™ empowers you to teach *your* students *your way*.

ACKNOWLEDGMENTS

We wish to acknowledge the many contributions made by the following people at McGraw-Hill, without whom this book would not exist. They have made working on the book a delight.

Editorial Director, Michael Lange

Global Publisher, Raghu Srinivasan

Senior Marketing Manager, Curt Reynolds

Developmental Editor, Robin Reed

Developmental Editor, Kathryn Neubauer

Senior Project Manager, Lisa Bruflodt

Design Coordinator, Brenda Rolwes

Production Editor, Rose Kernan

We would also like to thank the following reviewers for their many helpful comments, which were much appreciated.

Bill Barge, *Trine University*

Chris Bennett, *University of Maine–Farmington*

Augusto Casas, *St Thomas Aquinas College*

I-ping Chu, *DePaul University*

Vasil Hnatyshin, *Rowan University*

Rodney Hoffman, *Occidental College*

David Kamper Sr., *Northeastern Illinois University*

BJ Tjaden, *Anne Arundel Community College*

Richard Weiss, *Evergreen State College*

James Braman, *Towson University*

Steve Cooper, *Stanford University*

Michael Main, *University of Colorado—Boulder*

Jay McCarthy, *Brigham Young University*

Robert Moll, *University of Massachusetts—Amherst*

Jagadeesh Nandigam, *Grand Valley State University*

Gurpur Prabhu, *Iowa State University*

Daisy Sang, *California State Polytechnic University*

Mark Sherriff, *University of Virginia*

Joslyn Smith, *Florida International University*

James Young, *University of Manitoba*

Finally, and most importantly, we would like to thank our families for their support during the preparation of this book.

ABOUT THE AUTHORS

Herbert Schildt has been writing about programming since 1984 and is the author of several books on Java, C++, C, and C#. His programming books have sold millions of copies worldwide and have been widely translated. Although he is interested in all facets of computing, his primary focus is computer languages, including the standardization of languages. Schildt holds BA and MCS degrees from the University of Illinois, Urbana/Champaign. He provided the initial drafts for most of the chapters in this book.

Dale Skrien has been teaching mathematics and computer science at Colby College since 1980 and has been teaching Java since 1996. His interest in teaching students not just how to program, but how to program well, led to the publication of his textbook *Object-Oriented Design using Java* by McGraw-Hill. He holds a BA degree from St. Olaf College, MS degrees from the University of Illinois and the University of Washington, and a PhD degree from the University of Washington. In addition to contributions throughout the book, he provided Chapter 16, which introduces object-oriented design. He also provided the online supplements for this book.

A TOTAL SOLUTION

Key Skills & Concepts

Outlines the main topics and techniques presented in the chapter.

```
/*
    Try This 1-2

    This program displays a conversion
    table of gallons to liters.

    Call this program "GalToLitTable.java".
*/
class GalToLitTable {
  public static void main(String[] args) {
    double gallons, liters;              Line counter is initially set to zero.
    int counter;

    counter = 0;  ◄
    for(gallons = 1; gallons <= 100; gallons++) {
      liters = gallons * 3.7854; // convert to liters
      System.out.println(gallons + " gallons is " +
                         liters + " liters.");

      counter++;  ◄─────────────────── Increment the line counter
      // every 10th line, print a blank line with each loop iteration.
      if(counter == 10) {  ◄─────────── If counter is 10,
        System.out.println();            output a blank line.
        counter = 0; // reset the line counter
      }
    }
  }
}
```

Code Listings

Examples that show program elements and techniques in action. Call-outs point to key features, where appropriate.

Ask the Expert

Additional information or commentary from an "expert" perspective related to the topic at hand.

Ask the Expert

Q In the discussion of the **if** statement, you mentioned that a true/false expression is referred to as *Boolean* expression. Why is that term used?

A The term *Boolean* is named after George Boole (1815–1864). He developed and formalized the laws that govern true/false expressions. This became known as Boolean algebra. His work eventually came to form the basis of computer logic.

TRY THIS 3-1 START BUILDING A JAVA HELP SYSTEM

```
Help.java
```

This project builds a simple help system that displays the syntax for the Java control statements. In the process, it shows the **switch** statement in action. The program displays a menu containing the control statements and then waits for you to choose one. After one is chosen, the syntax of the statement is displayed. In this first version of the program, help is available for only the **if** and **switch** statements. The other control statements are added in subsequent examples.

STEP-BY-STEP

1. Create a file called **Help.java**.
2. The program begins by displaying the following menu:

```
Help on:
  1. if
  2. switch
Choose one:
```

To accomplish this, you will use the statement sequence shown here:

```
System.out.println("Help on:");
System.out.println("  1. if");
```

Try This

Step-by-step examples that demonstrate a key feature or technique.

Progress Check

These short self-tests let students test their understanding of the material as the chapter progresses.

Progress Check

1. What is the type of the literal 10? What is the type of the literal 10.0?
2. How do you specify a **long** literal?
3. Is "x" a string or a character literal?

EXERCISES

1. Given this fragment,

```
class X {
  private int count;
```

is the following fragment correct?

```
class Y {
  public static void main(String[] args) {
  X ob = new X();

  ob.count = 10;
```

2. An access modifier must _____ a member's declaration.
3. Given this class,

```
class Test {
  int a;
  Test(int i) { a = i; }
}
```

End-of-Chapter Exercises

Questions and coding exercises that test the student's grasp of the material discussed in the chapter.

Java Programming

PART ONE

The Java Language

P art One of this book describes the elements that comprise the Java programming language and the techniques required to use them. Chapter 1 begins by presenting several fundamental programming concepts, the history and design philosophy of Java, and an overview of some key Java features. The remaining chapters in Part One focus on specific aspects of Java, on a chapter-by-chapter basis. Part One concludes with an introduction to an important aspect of successful Java programming: object-oriented design.

CHAPTER 1

Java Programming Fundamentals

In the span of just a few decades, programming has gone from being an obscure discipline, practiced by a few, to becoming an integral part of the modern world, practiced by many. The reason for this development is easy to understand. If the modern world could be characterized by a single word, it might be *technology*. Supporting much of that technology is the computer. What makes a computer useful are the programs that it runs. Thus, in many ways it is programming that makes our technological world possible. Programming has become that important.

The purpose of this book is to teach the fundamentals of programming, using the Java programming language. As a discipline, programming is quite large. Not only does it involve many skills, concepts, and techniques, but there are also a number of specializations, such as those involving numeric analysis, information theory, networking, and device control. There are also many different computing environments in which programs are run. However, in all cases, mastery of the fundamentals of programming is required. What you will learn in this course forms the basis on which you will build your studies.

This chapter begins by defining several key terms, reviewing the concepts of bits, bytes, the binary number system, and the basic components of the computer. Although this will be familiar territory for many readers, it ensures that everyone begins with the necessary knowledge. Next, we introduce the Java language by presenting its history, design philosophy, and several of its most important attributes.

The chapter then discusses several core features of Java. One of the hardest things about learning to program is the fact that no element of a computer language exists in isolation. Instead, the components of the language are interrelated, working in conjunction with each other. In this regard, Java is no exception. It is difficult to discuss one aspect of Java without implicitly involving others. To help overcome this problem, this chapter provides a brief overview of several Java features, including the general form of a Java program, some basic control statements, a sampling of data types, and operators. It does not go into too many details but, rather, concentrates on the general concepts common to any Java program. Although many of these features will be examined in greater detail later in this book, this introduction helps you see how key parts of Java "fit together." It also enables you to begin creating and running Java programs.

COMPUTING BASICS

Since you are taking a programming course, it is very likely that you already have at least some general knowledge about the subject of computing. However, not everyone will necessarily have the same knowledge, or that knowledge may be imprecise. Therefore, before introducing the Java language, an overview of several core computing concepts is presented. In the process, a number of key terms are defined.

The Hardware Components of a Computer

Since it is the computer that ultimately runs a program that you write, it is helpful to understand in a general way what the pieces of a computer do. All computers consist of a set of components that work together to form the computer as a whole. Although it is true that the precise form of the computer has evolved over time, all computers still share certain key features. For example, the same basic elements contained in a desktop computer are also found in a smartphone.

To perform useful work, a computer must, at minimum, contain the following:

- A Central Processing Unit (CPU)
- Memory
- Input/output devices

Let's look at each of these, in turn.

The CPU provides the primary computational capabilities of the computer. It does so by executing the instructions that comprise a program. All CPUs are designed to understand a specific *instruction set*. The instruction set defines the various types of operations that the CPU can perform. For example, most CPUs support instructions that perform basic arithmetic operations, load data from and store data to memory, make logical comparisons, and alter program flow, to name a few. In addition to being able to access memory, most CPUs contain a limited number of *registers* that provide fast, short-term storage for data.

The instructions that a CPU executes, which are often called *machine instructions*, or *machine code*, perform very small operations. For example, an instruction might move a value from one register to another, move a value from a register to memory, or compare the contents of two registers. In general, the instruction set for one type of CPU differs from that of another. Thus, a set of instructions designed for one type of CPU can't normally be used with another type. Sometimes there are families of CPUs, which maintain backward compatibility, but unrelated CPUs normally differ in their instruction sets.

Machine instructions are not in a form that can be easily read by a person. Instead, they are encoded for use by the computer. It is possible, however, to represent machine code in a human-readable form by using mnemonic representations of the instructions. This is called *assembly language*. For example, the mnemonic representation of an instruction that moves data from one location to another might be called MOV. The instruction for comparing two values might be called CMP. Assembly language is converted into a form the computer can execute by a program called an *assembler*. However, very few people write assembly language today because languages such as Java usually provide a much better alternative.

The memory of the computer is used to store both instructions (in the form of machine code) and data. Memory is primarily intended to hold information only during the execution of a program. It is not for long-term storage. Memory in a computer is *addressable*. This means that the CPU can access a specific location in memory given its address. Memory is often referred to as RAM, which stands for Random Access Memory.

When the CPU executes a program, it does so by obtaining an instruction from memory and then performing the operation specified by that instruction. It then obtains the next instruction, executes it, and so on. By default, instructions are obtained from sequential locations in memory. However, some instructions can alter that flow by causing execution to "jump" to a different memory location.

Today, there are a wide variety of input/output (I/O) devices in use. These include such things as keyboards, monitors, the mouse, touch screens, voice input, and sound output. They all, however, perform the same function: they give the computer some way to receive or transmit information. Often, I/O devices enable humans to interact with the computer. However, in some cases, the computer uses I/O to communicate with another device, such as a storage device, a network adapter, or even a robotic control interface.

In addition to the three key components of a computer just described, many computers also include storage devices, such as disk drives, DVDs, and flash drives. Many computers are networked, either via the Internet or to a local area network. To support networking, a computer requires a network adapter.

Bits, Bytes, and Binary

Today, it is rare to find someone who has not heard the terms *bits*, *bytes*, and *binary*. They have entered the lexicon of common speech. However, because they describe some of the most fundamental aspects of computing, it is important that they be formally defined.

THE BINARY NUMBER SYSTEM

At the lowest level, computers work on 1's and 0's. As a result, a number system based on 1's and 0's is needed. This number system is called *binary*. Binary works just like our normal decimal number system, except that the meaning of each digit position is different. As you know, in decimal, when moving from right to left, each digit position represents values that are 10 times larger than the previous digit. Thus, decimal is based on powers of 10, with the rightmost digit being the 1's position, to its left is the 10's position, then the 100's position, and so on. For example, the number 423 means four hundred twenty three, because there are 4 hundreds, 2 tens, and 3 ones.

In binary, the process works the same way except that when moving left, each digit position increases by a factor of 2. Therefore, the first (rightmost) binary digit position represents 1's. To its left is the 2's position, then the 4's position, followed by the 8's position, and so on. This means that the first 8 binary digit positions represent the following values:

$$128 \quad 64 \quad 32 \quad 16 \quad 8 \quad 4 \quad 2 \quad 1$$

For example, the binary value 1010 is the decimal value 10. Why? Because it has no 1's, one 2, no 4's, and one 8. Thus, $0 + 2 + 0 + 8$ equals 10. Here is another example. The binary value 1101 is 13 in decimal because it has one 1's, no 2's, one 4, and one 8. Thus, $1 + 0 + 4 + 8$ equals 13. As you can see, to convert from binary to decimal, simply sum the values represented by the 1 digits.

BITS AND BYTES

In the computer, a single binary digit is represented by a *bit*. A bit can be either set or cleared. A set bit is 1 and a cleared bit is 0. Bits are organized into groups. The most common is the *byte*. Typically a byte consists of 8 bits. This means that it can represent the values 0 through 255.

Another organizational unit is the *word*. Typically, a word is sized to be compatible with a specific CPU architecture. For example, a 32-bit computer will typically use a 32-bit (4-byte) long word size.

For reasons of convenience, binary numbers are often shown grouped into units of 4 (or sometimes 8) digits—for example, 1011 1001. This makes it easier to keep track of the digits. Understand, however, that such visual groupings have no effect on the value being depicted.

The Operating System

The hardware components of the computer are managed and made accessible by the *operating system*. An operating system is a master program that controls the computer. Operating systems are one of the core subjects in computer science, and it isn't possible to describe them in detail here. Fortunately, a brief overview is sufficient for our purposes.

An operating system serves two primary functions. First, it provides a base level of functionality that other programs will use to access the computer's resources. For example, to save information to a disk drive, you will use a service provided by the operating system. Second, the operating system controls the execution of other programs.

For example, it provides memory space to hold the program while it is executing, schedules CPU time for its execution, and oversees its resource utilization.

A number of different operating systems are in common use. Here are some examples: Windows, Unix, Linux, Mac OS, iOS, and Android. As a general rule, a program must be designed to run under (targeted for) a specific operating system. For example, a program targeted for Windows can't be run under Unix unless it is specifically adapted.

Progress Check

1. The CPU executes _____ instructions.
2. What is 27 in binary?
3. What program oversees the operation of the computer?

THE PROGRAM

At the foundation of programming is the *program*. Since this book is about programming, it makes sense to formally define this term. Here is a very general definition: a program consists of a sequence of instructions that can be executed by a computer. However, the term *program* can mean different things, based on its context, because a program can have two basic forms. One is human readable, and the other is machine readable.

When you write a program, you will be creating a text file that holds the *source code* of your program. This is the human-readable form of the program. It is the form that programmers typically think of as "the program." However, it is not the form that is actually executed by the computer. Instead, the source code for a program must be converted into instructions that the computer can execute. This is called *object code*. An object code file is difficult (nearly impossible) for humans to read. This is why programmers work with the source code to their programs, converting it into object code only when it comes time to run it.

A program is converted from source code into object code by a *compiler*. In some cases, the compiler generates actual machine instructions that are directly executed by the CPU of the computer. (This is typically the way a compiler for programming languages like C++ works, for example.) A key point to understand about object code is that it is designed for a specific type of CPU. As explained earlier, the machine instructions for one type of CPU will not usually work with another type of CPU.

You may find it somewhat surprising that, in some cases, the instructions in the object code produced by a compiler are not designed for any actual CPU! Instead, they are designed to be executed by a *virtual machine*. A virtual machine is a program that emulates a CPU in software. Thus, it creates what is, essentially, a CPU in logic rather than in hardware. As such, it defines its own instruction set, which it is capable of executing.

Answers:

1. machine   **2.** 11011   **3.** The operating system.

The process of executing these instructions is commonly referred to as *interpreting*, and a virtual machine is sometimes referred to as an *interpreter*. As you will soon see, Java uses a virtual machine and there are significant advantages to this approach.

Whether your source code is compiled into directly executable machine code or into code to be run by a virtual machine, the process of converting source code into object code via a compiler is the same.

PROGRAMMING LANGUAGES

Precisely what constitutes the specific elements of a program's source code is defined by the programming language being used. There are two basic categories of languages: low-level and high-level. A low-level language is tied closely to the instruction set of the CPU. Assembly language is an example of a low-level language. As explained earlier, there is a one-to-one correspondence between each assembly code statement and a machine instruction. This makes writing assembly code a tedious job.

Most programming today is done using a high-level language. (For example, Java is a high-level language.) High-level languages enable you to write programs faster, easier, and more reliably. A high-level language defines constructs that help you organize, structure, and control the logic of your program. Each construct in a high-level language is translated into many machine instructions.

There are many different high-level programming languages, but nearly all define these three core elements:

- keywords
- operators
- punctuation

These elements must be combined according to the *syntax rules* defined by the language. The syntax rules specify quite precisely what constitutes a valid use of a program element. To be compiled, the source code must adhere to these rules.

As a general definition, keywords define the building blocks of the language. They are used to specify the high-level constructs supported by the language. For example, keywords are used to control the flow of execution, define various types of data, and provide options and mechanisms that let you manage the execution of a program.

Operators are used by expressions, with one of the most common being the arithmetic expression. For example, nearly all languages use + to specify addition. Punctuation comprises those elements of the language that are used to separate one element from another, group statements, prevent ambiguity, or otherwise clarify the syntax of the language.

Although many programming languages have been invented, only a few have become widely used. Among these are FORTRAN, COBOL, Pascal, various dialects of BASIC, C, C++, and, of course, Java. Fortunately, after you learn one programming language, it becomes much easier to learn another. So, the time you invest in learning Java will benefit you both now and in the future.

Progess Check

1. The human-readable form of a program is called _____.
2. The executable form of a program is called _____.
3. What are syntax rules?

Ask the Expert

Q I have heard programmers use the phrase "writing code." What does this mean?

A Professional programmers often refer to the act of programming (i.e., creating source code) as "writing code." Another phrase you will commonly hear is "coding a program." It too refers to creating source code. In fact, it's not uncommon to hear an excellent programmer referred to as a "great coder."

THE JAVA LANGUAGE

This book uses the Java language to teach the fundamentals of programming. Although other programming languages would also be suitable for this purpose, Java was chosen for two primary reasons. First, it is one of the world's most widely used computer languages. Thus, from a practical point of view, it is an excellent language to learn. Second, its features are designed and implemented in such a way that makes it easy to demonstrate the foundations of programming.

But there is also a third reason. Java represents much of what characterizes modern programming. An understanding of Java gives you insight into the way professional programmers think about the job of programming. It is one of the defining languages of our time.

Java is part of the ongoing, historical process of computer language evolution. As such, it is a blend of the best elements of its rich heritage combined with the innovative concepts inspired by its unique place in programming history. While the remainder of this book describes the practical aspects of Java, here we will examine the reasons behind its creation, the forces that shaped it, and the legacy that it inherits.

The Origins of Java

Java was conceived by James Gosling and others at Sun Microsystems in 1991. This language was initially called "Oak" but was renamed "Java" in 1995. Even though Java has become inexorably linked with the online environment, the original impetus for Java was not the Internet! Instead, the original motivation was the need for a

---

Answers:

1. source code
2. object code
3. The syntax rules determine how the elements of a language are used.

platform-independent language that could be used to create software to be embedded in various consumer electronic devices, such as microwave ovens and remote controls. As you can probably guess, many different types of CPUs are used as controllers. The trouble was, at that time most computer languages were designed to be compiled into machine code for a specific type of CPU. For example, consider C++, another language that was also very popular at the time (and still is).

Although it was possible to compile a C++ program for just about any type of CPU, to do so required a full C++ compiler targeted for that CPU. This is because C++ is normally compiled into machine instructions that are directly executed by the CPU, and each different CPU required a different set of machine instructions. The problem, however, is that compilers are expensive and time consuming to create. In an attempt to find a better solution, Gosling and others began work on a portable, cross-platform language that could produce code that would run on a variety of CPUs under differing environments. This effort ultimately led to the creation of Java.

About the time that the details of Java were being worked out, a second, and ultimately more important, factor emerged that would play a crucial role in the future of Java. This second force was, of course, the World Wide Web. Had the Web not taken shape at about the same time that Java was being implemented, Java might have remained a useful but obscure language for programming consumer electronics. However, with the emergence of the Web, Java was propelled to the forefront of computer language design because the Web, too, demanded portable programs. Why? Because the Internet is populated by various types of computers, using different types of CPUs and operating systems. Some means of letting this diverse group of computers run the same program was highly desired.

By 1993 it became obvious to members of the Java design team that the problems of portability frequently encountered when creating code for embedded controllers are also found when attempting to create code for the Internet. This realization caused the focus of Java to switch from consumer electronics to Internet programming. So, while it was the desire for an architecture-neutral programming language that provided the initial spark, it was the Internet that ultimately led to Java's large-scale success.

It is useful to note that Java is directly related to two older languages: C and C++. Java inherits its syntax from C. Its object model is adapted from C++. Java's relationship with C and C++ is important. At the time of Java's creation, many programmers were familiar with the C/C++ syntax. This made it easy for a C/C++ programmer to learn Java and, conversely, for a Java programmer to learn C/C++. Furthermore, Java's designers did not need to "reinvent the wheel." Instead, they were able to adapt, refine, and enrich an already highly successful programming paradigm.

Because of the similarities between Java and C++, especially their support for object-oriented programming, it is tempting to think of Java as simply the "Internet version of C++." To do so would be a mistake, however. Java has some significant differences. Although Java was influenced by C++, it is not an enhanced version of C++. For example, it is neither upwardly nor downwardly compatible with C++. Furthermore, Java was not designed to replace C++. Java was designed to solve a certain set of problems, and C++ was designed to solve a different set of problems. Both will coexist for many years to come.

Programming Fundamentals

Progress Check

1. Java is useful for the Internet because it can produce _____ programs.
2. Java is the direct descendant of what languages?

Java's Contribution to the Internet

The Internet helped catapult Java to the forefront of programming, and Java, in turn, had a profound effect on the Internet. In addition to simplifying Web programming in general, Java innovated a new type of networked program called the *applet* that, at the time, changed the way the online world thought about content. Java also addressed some of the thorniest issues associated with the Internet: portability and security. Let's look more closely at each of these.

Java Applets

An applet is a special kind of Java program that is designed to be transmitted over the Internet and automatically executed by a Java-compatible web browser. Furthermore, an applet is downloaded on demand. If the user clicks a link that contains an applet, the applet will be automatically downloaded and run in the browser. Applets are intended to be small programs. They are typically used to display data provided by the server, handle user input, or provide simple functions, such as a loan calculator, that execute locally rather than on the server. In essence, the applet allows some functionality to be moved from the server to the client. Thus, the creation of the applet changed Internet programming because it expanded the universe of objects that can move about freely in cyberspace.

As desirable as applets were, they also presented serious challenges in the areas of security and portability. Obviously, a program that downloads and executes automatically on the client computer must be prevented from doing harm. It must also be able to run in a variety of different environments and under different operating systems. As you will see, Java solved these problems in an effective and elegant way. Let's look a bit more closely at each.

Security

As you are likely aware, every time that you download a "normal" program, you are taking a risk because the code you are downloading might contain a virus, Trojan horse, or other harmful code. At the core of the problem is the fact that malicious code can cause its damage because it has gained unauthorized access to system resources. For example, a virus might gather private information, such as credit card numbers, bank account balances, and passwords, by searching the contents of your computer's local file system. In order for Java to enable applets to be safely downloaded and executed on the client computer, it was necessary to prevent an applet from launching such an attack.

Answers:

1. portable   **2.** C and C++.

Java achieved this protection by confining an applet to the Java execution environment and not allowing it access to other parts of the computer. (You will see how this is accomplished shortly.) The ability to download applets with confidence that no harm will be done and that no security will be breached is one of Java's most important features.

Portability

Portability is a major aspect of the Internet because many different types of computers and operating systems are connected to it. If a Java program were to be run on virtually any computer connected to the Internet, there needed to be some way to enable that program to execute on different systems. For example, in the case of an applet, the same applet must be able to be downloaded and executed by the wide variety of different CPUs, operating systems, and browsers. It is not practical to have different versions of the applet for different computers. The *same* code must work in *all* computers. Therefore, some means of generating portable executable code was needed. Happily, the same mechanism that helps ensure security also helps create portability.

Java's Solution: The Bytecode

The key that allows Java to solve both the security and the portability problems just described is that the output of a Java compiler is not directly executable machine code. Rather, it is bytecode. *Bytecode* is a highly optimized set of instructions designed to be executed by the *Java Virtual Machine* (JVM). In essence, the original JVM was designed as an *interpreter for bytecode*. The fact that a Java program is executed by the JVM helps solve the major problems of portability and security associated with Web-based programs. Here is why.

Compiling a Java program into bytecode makes it much easier to run a program in a wide variety of environments because only the JVM needs to be implemented for each platform. Once the JVM exists for a given system, any Java program can run on it. Although the details of the JVM will differ from platform to platform, all interpret the same Java bytecode. If a Java program were compiled to native code, then different versions of the same program would have to exist for each type of CPU connected to the Internet. This is, of course, not a feasible solution. Thus, the execution of bytecode by the JVM is the easiest way to create truly portable programs.

The fact that a Java program is executed by the JVM also helps to make it secure. Because the JVM is in control, it can contain the program and prevent it from generating side effects outside of the system. Safety is also enhanced by certain restrictions that exist in the Java language.

When a program is executed by a virtual machine, it generally runs slower than the same program would run if compiled to executable machine code. However, with Java, the differential between the two is not so great. Because bytecode has been highly optimized, the use of bytecode enables the JVM to execute programs much faster than you might expect. Furthermore, it is possible to use on-the-fly compilation of bytecode into machine code in order to boost performance. This is done through the use of a *just-in-time* (JIT) compiler for bytecode.

When a JIT compiler is part of the JVM, selected portions of bytecode are compiled into executable code in real time on a piece-by-piece, demand basis. It is important to emphasize that a JIT compiler does not compile an entire Java program into executable code all at once. Instead, a JIT compiler compiles code as it is needed, during execution. Furthermore, not all sequences of bytecode are compiled—only those that will benefit from compilation. Even when dynamic compilation is applied to bytecode, the portability and safety features still apply because the JVM is still in charge of the execution environment.

One last point: The JVM is part of the Java run-time system, which is also called the Java Runtime Environment, or JRE for short.

The Evolution of Java

Only a few languages have fundamentally reshaped the very essence of programming. In this elite group, Java stands out because its impact was both rapid and widespread. It is not an overstatement to say that the original release of Java 1.0 by Sun Microsystems, Inc. caused a revolution in programming. Not only did Java help transform the Web into a highly interactive environment, but it also set a new standard in computer language design.

Over the years, Java continued to grow, evolve, and otherwise redefine itself. Unlike some other languages, which are slow to incorporate new features, Java has often been at the forefront of computer language development. One reason for this is the culture of innovation and change that came to surround Java. As a result, Java has gone through several upgrades—some relatively small, others more significant.

At the time of this writing, the current release of Java is called Java SE 7, with the Java Development Kit being called JDK 7. The SE in Java SE 7 stands for Standard Edition. Java SE 7 is the first major release of Java since Sun Microsystems was acquired by Oracle. Java SE 7 contains many new features. Several of these new features are pointed out throughout this book.

Ask the Expert

Q You explained that applets run on the client (browser) side of the Internet. Is there a parallel type of Java program that runs on the server side?

A Yes. Not long after the initial release of Java it became obvious that Java would also be useful on the server side. The result was the *servlet*. A servlet is a small program that executes on the server. Just as applets dynamically extend the functionality of a web browser, servlets dynamically extend the functionality of a web server. Thus, with the advent of the servlet, Java spanned both sides of the client/server connection.

Progress Check

1. What is an applet?
2. What is Java bytecode?
3. The use of bytecode helps solve what two Internet programming problems?

THE KEY ATTRIBUTES OF OBJECT-ORIENTED PROGRAMMING

At the center of Java is *object-oriented programming* (OOP). The object-oriented methodology is inseparable from Java, and all Java programs are, to at least some extent, object-oriented. Because of OOP's importance to Java, it is useful to understand OOP's basic principles before you write even a simple Java program.

OOP is a powerful way to approach the job of programming. Programming methodologies have changed dramatically since the invention of the computer, primarily to accommodate the increasing complexity of programs. For example, when computers were first invented, programming was done by toggling in the binary machine instructions using the computer's front panel. As long as programs were just a few hundred instructions long, this approach worked. As programs grew, assembly language was invented so that a programmer could deal with larger, increasingly complex programs, using symbolic representations of the machine instructions. As programs continued to grow, high-level languages were introduced that gave the programmer more tools with which to handle complexity. The first widespread language was FORTRAN. Although it was a very impressive first step, large FORTRAN programs could still be quite difficult to understand.

The 1960s gave birth to structured programming. This is the method encouraged by languages such as C and Pascal. The use of structured languages made it possible to write moderately complex programs fairly easily. Structured languages are characterized by their support for stand-alone subroutines, local variables, rich control constructs, and their lack of reliance on the GOTO. Although structured languages are a powerful tool, they too can reach a limit.

Consider this: At each milestone in the development of programming, techniques and tools were created to allow the programmer to deal with increasingly greater complexity. Each step of the way, the new approach took the best elements of the previous methods

Answers:

1. An applet is a small program that is dynamically downloaded over the Web.
2. A highly optimized set of instructions that can be executed by the Java Virtual Machine.
3. Portability and security.

and moved forward. Prior to the invention of OOP, many projects were nearing (or exceeding) the breaking point. Object-oriented methods were created to help programmers overcome these barriers.

Object-oriented programming took the best ideas of structured programming and combined them with several new concepts. The result was a different way of organizing a program. In the most general sense, a program can be organized in one of two ways: around its code (what is happening) or around its data (what is being affected). Using only structured programming techniques, programs are typically organized around code. This approach can be thought of as "code acting on data."

Object-oriented programs work the other way around. They are organized around data, with the key principle being "data controlling access to code." In an object-oriented language, you define the data and the routines that are permitted to act on that data. Thus, a data type defines precisely what sort of operations can be applied to that data.

To support the principles of object-oriented programming, all OOP languages, including Java, have three traits in common: encapsulation, polymorphism, and inheritance. Let's examine each.

Encapsulation

Encapsulation is a programming mechanism that binds together code and the data it manipulates, and that keeps both safe from outside interference and misuse. In an object-oriented language, code and data can be bound together in such a way that a self-contained *black box* is created. Within the box are all necessary data and code. When code and data are linked together in this fashion, an object is created. In other words, an object is the device that supports encapsulation.

Within an object, code, data, or both may be *private* to that object or *public*. Private code or data is known to and accessible by only another part of the object. That is, private code or data cannot be accessed by a piece of the program that exists outside the object. When code or data is public, other parts of your program can access it even though it is defined within an object. Typically, the public parts of an object are used to provide a controlled interface to the private elements of the object.

Java's basic unit of encapsulation is the *class*. Although the class will be examined in great detail later in this book, the following brief discussion will be helpful now. A class defines the form of an object. It specifies both the data and the code that will operate on that data. Java uses a class specification to construct *objects*. Objects are *instances* of a class. Thus, a class is essentially a set of plans that specify how to build an object.

The code and data that constitute a class are called *members* of the class. Specifically, the data defined by the class are referred to as *member variables* or *instance variables*. The code that operates on that data is referred to as *member methods* or just *methods*.

Polymorphism

Polymorphism (from Greek, meaning "many forms") is the quality that allows one interface to access a general class of actions. The specific action is determined by the exact nature of the situation. A simple example of polymorphism is found in the steering wheel of an automobile. The steering wheel (i.e., the interface) is the same no matter what type of actual steering mechanism is used. That is, the steering wheel works the same whether your car has manual steering or power steering. Therefore, once you know how to operate the steering wheel, you can drive any type of car, regardless of how the steering is implemented.

The same principle can also apply to programming. Here is a simple example. You can create an interface that defines an operation called **get**, which obtains the next item of data from some form of list. This action, obtaining the next item, can be implemented in any number of ways, based on how the items are stored. For example, the items might be stored in first-in, first-out order; in first-in, last-out order; based on some priority; or in any of a number of different ways. However, as long as each storage mechanism implements your interface, then you can use **get** to retrieve the next item.

More generally, the concept of polymorphism is often expressed by the phrase "one interface, multiple methods." This means that it is possible to design a generic interface to a group of related activities. Polymorphism helps reduce complexity by allowing the same interface to be used to specify a *general class of action*. It is the compiler's job to select the *specific action* (i.e., method) as it applies to each situation. You, the programmer, don't need to do this selection manually. You need only utilize the general interface.

Inheritance

Inheritance is the process by which one object can acquire the properties of another object. This is important because it supports the concept of hierarchical classification. If you think about it, most knowledge is made manageable by hierarchical (i.e., top-down) classifications. For example, a Red Delicious apple is part of the classification *apple*, which in turn is part of the *fruit* class, which is under the larger class *food*. That is, the *food* class possesses certain qualities (edible, nutritious, etc.) which also, logically, apply to its subclass, *fruit*. In addition to these qualities, the *fruit* class has specific characteristics (juicy, sweet, etc.) that distinguish it from other food. The *apple* class defines those qualities specific to an apple (grows on trees, not tropical, etc.). A Red Delicious apple would, in turn, inherit all the qualities of all preceding classes and define only those qualities that make it unique.

Without the use of hierarchies, each object would have to explicitly define all of its characteristics. Using inheritance, an object need only define those qualities that make it unique within its class. It can inherit its general attributes from its parent. Thus, it is the inheritance mechanism that makes it possible for one object to be a specific instance of a more general case.

Progress Check

1. Name the principles of OOP.
2. What is the basic unit of encapsulation in Java?

THE JAVA DEVELOPMENT KIT

Now that the history and theoretical underpinning of Java have been discussed, it is time to start writing Java programs. Before you can compile and run those programs, however, the Java Development Kit (JDK) must be installed on the computer. Your instructor will explain how to access the JDK on the computers used by the course.

*Note: If you want to install the JDK on your own computer, the JDK can be downloaded from (at the time of this writing) **www.oracle.com/technetwork/java/ javase/downloads/index.html**. Follow the instructions for the type of computer that you have. After you have installed the JDK, you will be able to compile and run programs.*

The JDK supplies two primary programs. The first is **javac**, which is the Java compiler. It converts your source code into bytecode. The second is **java**. Sometimes referred to as the *application launcher*, this is the program you will use to run a Java program. It operates on the bytecode, using the JVM to execute your program.

One other point: the JDK runs in the command prompt environment and uses command-line tools. It is not a windowed application. It is also not an integrated development environment (IDE).

Note: In addition to the basic command-line tools supplied with the JDK, there are several high-quality integrated development environments available for Java. An IDE can be very helpful when developing and deploying commercial applications. As a general rule, you can also use an IDE to compile and run the programs in this book if you so choose. However, the instructions presented in this book for compiling and running a Java program describe only the JDK command-line tools. The reasons for this are easy to understand. First, the JDK is readily available. Second, the instructions for using the JDK are the same for all environments. Third, because of differences between IDEs, no general set of instructions can be given that will work for everyone. However, if your course is using an IDE, your instructor will provide the information needed to use it.

Answers:

1. Encapsulation, polymorphism, and inheritance.
2. The class.

Ask the Expert

Q You state that object-oriented programming is an effective way to manage large programs. However, it seems that it might add substantial overhead to relatively small ones. Since you say that all Java programs are, to some extent, object-oriented, does this impose a penalty for smaller programs?

A No. As you will see, for small programs, Java's object-oriented features are nearly transparent. Although it is true that Java follows a strict object model, you have wide latitude as to the degree to which you employ it. For smaller programs, their "object-orientedness" is barely perceptible. As your programs grow, you will integrate more object-oriented features effortlessly.

A FIRST SIMPLE PROGRAM

The best way to introduce several of the key elements of Java is to begin by compiling and running a short sample program. We will use the one shown here:

```
/*
   This is a simple Java program.

   Call this file Example.java.
*/
class Example {
  // A Java program begins with a call to main().
  public static void main(String[] args) {
    System.out.println("Java drives the Web.");
  }
}
```

You will follow these three steps:

1. Enter the program.
2. Compile the program.
3. Run the program.

Entering the Program

The first step in creating a program is to enter its source code into the computer. As explained earlier, a program's source code is the human-readable form of the program. You must enter the program into your computer using a text editor, not a word processor. Word processors typically store format information along with text. This format information will confuse the Java compiler. The source code must consist solely of text. If your course is using an IDE, it will provide a source code editor for you to use. Otherwise any simple text editor will work. For example, if you are using Windows, you can use Notepad.

For many computer languages, the name of the file that holds the source code to a program is arbitrary. However, this is not the case with Java. The first thing that you must learn about Java is that *the name you give to a source file is very important.* For this example, the name of the source file should be **Example.java**. Let's see why.

In Java, a source file is officially called a *compilation unit.* It is a text file that contains (among other things) one or more class definitions. (For now, we will be using source files that contain only one class.) The Java compiler requires that a source file use the **.java** filename extension. As you can see by looking at the program, the name of the class defined by the program is also **Example**. This is not a coincidence. In Java, all code must reside inside a class. By convention, the name of the main class should match the name of the file that holds the program. You should also make sure that the capitalization of the filename matches the class name. The reason for this is that Java is case sensitive. At this point, the convention that filenames correspond to class names may seem arbitrary, but following it makes maintaining and organizing your programs easier.

Compiling the Program

Before you can run the program, you must compile it using **javac**. To compile the **Example** program, execute **javac**, specifying the name of the source file on the command line, as shown here:

```
javac Example.java
```

The **javac** compiler creates a file called **Example.class** that contains the bytecode version of the program. Remember, bytecode is not executable code. Bytecode must be executed by a Java Virtual Machine. It cannot be directly executed by the CPU.

Running the Program

To actually run the program, you must use **java**. Recall that **java** operates on the bytecode form of your program. To execute the **Example** program, pass the class name **Example** as a command-line argument, as shown here:

```
java Example
```

When the program is run, the following output is displayed:

```
Java drives the Web.
```

When Java source code is compiled, each individual class is put into its own output file named after the class and using the **.class** extension. This is why it is a good idea to give a Java source file the same name as the class it contains—the name of the source file will match the name of the **.class** file. When you execute **java** as just shown, you are actually specifying the name of the class that you want to execute. **java** will automatically search for a file by that name that has the **.class** extension. If it finds the file, it will execute the code contained in the specified class.

The First Sample Program Line by Line

Although **Example.java** is quite short, it includes several key features that are common to all Java programs. Let's closely examine each part of the program.

The program begins with the following lines:

```
/*
   This is a simple Java program.

   Call this file Example.java.
*/
```

This is a *comment*. Like most other programming languages, Java lets you enter a remark into a program's source file. The compiler ignores the contents of a comment. Instead, a comment describes or explains the operation of the program to anyone who is reading its source code. In this case, the comment describes the program and reminds you that the source file should be called **Example.java**. Of course, in real applications, comments generally explain how some part of the program works or what a specific feature does.

The comment shown at the top of the program is called a *multiline comment*. This type of comment must begin with /* and end with */. The compiler ignores anything between these two comment symbols. As the name suggests, a multiline comment may be several lines long.

The next line of code in the program is shown here:

```
class Example {
```

This line uses the keyword **class** to declare that a new class is being defined. As mentioned, the class is Java's basic unit of encapsulation. **Example** is the name of the class. The class definition begins with the opening brace ({) and ends with the closing brace (}). The elements between the two braces are members of the class. For the moment, don't worry too much about the details of a class except to note that in Java, all program activity occurs within one. This is one reason all Java programs are (at least a little bit) object-oriented.

The next line in the program is the *single-line comment*, shown here:

```
// A Java program begins with a call to main().
```

This is the second type of comment supported by Java. A single-line comment begins with a // and ends at the end of the line. As a general rule, programmers use multiline comments for longer remarks and single-line comments for brief, line-by-line descriptions.

The next line of code is shown here:

```
public static void main (String[] args) {
```

This line begins the **main( )** method. As mentioned earlier, in Java, a subroutine is called a *method*. As the comment preceding it suggests, this is the line at which the program will begin executing. All Java applications begin execution by executing **main( )**. The exact meaning of each part of this line cannot be given now, since it involves a detailed understanding of several other of Java's features. However, since many of the examples in this book will use this line of code, a brief overview is warranted so that you have a general concept of what it means.

The line begins with the **public** keyword. This is an *access modifier*. An access modifier determines how other parts of the program can access the members of the class. When a class member is preceded by **public**, then that member can be accessed by code outside the class in which it is declared. (The opposite of **public** is **private**, which prevents a member from being used by code defined outside of its class.) The **main( )** method must be declared **public** because it is executed by code outside of the **Example** class. (In this case, it is the **java** application launcher that invokes **main( )**.)

The keyword **static** allows **main( )** to be executed independently of any object. This is necessary because **main( )** is executed by the JVM before any objects are made. The keyword **void** simply tells the compiler that **main( )** does not return a result. (As you will learn later, methods may also return values.) If all this seems a bit confusing, don't worry. All of these concepts will be discussed in detail in subsequent chapters.

As stated, **main( )** is the method called when a Java application begins. Any information that you need to pass to a method is received by variables specified within the set of parentheses that follow the name of the method. These variables are called *parameters*. (If no parameters are required for a given method, you still need to include the empty parentheses.) The **main( )** method requires that there be one parameter. This is specified in the **Example** program as **String[ ] args**, which declares a parameter named **args**. This is an array of objects of type **String**. *Arrays* are collections of similar objects. Objects of type **String** store sequences of characters. (Both arrays and the **String** type are discussed in detail in subsequent chapters.) In this case, **args** receives any command-line arguments present when the program is executed. The **Example** program does not use command-line arguments, but other programs shown later in this book will.

The last character on the line is the {. This signals the start of **main( )**'s body. All of the code included in a method will occur between the method's opening brace and its closing brace.

The next line of code is shown here. Notice that it occurs inside **main( )**.

```
| System.out.println("Java drives the Web.");
```

This line outputs the string "Java drives the Web." followed by a new line on the screen. Output is actually accomplished by the built-in **println( )** method. In this case, **println( )** displays the string that is passed to it. As you will see, **println( )** can be used to display other types of information, too. The line begins with **System.out**. While too complicated to explain in detail at this time, briefly, **System** is a predefined class that provides access to the system, and **out** is the output stream that is connected to the console. Thus, **System.out** is an object that encapsulates console output. The fact that Java uses an object to define console output is further evidence of its object-oriented nature.

As you might have guessed, console output (and input) is not used frequently in real-world Java applications. Since most modern computing environments are windowed and graphical in nature, console I/O is used mostly for simple utility programs, for demonstration programs (like those shown in this book), and for server-side code. Later, you will learn how to create graphical user interfaces (GUIs), but for now, we will continue to use the console I/O methods. Notice that the **println( )** statement ends with a semicolon. All statements in Java end with a semicolon. The reason that the other lines in the program do not end in a semicolon is that they are not, technically, statements.

The first } in the program ends **main( )**, and the last } ends the **Example** class definition.

One last point: Java is case sensitive. Forgetting this can cause you serious problems. For example, if you accidentally type **Main** instead of **main**, or **PrintLn** instead of **println**, the preceding program will be incorrect. Furthermore, although the Java compiler *will* compile classes that do not contain a **main( )** method, it has no way to execute them. So, if you had mistyped **main**, the compiler would still compile your program. However, **java** would report an error because it would be unable to find the **main( )** method.

Progress Check

1. Where does a Java program begin execution?
2. What does **System.out.println( )** do?
3. What is the name of the Java compiler? What do you use to run a Java program?

HANDLING SYNTAX ERRORS

If you have not yet done so, enter, compile, and run the preceding program. As you may know, it is quite easy to accidentally type something incorrectly when entering code into your computer. Fortunately, if you enter something incorrectly into your program, the compiler will report a *syntax error* message when it tries to compile it. The Java compiler attempts to make sense out of your source code no matter what you have written. For this reason, the error that is reported may not always reflect the actual cause of the problem. In the preceding program, for example, an accidental omission of the opening brace after the **main( )** method causes the compiler to report the following two errors.

```
Example.java:8: ';' expected
   public static void main(String[] args)
                                          ^
Example.java:11: class, interface, or enum expected
}
^
```

Clearly, the first error message is completely wrong because what is missing is not a semicolon but a brace. The second error message is not wrong, per se, but is simply the result of the compiler trying to make sense of the remainder of the program after its syntax has been distorted by the missing brace.

Answers:

1. **main( )**
2. Outputs information to the console.
3. The standard Java compiler is **javac**. To run a Java program, use **java**.

The point of this discussion is that when your program contains a syntax error, you shouldn't necessarily take the compiler's messages at face value. The messages may be misleading. You may need to "second-guess" an error message in order to find the real problem. Also, look at the last few lines of code in your program that precede the line being flagged. Sometimes an error will not be reported until several lines after the point at which the error actually occurred.

A SECOND SIMPLE PROGRAM

Perhaps no other construct is as important to a programming language as the assignment of a value to a variable. A *variable* is a named memory location that can be assigned a value. This value can then be accessed through the variable's name. Further, the value of a variable can be changed during the execution of a program. That is, the content of a variable is changeable, not fixed.

The following program creates two variables called **var1** and **var2**. Notice how they are used.

```java
/*
    This demonstrates a variable.

    Call this file Example2.java.
*/
class Example2 {
  public static void main(String[] args) {
    int var1; // this declares a variable         ←——————Declare variables.
    int var2; // this declares another variable

    var1 = 1024; // this assigns 1024 to var1  ←————Assign a variable a value.

    System.out.println("var1 contains" + var1);

    var2 = var1 / 2;

    System.out.print("var2 contains var1 / 2: ");
    System.out.println(var2);
  }
}
```

When you run this program, you will see the following output:

```
var1 contains 1024
var2 contains var1 / 2: 512
```

This program introduces several new concepts. First, the statement

```
int var1; // this declares a variable
```

declares a variable called **var1** of type integer. In Java, all variables must be declared before they are used. Further, the type of values that the variable can hold must also be specified. This is called the *type* of the variable. In this case, **var1** can hold integer values. These are whole-number values. In Java, to declare a variable to be of type integer, precede its name with the keyword **int**. Thus, the preceding statement declares a variable called **var1** of type **int**.

The next line declares a second variable called **var2**:

```
int var2; // this declares another variable
```

Notice that this line uses the same format as the first line except that the name of the variable is different.

In general, to declare a variable you will use a statement like this:

type var-name;

Here, *type* specifies the type of variable being declared, and *var-name* is the name of the variable. In addition to **int**, Java supports several other data types.

The following line of code assigns **var1** the value 1024:

```
var1 = 1024; // this assigns 1024 to var1
```

In Java, the assignment operator is the single equal sign. It copies the value on its right side into the variable on its left.

The next line of code outputs the value of **var1** preceded by the string "var1 contains":

```
System.out.println("var1 contains" + var1);
```

In this statement, the plus sign causes the value of **var1** to be displayed after the string that precedes it. This approach can be generalized. Using the + operator, you can chain together as many items as you want within a single **println( )** statement.

The next line of code assigns **var2** the value of **var1** divided by 2:

```
var2 = var1 / 2;
```

This line divides the value in **var1** by 2 and then stores that result in **var2**. Thus, after the line executes, **var2** will contain the value 512. The value of **var1** will be unchanged. Like most other computer languages, Java supports a full range of arithmetic operators, including those shown here:

+	Addition
−	Subtraction
*	Multiplication
/	Division

Here are the next two lines in the program:

```
System.out.print("var2 contains var1/2: ");
System.out.println(var2);
```

Two new things are occurring here. First, the built-in method **print( )** is used to display the string "var2 contains var1 / 2; ", This string is *not* followed by a new line. This means that when the next output is generated, it will start on the same line. The **print( )** method is just like **println( )**, except that it does not output a new line after each call. Second, in the call to **println( )**, notice that **var2** is used by itself. Both **print( )** and **println( )** can be used to output values of any of Java's built-in types.

One more point about declaring variables before we move on: It is possible to declare two or more variables using the same declaration statement. Just separate their names by commas. For example, **var1** and **var2** could have been declared like this:

```
int var1, var2; // both declared using one statement
```

ANOTHER DATA TYPE

In the preceding program, a variable of type **int** was used. However, a variable of type **int** can hold only whole numbers. Thus, it cannot be used when a fractional component is required. For example, an **int** variable can hold the value 18, but not the value 18.3. Fortunately, **int** is only one of several data types defined by Java. To allow numbers with fractional components, Java defines two floating-point types: **float** and **double**, which represent single- and double-precision values, respectively. Of the two, **double** is the most commonly used.

To declare a variable of type **double**, use a statement similar to that shown here:

```
double x;
```

Here, **x** is the name of the variable, which is of type **double**. Because **x** has a floating-point type, it can hold values such as 122.23, 0.034, or –19.0.

To better understand the difference between **int** and **double**, try the following program:

```
/*
    This program illustrates the differences
    between int and double.

    Call this file Example3.java.
*/
class Example3 {
  public static void main(String[] args) {
    int w; // this declares an int variable
    double x; // this declares a floating-point variable

    w = 10; // assign w the value 10

    x = 10.0; // assign x the value 10.0
```

```
      System.out.println("Original value of w: " + w);
      System.out.println("Original value of x: " + x);
      System.out.println(); // print a blank line ◄───────────Output a blank line.


      // now, divide both by 4
      w = w / 4;
      x = x / 4;


      System.out.println("w after division: " + w);
      System.out.println("x after division: " + x);
   }
}
```

The output from this program is shown here:

```
Original value of w: 10
Original value of x: 10.0


w after division: 2 ◄───────────Fractional component lost
x after division: 2.5 ◄───────────Fractional component preserved
```

As you can see, when **w** (an **int** variable) is divided by 4, a whole-number division is performed, and the outcome is 2—the fractional component is lost. However, when **x** (a **double** variable) is divided by 4, the fractional component is preserved, and the proper answer is displayed.

There is one other new thing to notice in the program. To print a blank line, simply call **println( )** without any arguments.

Ask the Expert

Q Why does Java have different data types for integers and floating-point values? That is, why aren't all numeric values just the same type?

A Java supplies different data types so that you can write efficient programs. For example, integer arithmetic is faster than floating-point calculations. Thus, if you don't need fractional values, then you don't need to incur the overhead associated with types **float** or **double**. Second, the amount of memory required for one type of data might be less than that required for another. By supplying different types, Java enables you to make best use of system resources. Finally, some algorithms require (or at least benefit from) the use of a specific type of data. In general, Java supplies a number of built-in types to give you the greatest flexibility.

TRY THIS 1-1 CONVERTING GALLONS TO LITERS

`GalToLit.java`

Although the preceding sample programs illustrate several important features of the Java language, they are not very useful. Even though you do not know much about Java at this point, you can still put what you have learned to work to create a practical program. In this project, we will create a program that converts gallons to liters. The program will work by declaring two **double** variables. One will hold the number of the gallons, and the second will hold the number of liters after the conversion. There are approximately 3.7854 liters in a gallon. Thus, to convert gallons to liters, the gallon value is multiplied by 3.7854. The program displays both the number of gallons and the equivalent number of liters.

STEP-BY-STEP

1. Create a new file called **GalToLit.java**.
2. Enter the following program into the file:

```
/*
   Try This 1-1

   This program converts gallons to liters.

   Call this program GalToLit.java.
*/
class GalToLit {
  public static void main(String[] args) {
    double gallons; // holds the number of gallons
    double liters; // holds conversion to liters

    gallons = 10; // start with 10 gallons

    liters = gallons * 3.7854; // convert to liters

    System.out.println(gallons + " gallons is " + liters +
                       " liters.");
  }
}
```

3. Compile the program using the following command line:

```
javac GalToLit.java
```

4. Run the program using this command:

```
java GalToLit
```

You will see this output:

```
10.0 gallons is 37.854 liters.
```

5. As it stands, this program converts 10 gallons to liters. However, by changing the value assigned to **gallons**, you can have the program convert a different number of gallons into its equivalent number of liters.

Progress Check

1. What is Java's keyword for the integer data type?
2. What is **double**?

TWO CONTROL STATEMENTS

Inside a method, execution proceeds in the sequence in which the statements occur. In other words, execution proceeds from one statement to the next, top to bottom. However, often you will want to alter this flow based on some condition. Such situations are extremely common in programming. Here is one example. A web site might require a password, and your code must not grant access to the site if the password is invalid. Thus, the code that grants access must not be executed if an invalid password is entered. Continuing with this example, if an invalid password is entered, you might want to give the user two (and only two) more tries to enter it correctly. To handle situations in which the flow of program execution is to be altered, Java provides a rich assortment of *control statements*. Although we will look closely at control statements in Chapter 3, two such statements, the **if** and the **for**, are briefly introduced here because we will be using them to write sample programs.

The if Statement

You can selectively execute part of a program through the use of the **if** statement. The **if** is Java's basic "decision making" statement. As such, the **if** is one of the foundational elements of Java and of programming in general. You would use an **if** statement to determine if one number is less than another, to check if a variable contains a target value, or to test for some error condition, to name just three examples among many.

The simplest form of the **if** is shown here:

if(*condition*) *statement*;

Here, *condition* is an expression that evaluates to either true or false. (Such an expression is called a *Boolean expression*.) If *condition* is true, then the statement is executed. If *condition* is false, then the statement is bypassed. Thus, the condition controls whether or not the following statement is executed. Here is an example:

```
if(10 < 11) System.out.println("10 is less than 11");
```

In this line, the less-than operator < is used to determine if 10 is less than 11. Since 10 is less than 11, the conditional expression is true, and **println( )** will execute. However, consider the following:

```
if(10 < 9) System.out.println("this won't be displayed");
```

Answers:

1. **int**
2. The keyword for the double floating-point data type.

In this case, 10 is not less than 9. Thus, the call to **println( )** will not take place.

The < is just one of Java's *relational operators*. A relational operator determines the relationship between two values. Java defines a full complement of relational operators that may be used in a conditional expression. They are shown here:

Operator	Meaning
<	Less than
<=	Less than or equal to
>	Greater than
>=	Greater than or equal to
==	Equal to
!=	Not equal

Notice that the test for equality is the double equal sign. In all cases, the outcome of a relational operator is a true or false value.

Here is a program that illustrates the **if** statement and several of the relational operators:

```
/*
   Demonstrate the if.

   Call this file IfDemo.java.
*/
class IfDemo {
   public static void main(String[] args) {
      int a, b, c;

      a = 2;
      b = 3;

      if(a < b) System.out.println("a is less than b");

      // this won't display anything
      if(a == b) System.out.println("you won't see this");

      System.out.println();

      c = a - b; // c contains -1

      System.out.println("c contains -1");
      if(c >= 0) System.out.println("c is non-negative");
      if(c < 0) System.out.println("c is negative");

      System.out.println();

      c = b - a; // c now contains 1
```

```
   System.out.println("c contains 1");
   if(c >= 0) System.out.println("c is non-negative");
   if(c < 0) System.out.println("c is negative");
 }
}
```

The output generated by this program is shown here:

```
a is less than b

c contains -1
c is negative

c contains 1
c is non-negative
```

Notice one other thing in this program. The line

```
int a, b, c;
```

declares three variables, **a**, **b**, and **c**, by use of a comma-separated list. As mentioned earlier, when you need two or more variables of the same type, they can be declared in one statement. Just separate the variable names by commas.

Ask the Expert

Q In the discussion of the **if** statement, you mentioned that a true/false expression is referred to as *Boolean* expression. Why is that term used?

A The term *Boolean* is named after George Boole (1815–1864). He developed and formalized the laws that govern true/false expressions. This became known as Boolean algebra. His work eventually came to form the basis of computer logic.

The for Loop

Many times a program will need to perform a task more than once. For example, you might want to display the time of day, with the time updated once every second. Obviously, it would not be practical to write such a program using hundreds of separate **println( )** statements, one for each possible time, in one-second intervals. Instead, such a repetitive operation would be accomplished by a *loop*. A loop is a control statement that repeatedly executes a sequence of code. Loops are used extensively by nearly all programs. Like the **if** statement, loops are a fundamental part of programming.

Java supplies a powerful assortment of loop constructs. The one we will introduce here is the **for** loop. The simplest form of the **for** loop is shown next:

for(*initialization*; *condition*; *iteration*) *statement*;

In its most common form, the *initialization* portion of the loop sets a *loop control variable* to an initial value. The *condition* is a Boolean expression that tests the loop control variable. If the outcome of that test is true, the **for** loop continues to iterate. If it is false, the loop terminates. The *iteration* expression determines how the loop control variable is changed each time the loop iterates. Here is a short program that illustrates the **for** loop:

```
/*
   Demonstrate the for loop.

   Call this file ForDemo.java.
*/
class ForDemo {
  public static void main(String[] args) {
    int count;

    for(count = 0; count < 5; count = count+1)◄─────── This loop iterates five times.
      System.out.println("This is count: " + count);

    System.out.println("Done!");
  }
}
```

The output generated by the program is shown here:

```
This is count: 0
This is count: 1
This is count: 2
This is count: 3
This is count: 4
Done!
```

In this example, **count** is the loop control variable. It is set to zero in the initialization portion of the **for**. At the start of each iteration (including the first one), the conditional test **count < 5** is performed. If the outcome of this test is true, the **println( )** statement is executed, and then the iteration portion of the loop is executed. This process continues until the conditional test is false, at which point execution picks up at the bottom of the loop. As a point of interest, in professionally written Java programs, you will almost never see the iteration portion of the loop written as shown in the preceding program. That is, you will seldom see statements like this:

```
count = count + 1;
```

The reason is that Java includes a special increment operator that performs this operation more efficiently. The increment operator is **++** (that is, two plus signs back to back). The increment operator increases its operand by one. By use of the increment operator, the preceding statement can be written like this:

```
count++;
```

Thus, the **for** in the preceding program will usually be written like this:

```
for(count = 0; count < 5; count++)
```

You might want to try this. As you will see, the loop still runs exactly the same as it did before.

Java also provides a decrement operator, which is specified as – –. This operator decreases its operand by one.

Progress Check

1. What does the **if** statement do?
2. What does the **for** statement do?
3. What are Java's relational operators?

CREATE BLOCKS OF CODE

Another key element of Java is the *code block*. A code block is a grouping of two or more statements. This is done by enclosing the statements between opening and closing braces. Once a block of code has been created, it becomes a logical unit that can be used any place that a single statement can. This is important because it lets you use a set of statements as the target of a control statement, such as the **if** or **for** described in the previous section. For example, consider this **if** statement:

```
if (w < h) {  ◄─────── Start of block
   v = w * h;
   w = 0;
}  ◄─────── End of block
```

Here, the target of the **if** statement is a block of code that contains two statements. If **w** is less than **h**, both statements inside the block will be executed. If **w** is not less than **h**, the block is bypassed and neither statement is executed. Thus, the two statements inside the block form a logical unit, and one statement cannot execute without the other also executing. This concept can be generalized: whenever you need to logically link two or more statements, you do so by creating a block.

The following program demonstrates a block of code by using it as the target of an **if** statement to prevent a division by zero:

```
/*
   Demonstrate a block of code.

   Call this file BlockDemo.java.
*/
class BlockDemo {
  public static void main(String[] args) {
```

Answers:

1. The **if** is Java's conditional statement.
2. The **for** is one of Java's loop statements.
3. The relational operators are = =, !=, <, >, <=, and >=.

```
   double i, j, d;


   i = 5;
   j = 10;

   // the target of this if is a block
   if(i != 0) {
     System.out.println("i does not equal zero");
     d = j / i;
     System.out.print("j / i is " + d);
   }
  }

 }
```

The target of the **if** is this entire block.

The output generated by this program is shown here:

```
i does not equal zero
j / i is 2.0
```

In this example, the target of the **if** statement is a block of code that is executed only if **i** does not equal zero. If the condition controlling the **if** is true (as it is in this case), the three statements inside the block will be executed. Try setting **i** to zero and observe the result. You will see that the entire block is skipped.

As you will learn later, blocks of code have additional properties and uses. However, the main reason for their existence is to create logically inseparable units of code.

Ask the Expert

Q Does the use of a code block introduce any run-time inefficiencies? In other words, does Java actually execute the { and }?

A No. Code blocks do not add any overhead whatsoever. In fact, because of their ability to simplify the coding of certain algorithms, their use generally increases speed and efficiency. Also, the { and } exist only in your program's source code. Java does not, per se, execute the { or }.

SEMICOLONS AND POSITIONING

In Java, the semicolon is a *separator* that is used to terminate a statement. That is, each individual statement must be ended with a semicolon. It indicates the end of one logical entity.

As you know, a block is a set of logically connected statements that are surrounded by opening and closing braces. A block is *not* terminated with a semicolon. Since a block is a group of statements, with a semicolon after each statement, it makes sense that a block is not terminated by a semicolon; instead, the end of the block is indicated by the closing brace.

Java does not recognize the end of the line as a terminator. For this reason, it does not matter where on a line you put a statement. For example,

```
x = y;
y = y + 1;
System.out.println(x + " " + y);
```

is the same as the following, to Java:

```
x = y; y = y + 1; System.out.println(x + " " + y);
```

Furthermore, the individual elements of a statement can also be put on separate lines. For example, the following is perfectly acceptable:

```
System.out.println("This is a long line of output" +
                   x + y + z +
                   "more output");
```

Breaking long lines in this fashion is often used to make programs more readable. It can also help prevent excessively long lines from wrapping.

INDENTATION PRACTICES

You may have noticed in the previous examples that certain statements were indented. Java is a free-form language, meaning that it does not matter where you place statements relative to each other on a line. However, over the years, a common and accepted indentation style has developed that allows for very readable programs. This book follows that style, and it is recommended that you do so as well. Using this style, you indent one level after each opening brace, and move back out one level after each closing brace. Certain statements encourage some additional indenting; these will be covered later.

Progress Check

1. How is a block of code created? What does it do?
2. In Java, statements are terminated by a _____ .
3. All Java statements must start and end on one line. True or False?

Answers:

1. A block is started by a {. It is ended by a }. A block creates a logical unit of code.
2. semicolon
3. False.

TRY THIS 1-2 IMPROVING THE GALLONS-TO-LITERS CONVERTER

GalToLitTable.java

You can use the **for** loop, the **if** statement, and code blocks to create an improved version of the gallons-to-liters converter that you developed in Try This 1-1. This new version will print a table of conversions, beginning with 1 gallon and ending at 100 gallons. After every 10 gallons, a blank line will be output. This is accomplished through the use of a variable called **counter** that counts the number of lines that have been output. Pay special attention to its use.

STEP-BY-STEP

1. Create a new file called **GalToLitTable.java**.
2. Enter the following program into the file:

```java
/*
    Try This 1-2

    This program displays a conversion
    table of gallons to liters.

    Call this program "GalToLitTable.java".
*/
class GalToLitTable {
  public static void main(String[] args) {
    double gallons, liters;
    int counter;                    Line counter is initially set to zero.

    counter = 0; ◄
    for(gallons = 1; gallons <= 100; gallons++) {
      liters = gallons * 3.7854; // convert to liters
      System.out.println(gallons + " gallons is " +
                         liters + " liters.");

      counter++; ◄──────────────────────Increment the line counter
      // every 10th line, print a blank line  with each loop iteration.
      if(counter == 10) { ◄──────────────── If counter is 10,
        System.out.println();                 output a blank line.
        counter = 0; // reset the line counter
      }
    }
  }
}
```

3. Compile the program using the following command line:

```
javac GalToLitTable.java
```

4. Run the program using this command:

```
java GalToLitTable
```

Here is a portion of the output that you will see:

```
1.0 gallons is 3.7854 liters.
2.0 gallons is 7.5708 liters.
3.0 gallons is 11.356200000000001 liters.
4.0 gallons is 15.1416 liters.
5.0 gallons is 18.927 liters.
6.0 gallons is 22.712400000000002 liters.
7.0 gallons is 26.4978 liters.
8.0 gallons is 30.2832 liters.
9.0 gallons is 34.0686 liters.
10.0 gallons is 37.854 liters.

11.0 gallons is 41.6394 liters.
12.0 gallons is 45.424800000000005 liters.
13.0 gallons is 49.2102 liters.
14.0 gallons is 52.9956 liters.
15.0 gallons is 56.781 liters.
16.0 gallons is 60.5664 liters.
17.0 gallons is 64.3518 liters.
18.0 gallons is 68.1372 liters.
19.0 gallons is 71.9226 liters.
20.0 gallons is 75.708 liters.

21.0 gallons is 79.49340000000001 liters.
22.0 gallons is 83.2788 liters.
23.0 gallons is 87.0642 liters.
24.0 gallons is 90.84960000000001 liters.
25.0 gallons is 94.635 liters.
26.0 gallons is 98.4204 liters.
27.0 gallons is 102.2058 liters.
28.0 gallons is 105.9912 liters.
29.0 gallons is 109.7766 liters.
30.0 gallons is 113.562 liters.
```

THE JAVA KEYWORDS

Fifty keywords are currently defined in the Java language (see Table 1-1). These keywords, combined with the syntax of the operators and separators, form the foundation of the Java language. These keywords cannot be used as names for things such as variables, classes, or methods.

TABLE 1-1: The Java Keywords					
abstract	assert	boolean	break	byte	case
catch	char	class	const	continue	default
do	double	else	enum	extends	final
finally	float	for	goto	if	implements
import	instanceof	int	interface	long	native
new	package	private	protected	public	return
short	static	strictfp	super	switch	synchronized
this	throw	throws	transient	try	void
volatile	while				

The keywords **const** and **goto** are reserved but not used. In the early days of Java, several other keywords were reserved for possible future use. However, the current specification for Java defines only the keywords shown in Table 1-1.

In addition to the keywords, Java reserves the following: **true**, **false**, and **null**. These are values defined by Java. You may not use these words for the names of a variable, class, and so on.

IDENTIFIERS IN JAVA

In Java an identifier is a name given to a method, a variable, or any other user-defined item. Identifiers can be from one to several characters long. Variable names may start with any letter of the alphabet, an underscore, or a dollar sign. Next may be either a letter, a digit, a dollar sign, or an underscore. The underscore can be used to enhance the readability of a variable name, as in **line_count**. Uppercase and lowercase are different; that is, to Java, **myvar** and **MyVar** are separate names. Here are some examples of legal identifiers:

Test	x	y2	maxLoad
$up	_top	my_var	sample23

Remember, you can't start an identifier with a digit. Thus, **12x** is invalid, for example.

As explained in the previous section, you cannot use any of the Java keywords or reserved words as identifier names. Also, you should not assign the name of any standard method, such as **println**, to an identifier. Beyond these two restrictions, good programming practice dictates that you use identifier names that reflect the meaning or usage of the items being named.

Ask the Expert

Q Can you give any guidelines to follow in choosing good variable names?

A Yes. In general, variables should be given names that describe their meaning as they are used in the program. For example, if you are creating variables that will hold the width and height of a rectangle, the names **width** and **height** are appropriate. Of course, sometimes a single word will not be adequate and a phrase is needed. For example, a variable that will hold the concentration of some material in parts per million might be called **partsPerMillion**, or perhaps shortened to **partsPerMil**. In these examples, notice the capitalization. After the first word, subsequent words are capitalized. This is referred to as *camel case* by programmers, and it is common style among Java programmers.

Although descriptive names are very important, sometimes the name of a variable is arbitrary and no descriptive name applies. This is commonly the case with loop control variables, variables that hold an interim result, and variables used in short example programs, such as those shown in this book, that simply demonstrate a feature of the language. In these cases, individual letters, such as **x**, **i**, or **v**, are frequently employed.

Progress Check

1. Which is the keyword: **for**, **For**, or **FOR**?
2. A Java identifier can contain what type of characters?
3. Are **index21** and **Index21** the same identifier?

THE JAVA CLASS LIBRARIES

The sample programs shown in this chapter make use of two of Java's built-in methods: **println( )** and **print( )**. These methods are members of the **System** class, which is a class predefined by Java that is automatically included in your programs. In the larger view, the Java environment relies on several built-in *class libraries* that contain many built-in methods that provide support for such things as I/O, string handling, networking, and a graphical user interface. Thus, Java as a totality is a combination of the Java language itself, plus its standard classes. As you will see, the class libraries provide much of the functionality that comes with Java. Indeed, part of becoming

---

Answers:

1. The keyword is **for**. In Java, all keywords are in lowercase.
2. Letters, digits, the underscore, and the $.
3. No; Java is case sensitive.

a Java programmer is learning to use the standard Java classes. Throughout this book, various elements of the standard library classes and methods are described. Understand, however, that the Java library is very large. It contains far more features than can be described in this book. It is something that you will also want to explore more on your own as you advance in your Java programming skills.

EXERCISES

1. Name the three necessary pieces of a computer.
2. What is source code? What is object code?
3. What is the value 14 in binary? What is the decimal equivalent of this binary number 1010 0110?
4. As a general rule, a byte is comprised of _____ bits.
5. What is bytecode and why is it important to Java's use for Internet programming?
6. What are the three main principles of object-oriented programming?
7. Where do Java programs begin execution?
8. What is a variable?
9. Which of the following variable names is invalid?
   A. **count**
   B. **$count**
   C. **count27**
   D. **67count**
10. How do you create a single-line comment? How do you create a multiline comment?
11. Show the general form of the **if** statement. Show the general form of the **for** loop.
12. How do you create a block of code?
13. The moon's gravity is about 17 percent that of earth's. Write a program that computes your effective weight on the moon.
14. Adapt Try This 1-2 so that it prints a conversion table of inches to meters. Display 12 feet of conversions, inch by inch. Output a blank line every 12 inches. (One meter equals approximately 39.37 inches.)
15. If you make a typing mistake when entering your program, what sort of error will result?
16. Does it matter where on a line you put a statement?

17. True or false:

    A. Comments contain important information for the compiler.

    B. You can have nested multiline comments of the form /*.../*...*/...*/.

    C. The equal sign = is used to test equality in **if** statements.

18. Name two I/O devices for computers that were not mentioned in this chapter.

19. Why don't programmers write code in a CPU's machine language? That is, why do almost all programmers use a higher level language like Java?

20. What is the difference between a compiler and an interpreter?

21. As mentioned in the text, a byte usually consists of 8 bits. Do a little research to determine what each of the following terms refer to:

    A. kilobyte

    B. megabyte

    C. gigabyte

    D. terabyte

22. Tell whether each of the following symbols or words is a Java keyword, operator, punctuation mark, or none of these.

    A. 33

    B. for

    C. ;

    D. int

    E. {}

23. Give an example, other than the food example in the chapter, of hierarchical classification where each classification inherits all the attributes of its parent classification.

24. What is wrong with each of the following commands?

```
javac Example.class
java Example.class
```

25. What is the difference between using x = 3; and { x = 3; } as the target of an **if** statement?

26. Use indentation, spacing and multiple lines to make the following program more readable.

```
/* This program computes and prints the sum of the first 10 positive
integers */ class SumFrom1To10{public static void main(String[] args){int
sum,i;sum=0;for(i=1;i<=10;i++) sum=sum+i;System.out.println("The sum
1 + 2+...+10 is "+sum);}}
```

27. Suggest more appropriate names for the class and the variables in the following program.

```
/* This program converts Fahrenheit to Celsius. */
class XXX {
```

```
  public static void main(String[] args) {
    double x, xx;


    x = 62;
    xx = (x-32) * 5.0/9.0;
    System.out.println(x + " degrees Fahrenheit is " +
                    xx + " degrees Celsius.");
  }
}
```

28. Assume **x** is a variable that is declared as type **int**. What is wrong with each of the following statements?

   A. `x = 3.5;`

   B. `if(x = 3) x = 4;`

   C. `x = "34";`

29. Write a program that prints out the first 20 squares (1, 4, 9, 16, ..., 400), one per line. Use a **for** loop.

30. Modify your answer to Exercise 29 so that it prints the sum of the first 20 squares $(1 + 4 + 9 + 16 + \cdots + 400)$.

31. Modify your answer to Exercise 30 so that it finds and displays the average of the first 20 squares.

Introducing Data Types and Operators

At the foundation of any programming language are its data types and operators, and Java is no exception. These elements define the limits of a language and determine the kind of tasks to which it can be applied. Fortunately, Java supports a rich assortment of both data types and operators, making it suitable for nearly any type of programming.

Data types and operators are a large subject. We will begin here with an examination of Java's foundational data types and its most commonly used operators. We will also take a closer look at variables and examine the expression.

WHY DATA TYPES ARE IMPORTANT

Data types are especially important in Java because it is a strongly typed language. This means that the compiler type-checks all operations for type compatibility. Illegal operations will not be compiled. Thus, strong type checking helps prevent errors and enhances reliability. To enable strong type checking, all variables, expressions,

TABLE 2-1: Java's Built-in Primitive Data Types	
Type	**Meaning**
boolean	Represents true/false values
byte	8-bit integer
char	Character
double	Double-precision floating point
float	Single-precision floating point
int	Integer
long	Long integer
short	Short integer

and values have a type. There is no concept of a "type-less" variable, for example. Furthermore, the type of a value determines what operations are allowed on it. An operation allowed on one type might not be allowed on another.

JAVA'S PRIMITIVE TYPES

Java contains two general categories of built-in data types: object-oriented and non-object-oriented. Java's object-oriented types are defined by classes, and a discussion of classes is deferred until later. However, at the core of Java are eight primitive (also called elemental or simple) types of data, which are shown in Table 2-1. The term *primitive* is used here to indicate that these types are not objects in an object-oriented sense, but rather, normal binary values. These primitive types are not objects because of efficiency concerns.

Java strictly specifies a range and behavior for each primitive type, which all implementations of the Java Virtual Machine must support. Because of Java's portability requirement, Java is uncompromising on this account. For example, an **int** is the same in all execution environments. This allows programs to be fully portable. There is no need to rewrite code to fit a specific platform. Although strictly specifying the range of the primitive types may cause a small loss of performance in some environments, it is necessary in order to achieve portability.

Integers

Java defines four integer types: **byte**, **short**, **int**, and **long**, which are shown here:

Type	Width in Bits	Range
byte	8	−128 to 127
short	16	−32,768 to 32,767
int	32	−2,147,483,648 to 2,147,483,647
long	64	−9,223,372,036,854,775,808 to 9,223,372,036,854,775,807

As the table shows, all of the integer types are signed positive and negative values. Java does not support unsigned (positive-only) integers. Many other computer languages support both signed and unsigned integers. However, Java's designers felt that unsigned integers were unnecessary.

Note: Technically, the Java run-time system can use any size it wants to store a primitive type. However, in all cases, types must act as specified.

The most commonly used integer type is **int**. Variables of type **int** are often employed to control loops, to index arrays, and to perform general-purpose integer math.

When you need an integer that has a range greater than **int**, use **long**. For example, here is a program that computes the number of cubic inches contained in a cube that is one mile, by one mile, by one mile:

```
/*
  Compute the number of cubic inches
  in 1 cubic mile.
*/
class Inches {
  public static void main(String[] args) {
    long cubicInches;
    long inchesPerMile;

    // compute the number of inches in a mile
    inchesPerMile = 5280 * 12;

    // compute the number of cubic inches
    cubicInches = inchesPerMile * inchesPerMile * inchesPerMile;

    System.out.println("There are " + cubicInches +
                       " cubic inches in a cubic mile.");
  }
}
```

Recall that a mile is 5,280 feet. Therefore, to compute the number of cubic inches in a cubic mile, first, the number of inches in a mile is obtained, and then that value is used to compute the volume. The output from the program is shown here:

```
There are 254358061056000 cubic inches in a cubic mile.
```

Clearly, the result could not have been held in an **int** variable.

The smallest integer type is **byte**. Variables of type **byte** are especially useful when working with raw binary data that may not be directly compatible with Java's other built-in types. The **short** type creates a short integer. Variables of type **short** are appropriate when you want to conserve memory and don't need the larger range offered by **int**.

Ask the Expert

Q You say that there are four integer types: **int**, **short**, **long**, and **byte**. However, I have heard that **char** can also be categorized as an integer type in Java. Can you explain?

A The formal specification for Java defines a type category called integral types, which include **byte**, **short**, **int**, **long**, and **char**. They are called integral types because they all hold whole-number, binary values. However, the purpose of the first four is to represent numeric integer quantities. The purpose of **char** is to represent characters. Therefore, the principal uses of **char** and the principal uses of the other integral types are fundamentally different. Because of the differences, the **char** type is treated separately in this book.

Floating-Point Types

As explained in Chapter 1, the floating-point types can represent numbers that have fractional components. There are two kinds of floating-point types, **float** and **double**, which represent single- and double-precision numbers, respectively. Type **float** is 32 bits wide and type **double** is 64 bits wide. The size differences mean that the largest **float** literal is approximately 3.4×10^{38} and the largest **double** literal is approximately 1.8×10^{308}.

Of the two, **double** is the most commonly used because all of the math functions in Java's class library use **double** values. For example, the **sqrt( )** method (which is defined by the standard **Math** class) returns a **double** value that is the square root of its **double** argument. Here, **sqrt( )** is used to compute the length of the hypotenuse, given the lengths of the two opposing sides:

```
/*
   Use the Pythagorean theorem to
   find the length of the hypotenuse
   given the lengths of the two opposing
   sides.
*/
class Hypotenuse {
  public static void main(String[] args) {
    double side1, side2, hypot;

    side1 = 3;
    side2 = 4;


    hypot = Math.sqrt(side1*side1 + side2*side2);

    System.out.println("Hypotenuse is " + hypot);
  }
}
```

Notice how **sqrt( )** is called. It is preceded by the name of the class of which it is a member.

The output from the program is shown here:

```
Hypotenuse is 5.0
```

One other point about the preceding example: As mentioned, **sqrt( )** is a member of the standard **Math** class. Notice how **sqrt( )** is called; it is preceded by the name **Math**. This is similar to the way **System.out** precedes **println( )**. Although not all standard methods are called by specifying their class name first, several are.

Characters

In Java, characters are not 8-bit quantities like they are in many other computer languages. Instead, Java uses 16-bit characters. The reason for this difference is that Java supports *Unicode* characters. *Unicode* defines a character set that can represent the characters found in all human languages. Originally, Unicode was designed as a 16-bit quantity, and Java reflected this fact by making **char** 16 bits long. In Java, **char** is an unsigned 16-bit type having a range of 0 to 65,535. The standard 8-bit ASCII character set is a subset of Unicode and ranges from 0 to 127. Thus, the ASCII characters are still valid Java characters. (ASCII stands for American Standard Code for Information Interchange.)

A character variable can be assigned a value by enclosing the character in single quotes. For example, this assigns the variable **ch** the letter X:

```
char ch;
ch = 'X';
```

You can output a **char** value using a **println( )** statement. For example, this line outputs the value in **ch**:

```
System.out.println("This is ch: " + ch);
```

Since **char** is an unsigned 16-bit type, it is possible to perform various arithmetic manipulations on a **char** variable. For example, consider the following program:

```
// Character variables can be handled like integers.
class CharArithDemo {
  public static void main(String[] args) {
    char ch;

    ch = 'X';
    System.out.println("ch contains " + ch);

    ch++; // increment ch  ←————————— A char can be incremented.
    System.out.println("ch is now " + ch);

    ch = 90; // give ch the value Z  ←————————— A char can be assigned an integer value.
    System.out.println("ch is now " + ch);
  }
}
```

The output generated by this program is shown here:

```
ch contains X
ch is now Y
ch is now Z
```

In the program, **ch** is first given the value X. Next, **ch** is incremented. This results in **ch** containing Y, the next character in the ASCII (and Unicode) sequence. Next, **ch** is assigned the value 90, which is the ASCII (and Unicode) value that corresponds to the letter Z. Since the ASCII character set occupies the first 127 values in the Unicode character set, all the "old tricks" that programmers have used with characters in other languages will work in Java, too.

Ask the Expert

Q Why does Java use Unicode?

A Java was designed for worldwide use. Thus, it needs to use a character set that can represent the world's languages. Unicode is the standard character set designed expressly for this purpose. Of course, the use of Unicode is inefficient for languages such as English, German, Spanish, or French, whose characters can be contained within 8 bits. But such is the price that must be paid for global portability.

The Boolean Type

The **boolean** type represents true/false values. Java defines the values true and false using the reserved words **true** and **false**. Thus, a variable or expression of type **boolean** will be one of these two values.

Here is a program that demonstrates the **boolean** type:

```
// Demonstrate boolean values.
class BoolDemo {
  public static void main(String[] args) {
    boolean b;

    b = false;
    System.out.println("b is " + b);
    b = true;
    System.out.println("b is " + b);

    // a boolean value can control the if statement
    if(b) System.out.println("This is executed.");

    b = false;
    if(b) System.out.println("This is not executed.");

    // outcome of a relational operator is a boolean value
    System.out.println("10 > 9 is " + (10 > 9));
  }
}
```

The output generated by this program is shown here:

```
b is false
b is true
This is executed.
10 > 9 is true
```

There are three interesting things to notice about this program. First, as you can see, when a **boolean** value is output by **println( )**, "true" or "false" is displayed. Second, the value of a **boolean** variable is sufficient, by itself, to control the **if** statement. There is no need to write an **if** statement like this:

```
if (b == true) ...
```

Third, the outcome of a relational operator, such as <, is a **boolean** value. This is why the expression **10 > 9** displays the value "true". Further, the extra set of parentheses around **10 > 9** is necessary because the + operator has a higher *precedence* than the >. When one operator has a higher precedence than another, it means that it is evaluated before the other in an expression.

Progress Check

1. What are Java's integer types?
2. What is Unicode?
3. What values can a **boolean** variable have?

TRY THIS 2-1 How Far Away Is the Lightning?

Sound.java

In this project you will create a program that computes how far away, in feet, a listener is from a lightning strike. Sound travels approximately 1,100 feet per second through air. Thus, knowing the interval between the time you see a lightning bolt and the time the sound reaches you enables you to compute the distance to the lightning. For this program, assume that the time interval is 7.2 seconds.

Answers:

1. Java's integer types are **byte**, **short**, **int**, and **long**.
2. Unicode is an international, multilingual character set.
3. Variables of type **boolean** can be either **true** or **false**.

STEP-BY-STEP

1. Create a new file called **Sound.java**.

2. To compute the distance, you will need to use floating-point values. Why? Because the time interval, 7.2, has a fractional component. Although it would be permissible to use a value of type **float**, we will use **double** in the example.

3. To compute the distance, you will multiply 7.2 by 1,100. You will then assign this value to a variable.

4. Finally, you will display the result.

5. Here is the entire **Sound.java** program:

```
/*
   Try This 2-1

   Compute the distance to a lightning
   strike whose sound takes 7.2 seconds
   to reach you.
*/
class Sound {
  public static void main(String[] args) {
    double distance;

    distance = 7.2 * 1100;

    System.out.println("The lightning is approximately " + distance +
                       " feet away.");
  }
}
```

6. Compile and run the program. The following result is displayed:

```
The lightning is approximately 7920.0 feet away.
```

7. Extra challenge: You can compute the distance to a large object, such as a rock wall, by timing the echo. For example, if you clap your hands and time how long it takes for you to hear the echo, then you know the total round-trip time. Dividing this value by 2 yields the time it takes the sound to go one way. You can then use this value to compute the distance to the object. Modify the preceding program so that it computes the distance, assuming that the time interval is that of an echo.

LITERALS

In Java, *literals* refer to fixed values that are represented in their human-readable form. For example, the number 100 is a literal. Literals are also commonly called *constants*. For the most part, literals, and their usage, are so intuitive that they have been used in one form or another by all the preceding sample programs. Now the time has come to explain them formally.

Java literals can be of any of the primitive data types. The way each literal is represented depends on its type. As explained earlier, character constants are enclosed in single quotes. For example, 'a' and '%' are both character constants.

Integer literals are specified as numbers without fractional components. For example, 10 and –100 are integer literals. Floating-point literals require the use of the decimal point followed by the number's fractional component. For example, 11.123 is a floating-point literal. Java also allows you to use scientific notation for floating-point numbers. To do so, specify the mantissa followed by either an **E** or an **e**, followed by the exponent (which must be an integer). For example, 1.234E2 represents the value 123.4, and 1.234E-2 represents the value 0.01234.

By default, integer literals are of type **int**. If you want to specify a **long** literal, append an l or an L. For example, 12 is an **int**, but 12L is a **long**.

By default, floating-point literals are of type **double**. To specify a **float** literal, append an F or f to the constant. For example, 10.19F is of type **float**.

Although integer literals create an **int** value by default, they can still be assigned to variables of type **char**, **byte**, or **short** as long as the value being assigned can be represented by the target type. An integer literal can always be assigned to a **long** variable.

Beginning with JDK 7, you can embed one or more underscores into an integer or floating-point literal. Doing so can make it easier to read values consisting of many digits. When the literal is compiled, the underscores are simply discarded. Here is an example:

```
123_45_1234
```

This specifies the value 123,451,234. The use of underscores is particularly useful when encoding things such as part numbers, customer IDs, and status codes that are commonly thought of as consisting of subgroups of digits.

Hexadecimal, Octal, and Binary Literals

In programming it is sometimes easier to use a number system based on 8 or 16 instead of 10. The number system based on 8 is called *octal*, and it uses the digits 0 through 7. In octal the number 10 is the same as 8 in decimal. The base 16 number system is called *hexadecimal* and uses the digits 0 through 9 plus the letters A through F (or, a through f), which stand for 10, 11, 12, 13, 14, and 15. For example, the hexadecimal number 10 is 16 in decimal. Because of the frequency with which these two number systems are used, Java allows you to specify integer literals in hexadecimal or octal instead of decimal. A hexadecimal literal must begin with **0x** or **0X** (a zero followed by an x or X). An octal literal begins with a zero. Here are some examples:

```
hex = 0xFF; // 255 in decimal
oct = 011; // 9 in decimal
```

As a point of interest, Java also allows hexadecimal floating-point literals, but they are seldom used.

Beginning with JDK 7, it is possible to specify an integer literal by use of binary. To do so, precede the binary number with a **0b** or **0B**. For example, this specifies the value 12 in binary: **0b1100**.

TABLE 2-2: Character Escape Sequences	
Escape Sequence	**Description**
\'	Single quote
\"	Double quote
\\	Backslash
\r	Carriage return
\n	Newline
\f	Form feed
\t	Horizontal tab
\b	Backspace
ddd	Octal constant (where *ddd* is an octal constant)
\u*xxxx*	Hexadecimal constant (where *xxxx* is a hexadecimal constant)

Character Escape Sequences

Enclosing character constants in single quotes works for most printing characters, but a few characters, such as the carriage return, pose a special problem when a text editor is used. In addition, certain other characters, such as the single and double quotes, have special meaning in Java, so you cannot use them directly. For these reasons, Java provides special *escape sequences*, sometimes referred to as backslash character constants, shown in Table 2-2. These sequences are used in place of the characters that they represent.

For example, this assigns **ch** the tab character:

```
ch = '\t';
```

The next example assigns a single quote to **ch**:

```
ch = '\'';
```

String Literals

Java supports one other type of literal: the string. A *string* is a set of characters enclosed by double quotes. For example,

```
"this is a test"
```

is a string. You have seen examples of strings in many of the **println( )** statements in the preceding sample programs.

In addition to normal characters, a string literal can also contain one or more of the escape sequences just described. For example, consider the following program. It uses the **\n** and **\t** escape sequences.

```
// Demonstrate escape sequences in strings.
class StrDemo {
  public static void main(String[] args) {
```

```
        System.out.println("First line\nSecond line");
      System.out.println("A\tB\tC");
      System.out.println("D\tE\tF") ;                      Use \n to generate a new line.
    }
  }
}
              Use tabs to align output.
```

The output is shown here:

```
First line
Second line
A          B          C
D          E          F
```

Notice how the **\n** escape sequence is used to generate a new line. You don't need to use multiple **println( )** statements to get multiline output. Just embed **\n** within a longer string at the points where you want the new lines to occur.

Progress Check

1. What is the type of the literal 10? What is the type of the literal 10.0?
2. How do you specify a **long** literal?
3. Is "x" a string or a character literal?

Ask the Expert

Q Is a string consisting of a single character the same as a character literal? For example, is "k" the same as 'k'?

A No. You must not confuse strings with characters. A character literal represents a single letter of type **char**. A string containing only one letter is still a string. Although strings consist of characters, they are not the same type.

A CLOSER LOOK AT VARIABLES

Variables were introduced in Chapter 1. Here, we will take a closer look at them. As you learned earlier, variables are declared using this form of statement,

type var-name;

Answers:

1. The literal 10 is an **int**, and 10.0 is a **double**.
2. A long literal is specified by adding the **L** or **l** suffix. For example, 100L.
3. The literal "x" is a string.

where *type* is the data type of the variable and *var-name* is its name. You can declare a variable of any valid type, including the simple types just described. When you declare a variable, you are creating an instance of its type. Thus, the capabilities of a variable are determined by its type. For example, a variable of type **boolean** can be used to store true/false values, but not floating-point values. Furthermore, the type of a variable cannot change during its lifetime. An **int** variable cannot turn into a **char** variable, for example.

All variables in Java must be declared prior to their use. This is necessary because the compiler must know what type of data a variable contains before it can properly compile any statement that uses the variable. It also enables Java to perform strict type checking.

Initializing a Variable

In general, you must give a variable a value prior to using it. One way to give a variable a value is through an assignment statement, as you have already seen. Another way is by giving it an initial value when it is declared. To do this, follow the variable's name with an equal sign and the value being assigned. The general form of initialization is shown here:

   type var = value;

Here, *value* is the value that is given to *var* when *var* is created. The value must be compatible with the specified type. Here are some examples:

```
int count = 10; // give count an initial value of 10
char ch = 'X'; // initialize ch with the letter X
float f = 1.2F; // f is initialized with 1.2
```

When declaring two or more variables of the same type using a comma-separated list, you can give one or more of those variables an initial value. For example:

```
int a, b = 8, c = 19, d; // b and c have initializations
```

In this case, only **b** and **c** are initialized.

Dynamic Initialization

Although the preceding examples have used only constants as initializers, Java allows variables to be initialized dynamically, using any expression valid at the time the variable is declared. For example, here is a short program that computes the volume of a cylinder given the radius of its base and its height:

```
// Demonstrate dynamic initialization.
class DynInit {
  public static void main(String[] args) {
    double radius = 4, height = 5;              volume is dynamically initialized at run time.

    // dynamically initialize volume
    double volume = 3.1416 * radius * radius * height;

    System.out.println("Volume is " + volume);
  }
}
```

Here, three local variables—**radius**, **height**, and **volume**—are declared. The first two, **radius** and **height**, are initialized by constants. However, **volume** is initialized dynamically to the volume of the cylinder. The key point here is that the initialization expression can use any element valid at the time of the initialization, including calls to methods, other variables, or literals.

THE SCOPE AND LIFETIME OF VARIABLES

So far, all of the variables that we have been using were declared at the start of the **main( )** method. However, Java allows variables to be declared within any block. As explained in Chapter 1, a block is begun with an opening brace and ended by a closing brace. A block defines a *scope*. Thus, each time you start a new block, you are creating a new scope. A scope determines what objects are visible to other parts of your program. It also determines the lifetime of those objects.

Many other computer languages define two general categories of scopes: global and local. Although supported by Java, these are not the best ways to categorize Java's scopes. The most important scopes in Java are those defined by a class and those defined by a method. A discussion of class scope (and variables declared within it) is deferred until later in this book, when classes are described. For now, we will examine only the scopes defined by or within a method.

The scope defined by a method begins with its opening brace. However, if that method has parameters, they too are included within the method's scope.

As a general rule, variables declared inside a scope are not visible (that is, accessible) to code that is defined outside that scope. Thus, when you declare a variable within a scope, you are localizing that variable and protecting it from unauthorized access and/or modification. Indeed, the scope rules provide the foundation for encapsulation.

Scopes can be nested. For example, each time you create a block of code, you are creating a new, nested scope. When this occurs, the outer scope encloses the inner scope. This means that objects declared in the outer scope will be visible to code within the inner scope. However, the reverse is not true. Objects declared within the inner scope will not be visible outside it.

To understand the effect of nested scopes, consider the following program:

```java
// Demonstrate block scope.
class ScopeDemo {
  public static void main(String[] args) {
    int x; // known to all code within main

    x = 10;
    if(x == 10) { // start new scope

      int y = 20; // known only to this block

      // x and y both known here.

      System.out.println("x and y: " + x + " " + y);
```

```
        x = y * 2;
    }
    // y = 100; // Error! y not known here  ◄────────── Here, y is outside of its scope.

    // x is still known here.
    System.out.println("x is " + x);
    }
}
```

As the comments indicate, the variable **x** is declared at the start of **main( )**'s scope and is accessible to all subsequent code within **main( )**. Within the **if** block, **y** is declared. Since a block defines a scope, **y** is visible only to other code within its block. This is why outside of its block, the line **y = 100;** is commented out. If you remove the leading comment symbol, a compile-time error will occur because **y** is not visible outside of its block. Within the **if** block, **x** can be used because code within a block (that is, a nested scope) has access to variables declared by an enclosing scope.

Within a block, variables can be declared at any point, but are valid only after they are declared. Thus, if you define a variable at the start of a method, it is available to all of the code within that method. Conversely, if you declare a variable at the end of a block, it is effectively useless because no code will have access to it.

Here is another important point to remember: variables are created when their scope is entered, and they are destroyed when their scope is left. This means that a variable will not hold its value once it has gone out of scope. Therefore, variables declared within a method will not hold their values between calls to that method. Also, a variable declared within a block will lose its value when the block is left. Thus, the lifetime of a variable is confined to its scope.

If a variable declaration includes an initializer, that variable will be reinitialized each time the block in which it is declared is entered. For example, consider this program:

```
// Demonstrate lifetime of a variable.
class VarInitDemo {
  public static void main(String[] args) {
    int x;

    for(x = 0; x < 3; x++) {
      int y = -1; // y is initialized each time block is entered
      System.out.println("y is: " + y); // this always prints -1
      y = 100;
      System.out.println("y is now: " + y);
    }
  }
}
```

The output generated by this program is shown here:

```
y is: -1
y is now: 100
y is: -1
y is now: 100
y is: -1
y is now: 100
```

As you can see, **y** is always reinitialized to –1 each time the **for** loop is entered. Even though it is subsequently assigned the value 100, this value is lost.

There is one quirk to Java's scope rules that may surprise you: although blocks can be nested, within a method no variable declared within an inner scope can have the same name as a variable declared by an enclosing scope. For example, the following program, which tries to declare two separate variables with the same name, will not compile.

```
/*
    This program attempts to declare a variable
    in an inner scope with the same name as one
    defined in an outer scope.

    *** This program will not compile. ***
*/
class NestVar {
  public static void main(String[] args) {
     int count;  ◄─────────────────────────────────┐
                                                     │
     for(count = 0; count < 10; count = count+1) {   │
       System.out.println("This is count: " + count);│
                                                     │
       int count; // illegal!!! ◄──────────────── Can't declare count again because
                                                  it's already declared.
       for(count = 0; count < 2; count++)
          System.out.println("This program is in error!");
     }
   }
}
```

As a point of interest, in some other languages (most notably, C/C++) there is no restriction on the names that you give variables declared in an inner scope. Thus, in C/C++ the declaration of **count** within the block of the outer **for** loop is completely valid, and such a declaration hides the outer variable. The designers of Java felt that this name hiding could easily lead to programming errors and disallowed it.

Progress Check

1. What is a scope? How can one be created?
2. Where in a block can variables be declared?
3. In a block, when is a variable created? When is it destroyed?

Answers:

1. A scope defines the visibility and lifetime of an object. A block defines a scope.
2. A variable can be declared at any point within a block.
3. Inside a block, a variable is created when its declaration is encountered. It is destroyed when the block exits.

OPERATORS

Java provides a rich operator environment. An *operator* is a symbol that tells the compiler to perform a specific mathematical, logical, or other manipulation. Java has four general classes of operators: arithmetic, bitwise, relational, and logical. Java also defines some additional operators that handle certain special situations. This chapter will examine the arithmetic, relational, and logical operators. We will also examine the assignment operator. The bitwise and other special operators are examined later.

ARITHMETIC OPERATORS

A basic set of arithmetic operators were introduced in Chapter 1. Here is the complete set:

Operator	Meaning
+	Addition (also unary plus)
−	Subtraction (also unary minus)
*	Multiplication
/	Division
%	Modulus
++	Increment
− −	Decrement

The operators +, −, *, and / all work the same way in Java as they do in any other computer language (or algebra, for that matter). These can be applied to any built-in numeric data type. They can also be used on objects of type **char**.

Although the actions of arithmetic operators are well known to all readers, a few special situations warrant some explanation. First, remember that when / is applied to an integer, any remainder will be truncated; for example, 10/3 will equal 3 in integer division. You can obtain the remainder of this division by using the modulus operator **%**. It yields the remainder of an integer division. For example, 10 % 3 is 1. In Java, the **%** can be applied to both integer and floating-point types. Thus, 10.0 % 3.0 is also 1.The following program demonstrates the modulus operator.

```
// Demonstrate the % operator.
class ModDemo {
  public static void main(String[] args) {
    int iresult, irem;
    double dresult, drem;

    iresult = 10 / 3;
    irem = 10 % 3;

    dresult = 10.0 / 3.0;
    drem = 10.0 % 3.0;
```

```
     System.out.println("Result and remainder of 10 / 3: " +
                        iresult + " " + irem);
     System.out.println("Result and remainder of 10.0 / 3.0: " +
                        dresult + " " + drem);
   }
}
```

The output from the program is shown here:

```
Result and remainder of 10 / 3: 3 1
Result and remainder of 10.0 / 3.0: 3.3333333333333335 1.0
```

As you can see, the **%** yields a remainder of 1 for both integer and floating-point operations.

Increment and Decrement

Introduced in Chapter 1, the **++** and the **−−** are Java's increment and decrement operators. As you will see, they have some special properties that make them quite interesting. Let's begin by reviewing precisely what the increment and decrement operators do.

The increment operator adds 1 to its operand, and the decrement operator subtracts 1. Therefore,

```
x = x + 1;
```

is the same as

```
x++;
```

and

```
x = x - 1;
```

is the same as

```
x--;
```

Both the increment and decrement operators can either precede (prefix) or follow (postfix) the operand. For example,

```
x = x + 1;
```

can be written as

```
++x; // prefix form
```

or as

```
x++; // postfix form
```

In the foregoing example, there is no difference whether the increment is applied as a prefix or a postfix. However, when an increment or decrement is used as part of a larger expression, there is an important difference. When an increment or decrement operator precedes its operand, Java will perform the corresponding operation prior to obtaining the operand's value for use by the rest of the expression. If the operator follows its operand, Java will obtain the operand's value before incrementing or decrementing it. Consider the following:

```
x = 10;
y = ++x;
```

In this case, **y** will be set to 11. However, if the code is written as

```
x = 10;
y = x++;
```

then **y** will be set to 10. In both cases, **x** is still set to 11; the difference is when it happens. In complicated arithmetic expressions, there can be significant advantages in being able to control when the increment or decrement operation takes place.

RELATIONAL AND LOGICAL OPERATORS

In the terms *relational operator* and *logical operator, relational* refers to the relationships that values can have with one another, and *logical* refers to the ways in which true and false values can be connected together. Since the relational operators produce true or false results, they often work with the logical operators. For this reason they will be discussed together here.

The relational operators were introduced in Chapter 1. They are shown again here for convenience:

Operator	Meaning
= =	Equal to
!=	Not equal to
>	Greater than
<	Less than
>=	Greater than or equal to
<=	Less than or equal to

The logical operators are shown next:

Operator	Meaning
&	AND
|	OR
^	XOR (exclusive OR)
||	Short-circuit OR
&&	Short-circuit AND
!	NOT

The outcome of the relational and logical operators is a **boolean** value.

In Java, all objects can be compared for equality or inequality using = = and !=. However, the comparison operators, <, >, <=, or >=, can be applied only to those types that support an ordering relationship. Therefore, all of the relational operators can be applied to all numeric types and to type **char**. However, values of type **boolean** can only be compared for equality or inequality, since the **true** and **false** values are not ordered. For example, **true** > **false** has no meaning in Java.

For the logical operators, the operands must be of type **boolean**, and the result of a logical operation is of type **boolean**. The logical operators, **&**, **|**, **^**, and **!**, support the basic logical operations AND, OR, XOR, and NOT, according to the following truth table.

p	q	p & q	p | q	p ^ q	!p
False	False	False	False	False	True
True	False	False	True	True	False
False	True	False	True	True	True
True	True	True	True	False	False

As the table shows, the outcome of an exclusive OR operation is true when exactly one and only one operand is true.

Here is a program that demonstrates several of the relational and logical operators:

```java
// Demonstrate the relational and logical operators.
class RelLogOps {
  public static void main(String[] args) {
    int i, j;
    boolean b1, b2;

    i = 10;
    j = 11;
    if(i < j) System.out.println("i < j");
    if(i <= j) System.out.println("i <= j");
    if(i != j) System.out.println("i != j");
    if(i == j) System.out.println("this won't execute");
    if(i >= j) System.out.println("this won't execute");
    if(i > j) System.out.println("this won't execute");

    b1 = true;
    b2 = false;
    if(b1 & b2) System.out.println("this won't execute");
    if(!(b1 & b2)) System.out.println("!(b1 & b2) is true");
    if(b1 | b2) System.out.println("b1 | b2 is true");
    if(b1 ^ b2) System.out.println("b1 ^ b2 is true");
  }
}
```

The output from the program is shown here:

```
i < j
i <= j
```

```
i != j
!(b1 & b2) is true
b1 | b2 is true
b1 ^ b2 is true
```

SHORT-CIRCUIT LOGICAL OPERATORS

Java supplies special *short-circuit* versions of its AND and OR logical operators that can be used to produce more efficient code. To understand why, consider the following. In an AND operation, if the first operand is false, the outcome is false no matter what value the second operand has. In an OR operation, if the first operand is true, the outcome of the operation is true no matter what the value of the second operand. Thus, in these two cases there is no need to evaluate the second operand. By not evaluating the second operand, time is saved and more efficient code is produced.

The short-circuit AND operator is **&&**, and the short-circuit OR operator is **||**. Their normal counterparts are **&** and **|**, respectively. The only difference between the normal and short-circuit versions is that the normal operands will always evaluate each operand, but short-circuit versions will evaluate the second operand only when necessary.

Here is a program that demonstrates the short-circuit AND operator. The program determines whether the value in **d** is a factor of **n**. It does this by performing a modulus operation. If the remainder of **n / d** is zero, then **d** is a factor. However, since the modulus operation involves a division, the short-circuit form of the AND is used to prevent a divide-by-zero error.

```java
// Demonstrate the short-circuit operators.
class SCops {
  public static void main(String[] args) {
    int n, d, q;

    n = 10;
    d = 2;
    if(d != 0 && (n % d) == 0)
      System.out.println(d + " is a factor of " + n);

    d = 0; // now, set d to zero

    // Since d is zero, the second operand is not evaluated.
    if(d != 0 && (n % d) == 0)                           The short-circuit opera-
      System.out.println(d + " is a factor of " + n);    tor prevents a division
                                                          by zero.
    /* Now, try same thing without short-circuit operator.
       This will cause a divide-by-zero error.
    */
    if(d != 0 & (n % d) == 0)                            Now both expressions
      System.out.println(d + " is a factor of " + n);    are evaluated, allowing a
  }                                                       division by zero to occur.
}
```

To prevent a divide-by-zero, the **if** statement first checks to see if **d** is equal to zero. If it is, the short-circuit AND stops at that point and does not perform the modulus division. Thus, in the first test, **d** is 2 and the modulus operation is performed. The second test fails because **d** is set to zero, and the modulus operation is skipped, avoiding a divide-by-zero error. Finally, the normal AND operator is tried. This causes both operands to be evaluated, which leads to a run-time error when the division by zero occurs.

One last point: the formal specification for Java refers to the short-circuit operators as the *conditional-or* and the *conditional-and* operators, but the term "short-circuit" is commonly used.

Progress Check

1. What does the % operator do? To what types can it be applied?
2. What type of values can be used as operands of the logical operators?
3. Does a short-circuit operator always evaluate both of its operands?

Ask the Expert

Q Since the short-circuit operators are, in some cases, more efficient than their normal counterparts, why does Java still offer the normal AND and OR operators?

A In some cases you will want both operands of an AND or OR operation to be evaluated because of the side effects produced. Consider the following:

```
// Side effects can be important.
class SideEffects {
  public static void main(String[] args) {
    int i;

    i = 0;

    /* Here, i is still incremented even though
       the if statement fails. */
    if(false & (++i < 100))
      System.out.println("this won't be displayed");
```

Answers:

1. The % is the modulus operator, which returns the remainder of an integer division. It can be applied to all of the numeric types.
2. The logical operators must have operands of type **boolean**.
3. No, a short-circuit operator evaluates its second operand only if the outcome of the operation cannot be determined solely by its first operand.

Ask the Expert (Continued)

```
      System.out.println("if statement executed: " + i); // displays 1


      /* In this case, i is not incremented because
         the short-circuit operator skips the increment. */
      if(false && (++i < 100))
        System.out.println("this won't be displayed");
      System.out.println("if statement executed: " + i); // still 1 !!
    }
}
```

As the comments indicate, in the first **if** statement, **i** is incremented whether the **if** succeeds or not. However, when the short-circuit operator is used, the variable **i** is not incremented when the first operand is false. The lesson here is that if your code expects the right-hand operand of an AND or OR operation to be evaluated, you must use Java's non-short-circuit forms of these operations.

THE ASSIGNMENT OPERATOR

You have been using the assignment operator since Chapter 1. Now it is time to take a formal look at it. The *assignment operator* is the single equal sign, =. This operator works in Java much as it does in any other computer language. It has this general form:

> *var = expression;*

Here, the type of *var* must be compatible with the type of *expression*.

The assignment operator does have one interesting attribute that you may not be familiar with: it allows you to create a chain of assignments. For example, consider this fragment:

```
int x, y, z;

x = y = z = 100; // set x, y, and z to 100
```

This fragment sets the variables **x**, **y**, and **z** to 100 using a single statement. This works because the = is an operator that yields the value of the right-hand expression. Thus, the value of **z = 100** is 100, which is then assigned to **y**, which in turn is assigned to **x**. Using a "chain of assignment" is an easy way to set a group of variables to a common value.

SHORTHAND ASSIGNMENTS

Java provides special *shorthand* assignment operators that simplify the coding of certain assignment statements. Let's begin with an example. The assignment statement shown here

```
x = x + 10;
```

can be written, using Java shorthand, as

```
x += 10;
```

The operator pair += tells the compiler to assign to **x** the value of **x** plus 10. Here is another example. The statement

```
x = x - 100;
```

is the same as

```
x -= 100;
```

Both statements assign to **x** the value of **x** minus 100.

This shorthand will work for all the binary operators in Java (that is, those that require two operands). The general form of the shorthand is

var op = expression;

Thus, the arithmetic and logical shorthand assignment operators are the following:

+=	– =	*=	/=
%=	&=	|=	^=

Because these operators combine an operation with an assignment, they are formally referred to as *compound assignment operators*.

The compound assignment operators provide two benefits. First, they are more compact than their "longhand" equivalents. Second, in some cases, more efficient bytecode can be generated. For these reasons, you will often see the compound assignment operators used in professionally written Java programs.

TYPE CONVERSION IN ASSIGNMENTS

In programming, it is common to assign one type of variable to another. For example, you might want to assign an **int** value to a **float** variable, as shown here:

```
int i;
float f;

i = 10;
f = i; // assign an int to a float
```

When compatible types are mixed in an assignment, the value of the right side is automatically converted to the type of the left side. Thus, in the preceding fragment, the valuc in **i** is converted into a **float** and then assigned to **f**. However, because of Java's strict type checking, not all types are compatible, and thus, not all type conversions are implicitly allowed. For example, **boolean** and **int** are not compatible.

When one type of data is assigned to another type of variable, an *automatic type conversion* will take place if

- The two types are compatible.
- The destination type is larger than the source type.

When these two conditions are met, a widening conversion takes place. For example, the **int** type is always large enough to hold all valid **byte** values, and both **int** and **byte** are integer types, so an automatic conversion from **byte** to **int** can be applied.

For widening conversions, the numeric types, including integer and floating-point types, are compatible with each other. For example, the following program is perfectly valid since **long** to **double** is a widening conversion that is automatically performed.

```
// Demonstrate automatic conversion from long to double.
class LtoD {
  public static void main(String[] args) {
    long longVar;
    double doubleVar;

    longVar = 100123285L;
    doubleVar = longVar;        ◄——————— Automatic conversion from long to double

    System.out.println("longVar and doubleVar: " +
                       longVar + " " + doubleVar);
  }
}
```

Although there is an automatic conversion from **long** to **double**, there is no automatic conversion from **double** to **long**, since this is not a widening conversion. Thus, the following version of the preceding program is invalid.

```
// *** This program will not compile. ***
class DtoL {
  public static void main(String[] args) {
    long longVar;
    double doubleVar;

    doubleVar = 100123285.0;
    longVar = doubleVar; // Illegal!!!  ◄——— No automatic conversion from double to long

    System.out.println("longVar and doubleVar: " +
                       longVar + " " + doubleVar);
  }
}
```

There are no automatic conversions from the numeric types to **char** or **boolean**. Also, **char** and **boolean** are not compatible with each other. However, an integer literal can be assigned to **char**.

USING A CAST

Although the automatic type conversions are helpful, they will not fulfill all programming needs because they apply only to widening conversions between compatible types. For all other cases you must employ a cast. A *cast* is an instruction to the compiler to convert one type into another. Thus, it requests an explicit type conversion. A cast has this general form:

(*target-type*) *expression*

Here, *target-type* specifies the desired type to convert the specified expression to. For example, if you want to convert the type of the expression **x/y** to **int**, you can write

```
double x, y;
// ...
int z = (int) (x / y);
```

Here, even though **x** and **y** are of type **double**, the cast converts the outcome of the expression to **int**. The parentheses surrounding **x / y** are necessary. Otherwise, the cast to **int** would apply only to the **x** and not to the outcome of the division. The cast is necessary here because there is no automatic conversion from **double** to **int**.

When a cast involves a *narrowing conversion*, information might be lost. For example, when casting a **long** into a **short**, information will be lost if the **long**'s value is greater than the range of a **short** because its high-order bits are removed. When a floating-point value is cast to an integer type, the fractional component will also be lost due to truncation. For example, if the value 1.23 is assigned to an integer, the resulting value will simply be 1. The 0.23 is lost.

The following program demonstrates some type conversions that require casts:

```
// Demonstrate casting.
class CastDemo {
  public static void main(String[] args) {
    double x, y;
    byte b;
    int i;
    char ch;

    x = 10.0;
    y = 3.0;                                         ── Truncation will occur in this conversion.

    i = (int) (x / y); // cast double to int
    System.out.println("Integer outcome of x / y: " + i);

    i = 100;
    b = (byte) i; ◄────── No loss of info here. A byte can hold the value 100.
    System.out.println("Value of b: " + b);

    i = 257;
    b = (byte) i; ◄────── Information loss this time. A byte cannot hold the value 257.
    System.out.println("Value of b: " + b);

    b = 88; // ASCII code for X
    ch = (char) b; ◄────── Cast byte to char.
    System.out.println("ch: " + ch);
  }
}
```

The output from the program is shown here:

```
Integer outcome of x / y: 3
Value of b: 100
Value of b: 1
ch: X
```

TABLE 2-3: The Precedence of the Java Operators							
Highest							
++ (postfix)	– – (postfix)						
++ (prefix)	– – (prefix)	~	!	+ (unary)	– (unary)	(*type-cast*)	
*	/	%					
+	–						
>>	>>>	<<					
>	>=	<	<=	instanceof			
==	!=						
&							
^							
|							
&&							
||							
?:							
=	*op=*						
Lowest							

In the program, the cast of **(x / y)** to **int** results in the truncation of the fractional component, and information is lost. Next, no loss of information occurs when **b** is assigned the value 100 because a **byte** can hold the value 100. However, when the attempt is made to assign **b** the value 257, information loss occurs because 257 exceeds a **byte**'s maximum value. Finally, no information is lost, but a cast is needed when assigning a **byte** value to a **char**.

Progress Check

1. What is a cast?
2. Can a **short** be assigned to an **int** without a cast? Can a **byte** be assigned to a **char** without a cast?
3. How can the following statement be rewritten?
   ```
   x = x + 23;
   ```

OPERATOR PRECEDENCE

Table 2-3 shows the order of precedence for all Java operators, from highest to lowest. Operators on the same line have the same precedence. This table includes several

---

Answers:

1. A cast is an explicit conversion.
2. Yes. No.
3. `x += 23;`

operators that will be discussed later in this book. An operator's precedence determines at what point it is evaluated in an expression. An operator with a higher precedence will be evaluated before an operator with a lower precedence. For example, given the expression

$$10 - 4 * 2$$

The result is 2, not 12, because multiplication has a higher precedence than does subtraction. Except for assignment, operators with equal precedence are evaluated left to right. A chain of assignments is evaluated right to left. Although they are technically called *separators*, if you consider the **[ ]**, **( )**, and **.** to be operators, then they would have the highest precedence.

TRY THIS 2-2 — DISPLAY A TRUTH TABLE FOR THE LOGICAL OPERATORS

`LogicalOpTable.java`

In this project, you will create a program that displays the truth table for Java's logical operators. You must make the columns in the table line up. This project makes use of several features covered in this chapter, including one of Java's escape sequences and the logical operators. It also illustrates the differences in the precedence between the arithmetic **+** operator and the logical operators.

STEP-BY-STEP

1. Create a new file called **LogicalOpTable.java**.
2. To ensure that the columns line up, you will use the **\t** escape sequence to embed tabs into each output string. For example, this **println( )** statement displays the header for the table:

```
System.out.println("P\tQ\tAND\tOR\tXOR\tNOT");
```

3. Each subsequent line in the table will use tabs to position the outcome of each operation under its proper heading.
4. Here is the entire **LogicalOpTable.java** program. Enter it at this time.

```
// Try This 2-2: A truth table for the logical operators.
class LogicalOpTable {
  public static void main(String[] args) {

    boolean p, q;

    System.out.println("P\tQ\tAND\tOR\tXOR\tNOT");

    p = true; q = true;
    System.out.print(p + "\t" + q +"\t");
    System.out.print((p&q) + "\t" + (p|q) + "\t");
    System.out.println((p^q) + "\t" + (!p));

    p = true; q = false;
    System.out.print(p + "\t" + q +"\t");
```

```
          System.out.print((p&q) + "\t" + (p|q) + "\t");
          System.out.println((p^q) + "\t" + (!p));

          p = false; q = true;
          System.out.print(p + "\t" + q +"\t");
          System.out.print((p&q) + "\t" + (p|q) + "\t");
          System.out.println((p^q) + "\t" + (!p));

          p = false; q = false;
          System.out.print(p + "\t" + q +"\t");
          System.out.print((p&q) + "\t" + (p|q) + "\t");
          System.out.println((p^q) + "\t" + (!p));
     }
}
```

Notice the parentheses surrounding the logical operations inside the print statements. They are necessary because of the precedence of Java's operators. The + operator is higher than the logical operators.

5. Compile and run the program. The following table is displayed.

P	Q	AND	OR	XOR	NOT
true	true	true	true	false	false
true	false	false	true	true	false
false	true	false	true	true	true
false	false	false	false	false	true

6. On your own, try modifying the program so that it uses and displays 1's and 0's, rather than true and false. This may involve a bit more effort than you might at first think!

EXPRESSIONS

Operators, variables, and literals are constituents of *expressions*. When an expression is encountered in a program, it is evaluated. You probably already have a fairly good, intuitive understanding of expressions because they have been used in the preceding programs. Furthermore, Java expressions are similar to those found in algebra. However, a few aspects of expressions will be discussed now.

Type Conversion in Expressions

Within an expression, it is possible to mix two or more different types of data as long as they are compatible with each other. For example, you can mix **short** and **long** within an expression because they are both numeric types. When different types of data are mixed within an expression, they are all converted to the same type. This is accomplished through the use of Java's *type promotion rules*.

First, all **char**, **byte**, and **short** values are promoted to **int**. Then, if one operand is a **long**, the whole expression is promoted to **long**. If one operand is a **float** operand, the entire expression is promoted to **float**. If any of the operands is **double**, the result is **double**.

It is important to understand that type promotions apply only to the values operated upon when an expression is evaluated. For example, if the value of a **byte** variable is promoted to **int** inside an expression, outside the expression, the variable is still a **byte**. Type promotion only affects the evaluation of an expression.

Type promotion can, however, lead to somewhat unexpected results. For example, when an arithmetic operation involves two **byte** values, the following sequence occurs: First, the **byte** operands are promoted to **int**. Then the operation takes place, yielding an **int** result. Thus, the outcome of an operation involving two **byte** values will be an **int**. This is not what you might intuitively expect. Consider the following program:

```java
// A promotion surprise!
class PromDemo {
  public static void main(String[] args) {
    byte b;
    int i;                       No cast needed because result is already elevated to int.

    b = 10;
    i = b * b; // OK, no cast needed
                                 Cast is needed here to assign an int to a byte!
    b = 10;
    b = (byte) (b * b); // cast needed!!

    System.out.println("i and b: " + i + " " + b);
  }
}
```

Somewhat counterintuitively, no cast is needed when assigning **b*b** to **i**, because **b** is promoted to **int** when the expression is evaluated. However, when you try to assign **b * b** to **b**, you do need a cast—back to **byte**! Keep this in mind if you get unexpected type-incompatibility error messages on expressions that would otherwise seem perfectly fine.

This same sort of situation also occurs when performing operations on **char**s. For example, in the following fragment, the cast back to **char** is needed because of the promotion of **ch1** and **ch2** to **int** within the expression.

```java
char ch1 = 'a', ch2 = 'b';

ch1 = (char) (ch1 + ch2);
```

Without the cast, the result of adding **ch1** to **ch2** would be **int**, which can't be assigned to a **char**.

Casts are not only useful when converting between types in an assignment. For example, consider the following program. It uses a cast to **double** to obtain a fractional component from an otherwise integer division.

```java
// Using a cast.
class UseCast {
  public static void main(String[] args) {
    int i;
```

```
    for(i = 0; i < 5; i++) {
        System.out.println(i + " / 3: " + i / 3);
        System.out.println(i + " / 3 with fractions: "
                             + (double) i / 3);
        System.out.println();
    }
  }
}
```

The output from the program is shown here:

```
0 / 3: 0
0 / 3 with fractions: 0.0

1 / 3: 0
1 / 3 with fractions: 0.3333333333333333

2 / 3: 0
2 / 3 with fractions: 0.6666666666666666

3 / 3: 1
3 / 3 with fractions: 1.0

4 / 3: 1
4 / 3 with fractions: 1.3333333333333333
```

Spacing and Parentheses

An expression in Java may have tabs and spaces in it to make it more readable. For example, the following two expressions are the same, but the second is easier to read:

```
x=10/y*(127/x);
```

```
x = 10 / y * (127/x);
```

Parentheses increase the precedence of the operations contained within them, just as in algebra. Use of redundant or additional parentheses will not cause errors or slow down the execution of the expression. You are encouraged to use parentheses to make clear the exact order of evaluation, both for yourself and for others who may have to figure out your program later. For example, which of the following two expressions is easier to read?

```
x = y/3-34*temp+127;
```

```
x = (y/3) - (34*temp) + 127;
```

EXERCISES

1. Why does Java strictly specify the range and behavior of its primitive types?
2. What is Java's character type, and how does it differ from the character type used by some other programming languages?
3. A **boolean** value can have any value you like because any non-zero value is true. True or False?
4. Given this output,

   ```
   One
   Two
   Three
   ```

   using a single string, show the **println( )** statement that produced it.
5. What is wrong with this fragment?

   ```
   for(i = 0; i < 10; i++) {
      int sum;

      sum = sum + i;
   }
   System.out.println("Sum is: " + sum);
   ```

6. Explain the difference between the prefix and postfix forms of the increment operator.
7. Show how a short-circuit AND can be used to prevent a divide-by-zero error.
8. In an expression, what type are **byte** and **short** promoted to?
9. In general, when is a cast needed?
10. Write a program that finds all of the prime numbers between 2 and 100.
11. Does the use of redundant parentheses affect program performance?
12. Does a block define a scope?
13. In some languages, variables can hold values of any type. Why doesn't Java allow this behavior? That is, why does Java restrict variables to hold values of only one type, namely, the declared type of the variable?
14. Write a program that assigns the value 50000 to an integer variable **x**, assigns the value of **x*x** to an integer variable **y**, and then prints out the value of **y**. Did you get a strange answer? If so, explain why.
15. In the **BoolDemo** example, the following line of code appears:

    ```
    System.out.println("10 > 9 is " + (10 > 9));
    ```

    What would be printed (if anything) if the parentheses were removed and it just read:

    ```
    System.out.println("10 > 9 is " + 10 > 9);
    ```

Explain your answer.

16. Which of the following assignment statements are legal in Java? For each one that is not legal, explain why.

A. `int x = false;`

B. `int x = 3 > 4;`

C. `int x = (3 > 4);`

D. `int x = int y = 3;`

E. `int x = 3.14;`

F. `int x = 3.14L;`

G. `int x = 5,000,000;`

H. `int x = 5_000_000;`

I. `int x = '350';`

J. `int x = "350";`

K. `int x = '3';`

L. `boolean b = (boolean) 5;`

M. `byte b = (byte) 5;`

N. `double d = 1E3.5;`

O. `char c = '\/';`

P. `char c = '\\';`

Q. `char c = 3;`

R. `char c = "3";`

17. Which of the following expressions are legal in Java? If an expression is not legal, explain why. If it is legal, give its value. Assume **x** is an **int** variable with the value 5, **y** is a **double** variable with value 3.5, and **b** is a **boolean** variable with value **false**.

A. `(3 + 4 / 5)/3`

B. `3 * 4 % 5 / 2 * 6`

C. `3 + x++`

D. `3 + ++x`

E. `0/0`

F. `y/x`

G. `'a' + 'b'`

H. `'a' + 'b' + "c"`

I. `"3" + 2 + 1`

J. `"3" + (2 + 1)`

K. `false < true`

L. `false == true`

M. `'c' == 99`

N. `(3+4 > 5) & (4=6) | b`

O. `!((3>4)|(5!=5))&(3<(4*0))`

P. `!(3>4|5!=5&3<4*0)`

18. Suppose **a**, **b**, and **c** are **boolean** variables. Find one set of values for **a**, **b**, and **c** so that both expressions `(a & b | c)` and `(!a | !b & c)` are true.

19. If **x** is a variable of type **int** and its value is 5, then what is its value after the following sequence of statements has been executed?

```
x += 4;
x *= 2;
x /= 3;
x %= 4;
```

20. If **x** is a variable of type **boolean** and its value is **true**, then what is its value after the following sequence of statements has been executed?

```
x |= false;
x &= true;
x ^= true;
```

21. **Math.random( )** is a method in the Java library that computes a random **double** value between 0 and 1. For example, the statement

```
double x = Math.random();
```

assigns to the variable **x** a random **double** between 0 and 1. Write a program that tests how well **Math.random( )** works. More precisely, write a program that calls **Math.random( )** 1,000 times to create 1,000 values, keeping track of how many of them are greater than 0.5, and then prints out the result. Your program should theoretically print out a number very close to 500.

22. Write a program that creates three random **double** variables **a**, **b**, and **c** and assigns them values between 0 and 1 using the **Math.random( )** method mentioned in the preceding exercise. It then does all of the following:

A. It prints out the three values.

B. It prints "All are tiny" if all three values are less than 0.2.

C. It prints out "One is tiny" if exactly one of the three values is less than 0.2.

CHAPTER 3

Program Control Statements

KEY SKILLS & CONCEPTS

- Input characters from the keyboard
- Know the complete form of the **if** statement
- Use the **switch** statement
- Know the complete form of the **for** loop
- Use the **while** loop
- Use the **do-while** loop
- Use **break** to exit a loop
- Use **break** as a form of goto
- Apply **continue**
- Nest loops

In this chapter you will learn about the statements that control a program's flow of execution. Java's program control statements can be organized into the following categories:

- Selection statements
- Iteration statements
- Jump statements

Selection statements allow your program to choose between different paths of execution. Iteration statements enable a section of code to be repeated. Jump statements directly transfer program control from one location to another. Java's selection statements include **if** and **switch**; iteration statements include **for**, **while**, and **do-while**; and jump statements include **break**, **continue**, and **return**. Except for **return**, which is discussed in Chapter 4, the remaining control statements, including the **if** and **for** statements to which you have already had a brief introduction, are examined in detail here.

The chapter begins not by presenting the control statements, however, but by explaining how to perform some simple keyboard input. This short digression will allow you to begin writing interactive programs.

Note: Java's exception handling mechanism can also affect the flow of program execution. It is discussed in Chapter 10.

INPUT CHARACTERS FROM THE KEYBOARD

Up to this point, the sample programs in this book have displayed information *to* the user, but they have not received information *from* the user. Thus, you have been using console output but not console (keyboard) input. The main reason for this is that many of Java's input capabilities rely on or make use of features that are not discussed until later in this book. Also, many real-world Java programs and applets will be graphical and window based, not console based. For these reasons, not much use of console input is found in this book. However, there is one type of console input that is relatively easy to use: reading a character from the keyboard. Since several of the examples in this chapter will make use of this feature, it is discussed here.

To read a character from the keyboard we will use **System.in.read( )**. **System.in** is the complement to **System.out**. It is the input object attached to the keyboard. The **read( )** method waits until the user presses a key and then returns the result. The character is returned as an integer, so it must be cast into a **char** to assign it to a **char** variable. By default, console input is *line buffered*. Here, the term *buffer* refers to a small portion of memory that is used to hold the characters before they are read by your program. In this case, the buffer holds a complete line of text. Because the entire line is buffered, you must press ENTER before any character that you type will be sent to your program. Here is a program that shows how to read a character from the keyboard:

```
// Read a character from the keyboard.
class KbIn {
  public static void main(String[] args)
    throws java.io.IOException {

    char ch;

    System.out.print("Press a key followed by ENTER: ");

    ch = (char) System.in.read(); // get a char  ←————————Read a character
                                                           from the keyboard.
    System.out.println("Your key is: " + ch);
  }
}
```

Here is a sample run:

```
Press a key followed by ENTER: t
Your key is: t
```

In the program, notice that **main( )** begins like this:

```
public static void main(String[] args)
  throws java.io.IOException {
```

Because **System.in.read( )** is being used, the program must specify the **throws java. io.IOException** clause. This line is necessary to handle input errors. It is part of Java's exception handling mechanism, which is discussed in Chapter 10. For now, don't worry about its precise meaning.

The fact that **System.in** is line buffered is a source of annoyance at times. When you press ENTER, a carriage return, line feed sequence is entered into the input stream. (In some environments, only a line feed is entered into the input stream.) Furthermore, these characters are left pending in the input buffer until you read them. Thus, for some applications, you may need to remove them (by reading them) before the next input operation. You will see an example of this later in this chapter.

Progress Check

1. What is **System.in**?
2. How can you read a character typed at the keyboard?

THE if STATEMENT

Chapter 1 introduced the **if** statement. It is examined in detail here. The complete form of the **if** statement is

> if(*condition*) *statement*;
> else *statement*;

where the targets of the **if** and **else** are single statements. The **else** clause is optional. The targets of both the **if** and **else** can be blocks of statements. The general form of the **if**, using blocks of statements, is

> if(*condition*)
> {
>   *statement sequence*
> }
> else
> {
>   *statement sequence*
> }

Answers:

1. **System.in** is the input object linked to standard input, which is usually the keyboard.
2. To read a character, call **System.in.read( )**.

If the conditional expression is true, the target of the **if** will be executed; otherwise, if it exists, the target of the **else** will be executed. At no time will both of them be executed. The conditional expression controlling the **if** must produce a **boolean** result. To demonstrate the **if** (and several other control statements), we will create and develop a simple computerized guessing game that would be suitable for young children. In the first version of the game, the program asks the player for a letter between A and Z. If the player presses the correct letter on the keyboard, the program responds by printing the message **** Right ****. The program is shown here:

```
// Guess the letter game.
class Guess {
  public static void main(String[] args)
    throws java.io.IOException {

    char ch, answer = 'K';

    System.out.println("I'm thinking of a letter between A and Z.");
    System.out.print("Can you guess it: ");

    ch = (char) System.in.read(); // read a char from the keyboard

    if(ch == answer) System.out.println("** Right **");
  }
}
```

This program prompts the player and then reads a character from the keyboard. Using an **if** statement, it then checks that character against the answer, which is K in this case. If K was entered, the message is displayed. When you try this program, remember that the K must be entered in uppercase.

Taking the guessing game further, the next version uses the **else** to print a message when the wrong letter is picked.

```
// Guess the letter game, 2nd version.
class Guess2 {
  public static void main(String[] args)
    throws java.io.IOException {

    char ch, answer = 'K';

    System.out.println("I'm thinking of a letter between A and Z.");
    System.out.print("Can you guess it: ");

    ch = (char) System.in.read(); // get a char

    if(ch == answer) System.out.println("** Right **");
    else System.out.println("...Sorry, you're wrong.");
  }
}
```

NESTED ifs

A *nested if* is an **if** statement that is the target of another **if** or **else**. Nested **if**s are very common in programming because they give you a way to make a follow-up selection based on the outcome of the previous selection. The main thing to remember about nested **if**s in Java is that an **else** statement always refers to the nearest **if** statement that is within the same block as the **else** and not already associated with an **else**. Here is an example:

```java
if(i == 10) {
  if(j < 20) a = b;
  if(k > 100) c = d;
  else a = c; // this else refers to if(k > 100)
}
else a = d; // this else refers to if(i == 10)
```

As the comments indicate, the final **else** is not associated with **if(j < 20)** because it is not in the same block (even though it is the nearest **if** without an **else**). Rather, the final **else** is associated with **if(i == 10)**. The inner **else** refers to **if(k > 100)**, because it is the closest **if** within the same block.

You can use a nested **if** to add a further improvement to the guessing game. This addition provides the player with feedback about a wrong guess.

```java
// Guess the letter game, 3rd version.
class Guess3 {
  public static void main(String[] args)
    throws java.io.IOException {

    char ch, answer = 'K';

    System.out.println("I'm thinking of a letter between A and Z.");
    System.out.print("Can you guess it: ");

    ch = (char) System.in.read(); // get a char

    if(ch == answer) System.out.println("** Right **");
    else {
      System.out.print("...Sorry, you're ");

      // a nested if
      if(ch < answer) System.out.println("too low");
      else System.out.println("too high");
    }
  }
}
```

A sample run is shown here:

```
I'm thinking of a letter between A and Z.
Can you guess it: Z
...Sorry, you're too high
```

THE if-else-if LADDER

A common programming construct that is based on the nested **if** is sometimes referred to as the **if-else-if** *ladder*. It looks like this:

> if(*condition*)
>> *statement*;
>
> else if(*condition*)
>> *statement*;
>
> else if(*condition*)
>> *statement*;
>
>> .
>
>> .
>
>> .
>
> else
>> *statement*;

The conditional expressions are evaluated from the top downward. As soon as a true condition is found, the statement associated with it is executed, and the rest of the ladder is bypassed. If none of the conditions is true, the final **else** statement will be executed. The final **else** often acts as a default condition; that is, if all other conditional tests fail, the last **else** statement is performed. If there is no final **else** and all other conditions are false, no action will take place.

The following program demonstrates the **if-else-if** ladder:

```
// Demonstrate an if-else-if ladder.
class Ladder {
  public static void main(String[] args) {
    int x;

    for(x=0; x<6; x++) {
      if(x==1)
        System.out.println("x is one");
      else if(x==2)
        System.out.println("x is two");
      else if(x==3)
        System.out.println("x is three");
      else if(x==4)
        System.out.println("x is four");
      else
        System.out.println("x is not between 1 and 4");   ◄————This is the default
    }                                                          statement.
  }
}
```

The program produces the following output:

```
x is not between 1 and 4
x is one
x is two
x is three
x is four
x is not between 1 and 4
```

As you can see, the default **else** is executed only if none of the preceding **if** statements succeeds.

Progress Check

1. The condition controlling the **if** must be of what type?
2. To what **if** does an **else** always associate?
3. What is an **if-else-if** ladder?

THE switch STATEMENT

The second Java selection statement is the **switch**. The **switch** provides for a multiway branch. Thus, it enables a program to select among several alternatives. Although a series of nested **if** statements can perform multiway tests, for many situations the **switch** is a more efficient approach. It works like this: the value of an expression is successively tested against a list of constants. When a match is found, the statement sequence associated with that match is executed. The general form of the **switch** statement is

```
switch(expression) {
    case constant1:
        statement sequence
        break;
    case constant2:
        statement sequence
        break;
    case constant3:
        statement sequence
        break;
```

Answers:

1. The condition controlling an **if** must be of type **boolean**.
2. An **else** always associates with the nearest **if** in the same block that is not already associated with an **else**.
3. An **if-else-if** ladder is a sequence of nested **if-else** statements.

```
    default:
      statement sequence
  }
```

For versions of Java prior to JDK 7, the *expression* controlling the **switch** must be of type **byte**, **short**, **int**, **char**, or an enumeration. (Enumerations are described in Chapter 13.) Beginning with JDK 7, *expression* can also be of type **String**. This means that modern versions of Java can use a string to control a **switch**. (This technique is demonstrated in Chapter 5, when **String** is described.) Frequently, the expression controlling a **switch** is simply a variable rather than a larger expression.

Each value specified in the **case** statements must be a unique constant expression (such as a literal value). Duplicate **case** values are not allowed. The type of each value must be compatible with the type of the controlling expression.

The **default** statement sequence is executed if no **case** constant matches the expression. The **default** is optional; if it is not present, no action takes place if all matches fail. When a match is found, the statements associated with that **case** are executed until the **break** is encountered or, in the case of **default** or the last **case**, until the end of the **switch** is reached.

The following program demonstrates the **switch**.

```java
// Demonstrate the switch.
class SwitchDemo {
  public static void main(String[] args) {
    int i;

    for(i=0; i<10; i++)
      switch(i) {
        case 0:
          System.out.println("i is zero");
          break;
        case 1:
          System.out.println("i is one");
          break;
        case 2:
          System.out.println("i is two");
          break;
        case 3:
          System.out.println("i is three");
          break;
        case 4:
          System.out.println("i is four");
          break;
        default:
          System.out.println("i is five or more");
      }
  }
}
```

The output produced by this program is shown here:

```
i is zero
i is one
i is two
i is three
i is four
i is five or more
i is five or more
i is five or more
i is five or more
i is five or more
```

As you can see, each time through the loop, the statements associated with the **case** constant that matches **i** are executed. All others are bypassed. When **i** is five or greater, no **case** statements match, so the **default** statement is executed.

Technically, the **break** statement is optional, although most applications of the **switch** will use it. When encountered within the statement sequence of a **case**, the **break** statement causes program flow to exit from the entire **switch** statement and resume at the next statement outside the **switch**. However, if a **break** statement does not end the statement sequence associated with a **case**, then all the statements *at and following* the matching **case** will be executed until a **break** (or the end of the **switch**) is encountered.

For example, study the following program carefully. Before looking at the output, can you figure out what it will display on the screen?

```
// Demonstrate the switch without break statements.
class NoBreak {
  public static void main(String[] args) {
    int i;

    for(i=0; i<=5; i++) {
      switch(i) {
        case 0:
          System.out.println("i is less than one");
        case 1:
          System.out.println("i is less than two");
        case 2:
          System.out.println("i is less than three");
        case 3:
          System.out.println("i is less than four");
        case 4:
          System.out.println("i is less than five");
      }
      System.out.println();
    }
  }
}
```

The **case** statements fall through here.

This program displays the following output:

```
i is less than one
i is less than two
i is less than three
i is less than four
i is less than five

i is less than two
i is less than three
i is less than four
i is less than five

i is less than three
i is less than four
i is less than five

i is less than four
i is less than five

i is less than five
```

As this program illustrates, execution will continue into the next **case** if no **break** statement is present.

You can also have empty **case**s, as shown in this example:

```
switch(i) {
  case 1:
  case 2:
  case 3: System.out.println("i is 1, 2 or 3");
    break;
  case 4: System.out.println("i is 4");
    break;
}
```

In this fragment, if **i** has the value 1, 2, or 3, the first **println( )** statement executes. If it is 4, the second **println( )** statement executes. The "stacking" of **case**s, as shown in this example, is common when several **case**s share common code.

NESTED switch STATEMENTS

It is possible to have a **switch** as part of the statement sequence of an outer **switch**. This is called a *nested* **switch**. Even if the **case** constants of the inner and outer **switch** contain common values, no conflicts will arise. For example, the following code fragment is perfectly acceptable.

```
switch(ch1) {
  case 'A': System.out.println("This A is part of outer switch.");
    switch(ch2) {
      case 'A':
        System.out.println("This A is part of inner switch");
```

```
      break;
   case 'B': // ...
 } // end of inner switch
   break;
case 'B': // ...
```

Progress Check

1. The expression controlling the **switch** can be of what type?
2. When the **switch** expression matches a **case** constant, what happens?
3. If a **case** sequence does not end in **break**, what happens?

TRY THIS 3-1   START BUILDING A JAVA HELP SYSTEM

```
Help.java
```

This project builds a simple help system that displays the syntax for the Java control statements. In the process, it shows the **switch** statement in action. The program displays a menu containing the control statements and then waits for you to choose one. After one is chosen, the syntax of the statement is displayed. In this first version of the program, help is available for only the **if** and **switch** statements. The other control statements are added in subsequent examples.

STEP-BY-STEP

1. Create a file called **Help.java**.
2. The program begins by displaying the following menu:

```
Help on:
  1. if
  2. switch
Choose one:
```

To accomplish this, you will use the statement sequence shown here:

```
System.out.println("Help on:");
System.out.println("  1. if");
```

Answers:

1. The **switch** expression can be of type **char**, **short**, **int**, **byte**, or an enumeration. Beginning with JDK 7, a **String** can also be used.
2. When a matching **case** constant is found, the statement sequence associated with that **case** is executed.
3. If a **case** sequence does not end with **break**, execution continues into the next **case** sequence, if one exists.

```
System.out.println("  2. switch");
System.out.print("Choose one: ");
```

3. Next, the program obtains the user's selection by calling **System.in.read( )**, as shown here:

```
choice = (char) System.in.read();
```

4. Once the selection has been obtained, the program uses the **switch** statement shown here to display the syntax for the selected statement.

```
switch(choice) {
  case '1':
    System.out.println("The if:\n");
    System.out.println("if(condition) statement;");
    System.out.println("else statement;");
    break;
  case '2':
    System.out.println("The switch:\n");
    System.out.println("switch(expression) {");
    System.out.println("  case constant:");
    System.out.println("    statement sequence");
    System.out.println("    break;");
    System.out.println("  // ...");
    System.out.println("}");
    break;
  default:
    System.out.print("Selection not found.");
}
```

Notice how the **default** clause catches invalid choices. For example, if the user enters 3, no **case** constants will match, causing the **default** sequence to execute.

5. Here is the entire **Help.java** program:

```
/*
    Try This 3-1

    A simple help system.
*/
class Help {
  public static void main(String[] args)
    throws java.io.IOException {
    char choice;

    System.out.println("Help on:");
    System.out.println("  1. if");
    System.out.println("  2. switch");
    System.out.print("Choose one: ");
    choice = (char) System.in.read();
```

```
      System.out.println("\n");

        switch(choice) {
          case '1':
            System.out.println("The if:\n");
            System.out.println("if(condition) statement;");
            System.out.println("else statement;");
            break;
          case '2':
            System.out.println("The switch:\n");
            System.out.println("switch(expression) {");
            System.out.println("  case constant:");
            System.out.println("    statement sequence");
            System.out.println("    break;");
            System.out.println("  // ...");
            System.out.println("}");
            break;
          default:
            System.out.print("Selection not found.");
        }
      }
    }
```

6. Here is a sample run.

```
Help on:
  1. if
  2. switch
Choose one: 1

The if:

if(condition) statement;
else statement;
```

Ask the Expert

Q Under what conditions should I use an **if-else-if** ladder rather than a **switch** when coding a multiway branch?

A In general, use an **if-else-if** ladder when the conditions controlling the selection process do not rely on a single value. For example, consider the following **if-else-if** sequence:

```
if(x < 10) // ...
else if(y != 0) // ...
else if(!done) // ...
```

Ask the Expert (Continued)

This sequence cannot be recoded into a **switch** because all three conditions involve different variables—and differing types. What variable would control the **switch**? Also, you will need to use an **if-else-if** ladder when testing floating-point values or other objects that are not of types valid for use in a **switch** expression.

THE for LOOP

You have been using a simple form of the **for** loop since Chapter 1. You might be surprised at just how powerful and flexible the **for** loop is. Let's begin by reviewing the basics, starting with the most traditional forms of the **for**.

The general form of the **for** loop for repeating a single statement is

for(*initialization*; *condition*; *iteration*) *statement*;

For repeating a block, the general form is

for(*initialization*; *condition*; *iteration*)
{
    statement sequence
}

The *initialization* is usually an assignment statement that sets the initial value of the *loop control variable*, which acts as the counter that controls the loop. The *condition* is a Boolean expression that determines whether or not the loop will repeat. The *iteration* expression defines the amount by which the loop control variable will change each time the loop is repeated. Notice that these three major sections of the loop must be separated by semicolons. The **for** loop will continue to execute as long as the condition tests true. Once the condition becomes false, the loop will exit, and program execution will resume on the statement following the **for**.

A **for** loop is most commonly used when you know that a loop will execute a predetermined number of times. It is also very useful when a sequence of values are required, since its loop control variable can often be used to produce the sequence. For example, if you want to display the square roots of the numbers between 1 and 99, a **for** loop is quite helpful, as this program illustrates.

```java
// Show square roots of 1 to 99.
class SqrRoot {
  public static void main(String[] args) {
    double num, sroot;

    for(num = 1.0; num < 100.0; num++) {
      sroot = Math.sqrt(num);
      System.out.println("Square root of " + num +
                         " is " + sroot);
    }
  }
}
```

Here, the sequence of values for which the square roots are obtained is produced by the **for**'s loop control variable.

The **for** loop can proceed in a positive or negative fashion, and it can change the loop control variable by any amount. For example, the following program prints the numbers from 100 to –95, in decrements of 5.

```
// A negatively running for loop.
class DecrFor {
  public static void main(String[] args) {
    int x;

    for(x = 100; x > -100; x -= 5)  ◄────── Loop control variable is
      System.out.println(x);                 decremented by 5 each time.
  }
}
```

An important point about **for** loops is that the conditional expression is always tested at the top of the loop. This means that the code inside the loop will not execute at all if the condition is false to begin with. Here is an example:

```
for(count=10; count < 5; count++)
  x += count; // this statement will not execute
```

This loop will never execute because its control variable, **count**, is greater than 5 when the loop is first entered. This makes the conditional expression, **count < 5**, false from the outset; thus, not even one iteration of the loop will occur.

SOME VARIATIONS ON THE for LOOP

The **for** is one of the most versatile statements in the Java language because it allows a wide range of variations. One of the most common is the use of multiple loop control variables. When using multiple loop control variables, the initialization and iteration expressions for each variable are separated by commas. Here is a simple example:

```
// Use multiple loop control variables in a for.
class MultipleLoopVars {
  public static void main(String[] args) {
    int i, j;

    for(i=0, j=10; i < j; i++, j--)  ◄────────── Notice the two loop control
      System.out.println("i and j: " + i + " " + j);   variables.
  }
}
```

The output from the program is shown here:

```
i and j: 0 10
i and j: 1 9
i and j: 2 8
i and j: 3 7
i and j: 4 6
```

Notice how commas separate the two initialization expressions and the two iteration expressions. When the loop begins, both **i** and **j** are initialized in the initialization portion of the loop. Each time the loop repeats, **i** is incremented and **j** is decremented. The loop terminates when **i** is equal to or greater than **j**. In principle, you can have any number of loop control variables, but in practice, more than two or three make the **for** loop unwieldy.

Another common **for** variation involves the nature of the loop control condition. This condition does not need to involve the loop control variable. It can be any valid **boolean** expression. In the next example, the loop continues to execute until the user types the letter S at the keyboard.

```java
// Loop until an S is typed.
class ForTest {
  public static void main(String[] args)
    throws java.io.IOException {

    int i;

    System.out.println("Press S to stop.");

    for(i = 0; (char) System.in.read() != 'S'; i++)
      System.out.println("Pass #" + i);
  }
}
```

Missing Pieces

Some interesting **for** loop variations are created by leaving pieces of the loop definition empty. In Java, it is possible for any or all of the initialization, condition, or iteration portions of the **for** loop to be blank. For example, consider the following program.

```java
// Parts of the for can be empty.
class Empty {
  public static void main(String[] args) {
    int i;

    for(i = 0; i < 10; ) {          ◄──────────── The iteration expression is missing.
      System.out.println("Pass #" + i);
      i++; // increment loop control var
    }
  }
}
```

Here, the iteration expression of the **for** is empty. Instead, the loop control variable **i** is incremented inside the body of the loop. This means that each time the loop repeats, **i** is tested to see whether it equals 10, but no further action takes place. Of course, since **i** is still incremented within the body of the loop, the loop runs normally, displaying the following output:

```
Pass #0
Pass #1
Pass #2
Pass #3
```

```
Pass #4
Pass #5
Pass #6
Pass #7
Pass #8
Pass #9
```

In the next example, the initialization portion is also moved out of the **for**.

```
// Move more out of the for loop.
class Empty2 {
  public static void main(String[] args) {
    int i;

    i = 0; // move initialization out of loop
    for(; i < 10; ) {
      System.out.println("Pass #" + i);
      i++; // increment loop control var
    }
  }
}
```

The initialization expression is moved out of the loop.

In this version, **i** is initialized before the loop begins, rather than as part of the **for**. Normally, you will want to initialize the loop control variable inside the **for**. Generally, the initialization is placed outside of the loop only when the initial value is derived through a process that does not lend itself to containment inside the **for** statement.

The Infinite Loop

You can create an *infinite loop* (a loop that never terminates) using the **for** by leaving the conditional expression empty. For example, the following fragment shows the way many Java programmers create an infinite loop.

```
for(;;) // intentionally infinite loop
{
  //...
}
```

This loop will run forever. Although there are some programming tasks, such as operating system command processors, that require an infinite loop, most "infinite loops" are really just loops with special termination requirements. Near the end of this chapter you will see how to halt a loop of this type. (*Hint*: it's done using the **break** statement.)

Loops with No Body

In Java, the body associated with a **for** loop (or any other loop) can be empty. This is because a *null statement* is syntactically valid. Body-less loops are often useful. For example, the following program uses one to sum the numbers 1 through 5.

```
// The body of a loop can be empty.
class Empty3 {
  public static void main(String[] args) {
```

```
      int i;
      int sum = 0;

      // sum the numbers through 5
      for(i = 1; i <= 5; sum += i++) ;        ←──────── No body in this loop!

      System.out.println("Sum is " + sum);
    }
  }
```

The output from the program is shown here:

```
Sum is 15
```

Notice that the summation process is handled entirely within the **for** statement, and no body is needed. Pay special attention to the iteration expression:

```
sum += i++
```

Don't be intimidated by statements like this. They are common in professionally written Java programs and are easy to understand if you break them down into their parts. In words, this statement says "assign to **sum** the value of **sum** plus **i**, then increment **i**." Thus, it is the same as this sequence of statements:

```
sum = sum + i;
i++;
```

DECLARING LOOP CONTROL VARIABLES INSIDE THE for STATEMENT

Often the variable that controls a **for** loop is needed only for the purposes of the loop and is not used elsewhere. When this is the case, it is possible to declare the variable inside the initialization portion of the **for**. For example, the following program computes both the sum and the product of the numbers 1 through 5. It declares its loop control variable **i** inside the **for**.

```
// Declare loop control variable inside the for.
class ForVar {
  public static void main(String[] args) {
    int sum = 0;
    int product = 1;

    // compute the sum and product of the numbers 1 through 5
    for(int i = 1; i <= 5; i++) {        ←──────── The variable i is declared
      sum += i; // i is known throughout the loop    inside the for statement.
      product *= i;
    }

    // but, i is not known here

    System.out.println("Sum is " + sum);
```

```
      System.out.println("Product is " + product);
  }
}
```

When you declare a variable inside a **for** loop, there is one important point to remember: the scope of that variable ends when the **for** statement does. (That is, the scope of the variable is limited to the **for** loop.) Outside the **for** loop, the variable will cease to exist. Thus, in the preceding example, **i** is not accessible outside the **for** loop. If you need to use the loop control variable elsewhere in your program, you will not be able to declare it inside the **for** loop.

Before moving on, you might want to experiment with your own variations on the **for** loop. As you will find, it is a fascinating loop.

THE ENHANCED for LOOP

There is another form of the **for** loop, called the *enhanced for*. The enhanced **for** provides a streamlined way to cycle through the contents of a collection of objects, such as an array. The enhanced **for** loop is discussed in Chapter 5, after arrays have been introduced.

Progress Check

1. Can portions of a **for** statement be empty?
2. Show how to create an infinite loop using **for**.
3. What is the scope of a variable declared within a **for** statement?

THE while LOOP

Another loop supported by Java is the **while**. The general form of the **while** loop is

>   while(*condition*) *statement*;

where *statement* may be a single statement or a block of statements, and *condition* defines the condition that controls the loop and it may be any valid Boolean expression. The loop repeats while the condition is true. When the condition becomes false, program control passes to the line immediately following the loop.

Here is a simple example in which a **while** is used to print the alphabet:

```
// Demonstrate the while loop.
class WhileDemo {
  public static void main(String[] args) {
```

Answers:

1. Yes. All three parts of the **for**—initialization, condition, and iteration—can be empty.
2. `for(;;)`
3. The scope of a variable declared within a **for** is limited to the loop. Outside the loop, it is unknown.

```
   char ch;

   // print the alphabet using a while loop
   ch = 'a';
   while(ch <= 'z') {
     System.out.print(ch);
     ch++;
   }
  }
}
```

Here, **ch** is initialized to the letter a. Each time through the loop, **ch** is output and then incremented. This process continues until **ch** is greater than z.

As with the **for** loop, the **while** checks the conditional expression at the top of the loop, which means that the loop code may not execute at all. This eliminates the need for performing a separate test before the loop. The following program illustrates this characteristic of the **while** loop. It computes the integer powers of 2, from 0 to 9.

```
// Compute integer powers of 2.
class Power {
  public static void main(String[] args) {
    int e;
    int result;

    for(int i=0; i < 10; i++) {
      result = 1;
      e = i;
      while(e > 0) {
        result *= 2;
        e--;
      }

      System.out.println("2 to the " + i +
                        " power is " + result);
    }
  }
}
```

The output from the program is shown here:

```
2 to the 0 power is 1
2 to the 1 power is 2
2 to the 2 power is 4
2 to the 3 power is 8
2 to the 4 power is 16
2 to the 5 power is 32
2 to the 6 power is 64
2 to the 7 power is 128
2 to the 8 power is 256
2 to the 9 power is 512
```

Notice that the **while** loop executes only when **e** is greater than 0. Thus, when **e** is zero, as it is in the first iteration of the **for** loop, the **while** loop is skipped.

Ask the Expert

Q Given the flexibility inherent in all of Java's loops, what criteria should I use when selecting a loop? That is, how do I choose the right loop for a specific job?

A Use a **for** loop when performing a predetermined number of iterations. Use the **do-while** when you need a loop that will always perform at least one iteration. The **while** is best used when the loop will repeat until some condition becomes false.

THE do-while LOOP

The last of Java's loops is the **do-while**. Unlike the **for** and the **while** loops, in which the condition is tested at the top of the loop, the **do-while** loop checks its condition at the bottom of the loop. This means that a **do-while** loop will always execute at least once. The general form of the **do-while** loop is

    do {
      statements;
    } while(*condition*);

Although the braces are not necessary when only one statement is present, they are often used to improve readability of the **do-while** construct, thus preventing confusion with the **while**. The **do-while** loop iterates as long as the conditional expression is true.

The following program demonstrates the **do-while** by looping until the user enters the letter q.

```
// Demonstrate the do-while loop.
class DWDemo {
  public static void main(String[] args)
    throws java.io.IOException {

    char ch;

    do {
      System.out.print("Press a key followed by ENTER: ");
      ch = (char) System.in.read(); // get a char
    } while(ch != 'q');
  }
}
```

Notice that body of the **do-while** loop prompts for a key press and then obtains the key that was entered. This character is then tested against the letter q in the conditional expression. If the key pressed was not a q, the loop repeats. Because this condition is tested at the bottom of the loop, the body of the loop will be executed at least once, ensuring that the user is prompted to press a key.

Using a **do-while** loop, we can further improve the guessing game program from earlier in this chapter. This time, the program loops until you guess the letter.

```java
// Guess the letter game, 4th version.
class Guess4 {
  public static void main(String[] args)
    throws java.io.IOException {

    char ch, ignore, answer = 'K';

    do {
      System.out.println("I'm thinking of a letter between A and Z.");
      System.out.print("Can you guess it: ");

      // read a character
      ch = (char) System.in.read();

      // discard any other characters in the input buffer
      do {
        ignore = (char) System.in.read();
      } while(ignore != '\n');

      if(ch == answer) System.out.println("** Right **");
      else {
        System.out.print("...Sorry, you're ");
        if(ch < answer) System.out.println("too low");
        else System.out.println("too high");
        System.out.println("Try again!\n");
      }
    } while(answer != ch);
  }
}
```

Here is a sample run:

```
I'm thinking of a letter between A and Z.
Can you guess it: A
...Sorry, you're too low
Try again!

I'm thinking of a letter between A and Z.
Can you guess it: Z
...Sorry, you're too high
Try again!

I'm thinking of a letter between A and Z.
Can you guess it: K
** Right **
```

Notice one other thing of interest in this program. There are two **do-while** loops in the program. The first loops until the user guesses the letter. Its operation and meaning should be clear. The second **do-while** loop, shown again here, warrants some explanation.

```
// discard any other characters in the input buffer
do {
   ignore = (char) System.in.read();
} while(ignore != '\n');
```

As explained earlier, console input is line buffered—you have to press ENTER before characters are sent. Pressing ENTER causes a carriage return and a line feed (newline) sequence to be generated. These characters are left pending in the input buffer. Also, if you typed more than one key before pressing ENTER, they too would still be in the input buffer. This loop discards those characters by continuing to read input until the end of the line is reached. If they were not discarded, then those characters would also be sent to the program as guesses, which is not what is wanted. (To see the effect of this, you might try removing the inner **do-while** loop.) In Chapter 11, after you have learned more about Java, some other, higher-level ways of handling console input are described. However, our use of **read( )** here gives you insight into how the foundation of Java's I/O system operates. It also shows another example of Java's loops in action.

Progress Check

1. What is the main difference between the **while** and the **do-while** loops?
2. The condition controlling the **while** can be of any type. True or False?

TRY THIS 3.2   IMPROVE THE JAVA HELP SYSTEM

`Help2.java`

This project expands on the Java help system that was created in Try This 3-1. This version adds the syntax for the **for**, **while**, and **do-while** loops. It also shows how a **do-while** loop can be used to check the user's menu selection, looping until a valid response is entered. Notice how the **switch** statement makes it very easy to add selections.

STEP-BY-STEP

1. Copy **Help.java** to a new file called **Help2.java**.

———————

Answers:

1. The **while** checks its condition at the top of the loop. The **do-while** checks its condition at the bottom of the loop. Thus, a **do-while** will always execute at least once.
2. False. The condition must be of type **boolean**.

2. Change the first part of **main( )** so that it uses a loop to display the choices, as shown here:

```
public static void main(String[] args)
  throws java.io.IOException {
  char choice, ignore;

  do {
    System.out.println("Help on:");
    System.out.println("  1. if");
    System.out.println("  2. switch");
    System.out.println("  3. for");
    System.out.println("  4. while");
    System.out.println("  5. do-while\n");
    System.out.print("Choose one: ");

    choice = (char) System.in.read();

    do {
      ignore = (char) System.in.read();
    } while(ignore != '\n');
  } while( choice < '1' | choice > '5');
```

Notice that a nested **do-while** loop is used to discard any unwanted characters remaining in the input buffer. After making this change, the program will loop, displaying the menu until the user enters a response that is between 1 and 5.

3. Expand the **switch** statement to include the **for**, **while**, and **do-while** loops, as shown here:

```
switch(choice) {
  case '1':
    System.out.println("The if:\n");
    System.out.println("if(condition) statement;");
    System.out.println("else statement;");
    break;
  case '2':
    System.out.println("The switch:\n");
    System.out.println("switch(expression) {");
    System.out.println("  case constant:");
    System.out.println("    statement sequence");
    System.out.println("    break;");
    System.out.println("  // ...");
    System.out.println("}");
    break;
  case '3':
    System.out.println("The for:\n");
    System.out.print("for(init; condition; iteration)");
    System.out.println(" statement;");
    break;
```

```
      case '4':
        System.out.println("The while:\n");
        System.out.println("while(condition) statement;");
        break;
      case '5':
        System.out.println("The do-while:\n");
        System.out.println("do {");
        System.out.println("  statement;");
        System.out.println("} while (condition);");
        break;
    }
```

Notice that no **default** statement is present in this version of the **switch**. Since the menu loop ensures that a valid response will be entered, it is no longer necessary to include a **default** statement to handle an invalid choice.

4. Here is the entire **Help2.java** program:

```
/*
    Try This 3-2

    An improved Help system that uses a
    do-while to process a menu selection.
*/
class Help2 {
  public static void main(String[] args)
    throws java.io.IOException {
    char choice, ignore;

    do {
      System.out.println("Help on:");
      System.out.println("  1. if");
      System.out.println("  2. switch");
      System.out.println("  3. for");
      System.out.println("  4. while");
      System.out.println("  5. do-while\n");
      System.out.print("Choose one: ");

      choice = (char) System.in.read();

      do {
        ignore = (char) System.in.read();
      } while(ignore != '\n');
    } while( choice < '1' | choice > '5');

    System.out.println("\n");

    switch(choice) {
      case '1':
        System.out.println("The if:\n");
```

```
           System.out.println("if(condition) statement;");
           System.out.println("else statement;");
           break;
        case '2':
           System.out.println("The switch:\n");
           System.out.println("switch(expression) {");
           System.out.println("  case constant:");
           System.out.println("    statement sequence");
           System.out.println("    break;");
           System.out.println("  // ...");
           System.out.println("}");
           break;
        case '3':
           System.out.println("The for:\n");
           System.out.print("for(init; condition; iteration)");
           System.out.println(" statement;");
           break;
        case '4':
           System.out.println("The while:\n");
           System.out.println("while(condition) statement;");
           break;
        case '5':
           System.out.println("The do-while:\n");
           System.out.println("do {");
           System.out.println("  statement;");
           System.out.println("} while (condition);");
           break;
      }
    }
  }
```

USE break TO EXIT A LOOP

It is possible to force an immediate exit from a loop, bypassing any remaining code in the body of the loop and the loop's conditional test, by using the **break** statement. When a **break** statement is encountered inside a loop, the loop is terminated and program control resumes at the next statement following the loop. Here is a simple example:

```
// Using break to exit a loop.
class BreakDemo {
  public static void main(String[] args) {
    int num;

    num = 100;

    // loop while i-squared is less than num
    for(int i=0; i < num; i++) {
      if(i*i >= num) break; // terminate loop if i*i >= 100
```

```
    System.out.print(i + " ");
  }
  System.out.println("Loop complete.");
  }
}
```

This program generates the following output:

```
0 1 2 3 4 5 6 7 8 9 Loop complete.
```

As you can see, although the **for** loop is designed to run from 0 to **num** (which in this case is 100), the **break** statement causes it to terminate early, when **i** squared is greater than or equal to **num**.

The **break** statement can be used with any of Java's loops, including intentionally infinite loops. For example, the following program simply reads input until the user types the letter q.

```
// Read input until a q is received.
class Break2 {
  public static void main(String[] args)
    throws java.io.IOException {

    char ch;

    for( ; ; ) {                                This "infinite" loop is
      ch = (char) System.in.read(); // get a char   terminated by the break.
      if(ch == 'q') break;
    }
    System.out.println("You pressed q!");
  }
}
```

When used inside a set of nested loops, the **break** statement will break out of only the innermost loop. For example:

```
// Using break with nested loops.
class Break3 {
  public static void main(String[] args) {

    for(int i=0; i<3; i++) {
      System.out.println("Outer loop count: " + i);
      System.out.print("    Inner loop count: ");

      int t = 0;
      while(t < 100) {
        if(t == 10) break; // terminate loop if t is 10
        System.out.print(t + " ");
        t++;
      }
      System.out.println();
    }
    System.out.println("Loops complete.");
  }
}
```

This program generates the following output:

```
Outer loop count: 0
    Inner loop count: 0 1 2 3 4 5 6 7 8 9
Outer loop count: 1
    Inner loop count: 0 1 2 3 4 5 6 7 8 9
Outer loop count: 2
    Inner loop count: 0 1 2 3 4 5 6 7 8 9
Loops complete.
```

As you can see, the **break** statement in the inner loop causes the termination of only that loop. The outer loop is unaffected.

Here are two other points to remember about **break**. First, more than one **break** statement may appear in a loop. However, be careful. Too many **break** statements have the tendency to destructure your code. Second, the **break** that terminates a **switch** statement affects only that **switch** statement and not any enclosing loops.

USE break AS A FORM OF goto

In addition to its uses with the **switch** statement and loops, the **break** statement can be employed by itself to provide a "civilized" form of the goto statement. Java does not have a goto statement, because it provides an unstructured way to alter the flow of program execution. Programs that make extensive use of the goto are usually hard to understand and hard to maintain. There are, however, a few places where the goto is a useful and legitimate device. For example, the goto can be helpful when exiting from a deeply nested set of loops. To handle such situations, Java defines an expanded form of the **break** statement. By using this form of **break**, you can, for example, break out of one or more blocks of code. These blocks need not be part of a loop or a **switch**. They can be any block. Further, you can specify precisely where execution will resume, because this form of **break** works with a label. The **break** statement gives you the benefits of a goto without some of its problems.

The general form of the labeled **break** statement is shown here:

break *label*;

Here, *label* is the name of a label that identifies a statement or a block of code. When this form of **break** executes, control is transferred out of the labeled statement or block. The labeled statement or block must enclose the **break** statement, but it does not need to be the immediately enclosing one. This means that you can use a labeled **break** statement to exit from a set of nested blocks, for example. But you cannot use **break** to transfer control to a block of code that does not enclose the **break** statement.

To name a statement or block, put a label at the start of it. A *label* is any valid Java identifier followed by a colon. Once you have labeled a statement or block, you can use this label as the target of a **break** statement. Doing so causes execution to resume at the *end* of the statement or block. For example, the following program shows three nested blocks.

```
// Using break with a label.
class Break4 {
  public static void main(String[] args) {
```

```
        int i;

        for(i=1; i<4; i++) {
one:      {
two:        {
three:        {
                System.out.println("\ni is " + i);
                if(i==1) break one;          ─────── Break to a label.
                if(i==2) break two;
                if(i==3) break three;

                // this is never reached
                System.out.println("won't print");
              }
              System.out.println("After block three.");
            }
            System.out.println("After block two.");
          }
          System.out.println("After block one.");
        }
        System.out.println("After for.");
      }
}
```

The output from the program is shown here:

```
i is 1
After block one.

i is 2
After block two.
After block one.

i is 3
After block three.
After block two.
After block one.
After for.
```

Let's look closely at the program to understand precisely why this output is produced. When **i** is 1, the first **if** statement succeeds, causing a **break** to the end of the block of code defined by label **one**. This causes **After block one.** to print. When **i** is 2, the second **if** succeeds, causing control to be transferred to the end of the block labeled by **two**. This causes the messages **After block two.** and **After block one.** to be printed, in that order. When **i** is 3, the third **if** succeeds, and control is transferred to the end of the block labeled by **three**. Now, all three messages are displayed.

Here is another example. This time, **break** is being used to jump outside of a series of nested **for** loops. When the **break** statement in the inner loop is executed, program control jumps to the end of the block defined by the outer **for** loop, which is labeled by **done**. This causes the remainder of all three loops to be bypassed.

```
// Another example of using break with a label.
class Break5 {
  public static void main(String[] args) {

done:
    for(int i=0; i<10; i++) {
      for(int j=0; j<10; j++) {
        for(int k=0; k<10; k++) {
          System.out.println(k + " ");
          if(k == 5) break done; // jump to done
        }
        System.out.println("After k loop"); // won't execute
      }
      System.out.println("After j loop"); // won't execute
    }
    System.out.println("After i loop");
  }
}
```

The output from the program is shown here:

```
0
1
2
3
4
5
After i loop
```

Precisely where you put a label is very important—especially when working with loops. For example, consider the following program:

```
// Where you put a label is important.
class Break6 {
  public static void main(String[] args) {
    int x=0, y=0;

// here, put label before for statement.
stop1: for(x=0; x < 5; x++) {
        for(y = 0; y < 5; y++) {
          if(y == 2) break stop1;
          System.out.println("x and y: " + x + " " + y);
        }
      }

      System.out.println();

// now, put label immediately before {
      for(x=0; x < 5; x++)
stop2: {
        for(y = 0; y < 5; y++) {
          if(y == 2) break stop2;
```

```
                    System.out.println("x and y: " + x + " " + y);
                }
            }
        }
    }
```

The output from this program is shown here:

```
x and y: 0 0
x and y: 0 1

x and y: 0 0
x and y: 0 1
x and y: 1 0
x and y: 1 1
x and y: 2 0
x and y: 2 1
x and y: 3 0
x and y: 3 1
x and y: 4 0
x and y: 4 1
```

In the program, both sets of nested loops are the same except for one point. In the first set, the label precedes the outer **for** statement. In this case, when the **break** executes, it transfers control to the end of the entire **for** block, skipping the rest of the outer loop's iterations. In the second set, the label precedes the outer **for**'s opening curly brace. Thus, when **break stop2** executes, control is transferred to the end of the outer **for**'s block, rather than the end of the loop. This causes the next iteration to occur.

Keep in mind that you cannot **break** to any label that is not defined for a statement or block that encloses the **break** statement. For example, the following program is invalid and will not compile.

```
// This program contains an error.
class BreakErr {
  public static void main(String[] args) {

    one: for(int i=0; i<3; i++) {
      System.out.print("Pass " + i + ": ");
    }

    for(int j=0; j<100; j++) {
      if(j == 10) break one; // WRONG
      System.out.print(j + " ");
    }
  }
}
```

Since the **for** loop labeled **one** does not enclose the **break** statement in the second **for** loop, it is not possible to transfer control to that label.

Ask the Expert

Q You say that the **goto** is unstructured and that the **break** with a label offers a better alternative. But really, doesn't breaking to a label, which might be many lines of code and levels of nesting removed from the **break**, also destructure code?

A The short answer is yes! However, in those cases in which a jarring change in program flow is required, breaking to a label still retains some structure because you can only jump out of an enclosing, labeled block or statement. You can't jump into any arbitrary block or statement. In contrast, a **goto** has, essentially, no structure!

USE continue

It is possible to force an early iteration of a loop, bypassing the loop's normal control structure. This is accomplished using **continue**. The **continue** statement forces the next iteration of the loop to take place, skipping any code between itself and the conditional expression that controls the loop. Thus, **continue** is essentially the complement of **break**. For example, the following program uses **continue** to help print the even numbers between 0 and 100.

```
// Use continue.
class ContDemo {
  public static void main(String[] args) {
    int i;

    // print even numbers between 0 and 100
    for(i = 0; i<=100; i++) {
      if((i%2) != 0) continue; // iterate
      System.out.println(i);
    }
  }
}
```

Only even numbers are printed, because an odd one will cause the loop to iterate early, bypassing the call to **println( )**. This is accomplished by use of the **%** operator, which returns the remainder of a division. If the number is even, the remainder of a division by 2 is zero and the **if** fails. If the number is odd, then the remainder is 1, causing the **if** to execute the **continue** statement.

In **while** and **do-while** loops, a **continue** statement will cause control to go directly to the conditional expression and then continue the looping process. In the case of the **for**, the iteration expression of the loop is evaluated, next the conditional expression is executed, and then the loop continues.

A **continue** statement may specify a label to describe which enclosing loop to continue. Here is an example program that uses **continue** with a label:

```
// Use continue with a label.
class ContToLabel {
  public static void main(String[] args) {
```

```
outerloop:
    for(int i=1; i < 10; i++) {
        System.out.print("\nOuter loop pass " + i +
                         ", Inner loop: ");
        for(int j = 1; j < 10; j++) {
            if(j == 5) continue outerloop; // continue outer loop
            System.out.print(j);
        }
    }
}
```

The output from the program is shown here:

```
Outer loop pass 1, Inner loop: 1234
Outer loop pass 2, Inner loop: 1234
Outer loop pass 3, Inner loop: 1234
Outer loop pass 4, Inner loop: 1234
Outer loop pass 5, Inner loop: 1234
Outer loop pass 6, Inner loop: 1234
Outer loop pass 7, Inner loop: 1234
Outer loop pass 8, Inner loop: 1234
Outer loop pass 9, Inner loop: 1234
```

As the output shows, when the **continue** executes, control passes to the outer loop, skipping the remainder of the inner loop.

Good uses of **continue** are rare. One reason is that Java provides a rich set of loop statements that fit most applications. However, for those special circumstances in which early iteration is needed, the **continue** statement provides a structured way to accomplish it.

Progress Check

1. Within a loop, what happens when a **break** (with no label) is executed?
2. What happens when a **break** with a label is executed?
3. What does **continue** do?

Answers:

1. Within a loop, a **break** without a label causes immediate termination of the loop. Execution resumes at the first line of code after the loop.
2. When a labeled **break** is executed, execution resumes at the first line of code after the labeled statement or block.
3. The **continue** statement causes a loop to iterate immediately, bypassing any remaining code. If the **continue** includes a label, the labeled loop is continued.

TRY THIS 3-3 FINISH THE JAVA HELP SYSTEM

`Help3.java`

This project puts the finishing touches on the Java help system that was created in the previous projects. This version adds the syntax for **break** and **continue**. It also allows the user to request the syntax for more than one statement. It does this by adding an outer loop that runs until the user enters **q** as a menu selection.

STEP-BY-STEP

1. Copy **Help2.java** to a new file called **Help3.java**.
2. Surround all of the program code with an infinite **for** loop. Break out of this loop, using **break**, when a letter **q** is entered. Since this loop surrounds all of the program code, breaking out of this loop causes the program to terminate.
3. Change the menu loop as shown here:

```
do {
   System.out.println("Help on:");
   System.out.println("  1. if");
   System.out.println("  2. switch");
   System.out.println("  3. for");
   System.out.println("  4. while");
   System.out.println("  5. do-while");
   System.out.println("  6. break");
   System.out.println("  7. continue\n");
   System.out.print("Choose one (q to quit): ");

   choice = (char) System.in.read();

   do {
      ignore = (char) System.in.read();
   } while(ignore != '\n');
} while( choice < '1' | choice > '7' & choice != 'q');
```

Notice that this loop now includes the **break** and **continue** statements. It also accepts the letter **q** as a valid choice.

4. Expand the **switch** statement to include the **break** and **continue** statements, as shown here:

```
case '6':
   System.out.println("The break:\n");
   System.out.println("break; or break label;");
   break;
case '7':
   System.out.println("The continue:\n");
   System.out.println("continue; or continue label;");
   break;
```

5. Here is the entire **Help3.java** program:

```
/*
    Try This 3-3

    The finished Java statement Help system
    that processes multiple requests.
*/
class Help3 {
  public static void main(String[] args)
    throws java.io.IOException {
    char choice, ignore;

    for(;;) {
      do {
        System.out.println("Help on:");
        System.out.println("  1. if");
        System.out.println("  2. switch");
        System.out.println("  3. for");
        System.out.println("  4. while");
        System.out.println("  5. do-while");
        System.out.println("  6. break");
        System.out.println("  7. continue\n");
        System.out.print("Choose one (q to quit): ");

        choice = (char) System.in.read();

        do {
          ignore = (char) System.in.read();
        } while(ignore != '\n');
      } while( choice < '1' | choice > '7' & choice != 'q');

      if(choice == 'q') break;

      System.out.println("\n");

      switch(choice) {
        case '1':
          System.out.println("The if:\n");
          System.out.println("if(condition) statement;");
          System.out.println("else statement;");
          break;
        case '2':
          System.out.println("The switch:\n");
          System.out.println("switch(expression) {");
          System.out.println("  case constant:");
          System.out.println("    statement sequence");
          System.out.println("    break;");
          System.out.println("  // ...");
```

```
            System.out.println("}");
            break;
          case '3':
            System.out.println("The for:\n");
            System.out.print("for(init; condition; iteration)");
            System.out.println(" statement;");
            break;
          case '4':
            System.out.println("The while:\n");
            System.out.println("while(condition) statement;");
            break;
          case '5':
            System.out.println("The do-while:\n");
            System.out.println("do {");
            System.out.println("  statement;");
            System.out.println("} while (condition);");
            break;
          case '6':
            System.out.println("The break:\n");
            System.out.println("break; or break label;");
            break;
          case '7':
            System.out.println("The continue:\n");
            System.out.println("continue; or continue label;");
            break;
        }
        System.out.println();
      }
    }
}
```

6. Here is a sample run:

```
Help on:
  1. if
  2. switch
  3. for
  4. while
  5. do-while
  6. break
  7. continue

Choose one (q to quit): 1

The if:

if(condition) statement;
else statement;
```

```
Help on:
   1. if
   2. switch
   3. for
   4. while
   5. do-while
   6. break
   7. continue

Choose one (q to quit): 6

The break:

break; or break label;

Help on:
   1. if
   2. switch
   3. for
   4. while
   5. do-while
   6. break
   7. continue

Choose one (q to quit): q
```

NESTED LOOPS

As you have seen in some of the preceding examples, one loop can be nested inside of another. Nested loops are used to solve a wide variety of programming problems and are an essential part of programming. So, before leaving the topic of Java's loop statements, let's look at one more nested loop example. The following program uses a nested **for** loop to find all the factors (other than 1 and the number itself) of the numbers from 2 to 100. Notice that the outer loop produces the numbers for which the factors will be obtained. The inner loop determines the numbers' factors.

```java
/*
   Use nested loops to find factors of numbers
   between 2 and 100.
*/
class FindFac {
  public static void main(String[] args) {

    for(int i=2; i <= 100; i++) {
      System.out.print("Factors of " + i + ": ");
      for(int j = 2; j < i; j++)
        if((i%j) == 0) System.out.print(j + " ");
      System.out.println();
    }
  }
}
```

Here is a portion of the output produced by the program:

```
Factors of 2:
Factors of 3:
Factors of 4: 2
Factors of 5:
Factors of 6: 2 3
Factors of 7:
Factors of 8: 2 4
Factors of 9: 3
Factors of 10: 2 5
Factors of 11:
Factors of 12: 2 3 4 6
Factors of 13:
Factors of 14: 2 7
Factors of 15: 3 5
Factors of 16: 2 4 8
Factors of 17:
Factors of 18: 2 3 6 9
Factors of 19:
Factors of 20: 2 4 5 10
```

In the program, the outer loop runs **i** from 2 through 100. The inner loop successively tests all numbers from 2 up to **i**, printing those that evenly divide **i**. Notice the use of the % operator to determine when one value evenly divides another. If the result is zero, then the divisor is a factor. Extra challenge: The preceding program can be made more efficient. Can you see how? (*Hint*: the number of iterations in the inner loop can be reduced.)

EXERCISES

1. Write a program that reads characters from the keyboard until a period is received. Have the program count the number of spaces. Report the total at the end of the program.

2. Show the general form of the **if-else-if** ladder.

3. Given

```
if(x < 10)
   if(y > 100) {
      if(!done) x = z;
      else y = z;
   }
else System.out.println("error"); // what if?
```

to what **if** does the last **else** associate?

4. Show the **for** statement for a loop that counts from 1000 to 0 by −2.

5. Is the following fragment valid?

```
for(int i = 0; i < num; i++)
    sum += i;

count = i;
```

6. Explain what **break** does. Be sure to explain both of its forms.

7. In the following fragment, after the **break** statement executes, what is displayed?

```
for(i = 0; i < 10; i++) {
    while(running) {
        if(x<y) break;
        // ...
    }
    System.out.println("after while");
}
System.out.println("After for");
```

8. What does the following fragment print?

```
for(int i = 0; i<10; i++) {
    System.out.print(i + " ");
    if((i%2) == 0) continue;
    System.out.println();
}
```

9. The iteration expression in a **for** loop need not always alter the loop control variable by adding or subtracting a fixed amount. Instead, the loop control variable can change in any arbitrary way. Using this concept, write a program that uses a **for** loop to generate and display the progression 1, 2, 4, 8, 16, 32, and so on.

10. The ASCII lowercase letters are separated from the uppercase letters by 32. Thus, to convert a lowercase letter to uppercase, subtract 32 from it. Use this information to write a program that reads characters from the keyboard. Have it convert all lowercase letters to uppercase, and all uppercase letters to lowercase, displaying the result. Make no changes to any other character. Have the program stop when the user presses period. At the end, have the program display the number of case changes that have taken place.

11. What is an infinite loop?

12. When using **break** with a label, must the label be on a statement or block that contains the **break**?

13. What is the difference between the following three literal values: 5, '5', "5"?

14. Suppose **c** is a variable of type **char**. How would you test whether the value of **c** is the single quote character?

15. The class **ContDemo** in this chapter shows one way to use a **for** loop to print the even numbers from 0 to 100. Write programs that print the same output as that program, but do it in the following ways:

     A. Using a **for** loop that increments the loop control variable by 2 each iteration.

     B. Using a **for** loop whose loop control variable goes from 0 to 50.

     C. Using a **for** loop whose loop control variable goes from 100 down to 0.

     D. Using an infinite **for** loop with no conditional expression and exiting the loop with a **break** statement.

     E. Using a **while** loop.

     F. Using a **do-while** loop.

16. Write program that uses a loop to print the powers of 3 from 3^0 up to and including 3^9.

17. Write a program that uses a loop to print a list of 100 numbers consisting of alternating 1's and −1's, starting with 1.

18. The class **FindFac** discussed in this chapter prints the factors of all numbers from 1 to 100. Modify this class so that, instead of stopping at 100, it keeps going until it finds a number with exactly nine factors.

19. Write a program that reads in characters from the keyboard until it reads a line feed character '\n'. Then have it print the number of vowels, the number of consonants, the number of digits, and the number of other characters. Include the final line feed character in your count of other characters.

20. The **StarPattern** program below prints out the pattern of stars underneath it. Modify the program so that it prints out the other patterns below using nested loops.

```
class StarPattern {
  public static void main(String[] args) {

    for(int i = 1; i <= 5; i++) {
      for(int j = 1; j <= i; j++)
        System.out.print('*');
      System.out.println();
    }
  }
}
```

```
*
**
***
****
*****
```

  A.
```
*****
****
***
**
*
```

B.
```
    *
   **
  ***
 ****
*****
```

C.
```
**********
 ********
  ******
   ****
    **
```

21. As mentioned in the text, a Java identifier consists of one or more characters. The first character must be an uppercase or lowercase letter of the alphabet, an underscore _, or a dollar sign $. Each remaining character must be an uppercase or lowercase letter of the alphabet, a digit 0-9, an underscore, or a dollar sign. Write a Java program that reads in a line of characters and prints out whether the line of characters is a legal Java identifier.

22. Unfortunately, the Unicode values of the characters '0'-'9' do not correspond to the integer value of the characters. That is, the Unicode values of '0'-'9' are 48-57, not 0-9. But we can easily convert these characters to their integer values by subtracting 48. In particular, if **c** is a variable of type **char** containing a digit '0'-'9', then we can create a variable **x** of type **int** with the corresponding integer value as follows:

```
int x = c - 48;
```

Use this conversion technique in a program that reads in three digits, converts them to a three-digit integer, doubles the value of the integer, and then prints out the result. For example, if the input is '3', '4', and '5', then the output is 690.

23. If you divide 1 by 2, you get 0.5. If you divide it again by 2, you get 0.25. Write a program that calculates and outputs the number of times you have to divide 1 by 2 to get a value less than one ten-thousandth (0.0001).

CHAPTER 4

Introducing Classes, Objects, and Methods

KEY SKILLS & CONCEPTS

- Know the fundamentals of the class
- Understand how objects are created
- Understand how reference variables are assigned
- Create a method
- Use the **return** keyword
- Return a value from a method
- Add parameters to a method
- Utilize constructors
- Create parameterized constructors
- Understand **new**
- Understand garbage collection and finalizers
- Use the **this** keyword

Before you can go much further in your study of Java, you need to learn about the class. The class is the essence of Java. It is the logical construct on which the Java language is built because the class defines the nature of an object. As such, the class forms the basis for object-oriented programming in Java. Within a class are defined data and code that acts upon that data. The code is contained in methods. Because classes, objects, and methods are fundamental to Java, they are introduced in this chapter. Having a basic understanding of these features will allow you to write more sophisticated programs and better understand certain key Java features described in the following chapter.

CLASS FUNDAMENTALS

Since all Java program activity occurs within a class, we have been using classes since the start of this book. Of course, only extremely simple classes have been used, and we have not taken advantage of the majority of their features. As you will see, classes are substantially more powerful than the limited ones presented so far.

Let's begin by reviewing the basics. A class is a template that defines the form of an object. It specifies both data and the code that will operate on that data. Java uses a class specification to construct *objects*. Objects are *instances* of a class. Thus, a class is essentially a set of plans that specify how to build an object. It is important to be clear on one issue: a class is a logical abstraction. It is not until an object of that class has been created that a physical representation of that class exists in memory.

One other point: recall that the methods and variables that comprise a class are called *members* of the class. The data members associated with an instance of a class are also referred to as *instance variables*.

The General Form of a Class

When you define a class, you declare its exact form and nature. You do this by specifying the instance variables that it contains and the methods that operate on them. Although very simple classes might contain only methods or only instance variables, most real-world classes contain both.

A class is created by using the keyword **class**. A simplified general form of a **class** definition is shown here:

```
class classname {
    // declare instance variables
    type var1;
    type var2;
    // ...
    type varN;

    // declare methods
    type method1(parameters) {
        // body of method
    }
    type method2(parameters) {
        // body of method
    }
    // ...
    type methodN(parameters) {
        // body of method
    }
}
```

Although there is no syntactic rule that enforces it, a well-designed class should define one and only one logical entity. For example, a class that stores names and telephone numbers will not normally also store information about the stock market, average rainfall, sunspot cycles, or other unrelated information. The point here is that a well-designed class groups logically connected information. Putting unrelated information into the same class will quickly destructure your code!

Up to this point, the classes that we have been using have only had one method: **main( )**. Soon you will see how to create others. However, notice that the general form of a class does not specify a **main( )** method. A **main( )** method is required only if that class is the starting point for your program. Also, some types of Java applications, such as applets, don't require **main( )**.

Defining a Class

To illustrate classes, we will develop a class that encapsulates information about vehicles, such as cars, vans, and trucks. This class is called **Vehicle**, and it will store three items of information about a vehicle: the number of passengers that it can carry, its fuel capacity, and its average fuel consumption (in miles per gallon).

The first version of **Vehicle** is shown next. It defines three instance variables: **passengers**, **fuelCap**, and **mpg**. Notice that **Vehicle** does not contain any methods. Thus, it is currently a data-only class. (Subsequent sections will add methods to it.)

```
class Vehicle {
  int passengers; // number of passengers
  int fuelCap;    // fuel capacity in gallons
  int mpg;        // fuel consumption in miles per gallon
}
```

A **class** definition creates a new data type. In this case, the new data type is called **Vehicle**. You will use this name to declare objects of type **Vehicle**. Remember that a **class** declaration is only a type description; it does not create an actual object. Thus, the preceding code does not cause any objects of type **Vehicle** to come into existence.

To actually create a **Vehicle** object, you will use a statement such as the following:

```
Vehicle minivan = new Vehicle(); // create a Vehicle object called minivan
```

After this statement executes, **minivan** will be an instance of **Vehicle**. Thus, it will have "physical" reality. For the moment, don't worry about the details of this statement.

Each time you create an instance of a class, you are creating an object that contains its own copy of each instance variable defined by the class. Thus, every **Vehicle** object will contain its own copies of the instance variables **passengers**, **fuelCap**, and **mpg**. To access these variables, you will use what is commonly called the dot (.) operator. The *dot operator* links the name of an object with the name of a member. The general form of the dot operator is shown here:

> *object.member*

Thus, the object is specified on the left, and the member is put on the right. For example, to assign the **fuelCap** variable of **minivan** the value 16, use the following statement:

```
minivan.fuelCap = 16;
```

In general, the dot operator is used to access both instance variables and methods.

Here is a complete program that uses the **Vehicle** class:

```
/* A program that uses the Vehicle class.

   Call this file VehicleDemo.java
*/
class Vehicle {
  int passengers; // number of passengers
  int fuelCap; // fuel capacity in gallons
  int mpg; // fuel consumption in miles per gallon
}

// This class declares an object of type Vehicle.
class VehicleDemo {
  public static void main(String[] args) {
    Vehicle minivan = new Vehicle();
    int range;

    // assign values to fields in minivan
    minivan.passengers = 7;
    minivan.fuelCap = 16;        Notice the use of the dot
    minivan.mpg = 21;            operator to access a member.

    // compute the range assuming a full tank of gas
    range = minivan.fuelCap * minivan.mpg;
    System.out.println("Minivan can carry " + minivan.passengers +
                       " with a range of " + range);
  }
}
```

You should call the file that contains this program **VehicleDemo.java** because the **main( )** method is in the class called **VehicleDemo**, not the class called **Vehicle**. When you compile this program, you will find that two **.class** files have been created, one for **Vehicle** and one for **VehicleDemo**. The Java compiler automatically puts each class into its own **.class** file. It is not necessary for both the **Vehicle** and the **VehicleDemo** class to be in the same source file. You could put each class in its own file, called **Vehicle.java** and **VehicleDemo.java**, respectively.

To run this program, you must execute **VehicleDemo.class**. The following output is displayed:

```
Minivan can carry 7 with a range of 336
```

Before moving on, let's review a fundamental principle: each object has its own copies of the instance variables defined by its class. Thus, the contents of the variables in one object can differ from the contents of the variables in another. There is no connection between the two objects except for the fact that they are both objects of the same type. For example, if you have two **Vehicle** objects, each has its own copy of **passengers**, **fuelCap**, and **mpg**, and the contents of these can differ between the two objects. The following program demonstrates this fact. (Notice that the class with **main( )** is now called **TwoVehicles**.)

```
// This program creates two Vehicle objects.

class Vehicle {
  int passengers; // number of passengers
  int fuelCap; // fuel capacity in gallons
  int mpg; // fuel consumption in miles per gallon
}

// This class declares an object of type Vehicle.
class TwoVehicles {
  public static void main(String[] args) {
    Vehicle minivan = new Vehicle();
    Vehicle sportscar = new Vehicle();

    int range1, range2;

    // assign values to fields in minivan
    minivan.passengers = 7;
    minivan.fuelCap = 16;
    minivan.mpg = 21;

    // assign values to fields in sportscar
    sportscar.passengers = 2;
    sportscar.fuelCap = 14;
    sportscar.mpg = 12;

    // compute the ranges assuming a full tank of gas
    range1 = minivan.fuelCap * minivan.mpg;
    range2 = sportscar.fuelCap * sportscar.mpg;

    System.out.println("Minivan can carry " + minivan.passengers +
                       " with a range of " + range1);

    System.out.println("Sportscar can carry " + sportscar.passengers +
                       " with a range of " + range2);
  }
}
```

Remember, **minivan** and **sportscar** refer to separate objects.

The output produced by this program is shown here:

```
Minivan can carry 7 with a range of 336
Sportscar can carry 2 with a range of 168
```

As you can see, **minivan**'s data is completely separate from the data contained in **sportscar**. The following illustration depicts this situation.

	passengers	7
minivan ⟶	fuelCap	16
	mpg	21

	passengers	2
sportscar ⟶	fuelCap	14
	mpg	12

Progress Check

1. What two things does a class contain?
2. What is used to access the members of a class through an object?
3. Each object has its own copies of the class's _____.

HOW OBJECTS ARE CREATED

In the preceding programs, the following line was used to declare an object of type **Vehicle**:

```
Vehicle minivan = new Vehicle();
```

This declaration performs two functions. First, it declares a variable called **minivan** of the class type **Vehicle**. This variable does not define an object. Instead, it is simply a variable that can *refer to* an object. Second, the declaration creates a physical copy of the object and assigns to **minivan** a reference to that object. This is done by using the **new** operator.

The **new** operator dynamically allocates (that is, allocates at run time) memory for an object and returns a reference to it. This reference is, essentially, the address in memory of the object allocated by **new**. This reference is then stored in a variable. Thus, in Java, all class objects must be dynamically allocated.

The two steps combined in the preceding statement can be rewritten as follows to show each step individually:

```
Vehicle minivan; // declare reference to object
minivan = new Vehicle(); // allocate a Vehicle object
```

The first line declares **minivan** as a reference to an object of type **Vehicle**. Thus, **minivan** is a variable that can refer to an object, but it is not an object itself. At this point, **minivan** does not refer to an object. The next line creates a new **Vehicle** object and assigns a reference to it to **minivan**. Now, **minivan** is linked with an object.

REFERENCE VARIABLES AND ASSIGNMENT

In an assignment operation, object reference variables may act a bit differently than you would expect. To understand why, first consider what occurs when you assign one primitive-type variable to another. Assuming two **int** variables called **x** and **y**, the statement **x = y** means that **x** receives a *copy* of the *value* contained in **y**. Thus,

---

Answers:

1. Code and data. In Java, this means methods and instance variables.
2. The dot operator.
3. instance variables

after the assignment, both **x** and **y** contain their own, independent copies of the value. Changing one does not affect the other.

When you assign one object reference variable to another, the situation is a bit more complicated because you are assigning references. This means that you are changing the object that the reference variable refers to, not making a copy of that object. The effect of this difference may seem counterintuitive at first. For example, consider the following fragment:

```
Vehicle car1 = new Vehicle();
Vehicle car2 = car1;
```

At first glance, it is easy to think that **car1** and **car2** refer to different objects, but this is not the case because no copy of the object has been made. Instead, **car2** receives a copy of the *reference* in **car1**. As a result, **car1** and **car2** will both refer to the *same* object. In other words, the assignment of **car1** to **car2** simply makes **car2** refer to the same object as does **car1**. Thus, the object can be acted upon by either **car1** or **car2**. For example, after this assignment

```
car1.mpg = 26;
```

executes, both of these **println( )** statements

```
System.out.println(car1.mpg);
System.out.println(car2.mpg);
```

display the same value: 26.

Although **car1** and **car2** both refer to the same object, they are not linked in any other way. For example, a subsequent assignment to **car2** simply changes the object to which **car2** refers. For example:

```
Vehicle car1 = new Vehicle();
Vehicle car2 = car1;
Vehicle car3 = new Vehicle();

car2 = car3; // now car2 and car3 refer to the same object.
```

After this sequence executes, **car2** refers to the same object as **car3**. The object referred to by **car1** is unchanged.

Progress Check

1. Explain what occurs when one reference variable is assigned to another.
2. Assuming a class called **MyClass**, show how an object called **ob** is created.

Answers:

1. When one reference variable is assigned to another reference variable, both variables will refer to the same object. A copy of the object is not made.
2. `MyClass ob = new MyClass( );`

METHODS

As explained, instance variables and methods are constituents of classes. So far, the **Vehicle** class contains data, but no methods. Although data-only classes are perfectly valid, most classes will have methods. Methods are subroutines that manipulate the data defined by the class and, in many cases, control access to that data. In most cases, other parts of your program will interact with a class through its methods.

A method contains the statements that define its actions. In well-written Java code, each method performs only one task. Each method has a name, and it is this name that is used to call the method. In general, you can give a method whatever name you please as long as it is a valid identifier. However, good programming practice dictates that you use descriptive names. Remember that **main( )** is reserved for the method that begins execution of your program. Also, don't use Java's keywords for method names.

When denoting methods in text, this book has used and will continue to use a convention that has become common when writing about Java. A method will have parentheses after its name. For example, if a method's name is **getVal**, it will be written **getVal( )** when its name is used in a sentence. This notation will help you distinguish variable names from method names in this book.

The general form of a method is shown here:

```
ret-type name( parameter-list ) {
   // body of method
}
```

Here, *ret-type* specifies the type of data returned by the method. This can be any valid type, including class types that you create. If the method does not return a value, its return type must be **void**. The name of the method is specified by *name*. This can be any legal identifier other than those already used by other items within the current scope. The *parameter-list* is a sequence of type and identifier pairs separated by commas. Parameters are essentially variables that receive the value of the *arguments* passed to the method when it is called. If the method has no parameters, the parameter list will be empty.

Adding a Method to the Vehicle Class

As just explained, the methods of a class typically manipulate and provide access to the data of the class. With this in mind, recall that **main( )** in the preceding examples computed the range of a vehicle by multiplying its fuel consumption rate by its fuel capacity. While technically correct, this is not the best way to handle this computation. The calculation of a vehicle's range is something that is best handled by the **Vehicle** class itself. The reason for this conclusion is easy to understand: the range of a vehicle is dependent on the capacity of the fuel tank and the rate of fuel consumption, and both of these quantities are encapsulated by **Vehicle**. By adding a method to **Vehicle** that computes the range, you are enhancing its object-oriented structure. To add a method to **Vehicle**, specify it within **Vehicle**'s declaration. For example, the following version of **Vehicle** contains a method called **range( )** that displays the range of the vehicle.

```
// Add range to Vehicle.

class Vehicle {
  int passengers; // number of passengers
  int fuelCap; // fuel capacity in gallons
  int mpg; // fuel consumption in miles per gallon

  // Display the range.
  void range() {
    System.out.println("Range is " + fuelCap * mpg);
  }
}
```

The **range( )** method is contained within the **Vehicle** class.

Notice that **fuelCap** and **mpg** are used directly, without the dot operator.

```
class AddMeth {
  public static void main(String[] args) {
    Vehicle minivan = new Vehicle();
    Vehicle sportscar = new Vehicle();

    int range1, range2;

    // assign values to fields in minivan
    minivan.passengers = 7;
    minivan.fuelCap = 16;
    minivan.mpg = 21;

    // assign values to fields in sportscar
    sportscar.passengers = 2;
    sportscar.fuelCap = 14;
    sportscar.mpg = 12;


    System.out.print("Minivan can carry " + minivan.passengers + ". ");

    minivan.range(); // display range of minivan

    System.out.print("Sportscar can carry " + sportscar.passengers + ". ");

    sportscar.range(); // display range of sportscar.
  }
}
```

This program generates the following output:

```
Minivan can carry 7. Range is 336
Sportscar can carry 2. Range is 168
```

Let's look at the key elements of this program, beginning with the **range( )** method itself. The first line of **range( )** is

```
void range() {
```

This line declares a method called **range** that has no parameters. Its return type is **void**. Thus, **range( )** does not return a value to the caller. The line ends with the opening brace of the method body.

The body of **range( )** consists solely of this line:

```
System.out.println("Range is " + fuelCap * mpg);
```

This statement displays the range of the vehicle by multiplying **fuelCap** by **mpg**. Since each object of type **Vehicle** has its own copy of **fuelCap** and **mpg**, when **range( )** is called, the range computation uses the calling object's copies of those variables.

The **range( )** method ends when its closing brace is encountered. This causes program control to transfer back to the caller.

Next, look closely at this line of code from inside **main( )**:

```
minivan.range();
```

This statement invokes the **range( )** method on **minivan**. That is, it calls **range( )** relative to the **minivan** object, using the object's name followed by the dot operator. When a method is called, program control is transferred to the method. When the method terminates, control is transferred back to the caller, and execution resumes with the line of code following the call.

In this case, the call to **minivan.range( )** displays the range of the vehicle defined by **minivan**. In similar fashion, the call to **sportscar.range( )** displays the range of the vehicle defined by **sportscar**. Each time **range( )** is invoked, it displays the range for the specified object.

There is something very important to notice inside the **range( )** method: the instance variables **fuelCap** and **mpg** are referred to directly, without preceding them with an object name or the dot operator. When a method uses an instance variable that is defined by its class, it can do so directly, without explicit reference to an object and without use of the dot operator. This is easy to understand if you think about it. A method is always invoked relative to some object of its class. Once this invocation has occurred, the object is known. Thus, within a method, there is no need to specify the object a second time. This means that **fuelCap** and **mpg** inside **range( )** implicitly refer to the copies of those variables found in the object on which **range( )** is called.

RETURNING FROM A METHOD

In general, two conditions can cause a method to return—first, as the **range( )** method in the preceding example shows, when the method's closing brace is encountered. The second is when a **return** statement is executed. There are two forms of **return**—one for use in **void** methods (those that do not return a value) and one for returning values. The first form is examined here. The next section explains how to return values.

In a **void** method, you can cause the immediate termination of a method by using this form of **return**:

```
return;
```

When this statement executes, program control returns to the caller, skipping any remaining code in the method. For example, consider this method:

```java
void myMeth() {
  for(int i=0; i < 10; i++) {
    if(i == 5) return; // stop at 5
    System.out.println(i);
  }
}
```

Here, the **for** loop will only run from 0 to 5 because once **i** equals 5, the method returns. It is permissible to have multiple **return** statements in a method, especially when there are two or more routes out of it. For example:

```java
void myMeth() {
  // ...
  if(done) return;
  // ...
  if(error) return;
  // ...
}
```

Here, the method returns if it is done or if an error occurs. Be careful, however, because having too many exit points in a method can destructure your code; so avoid using them casually. A well-designed method has well-defined exit points.

To review: a **void** method can return in one of two ways—its closing brace is reached, or a **return** statement is executed.

RETURNING A VALUE

Although methods with a return type of **void** are not rare, most methods will return a value. In fact, the ability to return a value is one of the most useful features of a method. You have already seen one example of a return value: when we used the **sqrt( )** function to obtain a square root.

Return values are used for a variety of purposes in programming. In some cases, such as with **sqrt( )**, the return value contains the outcome of some calculation. In other cases, the return value may simply indicate success or failure. In still others, it may contain a status code. Whatever the purpose, using method return values is an integral part of Java programming.

Methods return a value to the calling routine using this form of **return**:

   return *value*;

Here, *value* is the value returned. This form of **return** can be used only with methods that have a non-**void** return type. Furthermore, a non-**void** method *must* return a value by using this form of **return**.

You can use a return value to improve the implementation of **range( )**. Instead of displaying the range, a better approach is to have **range( )** compute the range and return this value. Among the advantages of this approach is that you can use the value for other calculations. The following example modifies **range( )** to return the range rather than displaying it.

```
// Use a return value.

class Vehicle {
  int passengers; // number of passengers
  int fuelCap; // fuel capacity in gallons
  int mpg; // fuel consumption in miles per gallon

  // Return the range.
  int range() {
    return mpg * fuelCap;                    Return the range for a given vehicle.
  }
}

class RetMeth {
  public static void main(String[] args) {
    Vehicle minivan = new Vehicle();
    Vehicle sportscar = new Vehicle();

    int range1, range2;

    // assign values to fields in minivan
    minivan.passengers = 7;
    minivan.fuelCap = 16;
    minivan.mpg = 21;

    // assign values to fields in sportscar
    sportscar.passengers = 2;
    sportscar.fuelCap = 14;
    sportscar.mpg = 12;

    // get the ranges                          Assign the value
    range1 = minivan.range();                  returned to a
    range2 = sportscar.range();                variable.

    System.out.println("Minivan can carry " + minivan.passengers +
                       " with range of " + range1 + " miles");

    System.out.println("Sportscar can carry " + sportscar.passengers +
                       " with range of " + range2 + " miles");
  }
}
```

The output is shown here:

```
Minivan can carry 7 with range of 336 miles
Sportscar can carry 2 with range of 168 miles
```

In the program, notice that when **range( )** is called, it is put on the right side of an assignment statement. On the left is a variable that will receive the value returned by **range( )**. Thus, after

```
range1 = minivan.range();
```

executes, the range of the **minivan** object is stored in **range1**. In other words, the call to **minivan.range( )** results in the range of **minivan** being computed. The result is then returned via the **return** statement in **range( )**. This value is then assigned to **range1**. Thus, the value returned by **range( )** becomes the value of the method call. In this case, it acts as if you had written **range1 = 336** because 336 is the value returned by **minivan.range( )**.

Notice that **range( )** now has a return type of **int**. This means that it will return an integer value to the caller. The return type of a method is important because the type of data returned by a method must be compatible with the return type specified by the method. Thus, if you want a method to return data of type **double**, its return type must be type **double**.

Although the preceding program is correct, it is not written as efficiently as it could be. Specifically, there is no need for the **range1** or **range2** variables. A call to **range( )** can be used in the **println( )** statement directly, as shown here:

```
System.out.println("Minivan can carry " + minivan.passengers +
                  " with range of " + minivan.range() + " miles");
```

In this case, when **println( )** is executed, **minivan.range( )** is called automatically and its return value will be passed to **println( )**. Furthermore, you can use a call to **range( )** whenever the range of a **Vehicle** object is needed. For example, this statement compares the ranges of two vehicles:

```
if(v1.range() > v2.range()) System.out.println("v1 has greater range");
```

USING PARAMETERS

It is possible to pass one or more values to a method when the method is called. Recall that a value passed to a method is called an *argument*. Inside the method, the variable that receives the argument is called a *parameter*. Parameters are declared inside the parentheses that follow the method's name. The parameter declaration syntax is the same as that used for variables. A parameter is within the scope of its method, and aside from its special task of receiving an argument, it acts like any other local variable.

Here is a simple example that uses a parameter. Inside the **ChkNum** class, the method **isEven( )** returns **true** if the value that it is passed is even. It returns **false** otherwise. Therefore, **isEven( )** has a return type of **boolean**.

```
// A simple example that uses a parameter.

class ChkNum {

  // Return true if x is even.
```

```
    boolean isEven(int x) {              Here, x is an integer parameter of isEven( ).
      if((x%2) == 0) return true;
      else return false;
    }
}

class ParmDemo {
  public static void main(String[] args) {
    ChkNum e = new ChkNum();
                                         Pass arguments to isEven( ).
    if(e.isEven(10)) System.out.println("10 is even.");

    if(e.isEven(9)) System.out.println("9 is even.");

    if(e.isEven(8)) System.out.println("8 is even.");
  }
}
```

Here is the output produced by the program:

```
10 is even.
8 is even.
```

In the program, **isEven( )** is called three times, and each time a different value is passed. Let's look at this process closely. First, notice how **isEven( )** is called. The argument is specified between the parentheses. When **isEven( )** is called the first time, it is passed the value 10. Thus, when **isEven( )** begins executing, the parameter **x** receives the value 10. In the second call, 9 is the argument, and **x**, then, has the value 9. In the third call, the argument is 8, which is the value that **x** receives. The point is that the value passed as an argument when **isEven( )** is called is the value received by its parameter, **x**.

Now that you have seen a parameter in action, an important concept needs to be stated. Parameters are important to Java programming because they give you a means of supplying the data on which a method will operate. This enables many types of methods to be more useful, and more general. For example, if the **isEven( )** method just shown did not have a parameter and only returned the result of testing the value 19, it would be of very limited use. However, by passing the value to be tested, the utility of **isEven( )** is greatly expanded because it can now test any value. Thus, by parameterizing a method, you enable that method to address the *general* case rather than just one *specific* situation.

A key point to understand about argument passing is that the type of the argument must be compatible with the type of the parameter that receives it. This means, for example, that it would be an error to attempt to call **isEven( )** with a **boolean** argument. Because a **boolean** value cannot be converted into an **int** value, the Java compiler will flag an error and not compile the program.

A method can have more than one parameter. Simply declare each parameter, separating one from the next with a comma. For example, the **Factor** class defines a method called **isFactor( )** that determines whether the first parameter is a factor of the second.

```
class Factor {

  // Return true if a is a factor of b.
  boolean isFactor(int a, int b) {  ◄─────────────── This method has two parameters.
    if( (b % a) == 0) return true;
    else return false;
  }
}

class IsFact {
  public static void main(String[] args) {
    Factor x = new Factor();
                                               ──── Pass two arguments to isFactor( ).
    if(x.isFactor(2, 20)) System.out.println("2 is factor");
    if(x.isFactor(3, 20)) System.out.println("this won't be displayed");
  }
}
```

Notice that when **isFactor( )** is called, the arguments are also separated by commas.

When using multiple parameters, each parameter specifies its own type, which can differ from the others. For example, this is perfectly valid:

```
int myMeth(int a, double b, float c) {
// ...
```

Adding a Parameterized Method to Vehicle

You can use a parameterized method to add a new feature to the **Vehicle** class: the ability to compute the amount of fuel needed for a given distance. This new method is called **fuelNeeded( )**. This method takes the number of miles that you want to drive and returns the number of gallons of gas required. The **fuelNeeded( )** method is defined like this:

```
double fuelNeeded(int miles) {
  return (double) miles / mpg;
}
```

Notice that this method returns a value of type **double**. This is useful since the amount of fuel needed for a given distance might not be a whole number. The entire **Vehicle** class that includes **fuelNeeded( )** is shown here:

```
/*
   Add a parameterized method that computes the
   fuel required for a given distance.
*/
```

```
class Vehicle {
  int passengers; // number of passengers
  int fuelCap; // fuel capacity in gallons
  int mpg; // fuel consumption in miles per gallon

  // Return the range.
  int range() {
    return mpg * fuelCap;
  }

  // Compute fuel needed for a given distance.
  double fuelNeeded(int miles) {
    return (double) miles / mpg;
  }
}

class CompFuel {
  public static void main(String[] args) {
    Vehicle minivan = new Vehicle();
    Vehicle sportscar = new Vehicle();
    double gallons;
    int dist = 252;

    // assign values to fields in minivan
    minivan.passengers = 7;
    minivan.fuelCap = 16;
    minivan.mpg = 21;

    // assign values to fields in sportscar
    sportscar.passengers = 2;
    sportscar.fuelCap = 14;
    sportscar.mpg = 12;

    gallons = minivan.fuelNeeded(dist);

    System.out.println("To go " + dist + " miles minivan needs " +
                       gallons + " gallons of fuel.");

    gallons = sportscar.fuelNeeded(dist);

    System.out.println("To go " + dist + " miles sportscar needs " +
                       gallons + " gallons of fuel.");
  }
}
```

The output from the program is shown here:

```
To go 252 miles minivan needs 12.0 gallons of fuel.
To go 252 miles sportscar needs 21.0 gallons of fuel.
```

Progress Check

1. When must an instance variable or method be accessed through an object reference using the dot operator? When can a variable or method be used directly?
2. Explain the difference between an argument and a parameter.
3. Explain the two ways that a method can return to its caller.

TRY THIS 4-1   CREATING A HELP CLASS

`HelpClassDemo.java`

If one were to try to summarize the essence of the class in one sentence, it might be this: a class encapsulates functionality. Of course, sometimes the trick is knowing where one functionality ends and another begins. As a general rule, you will want your classes to be the building blocks of your larger application. In order to do this, each class must represent a single functional unit that performs clearly delineated actions. Thus, you will want your classes to be as small as possible—but no smaller! That is, classes that contain extraneous functionality confuse and destructure code, but classes that contain too little functionality are fragmented. What is the balance? It is at this point that the science of programming becomes the *art* of programming. Fortunately, most programmers find that this balancing act becomes easier with experience.

To begin to gain that experience you will convert the help system from Try This 3-3 in the preceding chapter into a Help class. Let's examine why this is a good idea. First, the help system defines one logical unit. It simply displays the syntax for Java's control statements. Thus, its functionality is compact and well defined. Second, putting help in a class is an aesthetically pleasing approach. Whenever you want to offer the help system to a user, simply instantiate a help-system object. Finally, because help is encapsulated, it can be upgraded or changed without causing unwanted side effects in the programs that use it.

Answers:

1. When an instance variable is accessed by code that is not part of the class in which that instance variable is defined, it must be done through an object, by use of the dot operator. When an instance variable is accessed by code that is part of the same class as the instance variable, that variable can be referred to directly. The same thing applies to methods.
2. An argument is a value that is passed to a method when it is invoked. A parameter is a variable defined by a method that receives the value of the argument.
3. A method can be made to return through use of the **return** statement. If the method has a **void** return type, it will also return when its closing brace is reached. Non-**void** methods must return a value, so returning by reaching the closing brace is not an option.

STEP-BY-STEP

1. Create a new file called **HelpClassDemo.java**. To save you some typing, you might want to copy the file from Try This 3-3, **Help3.java**, into **HelpClassDemo.java**.

2. To convert the help system into a class, you must first determine precisely what constitutes the help system. For example, in **Help3.java**, there is code to display a menu, input the user's choice, check for a valid response, and display information about the item selected. The program also loops until the letter q is pressed. If you think about it, it is clear that the menu, the check for a valid response, and the display of the information are integral to the help system. How user input is obtained, and whether repeated requests should be processed, are not. Thus, you will create a class that displays the help information, the help menu, and checks for a valid selection. Its methods will be called **helpOn( )**, **showMenu( )**, and **isValid( )**, respectively.

3. Create the **helpOn( )** method as shown here:

```
// Display help.
void helpOn(int what) {
  switch(what) {
    case '1':
      System.out.println("The if:\n");
      System.out.println("if(condition) statement;");
      System.out.println("else statement;");
      break;
    case '2':
      System.out.println("The switch:\n");
      System.out.println("switch(expression) {");
      System.out.println("  case constant:");
      System.out.println("    statement sequence");
      System.out.println("    break;");
      System.out.println("  // ...");
      System.out.println("}");
      break;
    case '3':
      System.out.println("The for:\n");
      System.out.print("for(init; condition; iteration)");
      System.out.println(" statement;");
      break;
    case '4':
      System.out.println("The while:\n");
      System.out.println("while(condition) statement;");
      break;
    case '5':
      System.out.println("The do-while:\n");
      System.out.println("do {");
      System.out.println("  statement;");
      System.out.println("} while (condition);");
      break;
```

```
      case '6':
        System.out.println("The break:\n");
        System.out.println("break; or break label;");
        break;
      case '7':
        System.out.println("The continue:\n");
        System.out.println("continue; or continue label;");
        break;
    }
    System.out.println();
}
```

4. Next, create the **showMenu( )** method:

```
// Display menu.
void showMenu() {
  System.out.println("Help on:");
  System.out.println("  1. if");
  System.out.println("  2. switch");
  System.out.println("  3. for");
  System.out.println("  4. while");
  System.out.println("  5. do-while");
  System.out.println("  6. break");
  System.out.println("  7. continue\n");
  System.out.print("Choose one (q to quit): ");
}
```

5. Create the **isValid( )** method, shown here:

```
// Return true if ch is a valid selection.
boolean isValid(int ch) {
  if(ch < '1' | ch > '7' & ch != 'q') return false;
  else return true;
}
```

6. Assemble the foregoing methods into the **Help** class, shown here:

```
class Help {

  // Display help.
  void helpOn(int what) {
    switch(what) {
      case '1':
        System.out.println("The if:\n");
        System.out.println("if(condition) statement;");
        System.out.println("else statement;");
        break;
      case '2':
        System.out.println("The switch:\n");
        System.out.println("switch(expression) {");
        System.out.println("  case constant:");
```

```
        System.out.println("    statement sequence");
        System.out.println("    break;");
        System.out.println("  // ...");
        System.out.println("}");
        break;
      case '3':
        System.out.println("The for:\n");
        System.out.print("for(init; condition; iteration)");
        System.out.println(" statement;");
        break;
      case '4':
        System.out.println("The while:\n");
        System.out.println("while(condition) statement;");
        break;
      case '5':
        System.out.println("The do-while:\n");
        System.out.println("do {");
        System.out.println("  statement;");
        System.out.println("} while (condition);");
        break;
      case '6':
        System.out.println("The break:\n");
        System.out.println("break; or break label;");
        break;
      case '7':
        System.out.println("The continue:\n");
        System.out.println("continue; or continue label;");
        break;
    }
    System.out.println();
  }

  // Display menu.
  void showMenu() {
    System.out.println("Help on:");
    System.out.println("  1. if");
    System.out.println("  2. switch");
    System.out.println("  3. for");
    System.out.println("  4. while");
    System.out.println("  5. do-while");
    System.out.println("  6. break");
    System.out.println("  7. continue\n");
    System.out.print("Choose one (q to quit): ");
  }

  // Return true if ch is a valid selection.
  boolean isValid(int ch) {
```

```
      if(ch < '1' | ch > '7' & ch != 'q') return false;
      else return true;
   }
}
```

7. Finally, rewrite the **main( )** method from Try This 3-3 so that it uses the new **Help** class. Call this class **HelpClassDemo.java**. The entire program for **HelpClassDemo.java** is shown here:

```java
/*
    Try This 4-1

    Convert the help system from Try This 3-3 into
    a Help class.
*/

class Help {

  // Display help.
  void helpOn(int what) {
    switch(what) {
      case '1':
        System.out.println("The if:\n");
        System.out.println("if(condition) statement;");
        System.out.println("else statement;");
        break;
      case '2':
        System.out.println("The switch:\n");
        System.out.println("switch(expression) {");
        System.out.println("  case constant:");
        System.out.println("    statement sequence");
        System.out.println("    break;");
        System.out.println("  // ...");
        System.out.println("}");
        break;
      case '3':
        System.out.println("The for:\n");
        System.out.print("for(init; condition; iteration)");
        System.out.println(" statement;");
        break;
      case '4':
        System.out.println("The while:\n");
        System.out.println("while(condition) statement;");
        break;
      case '5':
        System.out.println("The do-while:\n");
        System.out.println("do {");
        System.out.println("  statement;");
        System.out.println("} while (condition);");
        break;
```

```java
         case '6':
           System.out.println("The break:\n");
           System.out.println("break; or break label;");
           break;
         case '7':
           System.out.println("The continue:\n");
           System.out.println("continue; or continue label;");
           break;
       }
     System.out.println();
   }

   // Display menu.
   void showMenu() {
     System.out.println("Help on:");
     System.out.println("  1. if");
     System.out.println("  2. switch");
     System.out.println("  3. for");
     System.out.println("  4. while");
     System.out.println("  5. do-while");
     System.out.println("  6. break");
     System.out.println("  7. continue\n");
     System.out.print("Choose one (q to quit): ");
   }

   // Return true if ch is a valid selection.
   boolean isValid(int ch) {
     if(ch < '1' | ch > '7' & ch != 'q') return false;
     else return true;
   }
}

class HelpClassDemo {
   public static void main(String[] args)
     throws java.io.IOException {

     char choice, ignore;
     Help hlpobj = new Help();

     for(;;) {
       do {
         hlpobj.showMenu();

         choice = (char) System.in.read();

         do {
           ignore = (char) System.in.read();
         } while(ignore != '\n');
```

```
        } while( !hlpobj.isValid(choice) );

        if(choice == 'q') break;

        System.out.println("\n");

        hlpobj.helpOn(choice);
      }
    }
  }
```

When you try the program, you will find that it is functionally the same as before. The advantage of this approach is that you now have a help system component that can be reused whenever it is needed.

CONSTRUCTORS

In the preceding examples, the instance variables of each **Vehicle** object had to be set manually using a sequence of statements, such as:

```
minivan.passengers = 7;
minivan.fuelCap = 16;
minivan.mpg = 21;
```

An approach like this would never be used in professionally written Java code. Aside from being error prone (you might forget to set one of the fields), there is simply a better way to accomplish this task: the constructor.

A *constructor* initializes an object when it is created. It has the same name as its class and is syntactically similar to a method. However, constructors have no explicit return type. Typically, you will use a constructor to give initial values to the instance variables defined by the class, or to perform any other startup procedures required to create a fully formed object.

All classes have constructors, whether you define one or not, because Java automatically provides a default constructor. However, once you define your own constructor, the default constructor is no longer used.

Here is a simple example that uses a constructor:

```
// A simple constructor.

class MyClass {
  int x;

  MyClass() {          ◄──────────── This is the constructor
    x = 10;                           for MyClass.
  }
```

```
  }

class ConsDemo {
  public static void main(String[] args) {
    MyClass t1 = new MyClass();
    MyClass t2 = new MyClass();

    System.out.println(t1.x + " " + t2.x);
  }
}
```

In this example, the constructor for **MyClass** is

```
MyClass() {
  x = 10;
}
```

This constructor assigns the instance variable **x** of **MyClass** the value 10. This constructor is called by **new** when an object is created. For example, in the line

```
MyClass t1 = new MyClass();
```

the constructor **MyClass( )** is called and the resulting object is assigned to **t1**, giving **t1.x** the value 10. The same is true for **t2**. After construction, **t2.x** has the value 10. Thus, the output from the program is

```
10 10
```

PARAMETERIZED CONSTRUCTORS

In the preceding example, a parameter-less constructor was used. Although this is fine for some situations, most often you will need a constructor that accepts one or more parameters. Parameters are added to a constructor in the same way that they are added to a method: just declare them inside the parentheses after the constructor's name. For example, here, **MyClass** is given a parameterized constructor:

```
// A parameterized constructor.

class MyClass {
  int x;

  MyClass(int i) {          ←——————————— This constructor has a parameter.
    x = i;
  }
}

class ParmConsDemo {
  public static void main(String[] args) {
    MyClass t1 = new MyClass(10);
    MyClass t2 = new MyClass(88);

    System.out.println(t1.x + " " + t2.x);
```

```
   }
}
```

The output from this program is shown here:

```
10 88
```

In this version of the program, the **MyClass( )** constructor defines one parameter called **i**, which is used to initialize the instance variable, **x**. Thus, when the line

```
MyClass t1 = new MyClass(10);
```

executes, the value 10 is passed to **i**, which is then assigned to **x**.

Ask the Expert

Q If I don't initialize an instance variable, what value does it have?

A If you don't initialize an instance variable, then it will be given a default value. For numeric types, the default is zero. For reference types, the default is **null**, which indicates that no object is referred to, and for **boolean** variables, the default is **false**.

Adding a Constructor to the Vehicle Class

We can improve the **Vehicle** class by adding a constructor that automatically initializes the **passengers**, **fuelCap**, and **mpg** fields when an object is constructed. Pay special attention to how **Vehicle** objects are created.

```
// Add a constructor.

class Vehicle {
  int passengers; // number of passengers
  int fuelCap;    // fuel capacity in gallons
  int mpg;        // fuel consumption in miles per gallon

  // This is a constructor for Vehicle.
  Vehicle(int p, int f, int m) {  ◄─────────────── Constructor for Vehicle.
    passengers = p;
    fuelCap = f;
    mpg = m;
  }

  // Return the range.
  int range() {
    return mpg * fuelCap;
  }

  // Compute fuel needed for a given distance.
```

```
   double fuelNeeded(int miles) {
     return (double) miles / mpg;
   }
}

class VehConsDemo {
  public static void main(String[] args) {

    // construct complete vehicles
    Vehicle minivan = new Vehicle(7, 16, 21);
    Vehicle sportscar = new Vehicle(2, 14, 12);

    double gallons;
    int dist = 252;

    gallons = minivan.fuelNeeded(dist);

    System.out.println("To go " + dist + " miles minivan needs " +
                        gallons + " gallons of fuel.");

    gallons = sportscar.fuelNeeded(dist);

    System.out.println("To go " + dist + " miles sportscar needs " +
                        gallons + " gallons of fuel.");
  }
}
```

Both **minivan** and **sportscar** are initialized by the **Vehicle( )** constructor when they are created. Each object is initialized as specified in the parameters to its constructor. For example, in the following line,

```
Vehicle minivan = new Vehicle(7, 16, 21);
```

the values 7, 16, and 21 are passed to the **Vehicle( )** constructor when **new** creates the object. Thus, **minivan**'s copy of **passengers**, **fuelCap**, and **mpg** will contain the values 7, 16, and 21, respectively. The output from this program is the same as for the previous version.

Progress Check

1. When is a constructor executed?
2. Does a constructor have a return type?

———

Answers:

1. A constructor is executed when an object of its class is instantiated. A constructor is used to initialize the object being created.
2. No.

THE new OPERATOR REVISITED

Now that you know more about classes and their constructors, let's take a closer look at the **new** operator. In the context of an assignment, the **new** operator has this general form:

    class-var = new *class-name*(*arg-list*);

Here, *class-var* is a variable of the class type being created. The *class-name* is the name of the class that is being instantiated. The class name followed by a parenthesized argument list (which can be empty) specifies the constructor for the class. If a class does not define its own constructor, **new** will use the default constructor supplied by Java. Thus, **new** can be used to create an object of any class type. The **new** operator returns a reference to the newly created object, which (in this case) is assigned to *class-var*.

Since memory is finite, it is possible that **new** will not be able to allocate memory for an object because insufficient memory exists. If this happens, a run-time exception will occur. (You will learn about exceptions in Chapter 10.) For the sample programs in this book, you won't need to worry about running out of memory, but you will need to consider this possibility in real-world programs that you write.

Ask the Expert

Q Why don't I need to use **new** for variables of the primitive types, such as **int** or **float**?

A Java's primitive types are not implemented as objects. Rather, because of efficiency concerns, they are implemented as "normal" variables. A variable of a primitive type directly contains the value that you have given it. As explained, a reference variable contains a reference to the object. This layer of indirection (and other object features) adds overhead to an object that is avoided by a primitive type.

GARBAGE COLLECTION AND FINALIZERS

As you have seen, objects are dynamically allocated from a pool of free memory by using the **new** operator. As explained, memory is not infinite, and the free memory can be exhausted. Thus, it is possible for **new** to fail because there is insufficient free memory to create the desired object. For this reason, a key component of any dynamic allocation scheme is the recovery of free memory from unused objects, making that memory available for subsequent reallocation. In some programming languages, the release of previously allocated memory is handled manually. (For example, in C++, you use the **delete** operator to free memory that was allocated.) However, Java uses a different, more trouble-free approach: *garbage collection*.

Java's garbage collection system reclaims objects automatically—occurring transparently, behind the scenes, without any programmer intervention. It works like this:

when no references to an object exist, that object is assumed to be no longer needed, and the memory occupied by the object is released. This recycled memory can then be used for a subsequent allocation.

Garbage collection occurs only sporadically during the execution of your program. It will not occur simply because one or more objects exist that are no longer used. For efficiency, the garbage collector will usually run only when two conditions are met: there are objects to recycle, and there is a need to recycle them. Remember, garbage collection takes time, so the Java run-time system does it only when it is appropriate. Thus, you can't know precisely when garbage collection will take place.

The finalize( ) Method

It is possible to define a method called a *finalizer* that will be called just before an object's final destruction by the garbage collector. This method is called **finalize( )**, and it can be used in very specialized cases to ensure that an object terminates cleanly. For example, **finalize( )** might be used to make sure that some system resource not managed by the Java run time is properly released. Although the vast majority of Java programs do not need finalizers, the topic is covered here for completeness and because a finalizer will be used to demonstrate Java's garbage collection mechanism.

To add a finalizer to a class, you must define the **finalize( )** method. The Java run-time system calls that method whenever it is about to recycle an object of that class. Inside the **finalize( )** method you will specify those actions that must be performed before an object is destroyed.

The **finalize( )** method has this general form:

```
protected void finalize( )
{
  // finalization code here
}
```

Here, the keyword **protected** is a modifier that governs access to **finalize( )** by code defined outside its class. This and the other access modifers are explained in Chapter 6.

It is important to understand that **finalize( )** is called just before garbage collection. It is not called when an object goes out of scope, for example. This means that you cannot know when—or even if—**finalize( )** will be executed. For example, if your program ends before garbage collection occurs, **finalize( )** will not execute. Therefore, it should be used only as a "backup" procedure to ensure the proper handling of some resource, or for special-use applications, not as the means that your program uses in its normal operation. In short, **finalize( )** is a specialized method that is seldom needed.

TRY THIS 4-2   DEMONSTRATE GARBAGE COLLECTION

GCDemo.java

Because garbage collection runs sporadically, in the background, it is not easy to see it in action. However, one way it can be done is through the use of the **finalize( )** method. Recall that **finalize( )** is called when an object is about to be recycled. As explained, objects are not necessarily recycled as soon as they are no longer needed. Instead, the garbage collector waits until it can perform its collection efficiently, usually when there are many unused objects. Thus, to demonstrate garbage collection via the **finalize( )** method, you often need to create and destroy a large number of objects—and this is precisely what you will do in this project.

STEP-BY-STEP

1. Create a new file called **GCDemo.java**.
2. Create the **MyClass** class shown here:

```
class MyClass {
  int x;

  MyClass(int i) {
    x = i;
  }

  // Called when object is recycled.
  protected void finalize() {
    System.out.println("Finalizing " + x);
  }

  // Generates an object that is immediately abandoned.
  void generate(int i) {
    MyClass o = new MyClass(i);
  }
}
```

The constructor sets the instance variable **x** to a known value. In this example, **x** is used as an object ID. The **finalize( )** method displays the value of **x** when an object is recycled. Of special interest is **generate( )**. This method creates and then promptly abandons a **MyClass** object. This makes that object subject to garbage collection. You will see how this is used in the next step.

3. Create the **GCDemo** class, shown here:

```
class GCDemo {
  public static void main(String[] args) {
    MyClass ob = new MyClass(0);

    /* Now, generate a large number of objects. At
       some point, garbage collection will occur.
       Note: you might need to increase the number
       of objects generated in order to force
       garbage collection. */

    for(int count=1; count < 1000000; count++)
      ob.generate(count);
  }
}
```

This class creates an initial **MyClass** object called **ob**. Then, using **ob**, it creates 1,000,000 objects by calling **generate( )** on **ob**. This has the net effect of creating and discarding 1,000,000 objects. At various points in the middle of this process, garbage collection will take place. Precisely how often or when depends on several factors, such as the initial amount of free memory and the current task load of the operating system. However, at some point, you will start to see the messages generated by **finalize( )**. If you don't see the messages, try increasing the number of objects being generated by raising the count in the **for** loop.

4. Here is the entire **GCDemo.java** program:

```
/*
    Try This 4-2

    Demonstrate garbage collection and the finalize() method.
*/

class MyClass {
  int x;

  MyClass(int i) {
    x = i;
  }

  // Called when object is recycled.
  protected void finalize() {
    System.out.println("Finalizing " + x);
  }

  // Generates an object that is immediately abandoned.
  void generate(int i) {
    MyClass o = new MyClass(i);
```

```
      }
    }

class GCDemo {
  public static void main(String[] args) {
    MyClass ob = new MyClass(0);

      /* Now, generate a large number of objects. At
         some point, garbage collection will occur.
         Note: you might need to increase the number
         of objects generated in order to force
         garbage collection. */

      for(int count=1; count < 1000000; count++)
        ob.generate(count);
  }
}
```

THE this KEYWORD

Before concluding this chapter it is necessary to introduce **this**. When a method is called, it is automatically passed an *implicit argument* that is a reference to the invoking object (that is, the object on which the method is called). This reference is called **this**. To understand **this**, first consider a program that creates a class called **Power** that computes the result of a number raised to some integer power:

```
class Power {
  double b;
  int e;
  double val;

  Power(double base, int exp) {
    b = base;
    e = exp;

    val = 1;
    if(exp==0) return;
    for( ; exp>0; exp--) val = val * base;
  }

  double getPwr() {
    return val;
  }
}

class DemoPower {
  public static void main(String[] args) {
    Power x = new Power(4.0, 2);
    Power y = new Power(2.5, 1);
```

```
      Power z = new Power(5.7, 0);

    System.out.println(x.b + " raised to the " + x.e +
                            " power is " + x.getPwr());
    System.out.println(y.b + " raised to the " + y.e +
                            " power is " + y.getPwr());
    System.out.println(z.b + " raised to the " + z.e +
                            " power is " + z.getPwr());
  }
}
```

The output from the program is shown here:

```
4.0 raised to the 2 power is 16.0
2.5 raised to the 1 power is 2.5
5.7 raised to the 0 power is 1.0
```

In each case, the value of **Power**'s instance variable **b** is raised to the power passed to **e**.

As you know, within a method, the other members of a class can be accessed directly, without any object or class qualification. Thus, inside **getPwr( )**, the statement

```
return val;
```

means that the copy of **val** associated with the invoking object will be returned. However, the same statement can also be written like this:

```
return this.val;
```

Here, **this** refers to the object on which **getPwr( )** was called. Thus, **this.val** refers to that object's copy of **val**. For example, if **getPwr( )** had been invoked on **x**, then **this** in the preceding statement would have been referring to **x**. Writing the statement without using **this** is really just shorthand.

Here is the entire **Power** class written using the **this** reference:

```
class Power {
  double b;
  int e;
  double val;

  Power(double base, int exp) {
    this.b = base;
    this.e = exp;

    this.val = 1;
    if(exp==0) return;
    for( ; exp>0; exp--) this.val = this.val * base;
  }

  double getPwr() {
    return this.val;
  }
}
```

If you substitute this version of **Power** for the previous version in the preceding program, the same results will be produced because both versions of **Power** are functionally equivalent.

Actually, no Java programmer would write **Power** as just shown because nothing is gained, and the standard form is easier. However, **this** has some important uses. For example, the Java syntax permits the name of a parameter or a local variable to be the same as the name of an instance variable. When this happens, the local name *hides* the instance variable. You can gain access to the hidden instance variable by referring to it through **this**. For example, the following is a syntactically valid way to write the **Power( )** constructor.

```
Power(double b, int e) {
   this.b = b;
   this.e = e;                          This refers to the b instance
                                        variable, not the parameter.
   val = 1;
   if(e==0) return;
   for( ; e>0; e--) val = val * b;
}
```

In this version, the names of the parameters are the same as the names of the instance variables, thus hiding them. However, **this** is used to "uncover" the instance variables.

EXERCISES

1. What is the difference between a class and an object?
2. How is a class defined?
3. What does each object have its own copy of?
4. Using two separate statements, show how to declare a variable called **counter** of a class called **MyCounter** and assign it a new object of that class.
5. Show how a method called **myMeth( )** is declared if it has a return type of **double** and has two **int** parameters called **a** and **b**.
6. How must a method return if it returns a value?
7. What name does a constructor have?
8. What does **new** do?
9. What is garbage collection, and how does it work? What is **finalize( )**?
10. What is **this**?
11. Can a constructor have one or more parameters?
12. If a method returns no value, what must its return type be?
13. Create a **Die** class with one integer instance variable called **sideUp**. Give it a constructor and a **getSideUp( )** method that returns the value of **sideUp** and a **void roll( )** method that changes **sideUp** to a random value from

1 to 6. (To see how to generate a random integer between 1 and 6, look at the last exercise in Chapter 2.) Then create a **DieDemo** class with a main method that creates two **Die** objects, rolls them, and prints the sum of the two sides up.

14. Create a **Card** class that represents a playing card. It should have an **int** instance variable named **rank** and a **char** variable named **suit**. Give it a constructor with two parameters for initializing the two instance variables and give it a **getSuit( )** method and a **getRank( )** method that return the values of the two instance variables. Then create a **CardTester** class with a main method that creates five **Card**s that make up a full house (that is, three of the cards have the same rank and the other two cards have the same rank) and prints out the ranks and suits of the five **Card**s using the **getSuit( )** and **getRank( )** methods.

15. Suppose you have a class **MyClass** with one instance variable x. What will be printed by the following code segment? Explain your answer.

```
MyClass c1 = new MyClass();
c1.x = 3;
MyClass c2 = c1;
c2.x = 4;
System.out.println(c1.x);
```

16. Suppose a class has an instance variable **x** and a method with a local variable **x**.
    A. If **x** is used in a calculation in the body of the method, which **x** is being referred to?
    B. Suppose you needed to add the local variable **x** to the instance variable **x** in the body of the method. How would you do so?

17. The following method has a flaw (in fact, due to this flaw it will not compile). What is the flaw?

```
void displayAbsX(int x) {
  if (x > 0) {
    System.out.println(x);
    return;
  }
  else {
    System.out.println(-x);
    return;
  }
  System.out.println("Done");
}
```

18. Create a method **max( )** that has two integer parameters **x** and **y** and returns the larger of **x** and **y**.

19. Create a method **max( )** that has three integer parameters **x**, **y**, and **z** and it returns the largest of the three. Do it two ways: once using an **if-else-if** ladder and once using nested **if** statements.

20. Suppose a class needs to compute a value and then print it. To modularize the code, the programmer wants to create a new method in the class to handle this work. Would it be better for the new method to compute and print the value or just compute and return the value, leaving the printing of the value to the code that calls the new method?

21. Find all the errors (if any) in the following class declaration:

```
Class MyCla$$ {
    integer x = 3.0;
    boolean b == false

    //constructor
    MyClass(boolean b) { b = b; }

    int doIt() {}

    int don'tDoIt() { return this; }
}
```

22. Create a **Swapper** class with two integer instance variables **x** and **y** and a constructor with two parameters that initialize the two variables. Also include three methods: A **getX( )** method that returns **x**, a **getY( )** method that returns **y**, and a **void swap( )** method that swaps the values of **x** and **y**. Then create a **SwapperDemo** class that tests all the methods.

23. Suppose you are writing a genealogy program. One useful class might be a **Person** class, where each person in the family tree is represented by a **Person** object. List at least five appropriate instance variables to include in such a class. Don't worry about the type of the instance variables.

24. Create a **USMoney** class with two integer instance variables **dollars** and **cents**. Add a constructor with two parameters for initializing a **USMoney** object. The constructor should check that the **cents** value is between 0 and 99 and, if not, transfer some of the **cents** to the **dollars** variable to make it between 0 and 99. Add a **plus** method to the class that takes a **USMoney** object as its parameter. It creates and returns a new **USMoney** object representing the sum of the object whose **plus( )** method is being invoked and the parameter. It does not modify the values of the two existing objects. It should also ensure that the value of the **cents** instance variable of the new object is between 0 and 99. For example, if **x** is a **USMoney** object with 5 dollars and 80 cents, and if **y** is a **USMoney** object with 1 dollar and 90 cents, then **x.plus(y)** will return a new **USMoney** object with 7 dollars and 70 cents. Also, create a **USMoneyDemo** class that tests the **USMoney** class.

25. Create a **Date** class with three integer instance variables named **day**, **month**, **year**. It has a constructor with three parameters for initializing the instance variables, and it has one method named **daysSinceJan1( )**. It computes and returns the number of days since January 1 of the same year, including January 1 and the day in the **Date** object. For example, if **day** is a **Date** object with **day** = 1, **month** = 3, and **year** = 2000, then the call

date.daysSinceJan1( ) should return 61 since there are 61 days between the dates of January 1, 2000, and March 1, 2000, including January 1 and March 1. Include a **DateDemo** class that tests the **Date** class. Don't forget leap years.

26. What is the difference, if anything, between the following two implementations of the method **doIt( )**?

```java
void doIt(int x) {
  if(x > 0)
    System.out.println("Pos");
  else
    System.out.println("Neg");
}

void doIt(int x) {
  if(x > 0) {
    System.out.println("Pos");
    return;
  }
  System.out.println("Neg");
}
```

CHAPTER 5

More Data Types and Operators

This chapter returns to the subject of Java's data types and operators. It discusses arrays, the **String** type, the bitwise operators, and the **?** ternary operator. It also covers Java's for-each style **for** loop. Along the way, command-line arguments are described.

ARRAYS

It is common in programming to have a group of related variables. For example, you might want to keep a list of the daily high temperatures for the month of April. Although you could use 30 separate variables for this purpose, doing so would both be clumsy and inefficient. Just imagine how difficult it would be to compute the average high temperature. You would need to first add together all 30 individual variables and then divide that value by 30. This would make for a very long, tedious expression. It would also make for an inflexible solution. Fortunately, Java supports a much better way to handle groups of related variables: the *array*.

An array is a collection of variables of the same type, referred to by a common name. In Java, arrays can have one or more dimensions, although the one-dimensional array is the most common. Arrays offer a convenient means of grouping together related variables. For example, using an array to hold the daily high temperatures for a month is much better than using 30 separate values. Other things you might use an array to hold include a list of stock prices, the titles of your collection of programming books, or a product inventory.

The principal advantage of an array is that it organizes data in such a way that it can be easily manipulated. For example, if you have an array containing a list of account balances, it is an easy task to compute the total value by cycling through the array. Also, arrays organize data in such a way that it can be easily sorted.

Although arrays in Java can be used just like arrays in other programming languages, they have one special attribute: they are implemented as objects. This fact is one reason that a discussion of arrays was deferred until objects had been introduced. By implementing arrays as objects, several important advantages are gained, not the least of which is that unused arrays can be garbage collected.

One-Dimensional Arrays

A one-dimensional array is a list of related variables. Such lists are common in programming. For example, you might use a one-dimensional array to store the account numbers of the active users on a network. To declare a one-dimensional array, you will use this general form:

type[ ] *array-name* = new *type*[*size*];

Here, *type* declares the *element type* of the array. (The element type is also sometimes referred to as the base type.) The element type determines the data type of each element contained in the array. The number of elements that the array will hold is determined by *size*. Since arrays are implemented as objects, the creation of an array is a two-step process. First, you declare an array reference variable. Second, you allocate memory for the array, assigning the reference to that memory to the array variable. Thus, arrays in Java are dynamically allocated using the **new** operator.

Here is an example. The following creates an **int** array of 10 elements and links it to an array reference variable named **sample**.

```
int[] sample = new int[10];
```

This declaration works just like an object declaration. The **sample** variable holds a reference to the memory allocated by **new**. This memory is large enough to hold 10 elements of type **int**. As with objects, it is possible to break the preceding declaration in two. For example:

```
int[] sample;
sample = new int[10];
```

In this case, when **sample** is first created, it refers to no physical object. It is only after the second statement executes that **sample** is linked with an array.

An individual element within an array is accessed by use of an index. An *index* describes the position of an element within an array. In Java, all arrays have zero as the index of their first element. Because **sample** has 10 elements, it has index values of 0 through 9. To index an array, specify the number of the element you want, surrounded by square brackets. Thus, the first element in **sample** is **sample[0]**, and the last element is **sample[9]**.

An important point to understand is that each individual array element is used in the same way as a "normal" variable. For example, you can assign a value to an element, as shown here:

```
sample[0] = 3;
```

After this statement executes, the first element in **sample** will have the value 3. You can obtain an element's value for use in an expression, as shown next:

```
2 * sample[0]
```

Here, if **sample[0]** contains 3, then the result of the preceding expression is 6.

The following program demonstrates **sample** by loading it with the numbers 0 through 9 and then displaying its contents.

```java
// Demonstrate a one-dimensional array.
class ArrayDemo {
  public static void main(String[] args) {
    int[] sample = new int[10];
    int i;

    for(i = 0; i < 10; i = i+1)            ←
      sample[i] = i;
                                    Arrays are indexed from zero.
    for(i = 0; i < 10; i = i+1)            ←
      System.out.println("This is sample[" + i + "]: " + sample[i]);
  }
}
```

The output from the program is shown here:

```
This is sample[0]: 0
This is sample[1]: 1
This is sample[2]: 2
This is sample[3]: 3
This is sample[4]: 4
This is sample[5]: 5
This is sample[6]: 6
This is sample[7]: 7
This is sample[8]: 8
This is sample[9]: 9
```

Conceptually, the **sample** array looks like this:

0	1	2	3	4	5	6	7	8	9
sample [0]	sample [1]	sample [2]	sample [3]	sample [4]	sample [5]	sample [6]	sample [7]	sample [8]	sample [9]

Arrays are common in programming because they let you deal easily with large numbers of related variables. For example, the following program finds the minimum and maximum values stored in the **nums** array by cycling through the array using a **for** loop.

```
// Find the minimum and maximum values in an array.
class MinMax {
  public static void main(String[] args) {
    int[] nums = new int[10];
    int min, max;

    nums[0] = 99;
    nums[1] = -10;
    nums[2] = 100123;
    nums[3] = 18;
    nums[4] = -978;
    nums[5] = 5623;
    nums[6] = 463;
    nums[7] = -9;
    nums[8] = 287;
    nums[9] = 49;

    min = max = nums[0];
    for(int i=1; i < 10; i++) {
      if(nums[i] < min) min = nums[i];
      if(nums[i] > max) max = nums[i];
    }
    System.out.println("min and max: " + min + " " + max);

  }
}
```

The output from the program is shown here:

```
min and max: -978 100123
```

Notice how the program works. It first gives both **min** and **max** the value of **nums[0]**. It then cycles through the **nums** array, one element at a time, starting with the second element. Inside the loop, if the value of **nums[i]** is less than **min**, then that value becomes the new minimum value. Similarly, if the value **nums[i]** is greater than **max**, then that value becomes the new maximum value. The process continues until all elements in **nums** have been tested. As a result, when the loop ends, **min** will contain the smallest value in the array and **max** will contain the largest.

In the preceding program, the **nums** array was given values by hand, using 10 separate assignment statements. Although perfectly correct, there is an easier way to accomplish this. Arrays can be initialized when they are created. The general form for initializing a one-dimensional array is shown here:

type[ ] *array-name* = { *val1, val2, val3,…, valN* };

Here, the initial values are specified by *val1* through *valN*. They are assigned in sequence, left to right, in index order. Java automatically allocates an array large enough to hold the initializers that you specify. There is no need to explicitly use the **new** operator. For example, here is a better way to write the **MinMax** program:

```
// Use array initializers.
class MinMax2 {
  public static void main(String[] args) {
    int[] nums = { 99, -10, 100123, 18, -978,
                   5623, 463, -9, 287, 49 };    ◄──────── Array initializers
    int min, max;

    min = max = nums[0];
    for(int i=1; i < 10; i++) {
      if(nums[i] < min) min = nums[i];
      if(nums[i] > max) max = nums[i];
    }
    System.out.println("Min and max: " + min + " " + max);
  }
}
```

Array boundaries are strictly enforced in Java; it is a run-time error to overrun or underrun the end of an array. If you want to confirm this for yourself, try the following program that purposely overruns an array.

```
// Demonstrate an array overrun.
class ArrayErr {
  public static void main(String[] args) {
    int[] sample = new int[10];
    int i;

    // generate an array overrun
    for(i = 0; i < 100; i++)
      sample[i] = i;
  }
}
```

As soon as **i** reaches 10, an **ArrayIndexOutOfBoundsException** is generated and the program is terminated.

TRY THIS 5-1   SORTING AN ARRAY

Bubble.java

Because a one-dimensional array organizes data into an indexable linear list, it makes it easy to sort. In this project you will learn a simple way to sort an array. As you may know, there are a number of different sorting algorithms. There are the quicksort, the shaker sort, and the shell sort, to name just three. However, the best known, simplest, and easiest to understand is called the bubble sort. Although the bubble sort is not very efficient for most cases—in fact, its performance is generally unacceptable for sorting large arrays—it can sometimes be effective for sorting small arrays. It is used here, however, because it offers an excellent example that demonstrates the power of arrays.

STEP-BY-STEP

1. Create a file called **Bubble.java**.

2. The bubble sort gets its name from the way it performs the sorting operation. It uses the repeated comparison and, if necessary, exchange of adjacent elements in the array. In this process, small values move toward one end and large ones toward the other end. The bubble sort operates by making several passes through the array, exchanging out-of-place elements when necessary.

    Here is the code that forms the core of the bubble sort. The array being sorted is called **nums**.

```
// This is the Bubble sort.
for(a=1; a < size; a++)
  for(b=size-1; b >= a; b--) {
    if(nums[b-1] > nums[b]) { // if out of order
      // exchange elements
      t = nums[b-1];
      nums[b-1] = nums[b];
      nums[b] = t;
    }
  }
```

    Notice that the sort relies on two **for** loops. The inner loop checks adjacent elements in the array, looking for out-of-order elements. When an out-of-order element pair is found, the two elements are exchanged. With each pass, the smallest of the remaining elements moves into its proper location. The outer loop causes this process to repeat until the entire array has been sorted.

3. Here is the entire **Bubble** program:

```
/*
    Try This 5-1

    Demonstrate the Bubble sort.
*/

class Bubble {
  public static void main(String[] args) {
    int[] nums = { 99, -10, 100123, 18, -978,
                   5623, 463, -9, 287, 49 };
    int a, b, t;
    int size;

    size = 10; // number of elements to sort

    // display original array
    System.out.print("Original array is:");
    for(int i=0; i < size; i++)
      System.out.print(" " + nums[i]);
    System.out.println();
```

```
      // This is the Bubble sort.
      for(a=1; a < size; a++)
        for(b=size-1; b >= a; b--) {
          if(nums[b-1] > nums[b]) { // if out of order
            // exchange elements
            t = nums[b-1];
            nums[b-1] = nums[b];
            nums[b] = t;
          }
        }


      // display sorted array
      System.out.print("Sorted array is:");
      for(int i=0; i < size; i++)
        System.out.print(" " + nums[i]);
      System.out.println();
    }
  }
```

The output from the program is shown here:

```
Original array is: 99 -10 100123 18 -978 5623 463 -9 287 49
Sorted array is: -978 -10 -9 18 49 99 287 463 5623 100123
```

4. As mentioned, although the bubble sort can be useful for small arrays, it is not efficient when used on larger ones. One of the best general-purpose sorting algorithms is the quicksort. The quicksort, however, relies on features of Java that you have not yet learned about.

MULTIDIMENSIONAL ARRAYS

Although the one-dimensional array is used extensively in programming, multidimensional arrays (arrays of two or more dimensions) are certainly not rare. In Java, a multidimensional array is an array of arrays.

Two-Dimensional Arrays

The simplest form of the multidimensional array is the two-dimensional array. A two-dimensional array is, in essence, a list of one-dimensional arrays. A two-dimensional array can be thought of as creating a table of data, with the data organized by row and column. An individual item of data is accessed by specifying its row and column position.

To declare a two-dimensional array, you must specify the size of both dimensions. For example, here **table** is declared to be a two-dimensional array of **int** with the size 10 by 20:

```
int[][] table = new int[10][20];
```

Pay careful attention to the declaration. Unlike some other computer languages, which use commas to separate the array dimensions, Java places each dimension in its own set of brackets. Similarly, to access point 3, 5 of array **table**, you would use **table[3][5]**.

In the next example, a two-dimensional array is loaded with the numbers 1 through 12.

```
// Demonstrate a two-dimensional array.
class TwoD {
  public static void main(String[] args) {
    int t, i;
    int[][] table = new int[3][4];

    for(t=0; t < 3; ++t) {
      for(i=0; i < 4; ++i) {
        table[t][i] = (t*4)+i+1;
        System.out.print(table[t][i] + " ");
      }
      System.out.println();
    }
  }
}
```

In this example, **table[0][0]** will have the value 1, **table[0][1]** the value 2, **table[0][2]** the value 3, and so on. The value of **table[2][3]** will be 12. Conceptually, the array will look like that shown in Figure 5-1. Notice how the data is organized into a tabular form.

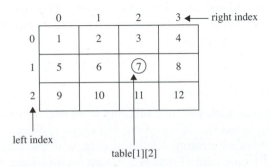

FIGURE 5-1: Conceptual view of the **table** array by the **TwoD** program.

Irregular Arrays

When you allocate memory for a multidimensional array, you need to specify only the memory for the first (leftmost) dimension. You can allocate the remaining dimensions separately. For example, the following code allocates memory for the first dimension of **table** when it is declared. It allocates the second dimension manually.

```
int[][] table = new int[3][];
table[0] = new int[4];
table[1] = new int[4];
table[2] = new int[4];
```

Although there is no advantage to individually allocating the second-dimension arrays in this situation, there can be in others. For example, when you allocate dimensions separately, you do not need to allocate the same number of elements for each index. Since multidimensional arrays are implemented as arrays of arrays, the length of each array is under your control.

For example, assume you are writing a program that stores the number of passengers who ride an airport shuttle. If the shuttle runs 10 times a day during the week and twice a day on Saturday and Sunday, you could use the **riders** array shown in the following program to store the information. Notice that the length of the second dimension for the first five indices is 10 and the length of the second dimension for the last two indices is 2.

```
// Manually allocate differing size second dimensions.
class Ragged {
  public static void main(String[] args) {
    int[][] riders = new int[7][];
    riders[0] = new int[10];          ←
    riders[1] = new int[10];
    riders[2] = new int[10];                Here, the second dimensions
    riders[3] = new int[10];                are 10 elements long.
    riders[4] = new int[10];          ←
    riders[5] = new int[2];    ←
    riders[6] = new int[2];    ←           But here, they are
                                           2 elements long.

    int i, j;

    // fabricate some data
    for(i=0; i < 5; i++)
      for(j=0; j < 10; j++)
        riders[i][j] = i + j + 10;
    for(i=5; i < 7; i++)
      for(j=0; j < 2; j++)
        riders[i][j] = i + j + 10;

    System.out.println("Riders per trip during the week:");
    for(i=0; i < 5; i++) {
      for(j=0; j < 10; j++)
        System.out.print(riders[i][j] + " ");
      System.out.println();
```

```
        }
      System.out.println();

      System.out.println("Riders per trip on the weekend:");
      for(i=5; i < 7; i++) {
        for(j=0; j < 2; j++)
          System.out.print(riders[i][j] + " ");
        System.out.println();
      }
    }
  }
```

The output from the program is shown here.

```
Riders per trip during the week:
10 11 12 13 14 15 16 17 18 19
11 12 13 14 15 16 17 18 19 20
12 13 14 15 16 17 18 19 20 21
13 14 15 16 17 18 19 20 21 22
14 15 16 17 18 19 20 21 22 23

Riders per trip on the weekend:
15 16
16 17
```

The use of irregular (or ragged) multidimensional arrays is not appropriate for all situations. Often, a regular two-dimensional array is the best choice. However, irregular arrays can be quite effective in some situations, such as the example just shown. In general, if you need a very large two-dimensional array that is sparsely populated (that is, one in which few of the elements will be used), an irregular array might be a perfect solution.

Arrays of Three or More Dimensions

Java allows arrays with more than two dimensions. Here is the general form of a multidimensional array declaration:

> *type*[ ][ ]...[ ] *name* = new *type*[*size1*][*size2*]...[*sizeN*];

For example, the following declaration creates a $4 \times 10 \times 3$ three-dimensional integer array.

```
int[][][] multidim = new int[4][10][3];
```

Given this array, the following statement assigns the value 10 to element 2, 7, 1:

```
multidim[2][7][1] = 10;
```

Initializing Multidimensional Arrays

A multidimensional array can be initialized by enclosing each dimension's initializer list within its own set of braces. For example, the general form of array initialization for a two-dimensional array is shown here:

```
type[ ] [ ] array_name = {
    { val, val, val, ..., val },
    { val, val, val, ..., val },
    .
    .
    .
    { val, val, val, ..., val }
};
```

Here, *val* indicates an initialization value. Each inner block designates a row. Within each row, the first value will be stored in the first position of the subarray, the second value in the second position, and so on. Notice that commas separate the initializer blocks and that a semicolon follows the closing }.

For example, the following program initializes an array called **sqrs** with the numbers 1 through 10 and their squares.

```
// Initialize a two-dimensional array.
class Squares {
  public static void main(String[] args) {
    int[][] sqrs = {
      { 1, 1 },
      { 2, 4 },
      { 3, 9 },
      { 4, 16 },
      { 5, 25 },
      { 6, 36 },
      { 7, 49 },
      { 8, 64 },
      { 9, 81 },
      { 10, 100 }
    };
    int i, j;

    for(i=0; i < 10; i++) {
      for(j=0; j < 2; j++)
        System.out.print(sqrs[i][j] + " ");
      System.out.println();
    }
  }
}
```

Notice how each row has its own set of initializers.

Here is the output from the program:

```
1 1
2 4
3 9
4 16
5 25
6 36
```

```
7  49
8  64
9  81
10 100
```

Progress Check

1. For multidimensional arrays, how is each dimension specified?
2. In a two-dimensional array, which is an array of arrays, can the length of each array differ?
3. How are multidimensional arrays initialized?

ALTERNATIVE ARRAY DECLARATION SYNTAX

There is a second form that can be used to declare an array:

type var-name[ ];

Here, the square brackets follow the name of the array variable, not the type specifier. For example, the following two declarations are equivalent:

```
int counter[] = new int[3];
int[] counter = new int[3];
```

The following declarations are also equivalent:

```
char table[][] = new char[3][4];
char[][] table = new char[3][4];
```

This alternative declaration lets you declare both array and nonarray variables of the same type in a single declaration. For example,

```
int alpha, beta[], gamma;
```

Here, **alpha** and **gamma** are of type **int**, but **beta** is an array of **int**.

ASSIGNING ARRAY REFERENCES

As with other objects, when you assign one array reference variable to another, you are simply changing what object that variable refers to. You are not causing a copy of

---

Answers:

1. Each dimension is specified within its own set of square brackets.
2. Yes.
3. Multidimensional arrays are initialized by putting each subarray's initializers inside their own set of braces.

the array to be made, nor are you causing the contents of one array to be copied to the other. For example, consider this program:

```java
// Assigning array reference variables.
class AssignARef {
  public static void main(String[] args) {
    int i;

    int[] nums1 = new int[10];
    int[] nums2 = new int[10];

    for(i=0; i < 10; i++)
      nums1[i] = i;

    for(i=0; i < 10; i++)
      nums2[i] = -i;

    System.out.print("Here is nums1: ");
    for(i=0; i < 10; i++)
      System.out.print(nums1[i] + " ");
    System.out.println();

    System.out.print("Here is nums2: ");
    for(i=0; i < 10; i++)
      System.out.print(nums2[i] + " ");
    System.out.println();

    nums2 = nums1; // now nums2 refers to nums1      ◄───────────── Assign an array reference.

    System.out.print("Here is nums2 after assignment: ");
    for(i=0; i < 10; i++)
      System.out.print(nums2[i] + " ");
    System.out.println();

    // now operate on nums1 array through nums2
    nums2[3] = 99;

    System.out.print("Here is nums1 after change through nums2: ");
    for(i=0; i < 10; i++)
      System.out.print(nums1[i] + " ");
    System.out.println();
  }
}
```

The output from the program is shown here:

```
Here is nums1: 0 1 2 3 4 5 6 7 8 9
Here is nums2: 0 -1 -2 -3 -4 -5 -6 -7 -8 -9
Here is nums2 after assignment: 0 1 2 3 4 5 6 7 8 9
Here is nums1 after change through nums2: 0 1 2 99 4 5 6 7 8 9
```

This example creates two arrays and gives them initial values. Thus, at the start, **nums1** and **nums2** refer to separate and distinct arrays. Next, **nums1** is assigned to **nums2**. After this assignment, both **nums1** and **nums2** now refer to the same array. Therefore, changing the array through **nums2** (as the example does) also affects the array referred to by **nums1** because they both refer to the same array.

USING THE length MEMBER

Because arrays are implemented as objects, each array has associated with it a **length** instance variable that contains the number of elements that the array can hold. In other words, **length** contains the size of the array. Here is a program that demonstrates this property:

```java
// Use the length array member.
class LengthDemo {
  public static void main(String[] args) {
    int[] list = new int[10];
    int[] nums = { 1, 2, 3 };
    int[][] table = { // a variable-length table
      {1, 2, 3},
      {4, 5},
      {6, 7, 8, 9}
    };

    System.out.println("length of list is " + list.length);
    System.out.println("length of nums is " + nums.length);
    System.out.println("length of table is " + table.length);
    System.out.println("length of table[0] is " + table[0].length);
    System.out.println("length of table[1] is " + table[1].length);
    System.out.println("length of table[2] is " + table[2].length);
    System.out.println();

    // use length to initialize list
    for(int i=0; i < list.length; i++)
      list[i] = i * i;

    System.out.print("Here is list: ");
    // now use length to display list
    for(int i=0; i < list.length; i++)
      System.out.print(list[i] + " ");
    System.out.println();
  }
}
```

Use **length** to control a **for** loop.

This program displays the following output:

```
length of list is 10
length of nums is 3
length of table is 3
length of table[0] is 3
```

```
length of table[1] is 2
length of table[2] is 4

Here is list: 0 1 4 9 16 25 36 49 64 81
```

Pay special attention to the way **length** is used with the two-dimensional array **table**. As explained, a two-dimensional array is an array of arrays. Thus, when the expression

```
table.length
```

is used, it obtains the number of arrays stored in **table**, which is 3 in this case. To obtain the length of any individual array in **table**, you will use an expression such as this,

```
table[0].length
```

which, in this case, obtains the length of the first array.

One other thing to notice in **LengthDemo** is the way that **list.length** is used by the **for** loops to govern the number of iterations that take place. Since each array carries with it its own length, you can use this information rather than manually keeping track of an array's size. Keep in mind that the value of **length** has nothing to do with the number of elements that are actually in use. It contains the number of elements that the array is capable of holding.

The inclusion of the **length** member simplifies many algorithms by making certain types of array operations easier—and safer—to perform. For example, the following program uses **length** to copy one array to another while preventing an array overrun and the run-time error that would result.

```java
// Use length variable to help copy an array.
class ACopy {
  public static void main(String[] args) {
    int i;
    int[] nums1 = new int[10];
    int[] nums2 = new int[10];

    for(i=0; i < nums1.length; i++)
      nums1[i] = i;

    // copy nums1 to nums2
    if(nums2.length >= nums1.length)    ← Use length to compare array sizes.
      for(i = 0; i < nums1.length; i++)
        nums2[i] = nums1[i];

    for(i=0; i < nums2.length; i++)
      System.out.print(nums2[i] + " ");
  }
}
```

Here, **length** helps perform two important functions. First, it is used to confirm that the target array is large enough to hold the contents of the source array. Second, it provides the termination condition of the **for** loop that performs the copy. Of course, in this simple example, the sizes of the arrays are easily known, but this same approach can be applied to a wide range of more challenging situations.

One more point about **length**: it is read-only. Therefore, you cannot assign it a new value. This means that you can't change the length of an array by changing the value of **length**.

TRY THIS 5-2   A SIMPLE STACK CLASS

`SimpleStackDemo.java`

One of the foundational elements of programming is the *data structure*. Although we will look more closely at data structures in Part Three, when those supported by the Java library are described, you now know enough about Java to be introduced to the concept.

At its core, a data structure provides a means of organizing data. The simplest data structure is the array. As you have just seen, an array is a linear list that supports random access to its elements. Arrays are often used as the underpinning for more sophisticated data structures, one of which is the stack. A *stack* is a list in which elements can be accessed in last-in, first-out (LIFO) order only. Thus, a stack is like a stack of plates on a table—the first down is the last to be used. Furthermore, a new plate can be added only to the top of the stack, and when a plate is needed, it must be removed from the top.

One thing that makes data structures such as stacks especially interesting is that they combine *storage* for information with the methods that *access* that information. Such a combination is, obviously, an excellent choice for encapsulation within a class. In fact, this is the way such data structures are normally implemented.

In this project, you will implement a simple stack. The stack is chosen for two reasons. First, a stack represents one of the quintessential examples of object-oriented programming because it shows a compact, yet realistic, application. Second, because our implementation is based on an array, it provides another example of array handling. Here you will create an initial implementation of the stack. Subsequent chapters will expand and enhance its capabilities as we introduce new elements of Java. For simplicity, the stack developed here stores characters, but it can be easily adapted to store other types of data.

In general, stacks support two basic operations, traditionally called *push* and *pop*. Each push operation puts a new element on the top of the stack. Each pop operation retrieves the top element from the stack. Thus, a new element is added to the stack by putting it on the top, and an element is removed from the stack by taking it off the top. No other access to a stack's elements is supported. For example, you can't remove an element from the middle of a stack. Furthermore, popping an element from the stack consumes that element. In other words, once an element has been retrieved, it cannot be retrieved again.

A stack has two boundary conditions: full and empty. A stack is full when there is no space available to store another item. It is empty when all of its elements have been removed.

One last point: As you will see in Part Three, the Java library provides a powerful, full-featured stack class that is part of the Collections Framework. Since our stack class is much simpler, we will call it **SimpleStack**.

STEP-BY-STEP

1. Create a file called **SimpleStackDemo.java**.

2. As explained, an array will provide the underlying storage for the stack. Since this version of the stack stores characters, a **char** array is used. This array is accessed through an index that indicates the top of the stack. With this in mind, begin creating the **SimpleStack** class with these lines:

```
class SimpleStack {
  char[] data; // this array holds the stack
  int tos; // index of top of stack
```

Here, **data** will refer to the array that holds the stack, and **tos** is the index of the top of the stack. In our implementation, the top of the stack indicates the next location at which a new item will be stored.

3. Add the constructor for **SimpleStack** shown here. It creates an empty stack of a given size.

```
// Construct an empty stack given its size.
SimpleStack(int size) {
  data = new char[size]; // create the array to hold the stack
  tos = 0;
}
```

The constructor creates an array of the specified size to hold the stack and assigns to **data** a reference to that array. Since the stack is initially empty, **tos** is initialized to zero. As just explained, **tos** is the index at which the next item will be stored.

4. **SimpleStack** uses four methods: **push( )**, **pop( )**, **isFull( )**, and **isEmpty( )**. These provide the basic functionality of the stack: putting an item on the stack, removing an item from the stack, and determining when the stack is full or empty. The following steps describe them.

5. Add the **push( )** method, which puts a new element on the top of the stack. It is shown here:

```
// Push a character onto the stack.
void push(char ch) {
  if(isFull()) {
    System.out.println(" -- Stack is full.");
    return;
  }
```

```
    data[tos] = ch;
    tos++;
}
```

Here is how it works. First, a check is made to ensure that the stack is not full. This is done by calling the **isFull( )** method. If the stack is full, then a message is displayed and the method returns. Otherwise, **ch** is added to the top of the stack by assigning it to the index indicated by **tos**, and then **tos** is incremented. As explained, **tos** contains the index at which the next item will be stored.

6. Add the **pop( )** method, shown next. It removes and returns the top element in the stack.

```
// Pop a character from the stack.
char pop() {
  if(isEmpty()) {
    System.out.println(" -- Stack is empty.");
    return (char) 0; // a placeholder value
  }

  tos--;
  return data[tos];
}
```

When **pop( )** is called, it first checks if the stack is empty by calling **isEmpty( )**. If the stack is empty, a message is displayed and a placeholder value of 0 is returned. If the stack is not empty, then **tos** is decremented and the character at that index is returned.

7. Before moving on, it is important to point out that displaying a message inside **push( )** and **pop( )** when a stack-full or a stack-empty condition occurs is simply for demonstration purposes at this time. Such an approach would never be used in a real-world application. The same applies to **pop( )** returning a placeholder value when the stack is empty. Later, in Chapter 10, you will learn a better way to handle errors. Until then, this approach is sufficient.

8. The **isFull( )** method, shown here, returns **true** when the stack is full. Add it to **SimpleStack**.

```
// Return true if the stack is full.
boolean isFull() {
  return tos==data.length;
}
```

The stack is full when **tos** is equal to the length of the array. Remember, array indexing begins at zero, so **data.length** is one beyond the last element in the array.

9. Conclude **SimpleStack** by adding the **isEmpty( )** method, shown next. It returns true when the stack is empty.

```java
// Return true if the stack is empty.
boolean isEmpty() {
  return tos==0;
}
}
```

The stack is empty when **tos** equals zero. This will be the case only when either no elements have yet been added to the stack or the last element has been removed.

10. Here is the entire **SimpleStack** class along with a class called **SimpleStackDemo.java** that demonstrates it.

```java
/*
    Try This 5-2

    A simple stack class for characters.
*/

class SimpleStack {
  char[] data; // this array holds the stack
  int tos; // index of top of stack

  // Construct an empty stack given its size.
  SimpleStack(int size) {
    data = new char[size]; // create the array to hold the stack
    tos = 0;
  }

  // Push a character onto the stack.
  void push(char ch) {
    if(isFull()) {
      System.out.println(" -- Stack is full.");
      return;
    }

    data[tos] = ch;
    tos++;
  }

  // Pop a character from the stack.
  char pop() {
    if(isEmpty()) {
      System.out.println(" -- Stack is empty.");
      return (char) 0; // a placeholder value
    }
```

```
      tos--;
      return data[tos];
    }

    // Return true if the stack is empty.
    boolean isEmpty() {
      return tos==0;
    }

    // Return true if the stack is full.
    boolean isFull() {
      return tos==data.length;
    }
  }

// Demonstrate the SimpleStack class.
class SimpleStackDemo {
  public static void main(String[] args) {
    int i;
    char ch;

    System.out.println("Demonstrate SimpleStack\n");

    // Construct 10-element empty stack.
    SimpleStack stack = new SimpleStack(10);

    System.out.println("Push 10 items onto a 10-element stack.");

    // Push the letters A through J onto the stack.
    System.out.print("Pushing: ");
    for(ch = 'A'; ch < 'K'; ch++) {
      System.out.print(ch);
      stack.push(ch);
    }

    System.out.println("\nPop those 10 items from stack.");

    // Now, pop the characters off the stack.
    // Notice that order will be the reverse of those pushed.
    System.out.print("Popping: ");
    for(i=0; i < 10; i++) {
      ch = stack.pop();
      System.out.print(ch);
    }

    System.out.println("\n\nNext, use isEmpty() and isFull() " +
                       "to fill and empty the stack.");

    // Push the letters until the stack is full.
    System.out.print("Pushing: ");
```

```
    for(ch = 'A'; !stack.isFull(); ch++) {
       System.out.print(ch);
       stack.push(ch);
    }

    System.out.println();

    // Now, pop the characters off the stack until it is empty.
    System.out.print("Popping: ");
    while(!stack.isEmpty()) {
      ch = stack.pop();
      System.out.print(ch);
    }

    System.out.println("\n\nNow, use a 4-element stack to generate" +
                        " some errors.");

    // Generate some errors.
    SimpleStack smallStack = new SimpleStack(4);

    // Attempt to push 5 characters onto a 4-character stack
    System.out.print("Pushing: ");
    for(ch = '1'; ch < '6'; ch++) {
      System.out.print(ch);
      smallStack.push(ch);
    }

    // Attempt to pop 5 elements from a 4-character stack.
    System.out.print("Popping: ");
    for(i=0; i < 5; i++) {
      ch = smallStack.pop();
      System.out.print(ch);
    }
   }
  }
}
```

11. The output produced by the program is shown here:

```
Demonstrate SimpleStack

Push 10 items onto a 10-element stack.
Pushing: ABCDEFGHIJ
Pop those 10 items from stack.
Popping: JIHGFEDCBA

Next, use isEmpty() and isFull() to fill and empty the stack.
Pushing: ABCDEFGHIJ
Popping: JIHGFEDCBA
```

```
Now, use a 4-element stack to generate some errors.
Pushing: 12345 -- Stack is full.
Popping: 4321 -- Stack is empty.
```

Notice in the output that elements are popped from the stack in the opposite order in which they are pushed onto the stack. Remember, a stack uses last-in, first-out ordering. Also notice how **isFull( )** and **isEmpty( )** can be used to manage a stack to avoid stack-full and stack-empty error conditions.

12. Before moving on, you might want to try an experiment. Although **SimpleStack** stores characters, its logic will work with other types of data. Try modifying **SimpleStack** so that it stores another type of data, such as **int** or **double**.

THE FOR-EACH STYLE for LOOP

When working with arrays, it is common to encounter situations in which each element in an array must be examined, from start to finish. For example, to compute the sum of the values held in an array, each element in the array must be examined. The same situation occurs when computing an average, searching for a value, copying an array, and so on. Because such "start to finish" operations are so common, Java defines a second form of the **for** loop that streamlines them.

The second form of the **for** implements a "for-each" style loop. A for-each loop cycles through a collection of objects, such as an array, in strictly sequential fashion, from start to finish. In recent years, for-each style loops have gained popularity among both computer language designers and programmers. Originally, Java did not offer a for-each style loop, but it was added with the JDK 5 release. The for-each style of **for** is also referred to as the *enhanced for loop.* Both terms are used in this book.

The general form of the for-each style **for** is shown here.

for(*type itr-var* : *collection*) *statement-block*

Here, *type* specifies the type, and *itr-var* specifies the name of an *iteration variable* that will receive the elements from a collection, one at a time, from beginning to end. The collection being cycled through is specified by *collection.* Various types of collections can be used with the **for**, but the only type used in this chapter is the array. With each iteration of the loop, the next element in the collection is retrieved and stored in *itr-var.* The loop repeats until all elements in the collection have been obtained. Thus, when iterating over an array of size N, the enhanced **for** obtains the elements in the array in index order, from 0 to $N-1$.

Because the iteration variable receives values from the collection, *type* must be the same as (or compatible with) the elements stored in the collection. Thus, when iterating over arrays, *type* must be compatible with the element type of the array.

Ask the Expert

Q Aside from arrays, what other types of collections can the for-each style **for** loop cycle through?

A One of the most important uses of the for-each style **for** is to cycle through the contents of a collection defined by the Collections Framework. The Collections Framework is a set of classes that implement various data structures, such as lists, vectors, sets, and maps. A discussion of the Collections Framework is found in Chapter 25.

To understand the motivation behind a for-each style loop, consider the type of **for** loop that it is designed to replace. The following fragment uses a traditional **for** loop to compute the sum of the values in an array:

```java
int[] nums = { 1, 2, 3, 4, 5, 6, 7, 8, 9, 10 };
int sum = 0;

for(int i=0; i < 10; i++) sum += nums[i];
```

To compute the sum, each element in **nums** is read, in order, from start to finish. Thus, the entire array is read in strictly sequential order. This is accomplished by manually indexing the **nums** array by **i**, the loop control variable. Furthermore, the starting and ending value for the loop control variable, and its increment, must be explicitly specified.

The for-each style **for** automates the preceding loop. Specifically, it eliminates the need to establish a loop counter, specify a starting and ending value, and manually index the array. Instead, it automatically cycles through the entire array, obtaining one element at a time, in sequence, from beginning to end. For example, here is the preceding fragment rewritten using a for-each version of the **for**:

```java
int[] nums = { 1, 2, 3, 4, 5, 6, 7, 8, 9, 10 };
int sum = 0;

for(int x : nums) sum += x;
```

With each pass through the loop, **x** is automatically given a value equal to the next element in **nums**. Thus, on the first iteration, **x** contains 1, on the second iteration, **x** contains 2, and so on. Not only is the syntax streamlined, it also prevents boundary errors.

Here is an entire program that demonstrates the for-each version of the **for** just described:

```java
// Use a for-each style for loop.
class ForEach {
  public static void main(String[] args) {
    int[] nums = { 1, 2, 3, 4, 5, 6, 7, 8, 9, 10 };
    int sum = 0;
```

```
// Use for-each style for to display and sum the values.
for(int x : nums) {
  System.out.println("Value is: " + x);
  sum += x;
}

  System.out.println("Summation: " + sum);
}
}
```

A for-each style **for** loop

The output from the program is shown here:

```
Value is: 1
Value is: 2
Value is: 3
Value is: 4
Value is: 5
Value is: 6
Value is: 7
Value is: 8
Value is: 9
Value is: 10
Summation: 55
```

As this output shows, the for-each style **for** automatically cycles through an array in sequence from the lowest index to the highest.

Although the for-each **for** loop iterates until all elements in an array have been examined, it is possible to terminate the loop early by using a **break** statement. For example, this loop sums only the first five elements of **nums**.

```
// Sum only the first 5 elements.
for(int x : nums) {
  System.out.println("Value is: " + x);
  sum += x;
  if(x == 5) break; // stop the loop when 5 is obtained
}
```

There is one important point to understand about the for-each style **for** loop. Its iteration variable is "read-only" as it relates to the underlying array. An assignment to the iteration variable has no effect on the underlying array. In other words, you can't change the contents of the array by assigning the iteration variable a new value. For example, consider this program:

```
// The for-each loop is essentially read-only.
class NoChange {
  public static void main(String[] args) {
    int[] nums = { 1, 2, 3, 4, 5, 6, 7, 8, 9, 10 };

    for(int x : nums) {
      System.out.print(x + " ");
      x = x * 10; // no effect on nums
```

This does not change **nums**.

```
    }

  System.out.println();

    for(int x : nums)
       System.out.print(x + " ");

    System.out.println();
  }
}
```

The first **for** loop increases the value of the iteration variable by a factor of 10. However, this assignment has no effect on the underlying array **nums**, as the output from the second **for** loop illustrates.

```
1 2 3 4 5 6 7 8 9 10
1 2 3 4 5 6 7 8 9 10
```

As you can see, the **nums** array is unchanged.

Iterating Over Multidimensional Arrays

The enhanced **for** also works on multidimensional arrays. Remember, however, that in Java, multidimensional arrays consist of *arrays of arrays*. (For example, a two-dimensional array is an array of one-dimensional arrays.) This is important when iterating over a multidimensional array because each iteration obtains the *next array*, not an individual element. Furthermore, the iteration variable in the **for** loop must be compatible with the type of array being obtained. For example, in the case of a two-dimensional array, the iteration variable must be a reference to a one-dimensional array. In general, when using the for-each **for** to iterate over an array of *N* dimensions, the objects obtained will be arrays of *N*–1 dimensions. To understand the implications of this, consider the following program. It uses nested **for** loops to obtain the elements of a two-dimensional array in row order, from first to last. Notice how **x** is declared.

```
// Use for-each style for on a two-dimensional array.
class ForEach2 {
  public static void main(String[] args) {
    int sum = 0;
    int[][] nums = new int[3][5];

    // give nums some values
    for(int i = 0; i < 3; i++)
      for(int j=0; j < 5; j++)
        nums[i][j] = (i+1)*(j+1);

    // Use for-each for loop to display and sum the values.
    for(int[] x : nums) {  ◄──────────┐
      for(int y : x) {                │
        System.out.println("Value is: " + y); │
        sum += y;                     │
    }                    Notice how x is declared.
```

```
      }
         System.out.println("Summation: " + sum);
      }
}
```

The output from this program is shown here:

```
Value is: 1
Value is: 2
Value is: 3
Value is: 4
Value is: 5
Value is: 2
Value is: 4
Value is: 6
Value is: 8
Value is: 10
Value is: 3
Value is: 6
Value is: 9
Value is: 12
Value is: 15
Summation: 90
```

In the program, pay special attention to this line:

```
for(int[] x : nums) {
```

Notice how **x** is declared. It is a reference to a one-dimensional array of integers. This is necessary because each iteration of the **for** obtains the next *array* in **nums**, beginning with the array specified by **nums[0]**. The inner **for** loop then cycles through each of these arrays, displaying the values of each element.

Applying the Enhanced for

Since the for-each style **for** can only cycle through an array sequentially, from start to finish, you might think that its use is limited. However, this is not true. A large number of algorithms require exactly this mechanism. One of the most common is searching. For example, the following program uses a **for** loop to search an unsorted array for a value. It stops if the value is found.

```
// Search an array using for-each style for.
class Search {
  public static void main(String[] args) {
    int[] nums = { 6, 8, 3, 7, 5, 6, 1, 4 };
    int val = 5;
    boolean found = false;

    // Use for-each style for to search nums for val.
    for(int x : nums) {
      if(x == val) {
        found = true;
        break;
```

```
        }
    }

    if(found)
      System.out.println("Value found!");
  }
}
```

The for-each style **for** is an excellent choice in this application because searching an unsorted array involves examining each element in sequence. Other types of applications that benefit from for-each style loops include computing an average, finding the minimum or maximum of a set, looking for duplicates, and so on.

Progress Check

1. What does the for-each style **for** loop do?
2. Given an array of **double** called **nums**, show a for-each style **for** that cycles through it.
3. Can the for-each style **for** cycle through the contents of a multidimensional array?

STRINGS

From a day-to-day programming standpoint, one of the most important of Java's data types is **String**. **String** defines and supports character strings. In many other programming languages a string is an array of characters. This is not the case with Java. In Java, strings are objects.

Actually, you have been using the **String** class since Chapter 1, but you did not know it. When you create a string literal, you are actually creating a **String** object. For example, in the statement

```
System.out.println("In Java, strings are objects.");
```

the string "In Java, strings are objects." is automatically made into a **String** object by Java. Thus, use of the **String** class has been "below the surface" in the preceding programs. In the following sections you will learn to handle it explicitly. Be aware, however, that the **String** class is quite large, and we will only scratch its surface here. It is examined in detail in Part Three.

Answers:

1. A for-each style **for** cycles through the contents of a collection, such as an array, from start to finish.
2. `for(double d : nums) ...`
3. Yes; however, each iteration obtains the next subarray.

Constructing Strings

You can construct a **String** just like you construct any other type of object: by using **new** and calling the **String** constructor. For example:

```
String str = new String("Hello");
```

This creates a **String** object called **str** that contains the character string "Hello". You can also construct a **String** from another **String**. For example:

```
String str = new String("Hello");
String str2 = new String(str);
```

After this sequence executes, **str2** will also contain the character string "Hello".

Another easy way to create a **String** is shown here:

```
String str = "Java strings are powerful.";
```

In this case, **str** is initialized to the character sequence "Java strings are powerful."

Once you have created a **String** object, you can use it anywhere that a quoted string is allowed. For example, you can use a **String** object as an argument to **println( )**, as shown in this example:

```
// Introduce String.
class StringDemo {
  public static void main(String[] args) {
    // declare strings in various ways
    String str1 = new String("Java strings are objects.");
    String str2 = "They are constructed various ways.";
    String str3 = new String(str2);

    System.out.println(str1);
    System.out.println(str2);
    System.out.println(str3);
  }
}
```

The output from the program is shown here:

```
Java strings are objects.
They are constructed various ways.
They are constructed various ways.
```

Operating on Strings

The **String** class contains several methods that operate on strings. Here are the general forms for a few:

boolean equals(*str*)	Returns true if the invoking string contains the same character sequence as *str*.
int length( )	Returns the number of characters in the string.
char charAt(*index*)	Returns the character at the index specified by *index*.

int compareTo(*str*)	Returns less than zero if the invoking string is less than *str*, greater than zero if the invoking string is greater than *str*, and zero if the strings are equal.
int indexOf(*str*)	Searches the invoking string for the substring specified by *str*. Returns the index of the first match or –1 on failure.
int lastIndexOf(*str*)	Searches the invoking string for the substring specified by *str*. Returns the index of the last match or –1 on failure.

Here is a program that demonstrates these methods:

```java
// Some String operations.
class StrOps {
  public static void main(String[] args) {
    String str1 =
      "When it comes to Web programming, Java is #1.";
    String str2 = new String(str1);
    String str3 = "Java strings are powerful.";
    int result, idx;
    char ch;

    System.out.println("Length of str1: " + str1.length());

    // display str1, one char at a time.
    for(int i=0; i < str1.length(); i++)
      System.out.print(str1.charAt(i));
    System.out.println();

    if(str1.equals(str2))
      System.out.println("str1 equals str2");
    else
      System.out.println("str1 does not equal str2");

    if(str1.equals(str3))
      System.out.println("str1 equals str3");
    else
      System.out.println("str1 does not equal str3");

    result = str1.compareTo(str3);
    if(result == 0)
      System.out.println("str1 and str3 are equal");
    else if(result < 0)
      System.out.println("str1 is less than str3");
    else
      System.out.println("str1 is greater than str3");

    // assign a new string to str2
    str2 = "One Two Three One";

    idx = str2.indexOf("One");
    System.out.println("Index of first occurrence of One: " + idx);
```

```
      idx = str2.lastIndexOf("One");
      System.out.println("Index of last occurrence of One: " + idx);
  }
}
```

This program generates the following output:

```
Length of str1: 45
When it comes to Web programming, Java is #1.
str1 equals str2
str1 does not equal str3
str1 is greater than str3
Index of first occurrence of One: 0
Index of last occurrence of One: 14
```

You can *concatenate* (join together) two strings using the + operator. For example, this sequence

```
String str1 = "One";
String str2 = "Two";
String str3 = "Three";
String str4 = str1 + str2 + str3;
```

initializes **str4** with the string "OneTwoThree".

Ask the Expert

Q Why does **String** define the **equals( )** method? Can't I just use **==**?

A The **equals( )** method compares the character sequences of two **String** objects for equality. Applying the **==** to two **String** references simply determines whether the two references refer to the same object.

Arrays of Strings

Like any other data type, strings can be assembled into arrays. For example:

```
// Demonstrate String arrays.
class StringArrays {
  public static void main(String[] args) {
    String[] strs = { "This", "is", "a", "test." };

    System.out.println("Original array: ");
    for(String s : strs)
      System.out.print(s + " ");
    System.out.println("\n");

    // change a string in the array
    strs[1] = "was";
    strs[3] = "test, too!";
```

```
      System.out.println("Modified array: ");
      for(String s : strs)
        System.out.print(s + " ");
  }
}
```

Here is the output from this program:

```
Original array:
This is a test.

Modified array:
This was a test, too!
```

In the program, pay special attention to this line:

```
String[] strs = { "This", "is", "a", "test." };
```

It creates an array of strings called **strs** that consists of the strings specified in its initializer list. As the program illustrates, other than containing strings, **strs** works just like any other array in Java.

Strings Are Immutable

The contents of a **String** object are immutable. That is, once created, the character sequence that makes up the string cannot be altered. This restriction allows Java to implement strings more efficiently. Even though this probably sounds like a serious drawback, it isn't. When you need a string that is a variation on one that already exists, simply create a new string that contains the desired changes. Since unused **String** objects are automatically garbage collected, you don't even need to worry about what happens to the discarded strings. It must be made clear, however, that a **String** reference variable may, of course, be assigned a reference to a different **String** object. It is just that the contents of a specific **String** object cannot be changed after it is created.

Ask the Expert

Q You say that once created, **String** objects are immutable. I understand that, from a practical point of view, this is not a serious restriction, but what if I want to create a string that can be changed?

A You're in luck because the Java library provides classes that support mutable strings. One is called **StringBuffer**. It adds methods that modify the string it holds. For example, in addition to the **charAt( )** method, which obtains the character at a specific location, **StringBuffer** defines **setCharAt( )**, which sets a character within the string. However, for most purposes you will want to use **String**, not **StringBuffer**.

To fully understand why immutable strings are not a hindrance, we will use another of **String**'s methods: **substring( )**. The **substring( )** method returns a new string that contains a specified portion of the invoking string. Because a new **String** object is manufactured that contains the substring, the original string is unaltered, and the rule of immutability remains intact. The form of **substring( )** that we will be using is shown here:

String substring(int *startIndex*, int *endIndex*)

Here, *startIndex* specifies the beginning index, and *endIndex* specifies the stopping point. The string returned contains all the characters from the beginning index, up to, but not including, the ending index. Here is a program that demonstrates **substring( )** and the principle of immutable strings:

```
// Use substring().
class SubStr {
  public static void main(String[] args) {
    String orgstr = "Java makes the Web move.";

    // construct a substring
    String substr = orgstr.substring(5, 18);   ← This creates a new string that contains the desired substring.

    System.out.println("orgstr: " + orgstr);
    System.out.println("substr: " + substr);
  }
}
```

Here is the output from the program:

```
orgstr: Java makes the Web move.
substr: makes the Web
```

As you can see, the original string **orgstr** is unchanged, and **substr** contains the substring.

Using a String to Control a switch Statement

As mentioned in Chapter 3, prior to JDK 7, a **switch** had to be controlled by an integer type, such as **int** or **char**. This precluded the use of a **switch** in situations in which one of several actions is selected based on the contents of a string. Instead, an **if-else-if** ladder was the typical solution. Although an **if-else-if** ladder is semantically correct, a **switch** statement would be the more natural idiom for such a selection. Fortunately, this situation has been remedied. Beginning with JDK 7, you can now use a **String** to control a switch. This results in more readable, streamlined code in many situations.

One good use for a **String**-controlled **switch** is when some action must be taken based on a command given in string form. Imagine a **switch** statement that manages a connection to the Internet based on the command that is in string form. For example, the command might have been entered by the user or obtained from an external script.

The following program illustrates how you could easily handle the situation through the use of a **switch** controlled by a **String**:

```java
// Use a string to control a switch statement.

class StringSwitch {
  public static void main(String[] args) {

    String command = "cancel";

    switch(command) {
      case "connect":
        System.out.println("Connecting");
        // ...
        break;
      case "cancel":
        System.out.println("Canceling");
        // ...
        break;
      case "disconnect":
        System.out.println("Disconnecting");
        // ...
        break;
      default:
        System.out.println("Command Error!");
        break;
    }
  }
}
```

As you would expect, the output from the program is

```
Canceling
```

The string contained in **command** (which is "cancel" in this program) is tested against the **case** constants. When a match is found (as it is in the second **case**), the code sequence associated with that string is executed.

Being able to use strings in a **switch** statement can be very convenient and can improve the readability of some code. For example, using a string-based **switch** is an improvement over using the equivalent sequence of **if/else** statements. However, switching on strings is more expensive than switching on integers. Therefore, it is best to switch on strings only in cases in which the controlling data is already in string form, such as when the string is entered by the user or is obtained from an external source.

USING COMMAND-LINE ARGUMENTS

Now that you know about the **String** class, you can understand the **args** parameter to **main( )** that has been in every program shown so far. Many programs accept what are called *command-line arguments*. A command-line argument is the information that directly follows the program's name on the command line when it is executed. To access the command-line arguments inside a Java program is quite easy—they are stored as strings in the **String** array passed to **main( )**. For example, the following program displays all of the command-line arguments that it is called with:

```
// Display all command-line information.
class CLDemo {
  public static void main(String[] args) {
    System.out.println("There are " + args.length +
                       " command-line arguments.");

    System.out.println("They are: ");
    for(int i=0; i<args.length; i++)
      System.out.println("arg[" + i + "]: " + args[i]);
  }
}
```

If **CLDemo** is executed like this,

```
java CLDemo one two three
```

you will see the following output:

```
There are 3 command-line arguments.
They are:
arg[0]: one
arg[1]: two
arg[2]: three
```

Notice that the first argument is stored at index 0, the second argument is stored at index 1, and so on.

To get an idea of the way command-line arguments can be used, consider the next program. It takes one command-line argument that specifies a person's name. It then searches through a two-dimensional array of strings for that name. If it finds a match, it displays that person's telephone number.

```
// A simple automated telephone directory.
class Phone {
  public static void main(String[] args) {
    String[][] numbers = {
      { "Tom", "555-3322" },
      { "Mary", "555-8976" },
      { "Jon", "555-1037" },
      { "Rachel", "555-1400" }
    };
    int i;

    if(args.length != 1)          ◄———————————— To use the program,
      System.out.println("Usage: java Phone <name>");   one command-line
    else {                                              argument must be
      for(i=0; i<numbers.length; i++) {                 present.
        if(numbers[i][0].equals(args[0])) {
          System.out.println(numbers[i][0] + ": " +
```

```
                            numbers[i][1]);
            break;
          }
        }
      if(i == numbers.length)
        System.out.println("Name not found.");
    }
  }
}
```

Here is a sample run:

```
C>java Phone Mary
Mary: 555-8976
```

Progress Check

1. In Java, all strings are objects. True or False?
2. How can you obtain the length of a string?
3. What are command-line arguments?

THE BITWISE OPERATORS

In Chapter 2 you learned about Java's arithmetic, relational, and logical operators. Although these are some of the most commonly used, Java provides additional operators that expand the set of problems to which Java can be applied. Among these are the bitwise operators. The bitwise operators can be applied to values of type **long, int, short, char**, or **byte**. Bitwise operations cannot be used on **boolean, float**, or **double**, or class types. They are called the bitwise operators because they are used to test, set, or shift the individual bits that make up a value. Bitwise operations are important to a wide variety of programming tasks, such as when status information from a device must be interrogated or constructed. Table 5-1 lists the bitwise operators.

The Bitwise AND, OR, XOR, and NOT Operators

The bitwise operators AND, OR, XOR, and NOT are **&, |, ^**, and **~**. They perform the same operations as their Boolean logical equivalents described in Chapter 2. The

---

Answers:

1. True.
2. The length of a string can be obtained by calling the **length( )** method.
3. Command-line arguments are specified on the command line when a program is executed. They are passed as strings to the **args** parameter of **main( )**.

TABLE 5-1: The Bitwise Operators	
Operator	**Result**
&	Bitwise AND
|	Bitwise OR
^	Bitwise exclusive OR
>>	Shift right
>>>	Unsigned shift right
<<	Shift left
~	One's complement (unary NOT)

difference is that the bitwise operators work on a bit-by-bit basis. The following table shows the outcome of each operation using 1's and 0's.

p	q	p & q	p | q	p ^ q	~p
0	0	0	0	0	1
1	0	0	1	1	0
0	1	0	1	1	1
1	1	1	1	0	0

It is sometimes helpful to think of the bitwise AND as a way to turn bits off. That is, any bit that is 0 in either operand will cause the corresponding bit in the outcome to be set to 0. For example:

```
  1 1 0 1  0 0 1 1
& 1 0 1 0  1 0 1 0
  1 0 0 0  0 0 1 0
```

The following program demonstrates the **&** by turning any lowercase letter into uppercase by resetting the 6th bit to 0. As the Unicode/ASCII character set is defined, the lowercase letters are the same as the uppercase ones except that the lowercase ones are greater in value by exactly 32. Therefore, to transform a lowercase letter to uppercase, just turn off the 6th bit, as this program illustrates.

```java
// Uppercase letters.
class UpCase {
  public static void main(String[] args) {
    char ch;

    for(int i=0; i < 10; i++) {
      ch = (char) ('a' + i);
      System.out.print(ch);

      // This statement turns off the 6th bit.
      ch = (char) ((int) ch & 65503); // ch is now uppercase
```

```
        System.out.print(ch + " ");
      }
    }
}
```

The output from this program is shown here:

```
aA bB cC dD eE fF gG hH iI jJ
```

The value 65,503 used in the AND statement is the decimal representation of the binary value 1111 1111 1101 1111. Thus, the AND operation leaves all bits in **ch** unchanged except for the 6th one, which is set to 0.

The AND operator is also useful when you want to determine whether a bit is on or off. For example, this statement determines whether bit 4 in **status** is set:

```
if((status & 8) != 0) System.out.println("bit 4 is on");
```

The number 8 is used because it translates into a binary value that has only the 4th bit set. Therefore, the **if** statement can succeed only when bit 4 of **status** is also on. An interesting use of this concept is to show the bits of a **byte** value in binary format.

```
// Display the bits within a byte.
class ShowBitsInByte {
  public static void main(String[] args) {
    int t;
    byte val;

    val = 123;
    for(t=128; t > 0; t = t/2) {
      if((val & t) != 0) System.out.print("1 ");
      else System.out.print("0 ");
    }
  }
}
```

The output is shown here:

```
0 1 1 1 1 0 1 1
```

The **for** loop successively tests each bit in **val**, using the bitwise AND, to determine whether it is on or off. If the bit is on, the digit **1** is displayed; otherwise, **0** is displayed. In Try This 5-3, you will see how this basic concept can be expanded to create a class that will display the bits in any type of integer.

The bitwise OR, as the reverse of AND, can be used to turn bits on. Any bit that is set to 1 in either operand will cause the corresponding bit in the result to be set to 1. For example:

```
  1 1 0 1 0 0 1 1
| 1 0 1 0 1 0 1 0
  1 1 1 1 1 0 1 1
```

We can make use of the OR to change the uppercasing program into a lowercasing program, as shown here:

```
// Lowercase letters.
class LowCase {
  public static void main(String[] args) {
    char ch;

    for(int i=0; i < 10; i++) {
      ch = (char) ('A' + i);
      System.out.print(ch);

      // This statement turns on the 6th bit.
      ch = (char) ((int) ch | 32); // ch is now lowercase

      System.out.print(ch + " ");
    }
  }
}
```

The output from this program is shown here:

```
Aa Bb Cc Dd Ee Ff Gg Hh Ii Jj
```

The program works by ORing each character with the value 32, which is 0000 0000 0010 0000 in binary. Thus, 32 is the value that, in binary, has only the 6th bit set. When this value is ORed with any other value, it produces a result in which the 6th bit is set and all other bits remain unchanged. As explained, for characters this means that each uppercase letter is transformed into its lowercase equivalent.

An exclusive OR, usually abbreviated XOR, will result in a set bit if, and only if, the bits being compared are different, as illustrated here:

```
    0 1 1 1 1 1 1 1
^   1 0 1 1 1 0 0 1
    1 1 0 0 0 1 1 0
```

The XOR operator has an interesting property. When some value X is XORed with another value Y, and then that result is XORed with Y again, X is produced. That is, given the sequence

```
R1 = X ^ Y; R2 = R1 ^ Y;
```

then R2 is the same value as X. Thus, the outcome of a sequence of two XORs produces the original value.

You can use this principle to create a simple cipher program in which some integer is the key that is used to both encode and decode a message by XORing the characters in that message. To encode, the XOR operation is applied the first time, yielding the cipher text. To decode, the XOR is applied a second time, yielding the plain text. Of course, such a cipher has no practical value, being trivially easy to break. It does, however, provide an interesting way to demonstrate the XOR. Here is a program that uses this approach to encode and decode a short message:

```java
// Use XOR to encode and decode a message.
class SimpleCipher {
  public static void main(String[] args) {
    String msg = "This is a test";
    String encMsg = "";
    String decMsg = "";
    int key = 88;

    System.out.print("Original message: ");
    System.out.println(msg);

    // encode the message
    for(int i=0; i < msg.length(); i++)
      encMsg = encMsg + (char) (msg.charAt(i) ^ key);

    System.out.print("Encoded message: ");
    System.out.println(encMsg);

    // decode the message
    for(int i=0; i < msg.length(); i++)
      decMsg = decMsg + (char) (encMsg.charAt(i) ^ key);

    System.out.print("Decoded message: ");
    System.out.println(decMsg);
  }
}
```

This constructs the encoded string.

This constructs the decoded string.

Here is the output:

```
Original message: This is a test
Encoded message: 01+x1+x9x,=+,
Decoded message: This is a test
```

As you can see, the result of two XORs using the same key produces the decoded message.

The unary one's complement (NOT) operator reverses the state of all the bits of the operand. For example, if some integer called **A** has the bit pattern 1001 0110, then ~A produces a result with the bit pattern 0110 1001.

The following program demonstrates the NOT operator by displaying a number and its complement in binary.

```java
// Demonstrate the bitwise NOT.
class NotDemo {
  public static void main(String[] args) {
    byte b = -34;

    for(int t=128; t > 0; t = t/2) {
      if((b & t) != 0) System.out.print("1 ");
      else System.out.print("0 ");
```

```
    }
    System.out.println();

    // reverse all bits
    b = (byte) ~b;

    for(int t=128; t > 0; t = t/2) {
      if((b & t) != 0) System.out.print("1 ");
      else System.out.print("0 ");
    }
  }
}
```

Here is the output:

```
1 1 0 1 1 1 1 0
0 0 1 0 0 0 0 1
```

The Shift Operators

In Java it is possible to shift the bits that make up a value to the left or to the right by a specified amount. Java defines the three bit-shift operators shown here:

<<	Left shift
>>	Right shift
>>>	Unsigned right shift

The general forms for these operators are shown here:

> *value* << *num-bits*
> *value* >> *num-bits*
> *value* >>> *num-bits*

Here, *value* is the value being shifted by the number of bit positions specified by *num-bits*.

Each left shift causes all bits within the specified value to be shifted left one position and a 0 bit to be brought in on the right. Each right shift shifts all bits to the right one position and preserves the sign bit. As you may know, negative numbers are usually represented by setting the high-order bit of an integer value to 1, and this is the approach used by Java. Thus, if the value being shifted is negative, each right shift brings in a 1 on the left. If the value is positive, each right shift brings in a 0 on the left.

In addition to the sign bit, there is something else to be aware of when right shifting. Java uses *two's complement* to represent negative values. In this approach negative values are stored by first reversing the bits in the equivalent positive value and then adding 1. Thus, the byte value for −1 in binary is 1111 1111. Right shifting this value will always produce −1!

If you don't want to preserve the sign bit when shifting right, you can use an unsigned right shift (>>>), which always brings in a 0 on the left. For this reason, the >>> is also called the *zero-fill* right shift. You will use the unsigned right shift when shifting bit patterns, such as status codes, that do not represent integers.

For all of the shifts, the bits shifted out are lost. Thus, a shift is not a rotate. Once a bit has been shifted out, it is gone.

Shown next is a program that graphically illustrates the effect of a left and right shift. Here, an integer is given an initial value of 1, which means that its low-order bit is set. Then, a series of eight shifts are performed on the integer. After each shift, the lower 8 bits of the value are shown. The process is then repeated, except that a 1 is put in the 8th bit position, and right shifts are performed.

```java
// Demonstrate the shift << and >> operators.
class ShiftDemo {
  public static void main(String[] args) {
    int val = 1;

    for(int i = 0; i < 8; i++) {
      for(int t=128; t > 0; t = t/2) {
        if((val & t) != 0) System.out.print("1 ");
        else System.out.print("0 ");
      }
      System.out.println();
      val = val << 1; // left shift
    }
    System.out.println();

    val = 128;
    for(int i = 0; i < 8; i++) {
      for(int t=128; t > 0; t = t/2) {
        if((val & t) != 0) System.out.print("1 ");
        else System.out.print("0 ");
      }
      System.out.println();
      val = val >> 1; // right shift
    }
  }
}
```

The output from the program is shown here:

```
0 0 0 0 0 0 0 1
0 0 0 0 0 0 1 0
0 0 0 0 0 1 0 0
0 0 0 0 1 0 0 0
0 0 0 1 0 0 0 0
0 0 1 0 0 0 0 0
0 1 0 0 0 0 0 0
1 0 0 0 0 0 0 0

1 0 0 0 0 0 0 0
0 1 0 0 0 0 0 0
0 0 1 0 0 0 0 0
0 0 0 1 0 0 0 0
0 0 0 0 1 0 0 0
```

```
0 0 0 0 0 1 0 0
0 0 0 0 0 0 1 0
0 0 0 0 0 0 0 1
```

You need to be careful when shifting **byte** and **short** values because Java will automatically promote these types to **int** when evaluating an expression. For example, if you right shift a **byte** value, it will first be promoted to **int** and then shifted. The result of the shift will also be of type **int**. Often this conversion is of no consequence. However, if you shift a negative **byte** or **short** value, it will be sign-extended when it is promoted to **int**. Thus, the high-order bits of the resulting integer value will be filled with ones. This is fine when performing a normal right shift. But when you perform a zero-fill right shift, there are 24 ones to be shifted before the byte value begins to see zeros.

Ask the Expert

Q Since binary is based on powers of two, can the shift operators be used as a shortcut for multiplying or dividing an integer by two?

A Yes. The bitwise shift operators can be used to perform very fast multiplication or division by 2. A shift left doubles a value. A shift right halves it.

Bitwise Shorthand Assignments

All of the binary bitwise operators have a shorthand form that combines an assignment with the bitwise operation. For example, the following two statements both assign to **x** the outcome of an XOR of **x** with the value 127.

```
x = x ^ 127;
x ^= 127;
```

TRY THIS 5-3   A GENERAL-PURPOSE BIT DISPLAY CLASS

```
ShowBitsDemo.java
```

This project creates a utility class called **BitOut** that enables you to display in binary the bit pattern for any integer value. Such a class can be quite useful in programming. For example, if you are debugging an Internet connection, then being able to monitor the data stream in binary might be a benefit. It also provides a framework to which you could add other bit display options.

STEP-BY-STEP

1. Create a file called **ShowBitsDemo.java**.

2. Begin a class called **BitOut** as shown here:

```
class BitOut {
  int numBits; // number of bits to display

  BitOut(int n) {
    if(n < 1) n = 1;
    if(n > 64) n = 64;
    numBits = n;
  }
```

BitOut creates an object that can display a specified number of bits, which must be between 1 and 64. For example, to create an object that will display the low-order 8 bits of some value, use

```
BitOut byteval = new BitOut(8)
```

The number of bits to display is stored in **numBits**.

3. To actually display the bit pattern, **BitOut** provides the method **showBits( )**, which is shown here:

```
// Display the sequence of bits.
void showBits(long val) {
  long mask = 1;

  // left-shift a 1 into the proper position
  mask <<= numBits-1;

  int spacer = 8 - (numBits % 8);
  for(; mask != 0; mask >>>= 1) {
    if((val & mask) != 0) System.out.print("1");
    else System.out.print("0");

    spacer++;

    if((spacer % 8) == 0) {
      System.out.print(" ");
      spacer = 0;
    }
  }
  System.out.println();
}
```

Notice that **showBits( )** specifies one **long** parameter. This does not mean that you always have to pass **showBits( )** a **long** value, however. Because of Java's automatic type promotions, any integer type can be passed to **showBits( )**. The number of bits displayed is determined by the value stored in **numBits**. The bits are displayed in units of 8, starting on the right. This makes it easier to read the binary values of long bit patterns.

4. The following program assembles the pieces and adds the class **ShowBitsDemo**, which demonstrates the use of **BitOut** and **showBits( )**.

```
/*
    Try This 5-3

    A class that stores the number of bits that will be
    displayed. It then implements the showBits() method,
    which displays that number of bits for the binary
    representation of the value that it is passed.
*/

class BitOut {
  int numBits; // number of bits to display

  BitOut(int n) {
    if(n < 1) n = 1;
    if(n > 64) n = 64;
    numBits = n;
  }

  // Display the sequence of bits.
  void showBits(long val) {
    long mask = 1;

    // left-shift a 1 into the proper position
    mask <<= numBits-1;

    int spacer = 8 - (numBits % 8);
    for(; mask != 0; mask >>>= 1) {
      if((val & mask) != 0) System.out.print("1");
      else System.out.print("0");

      spacer++;

      if((spacer % 8) == 0) {
        System.out.print(" ");
        spacer = 0;
      }
    }
    System.out.println();
  }
}

// Demonstrate showBits().
class ShowBitsDemo {
  public static void main(String[] args) {
```

```
    BitOut b = new BitOut(8);
    BitOut i = new BitOut(32);
    BitOut li = new BitOut(64);

    System.out.println("123 in binary: ");
    b.showBits(123);

    System.out.println("\n87987 in binary: ");
    i.showBits(87987);

    System.out.println("\n237658768 in binary: ");
    li.showBits(237658768);

    // you can also show low-order bits of any integer
    System.out.println("\nLow order 8 bits of 87987 in binary: ");
    b.showBits(87987);
  }
}
```

5. The output from **ShowBitsDemo** is shown here:

```
123 in binary:
01111011

87987 in binary:
00000000 00000001 01010111 10110011

237658768 in binary:
00000000 00000000 00000000 00000000 00001110 00101010 01100010 10010000

Low order 8 bits of 87987 in binary:
10110011
```

6. You might try adding additional methods to the **BitOut** class that display bits in different ways. For example, you could show the bits in reverse or show just a subrange of the bits.

Progress Check

1. To what types can the bitwise operators be applied?
2. What is >>>?

Answers:

1. **byte**, **short**, **int**, **long**, and **char**.
2. >>> performs an unsigned right shift. This causes a zero to be shifted into the leftmost bit position. It differs from >>, which preserves the sign bit.

THE ? OPERATOR

One of Java's most fascinating operators is the **?**. The **?** operator is often used to replace **if-else** statements of this general form:

> if (*condition*)
>   *var* = *expression1*;
> else
>   *var* = *expression2*;

Here, the value assigned to *var* depends on the outcome of the condition controlling the **if**.

The **?** is called a *ternary operator* because it requires three operands. It takes the general form

> *condition* ? *expression1* : *expression2*

where *condition* is a **boolean** expression, and *expression1* and *expression2* are expressions of any type other than **void**. The type of *expression1* and *expression2* must be the same (or compatible), though. Notice the use and placement of the colon.

The value of a **?** expression is determined like this: *condition* is evaluated. If it is true, then *expression1* is evaluated and becomes the value of the entire **?** expression. If *condition* is false, then *expression2* is evaluated and its value becomes the value of the expression. Consider this example, which assigns **absval** the absolute value of **val**:

```
absval = val < 0 ? -val : val; // get absolute value of val
```

Here, **absval** will be assigned the value of **val** if **val** is zero or greater. If **val** is negative, then **absval** will be assigned the negative of that value (which yields a positive value). The same code written using the **if-else** structure would look like this:

```
if(val < 0) absval = -val;
else absval = val;
```

Here is another example of the **?** operator. This program divides two numbers but will not allow a division by zero.

```
// Prevent a division by zero using the ?.
class NoZeroDiv {
  public static void main(String[] args) {
    int result;

    for(int i = -5; i < 6; i++) {
      result = i != 0 ? 100 / i : 0;    ◄─────────────This prevents a divide-by-zero.
      if(i != 0)
        System.out.println("100 / " + i + " is " + result);
    }
  }
}
```

The output from the program is shown here:

```
100 / -5 is -20
100 / -4 is -25
```

```
100 / -3 is -33
100 / -2 is -50
100 / -1 is -100
100 / 1 is 100
100 / 2 is 50
100 / 3 is 33
100 / 4 is 25
100 / 5 is 20
```

Pay special attention to this line from the program:

```
result = i != 0 ? 100 / i : 0;
```

Here, **result** is assigned the outcome of the division of 100 by **i**. However, this division takes place only if **i** is not zero. When **i** is zero, a placeholder value of zero is assigned to **result**.

You don't actually have to assign the value produced by the **?** to some variable. For example, you could use the value as an argument in a call to a method. Or if the expressions are all of type **boolean**, the **?** can be used as the conditional expression in a loop or **if** statement. For example, here is the preceding program rewritten a bit more compactly. It produces the same output as before.

```
// Prevent a division by zero using the ?.
class NoZeroDiv2 {
  public static void main(String[] args) {

    for(int i = -5; i < 6; i++)
      if(i != 0 ? true : false)
        System.out.println("100 / " + i +
                          " is " + 100 / i);

  }
}
```

Notice the **if** statement. If **i** is zero, then the conditional expression of the **if** is false, the division by zero is prevented, and no result is displayed. Otherwise the division takes place.

EXERCISES

1. Show two ways to declare a one-dimensional array of 12 **double**s.
2. Show how to initialize a one-dimensional array of integers to the values 1 through 5.
3. Write a program that uses an array to find the average of 10 **double** values. Use any 10 values you like.
4. Change the sort in Try This 5-1 so that it sorts an array of strings. Demonstrate that it works.
5. What is the difference between the **String** methods **indexOf( )** and **lastIndexOf( )**?

6. Since all strings are objects of type **String**, show how you can call the **length( )** and **charAt( )** methods on this string literal: "I like Java".

7. Expanding on the **SimpleCipher** class, modify it so that it uses an eight-character string as the key.

8. Can the bitwise operators be applied to the **double** type?

9. Show how this sequence can be rewritten using the **?** operator.

```
if(x < 0) y = 10;
else y = 20;
```

10. In the following fragment, is the **&** a bitwise or logical operator? Why?

```
boolean a, b;
// ...
if(a & b) ...
```

11. Is it an error to overrun the end of an array? Is it an error to index an array with a negative value?

12. What is the symbol used for the unsigned right-shift operator?

13. Rewrite the **MinMax** class shown earlier in this chapter so that it uses a for-each style **for** loop.

14. Can the **for** loops that perform sorting in the **Bubble** class shown in Try This 5-1 be converted into for-each style loops? If not, why not?

15. Can a **String** control a **switch** statement?

16. Write a program that creates an integer array of length 30, fills the array with the sequence of values (shown below) using a **for** loop, and then loops through the array printing out the values. Use a for-each style **for** loop to print out the values.

A. 1, −2, 3, −4, 5, −6,..., 29, −30

B. 1, 1, 2, 2, 3, 3,..., 15, 15

C. 1, 2, 4, 8, 16,...

D. 1, 1, 2, 3, 5, 8, 13, ... (Except for the first two values, each value is the sum of the two preceding values)

17. Write a program that creates an array of **doubles** of length 50. It then fills the array with the sequence of values $2^{1/2}$, $2^{1/4}$, $2^{1/8}$, $2^{1/16}$, ... and then loops through the array printing out the values. Use the **Math.sqrt( )** function to compute the square roots of the values.

18. Can you have an array of length 0? If so, how would you create one?

19. Change the bubble sort code in Try This 5-1 so that it sorts the array of integers from largest down to smallest instead of from smallest to largest.

20. Change the bubble sort code in Try This 5-1 so that it sorts an array of strings by their lengths (instead of sorting them alphabetically). Demonstrate that it works.

21. Note that, if the bubble sort's inner loop never exchanges any pairs of values, then the array is sorted and so the sorting routine can stop. Modify the code

in Try This 5-1 so that the bubble sort stops sorting as soon as the inner loop never exchanges any values.

22. Write a program that creates a "triangular" two-dimensional array **A** of 10 rows. The first row has length 1, the second row has length 2, the third row has length 3, and so on. Then initialize the array using nested **for** loops so that the value of **A[i][j]** is **i+j**. Finally, print out the array in a nice triangular form.

23. Write a program that creates an array of integers and then uses a **for** loop to reverse the order of the elements in the array.

24. Fill in the **indexOf( )** method in the class below so that it uses a **for** loop to find the index of **x** in **data**. It returns the index or −1 if **x** does not appear in **data**. For example, **indexOf(3)** returns 2. Demonstrate your solution.

```
class MyClass {
   int[] data = { 1, 8, 3, 5, 4, 6, 10, 9, 2, 7 };

   int indexOf(int x) {
     // ... add your code here
   }
}
```

25. Write a program that creates an integer array **data** and then uses a **for** loop to create a new **String** that displays the contents of the **data** array surrounded by braces and separated by commas. For example, if the **data** array is of length 4 and contains the values 3, 4, 1, 5, then the **String** "{3, 4, 1, 5}" should be created and printed.

26. Write a program that creates two integer arrays **data1** and **data2**, possibly of different lengths. Then it uses **for** loops to create a new array **data3** whose length is the sum of the lengths of **data1** and **data2** and whose contents consist of the contents of **data1** followed by the contents of **data2**. For example, if the two arrays are {1,2,3} and {4,5,6,7}, then the code should create the new array {1,2,3,4,5,6,7}.

27. Write a program that creates an integer array and then uses a **for** loop to check whether the array is sorted from smallest to largest. If so, it prints "Sorted". Otherwise, it prints "Not sorted".

28. Write a program that creates a **String** and then uses a **for** loop to test whether the **String** is a palindrome, which means that if you reverse the order of the characters in the **String**, you get the same **String** back. For example, "abcdcba" is a palindrome.

29. Write a program that creates a string and then uses a **for** loop to split the **String** into an array of substrings, using the comma character as the separator. For example, if the string was "abc,def,hi", then the array it creates would be {"abc", "def", "hi"}. It then prints out the string and the new array. Don't use the **split( )** method in the **String** class.

30. Rewrite the following statements without using the **?** operator. Assume that **y** is an integer variable previously declared and initialized.

```
a. int x = y > 0 ? 3 : 4;
b. int x = ((y > 0) ? (y > 5) : (y < -5)) ? 3 : 4;
c. int x = y > 0 ? ( y > 5 ? 3 : 4) : (y < -5 ? 6 : 7);
```

31. Implement a method **cyclicShift( )** that takes two integers **x** and **dist** as its parameters. It cyclically shifts the bits in the representation of **x** the distance given by **dist** and returns the result. If **dist** ≥ 0, then it shifts right, and otherwise it shifts left. A *cyclic shift* shifts the bits to the left or right and the bits that are shifted off one end are inserted on the other end to fill the vacated bits. (A cyclic shift is also commonly referred to as a *rotate*.) For example, a right cyclic shift of 10010111 a distance 3 would give you 11110010. Use the OR and shift operators to perform the cyclic shift. *Hint:* Shift one copy of **x** to the right and shift another copy of **x** to the left, using the fact that an integer has 32 bits, and then use the OR operator to combine them. Demonstrate your method using the **BitOut** class from Try This 5-3 to display the results.

32. Suppose a **SimpleStack** is created with the name **stack** and then the following sequence of statements is executed. When it is done, what characters are left on the stack and in what order?

```
stack.push('a');
stack.push('b');
stack.pop();
stack.push('c');
stack.push('d');
stack.pop();
stack.push('e');
stack.pop();
stack.pop();
```

CHAPTER 6

A Closer Look at Methods and Classes

This chapter resumes our examination of classes and methods. It begins by explaining how to control access to the members of a class. It then discusses the passing and returning of objects, method overloading, recursion, and use of the keyword **static**. Also described are nested classes and variable-length arguments.

CONTROLLING ACCESS TO CLASS MEMBERS

In its support for encapsulation, the class provides two major benefits. First, it links data with the code that manipulates it. You have been taking advantage of this aspect of the class since Chapter 4. Second, it provides the means by which access to members can be controlled. It is this feature that is examined here.

Although Java's approach is a bit more sophisticated, in essence, there are two basic types of class members: public and private. A public member can be freely accessed by code defined outside of its class. This is the type of class member that we have been using up to this point. A private member can be accessed only by other methods defined by its class. It is through the use of private members that access is controlled.

Restricting access to a class's members is a fundamental part of object-oriented programming because it helps prevent the misuse of an object. By allowing access to private data only through a well-defined set of methods, you can prevent improper values from being assigned to that data—by performing a range check, for example. It is not possible for code outside the class to set the value of a private member directly. You can also control precisely how and when the data within an object is used. Thus, when correctly implemented, a class creates a "black box" that can be used, but its inner workings are not open to tampering.

Up to this point, you haven't had to worry about access control because Java provides a default access setting in which, for the programs seen so far, the members of a class are freely available to the other code in your program. (Thus, for these programs, the default access setting is essentially public.) Although convenient for simple classes (and example programs in books such as this one), this default setting is inadequate for many real-world situations. Here you will see how to use Java's other access control features.

Java's Access Modifiers

Member access control is achieved through the use of three *access modifiers*: **public**, **private**, and **protected**. As explained, if no access modifier is used, the default access setting is assumed. In this chapter we will be concerned with **public** and **private**. The **protected** modifier is useful only when inheritance is involved; it is described in Chapter 9.

When a member of a class is modified by the **public** modifier, that member can be accessed by any other code in your program. This includes methods defined inside other classes.

When a member of a class is specified as **private**, that member can be accessed only by other members of its class. Thus, methods in other classes cannot access a **private** member of another class.

The default access setting (in which no access modifier is used) is the same as **public** unless two or more packages are involved. A *package* is, essentially, a grouping of classes. Packages are both an organizational and an access control feature, but a discussion of packages must wait until Chapter 9. For the types of programs shown in this and the preceding chapters, **public** access is the same as default access.

An access modifier precedes the rest of a member's type specification. That is, it must begin a member's declaration statement. Here are some examples:

```
public String errMsg;
private accountBalance bal;

private boolean isError(byte status) { // ...
```

To understand the effects of **public** and **private**, consider the following program:

```
// Public vs private access.
class MyClass {
  private int alpha; // private access
  public int beta; // public access
  int gamma; // default access
```

```
/* Methods to access alpha. It is OK for a
   member of a class to access a private member
   of the same class.
*/
void setAlpha(int a) {
  alpha = a;
}

int getAlpha() {
  return alpha;
}
}

class AccessDemo {
  public static void main(String[] args) {
    MyClass ob = new MyClass();

    /* Access to alpha is allowed only through
       its accessor methods. */
    ob.setAlpha(-99);
    System.out.println("ob.alpha is " + ob.getAlpha());

    // You cannot access alpha like this:
//  ob.alpha = 10; // Wrong! alpha is private! ◄──────────Wrong—alpha is private!

    // These are OK because beta and gamma are accessible.
    ob.beta = 88; ◄──────────OK because these are accessible.
    ob.gamma = 99;
  }
}
```

As you can see, inside the **MyClass** class, **alpha** is specified as **private**, **beta** is explicitly specified as **public**, and **gamma** uses the default access, which for this example is, essentially, the same as specifying **public**. Because **alpha** is private, it cannot be accessed by code outside of its class. Therefore, inside the **AccessDemo** class, **alpha** cannot be used directly. It must be accessed through its public accessor methods: **setAlpha( )** and **getAlpha( )**. If you were to remove the comment symbol from the beginning of the following line,

```
//  ob.alpha = 10; // Wrong! alpha is private!
```

you would not be able to compile this program because of the access violation. Although access to **alpha** by code outside of **MyClass** is not allowed, methods defined within **MyClass** can freely access it, as the **setAlpha( )** and **getAlpha( )** methods show.

The key point is this: a private member can be used freely by other members of its class, but it cannot be accessed by code outside its class.

To see how access control can be applied to a more practical example, consider the following program that implements a "fail-soft" **int** array, in which boundary errors are prevented, thus avoiding a run-time exception from being generated. This is accomplished by encapsulating the array as a private member of a class, allowing access to the array only through member methods. With this approach, any attempt to access the array beyond its boundaries can be prevented, with such an attempt failing gracefully (resulting in a "soft" landing rather than a "crash"). The fail-soft array is implemented by the **FailSoftArray** class, shown here:

```java
/* This class implements a "fail-soft" array which prevents
   runtime errors.
*/
class FailSoftArray {
  private int[] a; // reference to array
  private int errval; // value to return if get() fails
  public int length; // length is public

  /* Construct array given its size and the value to
     return if get() fails. */
  public FailSoftArray(int size, int errv) {
    a = new int[size];
    errval = errv;
    length = size;
  }

  // Return value at given index.
  public int get(int index) {
    if(ok(index)) return a[index];    ←————— Trap an out-of-bounds index.
    return errval;
  }

  // Put a value at an index. Return false on failure.
  public boolean put(int index, int val) {
    if(ok(index)) {←
      a[index] = val;
      return true;
    }
    return false;
  }

  // Return true if index is within bounds.
  private boolean ok(int index) {
    if(index >= 0 & index < length) return true;
    return false;
  }
}

// Demonstrate the fail-soft array.
class FSDemo {
  public static void main(String[] args) {
    FailSoftArray fs = new FailSoftArray(5, -1);
    int x;

    // show quiet failures
```

```
    System.out.println("Fail quietly.");
    for(int i=0; i < (fs.length * 2); i++)
      fs.put(i, i*10);  ◄─────── Access to array must be through its accessor methods.

    for(int i=0; i < (fs.length * 2); i++) {
      x = fs.get(i);  ◄─────
      if(x != -1) System.out.print(x + " ");
    }
    System.out.println("");

    // now, handle failures
    System.out.println("\nFail with error reports.");
    for(int i=0; i < (fs.length * 2); i++)
      if(!fs.put(i, i*10))
        System.out.println("Index " + i + " out-of-bounds");

    for(int i=0; i < (fs.length * 2); i++) {
      x = fs.get(i);
      if(x != -1) System.out.print(x + " ");
      else
        System.out.println("Index " + i + " out-of-bounds");
    }
  }
}
```

The output from the program is shown here:

```
Fail quietly.
0 10 20 30 40

Fail with error reports.
Index 5 out-of-bounds
Index 6 out-of-bounds
Index 7 out-of-bounds
Index 8 out-of-bounds
Index 9 out-of-bounds
0 10 20 30 40 Index 5 out-of-bounds
Index 6 out-of-bounds
Index 7 out-of-bounds
Index 8 out-of-bounds
Index 9 out-of-bounds
```

Let's look closely at this example. Inside **FailSoftArray** are defined three **private** members. The first is **a**, which stores a reference to the array that will actually hold information. The second is **errval**, which is the value that will be returned when a call to **get( )** fails. The third is the **private** method **ok( )**, which determines whether an index is within bounds. Thus, these three members can be used only by other members of the **FailSoftArray** class. Specifically, **a** and **errval** can be used only by other methods in the class, and **ok( )** can be called only by other members of **FailSoftArray**. The rest of the class members are **public** and can be called by any other code in a program that uses **FailSoftArray**.

When a **FailSoftArray** object is constructed, you must specify the size of the array and the value that you want to return if a call to **get( )** fails. The error value must be a value that would otherwise not be stored in the array. Once constructed, the actual array referred to by **a** and the error value stored in **errval** cannot be accessed by users of the **FailSoftArray** object. Thus, they are not open to misuse. For example, the user cannot try to index **a** directly, possibly exceeding its bounds. Access is available only through the **get( )** and **put( )** methods.

The **ok( )** method is **private** mostly for the sake of illustration. It would be harmless to make it **public** because it does not modify the object. However, since it is used internally by the **FailSoftArray** class, it can be **private**.

Notice that the **length** instance variable is **public**. This is in keeping with the way Java implements arrays. To obtain the length of a **FailSoftArray**, simply use its **length** member. It is important to point out, however, that because **length** is public, it is open to misuse. For example, it could be set to an improper value. In Chapter 7, you will see another feature of Java that can be used to prevent such misuse.

To use a **FailSoftArray** array, call **put( )** to store a value at the specified index. Call **get( )** to retrieve a value from a specified index. If the index is out-of-bounds, **put( )** returns **false** and **get( )** returns **errval**.

For the sake of convenience, the majority of the examples in this book will continue to use default access for most members. Remember, however, that in the real world, restricting access to members—especially instance variables—is an important part of successful object-oriented programming. As you will see in Chapter 7, access control is even more vital when inheritance is involved.

Progress Check

1. Name Java's access modifiers.
2. Explain what **private** does.

TRY THIS 6-1   IMPROVING SimpleStack

`SimpleStack.java`
You can use the **private** modifier to make a rather important improvement to the **SimpleStack** class developed in Try This 5-2 in the previous chapter. In that version, all members of **SimpleStack** use the default access. This means that it would be possible for a program that uses a **SimpleStack** to directly access the underlying array, possibly using its elements out of turn. Since the entire point of a stack

Answers:
1. **private**, **public**, and **protected**. A default access is also available.
2. When a member is specified as **private**, it can be accessed only by other members of its class.

is to provide a last-in, first-out list, allowing out-of-order access is not desirable. Furthermore, the values in the underlying array could be changed directly, bypassing the use of **push( )** and **pop( )**, thus corrupting the stack. It would also be possible for a malicious programmer to alter the value stored in the **tos** variable. This too would corrupt the stack. Fortunately, these types of problems are easy to prevent by applying the **private** specifier.

STEP-BY-STEP

1. Begin with the original **SimpleStack** class in Try This 5-2.
2. In **SimpleStack**, add the **private** modifier to the **data** array and the **tos** variable, as shown here:

```
private char[] data; // this array holds the stack
private int tos; // index of top of stack
```

3. Changing **data** and **tos** from default access to **private** access has no effect on a program that properly uses **SimpleStack**. For example, it still works fine with the **SimpleStackDemo** class from Try This 5-2. However, the use of **private** prevents the improper use of a **SimpleStack**. For example, given

```
SimpleStack myStack = new SimpleStack(10);
```

the following types of statements are illegal:

```
myStack.data[0] = 'X'; // wrong!
myStack.tos = -100; // won't work!
```

4. Now that **tos** and **data** are private, the **SimpleStack** class strictly enforces the last-in, first-out attribute of a stack. It also prevents the stack from being either maliciously or accidentally corrupted by the improper use of **data** or **tos**. The simple addition of **private** to these two fields is one of the easiest, yet most effective, ways to improve the robustness of **SimpleStack**.

PASS OBJECTS TO METHODS

Up to this point, the examples in this book have been using primitive types, such as **int**, as parameters to methods. However, it is both correct and common to pass objects to methods. For example, the following program defines a class called **Block** that stores the dimensions of a three-dimensional block:

```
// Objects can be passed to methods.
class Block {
  int a, b, c;
  int volume;

  Block(int i, int j, int k) {
    a = i;
    b = j;
```

```
      c = k;
      volume = a * b * c;
    }

    // Return true if ob defines same block.
    boolean sameBlock(Block ob) {  ←——————Use object type for parameter.
      if((ob.a == a) & (ob.b == b) & (ob.c == c)) return true;
      else return false;
    }

    // Return true if ob has same volume.
    boolean sameVolume(Block ob) {  ←
      if(ob.volume == volume) return true;
      else return false;
    }
}

class PassOb {
  public static void main(String[] args) {
    Block ob1 = new Block(10, 2, 5);
    Block ob2 = new Block(10, 2, 5);
    Block ob3 = new Block(4, 5, 5);

    System.out.println("ob1 same dimensions as ob2: " +
                        ob1.sameBlock(ob2));  ←————————Pass an object.
    System.out.println("ob1 same dimensions as ob3: " +
                        ob1.sameBlock(ob3));  ←
    System.out.println("ob1 same volume as ob3: " +
                        ob1.sameVolume(ob3));  ←

  }
}
```

This program generates the following output:

```
ob1 same dimensions as ob2: true
ob1 same dimensions as ob3: false
ob1 same volume as ob3: true
```

The **sameBlock( )** and **sameVolume( )** methods compare the **Block** object passed as a parameter to the invoking object. For **sameBlock( )**, the dimensions of the objects are compared, and **true** is returned only if the two blocks are the identical. For **sameVolume( )**, the two blocks are compared only to determine whether they have the same volume. In both cases, notice that the parameter **ob** specifies **Block** as its type. Although **Block** is a class type created by the program, it is used in the same way as Java's built-in types.

HOW ARGUMENTS ARE PASSED

As the preceding example demonstrated, passing an object to a method is a straightforward task. However, there are some nuances of passing an object that are not shown in the example. In certain cases, the effects of passing an object will be different from those experienced when passing non-object arguments. To see why, it's helpful to begin by describing in general two of the ways in which a computer language can pass an argument to a subroutine.

The first way is *call-by-value*. This approach copies the *value* of an argument into the formal parameter of the subroutine. Therefore, changes made to the parameter of the subroutine have no effect on the argument in the call. The second way an argument can be passed is *call-by-reference*. In this approach, a reference to an argument (not the value of the argument) is passed to the parameter. Inside the subroutine, this reference is used to access the actual argument specified in the call. This means that changes made to the parameter *will* affect the argument used to call the subroutine. As you will see, although Java uses call-by-value to pass arguments, the precise effect differs between whether a primitive type or a reference type is passed.

When you pass a primitive type, such as **int** or **double**, to a method, its value is passed to the parameter. Thus, a copy of the argument is made, and what occurs to the parameter that receives the argument has no effect outside the method. For example, consider the following program:

```java
// Primitive types are passed by value.
class Test {
  /* This method causes no change to the arguments
     used in the call. */
  void noChange(int i, int j) {
    i = i + j;
    j = -j;
  }
}

class CallByValue {
  public static void main(String[] args) {
    Test ob = new Test();

    int a = 15, b = 20;

    System.out.println("a and b before call: " +
                   a + " " + b);

    ob.noChange(a, b);

    System.out.println("a and b after call: " +
                   a + " " + b);
  }
}
```

The output from this program is shown here:

```
a and b before call: 15 20
a and b after call: 15 20
```

As you can see, the operations that occur inside **noChange( )** have no effect on the values of **a** and **b** used in the call.

When you pass an object to a method, the situation changes dramatically. First, recall that when you create a variable of a class type, you are creating a reference. When you pass an object as an argument, you are, in reality, not passing the object itself, but only the reference that refers to that object. This means that when you pass an object reference to a method, the parameter that receives it will refer to the *same object* as that referred to by the argument. Therefore, objects are passed to methods by what is effectively call-by-reference (since only a reference is passed). Changes to the object inside the method *do* affect the object used as an argument. For example, consider the following program:

```
// Objects are passed through their references.
class Test {
  int a, b;

  Test(int i, int j) {
    a = i;
    b = j;
  }
  /* Pass an object. Now, ob.a and ob.b in object
     used in the call will be changed. */
  void change(Test ob) {
    ob.a = ob.a + ob.b;
    ob.b = -ob.b;
  }
}

class PassObjRef {
  public static void main(String[] args) {
    Test ob = new Test(15, 20);

    System.out.println("ob.a and ob.b before call: " +
                         ob.a + " " + ob.b);

    ob.change(ob);

    System.out.println("ob.a and ob.b after call: " +
                         ob.a + " " + ob.b);
  }
}
```

This program generates the following output:

```
ob.a and ob.b before call: 15 20
ob.a and ob.b after call: 35 -20
```

As you can see, in this case, the actions inside **change( )** have affected the object passed to the method.

To review: When an object reference is passed to a method, the reference itself is passed by use of call-by-value. Therefore, the parameter receives a *copy* of the reference used as the argument. As a result, a change *to* the parameter (such as making it refer to a different object) will not affect the reference used as an argument. However, since the parameter and the argument both refer to the *same object*, a change *through* the parameter will affect the object referred to by the argument.

Ask the Expert

Q Is there any way that I can pass a primitive type by reference?

A Not directly. However, Java defines a set of classes that *wrap* the primitive types in objects. These are **Double**, **Float**, **Byte**, **Short**, **Integer**, **Long**, and **Character**. In addition to allowing a primitive type to be passed by reference, these wrapper classes define several methods that enable you to manipulate their values. For example, the numeric type wrappers include methods that convert a numeric value from its binary form into its human-readable **String** form, and vice versa.

Progress Check

1. What is the difference between call-by-value and call-by-reference?
2. How does Java pass primitive types? How does it pass objects?

RETURNING OBJECTS

A method can return any type of data, including class types. For example, the class **ErrorMsg** shown here could be used to report errors. Its method, **getErrorMsg( )**, returns a reference to a **String** object that contains a description of an error based on the error code that it is passed.

```
// Return a String object.
class ErrorMsg {
  String[] msgs = {
    "Output Error",
    "Input Error",
    "Disk Full",
    "Index Out-Of-Bounds"
  };

  // Return the error message.
  String getErrorMsg(int i) {  ◄──────── Return an object of type String.
    if(i >=0 & i < msgs.length)
```

Answers:

1. In call-by-value, a copy of the argument is passed to a subroutine. In call-by-reference, a reference to the argument is passed.
2. Java passes primitive types by value. An object is passed through its reference. (The reference itself is passed by value.).

```
        return msgs[i];
      else
        return "Invalid Error Code";
    }
}

class ErrMsgDemo {
  public static void main(String[] args) {
    ErrorMsg err = new ErrorMsg();

    System.out.println(err.getErrorMsg(2));
    System.out.println(err.getErrorMsg(19));
  }
}
```

Its output is shown here:

```
Disk Full
Invalid Error Code
```

You can, of course, also return objects of classes that you create. For example, here is a reworked version of the preceding program that creates two error classes. One is called **Err**, and it encapsulates an error message along with a severity code. The second is called **ErrorInfo**. It defines a method called **getErrorInfo( )**, which returns a reference to an **Err** object.

```
// Return a programmer-defined object.

class Err {
  String msg; // error message
  int severity; // code indicating severity of error

  Err(String m, int s) {
    msg = m;
    severity = s;
  }
}

class ErrorInfo {
  String[] msgs = {
    "Output Error",
    "Input Error",
    "Disk Full",
    "Index Out-Of-Bounds"
  };
  int[] howbad = { 3, 3, 2, 4 };

  Err getErrorInfo(int i) {            ←——— Return an object of type Err.
    if(i >= 0 & i < msgs.length)
      return new Err(msgs[i], howbad[i]);
    else
```

```
        return new Err("Invalid Error Code", 0);
   }
}

class ErrInfoDemo {
  public static void main(String[] args) {
    ErrorInfo err = new ErrorInfo();
    Err e;

    e = err.getErrorInfo(2);
    System.out.println(e.msg + " severity: " + e.severity);

    e = err.getErrorInfo(19);
    System.out.println(e.msg + " severity: " + e.severity);
  }
}
```

Here is the output:

```
Disk Full severity: 2
Invalid Error Code severity: 0
```

Each time **getErrorInfo( )** is invoked, a new **Err** object is created, and a reference to it is returned to the calling routine. This object is then used within **main( )** to display the error message and severity code.

When an object is returned by a method, it remains in existence until there are no more references to it. At that point it is subject to garbage collection. Thus, an object won't be destroyed just because the method that created it terminates.

METHOD OVERLOADING

In this section, you will learn about an exciting feature of Java: method overloading. In Java, two or more methods within the same class can share the same name, as long as their parameter declarations are different. When this is the case, the methods are said to be *overloaded,* and the process is referred to as *method overloading.* Method overloading is one of the ways that Java implements polymorphism.

In general, to overload a method, simply declare different versions of it. The compiler takes care of the rest. You must observe one important restriction: the type and/or number of the parameters of each overloaded method must differ. It is not sufficient for two methods to differ only in their return types. (Return types do not provide sufficient information in all cases for Java to decide which method to use.) Of course, overloaded methods *may* differ in their return types, too. When an overloaded method is called, the version of the method whose parameters match the arguments is executed.

Here is a simple example that illustrates method overloading:

```
// Demonstrate method overloading.
class Overload {
  void ovlDemo() {◄────────────────── First version
    System.out.println("No parameters");
  }
```

```
   // Overload ovlDemo for one integer parameter.
   void ovlDemo(int a) {◄────────────────────Second version
     System.out.println("One parameter: " + a);
   }

   // Overload ovlDemo for two integer parameters.
   int ovlDemo(int a, int b) {◄────────────── Third version
     System.out.println("Two parameters: " + a + " " + b);
     return a + b;
   }

   // Overload ovlDemo for two double parameters.
   double ovlDemo(double a, double b) {◄───── Fourth version
     System.out.println("Two double parameters: " +
                          a + " " + b);
     return a + b;
   }
}

class OverloadDemo {
  public static void main(String[] args) {
    Overload ob = new Overload();
    int resI;
    double resD;

    // call all versions of ovlDemo()
    ob.ovlDemo();
    System.out.println();

    ob.ovlDemo(2);
    System.out.println();

    resI = ob.ovlDemo(4, 6);
    System.out.println("Result of ob.ovlDemo(4, 6): " +
                        resI);
    System.out.println();

    resD = ob.ovlDemo(1.1, 2.32);
    System.out.println("Result of ob.ovlDemo(1.1, 2.32): " +
                        resD);
  }
}
```

This program generates the following output:

```
No parameters

One parameter: 2

Two parameters: 4 6
```

```
Result of ob.ovlDemo(4, 6): 10

Two double parameters: 1.1 2.32
Result of ob.ovlDemo(1.1, 2.32): 3.42
```

As you can see, **ovlDemo( )** is overloaded four times. The first version takes no parameters, the second takes one integer parameter, the third takes two integer parameters, and the fourth takes two **double** parameters. Notice that the first two versions of **ovlDemo( )** return **void**, and the second two return a value. This is perfectly valid, but as explained, overloading is not affected one way or the other by the return type of a method. Thus, attempting to use the following two versions of **ovlDemo( )** will cause an error:

```
// One ovlDemo(int) is OK.
void ovlDemo(int a) {◄─────────────────── Return types cannot be used to
  System.out.println("One parameter: " + a);  differentiate overloaded methods.
}

/* Error! Two ovlDemo(int)s are not OK even though
   return types differ.
*/
int ovlDemo(int a) {◄───────────────────
  System.out.println("One parameter: " + a);
  return a * a;
}
```

As the comments suggest, the difference in their return types is insufficient for the purposes of overloading.

As you will recall from Chapter 2, Java provides certain automatic type conversions. These conversions also apply to parameters of overloaded methods. For example, consider the following:

```
/* Automatic type conversions can affect
   overloaded method resolution.
*/
class Overload2 {
  void f(int x) {
    System.out.println("Inside f(int): " + x);
  }

  void f(double x) {
    System.out.println("Inside f(double): " + x);
  }
}

class TypeConv {
  public static void main(String[] args) {
    Overload2 ob = new Overload2();

    int i = 10;
    double d = 10.1;
```

```
     byte b = 99;
     short s = 10;
     float f = 11.5F;

     ob.f(i); // calls ob.f(int)
     ob.f(d); // calls ob.f(double)

     ob.f(b); // calls ob.f(int) - type conversion
     ob.f(s); // calls ob.f(int) - type conversion
     ob.f(f); // calls ob.f(double) - type conversion
   }
}
```

The output from the program is shown here:

```
Inside f(int): 10
Inside f(double): 10.1
Inside f(int): 99
Inside f(int): 10
Inside f(double): 11.5
```

In this example, only two versions of **f( )** are defined: one that has an **int** parameter and one that has a **double** parameter. However, it is possible to pass **f( )** a **byte**, **short**, or **float** value. In the case of **byte** and **short**, Java automatically converts them to **int**. Thus, **f(int)** is invoked. In the case of **float**, the value is converted to **double** and **f(double)** is called.

It is important to understand, however, that the automatic conversions apply only if there is no direct match between a parameter and an argument. For example, here is the preceding program with the addition of a version of **f( )** that specifies a **byte** parameter:

```
// Add f(byte).
class Overload2 {
  void f(byte x) {
    System.out.println("Inside f(byte): " + x);
  }

  void f(int x) {
    System.out.println("Inside f(int): " + x);
  }

  void f(double x) {
    System.out.println("Inside f(double): " + x);
  }
}

class TypeConv {
  public static void main(String[] args) {
    Overload2 ob = new Overload2();

    int i = 10;
    double d = 10.1;
```

```
        byte b = 99;
        short s = 10;
        float f = 11.5F;

     ob.f(i); // calls ob.f(int)
     ob.f(d); // calls ob.f(double)

     ob.f(b); // calls ob.f(byte) - now, no type conversion

     ob.f(s); // calls ob.f(int) - type conversion
     ob.f(f); // calls ob.f(double) - type conversion
   }
}
```

Now when the program is run, the following output is produced:

```
Inside f(int): 10
Inside f(double): 10.1
Inside f(byte): 99
Inside f(int): 10
Inside f(double): 11.5
```

In this version, since there is a version of **f( )** that takes a **byte** argument, when **f( )** is called with a **byte** argument, **f(byte)** is invoked and the automatic conversion to **int** does not occur.

Method overloading supports polymorphism because it is one way that Java implements the "one interface, multiple methods" paradigm. To understand how, consider the following: In languages that do not support method overloading, each method must be given a unique name. The trouble is that, often, you will want to implement a set of related methods, such as when each method differs from the next only in terms of the data being acted upon. Consider the method that returns the absolute value of its argument. In languages that do not support overloading, there are usually three or more versions of this method, each with a slightly different name. For instance, in the C language (which does not support method overloading), the method **abs( )** returns the absolute value of an integer, **labs( )** returns the absolute value of a long integer, and **fabs( )** returns the absolute value of a floating-point value. Since C does not support overloading, each method must have its own name, even though all three methods do essentially the same thing.

Of course, the use of three names makes the situation more complex, conceptually, than it actually is. Although the underlying concept of each method is the same (return the absolute value), you still have three names to remember. This situation does not occur in Java because each absolute value method can use the same name. Indeed, Java's standard class library includes an absolute value method, called **abs( )**. This method is overloaded by Java's **Math** class to handle all of the numeric types. Java determines which version of **abs( )** to call based on the type of argument.

The value of overloading is that it allows related methods to be accessed by use of a common name. Thus, the name **abs** represents the *general action* that is being performed. It is left to the compiler to choose the correct *specific* version for a particular circumstance. You, the programmer, need be concerned with only the general operation. Through the application of polymorphism, several names have been reduced to one. Although this example is fairly simple, if you expand the concept, you can see how overloading can help manage greater complexity.

When you overload a method, each version of that method can perform any activity you desire. There is no rule stating that overloaded methods must relate to one another. However, from a stylistic point of view, method overloading implies a relationship. Thus, while you can use the same name to overload unrelated methods, you should not. For example, you could use the name **sqr** to create methods that return the *square* of an integer and the *square root* of a floating-point value. But these two operations are fundamentally different. Applying method overloading in this manner defeats its original purpose. In practice, you should overload only closely related operations.

Ask the Expert

Q I've heard the term *signature* used by Java programmers. What is it?

A As it applies to Java, a signature is the name of a method plus its parameter list. Thus, for the purposes of overloading, no two methods within the same class can have the same signature. Notice that a signature does not include the return type, since it is not used by Java for overload resolution.

OVERLOADING CONSTRUCTORS

Like methods, constructors can also be overloaded. Doing so allows you to construct objects in a variety of ways. For example, consider the following program:

```
// Demonstrate an overloaded constructor.
class MyClass {
  int x;

  MyClass() {                                              ← Construct objects in a variety of ways.
    System.out.println("Inside MyClass().");
    x = 0;
  }

  MyClass(int i) {  ←
    System.out.println("Inside MyClass(int).");
    x = i;
  }

  MyClass(double d) {  ←
    System.out.println("Inside MyClass(double).");
    x = (int) d;
  }

  MyClass(int i, int j) {  ←
    System.out.println("Inside MyClass(int, int).");
```

```
      x = i * j;
  }
}
```

```
class OverloadConsDemo {
  public static void main(String[] args) {
    MyClass t1 = new MyClass();
    MyClass t2 = new MyClass(88);
    MyClass t3 = new MyClass(17.23);
    MyClass t4 = new MyClass(2, 4);

    System.out.println("t1.x: " + t1.x);
    System.out.println("t2.x: " + t2.x);
    System.out.println("t3.x: " + t3.x);
    System.out.println("t4.x: " + t4.x);
  }
}
```

The output from the program is shown here:

```
Inside MyClass().
Inside MyClass(int).
Inside MyClass(double).
Inside MyClass(int, int).
t1.x: 0
t2.x: 88
t3.x: 17
t4.x: 8
```

MyClass( ) is overloaded four ways, each constructing an object differently. The proper constructor is called based on the parameters specified when **new** is executed. By overloading a class's constructor, you give the user of your class flexibility in the way objects are constructed.

One reason that constructors are overloaded is to allow one object to initialize another. For example, consider this program that uses the **Summation** class to compute the summation of an integer value.

```
// Initialize one object with another.
class Summation {
  int sum;

  // Construct from an int.
  Summation(int num) {
    sum = 0;
    for(int i=1; i <= num; i++)
      sum += i;
  }

  // Construct from another object.
  Summation(Summation ob) {          Construct one object from another.
    sum = ob.sum;
  }
}
```

```
class SumDemo {
  public static void main(String[] args) {
    Summation s1 = new Summation(5);
    Summation s2 = new Summation(s1);

    System.out.println("s1.sum: " + s1.sum);
    System.out.println("s2.sum: " + s2.sum);
  }
}
```

The output is shown here:

```
s1.sum: 15
s2.sum: 15
```

Often, as this example shows, an advantage of providing a constructor that uses one object to initialize another is efficiency. In this case, when **s2** is constructed, it is not necessary to recompute the summation. Of course, even in cases when efficiency is not an issue, it is often useful to provide a constructor that makes a copy of an object.

Progress Check

1. Can a constructor take an object of its own class as a parameter?
2. Why might you want to provide overloaded constructors?

TRY THIS 6-2 OVERLOADING THE SimpleStack CONSTRUCTOR

```
SimpleStackDemo2.java
```

In this project you will enhance the **SimpleStack** class by giving it two additional constructors. The first will construct a new stack from another stack. The second will construct a stack, giving it initial values. As you will see, adding these constructors enhances the usability of **SimpleStack**.

STEP-BY-STEP

1. Create a file called **SimpleStackDemo2.java** and copy the updated **SimpleStack** class you created in Try This 6-1 into it.
2. Add the following constructor, which constructs a stack from a stack.

Answers:

1. Yes.
2. To provide convenience and flexibility to the user of your class.

```
// Construct a stack from a stack.
SimpleStack(SimpleStack otherStack) {
  // size of new stack equals that of otherStack
  data = new char[otherStack.data.length];

  // set tos to the same position
  tos = otherStack.tos;

  // copy the contents
  for(int i = 0; i < tos; i++)
    data[i] = otherStack.data[i];
}
```

Look closely at this constructor. It initializes **tos** to the value contained in the **otherStack.tos** parameter. It also allocates a new array to hold the stack and copies the elements from **otherStack** into that array. Once constructed, the new stack will be an identical copy of the original, but both will be completely separate objects.

3. Add the constructor that initializes the stack from a character array, as shown here:

```
// Construct a stack with initial values.
SimpleStack(char[] chrs) {
  // create the array to hold the initial values
  data = new char[chrs.length];
  tos = 0;

  // initialize the stack by pushing the contents
  // of chrs onto it
  for(char ch : chrs)
    push(ch);
}
```

This constructor creates a stack large enough to hold the characters in **chrs** and then stores those characters in the stack by calling **push( )**.

4. Here is the complete updated **SimpleStack** along with a **SimpleStackDemo2** class, which demonstrates it. Notice that this version includes the addition of **private** to **data** and **tos** as described in Try This 6-1.

```
/*
    Try This 6-2

    Add overloaded constructors to SimpleStack.
*/

class SimpleStack {
  // the following members are now private
  private char[] data; // this array holds the stack
```

```java
private int tos; // index of top of stack

// Construct an empty stack given its size.
SimpleStack(int size) {
  data = new char[size]; // create the array to hold the stack
  tos = 0;
}

// Construct a stack from a stack.
SimpleStack(SimpleStack otherStack) {
  // size of new stack equals that of otherStack
  data = new char[otherStack.data.length];

  // set tos to the same position
  tos = otherStack.tos;

  // copy the contents
  for(int i = 0; i < tos; i++)
    data[i] = otherStack.data[i];
}

// Construct a stack with initial values.
SimpleStack(char[] chrs) {
  // create the array to hold the initial values
  data = new char[chrs.length];
  tos = 0;

  // initialize the stack by pushing the contents
  // of chrs onto it
  for(char ch : chrs)
    push(ch);
}

// Push a character onto the stack.
void push(char ch) {
  if(isFull()) {
    System.out.println(" -- Stack is full.");
    return;
  }

  data[tos] = ch;
  tos++;
}

// Pop a character from the stack.
char pop() {
  if(isEmpty()) {
    System.out.println(" -- Stack is empty.");
    return (char) 0; // a placeholder value
```

```
    }
    tos--;
    return data[tos];
  }

  // Return true if the stack is empty.
  boolean isEmpty() {
    return tos==0;
  }

  // Return true if the stack is full.
  boolean isFull() {
    return tos==data.length;
  }
}

// Demonstrate the overloaded SimpleStack class constructors.
class SimpleStackDemo2 {
  public static void main(String[] args) {
    int i;
    char ch;

    char[] chrs = { 'A', 'B', 'C', 'D' };

    // Initialize stack1 with chrs.
    SimpleStack stack1 = new SimpleStack(chrs);

    // Initialize stack2 with the contents of stack1.
    SimpleStack stack2 = new SimpleStack(stack1);

    System.out.print("Popping contents of stack1: ");
    while(!stack1.isEmpty()) {
      ch = stack1.pop();
      System.out.print(ch);
    }

    System.out.print("\nPopping contents of stack2: ");
    while(!stack2.isEmpty()) {
      ch = stack2.pop();
      System.out.print(ch);
    }
  }
}
```

The output from the program is shown here:

```
Popping contents of stack1: DCBA
Popping contents of stack2: DCBA
```

RECURSION

In Java, a method can call itself. This process is called *recursion,* and a method that calls itself is said to be *recursive.* In general, recursion is the process of defining something in terms of itself and is somewhat similar to a circular definition. The key component of a recursive method is a statement that executes a call to that method. Recursion is a powerful control mechanism.

Let's begin with a very simple example that demonstrates the key elements of recursion. The following **drawStars( )** method takes an integer parameter called **n** and then draws a row of **n** stars (actually, asterisks). It uses recursion to control the process.

```
// Use recursion to draw a line of n stars.
void drawStars(int n) {
  if(n == 1)
    System.out.print("*");
  else {
    System.out.print("*");
    drawStars(n-1); // a recursive call
  }
}
```

Notice that inside **drawStars( )** a call to **drawStars( )** is made. This is what is meant by a *recursive call.*

Before we look closely at how **drawStars( )** works, it will be helpful to describe the problem of drawing a line of stars in terms of its recursive solution. To begin, think of the act of drawing stars as a job. After the first star is drawn, what's left to do? The answer: draw the remaining stars. In other words, the job of drawing *N* stars can be broken down into the job of drawing one star, followed by the job of drawing the remaining *N*–1 stars. Of course, the job of drawing *N*–1 stars is simply the process of drawing one star followed by the job of drawing the remaining *N*–2 stars. This process is then repeated until there are no more stars to draw. This general idea is the essence of recursion. Of course, the process must end at some point. In the case of drawing stars, it ends when *N* equals 1 and the final star is drawn.

Now let's look at how the process is implemented in Java code. First, **drawStars ( )** is passed the number of stars to draw in its **n** parameter. Inside the method, if **n** equals 1, then **drawStars( )** draws one star and returns. Thus, when **n** equals 1, the recursive call is *not made.* The point at which the recursive call is not made is called the *base case.* For all cases in which **n** is greater than 1, **drawStars( )** draws one star and then recursively calls itself, passing **n**–1 as an argument. This process repeats until the value passed to **n** is 1 and the recursive calls begin returning. For example, a call to **drawStars(3)** displays one star and then calls **drawStars(2)**, which displays one star and then calls **drawStars(1)**. Since **drawStars(1)** is the base case, the star is displayed and the recursive calls begin to return. After the initial call to **drawStars( )** returns, a line of **n** stars will have been drawn.

There is one more important point that needs to be made about **drawStars( )**. The recursive calls stop when the base case is encountered. As explained, in **drawStars( )**, this is when **n** is passed 1. If the base case were not present to prevent the recursive call, then

drawStars( ) would simply call itself forever (until a run-time error occurred). This is why the base case is important and why every recursive method needs one.

Here is a complete program that demonstrates the **drawStars( )** method.

```java
class StarDrawer {
  void drawStars(int n) {
    if(n == 1)
      System.out.print("*");
    else {
      System.out.print("*");
      drawStars(n-1); // a recursive call
    }
  }
}

class StarDrawingDemo {
  public static void main(String[] args) {
    StarDrawer drawer = new StarDrawer();

    drawer.drawStars(1); // just base case
    System.out.println();
    drawer.drawStars(2); // one recursive call
    System.out.println();
    drawer.drawStars(3); // two recursive calls
    System.out.println();
    drawer.drawStars(10); // nine recursive calls
    System.out.println();
  }
}
```

The output from this program is shown here:

```
*
**
***
**********
```

Let's now look at a slightly more complicated example of recursion. As a general rule, a recursive method requires the use of a parameter that helps determine when a recursive call will take place. In the case of **drawStars( )**, this was **n**, and it was passed the number of stars to draw. However, sometimes the most natural form of a method does not have such a parameter. For example, consider a method called **printArray( )** that takes an integer array as its parameter and displays the elements of the array. This method is easy to implement iteratively using a **for** loop, but how would you implement it recursively? To do so, you would need a base case to stop the recursive calls. What would the base case be? Since the array never changes, the parameter to the method never changes and so each recursive call to the method would use the same parameter, resulting in a never-ending succession of recursive calls. The only thing that changes during the printing of the array is the index of the next element to be printed.

The solution to this type of problem is to use an auxiliary method that adds a parameter that controls the recursion. For example, in the case of **printArray( )**, the auxiliary method might be called **printArrayAux( )**. It would have the array as its first parameter and, as its second parameter, an integer giving the index of the element of the array to be printed next. This auxiliary method reaches the base case when the second parameter is one greater than the index of the last element of the array. Here is a complete program that shows an implementation of these methods and demonstrates how they work:

```
class Printer {
  void printArray(int[] array) {
    printArrayAux(array, 0); // start at the 0th element
    System.out.println();
  }

  void printArrayAux(int[] array, int index) {
    if(index == array.length)
      return; // we are done
    else { // there are more elements to print
      System.out.print(array[index] + " ");
      printArrayAux(array, index+1);
    }
  }
}

class PrinterDemo {
  public static void main(String[] args) {
    Printer printer = new Printer();
    int[] array = { 3,1,4,2,5,7,6,8 };

    printer.printArray(array);
  }
}
```

The output from this program is shown here:

```
3 1 4 2 5 7 6 8
```

So far, the examples of recursive methods have had a **void** return type. However, a recursive method can also return a value. A classic example of such a method is one that computes and returns the factorial of a number. The *factorial* of a number N is the product of all the whole numbers between 1 and N. For example, 3 factorial is $1 \times 2 \times 3$, or 6. The following program shows a recursive way to compute the factorial of a number. For comparison purposes, a nonrecursive equivalent is also shown.

```
// A simple example of recursion.
class Factorial {
  // This is a recursive function.
  int factR(int n) {
    int result;
```

```
     if(n==1) return 1;
     result = factR(n-1) * n;
     return result;  ┐
   }              └──────── Execute the recursive call to factR( ).

   // This is an iterative equivalent.
   int factI(int n) {
     int t, result;

     result = 1;
     for(t=1; t <= n; t++) result *= t;
     return result;
   }
}

class Recursion {
   public static void main(String[] args) {
     Factorial f = new Factorial();

     System.out.println("Factorials using recursive method.");
     System.out.println("Factorial of 3 is " + f.factR(3));
     System.out.println("Factorial of 4 is " + f.factR(4));
     System.out.println("Factorial of 5 is " + f.factR(5));
     System.out.println();

     System.out.println("Factorials using iterative method.");
     System.out.println("Factorial of 3 is " + f.factI(3));
     System.out.println("Factorial of 4 is " + f.factI(4));
     System.out.println("Factorial of 5 is " + f.factI(5));
   }
}
```

The output from this program is shown here:

```
Factorials using recursive method.
Factorial of 3 is 6
Factorial of 4 is 24
Factorial of 5 is 120

Factorials using iterative method.
Factorial of 3 is 6
Factorial of 4 is 24
Factorial of 5 is 120
```

The operation of the nonrecursive method **factI( )** should be clear. It uses a loop starting at 1 and progressively multiplies each number by the moving product.

The operation of the recursive **factR( )** is a bit more complex. When **factR( )** is called with an argument of 1, the method returns 1; otherwise, it returns the product of **factR(n–1)*n**. To evaluate this expression, **factR( )** is called with **n–1**. This process repeats until **n** equals 1 and the calls to the method begin returning. For example, when the factorial of 2 is calculated, the first call to **factR( )** will cause a second call to be made with an argument of 1. This call will return 1, which is then multiplied by 2 (the original value of **n**). The answer is then 2. You might find it interesting to insert **println( )** statements into **factR( )** that show at what level each call is, and what the intermediate results are.

Although recursion can be quite useful, it is not without its costs. Each time you call a method, some overhead is added to your program. As a result, a recursive method will incur this overhead each time the recursive call executes. In some cases, this may impact performance to such an extent that an iterative solution is better. A principal advantage to recursion is that some types of algorithms can be implemented more clearly and simply recursively than they can be iteratively. For example, the quicksort sorting algorithm is quite difficult to implement in an iterative way. Furthermore, in some cases, the use of recursion provides the most natural way to approach a problem.

When writing recursive methods, it is important to remember one thing: you must have a conditional statement, such as an **if**, somewhere that causes the method to return without the recursive call being executed. (In other words, you must establish a base case.) If you don't do this, once you call the method, it will never return. This will result in a run-time error. Runaway recursion is very common when you first begin to develop recursive methods. Use **println( )** statements liberally so that you can watch what is going on and cancel execution if you see that you have made a mistake.

Ask the Expert

Q Recursion is fascinating, but I don't understand how Java can keep all the recursive calls straight. Won't the values of the parameters and variables get mixed up from one call to the next?

A Although the details on how recursion is handled by a compiler is the subject of a more advanced programming course, here is a brief description. Each time a method is called, storage for its parameters and local variables is created, with the parameters being assigned the values of the arguments. Thus, each invocation of a method begins with its own set of parameters and local variables. When a method calls itself, the same process occurs. For each recursive call, a new set of parameters and local variables is allocated storage, and then the method code is executed from the top. A recursive call *does not* make a new copy of the method. Only the parameters and local variables are new. As each recursive call returns, its local variables and parameters are removed from storage, and execution resumes at the point of the recursive call inside the method. Recursive methods could be said to "telescope" out and back.

UNDERSTANDING static

You can define a class member that will be used independently of any object of that class. As you know, normally a class member must be accessed through an object of its class, but it is possible to create a member that can be used without reference to a specific instance. Such a member can be thought of as applying to the class as a whole. To create this type of a member, precede its declaration with the keyword **static**.

When a member is declared **static**, it can be accessed before any objects of its class are created and without reference to any object. You can declare both methods and variables to be **static**. The most common example of a **static** member is **main( )**. **main( )** is declared as **static** because it must be called by the JVM when your program begins. Outside the class, to use a **static** member, you need only specify the name of its class followed by the dot operator. No object needs to be created. For example, if you want to assign the value 10 to a **static** variable called **count** that is part of a class called **MyTimer**, use this line:

```
MyTimer.count = 10;
```

This format is similar to that used to access normal instance variables through an object, except that the class name is used. A **static** method can be called in the same way—by use of the dot operator on the name of the class.

Static Variables

Variables declared **static** are, essentially, global variables. When an object is created, no copy of a **static** variable is made. Instead, all instances of the class share the same **static** variable. Here is an example that shows the differences between a **static** variable and an instance variable:

```java
// Use a static variable.
class StaticDemo {
  int x; // a normal instance variable
  static int y; // a static variable ◄───────────── There is one copy of y for all
                                                     objects to share.
  // Return the sum of the instance variable x
  // and the static variable y.
  int sum() {
    return x + y;
  }
}

class SDemo {
  public static void main(String[] args) {
    StaticDemo ob1 = new StaticDemo();
    StaticDemo ob2 = new StaticDemo();

    // Each object has its own copy of an instance variable.
    ob1.x = 10;
    ob2.x = 20;
    System.out.println("Of course, ob1.x and ob2.x " +
                       "are independent.");
    System.out.println("ob1.x: " + ob1.x +
                       "\nob2.x: " + ob2.x);
    System.out.println();

    // Each object shares one copy of a static variable.
```

```
        System.out.println("The static variable y is shared.");
        StaticDemo.y = 19;
        System.out.println("Set StaticDemo.y to 19.");

        System.out.println("ob1.sum(): " + ob1.sum());
        System.out.println("ob2.sum(): " + ob2.sum());
        System.out.println();

        StaticDemo.y = 100;
        System.out.println("Change StaticDemo.y to 100");
        System.out.println("ob1.sum(): " + ob1.sum());
        System.out.println("ob2.sum(): " + ob2.sum());
        System.out.println();
    }
}
```

The output from the program is shown here:

```
Of course, ob1.x and ob2.x are independent.
ob1.x: 10
ob2.x: 20

The static variable y is shared.
Set StaticDemo.y to 19.
ob1.sum(): 29
ob2.sum(): 39

Change StaticDemo.y to 100
ob1.sum(): 110
ob2.sum(): 120
```

As the output shows, the **static** variable **y** is shared by both **ob1** and **ob2**. Thus, **sum( )** adds the same value of **y** to each object's **x**. Furthermore, changing **y** affects all objects (that is, the entire class), not just a specific instance. Pay special attention to how **y** is accessed through its class name, as shown here:

```
StaticDemo.y = 19;
```

Since **y** is shared by all objects, it is accessed via its class name, not an object reference.

Because **static** variables are independent of any specific object, they are useful when you need to maintain information that is applicable to an entire class. Here is a simple example. It uses a **static** member called **count** to keep a count of the number of **MyClass** objects that have been created.

```
// Count instances.
class MyClass {
    // This static variable will be incremented each
    // time a MyClass object is made.
    static int count = 0;

    MyClass() {
        count++; // increment the count
    }
}
```

```
class UseStatic {
  public static void main(String[] args) {
    for(int i=0; i < 3; i++) {
      MyClass obj = new MyClass();
      System.out.println("Number of objects created: " + MyClass.count);
    }
  }
}
```

The output is shown here:

```
Number of objects created: 1
Number of objects created: 2
Number of objects created: 3
```

Each time that a **MyClass** object is created, the **count** variable is incremented. Because it is **static**, it is used by all instances of **MyClass**. As a result, it stores a running count of the number of **MyClass** objects that have been instantiated. There is no way that this can be accomplished using an instance variable because each object has its own copy of each instance variable. A **static** variable applies to the entire class.

Static Methods

Methods declared **static** are, essentially, global methods. They are called independently of any object. Instead, a **static** method is called through its class name. Here is an example that creates a **static** method. Notice how it is called inside **main( )**.

```
// Use a static method.
class StaticMeth {
  static int val = 1024; // a static variable

  // A static method.
  static int valDiv2() {
    return val/2;
  }
}

class SDemo2 {
  public static void main(String[] args) {

    System.out.println("val is " + StaticMeth.val);
    System.out.println("StaticMeth.valDiv2(): " +
                       StaticMeth.valDiv2());

    StaticMeth.val = 4;
    System.out.println("val is " + StaticMeth.val);
    System.out.println("StaticMeth.valDiv2(): " +
                       StaticMeth.valDiv2());

  }
}
```

The output is shown here:

```
val is 1024
StaticMeth.valDiv2(): 512
val is 4
StaticMeth.valDiv2(): 2
```

As the program shows, because **valDiv2( )** is declared **static**, it can be called without any instances of its class, **StaticMeth**, being created.

Static methods are particularly useful for creating utility methods that perform useful functions not related to a specific object. Several examples are found in the standard **Math** class. It defines a large number of **static** methods that perform various mathematical computations. You have seen an example of this already: the **sqrt( )** method. Others include trigonometric functions such as **cos( )**, **sin( )**, and **tan( )**, the **abs( )** method, which returns the absolute value, and **log( )**, which returns the natural logarithm of a value. Later in this course, you will encounter other examples of **static** methods from the Java library.

Methods declared as **static** have several restrictions:

■ They can directly call only other **static** methods.

■ They can directly access only **static** data.

■ They do not have a **this** reference.

For example, in the following class, the **static** method **valDivDenom( )** is illegal.

```
class StaticError {
  int denom = 3; // a normal instance variable
  static int val = 1024; // a static variable

  /* Error! Can't access a non-static variable
     from within a static method. */
  static int valDivDenom() {
    return val/denom; // won't compile!
  }
}
```

Here, **denom** is a normal instance variable that cannot be accessed within a **static** method.

Static Blocks

Sometimes a class will require some type of initialization before it is ready to create objects. For example, it might need to establish a connection to a remote site. It also might need to initialize certain **static** variables before any of the class's **static** methods are used. To handle these types of situations, Java allows you to declare a **static** block. A **static** block is executed when the class is first loaded. Thus, it is executed before the class can be used for any other purpose. Here is an example of a **static** block:

```
// Use a static block
class StaticBlock {
  static double rootOf2;
  static double rootOf3;

  static {  ←────────────────────────── This block is executed
    System.out.println("Inside static block.");    when the class is loaded.
    rootOf2 = Math.sqrt(2.0);
    rootOf3 = Math.sqrt(3.0);
  }

  StaticBlock(String msg) {
    System.out.println(msg);
  }
}

class SDemo3 {
  public static void main(String[] args) {
    StaticBlock ob = new StaticBlock("Inside Constructor");

    System.out.println("Square root of 2 is " +
                        StaticBlock.rootOf2);
    System.out.println("Square root of 3 is " +
                        StaticBlock.rootOf3);

  }
}
```

The output is shown here:

```
Inside static block.
Inside Constructor
Square root of 2 is 1.4142135623730951
Square root of 3 is 1.7320508075688772
```

As you can see, the **static** block is executed before any objects are constructed.

Progress Check

1. Define recursion.
2. Explain the difference between **static** variables and instance variables.
3. When is a **static** block executed?

———

Answers:

1. Recursion is the process of a method calling itself.
2. Each object of a class has its own copy of the instance variables defined by the class. Each object of a class shares one copy of a **static** variable.
3. A **static** block is executed when its class is first loaded, before its first use.

TRY THIS 6-3   THE QUICKSORT

QSDemo.java

In Chapter 5 you were shown a simple sorting method called the bubble sort. It was mentioned at the time that substantially better sorts exist. Here you will develop a version of one of the best: the quicksort, invented by C.A.R. Hoare. The reason it could not be shown in Chapter 5 is that the cleanest implementations of the quicksort rely on recursion. The version we will develop sorts a character array, but the logic can be adapted to sort any type of object you like.

The quicksort is built on the idea of partitions. The general procedure is to select a value, called the *comparand,* and then to partition the array into two sections. All elements greater than or equal to the comparand are put on one side, and those less than the comparand are put on the other. This process is then repeated for each remaining section until the array is sorted. For example, given the array **fedacb** and using the value **d** as the comparand, the first pass of the quicksort would rearrange the array as follows:

Initial	f e d a c b
Pass1	b c a d e f

This process is then repeated for each section—that is, **bca** and **def**. As you can see, the process is essentially recursive in nature, which is why the cleanest implementation of quicksort is recursive.

You can select the comparand value in a variety of ways. Here are two. You can choose it at random, or you can select it by averaging a small set of values taken from the array. For optimal sorting, you should select a value that is precisely in the middle of the range of values. However, this is not easy to do for most sets of data. In the worst case, the value chosen is at one extremity. Even in this case, however, quicksort still performs correctly. The version of quicksort that we will develop selects the middle element of the array as the comparand.

STEP-BY-STEP

1. Create a file called **QSDemo.java**.
2. First, create the **Quicksort** class shown here:

```
// Try This 6-3: A simple version of the quicksort.
class Quicksort {

  // Set up a call to the actual quicksort method.
  static void qsort(char[] items) {
    qs(items, 0, items.length-1);
  }

  // A recursive version of quicksort for characters.
```

```
private static void qs(char[] items, int left, int right)
{
    int i, j;
    char x, y;

    i = left; j = right;
    x = items[(left+right)/2];

    do {
        while((items[i] < x) && (i < right)) i++;
        while((x < items[j]) && (j > left)) j--;

        if(i <= j) {
            y = items[i];
            items[i] = items[j];
            items[j] = y;
            i++; j--;
        }
    } while(i <= j);

    if(left < j) qs(items, left, j);
    if(i < right) qs(items, i, right);
}
}
```

To keep the interface to the quicksort simple, the **Quicksort** class provides the **qsort( )** method, which sets up a call to the actual quicksort method, **qs( )**. This enables the quicksort to be called with just the name of the array to be sorted, without having to provide an initial partition. Since **qs( )** is only used internally, it is specified as **private**.

3. To use the **Quicksort**, simply call **Quicksort.qsort( )**. Since **qsort( )** is specified as **static**, it can be called through its class rather than on an object. Thus, there is no need to create a **Quicksort** object. After the call returns, the array will be sorted. Remember, this version works only for character arrays, but you can adapt the logic to sort any type of arrays you want.

4. Here is a program that demonstrates **Quicksort**:

```
// Try This 6-3: A simple version of the quicksort.

class Quicksort {

    // Set up a call to the actual quicksort method.
    static void qsort(char[] items) {
        qs(items, 0, items.length-1);
    }

    // A recursive version of quicksort for characters.
    private static void qs(char[] items, int left, int right)
    {
```

```
    int i, j;
    char x, y;

    i = left; j = right;
    x = items[(left+right)/2];

    do {
      while((items[i] < x) && (i < right)) i++;
      while((x < items[j]) && (j > left)) j--;

      if(i <= j) {
        y = items[i];
        items[i] = items[j];
        items[j] = y;
        i++; j--;
      }
    } while(i <= j);

    if(left < j) qs(items, left, j);
    if(i < right) qs(items, i, right);
  }
}

class QSDemo {
  public static void main(String[] args) {
    char[] a = { 'd', 'x', 'a', 'r', 'p', 'j', 'i' };
    int i;

    System.out.print("Original array: ");
    for(i=0; i < a.length; i++)
      System.out.print(a[i]);

    System.out.println();

    // now, sort the array
    Quicksort.qsort(a);

    System.out.print("Sorted array: ");
    for(i=0; i < a.length; i++)
      System.out.print(a[i]);
  }
}
```

INTRODUCING NESTED AND INNER CLASSES

In Java you can define a *nested class*. This is a class that is declared within another class. A nested class does not exist independently of its enclosing class. Thus, the scope of a nested class is bounded by its outer class. A nested class that is declared directly within its enclosing class scope is a member of its enclosing class. It is also possible to declare a nested class that is local to a block.

There are two general types of nested classes: those that are preceded by the **static** modifier and those that are not. The only type that we are concerned about in this book is the non-**static** variety. This type of nested class is also called an *inner class*. It has access to all of the variables and methods of its outer class and may refer to them directly in the same way that other non-**static** members of the outer class do.

Sometimes an inner class is used to provide a set of services that are used only by its enclosing class. Here is an example that uses an inner class to compute various values for its enclosing class:

```java
// Use an inner class.
class Outer {
  int[] nums;

  Outer(int[] n) {
    nums = n;
  }

  void analyze() {
    Inner inOb = new Inner();

    System.out.println("Minimum: " + inOb.min());
    System.out.println("Maximum: " + inOb.max());
    System.out.println("Average: " + inOb.avg());
  }

  // This is an inner class.
  class Inner {                          ← An inner class
    // Return the minimum value.
    int min() {
      int m = nums[0];

      for(int i=1; i < nums.length; i++)
        if(nums[i] < m) m = nums[i];

      return m;
    }

    // Return the maximum value.
    int max() {
      int m = nums[0];
      for(int i=1; i < nums.length; i++)
        if(nums[i] > m) m = nums[i];

      return m;
    }

    // Return the average.
    int avg() {
```

```
        int a = 0;
        for(int i=0; i < nums.length; i++)
          a += nums[i];

        return a / nums.length;
      }
    }
}

class NestedClassDemo {
  public static void main(String[] args) {
    int[] x = { 3, 2, 1, 5, 6, 9, 7, 8 };
    Outer outOb = new Outer(x);

    outOb.analyze();
  }
}
```

The output from the program is shown here:

```
Minimum: 1
Maximum: 9
Average: 5
```

In this example, the inner class **Inner** computes various values from the array **nums**, which is a member of **Outer**. As explained, an inner class has access to the members of its enclosing class, so it is perfectly acceptable for **Inner** to access the **nums** array directly. The opposite, however, is not true. For example, it would not be possible for **analyze( )** to invoke the **min( )** method directly, without creating an **Inner** object.

As mentioned, it is possible to nest a class within a block scope. Doing so simply creates a localized class that is not known outside its block. The following example adapts the **BitOut** class developed in Try This 5-3 for use as a local class.

```
// Use BitOut as a local class.
class LocalClassDemo {
  public static void main(String[] args) {

    // An inner class version of BitOut.
    class BitOut {            ←——————— A local class nested within a method
      int numBits;

      BitOut(int n) {
        if(n < 1) n = 1;
        if(n > 64) n = 64;
        numBits = n;
      }
```

```
      void show(long val) {
         long mask = 1;

         // left-shift a 1 into the proper position
         mask <<= numBits-1;

         int spacer =  8 - (numBits % 8);
         for(; mask != 0; mask >>>= 1) {
            if((val & mask) != 0) System.out.print("1");
            else System.out.print("0");
            spacer++;
            if((spacer % 8) == 0) {
               System.out.print(" ");
               spacer = 0;
            }
         }
         System.out.println();
      }
   }

   for(byte b = 0; b < 10; b++) {
      BitOut byteval = new BitOut(8);

      System.out.print(b + " in binary: ");
      byteval.show(b);
   }
  }
}
```

The output from this version of the program is shown here:

```
0 in binary: 00000000
1 in binary: 00000001
2 in binary: 00000010
3 in binary: 00000011
4 in binary: 00000100
5 in binary: 00000101
6 in binary: 00000110
7 in binary: 00000111
8 in binary: 00001000
9 in binary: 00001001
```

In this example, the **BitOut** class is not known outside of **main( )**, and any attempt to access it by any method other than **main( )** will result in an error.

One last point: you can create an inner class that does not have a name. This is called an *anonymous inner class*. An object of an anonymous inner class is instantiated when the class is declared, using **new**. Anonymous inner classes are discussed further in Part Two of this book, when Swing event handling is described.

Ask the Expert

Q What makes a **static** nested class different from a non-**static** one?

A A **static** nested class is one that has the **static** modifier applied. Because it is **static**, it can access only other **static** members of the enclosing class directly. It must access other members of its outer class through an object reference.

Progress Check

1. An inner class has access to the other members of its enclosing class. True or False?
2. A nested class does not exist independently of its enclosing class. True or False?

VARARGS: VARIABLE-LENGTH ARGUMENTS

Sometimes you will want to create a method that takes a variable number of arguments, based on its precise usage. For example, a method that opens an Internet connection might take a user name, password, file name, protocol, and so on, but supply defaults if some of this information is not provided. In this situation, it would be convenient to pass only the arguments to which the defaults did not apply. To create such a method implies that there must be some way to create a list of arguments that is variable in length, rather than fixed.

In the past, methods that required a variable-length argument list could be handled in two ways, neither of which was particularly pleasing. First, if the maximum number of arguments was small and known, then you could create overloaded versions of the method, one for each way the method could be called. Although this works and is suitable for some situations, it applies to only a narrow class of situations. In cases where the maximum number of potential arguments is larger, or unknowable, a second approach was used in which the arguments were put into an array, and then the array was passed to the method. Frankly, both of these approaches often resulted in clumsy solutions, and it was widely acknowledged that a better approach was needed.

Beginning with JDK 5, this need was addressed by the inclusion of a feature that simplified the creation of methods that require a variable number of arguments. This feature is called *varargs,* and it is short for variable-length arguments. A method that takes a variable number of arguments is called a *variable-arity method,* or simply a *varargs method.* The parameter list for a varargs method is not fixed, but rather variable in length. Thus, a varargs method can take a variable number of arguments.

Answers:

1. True.
2. True.

Varargs Basics

A variable-length argument is specified by three periods (**...**). For example, here is how to write a method called **vaTest( )** that takes a variable number of arguments:

```
// vaTest() uses a vararg.              Declare a variable-length argument list.
static void vaTest(int ... v) {◄─────────────────┐
  System.out.println("Number of args: " + v.length);
  System.out.println("Contents: ");

  for(int i=0; i < v.length; i++)
    System.out.println(" arg " + i + ": " + v[i]);

  System.out.println();
}
```

Notice that **v** is declared as shown here:

```
int ... v
```

This syntax tells the compiler that **vaTest( )** can be called with zero or more arguments. Furthermore, it causes **v** to be implicitly declared as an array of type **int[ ]**. Thus, inside **vaTest( )**, **v** is accessed using the normal array syntax.

Here is a complete program that demonstrates **vaTest( )**:

```
// Demonstrate variable-length arguments.
class VarArgs {

  // vaTest() uses a vararg.
  static void vaTest(int ... v) {
    System.out.println("Number of args: " + v.length);
    System.out.println("Contents: ");

    for(int i=0; i < v.length; i++)
      System.out.println("  arg " + i + ": " + v[i]);

    System.out.println();
  }

  public static void main(String[] args)
  {

    // Notice how vaTest() can be called with a
    // variable number of arguments.
    vaTest(10);        // 1 arg
    vaTest(1, 2, 3); //  3 args        Call with different numbers
    vaTest();          //   no args    of arguments.
  }
}
```

The output from the program is shown here:

```
Number of args: 1
Contents:
  arg 0: 10

Number of args: 3
Contents:
  arg 0: 1
  arg 1: 2
  arg 2: 3

Number of args: 0
Contents:
```

There are two important things to notice about this program. First, as explained, inside **vaTest( )**, **v** is operated on as an array. This is because **v** *is an array*. The **...** syntax simply tells the compiler that a variable number of arguments will be used and that these arguments will be stored in the array referred to by **v**. Second, in **main( )**, **vaTest( )** is called with different numbers of arguments, including no arguments at all. The arguments are automatically put in an array and passed to **v**. In the case of no arguments, the length of the array is zero.

A method can have "normal" parameters along with a variable-length parameter. However, the variable-length parameter must be the last parameter declared by the method. For example, this method declaration is perfectly acceptable:

```
int doIt(int a, int b, double c, int ... vals) {
```

In this case, the first three arguments used in a call to **doIt( )** are matched to the first three parameters. Then, any remaining arguments are assumed to belong to **vals**.

Here is a reworked version of the **vaTest( )** method that takes a regular argument and a variable-length argument:

```
// Use varargs with standard arguments.
class VarArgs2 {

  // Here, msg is a normal parameter and v is a
  // varargs parameter.
  static void vaTest(String msg, int ... v) {       A "normal" and vararg
    System.out.println(msg + v.length);             parameter
    System.out.println("Contents: ");

    for(int i=0; i < v.length; i++)
      System.out.println("  arg " + i + ": " + v[i]);

    System.out.println();
  }

  public static void main(String[] args)
  {
```

```
    vaTest("One vararg: ", 10);
    vaTest("Three varargs: ", 1, 2, 3);
    vaTest("No varargs: ");
  }
}
```

The output from this program is shown here:

```
One vararg: 1
Contents:
  arg 0: 10

Three varargs: 3
Contents:
  arg 0: 1
  arg 1: 2
  arg 2: 3

No varargs: 0
Contents:
```

Remember, the varargs parameter must be last. For example, the following declaration is incorrect:

```
int doIt(int a, int b, double c, int ... vals, boolean stopFlag) { // Error!
```

Here, there is an attempt to declare a regular parameter after the varargs parameter, which is illegal. There is one more restriction to be aware of: there must be only one varargs parameter. For example, this declaration is also invalid:

```
int doIt(int a, int b, double c, int ... vals, double ... morevals) { // Error!
```

The attempt to declare the second varargs parameter is illegal.

Progress Check

1. Show how to declare a method called **sum( )** that takes a variable number of **int** arguments. (Use a return type of **int**.)
2. Given this declaration,

   ```
   void m(double ... x)
   ```

   the parameter **x** is implicitly declared as a/an _____.

Overloading Varargs Methods

You can overload a method that takes a variable-length argument. For example, the following program overloads **vaTest( )** three times:

_____

Answers:

1. `int sum(int ... n)`
2. array of **double**

```
// Varargs and overloading.
class VarArgs3 {
                                                First version of vaTest( )
  static void vaTest(int ... v) {
    System.out.println("vaTest(int ...): " +
                        "Number of args: " + v.length);
    System.out.println("Contents: ");

    for(int i=0; i < v.length; i++)
      System.out.println("  arg " + i + ": " + v[i]);

    System.out.println();
  }                                             Second version of vaTest( )

  static void vaTest(boolean ... v) {
    System.out.println("vaTest(boolean ...): " +
                        "Number of args: " + v.length);
    System.out.println("Contents: ");

    for(int i=0; i < v.length; i++)
      System.out.println("  arg " + i + ": " + v[i]);

    System.out.println();
  }                                             Third version of vaTest( )

  static void vaTest(String msg, int ... v) {
    System.out.println("vaTest(String, int ...): " +
                        msg + v.length);
    System.out.println("Contents: ");

    for(int i=0; i < v.length; i++)
      System.out.println("  arg " + i + ": " + v[i]);

    System.out.println();
  }

  public static void main(String[] args)
  {
    vaTest(1, 2, 3);
    vaTest("Testing: ", 10, 20);
    vaTest(true, false, false);
  }
}
```

The output produced by this program is shown here:

```
vaTest(int ...): Number of args: 3
Contents:
  arg 0: 1
  arg 1: 2
  arg 2: 3
```

```
vaTest(String, int ...): Testing: 2
Contents:
  arg 0: 10
  arg 1: 20

vaTest(boolean ...): Number of args: 3
Contents:
  arg 0: true
  arg 1: false
  arg 2: false
```

This program illustrates both ways that a varargs method can be overloaded. First, the types of its vararg parameter can differ. This is the case for **vaTest(int ...)** and **vaTest(boolean ...)**. Remember, the **...** causes the parameter to be treated as an array of the specified type. Therefore, just as you can overload methods by using different types of array parameters, you can overload varargs methods by using different types of varargs. In this case, Java uses the type difference to determine which overloaded method to call.

The second way to overload a varargs method is to add one or more normal parameters. This is what was done with **vaTest(String, int ...)**. In this case, Java uses both the number of arguments and the type of the arguments to determine which method to call.

Varargs and Ambiguity

Somewhat unexpected errors can result when overloading a method that takes a variable-length argument. These errors involve ambiguity because it is possible to create an ambiguous call to an overloaded varargs method. For example, consider the following program:

```
// Varargs, overloading, and ambiguity.
//
// This program contains an error and will not compile!
class VarArgs4 {

  // Use an int vararg parameter.
  static void vaTest(int ... v) {          ◄———————— An int vararg
    // ...
  }

  // Use a boolean vararg parameter.
  static void vaTest(boolean ... v) {      ◄———————— A boolean vararg
    // ...
  }

  public static void main(String[] args)
  {
    vaTest(1, 2, 3); // OK
    vaTest(true, false, false); // OK

    vaTest(); // Error: Ambiguous!   ◄———————— Ambiguous!
  }
}
```

In this program, the overloading of **vaTest( )** is perfectly correct. However, this program will not compile because of the following call:

```
vaTest(); // Error: Ambiguous!
```

Because the vararg parameter can be empty, this call could be translated into a call to **vaTest(int ...)** or to **vaTest(boolean ...)**. Both are equally valid. Thus, the call is inherently ambiguous.

Here is another example of ambiguity. The following overloaded versions of **vaTest( )** are inherently ambiguous even though one takes a normal parameter:

```
static void vaTest(int ... v) { // ...
```

```
static void vaTest(int n, int ... v) { // ...
```

Although the parameter lists of **vaTest( )** differ, there is no way for the compiler to resolve the following call:

    vaTest(1)

Does this translate into a call to **vaTest(int ...)**, with one varargs argument, or into a call to **vaTest(int, int ...)** with no varargs arguments? There is no way for the compiler to answer this question. Thus, the situation is ambiguous.

Because of ambiguity errors like those just shown, sometimes you will need to forego overloading and simply use two different method names. Also, in some cases, ambiguity errors expose a conceptual flaw in your code, which you can remedy by more carefully crafting a solution.

EXERCISES

1. Given this fragment,

   ```
   class X {
     private int count;
   ```

   is the following fragment correct?

   ```
   class Y {
     public static void main(String[] args) {
       X ob = new X();

       ob.count = 10;
   ```

2. An access modifier must _____ a member's declaration.

3. Given this class,

   ```
   class Test {
     int a;
     Test(int i) { a = i; }
   }
   ```

write a method called **swap( )** that exchanges the contents of the objects referred to by two **Test** object references.

4. Is the following fragment correct?

```
class X {
   int meth(int a, int b) { ... }
   String meth(int a, int b) { ... }
```

5. Write a recursive method that displays the contents of a string backwards.

6. If all objects of a class need to share the same variable, how must you declare
   that variable?

7. Why might you need to use a **static** block?

8. What is an inner class?

9. To make a member accessible by only other members of its class, what access
   modifier must be used?

10. The name of a method plus its parameter list constitutes the method's

    _____.

11. An **int** argument is passed to a method by using call-by-_____.

12. Create a varargs method called **sum( )** that sums the **int** values passed to it.
    Have it return the result. Demonstrate its use.

13. Can a varargs method be overloaded?

14. Show an example of an overloaded varargs method that is ambiguous.

15. Modify the **showBits( )** method in the **BitOut** class in Try This 5-3 in Chapter
    5 so that it doesn't print the bits and instead it returns a **String** containing the
    bits that would otherwise have been printed. Also modify the **main( )** method
    in the **ShowBitsDemo** class so that it tests the new **showBits( )** method.

16. Implement a **string2charArray( )** method that takes a **String** as its parameter.
    It creates and returns a **char** array containing the same characters in the same
    order as in the string.

17. Implement a **charArray2string( )** method that takes a **char** array as its param-
    eter. It creates and returns a **String** that contains the same characters in the
    same order as in the array.

18. Implement a method **readString( )** that uses **System.in.read( )** to read in a line
    of characters. It then combines the characters into a **String** which it returns.
    The string that is returned should include the end of line character **'\n'**.

19. The method **hasDuplicateValues( )** shown below is supposed to return **true**
    if the array contains any repeated integers and return **false** if all integers in
    the array are unique. However, it doesn't work correctly. Explain why it is
    wrong and then fix it.

```
boolean hasDuplicateValues(int[] data) {
   for(int i = 0; i < data.length; i++)
      for(int j = 0; j < data.length; j++)
         if(data[i] == data[j]) return true;
   return false;
}
```

20. Implement a method **addAtEnd( )** that takes an integer array **data** and an integer **x** as its parameters. It creates a new array whose length is one greater than **data**'s length. It then copies all of **data**'s elements into the new array and lastly adds the value of **x** into the last element of the array. It returns the new array.

21. Implement a method **insert( )** that takes an integer array **data**, an integer **x**, and an integer **idx** as its parameters. It creates a new array whose length is one greater than **data**'s length. It then copies all of **data**'s elements and **x** into the new array. The value of **x** is inserted into the new array at the index **idx,** and the values of **data** are added to the new array to fill the other elements around **x** in the order they are in **data**. It returns the new array.

22. Implement a method **remove( )** that takes an integer array **data** and an integer **idx** as its parameters. It creates a new array whose length is one less than **data**'s length. It then copies all of **data**'s elements into the new array except for the value at the index **idx**. It returns the new array.

23. Suppose you have a method that takes as its parameters two integer arrays **data1** and **data2** of the same length and it copies all the data from **data1** to **data2** and then clears **data1** (that is, it sets all the values in **data1** to 0). What would happen if someone invoked this method and passed in the same array for both arguments rather than passing in two distinct arrays?

24. Suppose that a class has an overloaded method named **add** with the following two implementations:

```
double add(int x, double y) { return x + y; }

double add(double x, int y) { return x + y + 1; }
```

What, if anything, will be returned by the following method calls?

 A. add(3, 3.14)

 B. (3.14, 3)

 C. add(3, 3)

 D. add(3.14, 3.14)

25. The **drawStars( )** method described in the section on recursion draws one star and then recursively calls itself to draw the remaining **n**-1 stars. Could it also do things in the opposite order? That is, could it recursively call itself to draw **n**-1 of the stars and then draw the last star?

26. What would happen if the **drawStars( )** method described in the section on recursion were invoked using as its argument the integer -1? Modify the method so that if a negative integer is passed in as its argument, nothing is printed.

27. Write a recursive method **countDown( )** that takes an integer **n** as its parameter. It prints the integers from **n** down to 0, one per line, and then it prints "Blast off!".

28. Write a recursive method **add1toN( )** that takes an integer **n** as its parameter. It returns the sum $1 + 2 + 3 + \cdots + n$.

29. Here is the code for a recursive method named **mystery**. What is printed when **mystery(1, 2)** is called? How many recursive calls were made?

```
void mystery(int a, int b)
{
  if(a == 0 && b == 0)
    System.out.println(0);
  else if(a == 0) {
    System.out.println(b);
    mystery(a, b-1);
  }
  else {
    mystery(a-1, b);
    System.out.println(b);
  }
}
```

30. Implement an **equalArrays( )** method that takes two integer arrays as parameters and returns **true** if both arrays are the same length and have equal values at corresponding indices. Implement it two ways:

   A. iteratively
   B. recursively (*Hint:* Create an auxiliary function with an extra parameter.)

31. Write a method **reverse( )** that takes an integer array as its parameter and reverses the order of the elements in the array. Implement it two ways:

   A. iteratively
   B. recursively (*Hint:* Create an auxiliary function with an extra parameter.)

32. Implement a **numTimes( )** method that takes two parameters: an integer array called **data** and an integer called **x**. It returns the number of times that **x** appears in the array. Implement it two ways:

   A. iteratively
   B. recursively (*Hint*: Create an auxiliary function with an extra parameter.)

33. The following code will not compile. Explain what is wrong.

```
class Oops {
  int x = 3;

  static void changeX() { x = 4; }
}
```

34. In Try This 6-3, a quicksort method **qsort( )** is implemented and demonstrated. It calls a recursive method **qs( )**. How many times is **qs( )** called altogether if **qsort( )** is called to sort each of the following arrays? To answer the question, create a **counter** variable and add a statement that increments **counter** at the beginning of the body of **qs( )** so that it keeps track of the number of times **qs( )** is called.

   A. {'a', 'b', 'c', 'd', 'e', 'f', 'g'} // an already sorted array

   B. {'g', 'f', 'e', 'd', 'c', 'b', 'a'} // a reverse sorted array

C. {'a', 'c', 'e', 'g', 'i', 'k', 'm', 'o', 'q', 's', 'u', 'w', 'y', 'b', 'd', 'f', 'h', 'j', 'l', 'n', 'p', 'r', 't', 'v', 'x', 'z'}

35. In Try This 6-3, the recursive quicksort method **qs ( )** selects the middle value of the array as the comparand. Modify the method so that it selects the first element of the array as the comparand, and then answer the same questions as in the preceding exercise.

36. If an inner class has an instance variable named **x** and the outer class also has an instance variable named **x**, which variable is being referred to when **x** is used in a method in the inner class? Why?

37. What is the difference between the following two methods? More precisely, the bodies of the methods are the same, but the parameters aren't. What does the vararg version **addUp1** allow us to do differently than the array version **addUp2**?

```
int addUp1(int ... v) {
    int sum = 0;

    for(int x : v)
        sum += x;
    return sum;
}

int addUp2(int[] v) {
    int sum = 0;

    for(int x : v)
        sum += x;
    return sum;
}
```

38. In Try This 6-2, a new **SimpleStack** constructor was implemented that takes another stack as its argument and creates a copy of it. Here is the code:

```
// Construct a stack from a stack.
SimpleStack(SimpleStack otherStack) {
    // size of new stack equals that of otherStack
    data = new char[otherStack.data.length];

    // set tos to the same position
    tos = otherStack.tos;

    // copy the contents
    for(int i = 0; i < tos; i++)
        data[i] = otherStack.data[i];
}
```

What is wrong with implementing the constructor the following way, which is much simpler?

```
// Construct a stack from a stack.
SimpleStack(SimpleStack otherStack) {
   // set data & tos to otherStack's data & tos
   data = otherStack.data;
   tos = otherStack.tos;
}
```

CHAPTER 7

Inheritance

KEY SKILLS & CONCEPTS

- ◼ Understand inheritance basics
- ◼ Call superclass constructors
- ◼ Use **super** to access superclass members
- ◼ Create a multilevel class hierarchy
- ◼ Know when constructors are executed
- ◼ Understand superclass references to subclass objects
- ◼ Override methods
- ◼ Use overridden methods to support polymorphism
- ◼ Use abstract classes
- ◼ Use **final**
- ◼ Know the **Object** class

Inheritance is one of the three foundational principles of object-oriented programming because it allows the creation of hierarchical classifications. Using inheritance, you can create a general class that defines traits common to a set of related items. This class can then be inherited by other, more specific classes, each adding those things that are unique to it.

In the language of Java, a class that is inherited is called a *superclass*. The class that does the inheriting is called a *subclass*. Therefore, a subclass is a specialized version of a superclass. It inherits all of the variables and methods defined by the superclass and adds its own, unique elements.

INHERITANCE BASICS

Java supports inheritance by allowing one class to incorporate another class into its declaration. This is done by using the **extends** keyword. Thus, the subclass adds to (extends) the superclass.

Let's begin with a short example that illustrates several of the key features of inheritance. The following program creates a superclass called **TwoDShape**, which stores the width and height of a two-dimensional object, and a subclass called **Triangle**. Notice how the keyword **extends** is used to create a subclass.

```java
// A simple class hierarchy.

// A class for two-dimensional objects.
class TwoDShape {
  double width;
  double height;

  void showDim() {
    System.out.println("Width and height are " +
                       width + " and " + height);
  }
}

// A subclass of TwoDShape for triangles.
class Triangle extends TwoDShape {
  String style;

  double area() {
    return width * height / 2;
  }

  void showStyle() {
    System.out.println("Triangle is " + style);
  }
}

class Shapes {
  public static void main(String[] args) {
    Triangle t1 = new Triangle();
    Triangle t2 = new Triangle();

    t1.width = 4.0;
    t1.height = 4.0;
    t1.style = "filled";

    t2.width = 8.0;
    t2.height = 12.0;
    t2.style = "outlined";

    System.out.println("Info for t1: ");
    t1.showStyle();
    t1.showDim();
    System.out.println("Area is " + t1.area());

    System.out.println();
```

Triangle inherits **TwoDShape**.

Triangle can refer to the members of **TwoDShape** as if they were part of **Triangle**.

All members of **Triangle** are available to **Triangle** objects, even those inherited from **TwoDShape**.

```
        System.out.println("Info for t2: ");
        t2.showStyle();
        t2.showDim();
        System.out.println("Area is " + t2.area());
    }
}
```

The output from this program is shown here:

```
Info for t1:
Triangle is filled
Width and height are 4.0 and 4.0
Area is 8.0

Info for t2:
Triangle is outlined
Width and height are 8.0 and 12.0
Area is 48.0
```

Here, **TwoDShape** defines the attributes of a "generic" two-dimensional shape, such as a square, rectangle, or triangle. The **Triangle** class creates a specific type of **TwoDShape**, in this case, a triangle. The **Triangle** class includes all of **TwoDShape** and adds the field **style**, the method **area( )**, and the method **showStyle( )**. The triangle's style is stored in **style**. This can be any string that describes the triangle, such as "filled", "outlined", "transparent", or even something like "warning symbol", "isosceles", or "rounded". The **area( )** method computes and returns the area of the triangle, and **showStyle( )** displays the triangle style.

Because **Triangle** includes all of the members of its superclass, **TwoDShape**, it can access **width** and **height** inside **area( )**. Also, inside **main( )**, objects **t1** and **t2** can refer to **width** and **height** directly, as if they were part of **Triangle**. Figure 7-1 depicts conceptually how **TwoDShape** is incorporated into **Triangle**.

Even though **TwoDShape** is a superclass for **Triangle**, it is also a completely independent, stand-alone class. Being a superclass for a subclass does not mean that the superclass cannot be used by itself. For example, the following is perfectly valid.

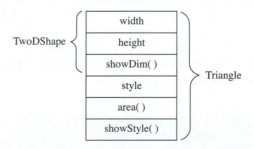

FIGURE 7-1: A conceptual depiction of the **Triangle** class

```
TwoDShape shape = new TwoDShape();

shape.width = 10;
shape.height = 20;

shape.showDim();
```

Of course, an object of **TwoDShape** has no knowledge of or access to any subclasses of **TwoDShape**.

The general form of a **class** declaration that inherits a superclass is shown here:

class *subclass-name* extends *superclass-name* {

// body of class

}

You can specify only one superclass for any subclass that you create. Java does not support the inheritance of multiple superclasses into a single subclass. You can, however, create a hierarchy of inheritance in which a subclass becomes a superclass of another subclass. Of course, no class can be a superclass of itself.

A major advantage of inheritance is that once you have created a superclass that defines the attributes common to a set of objects, it can be used to create any number of more specific subclasses. Each subclass can precisely tailor its own classification. For example, here is another subclass of **TwoDShape** that encapsulates rectangles.

```
// A subclass of TwoDShape for rectangles.
class Rectangle extends TwoDShape {
  boolean isSquare() {
    if(width == height) return true;
    return false;
  }

  double area() {
    return width * height;
  }
}
```

The **Rectangle** class includes **TwoDShape** and adds the methods **isSquare( )**, which determines if the rectangle is square, and **area( )**, which computes the area of a rectangle. Notice that **Rectangle** does not have a **style** field or a **showStyle( )** method. Although **Triangle** adds those members, it does not mean that **Rectangle** (or any other subclass of **TwoDShape**) must also add them. Except for sharing a common superclass, each subclass is independent. Of course, subclasses can provide similar members, as is the case with the **area( )** method. Although it is implemented differently, both **Triangle** and **Rectangle** provide this method.

MEMBER ACCESS AND INHERITANCE

As you learned in Chapter 6, often an instance variable of a class will be declared **private** to prevent its unauthorized use or tampering. Inheriting a class *does not* overrule the **private** access restriction. Thus, even though a subclass includes all of the members of its superclass, it cannot access those members of the superclass that have been declared **private**. For example, if, as shown here, **width** and **height** are made private in **TwoDShape**, then **Triangle** will not be able to access them.

```java
// Private members of a superclass are not accessible by a subclass.

// This example will not compile.

// A class for two-dimensional objects.
class TwoDShape {
  private double width; // these are
  private double height; // now private

  void showDim() {
    System.out.println("Width and height are " +
                        width + " and " + height);
  }
}

// A subclass of TwoDShape for triangles.
class Triangle extends TwoDShape {
  String style;

  double area() {
    return width * height / 2; // Error! can't access
  }

  void showStyle() {
    System.out.println("Triangle is " + style);
  }
}
```

Can't access a **private** member of a superclass.

The **Triangle** class will not compile because the reference to **width** and **height** inside the **area( )** method causes an access violation. Since **width** and **height** are now declared **private** in **TwoDShape**, they are accessible only by other members of **TwoDShape**. Subclasses have no access to them.

Remember that a class member that has been declared **private** will remain private to its class. It is not accessible by any code outside its class, including subclasses.

At first, you might think that the fact that subclasses do not have access to the private members of superclasses is a serious restriction that would prevent the use of private members in many situations. However, this is not true. As explained in Chapter 6, Java programmers typically use accessor methods to provide access to the private instance variables of a class. Here is a rewrite of the **TwoDShape** and **Triangle** classes that uses methods to access the private instance variables **width** and **height**.

```java
// Use accessor methods to set and get private members.

// A class for two-dimensional objects.
class TwoDShape {
  private double width; // these are
  private double height; // now private
```

```
    // Accessor methods for width and height.
    double getWidth() { return width; }
    double getHeight() { return height; }  ◄──────── Accessor methods for width and height
    void setWidth(double w) { width = w; }
    void setHeight(double h) { height = h; }

  void showDim() {
    System.out.println("Width and height are " +
                        width + " and " + height);

  }
}


// A subclass of TwoDShape for triangles.
class Triangle extends TwoDShape {
  String style;
                            ┌──────── Use accessor methods provided by superclass.
  double area() {          │
    return getWidth() * getHeight() / 2;
  }

  void showStyle() {
    System.out.println("Triangle is " + style);
  }
}

class Shapes2 {
  public static void main(String[] args) {
    Triangle t1 = new Triangle();
    Triangle t2 = new Triangle();

    t1.setWidth(4.0);
    t1.setHeight(4.0);
    t1.style = "filled";

    t2.setWidth(8.0);
    t2.setHeight(12.0);
    t2.style = "outlined";

    System.out.println("Info for t1: ");
    t1.showStyle();
    t1.showDim();
    System.out.println("Area is " + t1.area());

    System.out.println();

    System.out.println("Info for t2: ");
    t2.showStyle();
    t2.showDim();
    System.out.println("Area is " + t2.area());
  }
}
```

Ask the Expert

Q When should I make an instance variable private?

A There are no hard and fast rules that fit every situation, but here are two general principles. If an instance variable is to be used only by methods defined within its class, then it should be made private. If an instance variable must be within certain bounds, then it should be private and made available only through accessor methods. This way, you can prevent invalid values from being assigned. Furthermore, using accessor methods to access data lets you more easily change your class's implementation without affecting the users of your class.

Progress Check

1. When creating a subclass, what keyword is used to include a superclass?
2. Does a subclass include the members of its superclass?
3. Does a subclass have access to the private members of its superclass?

CONSTRUCTORS AND INHERITANCE

In a hierarchy, it is possible for both superclasses and subclasses to have their own constructors. This raises an important question: what constructor is responsible for building an object of the subclass—the one in the superclass, the one in the subclass, or both? The answer is this: the constructor for the superclass constructs the superclass portion of the object, and the constructor for the subclass constructs the subclass part. This makes sense because the superclass has no knowledge of or access to any element in a subclass. Thus, their construction must be separate. The preceding examples have relied on the default constructors created automatically by Java, so this was not an issue. However, in practice, most classes will have explicit constructors. Here you will see how to handle this situation.

When only the subclass defines a constructor, the process is straightforward: simply construct the subclass object. The superclass portion of the object is constructed automatically using its default constructor. For example, here is a reworked version of **Triangle** that defines a constructor. It also makes **style** private, since it is now set by the constructor.

Answers:

1. **extends**
2. Yes.
3. No.

```
// Add a constructor to Triangle.

// A class for two-dimensional objects.
class TwoDShape {
  private double width; // these are
  private double height; // now private

  // Accessor methods for width and height.
  double getWidth() { return width; }
  double getHeight() { return height; }
  void setWidth(double w) { width = w; }
  void setHeight(double h) { height = h; }

  void showDim() {
    System.out.println("Width and height are " +
                       width + " and " + height);
  }
}

// A subclass of TwoDShape for triangles.
class Triangle extends TwoDShape {
  private String style;

  // Constructor
  Triangle(String s, double w, double h) {
    setWidth(w);                        ← Initialize TwoDShape portion of object.
    setHeight(h);

    style = s;
  }

  double area() {
    return getWidth() * getHeight() / 2;
  }

  void showStyle() {
    System.out.println("Triangle is " + style);
  }
}

class Shapes3 {
  public static void main(String[] args) {
    Triangle t1 = new Triangle("filled", 4.0, 4.0);
    Triangle t2 = new Triangle("outlined", 8.0, 12.0);

    System.out.println("Info for t1: ");
    t1.showStyle();
    t1.showDim();
    System.out.println("Area is " + t1.area());

    System.out.println();
```

```
      System.out.println("Info for t2: ");
      t2.showStyle();
      t2.showDim();
      System.out.println("Area is " + t2.area());
   }
}
```

Here, **Triangle**'s constructor initializes the members of **TwoDClass** that it inherits along with its own **style** field.

When both the superclass and the subclass define constructors, the process is a bit more complicated because both the superclass and subclass constructors must be executed. In this case you must use another of Java's keywords, **super**, which has two general forms. The first calls a superclass constructor. The second is used to access a member of the superclass that has been hidden by a member of a subclass. Here, we will look at its first use.

USING super TO CALL SUPERCLASS CONSTRUCTORS

A subclass can call a constructor defined by its superclass by use of the following form of **super**:

> super(*parameter-list*);

Here, *parameter-list* specifies any parameters needed by the constructor in the superclass. **super( )** must always be the first statement executed inside a subclass constructor. To see how **super( )** is used, consider the version of **TwoDShape** in the following program. It defines a constructor that initializes **width** and **height**.

```
// Add constructors to TwoDShape.
class TwoDShape {
  private double width;
  private double height;

  // Parameterized constructor.
  TwoDShape(double w, double h) {  ◄──────── A constructor for TwoDShape
    width = w;
    height = h;
  }

  // Accessor methods for width and height.
  double getWidth() { return width; }
  double getHeight() { return height; }
  void setWidth(double w) { width = w; }
  void setHeight(double h) { height = h; }

  void showDim() {
    System.out.println("Width and height are " +
                       width + " and " + height);
  }
}
```

```
}

// A subclass of TwoDShape for triangles.
class Triangle extends TwoDShape {
  private String style;

  Triangle(String s, double w, double h) {
    super(w, h); // call superclass constructor

    style = s;
  }
```

Use **super( )** to execute the
TwoDShape constructor.

```
  double area() {
    return getWidth() * getHeight() / 2;
  }

  void showStyle() {
    System.out.println("Triangle is " + style);
  }
}

class Shapes4 {
  public static void main(String[] args) {
    Triangle t1 = new Triangle("filled", 4.0, 4.0);
    Triangle t2 = new Triangle("outlined", 8.0, 12.0);

    System.out.println("Info for t1: ");
    t1.showStyle();
    t1.showDim();
    System.out.println("Area is " + t1.area());

    System.out.println();

    System.out.println("Info for t2: ");
    t2.showStyle();
    t2.showDim();
    System.out.println("Area is " + t2.area());
  }
}
```

Here, **Triangle( )** calls **super( )** with the parameters **w** and **h**. This causes the **TwoDShape( )** constructor to be called, which initializes **width** and **height** using these values. **Triangle** no longer initializes these values itself. It need only initialize the value unique to it: **style**. This leaves **TwoDShape** free to construct its portion in any manner that it so chooses. Furthermore, **TwoDShape** can add functionality about which existing subclasses have no knowledge, thus preventing existing code from breaking.

Any form of constructor defined by the superclass can be called by **super( )**. The constructor executed will be the one that matches the arguments. For example, here are expanded versions of both **TwoDShape** and **Triangle** that include default constructors and constructors that take one argument.

```java
// Add more constructors to TwoDShape.
class TwoDShape {
  private double width;
  private double height;

  // A default constructor.
  TwoDShape() {
    width = height = 0.0;
  }

  // Parameterized constructor.
  TwoDShape(double w, double h) {
    width = w;
    height = h;
  }

  // Construct object with equal width and height.
  TwoDShape(double x) {
    width = height = x;
  }

  // Accessor methods for width and height.
  double getWidth() { return width; }
  double getHeight() { return height; }
  void setWidth(double w) { width = w; }
  void setHeight(double h) { height = h; }

  void showDim() {
    System.out.println("Width and height are " +
                       width + " and " + height);
  }
}

// A subclass of TwoDShape for triangles.
class Triangle extends TwoDShape {
  private String style;

  // A default constructor.
  Triangle() {
    super();  ◄
    style = "none";
  }

  // Constructor
  Triangle(String s, double w, double h) {
    super(w, h); // call superclass constructor ◄

    style = s;
  }

  // One argument constructor.
  Triangle(double x) {
    super(x); // call superclass constructor ◄
```

Use **super( )** to call the various forms of the **TwoDShape** constructor.

```
      // default style to filled
      style = "filled";
   }

   double area() {
      return getWidth() * getHeight() / 2;
   }

   void showStyle() {
      System.out.println("Triangle is " + style);
   }
}

class Shapes5 {
   public static void main(String[] args) {
      Triangle t1 = new Triangle();
      Triangle t2 = new Triangle("outlined", 8.0, 12.0);
      Triangle t3 = new Triangle(4.0);

      t1 = t2;

      System.out.println("Info for t1: ");
      t1.showStyle();
      t1.showDim();
      System.out.println("Area is " + t1.area());

      System.out.println();

      System.out.println("Info for t2: ");
      t2.showStyle();
      t2.showDim();
      System.out.println("Area is " + t2.area());

      System.out.println();

      System.out.println("Info for t3: ");
      t3.showStyle();
      t3.showDim();
      System.out.println("Area is " + t3.area());

      System.out.println();
   }
}
```

Here is the output from this version.

```
Info for t1:
Triangle is outlined
Width and height are 8.0 and 12.0
Area is 48.0
```

```
Info for t2:
Triangle is outlined
Width and height are 8.0 and 12.0
Area is 48.0

Info for t3:
Triangle is filled
Width and height are 4.0 and 4.0
Area is 8.0
```

Let's review the key concepts behind **super( )**. When a subclass calls **super( )**, it is calling the constructor of its immediate superclass. Thus, **super( )** always refers to the superclass immediately above the calling class. This is true even in a multilevel hierarchy. Also, **super( )** must always be the first statement executed inside a subclass constructor.

Progress Check

1. How does a subclass execute its superclass's constructor?
2. Can parameters be passed via **super( )**?
3. Can a call to **super( )** go anywhere within a subclass's constructor?

USING super TO ACCESS SUPERCLASS MEMBERS

There is a second form of **super** that acts somewhat like **this**, except that it always refers to the superclass of the subclass in which it is used. This usage has the following general form:

> super.*member*

Here, *member* can be either a method or an instance variable. This form of **super** is most applicable to situations in which member names of a subclass hide members by the same name in the superclass. Consider this simple class hierarchy:

```
// Using super to overcome name hiding.
class A {
  int i;
}

// Create a subclass by extending class A.
class B extends A {
  int i; // this i hides the i in A
```

Answers:

1. It calls **super( )**.
2. Yes.
3. No, it must be the first statement executed.

```
    B(int a, int b) {
      super.i = a; // i in A ◄─────────  Here, super.i refers to the i in A.
      i = b; // i in B
    }

    void show() {
      System.out.println("i in superclass: " + super.i);
      System.out.println("i in subclass: " + i);
    }
}

class UseSuper {
  public static void main(String[] args) {
    B subOb = new B(1, 2);

    subOb.show();
  }
}
```

This program displays the following:

```
i in superclass: 1
i in subclass: 2
```

Although the instance variable **i** in **B** hides the **i** in **A**, **super** allows access to the **i** defined in the superclass. **super** can also be used to call methods that are hidden by a subclass.

TRY THIS 7-1   EXTENDING THE Vehicle CLASS

TruckDemo.java

To illustrate the power of inheritance, we will extend the **Vehicle** class first developed in Chapter 4. As you should recall, **Vehicle** encapsulates information about vehicles, including the number of passengers they can carry, their fuel capacity, and their fuel consumption rate. We can use the **Vehicle** class as a starting point from which more specialized classes are developed. For example, one type of vehicle is a truck. An important attribute of a truck is its cargo capacity. Thus, to create a **Truck** class, you can extend **Vehicle**, adding an instance variable that stores the carrying capacity. This project shows how. In the process, the instance variables in **Vehicle** will be made **private**, and accessor methods are provided to get and set their values.

STEP-BY-STEP

1. Create a file called **TruckDemo.java** and copy the last implementation of **Vehicle** from Chapter 4 into the file.

2. Create the **Truck** class as shown here.

```
// Extend Vehicle to create a Truck specialization.
class Truck extends Vehicle {
  private int cargoCap; // cargo capacity in pounds

  // This is a constructor for Truck.
  Truck(int p, int f, int m, int c) {
    /* Initialize Vehicle members using
       Vehicle's constructor. */
    super(p, f, m);

    cargoCap = c;
  }

  // Accessor methods for cargoCap.
  int getCargo() { return cargoCap; }
  void putCargo(int c) { cargoCap = c; }
}
```

Here, **Truck** inherits **Vehicle**, adding **cargoCap**, **getCargo( )**, and **putCargo( )**. Thus, **Truck** includes all of the general vehicle attributes defined by **Vehicle**. It need add only those items that are unique to its own class.

3. Next, make the instance variables of **Vehicle** private, as shown here.

```
private int passengers; // number of passengers
private int fuelCap;     // fuel capacity in gallons
private int mpg;         // fuel consumption in miles per gallon
```

4. Because the instance variables of **Vehicle** are now private, you will need the following accessor methods to set or get their values.

```
int getPassengers() { return passengers; }
void setPassengers(int p) { passengers = p; }

int getFuelCap() { return fuelCap; }
void setFuelCap(int f) { fuelCap = f; }

int getMpg() { return mpg; }
void setMpg(int m) { mpg = m; }
```

5. Here is an entire program that demonstrates the **Truck** class and the changes to **Vehicle**.

```
// Try This 7-1
//
// Build a subclass of Vehicle for trucks.
class Vehicle {
  private int passengers; // number of passengers
  private int fuelCap;     // fuel capacity in gallons
  private int mpg;         // fuel consumption in miles per gallon
```

```java
    // This is a constructor for Vehicle.
    Vehicle(int p, int f, int m) {
      passengers = p;
      fuelCap = f;
      mpg = m;
    }

    // Return the range.
    int range() {
      return mpg * fuelCap;
    }

    // Compute fuel needed for a given distance.
    double fuelNeeded(int miles) {
      return (double) miles / mpg;
    }

    // Accessor methods for instance variables.
    int getPassengers() { return passengers; }
    void setPassengers(int p) { passengers = p; }

    int getFuelCap() { return fuelCap; }
    void setFuelCap(int f) { fuelCap = f; }

    int getMpg() { return mpg; }
    void setMpg(int m) { mpg = m; }
}

// Extend Vehicle to create a Truck specialization.
class Truck extends Vehicle {
  private int cargoCap; // cargo capacity in pounds

  // This is a constructor for Truck.
  Truck(int p, int f, int m, int c) {
    /* Initialize Vehicle members using
       Vehicle's constructor. */
    super(p, f, m);

    cargoCap = c;
  }

  // Accessor methods for cargoCap.
  int getCargo() { return cargoCap; }
  void putCargo(int c) { cargoCap = c; }
}

class TruckDemo {
  public static void main(String[] args) {
```

```
             // construct some trucks
             Truck semi = new Truck(2, 200, 7, 44000);
             Truck pickup = new Truck(3, 20, 15, 2000);
             double gallons;
             int dist = 252;

             gallons = semi.fuelNeeded(dist);

             System.out.println("Semi can carry " + semi.getCargo() +
                             " pounds.");
             System.out.println("To go " + dist + " miles semi needs " +
                             gallons + " gallons of fuel.\n");

             gallons = pickup.fuelNeeded(dist);

             System.out.println("Pickup can carry " + pickup.getCargo() +
                             " pounds.");
             System.out.println("To go " + dist + " miles pickup needs " +
                             gallons + " gallons of fuel.");
         }
}
```

6. The output from this program is shown here:

```
Semi can carry 44000 pounds.
To go 252 miles semi needs 36.0 gallons of fuel.

Pickup can carry 2000 pounds.
To go 252 miles pickup needs 16.8 gallons of fuel.
```

7. Many other types of classes can be derived from **Vehicle**. For example, the following skeleton creates an off-road class that stores the ground clearance of the vehicle.

```
// Create an off-road vehicle class
class OffRoad extends Vehicle {
   private int groundClearance; // ground clearance in inches

   // ...
}
```

The key point is that once you have created a superclass that defines the general aspects of an object, that superclass can be inherited to form specialized classes. Each subclass simply adds its own, unique attributes. This is the essence of inheritance.

CREATING A MULTILEVEL HIERARCHY

Up to this point, we have been using simple class hierarchies that consist of only a superclass and a subclass. However, you can build hierarchies that contain as many layers of inheritance as you like. As mentioned, it is perfectly acceptable to use a subclass as a superclass of another. For example, given three classes called **A**, **B**, and **C**, **C** can be a subclass of **B**, which is a subclass of **A**. When this type of situation occurs, each subclass inherits all of the traits found in all of its superclasses. In this case, **C** inherits all aspects of **B** and **A**.

To see how a multilevel hierarchy can be useful, consider the following program. In it, the subclass **Triangle** is used as a superclass to create the subclass called **ColorTriangle**. **ColorTriangle** inherits all of the traits of **Triangle** and **TwoDShape** and adds a field called **color**, which holds the color of the triangle.

```java
// A multilevel hierarchy.
class TwoDShape {
  private double width;
  private double height;

  // A default constructor.
  TwoDShape() {
    width = height = 0.0;
  }

  // Parameterized constructor.
  TwoDShape(double w, double h) {
    width = w;
    height = h;
  }

  // Construct object with equal width and height.
  TwoDShape(double x) {
    width = height = x;
  }

  // Accessor methods for width and height.
  double getWidth() { return width; }
  double getHeight() { return height; }
  void setWidth(double w) { width = w; }
  void setHeight(double h) { height = h; }

  void showDim() {
    System.out.println("Width and height are " +
                        width + " and " + height);
  }
}

// Extend TwoDShape.
class Triangle extends TwoDShape {
  private String style;

  // A default constructor.
  Triangle() {
    super();
```

```
      style = "none";
    }

    Triangle(String s, double w, double h) {
      super(w, h); // call superclass constructor

      style = s;
    }

    // One argument constructor.
    Triangle(double x) {
      super(x); // call superclass constructor

      // default style to filled
      style = "filled";
    }

    double area() {
      return getWidth() * getHeight() / 2;
    }

    void showStyle() {
      System.out.println("Triangle is " + style);
    }
}

// Extend Triangle.
class ColorTriangle extends Triangle {
  private String color;

  ColorTriangle(String c, String s,
                double w, double h) {
    super(s, w, h);

    color = c;
  }

  String getColor() { return color; }

  void showColor() {
    System.out.println("Color is " + color);
  }
}

class Shapes6 {
  public static void main(String[] args) {
    ColorTriangle t1 =
        new ColorTriangle("Blue", "outlined", 8.0, 12.0);
    ColorTriangle t2 =
        new ColorTriangle("Red", "filled", 2.0, 2.0);
```

ColorTriangle inherits **Triangle**, which is descended from **TwoDShape**, so **ColorTriangle** includes all members of **Triangle** and **TwoDShape**.

```
    System.out.println("Info for t1: ");
    t1.showStyle();
    t1.showDim();
    t1.showColor();
    System.out.println("Area is " + t1.area());

    System.out.println();

    System.out.println("Info for t2: ");
    t2.showStyle(); ←———————  A ColorTriangle object can call methods
    t2.showDim();                      defined by itself and its superclasses.
    t2.showColor();
    System.out.println("Area is " + t2.area());
  }
}
```

The output of this program is shown here:

```
Info for t1:
Triangle is outlined
Width and height are 8.0 and 12.0
Color is Blue
Area is 48.0

Info for t2:
Triangle is filled
Width and height are 2.0 and 2.0
Color is Red
Area is 2.0
```

Because of inheritance, **ColorTriangle** can make use of the previously defined classes of **Triangle** and **TwoDShape**, adding only the extra information it needs for its own, specific application. This is part of the value of inheritance; it allows the reuse of code.

This example illustrates one other important point: **super( )** always refers to the constructor in the closest superclass. The **super( )** in **ColorTriangle** calls the constructor in **Triangle**. The **super( )** in **Triangle** calls the constructor in **TwoDShape**. In a class hierarchy, if a superclass constructor requires parameters, then all subclasses must pass those parameters "up the line." This is true whether or not a subclass needs parameters of its own.

WHEN ARE CONSTRUCTORS EXECUTED?

In the foregoing discussion of inheritance and class hierarchies, an important question may have occurred to you: When a subclass object is created, whose constructor is executed first, the one in the subclass or the one defined by the superclass? For example, given a subclass called **B** and a superclass called **A**, is **A**'s constructor executed before **B**'s, or vice versa? The answer is that in a class hierarchy, constructors complete their execution in order of derivation, from superclass to subclass. Further, since **super( )** must be the first statement executed in a subclass's constructor, this order is the same whether or not **super( )** is used. If **super( )** is not used, then the default (parameterless) constructor of each superclass will be executed. The following program illustrates when constructors are executed:

```java
// Demonstrate when constructors are executed.

// Create a super class.
class A {
  A() {
    System.out.println("Constructing A.");
  }
}

// Create a subclass by extending class A.
class B extends A {
  B() {
    System.out.println("Constructing B.");
  }
}

// Create another subclass by extending B.
class C extends B {
  C() {
    System.out.println("Constructing C.");
  }
}

class OrderOfConstruction {
  public static void main(String[] args) {
    C c = new C();  ←——————————————— Construct a C object.
  }
}
```

The output from this program is shown here:

```
Constructing A.
Constructing B.
Constructing C.
```

As you can see, the constructors are executed in order of derivation.

If you think about it, it makes sense that constructors are executed in order of derivation. Because a superclass has no knowledge of any subclass, any initialization it needs to perform is separate from and possibly prerequisite to any initialization performed by the subclass. Therefore, it must complete its execution first.

SUPERCLASS REFERENCES AND SUBCLASS OBJECTS

As you know, Java is a strongly typed language. Aside from the standard conversions and automatic promotions that apply to its primitive types, type compatibility is strictly enforced. Therefore, a reference variable for one class type cannot normally refer to an object of another class type. For example, consider the following program.

```
// This will not compile.
class X {
  int a;

  X(int i) { a = i; }
}

class Y {
  int a;

  Y(int i) { a = i; }
}

class IncompatibleRef {
  public static void main(String[] args) {
    X x = new X(10);
    X x2;
    Y y = new Y(5);

    x2 = x; // OK, both of same type

    x2 = y; // Error, not of same type
  }
}
$eol
```

Here, even though class **X** and class **Y** are physically the same, it is not possible to assign to an **X** variable a reference to a **Y** object because they have different types. In general, an object reference variable can refer only to objects of its type.

There is, however, an important exception to Java's strict type enforcement. A reference variable of a superclass can be assigned a reference to an object of any subclass derived from that superclass. In other words, a superclass reference can refer to a subclass object. Here is an example:

```
// A superclass reference can refer to a subclass object.
class X {
  int a;

  X(int i) { a = i; }
}

class Y extends X {
  int b;

  Y(int i, int j) {
    super(j);
    b = i;
  }
```

```
}

class SupSubRef {
  public static void main(String[] args) {
    X x = new X(10);
    X x2;
    Y y = new Y(5, 6);

    x2 = x; // OK, both of same type
    System.out.println("x2.a: " + x2.a);

    x2 = y; // still OK because Y is derived from X
    System.out.println("x2.a: " + x2.a);

    // X references know only about X members
    x2.a = 19; // OK
//  x2.b = 27; // Error, X doesn't have a b member
  }
}
```

OK because **Y** is a subclass of **X**; thus **x2** can refer to **y**.

Here, **Y** is now derived from **X**; thus it is permissible for **x2** to be assigned a reference to a **Y** object.

It is important to understand that it is the type of the reference variable—not the type of the object that it refers to—that determines what members can be accessed. That is, when a reference to a subclass object is assigned to a superclass reference variable, you will have access only to those parts of the object defined by the superclass. This is why **x2** can't access **b** even when it refers to a **Y** object. If you think about it, this makes sense, because the superclass has no knowledge of what a subclass adds to it. This is why the last line of code in the program is commented out.

Although the preceding discussion may seem a bit esoteric, it has some important practical applications. One is described here. The other is discussed later in this chapter, when method overriding is covered.

An important place where subclass references are assigned to superclass variables is when constructors are called in a class hierarchy. As you know, it is common for a class to define a constructor that takes an object of the class as a parameter. This allows the class to construct a copy of an object. Subclasses of such a class can take advantage of this feature. For example, consider the following versions of **TwoDShape** and **Triangle**. Both add constructors that take an object as a parameter.

```
class TwoDShape {
  private double width;
  private double height;

  // A default constructor.
  TwoDShape() {
    width = height = 0.0;
  }

  // Parameterized constructor.
  TwoDShape(double w, double h) {
```

```
    width = w;
    height = h;
  }

  // Construct an object with equal width and height.
  TwoDShape(double x) {
    width = height = x;
  }

  // Construct an object from an object.
  TwoDShape(TwoDShape ob) {
    width = ob.width;
    height = ob.height;
  }

  // Accessor methods for width and height.
  double getWidth() { return width; }
  double getHeight() { return height; }
  void setWidth(double w) { width = w; }
  void setHeight(double h) { height = h; }

  void showDim() {
    System.out.println("Width and height are " +
                        width + " and " + height);
  }
}

// A subclass of TwoDShape for triangles.
class Triangle extends TwoDShape {
  private String style;

  // A default constructor.
  Triangle() {
    super();
    style = "none";
  }

  // Constructor for Triangle.
  Triangle(String s, double w, double h) {
    super(w, h); // call superclass constructor

    style = s;
  }

  // One argument constructor.
  Triangle(double x) {
    super(x); // call superclass constructor

    // default style to filled
    style = "filled";
  }
```

(arrow annotation on `TwoDShape(TwoDShape ob) {`): Construct object from an object.

```
   // Construct an object from an object.
   Triangle(Triangle ob) {
     super(ob); // pass object to TwoDShape constructor
     style = ob.style;
   }
```
Pass a **Triangle** reference to
TwoDShape's constructor.

```
   double area() {
     return getWidth() * getHeight() / 2;
   }

   void showStyle() {
     System.out.println("Triangle is " + style);
   }
}

class Shapes7 {
  public static void main(String[] args) {
    Triangle t1 =
        new Triangle("outlined", 8.0, 12.0);

    // make a copy of t1
    Triangle t2 = new Triangle(t1);

    System.out.println("Info for t1: ");
    t1.showStyle();
    t1.showDim();
    System.out.println("Area is " + t1.area());

    System.out.println();

    System.out.println("Info for t2: ");
    t2.showStyle();
    t2.showDim();
    System.out.println("Area is " + t2.area());
  }
}
```

In this program, **t2** is constructed from **t1** and is, thus, identical. The output is shown here.

```
Info for t1:
Triangle is outlined
Width and height are 8.0 and 12.0
Area is 48.0

Info for t2:
Triangle is outlined
Width and height are 8.0 and 12.0
Area is 48.0
```

Pay special attention to this **Triangle** constructor:

```
// Construct an object from an object.
Triangle(Triangle ob) {
   super(ob); // pass object to TwoDShape constructor
   style = ob.style;
}
```

It receives an object of type **Triangle,** and it passes that object (through **super**) to this **TwoDShape** constructor:

```
// Construct an object from an object.
TwoDShape(TwoDShape ob) {
   width = ob.width;
   height = ob.height;
}
```

The key point is that **TwoDshape( )** is expecting a **TwoDShape** object. However, **Triangle( )** passes it a **Triangle** object. The reason this works is because, as explained, a superclass reference can refer to a subclass object. Thus it is perfectly acceptable to pass **TwoDShape( )** a reference to an object of a class derived from **TwoDShape**. Because the **TwoDShape( )** constructor is initializing only those portions of the subclass object that are members of **TwoDShape**, it doesn't matter that the object might also contain other members added by derived classes.

Progress Check

1. Can a subclass be used as a superclass for another subclass?
2. In a class hierarchy, in what order are the constructors called?
3. Given that **Jet** extends **Airplane**, can an **Airplane** reference refer to a **Jet** object?

METHOD OVERRIDING

In a class hierarchy, when a method in a subclass has the same return type and signature as a method in its superclass, then the method in the subclass is said to *override* the method in the superclass. When an overridden method is called from within a subclass, it will always refer to the version of that method defined by that subclass.

———————

Answers:

1. Yes.
2. Constructors are called in order of derivation.
3. Yes. In all cases, a superclass reference can refer to a subclass object, but not vice versa.

The version of the method defined by the superclass will be hidden. Consider the following:

```
// Method overriding.
class A {
  int i, j;
  A(int a, int b) {
    i = a;
    j = b;
  }

  // display i and j
  void show() {
    System.out.println("i and j: " + i + " " + j);
  }
}

class B extends A {
  int k;

  B(int a, int b, int c) {
    super(a, b);
    k = c;
  }

  // display k - this overrides show() in A
  void show() {  ◄──────────── This show( ) in B overrides the one defined by A.
    System.out.println("k: " + k);
  }
}

class Override {
  public static void main(String[] args) {
    B subOb = new B(1, 2, 3);

    subOb.show(); // this calls show() in B
  }
}
```

The output produced by this program is shown here:

```
k: 3
```

When **show( )** is invoked on an object of type **B**, the version of **show( )** defined within **B** is used. That is, the version of **show( )** inside **B** overrides the version declared in **A**.

If you want to access the superclass version of an overridden method, you can do so by using **super**. For example, in this version of **B**, the superclass version of **show( )** is invoked within the subclass's version. This allows all instance variables to be displayed.

```
class B extends A {
  int k;

  B(int a, int b, int c) {
    super(a, b);
    k = c;
  }

  void show() {
    super.show(); // this calls A's show()
    System.out.println("k: " + k);
  }
}
```

Use **super** to call the version of **show( )** defined by superclass **A**.

If you substitute this version of **show( )** into the previous program, you will see the following output:

```
i and j: 1 2
k: 3
```

Here, **super.show( )** calls the superclass version of **show( )**.

Method overriding occurs only when the signatures of the two methods are identical. If they are not, then the two methods are simply overloaded. For example, consider this modified version of the preceding example:

```
/* Methods with differing signatures are
   overloaded and not overridden. */
class A {
  int i, j;

  A(int a, int b) {
    i = a;
    j = b;
  }

  // display i and j
  void show() {
    System.out.println("i and j: " + i + " " + j);
  }
}

// Create a subclass by extending class A.
class B extends A {
  int k;

  B(int a, int b, int c) {
    super(a, b);
    k = c;
  }

  // overload show()
  void show(String msg) {
```

Because signatures differ, this **show( )** simply overloads **show( )** in superclass **A**.

```
      System.out.println(msg + k);
   }
}

class Overload {
  public static void main(String[] args) {
    B subOb = new B(1, 2, 3);

    subOb.show("This is k: "); // this calls show() in B
    subOb.show(); // this calls show() in A
  }
}
```

The output produced by this program is shown here:

```
This is k: 3
i and j: 1 2
```

The version of **show( )** in **B** takes a string parameter. This makes its signature different from the one in **A**, which takes no parameters. Therefore, no overriding (or name hiding) takes place.

OVERRIDDEN METHODS SUPPORT POLYMORPHISM

While the examples in the preceding section demonstrate the mechanics of method overriding, they do not show its power. Indeed, if there were nothing more to method overriding than a name space convention, then it would be, at best, an interesting curiosity but of little real value. However, this is not the case. Method overriding forms the basis for one of Java's most powerful concepts: *dynamic method dispatch.* Dynamic method dispatch is the mechanism by which a call to an overridden method is resolved at run time rather than compile time. Dynamic method dispatch is important because this is how Java implements run-time polymorphism.

Let's begin by restating an important principle: a superclass reference variable can refer to a subclass object. Java uses this fact to resolve calls to overridden methods at run time. Here's how. When an overridden method is called through a superclass reference, Java determines which version of that method to execute based on the type of the object being referred to at the time the call occurs. Thus, this determination is made at run time. When different types of objects are referred to, different versions of an overridden method will be called. In other words, *it is the type of the object being referred to* (not the type of the reference variable) that determines which version of an overridden method will be executed. Therefore, if a superclass contains a method that is overridden by a subclass, then when different types of subclass objects are referred to through a superclass reference variable, different versions of the method are executed.

Here is an example that illustrates dynamic method dispatch:

```
// Demonstrate dynamic method dispatch.

class Sup {
  void who() {
    System.out.println("who() in Sup");
  }
}

class Sub1 extends Sup {
  void who() {
    System.out.println("who() in Sub1");
  }
}

class Sub2 extends Sup {
  void who() {
    System.out.println("who() in Sub2");
  }
}

class DynDispDemo {
  public static void main(String[] args) {
    Sup superOb = new Sup();
    Sub1 subOb1 = new Sub1();
    Sub2 subOb2 = new Sub2();

    Sup supRef;

    supRef = superOb;
    supRef.who();          ←—  In each case,
                               the version of
                               who( ) to call
    supRef = subOb1;           is determined
    supRef.who();          ←—  at run time by
                               the type of
                               object being
    supRef = subOb2;           referred to.
    supRef.who();          ←—  referred to.
  }
}
```

The output from the program is shown here:

```
who() in Sup
who() in Sub1
who() in Sub2
```

This program creates a superclass called **Sup** and two subclasses of it, called **Sub1** and **Sub2**. **Sup** declares a method called **who( )**, and the subclasses override it. Inside the **main( )** method, objects of type **Sup**, **Sub1**, and **Sub2** are declared. Also, a reference of type **Sup**, called **supRef**, is declared. The program then assigns a reference to each type of object to **supRef** and uses that reference to call **who( )**. As the output shows, the version of **who( )** executed is determined by the type of object being referred to at the time of the call, not by the class type of **supRef**.

Ask the Expert

Q Are there any other object-oriented programming languages that support method overriding? Or is it unique to Java?

A Method overriding is not unique to Java. For example, both C++ and C# support method overriding. In C++, it is through the use of virtual functions. In C#, it is through the use of virtual methods. However, in both, the effect is similar to that found in Java.

WHY OVERRIDDEN METHODS?

As stated earlier, overridden methods allow Java to support run-time polymorphism. Polymorphism is essential to object-oriented programming for one reason: it allows a general class to specify methods that will be common to all of its derivatives, while allowing subclasses to define the specific implementation of some or all of those methods. Overridden methods are another way that Java implements the "one interface, multiple methods" aspect of polymorphism. Part of the key to successfully applying polymorphism is understanding that the superclasses and subclasses form a hierarchy that moves from lesser to greater specialization. Used correctly, the superclass provides all elements that a subclass can use directly. It also specifies those methods that the derived class must implement on its own. This allows the subclass the flexibility to define its own methods, yet still enforces a consistent interface. Thus, by combining inheritance with overridden methods, a superclass can define the general form of the methods that will be used by all of its subclasses.

Applying Method Overriding to TwoDShape

To better understand the power of method overriding, we will apply it to the **TwoDShape** class. In the preceding examples, each class derived from **TwoDShape** defines a method called **area( )**. This suggests that it might be better to make **area( )** part of the **TwoDShape** class, allowing each subclass to override it, defining how the area is calculated for the type of shape that the class encapsulates. The following program does this. For convenience, it also adds a name field to **TwoDShape**. (This makes it easier to write demonstration programs.)

```
// Use dynamic method dispatch.
class TwoDShape {
  private double width;
  private double height;
  private String name;

  // A default constructor.
  TwoDShape() {
```

```
    width = height = 0.0;
    name = "none";
  }

  // Parameterized constructor.
  TwoDShape(double w, double h, String n) {
    width = w;
    height = h;
    name = n;
  }

  // Construct object with equal width and height.
  TwoDShape(double x, String n) {
    width = height = x;
    name = n;
  }

  // Construct an object from an object.
  TwoDShape(TwoDShape ob) {
    width = ob.width;
    height = ob.height;
    name = ob.name;
  }

  // Accessor methods for width and height.
  double getWidth() { return width; }
  double getHeight() { return height; }
  void setWidth(double w) { width = w; }
  void setHeight(double h) { height = h; }

  String getName() { return name; }

  void showDim() {
    System.out.println("Width and height are " +
                        width + " and " + height);
  }
```

The **area( )** method defined by **TwoDShape**

```
  double area() {
    System.out.println("area() must be overridden");
    return 0.0;
  }
}

// A subclass of TwoDShape for triangles.
class Triangle extends TwoDShape {
  private String style;

  // A default constructor.
  Triangle() {
    super();
```

```java
      style = "none";
    }

    // Constructor for Triangle.
    Triangle(String s, double w, double h) {
      super(w, h, "triangle");

      style = s;
    }

    // One argument constructor.
    Triangle(double x) {
      super(x, "triangle"); // call superclass constructor

      // default style to filled
      style = "filled";
    }

    // Construct an object from an object.
    Triangle(Triangle ob) {
      super(ob); // pass object to TwoDShape constructor
      style = ob.style;
    }

    // Override area() for Triangle.
    double area() {  ◄──────── Override area( ) for Triangle.
      return getWidth() * getHeight() / 2;
    }

    void showStyle() {
      System.out.println("Triangle is " + style);
    }
}

// A subclass of TwoDShape for rectangles.
class Rectangle extends TwoDShape {
    // A default constructor.
    Rectangle() {
      super();
    }

    // Constructor for Rectangle.
    Rectangle(double w, double h) {
      super(w, h, "rectangle"); // call superclass constructor
    }

    // Construct a square.
    Rectangle(double x) {
      super(x, "rectangle"); // call superclass constructor
    }
```

```
    // Construct an object from an object.
    Rectangle(Rectangle ob) {
      super(ob); // pass object to TwoDShape constructor
    }

    boolean isSquare() {
      if(getWidth() == getHeight()) return true;
      return false;
    }

    // Override area() for Rectangle.
    double area() {  ◄─────────  Override area( ) for Rectangle.
      return getWidth() * getHeight();
    }
}

class DynShapes {
  public static void main(String[] args) {
    TwoDShape[] shapes = new TwoDShape[5];

    shapes[0] = new Triangle("outlined", 8.0, 12.0);
    shapes[1] = new Rectangle(10);
    shapes[2] = new Rectangle(10, 4);
    shapes[3] = new Triangle(7.0);                    The proper version of area( )
    shapes[4] = new TwoDShape(10, 20, "generic");     is called for each shape.

    for(TwoDShape shape : shapes) {
      System.out.println("object is " + shape.getName());
      System.out.println("Area is " + shape.area());  ◄───────┐
      System.out.println();
    }
  }
}
```

The output from the program is shown here:

```
object is triangle
Area is 48.0

object is rectangle
Area is 100.0

object is rectangle
Area is 40.0

object is triangle
Area is 24.5

object is generic
area() must be overridden
Area is 0.0
```

Let's examine this program closely. First, as explained, **area( )** is now part of the **TwoDShape** class and is overridden by **Triangle** and **Rectangle**. Inside **TwoDShape**, **area( )** is given a placeholder implementation that simply informs the user that this method must be overridden by a subclass. Each override of **area( )** supplies an implementation that is suitable for the type of object encapsulated by the subclass. Thus, if you were to implement an ellipse class, for example, then **area( )** would need to compute the area of an ellipse.

There is one other important feature in the preceding program. Notice in **main( )** that **shapes** is declared as an array of **TwoDShape** objects. However, the elements of this array are assigned **Triangle**, **Rectangle**, and **TwoDShape** references. This is valid because, as explained, a superclass reference can refer to a subclass object. The program then cycles through the array, displaying information about each object. Although quite simple, this illustrates the power of both inheritance and method overriding. The type of object referred to by a superclass reference variable is determined at run time and acted on accordingly. If an object is derived from **TwoDShape**, then its area can be obtained by calling **area( )**. The interface to this operation is the same no matter what type of shape is being used.

Progress Check

1. What is method overriding?
2. Why is method overriding important?
3. When an overridden method is called through a superclass reference, which version of the method is executed?

USING ABSTRACT CLASSES

Sometimes you will want to create a superclass that defines only a generalized form that will be shared by all of its subclasses, leaving it to each subclass to fill in the details. Such a class determines the nature of the methods that the subclasses must implement but does not itself provide an implementation of one or more of these methods. One way this situation can occur is when a superclass is unable to create a meaningful implementation for a method. This is the case with the version of **TwoDShape** used in the preceding example. The definition of **area( )** is simply a placeholder. It will not compute and display the area of any type of object.

———

Answers:

1. Method overriding occurs when a subclass defines a method that has the same signature and return type as a method in its superclass.
2. Overridden methods allow Java to support run-time polymorphism.
3. The version of an overridden method that is executed is determined by the type of the object being referred to at the time of the call. Thus, this determination is made at run time.

As you will see as you create your own class hierarchies, it is not uncommon for a method to have no meaningful definition in the context of its superclass. You can handle this situation in two ways. One way, as shown in the previous example, is to simply have it report a warning message. While this approach can be useful in certain situations—such as debugging—it is not usually appropriate. You may have methods that must be overridden by the subclass in order for the subclass to have any meaning. Consider the class **Triangle**. It is incomplete if **area( )** is not defined. In this case, you want some way to ensure that a subclass does indeed override all necessary methods. Java's solution to this problem is the *abstract method*.

An abstract method is created by specifying the **abstract** type modifier. An abstract method contains no body and is, therefore, not implemented by the superclass. Thus, a subclass must override it—it cannot simply use the version defined in the superclass. To declare an abstract method, use this general form:

> abstract *type name*(*parameter-list*);

As you can see, no method body is present. The **abstract** modifier can be used only on normal methods. It cannot be applied to **static** methods or to constructors.

A class that contains one or more abstract methods must also be declared as abstract by preceding its **class** declaration with the **abstract** specifier. Since an abstract class does not define a complete implementation, there can be no objects of an abstract class. Thus, attempting to create an object of an abstract class by using **new** will result in a compile-time error.

When a subclass inherits an abstract class, it must implement all of the abstract methods in the superclass. If it doesn't, then the subclass must also be specified as **abstract**. Thus, the **abstract** attribute is inherited until such time as a complete implementation is achieved.

Using an abstract class, you can improve the **TwoDShape** class. Since there is no meaningful concept of area for an undefined two-dimensional figure, the following version of the preceding program declares **area( )** as **abstract** inside **TwoDShape** and **TwoDShape** as **abstract**. This, of course, means that all classes derived from **TwoDShape** must override **area( )**.

```
// Create an abstract class.
abstract class TwoDShape {  ◄─────────── TwoDShape is now abstract.
  private double width;
  private double height;
  private String name;

  // A default constructor.
  TwoDShape() {
    width = height = 0.0;
    name = "none";
  }

  // Parameterized constructor.
  TwoDShape(double w, double h, String n) {
    width = w;
    height = h;
```

```
    name = n;
  }

  // Construct object with equal width and height.
  TwoDShape(double x, String n) {
    width = height = x;
    name = n;
  }

  // Construct an object from an object.
  TwoDShape(TwoDShape ob) {
    width = ob.width;
    height = ob.height;
    name = ob.name;
  }

  // Accessor methods for width and height.
  double getWidth() { return width; }
  double getHeight() { return height; }
  void setWidth(double w) { width = w; }
  void setHeight(double h) { height = h; }

  String getName() { return name; }

  void showDim() {
    System.out.println("Width and height are " +
                       width + " and " + height);
  }

  // Now, area() is abstract.
  abstract double area();  ◄─────── Make area( ) into an abstract method.
}

// A subclass of TwoDShape for triangles.
class Triangle extends TwoDShape {
  private String style;

  // A default constructor.
  Triangle() {
    super();
    style = "none";
  }

  // Constructor for Triangle.
  Triangle(String s, double w, double h) {
    super(w, h, "triangle");

    style = s;
  }

  // One argument constructor.
```

```
    Triangle(double x) {
      super(x, "triangle"); // call superclass constructor

      // default style to filled
      style = "filled";
    }

    // Construct an object from an object.
    Triangle(Triangle ob) {
      super(ob); // pass object to TwoDShape constructor
      style = ob.style;
    }

    double area() {
      return getWidth() * getHeight() / 2;
    }

    void showStyle() {
      System.out.println("Triangle is " + style);
    }
  }

  // A subclass of TwoDShape for rectangles.
  class Rectangle extends TwoDShape {
    // A default constructor.
    Rectangle() {
      super();
    }

    // Constructor for Rectangle.
    Rectangle(double w, double h) {
      super(w, h, "rectangle"); // call superclass constructor
    }

    // Construct a square.
    Rectangle(double x) {
      super(x, "rectangle"); // call superclass constructor
    }

    // Construct an object from an object.
    Rectangle(Rectangle ob) {
      super(ob); // pass object to TwoDShape constructor
    }

    boolean isSquare() {
      if(getWidth() == getHeight()) return true;
      return false;
    }

    double area() {
      return getWidth() * getHeight();
```

```
    }
}

class AbsShape {
  public static void main(String[] args) {
    TwoDShape[] shapes = new TwoDShape[4];

    shapes[0] = new Triangle("outlined", 8.0, 12.0);
    shapes[1] = new Rectangle(10);
    shapes[2] = new Rectangle(10, 4);
    shapes[3] = new Triangle(7.0);

    for(TwoDShape shape : shapes) {
      System.out.println("object is " + shape.getName());
      System.out.println("Area is " + shape.area());
      System.out.println();
    }
  }
}
```

As the program illustrates, all subclasses of **TwoDShape** must override **area( )**. To prove this to yourself, try creating a subclass that does not override **area( )**. You will receive a compile-time error. Of course, it is still possible to create an object reference of type **TwoDShape**, which the program does. However, it is no longer possible to declare objects of type **TwoDShape**. Because of this, in **main( )** the **shapes** array has been shortened to 4, and a **TwoDShape** object is no longer created.

One last point: notice that **TwoDShape** still includes the **showDim( )** and **getName( )** methods and that these are not modified by **abstract**. It is perfectly acceptable—indeed, quite common—for an abstract class to contain concrete methods that a subclass is free to use as is. Only those methods declared as **abstract** need be overridden by subclasses.

Progress Check

1. What is an abstract method? How is one created?
2. When must a class be declared abstract?
3. Can an object of an abstract class be instantiated?

Answers:

1. An abstract method is a method without a body. Thus it consists of a return type, name, and parameter list and is preceded by the keyword **abstract**.
2. When it contains at least one abstract method.
3. No.

USING final

As powerful and useful as method overriding and inheritance are, sometimes you will want to prevent them. For example, you might have a class that encapsulates control of some hardware device. Further, this class might offer the user the ability to initialize the device, making use of private, proprietary information. In this case, you don't want users of your class to be able to override the initialization method. Whatever the reason, in Java it is easy to prevent a method from being overridden or a class from being inherited by using the keyword **final**.

final Prevents Overriding

To prevent a method from being overridden, specify **final** as a modifier at the start of its declaration. Methods declared as **final** cannot be overridden. The following fragment illustrates **final**:

```
class A {
  final void meth() {
    System.out.println("This is a final method.");
  }
}

class B extends A {
  void meth() { // ERROR! Can't override.
    System.out.println("Illegal!");
  }
}
```

Because **meth( )** is declared as **final**, it cannot be overridden in **B**. If you attempt to do so, a compile-time error will result.

final Prevents Inheritance

You can prevent a class from being inherited by preceding its declaration with **final**. Declaring a class as **final** implicitly declares all of its methods as **final**, too. As you might expect, it is illegal to declare a class as both **abstract** and **final** since an abstract class is incomplete by itself and relies on its subclasses to provide complete implementations.

Here is an example of a **final** class:

```
final class A {
  // ...
}

// The following class is illegal.
class B extends A { // ERROR! Can't subclass A
  // ...
}
```

As the comments imply, it is illegal for **B** to inherit **A** since **A** is declared as **final**.

Using final with Data Members

In addition to the uses of **final** just shown, **final** can also be applied to member variables to create what amounts to named constants. If you precede a class variable's name with **final**, its value cannot be changed throughout the lifetime of your program. You can, of course, give that variable an initial value. For example, in Chapter 6 a simple error-management class called **ErrorMsg** was shown. That class mapped a human-readable string to an error code. Here, that original class is improved by the addition of **final** constants that stand for the errors. Now, instead of passing **getErrorMsg( )** a number such as 2, you can pass the named integer constant **DISKERR**.

```java
// Return a String object.
class ErrorMsg {
  // Error codes.
  final int OUTERR    = 0;
  final int INERR    = 1;              ◄─────── Declare final constants.
  final int DISKERR  = 2;
  final int INDEXERR = 3;

  String[] msgs = {
    "Output Error",
    "Input Error",
    "Disk Full",
    "Index Out-Of-Bounds"
  };

  // Return the error message.
  String getErrorMsg(int i) {
    if(i >=0 & i < msgs.length)
      return msgs[i];
    else
      return "Invalid Error Code";
  }
}

class FinalD {
  public static void main(String[] args) {
    ErrorMsg err = new ErrorMsg();                    ─── Use final constants.

    System.out.println(err.getErrorMsg(err.OUTERR));
    System.out.println(err.getErrorMsg(err.DISKERR));
  }
}
```

Notice how the **final** constants are used in **main( )**. Since they are members of the **ErrorMsg** class, they must be accessed via an object of that class. (See the following Ask the Expert for an alternative approach.) Of course, they can also be inherited by subclasses and accessed directly inside those subclasses.

As a point of style, many Java programmers use uppercase identifiers for **final** constants, as does the preceding example. But this is not a hard and fast rule.

Ask the Expert

Q Can **final** member variables be made **static**? Can **final** be used on method parameters and local variables?

A The answer to both is Yes. Making a **final** member variable **static** lets you refer to the constant through its class name rather than through an object. For example, if the constants in **ErrorMsg** were modified by **static**, then the **println( )** statements in **main( )** could look like this:

```
System.out.println(err.getErrorMsg(ErrorMsg.OUTERR));
System.out.println(err.getErrorMsg(ErrorMsg.DISKERR));
```

The use of a **static final** variable is often a better approach for these types of constants, and it is the approach that you will typically see.

Declaring a parameter **final** prevents it from being changed within the method. Declaring a local variable **final** prevents it from being assigned a value more than once.

Progress Check

1. How do you prevent a method from being overridden?
2. If a class is declared as **final**, can it be inherited?

THE Object CLASS

Java defines one special class called **Object** that is an implicit superclass of all other classes. In other words, all other classes are subclasses of **Object**. This means that a reference variable of type **Object** can refer to an object of any other class. Also, since arrays are implemented as classes, a variable of type **Object** can also refer to any array.

Object defines the following methods, which means that they are available in every object.

Answers:

1. Precede its declaration with the keyword **final**.
2. No.

Method	Purpose
Object clone( )	Creates a new object that is the same as the object being cloned.
boolean equals(Object *object*)	Determines whether one object is equal to another.
void finalize( )	Called before an unused object is recycled.
Class<?> getClass( )	Obtains the class of an object at run time.
int hashCode( )	Returns the hash code associated with the invoking object.
void notify( )	Resumes execution of a thread waiting on the invoking object.
void notifyAll( )	Resumes execution of all threads waiting on the invoking object.
String toString( )	Returns a string that describes the object.
void wait( ) void wait(long *milliseconds*) void wait(long *milliseconds*, int *nanoseconds*)	Waits on another thread of execution.

The methods **getClass( )**, **notify( )**, **notifyAll( )**, and **wait( )** are declared as **final**. You can override the others. Several of these methods are described later in this book. However, notice two methods now: **equals( )** and **toString( )**. The **equals( )** method compares two objects. It returns **true** if the objects are equivalent, and **false** otherwise. The **Object** implementation of **equals( )** simply checks if the invoking reference refers to the same object as the one passed as an argument. However, **equals( )** is frequently overridden to determine if two objects are equal in their contents. The **toString( )** method returns a string that contains a description of the object on which it is called. Also, this method is automatically called when an object is output using **println( )**. Many classes override this method. Doing so allows them to tailor a description specifically for the types of objects that they create.

One last point: notice the unusual syntax in the return type for **getClass( )**. This relates to Java's *generics* feature. Generics allow the type of data used by a class or method to be specified as a parameter. Generic types are discussed in Chapter 14.

EXERCISES

1. Does a superclass have access to the members of a subclass? Does a subclass have access to the members of a superclass?

2. Create a subclass of **TwoDShape** called **Circle**. Include an **area( )** method that computes the area of the circle and a constructor that uses **super** to initialize the **TwoDShape** portion.

3. How do you prevent a subclass from having access to a member of a superclass?

4. Describe the purpose and use of both versions of **super**.

5. Given the following hierarchy:

```
class Alpha { ...

class Beta extends Alpha { ...

Class Gamma extends Beta { ...
```

   In what order are the constructors for these classes executed when a **Gamma** object is instantiated?

6. A superclass reference can refer to a subclass object. Explain why this is important as it relates to method overriding.

7. What is an abstract class?

8. How do you prevent a method from being overridden? How do you prevent a class from being inherited?

9. Explain how inheritance, method overriding, and abstract classes are used to support polymorphism.

10. What class is a superclass of every other class?

11. A class that contains at least one abstract method must itself be declared abstract. True or False?

12. What keyword is used to create a named constant?

13. Suppose a class **A** has methods **m1( )**, **m2( )**, and **m3( )** and a subclass **B** has methods **m4( )** and **m5( )**.

   A. Which of the five methods are accessible by objects of class **A**?
   B. Which of the five methods are accessible by objects of class **B**?
   C. Which of the five methods can be called using a variable of type **A** that refers to an object of type **B**?
   D. Suppose **m1( )** is declared **private**. Which of the five methods are now accessible by objects of class **B**?

14. Create a **Person** class with private instance variables for the person's name and birth date. Add appropriate accessor methods for these variables. Then create a subclass **CollegeGraduate** with private instance variables for the student's GPA and year of graduation and appropriate accessors for these variables. Don't forget to include appropriate constructors for your classes. Then create a class with a **main( )** method that demonstrates your classes.

15. Standard practice in many situations is to declare all nonfinal instance variables to be **private** and then provide appropriate accessor methods for accessing the variables. For some instance variables it is appropriate to have a "getter" method for getting the value of the variable but no "setter" method for changing the value of the variable. Think of an example of a class and an instance variable where this situation occurs and explain why it is not appropriate to have a "setter" method for the variable.

16. In Chapter 6, a **FailSoftArray** class was created to prevent boundary errors from occurring when the array was accessed. However, the class is not totally fail-soft due to the fact that the **length** instance variable is **public**. If you were

to purposely misuse the class by assigning **length** a value greater than the size of the underlying array, an attempt to access the array beyond its bounds would not be prevented. What should be done to the **length** variable to prevent this type of misuse from occurring? Remember: **length** needs to remain **public** so that users can determine the length of the array.

17. Override the inherited **toString( )** method of the **FailSoftArray** class from Chapter 6 so that it returns a string displaying the contents of the array. For example, if the array contains 1,2,3, and 4, then the **toString( )** method should return the string "{1, 2, 3, 4}". (For more information about overriding **toString( )**, see Chapter 22.)

18. Suppose we were to enhance our modeling of vehicles by creating **Tire** objects to represent the tires of the vehicle. How should the **Tire** class be related to the **Vehicle** class? Should it be a subclass of **Vehicle**? Why or why not?

19. Suppose you have classes **Boat**, **House**, **HouseBoat**, and **BoatHouse** for representing boats, houses, houseboats (a floating house), and boathouses (a building for storing boats), respectively. Should any of the classes be subclasses of any of the other classes? Why or why not?

20. Is the following code segment legal in Java? Why or why not?

```
int[] array = {1,2,3};
Object[] data = {"hello", new Object(), array};
```

21. Suppose you are writing a Java program that does a lot of mathematical calculations involving π. If you only need 2 decimal places of accuracy, you could use 3.14 everywhere π is needed in your code (for example, in formulas such as `area = 3.14*r*r`), or you could declare a constant **PI** equal to 3.14 and then use **PI** instead of 3.14 everywhere π is needed (and so use formulas such as `area = PI*r*r`).

   A. Show what the declaration of such a constant **PI** would look like in Java.
   B. Give at least two reasons why using the declared constant **PI** is better than using 3.14.

22. One of the uses of inheritance is to eliminate code duplication. For example, suppose you have two classes **A** and **B** and both have identical **getData( )** methods that extract data from files, but both classes do different things with the data once they've extracted it. Describe one way that inheritance can be used to avoid the duplicate code.

23. Suppose a class **A** declares an **equals( )** method that takes a parameter of type **A**. Such a class will also inherit the **equals( )** method from the **Object** class. Does the **equals( )** method in class **A** override the inherited **equals( )** method, or is the **equals( )** method overloaded in class **A**?

CHAPTER 8

Interfaces

KEY SKILLS & CONCEPTS

- Understand interface fundamentals
- Know the general form of an interface
- Implement an interface
- Apply interface references
- Use interface constants
- Extend interfaces
- Nest interfaces

In object-oriented programming, it is sometimes helpful to define what a class must do but not how it will do it. You have already seen one way to accomplish this: the abstract method. An abstract method defines the signature for a method but provides no implementation. A subclass must provide its own implementation of each abstract method defined by its superclass. Thus, an abstract method specifies the *interface* to the method but not the *implementation*. While abstract classes and methods are useful, it is possible to take this concept a step further. In Java, you can fully separate a class's interface from its implementation by using the keyword **interface**, and that is the subject of this chapter.

INTERFACE FUNDAMENTALS

In Java, an **interface** defines a set of methods that will be implemented by a class. Syntactically, interfaces are similar to abstract classes, except that no method can include a body. This means that an interface provides no implementation whatsoever of the methods it defines. Therefore, an interface simply specifies what must be done, but not how. Put more formally, an interface is a construct that describes functionality without specifying implementation.

Once an interface is defined, any number of classes can implement it. This makes it possible for two or more classes to provide the same functionality even though they might do so in different ways. Furthermore, one class can implement any number of interfaces. This makes it possible for a single class to provide a wide range of well-defined functionality.

To implement an interface, a class must provide bodies (implementations) for the methods described by the interface. Each class is free to determine the details of its own implementation. Two classes might implement the methods defined by an interface differently, but each class still supports the same set of methods. Thus, code that has knowledge of the interface can use objects of either class since the interface to those objects is the same. By providing the interface, Java allows you to fully utilize the "one interface, multiple methods" aspect of polymorphism.

An interface is declared by use of the **interface** keyword. Here is a simplified general form of an interface declaration:

```
access interface name {
    ret-type method-name1(param-list);
    ret-type method-name2(param-list);
    // ...
    ret-type method-nameN(param-list);
}
```

Here, *access* is either **public** or not used. When no access modifier is included, then default access results. Although default access is proper for many applications, interfaces are often declared **public** because it makes them accessible to the widest range of code. (When an **interface** is declared **public**, it must be in a file of the same name.) The name of the interface is specified by *name*, and it can be any valid identifier.

In an **interface**, methods are declared using only their return type and signature. They are, essentially, abstract methods. As explained, in an **interface**, no method can have an implementation. It is the responsibility of each class that includes an **interface** to provide the implementations. In an interface, methods are implicitly **public**.

CREATING AN INTERFACE

As just explained, the core purpose of an interface is to specify what must be done, but not how it will do it. This is a powerful concept in programming. To understand why, let's work through a simple example. Assume you want to create a set of classes that generate different types of number series. These series might be the even numbers beginning with 2, random numbers, or the set of prime numbers, to name a few. However, in all cases, you want the classes to work the same way, with each having methods that obtain the next number in the series, reset the series to its start, and specify a starting value. This way, the code that uses one number series generator can easily be changed to use a different one. This type of situation is ideal for an interface, because the interface can declare the methods that each number series generator will support, but each class can implement its own specific number series.

Putting the preceding example into concrete terms, here is an example of a simple **interface** definition. It specifies an interface called **Series** that describes the methods used to generate a series of numbers.

```
public interface Series {
  int getNext(); // return next number in series
  void reset(); // restart
  void setStart(int x); // set starting value
}
```

Notice that **Series** defines three methods. The first is **getNext( )**, which will obtain the next number in the series. The second is **reset( )**, which will reset the series to its starting point. The last one is **setStart( )**, which is used to set the starting point. All classes that implement **Series** must provide these three methods. Because of this, all classes that implement **Series** can be used in the same way, by calling the same set of methods. One other point: Here, **Series** is declared **public**, so it must be held in a file called **Series.java**.

IMPLEMENTING AN INTERFACE

Once an **interface** has been defined, one or more classes can implement the interface. To implement an interface, follow these two steps:

1. In a class declaration, include an **implements** clause that specifies the interface being implemented.
2. Inside the class, implement the methods defined by the interface.

The **implements** clause specifies the name of an interface that a class will implement. The general form of a class that includes the **implements** clause looks like this:

```
class classname extends superclass implements interface {
  // class-body
}
```

To implement more than one interface, the interfaces are separated with a comma. Of course, the **extends** clause is optional, but using it enables you to inherit a class and implement one or more interfaces at the same time.

Inside the class, you must define each of the methods specified by the interface being implemented. The methods that implement an interface must be declared **public**. Also, the return type and signature of the implementing method must match exactly the return type and signature specified in the **interface** declaration.

Here is an example that shows an implementation of the **Series** interface shown earlier. It creates a class called **ByTwos**, which generates a series of numbers, each two greater than the previous one. Notice the use of the **implements** clause.

```
// Implement Series.
class ByTwos implements Series {
  int start;
  int val;

  ByTwos() {
    start = 0;
```

Implement the **Series** interface.

```
    val = 0;
}

// Implement the methods specified by Series.
public int getNext() {
  val += 2;
  return val;
}

public void reset() {
  val = start;
}

public void setStart(int x) {
  start = x;
  val = x;
}
}
```

Notice that the methods **getNext( )**, **reset( )**, and **setStart( )** are declared **public**. As explained, this is necessary. Whenever you implement a method defined by an interface, it must be implemented as **public** because all methods specified by an interface are implicitly **public**.

Here is a class that demonstrates **ByTwos**:

```
// Demonstrate the use of Series.
class SeriesDemo {
  public static void main(String[] args) {
    ByTwos ob = new ByTwos();

    for(int i=0; i < 5; i++)
      System.out.println("Next value is " + ob.getNext());

    System.out.println("\nResetting");
    ob.reset();
    for(int i=0; i < 5; i++)
      System.out.println("Next value is " + ob.getNext());

    System.out.println("\nStarting at 100");
    ob.setStart(100);
    for(int i=0; i < 5; i++)
      System.out.println("Next value is " + ob.getNext());
  }
}
```

The output from this program is shown here.

```
Next value is 2
Next value is 4
Next value is 6
Next value is 8
Next value is 10
```

```
Resetting
Next value is 2
Next value is 4
Next value is 6
Next value is 8
Next value is 10

Starting at 100
Next value is 102
Next value is 104
Next value is 106
Next value is 108
Next value is 110
```

It is both permissible and common for classes that implement an interface to define additional members of their own. For example, the following version of **ByTwos** adds the method **getPriorVal( )**, which returns the previous value generated.

```
// Implement Series and add getPriorVal().
class ByTwos implements Series {
  int start;
  int val;
  int priorVal;

  ByTwos() {
    start = 0;
    val = 0;
    priorVal = -2;
  }

  // Implement the methods specified by Series.
  public int getNext() {
    priorVal = val;
    val += 2;
    return val;
  }

  public void reset() {
    val = start;
    priorVal = start - 2;
  }

  public void setStart(int x) {
    start = x;
    val = x;
    priorVal = x - 2;
  }

  // Return the previous value. This method is not
  // defined by Series.
  int getPriorVal() {            Add a method not defined by Series.
```

```
      return priorVal;
  }
}
```

Even though **ByTwos** adds the **getPriorVal( )** method, it does not alter the fact that **ByTwos** implements **Series**. The key point is that the only obligation a class has when implementing an interface is to provide the methods defined by the interface. It is *not* limited to providing *only* those methods. The class can provide whatever additional functionality is desired. Thus, you can use the same **SeriesDemo** class with the new version of **ByTwos**.

There is something else to notice in this version of **ByTwos**. The addition of **getPriorVal( )** required a change to the implementations of the methods defined by **Series**. However, since the interface to those methods stays the same, the change is seamless and does not break preexisting code. This is one of the principal advantages of interfaces.

Any number of classes can implement an **interface**. For example, here is a class called **ByThrees** that generates a series that consists of multiples of three. Thus, it implements a different series.

```
// Implement Series a different way.
class ByThrees implements Series {        ──── Implement Series a different way.
  int start;
  int val;

  ByThrees() {
    start = 0;
    val = 0;
  }

  // Implement the methods specified by Series.
  public int getNext() {
    val += 3;
    return val;
  }

  public void reset() {
    val = start;
  }

  public void setStart(int x) {
    start = x;
    val = x;
  }
}
```

Although the implementation of **ByThrees** differs from that of **ByTwos**, both implement the same **Series** interface. This means that the two classes can be used in the same way. For example, in both cases, **getNext( )** obtains the next element in the series.

As a general rule, a class will define all of the methods specified by an interface that it is implementing. However, if a class implements an interface but does not define every method, then that class must be declared as **abstract**. No objects of such a class can be created, but it can be used as an abstract superclass, allowing subclasses to provide the complete implementation.

Progress Check

1. What is an interface? What keyword is used to declare one?
2. What is **implements** for?

USING INTERFACE REFERENCES

As you know, when you define a class, you are creating a new reference type. The same is true of interfaces. An interface declaration also creates a new reference type. When a class implements an interface, it is adding that interface's type to its type. As a result, an instance of a class that implements an interface is also an instance of that interface type. For example, an instance of **ByTwos** is also an instance of **Series**.

Because an interface defines a type, you can declare a reference variable of an interface type. In other words, you can create an interface reference variable. Such a variable has a very important property: It can refer to any object that implements the interface. (In other words, it can refer to any instance of its type.) When you call a method on an object through an interface reference, it is the version of the method implemented by the object that is executed. This process is similar to using a super-class reference to access a subclass object, as described in Chapter 7.

The following example illustrates this process. The **SeriesDemo2** class uses the same interface reference variable to call methods on objects of both **ByTwos** and **ByThrees**.

```
class SeriesDemo2 {
  public static void main(String[] args) {
    ByTwos twoOb = new ByTwos();
    ByThrees threeOb = new ByThrees();

    Series iRef; // an interface reference

    for(int i=0; i < 5; i++) {
      iRef = twoOb; // refers to a ByTwos object
      System.out.println("Next ByTwos value is " +
                    iRef.getNext());
      iRef = threeOb; // refers to a ByThrees object
      System.out.println("Next ByThrees value is " +
                    iRef.getNext());
```

Access an object via an interface reference.

Answers:

1. An interface defines methods that a class must implement but defines no implementation of its own. It is declared by the keyword **interface**.
2. To implement an interface, include that interface in a class by using the **implements** keyword.

```
      }
   }
}
```

The output is shown here:

```
Next ByTwos value is 2
Next ByThrees value is 3
Next ByTwos value is 4
Next ByThrees value is 6
Next ByTwos value is 6
Next ByThrees value is 9
Next ByTwos value is 8
Next ByThrees value is 12
Next ByTwos value is 10
Next ByThrees value is 15
```

In **main( )**, **iRef** is declared to be a reference to the **Series** interface. This means that it can be used to store a reference to any object that implements **Series**. In this case, it is used to refer to **twoOb** and **threeOb**, which are objects of type **ByTwos** and **ByThrees**, respectively. This is possible because both implement **Series**. Each time one of the methods defined by **Series** is called through **iRef**, the version of the method implemented by the object being referred to is executed.

One other point about this example: An interface reference variable has knowledge only of the methods declared by its **interface** declaration. Thus, **iRef** could not be used to access any other variables or methods that might be provided by an implementing class. For example, if **ByTwos** included the **getPriorVal( )** method shown earlier, it could not have been accessed via **iRef**.

Although the preceding example shows the mechanics of calling methods through an interface reference, it does not show one of its most important benefits. As you know, polymorphism is a key tenet of object-oriented programming. Its defining principle is that related functionality can be accessed through a common interface. Once you understand the interface, you can use any specific implementation of that interface. But perhaps more importantly, the implementation can change without affecting code that uses the interface. Calling interface methods through an interface reference helps you fully realize this benefit of the "one interface, multiple methods" philosophy.

To understand why, consider a class that simulates some physical process, such as the movement of lines of customers at a bank or crop yield differences based on rainfall. To perform the simulation, the class might require the use of a number series generator. However, you might want to change the precise nature of the series so that you can observe different outcomes. You might create such a class as shown here.

```
class Simulation {
   // numSeq refers to the number series generator
   // that will be used by the simulation.
   Series numSeq;

   // Pass the number series generator that will be used
   // by the instance of Simulation being constructed.
```

```
  Simulation(Series s) {
    numSeq = s;
  }

  // ...

}
```

Notice that the series generator is passed to **Simulation**, via its constructor, as a parameter of type **Series**. Also notice that a reference to that object is held in an instance variable called **numSeq**, which is also a reference of type **Series**. Because **Simulation** specifies the number generator by the interface type **Series**, rather than hard-coding a specific type of generator, you can easily change the specific type of number generator used. For example, both of these declarations are valid:

```
Simulation sim = new Simulation(new ByTwos());
Simulation sim2 = new Simulation(new ByThrees());
```

In the first one, the number generator is a **ByTwos** instance. In the second, it is a **ByThrees** object. Of course, it could have been any type of object as long as it implemented **Series**. For example, if a series that reflected a normal (bell-shaped) distribution is needed, you could create a class called **NormalDist** that implements **Series**, and then pass a **NormalDist** instance to **Simulation**. Since all implementations of **Series** are used in the same way, no changes to **Simulation** would be required.

To summarize: By specifying the functionality of the number generator by its interface type (rather than a specific implementation class type), an interface makes it possible to design code that is easily adaptable. You can simply change the type of object passed to **Simulation** when an instance is constructed. No other changes are needed.

The above example can be generalized. Specifying functionality by use of an interface reference lets you gracefully migrate code over time, without breaking it. As long as the interface remains unchanged, both the implementation of the interface and the code that uses it can evolve as required. Through the use of the interface, your code gains flexibility.

IMPLEMENTING MULTIPLE INTERFACES

As mentioned, a class can implement more than one interface. To do so, simply specify each interface in a comma-separated list. The class must, of course, implement all of the methods specified by each interface. Here is a simple example:

```
interface IfA {
  void doSomething();
}

interface IfB {
  void doSomethingElse();
}

// Implement both IfA and IfB.
class MyClass implements IfA, IfB {
```

```
  public void doSomething() {
    System.out.println("Doing something.");
  }

  public void doSomethingElse() {
    System.out.println("Doing something else.");
  }
}
```

In this example, **MyClass** specifies both **IfA** and **IfB** in its **implements** clause. It then implements the method specified by each.

In real-world applications, it is not uncommon for a class to implement more than one interface. Doing so enables a class to provide a variety of well-defined functionality without having to use class inheritance. As you know, one class can directly inherit only one other class. As a result, it can be difficult to specify additional functionality without resorting to top-heavy hierarchies. Interfaces address this problem, letting a class specify the additional functionality without impacting the inheritance hierarchy.

Ask the Expert

Q When implementing multiple interfaces, what happens if both interfaces declare the same method? For example, what if two interfaces both specify a method called **doSomething( )**?

A If a class implements two interfaces that declare the same method, then the same method implementation will be used for both interfaces. This means that only one version of the method is defined by the class. For example, consider this variation on the example just shown:

```
// Both IfA and IfB declare the method doSomething().
interface IfA {
  void doSomething();
}

interface IfB {
  void doSomething();
}

// Implement both IfA and IfB
class MyClass implements IfA, IfB {

  // This method implements both IfA and IfB.
  public void doSomething() {
    System.out.println("Doing something.");
  }
}
```

```
class MultiImpDemo {
  public static void main(String[] args) {
    IfA aRef;
    IfB bRef;
    MyClass obj = new MyClass();

    // Both interfaces use the same doSomething().
    aRef = obj;
    aRef.doSomething();

    bRef = obj;
    bRef.doSomething();
  }
}
```

The output is shown here:

```
Doing something.
Doing something.
```

In this case, both **IfA** and **IfB** declare the same method, **doSomething( )**. When **MyClass** implements these interfaces, both will use the same **doSomething( )**. Thus, whether **doSomething( )** is called through an **IfA** reference or an **IfB** reference, the same method is executed.

Progress Check

1. Can an interface reference variable refer to an object that implements that interface?
2. A class can implement only one interface. True or False?

TRY THIS 8-1   CREATE A SIMPLE STACK INTERFACE

ISimpleStack.java
FixedLengthStack.java
DynamicStack.java
ISimpleStackDemo.java

To better understand the power of interfaces and the "one interface, multiple methods" principle of object-oriented programming, it is helpful to look at a practical example. In earlier chapters, you developed a class called **SimpleStack** that implemented a fixed-length stack for characters. However, there are other ways to implement a stack.

Answers:

1. Yes.
2. False.

For example, a stack can be dynamic, meaning that its size will be expanded when necessary to accommodate additional items. It is also possible to use a data structure other than an array to hold the contents of a stack. No matter how the stack is implemented, the interface to the stack remains the same. In other words, methods such as **push( )** and **pop( )** define the interface to the stack independently of the details of the implementation. Therefore, once you have created a stack interface, all stacks that implement that interface can be used in the same way. Furthermore, they can be used through an interface reference, enabling you to change the specific implementation that you use without fear of breaking existing code.

In this project, you will create an interface for a simple stack that is based on the functionality provided by the **SimpleStack** class first developed in Try This 5-2, and enhanced in Try This 6-1 and Try This 6-2. This interface will be called **ISimpleStack**. Then, two implementations of **ISimpleStack** are developed. The first is adapted from **SimpleStack**. Because it is a fixed-length stack, it will be called **FixedLengthStack**. The second implementation, called **DynamicStack**, will be a dynamic stack, which grows as necessary when its underlying array size is exceeded.

STEP-BY-STEP

1. Because an interface defines the functionality of an implementation, the first step is to create the interface that describes a simple stack. To do so, we take a lead from the methods defined by **SimpleStack**. Recall that it declares the four stack methods, **push( )**, **pop( )**, **isFull( )**, and **isEmpty( )**. These methods are declared in **ISimpleStack**, shown here. Put this interface in a file called **ISimpleStack.java**.

   ```
   // An interface for a simple stack that stores characters.
   public interface ISimpleStack {

     // Push a character onto the stack.
     void push(char ch);

     // Pop a character from the stack.
     char pop();

     // Return true if the stack is empty.
     boolean isEmpty();

     // Return true if the stack is full.
     boolean isFull();
   }
   ```

   This interface describes the operations of a simple stack. Each class that implements **ISimpleStack** will need to implement these methods.

   One point of interest before moving on: At this time, **ISimpleStack** specifies the interface for a stack of characters. In Chapter 14, you see how to adapt **ISimpleStack** so that it can specify a stack that holds any type of data.

2. You will now create two stacks that implement **ISimpleStack**. The first is adapted from the version of **SimpleStack** shown in Try This 6-2. Because **SimpleStack** already implements the methods specified by **ISimpleStack**, only three changes are necessary. First, the name must be changed to **FixedLengthStack**. Second, an **implements ISimpleStack** clause must be added to its declaration. Third, **push( )**, **pop( )**, **isFull( )**, and **isEmpty( )** need to specified **public** since they now provide the implementations for **ISimpleStack**. For clarity, the entire **FixedLengthStack** is shown here. Put it in a file called **FixedLengthStack.java**:

```java
// A fixed-length stack for characters.
class FixedLengthStack implements ISimpleStack {
  private char[] data; // this array holds the stack
  private int tos; // index of top of stack

  // Construct an empty stack given its size.
  FixedLengthStack(int size) {
    data = new char[size]; // create the array to hold the stack
    tos = 0;
  }

  // Construct a stack from a stack.
  FixedLengthStack(FixedLengthStack otherStack) {
    // size of new stack equals that of otherStack
    data = new char[otherStack.data.length];

    // set tos to the same position
    tos = otherStack.tos;

    // copy the contents
    for(int i = 0; i < tos; i++)
      data[i] = otherStack.data[i];
  }

  // Construct a stack with initial values.
  FixedLengthStack(char[] chrs) {
    // create the array to hold the initial values
    data = new char[chrs.length];
    tos = 0;

    // initialize the stack by pushing the contents
    // of chrs onto it
    for(char ch : chrs)
      push(ch);
  }

  // Push a character onto the stack.
  public void push(char ch) {
    if(isFull()) {
      System.out.println(" -- Stack is full.");
```

```
      return;
    }

    data[tos] = ch;
    tos++;
  }

  // Pop a character from the stack.
  public char pop() {
    if(isEmpty()) {
      System.out.println(" -- Stack is empty.");
      return (char) 0; // a placeholder value
    }

    tos--;
    return data[tos];
  }

  // Return true if the stack is empty.
  public boolean isEmpty() {
    return tos==0;
  }

  // Return true if the stack is full.
  public boolean isFull() {
    return tos==data.length;
  }
}
```

3. **Create** the **DynamicStack** class shown next. It implements a "growable" stack that expands its size when space is exhausted. Put it in a file called **DynamicStack.java**.

```
// A growable stack for characters.
class DynamicStack implements ISimpleStack {
  private char[] data; // this array holds the stack
  private int tos; // index of top of stack

  // Construct an empty stack given its size.
  DynamicStack(int size) {
    data = new char[size]; // create the array to hold the stack
    tos = 0;
  }

  // Construct a stack from a stack.
  DynamicStack(DynamicStack otherStack) {
    // size of new stack equals that of otherStack
    data = new char[otherStack.data.length];

    // set tos to the same position
```

```java
    tos = otherStack.tos;

  // copy the contents
  for(int i = 0; i < tos; i++)
    data[i] = otherStack.data[i];
}

// Construct a stack with initial values.
DynamicStack(char[] chrs) {
  // create the array to hold the initial values
  data = new char[chrs.length];
  tos = 0;

  // initialize the stack by pushing the contents
  // of chrs onto it
  for(char ch : chrs)
    push(ch);
}

// Push a character onto the stack.
public void push(char ch) {

  // if there is no more room in the array,
  // expand the size of the stack
  if(tos == data.length) {
    // double the size of the existing array
    char[] t = new char[data.length * 2];

    // copy the contents of the stack into the larger array
    for(int i = 0; i < tos; i++)
      t[i] = data[i];

    // set data to refer to the new array
    data = t;
  }

  data[tos] = ch;
  tos++;
}

// Pop a character from the stack.
public char pop() {
  if(isEmpty()) {
    System.out.println(" -- Stack is empty.");
    return (char) 0; // a placeholder value
  }

  tos--;
  return data[tos];
}
```

```
    // Return true if the stack is empty.
    public boolean isEmpty() {
      return tos==0;
    }

    // Return true if the stack is full. For DynamicStack,
    // this method always returns false.
    public boolean isFull() {
      return false;
    }
}
```

In this implementation, when the limit of the **data** array has been reached, an attempt to store another element causes a new array to be allocated that is twice as large as the original. Then, the current contents of the stack are copied into the new array. Finally, a reference to the new array is stored in **data**. There is one other thing to note in the dynamic stack implementation: the **isFull( )** method always returns **false**. Since the stack size will be automatically increased as needed, the stack can never be full. (Of course, at some point in an extreme case, memory will be exhausted, resulting in a run-time error, but the handling of this type of error is beyond the scope of this discussion.)

4. To demonstrate the two **ISimpleStack** implementations, enter the following class into **ISimpleStackDemo.java**. It uses an **ISimpleStack** reference to access both stacks.

```
// Demonstrate ISimpleStack.
class ISimpleStackDemo {
  public static void main(String[] args) {
    int i;
    char ch;

    // create an ISimpleStack interface variable
    ISimpleStack iStack;

    // Now, construct a FixedLengthStack and a DynamicStack
    FixedLengthStack fixedStack = new FixedLengthStack(10);
    DynamicStack dynStack = new DynamicStack(5);

    // first, use fixedStack through iStack
    iStack = fixedStack;

    // push characters onto fixedStack
    for(i = 0; !iStack.isFull(); i++)
      iStack.push((char) ('A'+i));

    // pop characters off fixedStack
    System.out.print("Contents of fixedStack: ");
```

```
      while(!iStack.isEmpty()) {
        ch = iStack.pop();
        System.out.print(ch);
      }

      System.out.println();

      // next, use dynStack through iStack
      iStack = dynStack;

      // push A through Z onto dynStack
      // this will result in three increases in its size
      for(i = 0; i < 26; i++)
        iStack.push((char) ('A'+i));

      // pop characters off dynStack
      System.out.print("Contents of dynStack: ");
      while(!iStack.isEmpty()) {
        ch = iStack.pop();
        System.out.print(ch);
      }
    }
}
```

5. Compile all of the files and then run **ISimpleStackDemo**. The output is shown here.

```
Contents of fixedStack: JIHGFEDCBA
Contents of dynStack: ZYXWVUTSRQPONMLKJIHGFEDCBA
```

6. Several other methods could be added to the **ISimpleStack** interface to enhance the functionality that it specifies. For example, you could add a **reset( )** method that resets the stack and a **peek( )** method that obtains, but does not remove, the top element on the stack. A **size( )** method that returns the number of elements in the stack would also be a useful addition. The implementation of these methods is the subject of Exercise 12 at the end of this chapter.

CONSTANTS IN INTERFACES

Although the primary purpose of an **interface** is to declare methods that provide a well-defined interface to functionality, an interface can also include "variables." However, such "variables" are not instance variables. Instead, they are implicitly **public**, **final**, and **static** and must be initialized. Thus, they are essentially constants. At first glance, you might think that there would be very limited use for them, but the opposite is true. Large programs often make use of several constant values that describe such things as array size, various limits, and special values. Since a large program typically uses a number of separate classes, there needs to be a convenient way to make these constants available to each class. In Java, interface constants offer a solution.

To define a set of shared constants, simply create an **interface** that contains only those constants, without any methods. Each class that needs access to the constants simply "implements" the interface. This brings the constants into view. Here is a simple example that gives you an idea of how the process works:

```
// An interface that contains constants.
interface IConst {
  int MIN = 0;
  int MAX = 10;                                    These are constants.
  String ERRORMSG = "Boundary Error";
}


// Gain access to the constants by implementing IConst.
class IConstDemo implements IConst {
  public static void main(String[] args) {
    int[] nums = new int[MAX];

    for(int i=MIN; i < (MAX + 1); i++) {
      if(i >= MAX) System.out.println(ERRORMSG);
      else {
        nums[i] = i;
        System.out.print(nums[i] + " ");
      }
    }
  }
}
```

In this example, the **IConst** interface defines three constants. **MIN** and **MAX** are of type **int**, and **ERRORMSG** is of type **String**. As required, they are given initial values. The **IConstDemo** class gains access to these constants by implementing **IConst**. This means that they can be used directly by **IConstDemo**, as if they had been defined by **IConstDemo**. Since **IConst** can be implemented by any number of classes, it can be used by any class that needs access to its constants.

Ask the Expert

Q Must an interface actually define any members? The reason I ask is that I was looking through Java's API documentation and I noticed an interface called **Cloneable**. It did not appear to have any members. Can you explain?

A It is not necessary for an interface to define any members. Such an interface is sometimes called a "marker interface" because its sole purpose is to indicate that a class is capable of supporting some action. The marker interface becomes part of the implementing class's type, even though it does nothing. As you will see later in this book, it is possible for an object's type to be queried at run time, and the presence of the marker interface can be checked. In the case of **Cloneable**, it means that a bitwise, exact copy of an object of that class is legal. As you explore Java's API library, you will find other examples of marker interfaces.

INTERFACES CAN BE EXTENDED

One interface can inherit another by use of the keyword **extends**. The syntax is the same as for inheriting classes. When a class implements an interface that inherits another interface, it must provide implementations for all methods defined within the interface inheritance chain. Following is an example:

```java
// One interface can extend another.
interface A {
  void meth1();
  void meth2();
}

// B inherits meth1() and meth2() - it adds meth3().
interface B extends A {
  void meth3();
}
                                    B inherits A.

// This class must implement all of A and B.
class MyClass implements B {
  public void meth1() {
    System.out.println("Implement meth1().");
  }

  public void meth2() {
    System.out.println("Implement meth2().");
  }

  public void meth3() {
    System.out.println("Implement meth3().");
  }
}

class IFExtend {
  public static void main(String[] args) {
    MyClass ob = new MyClass();

    ob.meth1();
    ob.meth2();
    ob.meth3();
  }
}
```

In this example, interface **A** is extended by interface **B**. Next, **MyClass** implements **B**. This means that **MyClass** must implement all of the methods defined by both interfaces **A** and **B**, since **A** has been inherited by **B**. As an experiment, you might try removing the implementation for **meth1( )** in **MyClass**. This will cause a compile-time error. Remember, any class that implements an interface must implement all methods defined by that interface, including any that are inherited from other interfaces.

NESTED INTERFACES

An interface can be declared a member of another interface or of a class. Such an interface is called a *member interface* or a *nested interface*. An interface nested in a class can use any access modifier. An interface nested in another interface is implicitly public. When a nested interface is used outside of its enclosing scope, it must be qualified by the name of the class or interface of which it is a member. Thus, outside of the interface or class in which a nested interface is declared, its name must be fully qualified.

Here is an example that demonstrates a nested interface:

```java
// A nested interface example.

// This interface contains a nested interface.
interface A {
  // this is a nested interface
  public interface NestedIF {
    boolean isNotNegative(int x);
  }

  void doSomething();
}

// This class implements the nested interface.
class B implements A.NestedIF {
  public boolean isNotNegative(int x) {
    return x < 0 ? false: true;
  }
}

class NestedIFDemo {
  public static void main(String[] args) {

    // use a nested interface reference
    A.NestedIF nif = new B();

    if(nif.isNotNegative(10))
      System.out.println("10 is not negative");
    if(nif.isNotNegative(-12))
      System.out.println("this won't be displayed");
  }
}
```

A defines a member interface called **NestedIF** that is declared **public**. Next, **B** implements the nested interface by specifying

```java
implements A.NestedIF
```

Notice that the name is fully qualified by the enclosing interface name. Inside the **main( )** method, an **A.NestedIF** reference called **nif** is created, and it is assigned a reference to a **B** object. Because **B** implements **A.NestedIF**, this is legal.

One other point. In the program, notice that **A** also specifies a method, called **doSomething( )**. Because **B** implements only the nested interface **NestedIF**, it does not need to implement **doSomething( )**.

Progress Check

1. A "variable" declared in an interface creates a constant because it is implicitly _____, _____, and _____.
2. Must an interface constant be initialized?

FINAL THOUGHTS ON INTERFACES

Although the examples we show in this book do not make frequent use of interfaces, they are an important part of real-world Java programming. Furthermore, many interfaces are found in the Java library, and many of the standard classes implement one or more of the standard interfaces. This enables a great deal of functionality to be shared among a wide range of classes. It is important, therefore, that you be comfortable with interface usage.

EXERCISES

1. "One interface, multiple methods" is a key tenet of Java. What feature best exemplifies it?
2. How many classes can implement an interface?
3. How many interfaces can a class implement?
4. A class declares that it implements an interface by use of a/an _____ _____.
5. Can interfaces be extended?
6. Create an interface for the **Vehicle** class from Chapter 7. Call the interface **IVehicle**.
7. Variables declared in an interface are implicitly **static** and **final**. What good are they?
8. Can one interface be a member of another?

_____

Answers:

1. **public**, **static**, and **final**
2. Yes.

9. Given two interfaces called **Alpha** and **Beta**, show how a class called **MyClass** specifies that it implements each.

10. Create a new class **Constants** that implements the **Series** interface discussed at the beginning of this chapter. Its **getNext( )** method repeatedly returns the last value passed in as an argument to the **setStart( )** method. Until **setStart( )** is called, it returns 0.

11. Consider the following class that claims to implement the **ISimpleStack** interface defined in Try This 8-1. Does it? Why or why not?

```
class MockStack implements ISimpleStack {
    public char pop() { return ' '; }
    public void push(char c) { }
    public boolean isEmpty() { return false; }
    public boolean isFull() { return false; }
}
```

12. Add the following methods to the **ISimpleStack** interface given in Try This 8-1. Then implement these methods in both of the classes **FixedLengthStack** and **DynamicStack**.

    A. `void reset(); // empties the stack`
    B. `char peek(); // like pop() but the char remains on the stack`
    C. `int size(); // the number of chars currently on the stack`

13. True or false: A class that implements an interface must

    A. use the same method names as those used by the interface.
    B. use the same method return types as those used by the interface.
    C. use the same parameter names as those used by the interface.
    D. make **public** all the methods that are specified by the interface.

14. A standard electrical outlet is extremely versatile in the sense that any electric appliance with a standard plug that fits the outlet can be run from the outlet, regardless of whether the appliance is, for example, a lamp, a toaster, an air conditioner, or a computer and regardless of the brand of appliance. A much less versatile outlet would be one that requires a special plug that only one brand of one kind of appliance used. How does this relate to the subject of this chapter?

15. True or false:

    A. An interface with an empty body can extend an interface with a non-empty body.
    B. An interface with a non-empty body can extend an interface with an empty body.

16. Suppose that a class **Class1** extends a class **Class2** and implements an interface **Interface1** that extends an interface **Interface2**. Also assume **Class1** has a no-argument constructor. Which of the following statements are legal?

    A. `Class1 x = new Class1();`
    B. `Class2 x = new Class1();`
    C. `Interface1 x = new Class1();`
    D. `Interface2 x = new Class1();`
    E. `Object x = new Class1();`

17. True or false: If **MyInterface** is an interface, and **x** and **y** are variables declared to be of type **MyInterface**, then

    A. neither **x** nor **y** can have the value **null**.
    B. if **x** and **y** both refer to objects, then those objects must be instances of the same class.

18. In Try This 8-1, a **FixedLengthStack** class is created and tested using an **ISimpleStackDemo** class. The class declaration of **FixedLengthStack** included an **implements** clause:

    ```
    class FixedLengthStack implements ISimpleStack {
    ```

    Suppose the class implements all the methods of the **ISimpleStack** interface but the **implements** clause is omitted.

    A. Would the **FixedLengthStack** class still compile?
    B. Would the **ISimpleStackDemo** class still compile?

CHAPTER 9

Packages

KEY SKILLS & CONCEPTS

- Know the purpose of a package
- Create a package
- Understand how packages affect access
- Apply the **protected** access modifier
- Import packages
- Import Java's standard packages
- Use static import

This chapter examines another powerful Java feature: the package. A *package* is a group of related classes and interfaces. Packages help organize your code and provide another layer of encapsulation. Through the use of packages you gain greater control over the organization of your program.

PACKAGE FUNDAMENTALS

In programming, it is often helpful to group related pieces of a program together. In Java, this is accomplished by using a package. A package serves two purposes. First, it provides a mechanism by which related pieces of a program can be organized as a unit. For example, if you are developing an order-entry system for an online store, then you would very likely want to create a package that contains those classes and interfaces. Classes defined within a package must be accessed through their package name. Thus, a package provides a way to name a collection of classes. Second, a package participates in Java's access control mechanism. Classes defined within a package can be made private to that package and not accessible by outside code. Thus, the package provides a means by which classes can be encapsulated. Let's examine each feature a bit more closely.

In general, when you name a class, you are allocating a name from the *namespace*. A namespace defines a declarative region. In Java, no two classes can use the same name from the same namespace. Thus, within a given namespace, each class name must be unique. The examples shown in the preceding chapters have all used the default or global namespace. While this is fine for short sample programs, it becomes a problem as programs grow and the default namespace becomes crowded. In large programs, finding unique names for each class can be difficult. Furthermore, you must avoid name collisions with code created by other programmers working on the same project, and with Java's library. The solution to these problems is the package because it gives you a way to partition the namespace. When a class is defined within a package, the name of that package is attached to the class, thus avoiding name collisions with other classes that have the same name but are in other packages.

Since a package usually contains related classes, Java defines special access rights to code within a package. In a package, you can define code that is accessible by other code within the same package but not by code outside the package. This enables you to create self-contained groups of related classes that keep their operation private.

Defining a Package

All classes in Java belong to some package. When no package has been explicitly specified, the default (or global) package is used. Furthermore, the default package has no name, which makes the default package transparent. This is why you haven't had to worry about packages before now. While the default package is fine for short, sample programs, it is inadequate for real applications. Most of the time, you will define one or more packages for your code.

To create a package, you will use the **package** statement, which is located at the top of a Java source file. A class declared within that file will belong to the specified package. Since a package defines a namespace, the name of a class that you put into the package will be in that package's namespace.

This is the general form of the **package** statement:

package *pkg*;

Here, *pkg* is the name of the package. For example, the following statement creates a package called **mypack**.

```
package mypack;
```

Java uses the file system to manage packages, with each package stored in its own directory. For example, the **.class** files for any classes you declare to be part of **mypack** must be stored in a directory called **mypack**.

Like the rest of Java, package names are case sensitive. This means that the directory in which a package is stored must be precisely the same as the package name. If you have trouble trying the examples in this chapter, remember to check your package and directory names carefully. Often, lowercase is used for package names.

More than one file can include the same **package** statement. The **package** statement simply specifies to which package the file belongs. It does not exclude other classes in other files from being part of that same package. Most real-world packages are spread across many files.

You can create a hierarchy of packages. To do so, simply separate each package name from the one above it by use of a period. The general form of a multileveled package statement is shown here:

package *pack1.pack2.pack3...packN*;

Of course, you must create directories that support the package hierarchy that you create. For example,

```
package alpha.beta.gamma;
```

must be stored in .../alpha/beta/gamma, where ... specifies the path to the specified directories.

Finding Packages and CLASSPATH

As just explained, packages are mirrored by directories. This raises an important question: How does the Java run-time system know where to look for packages that you create? The answer has three parts. First, by default, the run-time system uses the current working directory as its starting point. Therefore, if your package is in a sub-directory of the current directory, it will be found. Second, you can specify a directory path or paths by setting the **CLASSPATH** environmental variable. Third, you can use the **-classpath** option with **java** and **javac** to specify the path to your classes.

For example, consider the following package specification:

```
package mypack;
```

In order for a program to find **mypack**, one of three things must be true: The program can be executed from a directory immediately above **mypack**, or **CLASSPATH** must be set to include the path to **mypack**, or the **-classpath** option must specify the path to **mypack** when the program is run via **java**.

The easiest way to try the examples shown in this book is to create the package directories below your current development directory, put the **.class** files into the appropriate directories, and then execute the programs from the development directory. This is the approach used by the following examples.

One last point: To avoid problems, it is best to keep all **.java** and **.class** files associated with a package in that package's directory. Also, compile each file from the directory above the package directory.

A Short Package Example

Keeping the preceding discussion in mind, try this short package example. It creates a simple book database that is contained within a package called **bookpack**.

```
// A short package demonstration.
package bookpack; ◄————— This file is part of the bookpack package.

class Book { ◄————— Thus, Book is part of bookpack.
  private String title;
  private String author;
  private int pubDate;
```

```
  Book(String t, String a, int d) {
    title = t;
    author = a;
    pubDate = d;
  }

  void show() {
    System.out.println(title);
    System.out.println(author);
    System.out.println(pubDate);
  }
}

class BookDemo {          ◄────── BookDemo is also part of bookpack.
  public static void main(String[] args) {
    Book[] books = new Book[5];

    books[0] = new Book("The Art of Computer Programming, Vol 3",
                        "Knuth", 1973);
    books[1] = new Book("Moby Dick",
                        "Melville", 1851);
    books[2] = new Book("Thirteen at Dinner",
                        "Christie", 1933);
    books[3] = new Book("Red Storm Rising",
                        "Clancy", 1986);
    books[4] = new Book("On the Road",
                        "Kerouac", 1955);

    for(int i=0; i < books.length; i++) {
      books[i].show();
      System.out.println();
    }
  }
}
```

Call this file **BookDemo.java** and put it in a directory called **bookpack**.

Next, compile the file. You can do this by specifying

```
javac bookpack/BookDemo.java
```

from the directory directly above **bookpack**. Then try executing the class, using the following command line:

```
java bookpack.BookDemo
```

Remember, you will need to be in the directory above **bookpack** when you execute this command. (Or, use one of the other two options described in the preceding section to specify the path to **bookpack**.)

As explained, **BookDemo** and **Book** are now part of the package **bookpack**. This means that **BookDemo** cannot be executed by itself. That is, you cannot use this command line:

```
java BookDemo
```

Instead, **BookDemo** must be qualified with its package name.

1. What is a package?
2. Show how to declare a package called **tools**.
3. What is **CLASSPATH**?

PACKAGES AND MEMBER ACCESS

The preceding chapters have introduced the fundamentals of access control, including the **private** and **public** modifiers, but they have not told the entire story. The reason for this is that packages also participate in Java's access control mechanism, and a complete discussion had to wait until packages were covered.

The visibility of an element is determined by its access specification—**private**, **public**, **protected**, or default—and the package in which it resides. Thus, the visibility of an element is determined by its visibility within a class and its visibility within a package. This multilayered approach to access control supports a rich assortment of access privileges. Table 9-1 summarizes the various access levels. Let's examine each access option individually.

If a member of a class has no explicit access modifier, then it is visible within its package but not outside its package. Therefore, you will use the default access specification for elements that you want to keep private to a package but public within that package.

Members explicitly declared **public** are visible everywhere, including in different classes and different packages. There is no restriction on their use or access. A **private** member is accessible only to the other members of its class. A **private** member is unaffected by its membership in a package. A member specified as **protected** is accessible within its package and to all subclasses, including subclasses in other packages.

Table 9-1 applies only to members of classes. A top-level class has only two possible access levels: default and public. When a class is declared as **public**, it is accessible by any other code. If a class has default access, it can be accessed only by other code within its same package. The same is true of interfaces. Also, a class or interface that is declared **public** must reside in a file by the same name.

Answers:

1. A package is a container for classes. It performs both an organization and an encapsulation role.
2. `package tools;`
3. **CLASSPATH** is the environmental variable that specifies the path to classes.

TABLE 9-1: Class Member Access

	Private Member	Default Member	Protected Member	Public Member
Visible within same class	Yes	Yes	Yes	Yes
Visible within same package by subclass	No	Yes	Yes	Yes
Visible within same package by non-subclass	No	Yes	Yes	Yes
Visible within different package by subclass	No	No	Yes	Yes
Visible within different package by non-subclass	No	No	No	Yes

Progress Check

1. If a class member has default access inside a package, is that member accessible by other packages?
2. What does **protected** do?
3. A **private** member can be accessed by subclasses within its packages. True or False?

A Package Access Example

In the package example shown earlier, both **Book** and **BookDemo** were in the same package, so there was no problem with **BookDemo** using **Book** because the default access privilege grants all members of the same package access. However, if **Book** were in one package and **BookDemo** were in another, the situation would be different. In this case, access to **Book** would be denied. To make **Book** available to other packages, you must make three changes. First, **Book** needs to be declared **public**. This makes **Book** visible outside of **bookpack**. Second, its constructor must be made **public**, and finally its **show( )** method needs to be **public**. This allows them to be visible outside of **bookpack**, too. Thus, to make **Book** usable by other packages, it must be recoded as shown here.

Answers:

1. No.
2. It allows a member to be accessible by other code in its package and by all subclasses, no matter what package the subclass is in.
3. False.

```
// Book recoded for public access.
package bookpack;

public class Book {        ◄────────────  Book and its members must be public
  private String title;                   in order to be used by other packages.
  private String author;
  private int pubDate;

  // Now public.
  public Book(String t, String a, int d) {
    title = t;
    author = a;
    pubDate = d;
  }

  // Now public.
  public void show() {
    System.out.println(title);
    System.out.println(author);
    System.out.println(pubDate);
  }
}
```

To use **Book** from another package, either you must use the **import** statement described later in this chapter, or you must fully qualify its name to include its full package specification. For example, here is a class called **UseBook**, which is contained in a different package, called **mypack** package. It fully qualifies **Book** in order to use it.

```
// This class is in package mypack.
package mypack;
                                          Qualify Book with its
// Use the Book Class from bookpack.      package name: bookpack.
class UseBook {
  public static void main(String[] args) {
    bookpack.Book[] books = new bookpack.Book[5];  ◄─────

    books[0] = new bookpack.Book("The Art of Computer Programming, Vol 3",
                  "Knuth", 1973);
    books[1] = new bookpack.Book("Moby Dick",
                  "Melville", 1851);
    books[2] = new bookpack.Book("Thirteen at Dinner",
                  "Christie", 1933);
    books[3] = new bookpack.Book("Red Storm Rising",
                  "Clancy", 1986);
    books[4] = new bookpack.Book("On the Road",
                  "Kerouac", 1955);

    for(int i=0; i < books.length; i++) {
      books[i].show();
      System.out.println();
```

```
      }
    }
  }
```

Notice how every use of **Book** is preceded with the **bookpack** qualifier. Without this specification, **Book** would not be found when you tried to compile **UseBook**.

Understanding Protected Members

Newcomers to Java are sometimes confused by the meaning and use of **protected**. As explained, the **protected** modifier creates a member that is accessible within its package and to subclasses in other packages. Thus, a **protected** member is available for all subclasses to use but is still protected from arbitrary access by code outside its package.

To better understand the effects of **protected**, let's work through an example. First, change the **Book** class so that its instance variables are **protected**, as shown here.

```
// Make the instance variables in Book protected.
package bookpack;

public class Book {
  // these are now protected
  protected String title;          These are now protected.
  protected String author;
  protected int pubDate;

  public Book(String t, String a, int d) {
    title = t;
    author = a;
    pubDate = d;
  }

  public void show() {
    System.out.println(title);
    System.out.println(author);
    System.out.println(pubDate);
  }
}
```

Next, create a subclass of **Book**, called **ExtBook**, and a class called **ProtectDemo** that uses **ExtBook**. **ExtBook** adds a field that stores the book's condition and several accessor methods. Both of these classes will be in their own package called **bookpackext**. They are shown here.

```
// Demonstrate protected.
package bookpackext;

class ExtBook extends bookpack.Book {
  private String condition;

  public ExtBook(String t, String a, int d, String c) {
```

```
      super(t, a, d);
      condition = c;
    }

  public void show() {
    super.show();
    System.out.print("Condition is " + condition);
    System.out.println();
  }

  public String getCondition() { return condition; }
  public void setCondition(String c) { condition = c; }

  /* These are OK because subclass can access
     a protected member. */
  public String getTitle() { return title; }
  public void setTitle(String t) { title = t; }
  public String getAuthor() { return author; }
  public void setAuthor(String a) { author = a; }
  public int getPubDate() { return pubDate; }
  public void setPubDate(int d) { pubDate = d; }
}
```

Access to **Book**'s members is allowed for subclasses.

```
class ProtectDemo {
  public static void main(String[] args) {
    ExtBook[] books = new ExtBook[5];

    books[0] = new ExtBook("The Art of Computer Programming, Vol 3",
                     "Knuth", 1973, "well used");
    books[1] = new ExtBook("Moby Dick",
                     "Melville", 1851, "like new");
    books[2] = new ExtBook("Thirteen at Dinner",
                     "Christie", 1933, "fair");
    books[3] = new ExtBook("Red Storm Rising",
                   "Clancy", 1986, "good");
    books[4] = new ExtBook("On the Road",
                   "Kerouac", 1955, "fair");

    for(int i=0; i < books.length; i++) {
      books[i].show();
      System.out.println();
    }

    // Find condition of Moby Dick.
    System.out.print("Condition of Moby Dick is ");
    for(int i=0; i < books.length; i++)
      if(books[i].getTitle() == "Moby Dick")
        System.out.println(books[i].getCondition());

//    books[0].title = "test title"; // Error - not accessible
  }
}
```

Access to **protected** field not allowed by non-subclass.

Look first at the code inside **ExtBook**. Because **ExtBook** extends **Book**, it has access to the **protected** members of **Book** even though **ExtBook** is in a different package. Thus, it can access **title**, **author**, and **pubDate** directly, as it does in the accessor methods it creates for those variables. However, in **ProtectDemo**, access to these variables is denied because **ProtectDemo** is not a subclass of **Book**. For example, if you remove the comment symbol from the following line, the program will not compile.

```
//     books[0].title = "test title"; // Error - not accessible
```

Ask the Expert

Q Are there any restrictions on the way that a subclass can access a **protected** member?

A As the **ProtectDemo** example shows, a subclass in a different package has access to a **protected** member of its superclass for the purposes of extending the superclass. However, a subclass in a different package *does not* have the ability to access a **protected** member of its superclass through an object of that superclass. For example, if the following method is added to **ExtBook**

```
void wontWork() {
   bookpack.Book b = new bookpack.Book("sometitle", "someauthor", 1961);
   b.title = "newtitle"; // Error!
}
```

the attempt to access **title** through **b** will fail. If you think about it, this restriction makes sense. A subclass can use a **protected** member for the purpose of implementing the subclass, but not as a means of getting around the **protected** access limitation in general.

IMPORTING PACKAGES

When you use a class from another package, you can fully qualify the name of the class with the name of its package, as the preceding examples have done. However, such an approach could easily become tiresome and awkward, especially if the classes you are qualifying are deeply nested in a package hierarchy. Since Java was invented by programmers for programmers—and programmers don't like tedious constructs—it should come as no surprise that a more convenient method exists for using the contents of packages: the **import** statement. Using **import**, you can bring one or more members of a package into view. This allows you to use those members directly, without explicit package qualification.

Here is the general form of the **import** statement:

import *pkg.classname*;

Here, *pkg* is the name of the package, which can include its full path, and *classname* is the name of the class being imported. If you want to import the entire contents of a package, use an asterisk (*) for the class name. Here are examples of both forms:

```
import mypack.MyClass;
import mypack.*;
```

In the first case, the **MyClass** class is imported from **mypack**. In the second, all of the classes in **mypack** are imported. In a Java source file, **import** statements occur immediately following the **package** statement (if it exists) and before any class definitions.

You can use **import** to bring the **bookpack** package into view so that the **Book** class can be used without qualification. To do so, simply add this **import** statement to the top of any file that uses **Book**.

```
import bookpack.*;
```

For example, here is the **UseBook** class recoded to use **import**.

```
// Demonstrate import.
package mypack;
import bookpack.*;  ◄─────────── Import bookpack.

// Use the Book Class from bookpack.
class UseBook {
  public static void main(String[] args) {
    Book[] books = new Book[5];  ◄───────────── Now, you can refer to Book
                                                 directly, without qualification.
    books[0] = new Book("The Art of Computer Programming, Vol 3",
                        "Knuth", 1973);
    books[1] = new Book("Moby Dick",
                        "Melville", 1851);
    books[2] = new Book("Thirteen at Dinner",
                        "Christie", 1933);
    books[3] = new Book("Red Storm Rising",
                        "Clancy", 1986);
    books[4] = new Book("On the Road",
                        "Kerouac", 1955);

    for(int i=0; i < books.length; i++) {
      books[i].show();
      System.out.println();
    }
  }
}
```

Notice that you no longer need to qualify **Book** with its package name.

Importing Java's Standard Packages

As explained earlier in this book, Java defines a large number of standard classes that are available to all programs. This class library is often referred to as the Java API (Application Programming Interface). The Java API is stored in packages. At the top of the package hierarchy is **java**. Descending from **java** are several subpackages, including these:

Subpackage	Description
java.lang	Contains a large number of general-purpose classes
java.io	Contains the I/O classes
java.net	Contains those classes that support networking
java.applet	Contains classes for creating applets
java.awt	Contains classes that support the Abstract Window Toolkit
java.util	Contains various utility classes, plus the Collections Framework

Since the beginning of this book, you have been using **java.lang**. It contains, among several others, the **System** class, which you have been using when performing output using **println( )**. The **java.lang** package is unique because it is imported automatically into every Java program. This is why you did not have to import **java.lang** in the preceding sample programs.

You must, however, explicitly import the other packages in the API. The standard packages are imported in the same way as those shown in the preceding examples. For example, to import all of **java.net**, use the following statement:

```
import java.net.*;
```

Later in this book, several packages in the Java API will be examined. As you will see, the API offers a vast assortment of predefined functionality that your program can access, simply by importing the relevant package.

Progress Check

1. How do you include another package in a source file?
2. Show how to include all of the classes in a package called **toolpack**.
3. Do you need to include **java.lang** explicitly?

TRY THIS 9-1   MOVING A CLASS TO ANOTHER PACKAGE

```
Dog.java
Owner.java
DogOwnerDemo.java
```

This project shows what is involved in moving a class to another package. As you can probably guess, it requires more than just changing the package statement at the beginning of the file containing the class. We will use three classes in this project: an **Owner** class, a **Dog** class, and a **DogOwnerDemo** class. Initially, the **Owner** and **Dog** classes will be in an **owner** package, and the **DogOwnerDemo** class will be in its own package. Then we will move the **Dog** class to a new **dog** package.

Answers:

1. Use the **import** statement.
2. `import toolpack.*;`
3. No.

STEP-BY-STEP

1. Under your current working directory, create the following three directories: **owner**, **dogownerdemo**, and **dog**.

2. In the **owner** directory, create a file called **Dog.java**. Into **Dog.java**, add the following code.

```
package owner;

public class Dog {
   String name;

   public Dog(String n) { name = n; }

   public String toString() {
      return name;
   }
}
```

3. In the **owner** directory, create a file called **Owner.java**. Into **Owner.java**, add the following code.

```
package owner;

public class Owner {
   String name;
   Dog dog;

   public Owner(String n, Dog d) {
      name = n; dog = d;
   }

   public String toString() {
      return name + " owns " + dog;
   }
}
```

4. In the **dogownerdemo** directory, create a file called **DogOwnerDemo.java**. Into **DogOwnerDemo.java**, add the following program.

```
package dogownerdemo;

import owner.*;

class DogOwnerDemo {
   public static void main(String[] args) {
      Owner owner = new Owner("Fred", new Dog("Sam"));
      System.out.println(owner);
   }
}
```

5. Compile all the files from the current working directory using this sequence:

```
javac owner/Dog.java
javac owner/Owner.java
javac dogownerdemo/DogOwnerDemo.java
```

Then, use this line

```
java dogownerdemo.DogOwnerDemo
```

to run the **DogOwnerDemo** class to make sure everything is working properly. You should get the following output.

```
Fred owns Sam
```

6. Now we will move the **Dog** class to a new **dog** package. There are three steps.

   A. Change the first line of **Dog.java** to read **package dog;** instead of **package owner;**.

   B. Move **Dog.java** to the directory named **dog**. (Be sure to remove both its source file and class file from the **owner** directory.)

   C. Add the line **import dog.*;** to both of the other files, since they both use the **Dog** class.

7. Compile all files as just shown, except that now **Dog.java** is compiled using this line:

```
javac dog/Dog.java
```

Next, again run **DogOwnerDemo** as shown earlier. You should get the same output as before.

8. It is important to understand that it was relatively simple to move **Dog** from one package to another due to a variety of factors. First, the **import** statement made it easy for other classes to still access the **Dog** class, even though it was moved to a different package—only one new line of code needed to be added to those classes. Second, the fact that the **Dog** class and its method and constructor are **public** made it possible for the class to be moved and still be accessible by other classes. In contrast, if other classes in the **owner** package had directly accessed the **Dog**'s **name** instance variable, which is not **public**, then, after the move, they would no longer have been able do so. Thus, a change to their code would have been required. Similarly, if the **Dog** class had accessed any non-public member of a class in the **owner** package, it would no longer be able to do so after the move, and so its code would also have needed to be changed. In summary, moving a class to a new package can raise several issues. The key to preventing problems is to spend time up front, carefully designing your classes and packages to minimize the number of times that a package needs to be changed.

STATIC IMPORT

Java supports an expanded use of the **import** keyword. By following **import** with the keyword **static**, an **import** statement can be used to import the static members of a class or interface. This is called *static import*, and it was added to Java by JDK 5. When using static import, it is possible to refer to static members directly by their names, without having to qualify them with the name of their class. This simplifies and shortens the syntax required to use a static member.

To understand the usefulness of static import, let's begin with an example that *does not* use it. The following program computes the solutions to a quadratic equation, which has this form:

$$ax^2 + bx + c = 0$$

The program uses two static methods from Java's built-in math class **Math**, which is part of **java.lang**. The first is **Math.pow( )**, which returns a value raised to a specified power. The second is **Math.sqrt( )**, which returns the square root of its argument.

```
// Find the solutions to a quadratic equation.
class Quadratic {
  public static void main(String[] args) {

    // a, b, and c represent the coefficients in the
    // quadratic equation: ax2 + bx + c = 0
    double a, b, c, x;

    // Solve 4x2 + x - 3 = 0 for x.
    a = 4;
    b = 1;
    c = -3;

    // Find first solution.
    x = (-b + Math.sqrt(Math.pow(b, 2) - 4 * a * c)) / (2 * a);
    System.out.println("First solution: " + x);

    // Find second solution.
    x = (-b - Math.sqrt(Math.pow(b, 2) - 4 * a * c)) / (2 * a);
    System.out.println("Second solution: " + x);
  }
}
```

Because **pow( )** and **sqrt( )** are static methods, they must be called through the use of their class's name, **Math**. This results in a somewhat unwieldy expression:

```
x = (-b + Math.sqrt(Math.pow(b, 2) - 4 * a * c)) / (2 * a);
```

Furthermore, having to specify the class name each time **pow( )** or **sqrt( )** (or any of Java's other math methods, such as **sin( )**, **cos( )**, and **tan( )**) are used can become tedious.

You can eliminate the tedium of specifying the class name through the use of static import, as shown in the following version of the preceding program.

```
// Use static import to bring sqrt() and pow() into view.
import static java.lang.Math.sqrt; ◄─────────────┐  Use static import to bring
import static java.lang.Math.pow; ◄──────────────┘  sqrt( ) and pow( ) into view.

class Quadratic {
  public static void main(String[] args) {

    // a, b, and c represent the coefficients in the
    // quadratic equation: ax2 + bx + c = 0
    double a, b, c, x;

    // Solve 4x2 + x - 3 = 0 for x.
    a = 4;
    b = 1;
    c = -3;

    // Find first solution.
    x = (-b + sqrt(pow(b, 2) - 4 * a * c)) / (2 * a);
    System.out.println("First solution: " + x);

    // Find second solution.
    x = (-b - sqrt(pow(b, 2) - 4 * a * c)) / (2 * a);
    System.out.println("Second solution: " + x);
  }
}
```

In this version, the names **sqrt** and **pow** are brought into view by these static import statements:

```
import static java.lang.Math.sqrt;
import static java.lang.Math.pow;
```

After these statements, it is no longer necessary to qualify **sqrt( )** or **pow( )** with its class name. Therefore, the expression can more conveniently be specified, as shown here:

```
x = (-b + sqrt(pow(b, 2) - 4 * a * c)) / (2 * a);
```

As you can see, this form is considerably shorter and easier to read.

There are two general forms of the **import static** statement. The first, which is used by the preceding example, brings into view a single name. Its general form is shown here:

import static *pkg.type-name.static-member-name*;

Here, *type-name* is the name of a class or interface that contains the desired static member. Its full package name is specified by *pkg*. The name of the member is specified by *static-member-name*.

The second form of static import imports all static members. Its general form is shown here:

    import static *pkg.type-name*.*;

If you will be using many static methods or fields defined by a class, then this form lets you bring them into view without having to specify each individually. Therefore, the preceding program could have used this single **import** statement to bring both **pow( )** and **sqrt( )** (and *all other* static members of **Math**) into view:

```
import static java.lang.Math.*;
```

Of course, static import is not limited just to the **Math** class or just to methods. For example, this brings the static field **System.out** into view:

```
import static java.lang.System.out;
```

After this statement, you can output to the console without having to qualify **out** with **System**, as shown here:

```
out.println("After importing System.out, you can use out directly.");
```

Whether importing **System.out** as just shown is a good idea is subject to debate. Although it does shorten the statement, it is no longer instantly clear to anyone reading the program that the **out** being referred to is **System.out**.

As convenient as static import can be, it is important not to abuse it. Remember, one reason that Java organizes its libraries into packages is to avoid namespace collisions. When you import static members, you are bringing those members into the global namespace. Thus, you are increasing the potential for namespace conflicts and the inadvertent hiding of other names. If you are using a static member once or twice in the program, it's best not to import it. Also, some static names, such as **System.out**, are so recognizable that you might not want to import them. Static import is designed for those situations in which you are using a static member repeatedly, such as when performing a series of mathematical computations. In essence, you should use, but not abuse, this feature.

Ask the Expert

Q Is static import only for use with classes in the Java library, or can I use static import with classes that I create?

A You can use static import to import the static members of classes and interfaces you create. Doing so is especially convenient when you define several static members that are used frequently throughout a large program. For example, if a class defines a number of **static final** constants that specify various limits, then using static import to bring them into view will save you a lot of tedious typing. However, the same caution given earlier still applies: use, but don't abuse, this feature.

EXERCISES

1. Using the code from Try This 8-1, put the **ISimpleStack** interface and its two implementations into a package called **stackpack**. Keeping the stack demonstration class **ISimpleStackDemo** in the default package, show how to import and use the classes in **stackpack**.

2. What is a namespace? Why is it important that Java allows you to partition the namespace?

3. Packages are stored in _____.

4. Explain the difference between **protected** and default access.

5. Explain the two ways that the members of a package can be accessed by other packages.

6. A package is, in essence, a container for classes. True or False?

7. What standard Java package is automatically imported into a program?

8. In your own words, what does static import do?

9. What does this statement do?

```
import static somepack.SomeClass.myMethod;
```

10. Is static import designed for special-case situations, or is it good practice to bring all static members of all classes into view?

11. It is fine for the Java library to divide classes and interfaces into packages, but why do you need to do so for your programs? What is wrong with just giving all your classes unique names so that there is never a name conflict?

12. True or false:

   A. If you don't include a **package** statement in a Java source file, then all classes declared in the file do not belong to any package.

   B. If a class **A** is in one package **pkg** and a second class **B** is in a subpackage **pkg.subpkg**, then class **A** automatically has access to all members of class **B** that use the **protected** modifier.

13. Rank the three access modifiers **public**, **private**, and **protected**, and the default access in order from most restrictive to least restrictive.

14. Suppose a class **A** has four instance variables with four different access levels as follows:

```
class A {
   private int x;
   public int y;
   protected int z;
   int w;
}
```

and suppose a class **B** attempts to access those four variables as follows:

```
class B {
  public static void main(String[] args) {
    A a = new A();
    System.out.println(a.x);
    System.out.println(a.y);
    System.out.println(a.z);
    System.out.println(a.w);
  }
}
```

Which of the four calls to **println( )** in class **B**'s **main( )** method are legal if:

A. classes **A** and **B** are in the same package?
B. classes **A** and **B** are in different packages?
C. class **B** is a subclass of class **A** and in the same package?
D. class **B** is a subclass of class **A** and in a different package?

15. Suppose an interface **MyConstants** is defined as follows:

```
package mypackage;

public interface MyConstants {
  public static final int ANSWER = 42;
}
```

There are two ways to bring the constant **ANSWER** into view for use in another class: (1) have your class implement the **MyConstants** interface and (2) use a static import statement. Demonstrate how to use each of these approaches to get the following code to compile:

```
class MyClass {
  public static void main(String[] args) {
    System.out.println(ANSWER);
  }
}
```

16. Suppose you have a file **MyClass.java** containing the declaration of the class **MyClass** and suppose you want to move **MyClass** into a different package. What are two changes that need to be made to **MyClass.java**?

17. When you import a class, you are adding the class name to the current namespace. What if there is already a class of that name? For example, suppose you define the following class. What will happen when you try to compile it?

```
import java.util.Date;

public class Date {
  public static String getDate() { return "Jan 1, 1970"; }
}
```

18. Suppose a package **pkg1** contains a class named **MyClass** and another package **pkg2** contains a different class named **MyClass**. What happens when you import both classes? In particular, what would happen if you attempt to compile the following code?

```
import pkg1.MyClass;
import pkg2.MyClass;

public class AnotherClass {
  public static void main(String[] args) {
    MyClass c = new MyClass();
  }
}
```

19. When you import a whole package instead of just one class or interface, you are adding all the class and interface names in that package to the current namespace. What if there is already a class or interface of one of the imported names? For example, suppose you define the following classes. What happens when you try to compile and run the **Test** class? Note that the **java.util** package already has a **Date** class.

```
import java.util.*;

public class Date {
  public static String getDate() { return "Jan 1, 1970"; }
}

class Test {
  public static void main(String[] args) {
    System.out.println(Date.getDate());
  }
}
```

CHAPTER 10

Exception Handling

KEY SKILLS & CONCEPTS

- Know the exception hierarchy
- Use **try** and **catch**
- Understand the effects of an uncaught exception
- Use multiple **catch** clauses
- Catch subclass exceptions
- Nest **try** blocks
- Throw an exception
- Know the members of **Throwable**
- Use **finally**
- Use **throws**
- Know Java's built-in exceptions
- Create custom exception classes

This chapter discusses exception handling. An exception is an error that occurs at run time. Using Java's exception handling subsystem, you can, in a structured and controlled manner, handle run-time errors. A principal advantage of exception handling is that it automates much of the error handling code that previously had to be entered "by hand" into any large program. For example, in some older computer languages, error codes are returned when a method fails, and these values must be checked manually, each time the method is called. This approach is both tedious and error-prone. Exception handling streamlines error handling by allowing your program to define a block of code, called an *exception handler*, that is executed automatically when an error occurs. It is not necessary to manually check the success or failure of each specific operation or method call. If an error occurs, it will be processed by the exception handler.

Another reason that exception handling is important is that Java defines standard exceptions for common program errors, such as divide-by-zero or an out-of-bounds array index. To respond to these errors, your program must watch for and handle these exceptions. Also, Java's API library makes extensive use of exceptions. In general, to be a successful Java programmer means that you are fully capable of navigating Java's exception handling subsystem.

THE EXCEPTION HIERARCHY

In Java, all exceptions are represented by classes. All exception classes are derived from a class called **Throwable**. Thus, when an exception occurs in a program, an object of some type of exception class is generated. There are two direct subclasses of **Throwable**: **Exception** and **Error**. Exceptions of type **Error** are related to errors that are beyond your control, such as those that occur in the Java virtual machine itself. Your program will not usually deal with them. Thus, these types of exceptions are not described here.

Errors that result from program activity are represented by subclasses of **Exception**. For example, divide-by-zero, array boundary, and I/O errors fall into this category. In general, your program should handle exceptions of these types. An important subclass of **Exception** is **RuntimeException**, which is used to represent various common types of run-time errors.

EXCEPTION HANDLING FUNDAMENTALS

Java exception handling is managed via five keywords: **try**, **catch**, **throw**, **throws**, and **finally**. They form an interrelated subsystem in which the use of one implies the use of another. Throughout the course of this chapter, each keyword is examined in detail. However, it is useful at the outset to have a general understanding of the role each plays in exception handling. Briefly, here is how they work.

Program statements that you want to monitor for exceptions are contained within a **try** block. If an exception occurs within the **try** block, it is thrown. Your code can catch this exception using **catch** and handle it in some rational manner. System-generated exceptions are automatically thrown by the Java run-time system. To manually throw an exception, use the keyword **throw**. In some cases, an exception that is thrown out of a method must be specified as such by a **throws** clause. Any code that absolutely must be executed upon exiting from a **try** block is put in a **finally** block.

Ask the Expert

Q Just to be sure, could you review the conditions that cause an exception to be generated?

A Exceptions are generated in three different ways. First, the JVM or the run-time support system can generate an exception in response to some internal error that is beyond your control. Normally, your program won't handle these types of exceptions. Second, standard exceptions, such as those corresponding to divide-by-zero or array index out-of-bounds, are generated by errors in program code. You will often need to handle these exceptions. Third, you can manually generate an exception by using the **throw** statement. No matter how an exception is generated, it is caught in the same way.

Using try and catch

At the core of exception handling are **try** and **catch**. These keywords work together; you can't have a **catch** without a **try**. Here is the general form of the **try/catch** exception handling blocks:

```
try {
  // block of code to monitor for errors
}
catch (ExcepType1 exOb) {
  // handler for ExcepType1
}
catch (ExcepType2 exOb) {
  // handler for ExcepType2
}
    .
    .
    .
```

Here, *ExcepType* is the type of exception that has occurred. When an exception is thrown, it is caught by its corresponding **catch** clause, which then processes the exception. As the general form shows, there can be more than one **catch** clause associated with a **try**. The type of the exception determines which **catch** is executed. That is, if the exception type specified by a **catch** matches that of the exception, then that **catch** clause is executed (and all others are bypassed). When an exception is caught, *exOb* will receive its value.

Here is an important point: If no exception is thrown, then a **try** block ends normally, and all of its **catch** clauses are bypassed. Execution resumes with the first statement following the last **catch**. Thus, **catch** clauses are executed only if an exception is thrown.

*Note: JDK 7 adds a new form of the **try** statement that supports automatic resource management. This new form of **try** is called **try**-with-resources. It is described in Chapter 11, in the context of managing I/O streams (such as those connected to a file) because streams are some of the most commonly used resources.*

A Simple Exception Example

Here is a simple example that illustrates how to watch for and catch an exception. As you know, it is an error to attempt to index an array beyond its boundaries. When this occurs, the JVM throws an **ArrayIndexOutOfBoundsException**. The following program purposely generates such an exception and then catches it.

```
// Demonstrate exception handling.
class ExcDemo1 {
  public static void main(String[] args) {
    int[] nums = new int[4];

    try {  ◄————————Create a try block.
```

```
          System.out.println("Before exception is generated.");

          // generate an index out-of-bounds exception
          nums[7] = 10;                                          Attempt to index past
          System.out.println("this won't be displayed");         nums boundary.
        }
      catch (ArrayIndexOutOfBoundsException exc) {               Catch array boundary errors.
        // catch the exception
        System.out.println("Index out-of-bounds!");
      }
      System.out.println("After catch.");
    }
}
```

This program displays the following output:

```
Before exception is generated.
Index out-of-bounds!
After catch.
```

Although quite short, the preceding program illustrates several key points about exception handling. First, the code that you want to monitor for errors is contained within a **try** block. Second, when an exception occurs (in this case, because of the attempt to index **nums** beyond its bounds), the exception is thrown out of the **try** block and caught by the **catch**. At this point, control passes to the **catch**, and the **try** block is terminated. That is, **catch** is *not* called. Rather, program execution is transferred to it. This means that the **println( )** statement following the out-of-bounds index will never execute. After the **catch** clause executes, program control continues with the statements following the **catch**. Thus, it is the job of your exception handler to remedy the problem that caused the exception (if possible) so that program execution can continue normally. If the problem can't be remedied, then your exception handler must take some other appropriate action, such as informing the user and terminating the program.

Remember, if no exception is thrown by a **try** block, no **catch** clauses will be executed and program control will resume after the **catch**. To confirm this, in the preceding program, change the line

```
nums[7] = 10;
```

to

```
nums[0] = 10;
```

Now, no exception is generated, and the **catch** block is not executed.

It is important to understand that all code within a **try** block is monitored for exceptions. This includes exceptions that might be generated by a method called from within the **try** block. An exception thrown by a method called from within a **try** block can be caught by the **catch** clauses associated with that **try** block—assuming, of course, that the method did not catch the exception itself. For example, this is a valid program:

```
/* An exception can be generated by one
   method and caught by another. */
```

```
class ExcTest {
  // Generate an exception.
  static void genException() {
    int[] nums = new int[4];

    System.out.println("Before exception is generated.");

    // generate an index out-of-bounds exception
    nums[7] = 10; ◄──────────────────── Exception generated here.
    System.out.println("this won't be displayed");
  }
}

class ExcDemo2 {
  public static void main(String[] args) {

    try {                                    Exception caught here.
      ExcTest.genException();
    } catch (ArrayIndexOutOfBoundsException exc) { ◄──┘
      // catch the exception
      System.out.println("Index out-of-bounds!");
    }
    System.out.println("After catch.");
  }
}
```

This program produces the following output, which is the same as that produced by the first version of the program shown earlier.

```
Before exception is generated.
Index out-of-bounds!
After catch.
```

Since **genException( )** is called from within a **try** block, the exception that it generates (and does not catch) is caught by the **catch** in **main( )**. Understand, however, that if **genException( )** had caught the exception itself, it never would have been passed back to **main( )**.

Progress Check

1. What is an exception?
2. Code monitored for exceptions must be part of what statement?
3. What does **catch** do? After a **catch** executes, what happens to the flow of execution?

Answers:

1. An exception is a run-time error.
2. To monitor code for exceptions, it must be part of a **try** block.
3. The **catch** receives exceptions. A **catch** is not called; thus execution does not return to the point at which the exception was generated. Rather, execution continues after the **catch** block.

THE CONSEQUENCES OF AN UNCAUGHT EXCEPTION

Catching one of Java's standard exceptions, as the preceding program does, has a side benefit: It prevents abnormal program termination. When an exception is thrown, it must be caught by some piece of code, somewhere. In general, if your program does not catch an exception, then it will be caught by the JVM. The trouble is that the JVM's default exception handler terminates execution and displays an error message followed by a list of the method calls that lead to the exception. (This list is commonly referred to as a *stack trace*.) For example, in this version of the preceding example, the program does not catch the index out-of-bounds exception.

```
// Let JVM handle the error.
class NotHandled {
  public static void main(String[] args) {
    int[] nums = new int[4];

    System.out.println("Before exception is generated.");

    // generate an index out-of-bounds exception
    nums[7] = 10;
  }
}
```

When the array index error occurs, execution is halted, and the following error message is displayed.

```
Exception in thread "main" java.lang.ArrayIndexOutOfBoundsException: 7
        at NotHandled.main(NotHandled.java:9)
```

Although such a message is useful for you while debugging, it would not be something that you would want others to see, to say the least! This is why it is important for your program to handle exceptions itself, rather than rely on the JVM.

As mentioned earlier, the type of the exception must match the type specified in a **catch**. If it doesn't, the exception won't be caught. For example, the following program tries to catch an array boundary error with a **catch** for an **ArithmeticException** (another of Java's built-in exceptions). When the array boundary is overrun, an **ArrayIndexOutOfBoundsException** is generated, but it won't be caught by the **catch**. This results in abnormal program termination.

```
// This won't work!
class ExcTypeMismatch {
  public static void main(String[] args) {
    int[] nums = new int[4];

    try {
      System.out.println("Before exception is generated.");

      //generate an index out-of-bounds exception
      nums[7] = 10;    ◄
      System.out.println("this won't be displayed");
```

This throws an **ArrayIndexOutOfBoundsException**.

```
    }

    /* Can't catch an array boundary error with an
       ArithmeticException. */
    catch (ArithmeticException exc) {          This tries to catch it with an
      // catch the exception                   ArithmeticException.
      System.out.println("Index out-of-bounds!");
    }
    System.out.println("After catch.");
  }
}
```

The output is shown here.

```
Before exception is generated.
Exception in thread "main" java.lang.ArrayIndexOutOfBoundsException: 7
        at ExcTypeMismatch.main(ExcTypeMismatch.java:10)
```

As the output demonstrates, a **catch** for **ArithmeticException** won't catch an **ArrayIndexOutOfBoundsException**.

EXCEPTIONS ENABLE YOU TO HANDLE ERRORS GRACEFULLY

One of the key benefits of exception handling is that it enables your program to respond to an error in a graceful, rational way. In some cases, it may be possible to fix the problem and allow the program to continue running. For example, if the user attempts to open a file, but specifies an invalid file name, you could reprompt the user, asking for a new file name. In other cases, the error can't be fixed, but program execution can continue. For example, a network connection might time-out, but a program using that connection may be performing other tasks that are not dependent on that connection. In such a case, you can inform the user about the problem, cancel the operation that caused the exception, but let the other parts of the program continue. Of course, in some cases, there is no way to fix or bypass a problem and program execution must be terminated. However, even in these cases, you should do an orderly shutdown.

To give you a sense of how an exception handler can prevent abrupt program termination, consider the following example. It divides the elements of one array by the elements of another. If a division by zero occurs, an **ArithmeticException** is generated. In the program, this exception is handled by reporting the error and then continuing with execution. Thus, attempting to divide by zero does not cause an abrupt run-time error resulting in the termination of the program. Instead, it is handled and program execution is allowed to continue. Of course, it is trivially easy to prevent a divide-by-zero error in the first place by ensuring that the denominator is not zero prior to the division. However, producing divide-by-zero errors gives us an easy way to generate exceptions for the purposes of demonstration.

```
// Handle error and continue.
class ExcDemo3 {
  public static void main(String[] args) {
    int[] numer = { 4, 8, 16, 32, 64, 128 };
    int[] denom = { 2, 0, 4, 4, 0, 8 };

    for(int i=0; i<numer.length; i++) {
      try {
        System.out.println(numer[i] + " / " +
                          denom[i] + " is " +
                          numer[i]/denom[i]);
      }
      catch (ArithmeticException exc) {
        // catch the exception
        System.out.println("Can't divide by Zero!");
      }
    }
  }
}
```

The output from the program is shown here.

```
4 / 2 is 2
Can't divide by Zero!
16 / 4 is 4
32 / 4 is 8
Can't divide by Zero!
128 / 8 is 16
```

This example makes another important point: Once an exception has been handled, it is removed from the system. Therefore, in the program, each pass through the loop enters the **try** block anew; any prior exceptions have been handled. This enables your program to handle repeated errors.

Progress Check

1. Does the exception type in a **catch** clause matter?
2. What happens if an exception is not caught?
3. When an exception occurs, what should your program do?

Answers:

1. The type of exception in a **catch** must match the type of exception that you want to catch.
2. An uncaught exception ultimately leads to abnormal program termination.
3. A program should handle exceptions in a rational, graceful manner, eliminating the cause of the exception if possible and then continuing.

USING MULTIPLE catch CLAUSES

As stated earlier, you can associate more than one **catch** clause with a **try**. In fact, it is common to do so. However, each **catch** must catch a different type of exception. For example, the program shown here is a variation on the previous one. It catches both array boundary and divide-by-zero errors. In this version, the length of **numer** is longer than that of **denom**. Thus, at some point, an array boundary error will be produced. The additional **catch** clause will handle it.

```java
// Use multiple catch clauses.
class ExcDemo4 {
  public static void main(String[] args) {
    // Here, numer is longer than denom.
    int[] numer = { 4, 8, 16, 32, 64, 128, 256, 512 };
    int[] denom = { 2, 0, 4, 4, 0, 8 };

    for(int i=0; i<numer.length; i++) {
      try {
        System.out.println(numer[i] + " / " +
                           denom[i] + " is " +
                           numer[i]/denom[i]);
      }
      catch (ArithmeticException exc) {        ◄——————————— Multiple catch clauses
        // catch the exception
        System.out.println("Can't divide by Zero!");
      }
      catch (ArrayIndexOutOfBoundsException exc) {◄
        // catch the exception
        System.out.println("No matching element found.");
      }
    }
  }
}
```

This program produces the following output:

```
4 / 2 is 2
Can't divide by Zero!
16 / 4 is 4
32 / 4 is 8
Can't divide by Zero!
128 / 8 is 16
No matching element found.
No matching element found.
```

As the output confirms, each **catch** responds only to its own type of exception.

In general, **catch** clauses are checked in the order in which they occur in a program. Only a matching clause is executed. All other **catch** blocks are ignored.

CATCHING SUBCLASS EXCEPTIONS

There is one important point about multiple **catch** clauses that relates to subclasses. A **catch** clause for a superclass will also match any of its subclasses. If you want to catch exceptions of both a superclass type and a subclass type, put the subclass first in the **catch** sequence. If you don't, then the superclass **catch** will also catch all derived classes. This rule is self-enforcing because putting the superclass first causes unreachable code to be created, since the subclass **catch** clause can never execute. In Java, unreachable code causes a compile-time error.

For example, consider the following program. It generates both an **ArrayIndexOutOfBoundsException** and an **ArithmeticException**. However, it catches **ArrayIndexOutOfBoundsException** and **Exception**. This works because **Exception** is the superclass for all program-related exceptions. These include **ArrayIndexOutOfBoundsException** and **ArithmeticException**, among many others. This means that catching **Exception** also catches **ArithmeticException**.

```
// Subclasses must precede superclasses in catch clauses.
class ExcDemo5 {
  public static void main(String[] args) {
    // Here, numer is longer than denom.
    int[] numer = { 4, 8, 16, 32, 64, 128, 256, 512 };
    int[] denom = { 2, 0, 4, 4, 0, 8 };

    for(int i=0; i<numer.length; i++) {
      try {
        System.out.println(numer[i] + " / " +
                           denom[i] + " is " +
                           numer[i]/denom[i]);
      }
      catch (ArrayIndexOutOfBoundsException exc) {  ◀———————Catch subclass
        // catch the exception
        System.out.println("No matching element found.");
      }
      catch (Exception exc) {  ◀———————Catch superclass
        System.out.println("Some exception occurred.");
      }
    }
  }
}
```

The output from the program is shown here.

```
4 / 2 is 2
Some exception occurred.
16 / 4 is 4
32 / 4 is 8
```

```
Some exception occurred.
128 / 8 is 16
No matching element found.
No matching element found.
```

In this case, the first **catch** clause handles **ArrayIndexOutOfBoundsException**. The second one catches all other program-related exceptions, including **ArithmeticException** generated when a division by zero occurs.

The order of the **catch** clauses in the preceding example is important. As explained, a subclass exception must be caught before its superclass exception. As an experiment, try reversing the two **catch** clauses like this:

```java
// This looks right, but is actually wrong!
catch (Exception exc) {
   System.out.println("Some exception occurred.");
}
catch (ArrayIndexOutOfBoundsException exc) {
   // catch the exception
   System.out.println("No matching element found.");
}
```

Although it "looks right," this sequence won't compile. The first **catch** statement will catch all exceptions and the second **catch** will never be reached, thus producing a compile-time error.

Ask the Expert

Q Why would I want to catch superclass exceptions?

A There are, of course, a variety of reasons. Here are a couple. First, if you add a **catch** clause that catches exceptions of type **Exception**, then you have effectively added a "catch all" clause to your exception handler that deals with all program-related exceptions. Although not recommended for normal use, such a "catch all" clause might be useful in a situation in which abnormal program termination must be avoided no matter what happens, such as during debugging. Second, in some situations, the same clause can handle an entire category of exceptions. Catching the superclass of these exceptions allows you to handle all without duplicated code.

try BLOCKS CAN BE NESTED

One **try** block can be nested within another. An exception generated within the inner **try** block that is not caught by a **catch** associated with that **try** is propagated to the outer **try** block. For example, here the **ArrayIndexOutOfBoundsException** is not caught by the inner **catch**, but by the outer **catch**.

```
// Use a nested try block.
class NestTrys {
  public static void main(String[] args) {
    // Here, numer is longer than denom.
    int[] numer = { 4, 8, 16, 32, 64, 128, 256, 512 };
    int[] denom = { 2, 0, 4, 4, 0, 8 };

    try { // outer try  ◄──────────────────────── Nested try blocks
      for(int i=0; i<numer.length; i++) {
        try { // nested try ◄───────────────────────────┐
          System.out.println(numer[i] + " / " +
                             denom[i] + " is " +
                             numer[i]/denom[i]);
        }
        catch (ArithmeticException exc) {
          // catch the exception
          System.out.println("Can't divide by Zero!");
        }
      }
    }
    catch (ArrayIndexOutOfBoundsException exc) {
      // catch the exception
      System.out.println("No matching element found.");
      System.out.println("Fatal error - program terminated.");
    }
  }
}
```

The output from the program is shown here.

```
4 / 2 is 2
Can't divide by Zero!
16 / 4 is 4
32 / 4 is 8
Can't divide by Zero!
128 / 8 is 16
No matching element found.
Fatal error - program terminated.
```

In this example, an exception that can be handled by the inner **try**—in this case, a divide-by-zero error—allows the program to continue. However, an array boundary error is caught by the outer **try**, which causes the program to terminate.

Although certainly not the only reason for nested **try** statements, the preceding program makes an important point that can be generalized. Often nested **try** blocks are used to allow different categories of errors to be handled in different ways. Some types of errors are catastrophic and cannot be fixed. Some are minor and can be handled immediately. Many programmers use an outer **try** block to catch the most severe errors, allowing inner **try** blocks to handle less serious ones, if possible.

Progress Check

1. Can one **try** block be used to handle two or more different types of exceptions?
2. Can a **catch** for a superclass exception also catch subclasses of that superclass?
3. In nested **try** blocks, what happens to an exception that is not caught by the inner block?

THROWING AN EXCEPTION

The preceding examples have been catching exceptions generated automatically by the JVM. However, it is possible to manually throw an exception by using the **throw** statement. Its general form is shown here.

throw *exceptOb*;

Here, *exceptOb* must be an object of an exception class derived from **Throwable**.

Here is an example that illustrates the **throw** statement by manually throwing an **ArithmeticException**.

```java
// Manually throw an exception.
class ThrowDemo {
  public static void main(String[] args) {
    try {
      System.out.println("Before throw.");
      throw new ArithmeticException();  // ←——— Throw an exception.
    }
    catch (ArithmeticException exc) {
      // catch the exception
      System.out.println("Exception caught.");
    }
    System.out.println("After try/catch block.");
  }
}
```

The output from the program is shown here.

```
Before throw.
Exception caught.
After try/catch block.
```

Answers:

1. Yes.
2. Yes.
3. An exception not caught by an inner **try/catch** block moves outward to the enclosing **try** block.

Notice how the **ArithmeticException** was created using **new** in the **throw** statement. Remember, **throw** throws an object. Thus, you must create an object for it to throw. That is, you can't just throw a type.

Ask the Expert

Q Why would I want to manually throw an exception?

A Most often, the exceptions that you will throw will be instances of exception classes that you created. As you will see later in this chapter, creating your own exception classes allows you to handle errors in your code as part of your program's overall exception handling strategy.

Rethrowing an Exception

An exception caught by one **catch** can be rethrown so that it can be caught by an outer **catch**. The most likely reason for rethrowing this way is to allow multiple handlers access to the exception. For example, perhaps one exception handler manages one aspect of an exception, and a second handler copes with another aspect. Remember, when you rethrow an exception, it will not be recaught by the same **catch** clause. It will propagate to an outer **catch**. To rethrow an exception, use a **throw** statement inside a **catch** clause, throwing the exception passed as an argument.

The following program illustrates rethrowing an exception.

```
// Rethrow an exception.
class Rethrow {
  public static void genException() {
    // here, numer is longer than denom
    int[] numer = { 4, 8, 16, 32, 64, 128, 256, 512 };
    int[] denom = { 2, 0, 4, 4, 0, 8 };

    for(int i=0; i<numer.length; i++) {
      try {
        System.out.println(numer[i] + " / " +
                           denom[i] + " is " +
                           numer[i]/denom[i]);
      }
      catch (ArithmeticException exc) {
        // catch the exception
        System.out.println("Can't divide by Zero!");
      }
      catch (ArrayIndexOutOfBoundsException exc) {
        // catch the exception
        System.out.println("No matching element found.");
        throw exc; // rethrow the exception    ———— Rethrow the exception.
      }
```

```
        }
      }
   }

class RethrowDemo {
   public static void main(String[] args) {
      try {
         Rethrow.genException();
      }
      catch(ArrayIndexOutOfBoundsException exc) {    ◄─────── Catch rethrown exception.
         // recatch exception
         System.out.println("Fatal error - " +
                            "program terminated.");
      }
   }
}
```

In this program, divide-by-zero errors are handled locally, by **genException( )**, but an array boundary error is rethrown. In this case, it is caught by **main( )**.

Progress Check

1. What does **throw** do?
2. Does **throw** throw types or objects?
3. Can an exception be rethrown after it is caught?

A CLOSER LOOK AT Throwable

Up to this point, we have been catching exceptions, but we haven't been doing anything with the exception object itself. As the preceding examples all show, a **catch** clause specifies an exception type and a parameter. The parameter receives the exception object. Since all exceptions are subclasses of **Throwable**, all exceptions support the methods defined by **Throwable**. Several commonly used ones are shown in Table 10-1.

Of the methods defined by **Throwable**, two of the most interesting are **printStackTrace( )** and **toString( )**. You can display the standard error message plus a record of the method calls that lead up to the exception by calling **printStackTrace( )**. You can use **toString( )** to retrieve the standard error message associated with the exception. The **toString( )** method is also called when an exception is used as an argument to **println( )**. The following program demonstrates these methods.

Answers:

1. **throw** generates an exception.
2. **throw** throws objects. These objects must be instances of valid exception classes, of course.
3. Yes.

TABLE 10-1: Several Commonly Used Methods Defined by Throwable	
Method	**Description**
Throwable fillInStackTrace( )	Returns a **Throwable** object that contains a completed stack trace. This object can be rethrown.
String getLocalizedMessage( )	Returns a localized description of the exception.
String getMessage( )	Returns a description of the exception.
void printStackTrace( )	Displays the stack trace.
void printStackTrace(PrintStream *stream*)	Sends the stack trace to the specified stream.
void printStackTrace(PrintWriter *stream*)	Sends the stack trace to the specified stream.
String toString( )	Returns a **String** object containing a complete description of the exception. This method is called by **println( )**, for example, when outputting a **Throwable** object.

```java
// Using two Throwable methods.

class ExcTest {
  static void genException() {
    int[] nums = new int[4];

    System.out.println("Before exception is generated.");

    // generate an index out-of-bounds exception
    nums[7] = 10;
    System.out.println("this won't be displayed");
  }
}

class UseThrowableMethods {
  public static void main(String[] args) {

    try {
      ExcTest.genException();
    }
    catch (ArrayIndexOutOfBoundsException exc) {
      // catch the exception
      System.out.println("Standard message is: ");
      System.out.println(exc);
      System.out.println("\nStack trace: ");
      exc.printStackTrace();
    }
    System.out.println("After catch.");
  }
}
```

The output from this program is shown here.

```
Before exception is generated.
Standard message is:
java.lang.ArrayIndexOutOfBoundsException: 7

Stack trace:
java.lang.ArrayIndexOutOfBoundsException: 7
    at ExcTest.genException(UseThrowableMethods.java:10)
    at UseThrowableMethods.main(UseThrowableMethods.java:19)
After catch.
```

Pay special attention to the stack trace. It shows the order in which the methods that lead to the exception are called, with the last method called on top. Here, the stack trace shows that **main( )** called **genException( )**. Since **genException( )** is on top, it is the method in which the exception occurred.

USING finally

Sometimes you will want to define a block of code that will execute when a **try/catch** block is left. For example, an exception might cause an error that terminates the current method, causing its premature return. However, the method may need to perform some action before it ends. For example, it may have allocated some resource that needs to be released. It is important that an exception not prevent the resource from being released. Circumstances of this type are common in programming, and Java provides a convenient way to handle them: **finally**.

A **finally** block will be executed whenever execution leaves a **try/catch** block, no matter what condition causes it. That is, whether the **try** block ends normally, or because of an exception, the last code executed is that defined by **finally**. The **finally** block is also executed if any code within the **try** block or any of its **catch** clauses return from a method.

To specify a **finally** block, add it to the end of a **try/catch** sequence. The general form of a **try/catch** that includes **finally** is shown here.

```
try {
  // block of code to monitor for errors
}
catch (ExcepType1 exOb) {
  // handler for ExcepType1
}
catch (ExcepType2 exOb) {
  // handler for ExcepType2
}
//...
finally {
  // finally code
}
```

Here is an example of **finally**.

```
// Use finally.
class UseFinally {
  public static void genException(int what) {
    int t;
    int[] nums = new int[2];

    System.out.println("Receiving " + what);
    try {
      switch(what) {
        case 0:
          t = 10 / what; // generate div-by-zero error
          break;
        case 1:
          nums[4] = 4; // generate array index error.
          break;
        case 2:
          return; // return from try block
      }
    }
    catch (ArithmeticException exc) {
      // catch the exception
      System.out.println("Can't divide by Zero!");
      return; // return from catch
    }
    catch (ArrayIndexOutOfBoundsException exc) {
      // catch the exception
      System.out.println("No matching element found.");
    }
    finally { ◄─────────────────────── This is executed on way out of try/catch blocks.
      System.out.println("Leaving try.");
    }
  }
}

class FinallyDemo {
  public static void main(String[] args) {

    for(int i=0; i < 3; i++) {
      UseFinally.genException(i);
      System.out.println();
    }
  }
}
```

Here is the output produced by the program.

```
Receiving 0
Can't divide by Zero!
Leaving try.
```

```
Receiving 1
No matching element found.
Leaving try.

Receiving 2
Leaving try.
```

As the output shows, no matter how the **try** block is exited, the **finally** block is executed.

Progress Check

1. Exception classes are subclasses of what class?
2. When is the code within a **finally** block executed?
3. How can you display a stack trace of the events leading up to an exception?

USING throws

In some cases, if a method generates an exception that it does not handle, it must declare that exception in a **throws** clause. Here is the general form of a method that includes a **throws** clause.

> *ret-type methName(param-list)* throws *except-list* {
>
>   // body
>
> }

Here, *except-list* is a comma-separated list of exceptions that the method might throw outside of itself.

You might be wondering why you did not need to specify a **throws** clause for some of the preceding examples, which threw exceptions outside of methods. The answer is that exceptions that are subclasses of **Error** or **RuntimeException** don't need to be specified in a **throws** list. Java simply assumes that a method may throw one. All other types of exceptions *do* need to be declared. Failure to do so causes a compile-time error.

Actually, you saw an example of a **throws** clause earlier in this book. As you will recall, when performing keyboard input, you needed to add the clause

```
throws java.io.IOException
```

to **main( )**. Now you can understand why. An input statement might generate an **IOException**, and at that time, we weren't able to handle that exception. Thus, such

---

Answers:

1. **Throwable**
2. A **finally** block is the last thing executed when a **try/catch** block is exited.
3. To print a stack trace, call **printStackTrace( )**, which is defined by **Throwable**.

an exception would be thrown out of **main( )** and needed to be specified as such. Now that you know about exceptions, you can easily handle **IOException**.

Let's look at an example that handles **IOException**. It creates a method called **prompt( )**, which displays a prompting message and then reads a character from the keyboard. Since input is being performed, an **IOException** might occur. However, the **prompt( )** method does not handle **IOException** itself. Instead, it uses a **throws** clause, which means that the calling method must handle it. In this example, the calling method is **main( )**, and it deals with the error.

```
// Use throws.
class ThrowsDemo {
  public static char prompt(String str)
    throws java.io.IOException {          Notice the throws clause.

    System.out.print(str + ": ");
    return (char) System.in.read();
  }

  public static void main(String[] args) {
    char ch;

    try {
      ch = prompt("Enter a letter");      Since prompt( ) might throw an
    }                                      exception, a call to it must be
    catch(java.io.IOException exc) {       enclosed within a try block.
      System.out.println("I/O exception occurred.");
      ch = 'X';
    }

    System.out.println("You pressed " + ch);
  }
}
```

On a related point, notice that **IOException** is fully qualified by its package name **java.io**. As you will learn in Chapter 11, Java's I/O system is contained in the **java.io** package. Thus, the **IOException** is also contained there. It would also have been possible to import **java.io** and then refer to **IOException** directly.

JAVA'S BUILT-IN EXCEPTIONS

Inside the standard package **java.lang**, Java defines several exception classes. A few have been used by the preceding examples. The most general of these exceptions are subclasses of the standard type **RuntimeException**. Since **java.lang** is implicitly imported into all Java programs, most exceptions derived from **RuntimeException** are automatically available. Furthermore, they need not be included in any method's **throws** list. In the language of Java, these are called *unchecked exceptions* because the compiler does not check to see if a method handles or throws these exceptions. The unchecked exceptions defined in **java.lang** are listed in Table 10-2. Table 10-3 lists

TABLE 10-2: The Unchecked Exceptions Defined in java.lang

Exception	Meaning
ArithmeticException	Arithmetic error, such as divide by zero.
ArrayIndexOutOfBoundsException	Array index is out-of-bounds.
ArrayStoreException	Assignment to an array element of an incompatible type.
ClassCastException	Invalid cast.
EnumConstantNotPresentException	An attempt is made to use an undefined enumeration value.
IllegalArgumentException	Illegal argument used to invoke a method.
IllegalMonitorStateException	Illegal monitor operation, such as waiting on an unlocked thread.
IllegalStateException	Environment or application is in incorrect state.
IllegalThreadStateException	Requested operation not compatible with current thread state.
IndexOutOfBoundsException	Some type of index is out of bounds.
NegativeArraySizeException	Array created with a negative size.
NullPointerException	Invalid use of a null reference.
NumberFormatException	Invalid conversion of a string to a numeric format.
SecurityException	Attempt to violate security.
StringIndexOutOfBoundsException	Attempt to index outside the bounds of a string.
TypeNotPresentException	Type not found.
UnsupportedOperationException	An unsupported operation was encountered.

TABLE 10-3: The Checked Exceptions Defined in java.lang

Exception	Meaning
ClassNotFoundException	Class not found.
CloneNotSupportedException	Attempt to clone an object that does not implement the **Cloneable** interface.
IllegalAccessException	Access to a class is denied.
InstantiationException	Attempt to create an object of an abstract class or interface.
InterruptedException	One thread has been interrupted by another thread.
NoSuchFieldException	A requested field does not exist.
NoSuchMethodException	A requested method does not exist.
ReflectiveOperationException	Superclass of reflection-related exceptions (added by JDK 7).

those exceptions defined by **java.lang** that must be included in a method's **throws** list if that method can generate one of these exceptions and does not handle it, itself. These are called *checked exceptions*. Java defines several other types of exceptions that relate to its various class libraries, such as **IOException** mentioned earlier.

Ask the Expert

Q I have heard that Java supports something called *chained exceptions*. What are they?

A Chained exceptions were added to Java by JDK 1.4. The chained exception feature allows you to specify one exception as the underlying cause of another. For example, imagine a situation in which a method throws an **ArithmeticException** because of an attempt to divide by zero. However, the actual cause of the problem was that an I/O error occurred, which caused the divisor to be set improperly. Although the method must certainly throw an **ArithmeticException**, since that is the error that occurred, you might also want to let the calling code know that the underlying cause was an I/O error. Chained exceptions let you handle this, and any other situation, in which layers of exceptions exist.

To allow chained exceptions, two constructors and two methods were added to **Throwable**. The constructors are shown here:

Throwable(Throwable *causeExc*)
Throwable(String *msg*, Throwable *causeExc*)

In the first form, *causeExc* is the exception that causes the current exception. That is, *causeExc* is the underlying reason that an exception occurred. The second form allows you to specify a description at the same time that you specify a cause exception. These two constructors have also been added to the **Error**, **Exception**, and **RuntimeException** classes.

The chained exception methods added to **Throwable** are **getCause( )** and **initCause( )**. These methods are shown here:

Throwable getCause( )
Throwable initCause(Throwable *causeExc*)

The **getCause( )** method returns the exception that underlies the current exception. If there is no underlying exception, **null** is returned. The **initCause( )** method associates *causeExc* with the invoking exception and returns a reference to the exception. Thus, you can associate a cause with an exception after the exception has been created. In general, **initCause( )** is used to set a cause for legacy exception classes that don't support the two additional constructors described earlier.

Chained exceptions are not something that many programs will need. However, in cases in which knowledge of an underlying cause is useful, they offer an elegant solution.

Progress Check

1. What is **throws** used for?
2. What is the difference between checked and unchecked exceptions?
3. If a method generates an exception that it handles, must it include a **throws** clause for the exception?

NEW EXCEPTION FEATURES ADDED BY JDK 7

With the release of JDK 7, Java's exception handling mechanism has been expanded by the addition of three new features. The first automates the process of releasing a resource, such as a file, when it is no longer needed. It is based on an expanded form of **try**, called the *try-with-resources* statement, and it is described in Chapter 11, when files are discussed. The second new feature is called *multi-catch*, and the third is sometimes called *final rethrow* or *more precise rethrow*. These two features are described here.

Multi-catch allows two or more exceptions to be caught by the same **catch** clause. As you learned earlier, it is possible (indeed, common) for a **try** to be followed by two or more **catch** clauses. Although each **catch** clause often supplies its own unique code sequence, it is not uncommon to have situations in which two or more **catch** clauses execute *the same code sequence* even though they catch different exceptions. Instead of having to catch each exception type individually, you can now use a single **catch** clause to handle them without code duplication.

To create a multi-catch, specify a list of exceptions within a single **catch** clause. You do this by separating each exception type in the list with the OR operator. Each multi-catch parameter is implicitly **final**. (You can explicitly specify **final**, if desired, but it is not necessary.) Because each multi-catch parameter is implicitly **final**, it can't be assigned a new value.

Here is how you can use the multi-catch feature to catch both **ArithmeticException** and **ArrayIndexOutOfBoundsException** with a single **catch** clause:

```
catch(final ArithmeticException | ArrayIndexOutOfBoundsException e) {
```

Here is a simple program that demonstrates the use of this multi-catch:

```
// Use the multi-catch feature.  Note: This code requires JDK 7 or
// later to compile.
class MultiCatch {
  public static void main(String[] args) {
    int a=88, b=0;
    int result;
```

Answers:

1. When a method generates a checked exception that it does not handle, it must state this fact using a **throws** clause.
2. No **throws** clause is needed for unchecked exceptions.
3. No. A **throws** clause is needed only when the method does not handle the exception.

```
      char[] chrs = { 'A', 'B', 'C' };

    for(int i=0; i < 2; i++) {
      try {
        if(i == 0)
          result = a / b; // generate an ArithmeticException
        else
          chrs[5] = 'X'; // generate an ArrayIndexOutOfBoundsException

        // This catch clause catches both exceptions.
      }
      catch(ArithmeticException | ArrayIndexOutOfBoundsException e) {
        System.out.println("Exception caught: " + e);
      }
    }

    System.out.println("After multi-catch.");
  }
}
```

The program will generate an **ArithmeticException** when the division by zero is attempted. It will generate an **ArrayIndexOutOfBoundsException** when the attempt is made to access outside the bounds of **chrs**. Both exceptions are caught by the single **catch**.

The more precise rethrow feature restricts the type of exceptions that can be rethrown to only those checked exceptions that the associated **try** block throws, that are not handled by a preceding **catch** clause, and that are a subtype or supertype of the parameter. While this capability might not be needed often, it is now available for use. For the final rethrow feature to be in force, the **catch** parameter must be effectively final. This means that it must not be assigned a new value inside the **catch** block. It can also be explicitly specified as **final**, but this is not necessary.

CREATING EXCEPTION SUBCLASSES

Although Java's built-in exceptions handle most common errors, Java's exception handling mechanism is not limited to these errors. In fact, part of the power of Java's approach to exceptions is its ability to handle exceptions that you create which correspond to errors in your own code. Creating an exception is easy. Just define a subclass of **Exception** (which is, of course, a subclass of **Throwable**). Your subclasses don't need to actually implement anything—it is their existence in the type system that allows you to use them as exceptions.

The **Exception** class does not define any methods of its own. It does, of course, inherit those methods provided by **Throwable**. Thus, all exceptions, including those that you create, have the methods defined by **Throwable** available to them. You can override one or more of these methods in exception subclasses that you create.

Two commonly used **Exception** constructors are shown here:

    Exception( )
    Exception(String *msg*)

The first form creates an exception that has no description. The second form lets you specify a description of the exception.

Although specifying a description when an exception is created is often useful, sometimes it is better to override **toString( )**. Here's why: The version of **toString( )** defined by **Throwable** (and inherited by **Exception**) first displays the name of the exception followed by a colon, which is then followed by your description. By overriding **toString( )**, you can prevent the exception name and colon from being displayed. This makes for a cleaner output, which is desirable in some cases. Of course, you can specify a message *and* override **toString( )**. This way, the **getMessage( )** method defined by **Throwable** will return something other than null.

Here is an example that creates an exception called **NonIntResultException**, which is generated when the result of dividing two integer values produces a result with a fractional component. **NonIntResultException** has two fields that hold the integer values; a constructor; and an override of the **toString( )** method, allowing a friendlier description of the exception to be displayed using **println( )**. It also passes a message string to the **Exception** constructor for the sake of completeness, but it is not used in the program.

```java
// Use a custom exception.

// Create an exception.
class NonIntResultException extends Exception {
  int n;
  int d;

  NonIntResultException(int i, int j) {
    super("Result is not an integer.");
    n = i;
    d = j;
  }

  public String toString() {
    return "Result of " + n + " / " + d +
           " is non-integer.";
  }
}

class CustomExceptDemo {
  public static void main(String[] args) {

    // Here, numer contains some odd values.
    int[] numer = { 4, 8, 15, 32, 64, 127, 256, 512 };
    int[] denom = { 2, 0, 4, 4, 0, 8 };

    for(int i=0; i<numer.length; i++) {
```

```
        try {
          if((numer[i]%denom[i]) != 0)
             throw new
               NonIntResultException(numer[i], denom[i]);

          System.out.println(numer[i] + " / " +
                                denom[i] + " is " +
                                numer[i]/denom[i]);
        }
        catch (ArithmeticException exc) {
          // catch the exception
          System.out.println("Can't divide by Zero!");
        }
        catch (ArrayIndexOutOfBoundsException exc) {
          // catch the exception
          System.out.println("No matching element found.");
        }
        catch (NonIntResultException exc) {
          System.out.println(exc);
        }
      }
    }
}
```

The output from the program is shown here.

```
4 / 2 is 2
Can't divide by Zero!
Result of 15 / 4 is non-integer.
32 / 4 is 8
Can't divide by Zero!
Result of 127 / 8 is non-integer.
No matching element found.
No matching element found.
```

Ask the Expert

Q When should I use exception handling in a program? When should I create my own custom exception classes?

A Since the Java API makes extensive use of exceptions to report errors, nearly all real-world programs will make use of exception handling. This is the part of exception handling that most new Java programmers find easy. It is harder to decide when and how to use your own custom-made exceptions. In general, errors can be reported in two ways: return values and exceptions. When is one approach better than the other? Simply put, in Java, exception handling should be the norm. Certainly, returning an error code is a valid alternative in some cases, but exceptions provide a more powerful, structured way to handle errors. They are the way professional Java programmers handle errors in their code.

TRY THIS 10-1   ADD EXCEPTIONS TO THE SIMPLE STACK CLASSES

```
SimpleStackExc.java
FixedLengthStack.java
ISimpleStack.java
SimpleStackExcDemo.java
```

In this project, you will create two exception classes that can be used by the stack classes developed by Try This 8-1. They will indicate the stack-full and stack-empty conditions. These exceptions will be thrown, respectively, by the **push( )** and **pop( )** methods to report errors. This project will then add these exceptions to the **FixedLengthStack** class. In Exercise 19, you will be asked to add them to **DynamicStack**. As you will see, using exceptions to report errors is a substantial improvement to the stack classes.

STEP-BY-STEP

1. Create a file called **SimpleStackExc.java**. Into this file, add the following exceptions.

```java
/*
    Try This 10-1

    Add exception handling to the stack classes.
*/

// An exception for stack-full errors.
class StackFullException extends Exception {
  int size;

  StackFullException(int s) {
    super("Stack Full");
    size = s;
  }

  public String toString() {
    return "\nStack is full. Maximum size is " + size;
  }
}

// An exception for stack-empty errors.
class StackEmptyException extends Exception {

  StackEmptyException() {
    super("Stack Empty");
  }

  public String toString() {
```

```
      return "\nStack is empty.";
    }
}
```

A **StackFullException** is generated when an attempt is made to store an item in an already full stack. Notice that the maximum size of the stack is passed to the constructor so that this information can be reported to the user. A **StackEmptyException** is generated when an attempt is made to remove an element from an empty stack. For completeness, each passes a message string to the **Exception** constructor, but both also override **toString( )**.

2. Modify the **FixedLengthStack** class so that it throws exceptions when an error occurs, as shown here.

```
// A fixed-length stack for characters that uses exceptions.
class FixedLengthStack implements ISimpleStack {
  private char[] data; // this array holds the stack
  private int tos; // index of top of stack

  // Construct an empty stack given its size.
  FixedLengthStack(int size) {
    data = new char[size]; // create the array to hold the stack
    tos = 0;
  }

  // Construct a stack from a stack.
  FixedLengthStack(FixedLengthStack otherStack) {
    // size of new stack equals that of otherStack
    data = new char[otherStack.data.length];

    // set tos to the same position
    tos = otherStack.tos;

    // copy the contents
    for(int i = 0; i < tos; i++)
      data[i] = otherStack.data[i];
  }

  // Construct a stack with initial values.
  FixedLengthStack(char[] chrs) throws StackFullException {
    // create the array to hold the initial values
    data = new char[chrs.length];
    tos = 0;

    // initialize the stack by pushing the contents
    // of chrs onto it
    for(char ch : chrs)
      push(ch);
  }

  // Push a character onto the stack.
```

```
public void push(char ch) throws StackFullException {
  if(isFull())
    throw new StackFullException(data.length);

  data[tos] = ch;
  tos++;
}

// Pop a character from the stack.
public char pop() throws StackEmptyException {
  if(isEmpty())
    throw new StackEmptyException();

  tos--;
  return data[tos];
}

// Return true if the stack is empty.
public boolean isEmpty() {
  return tos==0;
}

// Return true if the stack is full.
public boolean isFull() {
  return tos==data.length;
}
}
```

Notice that two steps are required to add exceptions to **push( )** and **pop( )**. First, each must have a **throws** clause added to its declaration. Second, when an error occurs, these methods throw the appropriate exception. Using exceptions allows the calling code to handle the error in a rational fashion. You might recall that the previous version simply reported the error. Throwing an exception is a much better approach. Moreover, it is the *proper* approach.

One other point: Notice that the constructor **FixedLengthStack(char[ ] chrs)** also has a **throws StackFullException** clause. This is because **push( )** is used to initialize the stack with the characters in **chrs**. Because **push( )** can throw an exception, any method that uses **push( )** must either handle that exception or pass it along to the calling code. In this case, the constructor simply passes it along. Of course, in this constructor, no such exception should occur because **data** is large enough to accommodate the characters in **chrs**, but the compiler still requires us to handle the possibility.

3. Since **FixedLengthStack** implements the **ISimpleStack** interface, **ISimpleStack** will need to be changed to reflect the **throws** clause. Here is the updated **ISimpleStack**. Remember, this must remain in a file by itself called **ISimpleStack.java**.

```
// A simple stack interface that throws exceptions.
public interface ISimpleStack {

  // Push a character onto the stack.
  void push(char ch) throws StackFullException;

  // Pop a character from the stack.
  char pop() throws StackEmptyException;

  // Return true if the stack is empty.
  boolean isEmpty();

  // Return true if the stack is full.
  boolean isFull();
}
```

4. To try the updated **FixedLengthStack** class, create the **SimpleStack-ExcDemo** class shown here and put it in a file called **SimpleStack-ExcDemo.java**.

```java
// Demonstrate the stack exceptions.
class SimpleStackExcDemo {
  public static void main(String[] args) {
    FixedLengthStack stack = new FixedLengthStack(5);
    char ch;
    int i;

    try {
      // overrun the stack
      for(i=0; i < 6; i++) {
        System.out.print("Attempting to push : " +
                          (char) ('A' + i));
        stack.push((char) ('A' + i));
        System.out.println(" - OK");
      }
      System.out.println();
    }
    catch (StackFullException exc) {
      System.out.println(exc);
    }

    System.out.println();

    try {
      // over-empty the stack
      for(i=0; i < 6; i++) {
        System.out.print("Popping next char: ");
        ch = stack.pop();
        System.out.println(ch);
      }
    }
```

```
        catch (StackEmptyException exc) {
          System.out.println(exc);
        }
      }
  }
```

5. Now, compile **SimpleStackExc.java**, **ISimpleStack.java**, and **Fixed-LengthStack.java**. Finally, compile and run **SimpleStackExcDemo.java**. You will see the following output.

```
Attempting to push : A - OK
Attempting to push : B - OK
Attempting to push : C - OK
Attempting to push : D - OK
Attempting to push : E - OK
Attempting to push : F
Stack is full. Maximum size is 5

Popping next char: E
Popping next char: D
Popping next char: C
Popping next char: B
Popping next char: A
Popping next char:
Stack is empty.
```

EXERCISES

1. What class is at the top of the exception hierarchy?
2. Briefly explain how to use **try** and **catch**.
3. What is wrong with this fragment?

```
// ...
vals[18] = 10;
catch (ArrayIndexOutOfBoundsException exc) {
  // handle error
}
```

4. What happens if an exception is not caught?
5. What is wrong with this fragment?

```
class A extends Exception { ...

class B extends A { ...
```

```
// ...

try {
  // ...
}
catch (A exc) { ... }
catch (B exc) { ... }
```

6. Can an inner **catch** rethrow an exception to an outer **catch**?

7. The **finally** block is the last bit of code executed before your program ends. True or False? Explain your answer.

8. What type of exceptions must be explicitly declared in a **throws** clause of a method?

9. What is wrong with this fragment?

```
class MyClass { // ... }
// ...
throw new MyClass();
```

10. What are the three ways that an exception can be generated?

11. What are the two direct subclasses of **Throwable**?

12. What is the multi-catch feature?

13. Should your code typically catch exceptions of type **Error**?

14. In Try This 10-1, it is mentioned that throwing an exception is preferable to printing an error message. Why is that the case?

15. Suppose **methodA( )** calls **methodB( )**, which calls **methodC( )**, which calls **methodD( )**. Also suppose that **methodA( )** catches all exceptions, **methodB( )** catches **RuntimeExceptions**, **methodC( )** catches **Arithmetic-Exceptions**, and **methodD( )** catches no exceptions. Who catches an exception or error thrown by **methodD( )** if:

    A. what is thrown is a **NullPointerException**?
    B. what is thrown is an **ArithmeticException**?
    C. what is thrown is an **Error**?

16. What is wrong with this method declaration?

```
void methodA() {
  throw new ClassNotFoundException();
}
```

17. What is wrong with this method declaration?

```
void methodB() {
  throw new RuntimeException();
  System.out.println("Exception thrown.");
}
```

18. Is it legal for a method to create a new **ArrayIndexOutOfBoundsException** and throw it even though there is no array being used anywhere by the method?

19. In Try This 10-1, two new exceptions were created for use by the **FixedLengthStack** class. Modify the **DynamicStack** class from Try This 8-1 so that it also uses these new exceptions as appropriate.

20. Simplify the following method as much as possible but in a way so that, to the user, it still behaves the same. Also rename the method to something more appropriate.

```java
int messy(int[] data) {
   int c = 0;

   for(int x : data)
      try {
         int y = 1/x;
      } catch (ArithmeticException exc) { c++; }
   return c;
}
```

21. What will be the output of the following program? Explain why.

```java
class Prog1 {
   public static void main(String[] args) {
      String[] data = {"Larry", "Moe", null, "Curly"};

      try {
         for(String s : data)
            System.out.println(s.length());
      }
      catch (Exception exc) { }
   }
}
```

22. What will be the output of the following program? Explain why.

```java
class Prog2 {
   public static void main(String[] args) {
      String[] data = {"Larry", "Moe", null, "Curly"};
      int sum = 0;

      try {
         for(String s : data)
            sum += s.length();
      }
      catch (Exception exc) { }
      System.out.println(sum);
   }
}
```

23. What will be the output of the following program? Explain why.

```java
class Prog3 {
  public static void main(String[] args) {
    String[] data = {"Larry", "Moe", null, "Curly"};
    int sum = 0;

    try {
      for(String s : data)
        sum += s.length();
      System.out.println(sum);
    }
    catch (Exception exc) { }
  }
}
```

24. What will be the output of the following program? Explain why.

```java
class Prog4 {
  public static void main(String[] args) {
    String[] data = {"Larry", "Moe", null, "Curly"};
    int sum = 0;

    for(String s : data)
      sum += s.length();
    System.out.println(sum);
  }
}
```

25. What will be the output of the following program? Explain why.

```java
class Prog5 {
  public static void main(String[] args) {
    Object[] data = {"Larry", new Prog5(), "Moe", null, "Curly"};

    try {
      for(Object s : data)
        System.out.println((String) s);
    }
    catch (Exception exc) {}
  }
}
```

26. Simplify the following method as much as possible but in such a way that, to the user of the method, it still behaves the same. Also rename the method to something more appropriate.

```java
int foolish(int x) {
  try {
    throw new RuntimeException();
  } catch (RuntimeException exc) { }
  finally { return x+3; }
}
```

27. The **finally** clause is designed for cleaning things up after handling an exception. But what happens if the code in the **finally** clause throws an exception? Is that legal? Try it and explain what happened.

CHAPTER 11

Using I/O

KEY SKILLS & CONCEPTS

- Understand the stream
- Know the difference between byte and character streams
- Know Java's byte stream classes
- Know Java's character stream classes
- Know the predefined streams
- Use byte streams
- Use byte streams for file I/O
- Automatically close a file by using **try**-with-resources
- Read and write binary data
- Use random access files
- Use character streams
- Use character streams for file I/O
- Use the **File** class
- Apply Java's type wrappers to convert numeric strings

Since the beginning of this book, you have been using parts of the Java I/O system, such as **println( )**. However, you have been doing so without much formal explanation. Because the Java I/O system is based on a hierarchy of classes, it was not possible to present its theory and details without first discussing classes, inheritance, and exceptions. Now it is time to examine Java's approach to I/O in detail.

Be forewarned, Java's I/O system is quite large, containing many classes, interfaces, and methods. Part of the reason for its size is that Java defines two complete I/O systems: one for byte I/O and the other for character I/O. It won't be possible to discuss every aspect of Java's I/O here. (An entire book could easily be dedicated to Java's I/O system!) This chapter will, however, introduce you to some of the most important and commonly used features. Fortunately, Java's I/O system is cohesive and consistent; once you understand its fundamentals, the rest of the I/O system is easy to master.

Before we begin, an important point needs to be made. The I/O classes described in this chapter support text-based console I/O and file I/O. They are not used to create graphical user interfaces (GUIs). Thus, you will not use them to create windowed applications, for example. However, Java *does* include substantial support for building graphical user interfaces. The basics of GUI programming are found in Chapter 15, where applets are introduced, and Part Two, which offers an introduction to Swing. (Swing is Java's modern GUI toolkit.)

JAVA'S I/O IS BUILT ON STREAMS

Java programs perform I/O through streams. A *stream* is an abstraction that either produces or consumes information. A stream is linked to a physical device by the Java I/O system. All streams behave in the same manner, even if the actual physical devices they are linked to differ. Thus, the same I/O classes and methods can be applied to different types of devices. For example, the same methods that you use to write to the console can also be used to write to a disk file. Java implements streams within class hierarchies defined in the **java.io** package.

BYTE STREAMS AND CHARACTER STREAMS

Modern versions of Java define two types of streams: byte and character. (The original version of Java defined only the byte stream, but character streams were quickly added.) Byte streams provide a convenient means for handling the input and output of bytes. They are used, for example, when reading or writing binary data. They are especially helpful when working with files. Character streams are designed for handling the input and output of characters. They use Unicode and, therefore, can be internationalized. Also, in some cases, character streams are more efficient than byte streams.

The fact that Java defines two different types of streams makes the I/O system quite large because two separate sets of class hierarchies (one for bytes, one for characters) are needed. The sheer number of I/O classes can make the I/O system appear more intimidating than it actually is. Just remember, for the most part, the functionality of byte streams is paralleled by that of the character streams.

One other point: at the lowest level, all I/O is still byte-oriented. The character-based streams simply provide a convenient and efficient means for handling characters.

THE BYTE STREAM CLASSES

Byte streams are defined by using two class hierarchies. At the top of these are two abstract classes: **InputStream** and **OutputStream**. **InputStream** defines the characteristics common to byte input streams, and **OutputStream** describes the behavior of byte output streams.

TABLE 11-1: The Byte Stream Classes	
Byte Stream Class	**Meaning**
BufferedInputStream	Buffered input stream
BufferedOutputStream	Buffered output stream
ByteArrayInputStream	Input stream that reads from a byte array
ByteArrayOutputStream	Output stream that writes to a byte array
DataInputStream	An input stream that contains methods for reading the primitive data types
DataOutputStream	An output stream that contains methods for writing the primitive data types
FileInputStream	Input stream that reads from a file
FileOutputStream	Output stream that writes to a file
FilterInputStream	Filtered **InputStream**
FilterOutputStream	Filtered **OutputStream**
InputStream	Abstract class that describes stream input
ObjectInputStream	Input stream for objects
ObjectOutputStream	Output stream for objects
OutputStream	Abstract class that describes stream output
PipedInputStream	Input pipe
PipedOutputStream	Output pipe
PrintStream	Output stream that contains **print( )** and **println( )**
PushbackInputStream	Input stream that allows bytes to be returned to the stream
SequenceInputStream	Input stream that is a combination of two or more input streams that will be read sequentially, one after the other

From **InputStream** and **OutputStream** are created several concrete subclasses that offer varying functionality and handle the details of reading and writing to various devices, such as disk files. The byte stream classes are shown in Table 11-1.

THE CHARACTER STREAM CLASSES

Character streams are defined by using two class hierarchies topped by these two abstract classes: **Reader** and **Writer**. **Reader** is used for input, and **Writer** is used for output. Concrete classes derived from **Reader** and **Writer** operate on Unicode character streams.

From **Reader** and **Writer** are derived several concrete subclasses that handle various I/O situations. In general, the character-based classes parallel the byte-based classes. The character stream classes are shown in Table 11-2.

TABLE 11-2: The Character Stream Classes	
Character Stream Class	**Meaning**
BufferedReader	Buffered input character stream
BufferedWriter	Buffered output character stream
CharArrayReader	Input stream that reads from a character array
CharArrayWriter	Output stream that writes to a character array
FileReader	Input stream that reads from a file
FileWriter	Output stream that writes to a file
FilterReader	Filtered reader
FilterWriter	Filtered writer
InputStreamReader	Input stream that translates bytes to characters
LineNumberReader	Input stream that counts lines
OutputStreamWriter	Output stream that translates characters to bytes
PipedReader	Input pipe
PipedWriter	Output pipe
PrintWriter	Output stream that contains **print( )** and **println( )**
PushbackReader	Input stream that allows characters to be returned to the input stream
Reader	Abstract class that describes character stream input
StringReader	Input stream that reads from a string
StringWriter	Output stream that writes to a string
Writer	Abstract class that describes character stream output

THE PREDEFINED STREAMS

As you know, all Java programs automatically import the **java.lang** package. This package defines a class called **System**, which encapsulates several aspects of the runtime environment. Among other things, it contains three predefined stream variables, called **in**, **out**, and **err**. These fields are declared as **public**, **final**, and **static** within **System**. This means that they can be used by any other part of your program and without reference to a specific **System** object.

System.out refers to the standard output stream. By default, this is the console. **System.in** refers to standard input, which is by default the keyboard. **System.err** refers to the standard error stream, which is also the console by default. However, these streams can be redirected to any compatible I/O device.

System.in is an object of type **InputStream**; **System.out** and **System.err** are objects of type **PrintStream**. These are byte streams, even though they are typically used to read and write characters from and to the console. The reason they are byte and not character streams is that the predefined streams were part of the original specification for Java, which did not include the character streams. As you will see, it is possible to wrap these within character-based streams if desired.

TABLE 11-3: The Methods Defined by InputStream

Method	Description
int available( )	Returns the number of bytes of input currently available for reading.
void close( )	Closes the input source. Further read attempts will generate an **IOException**.
void mark(int *numBytes*)	Places a mark at the current point in the input stream that will remain valid until *numBytes* bytes are read.
boolean markSupported( )	Returns **true** if **mark( )/reset( )** are supported by the invoking stream.
int read( )	Returns an integer representation of the next available byte of input. If the end of the stream is encountered, −1 is returned.
int read(byte[ ] *buffer*)	Attempts to read up to *buffer*.length bytes into *buffer* and returns the actual number of bytes that were successfully read. If the end of the stream is encountered when first attempting to read, −1 is returned.
int read(byte[ ] *buffer*, int *offset*, int *numBytes*)	Attempts to read up to *numBytes* bytes into *buffer* starting at *buffer*[*offset*], returning the number of bytes successfully read. If the end of the stream is encountered when first attempting to read, −1 is returned.
void reset( )	Resets the input pointer to the previously set mark.
long skip(long *numBytes*)	Ignores (that is, skips) *numBytes* bytes of input, returning the number of bytes actually ignored.

Progress Check

1. What is a stream?
2. What types of streams does Java define?
3. What are the built-in streams?

USING THE BYTE STREAMS

We will begin our examination of Java's I/O with the byte streams. As explained, at the top of the byte stream hierarchy are the **InputStream** and **OutputStream** classes. Table 11-3 shows the methods in **InputStream**, and Table 11-4 shows the methods in **OutputStream**. In general, the methods in **InputStream** and **OutputStream** can

---

Answers:

1. A stream is an abstraction that either produces or consumes information.
2. Java defines both byte and character streams.
3. **System.in**, **System.out**, and **System.err**

TABLE 11-4: The Methods Defined by OutputStream

Method	Description
void close( )	Closes the output stream. Further write attempts will generate an **IOException**.
void flush( )	Causes any output that has been buffered to be sent to its destination. That is, it flushes the output buffer.
void write(int *b*)	Writes a single byte to an output stream. Note that the parameter is an **int**, which allows you to call **write( )** with expressions without having to cast them back to **byte**.
void write(byte[ ] *buffer*)	Writes a complete array of bytes to an output stream.
void write(byte[ ] *buffer*, int *offset*, int *numBytes*)	Writes a subrange of *numBytes* bytes from the array *buffer*, beginning at *buffer[offset]*.

throw an **IOException** on error. The methods defined by these two abstract classes are available to all of their subclasses. Thus, they form a minimal set of I/O functions that all byte streams will have.

Reading Console Input

Originally, the only way to perform console input was to use a byte stream, and much Java code still uses the byte streams exclusively. Today, you can use byte or character streams. For commercial code, the preferred method of reading console input is to use a character-oriented stream. Doing so makes your program easier to internationalize and easier to maintain. It is also more convenient to operate directly on characters rather than converting back and forth between characters and bytes. However, for sample programs, simple utility programs for your own use, and applications that deal with raw keyboard input, using the byte streams is acceptable. For this reason, console I/O using byte streams is examined here.

Because **System.in** is an instance of **InputStream**, you automatically have access to the methods defined by **InputStream**. Unfortunately, **InputStream** defines only one input method, **read( )**, which reads bytes. There are three versions of **read( )**, which are shown here:

> int read( ) throws IOException
> int read(byte[ ] *buffer*) throws IOException
> int read(byte[ ] *buffer*, int *offset*, int *numBytes*) throws IOException

In Chapter 3 you saw how to use the first version of **read( )** to read a single character from the keyboard (from **System.in**). It returns –1 when the end of the stream is encountered. The second version reads bytes from the input stream and puts them into *buffer* until either the array is full, the end of stream is reached, or an error occurs. It returns the number of bytes read, or –1 when the end of the stream is encountered. The third version reads input into *buffer* beginning at the location specified by *offset*. Up to *numBytes* bytes are stored. It returns the number of bytes read, or –1 when the end of the stream is encountered. All throw an **IOException** when an error occurs. When reading from **System.in**, pressing ENTER generates an end-of-stream condition.

Here is a program that demonstrates reading an array of bytes from **System.in**. Notice that any I/O exceptions that might be generated are simply thrown out of **main( )**. Such an approach is common when reading from the console, but you can handle these types of errors yourself, if you choose.

```java
// Read an array of bytes from the keyboard.

import java.io.*;

class ReadBytes {
  public static void main(String[] args)
    throws IOException {
      byte[] data = new byte[10];

      System.out.println("Enter some characters.");
      int numRead = System.in.read(data);  //⟵————— Read an array of bytes
      System.out.print("You entered: ");    //         from the keyboard.
      for(int i=0; i < numRead; i++)
        System.out.print((char) data[i]);
  }
}
```

Here is a sample run:

```
Enter some characters.
Read Bytes
You entered: Read Bytes
```

Writing Console Output

As is the case with console input, Java originally provided only byte streams for console output. Java 1.1 added character streams. For the most portable code, character streams are recommended. Because **System.out** is a byte stream, however, byte-based console output is still widely used. In fact, all of the programs in this book up to this point have used it! Thus, it is examined here.

Console output is most easily accomplished with **print( )** and **println( )**, with which you are already familiar. These methods are defined by the class **PrintStream** (which is the type of the object referenced by **System.out**). Even though **System.out** is a byte stream, it is still acceptable to use this stream for simple console output.

Since **PrintStream** is an output stream derived from **OutputStream**, it also implements the low-level method **write( )**. Thus, it is possible to write to the console by using **write( )**. The simplest form of **write( )** defined by **PrintStream** is shown here:

      void write(int *b*)

This method writes the byte specified by *b*. Although *b* is declared as an integer, only the low-order 8 bits are written. Here is a short example that uses **write( )** to output the character X followed by a new line:

```
// Demonstrate System.out.write().
class WriteDemo {
  public static void main(String[] args) {
    int b;

    b = 'X';
    System.out.write(b);                    Write a byte to the screen.
    System.out.write('\n');
  }
}
```

You will not often use **write( )** to perform console output (although it might be useful in some situations), since **print( )** and **println( )** are substantially easier to use.

PrintStream supplies two additional output methods: **printf( )** and **format( )**. Both give you detailed control over the precise format of data that you output. For example, you can specify the number of decimal places displayed, a minimum field width, or the format of a negative value. These methods are examined in Chapter 24, when formatting is discussed.

Progress Check

1. What method is used to read a byte from **System.in**?
2. Other than **print( )** and **println( )**, what method can be used to write a byte to **System.out**?

READING AND WRITING FILES USING BYTE STREAMS

Java provides a number of classes and methods that allow you to read and write files. Of course, the most common types of files are disk files. In Java, all files are byte-oriented, and Java provides methods to read and write bytes from and to a file. Thus, reading and writing files using byte streams is very common. However, Java allows you to wrap a byte-oriented file stream within a character-based object, which is shown later in this chapter.

To create a byte stream linked to a file, use **FileInputStream** or **FileOutputStream**. To open a file, simply create an object of one of these classes, specifying the name of the file as an argument to the constructor. Once the file is open, you can read from or write to it.

Answers:

1. To read a byte, call **read( )**.
2. You can write a byte to **System.out** by calling **write( )**.

Inputting from a File

A file is opened for input by creating a **FileInputStream** object. One commonly used constructor is shown here:

>FileInputStream(String *fileName*) throws FileNotFoundException

Here, *fileName* specifies the name of the file you want to open. If the file does not exist, then **FileNotFoundException** is thrown. **FileNotFoundException** is a subclass of **IOException**.

To read from a file, you can use **read( )**. The version that we will use is shown here:

>int read( ) throws IOException

Each time it is called, **read( )** reads a single byte from the file and returns it as an integer value. It returns −1 when the end of the file is encountered. It throws an **IOException** when an error occurs. Thus, this version of **read( )** is the same as the one used to read from the console.

When you are done with a file, you must close it by calling **close( )**. Its general form is shown here:

>void close( ) throws IOException

Closing a file releases the system resources allocated to the file, allowing them to be used by another file. Failure to close a file can result in unused resources remaining allocated.

The following program uses **read( )** to input and display the contents of a file, the name of which is specified as a command-line argument. Notice how the **try/catch** blocks handle I/O errors that might occur.

```
/* Display a text file.

   To use this program, specify the name
   of the file that you want to see.
   For example, to see a file called TEST.TXT,
   use the following command line.

   java ShowFile TEST.TXT
*/

import java.io.*;

class ShowFile {
  public static void main(String[] args)
  {
    int i;
    FileInputStream fin;

    // First make sure that a file has been specified.
    if(args.length != 1) {
      System.out.println("Usage: ShowFile File");
```

```
      return;
    }

    try {
      fin = new FileInputStream(args[0]);  ◄─────────── Open the file.
    } catch(FileNotFoundException exc) {
      System.out.println("File Not Found");
      return;
    }

    try {
      // read bytes until EOF is encountered
      do {
        i = fin.read();  ◄─────────── Read from the file.
        if(i != -1) System.out.print((char) i);
      } while(i != -1);  ◄─────────── When i equals −1, the end of
    } catch(IOException exc) {              the file has been reached.
      System.out.println("Error reading file.");
    }

    try {
      fin.close();  ◄─────────── Close the file.
    } catch(IOException exc) {
      System.out.println("Error closing file.");
    }
  }
}
```

Notice that the preceding example closes the file stream after the **try** block that reads the file has completed. Although this approach is occasionally useful, Java supports a variation that is often a better choice. The variation is to call **close( )** within a **finally** block. In this approach, all of the code that accesses the file is contained within a **try** block, and the **finally** block is used to close the file. This way, no matter how the **try** block terminates, the file is closed. Assuming the preceding example, here is how the **try** block that reads the file can be recoded:

```
try {
  do {
    i = fin.read();
    if(i != -1) System.out.print((char) i);
  } while(i != -1);
} catch(IOException exc) {
  System.out.println("Error Reading File");
} finally {  ◄───────────────────────────────┐
  // Close file on the way out of the try block.   │   Use a finally clause to
  try {                                            │   close the file.
    fin.close();  ◄──────────────────────────────┘
  } catch(IOException exc) {
    System.out.println("Error Closing File");
  }
}
```

One advantage to this approach in general is that if the code that accesses a file terminates because of some non-I/O-related exception, the file is still closed by the **finally** block. Although not an issue in this example (or most other example programs) because the program simply ends if an unexpected exception occurs, this can be a major source of trouble in larger programs. Using **finally** avoids this trouble.

Sometimes it's easier to wrap the portions of a program that open the file and access the file within a single **try** block (rather than separating the two), and then use a **finally** block to close the file if it was successfully opened. For example, here is another way to write the **ShowFile** program:

```java
/* This variation wraps the code that opens and
   accesses the file within a single try block.
   The file is closed by the finally block.
*/

import java.io.*;

class ShowFile {
  public static void main(String[] args)
  {
    int i;
    FileInputStream fin = null;          // Here, fin is initialized to null.

    // First, confirm that a file name has been specified.
    if(args.length != 1) {
      System.out.println("Usage: ShowFile filename");
      return;
    }

    // The following code opens a file, reads characters until EOF
    // is encountered, and then closes the file via a finally block.
    try {
      fin = new FileInputStream(args[0]);

      do {
        i = fin.read();
        if(i != -1) System.out.print((char) i);
      } while(i != -1);

    } catch(FileNotFoundException exc) {
      System.out.println("File Not Found.");
    } catch(IOException exc) {
      System.out.println("An I/O Error Occurred");
    } finally {
      // Close file in all cases.
      try {
        if(fin != null) fin.close();     // Close fin only if it is not null.
      } catch(IOException exc) {
```

```
            System.out.println("Error Closing File");
        }
      }
    }
}
```

In this approach, notice that **fin** is initialized to **null**. Then, in the **finally** block, the file is closed only if **fin** is not **null**. This works because **fin** will be non-**null** only if the file was successfully opened. Thus, **close( )** will not be called if an exception occurs while opening the file.

It is possible to make the **try**/**catch** sequence in the preceding example a bit more compact. Because **FileNotFoundException** is a subclass of **IOException**, it need not be caught separately. For example, this **catch** clause could be used to catch both exceptions, eliminating the need to catch **FileNotFoundException** separately. In this case, the standard exception message, which describes the error, is displayed.

```
...
} catch(IOException exc) {
  System.out.println("I/O Error: " + exc);
} finally {
...
```

In this approach, any error, including an error opening the file, will simply be handled by the single **catch** statement. Because of its compactness, many of the I/O examples in this book use this approach. Be aware, however, that it will not be appropriate in cases in which you want to deal separately with a failure to open a file, such as might be caused if a user mistypes a file name. In such a situation, you might want to prompt for the correct name, for example, before entering a **try** block that accesses the file.

Ask the Expert

Q I noticed that **read( )** returns –1 when the end of the file has been reached, but that it does not have a special return value for a file error. Why not?

A In Java, errors are handled by exceptions. Thus, if **read( )**, or any other I/O method, returns a value, it means that no error has occurred. This is a much cleaner way than handling I/O errors by using special error codes.

Writing to a File

To open a file for output, create a **FileOutputStream** object. Here are two commonly used constructors.

FileOutputStream(String *fileName*) throws FileNotFoundException
FileOutputStream(String *fileName*, boolean *append*)
    throws FileNotFoundException

If the file cannot be created, then **FileNotFoundException** is thrown. In the first form, when an output file is opened, any preexisting file by the same name is destroyed.

In the second form, if *append* is **true**, then output is appended to the end of the file. Otherwise, the file is overwritten.

To write to a file, you will use the **write( )** method. Its simplest form is shown here:

   void write(int *b*) throws IOException

This method writes the byte specified by *b* to the file. Although *b* is declared as an integer, only the low-order 8 bits are written to the file. If an error occurs during writing, an **IOException** is thrown.

Once you are done with an output file, you must close it using **close( )**, shown here:

   void close( ) throws IOException

Closing a file releases the system resources allocated to the file, allowing them to be used by another file. It also ensures that any output remaining in a buffer is actually written out.

The following example copies a text file. The names of the source and destination files are specified on the command line.

```java
/* Copy a text file.
   To use this program, specify the name
   of the source file and the destination file.
   For example, to copy a file called FIRST.TXT
   to a file called SECOND.TXT, use the following
   command line.

   java CopyFile FIRST.TXT SECOND.TXT
*/

import java.io.*;

class CopyFile {
  public static void main(String[] args)
  {
    int i;
    FileInputStream fin = null;
    FileOutputStream fout = null;

    // First, make sure that both files has been specified.
    if(args.length != 2) {
      System.out.println("Usage: CopyFile from to");
      return;
    }

    // Copy a File.
    try {
      // Attempt to open the files.
      fin = new FileInputStream(args[0]);
      fout = new FileOutputStream(args[1]);

      do {
```

```
            i = fin.read();                          Read bytes from one file and
            if(i != -1) fout.write(i);               write them to another.
        } while(i != -1);

    } catch(IOException exc) {
      System.out.println("I/O Error: " + exc);
    } finally {
      try {
        if(fin != null) fin.close();
      } catch(IOException exc) {
        System.out.println("Error Closing Input File");
      }
      try {
        if(fout != null) fout.close();
      } catch(IOException exc) {
        System.out.println("Error Closing Output File");
      }
    }
  }
}
```

Progress Check

1. What does **read( )** return when the end of the file is reached?
2. Must a file be closed after you done using it?
3. Can a **finally** block be used to close a file?

AUTOMATICALLY CLOSING A FILE

In the preceding section, the example programs have made explicit calls to **close( )** to close a file once it is no longer needed. This is the way files have been closed since Java was first created. As a result, this approach is widespread in existing code. Furthermore, this approach is still valid and useful. However, JDK 7 adds a new feature that offers another, more streamlined way to manage resources, such as file streams, by automating the closing process. It is based on a new version of the **try** statement called *try-with-resources* and is sometimes referred to as *automatic resource management*. The principal advantage of **try**-with-resources is that it prevents situations in which a file (or other resource) is inadvertently not released after it is no longer needed.

Answers:

1. A −1 is returned by **read( )** when the end of the file is encountered.
2. Yes.
2. Yes.

The *try-with-resources* statement has this general form:

```
try (resource-specification) {
    // use the resource

}
```

Here, *resource-specification* is a statement that declares and initializes a resource, such as a file. It consists of a variable declaration in which the variable is initialized with a reference to the object being managed. When the **try** block ends, the resource is automatically released. In the case of a file, this means that the file is automatically closed. (Thus, there is no need to call **close( )** explicitly.) A **try**-with-resources statement can also include **catch** and **finally** clauses.

The **try**-with-resources statement can only be used with those resources that implement the **AutoCloseable** interface defined by **java.lang**. This interface, which was added by JDK 7, defines the **close( )** method. **AutoCloseable** is inherited by the **Closeable** interface defined in **java.io**. Both interfaces are implemented by the stream classes, including **FileInputStream** and **FileOutputStream**. Thus, **try**-with-resources can be used when working with streams, including file streams.

As a first example of automatically closing a file, here is a reworked version of the **ShowFile** program that uses it:

```
/* This version of the ShowFile program uses a try-with-resources
   statement to automatically close a file when it is no longer needed.

   Note: This code requires JDK 7 or later.
*/

import java.io.*;

class ShowFile {
  public static void main(String[] args)
  {
    int i;

    // First, make sure that a file name has been specified.
    if(args.length != 1) {
      System.out.println("Usage: ShowFile filename");
      return;
    }

    // The following code uses try-with-resources to open a file
    // and then automatically close it when the try block is left.
    try(FileInputStream fin = new FileInputStream(args[0])) {     ←——— A try-with-resources block.

      do {
        i = fin.read();
        if(i != -1) System.out.print((char) i);
      } while(i != -1);
```

```
    } catch(IOException exc) {
      System.out.println("I/O Error: " + exc);
    }
  }
}
```

In the program, pay special attention to how the file is opened within the **try**-with-resources statement:

```
try(FileInputStream fin = new FileInputStream(args[0])) {
```

Notice how the resource-specification portion of the **try** declares a **FileInputStream** called **fin**, which is then assigned a reference to the file opened by its constructor. Thus, in this version of the program the variable **fin** is local to the **try** block, being created when the **try** is entered. When the **try** is exited, the file associated with **fin** is automatically closed by an implicit call to **close( )**. You don't need to call **close( )** explicitly, which means that you can't forget to close the file. This is a key advantage of the **try**-with-resources statement.

It is important to understand that the resource declared in the **try** statement is implicitly **final**. This means that you can't assign to the resource after it has been created. Also, the scope of the resource is limited to the **try**-with-resources statement.

You can manage more than one resource within a single **try** statement. To do so, simply separate each resource specification with a semicolon. The following program shows an example. It reworks the **CopyFile** program shown earlier so that it uses a single **try**-with-resources statement to manage both **fin** and **fout**.

```
/* A version of CopyFile that uses try-with-resources.
   It demonstrates two resources (in this case files) being
   managed by a single try statement.

   Note: This code requires JDK 7 or later.
*/

import java.io.*;

class CopyFile {
  public static void main(String[] args)
  {
    int i;

    // First, confirm that both files have been specified.
    if(args.length != 2) {
      System.out.println("Usage: CopyFile from to");
      return;
    }

    // Open and manage two files via the try statement.
    try (FileInputStream fin = new FileInputStream(args[0]);     ⟵┐ Manage two
         FileOutputStream fout = new FileOutputStream(args[1]))  ⟵┘ resources.
    {
```

```
        do {
           i = fin.read();
           if(i != -1) fout.write(i);
        } while(i != -1);

     } catch(IOException exc) {
        System.out.println("I/O Error: " + exc);
     }
   }
}
```

In this program, notice how the input and output files are opened within the **try**:

```
try (FileInputStream fin = new FileInputStream(args[0]);
     FileOutputStream fout = new FileOutputStream(args[1]))
{
```

After this **try** block ends, both **fin** and **fout** will have been closed. If you compare this version of the program to the previous version, you will see that it is much shorter. The ability to streamline source code is a side-benefit of **try**-with-resources.

One other aspect of **try**-with-resources needs to be mentioned. In general, when a **try** block executes, it is possible that an exception inside the **try** block will lead to another exception that occurs when the resource is closed in a **finally** clause. In the case of a "normal" **try** statement, the original exception is lost, being preempted by the second exception. However, with a **try**-with-resources statement, the second exception is *suppressed*. It is not, however, lost. Instead, it is added to the list of suppressed exceptions associated with the first exception. The list of suppressed exceptions can be obtained by use of the **getSuppressed( )** method defined by **Throwable**.

Because of its advantages, **try**-with-resources is expected to be used extensively in new code. As such, it will be used by the remaining examples in this chapter. However, it is still very important that you are familiar with the traditional approach shown earlier in which **close( )** is called explicitly. There are several reasons for this. First, there is a large amount of legacy code in widespread use that relies on the traditional approach. It is important that all Java programmers be fully versed in and comfortable with the traditional approach when maintaining or updating this older code. Second, for a period of time, you might need to program in an environment that predates JDK 7. In such a situation, the **try**-with-resources statement will not be available and, therefore, the traditional approach must be employed. Finally, there may be cases in which explicitly closing a resource is more appropriate than the automated approach. The foregoing notwithstanding, if you are using JDK 7 or later, then you will usually want to use the new, automated approach to resource management. It offers a streamlined, robust alternative to the traditional approach.

READING AND WRITING BINARY DATA

So far, we have just been reading and writing bytes containing ASCII characters, but it is possible—indeed, common—to read and write other types of data. For example, you might want to create a file that contains **int**s, **double**s, or **short**s. To read and

TABLE 11-5: A Sampling of Output Methods Defined by DataOutputStream	
Output Method	**Purpose**
void writeBoolean(boolean *val*)	Writes the **boolean** specified by *val*.
void writeByte(int *val*)	Writes the low-order byte specified by *val*.
void writeChar(int *val*)	Writes the value specified by *val* as a **char**.
void writeDouble(double *val*)	Writes the **double** specified by *val*.
void writeFloat(float *val*)	Writes the **float** specified by *val*.
void writeInt(int *val*)	Writes the **int** specified by *val*.
void writeLong(long *val*)	Writes the **long** specified by *val*.
void writeShort(int *val*)	Writes the value specified by *val* as a **short**.

write binary values of the Java primitive types, you will use **DataInputStream** and **DataOutputStream**.

DataOutputStream implements the **DataOutput** interface. This interface defines methods that write all of Java's primitive types to a file. It is important to understand that this data is written using its internal, binary format, not its human-readable text form. Several commonly used output methods for Java's primitive types are shown in Table 11-5. Each throws an **IOException** on failure.

Here is the constructor for **DataOutputStream**. Notice that it is built on an instance of **OutputStream**.

DataOutputStream(OutputStream *outputStream*)

Here, *outputStream* is the stream to which data is written. To write output to a file, you can use the object created by **FileOutputStream** for this parameter.

DataInputStream implements the **DataInput** interface, which provides methods for reading all of Java's primitive types. A sampling of these methods is shown in Table 11-6, and each can throw an **IOException**. **DataInputStream** uses an **InputStream** instance as its foundation, overlaying it with methods that read the various Java data types. Remember that **DataInputStream** reads data in its binary format, not its human-readable form. The constructor for **DataInputStream** is shown here.

DataInputStream(InputStream *inputStream*)

TABLE 11-6: A Sampling of Input Methods Defined by DataInputStream	
Input Method	**Purpose**
boolean readBoolean( )	Reads a **boolean**.
byte readByte( )	Reads a **byte**.
char readChar( )	Reads a **char**.
double readDouble( )	Reads a **double**.
float readFloat( )	Reads a **float**.
int readInt( )	Reads an **int**.
long readLong( )	Reads a **long**.
short readShort( )	Reads a **short**.

Here, *inputStream* is the stream that is linked to the instance of **DataInputStream** being created. To read input from a file, you can use the object created by **FileInputStream** for this parameter. Here is a program that demonstrates **DataOutputStream** and **DataInputStream**. It writes and then reads back various types of data to and from a file.

```java
// Write and then read back binary data.

// This code requires JDK 7 or later.

import java.io.*;

class RWData {
  public static void main(String[] args)
  {
    int i = 10;
    double d = 1023.56;
    boolean b = true;

    // Write some values.
    try (DataOutputStream dataOut =
            new DataOutputStream(new FileOutputStream("testdata")))
    {
      System.out.println("Writing " + i);
      dataOut.writeInt(i);

      System.out.println("Writing " + d);
      dataOut.writeDouble(d);

      System.out.println("Writing " + b);
      dataOut.writeBoolean(b);

      System.out.println("Writing " + 12.2 * 7.4);
      dataOut.writeDouble(12.2 * 7.4);
    }
    catch(IOException exc) {
      System.out.println("Write error.");
      return;
    }

    System.out.println();

    // Now, read them back.
    try (DataInputStream dataIn =
            new DataInputStream(new FileInputStream("testdata")))
    {
      i = dataIn.readInt();
      System.out.println("Reading " + i);

      d = dataIn.readDouble();
      System.out.println("Reading " + d);
```

Write binary data.

Read binary data.

```
      b = dataIn.readBoolean();
      System.out.println("Reading " + b);

      d = dataIn.readDouble();
      System.out.println("Reading " + d);
    }
    catch(IOException exc) {
      System.out.println("Read error.");
    }
  }
}
```

Read binary data.

The output from the program is shown here.

```
Writing 10
Writing 1023.56
Writing true
Writing 90.28

Reading 10
Reading 1023.56
Reading true
Reading 90.28
```

Progress Check

1. What statement automates the closing of a file?
2. What streams are used to read and write binary data?

TRY THIS 11-1   A FILE COMPARISON UTILITY

CompFiles.java

This project develops a simple, yet useful, file comparison utility. It works by opening both files to be compared and then reading and comparing each corresponding set of bytes. If a mismatch is found, the files differ. If the end of each file is reached at the same time and if no mismatches have been found, then the files are the same. Notice that the program uses the new **try**-with-resources statement to automatically close the files.

Answers:

1. **try**-with-resources
2. **DataInputStream** and **DataOutputStream**

STEP-BY-STEP

1. Create a file called **CompFiles.java**.
2. Into **CompFiles.java**, add the following program.

```java
/*
    Try This 11-1

    Compare two files.

    To use this program, specify the names
    of the files to be compared on the command line.

    java CompFiles FIRST.TXT SECOND.TXT

    This code requires JDK 7 or later.
*/

import java.io.*;

class CompFiles {
  public static void main(String[] args)
  {
    int i=0, j=0;

    // First make sure that both files have been specified.
    if(args.length !=2 ) {
      System.out.println("Usage: CompFiles f1 f2");
      return;
    }

    // Compare the files.
    try (FileInputStream f1 = new FileInputStream(args[0]);
         FileInputStream f2 = new FileInputStream(args[1]))
    {
      // Check the contents of each file.
      do {
        i = f1.read();
        j = f2.read();
        if(i != j) break;
      } while(i != -1 && j != -1);

      if(i != j)
        System.out.println("Files differ.");
      else
        System.out.println("Files are the same.");
    } catch(IOException exc) {
      System.out.println("I/O Error: " + exc);
    }
  }
}
```

3. To try **CompFiles**, first copy **CompFiles.java** to a file called **temp**. Then, try this command line:

```
|java CompFiles CompFiles.java temp
```

The program will report that the files are the same. Next, compare **CompFiles.java** to **CopyFile.java** (shown earlier) using this command line:

```
|java CompFiles CompFiles.java CopyFile.java
```

These files differ, and **CompFiles** will report this fact.

4. On your own, try enhancing **CompFiles** with various options. For example, add an option that ignores the case of letters. Another idea is to have **CompFiles** display the position within the file where the files differ.

RANDOM-ACCESS FILES

Up to this point, we have been using *sequential files*, which are files that are accessed in a strictly linear fashion, one byte after another. However, Java also allows you to access the contents of a file in random order. To do this you will use **RandomAccessFile**, which encapsulates a random-access file. **RandomAccessFile** is not derived from **InputStream** or **OutputStream**. Instead, it implements the interfaces **DataInput** and **DataOutput**, which define the basic I/O methods. It also supports positioning requests—that is, you can position the *file pointer* within the file. The constructor that we will be using is shown here.

RandomAccessFile(String *fileName*, String *access*)
throws FileNotFoundException

Here, the name of the file is passed in *fileName*, and *access* determines what type of file access is permitted. In this chapter, the following values for *access* are used: "r" and "rw". If it is "r", the file can be read but not written. If it is "rw", the file is opened in read-write mode. (Other modes include "rwd", which causes data to be written immediately to the device, and "rws", which causes data and metadata to be written immediately to the device.)

The method **seek( )**, shown here, is used to set the current position of the file pointer within the file:

void seek(long *newPos*) throws IOException

Here, *newPos* specifies the new position, in bytes, of the file pointer from the beginning of the file. After a call to **seek( )**, the next read or write operation will occur at the new file position.

RandomAccessFile implements the **read( )** and **write( )** methods. It also implements the **DataInput** and **DataOuput** interfaces, which means that methods to read and write the primitive types, such as **readInt( )** and **writeDouble( )**, are available.

Here is an example that demonstrates random-access I/O. It writes six **doubles** to a file and then reads them back in nonsequential order.

```java
// Demonstrate random access files.
// This code requires JDK 7 or later.

import java.io.*;

class RandomAccessDemo {
  public static void main(String[] args)
  {
    double[] data = { 19.4, 10.1, 123.54, 33.0, 87.9, 74.25 };
    double d;

    // Open and use a random access file.
    try (RandomAccessFile raf = new RandomAccessFile("random.dat", "rw"))
    {
      // Write values to the file.
      for(int i=0; i < data.length; i++) {
        raf.writeDouble(data[i]);
      }

      // Now, read back specific values
      raf.seek(0); // seek to first double
      d = raf.readDouble();
      System.out.println("First value is " + d);

      raf.seek(8); // seek to second double
      d = raf.readDouble();
      System.out.println("Second value is " + d);

      raf.seek(8 * 3); // seek to fourth double
      d = raf.readDouble();
      System.out.println("Fourth value is " + d);

      System.out.println();

      // Now, read every other value.
      System.out.println("Here is every other value: ");
      for(int i=0; i < data.length; i+=2) {
        raf.seek(8 * i); // seek to ith double
        d = raf.readDouble();
        System.out.print(d + " ");
      }
    }
    catch(IOException exc) {
      System.out.println("I/O Error: " + exc);
    }
  }
}
```

Open random-access file.

Use **seek( )** to set the file pointer.

The output from the program is shown here.

```
First value is 19.4
Second value is 10.1
Fourth value is 33.0


Here is every other value:
19.4 123.54 87.9
```

Notice how each value is located. Since each double value is 8 bytes long, each value starts on an 8-byte boundary. Thus, the first value is located at zero, the second begins at byte 8, the third starts at byte 16, and so on. Thus, to read the fourth value, the program seeks to location 24.

Progress Check

1. What class do you use to create a random-access file?
2. How do you position the file pointer?

Ask the Expert

Q In looking through the documentation provided by the JDK, I noticed a class called **Console**. Is this a class that I can use to perform console-based I/O?

A The short answer is Yes. The **Console** class was added by JDK 6, and it is used to read from and write to the console. **Console** is primarily a convenience class because most of its functionality is available through **System.in** and **System.out**. However, its use can simplify some types of console interactions, especially when reading strings from the console.

Console supplies no constructors. Instead, a **Console** object is obtained by calling **System.console( )**. It is shown here.

```
static Console console( )
```

If a console is available, then a reference to it is returned. Otherwise, null is returned. A console may not be available in all cases, such as when a program runs as a background task. Therefore, if null is returned, no console I/O is possible.

Console defines several methods that perform I/O, such as **readLine( )** and **printf( )**. It also defines a method called **readPassword( )**, which can be used to obtain a password. It lets your application read a password without echoing what is typed. You can also obtain a reference to the **Reader** and the **Writer** that is attached to the console. In general, **Console** is a class that you may find useful for some types of applications.

Answers:

1. To create a random-access file, use **RandomAccessFile**.
2. To position the file pointer, use **seek( )**.

TABLE 11-7: The Methods Defined by Reader	
Method	**Description**
abstract void close( )	Closes the input source. Further read attempts will generate an **IOException**.
void mark(int *numChars*)	Places a mark at the current point in the input stream that will remain valid until *numChars* characters are read.
boolean markSupported( )	Returns **true** if **mark( )/reset( )** are supported on this stream.
int read( )	Returns an integer representation of the next available character from the invoking input stream. If the end of the stream is encountered, −1 is returned.
int read(char[ ] *buffer*)	Attempts to read up to *buffer*.length characters into *buffer* and returns the actual number of characters that were successfully read. If the end of the stream is encountered when first attempting to read, −1 is returned.

abstract int read(char[ ] *buffer*,
            int *offset*,
            int *numChars*)
	Attempts to read up to *numChars* characters into *buffer* starting at *buffer*[*offset*], returning the number of characters successfully read. If the end of the stream is encountered when first attempting to read, −1 is returned.

int read(CharBuffer *buffer*)	Attempts to fill the buffer specified by *buffer*, returning the number of characters successfully read. If the end of the stream is encountered when first attempting to read, −1 is returned. **CharBuffer** is a class that encapsulates a sequence of characters, such as a string.
boolean ready( )	Returns **true** if the next input request will not wait. Otherwise, it returns **false**.
void reset( )	Resets the input pointer to the previously set mark.
long skip(long *numChars*)	Ignores (that is, skips) *numChars* characters of input, returning the number of characters actually ignored

USING JAVA'S CHARACTER-BASED STREAMS

As the preceding sections have shown, Java's byte streams are both powerful and flexible. However, they are not the ideal way to handle character-based I/O. For this purpose, Java defines the character stream classes. At the top of the character stream hierarchy are the abstract classes **Reader** and **Writer**. Table 11-7 shows the methods in **Reader**, and Table 11-8 shows the methods in **Writer**. Most of the methods can throw an **IOException** on error. The methods defined by these two abstract classes are available to all of their subclasses. Thus, they form a minimal set of I/O functions that all character streams will have.

Console Input Using Character Streams

For code that will be internationalized, inputting from the console using Java's character-based streams is a better, more convenient way to read characters from the keyboard than is using the byte streams. However, since **System.in** is a byte stream, you

TABLE 11-8: The Methods Defined by Writer

Method	Description
Writer append(char *ch*)	Appends *ch* to the end of the invoking output stream. Returns a reference to the invoking stream.
Writer append(CharSequence *chars*)	Appends *chars* to the end of the invoking output stream. Returns a reference to the invoking stream. **CharSequence** is an interface that defines read-only operations on a sequence of characters.
Writer append(CharSequence *chars*, int *begin*, int *end*)	Appends the sequence of *chars* starting at *begin* and stopping with *end* to the end of the invoking output stream. Returns a reference to the invoking stream. **CharSequence** is an interface that defines read-only operations on a sequence of characters.
abstract void close( )	Closes the output stream. Further write attempts will generate an **IOException**.
abstract void flush( )	Causes any output that has been buffered to be sent to its destination. That is, it flushes the output buffer.
void write(int *ch*)	Writes a single character to the invoking output stream. Note that the parameter is an **int**, which allows you to call **write( )** with expressions without having to cast them back to **char**.
void write(char[ ] *buffer*)	Writes a complete array of characters to the invoking output stream.
abstract void write(char[ ] *buffer*, int *offset*, int *numChars*)	Writes a subrange of *numChars* characters from the array *buffer*, beginning at *buffer[offset]* to the invoking output stream.
void write(String *str*)	Writes *str* to the invoking output stream.
void write(String *str*, int *offset*, int *numChars*)	Writes a subrange of *numChars* characters from the array *str*, beginning at the specified *offset*.

will need to wrap **System.in** inside some type of **Reader**. The best class for reading console input is **BufferedReader**, which supports a buffered input stream. However, you cannot construct a **BufferedReader** directly from **System.in**. Instead, you must first convert it into a character stream. To do this, you will use **InputStreamReader**, which converts bytes to characters. To obtain an **InputStreamReader** object that is linked to **System.in**, use the constructor shown next.

InputStreamReader(InputStream *inputStream*)

Since **System.in** refers to an object of type **InputStream**, it can be used for *inputStream*.

Next, using the object produced by **InputStreamReader**, construct a **BufferedReader** using the constructor shown here:

BufferedReader(Reader *inputReader*)

Here, *inputReader* is the stream that is linked to the instance of **BufferedReader** being created. Putting it all together, the following line of code creates a **BufferedReader** that is connected to the keyboard.

```
BufferedReader br = new BufferedReader(new
                        InputStreamReader(System.in));
```

After this statement executes, **br** will be a character-based stream that is linked to the console through **System.in**.

READING CHARACTERS

Characters can be read from **System.in** using the **read( )** method defined by **BufferedReader** in much the same way as they were read using byte streams. Here are three versions of **read( )** supported by **BufferedReader**.

> int read( ) throws IOException
> int read(char[ ] *buffer*) throws IOException
> int read(char[ ] *buffer*, int *offset*, int *numChars*) throws IOException

The first version of **read( )** reads a single character. It returns –1 when the end of the stream is encountered. The second version reads characters from the input stream and puts them into *buffer* until either the array is full, the end of file is encountered, or an error occurs. It returns the number of characters read or –1 at the end of the stream. The third version reads input into *buffer* beginning at the location specified by *offset*. Up to *numChars* characters are stored. It returns the number of characters read or –1 when the end of the stream is encountered. All throw an **IOException** on error. When reading from **System.in**, pressing ENTER generates an end-of-stream condition.

The following program demonstrates **read( )** by reading characters from the console until the user types a period. Notice that any I/O exceptions that might be generated are simply thrown out of **main( )**. As mentioned earlier in this chapter, such an approach is common when reading from the console. Of course, you can handle these types of errors under program control, if you choose.

```
// Use a BufferedReader to read characters from the console.
import java.io.*;

class ReadChars {
  public static void main(String[] args)
    throws IOException                    Create BufferedReader
  {                                       linked to System.in.
    char c;
    BufferedReader br = new ◄──────────────────┐
            BufferedReader(new
                    InputStreamReader(System.in));

    System.out.println("Enter characters, period to quit.");

    // read characters
    do {
      c = (char) br.read();
```

```
      System.out.println(c);
    } while(c != '.');
  }
}
```

Here is a sample run.

```
Enter characters, period to quit.
One Two.
O
n
e

T
w
o
.
```

Reading Strings

To read a string from the keyboard, use the version of **readLine( )** that is a member of the **BufferedReader** class. Its general form is shown here:

> String readLine( ) throws IOException

It returns a **String** object that contains the characters read. It returns null if an attempt is made to read when at the end of the stream.

The following program demonstrates **BufferedReader** and the **readLine( )** method. The program reads and displays lines of text until you enter the word "stop".

```java
// Read a string from console using a BufferedReader.
import java.io.*;

class ReadLines {
  public static void main(String[] args)
    throws IOException
  {
    // create a BufferedReader using System.in
    BufferedReader br = new BufferedReader(new
                          InputStreamReader(System.in));
    String str;

    System.out.println("Enter lines of text.");
    System.out.println("Enter 'stop' to quit.");
    do {
      str = br.readLine();  ←——————  Use readLine( ) from BufferedReader
      System.out.println(str);           to read a line of text.
    } while(!str.equals("stop"));
  }
}
```

Console Output Using Character Streams

While it is still permissible to use **System.out** to write to the console under Java, its use is recommended mostly for debugging purposes or for sample programs such as those found in this book. For real-world programs, the preferred method of writing to the console when using Java is through a **PrintWriter** stream. **PrintWriter** is one of the character-based classes. As explained, using a character-based class for console output makes it easier to internationalize your program.

PrintWriter defines several constructors. The one we will use is shown here:

> PrintWriter(OutputStream *outputStream*, boolean *flushOnNewline*)

Here, *outputStream* is an object of type **OutputStream** and *flushOnNewline* controls whether Java flushes the output stream every time a **println( )** method is called. If *flushOnNewline* is **true**, flushing automatically takes place. If **false**, flushing is not automatic.

PrintWriter supports the **print( )** and **println( )** methods for all types including **Object**. Thus, you can use these methods in just the same way as they have been used with **System.out**. If an argument is not a primitive type, the **PrintWriter** methods will call the object's **toString( )** method and then print out the result.

To write to the console using a **PrintWriter**, specify **System.out** for the output stream and flush the stream after each call to **println( )**. For example, this line of code creates a **PrintWriter** that is connected to console output.

```
PrintWriter pw = new PrintWriter(System.out, true);
```

The following application illustrates using a **PrintWriter** to handle console output.

Create a **PrintWriter** linked to **System.out**.

```
// Demonstrate PrintWriter.
import java.io.*;

public class PrintWriterDemo {
   public static void main(String[] args) {
      PrintWriter pw = new PrintWriter(System.out, true);
      int i = 10;
      double d = 123.65;

      pw.println("Using a PrintWriter.");
      pw.println(i);
      pw.println(d);

      pw.println(i + " + " + d + " is " + (i+d));
   }
}
```

The output from this program is:

```
Using a PrintWriter.
10
123.65
10 + 123.65 is 133.65
```

Remember that there is nothing wrong with using **System.out** to write simple text output to the console when you are learning Java or debugging your programs. However, using a **PrintWriter** will make your real-world applications easier to internationalize. Since no advantage is to be gained by using a **PrintWriter** in the sample programs shown in this book, for convenience we will continue to use **System.out** to write to the console.

Progress Check

1. What classes top the character-based stream classes?
2. To read from the console, you will open what type of reader?
3. To write to the console, you will open what type of writer?

FILE I/O USING CHARACTER STREAMS

Although byte-oriented file handling is quite common, it is possible to use character-based streams for this purpose. The advantage of the character streams is that they operate directly on Unicode characters. Thus, if you want to store Unicode text, the character streams are certainly your best option. In general, to perform character-based file I/O, you will use the **FileReader** and **FileWriter** classes.

Using a FileWriter

FileWriter creates a **Writer** that you can use to write to a file. Two commonly used constructors are shown here:

FileWriter(String *fileName*) throws IOException
FileWriter(String *fileName*, boolean *append*) throws IOException

Here, *fileName* is the name of a file. If *append* is **true**, then output is appended to the end of the file. Otherwise, the file is overwritten. Either throws an **IOException** on failure. **FileWriter** is derived from **OutputStreamWriter** and **Writer**. Thus, it has access to the methods defined by those classes.

Here is a simple key-to-disk utility that reads lines of text entered at the keyboard and writes them to a file called "test.txt". Text is read until the user enters the word "stop". It uses a **FileWriter** to output to the file.

```
// A simple key-to-disk utility that demonstrates a FileWriter.
// This code requires JDK 7 or later.

import java.io.*;
```

Answers:

1. At the top of the character-based stream classes are **Reader** and **Writer**.
2. To read from the console, open a **BufferedReader**.
3. To write to the console, open a **PrintWriter**.

```
class KtoD {
  public static void main(String[] args)
  {

    String str;
    BufferedReader br =
            new BufferedReader(
                new InputStreamReader(System.in));

    System.out.println("Enter text ('stop' to quit).");

    try (FileWriter fw = new FileWriter("test.txt"))    ◄────────  Create a FileWriter.
    {
      do {
        System.out.print(": ");
        str = br.readLine();

        if(str.compareTo("stop") == 0) break;

        str = str + "\r\n"; // add newline
        fw.write(str);  ◄──────────────────────────────  Write strings to the file.
      } while(str.compareTo("stop") != 0);
    } catch(IOException exc) {
      System.out.println("I/O Error: " + exc);
    }
  }
}
```

Using a FileReader

The **FileReader** class creates a **Reader** that you can use to read the contents of a file. A commonly used constructor is shown here:

>   FileReader(String *fileName*) throws FileNotFoundException

Here, *fileName* is the name of a file. It throws a **FileNotFoundException** if the file does not exist. **FileReader** is derived from **InputStreamReader** and **Reader**. Thus, it has access to the methods defined by those classes.

The following program creates a simple disk-to-screen utility that reads a text file called "test.txt" and displays its contents on the screen. Thus, it is the complement of the key-to-disk utility shown in the previous section.

```
// A simple disk-to-screen utility that demonstrates a FileReader.
// This code requires JDK 7 or later.

import java.io.*;

class DtoS {
  public static void main(String[] args) {
    String s;
```

```
                                                                    Create a
    // Create and use a FileReader wrapped in a BufferedReader.     FileReader.
    try (BufferedReader br = new BufferedReader(new FileReader("test.txt")))
    {
                                                     Read lines from the file and
      while((s = br.readLine()) != null) {           display them on the screen.
        System.out.println(s);
      }
    } catch(IOException exc) {
      System.out.println("I/O Error: " + exc);
    }
  }
}
```

In this example, notice that the **FileReader** is wrapped in a **BufferedReader**. This gives it access to **readLine( )**. Also, closing the **BufferedReader**, **br** in this case, automatically closes the file.

Progress Check

1. What class is used to read characters from a file?
2. What class is used to write characters to a file?

Ask the Expert

Q I have heard about another I/O package called NIO. Can you tell me about it?

A Originally called *New I/O*, NIO was added to Java by JDK 1.4. It supports a channel-based approach to I/O operations. The NIO classes are contained in **java.nio** and its subordinate packages, such as **java.nio.channels** and **java.nio.charset**. NIO is built on two foundational items: *buffers* and *channels*. A buffer holds data. A channel represents an open connection to an I/O device, such as a file or a socket. In general, to use the new I/O system, you obtain a channel to an I/O device and a buffer to hold data. You then operate on the buffer, inputting or outputting data as needed.

Beginning with JDK 7, NIO was substantially enhanced, so much so that the term *NIO.2* is often used. The improvements include three new packages (**java.nio.file**, **java.nio.file.attribute**, and **java.nio.file.spi**); several new classes, interfaces, and methods; and direct support for stream-based I/O. The additions have greatly expanded the ways in which NIO can be used, especially with files.

It is important to understand that NIO does not replace the I/O classes found in **java.io**, which are discussed in this chapter. Instead, the NIO classes are designed to supplement the standard I/O system, offering an alternative approach, which can be beneficial in some circumstances.

Answers:

1. To read characters, use a **FileReader**.
2. To write characters, use a **FileWriter**.

File

Before leaving the topic of I/O, there is one more class that needs to be discussed. This is the **File** class. Instead of operating on streams, **File** deals directly with files and the file system. That is, the **File** class does not specify how information is retrieved from or stored in files; it describes the properties of a file itself. A **File** object is used to obtain or manipulate the information associated with a disk file, such as the permissions, time, date, and directory path, and to navigate subdirectory hierarchies.

File defines several constructors, including the two shown here:

File(String *path*)
File(String *directoryPath*, String *filename*)

In the first form, *path* specifies the complete path to the file or directory. In the second form, *directoryPath* is the path name of a directory and *filename* is the name of the file or subdirectory. For example, the following example creates two **File** objects called **myFileA** and **myFileB**. The first object is constructed with a path (which includes a file name) as the only argument. The second includes two arguments—the path and the file name.

```
File myFileA = new File("/javafiles/MyClass.java");
File myFileB = new File("/javafiles","MyClass.java");
```

Note: In general, Java does the right thing with path separators between UNIX and Windows conventions. If you use a forward slash (/) on a Windows version of Java, the path will still resolve correctly. Remember, if you are using the Windows convention of a backslash character (\), you will need to use its escape sequence (\\) within a string. For convenience, the examples in this chapter use forward slashes.

Obtaining a File's Properties

File defines many methods that obtain the standard properties of a **File** object. Several are shown here:

Method	Description
boolean canRead( )	Returns **true** if the file can be read.
boolean canWrite( )	Returns **true** if the file can be written.
boolean exists( )	Returns **true** if the file exists.
String getAbsolutePath( )	Returns the absolute path to the file.
String getName( )	Returns the file's name.
String getParent( )	Returns name of the file's parent directory, or null if no parent exists.
boolean isAbsolute( )	Returns **true** if the path is absolute. It returns **false** if the path is relative.
boolean isDirectory( )	Returns **true** if the file is a directory.

boolean isFile( )	Returns true if the file is a "normal" file. It returns false if the file is a directory, or some other nonfile object.
boolean isHidden( )	Returns true if the invoking file is hidden. Returns false otherwise.
long length( )	Returns the length of the file, in bytes.

The following example demonstrates these **File** methods. It assumes that a directory called **javafiles** exists off the root directory and that it contains a file called **MyClass.java**.

```java
// Obtain information about a file.
import java.io.*;

class FileDemo {
  public static void main(String[] args) {
    File myFile = new File("/javafiles/MyClass.java");

    System.out.println("File Name: " + myFile.getName());
    System.out.println("Path: " + myFile.getPath());
    System.out.println("Abs Path: " + myFile.getAbsolutePath());
    System.out.println("Parent: " + myFile.getParent());
    System.out.println(myFile.exists() ? "exists" : "does not exist");
    System.out.println(myFile.isHidden() ? "is hidden" :
                        "is not hidden");
    System.out.println(myFile.canWrite() ? "is writeable" :
                        "is not writeable");
    System.out.println(myFile.canRead() ? "is readable" :
                        "is not readable");
    System.out.println("is " + (myFile.isDirectory() ? "" :
                        "not" + " a directory"));
    System.out.println(myFile.isFile() ? "is normal file" :
                        "might be a named pipe");
    System.out.println(myFile.isAbsolute() ? "is absolute" :
                        "is not absolute");
    System.out.println("File size: " + myFile.length() + " Bytes");
  }
}
```

This program will produce output similar to this:

```
File Name: MyClass.java
Path: \javafiles\MyClass.java
Abs Path: C:\javafiles\MyClass.java
Parent: \javafiles
exists
is not hidden
is writeable
is readable
is not a directory
is normal file
is not absolute
File size: 369 Bytes
```

Obtaining a Directory Listing

A directory is a file that contains a list of other files and directories. When you create a **File** object that is a directory, the **isDirectory( )** method will return **true**. In this case, you can obtain a list of the files in the directory. One way to do this is to call **list( )** on that object. It has two forms. The first is shown here:

String[ ] list( )

The list of files is returned in an array of **String** objects.

The program shown here illustrates how to use **list( )** to examine the contents of a directory:

```java
// Using directories.
import java.io.*;

class DirList {
  public static void main(String[] args) {
    String dirname = "/javafiles";
    File myDir = new File(dirname);

    if (myDir.isDirectory()) {
      System.out.println("Directory of " + dirname);
      String[] s = myDir.list();

      for (int i=0; i < s.length; i++) {
        File f = new File(dirname + "/" + s[i]);
        if (f.isDirectory()) {
          System.out.println(s[i] + " is a directory");
        } else {
          System.out.println(s[i] + " is a file");
        }
      }
    } else {
      System.out.println(dirname + " is not a directory");
    }
  }
}
```

Here is sample output from the program. (Of course, the output you see will be different, based on what is in the directory.)

```
Directory of /javafiles
examples is a directory
MyClass.class is a file
MyClass.java is a file
ReadMe.txt is a file
SampleClass.class is a file
SampleClass.java is a file
temp is a directory
```

Using FilenameFilter

Sometimes you might want to limit the number of files returned by the **list( )** method to include only those files that match a certain file name pattern, or *filter*. To do this, you can use a second form of **list( )**, shown here:

String[ ] list(FilenameFilter *FFObj*)

In this form, *FFObj* is an object of a class that implements the **FilenameFilter** interface.

FilenameFilter defines only a single method, **accept( )**, which is called once for each file in a list. Its general form is given here:

boolean accept(File *directory*, String *filename*)

The **accept( )** method returns **true** if the file specified by *filename* in the directory specified by *directory* should be included in the list, and returns **false** if the file should be excluded.

The **FilterExt** class, shown next, implements **FilenameFilter**. It will be used to modify the preceding program to restrict the visibility of the file names returned by **list( )** to files with names that end in the file extension specified when the object is constructed.

```java
import java.io.*;

public class FilterExt implements FilenameFilter {
  String ext;

  public FilterExt(String ext) {
    this.ext = "." + ext;
  }

  public boolean accept(File dir, String name) {
    return name.endsWith(ext);
  }
}
```

The modified directory listing program is shown here. Now it will only display files that use the **.java** extension.

```java
// Directory of .java files.
import java.io.*;

class DirListFiltered {
  public static void main(String[] args) {
    FilenameFilter only = new FilterExt("java");
    String dirname = "/javafiles";
    File myDir = new File(dirname);


    if (myDir.isDirectory()) {
      System.out.println("Java source files in " + dirname);

      String[] s = myDir.list(only);
```

```
    for (int i=0; i < s.length; i++) {
        System.out.println(s[i]);
      }
    }
  }
}
```

When run on the same directory as shown in the earlier example, the following output is produced:

```
Java source files in /javafiles
MyClass.java
SampleClass.java
```

The listFiles( ) Alternative

There is a variation to the **list( )** method, called **listFiles( )**, which you might find useful. Its three forms are shown here:

```
File[ ] listFiles( )
File[ ] listFiles(FilenameFilter FFObj)
File[ ] listFiles(FileFilter FObj)
```

These methods return the file list as an array of **File** objects instead of strings. The first method returns all files, and the second returns those files that satisfy the specified **FilenameFilter**. Aside from returning an array of **File** objects, these two versions of **listFiles( )** work like their equivalent **list( )** methods.

The third version of **listFiles( )** returns those files with path names that satisfy the specified **FileFilter**. **FileFilter** defines only a single method, **accept( )**, which is called once for each file in a list. Its general form is given here:

```
boolean accept(File path)
```

The **accept( )** method returns **true** if the file specified by *path* should be included in the list, and **false** if the file should be excluded.

Various File Utility Methods

In addition to the **list( )** and **listFiles( )** methods just described, **File** includes several other utility methods that let you perform various actions on a file or the file system. A sampling is shown in Table 11-9. A particularly interesting one is **getFreeSpace( )**. It returns the number of bytes of free space remaining on the current partition of the storage device. Here is a program that shows it in action.

```
// Show the free space on the current drive partition.
import java.io.*;

class FreeSpace {
  public static void main(String[] args) {
    File myFile = new File("\\");
```

```
        System.out.println("Free Space: " + myFile.getFreeSpace());
    }
}
```

JDK 7 adds a new method to **File** called **toPath( )**, which is shown here:

Path toPath( )

toPath( ) returns a **Path** object that represents the file encapsulated by the invoking **File** object. (In other words, **toPath( )** converts a **File** into a **Path**.) **Path** is a new

TABLE 11-9: A Sampling of Utility Methods Provided by File.	
Method	**Description**
boolean delete( )	Deletes the file specified by the invoking object. Returns **true** if the file was deleted and **false** if the file cannot be removed.
void deleteOnExit( )	Removes the file associated with the invoking object when the Java Virtual Machine terminates.
long getFreeSpace( )	Returns the number of free bytes of storage available on the partition associated with the invoking object.
long getTotalSpace( )	Returns the storage capacity of the partition associated with the invoking object.
long getUsableSpace( )	Returns the number of usable free bytes of storage available on the partition associated with the invoking object.
long lastModified( )	Obtains the time stamp on the invoking file. The value returned is the number of milliseconds from January 1, 1970, Coordinated Universal Time (UTC). If no time stamp is available, zero is returned.
boolean mkdir( )	Creates the directory specified by the invoking object. Returns **true** if the directory was created and **false** if the directory could not be created. Failure can occur for various reasons, such as the path specified in the **File** object already exists, or the directory cannot be created because the entire path does not exist yet.
boolean mkdirs( )	Creates the directory and all required parent directories specified by the invoking object. Returns **true** if the entire path was created and **false** otherwise.
boolean renameTo(File *newName*)	Renames the file specified by the invoking object to *newName*. Returns **true** if successful and **false** if the file cannot be renamed.
boolean setLastModified(long *millisec*)	Sets the time stamp on the invoking file to that specified by *millisec*, which is the number of milliseconds from January 1, 1970, Coordinated Universal Time (UTC).
boolean setReadOnly( )	Sets the file to read-only.
boolean setWritable(boolean *how*)	If *how* is true, the file is set to writable. If *how* is false, the file is set to read-only. Returns **true** if the status of the file was modified and **false** if the write status cannot be changed.

interface added by JDK 7. It is packaged in **java.nio.file** and is part of NIO. Thus, **toPath( )** forms a bridge between the **File** class and the new **Path** interface.

Progress Check

1. Does **File** open a file?
2. What **File** method is used to determine if a file is hidden?
3. What method is used to list the files in a directory?

USING JAVA'S TYPE WRAPPERS TO CONVERT NUMERIC STRINGS

Before concluding this chapter, we will examine a technique useful when reading numeric strings. As you know, Java's **println( )** method provides a convenient way to output various types of data to the console, including numeric values of the built-in types, such as **int** and **double**. Thus, **println( )** automatically converts numeric values into their human-readable form. However, methods like **read( )** do not provide a parallel functionality that reads and converts a string containing a numeric value into its internal, binary format. For example, there is no version of **read( )** that reads a string such as "100" and then automatically converts it into its corresponding binary value that is able to be stored in an **int** variable. Instead, Java provides various other ways to accomplish this task. The way we will examine here uses Java's *type wrappers*.

Java's type wrappers are classes that encapsulate, or *wrap*, the primitive types. Type wrappers are needed because the primitive types are not objects. This limits their use to some extent. For example, a primitive type cannot be passed by reference. To address this kind of need, Java provides classes that correspond to each of the primitive types.

The type wrappers are **Double**, **Float**, **Long**, **Integer**, **Short**, **Byte**, **Character**, and **Boolean**. These classes offer a wide array of methods that allow you to fully integrate the primitive types into Java's object hierarchy. As a side-benefit, the numeric wrappers also define methods that convert a numeric string into its corresponding binary equivalent. Several of these conversion methods are shown here. Each returns a binary value that corresponds to the string.

Wrapper	Conversion Method
Double	static double parseDouble(String *str*) throws NumberFormatException
Float	static float parseFloat(String *str*) throws NumberFormatException
Long	static long parscLong(String *str*) throws NumberFormatException

---

Answers:

1. No.
2. **isHidden( )**
3. **list( )** or **listFiles( )**

Wrapper	Conversion Method
Integer	static int parseInt(String *str*) throws NumberFormatException
Short	static short parseShort(String *str*) throws NumberFormatException
Byte	static byte parseByte(String *str*) throws NumberFormatException

The integer wrappers also offer a second parsing method that allows you to specify the radix.

The parsing methods give us an easy way to convert a numeric value, read as a string from the keyboard or a text file, into its proper internal format. For example, the following program demonstrates **parseInt( )** and **parseDouble( )**. It averages a list of numbers entered by the user. It first asks the user for the number of values to be averaged. It then reads that number using **readLine( )** and uses **parseInt( )** to convert the string into an integer. Next, it inputs the values, using **parseDouble( )** to convert the strings into their **double** equivalents.

```java
// This program averages a list of numbers entered by the user.

import java.io.*;

class AvgNums {
  public static void main(String[] args)
    throws IOException
  {
    // create a BufferedReader using System.in
    BufferedReader br = new
      BufferedReader(new InputStreamReader(System.in));
    String str;
    int n;
    double sum = 0.0;
    double avg, t;

    System.out.print("How many numbers will you enter: ");
    str = br.readLine();
    try {
      n = Integer.parseInt(str);  ◄──────── Convert string to int.
    }
    catch(NumberFormatException exc) {
      System.out.println("Invalid format");
      n = 0;
    }

    System.out.println("Enter " + n + " values.");
    for(int i=0; i < n ; i++) {
      System.out.print(": ");
      str = br.readLine();
      try {
        t = Double.parseDouble(str);  ◄──────── Convert string to double.
      } catch(NumberFormatException exc) {
        System.out.println("Invalid format");
```

```
      t = 0.0;
    }
    sum += t;
  }
  avg = sum / n;
  System.out.println("Average is " + avg);
  }
}
```

Here is a sample run.

```
How many numbers will you enter: 5
Enter 5 values.
 : 1.1
 : 2.2
 : 3.3
 : 4.4
 : 5.5
Average is 3.3
```

Ask the Expert

Q What else can the primitive type wrapper classes do?

A The primitive type wrappers provide a number of methods that help integrate the primitive types into the object hierarchy. For example, various storage mechanisms provided by the Java library, including maps, lists, and sets, work only with objects. Thus, to store an **int**, for example, in a list, it must be wrapped in an object. Also, all type wrappers have a method called **compareTo( )**, which compares the value contained within the wrapper; **equals( )**, which tests two values for equality; and methods that return the value of the object in various forms. The topic of type wrappers is taken up again in Chapter 13, when autoboxing is discussed.

TRY THIS 11-2   CREATING A DISK-BASED HELP SYSTEM

FileHelp.java

In Try This 4-1 you created a **Help** class that displayed information about Java's control statements. In that implementation, the help information was stored within the class itself, and the user selected help from a menu of numbered options.

Although this approach was fully functional, it is certainly not the ideal way of creating a Help system. For example, to add to or change the help information, the source code of the program needed to be modified. Also, the selection of the topic by number rather than by name is tedious and is not suitable for long lists of topics. Here, we will remedy these shortcomings by creating a disk-based Help system.

The disk-based Help system stores help information in a help file. The help file is a standard text file that can be changed or expanded at will, without changing the Help program. The user obtains help about a topic by typing in its name. The Help system searches the help file for the topic. If it is found, information about the topic is displayed.

STEP-BY-STEP

1. Create the help file that will be used by the Help system. The help file is a standard text file that is organized like this:

   #topic-name1
   topic info

   #topic-name2
   topic info

   .

   .

   .

   #topic-nameN
   topic info

   The name of each topic must be preceded by a #, and the topic name must be on a line of its own. Preceding each topic name with a # allows the program to quickly find the start of each topic. Following the topic name are any number of information lines about the topic. However, there must be a blank line between the end of one topic's information and the start of the next topic.

   Here is a simple help file that you can use to try the disk-based Help system. It stores information about Java's control statements.

   ```
   #if
   if(condition) statement;
   else statement;

   #switch
   switch(expression) {
     case constant:
       statement sequence
       break;
       // ...
   }

   #for
   for(init; condition; iteration) statement;

   #while
   while(condition) statement;
   ```

```
#do
do {
   statement;
} while (condition);

#break
break; or break label;

#continue
continue; or continue label;
```

Call this file **helpfile.txt**.

2. Create a file called **FileHelp.java**.

3. Begin creating the new **Help** class with these lines of code.

```java
class Help {
   String helpfile; // name of help file

   Help(String fname) {
      helpfile = fname;
   }
```

The name of the help file is passed to the **Help** constructor and stored in the instance variable **helpfile**. Since each instance of **Help** will have its own copy of **helpfile**, each instance can use a different file. Thus, you can create different sets of help files for different sets of topics.

4. Add the **helpOn( )** method shown here to the **Help** class. This method retrieves help on the specified topic.

```java
// Display help on a topic.
boolean helpOn(String what) {
   int ch;
   String topic, info;

   // Open the help file.
   try (BufferedReader helpRdr =
           new BufferedReader(new FileReader(helpfile)))
   {
      do {
         // read characters until a # is found
         ch = helpRdr.read();

         // now, see if topics match
         if(ch == '#') {
            topic = helpRdr.readLine();
            topic = topic.trim(); // remove leading and trailing
                                  // whitespace
```

```
            if(what.compareTo(topic) == 0) { // found topic
              do {
                info = helpRdr.readLine();
                if(info != null) System.out.println(info);
              } while((info != null) &&
                      (info.trim().compareTo("") != 0));
              return true;
            }
          }
        } while(ch != -1);
      }
      catch(IOException exc) {
        System.out.println("Error accessing help file.");
        return false;
      }
      return false; // topic not found
    }
```

The first thing to notice is that **helpOn( )** handles all possible I/O exceptions itself and does not include a **throws** clause. By handling its own exceptions, it prevents this burden from being passed on to all code that uses it. Thus, other code can simply call **helpOn( )** without having to wrap that call in a **try**/**catch** block.

The help file is opened using a **FileReader** that is wrapped in a **BufferedReader**. Since the help file contains text, using a character stream allows the Help system to be more efficiently internationalized.

The **helpOn( )** method works like this. A string containing the name of the topic is passed in the **what** parameter. The help file is then opened. Next, the file is searched, looking for a match between **what** and a topic in the file. Remember, in the file, each topic is preceded by a #, so the search loop scans the file for #s. When it finds one, it checks to see if the topic following that # matches the one passed in **what**. If it does, the information associated with that topic is displayed. If a match is found, **helpOn( )** returns **true**. Otherwise, it returns **false**.

One other point: Notice that **helpOn( )** uses another of **String**'s methods called **trim( )**. It removes any leading or trailing whitespace (such as spaces and tabs) from the string.

5. The **Help** class also provides a method called **getSelection( )**. It prompts the user for a topic and returns the topic string entered by the user.

```
// Get a Help topic.
String getSelection() {
  String topic = "";

  BufferedReader br = new BufferedReader(
                new InputStreamReader(System.in));
```

```
    System.out.print("Enter topic: ");
    try {
      topic = br.readLine();
    }
    catch(IOException exc) {
      System.out.println("Error reading console.");
    }
    return topic;
  }
```

This method creates a **BufferedReader** attached to **System.in**. It then prompts for the name of a topic, reads the topic, and returns it to the caller.

6. The entire disk-based Help system is shown here.

```
/*
   Try This 11-2

   A help program that uses a disk file
   to store help information.

   This code requires JDK 7 or later.
*/

import java.io.*;

/* The Help class opens a help file,
   searches for a topic, and then displays
   the information associated with that topic.
   Notice that it handles all I/O exceptions
   itself, avoiding the need for calling
   code to do so. */
class Help {
  String helpfile; // name of help file

  Help(String fname) {
    helpfile = fname;
  }

  // Display help on a topic.
  boolean helpOn(String what) {
    int ch;
    String topic, info;

    // Open the help file.
    try (BufferedReader helpRdr =
            new BufferedReader(new FileReader(helpfile)))
    {
      do {
        // read characters until a # is found
        ch = helpRdr.read();
```

```
            // now, see if topics match
            if(ch == '#') {
              topic = helpRdr.readLine();
              topic = topic.trim(); // remove leading and trailing
                                    // whitespace

              if(what.compareTo(topic) == 0) { // found topic
                do {
                  info = helpRdr.readLine();
                  if(info != null) System.out.println(info);
                } while((info != null) &&
                          (info.trim().compareTo("") != 0));
                return true;
              }
            }
          } while(ch != -1);
        }
        catch(IOException exc) {
          System.out.println("Error accessing help file.");
          return false;
        }
        return false; // topic not found
      }

      // Get a Help topic.
      String getSelection() {
        String topic = "";

        BufferedReader br = new BufferedReader(
                      new InputStreamReader(System.in));

        System.out.print("Enter topic: ");
        try {
          topic = br.readLine();
        }
        catch(IOException exc) {
          System.out.println("Error reading console.");
        }
        return topic;
      }
    }

    // Demonstrate the file-based Help system.
    class FileHelp {
      public static void main(String[] args) {
        Help hlpobj = new Help("helpfile.txt");
        String topic;

        System.out.println("Try the help system. " +
```

```
                        "Enter 'stop' to end.");
      do {
        topic = hlpobj.getSelection();

        if(!hlpobj.helpOn(topic))
          System.out.println("Topic not found.\n");

      } while(topic.compareTo("stop") != 0);
    }
  }
```

Ask the Expert

Q In addition to the **parse** methods defined by the primitive type wrappers, is there another easy way to convert a numeric string entered at the keyboard into its equivalent binary format?

A Yes! Another way to convert a numeric string into its internal, binary format is to use one of the methods defined by the **Scanner** class, packaged in **java.util**. Added by JDK 5, **Scanner** reads formatted (that is, human-readable) input and converts it into its binary form. **Scanner** can be used to read input from a variety of sources, including the console and files. Therefore, you can use **Scanner** to read a numeric string entered at the keyboard and assign its value to a variable. **Scanner** is described in detail in Chapter 24, when **java.util** is explored. However, the following illustrates its basic usage for reading keyboard input. You might enjoy experimenting with it now.

To use **Scanner** to read from the keyboard, you must first create a **Scanner** linked to console input. You can do this using one of **Scanner**'s constructors, as shown here:

```
Scanner conin = new Scanner(System.in);
```

After this line executes, **conin** can be used to read input from the keyboard.

Once you have created the **Scanner**, it is a simple matter to use it to read numeric input. Here is the general procedure:

1. Determine if a specific type of input is available by calling one of **Scanner**'s **hasNext**X methods, where X is the type of data desired.
2. If input is available, read it by calling one of **Scanner**'s **next**X methods.

As the preceding indicates, **Scanner** defines two sets of methods that enable you to read input. The first are the **hasNext** methods. These include methods such as **hasNextInt( )** and **hasNextDouble( )**, for example. Each of the **hasNext** methods returns **true** if the desired data type is the next available item in the data stream, and **false** otherwise. For example, calling **hasNextInt( )** returns **true** only if the next item in

Ask the Expert (Continued)

the stream is the human-readable form of an integer. If the desired data is available, you can read it by calling one of **Scanner**'s **next** methods, such as **nextInt( )** or **nextDouble( )**. These methods convert the human-readable form of the data into its internal, binary representation and return the result. For example, to read an integer, call **nextInt( )**.

The following sequence shows how to read an integer from the keyboard.

```
Scanner conin = new Scanner(System.in);
int i;

if (conin.hasNextInt()) i = conin.nextInt();
```

Using this code, if you enter the number **123** on the keyboard, then **i** will contain the value 123.

Technically, you can call a **next** method without first calling a **hasNext** method. However, doing so is not usually a good idea. If a **next** method cannot find the type of data it is looking for, it throws a **InputMismatchException**. For this reason, it is best to first confirm that the desired type of data is available by calling a **hasNext** method before calling its corresponding **next** method.

EXERCISES

1. Why does Java define both byte and character streams?
2. Even though console input and output is text-based, why does Java still use byte streams for this purpose?
3. Show how to open a file for reading bytes.
4. Show how to open a file for reading characters.
5. Show how to open a file for random-access I/O.
6. How can you convert a numeric string such as "123.23" into its binary equivalent?
7. Write a program that copies a text file. In the process, have it convert all spaces into hyphens. Use the byte stream file classes. Use the traditional approach to closing a file by explicitly calling **close( )**.
8. Rewrite the program described in exercise 7 so that it uses the character stream classes. This time, use the **try**-with-resources statement to automatically close the file.
9. What type of stream is **System.in**?
10. What does the **read( )** method of **InputStream** return when the end of the stream is reached?
11. What type of stream is used to read binary data?
12. **Reader** and **Writer** are at the top of the _____ class hierarchies.

13. The **try**-with-resources statement is used for _____ _____
_____ .

14. If you are using the traditional method of closing a file, then closing a file within a **finally** block is generally a good approach. True or False?

15. What class gives you access to the attributes of a file?

16. Can you use the **File** class to delete a file?

17. Create a method **nameFromPath( )** that takes as its parameter a string containing the full path name of a file or directory. Have it return just the name of the file or directory. For example, the call **nameFromPath("/usr/etc/abc.txt")** returns "abc.txt".

18. Rewrite the following program so that it uses **try**-with-resources to eliminate the calls to **close( )**. Use only one **try** block.

```java
import java.io.*;

class NoTryWithResources {
  public static void main(String[] args) {
    FileInputStream fin = null;
    FileOutputStream fout = null;

    // First make sure that both files have been specified.
    if(args.length != 2) {
      System.out.println("Usage: NoTryWithResources From To");
      return;
    }

    try {
      fin = new FileInputStream(args[0]);
    }
    catch (IOException exc) {
      System.out.println("IOException: program halted.");
    }
    try {
      fout = new FileOutputStream(args[1]);
    }
    catch (IOException exc) {
      System.out.println("IOException: program halted.");
    }
    try {
      if(fin != null && fout != null) {
        int c = fin.read();
        fout.write(c);
      }
    }
    catch (IOException exc) {
      System.out.println("IOException: program halted.");
    }
    finally {
      try {
```

```
          if(fin != null)
              fin.close();
        }
        catch (IOException exc) {
            System.out.println("IOException: program halted.");
        }
        try {
            if(fout != null)
                fout.close();
        }
        catch (IOException exc) {
            System.out.println("IOException: program halted.");
        }
    }

  }
}
```

19. Write a program that takes a file name as its command line argument. It assumes the file is a binary data file and checks the first 4 bytes of the file to see whether they contain the integer −889275714. It outputs "yes" or "no" or an error message if there was an **IOException** generated. (Trivia question: Why test for that particular value? *Hint*: Try it on several **.class** files.)

20. Write a code segment that prints only the thousandth byte of a binary data file named "datafile". Use a **RandomAccessFile**.

21. Write a program that takes the name of a binary data file as its command-line argument. Assume the file contains only integers. Using a **RandomAccessFile**, sort the data in the file from smallest to largest. Use any sorting algorithm you wish. Note that you should not load the data from the file into an array in memory and then sort the array. Instead you should sort the data in place in the file, using memory for only a small fixed number of variables. Display the integers in the file before and after sorting to verify that the sort worked correctly. *Hint:* The **RandomAccessFile** class has a **length( )** method that returns the number of bytes in the file as a **long** value.

22. A common file format for storing data from a table (such as obtained from a spreadsheet) as text is CSV or "comma-separated values." All the data in the table is stored in the file as rows of text and the data in each row are separated from each other by commas. Write a **CSVConverter** program that takes two file names as its command-line arguments. The first file is a binary data file (not a text file). The first line of this file contains two integers and a new-line '**\n**' character. The first integer is the number of rows of data in the file and the second integer is the number of columns of data in the file. The rest of the file contains rows of integers, separated by commas, and ending with new-line '**\n**' characters. The **CSVConverter** program must extract all the data from the data file and store it in the second file as text in CSV format. Use a **DataInputStream** and a **FileWriter**.

Here is a program you can use to create a data file to use as test input for your **CSVConverter** program. If you run this program to create a data file and then run your **CSVConverter** program on the data file, you will get a new text file with two lines of text, the first containing "1,2,3" and the second containing "4,5,6".

```java
import java.io.*;

public class DataFileCreator {
  public static void main(String[] args) {
     if(args.length != 1) {
        System.out.println("Usage: DataFileCreator File");
        return;
     }

     try (DataOutputStream out =
               new DataOutputStream(new FileOutputStream(args[0]))){
        out.writeInt(2); out.writeInt(3); out.writeChar('\n');
        out.writeInt( 1 ); out.writeChar(',');
        out.writeInt( 2 ); out.writeChar(',');
        out.writeInt( 3 ); out.writeChar('\n');
        out.writeInt( 4 ); out.writeChar(',');
        out.writeInt( 5 ); out.writeChar(',');
        out.writeInt( 6 ); out.writeChar('\n');
     } catch (IOException exc) {
        System.out.println("IOException:   file creation cancelled.");
     }
  }
}
```

23. Write a program that reads all the data from a CSV-formatted text file (see the preceding problem for a definition of CSV format) and displays the average of all the numbers in the file. For example, if the file contains the following characters:

```
1,26,7
444,50,6
```

then the output should report that the average of the values in the file is 89. The name of the CSV file should be provided as a command-line argument. You can assume that the CSV file has at least one row and column. Implement your program either

A. using a **BufferedReader** or
B. using a **Scanner**, as described in the Ask the Expert section at the end of the chapter. *Note: You will need to use methods in the **Scanner** class not discussed in this chapter.*

24. Can you create a **File** object that doesn't correspond to an actual physical file? For example, suppose there is no file named "file.txt" in the **/usr/bin**

directory. In that case, is the following code legal? If so, how do you tell whether the file actually exists?

```
File file = new File("/usr/bin/file.txt");
```

25. Create a class called **FileUtilities** and add to it the following **static** methods:

   A. A method called **moveFile( )** that takes a **File** and a directory (a **String**) as its parameters and moves the file into the directory. Do it by using the **renameTo( )** method in the **File** class that was mentioned in this chapter. The file should be renamed using the same file name but with a different directory. The **moveFile( )** method must return **true** if it was successful and **false** otherwise. The method should work with all files, not just text files. The directory string should end in a slash '/' character.

   B. A method called **moveFile( )** that takes two **String**s as parameters, the first being the name of a file and the second being the name of a directory. It moves the file into the directory. Do it by copying the file into the new directory and then deleting it from the old directory. It must return **true** if it was successful and **false** otherwise. The method should work with all files, not just text files. The directory string should end in a slash '/' character.

   C. A method called **appendFile( )** that takes two **File**s as its parameters. It modifies the first file by appending the contents of the second file to it. The method must return **true** if it was successful and **false** otherwise.

26. The primitive wrapper classes **Byte**, **Short**, **Int**, **Long**, **Float**, **Double**, **Boolean**, and **Character** provide simple ways of converting their binary value to a numerical string equivalent and vice versa. In particular, if **bObj** is a **Byte** object, then the instruction

```
String bString = bObj.toString();
```

assigns to **bString** the numerical string equivalent to the binary value of **bObj**. For example, if **bObj** has the value 24, then **bString** will be assigned the string "24". Conversely, given a string **bString**, you can convert it into an equivalent binary value by

```
byte b = _____;
```

CHAPTER 12

Multithreaded Programming

KEY SKILLS & CONCEPTS

- Understand multithreading fundamentals
- Know the **Thread** class and the **Runnable** interface
- Create a thread
- Create multiple threads
- Determine when a thread ends
- Know thread priorities
- Understand thread synchronization
- Use synchronized methods
- Use synchronized blocks
- Communicate between threads
- Suspend, resume, and stop threads

One of Java's most impressive features is its built-in support for *multithreaded programming*. A multithreaded program contains two or more parts that can run concurrently. Each part of such a program is called a *thread*, and each thread defines a separate path of execution. Thus, multithreading is a specialized form of multitasking. Multithreading can have a dramatic impact on a program's run-time characteristics.

MULTITHREADING FUNDAMENTALS

There are two distinct types of multitasking: process-based and thread-based. It is important to understand the difference between the two. As the terms are used in this book, a process is, in essence, a program that is executing. Thus, *process-based* multitasking is the feature that allows your computer to run two or more programs concurrently. For example, it is process-based multitasking that allows you to run the Java compiler at the same time you are using a text editor or browsing the Internet. In process-based multitasking, a program is the smallest unit of code that can be dispatched by the scheduler.

In a *thread-based* multitasking environment, the thread is the smallest unit of dispatchable code. This means that a single program can perform two or more tasks at once. For instance, a text editor can be formatting text at the same time that it is printing, as long as these two actions are being performed by two separate threads. Although Java programs make use of process-based multitasking environments, process-based multitasking is not under the control of Java. Multithreaded multitasking is.

A principal advantage of multithreading is that it enables you to write very efficient programs because it lets you utilize the idle time that is present in most programs. Most I/O devices, whether they be network ports, disk drives, or the keyboard, are much slower than the CPU. Thus, a program will often spend a majority of its execution time waiting to send or receive information to or from a device. By using multithreading, your program can execute another task during this idle time. For example, while one part of your program is sending a file over the Internet, another part can be reading keyboard input, and still another can be buffering the next block of data to send.

As you probably know, over the past few years, multiprocessor and multicore systems have become commonplace. Of course, single-processor systems are still in widespread use. It is important to understand that Java's multithreading features work in both types of systems. In a single-core system, concurrently executing threads share the CPU, with each thread receiving a slice of CPU time. Therefore, in a single-core system, two or more threads do not actually run at the same time, but idle CPU time is utilized. However, in multiprocessor/multicore systems, it is possible for two or more threads to actually execute simultaneously. In many cases, this can further improve program efficiency and increase the speed of certain operations.

A thread can be in one of several states. In general terms, a thread can be *running*. It can be *ready to run* as soon as it gets CPU time. A running thread can be *suspended*, which is a temporary halt to its execution. It can later be *resumed*. A thread can be *blocked* when waiting for a resource. A thread can be *terminated,* in which case its execution ends and cannot be resumed.

Along with thread-based multitasking comes the need for a special type of feature called *synchronization*, which allows the execution of threads to be coordinated in certain well-defined ways. Java has a complete subsystem devoted to synchronization, and its key features are also described here.

One last point: although multithreading adds another dimension to your programs, the fact that Java manages threads through language elements makes multithreading convenient and easy to use. Many of the details are handled for you.

THE Thread CLASS AND Runnable INTERFACE

Java's multithreading system is built on the **Thread** class and its companion interface, **Runnable**. Both are packaged in **java.lang**. **Thread** encapsulates a thread of execution. It also provides methods that are used to manage thread execution, and several are examined in this chapter. To create a new thread, your program will either extend **Thread** or implement the **Runnable** interface.

All processes have at least one thread of execution, which is usually called the *main thread*, because it is the one that is executed when your program begins. Thus, the main thread is the thread that all of the preceding example programs in the book have been using. From the main thread, you can create other threads.

Progress Check

1. What is the difference between process-based multitasking and thread-based multitasking?
2. In general, in what states can a thread exist?
3. What class encapsulates a thread?

CREATING A THREAD

You create a thread by instantiating an object of type **Thread**. The **Thread** class encapsulates an object that is runnable. As mentioned, Java defines two ways in which you can create a runnable object:

- You can implement the **Runnable** interface.
- You can extend the **Thread** class.

Most of the examples in this chapter will use the approach that implements **Runnable**. However, Try This 12-1 shows how to implement a thread by extending **Thread**. Remember: Both approaches still use the **Thread** class to instantiate, access, and control the thread. The only difference is how a thread-enabled class is created.

The **Runnable** interface abstracts a unit of executable code. You can construct a thread on any object that implements the **Runnable** interface. **Runnable** defines only one method called **run( )**, which is declared like this:

```
public void run( )
```

Inside **run( )**, you will define the code that constitutes the new thread. It is important to understand that **run( )** can call other methods, use other classes, and declare variables just like the main thread. The only difference is that **run( )** establishes the entry point for another, concurrent thread of execution within your program. This thread will end when **run( )** returns.

After you have created a class that implements **Runnable**, you will instantiate an object of type **Thread** on an object of that class. **Thread** defines several constructors. The one that we will use first is shown here:

```
Thread(Runnable threadOb)
```

Answers:

1. Process-based multitasking is used to run two or more programs concurrently. Thread-based multitasking, called multithreading, is used to run pieces of one program concurrently.
2. The thread states are running, ready-to-run, suspended, blocked, and terminated. When a suspended thread is restarted, it is said to be resumed.
3. **Thread**

In this constructor, *threadOb* is an instance of a class that implements the **Runnable** interface. This defines where execution of the thread will begin.

Once created, the new thread will not start running until you call its **start( )** method, which is declared by **Thread**. The **start( )** method causes the JVM to call **run( )**. The **start( )** method is shown here:

      void start( )

Here is an example that creates a new thread and starts it running:

```
// Create a thread by implementing Runnable.

class MyThread implements Runnable {        ← Objects of MyThread can be run
  String thrdName;                                 in their own threads because
                                                   MyThread implements Runnable.
  MyThread(String name) {
    thrdName = name;
  }

  // Entry point of thread.
  public void run() {        ← Threads start executing here.
    System.out.println(thrdName + " starting.");
    try {
      for(int count=0; count < 10; count++) {
        Thread.sleep(400);
        System.out.println("In " + thrdName +
                           ", count is " + count);
      }
    }
    catch(InterruptedException exc) {
      System.out.println(thrdName + " interrupted.");
    }
    System.out.println(thrdName + " terminating.");
  }
}

class UseThreads {
  public static void main(String[] args) {
    System.out.println("Main thread starting.");

    // First, construct a MyThread object.
    MyThread mt = new MyThread("Child #1");        ← Create a runnable object.

    // Next, construct a thread from that object.
    Thread newThrd = new Thread(mt);        ← Construct a thread on that object.

    // Finally, start execution of the thread.
    newThrd.start();        ← Start running the thread.

    for(int i=0; i < 50; i++) {
      System.out.print(".");
      try {
```

```
      Thread.sleep(100);
    }
    catch(InterruptedException exc) {
      System.out.println("Main thread interrupted.");
    }
  }

  System.out.println("Main thread ending.");
  }
}
```

Let's look closely at this program. First, **MyThread** implements **Runnable**. This means that an object of type **MyThread** is suitable for use as a thread and can be passed to the **Thread** constructor.

Inside **run( )**, a loop is established that counts from 0 to 9. Notice the call to **sleep( )**. The **sleep( )** method causes the thread from which it is called to suspend execution for the specified period of milliseconds. Its general form is shown here:

static void sleep(long *milliseconds*) throws InterruptedException

The number of milliseconds to suspend is specified in *milliseconds*. This method can throw an **InterruptedException**. Thus, calls to it must be wrapped in a **try** block. The **sleep( )** method also has a second form, which allows you to specify the period in terms of milliseconds and nanoseconds if you need that level of precision. In **run( )**, **sleep( )** pauses the thread for 400 milliseconds each time through the loop. This lets the thread run slow enough for you to watch it execute.

Inside **main( )**, a new **Thread** object is created by the following sequence of statements:

```
// First, construct a MyThread object.
MyThread mt = new MyThread("Child #1");

// Next, construct a thread from that object.
Thread newThrd = new Thread(mt);

// Finally, start execution of the thread.
newThrd.start();
```

As the comments suggest, first an object of **MyThread** is created. This object is then used to construct a **Thread** object. This is possible because **MyThread** implements **Runnable**. Finally, execution of the new thread is started by calling **start( )**. This causes the child thread's **run( )** method to begin. After calling **start( )**, execution returns to **main( )**, and it enters **main( )**'s **for** loop. Notice that this loop iterates 50 times, pausing 100 milliseconds each time through the loop. Both threads continue running, sharing the CPU in single-CPU systems, until their loops finish. The output produced by this program is as follows. Because of differences between computing environments, the precise output that you see may differ slightly from that shown here.

```
Main thread starting.
.Child #1 starting.
...In Child #1, count is 0
```

```
....In Child #1, count is 1
....In Child #1, count is 2
...In Child #1, count is 3
....In Child #1, count is 4
....In Child #1, count is 5
....In Child #1, count is 6
...In Child #1, count is 7
....In Child #1, count is 8
....In Child #1, count is 9
Child #1 terminating.
...........Main thread ending.
```

There is one other point of interest to notice in this first threading example. To illustrate the fact that the main thread and **mt** execute concurrently, it is necessary to keep **main( )** from terminating until **mt** is finished. Here, this is done through the timing differences between the two threads. Because the calls to **sleep( )** inside **main( )**'s **for** loop cause a total delay of 5 seconds (50 iterations times 100 milliseconds), but the total delay within **run( )**'s loop is only 4 seconds (10 iterations times 400 milliseconds), **run( )** will finish approximately 1 second before **main( )**. As a result, both the main thread and **mt** will execute concurrently until **mt** ends. Then, about 1 second later **main( )** ends.

Although this use of timing differences to ensure that **main( )** finishes last is sufficient for this and the next few examples, it is not something that you would normally use in practice. As you will see later in this chapter, Java provides much better ways of waiting for a thread to end.

It is important to point out that having the main thread finish last is not necessarily a requirement when using multiple threads. For the type of threads created in this chapter, a program will continue to run until all of its child threads have ended. Having the main thread finish last is, however, often useful when you are first learning about threads.

Some Simple Improvements

While the preceding program is perfectly valid, some simple improvements will make it more efficient and easier to use. First, it is possible to have a thread begin execution as soon as it is created. In the case of **MyThread**, this is done by instantiating a **Thread** object inside **MyThread**'s constructor. Second, there is no need for **MyThread** to store the name of the thread since it is possible to give a name to a thread when it is created. To do so, use this version of **Thread**'s constructor.

Thread(Runnable *threadOb*, String *name*)

Here, *name* becomes the name of the thread.

You can obtain the name of a thread by calling **getName( )** defined by **Thread**. Its general form is shown here:

final String getName( )

Although not needed by the following program, you can set the name of a thread after it is created by using **setName( )**, which is shown here:

final void setName(String *threadName*)

Here, *threadName* specifies the name of the thread.

Here is the improved version of the preceding program:

```
// Improved MyThread.

class MyThread implements Runnable {
  Thread thrd; ◄──────────A reference to the thread is stored in thrd.

  // Construct a new thread.
  MyThread(String name) {
    thrd = new Thread(this, name); ◄──────────The thread is named when it is created.
    thrd.start(); // start the thread ◄──────────Begin executing the thread.
  }

  // Begin execution of new thread.
  public void run() {
    System.out.println(thrd.getName() + " starting.");
    try {
      for(int count=0; count < 10; count++) {
        Thread.sleep(400);
        System.out.println("In " + thrd.getName() +
                         ", count is " + count);

      }
    }
    catch(InterruptedException exc) {
      System.out.println(thrd.getName() + " interrupted.");
    }
    System.out.println(thrd.getName() + " terminating.");
  }
}

class UseThreadsImproved {
  public static void main(String[] args) {
    System.out.println("Main thread starting.");

    MyThread mt = new MyThread("Child #1"); ◄──────────┐
                                                        │  Now the thread starts when it is created.
    for(int i=0; i < 50; i++) {
      System.out.print(".");
      try {
        Thread.sleep(100);
      }
      catch(InterruptedException exc) {
        System.out.println("Main thread interrupted.");
      }
    }

    System.out.println("Main thread ending.");
  }
}
```

This version produces the same output as before. Notice that the thread instance is stored in **thrd** inside **MyThread**.

Progress Check

1. In what two ways can you create a class that can act as a thread?
2. What is the purpose of the **run( )** method defined by **Runnable**?
3. What does the **start( )** method defined by **Thread** do?

Ask the Expert

Q Are there different types of threads?

A Java defines two basic types of threads: user and daemon. The type of threads created by the programs in this chapter are user threads. A user thread will continue to execute until it concludes. A daemon thread will be automatically terminated when all user threads have terminated. By default, a new thread is of the same type as its creating thread. Because the main thread is a user thread, the threads created in this chapter are user threads. You can change a thread to a daemon thread by calling **setDaemon( )**, shown here:

```
final void setDaemon(boolean isDaemon)
```

If *isDaemon* is **true**, the thread becomes a daemon thread. Otherwise, it becomes a user thread. This method must be called before the thread's **start( )** method is called.

TRY THIS 12-1 EXTENDING Thread

`ExtendThread.java`

Implementing **Runnable** is one way to create a class that can instantiate thread objects. Extending **Thread** is the other. In this project, you will see how to extend **Thread** by creating a program functionally identical to the **UseThreadsImproved** program.

When a class extends **Thread**, it must override the **run( )** method, which is the entry point for the new thread. It must also call **start( )** to begin execution of the new thread. It is possible to override other **Thread** methods, but doing so is not required.

Answers:

1. To create a thread, either implement **Runnable** or extend **Thread**.
2. The **run( )** method is the entry point to a thread.
3. The **start( )** method starts the execution of a thread.

STEP-BY-STEP

1. Create a file called **ExtendThread.java**. Into this file, copy the code from the second threading example (**UseThreadsImproved.java**).

2. Change the declaration of **MyThread** so that it extends **Thread** rather than implementing **Runnable**, as shown here.

```
class MyThread extends Thread {
```

3. Remove this line:

```
Thread thrd;
```

The **thrd** variable is no longer needed, since **MyThread** includes an instance of **Thread** and can refer to itself.

4. Change the **MyThread** constructor so that it looks like this:

```
// Construct a new thread.
MyThread(String name) {
  super(name); // name thread
  start(); // start the thread
}
```

As you can see, first **super** is used to call this version of **Thread**'s constructor:

   Thread(String *name*);

Here, *name* is the name of the thread. Therefore, this constructor sets the name of the thread.

5. Change **run( )** so it calls **getName( )** directly, without qualifying it with the **thrd** variable. It should look like this:

```
// Begin execution of new thread.
public void run() {
  System.out.println(getName() + " starting.");
  try {
    for(int count=0; count < 10; count++) {
      Thread.sleep(400);
      System.out.println("In " + getName() +
                         ", count is " + count);
    }
  }
  catch(InterruptedException exc) {
    System.out.println(getName() + " interrupted.");
  }

  System.out.println(getName() + " terminating.");
}
```

6. Here is the completed program that now extends **Thread** rather than implementing **Runnable**. The output is the same as before.

```java
/*
   Try This 12-1

   Extend Thread.
*/
class MyThread extends Thread {

  // Construct a new thread.
  MyThread(String name) {
    super(name); // name thread
    start(); // start the thread
  }

  // Begin execution of new thread.
  public void run() {
    System.out.println(getName() + " starting.");
    try {
      for(int count=0; count < 10; count++) {
        Thread.sleep(400);
        System.out.println("In " + getName() +
                           ", count is " + count);
      }
    }
    catch(InterruptedException exc) {
      System.out.println(getName() + " interrupted.");
    }

    System.out.println(getName() + " terminating.");
  }
}

class ExtendThread {
  public static void main(String[] args) {
    System.out.println("Main thread starting.");

    MyThread mt = new MyThread("Child #1");

    for(int i=0; i < 50; i++) {
      System.out.print(".");
      try {
        Thread.sleep(100);
      }
      catch(InterruptedException exc) {
        System.out.println("Main thread interrupted.");
      }
    }

    System.out.println("Main thread ending.");
  }
}
```

CREATING MULTIPLE THREADS

The preceding examples have created only one child thread. However, your program
can spawn as many threads as it needs. For example, the following program creates
three child threads:

```java
// Create multiple threads.

class MyThread implements Runnable {
  Thread thrd;

  // Construct a new thread.
  MyThread(String name) {
    thrd = new Thread(this, name);

    thrd.start(); // start the thread
  }

  // Begin execution of new thread.
  public void run() {
    System.out.println(thrd.getName() + " starting.");
    try {
      for(int count=0; count < 10; count++) {
        Thread.sleep(400);
        System.out.println("In " + thrd.getName() +
                           ", count is " + count);
      }
    }
    catch(InterruptedException exc) {
      System.out.println(thrd.getName() + " interrupted.");
    }
    System.out.println(thrd.getName() + " terminating.");
  }
}

class MoreThreads {
  public static void main(String[] args) {
    System.out.println("Main thread starting.");

    MyThread mt1 = new MyThread("Child #1");
    MyThread mt2 = new MyThread("Child #2");
    MyThread mt3 = new MyThread("Child #3");

    for(int i=0; i < 50; i++) {
      System.out.print(".");
      try {
        Thread.sleep(100);
      }
      catch(InterruptedException exc) {
        System.out.println("Main thread interrupted.");
      }
```

Create and start executing three threads.

```
    }

        System.out.println("Main thread ending.");
    }
}
```

Sample output from this program follows.

```
Main thread starting.
Child #1 starting.
.Child #2 starting.
Child #3 starting.
...In Child #3, count is 0
In Child #2, count is 0
In Child #1, count is 0
....In Child #1, count is 1
In Child #2, count is 1
In Child #3, count is 1
....In Child #2, count is 2
In Child #3, count is 2
In Child #1, count is 2
...In Child #1, count is 3
In Child #2, count is 3
In Child #3, count is 3
....In Child #1, count is 4
In Child #3, count is 4
In Child #2, count is 4
....In Child #1, count is 5
In Child #3, count is 5
In Child #2, count is 5
...In Child #3, count is 6
.In Child #2, count is 6
In Child #1, count is 6
...In Child #3, count is 7
In Child #1, count is 7
In Child #2, count is 7
....In Child #2, count is 8
In Child #1, count is 8
In Child #3, count is 8
....In Child #1, count is 9
Child #1 terminating.
In Child #2, count is 9
Child #2 terminating.
In Child #3, count is 9
Child #3 terminating.
...........Main thread ending.
```

As you can see, once started, all three child threads execute concurrently. Notice that the threads are started in the order in which they are created. However, this may not always be the case. Java is free to schedule the execution of threads in its own way. Of course, because of differences in timing or environment, the precise output from the program may differ, so don't be surprised if you see slightly different results when you try the program.

Ask the Expert

Q Why does Java have two ways to create child threads (by extending **Thread** or implementing **Runnable**) and which approach is better?

A The **Thread** class defines several methods that can be overridden by a derived class. Of these methods, the only one that *must* be overridden is **run( )**. This is, of course, the same method required when you implement **Runnable**. Some Java programmers feel that classes should be extended only when they are being enhanced or modified in some way. So, if you will not be overriding any of **Thread**'s other methods, it is probably best to simply implement **Runnable**. Also, by implementing **Runnable**, you enable your thread to inherit a class other than **Thread**.

DETERMINING WHEN A THREAD ENDS

It is often useful to know when a thread has ended. For example, in the preceding examples, for the sake of illustration it was useful to keep the main thread alive until the other threads ended. In those examples, this was accomplished by having the main thread sleep longer than the child threads that it spawned. This is, of course, hardly a satisfactory or generalizable solution!

Fortunately, **Thread** provides two means by which you can determine if a thread has ended. First, you can call **isAlive( )** on the thread. Its general form is shown here:

```
final boolean isAlive( )
```

The **isAlive( )** method returns **true** if the thread on which it is called is still running. It returns **false** otherwise. To try **isAlive( )**, substitute this version of **MoreThreads** for the one shown in the preceding program.

```java
// Use isAlive().
class MoreThreads {
  public static void main(String[] args) {
    System.out.println("Main thread starting.");

    MyThread mt1 = new MyThread("Child #1");
    MyThread mt2 = new MyThread("Child #2");
    MyThread mt3 = new MyThread("Child #3");

    do {
      System.out.print(".");
      try {
        Thread.sleep(100);
      }
      catch(InterruptedException exc) {
        System.out.println("Main thread interrupted.");
      }
```

```
     } while (mt1.thrd.isAlive() ||
              mt2.thrd.isAlive() ||          This waits until all threads terminate.
              mt3.thrd.isAlive());

    System.out.println("Main thread ending.");
  }
}
```

This version uses **isAlive( )** to wait for the child threads to terminate. It produces output similar to that produced by the earlier example, except that **main( )** terminates as soon as the child threads end.

Another way to wait for a thread to finish is to call **join( )**, shown here:

final void join( ) throws InterruptedException

This method waits until the thread on which it is called terminates. Its name comes from the concept of the calling thread waiting until the specified thread *joins* it. Additional forms of **join( )** allow you to specify a maximum amount of time that you want to wait for the specified thread to terminate.

Here is a program that uses **join( )** to ensure that the main thread is the last to stop.

```
// Use join().

class MyThread implements Runnable {
  Thread thrd;

  // Construct a new thread.
  MyThread(String name) {
    thrd = new Thread(this, name);
    thrd.start(); // start the thread
  }

  // Begin execution of new thread.
  public void run() {
    System.out.println(thrd.getName() + " starting.");
    try {
      for(int count=0; count < 10; count++) {
        Thread.sleep(400);
        System.out.println("In " + thrd.getName() +
                           ", count is " + count);
      }
    }
    catch(InterruptedException exc) {
      System.out.println(thrd.getName() + " interrupted.");
    }
    System.out.println(thrd.getName() + " terminating.");
  }
}

class JoinThreads {
```

```
public static void main(String[] args) {
    System.out.println("Main thread starting.");

    MyThread mt1 = new MyThread("Child #1");
    MyThread mt2 = new MyThread("Child #2");
    MyThread mt3 = new MyThread("Child #3");

    try {
        mt1.thrd.join();
        System.out.println("Child #1 joined.");
        mt2.thrd.join();
        System.out.println("Child #2 joined.");
        mt3.thrd.join();
        System.out.println("Child #3 joined.");
    }
    catch(InterruptedException exc) {
        System.out.println("Main thread interrupted. ");
    }
    System.out.println("Main thread ending.");
  }
}
```

Wait until the specified thread ends.

Sample output from this program is shown here. Remember that when you try the program, your precise output may vary slightly.

```
Main thread starting.
Child #1 starting.
Child #2 starting.
Child #3 starting.
In Child #2, count is 0
In Child #3, count is 0
In Child #1, count is 0
In Child #1, count is 1
In Child #2, count is 1
In Child #3, count is 1
In Child #1, count is 2
In Child #2, count is 2
In Child #3, count is 2
In Child #3, count is 3
In Child #2, count is 3
In Child #1, count is 3
In Child #2, count is 4
In Child #3, count is 4
In Child #1, count is 4
In Child #2, count is 5
In Child #3, count is 5
In Child #1, count is 5
In Child #3, count is 6
In Child #2, count is 6
In Child #1, count is 6
In Child #1, count is 7
```

```
In Child #3, count is 7
In Child #2, count is 7
In Child #1, count is 8
In Child #3, count is 8
In Child #2, count is 8
In Child #2, count is 9
In Child #3, count is 9
Child #3 terminating.
In Child #1, count is 9
Child #1 terminating.
Child #2 terminating.
Child #1 joined.
Child #2 joined.
Child #3 joined.
Main thread ending.
```

As you can see, after the calls to **join( )** return, the threads have stopped executing. Then, the main thread ends.

Progress Check

1. What are the two ways in which you can determine whether a thread has ended?
2. Explain **join( )**.

THREAD PRIORITIES

Each thread has associated with it a priority setting. A thread's priority determines, in part, how much CPU time a thread receives relative to the other active threads. In general, low-priority threads receive little, whereas high-priority threads receive a lot. As you might expect, how much CPU time a thread receives has a profound impact on its execution characteristics and its interaction with other threads currently executing in the system.

It is important to understand that factors other than a thread's priority also affect how much CPU time a thread receives. For example, if a high-priority thread is waiting on some resource, perhaps for keyboard input, then it will be blocked, and a lower priority thread will run. However, when that high-priority thread gains access to the resource, it can preempt the low-priority thread and resume execution. Another factor that affects the scheduling of threads is the way the operating system implements multitasking. (See "Ask the Expert," at the end of this section.) Thus, just because you give one thread a high priority and another a low priority does not necessarily mean

---

Answers:

1. To determine whether a thread has ended, you can call **isAlive( )** or use **join( )** to wait for the thread to join the calling thread.
2. The **join( )** method suspends execution of the calling thread until the thread on which **join( )** is called ends.

that one thread will run faster or more often than the other. It's just that the high-priority thread has greater potential access to the CPU.

When a child thread is started, its priority setting is equal to that of its parent thread. You can change a thread's priority by calling **setPriority( )**, which is a member of **Thread**. This is its general form:

final void setPriority(int *level*)

Here, *level* specifies the new priority setting for the calling thread. The value of *level* must be within the range **MIN_PRIORITY** and **MAX_PRIORITY**. Currently, these values are 1 and 10, respectively. To return a thread to default priority, specify **NORM_PRIORITY**, which is currently 5. These priorities are defined as **static final** variables within **Thread**.

You can obtain the current priority setting by calling the **getPriority( )** method of **Thread**, shown here:

final int getPriority( )

Although there may be situations in which setting a thread's priority is helpful, often it is best to simply use the default setting—especially when you're just beginning to use multithreading. One reason for this is that in today's multicore environments, sometimes increasing or decreasing a thread's priority has little impact on its run-time characteristics. Furthermore, you should never try to use a thread's priority setting as a means of managing the interaction between threads. To handle thread interaction, you must use one of Java's synchronization features, which are described in the next section.

Ask the Expert

Q Does the operating system's implementation of multitasking affect how much CPU time a thread receives?

A One of the most important factors affecting thread execution is the way the operating system implements multitasking and scheduling. For example, it is common for an operating system to use preemptive multitasking in which each thread receives a time slice, at least occasionally. However, it is also possible for an operating system to use nonpreemptive scheduling in which one thread must yield execution before another thread will execute. If your multithreaded program is running in a nonpreemptive environment, it is easy for one thread to dominate, preventing others from running.

SYNCHRONIZATION

When using multiple threads, it is sometimes necessary to coordinate the activities of two or more. The process by which this is achieved is called *synchronization*. The most common reason for synchronization is when two or more threads need access to a shared resource that can be used by only one thread at a time. For example, when one thread is writing to a file, a second thread must be prevented from doing so at the same time. Another reason for synchronization is when one thread is waiting for an event that is caused by another thread. In this case, there must be some means by which the first thread is held in a suspended state until the event has occurred. Then, the waiting thread must resume execution.

Key to synchronization in Java is the concept of the *monitor*, which controls access to an object. A monitor works by implementing the concept of a *lock*. When an object is locked by one thread, access to the object by another thread is restricted. When the thread exits, the object is unlocked and is available for use by another thread.

All objects in Java have a monitor. This feature is built into the Java language itself. Thus, all objects support synchronization. Synchronization is supported by the keyword **synchronized** and a few well-defined methods that all objects have. Since synchronization was designed into Java from the start, it is much easier to use than you might first expect. In fact, for many programs, synchronization is almost transparent.

You can synchronize your code in two ways. Both involve the use of the **synchronized** keyword, and both are examined here.

USING SYNCHRONIZED METHODS

You can synchronize access to a method by modifying it with the **synchronized** keyword. When that method is called, the calling thread enters the object's monitor, which then locks the object. While locked, no other thread can enter the method (or enter any other synchronized method defined by the object's class) on that object. When the thread returns from the method, the monitor unlocks the object, allowing it to be used by the next thread. Thus, synchronization is achieved with virtually no programming effort on your part.

The following program demonstrates synchronization by controlling access to a method called **sumArray( )**, which sums the elements of an integer array.

```
// Use synchronize to control access.

class SumArray {
  private int sum;

  synchronized int sumArray(int[] nums) {          sumArray( ) is synchronized.
    sum = 0; // reset sum

    for(int i=0; i<nums.length; i++) {
      sum += nums[i];
      System.out.println("Running total for " +
            Thread.currentThread().getName() +
            " is " + sum);
      try {
        Thread.sleep(10); // allow task-switch
      }
      catch(InterruptedException exc) {
        System.out.println("Thread interrupted.");
```

```
      }
    }
    return sum;
  }
}

class MyThread implements Runnable {
  Thread thrd;
  static SumArray sa = new SumArray();
  int[] a;
  int answer;

  // Construct a new thread.
  MyThread(String name, int[] nums) {
    thrd = new Thread(this, name);
    a = nums;
    thrd.start(); // start the thread
  }

  // Begin execution of new thread.
  public void run() {
    int sum;

    System.out.println(thrd.getName() + " starting.");

    answer = sa.sumArray(a);
    System.out.println("Sum for " + thrd.getName() +
                       " is " + answer);

    System.out.println(thrd.getName() + " terminating.");
  }
}

class Sync {
  public static void main(String[] args) {
    int[] a = {1, 2, 3, 4, 5};

    MyThread mt1 = new MyThread("Child #1", a);
    MyThread mt2 = new MyThread("Child #2", a);

    try {
      mt1.thrd.join();
      mt2.thrd.join();
    }
    catch(InterruptedException exc) {
      System.out.println("Main thread interrupted.");
    }
  }
}
```

The output from the program is shown here. (The precise output may differ on your computer.)

```
Child #1 starting.
Running total for Child #1 is 1
Child #2 starting.
Running total for Child #1 is 3
Running total for Child #1 is 6
Running total for Child #1 is 10
Running total for Child #1 is 15
Sum for Child #1 is 15
Child #1 terminating.
Running total for Child #2 is 1
Running total for Child #2 is 3
Running total for Child #2 is 6
Running total for Child #2 is 10
Running total for Child #2 is 15
Sum for Child #2 is 15
Child #2 terminating.
```

Let's examine this program in detail. The program creates three classes. The first is **SumArray**. It contains the method **sumArray( )**, which sums an integer array. The second class is **MyThread**, which uses a **static** object of type **SumArray** to obtain the sum of an integer array. This object is called **sa**, and because it is **static**, there is only one copy of it, which is shared by all instances of **MyThread**. Finally, the class **Sync** creates two threads and has each compute the sum of an integer array.

Inside **sumArray( )**, **sleep( )** is called to purposely allow a task switch to occur, if one can—but it can't. Because **sumArray( )** is synchronized, it can be used by only one thread at a time on any given object. Thus, when the second child thread begins execution, it does not enter **sumArray( )** until after the first child thread is done. This ensures that the correct result is produced.

To fully understand the effects of **synchronized**, try removing it from the declaration of **sumArray( )**. After doing this, **sumArray( )** is no longer synchronized, and any number of threads may execute it concurrently. The problem with this change is that the running total is stored in **sum**, which will be changed by each thread that calls **sumArray( )** through the **static** object **sa**. Thus, when two threads call **sa.sumArray( )** at the same time, incorrect results are produced because **sum** reflects the summation of both threads, mixed together. For example, here is sample output from the program after **synchronized** has been removed from **sumArray( )**'s declaration. (The precise output may differ on your computer.)

```
Child #1 starting.
Running total for Child #1 is 1
Child #2 starting.
Running total for Child #2 is 1
Running total for Child #1 is 3
Running total for Child #2 is 5
Running total for Child #2 is 8
Running total for Child #1 is 11
Running total for Child #2 is 15
```

```
Running total for Child #1 is 19
Running total for Child #2 is 24
Sum for Child #2 is 24
Child #2 terminating.
Running total for Child #1 is 29
Sum for Child #1 is 29
Child #1 terminating.
```

As the output shows, both child threads are calling **sa.sumArray( )** concurrently, and the value of **sum** is corrupted. Before moving on, let's review the key points of a synchronized method:

- A synchronized method is created by preceding its declaration with **synchronized**.
- For any given object, once a synchronized method has been called, the object is locked and no synchronized methods on the same object can be used by another thread of execution.
- Other threads trying to call a synchronized method on a locked object will enter a wait state until the object is unlocked.
- When a thread leaves the synchronized method, the object is unlocked.

THE synchronized STATEMENT

Although creating **synchronized** methods within classes that you create is an easy and effective means of achieving synchronization, it will not work in all cases. For example, you might want to synchronize access to some method that is not modified by **synchronized**. This can occur because you want to use a class that was not created by you but by a third party, and you do not have access to the source code. Thus, it is not possible for you to add **synchronized** to the appropriate methods within the class. How can access to an object of this class be synchronized? Fortunately, the solution to this problem is easy: You simply put calls to the methods defined by this class inside a **synchronized** block.

This is the general form of a **synchronized** block:

```
synchronized(objref) {
    // statements to be synchronized
}
```

Here, *objref* is a reference to the object for which synchronization is needed. Once a synchronized block has been entered, no other thread can call a synchronized method or enter a synchronized block on the object *objref* refers to until the block has been exited.

For example, another way to synchronize calls to **sumArray( )** is to call it from within a synchronized block, as shown in this version of the program.

```
// Use a synchronized block to control access to SumArray.
class SumArray {
  private int sum;

  int sumArray(int[] nums) {          ———————Here, sumArray( ) is not synchronized.
```

```
      sum = 0; // reset sum

   for(int i=0; i<nums.length; i++) {
     sum += nums[i];
     System.out.println("Running total for " +
              Thread.currentThread().getName() +
              " is " + sum);
     try {
       Thread.sleep(10); // allow task-switch
     }
     catch(InterruptedException exc) {
       System.out.println("Thread interrupted.");
     }
   }
   return sum;
 }
}

class MyThread implements Runnable {
  Thread thrd;
  static SumArray sa = new SumArray();
  int[] a;
  int answer;

  // Construct a new thread.
  MyThread(String name, int[] nums) {
    thrd = new Thread(this, name);
    a = nums;
    thrd.start(); // start the thread
  }

  // Begin execution of new thread.
  public void run() {
    System.out.println(thrd.getName() + " starting.");

    // synchronize calls to sumArray()
    synchronized(sa) {  ◄──────────Here, calls to sumArray( ) on sa are synchronized.
      answer = sa.sumArray(a);
    }
    System.out.println("Sum for " + thrd.getName() +
                " is " + answer);

    System.out.println(thrd.getName() + " terminating.");
  }
}

class Sync {
  public static void main(String[] args) {
    int[] a = {1, 2, 3, 4, 5};

    MyThread mt1 = new MyThread("Child #1", a);
```

```
      MyThread mt2 = new MyThread("Child #2", a);

      try {
        mt1.thrd.join();
        mt2.thrd.join();
      } catch(InterruptedException exc) {
        System.out.println("Main Thread interrupted.");
      }
    }
  }
}
```

This version produces the same, correct output as the one shown earlier that uses a synchronized method.

Progress Check

1. How do you set a thread's priority?
2. How do you restrict access to an object to one thread at a time?
3. The **synchronized** keyword can be used to modify a method or to create a _____ block.

Ask the Expert

Q A friend was telling me about something called the "concurrency utilities." What are these? Also, what is the Fork/Join Framework?

A The concurrency utilities, which are packaged in **java.util.concurrent** (and its subpackages), support concurrent programming. Among several other items, they offer various synchronizers, thread pools, execution managers, and locks that expand your control over thread execution. One of the most exciting features of the concurrent API is the Fork/Join Framework, which was added by JDK 7.

The Fork/Join Framework supports what is often termed *parallel programming*. This is the name commonly given to the techniques that take advantage of computers that contain two or more processors (including multicore systems) by subdividing a task into subtasks, with each subtask executing on its own processor. As you can imagine, such an approach can lead to significantly higher throughput and performance. The key advantage of the Fork/Join Framework is ease of use; it streamlines the development of multithreaded code that automatically scales to utilize the number of processors in a system. After you learn the fundamentals of multithreading, you will be ready to move on to the concurrency utilities. They are described in depth in Chapter 27.

Answers:

1. To set a thread's priority, call **setPriority( )**.
2. To restrict access to an object to one thread at a time, use the **synchronized** keyword.
3. synchronized

THREAD COMMUNICATION USING notify( ), wait( ), AND notifyAll( )

Consider the following situation. A thread called T is executing inside a synchronized method and needs access to a resource called R that is temporarily unavailable. What should T do? If T enters some form of polling loop that waits for R, T ties up the object, preventing other threads access to it. This is a less than optimal solution because it partially defeats the advantages of programming for a multithreaded environment. A better solution is to have T temporarily relinquish control of the object, allowing another thread to run. When R becomes available, T can be notified and resume execution. Such an approach relies on some form of interthread communication in which one thread can notify another that it is blocked and later be notified that it can resume execution. Java supports interthread communication with the **wait( )**, **notify( )**, and **notifyAll( )** methods.

The **wait( )**, **notify( )**, and **notifyAll( )** methods are part of all objects because they are implemented by the **Object** class. These methods can be called only from within a **synchronized** context. Here is how they are used. When a thread is temporarily blocked from running, it calls **wait( )**. This causes the thread to go to sleep and the monitor for that object to be released, allowing another thread to use the object. At a later point, the sleeping thread is awakened when some other thread enters the same monitor and calls **notify( )**, or **notifyAll( )**.

Following are the various forms of **wait( )** defined by **Object**.

```
final void wait( ) throws InterruptedException
final void wait(long millis) throws InterruptedException
final void wait(long millis, int nanos) throws InterruptedException
```

The first form waits until notified. The second form waits until notified or until the specified period of milliseconds has expired. The third form allows you to specify the wait period in terms of milliseconds and nanoseconds.

Here are the general forms for **notify( )** and **notifyAll( )**.

```
final void notify( )
final void notifyAll( )
```

A call to **notify( )** resumes one waiting thread. A call to **notifyAll( )** notifies all threads, with the highest priority thread gaining access to the object.

Before looking at an example that uses **wait( )**, an important point needs to be made. Although **wait( )** normally waits until **notify( )** or **notifyAll( )** is called, there is a possibility that in very rare cases the waiting thread could be awakened due to a *spurious wakeup*. The conditions that lead to a spurious wakeup are complex and beyond the scope of this book. However, Oracle recommends that because of the remote possibility of a spurious wakeup, calls to **wait( )** should take place within a loop that checks the condition on which the thread is waiting. The following example shows this technique.

An Example That Uses wait( ) and notify( )

To understand the need for and the application of **wait( )** and **notify( )**, we will create a program that simulates the ticking of a clock by displaying the words "Tick" and "Tock" on the screen. To accomplish this, we will create a class called **TickTock** that contains two methods: **tick( )** and **tock( )**. The **tick( )** method displays the word "Tick", and **tock( )** displays "Tock". To run the clock, two threads are created, one that calls **tick( )** and one that calls **tock( )**. The goal is to make the two threads execute in a way that the output from the program displays a consistent "Tick Tock"—that is, a repeated pattern of one tick followed by one tock.

```java
// Use wait() and notify() to create a ticking clock.

class TickTock {

  String state; // contains the state of the clock

  synchronized void tick(boolean running) {
    if(!running) { // stop the clock
      state = "ticked";
      notify(); // notify any waiting threads
      return;
    }

    System.out.print("Tick ");

    state = "ticked"; // set the current state to ticked

    notify(); // let tock() run              ————————tick( ) notifies tock( ).
    try {
      while(!state.equals("tocked"))
        wait(); // wait for tock() to complete  ————————tick( ) waits for tock( ).
    }
    catch(InterruptedException exc) {
      System.out.println("Thread interrupted.");
    }
  }

  synchronized void tock(boolean running) {
    if(!running) { // stop the clock
      state = "tocked";
      notify(); // notify any waiting threads
      return;
    }

    System.out.println("Tock");

    state = "tocked"; // set the current state to tocked

    notify(); // let tick() run              ————————tock( ) notifies tick( ).
    try {
      while(!state.equals("ticked"))
        wait(); // wait for tick to complete  ————————tock( ) waits for tick( ).
    }
    catch(InterruptedException exc) {
```

```
          System.out.println("Thread interrupted.");
      }
    }
}

class MyThread implements Runnable {
  Thread thrd;
  TickTock ttOb;

  // Construct a new thread.
  MyThread(String name, TickTock tt) {
    thrd = new Thread(this, name);
    ttOb = tt;
    thrd.start(); // start the thread
  }

  // Begin execution of new thread.
  public void run() {

    if(thrd.getName().compareTo("Tick") == 0) {
      for(int i=0; i<5; i++) ttOb.tick(true);
      ttOb.tick(false);
    }
    else {
      for(int i=0; i<5; i++) ttOb.tock(true);
      ttOb.tock(false);
    }
  }
}

class ThreadCom {
  public static void main(String[] args) {
    TickTock tt = new TickTock();
    MyThread mt1 = new MyThread("Tick", tt);
    MyThread mt2 = new MyThread("Tock", tt);

    try {
      mt1.thrd.join();
      mt2.thrd.join();
    } catch(InterruptedException exc) {
      System.out.println("Main thread interrupted.");
    }
  }
}
```

Here is the output produced by the program:

```
Tick Tock
Tick Tock
Tick Tock
Tick Tock
Tick Tock
```

Let's take a close look at this program. The heart of the clock is the **TickTock** class. It contains two methods, **tick( )** and **tock( )**, which communicate with each other to ensure that a Tick is always followed by a Tock, which is always followed by a Tick, and so on. Notice the **state** field. When the clock is running, **state** will hold either the string "ticked" or "tocked", which indicates the current state of the clock. In **main( )**, a **TickTock** object called **tt** is created, and this object is used to start two threads of execution.

The threads are based on objects of type **MyThread**. The **MyThread** constructor is passed two arguments. The first becomes the name of the thread. This will be either "Tick" or "Tock". The second is a reference to the **TickTock** object, which is **tt** in this case. Inside the **run( )** method of **MyThread**, if the name of the thread is "Tick", then calls to **tick( )** are made. If the name of the thread is "Tock", then the **tock( )** method is called. Five calls that pass **true** as an argument are made to each method. The clock runs as long as **true** is passed. A final call that passes **false** to each method stops the clock.

The most important part of the program is found in the **tick( )** and **tock( )** methods of **TickTock**. We will begin with the **tick( )** method, which, for convenience, is shown again here.

```java
synchronized void tick(boolean running) {
  if(!running) { // stop the clock
    state = "ticked";
    notify(); // notify any waiting threads
    return;
  }

  System.out.print("Tick ");

  state = "ticked"; // set the current state to ticked

  notify(); // let tock() run
  try {
    while(!state.equals("tocked"))
      wait(); // wait for tock() to complete
  }
  catch(InterruptedException exc) {
    System.out.println("Thread interrupted.");
  }
}
```

First, notice that **tick( )** is modified by **synchronized**. Remember, **wait( )** and **notify( )** apply only to synchronized methods and synchronized blocks. The method begins by checking the value of the **running** parameter. This parameter is used to provide a clean shutdown of the clock. If it is **false**, then the clock has been stopped. If this is the case, **state** is set to "ticked" and a call to **notify( )** is made to enable any waiting thread to run. We will return to this point in a moment.

Assuming that the clock is running when **tick( )** executes, the word "Tick" is displayed, **state** is set to "ticked", and then a call to **notify( )** takes place. The call to **notify( )** allows a thread waiting on the same object to run. Next, **wait( )** is called within a while loop. The call to **wait( )** causes **tick( )** to suspend until another thread calls **notify( )**. Therefore, the loop will not iterate until another thread calls **notify( )** on the same object. As a result, when **tick( )** is called, it displays one "Tick", lets another thread run, and then suspends.

The **while** loop that calls **wait( )** checks the value of **state**, waiting for it to equal "tocked", which will be the case only after the **tock( )** method executes. As explained, using a **while** loop to check this condition prevents a spurious wakeup from incorrectly restarting the thread. If **state** does not equal "tocked" when **wait( )** returns, it means that a spurious wakeup occurred, and **wait( )** is simply called again.

The **tock( )** method is an exact copy of **tick( )** except that it displays "Tock" and sets **state** to "tocked". Thus, when entered, it displays "Tock", calls **notify( )**, and then waits. When viewed as a pair, a call to **tick( )** can only be followed by a call to **tock( )**, which can only be followed by a call to **tick( )**, and so on. Therefore, the two methods are mutually synchronized.

The reason for the call to **notify( )** when the clock is stopped is to allow a final call to **wait( )** to succeed. Remember, both **tick( )** and **tock( )** execute a call to **wait( )** after displaying their message. The problem is that when the clock is stopped, one of the methods will still be waiting. Thus, a final call to **notify( )** is required in order for the waiting method to run. As an experiment, try removing this call to **notify( )** and watch what happens. As you will see, the program will "hang," and you will need to press CTRL-C to exit. The reason for this is that when the final call to **tock( )** calls **wait( )**, there is no corresponding call to **notify( )** that lets **tock( )** conclude. Thus, **tock( )** just sits there, waiting forever.

Before moving on, if you have any doubt that the calls to **wait( )** and **notify( )** are actually needed to make the "clock" run right, substitute this version of **TickTock** into the preceding program. It has all calls to **wait( )** and **notify( )** removed.

```
// No calls to wait() or notify().
class TickTock {

  String state; // contains the state of the clock

  synchronized void tick(boolean running) {
    if(!running) { // stop the clock
      state = "ticked";
      return;
    }

    System.out.print("Tick ");

    state = "ticked"; // set the current state to ticked
  }

  synchronized void tock(boolean running) {
    if(!running) { // stop the clock
      state = "tocked";
      return;
    }
```

```
    System.out.println("Tock");

    state = "tocked"; // set the current state to tocked
  }
}
```

After the substitution, the output produced by the program will look like this:

```
Tick Tick Tick Tick Tick Tock
Tock
Tock
Tock
Tock
```

Clearly, the **tick( )** and **tock( )** methods are no longer working together!

Progress Check

1. What methods support interthread communication?
2. Do all objects support interthread communication?
3. What happens when **wait( )** is called?

Ask the Expert

Q I have heard the term *deadlock* applied to misbehaving multithreaded programs. What is it, and how can I avoid it? Also, what is a *race condition*, and how can I avoid that, too?

A Deadlock is, as the name implies, a situation in which one thread is waiting for another thread to do something, but that other thread is waiting on the first. Thus, both threads are suspended, waiting on each other, and neither executes. This situation is analogous to two overly polite people, both insisting that the other step through a door first!

Avoiding deadlock seems easy, but sometimes it's not. For example, deadlock can occur in roundabout ways. The cause of the deadlock often is not readily understood just by looking at the source code to the program because concurrently executing threads can interact in complex ways at run time. To avoid deadlock, careful programming and thorough testing is required. Remember, if a multithreaded program occasionally "hangs," deadlock is the likely cause.

Answers:

1. The interthread communication methods are **wait( )**, **notify( )**, and **notifyAll( )**.
2. Yes, all objects support interthread communication because this support is part of **Object**.
3. When **wait( )** is called, the calling thread relinquishes control of the object and suspends until it receives a notification.

Ask the Expert (Continued)

A race condition occurs when two (or more) threads attempt to access a shared resource at the same time, without proper synchronization. For example, one thread may be writing a new value to a variable while another thread is incrementing the variable's current value. Without synchronization, the new value of the variable will depend on the order in which the threads execute. (Does the second thread increment the original value or the new value written by the first thread?) In situations like this, the two threads are said to be "racing each other," with the final outcome determined by which thread finishes first. Like deadlock, a race condition can occur in difficult-to-discover ways. The solution is prevention: careful programming that properly synchronizes access to shared resources.

SUSPENDING, RESUMING, AND STOPPING THREADS

It is sometimes useful to suspend execution of a thread. For example, a separate thread can be used to display the time of day. If the user does not desire a clock, then its thread can be suspended. Whatever the case, it is a simple matter to suspend a thread. Once suspended, it is also a simple matter to restart the thread.

The mechanisms to suspend, stop, and resume threads differ between early versions of Java and more modern versions, beginning with Java 2. Prior to Java 2, a program used **suspend( )**, **resume( )**, and **stop( )**, which are methods defined by **Thread**, to pause, restart, and stop the execution of a thread. Although these methods seem to be a perfectly reasonable and convenient approach to managing the execution of threads, they must no longer be used. Here's why. The **suspend( )** method of the **Thread** class was deprecated by Java 2. This was done because **suspend( )** can sometimes cause serious problems that involve deadlock. The **resume( )** method is also deprecated. It cannot be used without the **suspend( )** method as its counterpart. The **stop( )** method of the **Thread** class was also deprecated by Java 2. This was done because this method, too, can sometimes cause serious problems.

Since you cannot now use the **suspend( )**, **resume( )**, or **stop( )** methods to control a thread, you might at first be thinking that there is no way to pause, restart, or terminate a thread. But, fortunately, this is not true. Instead, a thread must be designed so that the **run( )** method periodically checks to determine if that thread should suspend, resume, or stop its own execution. Typically, this is accomplished by establishing two flag variables: one for suspend and resume, and one for stop. For suspend and resume, as long as the flag is set to "running," the **run( )** method must continue to let the thread execute. If this variable is set to "suspend," the thread must pause. For the stop flag, if it is set to "stop," the thread must terminate.

The following example shows one way to implement your own versions of **suspend( )**, **resume( )**, and **stop( )**.

```
// Suspending, resuming, and stopping a thread.

class MyThread implements Runnable {
  Thread thrd;

  boolean suspended;  ◄───────────Suspends thread when true.
  boolean stopped;  ◄───────────Stops thread when true.

  MyThread(String name) {
    thrd = new Thread(this, name);
    suspended = false;
    stopped = false;
    thrd.start();
  }

  // This is the entry point for thread.
  public void run() {
    System.out.println(thrd.getName() + " starting.");
    try {
      for(int i = 1; i < 1000; i++) {
        System.out.print(i + " ");
        if((i%10)==0) {
          System.out.println();
          Thread.sleep(250);
        }

        // Use synchronized block to check suspended and stopped.
        synchronized(this) {  ◄─────────────────────┐
          while(suspended) {                         │
            wait();                This synchronized block checks **suspended** and
          }                       **stopped**.
          if(stopped) break;
        }
      }
    } catch (InterruptedException exc) {
      System.out.println(thrd.getName() + " interrupted.");
    }
    System.out.println(thrd.getName() + " exiting.");
  }

  // Stop the thread.
  synchronized void myStop() {
    stopped = true;

    // The following ensures that a suspended thread can be stopped.
    suspended = false;
    notify();
  }

  // Suspend the thread.
  synchronized void mySuspend() {
```

```
      suspended = true;
  }

  // Resume the thread.
  synchronized void myResume() {
    suspended = false;
    notify();
  }
}

class Suspend {
  public static void main(String[] args) {
    MyThread ob1 = new MyThread("My Thread");

    try {
      Thread.sleep(1000); // let ob1 thread start executing

      ob1.mySuspend();
      System.out.println("Suspending thread.");
      Thread.sleep(1000);

      ob1.myResume();
      System.out.println("Resuming thread.");
      Thread.sleep(1000);

      ob1.mySuspend();
      System.out.println("Suspending thread.");
      Thread.sleep(1000);

      ob1.myResume();
      System.out.println("Resuming thread.");
      Thread.sleep(1000);

      ob1.mySuspend();
      System.out.println("Stopping thread.");
      ob1.myStop();
    } catch (InterruptedException e) {
      System.out.println("Main thread Interrupted");
    }

    // wait for thread to finish
    try {
      ob1.thrd.join();
    } catch (InterruptedException e) {
      System.out.println("Main thread Interrupted");
    }

    System.out.println("Main thread exiting.");
  }
}
```

Sample output from this program is shown here. (Your output may differ slightly.)

```
My Thread starting.
1 2 3 4 5 6 7 8 9 10
11 12 13 14 15 16 17 18 19 20
21 22 23 24 25 26 27 28 29 30
31 32 33 34 35 36 37 38 39 40
Suspending thread.
Resuming thread.
41 42 43 44 45 46 47 48 49 50
51 52 53 54 55 56 57 58 59 60
61 62 63 64 65 66 67 68 69 70
71 72 73 74 75 76 77 78 79 80
Suspending thread.
Resuming thread.
81 82 83 84 85 86 87 88 89 90
91 92 93 94 95 96 97 98 99 100
101 102 103 104 105 106 107 108 109 110
111 112 113 114 115 116 117 118 119 120
Stopping thread.
My Thread exiting.
Main thread exiting.
```

Here is how the program works. The thread class **MyThread** defines two **boolean** variables, **suspended** and **stopped**, which govern the suspension and termination of a thread. Both are initialized to **false** by the constructor. The **run( )** method contains a **synchronized** statement block that checks **suspended**. If that variable is **true**, the **wait( )** method is invoked to suspend the execution of the thread. To suspend execution of the thread, call **mySuspend( )**, which sets **suspended** to **true**. To resume execution, call **myResume( )**, which sets **suspended** to **false** and invokes **notify( )** to restart the thread.

To stop the thread, call **myStop( )**, which sets **stopped** to **true**. In addition, **myStop( )** sets **suspended** to **false** and then calls **notify( )**. These steps are necessary to ensure that a suspended thread is stopped.

Ask the Expert

Q Multithreading seems like a great way to improve the efficiency of my programs. Can you give me any tips on effectively using it?

A The key to effectively utilizing multithreading is to think concurrently rather than serially. For example, when you have two subsystems within a program that are fully independent of each other, consider making them into individual threads. A word of caution is in order, however. If you create too many threads, you can actually degrade the performance of your program rather than enhance it. Remember, overhead is associated with context switching. If you create too many threads, more CPU time will be spent changing contexts than in executing your program!

TRY THIS 12-2 USING THE MAIN THREAD

UseMain.java

All Java programs have at least one thread of execution, called the *main thread*, which is given to the program automatically when it begins running. So far, we have been taking the main thread for granted. In this project, you will see that the main thread can be handled just like all other threads.

STEP-BY-STEP

1. Create a file called **UseMain.java**.
2. To access the main thread, you must obtain a **Thread** object that refers to it. You do this by calling the **currentThread( )** method, which is a **static** member of **Thread**. Its general form is shown here:

   static Thread currentThread( )

   This method returns a reference to the thread in which it is called. Therefore, if you call **currentThread( )** while execution is inside the main thread, you will obtain a reference to the main thread. Once you have this reference, you can control the main thread just like any other thread.

3. Enter the following program into the file. It obtains a reference to the main thread, and then gets and sets the main thread's name, and displays its priority.

```
/*
    Try This 12-2

    Controlling the main thread.
*/

class UseMain {
  public static void main(String[] args) {
    Thread thrd;

    // Get the main thread.
    thrd = Thread.currentThread();

    // Display main thread's name.
    System.out.println("Main thread is called: " +
                         thrd.getName());

    // Display main thread's priority.
    System.out.println("Priority: " +
                         thrd.getPriority());
```

```
        System.out.println();

        // Set the name.
        System.out.println("Setting name.\n");
        thrd.setName("Thread #1");

        System.out.println("Main thread is now called: " +
                        thrd.getName());
    }
}
```

4. The output from the program is shown here.

```
Main thread is called: main
Priority: 5

Setting name.

Main thread is now called: Thread #1
```

5. You need to be careful about what operations you perform on the main thread. For example, if you add the following code to the end of **main( )**, the program will never terminate because the main thread will be waiting for itself to end!

```
try {
    thrd.join();
} catch(InterruptedException exc) {
    System.out.println("Interrupted");
}
```

EXERCISES

1. How does Java's multithreading capability enable you to write more efficient programs?
2. Multithreading is supported by the _____ class and the _____ interface.
3. When creating a runnable object, why might you want to extend **Thread** rather than implement **Runnable**?
4. Show how to use **join( )** to wait for a thread object called **MyThrd** to end.
5. Show how to set a thread called **MyThrd** to three levels above normal priority.
6. What is the effect of adding the **synchronized** keyword to a method?
7. The **wait( )** and **notify( )** methods are used to perform

    _____.

8. Change the **TickTock** class so that it actually keeps time. That is, have each tick take one half second, and each tock take one half second. Thus, each tick-tock will take one second. (Don't worry about the time it takes to switch tasks, etc.)

9. Why can't you use **suspend( )**, **resume( )**, and **stop( )** for new programs?

10. What method defined by **Thread** obtains the name of a thread?

11. What does **isAlive( )** return?

12. If by synchronizing methods you can prevent concurrent access problems from occurring, why aren't all methods automatically synchronized?

13. By the end of this chapter, all of the **main( )** methods in the examples ended with a **try** block containing one or more calls to **join( )** on threads. Explain why.

14. In applications that use GUIs (graphical user interfaces with windows, buttons, menus, etc.), it is important that the interface always be responsive to mouse clicks and key presses. But sometimes a click on a button causes a method to execute that needs a lot of processing time, such as rendering a complex picture or loading a large file. While that method is working, how can the GUI remain responsive?

15. If **t** is a **Thread**, does **t.start( )** call **t.run( )**? That is, does **t**'s **run( )** method necessarily start executing before **t.start( )** returns?

16. Suppose you created a subclass **MyThread** of **Thread** in which the **run( )** method just displays the thread's name 50 times using a loop and then returns. Further, suppose you created 20 **MyThread** objects with different names and started them running.

A. Describe what the output would look like as precisely as possible.

B. What if the **run( )** method were declared **synchronized** in the **MyThread** class? Explain the difference you would see, if any.

C. What if the **run( )** method were declared **synchronized** in the **MyThread** class and the output statement inside the **run( )** method were surrounded by the synchronized block **synchronized(this) {...}**? Explain the difference you would see, if any.

17. In the synchronized block examples in this chapter, we always used the monitor associated with **this**. Can you use the monitor associated with some object other than the one whose methods you are using? For example, can you create an object with no methods or instance variables and use that object's monitor?

18. In the section of this chapter entitled "The **synchronized** Statement," an example is given using classes **SumArray**, **MyThread**, and **Sync**. In each of the following variations, explain what would happen if the proposed change were made.

A. Add a **synchronized(this)** block around the **for** loop in the **sumArray( )** method of **SumArray**.

B. Remove the synchronized block around the statement

```
answer = sa.sumArray(a)
```

in the body of the **run( )** method in **MyThread** and add a **synchronized(this)** block around the **for** loop in the **sumArray( )** method of **SumArray**.

C. Remove the keyword **static** in front of the instance variable **sa** in **MyThread**.

D. Remove the synchronized block around the statement

```
answer = sa.sumArray(a)
```

in the body of the **run( )** method in **MyThread** and add the modifier **synchronized** to the declaration of the **run( )** method of **MyThread**.

19. This exercise demonstrates how two synchronized methods need to communicate to keep a counter between 0 and 3 when one thread repeatedly tries to increase the counter and the other thread repeatedly tries to decrease the counter. It uses the **Math.random( )** method that takes no parameters and returns a random **double** value between 0 and 1. Do all of the following steps:

A. Create a **Counter** class with a private **count** instance variable and two methods. The first method:

   synchronized void increment( )

tries to increment **count** by 1. If **count** is already at its maximum of 3, then it waits until **count** is less than 3 before incrementing it. The other method:

   synchronized void decrement( )

attempts to decrement **count** by 1. If **count** is already at its minimum of 0, then it waits until **count** is greater than 0 before decrementing it. Every time either method has to wait, it displays a statement saying why it is waiting. Also, every time an increment or decrement occurs, the counter displays a statement that says what occurred and shows **count**'s new value.

B. Create one thread class whose **run( )** method calls the **Counter**'s **increment( )** method 20 times. In between each call, it sleeps for a random amount of time between 0 and 500 milliseconds.

C. Create one thread class whose **run( )** method calls the **Counter**'s **decrement( )** method 20 times. In between each call, it sleeps for a random amount of time between 0 and 500 milliseconds.

D. Write a **CounterUser** class with a **main( )** method that creates one **Counter** and the two threads and starts the threads running.

   Note: Instead of creating two thread classes, you are free to create just one thread class that either increments or decrements the counter, depending on a parameter passed to the thread class's constructor.

20. The following program tests the efficiency of threads. It should be run with two command-line arguments. The first argument is the size of an array to be sorted. The second argument is the number of times, **m**, such an array is to be sorted. The program first creates an array of the specified size and then copies and sorts the array **m** times consecutively using just one thread. It then starts **m** threads in parallel, each doing one copy and sort. Enter the program

on your computer and run the program with various arguments, timing the program to see how much faster the **m** threads can do the sorting in parallel. It is helpful to choose a large enough array size and large enough **m** so that it takes 10 or more seconds to do the parallel sorts. Write a summary of your results, including an explanation of any differences you observed between the **m** consecutive sorts in one thread and the parallel sorts using **m** threads.

```java
// Test the efficiency of threads.

class ThreadSpeedUp {
  public static void main(String[] args) {
    if (args.length != 2) {
      System.out.println("Usage: ThreadSpeedUp size numReps");
      return;
    }

    // create all the data and the threads
    int[] data = new int[Integer.parseInt(args[0])];
    for (int i = 0; i < data.length; i++)
      data[i] = data.length - i;

    int numReps = Integer.parseInt(args[1]);
    Thread[] threads = new Thread[numReps];
    for(int i = 0; i < numReps; i++)
      threads[i] = new CopyAndSortThread(data);

    // now sort consecutively in one thread
    System.out.println("Starting sorting array of length " + args[0] +
                       " in one thread " + numReps + " times.");

    for (int i = 0; i < numReps; i++) {
      copyAndSort(data);
    }

    System.out.println("Done sorting in one thread. ");
    System.out.println("Starting sorting arrays of length " +
                       args[0] + " using " + numReps + " threads.");

    // start all threads sorting in parallel
    for(Thread thd : threads)
      thd.start();

    // wait for all threads to stop
    try {
      for(Thread thd: threads)
        thd.join();
    }
    catch (InterruptedException e) {
      System.out.println("InterruptedException occurred.");
    }
    System.out.println("Done sorting using " + numReps + " threads.");
```

```
    }

    static void copyAndSort(int[] data) {
       // copy data to a new array
       int[] nums = new int[data.length];

       for (int j = 0; j < data.length; j++)
          nums[j] = data[j];

       // now sort the new array using bubble sort
       for (int a = 1; a < nums.length; a++)
          for (int b = nums.length - 1; b >= a; b--) {
             if (nums[b - 1] > nums[b]) { // swap if out of order
                int t = nums[b - 1];
                nums[b - 1] = nums[b];
                nums[b] = t;
             }
          }
    }
}

class CopyAndSortThread extends Thread {
   int[] data;

   CopyAndSortThread(int[] d) {
      data = d;
   }

   public void run() {
      ThreadSpeedUp.copyAndSort(data);
   }
}
```

CHAPTER 13

Enumerations, Autoboxing, and Annotations

KEY SKILLS & CONCEPTS

- Understand enumeration fundamentals
- Use the class-based features of enumerations
- Apply the **values( )** and **valueof( )** methods to enumerations
- Create enumerations that have constructors, instance variables, and methods
- Employ the **ordinal( )** and **compareTo( )** methods that enumerations inherit from **Enum**
- Use Java's type wrappers
- Know the basics of autoboxing and auto-unboxing
- Use autoboxing with methods
- Understand how autoboxing works with expressions
- Gain an overview of annotations

This chapter discusses three features that are relatively recent additions to Java. They are enumerations, autoboxing, and annotations. Although none of these were part of the original specification of Java, each expands the power and usability of the language. In the case of enumerations and autoboxing, both streamline the language, simplifying certain common constructs. Annotations expand the kinds of information that can be embedded within a source file. Collectively, all offer a better way to solve common programming problems. Also discussed in this chapter are Java's type wrappers because they relate to autoboxing.

ENUMERATIONS

Although the enumeration is a common programming feature that is found in several other computer languages, it was not part of the original specification for Java. One reason for this is that the enumeration is technically a convenience rather than a necessity. However, over the years, many programmers had wanted Java to support enumerations because they offer an elegant, structured solution to a variety of programming tasks. This request was granted by the release of JDK 5, which added enumerations to Java.

In its simplest form, an *enumeration* is a list of named constants that define a new data type. An object of an enumeration type can hold only the values that are defined by the list. Thus, an enumeration gives you a way to precisely define a new type of data that has a fixed number of valid values.

Enumerations are common in everyday life. For example, an enumeration of the coins used in the United States is penny, nickel, dime, quarter, half-dollar, and dollar. An enumeration of the months in the year consists of the names January through December. An enumeration of the days of the week is Sunday, Monday, Tuesday, Wednesday, Thursday, Friday, and Saturday.

From a programming perspective, enumerations are useful whenever you need to define a set of values that represent a collection of items. For example, you might use an enumeration to represent a set of status codes, such as success, waiting, failed, and retrying, which indicate the progress of a file transfer. In the past, such values were defined as **final** variables, but enumerations offer a more structured approach.

Enumeration Fundamentals

An enumeration is created using the **enum** keyword. For example, here is a simple enumeration that lists various forms of transportation:

```
// An enumeration of transportation.
enum Transport {
  CAR, TRUCK, AIRPLANE, TRAIN, BOAT
}
```

The identifiers **CAR**, **TRUCK**, and so on, are called *enumeration constants,* or *enum constants* for short. Each is implicitly declared as a public, static member of **Transport**. Furthermore, the enumeration constants' type is the type of the enumeration in which the constants are declared, which is **Transport** in this case. Thus, these constants are sometimes referred to as *self-typed*, where "self" refers to the enclosing enumeration.

Once you have declared an enumeration, you can create a variable of that type. However, even though enumerations define a class type, you do not instantiate an **enum** using **new**. Instead, you declare and use an enumeration variable in much the same way that you do one of the primitive types. For example, this declares **tp** as a variable of enumeration type **Transport**:

```
Transport tp;
```

Because **tp** is of type **Transport**, the only values that it can be assigned are those constants defined by the enumeration, or **null**. For example, this assigns **tp** the value **AIRPLANE**:

```
tp = Transport.AIRPLANE;
```

Notice that the symbol **AIRPLANE** is qualified by **Transport**.

Two enumeration constants can be compared for equality by using the == relational operator. For example, this statement compares the value in **tp** with the **TRAIN** constant:

```
if(tp == Transport.TRAIN) // ...
```

An enumeration value can also be used to control a **switch** statement. Of course, all of the **case** statements must use constants from the same **enum** as that used by the **switch** expression. For example, this **switch** is perfectly valid:

```
// Use an enum to control a switch statement.
switch(tp) {
  case CAR:
    // ...
  case TRUCK:
    // ...
```

Notice that in the **case** statements, the names of the enumeration constants are used without being qualified by their enumeration type name. That is, **TRUCK**, not **Transport.TRUCK**, is used. This is because the type of the enumeration in the **switch** expression has already implicitly specified the **enum** type of the **case** constants. There is no need to qualify the constants in the **case** statements with their **enum** type name. In fact, attempting to do so will cause a compilation error.

When an enumeration constant is displayed, such as in a **println( )** statement, its name is output. For example, given this statement:

```
System.out.println(Transport.BOAT);
```

the name **BOAT** is displayed.

The following program puts together all of the pieces and demonstrates the **Transport** enumeration.

```
// An enumeration of Transport varieties.
enum Transport {
  CAR, TRUCK, AIRPLANE, TRAIN, BOAT ◄————————Declare an enumeration.
}

class EnumDemo {
  public static void main(String[] args)
  {
    Transport tp; ◄————————Declare a Transport reference.

    tp = Transport.AIRPLANE; ◄————————Assign tp the constant AIRPLANE.

    // Output an enum value.
    System.out.println("Value of tp: " + tp);
    System.out.println();

    tp = Transport.TRAIN;

    // Compare two enum values.
    if(tp == Transport.TRAIN) ◄————————Compare two Transport
      System.out.println("tp contains TRAIN.\n");        objects for equality.
```

```
// Use an enum to control a switch statement.
switch(tp) {
  case CAR:
    System.out.println("A car carries people.");
    break;
  case TRUCK:
    System.out.println("A truck carries freight.");
    break;
  case AIRPLANE:
    System.out.println("An airplane flies.");
    break;
  case TRAIN:
    System.out.println("A train runs on rails.");
    break;
  case BOAT:
    System.out.println("A boat sails on water.");
    break;
  }
 }
}
```

Use an enumeration to control a **switch** statement.

The output from the program is shown here:

```
Value of tp: AIRPLANE

tp contains TRAIN.

A train runs on rails.
```

Before moving on, it's helpful to make one stylistic point. The constants in **Transport** use uppercase. (Thus, **CAR**, not **car**, is used.) However, the use of uppercase is not required. In other words, there is no rule that requires enumeration constants to be in uppercase. However, this is the style commonly used by Java programmers. (There are, of course, other viewpoints and styles.) The examples in this book will use uppercase for enumeration constants, for consistency.

Progress Check

1. An enumeration defines a list of _____ constants.
2. What keyword declares an enumeration?
3. Given

   ```
   enum Directions {
     LEFT, RIGHT, UP, DOWN
   }
   ```

   What is the data type of **UP**?

_____

Answers:

1. named
2. **enum**
3. The data type of **UP** is **Directions** because enumerated constants are self-typed.

JAVA ENUMERATIONS ARE CLASS TYPES

Although the preceding examples show the mechanics of creating and using an enumeration, they don't show all of its capabilities. The reason is that Java implements enumerations as class types. Although you don't instantiate an **enum** using **new**, it otherwise acts much like other classes. The fact that **enum** defines a class enables the Java enumeration to have powers that it otherwise would not. For example, you can give it constructors, add instance variables and methods, and even implement interfaces.

THE values( ) AND valueOf( ) METHODS

All enumerations automatically have two predefined methods: **values( )** and **valueOf( )**. Their general forms are shown here:

> public static *enum-type*[ ] values( )
> public static *enum-type* valueOf(String *str*)

The **values( )** method returns an array that contains a list of the enumeration constants. The **valueOf( )** method returns the enumeration constant whose value corresponds to the string passed in *str*. In both cases, *enum-type* is the type of the enumeration. For example, in the case of the **Transport** enumeration shown earlier, the return type of **Transport.valueOf("TRAIN")** is **Transport**. The value returned is **TRAIN**. The following program demonstrates the **values( )** and **valueOf( )** methods.

```
// Use the built-in enumeration methods.

// An enumeration of Transport varieties.
enum Transport {
  CAR, TRUCK, AIRPLANE, TRAIN, BOAT
}

class EnumDemo2 {
  public static void main(String[] args)
  {
    Transport tp;

    System.out.println("Here are all Transport constants");

    // use values()
    Transport[] allTransports = Transport.values();       Obtain an array of Transport constants.
    for(Transport t : allTransports)
      System.out.println(t);

    System.out.println();

    // use valueOf()
    tp = Transport.valueOf("AIRPLANE");        Obtain the constant with the name AIRPLANE.
    System.out.println("tp contains " + tp);
  }
}
```

The output from the program is shown here:

```
Here are all Transport constants
CAR
TRUCK
AIRPLANE
TRAIN
BOAT


tp contains AIRPLANE
```

Notice that this program uses a for-each style **for** loop to cycle through the array of constants obtained by calling **values( )**. For the sake of illustration, the variable **allTransports** was created and assigned a reference to the enumeration array. However, this step is not necessary because the **for** could have been written as shown here, eliminating the need for the **allTransports** variable:

```
for(Transport t : Transport.values())
  System.out.println(t);
```

Next, notice how the value corresponding to the name **AIRPLANE** was obtained by calling **valueOf( )**:

```
tp = Transport.valueOf("AIRPLANE");
```

As explained, **valueOf( )** returns the enumeration value associated with the name of the constant represented as a string.

CONSTRUCTORS, METHODS, INSTANCE VARIABLES, AND ENUMERATIONS

It is important to understand that each enumeration constant is an object of its enumeration type. Thus, an enumeration can define constructors, add methods, and have instance variables. When you define a constructor for an **enum**, the constructor is called when each enumeration constant is created. Each enumeration constant can call any method defined by the enumeration. Each enumeration constant has its own copy of any instance variables defined by the enumeration. The following version of **Transport** illustrates the use of a constructor, an instance variable, and a method. It gives each type of transportation a typical speed.

```
// Use an enum constructor, instance variable, and method.
enum Transport {
  CAR(65), TRUCK(55), AIRPLANE(600), TRAIN(70), BOAT(22);    ←———— Notice the
                                                                    initialization
  private int speed; // typical speed of each transport ←——┐       values.
                                                           └── Add an instance variable.
  // Constructor
  Transport(int s) { speed = s; } ←———————Add a constructor.

  int getSpeed() { return speed; } ←———————Add a method.
}
```

```
class EnumDemo3 {
  public static void main(String[] args)
  {
    Transport tp;

    // Display speed of an airplane.
    System.out.println("Typical speed for an airplane is " +
                    Transport.AIRPLANE.getSpeed() +
                    " miles per hour.\n");

    // Display all Transports and speeds.
    System.out.println("All Transport speeds: ");
    for(Transport t : Transport.values())
      System.out.println(t + " typical speed is " +
                        t.getSpeed() +
                        " miles per hour.");
  }
}
```

Obtain the speed by calling **getSpeed( )**.

The output is shown here:

```
Typical speed for an airplane is 600 miles per hour.

All Transport speeds:
CAR typical speed is 65 miles per hour.
TRUCK typical speed is 55 miles per hour.
AIRPLANE typical speed is 600 miles per hour.
TRAIN typical speed is 70 miles per hour.
BOAT typical speed is 22 miles per hour.
```

This version of **Transport** adds three things. The first is the instance variable **speed**, which is used to hold the speed of each kind of transport. The second is the **Transport** constructor, which is passed the speed of a transport. The third is the method **getSpeed( )**, which returns the value of **speed**.

When the variable **tp** is declared in **main( )**, the constructor for **Transport** is called once for each constant that is specified. Notice how the arguments to the constructor are specified, by putting them inside parentheses, after each constant, as shown here:

```
CAR(65), TRUCK(55), AIRPLANE(600), TRAIN(70), BOAT(22);
```

These values are passed to the **s** parameter of **Transport( )**, which then assigns this value to **speed**. There is something else to notice about the list of enumeration constants: it is terminated by a semicolon. That is, the last constant, **BOAT**, is followed by a semicolon. When an enumeration contains other members, the enumeration list must end in a semicolon.

Because each enumeration constant has its own copy of **speed**, you can obtain the speed of a specified type of transport by calling **getSpeed( )**. For example, in **main( )** the speed of an airplane is obtained by the following call:

```
Transport.AIRPLANE.getSpeed()
```

The speed of each transport is obtained by cycling through the enumeration using a **for** loop. Because there is a copy of **speed** for each enumeration constant, the value associated with one constant is separate and distinct from the value associated with another constant. This is a powerful concept, which is available only when enumerations are implemented as classes, as Java does.

Although the preceding example contains only one constructor, an **enum** can offer two or more overloaded forms, just as can any other class.

Ask the Expert

Q Since enumerations have been added to Java, should I avoid the use of **final** variables? In other words, have enumerations rendered **final** variables obsolete?

A No. Enumerations are appropriate when you are working with lists of items that must be represented by identifiers. A **final** variable is appropriate when you have a constant value, such as an array size, that will be used in many places. Thus, each has its own use. The advantage of enumerations is that **final** variables don't have to be pressed into service for a job for which they are not ideally suited.

Two Important Restrictions

Two restrictions apply to enumerations. First, an enumeration can't explicitly inherit another class. Second, an **enum** cannot be a superclass. This means that an **enum** can't be extended. Otherwise, **enum** acts much like any other class type. The key is to remember that each of the enumeration constants is an object of the enumeration in which it is defined.

ENUMERATIONS INHERIT Enum

Although you can't explicitly inherit a superclass when declaring an **enum**, all enumerations implicitly inherit one: **java.lang.Enum**. This class defines several methods that are available for use by all enumerations. Most often you won't need to use these methods, but there are two that you may find interesting: **ordinal( )** and **compareTo( )**.

The **ordinal( )** method obtains a value that indicates an enumeration constant's position in the list of constants. This is called its *ordinal value*. The **ordinal( )** method is shown here:

    final int ordinal( )

It returns the ordinal value of the invoking constant. Ordinal values begin at zero. Thus, in the **Transport** enumeration, **CAR** has an ordinal value of zero, **TRUCK** has an ordinal value of 1, **AIRPLANE** has an ordinal value of 2, and so on.

You can compare the ordinal value of two constants of the same enumeration by using the **compareTo( )** method. It has this general form:

    final int compareTo(*enum-type e*)

Here, *enum-type* is the type of the enumeration and *e* is the constant being compared to the invoking constant. Remember, both the invoking constant and *e* must be of the same enumeration. If the invoking constant has an ordinal value less than *e*'s, then **compareTo( )** returns a negative value. If the two ordinal values are the same, then zero is returned. If the invoking constant has an ordinal value greater than *e*'s, then a positive value is returned.

The following program demonstrates **ordinal( )** and **compareTo( )**.

```java
// Demonstrate ordinal() and compareTo().

// An enumeration of Transport varieties.
enum Transport {
  CAR, TRUCK, AIRPLANE, TRAIN, BOAT
}

class EnumDemo4 {
  public static void main(String[] args)
  {
    Transport tp, tp2, tp3;

    // Obtain all ordinal values using ordinal().
    System.out.println("Here are all Transport constants" +
                  " and their ordinal values: ");
    for(Transport t : Transport.values())
      System.out.println(t + " " + t.ordinal());     ←———————Obtain ordinal values.

    tp = Transport.AIRPLANE;
    tp2 = Transport.TRAIN;
    tp3 = Transport.AIRPLANE;

    System.out.println();
                              Compare ordinal values.
    // Demonstrate compareTo()
    if(tp.compareTo(tp2) < 0)  ←————┘
      System.out.println(tp + " comes before " + tp2);

    if(tp.compareTo(tp2) > 0)
      System.out.println(tp2 + " comes before " + tp);

    if(tp.compareTo(tp3) == 0)
      System.out.println(tp + " equals " + tp3);
  }
}
```

The output from the program is shown here:

```
Here are all Transport constants and their ordinal values:
CAR 0
TRUCK 1
AIRPLANE 2
TRAIN 3
```

```
BOAT 4

AIRPLANE comes before TRAIN
AIRPLANE equals AIRPLANE
```

Progress Check

1. What does **values( )** return?
2. Can an enumeration have a constructor?
3. What is the ordinal value of an enumeration constant?

TRY THIS 13-1   A COMPUTER-CONTROLLED TRAFFIC LIGHT

TrafficLightDemo.java

Enumerations are particularly useful when your program needs a set of constants, but the actual values of the constants are arbitrary, as long as all differ. This type of situation comes up quite often when programming. One common instance involves handling the states in which some device can exist. For example, imagine that you are writing a program that controls a traffic light. Your traffic light code must automatically cycle through the light's three states: green, yellow, and red. It also must enable other code to know the current color of the light and let the color of the light be set to a known initial value. This means that the three states must be represented in some way. Although it would be possible to represent these three states by integer values (for example, the values 1, 2, and 3) or by strings (such as "red", "green", and "yellow"), an enumeration offers a much better approach. Using an enumeration results in code that is more efficient than if strings represented the states and more structured than if integers represented the states.

In this project, you will create a simulation of an automated traffic light, as just described. This project not only demonstrates an enumeration in action, it also shows another example of multithreading and synchronization.

Answers:

1. The **values( )** method returns an array that contains a list of all the constants defined by the invoking enumeration.
2. Yes.
3. The ordinal value of an enumeration constant describes its position in the list of constants, with the first constant having the ordinal value of zero.

STEP-BY-STEP

1. Create a file called **TrafficLightDemo.java**.

2. Begin by defining an enumeration called **TrafficLightColor** that represents the three states of the light, as shown here:

```
// An enumeration of the colors of a traffic light.
enum TrafficLightColor {
  RED, GREEN, YELLOW
}
```

Whenever the color of the light is needed, its enumeration value is used.

3. Next, begin defining **TrafficLightSimulator**, as shown next. **TrafficLightSimulator** is the class that encapsulates the traffic light simulation.

```
// A computerized traffic light.
class TrafficLightSimulator implements Runnable {
  private Thread thrd; // holds the thread that runs the simulation
  private TrafficLightColor tlc; // holds the current color
  boolean stop = false; // set to true to stop the simulation
  boolean changed = false; // true when the light has changed

  TrafficLightSimulator(TrafficLightColor init) {
    tlc = init;

    thrd = new Thread(this);
    thrd.start();
  }

  TrafficLightSimulator() {
    tlc = TrafficLightColor.RED;

    thrd = new Thread(this);
    thrd.start();
  }
```

Notice that **TrafficLightSimulator** implements **Runnable**. This is necessary because a separate thread is used to run each traffic light. This thread will cycle through the colors. Two constructors are created. The first lets you specify the initial light color. The second defaults to red. Both start a new thread to run the light. Now look at the instance variables. A reference to the traffic light thread is stored in **thrd**. The current traffic light color is stored in **tlc**. The **stop** variable is used to stop the simulation. It is initially set to **false**. The light will run until this variable is set to **true**. The **changed** variable is **true** when the light has changed.

4. Next, add the **run( )** method, shown here, which begins running the traffic light.

```
// Start up the light.
public void run() {
```

```
while(!stop) {
  try {
    switch(tlc) {
      case GREEN:
        Thread.sleep(10000); // green for 10 seconds
        break;
      case YELLOW:
        Thread.sleep(2000); // yellow for 2 seconds
        break;
      case RED:
        Thread.sleep(12000); // red for 12 seconds
        break;
    }
  } catch(InterruptedException exc) {
    System.out.println(exc);
  }
  changeColor();
}
}
```

This method cycles the light through the colors. First, it sleeps an appropriate amount of time, based on the current color. Then, it calls **changeColor( )** to change to the next color in the sequence.

5. Now, add the **changeColor( )** method, as shown here:

```
// Change color.
synchronized void changeColor() {
  switch(tlc) {
    case RED:
      tlc = TrafficLightColor.GREEN;
      break;
    case YELLOW:
      tlc = TrafficLightColor.RED;
      break;
    case GREEN:
      tlc = TrafficLightColor.YELLOW;
  }

  changed = true;
  notify(); // signal that the light has changed
}
```

The **switch** statement examines the color currently stored in **tlc** and then assigns the next color in the sequence. Notice that this method is synchronized. This is necessary because it calls **notify( )** to signal that a color change has taken place. (Recall that **notify( )** can be called only from a synchronized context.)

6. The next method is **waitForChange( )**, which waits until the color of the light is changed.

```
// Wait until a light change occurs.
synchronized void waitForChange() {
  try {
    while(!changed)
      wait(); // wait for light to change
    changed = false;
  } catch(InterruptedException exc) {
    System.out.println(exc);
  }
}
```

This method simply calls **wait( )**. This call won't return until **changeColor( )** executes a call to **notify( )**. Thus, **waitForChange( )** won't return until the color has changed.

7. Finally, add the methods **getColor( )**, which returns the current light color, and **cancel( )**, which stops the traffic light thread by setting **stop** to **true**. These methods are shown here:

```
// Return current color.
synchronized TrafficLightColor getColor() {
  return tlc;
}

// Stop the traffic light.
synchronized void cancel() {
  stop = true;
}
```

8. Here is all the code assembled into a complete program that demonstrates the traffic light:

```
// Try This 13-1

// A simulation of a traffic light that uses
// an enumeration to describe the light's color.

// An enumeration of the colors of a traffic light.
enum TrafficLightColor {
  RED, GREEN, YELLOW
}

// A computerized traffic light.
class TrafficLightSimulator implements Runnable {
  private Thread thrd; // holds the thread that runs the simulation
  private TrafficLightColor tlc; // holds the current color
  boolean stop = false; // set to true to stop the simulation
  boolean changed = false; // true when the light has changed

  TrafficLightSimulator(TrafficLightColor init) {
    tlc = init;
```

```
      thrd = new Thread(this);
      thrd.start();
    }

    TrafficLightSimulator() {
      tlc = TrafficLightColor.RED;

      thrd = new Thread(this);
      thrd.start();
    }

    // Start up the light.
    public void run() {
      while(!stop) {
        try {
          switch(tlc) {
            case GREEN:
              Thread.sleep(10000); // green for 10 seconds
              break;
            case YELLOW:
              Thread.sleep(2000); // yellow for 2 seconds
              break;
            case RED:
              Thread.sleep(12000); // red for 12 seconds
              break;
          }
        } catch(InterruptedException exc) {
          System.out.println(exc);
        }
        changeColor();
      }
    }

    // Change color.
    synchronized void changeColor() {
      switch(tlc) {
        case RED:
          tlc = TrafficLightColor.GREEN;
          break;
        case YELLOW:
          tlc = TrafficLightColor.RED;
          break;
        case GREEN:
          tlc = TrafficLightColor.YELLOW;
      }

      changed = true;
      notify(); // signal that the light has changed
    }
```

```
    // Wait until a light change occurs.
    synchronized void waitForChange() {
      try {
        while(!changed)
          wait(); // wait for light to change
        changed = false;
      } catch(InterruptedException exc) {
        System.out.println(exc);
      }
    }

    // Return current color.
    synchronized TrafficLightColor getColor() {
      return tlc;
    }

    // Stop the traffic light.
    synchronized void cancel() {
      stop = true;
    }
}

class TrafficLightDemo {
  public static void main(String[] args) {
    TrafficLightSimulator tl =
      new TrafficLightSimulator(TrafficLightColor.GREEN);

    for(int i=0; i < 9; i++) {
      System.out.println(tl.getColor());
      tl.waitForChange();
    }

    tl.cancel();
  }
}
```

The following output is produced. As you can see, the traffic light cycles through the colors in the order of green, yellow, and red:

```
GREEN
YELLOW
RED
GREEN
YELLOW
RED
GREEN
YELLOW
RED
```

In the program, notice how the use of the enumeration simplifies and adds structure to the code that needs to know the state of the traffic light.

Because the light can have only three states (red, green, or yellow), use of an enumeration ensures that only these values are valid, thus preventing accidental misuse.

9. It is possible to improve the preceding program by taking advantage of the class capabilities of an enumeration. For example, by adding a constructor, instance variable, and method to **TrafficLightColor**, you can substantially improve the preceding program. This improvement is left as an exercise. See Exercise 4.

AUTOBOXING

Java has two very helpful features: *autoboxing* and *auto-unboxing*. These features were not part of the original specification for Java, but were added by JDK 5. Autoboxing/unboxing greatly simplifies and streamlines code that must convert primitive types into objects, and vice versa. Because such situations are found frequently in Java code, the benefits of autoboxing/unboxing affect nearly all Java programmers. As you will see in Chapter 14, autoboxing/unboxing also contributes greatly to the usability of generics.

Autoboxing/unboxing is directly related to Java's type wrappers and to the way that values are moved into and out of an instance of a wrapper. For this reason, we will begin with an overview of type wrappers and the process of manually boxing and unboxing values.

Type Wrappers and Boxing

As you know, Java uses primitive types, such as **int** or **double**, to hold the basic data types supported by the language. Primitive types, rather than objects, are used for these quantities for the sake of performance. Using objects for these basic types would add an unacceptable overhead to even the simplest of calculations. Thus, the primitive types are not part of the object hierarchy, and they do not inherit **Object**.

Despite the performance benefit offered by the primitive types, there are times when you will need an object representation. For example, you can't pass a primitive type by reference to a method. Also, many of the standard data structures implemented by Java operate on objects, which means that you can't use these data structures to store primitive types. To handle these (and other) situations, Java provides *type wrappers*, which are classes that encapsulate a primitive type within an object. The type wrapper classes were introduced briefly in Chapter 11. Here, we will look at them more closely.

The type wrappers are **Double**, **Float**, **Long**, **Integer**, **Short**, **Byte**, **Character**, and **Boolean**, which are packaged in **java.lang**. These classes offer a wide array of methods that allow you to fully integrate the primitive types into Java's object hierarchy.

Probably the most commonly used type wrappers are those that represent numeric values. These are **Byte**, **Short**, **Integer**, **Long**, **Float**, and **Double**. All of the numeric type wrappers inherit the abstract class **Number**. **Number** declares methods that return the value of an object in each of the different numeric types. These methods are shown here:

>   byte byteValue( )
>
>   double doubleValue( )
>
>   float floatValue( )
>
>   int intValue( )
>
>   long longValue( )
>
>   short shortValue( )

For example, **doubleValue( )** returns the value of an object as a **double**, **floatValue( )** returns the value as a **float**, and so on. These methods are implemented by each of the numeric type wrappers.

All of the numeric type wrappers define constructors that allow an object to be constructed from a given value, or a string representation of that value. For example, here are the constructors defined for **Integer** and **Double**:

>   Integer(int *num*)
>
>   Integer(String *str*) throws NumberFormatException
>
>   Double(double *num*)
>
>   Double(String *str*) throws NumberFormatException

If *str* does not contain a valid numeric value, then a **NumberFormatException** is thrown.

All of the type wrappers override **toString( )**. It returns the human-readable form of the value contained within the wrapper. This allows you to output the value by passing a type wrapper object to **println( )**, for example, without having to convert it into its primitive type.

The process of encapsulating a value within an object is called *boxing*. Prior to JDK 5, all boxing took place manually, with the programmer explicitly constructing an instance of a wrapper with the desired value. For example, this line manually boxes the value 100 into an **Integer**:

```
Integer iOb = new Integer(100);
```

In this example, a new **Integer** object with the value 100 is explicitly created, and a reference to this object is assigned to **iOb**.

The process of extracting a value from a type wrapper is called *unboxing*. Again, prior to JDK 5, all unboxing also took place manually, with the programmer explicitly calling a method on the wrapper to obtain its value. For example, this manually unboxes the value in **iOb** into an **int**.

```
int i = iOb.intValue();
```

Here, **intValue( )** returns the value encapsulated within **iOb** as an **int**.

The following program demonstrates the preceding concepts.

```
// Demonstrate manual boxing and unboxing with a type wrapper.
class Wrap {
```

```
    public static void main(String[] args) {

        Integer iOb = new Integer(100);  ◄─────────Manually box the value 100.

        int i = iOb.intValue();  ◄─────────Manually unbox the value in iOb.

        System.out.println(i + " " + iOb); // displays 100 100
    }
}
```

This program wraps the integer value 100 inside an **Integer** object called **iOb**. The program then obtains this value by calling **intValue( )** and stores the result in **i**. Finally, it displays the values of **i** and **iOb**, both of which are 100.

The same general procedure used by the preceding example to manually box and unbox values was required by all versions of Java prior to JDK 5 and is still widely used in legacy code. The problem is that it is both tedious and error-prone because it requires the programmer to manually create the appropriate object to wrap a value and to explicitly obtain the proper primitive type when its value is needed. Fortunately, autoboxing/unboxing fundamentally improves on these essential procedures.

Autoboxing Fundamentals

Autoboxing is the process by which a primitive type is automatically encapsulated (boxed) into its equivalent type wrapper whenever an object of that type is needed. There is no need to explicitly construct an object. Auto-unboxing is the process by which the value of a boxed object is automatically extracted (unboxed) from a type wrapper when its value is needed. There is no need to call a method such as **intValue( )** or **doubleValue( )**.

The addition of autoboxing and auto-unboxing greatly streamlines the coding of several algorithms, removing the tedium of manually boxing and unboxing values. It also helps prevent errors. With autoboxing it is not necessary to manually construct an object in order to wrap a primitive type. You need only assign that value to a type-wrapper reference. Java automatically constructs the object for you. For example, here is the modern way to construct an **Integer** object that has the value 100:

```
Integer iOb = 100; // autobox an int
```

Notice that the object is not explicitly created through the use of **new**. Java handles this for you, automatically.

To unbox an object, simply assign that object reference to a primitive-type variable. For example, to unbox **iOb**, you can use this line:

```
int i = iOb; // auto-unbox
```

Java handles the details for you.

The following program demonstrates the preceding statements.

```
// Demonstrate autoboxing/unboxing.
class AutoBox {
  public static void main(String[] args) {
```

```
    Integer iOb = 100; // autobox an int
```
                                                                          Autobox and then auto-
```
    int i = iOb; // auto-unbox
```
                                                                          unbox the value 100.

```
    System.out.println(i + " " + iOb); // displays 100 100
  }
}
```

Progress Check

1. What is the type wrapper for **double**?
2. When you box a primitive value, what happens?
3. Autoboxing is the feature that automatically boxes a primitive value into an object of its corresponding type wrapper. True or False?

Autoboxing and Methods

In addition to the simple case of assignments, autoboxing automatically occurs whenever a primitive type must be converted into an object, and auto-unboxing takes place whenever an object must be converted into a primitive type. Thus, autoboxing/unboxing might occur when an argument is passed to a method or when a value is returned by a method. For example, consider the following:

```
// Autoboxing/unboxing takes place with method parameters
// and return values.

class AutoBox2 {
  // This method has an Integer parameter.
  static void m(Integer v) {                      Receives an Integer.
    System.out.println("m() received " + v);
  }

  // This method returns an int.
  static int m2() {                      Returns an int.
    return 10;
  }
                                                  Returns an Integer.
  // This method returns an Integer.
  static Integer m3() {
    return 99; // autoboxing 99 into an Integer.
  }
```

Answers:

1. **Double**
2. When a primitive value is boxed, its value is placed inside an object of its corresponding type wrapper.
3. True.

```
public static void main(String[] args) {

   // Pass an int to m(). Because m() has an Integer
   // parameter, the int value passed is automatically boxed.
   m(199);

   // Here, iOb receives the int value returned by m2().
   // This value is automatically boxed so that it can be
   // assigned to iOb.
   Integer iOb = m2();
   System.out.println("Return value from m2() is " + iOb);

   // Next, m3() is called. It returns an Integer value
   // which is auto-unboxed into an int.
   int i = m3();
   System.out.println("Return value from m3() is " + i);

   // Next, Math.sqrt() is called with iOb as an argument.
   // In this case, iOb is auto-unboxed and its value promoted to
   // double, which is the type needed by sqrt().
   iOb = 100;
   System.out.println("Square root of iOb is " + Math.sqrt(iOb));
  }
}
```

This program displays the following result:

```
m() received 199
Return value from m2() is 10
Return value from m3() is 99
Square root of iOb is 10.0
```

In the program, notice that **m( )** specifies an **Integer** parameter. Inside **main( )**, **m( )** is passed the **int** value 199. Because **m( )** is expecting an **Integer**, this value is automatically boxed. Next, **m2( )** is called. It returns the **int** value 10. This **int** value is assigned to **iOb** in **main( )**. Because **iOb** is an **Integer**, the value returned by **m2( )** is autoboxed. Next, **m3( )** is called. It returns an **Integer** that is auto-unboxed into an **int**. Finally, **Math.sqrt( )** is called with **iOb** as an argument. In this case, **iOb** is auto-unboxed and its value promoted to **double**, since that is the type expected by **Math.sqrt( )**.

Autoboxing/Unboxing Occurs in Expressions

In general, autoboxing and unboxing take place whenever a conversion into an object or from an object is required. This applies to expressions. Within an expression, a numeric object is automatically unboxed. The outcome of the expression is reboxed, if necessary. For example, consider the following program.

```
// Autoboxing/unboxing occurs inside expressions.

class AutoBox3 {
  public static void main(String[] args) {
    Integer iOb, iOb2;
```

```
    int i;

    iOb = 99;
    System.out.println("Original value of iOb: " + iOb);

    // The following automatically unboxes iOb,
    // performs the increment, and then reboxes
    // the result back into iOb.
    ++iOb;
    System.out.println("After ++iOb: " + iOb);

    // Here, iOb is unboxed, its value is increased by 10,
    // and the result is boxed and stored back in iOb.
    iOb += 10;
    System.out.println("After iOb += 10: " + iOb);

    // Here, iOb is unboxed, the expression is
    // evaluated, and the result is reboxed and
    // assigned to iOb2.
    iOb2 = iOb + (iOb / 3);
    System.out.println("iOb2 after expression: " + iOb2);

    // The same expression is evaluated, but the
    // result is not reboxed.
    i = iOb + (iOb / 3);
    System.out.println("i after expression: " + i);
  }
}
```

Autoboxing/
unboxing occurs
in expressions.

The output is shown here:

```
Original value of iOb: 99
After ++iOb: 100
After iOb += 10: 110
iOb2 after expression: 146
i after expression: 146
```

In the program, pay special attention to this line:

```
++iOb;
```

This causes the value in **iOb** to be incremented. It works like this: **iOb** is unboxed, the value is incremented, and the result is reboxed.

Because of auto-unboxing, you can use integer numeric objects, such as an **Integer**, to control a **switch** statement. For example, consider this fragment:

```
Integer iOb = 2;

switch(iOb) {
  case 1: System.out.println("one");
    break;
  case 2: System.out.println("two");
    break;
```

```
    default: System.out.println("error");
}
```

When the **switch** expression is evaluated, **iOb** is unboxed and its **int** value is obtained.

As the examples in the program show, because of autoboxing/unboxing, using numeric objects in an expression is both intuitive and easy. In the past, such code would have involved casts and calls to methods such as **intValue( )**.

A Word of Warning

Because of autoboxing and auto-unboxing, one might be tempted to use objects such as **Integer** or **Double** exclusively, abandoning primitives altogether. For example, with autoboxing/unboxing it is possible to write code like this:

```
// A bad use of autoboxing/unboxing!
Double a, b, c;

a = 10.2;
b = 11.4;
c = 9.8;

Double avg = (a + b + c) / 3;
```

In this example, objects of type **Double** hold values, which are then averaged and the result is assigned to another **Double** object. Although this code is technically correct and does, in fact, work properly, it is a very bad use of autoboxing/unboxing. It is far less efficient than the equivalent code written using the primitive type **double**. The reason is that each autobox and auto-unbox adds overhead that is not present if the primitive type is used.

In general, you should restrict your use of the type wrappers to only those cases in which an object representation of a primitive type is required. Autoboxing/unboxing was not added to Java as a "back door" way of eliminating the primitive types.

Progress Check

1. Will a primitive value be autoboxed when it is passed as an argument to a method that is expecting a type wrapper object?
2. Because of the limits imposed by the Java run-time system, autoboxing/unboxing will not occur on objects used in expressions. True or False?
3. Because of autoboxing/unboxing, you should use objects rather than primitive types for performing most arithmetic operations. True or False?

Answers:

1. Yes.
2. False.
3. False.

ANNOTATIONS (METADATA)

Another feature added to Java by JDK 5 is the *annotation*. It enables you to embed supplemental information (an annotation) into a source file. For example, you might annotate a method with information about its version status. This information does not change the actions of a program. However, various tools can use this information, during both development and deployment. For example, an annotation might be processed by a source-code generator, by the compiler, or by a deployment tool. The term *metadata* is also used to refer to this feature, but the term *annotation* is the most descriptive and more commonly used.

Although most of the time you will probably use predefined annotations more often than you will define one of your own, it is still helpful to understand their syntax and basic concepts. Therefore, we begin with a brief overview of creating and using an annotation.

Creating and Using an Annotation

An annotation is created through a mechanism based on the **interface**. Here is a simple example:

```
// A simple annotation type.
@interface MyAnno {
  String str();
  int val();
}
```

This declares an annotation called **MyAnno**. Notice the **@** that precedes the keyword **interface**. This tells the compiler that an annotation type is being declared. Next, notice the two members **str( )** and **val( )**. All annotations consist solely of method declarations. However, you don't provide bodies for these methods. Instead, Java implements these methods. Moreover, the methods act much like fields.

All annotation types automatically extend the **Annotation** interface. Thus, **Annotation** is a super-interface of all annotations. It is declared within the **java.lang.annotation** package.

Once you have declared an annotation, you can use it to annotate a declaration. Any type of declaration can have an annotation associated with it. For example, classes, methods, fields, parameters, and **enum** constants can be annotated. Even an annotation can be annotated. In all cases, the annotation precedes the rest of the declaration.

When you apply an annotation, you give values to its members. For example, here is an example of **MyAnno** being applied to a method:

```
// Annotate a method.
@MyAnno(str = "Annotation Example", val = 100)
public static void myMeth() { // ...
```

This annotation is linked with the method **myMeth( )**. Look closely at the annotation syntax. The name of the annotation, preceded by an **@**, is followed by a parenthesized list of member initializations. To give a member a value, that member's name is assigned a value. Therefore, in the example, the string "Annotation Example" is assigned to the **str** member of **MyAnno**. Notice that no parentheses follow **str** in this assignment. When an annotation member is given a value, only its name is used. Thus, annotation members look like fields in this context.

You can give an annotation member a default value that will be used if no value is specified when the annotation is applied. A default value is indicated by adding a **default** clause to the member's declaration. It has this general form:

type member( ) default *value*;

Here, *value* must be of a type compatible with *type*. For example, here is **MyAnno**, with **val( )** given a default of 42:

```
// Give val() a default value
@interface MyAnno {
  String str();
  int val() default 42;
}
```

Now, you could use **MyAnno** like this:

```
@MyAnno(str = "Annotation Example")
```

Here, the value of **val( )** defaults to 42. Of course, you can still give **val( )** a different value, just as before. For example,

```
@MyAnno(str = "Annotation Example", val = 100)
```

is still valid.

If you have an annotation that has only a single member called **value**, then you can use a "shorthand" form to specify its value. You can simply pass the value for that member when the annotation is applied—you don't need to specify the name **value**. For example, given

```
@interface MySingle {
  int value();
}
```

then you can give **value( )** the value 100 when the annotation is applied like this:

```
@MySingle(100)
```

Notice that **value =** need not be specified.

One last point: Annotations that don't have parameters are called *marker annotations.* These are specified without passing any arguments and without using parentheses. Their sole purpose is to mark a declaration with some attribute.

Built-in Annotations

Java defines many built-in annotations. Most are specialized, but eight are general purpose. Four are imported from **java.lang.annotation**: **@Retention**, **@Documented**, **@Target**, and **@Inherited**. Four, **@Override**, **@Deprecated**, **@SafeVarargs**, and **@SuppressWarnings**, are included in **java.lang**. These are shown in Table 13-1.

Here is an example that uses **@Deprecated** to mark the **MyClass** class and the **getMsg( )** method as deprecated. (The term *deprecated* means obsolete and not for use in new code.) When you try to compile this program, warnings will report the use of these deprecated elements.

TABLE 13-1: The General Purpose Built-in Annotations	
Annotation	**Description**
@Retention	Specifies the retention policy that will be associated with the annotation. The retention policy determines how long an annotation is present during the compilation and deployment process.
@Documented	A marker annotation that tells a tool that an annotation is to be documented. It is designed to be used only as an annotation to an annotation declaration.
@Target	Specifies the types of declarations to which an annotation can be applied. It is designed to be used only as an annotation to another annotation. **@Target** takes one argument, which must be a constant from the **ElementType** enumeration, which defines various constants, such as **CONSTRUCTOR**, **FIELD**, and **METHOD**. The argument determines the types of declarations to which the annotation can be applied.
@Inherited	A marker annotation that causes the annotation for a superclass to be inherited by a subclass.
@Override	A method annotated with **@Override** must override a method from a superclass. If it doesn't, a compile-time error will result. It is used to ensure that a superclass method is actually overridden, and not simply overloaded. This is a marker annotation.
@Deprecated	A marker annotation that indicates that a feature is obsolete and has been replaced by a newer form.
@SafeVarargs	A marker annotation that indicates that no unsafe actions related to a varargs parameter in a method or constructor occur. Can only be applied to static or final methods or constructors. (Added by JDK 7.)
@SuppressWarnings	Specifies that one or more warnings that might be issued by the compiler are to be suppressed. The warnings to suppress are specified by name, in string form.

```
// An example that uses @Deprecated.

// Deprecate a class.
@Deprecated              Mark a class as deprecated.
class MyClass {
  private String msg;

  MyClass(String m) {
    msg = m;
  }

  // Deprecate a method within a class.
  @Deprecated              Mark a method as deprecated.
  String getMsg() {
    return msg;
  }
```

```
    // ...
  }

class AnnoDemo {
  public static void main(String[] args) {
    MyClass myObj = new MyClass("test");

    System.out.println(myObj.getMsg());
  }
}
```

EXERCISES

1. Enumeration constants are said to be *self-typed*. What does this mean?

2. What class do all enumerations automatically inherit?

3. Given the following enumeration, write a program that uses **values( )** to show a list of the constants and their ordinal values.

   ```
   enum Tools {
     SCREWDRIVER, WRENCH, HAMMER, PLIERS
   }
   ```

4. The traffic light simulation developed in Try This 13-1 can be improved with a few simple changes that take advantage of an enumeration's class features. In the version shown, the duration of each color was controlled by the **TrafficLightSimulator** class by hard-coding these values into the **run( )** method. Change this so that the duration of each color is stored by the constants in the **TrafficLightColor** enumeration. To do this, you will need to add a constructor, a private instance variable, and a method called **getDelay( )**.

5. Define boxing and unboxing. How does autoboxing/unboxing affect these actions?

6. Change the following fragment so that it uses autoboxing.

   ```
   Short val = new Short(123);
   ```

7. An annotation is syntactically based on a/an _____ .

8. What is a marker annotation?

9. An annotation can be applied only to methods. True or False?

10. Given an enumeration **MyEnum**, what is an easy way to find out how many values are in the enumeration?

11. Reimplement the **changeColor( )** method in the **TrafficLightSimulator** in Try This 13-1 so that, instead of a **switch** statement, it uses **values( )** and **ordinal( )** to determine the next color to assign to **tlc**.

12. Consider the following **Counter** class.

    ```
    class Counter {
      boolean up;
    ```

```
int count;

Counter(boolean b, int c) {
  up = b;
  count = c;
}

public int count() {
  if(up)
    return count++;
  else
    return count--;
}

// Test code
public static void main(String[] args) {
  Counter c1 = new Counter(true, 10);
  Counter c2 = new Counter(false, 10);

  for(int i = 0; i < 10; i++)
    System.out.println(c1.count() + ", " + c2.count());
}
}
```

As you can see, a **Counter** object counts either up or down, depending on the **boolean** argument passed to the constructor. An alternative implementation would not use a **boolean** parameter and instead would use an enumeration **Direction** with two values: **UP** and **DOWN**. Reimplement **Counter** this way. Give an advantage of each implementation over the other.

13. The following program uses named integer constants. Rewrite the program so that it uses an enumeration instead. It should still have the same input and output.

```
import java.io.*;

class Castle {
  public static final int NORTH = 0;
  public static final int SOUTH = 1;
  public static final int EAST = 2;
  public static final int WEST = 3;

  public static void main(String[] args) throws IOException {
    int direction;

    System.out.println("From which direction is the enemy attacking?");
    System.out.println(" 0 = North, 1 = South, 2 = East, 3 = West");
    direction = System.in.read() - '0';

    // now give them back their answer
    System.out.print("The attack is from the following direction: ");
    switch(direction) {
```

```
        case NORTH:
          System.out.println("NORTH");
          break;
        case SOUTH:
          System.out.println("SOUTH");
          break;
        case EAST:
          System.out.println("EAST");
          break;
        case WEST:
          System.out.println("WEST");
      }
    }
  }
```

14. Create an enumeration **DayOfWeek** with seven values **SUNDAY** through **SATURDAY**. Add a method **isWorkDay( )** to the **DayOfWeek** class that returns **true** if the value on which it is called is **MONDAY** through **FRIDAY**. For example, the call **DayOfWeek.SUNDAY.isWorkDay( )** returns **false**.

15. Since **Byte**, **Short**, **Integer**, **Long**, **Float**, and **Double** are subclasses of **Number**, they inherit all the methods of **Number**. So **Double**, for example, doesn't just have a **doubleValue( )** method, it also has **byteValue( )**, **shortValue( )**, **intValue( )**, **longValue( )**, and **floatValue( )** methods. What will be displayed by the following code segment? If any of the values are unusual, explain them.

```java
public class NumberTester {
  public static void main(String[] args) {
    Double d = new Double(123456.789);

    System.out.println(d.byteValue());
    System.out.println(d.shortValue());
    System.out.println(d.intValue());
    System.out.println(d.longValue());
    System.out.println(d.floatValue());
    System.out.println(d.doubleValue());
  }
}
```

16. In the code below, the variables **a** and **b** are initialized to refer to the same **Integer** object with value 3. Then the **Integer** object referred to by **b** is incremented to 4. Finally the values of **a** and **b** are displayed and we see "3 4". Why isn't the same value displayed for both **a** and **b**? Shouldn't **a** and **b** both have the same value since they refer to the same object? What's going on here?

```java
Integer a = 3;
Integer b = a;
b++;
System.out.println(a + " " + b); // prints "3 4"
```

17. Which of the following statements are legal?

    A. `Object o = 3;`

    B. `Number n = 3;`

    C. `Float f = (float) 3;`

    D. `Integer i = (Integer) 3;`

    E. `Integer j = o + i; // using the preceding variable declarations`

18. Consider the following two class declarations. Will they compile without error? Explain.

```java
class MySuper {
  void myHello(String s) {
    System.out.println(s);
  }
}

class MySub extends MySuper {
  @Override
  void myHello(int x) {
    System.out.println(x);
  }
}
```

CHAPTER 14

Generics

Since its original 1.0 version, many new features have been added to Java. All have enhanced and expanded the scope of the language, but perhaps the one that has had the most profound impact is *generics* because its effects were felt throughout the entire Java language. Introduced by JDK 5, generics added a completely new syntax element and caused changes to many of the classes and methods in the core API. It is not an overstatement to say that the inclusion of generics fundamentally reshaped the character of Java.

Today, generics are an integral part of Java programming, and a solid understanding is necessary for all Java programmers. Moreover, the concept of generic types has become part of the foundation of modern programming in general. Competency with generics is also required to effectively use the Collections Framework. Generics are not only one of Java's more sophisticated topics, but also one of its most important.

GENERICS FUNDAMENTALS

At its core, the term *generics* means *parameterized types*. Parameterized types are important because they enable you to create classes, interfaces, and methods in which the type of data on which they operate is specified as a parameter. A class, interface, or method that uses a type parameter is called *generic*, as in *generic class* or *generic method*.

A principal advantage of generic code is that it will automatically work with the type of data passed to its type parameter. Many algorithms are logically the same no matter what type of data they are being applied to. For example, the mechanism that supports a stack is the same whether it is storing items of type **Integer, String, Object**, or **Thread**. With generics, you can define an algorithm once, independently of any specific type of data, and then apply that algorithm to a wide variety of data types without any additional effort.

It is important to understand that Java has always given you the ability to create generalized classes, interfaces, and methods by operating through references of type **Object**. Because **Object** is the superclass of all other classes, an **Object** reference can refer to any type of object. Thus, in pre-generics code, generalized classes, interfaces, and methods used **Object** references to operate on various types of data. The problem was that they could not do so with *type safety* because casts were needed to explicitly convert from **Object** to the actual type of data being operated on. Thus, it was possible to accidentally create type mismatches. Generics add the type safety that was lacking because they make these casts automatic and implicit. In short, generics expand your ability to reuse code and let you do so safely and reliably.

A Simple Generics Example

Before discussing any more theory, it's best to look at a simple generics example. The following program defines two classes. The first is the generic class **Gen**, and the second is **GenDemo**, which uses **Gen**.

```
// A simple generic class.
// Here, T is a type parameter that will be replaced by a
// real type when an object of type Gen is created.
class Gen<T> {                                          Declare a generic class.
  T ob; // declare a reference to an object of type T   T is the generic type
                                                        parameter.
  // Pass the constructor a reference to
  // an object of type T.
  Gen(T o) {
    ob = o;
  }

  // Return ob.
  T getob() {
    return ob;
  }
```

```
    // Show type of T.
    void showType() {
      System.out.println("Type of T is " +
                       ob.getClass().getName());
    }
  }

// Demonstrate the generic class.
class GenDemo {
  public static void main(String[] args) {
    // Create a Gen reference for Integers.
    Gen<Integer> iOb;
```
Create a reference
to an object of type
Gen<Integer>.

```
    // Create a Gen<Integer> object and assign its
    // reference to iOb. Notice the use of autoboxing
    // to encapsulate the value 88 within an Integer object.
    iOb = new Gen<Integer>(88);
```
Instantiate an
object of type
Gen<Integer>.

```
    // Show the type of data used by iOb.
    iOb.showType();

    // Get the value in iOb. Notice that
    // no cast is needed.
    int v = iOb.getob();
    System.out.println("value: " + v);

    System.out.println();
```
Create a reference
and an object of
type **Gen<String>**.

```
    // Create a Gen object for Strings.
    Gen<String> strOb = new Gen<String>("Generics Test");

    // Show the type of data used by strOb.
    strOb.showType();

    // Get the value of strOb. Again, notice
    // that no cast is needed.
    String str = strOb.getob();
    System.out.println("value: " + str);
  }
}
```

The output produced by the program is shown here:

```
Type of T is java.lang.Integer
value: 88

Type of T is java.lang.String
value: Generics Test
```

Let's examine this program carefully. First, notice how **Gen** is declared by the following line:

```
class Gen<T> {
```

Here, **T** is the name of a *type parameter*. This name is used as a placeholder for the actual type that will be passed to **Gen** when an object is created. Thus, **T** is used within **Gen** whenever the type parameter is needed. Notice that **T** is contained within < >. This syntax can be generalized. Whenever a type parameter is being declared, it is specified within angle brackets. Because **Gen** uses a type parameter, **Gen** is a generic class.

In the declaration of **Gen**, there is no special significance to the name **T**. Any valid identifier could have been used, but **T** is traditional. Often parameter names are single-character, capital letters. Other commonly used type parameter names are **V** and **E**.

Next, **T** is used to declare an object called **ob**, as shown here:

```
T ob; // declare an object of type T
```

As explained, **T** is a placeholder for the actual type that will be specified when a **Gen** object is created. Thus, **ob** will be an object of the type passed to **T**. For example, if type **String** is passed to **T**, then in that instance, **ob** will be of type **String**.

Now consider **Gen**'s constructor:

```
Gen(T o) {
   ob = o;
}
```

Notice that its parameter, **o**, is of type **T**. This means that the actual type of **o** is determined by the type passed to **T** when a **Gen** object is created. Also, because both the parameter **o** and the member variable **ob** are of type **T**, they will both be of the same actual type when a **Gen** object is created.

The type parameter **T** can also be used to specify the return type of method, as is the case with the **getob( )** method, shown here:

```
T getob() {
   return ob;
}
```

Because **ob** is also of type **T**, its type is compatible with the return type specified by **getob( )**.

The **showType( )** method displays the type of **T**. It does this by calling **getName( )** on the **Class** object returned by the call to **getClass( )** on **ob**. We haven't used this feature before, so let's examine it closely. As you should recall from Chapter 7, the **Object** class defines the method **getClass( )**. Thus, **getClass( )** is a member of all class types. It returns a **Class** object that corresponds to the class type of the object on which it is called. **Class** is a class defined within **java.lang** that encapsulates information about a class. **Class** defines several methods that can be used to obtain information about a class at run time. Among these is the **getName( )** method, which returns a string representation of the class name.

The **GenDemo** class demonstrates the generic **Gen** class. It first creates a version of **Gen** for integers, as shown here:

```
Gen<Integer> iOb;
```

Look carefully at this declaration. First, notice that the type **Integer** is specified within the angle brackets after **Gen**. In this case, **Integer** is a *type argument* that is passed to **Gen**'s type parameter, **T**. This effectively creates a version of **Gen** in which all references to **T** are translated into references to **Integer**. Thus, for this declaration, **ob** is of type **Integer**, and the return type of **getob( )** is of type **Integer**.

Before moving on, it's necessary to state that the Java compiler does not actually create different versions of **Gen**, or of any other generic class. Although it's helpful to think in these terms, it is not what actually happens. Instead, the compiler removes all generic type information, substituting the necessary casts, to make your code *behave as if* a specific version of **Gen** was created. Thus, only one version of **Gen** actually exists in your program. The process of removing generic type information is called *erasure*, which is discussed later in this chapter.

The next line assigns to **iOb** a reference to an instance of an **Integer** version of the **Gen** class.

```
iOb = new Gen<Integer>(88);
```

Notice that when the **Gen** constructor is called, the type argument **Integer** is also specified. This is necessary because the type of the object (in this case **iOb**) to which the reference is being assigned is of type **Gen<Integer>**. Thus, the reference returned by **new** must also be of type **Gen<Integer>**. If it isn't, a compile-time error will result. For example, the following assignment will cause a compile-time error:

```
iOb = new Gen<Double>(88.0); // Error!
```

Because **iOb** is of type **Gen<Integer>**, it can't be used to refer to an object of **Gen<Double>**. This type checking is one of the main benefits of generics because it ensures type safety.

As the comments in the program state, the assignment

```
iOb = new Gen<Integer>(88);
```

makes use of autoboxing to encapsulate the value 88, which is an **int**, into an **Integer**. This works because **Gen<Integer>** creates a constructor that takes an **Integer** argument. Because an **Integer** is expected, Java will automatically box 88 inside one. Of course, the assignment could also have been written explicitly, like this:

```
iOb = new Gen<Integer>(new Integer(88));
```

However, there would be no benefit to using this version.

The program then displays the type of **ob** within **iOb**, which is **Integer**. Next, the program obtains the value of **ob** by use of the following line:

```
int v = iOb.getob();
```

Because the return type of **getob( )** is **T**, which was replaced by **Integer** when **iOb** was declared, the return type of **getob( )** is also **Integer**, which auto-unboxes into **int** when assigned to **v** (which is an **int**). Thus, there is no need to cast the return type of **getob( )** to **Integer**.

Next, **GenDemo** declares an object of type **Gen<String>**:

```
Gen<String> strOb = new Gen<String>("Generics Test");
```

Because the type argument is **String**, **String** is substituted for **T** inside **Gen**. This creates (conceptually) a **String** version of **Gen**, as the remaining lines in the program demonstrate.

Generics Work Only with Objects

When declaring an instance of a generic type, the type argument passed to the type parameter must be a reference type. You cannot use a primitive type, such as **int** or **char**. For example, with **Gen**, it is possible to pass any class type to **T**, but you cannot pass a primitive type to **T**. Therefore, the following declaration is illegal:

```
Gen<int> intOb = new Gen<int>(53); // Error, can't use primitive type
```

Of course, not being able to specify a primitive type is not a serious restriction because you can use the type wrappers (as the preceding example did) to encapsulate a primitive type. Further, Java's autoboxing and auto-unboxing mechanism makes the use of the type wrapper transparent.

Generic Types Differ Based on Their Type Arguments

A key point to understand about generic types is that a reference of one specific version of a generic type is not type-compatible with another version of the same generic type. For example, assuming the program just shown, the following line of code is in error and will not compile:

```
iOb = strOb; // Wrong!
```

Even though both **iOb** and **strOb** are of type **Gen<T>**, they are references to different types because their type parameters differ. This is part of the way that generics add type safety and prevent errors.

A Generic Class with Two Type Parameters

You can declare more than one type parameter in a generic type. To specify two or more type parameters, simply use a comma-separated list. For example, the following **TwoGen** class is a variation of the **Gen** class that has two type parameters.

```
// A simple generic class with two type parameters: T and V.
class TwoGen<T, V> {  ◄─────────────────────────── Use two type
  T ob1;                                            parameters.
  V ob2;

  // Pass the constructor references to
  // objects of type T and V.
  TwoGen(T o1, V o2) {
    ob1 = o1;
    ob2 = o2;
  }
```

```
    // Show types of T and V.
    void showTypes() {
      System.out.println("Type of T is " +
                            ob1.getClass().getName());

      System.out.println("Type of V is " +
                            ob2.getClass().getName());
    }

    T getob1() {
      return ob1;
    }

    V getob2() {
      return ob2;
    }
  }

  // Demonstrate TwoGen.
  class SimpGen {
    public static void main(String[] args) {

      TwoGen<Integer, String> tgObj =
        new TwoGen<Integer, String>(88, "Generics");

      // Show the types.
      tgObj.showTypes();

      // Obtain and show values.
      int v = tgObj.getob1();
      System.out.println("value: " + v);

      String str = tgObj.getob2();
      System.out.println("value: " + str);
    }
  }
```

Here, **Integer** is passed to **T**, and **String** is passed to **V**.

The output from this program is shown here:

```
Type of T is java.lang.Integer
Type of V is java.lang.String
value: 88
value: Generics
```

Notice how **TwoGen** is declared:

```
class TwoGen<T, V> {
```

It specifies two type parameters, **T** and **V**, separated by a comma. Because it has two type parameters, two type arguments must be passed to **TwoGen** when an object is created, as shown next:

```
TwoGen<Integer, String> tgObj =
  new TwoGen<Integer, String>(88, "Generics");
```

In this case, **Integer** is substituted for **T**, and **String** is substituted for **V**. Although the two type arguments differ in this example, it is possible for both types to be the same. For example, the following line of code is valid:

```
TwoGen<String, String> x = new TwoGen<String, String>("A", "B");
```

In this case, both **T** and **V** would be of type **String**. Of course, if the type arguments were always the same, then two type parameters would be unnecessary.

The General Form of a Generic Class

The generics syntax shown in the preceding examples can be generalized. Here is the syntax for declaring a generic class:

    class *class-name*<*type-param-list*> { // ...

In the context of an assignment, here is the syntax for declaring a reference to a generics class and creating an instance:

    class-name<*type-arg-list*> *var-name* =
         new *class-name*<*type-arg-list*>(*cons-arg-list*);

Progress Check

1. The type of data operated on by a generic class is passed to it through a/an _____.
2. Can a type parameter be passed a primitive type?
3. Assuming the **Gen** class shown in the preceding example, show how to declare a **Gen** reference that operates on data of type **Double**.

Ask the Expert

Q I can already see that generics are a powerful feature. Is it unique to Java, or do other computer languages support a similar concept?

A The general concept behind generics is supported by other languages. For example, C++ supports generic code through the use of *templates*. (In essence, what Java calls a parameterized type, C++ calls a template.) However, Java generics and C++ templates are not the same, and there are some fundamental differences between the two approaches. For the most part, Java's approach is simpler to use. Another language that supports generic code is C#. Its approach is more similar to Java's.

Answers:

1. type parameter
2. No.
3. `Gen<Double> d_ob;`

BOUNDED TYPES

In the preceding examples, the type parameters could be replaced by any class type. This is fine for many purposes, but sometimes it is useful to limit the types that can be passed to a type parameter. For example, assume that you want to create a generic class that stores a numeric value and is capable of performing various mathematical functions, such as computing the reciprocal or obtaining the fractional component. Furthermore, you want to use the class to compute these quantities for any type of number, including integers, **float**s, and **double**s. Thus, you want to specify the type of the numbers generically, using a type parameter. To create such a class, you might try something like this:

```java
// NumericFns attempts (unsuccessfully) to create
// a generic class that can compute various
// numeric functions, such as the reciprocal or the
// fractional component, given any type of number.
class NumericFns<T> {
  T num;

  // Pass the constructor a reference to
  // a numeric object.
  NumericFns(T n) {
    num = n;
  }

  // Return the reciprocal.
  double reciprocal() {
    return 1 / num.doubleValue(); // Error!
  }

  // Return the fractional component.
  double fraction() {
    return num.doubleValue() - num.intValue(); // Error!
  }

  // ...
}
```

Unfortunately, **NumericFns** will not compile as written because both methods will generate compile-time errors. First, examine the **reciprocal( )** method, which attempts to return the reciprocal of **num**. To do this, it must divide 1 by the value of **num**. The value of **num** is obtained by calling **doubleValue( )**, which obtains the **double** version of the numeric object stored in **num**. Because all numeric classes, such as **Integer** and **Double**, are subclasses of **Number**, and **Number** defines the **doubleValue( )** method, this method is available to all numeric wrapper classes. The trouble is that the compiler has no way to know that you are intending to create **NumericFns** objects using only numeric types. Thus, when you try to compile **NumericFns**, an error is reported that indicates that the **doubleValue( )** method is unknown. The same type of error occurs twice in **fraction( )**, which needs to call both **doubleValue( )** and **intValue( )**. Both calls result in error messages stating that these methods are unknown. To solve this problem, you need some way to tell the compiler that you intend to pass only numeric types to **T**. Furthermore, you need some way to *ensure* that *only* numeric types are actually passed.

To handle such situations, Java provides *bounded types*. When specifying a type parameter, you can create an upper bound that declares the superclass from which all type arguments must be derived. This is accomplished through the use of an **extends** clause when specifying the type parameter, as shown here:

<*T* extends *superclass*>

This specifies that *T* can be replaced only by *superclass*, or subclasses of *superclass*. Thus, *superclass* defines an inclusive, upper limit.

You can use an upper bound to fix the **NumericFns** class shown earlier by specifying **Number** as an upper bound, as shown here:

```java
// In this version of NumericFns, the type argument
// for T must be either Number, or a class derived
// from Number.
class NumericFns<T extends Number> {      // In this case, the type
  T num;                                  // argument must be
                                          // either Number or a
  // Pass the constructor a reference to  // subclass of Number.
  // a numeric object.
  NumericFns(T n) {
    num = n;
  }

  // Return the reciprocal.
  double reciprocal() {
    return 1 / num.doubleValue();
  }

  // Return the fractional component.
  double fraction() {
    return num.doubleValue() - num.intValue();
  }

  // ...
}

// Demonstrate NumericFns.
class BoundsDemo {
  public static void main(String[] args) {

    NumericFns<Integer> iOb =             // Integer is OK because it is a
                   new NumericFns<Integer>(5);    // subclass of Number.

    System.out.println("Reciprocal of iOb is " +
                   iOb.reciprocal());
    System.out.println("Fractional component of iOb is " +
                   iOb.fraction());
```

```
    System.out.println();

    NumericFns<Double> dOb =                              Double is also OK.
                    new NumericFns<Double>(5.25);

    System.out.println("Reciprocal of dOb is " +
                    dOb.reciprocal());
    System.out.println("Fractional component of dOb is " +
                    dOb.fraction());


    // This won't compile because String is not a
    // subclass of Number.
// NumericFns<String> strOb = new NumericFns<String>("Error");
    }
}
```

String is illegal because it is not a subclass of **Number**.

The output is shown here:

```
Reciprocal of iOb is 0.2
Fractional component of iOb is 0.0

Reciprocal of dOb is 0.19047619047619047
Fractional component of dOb is 0.25
```

Notice how **NumericFns** is now declared by this line:

```
class NumericFns<T extends Number> {
```

Because the type **T** is now bounded by **Number**, the Java compiler knows that all objects of type **T** can call **doubleValue( )** because it is a method declared by **Number**. This is in itself a major advantage. However, as an added bonus, the bounding of **T** also prevents nonnumeric **NumericFns** objects from being created. For example, if you remove the comments from the lines at the end of the program, and then try recompiling, you will receive compile-time errors because **String** is not a subclass of **Number**.

Bounded types are especially useful when you need to ensure that one type parameter is compatible with another. For example, consider the following class called **Pair**, which stores two objects that must be compatible with each other:

```
class Pair<T, V extends T> {               Here, V must be either
  T first;                                 the same type as T, or a
  V second;                                subclass of T.

  Pair(T a, V b) {
    first = a;
    second = b;
  }

  // ...
}
```

Notice that **Pair** uses two type parameters, **T** and **V**, and that **V** extends **T**. This means that **V** will either be the same as **T** or a subclass of **T**. This ensures that the two arguments to **Pair**'s constructor will be objects of the same type or of related types. For example, the following constructions are valid:

```
// This is OK because both T and V are Integer.
Pair<Integer, Integer> x = new Pair<Integer, Integer>(1, 2);

// This is OK because Integer is a subclass of Number.
Pair<Number, Integer> y = new Pair<Number, Integer>(10.4, 12);
```

However, the following is invalid:

```
// This causes an error because String is not
// a subclass of Number
Pair<Number, String> z = new Pair<Number, String>(10.4, "12");
```

In this case, **String** is not a subclass of **Number**, which violates the bound specified by **Pair**.

Progress Check

1. The keyword _____ specifies a bound for a type argument.
2. How do you declare a generic type **T** that must be a subclass of **Thread**?
3. Given

   ```
   class X<T, V extends T> {
   ```

   is the following declaration correct?

   ```
   X<Integer, Double> x = new X<Integer, Double>(10, 1.1);
   ```

USING WILDCARD ARGUMENTS

As useful as type safety is, sometimes it can get in the way of perfectly acceptable constructs. For example, given the **NumericFns** class shown at the end of the preceding section, assume that you want to add a method called **absEqual( )** that returns **true** if two **NumericFns** objects contain numbers whose absolute values are the same. Furthermore, you want this method to be able to work properly no matter what type of number each object holds. For example, if one object contains the **Double** value 1.25 and the other object contains the **Float** value −1.25, then **absEqual( )** would return **true**.

Answers:

1. **extends**
2. `T extends Thread`
3. No, because **Double** is not a subclass of **Integer**.

One way to implement **absEqual( )** is to pass it a **NumericFns** argument, and then compare the absolute value of that argument against the absolute value of the invoking object, returning true only if the values are the same. For example, you want to be able to call **absEqual( )** as shown here:

```
NumericFns<Double> dOb = new NumericFns<Double>(1.25);
NumericFns<Float> fOb = new NumericFns<Float>(-1.25);

if(dOb.absEqual(fOb))
  System.out.println("Absolute values are the same.");
else
  System.out.println("Absolute values differ.");
```

At first, creating **absEqual( )** seems like an easy problem. Unfortunately, trouble starts as soon as you try to declare a parameter of type **NumericFns**. What type do you specify for **NumericFns**'s type parameter? At first, you might think of a solution like this, in which **T** is used as the type parameter:

```
// This won't work!
// Determine if the absolute values of two objects are the same.
boolean absEqual(NumericFns<T> ob) {
  if(Math.abs(num.doubleValue()) ==
       Math.abs(ob.num.doubleValue()) return true;

  return false;
}
```

Here, the standard method **Math.abs( )** is used to obtain the absolute value of each number, and then the values are compared. The trouble with this attempt is that it will work only with other **NumericFns** objects whose type is the same as the invoking object. For example, if the invoking object is of type **NumericFns<Integer>**, then the parameter **ob** must also be of type **NumericFns<Integer>**. It can't be used to compare an object of type **NumericFns<Double>**, for example. Therefore, this approach does not yield a general (i.e., generic) solution.

To create a generic **absEqual( )** method, you must use another feature of Java generics: the *wildcard argument*. The wildcard argument is specified by the **?**, and it represents an unknown type. Using a wildcard, here is one way to write the **absEqual( )** method:

```
// Determine if the absolute values of two
// objects are the same.
boolean absEqual(NumericFns<?> ob) {  ◄———————— Notice the wildcard.
  if(Math.abs(num.doubleValue()) ==
       Math.abs(ob.num.doubleValue())) return true;

  return false;
}
```

Here, **NumericFns<?>** matches any type of **NumericFns** object, allowing any two **NumericFns** objects to have their absolute values compared. The following program demonstrates this.

```java
// Use a wildcard.
class NumericFns<T extends Number> {
  T num;

  // Pass the constructor a reference to
  // a numeric object.
  NumericFns(T n) {
    num = n;
  }

  // Return the reciprocal.
  double reciprocal() {
    return 1 / num.doubleValue();
  }

  // Return the fractional component.
  double fraction() {
    return num.doubleValue() - num.intValue();
  }

  // Determine if the absolute values of two
  // objects are the same.
  boolean absEqual(NumericFns<?> ob) {
    if(Math.abs(num.doubleValue()) ==
          Math.abs(ob.num.doubleValue())) return true;

    return false;
  }

  // ...
}

// Demonstrate a wildcard.
class WildcardDemo {
  public static void main(String[] args) {

    NumericFns<Integer> iOb =
                    new NumericFns<Integer>(6);

    NumericFns<Double> dOb =
                     new NumericFns<Double>(-6.0);

    NumericFns<Long> lOb =
                    new NumericFns<Long>(5L);

    System.out.println("Testing iOb and dOb.");
    if(iOb.absEqual(dOb))              ◄——————————— In this call, the wildcard
      System.out.println("Absolute values are equal."); type matches **Double**.
    else
      System.out.println("Absolute values differ.");
```

```
System.out.println();

System.out.println("Testing iOb and lOb.");
if(iOb.absEqual(lOb))            ← In this call, the wildcard
  System.out.println("Absolute values are equal.");  matches Long.
else
  System.out.println("Absolute values differ.");

  }
}
```

The output is shown here:

```
Testing iOb and dOb.
Absolute values are equal.

Testing iOb and lOb.
Absolute values differ.
```

In the program, notice these two calls to **absEqual( )**:

```
if(iOb.absEqual(dOb))

if(iOb.absEqual(lOb))
```

In the first call, **iOb** is an object of type **NumericFns<Integer>** and **dOb** is an object of type **NumericFns<Double>**. However, through use of a wildcard, it possible for **iOb** to pass **dOb** in the call to **absEqual( )**. The same applies to the second call, in which an object of type **NumericFns<Long>** is passed.

One last point: It is important to understand that the wildcard does not affect what type of **NumericFns** objects can be created. This is governed by the **extends** clause in the **NumericFns** declaration. The wildcard simply enables any *valid* **NumericFns** type to be matched.

BOUNDED WILDCARDS

Wildcard arguments can be bounded in much the same way that a type parameter can be bounded. A bounded wildcard is especially important when you are creating a method that is designed to operate only on objects that are subclasses of a specific superclass. To understand why, let's work through a simple example. Consider the following set of classes:

```
class A {
  // ...
}

class B extends A {
  // ...
}
```

```
class C extends A {
  // ...
}

// Note that D does NOT extend A.
class D {
  // ...
}
```

Here, class **A** is extended by classes **B** and **C**, but not by **D**.

Next, consider the following very simple generic class:

```
// A simple generic class.
class Gen<T> {
  T ob;

  Gen(T o) {
    ob = o;
  }
}
```

Gen takes one type parameter, which specifies the type of object stored in **ob**. Because **T** is unbounded, the type of **T** is unrestricted. That is, **T** can be of any class type.

Now, suppose that you want to create a method that takes as an argument any type of **Gen** object as long as its type parameter is **A** or a subclass of **A**. In other words, you want to create a method that operates only on objects of **Gen**<*type*>, where *type* is either **A** or a subclass of **A**. To accomplish this, you must use a bounded wildcard. For example, here is method called **test( )** that accepts as an argument only **Gen** objects whose type parameter is **A** or a subclass of **A**:

```
// Here, the ? will match A or any class type
// that extends A.
static void test(Gen<? extends A> o) {
  // ...
}
```

The following class demonstrates the types of **Gen** objects that can be passed to **test( )**.

```
class UseBoundedWildcard {
  // Here, the ? will match A or any class type
  // that extends A.
  static void test(Gen<? extends A> o) {  ◄──────── Use a bounded wildcard.
    // ...
  }

  public static void main(String[] args) {
    A a = new A();
    B b = new B();
    C c = new C();
    D d = new D();

    Gen<A> w = new Gen<A>(a);
    Gen<B> w2 = new Gen<B>(b);
```

```
Gen<C> w3 = new Gen<C>(c);
Gen<D> w4 = new Gen<D>(d);

// These calls to test() are OK.
test(w);
test(w2);
test(w3);

// Can't call test() with w4 because
// it is not an object of a class that
// inherits A.
//    test(w4); // Error!
  }
}
```

These are legal because **w**, **w2**, and **w3** are subclasses of **A**.

This is illegal because **w4** is not a subclass of **A**.

In **main( )**, objects of type **A**, **B**, **C**, and **D** are created. These are then used to create four **Gen** objects, one for each type. Finally, four calls to **test( )** are made, with the last call commented out. The first three calls are valid because **w**, **w2**, and **w3** are **Gen** objects whose type is either **A** or a subclass of **A**. However, the last call to **test( )** is illegal because **w4** is an object of type **D**, which is not derived from **A**. Thus, the method will not accept **w4** because of the wildcard's bound.

In general, to establish an upper bound for a wildcard, use the following type of wildcard expression:

>   *<? extends superclass>*

where *superclass* is the name of the class that serves as the upper bound. Remember, this is an inclusive clause because the class forming the upper bound (specified by *superclass*) is also within bounds.

You can also specify a lower bound for a wildcard by adding a **super** clause to a wildcard declaration. Here is its general form:

>   *<? super subclass>*

In this case, only classes that are superclasses of *subclass* are acceptable arguments. This is an inclusive clause.

Progress Check

1. To specify a wildcard argument, use _____.
2. A wildcard argument matches any reference type. True or False?
3. Can a wildcard be bounded?
4. In this expression, what types can be matched by the wildcard?

```
void myMeth(XYZ<? extends Thread> trdOb) { // ...
```

_____

Answers:

1. ?
2. True.
3. Yes.
4. The wildcard can match type **Thread** or a subclass of **Thread**.

Ask the Expert

Q: Can I cast one instance of a generic class into another?

A: Yes, but its use is somewhat limited. You can cast one instance of a generic class into another only if the two are otherwise compatible and their type arguments are the same. For example, assume a generic class called **Gen** that is declared like this:

```
class Gen<T> { // ...
```

Next, assume that **x** is declared as shown here:

```
Gen<Integer> x = new Gen<Integer>();
```

Then, this cast is legal:

```
(Gen<Integer>) x // legal
```

because **x** is an instance of **Gen<Integer>**. But, this cast

```
(Gen<Long>) x // illegal
```

is not legal because **x** is not an instance of **Gen<Long>**.

GENERIC METHODS

As the preceding examples have shown, methods inside a generic class can make use of a class's type parameter and are, therefore, automatically generic relative to the type parameter. However, it is possible to declare a generic method that uses one or more type parameters of its own. Furthermore, it is possible to create a generic method that is enclosed within a non-generic class.

The following program declares a non-generic class called **GenericMethodDemo** and a static generic method within that class called **arraysEqual( )**. This method determines if two arrays contain the same elements, in the same order. It can be used to compare any two arrays as long as the arrays are of the same or compatible types.

```
// Demonstrate a simple generic method.
class GenericMethodDemo {

  // Determine if the contents of two arrays are the same.
  static <T, V extends T> boolean arraysEqual(T[] x, V[] y) {    A generic method.
    // If array lengths differ, then the arrays differ.
    if(x.length != y.length) return false;

    for(int i=0; i < x.length; i++)
      if(!x[i].equals(y[i])) return false; // arrays differ

    return true; // contents of arrays are equivalent
  }
```

```
     public static void main(String[] args) {

        Integer[] nums = { 1, 2, 3, 4, 5 };
        Integer[] nums2 = { 1, 2, 3, 4, 5 };
        Integer[] nums3 = { 1, 2, 7, 4, 5 };
        Integer[] nums4 = { 1, 2, 7, 4, 5, 6 };

        if(arraysEqual(nums, nums))
           System.out.println("nums equals nums");

        if(arraysEqual(nums, nums2))
           System.out.println("nums equals nums2");

        if(arraysEqual(nums, nums3))
           System.out.println("nums equals nums3");

        if(arraysEqual(nums, nums4))
           System.out.println("nums equals nums4");


        // Create an array of Doubles
        Double[] dvals = { 1.1, 2.2, 3.3, 4.4, 5.5 };

        // This won't compile because nums and dvals
        // are not of the same type.
//      if(arraysEqual(nums, dvals))
//         System.out.println("nums equals dvals");
     }
}
```

The type arguments for **T** and **V** are implicitly determined when the method is called.

The output from the program is shown here:

```
nums equals nums
nums equals nums2
```

Let's examine **arraysEqual( )** closely. First, notice how it is declared by this line:

```
static <T, V extends T> boolean arraysEqual(T[] x, V[] y) {
```

The type parameters are declared *before* the return type of the method. Second, notice that the type **V** is upper-bounded by **T**. Thus, **V** must be either the same as type **T** or a subclass of **T**. This relationship enforces that **arraysEqual( )** can be called only with arguments that are compatible with each other. Also notice that **arraysEqual( )** is static, enabling it to be called independently of any object. Understand, though, that generic methods can be either static or nonstatic. There is no restriction in this regard.

Now, notice how **arraysEqual( )** is called within **main( )** by use of the normal call syntax, without the need to specify type arguments. This is because the types of the arguments are automatically discerned, and the types of **T** and **V** are adjusted accordingly. For example, in the first call:

```
if(arraysEqual(nums, nums))
```

the base type of the first argument is **Integer**, which causes **Integer** to be substituted for **T**. The base type of the second argument is also **Integer**, which makes **Integer** a substitute for **V**, too. Thus, the call to **arraysEqual( )** is legal, and the two arrays can be compared.

Now, notice the commented-out code, shown here:

```
//     if(arraysEqual(nums, dvals))
//         System.out.println("nums equals dvals");
```

If you remove the comments and then try to compile the program, you will receive an error. The reason is that the type parameter **V** is bounded by **T** in the **extends** clause in **V**'s declaration. This means that **V** must be either type **T** or a subclass of **T**. In this case, the first argument is of type **Integer**, making **T** into **Integer**, but the second argument is of type **Double**, which is not a subclass of **Integer**. This makes the call to **arraysEqual( )** illegal and results in a compile-time type-mismatch error.

The syntax used to create **arraysEqual( )** can be generalized. Here is the syntax for a generic method:

<type-param-list> ret-type meth-name(param-list) { // ...

In all cases, *type-param-list* is a comma-separated list of type parameters. Notice that for a generic method, the type parameter list precedes the return type.

GENERIC CONSTRUCTORS

A constructor can be generic, even if its class is not. For example, in the following program, the class **Summation** is not generic, but its constructor is.

```
// Use a generic constructor.
class Summation {
  private int sum;

  <T extends Number> Summation(T arg) {          ◄——————— A generic constructor
    sum = 0;

    for(int i=0; i <= arg.intValue(); i++)
      sum += i;
  }

  int getSum() {
    return sum;
  }
}

class GenConsDemo {
  public static void main(String[] args) {
    Summation ob = new Summation(4.0);

    System.out.println("Summation of 4.0 is " + ob.getSum());
  }
}
```

The **Summation** class computes and encapsulates the summation of the numeric value passed to its constructor. In this case, we are using a summation of N that is the sum of all the whole numbers between 0 and N. Because **Summation( )** specifies a type parameter that is bounded by **Number**, a **Summation** object can be constructed using any numeric type, including **Integer**, **Float**, or **Double**. No matter what numeric type is used, its value is converted to **Integer** by calling **intValue( )**, and the summation is computed. Therefore, it is not necessary for the class **Summation** to be generic; only a generic constructor is needed.

GENERIC CLASS HIERARCHIES

A generic class can be part of a class hierarchy in just the same way as a non-generic class. Thus, a generic class can act as a superclass or be a subclass. The key difference between generic and non-generic hierarchies is that in a generic hierarchy, any type arguments needed by a generic superclass must be passed up the hierarchy by all subclasses. This is similar to the way that constructor arguments must be passed up a hierarchy.

Here is a simple example of a hierarchy that uses a generic superclass:

```
// A simple generic class hierarchy.
class Gen<T> {
  T ob;

  Gen(T o) {
    ob = o;
  }

  // Return ob.
  T getob() {
    return ob;
  }
}

// A subclass of Gen.
class Gen2<T> extends Gen<T> {
  Gen2(T o) {
    super(o);
  }
}
```

In this hierarchy, **Gen2** extends the generic class **Gen**. Notice how **Gen2** is declared by the following line:

```
class Gen2<T> extends Gen<T> {
```

The type parameter **T** is specified by **Gen2** and is also passed to **Gen** in the **extends** clause. This means that whatever type is passed to **Gen2** will also be passed to **Gen**. For example, this declaration,

```
Gen2<Integer> num = new Gen2<Integer>(100);
```

passes **Integer** as the type parameter to **Gen**. Thus, the **ob** inside the **Gen** portion of **Gen2** will be of type **Integer**.

Notice also that **Gen2** does not use the type parameter **T** except to pass it to the **Gen** superclass. Thus, even if a subclass of a generic superclass would otherwise not need to be generic, it still must specify the type parameter(s) required by its generic superclass. Of course, a subclass is free to add its own type parameters, if needed.

It is also perfectly acceptable for a non-generic class to be the superclass of a generic subclass. For example:

```
// A non-generic class can be the superclass
// of a generic subclass.

// A non-generic class.
class NonGen {
  int num;

  NonGen(int i) {
    num = i;
  }

  int getnum() {
    return num;
  }
}

// A generic subclass.
class Gen<T> extends NonGen {
  T ob; // declare an object of type T

  // Pass the constructor a reference to
  // an object of type T.
  Gen(T o, int i) {
    super(i);
    ob = o;
  }

  // Return ob.
  T getob() {
    return ob;
  }
}
```

Notice how **Gen** inherits **NonGen** in the following declaration:

```
class Gen<T> extends NonGen {
```

Because **NonGen** is not generic, no type argument is specified. Thus, even though **Gen** declares the type parameter **T**, it is not needed by (nor can it be used by) **NonGen**. Thus, **NonGen** is inherited by **Gen** in the normal way. No special conditions apply.

Ask the Expert

Q In a generic class hierarchy, can a method with a type parameter be over-ridden?

A Yes. A generic method in a generic class hierarchy can be overridden just like any other method. For example, consider this example in which the method **getob( )** is overridden:

```java
// Overriding a generic method in a generic class.
class Gen<T> {
  T ob; // declare an object of type T

  // Pass the constructor a reference to
  // an object of type T.
  Gen(T o) {
    ob = o;
  }

  // Return ob.
  T getob() {
    System.out.print("Gen's getob(): " );
    return ob;
  }
}

// A subclass of Gen that overrides getob().
class Gen2<T> extends Gen<T> {

  Gen2(T o) {
    super(o);
  }

  // Override getob().
  T getob() {
    System.out.print("Gen2's getob(): ");
    return ob;
  }
}

// Demonstrate generic method override.
class OverrideDemo {
  public static void main(String[] args) {

    // A Gen reference that can refer to any type of Gen object.
    Gen<?> gRef;

    // Create a Gen object for Integers.
    Gen<Integer> iOb = new Gen<Integer>(88);
```

Ask the Expert (Continued)

```
    // Create a Gen2 object for Integers.
    Gen2<Integer> iOb2 = new Gen2<Integer>(99);

    // Create a Gen2 object for Strings.
    Gen2<String> strOb2 = new Gen2<String> ("Generics Test");

    gRef = iOb;
    System.out.println(gRef.getob());

    gRef = iOb2;
    System.out.println(gRef.getob());

    gRef = strOb2;
    System.out.println(gRef.getob());
  }
}
```

The output is shown here:

```
Gen's getob(): 88
Gen2's getob(): 99
Gen2's getob(): Generics Test
```

In the program, notice that the generic reference **gRef** is used to call **getob( )** on objects of both **Gen** and **Gen2**. As the output confirms, the overridden version of **getob( )** is called for objects of type **Gen2**, but the superclass version is called for objects of type **Gen**.

Progress Check

1. Can a method or constructor be generic even if its class is not?
2. Show how to declare a generic method called **myMeth( )** that takes one generic type argument. Have it return an argument of that generic type.
3. A generic class cannot be inherited. True or False?

GENERIC INTERFACES

In addition to generic classes and methods, you can also have generic interfaces. Generic interfaces are specified just like generic classes. Here is an example. It creates an interface called **Containment**, which can be implemented by classes that

---

Answers:

1. Yes.
2. `<T> T myMeth(T o)`
3. False.

store one or more values. It declares a method called **contains( )** that determines if a specified value is contained by the invoking object.

```java
// A generic interface example.

// A generic containment interface.
// This interface implies that an implementing
// class contains one or more values.
interface Containment<T> {        ◄──────────────── A generic interface.
  // The contains() method tests if a
  // specific item is contained within
  // an object that implements Containment.
  boolean contains(T o);
}

// Implement Containment using an array to
// hold the values.
class MyClass<T> implements Containment<T> { ◄──────── Any class that implements
  T[] arrayRef;                                         a generic interface must
                                                        itself be generic.
  MyClass(T[] o) {
    arrayRef = o;
  }

  // Implement Contains().
  public boolean contains(T o) {
    for(T x : arrayRef)
      if(x.equals(o)) return true;
    return false;
  }
}

class GenIFDemo {
  public static void main(String[] args) {
    Integer[] x = { 1, 2, 3 };

    MyClass<Integer> ob = new MyClass<Integer>(x);

    if(ob.contains(2))
      System.out.println("2 is in ob");
    else
      System.out.println("2 is NOT in ob");

    if(ob.contains(5))
      System.out.println("5 is in ob");
    else
      System.out.println("5 is NOT in ob");

    // The following is illegal because ob
    // is an Integer Containment and 9.25 is
    // a Double value.
```

```
//      if(ob.contains(9.25)) // Illegal!
//        System.out.println("9.25 is in ob");
    }
}
```

The output is shown here:

```
2 is in ob
5 is NOT in ob
```

Although most aspects of this program should be easy to understand, a couple of key points need to be made. First, notice that **Containment** is declared like this:

```
interface Containment<T> {
```

In general, a generic interface is declared in the same way as a generic class. In this case, the type parameter **T** specifies the type of objects that are contained.

Next, **Containment** is implemented by **MyClass**. Notice the declaration of **MyClass**, shown here:

```
class MyClass<T> implements Containment<T> {
```

In general, if a class implements a generic interface, then that class must also be generic, at least to the extent that it takes a type parameter that is passed to the interface. For example, the following attempt to declare **MyClass** is in error:

```
class MyClass implements Containment<T> { // Wrong!
```

This declaration is wrong because **MyClass** does not declare a type parameter, which means that there is no way to pass one to **Containment**. In this case, the identifier **T** is simply unknown and the compiler reports an error. Of course, if a class implements a *specific type* of generic interface, such as shown here:

```
class MyClass implements Containment<Double> { // OK
```

then the implementing class does not need to be generic.

As you might expect, the type parameter(s) specified by a generic interface can be bounded. This lets you limit the type of data for which the interface can be implemented. For example, if you wanted to limit **Containment** to numeric types, then you could declare it like this:

```
interface Containment<T extends Number> {
```

Now, any implementing class must pass to **Containment** a type argument also having the same bound. For example, now **MyClass** must be declared as shown here:

```
class MyClass<T extends Number> implements Containment<T> {
```

Pay special attention to the way the type parameter **T** is declared by **MyClass** and then passed to **Containment**. Because **Containment** now requires a type that extends

Number, the implementing class (**MyClass** in this case) must specify the same bound. Furthermore, once this bound has been established, there is no need to specify it again in the **implements** clause. In fact it would be wrong to do so. For example, this declaration is incorrect and won't compile:

```
// This is wrong!
class MyClass<T extends Number>
  implements Containment<T extends Number> { // Wrong!
```

Once the type parameter has been established, it is simply passed to the interface without further modification.

Here is the generalized syntax for a generic interface:

> interface *interface-name<type-param-list>* { // ...

Here, *type-param-list* is a comma-separated list of type parameters. When a generic interface is implemented, you must specify the type arguments, as shown here:

> class *class-name<type-param-list>*
>   implements *interface-name<type-param-list>* {

TRY THIS 14-1   CREATE A SIMPLE GENERIC STACK

```
IGenSimpleStack.java
SimpleStackExc.java
GenSimpleStack.java
GenSimpleStackDemo.java
```

One of the most powerful advantages that generics bring to programming is the ability to construct reliable, reusable code. As mentioned at the start of this chapter, many algorithms are the same no matter what type of data they are used on. For example, the basic functionality of a stack is the same no matter what type of objects are being stored. Instead of creating a separate stack class for each specific type of object, you can craft a single, generic solution that can be used with any type of object. Thus, the development cycle of design, code, test, and debug occurs only once when you create a generic solution—not repeatedly, each time a stack is needed for a new data type.

In this project you will adapt the simple stack example that has been evolving since Try This 5-2, making it generic. This project represents the final evolution of the stack. It includes a generic interface that defines the stack operations, a generic fixed-length stack implementation, and the stack exception classes. This version of the stack will be called **GenSimpleStack**.

STEP-BY-STEP

1. The first step in creating a generic stack is to create a generic interface that describes the stack's operations. The generic version of the stack

interface is called **IGenSimpleStack** and it is shown here. Put this interface into a file called **IGenSimpleStack.java**.

```
// A generic interface for a simple stack.
public interface IGenSimpleStack<T> {

  // Push an item onto the stack.
  void push(T item) throws StackFullException;

  // Pop an item from the stack.
  T pop() throws StackEmptyException;

  // Return true if the stack is empty.
  boolean isEmpty();

  // Return true if the stack is full.
  boolean isFull();
}
```

Notice that this interface is similar to the non-generic version developed in Try This 10-1 except that the data type is specified by **T** rather than **char**.

2. The generic stack can use the same, non-generic exception classes developed in Try This 10-1. Recall that they encapsulate the two stack errors: full or empty. They are not generic classes because they are the same no matter what type of data is stored in the stack. For your convenience, they are shown again here. They should be in the file **SimpleStackExc.java**.

```
// An exception for stack-full errors.
class StackFullException extends Exception {
  int size;

  StackFullException(int s) {
    super("Stack Full");
    size = s;
  }

  public String toString() {
    return "\nStack is full. Maximum size is " + size;
  }
}

// An exception for stack-empty errors.
class StackEmptyException extends Exception {

  StackEmptyException() {
    super("Stack Empty");
  }

  public String toString() {
    return "\nStack is empty.";
  }
}
```

3. Now, create a file called **GenSimpleStack.java**. Into that file, put the following code, which implements a simple fixed-size, generic stack.

```java
// A simple generic fixed-length stack.
class GenSimpleStack<T> implements IGenSimpleStack<T> {
  private T[] data; // this array holds the stack
  private int tos; // index of top of stack

  // Construct an empty stack with the given array as storage.
  GenSimpleStack(T[] arrayRef) {
    data = arrayRef;
    tos = 0;
  }

  // Push an item onto the stack.
  public void push(T obj) throws StackFullException {
    if(isFull())
      throw new StackFullException(data.length);

    data[tos] = obj;
    tos++;
  }

  // Pop an item from the stack.
  public T pop() throws StackEmptyException {
    if(isEmpty())
      throw new StackEmptyException();

    tos--;
    return data[tos];
  }

  // Return true if the stack is empty.
  public boolean isEmpty() {
    return tos==0;
  }

  // Return true if the stack is full.
  public boolean isFull() {
    return tos==data.length;
  }
}
```

GenSimpleStack is a generic class with type parameter **T**, which specifies the type of data stored in the stack. Notice that **T** is also passed to the **IGenSimpleStack** interface.

Pay special attention to the **GenSimpleStack** constructor. It is passed a reference to an array that will be used to hold the stack. Thus, to construct a **GenSimpleStack**, you will first create an array whose type is compatible with the objects that you will be storing in the stack and whose size is long enough to store the number of objects that will be placed in the stack. For example, the following sequence shows how to create a 10-element stack that holds strings:

```
String[] strArray = new String[10];
GenSimpleStack<String> strStack = new GenSimpleStack<String>(strArray);
```

4. To demonstrate **GenSimpleStack**, create a file called **GenSimpleStackDemo.java** and put the following code into it.

```
/*
    Try This 14-1

    Demonstrate a simple generic stack class.
*/

class GenSimpleStackDemo {
  public static void main(String[] args) {
    int i;
    Integer[] nums = new Integer[5];
    String[] strs = new String[3];

    // first create a stack for integers
    GenSimpleStack<Integer> intStack = newGenSimpleStack<Integer>(nums);

    System.out.println("Demonstrating Integer stack.");

    // use intStack
    try {

      System.out.print("Pushing: ");
      // push integers onto intStack
      for(i = 0; !intStack.isFull(); i++) {
        System.out.print(i);
        intStack.push(i);
      }

      System.out.println();

      // pop integers off intStack
      System.out.print("Popping: ");
      while(!intStack.isEmpty())
        System.out.print(intStack.pop());

      System.out.println();
    } catch (StackFullException exc) {
      System.out.println(exc);
    } catch (StackEmptyException exc) {
      System.out.println(exc);
    }
```

```
   // next, create a stack for strings
   GenSimpleStack<String> strStack = new GenSimpleStack<String>(strs);

   System.out.println("\nDemonstrating String stack.");

   // now, use strStack
   try {

     System.out.println("Pushing: alpha beta gamma");

     // push strings onto strStack
     strStack.push("alpha");
     strStack.push("beta");
     strStack.push("gamma");

     // pop Strings off strStack
     System.out.print("Popping: ");
     while(!strStack.isEmpty())
       System.out.print(strStack.pop() + " ");

     System.out.println();
   } catch (StackFullException exc) {
     System.out.println(exc);
   } catch (StackEmptyException exc) {
     System.out.println(exc);
   }    System.out.println();
   }
 }
}
```

5. Compile all the files and then run **GenSimpleStackDemo**. You will see the output shown here:

```
Demonstrating Integer stack.
Pushing: 01234
Popping: 43210

Demonstrating String stack.
Pushing: alpha beta gamma
Popping: gamma beta alpha
```

RAW TYPES AND LEGACY CODE

Because support for generics did not exist prior to JDK 5, it was necessary for Java to provide some transition path from existing, pre-generics code. Simply put: all pre-generics code needed to remain both functional and compatible with new code that used generics. This meant that pre-generics code must be able to work with generics, and generic code must be able to work with pre-generics code.

To handle the transition to generics, Java allows a generic class to be used without any type arguments. This creates a *raw type* for the class. This raw type is compatible with legacy code, which has no knowledge of generics. The main drawback to using the raw type is that the type safety of generics is lost.

Here is an example that shows a raw type in action.

```java
// Demonstrate a raw type.
class Gen<T> {
  T ob; // declare a reference to an object of type T

  // Pass the constructor a reference to
  // an object of type T.
  Gen(T o) {
    ob = o;
  }

  // Return ob.
  T getob() {
    return ob;
  }
}

// Demonstrate raw type.
class RawDemo {
  public static void main(String[] args) {

    // Create a Gen object for Integers.
    Gen<Integer> iOb = new Gen<Integer>(88);

    // Create a Gen object for Strings.
    Gen<String> strOb = new Gen<String>("Generics Test");

    // Create a raw-type Gen object and give it
    // a Double value.
    Gen raw = new Gen(new Double(98.6));    ⟵——————  When no type argument
                                                      is supplied, a raw type
                                                      is created.
    // Cast here is necessary because type is unknown.
    double d = (Double) raw.getob();
    System.out.println("value: " + d);

    // The use of a raw type can lead to run-time.
    // exceptions. Here are some examples.

    // The following cast causes a run-time error!
//    int i = (Integer) raw.getob(); // run-time error

    // This assignment overrides type safety.
    strOb = raw; // OK, but potentially wrong  ⟵————  Raw types override
//    String str = strOb.getob(); // run-time error      type safety.

    // This assignment also overrides type safety.
    raw = iOb; // OK, but potentially wrong
//    d = (Double) raw.getob(); // run-time error
  }
}
```

This program contains several interesting things. First, a raw type of the generic **Gen** class is created by the following declaration:

```
Gen raw = new Gen(new Double(98.6));
```

Notice that no type arguments are specified. In essence, this creates a **Gen** object whose type **T** is replaced by **Object**.

A raw type is not type safe. Thus, a variable of a raw type can be assigned a reference to any type of **Gen** object. The reverse is also allowed, in which a variable of a specific **Gen** type can be assigned a reference to a raw **Gen** object. However, both operations are potentially unsafe because the type checking mechanism of generics is circumvented.

This lack of type safety is illustrated by the commented-out lines at the end of the program. Let's examine each case. First, consider the following situation:

```
//    int i = (Integer) raw.getob(); // run-time error
```

In this statement, the value of **ob** inside **raw** is obtained, and this value is cast to **Integer**. The trouble is that **raw** contains a **Double** value, not an integer value. However, this cannot be detected at compile time because the type of **raw** is unknown. Thus, this statement fails at run time.

The next sequence assigns to a **strOb** (a reference of type **Gen<String>**) a reference to a raw **Gen** object:

```
    strOb = raw; // OK, but potentially wrong
//    String str = strOb.getob(); // run-time error
```

The assignment itself is syntactically correct, but questionable. Because **strOb** is of type **Gen<String>**, it is assumed to contain a **String**. However, after the assignment, the object referred to by **strOb** contains a **Double**. Thus, at run time, when an attempt is made to assign the contents of **strOb** to **str**, a run-time error results because **strOb** now contains a **Double**. Thus, the assignment of a raw reference to a generic reference bypasses the type-safety mechanism.

The following sequence inverts the preceding case:

```
    raw = iOb; // OK, but potentially wrong
//    d = (Double) raw.getob(); // run-time error
```

Here, a generic reference is assigned to a raw reference variable. Although this is syntactically correct, it can lead to problems, as illustrated by the second line. In this case, **raw** now refers to an object that contains an **Integer** object, but the cast assumes that it contains a **Double**. This error cannot be prevented at compile time. Rather, it causes a run-time error.

Because of the potential for danger inherent in raw types, **javac** displays *unchecked warnings* when a raw type is used in a way that might jeopardize type safety. In the preceding program, these lines generate unchecked warnings:

```
Gen raw = new Gen(new Double(98.6));

strOb = raw; // OK, but potentially wrong
```

In the first line, it is the call to the **Gen** constructor without a type argument that causes the warning. In the second line, it is the assignment of a raw reference to a generic variable that generates the warning.

At first, you might think that this line should also generate an unchecked warning, but it does not:

```
raw = iOb; // OK, but potentially wrong
```

No compiler warning is issued because the assignment does not cause any *further* loss of type safety than had already occurred when **raw** was created.

One final point: you should limit the use of raw types to those cases in which you must mix legacy code with newer, generic code. Raw types are simply a transitional feature and not something that should be used for new code.

TYPE INFERENCE WITH THE DIAMOND OPERATOR

Beginning with JDK 7, it is possible to shorten the syntax used to create an instance of a generic type. To begin, think back to the **TwoGen** class shown earlier in this chapter. A portion is shown here for convenience. Notice that it uses two generic types.

```
class TwoGen<T, V> {
  T ob1;
  V ob2;

  // Pass the constructor a reference to
  // an object of type T.
  TwoGen(T o1, V o2) {
    ob1 = o1;
    ob2 = o2;
  }
  // ...
}
```

For versions of Java prior to JDK 7, to create an instance of **TwoGen**, you must use a statement similar to the following:

```
TwoGen<Integer, String> tgOb =
  new TwoGen<Integer, String>(42, "testing");
```

Here, the type arguments (which are **Integer** and **String**) are specified twice: first, when **tgOb** is declared, and second, when a **TwoGen** instance is created when its constructor is called via **new**. Since generics were introduced by JDK 5, this is the form required by all versions of Java prior to JDK 7. While there is nothing wrong, per se, with this form, it is a bit more verbose than it needs to be. Since, in the **new** clause, the type of the type arguments can be readily inferred, there is really no reason that they need to be specified a second time. To address this situation, JDK 7 adds a syntactic element that lets you avoid the second specification.

In JDK 7, the preceding declaration can be rewritten as shown here:

```
TwoGen<Integer, String> tgOb = new TwoGen<>(42, "testing");
```

Notice that the instance creation portion simply uses < >, which is an empty type argument list. This is referred to as the *diamond* operator. It tells the compiler to infer the type arguments needed by the constructor. The principal advantage of this type-inference syntax is that it shortens what are sometimes quite long declaration statements. This is especially helpful for generic types that specify bounds.

The preceding example can be generalized. When type inference is used, the declaration syntax for a generic reference and instance creation has this general form:

class-name<type-arg-list> var-name = new *class-name< >(cons-arg-list)*;

Here, the type argument list of the **new** clause is empty.

Although mostly for use in declaration statements, type inference can also be applied to parameter passing. For example, if the following method is added to **TwoGen**:

```
boolean isSame(TwoGen<T, V> o) {
    if(ob1 == o.ob1 && ob2 == o.ob2) return true;
    else return false;
}
```

Then, the following call is legal in JDK 7:

```
if(tgOb.isSame(new TwoGen<>(42, "testing"))) System.out.println("Same");
```

In this case, the type arguments for the argument passed to **isSame( )** can be inferred. They don't need to be specified again.

Because the diamond operator is new to JDK 7 and it won't work with older compilers, the remaining examples of generics in this book will continue to use the full syntax when declaring instances of generic classes. This way, the examples will work with any Java compiler that supports generics. Using the full-length syntax also makes it very clear precisely what is being created, which is helpful when example code is shown. Of course, in your own code, use of the type inference syntax will streamline your declarations.

Progress Check

1. If a generic interface is implemented by a class, that class must also be generic. True or False?
2. A type parameter in a generic interface cannot be bounded. True or False?
3. Given

   ```
   class XYZ<T> { // ...
   ```

   show how to declare an object called **ob** that is **XYZ**'s raw type.
4. Type inference uses the _____ operator.

Answers:

1. True.
2. False.
3. `XYZ ob = new XYZ();`
4. diamond

ERASURE

Usually, it is not necessary for the programmer to know the details about how the Java compiler transforms source code into object code. However, in the case of generics, some general understanding of the process is important because it explains why the generic features work as they do—and why their behavior is sometimes a bit surprising. For this reason, a brief discussion of how generics are implemented in Java is in order.

An important constraint that governed the way generics were added to Java was the need for compatibility with previous versions of Java. Simply put: generic code had to be compatible with preexisting, non-generic code. Thus, any changes to the syntax of the Java language, or to the JVM, had to avoid breaking older code. The way Java implements generics while satisfying this constraint is through the use of *erasure*.

In general, here is how erasure works. When your Java code is compiled, all generic type information is removed (erased). This means replacing type parameters with their bound type, which is **Object** if no explicit bound is specified, and then applying the appropriate casts (as determined by the type arguments) to maintain type compatibility with the types specified by the type arguments. The compiler also enforces this type compatibility. This approach to generics means that no type parameters exist at run time. They are simply a source-code mechanism.

AMBIGUITY ERRORS

The inclusion of generics gives rise to a new type of error that you must guard against: *ambiguity*. Ambiguity errors occur when erasure causes two seemingly distinct generic declarations to resolve to the same erased type, causing a conflict. Here is an example that involves method overloading:

```
// Ambiguity caused by erasure on
// overloaded methods.
class MyGenClass<T, V> {
  T ob1;
  V ob2;

  // ...

  // These two overloaded methods are ambiguous
  // and will not compile.
  void set(T o) {
    ob1 = o;
  }

  void set(V o) {
    ob2 = o;
  }
}
```

These two methods are inherently ambiguous.

Notice that **MyGenClass** declares two generic types: **T** and **V**. Inside **MyGenClass**, an attempt is made to overload **set( )** based on parameters of type **T** and **V**. This looks reasonable because **T** and **V** appear to be different types. However, there are two ambiguity problems here.

First, as **MyGenClass** is written, there is no requirement that **T** and **V** actually be different types. For example, it is perfectly correct (in principle) to construct a **MyGenClass** object as shown here:

```
MyGenClass<String, String> obj = new MyGenClass<String, String>()
```

In this case, both **T** and **V** will be replaced by **String**. This makes both versions of **set( )** identical, which is, of course, an error.

Second, and more fundamental, is that the type erasure of **set( )** effectively reduces both versions to the following:

```
void set(Object o) { // ...
```

Thus, the overloading of **set( )** as attempted in **MyGenClass** is inherently ambiguous. The solution in this case is to use two separate method names rather than trying to overload **set( )**.

Progress Check

1. Erasure _____ all type parameters, substituting their bound types and applying appropriate casts.
2. By default, the bound type of a type parameter is _____.
3. Ambiguity can occur when type erasure causes two seemingly different declarations to resolve to the same erased type. True or False?

SOME GENERIC RESTRICTIONS

There are a few restrictions that you need to keep in mind when using generics. They involve creating objects of a type parameter, static members, exceptions, and arrays. Each is examined here.

Type Parameters Can't Be Instantiated

It is not possible to create an instance of a type parameter. For example, consider this class:

```java
// Can't create an instance of T.
class Gen<T> {
  T ob;
  Gen() {
    ob = new T(); // Illegal!!!
  }
}
```

Answers:

1. removes
2. **Object**
3. True.

Here, it is illegal to attempt to create an instance of **T**. The reason should be easy to understand: the compiler has no way to know what type of object to create. **T** is simply a placeholder.

Restrictions on Static Members

No **static** member can use a type parameter declared by the enclosing class. For example, both of the **static** members of this class are illegal:

```
class Wrong<T> {
  // Wrong, no static variables of type T.
  static T ob;

  // Wrong, no static method can use T.
  static T getob() {
    return ob;
  }
}
```

Although you can't declare **static** members that use a type parameter declared by the enclosing class, you *can* declare **static** generic methods, which define their own type parameters, as was done earlier in this chapter.

Generic Array Restrictions

There are two important generics restrictions that apply to arrays. First, you cannot instantiate an array whose element type is a type parameter. Second, you cannot create an array of type-specific generic references. The following short program shows both situations.

```
// Generics and arrays.
class Gen<T extends Number> {
  T ob;

  T[] vals; // OK

  Gen(T o, T[] nums) {
    ob = o;

    // This statement is illegal.
//   vals = new T[10]; // can't create an array of T

    // But, this statement is OK.
    vals = nums; // OK to assign reference to existent array
  }
}

class GenArrays {
  public static void main(String[] args) {
    Integer[] n = { 1, 2, 3, 4, 5 };
```

```
    Gen<Integer> iOb = new Gen<Integer>(50, n);

    // Can't create an array of type-specific generic references.
    // Gen<Integer>[] gens = new Gen<Integer>[10]; // Wrong!

    // This is OK.
    Gen<?>[] gens = new Gen<?>[10]; // OK
  }
}
```

As the program shows, it's valid to declare a reference to an array of type **T**, as this line does:

```
T[] vals; // OK
```

But you cannot instantiate an array of **T**, as this commented-out line attempts:

```
// vals = new T[10]; // can't create an array of T
```

The reason you can't create an array of **T** is that there is no way for the compiler to know what type of array to actually create. However, you can pass a reference to a type-compatible array to **Gen( )** when an object is created and assign that reference to **vals**, as the program does in this line:

```
vals = nums; // OK to assign reference to existent array
```

This works because the array passed to **Gen( )** has a known type, which will be the same type as **T** at the time of object creation. Inside **main( )**, notice that you can't declare an array of references to a specific generic type. That is, this line

```
// Gen<Integer>[] gens = new Gen<Integer>[10]; // Wrong!
```

won't compile.

Generic Exception Restriction

A generic class cannot extend **Throwable**. This means that you cannot create generic exception classes.

EXERCISES

1. Generics are important to Java because they enable the creation of code that is
   A. Type-safe
   B. Reusable
   C. Reliable
   D. All of the above
2. Can a primitive type be used as a type argument?
3. Show how to declare a class called **FlightSched** that takes two generic parameters.

4. Beginning with your answer to question 3, change **FlightSched**'s second type parameter so that it must extend **Thread**.

5. Now, change **FlightSched** so that its second type parameter must be a subclass of its first type parameter.

6. As it relates to generics, what is the **?** and what does it do?

7. Can the wildcard argument be bounded?

8. A generic method called **MyGen( )** has one type parameter. Furthermore, **MyGen( )** has one parameter whose type is that of the type parameter. It also returns an object of that type parameter. Show how to declare **MyGen( )**.

9. Given this generic interface

```
interface IGenIF<T, V extends T> { // ...
```

show the declaration of a class called **MyClass** that implements **IGenIF**.

10. Given a generic class called **Counter<T>**, show how to create an object of its raw type.

11. Do type parameters exist at run time?

12. When a generic class is inherited, its type parameters must also be specified by the subclass. True or False?

13. What is **< >**?

14. When using JDK 7, how can the following be simplified?

```
MyClass<Double,String> obj = new MyClass<Double,String>(1.1,"Hi");
```

15. Which of the following lines of code are legal declarations of generic methods? If any are not legal, explain why not.

A. `void print<T>(T x) { System.out.println(x); }`

B. `static <T> void print(T x) { System.out.println(x); }`

C. `<T> T getT(T t) { return null; }`

D. `<?> void print(Object x) { System.out.println(x); }`

E. `<V extends T> void print(V x) { System.out.println(x); }`

F. `<T extends Object> void print(T x) { System.out.println(x); }`

16. In the body of a generic method with parameter type **T**, you cannot use the assignment statement

```
T[] x = new T[10];
```

because you cannot create arrays of the parameter type **T**. Would it work to initialize **x** as follows?

```
T[] x = (T[]) new Object[10];
```

17. In this chapter, it was mentioned that a non-generic class can have a generic subclass. Is the opposite also true? That is, can a generic class have a non-generic subclass?

18. In this chapter, it was mentioned that a non-generic class can have a generic method. Is the opposite also true? That is, can a generic class have a non-generic method?

19. Is it legal to create a generic class with type parameter **T** and then never use **T** in the class implementation? For example, is the following class definition legal?

```
class MyClass<T> {
   MyClass() { }
   void printName() { System.out.println("MyClass"); }
}
```

20. In Try This 14-1, you saw how to create a simple generic stack class. You may be interested to know that the Java library already includes a full-featured stack class called **Stack**, which is in the **java.util** package. In the pre-generics versions of Java, that **Stack** class stored any kind of object. Its **push( )** method used **Object** as the type of its parameter and its **pop( )** method's return type was **Object**. To use such a stack to store strings, you had to do typecasting. For example, after pushing a string, you could retrieve it as a string only with statements of the form

```
String value = (String) stack.pop();
```

What are the disadvantages of doing it this way? That is, why is the generic **Stack** better?

21. If **Obj<T>** is a generic class that has a no-argument constructor, what are the differences, if any, between the following four statements?

A. `Obj x = new Obj<Object>();`

B. `Obj<Object> x = new Obj<Object>();`

C. `Obj<Object> x = new Obj<>();`

D. `Obj<Object> x = new Obj();`

22. Below is an attempt to make bubble sort a generic method so that it can sort all kinds of arrays, instead of just arrays of integers as was done in Chapter 5. However, it will not compile. Figure out what is illegal in the method.

```
<T> void bubbleSort(T[] data) {
   for(int a=1; a < data.length; a++)
      for(int b=data.length-1; b >= a; b--) {
         if(data[b-1] > data[b]) { // if out of order
            // exchange elements
            T x = data[b-1];
            data[b-1] = data[b];
            data[b] = x;
         }
      }
}
```

23. Consider the classes **C** and **CDemo** shown here.

```
class C<T> {
  T data;
  C(T t) { data = t; }
}

class CDemo {
  public static void main(String[] args) {
    C<Object> co = new C<String>("Hi");
    C<Integer> ci = new C<33>(44);
    C<int> cint = new C<>(3);
    C<String> cs = new C<>("Hi");
    String[] s = {"a", "b", "c"};
    C<String[]> csa = new C<>(s);
  }
}
```

Which of the statements in the **main( )** method of **CDemo** are illegal? Explain what is wrong with the illegal statements. Assume you are using JDK 7.

24. The following classes, one generic and one not, can be used to create an object that stores a **Number**. What are the advantages, if any, of each class over the other?

```
class C<T extends Number> {
  T data;

  C(T t) { data = t; }

  T getData() { return data; }
}

class C {
  Number data;

  C(Number t) { data = t; }

  Number getData() { return data; }
}
```

25. Implement a generic method **containsNull( )** that takes an array of type **T[ ]** as its parameter and returns **true** if any of the values in the array are **null**. What, if any, are the advantages of this method over a non-generic version of this method that you can implement by replacing **T** everywhere with **Object**?

26. If **A** is a superclass of **B** and **C** is a superclass of **D**, then which of the following are true?

A. **A<C>** is a superclass of **B<C>**

B. **A<C>** is a superclass of **A<D>**

C. **A<C>** is a superclass of **B<D>**

27. The following class definition will not compile. Why not?

```
class Keeper<T> {
  T t;

  Keeper(T t) {
    this.t = t;
  }

  public boolean equals(T other) {
    return other == t;
  }
}
```

28. Suppose that a class **B** is a subclass of class **A**. Also suppose that **A** has the following method

```
<T> void getX(T t) { ... }
```

and class **B** has the following method

```
<V> void getX(V v) { ... }
```

Is the **getX( )** method overloaded in **B**, or does the **getX( )** method in **B** override the inherited **getX( )** method?

29. Give an example where a lower-bounded wildcard type parameter **<? super T>** would be useful.

CHAPTER 15

Applets and the Remaining Java Keywords

KEY SKILLS & CONCEPTS

- Understand applet basics
- Create an applet skeleton
- Initialize and terminate applets
- Repaint applets
- Output to the status window
- Pass parameters to an applet
- Know the remaining Java keywords: **transient**, **volatile**, **instanceof**, **native**, **strictfp**, and **assert**

This chapter finishes our examination of the core Java language elements. It begins by describing the applet, which was a Java innovation. The applet helped shape the Internet in its early days, and applets are still in use today. Because applets are so closely associated with Java, no course in Java programming can be complete without an introduction to them. This chapter ends with a description of the remaining Java keywords, such as **instanceof** and **native**, that have not been described elsewhere in this book.

APPLET BASICS

Applets differ from the type of programs shown in the preceding chapters. As explained in Chapter 1, applets are small programs that are designed for transmission over the Internet and run within a browser. Because Java's virtual machine is in charge of executing all Java programs, including applets, applets offer a secure way to dynamically download and execute programs over the Web.

Before we begin, it is necessary to explain that there are two general varieties of applets: those based solely on the Abstract Window Toolkit (AWT) and those based on Swing. Both the AWT and Swing support the creation of a graphical user interface (GUI). The AWT is the original GUI toolkit, and Swing is Java's modern, lightweight alternative. This chapter used AWT-based applets to introduce the fundamentals of applet programming because they are the simplest to describe. Later, in Part Two,

Swing and Swing-based applets are covered. It is important to understand, however, that Swing-based applets are built on the same basic architecture as AWT-based applets. Furthermore, all of Swing is built on top of the AWT. Therefore, the information and techniques presented here describe the foundation of applet programming, and most of it applies to both types of applets.

Prior to discussing any theory or details, let's begin by examining a simple applet. It performs one function: It displays the string "Java makes applets easy." inside a window.

```
// A minimal AWT-based applet.
import java.awt.*; ◄───────────────── Notice these import statements.
import java.applet.*;

public class SimpleApplet extends Applet {
  public void paint(Graphics g) {
    g.drawString("Java makes applets easy.", 20, 20);
  }                        ▲──────────── This outputs to the
}                                        applet's window.
```

This applet begins with two **import** statements. The first imports the Abstract Window Toolkit classes. Applets interact with the user (either directly or indirectly) through the AWT, not through the console-based I/O classes. The AWT contains support for a window-based, graphical user interface. As you might expect, it is quite large and sophisticated, and a detailed discussion of the AWT is outside the scope of this book. Fortunately, for the simple applets that we will be creating, only a very limited use of the AWT is required. The next **import** statement imports the **java.applet** package. This package contains the class **Applet**. Every applet that you create must be a subclass (either directly or indirectly) of **Applet**.

The next line in the program declares the class **SimpleApplet**. This class must be declared as **public** because it will be accessed by external code.

Inside **SimpleApplet**, **paint( )** is declared. This method is part of the AWT **Component** class (which is a superclass of **Applet**) and is overridden by the applet. The **Component** class defines the core functionality common to all GUI components. It is a very large class, but the only piece of it that we need to use here is **paint( )**. The **paint( )** method is called each time the applet must redisplay its output. This can occur for several reasons. For example, the window in which the applet is running can be overwritten by another window and then uncovered. Or the applet window can be minimized and then restored. **paint( )** is also called when the applet begins execution. Whatever the cause, whenever the applet must redraw its output, **paint( )** is called. The **paint( )** method has one parameter of type **Graphics**. (**Graphics** is another AWT class.) This parameter will contain the *graphics context*, which describes the graphics environment in which the applet is running. This context is used whenever output to the applet is required.

*Note: The **paint( )** method is used only by AWT-based applets to output to a window. Swing applets use a different mechanism, which is described in Chapter 21.*

Inside **paint( )**, there is a call to **drawString( )**, which is a member of the **Graphics** class. This method outputs a string beginning at the specified X,Y location. It has the following general form:

void drawString(String *message*, int *x*, int *y*)

Here, *message* is the string to be output beginning at *x,y*. In a Java window, the upper-left corner is location 0,0. The call to **drawString( )** in the applet causes the message to be displayed beginning at location 20,20.

Notice that the applet does not have a **main( )** method. Unlike the programs shown earlier in this book, applets do not begin execution at **main( )**. In fact, most applets don't even have a **main( )** method. Instead, an applet begins execution when the name of its class is passed to a browser or other applet-enabled program.

After you have entered the source code for **SimpleApplet**, you compile in the same way that you have been compiling programs. However, running **SimpleApplet** involves a different process. There are two ways in which you can run an applet: inside a browser or with a special development tool that displays applets. The tool provided with the standard Java JDK is called **appletviewer**, and we will use it to run the applets developed in this chapter. Of course, you can also run them in a browser, but the **appletviewer** is much easier to use during development.

One way to execute an applet (in either a Web browser or **appletviewer**) is to write a short HTML text file that contains a tag that loads the applet. At the time of this writing, Oracle recommends using the APPLET tag for this purpose. (The OBJECT tag can also be used, and other deployment strategies are available. Consult the Java documentation for the latest information.) Using the APPLET tag, here is the HTML file that will execute **SimpleApplet**:

```
<applet code="SimpleApplet" width=200 height=60>
</applet>
```

The **width** and **height** statements specify the dimensions of the display area used by the applet.

To execute **SimpleApplet** with an applet viewer, you will execute this HTML file. For example, if the preceding HTML file is called **StartApp.html**, then the following command line will run **SimpleApplet**:

```
appletviewer StartApp.html
```

Although there is nothing wrong with using a stand-alone HTML file to execute an applet, there is an easier way when using **appletviewer**. Simply include a comment near the top of your applet's source code file that contains the APPLET tag. If you use this method, the **SimpleApplet** source file looks like this:

```
import java.awt.*;
import java.applet.*;
/*
<applet code="SimpleApplet" width=200 height=60>
</applet>
*/

public class SimpleApplet extends Applet {
  public void paint(Graphics g) {
    g.drawString("Java makes applets easy.", 20, 20);
  }
}
```

This HTML is used by **appletviewer** to run the applet.

Now you can execute the applet by passing the name of its source file to **appletviewer**. For example, this command line will now display **SimpleApplet**.

```
appletviewer SimpleApplet.java
```

The window produced by **SimpleApplet**, as displayed by **appletviewer**, is shown in the following illustration:

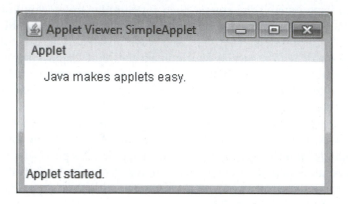

When using **appletviewer**, keep in mind that it provides the window frame. Applets run in a browser will not have a visible frame.

Let's review an applet's key points:

- All applets are, either directly or indirectly, subclasses of **Applet**.
- Applets do not need a **main( )** method.
- Applets must be run under an applet viewer or a Java-compatible browser.
- User I/O is not accomplished with Java's stream I/O classes. Instead, applets use the interface provided by the AWT (or by Swing).

Progress Check

1. What is an applet?
2. What does **paint( )** do?
3. What package must be included when creating an applet?
4. How are applets run?

Answers:

1. An applet is a special type of Java program that is designed for transmission over the Internet and that runs inside a browser.
2. The **paint( )** method displays output in an AWT-based applet's window.
3. The package **java.applet** must be included when creating an applet.
4. Applets are executed by a browser or by special tools, such as **appletviewer**.

A COMPLETE APPLET SKELETON

Although **SimpleApplet** shown earlier is a real applet, it does not contain all of the elements required by most applets. Actually, all but the most trivial applets override a set of methods that provide the basic mechanism by which the browser or applet viewer interfaces to the applet and controls its execution. These lifecycle methods are **init( )**, **start( )**, **stop( )**, and **destroy( )**, and they are defined by **Applet**. A fifth method, **paint( )**, is commonly overridden by AWT-based applets even though it is not a lifecycle method. As mentioned, it is inherited from the AWT **Component** class. Since default implementations for all of these methods are provided, applets do not need to override those methods they do not use. These four lifecycle methods plus **paint( )** can be assembled into the skeleton shown here:

```java
// An AWT-based Applet skeleton.
import java.awt.*;
import java.applet.*;
/*
<applet code="AppletSkel" width=300 height=100>
</applet>
*/

public class AppletSkel extends Applet {
  // Called first.
  public void init() {
    // initialization
  }

  /* Called second, after init(). Also called whenever
     the applet is restarted. */
  public void start() {
    // start or resume execution
  }

  // Called when the applet is stopped.
  public void stop() {
    // suspends execution
  }

  /* Called when applet is terminated. This is the last
     method executed. */
  public void destroy() {
    // perform shutdown activities
  }

  // Called when an AWT-based applet's window must be restored.
  public void paint(Graphics g) {
    // redisplay contents of window
  }
}
```

Although this skeleton does not do anything, it can be compiled and run.

*Note: Overriding **paint( )** applies mostly to AWT-based applets. Swing applets use a different painting mechanism.*

APPLET INITIALIZATION AND TERMINATION

It is important to understand the order in which the various methods shown in the preceding applet skeleton are executed. When an applet begins, the following methods are called in this sequence:

1. **init( )**
2. **start( )**
3. **paint( )**

When an applet is terminated, the following sequence of method calls takes place:

1. **stop( )**
2. **destroy( )**

Let's look more closely at these methods.

The **init( )** method is the first method to be called. In **init( )** the applet will initialize variables and perform any other startup activities.

The **start( )** method is called after **init( )**. It is also called to restart an applet after it has been stopped, such as when the user returns to a previously displayed Web page that contains an applet. Thus, **start( )** might be called more than once during the life cycle of an applet.

The **paint( )** method is called each time an AWT-based applet's output must be redrawn and was described earlier.

When the page containing the applet is left, the **stop( )** method is called. You will use **stop( )** to suspend any child threads created by the applet and to perform any other activities required to put the applet in a safe, idle state. Remember, a call to **stop( )** does not mean that the applet should be terminated because it might be restarted with a call to **start( )** if the user returns to the page.

The **destroy( )** method is called when the applet is no longer needed. It is used to perform any shutdown operations required of the applet.

A KEY ASPECT OF AN APPLET'S ARCHITECTURE

As the applet skeleton makes clear, the architecture of an applet is different from the console-based programs shown in the first part of this book. One of the key differences is that an applet waits for the run-time system to call one of its methods. For example, it displays output only if its **paint( )** method is called. Once a method defined by the applet has been called, the applet must take appropriate action and then quickly return control to the system. This is a crucial point. For the most part, the applet should not enter a "mode" of operation in which it maintains control for an extended period. Doing so could cause other parts of the applet to be unresponsive. In situations in which the applet needs to perform a repetitive task on its own (for example, displaying a scrolling message across its window), you must start an additional thread of execution.

Progress Check

1. What are the four lifecycle methods that most applets will override?
2. What must an applet do when **start( )** is called?
3. What must an applet do when **stop( )** is called?

REQUESTING REPAINTING

As a general rule, an AWT-based applet writes to its window only when its **paint( )** method is called by the run-time system. This raises an interesting question: How can the applet itself cause its window to be updated when its information changes? For example, if an applet displays a moving banner, what mechanism does the applet use to update the window each time this banner scrolls? As explained, a fundamental architectural constraint imposed on an applet is that it must quickly return control to the Java run-time system. It cannot create a loop inside **paint( )** that repeatedly scrolls the banner, for example. This would prevent control from passing back to the run-time system. Given this constraint, it may seem that output to an applet's window will be difficult at best. Fortunately, this is not the case. Whenever an applet needs to update the information displayed in its window, it simply calls **repaint( )**.

The **repaint( )** method is defined by the AWT's **Component** class and inherited by **Applet**. It causes the run-time system to execute a call to the applet's **paint( )** method. Thus, for another part of an applet to output to its window, simply store the output and then call **repaint( )**. This causes a call to **paint( )**, which can display the stored information. For example, if part of the applet needs to output a string, it can store this string in a **String** variable and then call **repaint( )**. Inside **paint( )**, you can output the string using **drawString( )**.

The simplest version of **repaint( )** is shown here:

```
void repaint( )
```

This version causes the entire window to be repainted. An example that demonstrates **repaint( )** is found in Try This 15-1.

Answers:

1. The lifecycle methods are **init( )**, **start( )**, **stop( )**, and **destroy( )**.
2. When **start( )** is called, the applet must be started, or restarted.
3. When **stop( )** is called, the applet must be paused.

Ask the Expert

Q Is it possible for a method other than **paint( )** to output to an applet's window?

A Yes. To do so, you must obtain a graphics context by calling **getGraphics( )** on the applet instance, and then use this context to output to the window. However, for most AWT-based applications, it is better and easier to route window output through **paint( )** and to call **repaint( )** when the contents of the window change.

TRY THIS 15-1 A SIMPLE BANNER APPLET

`Banner.java`

To demonstrate **repaint( )**, a simple banner applet is presented. This applet scrolls a message, from right to left, across the applet's window. Since the scrolling of the message is a repetitive task, it is performed by a separate thread, created by the applet when it is initialized. It also shows one way that a separate thread can be used to perform an ongoing task in an applet.

STEP-BY-STEP

1. Create a file called **Banner.java**.
2. Begin creating the banner applet with the following lines.

```
/*
    Try This 15-1

    A simple banner applet.

    This applet creates a thread that scrolls
    the message contained in msg right to left
    across the applet's window.
*/
import java.awt.*;
import java.applet.*;
/*
<applet code="Banner" width=300 height=50>
</applet>
*/

public class Banner extends Applet implements Runnable {
  String msg = " Java Rules the Web ";
  Thread t;
  boolean stopFlag;
```

```
// Initialize t to null.
public void init() {
  t = null;
}
```

Notice that **Banner** extends **Applet**, as expected, but it also implements **Runnable**. This is necessary since the applet will be creating a second thread of execution that will be used to a scroll the banner. The message that will be scrolled in the banner is contained in the **String** variable **msg**. A reference to the thread that runs the applet is stored in **t**. The Boolean variable **stopFlag** is used to stop the applet. Inside **init( )**, the thread reference variable **t** is set to **null**.

3. Add the **start( )** method shown next.

```
// Start thread when the applet is needed.
public void start() {
  t = new Thread(this);
  stopFlag = false;
  t.start();
}
```

The run-time system calls **start( )** to start the applet running. Inside **start( )**, a new thread of execution is created and assigned to the **Thread** variable **t**. Then, **stopFlag** is set to **false**. Next, the thread is started by a call to **t.start( )**. Remember that **t.start( )** is a call to a method defined by **Thread**, which causes **run( )** to begin executing. It does not cause a call to the version of **start( )** defined by **Applet**. These are two separate methods.

4. Add the **run( )** method, as shown here.

```
// Entry point for the thread that runs the banner.
public void run() {
  // Request a repaint every quarter second.
  for( ; ; ) {
    try {
      repaint();
      Thread.sleep(250);
      if(stopFlag) break;
    } catch(InterruptedException exc) {}
  }
}
```

In **run( )**, **repaint( )** is repeatedly called, with a delay of one quarter second between calls. Each call to **repaint( )** eventually causes the **paint( )** method to be called. The **stopFlag** variable is checked on each iteration. When it is **true**, the **run( )** method terminates.

5. Add the code for **stop( )** as shown here.

```
// Pause the banner.
public void stop() {
  stopFlag = true;
  t = null;
}
```

If a browser is displaying the applet when a new page is viewed, the **stop( )** method is called, which sets **stopFlag** to **true**, causing **run( )** to terminate. It also sets **t** to **null**. Thus, there is no longer a reference to the **Thread** object, and it can be recycled the next time the garbage collector runs. This is the mechanism used to stop the thread when its page is no longer in view. When the applet is brought back into view, **start( )** is once again called, which starts a new thread to execute the banner.

6. Finally, add the **paint( )** method shown here:

```
// Display the banner.
public void paint(Graphics g) {
   char ch;

   ch = msg.charAt(0);
   msg = msg.substring(1, msg.length());
   msg += ch;

   g.drawString(msg, 50, 30);
}
```

Inside **paint( )**, the characters in the string contained in **msg** are rotated left and then displayed. Because **paint( )** will be executed about every quarter second, the net effect is that the contents of **msg** are scrolled right to left in a constantly moving display.

7. The entire banner applet is shown here:

```
/*
   Try This 15-1

   A simple banner applet.

   This applet creates a thread that scrolls
   the message contained in msg right to left
   across the applet's window.
*/
import java.awt.*;
import java.applet.*;
/*
<applet code="Banner" width=300 height=50>
</applet>
*/

public class Banner extends Applet implements Runnable {
   String msg = " Java Rules the Web ";
   Thread t;
   boolean stopFlag;

   // Initialize t to null.
   public void init() {
      t = null;
   }
```

```
// Start thread when the applet is needed.
public void start() {
  t = new Thread(this);
  stopFlag = false;
  t.start();
}

// Entry point for the thread that runs the banner.
public void run() {
  // Request a repaint every quarter second.
  for( ; ; ) {
    try {
      repaint();
      Thread.sleep(250);
      if(stopFlag) break;
    } catch(InterruptedException exc) {}
  }
}

// Pause the banner.
public void stop() {
  stopFlag = true;
  t = null;
}

// Display the banner.
public void paint(Graphics g) {
  char ch;

  ch = msg.charAt(0);
  msg = msg.substring(1, msg.length());
  msg += ch;

  g.drawString(msg, 50, 30);
}
}
```

Sample output is shown here:

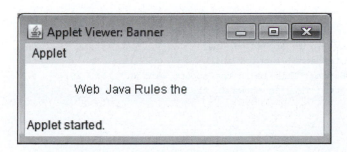

8. When you run the applet, you may notice that the scroll occasionally flickers. You can eliminate this flicker by use of a technique called *double buffering*. With double buffering, your program creates a second graphics context in which you prepare output. Then, the completed output is written to the screen all at once, thus eliminating flicker. The term *double buffering* comes from the fact that the screen is considered a buffer for pixels, and the off screen image is, therefore, a second buffer. The techniques required to implement a double buffer are beyond the scope of this chapter. Also, when using Swing, double buffering is implemented automatically, so it is not something that you will normally need to implement yourself. (This is one of the advantages of Swing.) However, as an extra challenge, you might do some research and try adding double buffering to this example on your own.

USING THE STATUS WINDOW

In addition to displaying information in its window, an applet can also output a message to the status window of the browser or applet viewer on which it is running. To do so, call **showStatus( )**, which is defined by **Applet**, with the string that you want displayed. The general form of **showStatus( )** is shown here:

    void showStatus(String *msg*)

Here, *msg* is the string to be displayed.

The status window is a good place to give the user feedback about what is occurring in the applet, suggest options, or possibly report some types of errors. The status window also makes an excellent debugging aid because it gives you an easy way to output information about your applet.

The following applet demonstrates **showStatus( )**:

```
// Using the Status Window.
import java.awt.*;
import java.applet.*;
/*
<applet code="StatusWindow" width=300 height=50>
</applet>
*/

public class StatusWindow extends Applet{
  // Display msg in applet window.
  public void paint(Graphics g) {
    g.drawString("This is in the applet window.", 10, 20);
    showStatus("This is shown in the status window.");
  }
}
```

Sample output from this program is shown here:

PASSING PARAMETERS TO APPLETS

You can pass parameters to an applet. In fact, doing so is quite common. Often a parameter specifies some setting or attribute associated with the applet. For example, thinking back to the **Banner** applet shown in Try This 15-1, you might control the scroll speed by passing in the delay rather than hard-coding it into the applet. You could also pass in the message to be displayed.

To pass a parameter to an applet, use the PARAM attribute of the APPLET tag, specifying the parameter's name and value. To retrieve a parameter, use the **getParameter( )** method, defined by **Applet**. Its general form is shown here:

String getParameter(String *paramName*)

Here, *paramName* is the name of the parameter. It returns the value of the specified parameter in the form of a **String** object. Thus, for numeric and **boolean** values, you will need to convert their string representations into their binary formats. (One way to do this is to use a **parse** method defined by a type wrapper, such as **Integer.parseInt( )**.) If the specified parameter cannot be found, **null** is returned. Therefore, be sure to confirm that the value returned by **getParameter( )** is valid. Also, check any parameter that is converted into a numeric value, confirming that a valid conversion took place.

Here is an example that demonstrates passing parameters:

```
// Pass a parameter to an applet.
import java.awt.*;
import java.applet.*;

/*
<applet code="Param" width=300 height=80>
<param name=author value="Herb and Dale">
<param name=purpose value="Demonstrate Parameters">
<param name=version value=2>
</applet>
*/
```

These HTML parameters are passed to the applet.

```
public class Param extends Applet {
  String author;
  String purpose;
  int ver;

  public void start() {
    String temp;

    author = getParameter("author");
    if(author == null) author = "not found";  ◄──────── It is important to check
                                                          that the parameter exists!
    purpose = getParameter("purpose");
    if(purpose == null) purpose = "not found";

    temp = getParameter("version");
    try {
      if(temp != null)
        ver = Integer.parseInt(temp);
      else
        ver = 0;
    } catch(NumberFormatException exc) {  ◄──────── It is also important to
      ver = -1; // error code                       make sure that numeric
    }                                               conversions succeed.
  }

  public void paint(Graphics g) {
    g.drawString("Purpose: " + purpose, 10, 20);
    g.drawString("By: " + author, 10, 40);
    g.drawString("Version: " + ver, 10, 60);
  }
}
```

Sample output from this program is shown here:

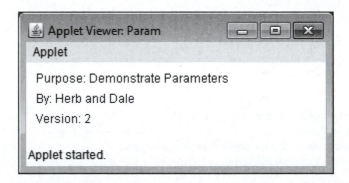

Progress Check

1. How do you cause an applet's **paint( )** method to be called?
2. Where does **showStatus( )** display a string?
3. What method is used to obtain a parameter specified in the APPLET tag?

Ask the Expert

Q Beyond what you have discussed, are there more features supported by **Applet**?

A Yes. In addition to the methods described in the preceding sections, **Applet** contains several others. For example, you can load a graphics image by use of **getImage( )**. To load an audio clip, use **getAudioClip( )**. You can play an audio clip by use of **play( )**. Furthermore, **Applet** inherits a very significant portion of the functionality supported by the AWT. As mentioned, **Applet** extends the **Component** class, which contains over 100 methods. It also inherits **Container** and **Panel**. These are two more AWT classes. **Container** specifies the features of a component that will be used to contain (that is, hold) other components. **Panel** is a simple container. You might want to explore these classes in Java's documentation. Doing so will give you insight into the rich functionality that underpins Java's support for graphical user interfaces.

THE REMAINING JAVA KEYWORDS

The preceding chapters have described the majority of the keywords defined by Java, but a few still remain. They are shown here:

- **volatile**
- **transient**
- **instanceof**
- **strictfp**
- **assert**
- **native**

Answers:

1. To cause **paint( )** to be called, call **repaint( )**.
2. **showStatus( )** displays output in the status window.
3. To obtain a parameter, call **getParameter( )**.

These keywords address specialized needs and are not used elsewhere in this book. However, for completeness each is described here.

The volatile Modifier

The **volatile** modifier tells the compiler that a variable can be changed unexpectedly by another thread. In a multithreaded program, sometimes two or more threads will share the same variable. For efficiency considerations, each thread can keep its own, private copy of such a shared variable, possibly in a register of the CPU. The actual (or *master*) copy of the variable is updated at various times, such as when a **synchronized** method is entered. While this approach works fine, in some cases, all that really matters is that the master copy of a variable always reflects the current state and that this current state is used by all threads. To ensure this, declare the variable as **volatile**.

The transient Modifier

The **transient** keyword is a type modifier that indicates that an instance variable is not part of the persistent state of an object. When an instance variable is declared as **transient**, then its value need not participate in *serialization*, which is the mechanism by which the state of an object is saved.

instanceof

Sometimes it is useful to know the type of an object during run time. For example, you might have one thread of execution that generates various types of objects and another thread that processes these objects. In this situation, it might be useful for the processing thread to know the type of each object when it receives it. Another situation in which knowledge of an object's type at run time is important involves casting. In Java, an invalid cast causes a run-time error. Many invalid casts can be caught at compile time. However, casts involving class hierarchies can produce invalid casts that can only be detected at run time. Because a superclass reference can refer to subclass objects, it is not always possible to know at compile time whether or not a cast involving a superclass reference is valid. The **instanceof** keyword addresses these types of situations.

In the formal Java syntax, **instanceof** is an operator. It has this general form:

objref instanceof *type*

Here, *objref* is a reference to an instance of a class, and *type* is a class or interface type. If *objref* is of the specified type or can be cast into the specified type, then the **instanceof** expression evaluates to **true**. Otherwise, the result is **false**. Thus, **instanceof** is the means by which a program can obtain run-time type information about an object.

strictfp

One of the more esoteric keywords is **strictfp**. It requires that Java's floating-point calculations strictly follow the IEEE 754 standard. Except for numeric constants, by default, Java's floating-point model does not require strict adherence to this standard in all cases. To ensure strict compliance, modify a class, method, or interface declaration with **strictfp**.

assert

The **assert** keyword is used during program development to create an *assertion*, which is a condition that is expected to be true during the execution of the program. For example, you might have a method that should always return a positive integer value. You might test this by asserting that the return value is greater than zero using an **assert** statement. At run time, if the condition actually is true, no other action takes place. However, if the condition is false, then an **AssertionError** is thrown. Assertions are often used during testing to verify that some expected condition is actually met. They are not usually used for released code.

The **assert** keyword has two forms. The first is shown here:

    assert *condition*;

Here, *condition* is an expression that must evaluate to a **boolean** result. If the result is true, then the assertion is true and no other action takes place. If the condition is false, then the assertion fails and a default **AssertionError** object is thrown. For example,

```
assert n > 0;
```

If **n** is less than or equal to zero, then an **AssertionError** is thrown. Otherwise, no action takes place.

The second form of **assert** is shown here:

    assert *condition* : *expr*;

In this version, *expr* is a value that is passed to the **AssertionError** constructor. This value is converted to its string format and displayed if an assertion fails. Typically, you will specify a string for *expr*, but any non-**void** expression is allowed as long as it defines a reasonable string conversion.

To enable assertion checking at run time, you must specify the **-ea** option. For example, to enable assertions for **Sample**, execute it using this line:

```
java -ea Sample
```

Native Methods

Although rare, there may occasionally be times when you will want to call a subroutine that is written in a language other than Java. Typically, such a subroutine will exist as executable code for the CPU and environment in which you are working—that is, native code. For example, you may wish to call a native code subroutine in order to achieve faster execution time. Or you may want to use a specialized, third-party library, such as a statistical package. However, since Java programs are compiled to bytecode, which is then interpreted (or compiled to machine code on the fly) by the Java run-time system, it would seem impossible to call a native code subroutine from within a Java program. This conclusion is, however, false. Java provides the **native** keyword, which is used to declare native code methods. Once declared, these methods can be called from inside a Java program just as you call any other Java method.

A native method is declared by preceding the declaration with the **native** modifier. However, no body for the method is supplied. For example:

```
public native int doSomething();
```

Once a native method has been declared, you must provide the native method. Native methods are often written in the C language. Once the native method has been created, it is necessary to follow a rather complex series of steps in order to link it with the Java code. The use of native methods is definitely an advanced programming technique, and is beyond the scope of this book.

Ask the Expert

Q While we are on the subject of keywords, I have a question about **this**. I was looking at some examples of Java code on the Internet and I noticed a form of **this** that takes parentheses. For example,

```
this(x);
```

Can you tell me what this does?

A The form of **this** that you refer to enables one constructor to invoke another constructor within the same class. The general form of this use of **this** is shown here:

this(*arg-list*)

When **this( )** is executed, the overloaded constructor that matches the parameter list specified by *arg-list* is executed first. Then, if there are any other statements inside the original constructor, they are executed. The call to **this( )** must be the first statement within the constructor. Here is a simple example.

```
class MyClass {
  int a;
  int b;

  // Initialize a and b individually.
  MyClass(int i, int j) {
    a = i;
    b = j;
  }

  // Use this() to initialize a and b to the same value.
  MyClass(int i) {
    this(i, i); // invokes MyClass(i, i)
  }
}
```

In **MyClass**, only the first constructor directly assigns a value to **a** and **b**. The second constructor simply invokes the first. Therefore, when this statement executes:

```
MyClass mc = new MyClass(8);
```

the call to **MyClass(8)** causes **this(8, 8)** to be executed, which translates into a call to **MyClass(8, 8)**.

Invoking overloaded constructors through **this( )** can be useful because it can prevent the unnecessary duplication of code. However, you need to be careful. Constructors that call **this( )** will execute a bit slower than those that contain all of their initialization code in-line. This is because the call and return mechanism used when the second constructor is invoked adds overhead. Remember that object creation affects all users of your class. If your class will be used to create large numbers of objects, then you must carefully balance the benefits of smaller code against the increased time it takes to create an object. As you gain more experience with Java, you will find these types of decisions easier to make.

There are two restrictions you need to keep in mind when using **this( )**. First, you cannot use any instance variable of the constructor's class in a call to **this( )**. Second, you cannot use **super( )** and **this( )** in the same constructor because each must be the first statement in the constructor.

EXERCISES

1. What method is called when an applet first begins running? What method is called when an applet is removed from the system?

2. Explain why an applet must use multithreading if it needs to run continually.

3. Enhance Try This 15-1 so that it displays the string passed to it as a parameter. Add a second parameter that specifies the time delay (in milliseconds) between each rotation.

4. Extra challenge: Create an applet that displays the current time, updated once per second. To accomplish this, you will need to do a little research. Here is a hint to help you get started: One way to obtain the current time is to use a **Calendar** object, which is part of the **java.util** package. (The **Calendar** class is described in Chapter 24.) You should now be at the point where you can examine the **Calendar** class on your own and use its methods to solve this problem.

5. To request that an applet's window be redisplayed, what method do you call?

6. Briefly describe the **assert** keyword.

7. Give one reason why a native method might be useful to some types of programs.

8. What operator can you use to determine the type of an object at run time?

9. Create an **Applet** that displays the following X pattern. Adjust the spacing between the asterisks and adjust the size of the **Applet** so that the pattern fills most of the **Applet**.

```
  *           *
    *       *
      *   *
        *
      *   *
    *       *
  *           *
```

10. The **paint( )** method of the **Applet** class has a **Graphics** object as its parameter. In the examples in this chapter, the **Graphics** object was used to draw a string. However, a **Graphics** object can do much more than draw strings. For example, it also has the following methods:

    void drawLine(int *startX*, int *startY*, int *endX*, int *endY*)

    void drawRect(int *left*, int *top*, int *width*, int *height*)

    Create an applet that uses these two methods to draw a house.

11. Modify the **Banner** applet in Try This 15-1 so that it displays two scrolling banners. Use any message you want in each banner but have one banner rotate forward and the other one rotate backward.

12. As mentioned in this chapter, five of the methods defined for the **Applet** class are **init( )**, **start( )**, **paint( )**, **stop( )**, and **destroy( )**. Now suppose a user opens a web page containing an applet and then covers and uncovers the applet. The user also switches among various web pages, frequently revisiting the page with the applet. Which of the five methods will be called most often, and which will be called least often?

13. The **getClass( )** method of **Object** can be used to tell you whether an object **x** is an instance of a class called **A** as follows:

    ```
    if( x.getClass() == A.class ) { ... }
    ```

    What is the main difference between that **if** statement and the following **if** statement?

    ```
    if( x instanceof A ) { ... }
    ```

14. What happens if you test to see whether **null** is an instance of a class using the **instanceof** operator? For example, is the following condition true?

    ```
    (null instanceof String)
    ```

15. Write a method **countTypes( )** that takes an array of **Object**s as its parameter. It uses **instanceof** to determine how many of the values in the array are **Integer**s, how many are **Number**s or a subclass of **Number** other than **Double**, how many are **String**s, and how many are some other type. It then displays the number of each that it found. The sum of the last three numbers displayed should equal the length of the array.

16. What will be displayed by the following program? Why?

    ```
    class Assertions {
      public static void main(String[] args) {
        assert 3 < 0 : "Oops";
        System.out.println("End of method.");
      }
    }
    ```

CHAPTER 16

Introduction to Object-Oriented Design

KEY SKILLS & CONCEPTS

- Know properties of high-quality software
- Use names properly
- Know how to maximize cohesion
- Know how to minimize coupling
- Know how to separate responsibilities
- Understand class invariants
- Write proper internal and external documentation
- Understand the Expert pattern
- Know how to use encapsulation and information hiding
- Know the Law of Demeter
- Know the Open-Closed Principle
- Know when to use inheritance versus delegation
- Understand the Adapter and Observer design patterns

The primary focus of the preceding 15 chapters has been on the core elements of the Java programming language, including its keywords, syntax, and basic techniques. At this point, you know how to write a program that compiles correctly and performs the actions you want. However, the programs that you have been writing are quite short. In this chapter, we will introduce you to another aspect of programming that becomes especially important as you start writing larger, more complex programs, whether in later courses or in the workplace. That aspect is the proper *design* of object-oriented programs. We will focus mostly on design issues such as which objects should interact with which other objects, which objects should maintain what data, which objects should have access to that data, and which objects should have the ability to manipulate the data. That is, we will focus on the proper way to divide up the responsibilities among the various objects in the system and how to get them to collaborate with each other to solve problems successfully. We will also address some implementation issues related to proper design.

ELEGANT SOFTWARE AND WHY IT MATTERS

How important is it to spend time properly designing your software before implementing it? Consider programmers who quickly throw together some code without doing any planning or design work first. They might justify their actions by saying that the programs are very short and they know what is going on in the code. Furthermore, they might say, the code is never going to be used again or viewed by anyone else, so why waste time needlessly on design before writing the code?

In the case of small "quick-and-dirty" programs, such as short shell scripts that are used only once, the programmers might be correct. It is usually not productive to spend a lot of time creating the most elegant possible version. All that is important is that the code work correctly. However, you also need to be aware that the code that the programmers thought of as "throw-away" is often not thrown away. It ends up being copied and pasted into another program, or it becomes the core of a more general, more complex program. In such cases, time devoted to designing the software properly would be time productively spent.

Designing software that is intended for long-term, heavy use requires a considerable investment of time and energy. For example, consider libraries of classes (such as Java's Swing package that we will visit in the next part of this book), which are used extensively by application developers. It is not sufficient that the library classes have no errors in them; it is also important that the classes have a good design. A poor design for any one of these classes can cause problems down the line for all of the developers using the package. For example, if a valuable or important feature was omitted, developers will have to write their own code, possibly in a very awkward way, to accomplish what the library classes should have provided.

For very large systems, in which many programmers are involved, it is even more important to spend a significant amount of time on the analysis of the problem and the design of the solution before doing any coding. In such cases, no one person can understand every part of the program, and instead each programmer works on one small part of it. If the solution has not been well designed, a change (a bug fix or an enhancement, for example) by one programmer in one line of code could easily introduce bugs in the code written by other programmers.

When a program has thousands or millions of lines of code, bugs are inevitable. The real issue is how to minimize the number of bugs that occur when the code is written in the first place, how to maximize the detection and removal of the bugs that do make it into the code, and how to minimize the number of new bugs that are accidentally introduced whenever the code is modified. Furthermore, this minimization and maximization process is not a one-time thing. Software continually changes due to patches introduced to fix bugs or due to enhancements added to the software. In other words, thorough testing to remove bugs is important in software development, but it is just as important to design and write the software so that as few bugs as possible are introduced in the first place and so that it is easy to modify the code later without introducing new bugs.

So why don't software developers design and write software in a way that minimizes bugs? The answer is that, try as they might, there are forces working against them. Doing the job right takes time and money in the short term, and the benefits do not appear until later. Meanwhile, software projects are under more and more pressure to be completed quickly and put into production before the window of opportunity for sales closes. As a result, the initial software design is often inadequately specified, and so a solid foundation has not been laid. In addition, after software has gone into production, the pressure to quickly fix the bugs and make enhancements works against major redesigns. As a result, a software system tends to become a "big ball of mud," that, as Foote and Yoder describe it on the web page <http://www.laputan.org/mud/>, is a "haphazardly structured, sprawling, sloppy, duct-tape and bailing wire, spaghetti code jungle." The degradation over time of software into such mud balls makes finding and fixing bugs and adding enhancements harder and harder, costing more time and money and resulting in more pressure to put off large-scale redesign. And so the vicious cycle continues.

There are other forces pushing software toward the same balls of mud. Those forces are the lack of skill, knowledge, and experience of the software developers regarding how to write high-quality software. If the developers have no experience with designing software systems of any size or complexity, or if the developers are writing a business application but have no knowledge of that particular business domain and its needs and requirements, then it is easy for the software to become muddy. Even if developers understand a system completely, the mud in the system will not go away if the developers don't have the tools (skills or knowledge) to clean it up.

What can be done to fight the tendency of software systems to turn into mud balls? Addressing the pressures of cost and time is beyond the scope of this chapter. Our focus concerns the skills, knowledge, and experience that developers need in order to do high-quality work. In this chapter, we will introduce you to some of the things a software developer should know in order to be able to design high-quality software systems in ways that fight the forces toward muddiness.

Properties of Elegant Software

How can you tell the difference between poorly designed and well-designed software? Unfortunately, there is no precise definition of "well-designed" software. Good software design is as much an art as a science. As people become more experienced in the software profession, they develop a feeling about the difference between high-quality and low-quality software. That is, they develop a sense of aesthetics about software design and implementation.

Even if well-designed software cannot be precisely defined, many properties of such software can be given. In this chapter, we will consider the following properties of high-quality software:

- Usable—It is easy for the client to use.
- Complete—It satisfies all the client's needs.
- Robust—It deals with unusual situations gracefully.
- Efficient—It uses a reasonable amount of time and other resources.
- Scalable—It will perform correctly and efficiently even when the problem grows in size by several orders of magnitude.
- Readable—It is easy for a software engineer to understand the design and the code.

- Reusable—It can be reused in other settings.
- Simple—It is not unnecessarily complex.
- Maintainable—Defects can be found and fixed easily without introducing new defects.
- Extensible—It can easily be enhanced without breaking existing code.

We will use the term *elegant* to describe software with these properties. This term is an appropriate one because a well-designed and well-implemented software system is a joy for software developers to maintain. Developers are easily able to find the places where changes need to be made and can make those changes with minimal worrying about whether the changes will introduce new bugs. In contrast, a poorly designed system may elicit shudders of revulsion from software engineers who are forced to maintain it.

In this chapter, we will be mostly concerned with the last six properties. We will discuss common guidelines and principles of design that can help give software such properties. These guidelines and principles evolved over the years, as practitioners noticed that certain things worked well and others worked poorly.

Progress Check

1. For large software systems, all that matters about the software is that it work correctly. True or false?
2. List three of the properties of elegant software.

Ask the Expert

Q Can you point me the in the right direction to learn more about design principles and patterns?

A If you want to learn more, there are several good places to start. *Effective Java* by Joshua Block (2nd ed., 2008, Addison-Wesley) is a good resource for learning best practices for writing elegant Java. A classic text on object-oriented design in general is *Obect-Oriented Software Construction* by Bertrand Meyer (2nd ed., 1997, Prentice Hall). The classical reference for design patterns (which are discussed at the end of this chapter) is *Design Patterns* by Eric Gamma, R. Helm, R. Johnson, and J. Vlissides (1995, Addison-Wesley). You can also find many excellent resources on the Internet.

Answers:

1. False.
2. Any three of the following properties: Complete, robust, efficient, scalable, readable, reusable, simple, maintainable, extensible.

ELEGANT METHODS

Before we can understand the proper way to design a large object-oriented software system, including the proper division of the system into classes with appropriate responsibilities and collaborations, we need to understand what makes an individual class elegant. What is the role of a class? What kind of responsibilities should it have? That is, what data should it maintain, and what should it be able to do to that data and other data? In other words, what should its behavior be? Also, once we have made that decision, how should we implement that behavior as methods?

Let's start with methods. Is the elegance of a method related to its return type or the name or the parameters or the body of the method? In fact, it is related to all of these parts. To help us understand the issues surrounding the elegance of methods, let us first consider a simple example.

Suppose we are developing a new **DataHolder** class that, when asked, should be able to insert new values into an integer array referenced by its private instance variable **data**. That is, this act of insertion needs to be part of the behavior of the class. As a result, we need to add one or more methods to the class to perform the insertion. There are a variety of methods we could create to give the class this behavior. For example, we could create a method **insert( )** that takes as its parameters the new integer value to be inserted and an integer index indicating where it is to be inserted. The method just inserts the value into the appropriate spot in the **data** array. Alternatively, we could break the process into three separate methods, where the first method **increaseCapacity( )** enlarges the array if necessary, the second method **shift( )** shifts the other integers out of the way to make room for the new integer, and the third method **put( )** puts the new integer in the newly freed up spot. Furthermore, we could leave it to the user to call the three methods individually, or we could create an additional **insert( )** method that calls these three other methods.

We could also use a different name for the method than "insert" or change the order or the number of parameters. For example, we could overload the method so that two values can be inserted at once. We also could have a variety of return types. The method could have **void** for its return type, or it could, for example, return information indicating whether it was successful in inserting the new value. Which of all these choices is best? We will repeatedly return to this example in this section of the chapter and, in the process, answer this question and the more general question of what makes a method elegant.

Naming Conventions

Several software principles can help us compare and judge the approaches mentioned in the preceding paragraph. One principle is *Use intention-revealing names*. Let's look at this principle in some detail because it doesn't just apply to methods. It applies to any part of the software that uses names, including methods, variables, classes, and interfaces.

A method name should indicate the intent of the method, that is, what the method is supposed to accomplish. The name should not indicate *how* the method accomplishes its goal but rather *what* that goal is. A method that does not return a value (a method with return type **void**) should have a name consisting of a verb or verb phrase, such as **print( )** or **setName( )**. Vague names like **doIt( )** are inadequate. A method that returns a value should have a name reflecting the value being returned, for example, **length( )** or **name( )**. Such a method could also have a verb phrase for a name, the convention being the word "get" followed by the value being returned. For example, a method that returns the size of some data structure could be named **size( )** or **getSize( )**. In regard to our **DataHolder** example, the name **insert( )** is a quite good one. It succinctly describes what the method intends to do.

Classes and interfaces should have names that reflect the role or intention of objects of those types. The name of a class is the reader's first clue as to the actual role the class plays in a design, and so it is worth spending time finding an appropriate name for the class. Class names typically are nouns, such as **Date** or **ComputerCard**. Interfaces often have names ending in "-able" or "-ible", such as **Cloneable** or **Iterable**.

Finally, variables need to be named appropriately to promote readability. Consider a program that has a variable in it called **nT**. An argument in favor of such a name is that it is short and therefore saves typing time and helps shorten your lines of code. However, the name is quite meaningless in terms of indicating the role of the variable, and so the reader is forced to memorize that role. In contrast, calling the variable **numberOfThreads** or **numThreads** or even **numThrds** instead of **nT** increases dramatically the ease with which your code can be understood.

A **boolean** variable should have an appropriate name for the value it represents. It usually should not represent the negation of a value, for example, don't call your variable **notYetDone**, which could possibly result in the need for expressions such as the double negative **!notYetDone**. Instead, it would be better to call it **done** and use the expression **!done** wherever **notYetDone** would have been used. Of course, the name **done** is not ideal either, since the word does not contain enough information to aid the reader in understanding the role of the variable. The variable name should say *what* activity is done or not done. For example, if this variable is being used to indicate that a graphic image is done loading and is now visible, a better name would be **doneLoading**.

Keep in mind that bad names are not just misleading; they make the whole system harder to understand, in opposition to our desire for readable software.

Method Cohesion

Another software principle is *Methods should do one thing only and do it well*. That is, a method should not do two or more tasks unless they are all part of a single cohesive action. For example, it makes sense for our **insert( )** method mentioned above to enlarge the array, move the other values to make room for the new value, and add the new value, because they are all part of one cohesive action. In contrast, a method that both inserts new items into a **data** array and determines whether a string is in the form of an e-mail address is not cohesive. The main reason to avoid creating such methods is that you often want to take one of the actions but not both. In that case, a method that does both is worthless. A method is much more reusable if it does only one thing.

Here's an example of a noncohesive method:

```java
void doThisOrThat(boolean flag) {
  if( flag ) {
    // ...twenty lines of code to do this...
  }
  else {
    // ...twenty lines of code to do that...
  }
}
```

This method is clearly trying to do two things and is using the flag to determine which of them to do. It would be better to have two separate auxiliary methods, such as **doThis( )** and **doThat( )**, neither of which needs a flag. Once we have these methods, then we can rewrite our method above to read:

```java
void doThisOrThat(boolean flag) {
  if( flag ) doThis();
  else doThat();
}
```

This code is now acceptable (except for the non-intention-revealing names **flag, this**, and **that**) since the method is just acting as a dispatch center and so is doing one thing only and doing it well.

An interesting corollary to the cohesiveness principle is the principle *A method should either modify the state of an existing object or objects or return a value, but not both*. By the *state* of an object, we mean the values of its instance variables. Again, the reasoning behind this principle is that sometimes you might want to modify the state of an object but not return any value, and other times you might want to return a value but not modify any objects. Therefore, for reusability, it is better to separate these actions into two separate methods. Note that the strict adherence to this principle requires that there be no code modification inside methods that return values. For example, a method that tells you whether an array is sorted or that tells you the largest value in the array is a method that returns a value, and so it shouldn't modify the array. Another way of stating this principle is that methods that return values should have no side effects and methods with side effects should not return values.

That said, note that we have been using the terminology "guidelines" and "principles," not "rules." That is, these guidelines should be taken into consideration when designing or implementing a software system, but they are not rules that absolutely must be followed. Occasionally, there are times when it is better for your design to ignore one or more of these principles. Also, some legacy code and library code do not follow them. For example, the **java.util** package has a **Stack** class with a **pop( )** method that both removes the top object from the stack and returns it. (And, of course, **SimpleStack** developed earlier in this book also works this way.) This behavior technically breaks the principle mentioned above, but it is acceptable because it is reasonable behavior in this case and, more importantly, because such a method has been in use for many years and so changing its behavior now would be much worse than letting it continue to break the guideline.

Ask the Expert

Q What about a method that attempts to modify an object's state and returns a **boolean** value indicating success or failure in the attempt? Is there anything wrong with that?

A This approach is a common one, especially in languages without exception handling mechanisms. It is therefore okay to create such a method even though it doesn't follow the guideline. But Java programmers should also consider alternate courses of action, such as throwing an exception if the method does not succeed. In any case, whether your system attains it or not, the guideline is worth striving for. Consider it a challenge to see whether you can design your methods better than previous designers have done with their methods.

Well-formed Objects

Here is another principle regarding elegant methods: *A non-private method should keep an object in a well-formed state.* For example, suppose you have a class with two instance variables: an integer array **data** and an integer **max** that stores the maximum value in the **data** array. You must be careful not to have any methods in the class that modify the data array without also updating the **max** variable. It is this kind of internal consistency that we refer to when we say a class is "well-formed."

How do we state the requirements of consistency for objects of a class? That is, how do we know whether an instance of a class is well-formed? A good way is to create a list of the class invariants. A *class invariant* is a statement giving requirements about the state of instances of the class between public method calls. An example of a class invariant is the statement "The value of **max** and the largest value in the **data** array must be equal."

For another example, consider the following implementation of the **DataHolder** class discussed earlier.

```java
class DataHolder {
  private int[] data;

  public DataHolder() {
    data = new int[0];
  }

  public void insert(int x, int index) {
    increaseCapacity();
    shift(index);
    put(x, index);
  }

  private void increaseCapacity() {
    int[] newData = new int[data.length+1];
    for(int i = 0; i < data.length; i++)
      newData[i] = data[i];
```

```
      data = newData;
   }

   private void shift(int index) {
      for(int i = index; i < data.length-1; i++)
         data[i+1] = data[i];
   }

   private void put(int x, int index) {
      data[index] = x;
   }
   public int get(int index) {
      return data[index];
   }
   public int size() {
      return data.length;
   }
}
```

Note that the **data** array is always full of data that had been inserted. That is, there are never unused spots in the array. This is a class invariant for objects of class **DataHolder**. If the invariant is broken, unexpected behavior can occur. To avoid that possibility, the three auxiliary methods **increaseCapacity( )**, **shift( )**, and **put( )** have been made private. As a result, objects of this class might be temporarily ill-formed, for example, after **increaseCapacity( )** has been called, but are restored to a well-formed state before any public methods return. If **increaseCapacity( )** or **shift( )** were made public, then any user of the object could call them in isolation, causing the object to become ill-formed.

For the purpose of maintaining class invariants, it should be noted that instance variables should be made private or final if they are involved in any of the class invariants. Otherwise, another object could unintentionally or maliciously change the instance variable's value, possibly rendering the object ill-formed.

Internal Documentation

The final principle we want to mention in this section is *Include complete external documentation for the user and internal documentation for the developer.*

A software package, no matter how well designed otherwise, is almost worthless if documentation is not included. Consider the frustration of a software designer who knows that a library almost surely has the tools she needs but she can't tell for sure because the library's documentation of its components is inadequate. Or consider the frustration of the person faced with the task of fixing a bug in a large section of code that contains little or no comments explaining why it does things the way it does. Elegant software avoids both of these situations by including appropriate documentation.

Internal documentation is the documentation for someone who is looking at the source code. Such documentation should provide information not readily available from the code itself. It should summarize what is being done, why it is being done, and why it is being done this particular way. For example, the documentation might explain that a method has been implemented a particular way to allow easy modification later or because the method is most efficient this way or because this way is the simplest way. It should explain the trade-offs that are involved among the various possible implementations.

Internal documentation should also clearly state any class or method invariants that exist. A person modifying an existing method without being aware of those invariants is very possibly going to write code that breaks them.

Internal documentation should not repeat what the code says. Instead, it should summarize the *intent* or purpose of the code. One reason to include the intent in the documentation is so that future maintainers of the code, when fixing errors in it, can understand what the method *should* have been doing rather than what it does.

Helpful internal documentation might also give an overview of the implementation. An internal method comment might explain the algorithm used by the method if the algorithm was not already mentioned in the external documentation. For example, a **sort( )** method's internal documentation might say that the recursive quick sort algorithm was used.

Internal documentation mostly consists of comments in the source code, but the code itself can be a useful part of the documentation if the code is well written. If the programmer uses intention-revealing names of methods and variables and appropriately combines them, the code can be almost self-documenting, and so there is less need for further documentation. Unfortunately, totally self-documenting code is an ideal that is rarely met, and so some additional comments are usually necessary.

Note that internal comments are supposed to be helpful in understanding code. However, they can also hinder the understanding if, for example, the comments are not also updated when the code is updated.

Internal documentation can also help you spot inelegant parts of your methods. For example, code needing a large number of comments usually indicates poor code. If you find yourself including many comments, then the code should probably be rewritten. In particular, if you write a lot of comments that summarize sections of code in a method, the method may be doing too many things.

External Documentation

External documentation is for users of the code who can't look at or don't care about the source code itself. It describes the public classes, interfaces, methods, fields, and packages and how to use them. External documentation might also include design documents indicating the relationships among and the roles played by the classes. Such documentation, if done correctly, describes all aspects of the behavior of each method on which the caller must rely.

It is important to understand that the only behavior of a method on which the user should rely is the documented behavior. Reliance should be limited in this way because, during maintenance of the system, a programmer might need to modify the method. The maintainer is free to change any undocumented behavior, which then can cause serious problems for anyone relying on that behavior.

What should be included in the external documentation of a method? This documentation must include the full method signature and return type so that the user knows the syntax to use in a method call, but much more is needed as well. For example, consider the method in the **java.lang.Math** class with the following header:

```
public static double rint(double a)
```

For an experienced programmer who already knows about **rint( )**, this header is sufficient to remind him or her of the type of the argument and the return type. But for everyone else, the method needs further documentation. A more descriptive name would go a long way toward clearing up any confusion, but, even with such a change, a textual description of what the method returns and how it uses the parameter is essential for proper usage.

For another example, consider the following documentation for an **nthRoot( )** function:

```
// returns the n-th root of the double value
public double nthRoot(double value, int n)
```

This documentation is inadequate. It explains the main behavior of the method, but it does not specify what happens in special cases, for example, when **value** is −1 and **n** is 2. Here is an example of more complete documentation:

```
// Returns the n-th root of the double value.
// If n is even, the positive n-th root is returned.
// If n is odd, the n-th root will have the same sign as the value.
// If n < 0 or if n is odd and value < 0 then an IllegalArgumentException
// is thrown
public double nthRoot(double value, int n)
```

External documentation should not specify too many details about the implementation of the method. These details are almost surely irrelevant to the user of the method and so just clutter up the documentation.

How do you determine when the external documentation for a method is just right? To answer this question, it is valuable to think of the method as a service an object of that class will perform for others who request/demand it. In order for users of your class to know what that service entails and therefore whether they want to use that service, you need to specify clearly what the users need to do (for example, the arguments they need to provide) and what your object will do in return when it executes the method. That is, think of the method as a contract. If a user provides appropriate arguments, then your method promises to perform a specific service. The appropriate arguments are often called *preconditions*. They indicate what must be true in order for the method to work. The specific service that is performed is often called the *postcondition*. It indicates what will happen when the method is executed.

Note that it is up to the client to make sure the preconditions are satisfied before attempting the method call. If the client attempts to use the method without satisfying the preconditions, then all bets are off and the method can have unspecified behavior, including crashing the program, running forever, or seeming to run correctly but actually generating garbage.

For an example, let's go back to our **insert( )** method in the **DataHolder** class. Recall that it takes two parameters: an integer value to be inserted and an integer index indicating where the value is to be inserted. At least two sets of preconditions and postconditions are possible for this method, depending on how the designer of the method wants it implemented. Here they are:

```
// Inserts the given value into the DataHolder at the given index
// If index < 0 or index > size()
//      an IllegalArgumentException is thrown
void insert(int value, int index)
```

This approach explains what will happen for all possible arguments and so there are no preconditions. An alternative approach is to specify preconditions and leave it up to the user to ensure that the arguments satisfy those preconditions. Here is how such documentation might look:

```
// Inserts the given value into the DataHolder at the given index
// Precondition: 0 <= index and index <= size()
void insert(int value, int index)
```

Although both approaches work, there are disadvantages to the second one. If a method specifies a precondition and the user accidentally calls that method with illegal arguments, the result may be that a value is inserted incorrectly. The user's program might then continue to execute with incorrect values, which can make it hard later to detect where the error occurred or even that one has occurred.

The first approach is one example of a practice called "defensive programming." You know errors are almost certainly going to occur and illegal input is going to be given to methods, so make sure that your methods can defend against such input by doing something explicit in a way that is helpful to the user.

As with internal documentation, one problem with writing external documentation is keeping it synchronized with the code as the design evolves. As the code is modified (e.g., errors are fixed, features are added), it is tempting, especially under time pressure, to postpone updating the documentation, resulting in documentation that no longer matches the code. One way to solve the problem of keeping documentation up to date is to generate external documentation from the source code or *vice versa*, so that they are always synchronized.

Javadoc is a tool and documentation technique designed for such document generation. It specifies a syntax to be used for comments in the source code that are then gathered by the Javadoc application and converted into external documentation. Javadoc was used to generate the Java API documentation that you can read online. Unfortunately, using Javadoc does not guarantee that the external documentation will always be synchronized with the source code, but only that the external documentation is synchronized with the Javadoc-formatted comments in the code.

For an example of Javadoc notation, the method header for the **nthRoot( )** method discussed earlier is presented here using that notation:

```
/**
 * Returns the n-th root of the double value.
 * If either n < 0 or n is even and value < 0,
 * then an IllegalArgumentException is thrown.
 *
 * @param value the double whose root is desired
 * @param n the integer indicating the root to be computed
```

```
 *
 * @return the n-th root of the value
 *     If n is even, the positive n-th root is returned.
 *     If n is odd, the n-th root will have the same sign as the value.
 *
 * @throws IllegalArgumentException
 *     if either n < 0 or n is even and value < 0.
 */
```

We are not using Javadoc notation to document the code in this book for reasons of space, but you are likely to use it in later courses or after college, in the workplace. A brief overview of Javadoc is found in Appendix A.

Progress Check

1. A method should do one thing only and do it well. True or False?
2. Statements specifying requirements about the state of objects of a class between method calls are called _____.
3. Documentation for the programmer who is charged with maintaining the source code is called _____ documentation.
4. A condition that must be true before a method call will work correctly is called a _____.

ELEGANT CLASSES

Now that you have a better understanding of what a high-quality method is, we can better explain what makes a class or a set of classes high quality. A class might have lots of responsibilities and lots of collaborators. Should such a class be broken into two or more smaller classes? Should extra responsibilities be given to it? Should it collaborate with other classes more or less than it does now? Should the class be moved into a different package? To help us answer these questions, we will present several more design principles.

Class Cohesion and the Expert Pattern

The main principle to consider is *Classes, like methods, should do one thing only and do it well*. That is, classes should model only one idea.

This guideline does not mean that each class should have exactly one method. Instead, it says that a class should model one concept and all the methods in the class should be related to and appropriate for that concept. That is, all the responsibilities

---

Answers:

1. True.
2. class invariants
3. internal
4. precondition

of the class should focus on the concept being modeled by the class. One advantage of following this guideline is that a class's behavior and its role in a software system is much clearer to everyone. Furthermore, the class is more reusable if it isn't encumbered with responsibilities and data irrelevant to its main purpose.

For example, a class that does one thing quite well is the **String** class. All the methods and data of that class refer to one and only one concept, namely, a sequence of characters. The methods of that class provide useful tools for manipulating that sequence.

A simple example of an ill-formed class would be one that is responsible for storing all the information relating to a person (e.g., name, address, age) and all the information relating to that person's current car (e.g., the brand, model, color, age). Instead, it would be more appropriate to have the person data and car data stored in separate objects, which, if necessary, have references to each other.

Another ill-formed class is a "god" class that controls all other objects in a large software system. Such a class is a master class with all the responsibilities and all other classes are just slave classes or just data holders. This approach is counter to the object orientation paradigm in which there should be decentralized control, with the responsibilities for various actions spread out among the cooperating classes.

Another term that can be used to describe the focused nature of a class is *cohesion*. When we say we want each class to "do one thing only," we mean that we want each class to have high cohesion in that all the class's behaviors and responsibilities are tightly related.

There is another general principle that can help you decide which class gets which responsibilities. Suppose an object stores a collection of data and suppose some of the data in the collection need to be deleted. Which object should do the deleting? The natural choice is the object that maintains the collection. That object has access to the necessary data to perform the desired task, and so it should be the one to do so. The principle here is *The object that contains the necessary data to perform a task should be the object that performs the task*. This principle is called the *Expert* pattern.

For example, consider a **CarDealer** object that stores, among other things, a collection of **Car** objects corresponding to the cars currently in stock. Suppose you want to know if there are any blue minivans in stock. You (the user) can do the work yourself by asking the **CarDealer** for a list of all cars and then traversing the list looking for a blue minivan. Or you can ask the **CarDealer** if it has any blue minivans in stock. The latter option is clearly preferable. The **CarDealer** is the object with the necessary data to perform the task, and so ideally it should be the one that does so.

In summary, the Expert pattern is being violated whenever class **A** has a method that gets several pieces of data from an object of class **B**, manipulates those pieces, and then possibly returns a result. The object of class **B** has all the necessary data, and so that object should be the one performing the manipulation rather than an object of class **A**. That is, the method in class **A** should probably be moved to class **B**.

One clue that your objects may not be doing their jobs properly is the existence of a lot of calls to accessor methods (**getX( )** methods). If there are many such calls, then you should ask yourself what the other objects are doing with the data they get when they call one of those methods? Shouldn't your class with the **getX( )** methods be doing that job for them?

Notice how this issue relates to our principle of a well-designed class doing one thing only and doing it well. An object that does its job well not only retrieves data for you, but also manipulates that data instead of expecting you to do all the manipulations yourself.

That said, there is a tension between the principle of doing one thing only and doing it well and the Expert pattern. For example, consider an application that is the front end of a database. The application gets some data from the database and then displays it in a window. The Expert pattern suggests that the database be responsible for displaying its own data. However, a database object should also have high cohesion, which suggests it should not be responsible for two completely different activities, namely, managing the data stored in it and displaying that data in a GUI. For many of your classes, you have to decide where to draw the line in terms of cohesiveness (doing one thing only) versus the Expert pattern (doing everything possible with the data for everyone else).

Avoiding Duplication

In the preceding section, we talked about separating the responsibilities among classes and, in particular, making sure that no class has too many different kinds of responsibilities. But there is another question about responsibilities that we haven't yet addressed: Is there anything wrong with two different classes having the same responsibility? Must there be one and only one class given each responsibility? The answer is easy to guess. It is another principle: *Avoid duplication*.

This guideline is also known as the "DRY" principle: *Don't repeat yourself.* It actually says much more than not to duplicate the responsibilities among classes. Duplication can occur in many forms. For example, there might be duplicate copies of the same information, there might be duplicated code within a method or between two methods, or there might be duplicate methods in two different classes. In addition, there might be duplication of processes, that is, unnecessary repeated execution of a piece of code. All of these forms of duplication result in inelegant designs and code.

What's actually wrong with duplication? In summary, code with duplication is less readable and less maintainable than code with no duplication.

To give you a better feeling for the problems that can occur, let us consider data duplication. Why should duplicate copies of the same data be avoided? If several classes need to know the same information—for example, if there are several school administration objects that need to access the same student records—doesn't it make sense to give them all copies of that information? In some cases it does make sense, if the information never changes (that is, it is immutable). In that case, duplicate copies are okay, although they can waste space, especially if they are large. However, if the information that is duplicated is modifiable, then it is very easy for the copies to become unsynchronized; that is, one copy might be updated while, for some reason, maybe accidentally, one or more of the other copies are not.

Instead of duplicating the data, how about keeping only one copy of the data but allowing duplicate points of access to that data? For example, suppose you have an object of class **Company** that is responsible for maintaining a collection of **Employee** objects. Suppose the **Company** class implements its collection with an array. Other objects may need to use the **Employee** objects, and so the **Company** might have a **getEmployees( )** method that returns the array of **Employee** objects. As a result, two objects may have references to the same array. Is that bad?

Duplicate references to the same piece of data occur often in software systems. However, one problem is that the other objects may maliciously or unintentionally render the data invalid. In our **Company** example, what if another object modified the array by removing **Employee**s who should be there or by adding new **Employee** objects to the array or even adding **null**? In this case, the **Company** is not properly maintaining the data against intentional or unintentional corruption by others.

What should the **Company** do instead of handing over its array to anyone who asks? There are several options:

1. Have the **getEmployees( )** method return a copy of the array of **Employee**s.

2. Assuming that other objects rarely need to see all the **Employee** objects, have a getter method that finds and returns just one employee at a time.

3. Have the **Company** class follow the Expert pattern and do all the manipulation of **Employee** objects for the other objects so that the **Employee**s are always hidden. That is, do not give other objects direct access to **Employee** objects and instead force those other objects to ask the **Company** to access the **Employee** objects for them.

The issue here relates to how much you trust your collaborators. A class's default behavior should be to trust no one. In particular, if the **Company** doesn't trust other objects, then it should never let them see the actual array itself, but only the data in the array.

In a good design, each set of data has an associated "gatekeeper" class that is responsible for maintaining the primary source of that data. Other objects must ask the gatekeeper for a reference to the data when they need access to it. The other objects can then temporarily use or even modify the data passed to them, if appropriate. But they should not, in general, have a permanent reference to the primary source of the data, nor should they create or maintain their own copy of it except on a temporary basis.

Also, just as methods should always keep objects in a well-formed state, so must the gatekeeper always keep its data in a well-formed state, which requires it to be the sole object with access to its data.

That said, duplication of data is sometimes preferable to the alternative. For example, consider the situation in which you have a gatekeeper of a massive collection of objects. If the collection changes infrequently but there are frequent requests for the size of the collection, then it makes little sense to traverse the collection counting the number of objects every time its size needs to be known. Instead, for efficiency, it makes sense to have a separate variable holding the size of the collection that can be returned when a request is made for the collection's size. This situation violates the guideline against duplication in that the collection itself contains the information concerning its size (although you have to traverse the collection to get that information), and the extra variable also contains information about the collection's size, thus duplicating that information. However, for efficiency reasons, the duplication is worth it in this case.

What about the other forms of duplication we mentioned above, such as code duplication within a method or method duplication? Like data duplication, the problem with code duplication is that copies can become unsynchronized when one copy is updated but not the others. If you have duplication of code within a class, it can be removed by extracting the duplicated section from all methods and moving it into a new auxiliary method that then gets called by the other methods. If you have two different classes with duplicate methods, you can give one class a reference to the other class and invoke the method indirectly by way of an instance of the other class. Alternatively, you could move the duplicate method up into a common superclass. Removing code duplication more generally, however, is not so easy because it can sometimes be subtly hidden.

As mentioned earlier, there is another form of duplication that can cause problems, namely, the duplication between the actual software itself and the documentation of that software. External and internal documentation must precisely reflect the design and the implementation of the software because, if they become out of sync, then the documentation becomes misleading, which can be worse than no documentation at all.

Duplication of processes should also be avoided for efficiency reasons. For example, it would be wasteful of resources to have one method do a complex calculation and then call another method that repeats the calculation. In that case, it would be better for the first method to pass the result of the calculation to the second method so that it can avoid duplication.

Finally, in addition to everything we have said so far about duplication of data, code, documentation, and processes, you should keep in mind that the appearance of any form of duplication in your software might be a symptom of a bigger problem. If you see a large amount of duplication, you should probably rethink the roles and responsibilities and relationships among the classes and components involved to see whether a better design can be found that eliminates or at least reduces the duplication.

Complete Interface

Up to this point in this chapter, our discussions have centered on determining the purpose of each class. That is, what concept should each class represent, or what role should a class play? The preceding sections argued that each class should play one and only one role in order to maximize cohesion and separate responsibilities. Furthermore, they argued that each responsibility should be assigned to exactly one class.

But once we have decided on the role of a class, then we still need to decide what behaviors (methods) the class should have with regard to that role. Do we include just the minimal necessary behavior? Or, while we are at it, should we add more behavior to the class in the hope of making it more reusable? What methods should we include to implement this behavior?

The answers to these questions vary from class to class. Some classes are very application specific. In particular, a class with just the **main( )** method that executes when an application starts running is not a class that will be reusable for other applications, and so it makes little sense to expend a lot of energy designing that class for reusability. However, considerable attention and energy should be devoted to the design of classes that will become part of a library on which many other applications will depend. For the rest of this section, we will assume we are talking about classes such as these.

For classes that you want to be as reusable as possible, there is a new guideline: *Give the class a complete interface.* By "complete," we mean that the class should have the full set of appropriate behavior so that it can perform any reasonable action related to the role that it plays. If, for example, we have a GUI component, and it has a **setSelected( )** method with no parameters that highlights the component, then it should have a **setUnselected( )** method with no parameters to remove the highlighting. Even better would be to have one method **setSelected( )** that takes a **boolean** parameter **b** and highlights the component if **b** is true and unhighlights it if **b** is false. For completeness, such a component should also have a **boolean isSelected( )** function that tells you whether the component is currently highlighted.

How full should the set of behaviors be? That is, how many public methods should be included? One extreme is to create the minimum number of essential methods. By *essential* methods, we mean methods that any class that does one thing well must have. Implementations of such methods typically are intimately tied to the representation of the data stored in the class. Informally, we can think of an essential method as one that cannot be implemented by calling other methods of the class. All nonessential methods we call *convenience* methods. At the other extreme from a class with only essential methods is a class that has a large number of convenience methods in addition to the essential methods.

For example, consider a rotatable **Rectangle** class with a **rotate( )** method that takes the number of degrees of rotation as its parameter. Suppose that a significant number of the rotations that are expected to be performed are actually 90-degree counterclockwise rotations. Then a **rotateLeft( )** method could be included in the **Rectangle** class for convenience. The **rotateLeft( )** method is not, however, essential since it can be implemented by a call to **rotate(90)**.

Finally, a designer needs to be careful not to overwhelm the users by adding too many methods to a class in an attempt to ensure completeness. In other words, don't try to anticipate all possible uses to which your class will be put. It is better to include a core set of essential methods and the most appropriate set of convenience methods and to let the users construct their own convenience methods or extend the class through subclassing if they need a larger range of methods. The key is to make sure that the core set is sufficiently large that users can create any convenience methods they need.

Design with Change in Mind

Much of our discussion so far has had to do with the reusability and readability of software. For example, we want intention-revealing names so that our code will be readable. We want our classes to have cohesion and a complete interface so that they can be easily reused. However, there are other, just as important, issues to consider when designing classes. These are the issues of maintainability, modifiability and extendibility.

There are many reasons why modifications to existing classes may be necessary, including fixing bugs, making optimizations, and adding new behavior. The hard part of making such changes is doing it in a way that does not introduce new bugs or make the code "brittle," which means easily breakable when attempting further modifications.

To have a maintainable, modifiable, and extendible system, you need to design it with the possibility of future modifications in mind. The new guideline is: *Design your classes so that they can handle change.*

The rule above is easier stated than achieved. How can you design for change when change can come in so many forms? In truth, you can't anticipate all the forms of change, but following some general guidelines as you design your code will greatly improve the ability of your classes to handle change as it occurs.

One such guideline is known as the *Open-Closed Principle*. It says that *You should design software so that it is easy to extend by adding new classes, extending existing classes, and reusing existing classes rather than by modifying existing classes.* Note that "extend" here does not just mean subclassing. Rather, we are referring more generally to extending a system by adding new features or new behavior.

The benefit of following this principle should be clear. When software needs to be changed, as it always does, one approach is to change the existing classes. For example, you can change your software by adding new methods or changing existing methods of your classes. Unfortunately, this approach will likely also require you to change other classes that depend on the changed classes, which in turn may require you to change classes that depend on these classes, and so on. Not only are all these cascading changes time consuming, but also they are likely to introduce new errors in the code. Clearly it is advantageous to minimize the modification of existing, working code and instead to extend that code by adding new classes that incorporate the changes, leaving the old classes alone.

How do you design classes so that the Open-Closed Principle holds? Consider an electrical outlet in your home that currently provides power to an electric clock you purchased from Acme ten years ago. There are at least three ways to view the outlet, with analogies in object-oriented design:

1. If we think of the outlet only as an Acme clock outlet (that is, if we reserve that outlet only for clocks of the brand of the current clock), then, if Acme stops making clocks, the outlet becomes useless when your clock breaks. The outlet in this case is analogous to an **AcmeClock** variable that can refer to (plug in) only clocks of type **AcmeClock**.

2. If we think of the outlet as an electric clock outlet, then, when our current clock breaks or becomes obsolete, we can buy a new electric clock of any brand or style and plug it into the outlet. The outlet in this case is analogous to a variable of type **ElectricClock** (an abstract class or interface) that can refer to objects of any subclass (brand) of **ElectricClock**. This view of the outlet is much more useful than the first view, but it is still restrictive in that only electric clocks are allowed to use the outlet.

3. If we think of the outlet as an electric appliance outlet, then, we can plug any appliance, not just a clock, into the outlet. The appliances need have no relationship with each other aside from the fact that they have a plug that fits the outlet (the electrical interface). This view corresponds to having an **ElectricAppliance** interface and a variable of type **ElectricAppliance** that can contain any object of any class that implements the **ElectricAppliance** interface.

It is clear that the third view provides much more flexibility to the users of your classes. In this case, it is much easier to change the value of the variable when necessary. The idea is to define your variables and values to have the widest possible type so that they can be used for as wide a range of values as possible. The widest possible type in Java is an interface type.

Therefore, we have another guideline: *Code to interfaces, not classes*. That is, wherever possible write your code so that objects are referred to by the interfaces they implement instead of by the concrete class to which they belong.

One way to view coding to interfaces or, more generally, designing your classes to handle change, is to think of it as a way of making it easy to back out of any design or implementation decision you made previously. For example, if you hard-wired your code to refer to an object of a particular class, then it is hard to back out of that design and instead use another class. In contrast, if you had written your code so that the object was stored in a variable of an interface type and only the interface's methods were used, then it would be easy to replace the object with an object of another class that implements the interface. Little or no other code would need to be modified.

Note that much of our discussion in this section can be thought of in terms of minimizing the interconnections between parts of the program. For example, by coding to interfaces instead of to a concrete class, you reduce the interdependence among the concrete classes. The concept of reducing such connections goes by the name of "minimizing coupling."

We can also consider interdependence on a larger scale, such as among groups of classes, rather than just between two classes. For example, suppose we decide that we need to replace a group of classes that work together to accomplish a task with another group of classes that accomplish the same task. If the classes had been designed so that each class is minimally coupled with the other classes, then it is easier to make the switch.

Two techniques that can help you design with change in mind are encapsulation and information hiding. As you learned in Chapter 1, *encapsulation* means grouping together related items and putting a wall around them or protecting them from access by others. Although encapsulation can be done in most programming languages, object-oriented languages such as Java provide a natural mechanism, the class, for encapsulating data and the methods that operate on that data. Java also provides a package mechanism for encapsulating groups of classes.

How can the encapsulated items be protected? One technique that is helpful is *information hiding*, which means keeping information hidden from others. In particular, it is helpful to keep the implementation of a class or group of classes hidden as much as possible from the users of the class or classes. If information in a class is exposed, then clients are likely to become dependent on the fact that it is exposed, resulting in tighter coupling between that class and the clients' classes. One way to hide information has been mentioned before: keep all instance variables private. This privacy is important for ensuring that objects of a class are always in a well-formed state. It is also necessary if, in the future, we want to be able to change the implementation of a class without requiring other classes to also change. If other classes need access to those instance variables, then, instead of making the variables public, provide *getter* and *setter* methods for each of them. One advantage of using such methods instead of making the variables public is that you can include code in the setter method that ensures the well-formed state of the object. For example, you might include a range check. Also, such methods can be overridden by subclasses, giving developers more flexibility in creating classes to fit their needs. In contrast, a public instance variable cannot be overridden in subclasses.

In summary, private instance variables and, if necessary, public getter and setter methods are almost always preferable to public instance variables.

How much of a class's implementation do you encapsulate and hide? The general rule is to encapsulate and hide as much as possible. For example, make private all methods that are intended only to be used internally to the class as auxiliary methods for other methods. It is far easier to expose something later if it no longer needs to be hidden than it is to hide something that was previously exposed. Hiding an item that has been exposed may require global changes to the system.

In summary, one of the most important things you can do to make your system elegant is to design it to handle change. The Open-Closed Principle states more specifically what you should strive for. Coding to interfaces, minimizing coupling, and using encapsulation and information hiding are guidelines to help you reach this goal.

Demeter's Law

There is one final topic we want to address in this section. It relates to the Expert pattern and the coupling between classes and how well your software can handle change. This topic is the *Law of Demeter*.

To understand the Law of Demeter, consider a general in an army that is setting up a base of operations in the field. One of the many jobs that need to be performed is the digging of foxholes. Here is one way that task could be accomplished. The general could get one of his colonels and tell him to get a major. The general would then tell the major to get a captain. The general would then tell the captain to get a sergeant. The general would then tell the sergeant to get a private. The general would then tell the private to dig some foxholes.

This approach is quite ridiculous, isn't it? And yet we might easily see the equivalent of that approach in code:

```
general.getColonel(c).getMajor(m).getCaptain(c).
        getSergeant(s).getPrivate(p).digFoxhole();
```

Hopefully you realize that, just as it is not appropriate for the general to go through all those steps for getting a foxhole dug, it is inappropriate for code to go down such a message chain to get a task done.

Consider a similar, but more realistic, chain that might appear in an ATM application, in which the program reads, from an ATM card, the bank name **b**, the branch number **r**, the customer name **c**, the account number **a**, and then attempts, starting with some associated **CentralControl** object, to get the customer's balance in that account:

```
Balance balance = centralControl.getBank(b).getBranch(r).
                getCustomer(c).getAccount(a).getBalance();
```

Do you see the problems with such code? One problem is that you have now strongly coupled the ATM application, **CentralControl**, **Bank**, **Branch**, **Customer**,

Account, and **Balance** classes. Any changes to the structure of any of the latter classes could affect the code in all the former classes. Just as important, such *getX* methods give the user access to the **Bank**, **Branch**, **Customer**, **Account**, and **Balance** objects, and so the user could manipulate them (that is, invoke methods on them) in ways that may not be intended for anyone other than those in a privileged subset.

What are better ways to handle these situations? Let us go back to the general in the army and consider what such a general would really do. Most likely he wouldn't even concern himself with details such as digging foxholes. But if he did, he would certainly call in one of his officers and tell him, "I don't care how it is done, but get someone to dig foxholes."

Similarly, one possible way to handle the request for an account balance would be to do something like the following:

```
Balance balance = centralControl.getBalance(b, r, c, a);
```

In this version, it is up to the **CentralControl** class to delegate or forward the responsibilities to other classes as necessary to get the desired balance. For example, the **CentralControl** could find the **Bank** with the name **b** and pass to it the values of **r**, **c**, and **a** and ask it for the balance. The **Bank** could continue similarly. As a result, the classes are less strongly coupled. The main application doesn't need to worry about the existence of **Customer** or **Account** objects and can leave those details to **CentralControl** or other classes with which the **CentralControl** communicates.

The method chaining seen in these examples is a violation of the *Law of Demeter*, which says: *Invoke methods only on objects that you either create yourself or have direct access to*. Informally, the law says, *Don't talk to strangers*. In particular, do not talk to (that is, invoke methods on) objects that are returned by methods invoked on other objects.

Here are some more examples in which this issue arises:

1. General contractors, when building a house or larger structure, often employ subcontractors. The subcontractors may in turn get other subcontractors to help them. The general contractor doesn't care about the second level of subcontractors. That is, the general contractor expects the first level of subcontractors to do the jobs for which they are contracted, and the general contractor doesn't care who they employ or how they get the job done.

2. Suppose you are accessing a bank's database and you need to find the customer with a given name. You could (a) ask the database for a collection of all the customers and then step through the collection looking for the one with the given name, (b) ask the database for a collection of all the customers and then ask the collection to find the desired customer for you, or (c) give the database the name and ask it to do the searching to find the customer for you. Version (c) is the preferable one from the perspective of the Law of Demeter.

It is important also to mention here that the Law of Demeter should really have been called a "Guideline" instead of a "Law." It is not an absolute that must always be followed. Otherwise, it would place a tremendous burden on the objects you have direct access to, in that all possible requests of any other objects would have to be handled through them. Given that you don't always know what kinds of requests will be made (remember that "change happens"), it is hard to anticipate all future requests.

Progress Check

1. What does the Expert pattern say?
2. The principle *Avoid duplication* applies only to data. True or False?
3. What does the Open-Closed Principle say?
4. What does Demeter's Law say in simple English?

INHERITANCE VERSUS DELEGATION

When designing a large system, it is very important to consider the role inheritance will play. Inheritance is one of the most significant features of object-oriented programming. It can greatly increase the reusability of classes and also minimize the duplication of code. However, if used improperly, it can also greatly decrease the quality of the design. In this section, we will address the question of how to use inheritance correctly.

UML Class Diagrams

As an aid in our discussion of the proper use of inheritance, it can be helpful to have a diagram showing the relationships among classes in any design. Therefore, before beginning that discussion, we will introduce UML Class diagrams. *UML* (which stands for "Unified Modeling Language") is a standard notation or language for diagramming the structure of a software system. UML is independent of the programming language used to implement the system. A UML *Class diagram* is one of more than a dozen diagrams in the UML. It shows classes and interfaces and the relationships between them in a language-independent fashion. Such a diagram provides a static view of classes, interfaces, and their relationships rather than a dynamic view of the interactions among objects of those classes.

A class is represented by a box divided into three sections. The top section gives the name of the class. The middle section gives the attributes or properties held by objects of the class. These properties are abstractions of the data or state of an object and are usually implemented using instance variables. The bottom section gives the operations of a class, which correspond in Java to methods and constructors.

Answers:

1. The object that contains the necessary data to perform a task should be the object that performs the task.
2. False.
3. Design software that is open to extension but closed to modification.
4. Don't talk to strangers. Talk only to your immediate neighbors.

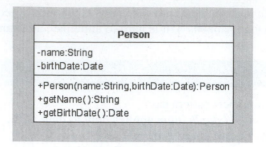

FIGURE 16-1. The Class diagram for a **Person** class.

For example, see Figure 16.1 for the Class diagram for a **Person** class. The diagram shows that this class has a **name** attribute that is a string and a **birthDate** attribute of type **Date**. In Java, these two attributes could be implemented by adding two instance variables to the **Person** class: a variable called **name** of type **String** and a variable called **birthDate** of type **Date**. The diagram also shows that this class has a constructor with two parameters, a method **getName( )** with no parameters that returns a **String**, and a **getBirthDate( )** method with no parameters that returns a **Date**.

Notice several other things about this diagram:

1. The "−" symbol in front of the attributes indicates that the attributes are private. Similarly, the "+" symbol in front of the operations indicates that they are public operations.

2. The types of the attributes, parameters, and return types of the operations are given after the names of the element and are separated from them by colons.

3. The implementation of these attributes and operations is not included in the box because a UML diagram is not usually concerned with such low-level details.

Any of the parts of a class except its name can be omitted from the diagram. To avoid clutter and confusion, it is strongly recommended that the diagram leave out all details of classes that are not relevant to the discussion. It is therefore important to remember that a class with no operations shown, for example, does not imply that the class has no operations. Rather, it implies that the operations are not relevant in this diagram.

UML Class diagrams show not just classes and interfaces, but relationships among them. The UML notation for subclassing is shown in Figure 16.2. The arrow pointing from the subclass to the superclass is called a *generalization* relationship in UML.

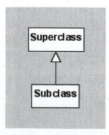

FIGURE 16-2. The UML notation for Subclass and Superclass.

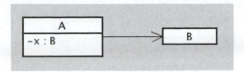

FIGURE 16-3.   An association between Classes A and B.

An *association* is a structural relationship between two classes. If objects of one class maintain a reference to objects of another class or if you need to navigate from objects of one class to objects of another, you would represent the connection between the classes by an association, which is drawn in UML Class diagrams as a line between the class boxes. See Figure 16.3 for an example. In this diagram, the association is implemented through an attribute **x** in **A** of type **B**.

Association lines can have many optional adornments, such as numbers at one or both ends, indicating multiplicity (the number of objects on that end of the association). They also might have an arrow at one end, as shown in the figure, to indicate one-way navigability or one-way awareness. From objects of the class at the tail of the arrow, you can easily "get to" or are "aware of" objects of the class at the arrow head. A plain line with no arrows could indicate two-way navigability, or it could mean that the direction of navigability is not important, and so was left out.

Ask the Expert

Q   What do all the other UML diagrams do?

A   UML 2.2 has 14 diagrams, which can be divided into two general categories: structural diagrams and behavioral diagrams. The Class diagram falls in the first group. It is beyond the scope of this book to discuss all the diagrams. Instead, we'll just mention three of them here. The *Use Case* diagram is a behavioral diagram that is useful for representing and managing all the uses to which the software will be put. For example, a digital music manager application might be used to listen to music, import music, create and edit music play lists, and copy music to an mp3 player. All these uses would be represented in a Use Case diagram. The UML *Sequence* diagram is a behavioral diagram. It is used for displaying the interactions among objects along a time line. The UML *State Machine* diagram is a behavioral diagram that represents how the state of an object or system changes over time. For example, consider the software in a low-cost digital watch. Initially, it may display the current time. But after you press the correct buttons, it will display a stopwatch or timer. The watch software is now in a new state. If the watch is in stopwatch mode and you press the correct button, the time will start advancing, which is another new state for the software. The State Machine diagram shows how all these states are related and what events need to occur to switch from one state to another.

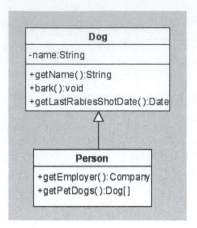

FIGURE 16-4.   A misuse of inheritance.

Code Reuse Perspective

Let us now return to the discussion of the proper use of inheritance. One of the real benefits of inheritance is code reuse. But is code reuse alone a sufficient reason for using inheritance?

Let us consider an example. Suppose your design includes a **Dog** class and a **Person** class, both of which have a **name** instance variable and a **getName( )** method. To avoid duplicating that field and method, you could remove the instance variable and method from the **Person** class and make the **Person** class a subclass of the **Dog** class. See Figure 16.4 for a UML diagram showing this relationship.

Unfortunately, in Java, subclasses inherit everything in their superclasses. Therefore, the **Person** class would also inherit the **bark( )** and **getLastRabiesShotDate( )** methods, which are rather inappropriate for **Person** objects.

Alternatively, you could put the **name** instance variable and **getName( )** method in the **Person** class and then make the **Dog** class a subclass of **Person**. Clearly this solution is just as inappropriate.

In situations such as these, you really want to reuse only some of the code. If a subclass could selectively choose which code to inherit and which not to inherit, an argument favoring the use of inheritance would have more merit.

What is a better way to avoid the code duplication in the **Dog** and **Person** classes? One way would be to create a **NamedObject** class with the **name** field and **getName( )** method and make **Dog** and **Person** both subclasses of **NamedObject**. This approach works well as long as you don't already have some other superclasses of **Dog** and **Person**. (Remember that, in Java, each class can have at most one superclass.)

In summary, being able to inherit code that would otherwise have to be duplicated is a useful feature of object-oriented languages. But code reuse in and of itself rarely justifies inheritance.

The *Is-a* Relationship

The problem with using inheritance for the **Dog** and **Person** class in the preceding section is that dogs are not people and people are not dogs. That is, there is no *is-a* relationship between the concepts that the classes model. Is the combination of code reuse and the *is-a* relationship among the classes a sufficient reason for using subclassing?

Let us consider another example. Suppose a software designer needs to model geometric shapes, and so creates a **Square** class and a **Rectangle** class. Should inheritance be used between these two classes? It is clearly the case that, from a geometrical perspective, every square "is a" rectangle. Furthermore, there are certainly good opportunities for code reuse between them. For example, the implementations of methods involving moving or finding the area or perimeter of the rectangles and squares are probably identical in both classes. Therefore it seems natural to make the **Square** class a subclass of the **Rectangle** class. But is this a good decision?

Consider the following Java implementation of the **Square** and **Rectangle** classes using inheritance. Notice how much code reuse we have—the **Square** class doesn't need to implement anything other than a constructor.

```java
public class Rectangle {

  private int x, y, width, height;

  public Rectangle(int x, int y, int w, int h) {
    this.x = x; this.y = y; width = w; height = h;
  }

  public int getWidth() { return width; }

  public int getHeight() { return height; }

  public int getArea() { return width * height; }

  public int getPerimeter() { return 2 * (width + height); }

  public void setTopLeft(int newx, int newy) { x = newx; y = newy; }

  public void setSize(int w, int h) { width = w; height = h; }
}

public class Square extends Rectangle
{
  public Square(int x, int y, int side) {
    super(x, y, side, side);
  }
}
```

However, as you may have noticed, there is a serious problem with this design. Because of the fact that subclasses inherit all methods of their superclasses, the **Square** class now inherits a **setSize( )** method that has two parameters. A call to this method can make the width and height of a square unequal, a rather undesirable outcome. A **setSize( )** method for squares should just take one parameter.

What can we do about this situation? Before throwing away inheritance, let's try to patch the problem up by other means. One way to do so is to nullify the negative effects of the inherited **setSize( )** method by overriding it in the subclass. For example, we might add the following method to the **Square** class:

```
public void setSize(int w, int h) { width = w; height = w; }
```

which ignores the parameter **h** and uses **w** for both the height and the width. This method allows users to modify the size of the square but only in a way that preserves its "squareness."

Unfortunately, this solution is not a very good one either. To see why, suppose that the user adds the following method to his program:

```
public int stretchAndFetch(Rectangle r, int dx) {
    r.setSize(r.getWidth() + dx, r.getHeight());
    return r.getHeight();
}
```

When this method is executed, the user expects that a rectangle will be stretched horizontally by the amount **dx**. But if, unbeknownst to the user, a **Square** object is passed as the first argument, then the height will be adjusted by **dx** as well, and the new height will be returned by the method. The user will be surprised or confused to see this new height because the user expected there to be only horizontal stretching. Code is not considered elegant if the user of that code is surprised or confused by the behavior of that code.

Our problem here is that the subclass does not have behavior consistent with the behavior of its superclass. Such consistent behavior is necessary for elegant code. This guideline can also be phrased in terms of astonishment: *If a client thinks she has a reference to an object of type A but actually has a reference to an object of subtype B, there should be no surprises when she invokes methods on the object.* This guideline is called the *principle of least astonishment.*

For example, a client using a **Square** object as the value of **r** in the **stretchAndFetch( )** method above will almost surely be surprised by its behavior, indicating a problem with the inheritance hierarchy.

What are the implications of following the principle of least astonishment? The answer depends on what we mean by a "surprise." There are two definitions of that word that we could use in this context. In the more restrictive case, a surprise is any difference in the behaviors of objects of the two classes. If we use this definition, then, by the principle of least astonishment, we are not allowed to change any of the inherited behavior in the subclass, which means that overriding superclass methods is pretty much prohibited. Therefore, subclasses can only add new behavior rather than modify existing behavior. The new behavior is invisible when the subclass objects are being treated as if they were of the type of the superclass. This restrictive version of the principle could better be called the *principle of no astonishment.*

A less restrictive definition of surprise would be to say that a surprise is any difference in the *documented* behavior of objects of the two classes. If the external documentation for the **stretchAndFetch( )** method says that only the width is stretched, then the behavior of this method when a square is the argument is breaking the guidelines. However, if the documentation mentions nothing about the behavior of the method with regard to the height of the rectangle, then the behavior with squares does not break the guideline. In that case, it is perfectly acceptable to have the square stretched both horizontally and vertically, and the principle of least astonishment will be satisfied.

You may have noticed another aspect of the square/rectangle example. The original *is-a* relationship between geometric squares and rectangles, as viewed by mathematicians, holds only because, in mathematics, all geometric shapes are fixed, or immutable. If a mathematician talks about stretching a rectangle, she is really talking about creating a new rectangle rather than modifying the old one. Therefore, if the **Rectangle** class and **Square** class were made immutable, they would more closely model the mathematician's idea of rectangles and squares. In fact, if the classes were made immutable by removing the **setTopLeft( )** and **setSize( )** methods, it would be perfectly acceptable to make the **Square** class a subclass of the **Rectangle** class.

Similar Behavior

As mentioned in the preceding section, the problem with the *is-a* relationship between the original **Square** and **Rectangle** classes was the fact that the **Square** and **Rectangle**'s behaviors didn't match. That is, a **Square** is not a **Rectangle** if a **Rectangle** has the ability to modify its width separately from its height. Another way of saying this is that the public methods of the **Rectangle** class were not all appropriate for the **Square** class. But what happens if we do have similar public interfaces with similar behaviors between two of our classes, in addition to code reuse and an *is-a* relationship? Do we now have a sufficient reason for using subclassing?

Consider a classical example often used to introduce the concept of inheritance, namely, the classes of **Student** and **Person**. Clearly, a student "is a" person (as long as the student is attending an elementary school, high school, or college, for example, and not dog obedience school). A student, like a person, has all the properties and behavior of a person, such as name, address, and date of birth, and, in addition, has other attributes like the school in which he or she is currently enrolled, the number of credits earned, the grade point average, and the class schedule. The student and person clearly have common behavior, and so there is an opportunity for code reuse.

Most naturally, you could argue that the **Student** class should be a subclass of **Person**. But should it? Let us suppose we include this inheritance in our design and consider a large university that uses our design to store its records on each student. Furthermore, suppose the university stores its employee records in **Employee** objects (where **Employee** is, by following the same line of reasoning, another subclass of **Person**). See Figure 16.5.

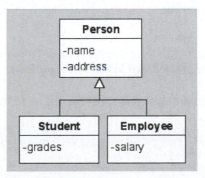

FIGURE 16-5. An inheritance hierarchy among **Person**, **Student**, and **Employee**.

Now, suppose one of the students graduates and starts to work for the university, and so becomes an employee. Or suppose the student becomes an employee of the university while still a student. What must the university do to update its records in this case?

In the case of a student graduating and becoming an employee, the university could just replace the **Student** object with an **Employee** object. However, this approach has two potential problems. If there are many references to the **Student** object in the university's records, those references will all need to be updated to refer to the new **Employee** object instead. Also, there might be data that needs to be preserved in the **Student** object, for example, the student's transcript, that is not included in the **Employee** object.

Alternatively, the university could create two distinct objects to represent the person: an active **Employee** object and an inactive **Student** object that might be archived. However, this approach is inelegant because it duplicates all the common **Person** data in both objects.

The problems could be resolved easily if it were possible to change an object dynamically to belong to a different class (and so change the **Student** object into an **Employee** object). However, such a change is not possible in Java.

A better approach avoids inheritance altogether and looks at the student and the employee as *roles* being played by the person. Roles are typically temporary aspects of an object. In our example, a person is not always a student or an employee, and so these are temporary roles. Because of the temporary nature of the roles but the more permanent nature of the person, inheritance is not an appropriate way to associate them.

A better design uses *delegation* (also called *referencing*), in which a **Student** object has an underlying **Person** to whom it refers. In this case, we could have exactly one **Person** object for each real person, which would be independent of all the roles currently played by that person.

For example, the **Person** class might be defined as follows:

```java
public class Person {
  private String name;
  private String address;

  public String getAddress() { return address; }

  // ...other methods and data...
}
```

Then, as new roles are played, objects representing those roles, such as **Student** or **Employee** objects, can be created that include a reference to the **Person** playing those roles.

For example, the **Student** class might be defined as follows:

```java
public class Student {
  private Person me;
  private AcademicRecord myRecord;

  public String getAddress() { return me.getAddress(); }
```

```
public float getGPA() {
    // ...compute it from the academic record...
}

// ...other methods and data...
}
```

Notice how any **Person**-specific behavior required of a **Student** is performed by forwarding the request to the **Person** object. For example, if **Student** objects are asked for their addresses, the **Student** objects, in turn, delegate that task to their underlying **Person** objects. The **Student** object handles student-specific tasks, such as computing GPAs and managing course schedules, and the underlying **Person** object handles all personal tasks.

Similarly, the **Employee** class might have a reference to the **Person** being employed. See Figure 16.6 for a diagram of these alternatives using the **Student**, **Employee**, and **Person** classes.

By using such delegation of responsibilities, it now becomes easy to keep track of the changing role of a person. When a person initially becomes a student, both a **Student** object and **Person** object are created, and the **Student** object is given a reference to the **Person** object. If and when the student becomes an employee, a new **Employee** object is created that refers to the same **Person** object. In this situation, it is perfectly acceptable to have both **Student** and **Employee** objects referring to the same **Person** object. When the person no longer plays one of the roles (e.g., if the student graduates or quits her job at the university), that role can be deleted or archived and the other roles can remain active. In this way, the **Person** object can be considered to exist permanently, but the person's roles can come and go. Furthermore, there is no duplication of data.

The following guideline summarizes this discussion: *If class B models a role played by class A, especially a temporary role, then B should not be a subclass of A. Instead objects of class B should have references to objects of class A.*

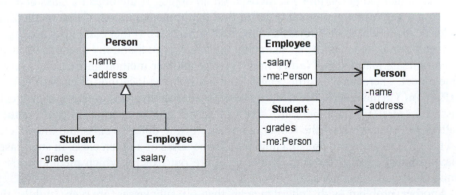

FIGURE 16-6. Inheritance (left) versus delegation (right).

Polymorphism

What if we have a situation in which we have code reuse, an *is-a* relationship, similar public behaviors between our classes, and we have the need for polymorphism? Do we now have a sufficient reason for using subclassing? Probably so.

For example, suppose you wish to create a new class **B** to be used as the argument to a method whose parameter is of type **A**, where **A** is a class. In that case, you have no choice but to make **B** a subclass of **A**.

This situation arises more often than you might at first think. For example, any method that doesn't care what type of object is passed in as an argument will have a parameter of type **Object**. Since all other classes automatically extend **Object**, polymorphism is being used here.

Abstract classes also naturally involve polymorphism. If you want to utilize the features of such a class, you must extend it.

Note that, in a well-designed system in which the guideline *Code to interfaces* has been followed, as many variables and parameters as possible will have an interface type instead of a class type, thus reducing the need for subclassing. But it is not always possible or appopriate to use interfaces everywhere. For example, the Java Swing package, discussed in the next part of this book, is a GUI framework in which much of the difficult work of dealing with buttons, windows, and menus has been implemented for you in several packages. Many of the classes in those packages extend other classes in the packages to give them needed functionality and to make it as easy as possible for the user to build a system from the provided components.

Costs of Inheritance

By now, you are hopefully realizing that inheritance, as wonderful as it may have first sounded, should not be used with abandon if you want a well-designed system. There are other costs to be considered when using inheritance, as well.

One problem with inheritance, especially a deep inheritance tree with many generations, is that the code for a method of a class low in the tree may be spread out among all its ancestors higher in the tree, which makes it harder for the reader of the code to follow the flow of execution. For example, suppose someone is reading code and sees that a method **getName( )** is invoked on an object. If the object's class does not implement **getName( )**, then, in order to find the implementation of that method, the reader needs to look to the object's immediate superclass. If that class does not implement **getName( )**, then a further search up the inheritance hierarchy needs to be made. To complicate matters, **getName( )** may invoke another method **getPerson( )** on the same object. There need be little relationship between the locations of **getName( )** and **getPerson( )** in the inheritance tree, and so the reader again needs to start at the object's class and search up the inheritance tree to find the implementation of **getPerson( )**. Matters are even worse if the reader is not sure of the object's class and knows only that the object belongs to one of a number of subclasses of a given class. In such cases, it is extremely hard, if not impossible, to figure out exactly which method body of which class gets executed at any given time.

Another problem with inheritance is that all subclasses are very tightly tied with their superclasses. This coupling comes from the fact that, to guarantee certain behavior in a subclass, that subclass needs to know significant parts of the implementation of the methods of the superclasses. However, the details of this problem are beyond the scope of this text.

Because of these costs and for all the other reasons mentioned in this section, a software designer should always carefully consider all the options when deciding on the relationships among classes. For example, sometimes two classes should be associated via a common interface, sometimes they should be connected by an association such as delegation, and sometimes inheritance is best.

TRY THIS 16-1 A PURE QUEUE IMPLEMENTED USING DELEGATION

```
PureQueue.java
PureQueueDemo.java
```

This project demonstrates how to use delegation instead of inheritance to implement a pure queue.

As you know from earlier in this book, a stack is a list in which elements can be accessed in last-in, first-out (LIFO) order only. A *queue* is a similar data structure except that its elements can be accessed in first-in, first-out (FIFO) order only. Queues are used in a multitude of places, including check-in lines at airline counters and check-out lines at supermarkets. Queues are used in computers in a variety of ways, such as managing processes. If there are several processes vying for one CPU, then they are lined up in a queue. The operation of adding an element to the end of the queue is traditionally called *enqueue*, and the operation of removing and obtaining the element at the head of the queue is called *dequeue*.

Suppose we are working in an industrial setting and we need a queue. Furthermore, we want the queue to be "pure;" that is, it must support only the queue operations just described. This will prevent the elements in the queue from being accessed out of order. In our pure queue, we want these methods to be called **enqueue( )** and **dequeue( )**. We also want our queue to have a **size( )** method that returns the number of elements in the queue and a **peek( )** method that obtains the element at the head of the queue but does not remove it from the queue. For convenience, an override of **toString( )** is also desired. How can we create such a queue? There are at least three ways to proceed.

One way is to implement a **PureQueue** class "from scratch," for example, using an array to hold the data, similar to the way that **SimpleStack** was implemented in several Try This examples in earlier chapters. For educational reasons, it was valuable to create such a stack class because it demonstrated several key aspects of Java. However, an important tenet in software development in the real world is *Don't reinvent the wheel*. In other words, if there is a class that already does what you want, don't create a new class to do it. Instead, reuse the existing class. It turns out that there is already an **ArrayDeque** class in the Java library in the **java.util** package that does everything we want our **PureQueue** class to do and more. Following the tenet mentioned above, it makes more sense to use that class instead of implementing our **PureQueue** class from scratch.

Therefore, a second way to proceed is to create a **PureQueue** class that inherits from **java.util.ArrayDeque**. However, the **ArrayDeque** class is not a pure FIFO queue. For example, it has methods such as **push( )** and **pop( )** that allow it to be used like a stack. If **PureQueue** were a subclass of **java.util.ArrayDeque**, then **PureQueue** would inherit more than just the desired five methods. Furthermore, the **ArrayDeque** class calls the enqueue and dequeue methods "offer" and "poll", which are not the names we want to use.

A third alternative is to use delegation. That is, create a **PureQueue** class that maintains a reference to an **ArrayDeque** from the **java.util** package. In this way, the **PureQueue** class can have only the desired set of methods, but it will implement those methods by delegating all the work to the **ArrayDeque** class that it references. We will use this third approach in this project.

STEP-BY-STEP

1. Create a file called **PureQueue.java** and type in the following code:

```java
import java.util.ArrayDeque;

class PureQueue<E> {
  private ArrayDeque<E> data;

  PureQueue() {
    data = new ArrayDeque<E>();
  }

  void enqueue(E o) { data.offer(o); }

  E dequeue() { return data.poll(); }

  E peek() { return data.peek(); }

  int size() { return data.size(); }

  public String toString() {
    return data.toString();
  }
}
```

Notice how the class has an instance variable **data** of type **java.util.ArrayDeque**. Notice also how easy it is to implement all of the methods. All the real work is being done by the **data** object. By using delegation in this way, we have created a class with only the methods we want and we can implement those methods very easily.

2. To test this class, create a file called **PureQueueDemo.java** and type in the following code:

```java
class PureQueueDemo {
```

```
    public static void main(String[] args) {
        PureQueue<String> q = new PureQueue<String>();
        System.out.println(q);
        q.enqueue("3");
        q.enqueue("abc");
        System.out.println(q);
        q.dequeue();
        System.out.println(q);
    }
}
```

3. Now compile both files and run the **PureQueueDemo** class's **main( )** method. You should see the following output:

```
[]
[3, abc]
[abc]
```

Progress Check

1. What does the principle of least astonishment say?
2. If **A** and **B** are classes and if a method has a parameter of type **A** and if you can use an object of type **B** as the argument for the method, then **B** must extend **A**. True or False?
3. An alternative to inheritance that one should always consider is _____.

DESIGN PATTERNS

We have now discussed the advantages and disadvantages of many software designs, and we have shown some guidelines and rules to follow that can help you develop good designs. In this section, we introduce more tools to help you create good software designs. These tools, which can be thought of as some of the software industry's best practices for solving problems within certain constraints, are called *design patterns*. The cataloging and organization of these patterns has been going on since the late 1980s. Names were given to these patterns so that software developers would have a vocabulary for talking about designs at a higher level of abstraction than would otherwise be possible. For example, designers on teams can now say things like "Let's use the Decorator pattern here to handle all the options."

Answers:

1. If a client thinks she has a reference to an object of type **A** but actually has a reference to an object of subtype **B**, there should be no surprises when she invokes methods on the object.
2. True.
3. delegation

In this section, we will introduce two of the simplest design patterns so that you can get a feeling for what design patterns are.

Adapter Pattern

One of the simplest, but very useful, patterns is the *Adapter* pattern. A non-software-related example of the Adapter pattern will be given first. In the United States, the electrical plugs for most appliances have two flat prongs and an optional third round prong that fit into standard American electrical outlets. However, in other countries, the outlets are designed for appliances with plugs that have two or three round prongs or flat prongs oriented in different directions or in different positions relative to each other. The voltage and frequency of the electrical current may also differ in other countries. In those countries, the electrical interface does not match the interface for American appliances. So how can you use American appliances abroad? The solution is to purchase adapter plugs, with slots on one side, into which American appliances fit, and prongs on the other side that fit into the other country's outlets. In other words, the solution is not to change the appliances or the outlets but instead create an adapter that allows the appliances to use the outlets. Let us now see how this pattern naturally appears in software design.

Suppose you are working on a team that built a large front end (for example, a web interface) for one of your company's main applications. The back end of the application is another large system that contains all the data (maybe in a database) and contains the tools and methods for fetching and for manipulating that data. The front end was designed to use the interface of the back end; that is, it was designed to call the methods of the back end to get and manipulate the back end data.

Now suppose another company likes your front end so much that they want to use it with their back end. But what if the other company's back end has a different interface than the back end for which your front end was designed? That is, suppose the other company's back end has a completely different set of methods for fetching and manipulating the data in the back end. What is the other company to do to get your front end working with their back end? The problem that you have is incompatible interfaces, and so your front end cannot communicate with the other company's back end.

One way for the other company to fix the problem would be to modify the front end so that it uses the interface of their back end. Alternatively, they could fix the problem by modifying their back end to use the interface expected by your front end. A third way would be to make some of the changes in your front end and some in their back end. However, you are asking for new bugs if you change the existing working code. How can the other company get your front end and their back end to communicate with the minimum changes to existing code?

An elegant way is to provide a new class to act as an "adapter" to adapt one interface to another interface. Objects of this class sit between the front end and back end. The front end communicates with the adapter class instead of the back end, and the adapter communicates with the back end. More precisely, the adapter will provide the interface that the front end expects, but it will actually get the data from the back end and transform it into the data that the front end expects.

The use of an adapter class, as in this example, to adapt an existing class to a different interface is what is meant by the Adapter pattern.

To show an example of such an adapter class, let's move away from large front ends and back ends. Instead, let's consider the following simple interface and classes:

```java
class Printer {
  void printRect(RectI r) {
    System.out.println(r.getWidth() + ", " + r.getHeight());
  }
}

interface RectI {
  int getWidth();
  int getHeight();
}

class SimpleRect implements RectI {
  int width, height;

  SimpleRect(int w, int h) {
    width = w; height = h;
  }

  public int getWidth() { return width; }
  public int getHeight() { return height; }
}

class NonConformingRect {
  int top, left, bottom, right;

  NonConformingRect(int a, int b, int c, int d) {
    top = a; left = b; bottom = c; right = d;
  }

  public int getTop() { return top; }
  public int getLeft() { return left; }
  public int getBottom() { return bottom; }
  public int getRight() { return right; }
}
```

The **Printer** class is our "front end." Its **printRect( )** method receives, as its argument, an object that implements the **RectI** interface. The **SimpleRect** class implements that interface, and so objects of that class can be passed as arguments to the **printRect( )** method. The **SimpleRect** class is our "back end."

Now suppose we want to pass **NonConformingRect** objects to **printRect( )**. This class does not implement the interface **RectI**, so instances cannot be passed as the argument to **printRect( )**. To be able to pass in **NonConformingRect**s, you could change the **Printer** class or the **RectI** interface, but changing existing, working code is not the way to handle this situation. Instead, we will use the following adapter class:

```java
class RectAdapter implements RectI {
  NonConformingRect ncRect;
```

```
RectAdapter(NonConformingRect r) {
  ncRect = r;
}

public int getWidth() { return ncRect.getRight() - ncRect.getLeft(); }
public int getHeight() { return ncRect.getBottom() - ncRect.getTop(); }
}
```

Notice that this class implements the **RectI** interface and so can be passed to **printRect( )**. Also note that it gets its data from a **NonConformingRect**.

When you use this adapter class, *no* changes need to be made to existing classes. Here is a complete program that demonstrates all these classes in action:

```
class Printer {
  void printRect(RectI r) {
    System.out.println(r.getWidth() + ", " + r.getHeight());
  }
}

interface RectI {
  int getWidth();
  int getHeight();
}

class SimpleRect implements RectI {
  int width, height;

  SimpleRect(int w, int h) {
    width = w; height = h;
  }

  public int getWidth() { return width; }
  public int getHeight() { return height; }
}


class NonConformingRect {
  int top, left, bottom, right;

  NonConformingRect(int a, int b, int c, int d) {
    top = a; left = b; bottom = c; right = d;
  }

  public int getTop() { return top; }
  public int getLeft() { return left; }
  public int getBottom() { return bottom; }
  public int getRight() { return right; }
}

class RectAdapter implements RectI {
  NonConformingRect ncRect;
```

```
RectAdapter(NonConformingRect r) {
    ncRect = r;
}

public int getWidth() { return ncRect.getRight() - ncRect.getLeft(); }
public int getHeight() { return ncRect.getBottom() - ncRect.getTop(); }
}

class AdapterDemo {
    public static void main(String[] args) {
        Printer prntr = new Printer();
        prntr.printRect(new SimpleRect(3,4));
        prntr.printRect(new RectAdapter(new NonConformingRect(1,2,3,4)));
    }
}
```

Notice how, in the main class, the **NonConformingRect** object is wrapped inside a **RectAdapter** object before being passed to the **printRect( )** method. When this program is run, you get the following output:

```
3, 4
2, 2
```

Observer Pattern

Consider a program that a bank might use to keep track of savings accounts. Suppose that it has the following **SavingsAccount** class for storing information about one account.

```
class SavingsAccount {
    private String owner;
    private int acctNumber;
    private int balance;   // in US dollars

    SavingsAccount(String o, int a) {
        owner = o;
        acctNumber = a;
        balance = 0;
    }

    // positive amount means deposit
    // negative amount means withdrawal
    void changeBalance(int amount) {
        balance += amount;
    }

    int getBalance() { return balance; }
    int getAcctNumber() { return acctNumber; }
    String getOwner() { return owner; }
}
```

Suppose also that many places access each savings account, such as ATMs, the various branches of the bank, and retail stores that accept a debit card on the account.

Now suppose that the bank decides to institute a new safety feature that flags all withdrawals over $1,000 so that the bank can check for fraud. How can such a feature be implemented?

One way would be to modify the code in all the places where transactions take place so that they flag large withdrawals. This approach requires far too many changes to existing code. A better way would be for the **SavingsAccount** class to handle the flagging. All we would need to do is modify the **changeBalance( )** method to test for large withdrawals and, if found, check for fraud. Under such a design, the class could use the following implementation of the **changeBalance( )** method:

```
void changeBalance(int amount) {
  balance += amount;
  if(amount < -1000)
    checkForFraud(amount);
}


void checkForFraud(int amount) {
  System.out.println("Checking for fraudulent " +
            "withdrawal of amount: " + amount);
}
```

Note that a change needed to be made to only one class because the **SavingsAccount** class handles the fraud using its **checkForFraud( )** method.

However, this version is not ideal because now the savings account is no longer cohesive. It both stores account information and checks for fraud. Instead, a separate **FraudHandler** class should handle checking for fraud:

```
class FraudHandler {
  void checkForFraud(int amount, SavingsAccount acct) {
    System.out.println("Checking for fraudulent withdrawal" +
                " of amount: " + amount + " from" +
                " account " + acct.getAcctNumber());
  }
}
```

Using this new class, the method **changeBalance( )** looks like this:

```
void changeBalance(int amount) {
  balance += amount;
  if(amount < -1000)
    fraudHandler.checkForFraud(amount, this);
}
```

In this version, the **SavingsAccount** class has an instance variable **fraudHandler** of type **FraudHandler** to which it delegates all fraud handling. Now the savings account is more cohesive. It is a bit inelegant for the savings account to have to maintain a reference to a fraud handler, since we would like to minimize coupling between classes, but we could live with this situation. Note that this division of labor has another advantage. The **FraudHandler** class can be reused if the bank wants to check other kinds of accounts for fraud.

However, suppose now that the bank decides to make more money by charging customers a fee every time they withdraw money from their savings account (after all, they are not saving much if they are always withdrawing money, right?). How can this new feature be implemented?

As before, we could modify the code in all the locations where transactions occur, but that involves changing too much code. Also, as before, we could have the savings account charge the fee, but, as before, that will reduce the cohesiveness of the **SavingsAccount** class by having it handle fees in addition to maintaining the account. A better solution would be to have a separate reusable **FeeHandler** class handle the fee, just as the **FraudHandler** deals with fraud. If the **SavingsAccount** class has an instance variable **feeHandler** of type **FeeHandler**, then the **changeBalance( )** method can be rewritten like this:

```java
void changeBalance(int amount) {
   balance += amount;
   if(amount < -1000)
      fraudHandler.checkForFraud(amount, this);
   if(amount < 0)
      feeHandler.handleWithdrawalFee(this);
}
```

This design nicely separates the responsibilities among various classes. However, the **SavingsAccount** class is now a bit more inelegant by having a reference to a fee handler.

But now, what if other actions need to be added, for example, a rewards program for people who maintain a balance of at least $10,000 every month, or an overdraft fee if the balance becomes less than 0? If we implement these new features in a similar way to the fraud detection and withdrawal fee features, our **SavingsAccount** class will have to be changed again and will be even more coupled to other classes. In addition, suppose the bank decides that $1,000 is not the appropriate limit for checking for fraud. In that case, the **SavingsAccount** class will need to be changed yet again. What can we do to minimize both the code changes and the coupling?

Let's summarize the situation. The **SavingsAccount** class needs to notify other classes when a special event occurs, namely, an amount being withdrawn or deposited. How can it do so without being tightly coupled to those classes?

Our solution is to use the *Observer* pattern. In this design pattern, there are *observers,* and there are *subjects* to be observed. The subjects are also called "publishers" or "broadcasters," and the observers are also called "subscribers" or "listeners." The publishers maintain a list of subscribers, and, whenever there is something to publish, they notify all the subscribers. In this pattern, a publisher can have any number of subscribers. (For an object to become a subscriber, it needs to ask the publisher to add it to the publisher's subscription list.)

In our example, the savings account is the publisher and the fraud and fee handlers are the subscribers. To use the Observer pattern here, the publisher (the savings account) needs to maintain a list of subscribers and notify them whenever the balance changes. It could maintain a list of subscribers using an array, for example. But what type should the array be? The answer is to use an interface. That is, define a new **BalanceChangeHandler** interface:

```
interface BalanceChangeHandler {
  void balanceChanged(int change, SavingsAccount acct);
}
```

and then add a new instance variable to the **SavingsAccount** class that refers to an array of **BalanceChangeHandler**s.

All the handlers, such as the fee and fraud-detection handlers, need to implement this interface and then register with the savings account. By registering, they get added to the array of subscribers. Then, whenever the balance changes, the savings account will notify all registered subscribers by calling their **balanceChanged( )** methods. In those methods, they can handle the change any way they want.

Here is the complete code, including a short demonstration program to test the classes.

```
class SavingsAccount {
  String owner;
  int acctNumber;
  int balance;   // in US dollars
  BalanceChangeHandler[] subscribers;
  int numSubscribers;

  SavingsAccount(String o, int a) {
    owner = o;
    acctNumber = a;
    balance = 0;
    subscribers = new BalanceChangeHandler[20];
    // At most 20 subscribers are allowed
    numSubscribers = 0;
  }

  void addHandler(BalanceChangeHandler h) {
    if(numSubscribers < 20) {
      subscribers[numSubscribers] = h;
      numSubscribers++;
    }
  }

  // positive amount means deposit
  // negative amount means withdrawal
  void changeBalance(int amount) {
    if(amount != 0) {

      // Change the balance
      balance += amount;

      // Notify all subscribers of the change
      for(int i = 0; i < numSubscribers; i++)
        subscribers[i].balanceChanged(amount, this);
    }
  }
}
```

```java
    int getBalance() { return balance; }
    int getAcctNumber() { return acctNumber; }
    String getOwner() { return owner; }
}


class FeeHandler implements BalanceChangeHandler {

  public void balanceChanged(int change, SavingsAccount acct) {
    System.out.println("Deducting a fee from account " +
                        acct.getAcctNumber());
  }
}

class FraudHandler implements BalanceChangeHandler {

  public void balanceChanged(int change, SavingsAccount acct) {
    System.out.println("Checking for fraudulent withdrawal" +
                        " of amount: " + change + " from" +
                        " account " + acct.getAcctNumber());
  }
}

interface BalanceChangeHandler {
  void balanceChanged(int change, SavingsAccount acct);
}

class SavingsAccountDemo {
  public static void main(String[] args) {
    SavingsAccount acct = new SavingsAccount("Sam", 1234);
    FeeHandler feeHandler = new FeeHandler();
    FraudHandler fraudHandler = new FraudHandler();

    acct.addHandler(feeHandler);
    acct.addHandler(fraudHandler);

    acct.changeBalance(0); // nothing happens
    acct.changeBalance(10);
    acct.changeBalance(-10);
  }
}
```

When the demo program is run, the following output appears:

```
Deducting a fee from account 1234
Checking for fraudulent withdrawal of amount: 10 from account 1234
Deducting a fee from account 1234
Checking for fraudulent withdrawal of amount: -10 from account 1234
```

Let us summarize all the advantages of using the Observer pattern. First, you can register many different handlers with the savings account without having to change the code of the **SavingsAccount** class. Second, the coupling is minimized between the savings account and the handlers. That is, the savings account need know nothing about the handlers other than that they implement the **BalanceChangeHandler** interface, which allows the account to call the handlers' **balanceChanged( )** methods.

It should be mentioned that the **java.util** package provides a framework that supports the Observer pattern. This framework is discussed in Chapter 24.

These two patterns (the Adapter and Observer) are just samples of the dozens of design patterns that provide best-practice solutions to common software problems. As you learn more about software development, you will want to learn more about these other patterns so that you can become conversant in the design pattern language.

Progress Check

1. The software industry's best practices for solving problems with certain constraints are called _____.
2. The use of a class to adapt an existing class to a different interface is the _____ pattern.
3. In the Observer pattern, there are two kinds of classes involved: the publishers and _____.

EXERCISES

1. For methods, classes, and variables, you should use _____ names.
2. All the principles discussed in this chapter are iron-clad rules that must be followed in order to have elegant software. True or False?
3. A good programmer writes self-documenting code and so never needs to add internal comments. True or False?
4. It is generally better to put all the important methods in one class and make most of the other classes simple servant classes. True or False?
5. Out-of-date documentation is better than no documentation at all. True or False?
6. A method with method chaining of the form **a.getB( ).getC( ).getD( ). doSomething( )** does not obey _____.
7. Suppose you have a **Person** class with instance variables containing the person's name, birth date, address, spouse, children, and occupation. According to the Expert pattern, this class should have methods that handle any manipulations of this data that are needed by other classes. However, an unlimited

Answers:

1. design patterns
2. Adapter
3. the subscribers

number of manipulations of a **Person** object can be performed. What is the correct number of methods that the **Person** class should have?

8. A class typically has both instance variables and methods. Consider the two extreme cases: a class **A** that has several instance variables but no methods and a class **B** that has several methods but no instance variables. Which one of the principles discussed in this chapter is most likely violated by such classes?

9. When you are trying to reach an executive in a company, you have at least three choices:

    A. Call and be put on hold until the executive is free.

    B. Keep calling back every few minutes until the executive is free.

    C. Leave a message asking the executive to call you back when she is free.

    Which one of these choices corresponds most closely to the Observer pattern?

10. What is one flaw in the following class that makes it inelegant?

```
class NamedObject {
    private String name;
    NamedObject(String n) { name = n; }
    void setName(String n) { name = n; }
}
```

11. Consider the following method in a class **B**. Assume that class **A** has methods **load( )**, **sort( )**, **store( )**.

```
void loadSortAndStore(A a) {
    a.load();
    a.sort();
    a.store();
}
```

    Is this method elegant? Why or why not? If not, explain what should be done to make it elegant.

12. If a class has an integer instance variable **x**, is it better to make **x** publicly accessible so that other objects can read and write it, or to make **x** private and add a **getX( )** and a **setX( )** method for reading and writing **x**?

13. Suppose you have **Person** objects and **Location** objects and you need to keep track of the place of birth of each **Person**. There are at least three ways to organize this information:

    A. Each **Person** object has an instance variable of type **Location** that stores the place of birth.

    B. Each **Location** keeps a collection of references to **Person** objects corresponding to the people born at that location.

    C. A third object keeps a table of **Person** objects and their place-of-birth **Location** objects.

    Discuss the advantages and disadvantages of each of these three designs.

14. To implement a **Rectangle** class that stores its position and size, you could use four integer instance variables **x**, **y**, **width**, and **height** where (x,y) is the

top left corner of the rectangle, or you could use eight variables **x1, y1, x2, y2, x3, y3, x4**, and **y4**, that store the (x,y) coordinates of the four corners of the rectangle. Which of these two implementations is better and why?

15. Suppose you are writing a method **getChildren( )** in a **Person** class that returns an array of **Person**s. Then, among other things, you need to deal with the case where the person on whom the method is invoked has no children. What should your method return in that case? Should it return **null** or an array of length 0?

16. A class designer is designing a **Person** class that he wants to be as popular and as reusable as the **String** class, and so he is attempting to maximize the reusability through the addition of as many methods as he can think of. The constructor and methods he has added are listed below. Which of the methods should not be included in a well-designed **Person** class?

A. **Person(int birthDate, String name, String address) // constructor**

B. **String getName( )**

C. **void setName(String name)**

D. **String toString( ) // returns the name of the person**

E. **int getSSN( ) // returns the person's Social Security Number**

F. **String getSSNAsString( ) // returns the SSN as a String**

G. **Person[] siblings( ) // returns an array of the siblings of the person**

H. **Race getRace( )**

I. **Person getBoss( ) // returns the person who is employing this person**

J. **boolean isDogOwner( )**

K. **boolean isUSCitizen( )**

L. **String getAddress( )**

M. **int numberOfCarsOwned( )**

N. **int getBirthdate( )**

O. **void setBirthdate(int date)**

17. Suppose you were told to implement a class whose objects need to store 20 pieces of data and the data are of several types. Some people might argue that you should store each piece of data in a separate instance variable. Others might argue that it is ludicrous to have one instance variable for each piece of data, and so it would be better to store all the data in one instance variable, such as an array **data** of type **Object**. For example, a **Person** object could store the person's first name in location **data[0]**, the last name in **data[1]**, the address in **data[2]**, the age in **data[3]**, and so on. Give your opinion on these two approaches. Discuss the approach you would use.

18. Come up with a non-software-related example of the Adapter pattern other than the example of electrical outlets mentioned in this chapter.

19. Consider the classes **ParttimeEmployee** and **FulltimeEmployee**. A part-time employee has fewer benefits than a full-time employee, and so the **FulltimeEmployee** class needs more fields than **ParttimeEmployee**. Therefore, to avoid duplication, it would seem to make sense to make

FullTimeEmployee a subclass of **ParttimeEmployee** so that it can inherit the superclass's instance variables. Is this approach elegant?

20. Tell what is inelegant about the following class. *Hint:* It relates to class invariants.

```java
/* Objects of this class store a random double between 0 and 1.*/
public class RandomDoubleStore {
  double value = 0.0;


  public RandomDoubleStore() { }

  public void initialize() {
    value = Math.random();
  }
}
```

21. The text mentioned that every method should return a value or modify the state of one or more objects, but not both. It also mentioned that the traditional **pop( )** method for a stack does not follow this convention since it both removes the top value from the stack and returns it. If you were forced to change a stack's implementation of **pop( )** so that it followed the convention, what is the simplest way to do so?

22. Suppose a **Person** object has a **getHeight( )** method that returns the person's height. Consider the following method:

```java
int getAverageHeight(Person p1, Person p2, Person p3) {
  int p1Height = p1.getHeight();
  int p2Height = p2.getHeight();
  int p3Height = p3.getHeight();


  return (p1Height + p2Height + p3Height) / 3;
}
```

As you can see, it computes and returns the average height of the three people. Why isn't this method very elegant? Suggest a change to make it more elegant.

23. Suppose there is a **Nameable** interface defining one method:

```java
interface Nameable {
  String getName();
}
```

and suppose there is a class **Person** that implements the **Nameable** interface. Finally, suppose, in another class, there is the following method:

```java
String nameOf(Person p) { return p.getName(); }
```

What is a simple way to make the **nameOf( )** method more useful?

24. Suppose a person needs to model the concept of balloons, and so, wishing to use inheritance to make an elegant design, the person creates a **RubberObject** class and a **Balloon** subclass. Can you see any problems with this design?

25. A person might say that "Fluffy is a cat" and "A cat is a mammal," and therefore **Fluffy** should be a subclass of **Cat** and **Cat** should be a subclass of **Mammal**, because we have two *is-a* relationships. What is wrong with this reasoning?

26. Suppose a **NamedObject** class has a constructor that takes, as its only parameter, a string that is the initial name of the object. It also has a **setName( )** method that takes a string as its parameter for changing the name of the object, and a **getName( )** method that returns the name. Now suppose you want to create an **ImmutableNamedObject** class whose initial name cannot be changed. One way to implement such a class is to make it a subclass of **NamedObject** and, in the subclass, override the **setName( )** method so that it does nothing. What do you think of the elegance of this approach?

27. Suppose a class **RentalCarCompany** has three integer instance variables, **numInUse**, **numAvail**, and **total**, that refer to the number of cars that are currently being rented, the number currently available to be rented, and the total number of cars (the sum of the other two amounts).
    A. Why is this class not elegant?
    B. Suppose it has the following method for updating the number of cars, for example, when some cars are wrecked, bought, or sold:

    ```
    void updateNumCars(int newInUse, int newAvail, int newTotal) {
        numInUse = newInUse; numAvail = newAvail; total = newTotal;
    }
    ```

    What is inelegant about this method?

28. There are two ways that information can be transferred from a source to a destination. In the *pull* model, the destination goes to the source and gets the information (the destination "pulls" the information from the source to itself). In the *push* model, the source sends the information to the destination (the source "pushes" the information from itself to the destination). Which model most closely corresponds to the Observer pattern?

PART TWO

Introducing GUI Programming With Swing

Part Two introduces the Swing toolkit. Swing is Java's modern approach to creating graphical user interfaces (GUIs). Part Two begins by presenting the Swing design philosophy and several core concepts. Subsequent chapters explore several Swing controls, the menu system, painting, and the creation of Swing-based applets.

Note: A full description of the Swing classes, interfaces, and methods is found in the JDK documentation, which is available on-line, from Oracle.

CHAPTER 17

Swing Fundamentals

With the exception of the applet examples shown in Chapter 15, all of the programs in Part One have been console-based. This means that they do not make use of a graphical user interface (GUI). While console-based programs are excellent for teaching the basics of Java, many real-world applications will be GUI-based. Therefore, this and the next four chapters explore Java's modern GUI toolkit: Swing.

Swing is a collection of classes and interfaces that offer a rich set of visual components, such as push buttons, text fields, scroll bars, check boxes, trees, tables, and menus, that can be tailored to fit nearly any need. By using Swing, your application will have a modern user interface based on GUI controls. This means that you can create programs that look like and act like other GUI applications with which you are familiar.

The purpose of this chapter is to introduce Swing, including its history, basic concepts, design philosophy, and core features. As you will see, Swing is comprised of many interrelated elements. This interrelatedness makes Swing a powerful, yet streamlined, framework. It also makes it important to understand how these elements work together. This chapter also introduces an important Java feature: the event. Among other uses, the event is the mechanism by which your program is notified about user interactions. The chapter ends by introducing two common Swing controls, the button and the text field, and using them to demonstrate the core elements of Swing programming.

THE ORIGINS AND DESIGN PHILOSOPHY OF SWING

Swing did not exist in the early days of Java. Rather, it was a response to deficiencies present in Java's original GUI subsystem: the Abstract Window Toolkit (AWT). The AWT defines a basic set of components that support a usable, but limited, graphical interface. One reason for the limited nature of the AWT is that its components rely on platform-specific native windows, or *peers*. Because of this they are referred to as *heavyweight*.

The use of native peers led to several problems. First, because of differences between operating systems, a component might look, or even act, differently on different platforms. Second, the look and feel of each component was fixed (because it is defined by the platform) and could not be (easily) changed. Third, the use of heavyweight components caused some frustrating restrictions. For example, a heavyweight component is always opaque.

Not long after Java's original release, it became apparent that the limitations and restrictions present in the AWT were sufficiently serious that a better approach was needed. The solution was Swing. Introduced in 1997, Swing was included as part of the Java Foundation Classes (JFC). Swing was initially available for use with Java 1.1 as a separate library. However, beginning with Java 1.2, Swing (and the rest of JFC) was fully integrated into the Java library.

Swing addresses the limitations associated with the AWT's components through the use of two key features: *lightweight components* and a *pluggable look and feel*. Although these two features are largely transparent to the programmer, they are at the foundation of Swing's design philosophy and the reason for much of its power and flexibility. Let's look at each.

With very few exceptions, Swing components are *lightweight*. This means that a component is written entirely in Java. Instead of having its own native peer, it uses the window provided by a heavyweight ancestor. Lightweight components have some important advantages, including efficiency and flexibility. For example, a lightweight component can be transparent, which enables nonrectangular shapes. Furthermore, because lightweight components do not translate into platform-specific peers, the look and feel of each component is determined by Swing. This means that each component can work in a consistent manner across all platforms.

Because each Swing component is rendered by Java code rather than by platform-specific peers, it is possible to separate the look and feel of a component from the logic of the component, and this is what Swing does. Separating out the look and feel provides a significant advantage: it becomes possible to change the way that a component is rendered without affecting any of its other aspects. In other words, it is possible to "plug-in" a new look and feel for any given component without creating any side effects in the code that uses that component.

Java provides look-and-feels, such as metal and Motif, that are available to all Swing users. The metal look and feel is also called the *Java look and feel*. It is a platform-independent look and feel that is available in all Java execution environments. It is also the default look and feel. For this reason, the examples in this book use the default Java look and feel (metal).

Swing's pluggable look-and-feel is made possible because Swing uses a modified version of a classic component architecture called *Model-View-Controller* (MVC). In MVC terminology, the *model* corresponds to the state information associated with the component. For example, in the case of a check box, the model contains a field that indicates if the box is checked or unchecked. The *view* determines how the component is displayed on the screen, including any aspects of the view that are affected by the current state of the model. The *controller* determines how the component reacts to the user. For example, when the user clicks on a check box, the controller reacts by changing the model to reflect the user's choice (checked or unchecked). This then results in the view being updated. By separating a component into a model, a view, and a controller, the specific implementation of each can be changed without affecting the other two. For instance, different view implementations can render the same component in different ways without affecting the model or the controller.

Although the MVC architecture and the principles behind it are conceptually sound, the high level of separation between the view and the controller was not beneficial for Swing components. Instead, Swing uses a modified version of MVC that combines the view and the controller into a single logical entity called the *UI delegate*. For this reason, Swing's approach is called either the *Model-Delegate* architecture or the *Separable Model* architecture. Therefore, although Swing's component architecture is based on MVC, it does not use a classical implementation of it. Although you won't work directly with models or UI delegates in this book, they are, nevertheless, present behind the scene.

In the course of this chapter, you will see that even though Swing embodies very sophisticated design concepts, it is easy to use. In fact, one could argue that Swing's ease of use is its most important advantage. Simply stated, Swing makes manageable the often difficult task of developing a program's user interface. This lets you concentrate on the GUI, itself, rather than on implementation details.

Ask the Expert

Q You say that Swing defines the look and feel of the modern Java GUI. Does this mean that Swing replaces the AWT?

A No, Swing does not replace the AWT. Rather, Swing builds on the foundation provided by the AWT. Thus, the AWT is still a crucial part of Java. Swing also uses the same event handling mechanism as the AWT. Although detailed knowledge of the AWT is not required to use Swing, those parts of the AWT required by Swing are described as needed throughout Part Two.

1. A lightweight component is written in highly optimized machine code. True or False?
2. What feature enables the look and feel of a Swing component to be changed?
3. Does Swing use a standard implementation of the MVC architecture?

COMPONENTS AND CONTAINERS

A Swing GUI consists of two key items: *components* and *containers*. However, this distinction is mostly conceptual because all containers are also components. The difference between the two is found in their intended purpose: As the term is commonly used, a *component* is an independent visual control, such as a push button or slider. A container holds a group of components. Thus, a container is a special type of component that is designed to hold other components. All Swing GUIs will have at least one container. Because containers are components, a container can also hold other containers. This enables Swing to define what is called a *containment hierarchy*, at the top of which must be a *top-level container*.

Let's look a bit more closely at components and containers.

Components

In general, Swing components are derived from the **JComponent** class. (The only exceptions to this are the four top-level containers, described in the next section.) **JComponent** provides the functionality that is common to all components. For example, **JComponent** supports the pluggable look and feel. **JComponent** inherits the AWT classes **Container** and **Component**. Thus, a Swing component is built on and compatible with an AWT component.

All of Swing's components are represented by classes defined within the package **javax.swing**. Here are the ones defined by Swing components (including those used as containers) at the time of this writing.

Answers:

1. False.
2. Pluggable look and feel
3. No, Swing uses a modified approach called Model-Delegate or Separable Model.

JApplet	JButton	JCheckBox	JCheckBoxMenuItem
JColorChooser	JComboBox	JComponent	JDesktopPane
JDialog	JEditorPane	JFileChooser	JFormattedTextField
JFrame	JInternalFrame	JLabel	JLayer
JLayeredPane	JList	JMenu	JMenuBar
JMenuItem	JOptionPane	JPanel	JPasswordField
JPopupMenu	JProgressBar	JRadioButton	JRadioButtonMenuItem
JRootPane	JScrollBar	JScrollPane	JSeparator
JSlider	JSpinner	JSplitPane	JTabbedPane
JTable	JTextArea	JTextField	JTextPane
JTogglebutton	JToolBar	JToolTip	JTree
JViewport	JWindow		

Notice that all component classes begin with the letter **J**. For example, the class for a label is **JLabel**, the class for a push button is **JButton**, and the class for a scroll bar is **JScrollBar**. Several of these are examined in this part of the book.

Containers

Swing defines two types of containers. The first are top-level containers: **JFrame**, **JApplet**, **JWindow**, and **JDialog**. These containers do not inherit **JComponent**. They do, however, inherit the AWT classes **Component** and **Container**. Unlike Swing's other components, which are lightweight, the top-level containers are heavyweight. This makes the top-level containers a special case in the Swing component library.

As the name implies, a top-level container must be at top of a containment hierarchy. A top-level container cannot be contained within any other container. Furthermore, every containment hierarchy must begin with a top-level container. The one commonly used for applications is **JFrame**. The one used for applets is **JApplet**.

The second type of containers supported by Swing are lightweight containers. Lightweight containers *do* inherit **JComponent**. Examples of lightweight containers are **JPanel** and **JRootPane**. Lightweight containers are often used to organize and manage groups of related components collectively because a lightweight container can be contained within another container. Thus, you can use lightweight containers to create subgroups of related controls that are contained within an outer container.

The Top-Level Container Panes

Each top-level container defines a set of *panes*. At the top of the hierarchy is an instance of **JRootPane**. **JRootPane** is a lightweight container whose purpose is to manage the other panes. It also helps manage the optional menu bar. The panes that compose the root pane are called the *glass pane*, the *content pane*, and the *layered pane*.

The glass pane is the top-level pane. It sits above and completely covers all other panes. The glass pane enables you to manage mouse events that affect the entire container (rather than an individual control) or to paint over any other component, for example. In most cases, you won't need to use the glass pane directly. The layered pane allows components to be given a depth value. This value determines which component overlays another. (Thus, the layered pane lets you specify a Z-order (depth) for a component, although this is not something that you will usually need to do.) The layered pane holds the content pane and the (optional) menu bar. Although the glass pane and the layered panes are integral to the operation of a top-level container and serve important purposes, much of what they provide occurs behind the scene. We won't be using them directly.

The pane with which your application will interact the most is the content pane, because this is the pane to which you will add visual components. In other words, when you add a component, such as a button, to a top-level container, you will add it to the content pane. Therefore, the content pane holds the components that the user interacts with.

Progress Check

1. All Swing components must be stored in a _____.
2. With only a few exceptions, Swing components are derived from **JComponent**. True or False?
3. In addition to the root pane, what other panes do all top-level containers have?
4. The top-level containers are a special case because they are heavyweight rather than lightweight components. True or False?

LAYOUT MANAGERS

Before you can begin writing a Swing program, there is one more thing that you need to be aware of: the *layout manager*. The layout manager controls the position of components within a container. In other words, a layout manager determines the location of controls within a container. Java offers several layout managers. Many are provided by the AWT (within **java.awt**), and Swing adds some of its own. All layout managers are instances of a class that implements the **LayoutManager** interface. (Some will also implement the **LayoutManager2** interface.) Here are a few of the layout managers available to the Swing programmer.

Answers:

1. Container
2. True.
3. The glass pane, the content pane, and the layered pane
4. True.

FlowLayout	A simple layout that positions components left-to-right, top-to-bottom. (Positions components right-to-left for some cultural settings.)
BorderLayout	Positions components within the center or the borders of the container. This is the default layout for a content pane.
GridLayout	Lays out components within a grid.
GridBagLayout	Lays out different size components within a flexible grid.
BoxLayout	Lays out components vertically or horizontally within a box.
SpringLayout	Lays out components subject to a set of constraints.

This chapter uses only two layout managers—**BorderLayout** and **FlowLayout**. Both are very easy to use, and they are described here. Other layout managers are described as needed.

BorderLayout is the default layout manager for the content pane. It implements a layout style that defines five locations to which a component can be added. The first is the center. The other four are the sides (i.e., borders), which are called north, south, east, and west. By default, when you add a component to the content pane, you are adding the component to the center. To add a component to one of the other regions, specify its name.

Although a border layout is useful is some situations, often another, more flexible layout manager is needed. One of the simplest is **FlowLayout**. A flow layout lays out components one row at a time, top to bottom. When one row is full, layout advances to the next row. Although this scheme gives you little control over the placement of components, it is quite simple to use. However, be aware that if you resize the frame, the position of the components will change.

A FIRST SIMPLE SWING PROGRAM

Swing programs differ from the console-based programs shown earlier in this book. They also differ from the AWT-based applets shown in Chapter 15. Not only do Swing programs use the Swing component set to handle user interaction, they also have special requirements that relate to threading. The best way to understand the structure of a Swing program is to work through an example. There are two types of Java programs in which Swing is typically used. The first is a desktop application, and the second is the applet. This section shows how to create a Swing application. The creation of a Swing applet is described in Chapter 21.

Although quite short, the following program shows one way to write a Swing application. In the process, it demonstrates several key features of Swing. It uses two Swing components: **JFrame** and **JLabel**. **JFrame** is the top-level container that is commonly used for Swing applications. **JLabel** is the Swing component that creates a label, which is a component that displays information. The label is Swing's simplest component because it is passive. That is, a label does not respond to user input. It just displays output. The program uses a **JFrame** container to hold an instance of a **JLabel**. The label displays a short text message.

```
// A simple Swing program.

import javax.swing.*;  ◀──────────Swing programs must import javax.swing.

class SwingDemo {

  SwingDemo() {                                              Create a top-level container.

    // Create a new JFrame container.
    JFrame jfrm = new JFrame("A Simple Swing Application"); ◀─

    // Give the frame an initial size.
    jfrm.setSize(275, 100); ◀──────────Set the container's size.

    // Terminate the program when the user closes the application.
    jfrm.setDefaultCloseOperation(JFrame.EXIT_ON_CLOSE); ◀──── Stop the program
                                                              when the user clicks
    // Create a text-based label.                              the close box.
    JLabel jlab = new JLabel(" Swing defines the modern Java GUI."); ◀─
                                                               Create a JLabel.
    // Add the label to the content pane.
    jfrm.add(jlab); ◀──────────Add the label to the content pane.

    // Display the frame.
    jfrm.setVisible(true); ◀──────────Make the frame visible.
  }

  public static void main(String[] args) {
    // Create the frame on the event dispatching thread.
    SwingUtilities.invokeLater(new Runnable() {
      public void run() {
        new SwingDemo(); ◀──────────Create the GUI on the event dispatching thread.
      }
    });
  }
}
```

Swing programs are compiled and run in the same way as other Java applications. Thus, to compile this program, you can use this command line:

```
javac SwingDemo.java
```

To run the program, use this command line:

```
java SwingDemo
```

When the program is run, it will produce the window shown in Figure 17-1.

The First Swing Example Line by Line

Because the **SwingDemo** program illustrates several key Swing concepts, we will examine it carefully, line by line. The program begins by importing the following package:

```
import javax.swing.*;
```

FIGURE 17-1   The window produced by the **SwingDemo** program.

This **javax.swing** package contains the components and models defined by Swing. For example, it defines classes that implement labels, buttons, edit controls, and menus. This package will be included in all programs that use Swing.

Next, the program declares the **SwingDemo** class and a constructor for that class. The constructor is where most of the action of the program occurs. It begins by creating a **JFrame**, using this line of code:

```
JFrame jfrm = new JFrame("A Simple Swing Application.");
```

This creates a container called **jfrm** that defines a rectangular window complete with a title bar; close, minimize, maximize, and restore buttons; and a system menu. Thus, it creates a standard, top-level window. The title of the window is passed to the constructor.

Next, the window is sized using this statement:

```
jfrm.setSize(275, 100);
```

The **setSize( )** method sets the dimensions of the window, which are specified in pixels. Its general form is shown here:

    void setSize(int *width*, int *height*)

In this example, the width of the window is set to 275 and the height is set to 100.

By default, when a top-level window is closed (such as when the user clicks the close box), the window is removed from the screen, but the application is not terminated. While this default behavior is useful in some situations, it is not what is needed for many applications. Instead, you will often want the entire application to terminate when its top-level window is closed. There are a couple of ways to achieve this. The easiest way is to call **setDefaultCloseOperation( )**, as the program does:

```
jfrm.setDefaultCloseOperation(JFrame.EXIT_ON_CLOSE);
```

After this call executes, closing the window causes the entire application to terminate. The general form of **setDefaultCloseOperation( )** is shown here:

    void setDefaultCloseOperation(int *what*)

The value passed in *what* determines what happens when the window is closed. There are several other options in addition to **JFrame.EXIT_ON_CLOSE**. They are shown here:

DISPOSE_ON_CLOSE	HIDE_ON_CLOSE	DO_NOTHING_ON_CLOSE

Their names reflect their actions. These constants are declared in **WindowConstants**, which is an interface declared in **javax.swing** that is implemented by **JFrame**.

The next line of code creates a **JLabel** component:

```
JLabel jlab = new JLabel(" Swing defines the modern Java GUI.");
```

JLabel is the easiest-to-use Swing component because it does not accept user input. It simply displays information, which can consist of text, an icon, or a combination of the two. The label created by the program contains only text, which is passed to its constructor.

The next line of code adds the label to the content pane of the frame:

```
jfrm.add(jlab);
```

As explained earlier, all top-level containers have a content pane in which components are stored. Thus, to add a component to a frame, you must add it to the frame's content pane. This is accomplished by calling **add( )** on the **JFrame** reference (**jfrm** in this case). The **add( )** method has several versions. The general form of the one used by the program is shown here:

Component add(Component *comp*)

By default, the content pane associated with a **JFrame** uses a border layout. This version of **add( )** adds the component (in this case, a label) to the center location. Other versions of **add( )** enable you to specify one of the border regions. When a component is added to the center, its size is automatically adjusted to fit the size of the center.

The last statement in the **SwingDemo** constructor causes the window to become visible.

```
jfrm.setVisible(true);
```

The **setVisible( )** method has this general form:

void setVisible(boolean *flag*)

If *flag* is **true**, the window will be displayed. Otherwise, it will be hidden. By default, a **JFrame** is invisible, so **setVisible(true)** must be called to show it.

Inside **main( )**, a **SwingDemo** object is created, which causes the window and the label to be displayed. Notice that the **SwingDemo** constructor is invoked using these lines of code:

```
SwingUtilities.invokeLater(new Runnable() {
  public void run() {
    new SwingDemo();
  }
});
```

This sequence causes a **SwingDemo** object to be created on the *event-dispatching thread* rather than on the main thread of the application. Here's why. In general, Swing programs are event-driven. For example, when a user interacts with a component, an event is generated. An event is passed to the application by calling an event handler defined by the application. However, the handler is executed on the event-dispatching thread provided by Swing and not on the main thread of the application. Thus, although event handlers are defined by your program, they are called on a thread that was not created by your program. To avoid problems (such as two different threads trying to update the same component at the same time), all Swing GUI components must be created and updated from the event-dispatching thread, not the main thread of the application. However, **main( )** is executed on the main thread. Thus, it cannot directly instantiate a **SwingDemo** object. Instead, it must create a **Runnable** object that executes on the event-dispatching thread, and have this object create the GUI.

To enable the GUI code to be created on the event-dispatching thread, you must use one of two methods that are defined by the **SwingUtilities** class. These methods are **invokeLater( )** and **invokeAndWait( )**. They are shown here:

static void invokeLater(Runnable *obj*)

static void invokeAndWait(Runnable *obj*)
      throws InterruptedException, InvocationTargetException

Here, *obj* is a **Runnable** object that will have its **run( )** method called by the event-dispatching thread. The difference between the two methods is that **invokeLater( )** returns immediately, but **invokeAndWait( )** waits until *obj*.**run( )** returns. You can use these methods to call a method that constructs the GUI for your Swing application, or whenever you need to modify the state of the GUI from code not executed by the event-dispatching thread. You will normally want to use **invokeLater( )**, as the preceding program does. However, when constructing the initial GUI for a Swing applet, you will want to use **invokeAndWait( )**.

Finally, notice the syntax that creates the new **Runnable**. This creates an anonymous inner class that causes an unnamed **Runnable** object to be created. We will look more closely at anonymous inner classes later in this chapter.

Ask the Expert

Q What is the **getContentPane( )** method, and do I need to use it?

A This question brings up an important historical point. Prior to JDK 5, when adding a component to the content pane, you could not invoke the **add( )** method directly on a **JFrame** instance. Instead, you needed to explicitly call **add( )** on the content pane of the **JFrame** object. The content pane can be obtained by calling **getContentPane( )** on a **JFrame** instance. The **getContentPane( )** method is shown here:

    Container getContentPane( )

Ask the Expert (Continued)

It returns a **Container** reference to the content pane. The **add( )** method was then called on that reference to add a component to a content pane. Thus, in the past, you had to use the following statement to add **jlab** to **jfrm**:

```
jfrm.getContentPane().add(jlab); // old-style
```

Here, **getContentPane( )** first obtains a reference to content pane, and then **add( )** adds the component to the container linked to this pane. This same procedure was also required to invoke **remove( )** to remove a component and **setLayout( )** to set the layout manager for the content pane. You will see explicit calls to **getContentPane( )** frequently throughout pre-5.0 code. Today, the use of **getContentPane( )** is no longer necessary for these purposes. You can simply call **add( )**, **remove( )**, and **setLayout( )** directly on **JFrame** because these methods have been changed so that they automatically operate on the content pane.

Progress Check

1. What Swing class creates a label?
2. What package must be included in all Swing programs?
3. All code that creates or modifies the GUI must be executed on the _____ thread.

Ask the Expert

Q Earlier, you stated that it is possible to add a component to the other regions of a border layout by using an overloaded version of **add( )**. Can you explain?

A As explained, **BorderLayout** implements a layout style that defines five locations to which a component can be added. The first is the center. The other four are the sides (i.e., borders), which are called north, south, east, and west. By default, when you add a component to the content pane, you are adding the component to the center. To specify one of the other locations, use this form of **add( )**:

> void add(Component *comp*, Object *loc*)

Here, *comp* is the component to add and *loc* specifies the location to which it is added. The *loc* value can be one of the following:

BorderLayout.CENTER	BorderLayout.EAST	BorderLayout.NORTH
BorderLayout.SOUTH	BorderLayout.WEST	

Answers:

1. **JLabel**
2. **javax.swing**
3. event-dispatching

In general, **BorderLayout** is most useful when you are creating a **JFrame** that contains a centered component (which might be a group of components held within one of Swing's lightweight containers) that has a header and/or footer component associated with it. In other situations, one of Java's other layout managers, such as **FlowLayout**, will be more appropriate.

EVENT HANDLING

The preceding example showed the basic form of a Swing program, but it left out one important part: event handling. Because **JLabel** does not take input from the user, it does not generate events, so no event handling was needed. However, the other Swing controls *do* respond to user input, and the events generated by those interactions need to be handled. For example, an event is generated when the user clicks a button, types a key on the keyboard, or selects an item from a list. Events are also generated in ways not directly related to user input. For example, an event is generated when a timer goes off. Whatever the case, event handling is a large part of any Swing-based application.

The event handling mechanism used by Swing is based on an approach called the *delegation event model*. Its concept is quite simple. A *source* generates an event and sends it to one or more *listeners*. In this scheme, the listener simply waits until it receives an event. Once an event arrives, the listener processes the event and then returns. The advantage of this design is that the application logic that processes events is cleanly separated from the user interface logic that generates the events. A user interface element is able to "delegate" the processing of an event to a separate piece of code. In the delegation event model, a listener must register with a source in order to receive an event notification. If this mechanism seems familiar, it should. It is, essentially, the Observer pattern described in Chapter 16.

Let's look at events, sources, and listeners a bit closer.

Events

In the delegation model, an event is an object that describes a state change in a source. It can be generated as a consequence of a person interacting with a control in a graphical user interface, or it can be generated under program control. The superclass for all events is **java.util.EventObject**. Many events are declared in **java.awt.event**. Others are found in **javax.swing.event**.

Event Sources

An event source is an object that generates an event. When a source generates an event, it must send that event to all registered listeners. Therefore, in order for a listener to receive an event, it must register with the source of that event. Listeners register with a source by calling an **add*Type*Listener( )** method on the event source object. Each type of event has its own registration method. Here is the general form:

    public void add*Type*Listener(*Type*Listener *el*)

Here, *Type* is the name of the event and *el* is a reference to the event listener. For example, the method that registers a listener that receives key stroke events is called **addKeyListener( )**. The method that registers a mouse motion listener is called **addMouseMotionListener( )**. When an event occurs, all registered listeners are notified.

A source must also provide a method that allows a listener to unregister an interest in a specific type of event. The general form of such a method is this:

public void remove*Type*Listener(*Type*Listener *el*)

Here, *Type* is the name of the event and *el* is a reference to the event listener. For example, to remove a key listener, you would call **removeKeyListener( )**.

The methods that add or remove listeners are provided by the source that generates events. For example, the **JButton** class, which supports a push button, provides a method to add and remove an *action listener,* which is notified when the button is pressed.

Event Listeners

A listener is an object that is notified when an event occurs. It has two major requirements. First, it must have registered with one or more sources to receive notifications about a specific type of event. Second, it must implement a method to receive and process that event.

The methods that receive and process events are defined in a set of interfaces. The ones we will use are found in **java.awt.event** and **javax.swing.event**. For example, the **ActionListener** interface defines a method that receives a notification when an action, such as clicking a button, takes place. Any object may receive and process this event if it provides an implementation of the **ActionListener** interface.

There is an important general principle that must be stated now. An event handler should do its job quickly and then return. In most cases, it should not engage in a long operation because doing so will slow down the entire application, rendering it unresponsive. If a time-consuming operation is required, then a separate thread will usually be created for this purpose.

Event Classes and Listener Interfaces

The classes that represent events are at the core of Java's event handling mechanism. At the root of the Java event class hierarchy is **EventObject**, which is in **java.util**. It is the superclass for all events. The class **AWTEvent**, declared in the **java.awt** package, is a subclass of **EventObject**. It is the superclass (either directly or indirectly) of all AWT-based events used by the delegation event model. Swing uses the AWT events. It also adds several of its own.

Table 17-1 shows a sampling of the event classes and listener interfaces defined in **java.awt.event**. Table 17-2 shows a sampling of the event classes and listener interfaces defined in **javax.swing.event**. The event classes and interfaces used by the examples are described as needed.

Adapter Classes

Although it isn't difficult to implement most of the event listener interfaces, Java offers a set of *adapter classes* that provide an empty implementation of event listener

TABLE 17-1: A Sampling of Event Classes in java.awt.event

Event Class	Description	Corresponding Event Listener
ActionEvent	Generated when an action occurs within a control, such as when a button is pressed.	ActionListener
AdjustmentEvent	Generated when a scroll bar is manipulated.	AdjustmentListener
FocusEvent	Generated when a component gains or loses focus.	FocusListener
ItemEvent	Generated when an item is selected, such as when a check box is clicked.	ItemListener
KeyEvent	Generated when input is received from the keyboard.	KeyListener
MouseEvent	Generated when the mouse is dragged or moved, clicked, pressed, or released; also generated when the mouse enters or exits a component.	MouseListener and MouseMotionListener
MouseWheelEvent	Generated when the mouse wheel is moved.	MouseWheelListener
WindowEvent	Generated when a window is activated, closed, deactivated, deiconified, iconified, opened, or quit.	WindowListener

TABLE 17-2: A Sampling of Event Classes in javax.swing.event

Event Class	Description	Corresponding Event Listener
AncestorEvent	Generated when an ancestor of a component has been added, moved, or removed.	AncestorListener
CaretEvent	Generated when the position of the caret in a text component changes.	CaretListener
ChangeEvent	Generated when a component changes its state.	ChangeListener
HyperlinkEvent	Generated when a hyperlink is accessed.	HyperlinkListener
ListDataEvent	Generated when the contents of a list changes.	ListDataListener
ListSelectionEvent	Generated when a list selection changes.	ListSelectionListener
MenuEvent	Generated when a menu selection occurs.	MenuListener
TableModelEvent	Generated when the table model changes.	TableModelListener
TreeExpansionEvent	Generated when a tree is expanded or collapsed.	TreeExpansionListener
TreeModelEvent	Generated when a tree model changes.	TreeModelListener
TreeSelectionEvent	Generated when a node on a tree is selected.	TreeSelectionListener

interface methods. Adapter classes are useful when you want to receive and process only some of the events that are associated with a particular listener interface. You can define a new class to act as an event listener by extending one of the adapter classes and implement only those methods in which you are interested. Not having to implement all of the methods defined by an event listener interface saves you a considerable amount of effort and prevents your code from becoming cluttered with empty methods. Also, it is common to implement an adapter through the use of an anonymous inner class, which can further simplify your code.

Not all listener interfaces have corresponding adapters. For example, there is no adapter for **ActionListener** because it defines only one method. In general, there are adapters for listeners that define two or more methods. For example, the **MouseMotionLister** class has two methods, **mouseDragged( )** and **mouseMoved( )**. Empty implementations of these methods are provided by **MouseMotionAdapter**. If you were interested in only mouse drag events, then you could simply extend **MouseMotionAdapter** and implement **mouseDragged( )**. The empty implementation of **mouseMoved( )** would handle the mouse motion events for you.

Here is a sampling of the adapter classes. Most are defined in **java.awt.event**, but **MouseInputAdapter** is defined in **javax.swing.event**.

Adapter Class	Implements
FocusAdapter	FocusListener
KeyAdapter	KeyListener
MouseAdapter	MouseListener
MouseMotionAdapter	MouseMotionListener
MouseInputAdapter	MouseListener and MouseMotionListener
WindowAdapter	WindowListener

Progress Check

1. The delegation event model is based on event sources and _____ _____.
2. What is the name of the event listener interface for action events?
3. What do adapter classes do?

_____

Answers:

1. event listeners
2. **ActionListener**
3. Adapter classes simplify the implementation of event listeners by providing empty implementations of all methods in the interface. Thus, you need only implement those methods in which you are interested.

USING A PUSH BUTTON

One of the simplest Swing controls is the push button. It is also one of the most commonly used. A push button is an instance of **JButton**. **JButton** inherits the abstract class **AbstractButton**, which defines the functionality common to all buttons. Swing push buttons can contain text, an image, or both. Here we will be using only text-based push buttons, but other types of buttons are discussed in Chapter 18.

JButton supplies several constructors. The one used here is

JButton(String *msg*)

The *msg* parameter specifies the string that will be displayed inside the button.

When a push button is pressed, it generates an **ActionEvent**. Thus, **JButton** provides the following methods (inherited from **AbstractButton**), which are used to add or remove an action listener:

void addActionListener(ActionListener *al*)

void removeActionListener(ActionListener *al*)

Here, *al* specifies an object that will receive event notifications. This object must be an instance of a class that implements the **ActionListener** interface.

The **ActionListener** interface defines only one method: **actionPerformed( )**. It is shown here:

void actionPerformed(ActionEvent *ae*)

This method is called when a button is pressed. In other words, it is the event handler that is called when a button press event has occurred. Your implementation of **actionPerformed( )** must quickly respond to that event and return. As mentioned earlier, as a general rule, event handlers must not engage in long operations because doing so will slow down the entire application. If a time-consuming procedure must be performed, then a separate thread should be created for that purpose.

Using the **ActionEvent** object passed to **actionPerformed( )**, you can obtain several useful pieces of information relating to the button-press event. The one used by this chapter is the *action command string* associated with the button. By default, this is the string displayed inside the button. The action command is obtained by calling **getActionCommand( )** on the event object. It is declared like this:

String getActionCommand( )

The action command identifies the button. Thus, when using two or more buttons within the same application, the action command gives you an easy way to determine which button was pressed.

The following program demonstrates how to create a push button and respond to button-press events. Figure 17-2 shows how the example appears on the screen.

```
// Demonstrate a button.

import java.awt.*;
import java.awt.event.*;
```

```java
import javax.swing.*;

class ButtonDemo implements ActionListener {

  JLabel jlab;

  ButtonDemo() {

    // Create a new JFrame container.
    JFrame jfrm = new JFrame("A Button Example");

    // Specify FlowLayout for the layout manager.
    jfrm.setLayout(new FlowLayout());         // ◄──── Note use of FlowLayout.

    // Give the frame an initial size.
    jfrm.setSize(220, 90);

    // Terminate the program when the user closes the application.
    jfrm.setDefaultCloseOperation(JFrame.EXIT_ON_CLOSE);

    // Make two buttons.
    JButton jbtnFirst = new JButton("First");     // ◄──┐
    JButton jbtnSecond = new JButton("Second");   // ◄──┘ Create two push buttons.

    // Add action listeners.
    jbtnFirst.addActionListener(this);            // ◄──┐ Set the action listeners
    jbtnSecond.addActionListener(this);           // ◄──┘ for the buttons.

    // Add the buttons to the content pane.
    jfrm.add(jbtnFirst);                          // ◄──┐ Add buttons to content pane.
    jfrm.add(jbtnSecond);                         // ◄──┘

    // Create a text-based label.
    jlab = new JLabel("Press a button.");

    // Add the label to the frame.
    jfrm.add(jlab);

    // Display the frame.
    jfrm.setVisible(true);
  }
                                              // This is the ActionEvent
                                              // handler for the push buttons.
  // Handle button events.
  public void actionPerformed(ActionEvent ae) {  // ◄──┐
    if(ae.getActionCommand().equals("First"))    // ◄──── Use the action
      jlab.setText("First button was pressed.");  //      command string to
    else                                          //      determine which
      jlab.setText("Second button was pressed. ");//      button was pressed.
  }

  public static void main(String[] args) {
```

FIGURE 17-2   Output from the **JButton** demonstration program.

```
    // Create the frame on the event dispatching thread.
    SwingUtilities.invokeLater(new Runnable() {
      public void run() {
        new ButtonDemo();
      }
    });
  }
}
```

Let's take a close look at the new things in this program. First, notice that, in addition to **javax.swing**, the program now imports both the **java.awt** and **java.awt.event** packages. The **java.awt** package is needed because it contains the **FlowLayout** class, which supports the standard flow layout manager used to lay out components in a frame. The **java.awt.event** package is needed because it defines the **ActionListener** interface and the **ActionEvent** class.

Next, the class **ButtonDemo** is declared. Notice that it implements **ActionListener**. This means that **ButtonDemo** objects can be used to receive action events. Next, a **JLabel** reference is declared. This reference will be used within the **actionPerformed( )** method to display which button has been pressed.

The **ButtonDemo** constructor begins by creating a **JFrame** called **jfrm**. It then sets the layout manager for the content pane of **jfrm** to **FlowLayout**, as shown here:

```
jfrm.setLayout(new FlowLayout());
```

As explained earlier, by default, the content pane uses **BorderLayout** as its layout manager, but for many applications, **FlowLayout** is more convenient. Recall that a flow layout lays out components one "line" at a time, top to bottom. When one "line" is full, layout advances to the next "line." Although this scheme gives you little control over the placement of components, it is quite simple to use. Remember, however, that if you resize the frame, the position of the components will change.

After setting the size and default close operation, **ButtonDemo( )** creates two buttons, as shown here:

```
JButton jbtnFirst = new JButton("First");
JButton jbtnSecond = new JButton("Second");
```

The first button will contain the text "First", and the second will contain "Second".

Next, the instance of **ButtonDemo** referred to via **this** is added as an action listener for the buttons by these two lines:

```
jbtnFirst.addActionListener(this);
jbtnSecond.addActionListener(this);
```

This approach means that the object that creates the buttons will also receive notifications when a button is pressed.

Next, the buttons are added to the content pane of **jfrm**:

```
jfrm.add(jbtnFirst);
jfrm.add(jbtnSecond);
```

This means that the buttons will be shown in the window provided by **jfrm**.

Each time a button is pressed, it generates an action event and all registered listeners are notified by calling the **actionPerformed( )** method. The **ActionEvent** object representing the button event is passed as a parameter. In the case of **ButtonDemo**, this event is passed to this implementation of **actionPerformed( )**.

```
public void actionPerformed(ActionEvent ae) {
  if(ae.getActionCommand().equals("First"))
    jlab.setText("First button was pressed.");
  else
    jlab.setText("Second button was pressed. ");
}
```

The event that occurred is passed via **ae**. Inside the method, the action command associated with the button that generated the event is obtained by calling **getActionCommand( )**. (Recall that, by default, the action command is the same as the text displayed by the button.) Based on the contents of that string, the text in the label is set appropriately by use of **setText( )**. This method is defined by **JLabel** as shown here:

void setText(String *msg*)

Here, *msg* specifies the text that will be shown inside the label. The **setText( )** method lets you set the text inside a label after it has been created.

One last point: Remember that **actionPerformed( )** is called on the event-dispatching thread as explained earlier. It must return quickly in order to avoid slowing down the application.

Progress Check

1. What class creates a Swing push button?
2. By default, the action command string associated with a button is the same as the text displayed within the button. True or False?

Answers:

1. **JButton**
2. True.

TRY THIS 17-1   A SIMPLE STOPWATCH

StopWatch.java

Although only two Swing controls have been introduced, **JLabel** and **JButton**, you can use these controls to create a fully functional and useful application: a stopwatch. The stopwatch contains two push buttons and one label. The push buttons are called Start and Stop and are used to start and stop the stopwatch. The label displays the elapsed time. Though quite simple, this project shows the ease with which GUI interfaces can be created using Swing.

STEP-BY-STEP

1. Begin by creating a file called **StopWatch.java** and then enter the following comment and **import** statements:

```
// Try This 17-1: A Simple stopwatch.

import java.awt.*;
import java.awt.event.*;
import javax.swing.*;
import java.util.*;
```

Notice that **java.util** is imported. This package is needed because it contains the **Calendar** class, which is used to obtain the current system time.

2. Begin the **StopWatch** class as shown here:

```
class StopWatch implements ActionListener {

  JLabel jlab;
  long start; // holds the start time in milliseconds
```

As the comment indicates, the **start** field is used to hold the start time in milliseconds. This value will be subtracted from the end time to obtain the elapsed time.

3. Begin the **StopWatch** constructor with the following lines:

```
StopWatch() {

  // Create a new JFrame container.
  JFrame jfrm = new JFrame("A Simple Stopwatch");

  // Specify FlowLayout for the layout manager.
  jfrm.setLayout(new FlowLayout());

  // Give the frame an initial size.
  jfrm.setSize(230, 90);

  // Terminate the program when the user closes the application.
  jfrm.setDefaultCloseOperation(JFrame.EXIT_ON_CLOSE);
```

These statements are similar to those used by the preceding examples and should be familiar to you.

4. Enter the following code, which creates the Start and Stop buttons, adds action listeners for the buttons, and then adds the buttons to the content pane.

```
// Make two buttons.
JButton jbtnStart = new JButton("Start");
JButton jbtnStop = new JButton("Stop");

// Add action listeners.
jbtnStart.addActionListener(this);
jbtnStop.addActionListener(this);

// Add the buttons to the content pane.
jfrm.add(jbtnStart);
jfrm.add(jbtnStop);
```

5. Create and add a label using the following statements:

```
// Create a text-based label.
jlab = new JLabel("Press Start to begin timing.");

// Add the label to the frame.
jfrm.add(jlab);
```

The label is used to indicate the status of the stopwatch and to display the elapsed time.

6. Conclude the **StopWatch** constructor by making the frame visible:

```
  // Display the frame.
  jfrm.setVisible(true);
}
```

7. Add the **actionPerformed( )** method shown here:

```
// Handle button events.
public void actionPerformed(ActionEvent ae) {
  // get the current system time
  Calendar cal = Calendar.getInstance();

  if(ae.getActionCommand().equals("Start")) {
    // Store start time.
    start = cal.getTimeInMillis();
    jlab.setText("Stopwatch is Running...");
  }
  else
    // Compute the elapsed time.
    jlab.setText("Elapsed time is "
        + (double) (cal.getTimeInMillis() - start)/1000);
}
```

Notice that a **Calendar** object called **cal** is created and initialized to the current system time by calling the static **Calendar** method **getInstance( )**. Thus, each time **actionPerformed( )** is called, **cal** will be initialized to the current system time. (For information on **Calendar**, see Chapter 24.)

Recall that, by default, the action command for a button is the text displayed by the button. Thus, the action command for the Start button is "Start". When the Start button is pressed, the current time (in milliseconds) is obtained (by calling **getTimeInMillis( )** on **cal**) and stored in the **start** field. When the Stop button is pressed, the current time is obtained and the start time is subtracted from it, yielding the elapsed time. This value is cast to **double** and divided by 1,000. This converts the elapsed time into seconds.

8. Conclude by adding this **main( )** method:

```
public static void main(String[] args) {

  // Create the frame on the event dispatching thread.
  SwingUtilities.invokeLater(new Runnable() {
    public void run() {
      new StopWatch();
    }
  });
}
```

9. Here is all the code assembled into a complete program. Sample output is shown here:

```
// Try This 17-1: A Simple stopwatch.

import java.awt.*;
import java.awt.event.*;
import javax.swing.*;
import java.util.*;

class StopWatch implements ActionListener {

  JLabel jlab;
  long start; // holds the start time in milliseconds

  StopWatch() {

    // Create a new JFrame container.
    JFrame jfrm = new JFrame("A Simple Stopwatch");
```

```java
    // Specify FlowLayout for the layout manager.
    jfrm.setLayout(new FlowLayout());

    // Give the frame an initial size.
    jfrm.setSize(230, 90);

    // Terminate the program when the user closes the application.
    jfrm.setDefaultCloseOperation(JFrame.EXIT_ON_CLOSE);

    // Make two buttons.
    JButton jbtnStart = new JButton("Start");
    JButton jbtnStop = new JButton("Stop");

    // Add action listeners.
    jbtnStart.addActionListener(this);
    jbtnStop.addActionListener(this);

    // Add the buttons to the content pane.
    jfrm.add(jbtnStart);
    jfrm.add(jbtnStop);

    // Create a text-based label.
    jlab = new JLabel("Press Start to begin timing.");

    // Add the label to the frame.
    jfrm.add(jlab);

    // Display the frame.
    jfrm.setVisible(true);
  }

  // Handle button events.
  public void actionPerformed(ActionEvent ae) {
    // get the current system time
    Calendar cal = Calendar.getInstance();

    if(ae.getActionCommand().equals("Start")) {
      // Store start time.
      start = cal.getTimeInMillis();
      jlab.setText("Stopwatch is Running...");
    }
    else
      // Compute the elapsed time.
      jlab.setText("Elapsed time is "
           + (double) (cal.getTimeInMillis() - start)/1000);
  }
```

```
public static void main(String[] args) {

  // Create the frame on the event dispatching thread.
  SwingUtilities.invokeLater(new Runnable() {
    public void run() {
      new StopWatch();
    }
  });
}
}
```

INTRODUCING JTextField

Another commonly used control is **JTextField**. It enables the user to enter a line of text. **JTextField** inherits the abstract class **JTextComponent**, which is the superclass of all text components. **JTextField** provides a convenient way to obtain text-based user input.

JTextField defines several constructors. The one we will use is shown here:

JTextField(int *cols*)

Here, *cols* specifies the width of the text field in columns. It is important to understand that you can enter a string that is longer than the number of columns. It's just that the physical size of the text field on the screen will be *cols* columns wide.

When a user presses ENTER when inputting into a text field, an **ActionEvent** is generated. Therefore, **JTextField** provides the **addActionListener( )** and **removeActionListener( )** methods. To handle action events, you must implement the **actionPerformed( )** method defined by the **ActionListener** interface. The process is similar to handling action events generated by a button, as described earlier.

To obtain the string that is currently displayed in the text field, call **getText( )** on the **JTextField** instance. It is declared as shown here:

String getText( )

You can set the text in a **JTextField** by calling **setText( )**, shown next:

void setText(String *text*)

Here, *text* is the string that will be put into the text field.

The following program demonstrates **JTextField**. It creates a text field that is 10 columns wide. Whenever you press ENTER while in the text field, the current contents are displayed via a **JLabel**. Its operation should be clear. Sample output is shown in Figure 17-3.

```
// Demonstrate a text field.

import java.awt.*;
import java.awt.event.*;
import javax.swing.*;

class JTextFieldDemo implements ActionListener {

  JTextField jtf;
  JLabel jlab;

  JTextFieldDemo() {

    // Create a new JFrame container.
    JFrame jfrm = new JFrame("A Text Field Example");

    // Specify FlowLayout for the layout manager.
    jfrm.setLayout(new FlowLayout());

    // Give the frame an initial size.
    jfrm.setSize(240, 90);

    // Terminate the program when the user closes the application.
    jfrm.setDefaultCloseOperation(JFrame.EXIT_ON_CLOSE);

    // Create a text field instance.
    jtf = new JTextField(10);           Create a 10-column text field.

    // Add an action listener for the text field.
    jtf.addActionListener(this);        Set the action listener for the text field.

    // Add the text field to the content pane.
    jfrm.add(jtf);

    // Create an empty text-based label.
    jlab = new JLabel("");

    // Add the label to the frame.
    jfrm.add(jlab);

    // Display the frame.
    jfrm.setVisible(true);
  }

  // Handle action events.
  public void actionPerformed(ActionEvent ae) {        An action event is
                                                       generated when the
                                                       user presses ENTER
                                                       when inside a text
                                                       field.
    // Obtain the current text and display it in a label.
    jlab.setText("Current contents: " + jtf.getText());
  }
```

FIGURE 17-3:   Sample output from the **JTextField** program.

```
public static void main(String[] args) {

    // Create the frame on the event dispatching thread.
    SwingUtilities.invokeLater(new Runnable() {
      public void run() {
        new JTextFieldDemo();
      }
    });
  }
}
```

Most of the program should be familiar, but notice this line from within the **actionPerformed( )** method:

```
jlab.setText("Current contents: " + jtf.getText());
```

As explained, when the user presses ENTER, an **ActionEvent** is generated and sent to all registered action listeners, through the **actionPerformed( )** method. For **TextFieldDemo**, this method simply obtains the text currently held in the text field by calling **getText( )** on **jtf**. It then displays the text through the label referred to by **jlab**.

Like a **JButton**, a **JTextField** has an action command string associated with it. By default, the action command is the current contents of the text field. However, you can set this to an action command of your choosing by calling the **setActionCommand( )** method, shown here:

     void setActionCommand(String *cmd*)

The string passed in *cmd* becomes the new action command. The text in the text field is unaffected. Once you set the action command string, it remains the same no matter what is entered into the text field. One reason that you might want to explicitly set the action command is to provide a way to recognize the text field as the source of an action event. This is helpful when another control in the same frame also generates action events and you want to use the same event handler to process both events. Setting the action command is one way you can tell them apart.

For example, in the following program, two text fields are used, and each is recognized based on its action command.

```
// Use two text fields.

import java.awt.*;
import java.awt.event.*;
import javax.swing.*;
```

```
class TwoTFDemo implements ActionListener {

  JTextField jtf1;
  JTextField jtf2;
  JLabel jlab;

  TwoTFDemo() {

    // Create a new JFrame container.
    JFrame jfrm = new JFrame("Use Two Text Fields");

    // Specify FlowLayout for the layout manager.
    jfrm.setLayout(new FlowLayout());

    // Give the frame an initial size.
    jfrm.setSize(240, 120);

    // Terminate the program when the user closes the application.
    jfrm.setDefaultCloseOperation(JFrame.EXIT_ON_CLOSE);

    // Create two text field instances.
    jtf1 = new JTextField(10);            ─┐  Create two text fields.
    jtf2 = new JTextField(10);            ─┘

    // Set the action commands.
    jtf1.setActionCommand("One");         ─┐  Set the action command strings
    jtf2.setActionCommand("Two");         ─┘  for the text fields.

    // Add action listeners for the text fields.
    jtf1.addActionListener(this);
    jtf2.addActionListener(this);

    // Add the text fields to the content pane.
    jfrm.add(jtf1);
    jfrm.add(jtf2);

    // Create an empty text-based label.
    jlab = new JLabel("");

    // Add the label to the frame.
    jfrm.add(jlab);

    // Display the frame.
    jfrm.setVisible(true);
  }

  // Handle action events.
  public void actionPerformed(ActionEvent ae) {      Use the action command string to
                                                     determine which text field fired
    if(ae.getActionCommand().equals("One"))      ◄── the event.
```

```
          jlab.setText("ENTER pressed in tf1: "
                      + jtf1.getText());
       else
          jlab.setText("ENTER pressed in jtf2: "
                      + jtf2.getText());
    }

    public static void main(String[] args) {

       // Create the frame on the event dispatching thread.
       SwingUtilities.invokeLater(new Runnable() {
          public void run() {
             new TwoTFDemo();
          }
       });
    }
}
```

Sample output is shown in Figure 17-4.

This program creates two **JTextField**s: **jtf1** and **jtf2**. Notice that the action commands associated with **jtf1** and **jtf2** are set using these lines of code:

```
jtf1.setActionCommand("One");
jtf2.setActionCommand("Two");
```

Next, inside **actionPerformed( )** notice how the action command is used to determine which text field generated the action event:

```
public void actionPerformed(ActionEvent ae) {

   if(ae.getActionCommand().equals("One"))
      jlab.setText("ENTER pressed in tf1: "
                  + jtf1.getText());
   else
      jlab.setText("ENTER pressed in jtf2: "
                  + jtf2.getText());
}
```

Because the action commands for each text field have been set to a known string, this string can be used to determine which text field generated the event.

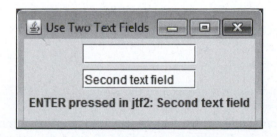

FIGURE 17-4: Sample output from the two text fields program.

Ask the Expert

Q You just explained that the action command associated with a text field can be set by calling **setActionCommand( )**. Can I use this method to set the action command associated with a push button?

A Yes. As you know, by default the action command associated with a push button is the name of the button. To set the action command to a different value, you can use the **setActionCommand( )** method. It works the same for **JButton** as it does for **JTextField**.

Progress Check

1. When using **JTextField**, if the text entered by the user is longer than the text field, the text is truncated. True or False?
2. When the user presses ENTER while within a **JTextField**, what event is generated?
3. Why is it a good idea to explicitly set the action command for a **JTextField**?

TRY THIS 17-2   CREATE A SIMPLE CODE MACHINE

`Coder.java`

This project uses **JLabel**, **JButton**, and **JTextField** to create a simple code machine. The code machine works by implementing a simple substitution cipher in which each character in a string is increased by one. For example, A becomes B, B becomes C, and so on. Of course, such a naive approach is trivially easy to break, but it provides an interesting means of illustrating the ways that push buttons and text fields can interact. It also shows how events generated by different components (in this case a text field and a button) can map to the same event handler.

Answers:

1. False. The width of the text can exceed the width of the field.
2. **ActionEvent**
3. If the action command is not set, then by default the action command is the text currently contained within the text field. Setting the action command explicitly identifies the text field independently of what it contains.

STEP-BY-STEP

1. Create a file called **Coder.java** and then enter the following comment and **import** statements:

```
// Try This 17-2: A simple code machine.

import java.awt.*;
import java.awt.event.*;
import javax.swing.*;
```

2. Begin creating the **Coder** class, like this:

```
class Coder implements ActionListener {

    JTextField jtfPlaintext;
    JTextField jtfCiphertext;
```

   Notice that **Coder** implements **ActionListener**. It also declares fields for two text fields. **jtfPlaintext** will hold the plain text message entered by the user. **jtfCiphertext** will hold the encoded version of the message.

3. Start the **Coder** constructor, as shown here:

```
Coder() {

    // Create a new JFrame container.
    JFrame jfrm = new JFrame("A Simple Code Machine");

    // Specify FlowLayout for the layout manager.
    jfrm.setLayout(new FlowLayout());

    // Give the frame an initial size.
    jfrm.setSize(340, 120);

    // Terminate the program when the user closes the application.
    jfrm.setDefaultCloseOperation(JFrame.EXIT_ON_CLOSE);
```

   This sequence is similar to that used by other examples in this chapter and should be familiar to you.

4. Add these two **JLabel**s:

```
// Create two labels.
JLabel jlabPlaintext = new JLabel("  Plain Text: ");
JLabel jlabCiphertext = new JLabel("Cipher Text: ");
```

5. Create two **JTextField** instances and assign them to the **jtfPlaintext** and **jtfCiphertext** fields.

```
// Create two text field instances.
jtfPlaintext = new JTextField(20);
jtfCiphertext = new JTextField(20);
```

6. Set the action command for the text fields and then add **this** as an action listener for both fields.

```
// Set the action commands for the text fields.
jtfPlaintext.setActionCommand("Encode");
jtfCiphertext.setActionCommand("Decode");

// Add action listeners for the text fields.
jtfPlaintext.addActionListener(this);
jtfCiphertext.addActionListener(this);
```

It is necessary to set the action command for both **JTextField** instances for three reasons. First, it gives a way to identify each text field. Second, if the action command is not set, then by default the current text is used. If, by happenstance, this text is the same as the action command used by another control, a conflict will arise. Setting the action command prevents this. Third, as you will see shortly, these two action commands are the same as the action commands for two of the push buttons. This means that the same code sequence can be used to handle events from both the push button and the text field.

7. Add the text fields and labels to the content pane.

```
// Add the text fields and labels to the content pane.
jfrm.add(jlabPlaintext);
jfrm.add(jtfPlaintext);
jfrm.add(jlabCiphertext);
jfrm.add(jtfCiphertext);
```

The order in which these components is added is important because the labels describe the text fields.

8. Create three push buttons called Encode, Decode, and Reset, as shown here:

```
// Create push button instances.
JButton jbtnEncode = new JButton("Encode");
JButton jbtnDecode = new JButton("Decode");
JButton jbtnReset =  new JButton("Reset");
```

9. Add **this** as an action listener for the buttons and then add the buttons to the content pane.

```
// Add action listeners for the buttons.
jbtnEncode.addActionListener(this);
jbtnDecode.addActionListener(this);
jbtnReset.addActionListener(this);

// Add the buttons to the content pane.
jfrm.add(jbtnEncode);
jfrm.add(jbtnDecode);
jfrm.add(jbtnReset);
```

10. Conclude the **Coder** constructor with a call to **setVisible( )**, as shown here:

```
   // Display the frame.
   jfrm.setVisible(true);
}
```

11. Begin coding the **actionPerformed( )** method, as shown here:

```
// Handle action events.
public void actionPerformed(ActionEvent ae) {

  // If action command is "Encode" then encode the string.
  if(ae.getActionCommand().equals("Encode")) {

    // This will hold the encoded string.
    String encStr = "";

    // Obtain the plain text.
    String str = jtfPlaintext.getText();

    // Add 1 to each character.
    for(int i=0; i<str.length(); i++)
      encStr += (char)(str.charAt(i) + 1);

    // Set the coded text into the Cipher Text field.
    jtfCiphertext.setText(encStr.toString());
  }
```

This **if** statement checks the action command against "Encode". The command will be "Encode" if the user pressed the **jbtnEncode** button, or if the user pressed ENTER while entering text inside the **jtfPlaintext** text field. Because the action command for both **jbtnEncode** and **jtfPlaintext** is "Encode", both events are handled by the same code. In other words, events generated by these two controls both map to the same handler because their action commands are the same. This handler encodes the string in the Plain Text field and puts it into the Cipher Text field.

12. Add the following **else if**, which determines if the action command is equal to "Decode":

```
// If action command is "Decode" then decode the string.
else if(ae.getActionCommand().equals("Decode")) {

  // This will hold the decoded string.
  String decStr = "";

  // Obtain the cipher text.
  String str = jtfCiphertext.getText();

  // Subtract 1 from each character.
  for(int i=0; i<str.length(); i++)
```

```
    decStr += (char)(str.charAt(i) - 1);

    // Set the decoded text into the Plain Text field.
    jtfPlaintext.setText(decStr.toString());
  }
```

This code works like the "Encode" handler except that it decodes the string in the Cipher Text field and puts it into the Plain Text field.

13. Finish the **actionPerformed( )** method by handling the "Reset" action command, which is linked to **jbtnReset**. Because there are only three action commands, there is no need to explicitly test for "Reset". If execution reaches this point, it is the only option left.

```
    // Otherwise, must be "Reset" command.
    else {
      jtfPlaintext.setText("");
      jtfCiphertext.setText("");
    }
  }
```

14. Conclude by adding this **main( )** method:

```
public static void main(String[] args) {

  // Create the frame on the event dispatching thread.
  SwingUtilities.invokeLater(new Runnable() {
    public void run() {
      new Coder();
    }
  });

}
```

15. Here is all the code assembled into a complete program. Sample output is shown here:

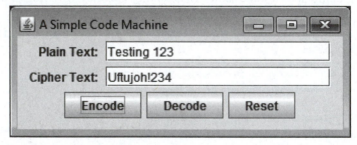

```
// Try This 17-2: A simple code machine.

import java.awt.*;
import java.awt.event.*;
import javax.swing.*;
```

```java
class Coder implements ActionListener {

  JTextField jtfPlaintext;
  JTextField jtfCiphertext;

  Coder() {

    // Create a new JFrame container.
    JFrame jfrm = new JFrame("A Simple Code Machine");

    // Specify FlowLayout for the layout manager.
    jfrm.setLayout(new FlowLayout());

    // Give the frame an initial size.
    jfrm.setSize(340, 130);

    // Terminate the program when the user closes the application.
    jfrm.setDefaultCloseOperation(JFrame.EXIT_ON_CLOSE);

    // Create two labels.
    JLabel jlabPlaintext = new JLabel("   Plain Text: ");
    JLabel jlabCiphertext = new JLabel("Cipher Text: ");

    // Create two text field instances.
    jtfPlaintext = new JTextField(20);
    jtfCiphertext = new JTextField(20);

    // Set the action commands for the text fields.
    jtfPlaintext.setActionCommand("Encode");
    jtfCiphertext.setActionCommand("Decode");

    // Add action listeners for the text fields.
    jtfPlaintext.addActionListener(this);
    jtfCiphertext.addActionListener(this);

    // Add the text fields and labels to the content pane.
    jfrm.add(jlabPlaintext);
    jfrm.add(jtfPlaintext);
    jfrm.add(jlabCiphertext);
    jfrm.add(jtfCiphertext);

    // Create push button instances.
    JButton jbtnEncode = new JButton("Encode");
    JButton jbtnDecode = new JButton("Decode");
    JButton jbtnReset =  new JButton("Reset");

    // Add action listeners for the buttons.
    jbtnEncode.addActionListener(this);
    jbtnDecode.addActionListener(this);
```

```
    jbtnReset.addActionListener(this);

    // Add the buttons to the content pane.
    jfrm.add(jbtnEncode);
    jfrm.add(jbtnDecode);
    jfrm.add(jbtnReset);

    // Display the frame.
    jfrm.setVisible(true);
  }

  // Handle action events.
  public void actionPerformed(ActionEvent ae) {

    // If action command is "Encode" then encode the string.
    if(ae.getActionCommand().equals("Encode")) {

      // This will hold the encoded string.
      String encStr = "";

      // Obtain the plain text.
      String str = jtfPlaintext.getText();

      // Add 1 to each character.
      for(int i=0; i<str.length(); i++)
        encStr += (char)(str.charAt(i) + 1);

      // Set the coded text into the Cipher Text field.
      jtfCiphertext.setText(encStr.toString());
    }

    // If action command is "Decode" then decode the string.
    else if(ae.getActionCommand().equals("Decode")) {

      // This will hold the decoded string.
      String decStr = "";

      // Obtain the cipher text.
      String str = jtfCiphertext.getText();

      // Subtract 1 from each character.
      for(int i=0; i<str.length(); i++)
        decStr += (char)(str.charAt(i) - 1);

      // Set the decoded text into the Plain Text field.
      jtfPlaintext.setText(decStr.toString());
    }

    // Otherwise, must be "Reset" command.
```

```
          else {
             jtfPlaintext.setText("");
             jtfCiphertext.setText("");
          }
       }

    public static void main(String[] args) {

       // Create the frame on the event dispatching thread.
       SwingUtilities.invokeLater(new Runnable() {
         public void run() {
           new Coder();
         }
       });
    }
  }
```

USE ANONYMOUS INNER CLASSES
TO HANDLE EVENTS

Up to this point, the programs in this chapter have used a simple, straightforward approach to handling events in which the main class of the application has implemented the listener interface itself and all events are sent to an instance of that class. While this is perfectly acceptable, it is not the only way to handle events. Two other approaches are commonly used. First, you can implement separate listener classes. Thus, different classes could handle different events, and these classes would be separate from the main class of the application. Second, you can implement listeners through the use of *anonymous inner classes*.

Recall from Chapter 6 that an inner class is a non-static class that is declared within another class. Anonymous inner classes are inner classes that don't have a name. Instead, an instance of the class is simply generated "on the fly" as needed. You have already been using anonymous inner classes in this chapter because they have been used to generate a call to the **invokeLater( )** method.

Anonymous inner classes make implementing some types of event handlers much easier. For example, given a **JButton** called **jbtn**, you could implement an action listener for it like this:

```
jbtn.addActionListener(new ActionListener() {
  public void actionPerformed(ActionEvent ae) {
    // Handle action event here.
  }
});
```

Here, an anonymous inner class is created that implements the **ActionListener** interface. Pay special attention to the syntax. The body of the inner class begins after the **{** that follows **new ActionListener( )**. Also notice that the call to **addActionListener( )** ends with a **)** and a **;** just like normal. The same basic syntax and approach is used to create an anonymous inner class for any event handler. Of course, for different events, you specify different event listeners and implement different methods.

One advantage to using an anonymous inner class is that the component that invokes the class's methods is already known. For instance, in the preceding example, there is no need to call **getActionCommand( )** to determine what component generated the event, because this implementation of **actionPerformed( )** will only be called by events generated by **jbtn**. You will see anonymous inner classes at work in subsequent examples.

EXERCISES

1. Most AWT components translate into native peers. Why is this a problem, and how does Swing fix it?

2. Most Swing components are written in 100 percent Java code. True or False?

3. What are the four top-level, heavyweight containers?

4. What is the most commonly used top-level container for an application?

5. **JFrame** contains several panes. To what pane are components added?

6. An event listener must _____ with a source in order to receive event notifications.

7. To receive an action event, a class must implement what interface?

8. When using a **JButton** or a **JTextField**, what method must be called to set the action command?

9. Name three layout managers.

10. The stopwatch example in Try This 17-1 uses two buttons, one to start the stopwatch and the other to stop it. However, it is possible to use only one button, which alternates between starting and stopping the stopwatch. One way to do this is to reset the text within the button after each press, alternating between Start and Stop. Because, by default, this text is also the action command associated with the button, you can use the same button for two different purposes. Your job is to rewrite Try This 17-1 so that it implements this approach.

    To solve this problem, you will use another **JButton** method: **setText( )**. This method sets the text in a button. It is shown here:

    void setText(String *msg*)

    Here, *msg* specifies the text that will be shown inside the button. This method lets you set the text inside a button during the execution of a program.

11. Modify the **SwingDemo** example in this chapter so that the **JFrame** displays five messages, one along each edge and one in the middle. Use the default **BorderLayout**. You can use whatever five messages you wish. Adjust the

size of the window and add appropriate spacing to the five messages so that they are centered nicely.

12. Modify the **ButtonDemo** example discussed in this chapter so that the **ButtonDemo** class is not an **ActionListener** and instead separate objects are used as the **ActionListeners** registered with the buttons. The two listener objects should be instances of the same class that implements **ActionListener**.

13. Modify the **ButtonDemo** example discussed in this chapter so that the **ButtonDemo** class is not an **ActionListener** and instead two anonymous inner classes are used as the **ActionListeners** registered with the buttons. Each button should have its own listener.

14. Create a Swing application that displays a window containing four buttons and a label. The first button says "Click here", and the other three buttons say "Not here". If one of the "Not here" buttons is clicked, the label displays the message "Wrong. Try again." If the "Click here" button is clicked, then the label displays "Good job. Do it again." Also, each time the "Click here" button is clicked, a new button is randomly chosen and given the text "Click here" and the other three buttons are given the text "Not here". The application quits when the user clicks the close box of the window. Use the **setText( )** method of the **JButton** class discussed in Exercise 10 and use the **Math.random( )** method that returns a random **double** value between 0 and 1.

15. Write a program that displays a **JFrame** with a label, two textboxes, and a button. The label says "Type the same thing in both boxes." When the user clicks the button, the contents of the two textboxes are compared. If the contents are different, the label displays the message "Try again. Type the same thing in both boxes." If the contents are the same, then a new **JFrame** appears with the message "They matched!" The close box of the new **JFrame** should just close the new window and not cause the program to quit.

16. True or False:

    A. If two or more action listeners register with the same button, only one of them is notified of a click in the button.

    B. A **JTextField** generates an **ActionEvent** every time the user clicks in the **JTextField**.

    C. A **JLabel** generates an **ActionEvent** every time the user clicks in the **JLabel**.

17. Suppose an action listener registers with three or four GUI controls, including at least one button and a text field. When its **actionPerformed( )** method is called, how can the action listener tell which of the controls generated the **ActionEvent**?

18. What are the main advantages of using an anonymous inner class as the action listener for one or more controls?

19. Implement a class with a **main( )** method that does the following:

A. creates an anonymous inner class implementing the **Nameable** interface below,

B. creates an instance **obj** of the anonymous inner class,

C. calls **obj.setName( )**,

D. calls **obj.getName( )** and prints the result.

```
public interface Nameable {
    // set the name of this object
    void setName(String name);

    // return the name of this object
    String getName();
```

CHAPTER 18

Exploring Swing Controls

The modern GUI is populated by a wide array of controls. Here, the term *controls* refers to components that directly interact with the user, such as buttons, text fields, and drop-down lists. To support the modern GUI, Swing provides a rich assortment of controls. Using them, you can construct applications that provide the contemporary look and feel with which you are familiar. Although a detailed description of each control is beyond the scope of this book, this chapter describes a representative sampling. Our purpose is to introduce several popular controls and describe the basic techniques required to use them. Once you understand how these components work, you will be able to use Java's API documentation to learn more about their capabilities and about Swing's other controls.

The Swing component classes described in this chapter are shown here:

JButton	JCheckBox	JComboBox
JLabel	JList	JRadioButton
JScrollPane	JTable	JTextField
JToggleButton	JTree	

These components are all lightweight, which means that they are all derived from **JComponent**.

Also discussed are the **ButtonGroup** class, which encapsulates a mutually exclusive set of buttons, and **ImageIcon**, which encapsulates a graphics image. Both are defined by Swing and packaged in **javax.swing**.

JLabel AND ImageIcon

JLabel is Swing's easiest-to-use component. It creates a label and was introduced in the preceding chapter. Here, we will look at **JLabel** a bit more closely. As you know, **JLabel** is a passive component, meaning that it does not respond to user input. In the preceding chapter, it was used to display a text message. However, it can also be used to display an icon (a graphics image) or both an icon and text. You can also specify the alignment of the label's contents. For example, here are three more of **JLabel**'s constructors:

> JLabel(String *str*, int *align*)
>
> JLabel(Icon *icon*, int *align*)
>
> JLabel(String *str*, Icon *icon*, int *align*)

Here, *str* specifies the text in the label, and *icon* specifies the graphics image. The horizontal alignment within the dimensions of the label is specified by *align*. The horizontal alignment must be one of the following values: **LEFT**, **RIGHT**, **CENTER**, **LEADING**, or **TRAILING**. (**LEADING** and **TRAILING** specify the leading or trailing edge, which is helpful when internationalizing a label for both left-to-right and right-to-left reading languages.) These constants are defined in the **SwingConstants** interface, along with several others used by the Swing classes.

Notice that icons are specified by objects of type **Icon**, which is an interface defined by Swing. The easiest way to obtain an icon is to use the **ImageIcon** class. **ImageIcon** implements **Icon** and encapsulates an image. Thus, an object of type **ImageIcon** can be passed as an argument to the **Icon** parameter of **JLabel**'s constructor. There are several ways to provide the image, including reading it from a file or downloading it from a URL. Here is the **ImageIcon** constructor used by the example in this section:

> ImageIcon(String *filename*)

It obtains the image in the file passed to *filename*. Files containing images commonly use extensions such as **gif**, **jpeg**, or **png**. These specify different image formats, but all can be loaded by **ImageIcon**.

The following program illustrates how to create and display labels that contain both an icon and a string, and use a specified alignment. The program creates three labels. Each label indicates a state of a traffic light: go, caution, and stop. They are instances of **ImageIcon** and are created by loading files called **Go.gif**, **Caution.gif**, and **Stop.gif** that contain the images. The text indicates the state of the light. In this example, the contents of each label are aligned differently, moving from left to right, but you might want to experiment with different alignments. One other point: notice that the content pane's default **BorderLayout** is used. Recall that **BorderLayout** defines five locations: center, north, south, east, and west. In this example, the first label goes into the north location, the second uses the center location, and the third the south location. **BorderLayout** makes it easy to show the alignment of the labels.

```java
// Demonstrate JLabel and ImageIcon.
// This example displays the three states of a traffic light.

import javax.swing.*;
import java.awt.*;

class JLabelDemo {

  JLabelDemo() {

    // Create a new JFrame container.
    JFrame jfrm = new JFrame("JLabel and ImageIcon Example");

    // Give the frame an initial size.
    jfrm.setSize(320, 280);

    // Terminate the program when the user closes the application.
    jfrm.setDefaultCloseOperation(JFrame.EXIT_ON_CLOSE);

    // Create an icon and label for Go.
    ImageIcon goIcon = new ImageIcon("Go.gif");              ←────────Make an icon from an image stored in a file.
    JLabel jlabGo = new JLabel(" Go ", goIcon, SwingConstants.LEFT);←─Create a label that
                                                                       contains an icon and text.
    // Create an icon and label for Caution.
    ImageIcon cautionIcon = new ImageIcon("Caution.gif");
    JLabel jlabCaution = new JLabel(" Caution ", cautionIcon,
                               SwingConstants.CENTER);

    // Create an icon and label for Stop.
    ImageIcon stopIcon = new ImageIcon("Stop.gif");
    JLabel jlabStop = new JLabel(" Stop ", stopIcon,
                               SwingConstants.RIGHT);

    // Add the labels to the content pane.
    jfrm.add(jlabGo, BorderLayout.NORTH);
    jfrm.add(jlabCaution, BorderLayout.CENTER);
    jfrm.add(jlabStop, BorderLayout.SOUTH);

    // Display the frame.
    jfrm.setVisible(true);
  }

  public static void main(String[] args) {
    // Create the GUI on the event dispatching thread.
    SwingUtilities.invokeLater(new Runnable() {
```

```
            public void run() {
               new JLabelDemo();
            }
         });
      }
   }
}
```

Output from the label example is shown here:

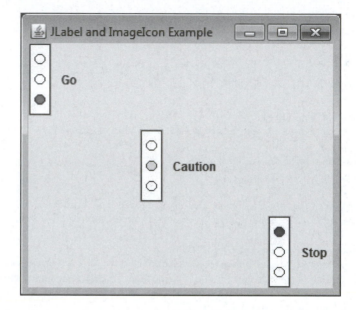

After a label has been created, you can change the text or icon that is displayed by using the **setText( )** or **setIcon( )** methods. The **setText( )** method was described in Chapter 17. The **setIcon( )** method is shown here:

     void setIcon(Icon *newIcon*)

Here, *newIcon* becomes the new image displayed within the label.

    Despite is relative simplicity, **JLabel** supports a number of other features you will want to explore. For example, you can set a keyboard mnemonic, set the vertical alignment, and obtain the text and/or icon in the label. **JLabel** is more powerful than you might first suspect.

Ask the Expert

Q How can I create a label that displays multiple lines of text?

A To show multiple lines in a label, you can use HTML as the label text. To do so, you must begin the text with the sequence **<html>**. When this is done, the text is automatically formatted as described by the markup. In addition to other benefits, using HTML enables you to create labels that span two or more lines. For example, this creates a label that displays two lines of text, with the string "Top" over the string "Bottom":

```
JLabel jlabhtml = new JLabel("<html>Top<br>Bottom");
```

Actually, HTML can be used in components other than labels. For example, you can use it in a button. In general, if a component displays text, then that text can be HTML.

Progress Check

1. Can a **JLabel** include a graphics image?
2. The contents of a **JLabel** must always be centered. True or False?
3. What class is commonly used to encapsulate an icon?

THE SWING BUTTONS

Chapter 17 introduced the button by describing the basics of the **JButton** class. However, **JButton** is just one of several Swing button types. Here is a list of the button classes that Swing provides:

JButton	A standard push button
JToggleButton	A two-state (on/off) button
JCheckBox	A standard check box
JRadioButton	A mutually exclusive check box

All buttons are subclasses of the **AbstractButton** class, which extends **JComponent**. **AbstractButton** contains many methods that provide the basic functionality common to all buttons.

Button events fall into three categories: action events, item events, and change events. An action event is generated when the user performs an action, such as clicking a button. An item event is generated when a button is selected or deselected. A change event is fired when the state of the button changes. Keep in mind that not all three events will necessarily be meaningful to all buttons, or all button applications. For example, **JButton** does not generate item events. In this chapter, only action and item events are used, and these two events are described here.

Answers:

1. Yes.
2. False.
3. **ImageIcon**

Handling Action Events

An action event is generated when the user clicks a button. The action event was introduced in Chapter 17. To review: An action event is represented by the **ActionEvent** class. Action events are handled by classes that implement the **ActionListener** interface. This interface specifies only one method, **actionPerformed( )**, which is shown here:

> void actionPerformed(ActionEvent *ae*)

The action event is received in *ae*.

The **ActionEvent** object passed to **actionPerformed( )** gives you access to several pieces of information. Perhaps most importantly, it enables you to identify what component has generated the event. There are two ways to identify the component: by its action command string (as shown in Chapter 17) or by its object reference. You can obtain the action command string for the component that generated the event by calling **getActionCommand( )** on the **ActionEvent** object. The action command identifies the button. You can set the action command by calling **setActionCommand( )**. Recall that these methods are declared as shown here:

> String getActionCommand( )

> void setActionCommand(String *cmd*)

The string passed in *cmd* becomes the new action command. The text in the button is unaffected.

The second way you can identify the component that generated an action event is by obtaining a reference to it by calling **getSource( )** on the **ActionEvent** object. This method is defined by **EventObject**, the superclass for all event objects. It is shown here:

> Object getSource( )

One advantage to using **getSource( )** is that if you need to act directly on the component, you can do so through this reference. Although we won't use this approach in the examples in this chapter, it is an option that may prove helpful in your own code.

Handling Item Events

An item event occurs when an item, such as a toggle button, check box, or radio button, is selected. Item events are represented by the **ItemEvent** class. Item events are handled by classes that implement the **ItemListener** interface. This interface specifies only one method: **itemStateChanged( )**, which is shown here:

> void itemStateChanged(ItemEvent *ie*)

The item event is received in *ie*.

To obtain a reference to the item that changed, call **getItem( )** on the **ItemEvent** object. This method is shown here:

> Object getItem( )

The reference returned must be cast to the component class being handled, such as **JCheckBox** or **JRadioButton**.

When an item event occurs, the component will be in one of two states: selected or deselected. The **ItemEvent** class defines the following **static final int** constants that represent these two states:

SELECTED	DESELECTED

To obtain the new state, call the **getStateChange( )** method defined by **ItemEvent**. It is shown here:

    int getStateChange( )

It returns either **ItemEvent.SELECTED** or **ItemEvent.DESELECTED**. You can also determine the selected/deselected state of a button by calling **isSelected( )**, which is defined by **AbstractButton**. It is shown here:

    boolean isSelected( )

It returns **true** if the button is selected and **false** otherwise.

JButton

The **JButton** class provides the functionality of a push button. You have already seen a simple form of it in the preceding chapter. Here we will use some of its additional features.

JButton allows an icon, a string, or both to be associated with the push button. Three of its constructors are shown here:

    JButton(Icon *icon*)
    JButton(String *str*)
    JButton(String *str*, Icon *icon*)

Here, *str* and *icon* are the string and icon used for the button.

As explained, when the button is pressed, an **ActionEvent** is generated. Using the **ActionEvent** object passed to the **actionPerformed( )** method of the registered **ActionListener**, you can obtain the action command string associated with the button. By default, this is the string displayed inside the button. However, you can set the action command by calling **setActionCommand( )** on the button. You can obtain the action command by calling **getActionCommand( )** on the event object. Thus, when using two or more buttons within the same application, the action command gives you an easy way to determine which button was pressed.

In the preceding chapter, you saw an example of a text-based button. The following demonstrates an icon-based button. It displays three push buttons and a label. Each button displays a traffic light state, using the same images as those used by the previous example. When a button is pressed, the state of the traffic light is displayed in the label. Notice the use of **setActionCommand( )** to set the action commands of the icon-based buttons.

```
// Demonstrate icon-based JButtons.
// This example displays traffic light icons inside buttons.

import java.awt.*;
import java.awt.event.*;
import javax.swing.*;

public class JButtonDemo implements ActionListener {
  JLabel jlab;

  JButtonDemo() {

    // Create a new JFrame container.
    JFrame jfrm = new JFrame("JButton Example");

    // Specify FlowLayout for the layout manager.
    jfrm.setLayout(new FlowLayout());

    // Give the frame an initial size.
    jfrm.setSize(300, 180);

    // Terminate the program when the user closes the application.
    jfrm.setDefaultCloseOperation(JFrame.EXIT_ON_CLOSE);

    // Create the buttons.
    ImageIcon goIcon = new ImageIcon("Go.gif");
    JButton jbtnGo = new JButton(goIcon);
    jbtnGo.setActionCommand("Go");
    jbtnGo.addActionListener(this);

    ImageIcon cautionIcon = new ImageIcon("Caution.gif");
    JButton jbtnCaution = new JButton(cautionIcon);
    jbtnCaution.setActionCommand("Caution");
    jbtnCaution.addActionListener(this);

    ImageIcon stopIcon = new ImageIcon("Stop.gif");
    JButton jbtnStop = new JButton(stopIcon);
    jbtnStop.setActionCommand("Stop");
    jbtnStop.addActionListener(this);

    // Add the buttons to the content pane.
    jfrm.add(jbtnGo);
    jfrm.add(jbtnCaution);
    jfrm.add(jbtnStop);

     // Create and add the label to content pane.
    jlab = new JLabel("Select a Traffic Light");
    jfrm.add(jlab);

    // Display the frame.
    jfrm.setVisible(true);
  }
```

Create an icon-based button.

```
// Handle button events.
public void actionPerformed(ActionEvent ae) {
  jlab.setText("You selected " + ae.getActionCommand() + ".");
}

public static void main(String[] args) {

  // Create the GUI on the event dispatching thread.
  SwingUtilities.invokeLater(new Runnable() {
    public void run() {
      new JButtonDemo();
    }
  });
}
}
```

Output from the button example is shown here:

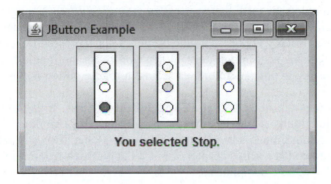

Sometimes it is useful to disable a button when it is not usable. To do so, call **setEnabled( )**, which is inherited from **JComponent**. Its general form is shown here:

    void setEnabled(boolean *state*)

If *state* is **true**, the button is enabled. If it is **false**, the button is disabled. A disabled button has its text and/or icon shown in gray. You might want to try disabling a button in the preceding program and observe the results.

In addition to the default icon specified by the **JButton** constructor, it is possible to specify icons that are displayed when certain button actions occur. Specifically, you can specify the icon that is displayed when the button is disabled, when it is pressed, and when it is rolled over by the mouse. To set these icons, you will use the following methods:

    void setDisabledIcon(Icon *disabledIcon*)

    void setPressedIcon(Icon *pressedIcon*)

    void setRolloverIcon(Icon *rolloverIcon*)

These methods are inherited by **JButton** from **AbstractButton**. Once the specified icon has been set, it will be displayed whenever one of the actions occurs. You might want to experiment with these on your own. Their addition can make for a very dynamic GUI.

JToggleButton

A useful variation on the push button is called a *toggle button*. A toggle button looks just like a push button, but it acts differently because it has two states: pushed and released. That is, when you press a toggle button, it stays pressed rather than popping back up as a regular push button does. When you press the toggle button a second time, it releases (pops up). Therefore, each time a toggle button is pushed, it toggles between its two states.

Toggle buttons are objects of the **JToggleButton** class. In addition to creating standard toggle buttons, **JToggleButton** is a superclass for two other Swing components that also represent two-state controls. These are **JCheckBox** and **JRadioButton**, which are described later in this chapter. Thus, **JToggleButton** defines the basic functionality of all two-state components.

JToggleButton defines several constructors. The one used by the example in this section is shown here:

JToggleButton(String *str*)

This creates a toggle button that contains the text passed in *str*. By default, the button is in the off position. Other constructors enable you to create a toggle button that contains images (or images and text) or set its state.

Like **JButton, JToggleButton** generates an action event each time it is pressed. Unlike **JButton,** however, **JToggleButton** also generates an item event. This event is used by those components that support the concept of selection. When a **JToggleButton** is pressed in, it is selected. When it is popped out, it is deselected.

To handle item events, you must implement the **ItemListener** interface. Each time an item event is generated, it is passed to the **itemStateChanged( )** method defined by **ItemListener**. Inside **itemStateChanged( )**, the **getItem( )** method can be called on the **ItemEvent** object to obtain a reference to the **JToggleButton** instance that generated the event.

Probably the easiest way to determine a toggle button's state is by calling the **isSelected( )** method on the button that generated the event, as described earlier. Recall that it returns **true** if the button is selected and **false** otherwise.

Here is an example that uses a toggle button. Notice how the item listener works. It simply calls **isSelected( )** to determine the button's state.

```java
// Demonstrate JToggleButton.
import java.awt.*;
import java.awt.event.*;
import javax.swing.*;

public class JToggleButtonDemo {

  JLabel jlab;
  JToggleButton jtbn;

  JToggleButtonDemo() {

    // Create a new JFrame container.
    JFrame jfrm = new JFrame("JToggleButton Example");

    // Specify FlowLayout for the layout manager.
    jfrm.setLayout(new FlowLayout());

    // Give the frame an initial size.
    jfrm.setSize(200, 100);

    // Terminate the program when the user closes the application.
    jfrm.setDefaultCloseOperation(JFrame.EXIT_ON_CLOSE);

    // Create a label.
    jlab = new JLabel("Button is off.");

    // Make a toggle button.
    jtbn =  new JToggleButton("On/Off");  ◄─────── Create a toggle button.

    // Add an item listener for the toggle button.
    jtbn.addItemListener(new ItemListener() {  ◄─────── Use an ItemListener to
      public void itemStateChanged(ItemEvent ie) {         handle toggle button events.
        if(jtbn.isSelected())  ◄─────── Use isSelected() to determine
          jlab.setText("Button is on.");   which state the button is in.
        else
          jlab.setText("Button is off.");
      }
    });

    // Add the toggle button and label to the content pane.
    jfrm.add(jtbn);
    jfrm.add(jlab);

    // Display the frame.
    jfrm.setVisible(true);
  }
```

```
public static void main(String[] args) {

  // Create the GUI on the event dispatching thread.
  SwingUtilities.invokeLater(new Runnable() {
    public void run() {
      new JToggleButtonDemo();
    }
  });
}
}
```

The output from the toggle button example is shown here:

Check Boxes

The **JCheckBox** class provides the functionality of a check box. Its immediate superclass is **JToggleButton**, which provides support for two-state buttons, as just described. **JCheckBox** defines several constructors. The one used here is

JCheckBox(String *str*)

It creates a check box that has the text specified by *str* as a label. Other constructors let you specify the initial selection state of the button and specify an icon.

When the user selects or deselects a check box, an **ItemEvent** is generated. You can obtain a reference to the **JCheckBox** that generated the event by calling **getItem( )** on the **ItemEvent** passed to the **itemStateChanged( )** method defined by **ItemListener**. The easiest way to determine the selected state of a check box is to call **isSelected( )** on the **JCheckBox** instance.

The following example illustrates check boxes. It displays four check boxes and a label. When the user clicks a check box, an **ItemEvent** is generated. Inside the **itemStateChanged( )** method, **getItem( )** is called to obtain a reference to the **JCheckBox** object that generated the event. Next, a call to **isSelected( )** determines if the box was selected or cleared. The **getText( )** method gets the text for that check box and uses it to set the text inside the label.

```
// Demonstrate JCheckbox.
import java.awt.*;
import java.awt.event.*;
import javax.swing.*;
```

```java
public class JCheckBoxDemo implements ItemListener {
  JLabel jlabChange;
  JLabel jlabSupported;

  JCheckBox cbWin;
  JCheckBox cbLinux;
  JCheckBox cbMac;

  JCheckBoxDemo() {
    // Create a new JFrame container.
    JFrame jfrm = new JFrame("JCheckBox Example");

    // Specify FlowLayout for the layout manager.
    jfrm.setLayout(new FlowLayout());

    // Give the frame an initial size.
    jfrm.setSize(340, 140);

    // Terminate the program when the user closes the application.
    jfrm.setDefaultCloseOperation(JFrame.EXIT_ON_CLOSE);

    // Add check boxes to the content pane.
    cbWin = new JCheckBox("Windows");
    cbWin.addItemListener(this);
    jfrm.add(cbWin);

    cbLinux = new JCheckBox("Linux");                    Create the check boxes.
    cbLinux.addItemListener(this);
    jfrm.add(cbLinux);

    cbMac = new JCheckBox("Mac OS");
    cbMac.addItemListener(this);
    jfrm.add(cbMac);

    // Create labels.
    jlabChange = new JLabel("Select Supported Operating Systems");
    jfrm.add(jlabChange);

    jlabSupported = new JLabel();
    jfrm.add(jlabSupported);

                                              Listen for item events
    // Display the frame.                      generated by the check
    jfrm.setVisible(true);                     boxes.
  }

  // Handle item events for the check boxes.
  public void itemStateChanged(ItemEvent ie) {
    JCheckBox cb = (JCheckBox)ie.getItem();

                                              Determine if the check box
    if(cb.isSelected())                       has been selected or cleared.
      jlabChange.setText(cb.getText() + " has been selected");
```

```
      else
        jlabChange.setText(cb.getText() + " has been cleared");

      // Build a string the indicate all selections.
      String supported = "Supported Operating Systems: ";
      if(cbWin.isSelected()) supported += "Windows  ";
      if(cbLinux.isSelected()) supported += "Linux  ";
      if(cbMac.isSelected()) supported += "Mac OS";

      jlabSupported.setText(supported);
    }

    public static void main(String[] args) {

      // Create the GUI on the event dispatching thread.
      SwingUtilities.invokeLater(new Runnable() {
        public void run() {
          new JCheckBoxDemo();
        }
      });
    }
  }
```

Output from this example is shown here:

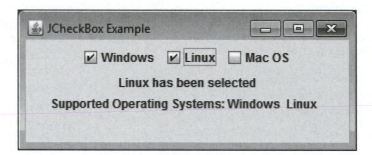

Radio Buttons

Radio buttons are a group of mutually exclusive buttons, in which only one button can be selected at any one time. They are supported by the **JRadioButton** class, which extends **JToggleButton**. **JRadioButton** provides several constructors. The one used in the example is shown here:

> JRadioButton(String *str*)

Here, *str* is the label for the button. Other constructors let you specify the initial selection state of the button and specify an icon.

In order for their mutually exclusive nature to be activated, radio buttons must be configured into a group. Only one of the buttons in the group can be selected at any time. For example, if a user presses a radio button that is in a group, any previously selected button in that group is automatically deselected. A button group is created by the **ButtonGroup** class. Its default constructor is invoked for this purpose. Elements are then added to the button group via the following method:

void add(AbstractButton *btn*)

Here, *btn* is a reference to the button to be added to the group.

A **JRadioButton** generates action events, item events, and change events each time the button selection changes. Often, it is the action event that is handled, which means that you will need to implement the **ActionListener** interface. Recall that the only method defined by **ActionListener** is **actionPerformed()**. Inside this method, you can use a number of different ways to determine which button was selected. Here are three. First, you can check its action command by calling **getActionCommand()**. By default, the action command is the same as the button label, but you can set the action command to something else by calling **setActionCommand()** on the radio button. Second, you can call **getSource()** on the **ActionEvent** object and check that reference against the buttons. Finally, you can simply check each radio button to find out which one is currently selected by calling **isSelected()** on each button. Remember, each time an action event occurs, it means that the button being selected has changed and that one and only one button will be selected.

The following example illustrates how to use radio buttons. Three radio buttons are created. The buttons are then added to a button group. As explained, this is necessary to cause their mutually exclusive behavior. Pressing a radio button generates an action event, which is handled by **actionPerformed()**. Within that handler, the **getActionCommand()** method gets the text that is associated with the radio button and uses it to set the text within a label.

```java
// Demonstrate JRadioButton
import java.awt.*;
import java.awt.event.*;
import javax.swing.*;

public class JRadioButtonDemo implements ActionListener {
  JLabel jlab;

  JRadioButtonDemo() {

    // Create a new JFrame container.
    JFrame jfrm = new JFrame("JRadioButton Example");

    // Specify FlowLayout for the layout manager.
    jfrm.setLayout(new FlowLayout());

    // Give the frame an initial size.
    jfrm.setSize(350, 100);

    // Terminate the program when the user closes the application.
    jfrm.setDefaultCloseOperation(JFrame.EXIT_ON_CLOSE);
```

```
    // Create radio buttons and add them to content pane.
    JRadioButton b1 = new JRadioButton("Debug");
    b1.addActionListener(this);
    jfrm.add(b1);

    JRadioButton b2 = new JRadioButton("Maximize Speed");
    b2.addActionListener(this);
    jfrm.add(b2);

    JRadioButton b3 = new JRadioButton("Minimize Size");
    b3.addActionListener(this);
    jfrm.add(b3);

    // Define a button group.
    ButtonGroup bg = new ButtonGroup();
    bg.add(b1);
    bg.add(b2);
    bg.add(b3);

    // Create a label and add it to the content pane.
    jlab = new JLabel("Select One");
    jfrm.add(jlab);

    // Display the frame.
    jfrm.setVisible(true);
  }

  // Handle button selection.
  public void actionPerformed(ActionEvent ae) {
    jlab.setText("You selected " + ae.getActionCommand());
  }

  public static void main(String[] args) {

    // Create the GUI on the event dispatching thread.
    SwingUtilities.invokeLater(new Runnable() {
      public void run() {
        new JRadioButtonDemo();
      }
    });
  }
}
```

Create the radio buttons.

Add radio buttons to a button group.

Output from the radio button example is shown here:

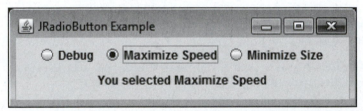

Progress Check

1. What type of event is typically handled when using **JCheckBox**?
2. **JToggleButton** creates a _____-state button.
3. For radio buttons to function correctly, they must be added to what class?

JTextField

JTextField was introduced in Chapter 17. To review, **JTextField** enables the user to enter a single line of text. It generates an **ActionEvent** when the user presses ENTER in the field. To handle action events, you must implement the **actionListener** interface. A **JTextField** has an action command string associated with it. By default, the action command is the current contents of the text field. However, you can set this to an action command of your choosing by calling the **setActionCommand( )** method. To obtain the string that is currently displayed in the text field, call **getText( )** on the **JTextField** instance. It is shown here:

String getText( )

You can set the text in a **JTextField** by calling **setText( )**, shown next:

void setText(String *text*)

Here, *text* is the string that will be put into the text field. In addition to these features with which you are already familiar, **JTextField** supports several others that you might find useful. A sampling is discussed here.

You can create a **JTextField** that contains an initial string by using one of these constructors:

JTextField(String *str*)

JTextField(String *str*, int *cols*)

In the first case, the text field is sized to fit the string. In the second form, the number of columns is specified.

You can obtain the portion of the text that has been selected by calling **getSelectedText( )**, shown here:

String getSelectedText( )

If no text has been selected, **null** is returned.

You can move text to or from the clipboard under program control by using the methods **cut( )**, **copy( )**, and **paste( )**, shown here:

void cut( )

void copy( )

void paste( )

Answers:

1. **ItemEvent**
2. two
3. **ButtonGroup**

The **cut( )** method removes any text that is selected within the text field and copies it to the clipboard. The **copy( )** method simply copies, but does not remove, the selected text. The **paste( )** method copies any text that may be in the clipboard to the text field. If the text field contains selected text, then that text is replaced by what is in the clipboard. Otherwise, the clipboard text is inserted immediately before the current cursor position.

The following program demonstrates **JTextField** and several of the methods just discussed. It creates a text field that is 15 columns wide. Whenever you press ENTER while in the text field, the current contents are displayed. If any part of the field has been selected, the selected text is also displayed. The program has two buttons called Cut and Paste. These buttons show how the standard cut and paste functions can be utilized under program control. If text has been selected, then pressing Cut removes the selected text and puts it in the clipboard. Pressing Paste copies any text in the clipboard to the text field. Of course, you can also perform cut and paste through standard keyboard commands, such as CTRL-X and CTRL-V in the Windows environment. Sample output is shown here:

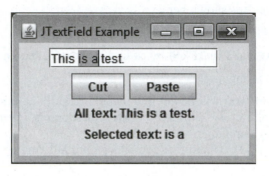

```
// Demonstrate various features of a text field.
import java.awt.*;
import java.awt.event.*;
import javax.swing.*;
import javax.swing.event.*;

class JTextFieldDemo {

  JLabel jlabAll;
  JLabel jlabSelected;

  JTextField jtf;

  JButton jbtnCut;
  JButton jbtnPaste;

  public JTextFieldDemo() {

    // Create a new JFrame container.
    JFrame jfrm = new JFrame("JTextField Example");
```

```
// Specify FlowLayout for the layout manager.
jfrm.setLayout(new FlowLayout());

// Give the frame an initial size.
jfrm.setSize(200, 150);

// Terminate the program when the user closes the application.
jfrm.setDefaultCloseOperation(JFrame.EXIT_ON_CLOSE);

// Create labels.
jlabAll = new JLabel("All text: ");
jlabSelected = new JLabel("Selected text: ");

// Create the text field.
jtf = new JTextField("This is a test.", 15);  ◄──────── Create a text field.

// Add an action listener for the text field.
// Each time the user presses enter, the contents
// of the field are displayed. Any currently
// selected text is also displayed.
jtf.addActionListener(new ActionListener() {
  public void actionPerformed(ActionEvent ae) {
    jlabAll.setText("All text: " + jtf.getText());  ◄──────── Each time the user
    if(jtf.getSelectedText() != null)                         presses ENTER, display
      jlabSelected.setText("Selected text: " +  ◄──────── the entire text and any
                        jtf.getSelectedText());              selected text.
  }
});

// Create the Cut and Paste buttons.
jbtnCut = new JButton("Cut");
jbtnPaste = new JButton("Paste");

// Add action listener for the Cut button.
jbtnCut.addActionListener(new ActionListener() {
  public void actionPerformed(ActionEvent ae) {
    // Cut any selected text and put it
    // on the clipboard.
    jtf.cut();  ◄──────────────────────────────────── Remove selected text
    jlabAll.setText("All text: " + jtf.getText());    and put it in the
    if(jtf.getSelectedText() != null)                 clipboard.
      jlabSelected.setText("Selected text: " +
                        jtf.getSelectedText());
  }
});

// Add action listener for the Paste button.
jbtnPaste.addActionListener(new ActionListener() {
  public void actionPerformed(ActionEvent ae) {
    // Paste text from the clipboard into
```

```
            // the text field.
            jtf.paste();  ◄───────────── Copy text from the clipboard.
        }
    });

    // Add the components to the content pane.
    jfrm.add(jtf);
    jfrm.add(jbtnCut);
    jfrm.add(jbtnPaste);
    jfrm.add(jlabAll);
    jfrm.add(jlabSelected);

    // Display the frame.
    jfrm.setVisible(true);
  }

  public static void main(String[] args) {
    // Create the GUI on the event dispatching thread.
    SwingUtilities.invokeLater(new Runnable() {
      public void run() {
        new JTextFieldDemo();
      }
    });
  }
}
```

Much of this program will be familiar, but there are a few key points that warrant a close look. First, when the text field **jtf** is created, it is given both an initial size of 15 and initial contents consisting of the string "This is a test."

Each time the user presses ENTER when inside the **jtf** text field, an **ActionEvent** is generated and sent to the **actionPerformed( )** method of **jtf**'s action listener. This method obtains the text currently held in the text field by calling **getText( )** on **jtf**. It then displays the text through the label referred to by **jlabAll**. It also obtains any selected text by calling **getSelectedText( )** and displays it through the **jlabSelected** label.

Next, look at the event handlers for the Cut and Paste buttons. The Cut button calls **cut( )** to remove any selected text and put it into the clipboard. The Paste button copies text from the clipboard into the text field by calling **paste( )**.

TRY THIS 18-1 A SWING-BASED FILE COMPARISON UTILITY

SwingFC.java

Although only a small number of controls have been introduced, you can still put them to use to create a practical application. In Try This 11-1 you created a console-based file comparison utility. This project creates a Swing-based version of the program. As you will see, giving this application a Swing-based user interface substantially improves its appearance and makes it easier to use. It also adds some additional functionality because it lets you display the position of the first mismatch when two files differ. Here is how the Swing version looks:

Because Swing streamlines the creation of GUI-based programs, you might be surprised by how easy it is to create this program.

STEP-BY-STEP

1. Begin by creating a file called **SwingFC.java** and then enter the following comment and **import** statements:

```
/*
    Try This 18-1

    A Swing-based file comparison utility.

    Requires JDK 7 or later.
*/

import java.awt.*;
import java.awt.event.*;
import javax.swing.*;
import java.io.*;
```

2. Next, begin the **SwingFC** class as shown here:

```
class SwingFC implements ActionListener {

    JTextField jtfFirst;  // holds the first file name
    JTextField jtfSecond; // holds the second file name

    JButton jbtnComp; // button to compare the files
```

```
JLabel jlabFirst, jlabSecond; // displays prompts
JLabel jlabResult; // displays results and error messages

JCheckBox jcbLoc; // check to display location of mismatch
```

The names of the files to compare are entered into the text fields defined by **jtfFirst** and **jtfSecond**. To compare the files, the user presses the **jbtnComp** button. Prompting messages are displayed in **jlabFirst** and **jlabSecond**. The results of the comparison, or any error messages, are displayed in **jlabResult**. The **jcbLoc** check box lets the user determine if the position of the first mismatch is displayed.

3. Code the **SwingFC** constructor like this:

```
SwingFC() {

  // Create a new JFrame container.
  JFrame jfrm = new JFrame("Compare Files");

  // Specify FlowLayout for the layout manager.
  jfrm.setLayout(new FlowLayout());

  // Give the frame an initial size.
  jfrm.setSize(200, 220);

  // Terminate the program when the user closes the application.
  jfrm.setDefaultCloseOperation(JFrame.EXIT_ON_CLOSE);

  // Create the text fields for the file names.
  jtfFirst = new JTextField(14);
  jtfSecond = new JTextField(14);

  // Create the Compare button.
  JButton jbtnComp = new JButton("Compare");

  // Add action listener for the Compare button.
  jbtnComp.addActionListener(this);

  // Create the labels.
  jlabFirst = new JLabel("First file: ");
  jlabSecond = new JLabel("Second file: ");
  jlabResult = new JLabel("");

  // Create check box.
  jcbLoc = new JCheckBox("Show position of mismatch");

  // Add the components to the content pane.
  jfrm.add(jlabFirst);
  jfrm.add(jtfFirst);
  jfrm.add(jlabSecond);
```

```
jfrm.add(jtfSecond);
jfrm.add(jcbLoc);
jfrm.add(jbtnComp);
jfrm.add(jlabResult);

// Display the frame.
jfrm.setVisible(true);
}
```

Most of the code in this constructor should be familiar to you. However, notice one thing: an action listener is added only to the push button **jbtnComp**.

Action listeners are not added to the text fields. Here's why: the contents of the text fields are needed only when the Compare button is pushed. At no other time are their contents required. Thus, there is no reason to respond to any text field events. As you begin to write more Swing programs, you will find that this is often the case when using a text field.

4. Begin creating the **actionPerformed( )** event handler as shown next. This method is called when the Compare button is pressed.

```
// Compare the files when the Compare button is pressed.
public void actionPerformed(ActionEvent ae) {
   int i = 0, j = 0;
   int count = 0;

   // First, confirm that both file names have been entered.
   if(jtfFirst.getText().equals("")) {
     jlabResult.setText("First file name missing.");
     return;
   }
   if(jtfSecond.getText().equals("")) {
     jlabResult.setText("Second file name missing.");
     return;
   }
```

The method begins by confirming that the user has entered a file name into each of the text fields. If this is not the case, the missing file name is reported and the handler returns.

5. Now, finish **actionPerformed( )** by adding the code that actually opens the files and then compares them.

```
// Compare files. Use try-with-resources to manage the files.
try (FileInputStream f1 =
        new FileInputStream(jtfFirst.getText());
     FileInputStream f2 =
        new FileInputStream(jtfSecond.getText()))
{

   // Check the contents of each file.
   do {
```

```
      i = f1.read();
      j = f2.read();
      if(i != j) break;
      count++;
    } while(i != -1 && j != -1);

    if(i != j) {
      if(jcbLoc.isSelected())
        jlabResult.setText("Files differ at location " + count);
      else
        jlabResult.setText("Files are not the same.");
    }
    else
      jlabResult.setText("Files compare equal.");

  } catch(IOException exc) {
    jlabResult.setText("File Error" + exc);
  }
}
```

Notice that the state of the check box is tested to determine if the location of the first mismatch is to be displayed.

6. Finish **SwingFC** by adding the following **main( )** method.

```
public static void main(String[] args) {

  // Create the GUI on the event dispatching thread.
  SwingUtilities.invokeLater(new Runnable() {
    public void run() {
    new SwingFC();
    }
  });
}
}
```

7. The entire Swing-based file comparison program is shown here:

```
/*
     Try This 18-1

     A Swing-based file comparison utility.

     It uses the try-with-resources statement and
     requires JDK 7 or later.
*/

import java.awt.*;
import java.awt.event.*;
import javax.swing.*;
import java.io.*;
```

```java
class SwingFC implements ActionListener {

  JTextField jtfFirst;  // holds the first file name
  JTextField jtfSecond; // holds the second file name

  JButton jbtnComp; // button to compare the files

  JLabel jlabFirst, jlabSecond; // displays prompts
  JLabel jlabResult; // displays results and error messages

  JCheckBox jcbLoc; // check to display location of mismatch

  SwingFC() {

    // Create a new JFrame container.
    JFrame jfrm = new JFrame("Compare Files");

    // Specify FlowLayout for the layout manager.
    jfrm.setLayout(new FlowLayout());

    // Give the frame an initial size.
    jfrm.setSize(200, 220);

    // Terminate the program when the user closes the application.
    jfrm.setDefaultCloseOperation(JFrame.EXIT_ON_CLOSE);

    // Create the text fields for the file names.
    jtfFirst = new JTextField(14);
    jtfSecond = new JTextField(14);

    // Create the Compare button.
    JButton jbtnComp = new JButton("Compare");

    // Add action listener for the Compare button.
    jbtnComp.addActionListener(this);

    // Create the labels.
    jlabFirst = new JLabel("First file: ");
    jlabSecond = new JLabel("Second file: ");
    jlabResult = new JLabel("");

    // Create check box.
    jcbLoc = new JCheckBox("Show position of mismatch");

    // Add the components to the content pane.
    jfrm.add(jlabFirst);
    jfrm.add(jtfFirst);
    jfrm.add(jlabSecond);
    jfrm.add(jtfSecond);
    jfrm.add(jcbLoc);
```

```
    jfrm.add(jbtnComp);
    jfrm.add(jlabResult);

    // Display the frame.
    jfrm.setVisible(true);
  }

  // Compare the files when the Compare button is pressed.
  public void actionPerformed(ActionEvent ae) {
    int i = 0, j = 0;
    int count = 0;

    // First, confirm that both file names have been entered.
    if(jtfFirst.getText().equals("")) {
      jlabResult.setText("First file name missing.");
      return;
    }
    if(jtfSecond.getText().equals("")) {
      jlabResult.setText("Second file name missing.");
      return;
    }

    // Compare files. Use try-with-resources to manage the files.
    try (FileInputStream f1 =
            new FileInputStream(jtfFirst.getText());
         FileInputStream f2 =
            new FileInputStream(jtfSecond.getText()))
    {

      // Check the contents of each file.
      do {
        i = f1.read();
        j = f2.read();
        if(i != j) break;
        count++;
      } while(i != -1 && j != -1);

      if(i != j) {
        if(jcbLoc.isSelected())
          jlabResult.setText("Files differ at location " + count);
        else
          jlabResult.setText("Files are not the same.");
      }
      else
        jlabResult.setText("Files compare equal.");

    } catch(IOException exc) {
      jlabResult.setText("File Error");
    }
  }
```

```
   public static void main(String[] args) {

     // Create the GUI on the event dispatching thread.
     SwingUtilities.invokeLater(new Runnable() {
       public void run() {
         new SwingFC();
       }
     });
   }
}
```

JScrollPane

JScrollPane is a lightweight container that automatically handles the scrolling of another lightweight component. The component being scrolled can either be an individual component, such as a table, or a group of components contained within another lightweight container, such as a **JPanel**. In either case, if the object being scrolled is larger than the viewable area, horizontal and/or vertical scroll bars are automatically provided, and the component can be scrolled through the pane. Because **JScrollPane** automates scrolling, it usually eliminates the need to manage individual scroll bars.

The viewable area of a scroll pane is called the *viewport*. It is a window in which the component being scrolled is displayed. Thus, the viewport displays the visible portion of the component being scrolled. The scroll bars scroll the component through the viewport. In its default behavior, a **JScrollPane** will dynamically add or remove a scroll bar as needed. For example, if the component is taller than the viewport, a vertical scroll bar is added. If the component will completely fit within the viewport, the scroll bars are removed.

JScrollPane defines several constructors. The one used in this chapter is shown here:

JScrollPane(Component *comp*)

The component to be scrolled is specified by *comp*. Scroll bars are automatically displayed when the content of the pane exceeds the dimensions of the viewport.

Here are the steps to follow to use a scroll pane:

1. Create the component to be scrolled.
2. Create an instance of **JScrollPane**, passing to it the object to scroll.
3. Add the scroll pane to the content pane.

The following example illustrates a scroll pane. It does so by creating a multiline label. As explained in the Ask the Expert box presented earlier, this is done by use of HTML-based text. The label is then added to a scroll pane, and the scroll pane is added to the content pane. Because the label contents are larger than the frame that holds them, vertical and horizontal scroll bars appear automatically. You can use the scroll bars to scroll the text into view.

```java
// A simple JScrollPane example.
import javax.swing.*;

class JScrollPaneDemo {

  JScrollPaneDemo() {

    // Create a new JFrame container.
    JFrame jfrm = new JFrame("JScrollPane Example");

    // Give the frame an initial size.
    jfrm.setSize(200, 120);

    // Terminate the program when the user closes the application.
    jfrm.setDefaultCloseOperation(JFrame.EXIT_ON_CLOSE);

    // Create a long, HTML-based label.
    JLabel jlab =
      new JLabel("<html>JScrollPane simplifies what would<br>" +
                 "otherwise be complicated tasks.<br>" +
                 "It can be used to scroll any lightweight <br>" +
                 "component or lightweight container. It is <br>" +
                 "especially useful when scrolling tables, lists,<br>" +
                 "or images.");

    // Create a scroll pane and have it scroll the label.
    JScrollPane jscrlp = new JScrollPane(jlab);

    // Add the scroll pane to the frame.
    jfrm.add(jscrlp);

    // Display the frame.
    jfrm.setVisible(true);
  }

  public static void main(String[] args) {

    // Create the GUI on the event dispatching thread.
    SwingUtilities.invokeLater(new Runnable() {
      public void run() {
        new JScrollPaneDemo();
      }
    });
  }
}
```

Create a multiline label.

Create a scroll pane that contains the multiline label.

Add the scroll pane to the content pane.

Output from the scroll pane example is shown here:

Progress Check

1. What method is called to obtain the selected text within a **JTextField**?
2. **JScrollPane** always shows both horizontal and vertical scroll bars. True or False?
3. In a **JScrollPane**, the viewable area is called the _____.

TRY THIS 18-2 SCROLL A JPanel

`ScrollJPanelDemo.java`

Because **JPanel** is a lightweight container that inherits **JComponent**, it too can be scrolled using **JScrollPane**. This capability makes it possible to scroll the entire contents of a **JPanel** with almost no effort on your part. When screen space is in short supply, scrolling a panel might be the solution to an otherwise difficult situation. You can simply add a set of components to the panel and then use a **JScrollPane** to scroll through the set.

Furthermore, **because JPanel** inherits **JComponent**, it is also a component. Thus, **JPanel** is a lightweight container that can also be used to hold other **JPanel**s. This makes **JPanel** perfect for creating a multilayered containment system.

Answers:

1. **getSelectedText( )**
2. False. Scroll bars are shown only when needed.
3. viewport

JPanel defines several constructors. In this example, only the default constructor is used. As the example will show, you can set the layout manager in just the same way as you do with a **JFrame**. By default, a **JPanel** is created with flow layout. It also uses double buffering. As mentioned in Chapter 15, double buffering is a mechanism that is commonly employed to achieve a better user experience when screen refreshes take place. Instead of drawing each component directly on the screen, which can lead to "flicker," the components are rendered to a separate buffer. When the rendering is complete, the buffer is copied to the screen in one fast, uninterrupted operation. In this way, the contents of a panel appear instantaneously and complete, rather than slowly and in pieces. You can turn off double buffering if desired, although you will seldom want to do so. Support for double buffering is inherited from **JComponent**.

This example demonstrates how to create a **JPanel**, add components to it, and then add the panel to a **JScrollPane**, to enable automatic scrolling of the panel. You will notice that the panel's layout manager is set to **GridLayout**. It lays out components in a two-dimensional grid. The size of the grid can be specified using this constructor:

GridLayout(int *numRows*, int *numCols*)

Here, the number of rows is passed in *numRows,* and the number of columns is passed in *numCols*. In this example, laying out the components in a grid makes the effects of scrolling quite apparent. (Understand, however, that in your own code, you will choose a layout manager appropriate to your needs. Neither **JPanel** nor **JScrollPane** requires the use of **GridLayout**.) In this example, the panel contains a label and a series of check boxes. However, you can use the basic technique whenever you need to scroll the contents of a panel. Sample output is shown here:

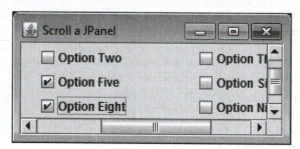

STEP-BY-STEP

1. Create a file called **ScrollJPanelDemo.java** and add the following comment and **import** statements:

```
// Try This 18-2: Use a JScrollPane to scroll a JPanel.

import java.awt.*;
import javax.swing.*;
```

2. Begin the **ScrollJPanelDemo** class like this:

```
class ScrollJPanelDemo {

  ScrollJPanelDemo() {

    // Create a new JFrame container.
    JFrame jfrm = new JFrame("Scroll a JPanel");

    // Give the frame an initial size.
    jfrm.setSize(280, 130);

    // Terminate the program when the user closes the application.
    jfrm.setDefaultCloseOperation(JFrame.EXIT_ON_CLOSE);
```

3. Add the following lines, which create the label and check boxes:

```
// Create a label.
JLabel jlabOptions = new JLabel("Select one or more options: ");

// Make some check boxes.
JCheckBox jcbOpt1 = new JCheckBox("Option One");
JCheckBox jcbOpt2 = new JCheckBox("Option Two");
JCheckBox jcbOpt3 = new JCheckBox("Option Three");
JCheckBox jcbOpt4 = new JCheckBox("Option Four");
JCheckBox jcbOpt5 = new JCheckBox("Option Five");
JCheckBox jcbOpt6 = new JCheckBox("Option Six");
JCheckBox jcbOpt7 = new JCheckBox("Option Seven");
JCheckBox jcbOpt8 = new JCheckBox("Option Eight");
JCheckBox jcbOpt9 = new JCheckBox("Option Nine");
JCheckBox jcbOpt10 = new JCheckBox("Option Ten");

// No event handlers used by this example, but as an
// exercise, you might try adding some.
```

Because the point of this program is to demonstrate scrolling a **JPanel**, no event handlers are included because the check boxes are simply used for their appearance. However, as an experiment, you can try adding event handlers of your own.

4. Add the code that constructs the **JPanel** that will be scrolled and then add the label and check boxes to it.

```
// Create a JPanel to hold the options check boxes.
JPanel jpnl = new JPanel();
jpnl.setLayout(new GridLayout(5, 3));

// Add check boxes and label to the JPanel.
jpnl.add(jlabOptions);
jpnl.add(new JLabel("")); // a placeholder label
jpnl.add(new JLabel("")); // a placeholder label
```

```
jpnl.add(jcbOpt1);
jpnl.add(jcbOpt2);
jpnl.add(jcbOpt3);
jpnl.add(jcbOpt4);
jpnl.add(jcbOpt5);
jpnl.add(jcbOpt6);
jpnl.add(jcbOpt7);
jpnl.add(jcbOpt8);
jpnl.add(jcbOpt9);
jpnl.add(jcbOpt10);
```

5. Create the **JScrollPane**, using the panel as the object to be scrolled. Then add the scroll pane to the content pane. Finally, make the frame visible.

```
// Create a scroll pane that will scroll the panel.
JScrollPane jscrlp = new JScrollPane(jpnl);

// Add that scroll pane to the frame.
jfrm.add(jscrlp);

// Display the frame.
jfrm.setVisible(true);
}
```

6. End the class in the usual way.

```
    public static void main(String[] args) {

        // Create the GUI on the event dispatching thread.
        SwingUtilities.invokeLater(new Runnable() {
          public void run() {
            new ScrollJPanelDemo();
          }
        });
    }
}
```

7. The entire program is shown here:

```
// Try This 18-2: Use a JScrollPane to scroll a JPanel.

import java.awt.*;
import javax.swing.*;

class ScrollJPanelDemo {

  ScrollJPanelDemo() {

    // Create a new JFrame container.
    JFrame jfrm = new JFrame("Scroll a JPanel");
```

```java
    // Give the frame an initial size.
    jfrm.setSize(280, 130);

    // Terminate the program when the user closes the application.
    jfrm.setDefaultCloseOperation(JFrame.EXIT_ON_CLOSE);

    // Create a label.
    JLabel jlabOptions = new JLabel("Select one or more options: ");

    // Make some check boxes.
    JCheckBox jcbOpt1 = new JCheckBox("Option One");
    JCheckBox jcbOpt2 = new JCheckBox("Option Two");
    JCheckBox jcbOpt3 = new JCheckBox("Option Three");
    JCheckBox jcbOpt4 = new JCheckBox("Option Four");
    JCheckBox jcbOpt5 = new JCheckBox("Option Five");
    JCheckBox jcbOpt6 = new JCheckBox("Option Six");
    JCheckBox jcbOpt7 = new JCheckBox("Option Seven");
    JCheckBox jcbOpt8 = new JCheckBox("Option Eight");
    JCheckBox jcbOpt9 = new JCheckBox("Option Nine");
    JCheckBox jcbOpt10 = new JCheckBox("Option Ten");

    // No event handlers used by this example, but as an
    // exercise, you might try adding some.

    // Create a JPanel to hold the options check boxes.
    JPanel jpnl = new JPanel();
    jpnl.setLayout(new GridLayout(5, 3));

    // Add check boxes and label to the JPanel.
    jpnl.add(jlabOptions);
    jpnl.add(new JLabel("")); // a placeholder label
    jpnl.add(new JLabel("")); // a placeholder label

    jpnl.add(jcbOpt1);
    jpnl.add(jcbOpt2);
    jpnl.add(jcbOpt3);
    jpnl.add(jcbOpt4);
    jpnl.add(jcbOpt5);
    jpnl.add(jcbOpt6);
    jpnl.add(jcbOpt7);
    jpnl.add(jcbOpt8);
    jpnl.add(jcbOpt9);
    jpnl.add(jcbOpt10);

    // Create a scroll pane that will scroll the panel.
    JScrollPane jscrlp = new JScrollPane(jpnl);

    // Add that scroll pane to the frame.
    jfrm.add(jscrlp);
```

```
      // Display the frame.
      jfrm.setVisible(true);
    }

    public static void main(String[] args) {

      // Create the GUI on the event dispatching thread.
      SwingUtilities.invokeLater(new Runnable() {
        public void run() {
          new ScrollJPanelDemo();
        }
      });
    }
  }
```

JList

In Swing, the basic list class is called **JList**. It supports the selection of one or more items from a list. Although the list often consists of strings, it is possible to create a list of just about any object that can be displayed. **JList** is so widely used in Java that it is likely that you have seen one before.

In the past, the items in a **JList** were represented as **Object** references. However, with the release of JDK 7, **JList** was made generic and is now declared like this:

> class JList<E>

Here, **E** represents the type of the items in the list. As a result, **JList** is now type-safe.

JList provides several constructors. The one used here is

> JList(E[ ] *items*)

This creates a **JList** that contains the items in the array specified by *items*.

Although a **JList** will work properly by itself, most of the time you will wrap a **JList** inside a **JScrollPane**. This way, long lists will automatically be scrollable, which simplifies GUI design. It also makes it easy to change the number of entries in a list without having to change the size of the **JList** component.

A **JList** generates a **ListSelectionEvent** when the user makes or changes a selection. This event is also generated when the user deselects an item. It is handled by implementing **ListSelectionListener**. This listener specifies only one method, called **valueChanged( )**, which is shown here:

> void valueChanged(ListSelectionEvent *le*)

Here, *le* is a reference to the event. Although **ListSelectionEvent** does provide some methods of its own, often you will interrogate the **JList** object itself to determine what has occurred. Both **ListSelectionEvent** and **ListSelectionListener** are packaged in **javax.swing.event**.

By default, a **JList** allows the user to select multiple ranges of items within the list, but you can change this behavior by calling **setSelectionMode( )**, which is defined by **JList**. It is shown here:

    void setSelectionMode(int *mode*)

Here, *mode* specifies the selection mode. It must be one of these values defined by **ListSelectionModel** (which is the model used by **JList**):

    SINGLE_SELECTION
    SINGLE_INTERVAL_SELECTION
    MULTIPLE_INTERVAL_SELECTION

The default, multiple-interval selection, lets the user select multiple ranges of items within a list. With single-interval selection, the user can select one range of items. With single selection, the user can select only a single item. Of course, a single item can be selected in the other two modes, too. It's just that they also allow a range to be selected.

You can obtain the index of the first item selected, which will also be the index of the only selected item when using single-selection mode, by calling **getSelectedIndex( )**, shown here:

    int getSelectedIndex( )

Indexing begins at zero. So, if the first item is selected, this method will return 0. If no item is selected, –1 is returned.

Instead of obtaining the index of a selection, you can obtain the value associated with the selection by calling **getSelectedValue( )**:

    E getSelectedValue( )

It returns a reference to the first selected value. If no value has been selected, it returns **null**.

The following program demonstrates a simple **JList**, which holds a list of apple varieties. Each time an apple is selected in the list, a **ListSelectionEvent** is generated, which is handled by the **valueChanged( )** method defined by **ListSelectionListener**. It responds by obtaining the index of the selected item and displaying the name of the selected apple in a label. Notice that it sets the preferred size of the list by calling **setPreferredSize( )**.

```
// Demonstrate a simple JList.

// This program requires JDK 7 or later.

import javax.swing.*;
import javax.swing.event.*;
import java.awt.*;
import java.awt.event.*;
```

```
class JListDemo {

  JList<String> jlst;
  JLabel jlab;
  JScrollPane jscrlp;

  // Create an array of apple varieties.
  String[] apples = { "Winesap", "Cortland", "Red Delicious",
                      "Golden Delicious", "Gala", "Fuji",
                      "Granny Smith", "Jonathan" };

  JListDemo() {
    // Create a new JFrame container.
    JFrame jfrm = new JFrame("JList Demo");

    // Specify FlowLayout manager.
    jfrm.setLayout(new FlowLayout());

    // Give the frame an initial size.
    jfrm.setSize(240, 200);

    // Terminate the program when the user closes the application.
    jfrm.setDefaultCloseOperation(JFrame.EXIT_ON_CLOSE);

    // Create a JList.
    jlst = new JList<String>(apples);          ◄———— Create a JList from an
                                                     array of strings.
    // Set the list selection mode to single- selection.
    jlst.setSelectionMode(ListSelectionModel.SINGLE_SELECTION); ◄— Set the selection
                                                                   mode to single
    // Add list to a scroll pane.                                  selection.
    jscrlp = new JScrollPane(jlst);            ◄———— Put the JList in a
                                                     scroll pane.
    // Set the preferred size of the scroll pane.
    jscrlp.setPreferredSize(new Dimension(120, 90));

    // Make a label that displays the selection.
    jlab = new JLabel("Please Choose an Apple.");

    // Add selection listener for the list.
    jlst.addListSelectionListener(new ListSelectionListener() { ◄— Listen for
      public void valueChanged(ListSelectionEvent le) {             selection events.
        // Get the index of the changed item.
        int idx = jlst.getSelectedIndex();     ◄———— Get the index of the
                                                     current selection.
        // Display selection, if item was selected.
        if(idx != -1)
          jlab.setText("Current selection: " + apples[idx]);
```

```
        else // Otherwise, reprompt.
           jlab.setText("Please Choose an Apple.");

     }
   });


   // Add the list and label to the content pane.
   jfrm.add(jscrlp);
   jfrm.add(jlab);

   // Display the frame.
   jfrm.setVisible(true);
 }

 public static void main(String[] args) {
   // Create the GUI on the event dispatching thread.
   SwingUtilities.invokeLater(new Runnable() {
     public void run() {
       new JListDemo();
     }
   });
 }
}
```

Output from the list example is shown here:

Something you might like to experiment with is selecting an item in a list under program control. This can be done by calling **setSelectedIndex( )**, which is shown here:

    void setSelectedIndex(int *index*)

Here, *index* specifies the index of the item in the list that you want to select. The index is zero-based, which means the first item in the list is at index zero. You can clear a selection under program control by calling **clearSelection( )**:

> void clearSelection( )

After this method executes, all selections are cleared.

Ask the Expert

Q You mention in the discussion of **JList** that the example sets the size of a component by use of **setPreferredSize( )**. Can you explain?

A Yes. By default, the size of a component is determined by its contents and by the layout manager. However, you can explicitly specify a preferred size for a component by calling **setPreferredSize( )**, which is defined by **JComponent**. It is shown here.

> void setPreferredSize(Dimension *newPS*)

Here, *newPS* specifies the new preferred dimension for the component. The **Dimension** class is part of the **java.awt** package. Here is one of its constructors:

> Dimension(int *w*, int *h*)

Here, *w* specifies the width and *h* specifies the height.

Once you have set the preferred size, a layout manager will use those dimensions as a guide to properly sizing the component. Understand, though, that some layout managers, such as **GridLayout**, will ignore those dimensions.

One last point: you can also specify a minimum size and a maximum size by calling **setMinimumSize( )** and **setMaximumSize( )**, also defined by **JComponent**. These are shown here.

> void setMaximumSize(Dimension *newSize*)

> void setMinimumSize(Dimension *newSize*)

As with **setPreferredSize( )**, the dimensions set by these methods are suggestions that can be ignored by the layout manager.

JComboBox

Swing provides a *combo box* (a combination of a text field and a drop-down list) through the **JComboBox** class. In the past, the items in a **JComboBox** were represented as **Object** references. However, with the release of JDK 7, **JComboBox** was made generic and is now declared like this:

> class JComboBox<E>

Here, **E** is the type of elements held in the list.

A combo box normally displays one entry, but it will also display a drop-down list that allows a user to select a different entry. You can also create a combo box that lets the user enter a selection into the text field, but we won't do so here.

The **JComboBox** constructor used by the example is shown here:

JComboBox(E[ ] *items*)

Here, *items* is an array that initializes the combo box. Other constructors are available.

JComboBox generates an action event when the user selects an item from the list. **JComboBox** also generates an item event when the state of selection changes, which occurs when an item is selected or deselected. Thus, changing a selection means that two item events will occur: one for the deselected item and another for the selected item. Often, it is sufficient to simply listen for action events, but both event types are available for your use.

One way to obtain the item selected in the list is to call **getSelectedItem( )** on the combo box. It is shown here:

Object getSelectedItem( )

You will need to cast the returned value into the type of object stored in the list.

The following example demonstrates **JComboBox** by reworking the previous **JList** example.

```java
// Demonstrate a simple combo box.

// This program requires JDK 7 or later.

import javax.swing.*;
import java.awt.*;
import java.awt.event.*;

class JComboBoxDemo {

  JComboBox<String> jcbb;
  JLabel jlab;

  // Create an array of apple varieties.
  String[] apples = { "Winesap", "Cortland", "Red Delicious",
                      "Golden Delicious", "Gala", "Fuji",
                      "Granny Smith", "Jonathan" };

  JComboBoxDemo() {
    // Create a new JFrame container.
    JFrame jfrm = new JFrame("JComboBox Demo");

    // Specify FlowLayout for the layout manager.
    jfrm.setLayout(new FlowLayout());

    // Give the frame an initial size.
    jfrm.setSize(380, 240);

    // Terminate the program when the user closes the application.
    jfrm.setDefaultCloseOperation(JFrame.EXIT_ON_CLOSE);
```

```
      // Create a JComboBox
      jcbb = new JComboBox<String>(apples);          Create a JComboBox
                                                      from an array of strings.
      // Make a label that displays the selection.
      jlab = new JLabel("Please Choose an Apple.");

      // Add action listener for the combo box.
      jcbb.addActionListener(new ActionListener() {    Listen for action
        public void actionPerformed(ActionEvent ae) {  events on the combo box.
          // Get a reference to the item selected.
          String item = (String) jcbb.getSelectedItem();    Get the selected item.

          // Display the selected item.
          jlab.setText("Current selection: " + item);
        }
      });

      // Add the combo box and label to the content pane.
      jfrm.add(jcbb);
      jfrm.add(jlab);

      // Display the frame.
      jfrm.setVisible(true);
    }

    public static void main(String[] args) {
      // Create the GUI on the event dispatching thread.
      SwingUtilities.invokeLater(new Runnable() {
        public void run() {
          new JComboBoxDemo();
        }
      });
    }
}
```

Output from the combo box example is shown here:

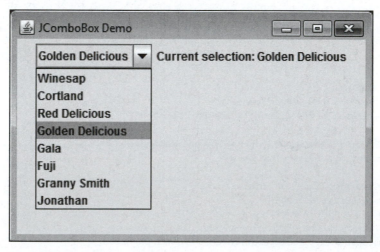

One useful combo box feature that you might like to try is its ability to add or remove items from the drop-down list dynamically, during program execution. This feature is supported by the methods **addItem( )** and **removeItem( )**, shown here:

void addItem(E *item*)

void removeItem(Object *item*)

Here, *item* is the item to be added or removed. One important point: These methods are available only to combo boxes that are mutable. Fortunately, this is the case by default for **JComboBox**. When an item is added, it is added to the end of the list.

Progress Check

1. What control creates a list?
2. In a **JList**, the index of the first selected item in a list can be obtained by using what method?
3. In a **JComboBox**, what method obtains the current selection?

TREES

A *tree* is a component that presents a hierarchical view of data. The user has the ability to expand or collapse individual subtrees in this display. Trees are implemented in Swing by the **JTree** class. Two of its constructors are shown here:

JTree(Object[ ] *obj*)

JTree(TreeNode *tn*)

In the first form, the tree is constructed from the elements in the array *obj*. In the second form, the tree whose root node is specified by *tn* specifies the tree.

Although **JTree** is packaged in **javax.swing**, its support classes and interfaces are packaged in **javax.swing.tree**. This is because the number of classes and interfaces needed to support **JTree** is quite large.

A **JTree** generates a variety of events. The one handled by the sample program shown in this section is **TreeSelectionEvent**. To listen for this event, implement **TreeSelectionListener**. It defines only one method, called **valueChanged( )**, which receives the **TreeSelectionEvent** object. It is shown here:

void valueChanged(TreeSelectionEvent *te*)

Answers:

1. **JList**
2. **getSelectedIndex( )**
3. **getSelectedItem( )**

You can obtain the path to the selected object by calling **getPath( )**, shown here, on the event object.

　　TreePath getPath( )

It returns a **TreePath** object that describes the path to the changed node. The **TreePath** class encapsulates information about a path to a particular node in a tree. It provides several constructors and methods. Here, only one is used: **getLastPathComponent( )**. Its general form is shown here:

　　Object getLastPathComponent( )

It returns the last node in the currently selected path.

　　The **TreeNode** interface declares methods that obtain information about a tree node. For example, it is possible to obtain a reference to the parent node or an enumeration of the child nodes. The **MutableTreeNode** interface extends **TreeNode**. It declares methods that can insert and remove child nodes or change the parent node.

　　The **DefaultMutableTreeNode** class implements the **MutableTreeNode** interface. It represents a node in a tree. One of its constructors is shown here:

　　DefaultMutableTreeNode(Object *obj*)

Here, *obj* is the object to be enclosed in this tree node. The new tree node doesn't have a parent or children.

　　To create a hierarchy of tree nodes, the **add( )** method of **DefaultMutableTreeNode** can be used. It is shown here:

　　void add(MutableTreeNode *child*)

Here, *child* is a mutable tree node that is to be added as a child to the current node.

　　JTree does not provide any scrolling capabilities of its own. Instead, a **JTree** is typically placed within a **JScrollPane**. This way, a large tree can be scrolled through a smaller viewport.

　　Here are the steps you can follow to use a tree:

1. Create an instance of **JTree**.
2. Add nodes to the tree.
3. Create a **JScrollPane** and specify the tree as the object to be scrolled.
4. Add the scroll pane to the content pane.

　　The following example illustrates how to create a tree and handle selections. It creates a tree that organizes several of Java's keywords. The program creates a **DefaultMutableTreeNode** instance labeled "Java Keywords". This is the root of the tree hierarchy. Additional subtrees for types and loops are created. Terminal nodes are added to these subtrees that correspond to keywords. In all cases, the **add( )** method is called to connect these nodes to the tree. A reference to the root node in the tree is passed as the argument to the **JTree** constructor. The tree is then provided as the argument to the **JScrollPane** constructor. This scroll pane is then added to the content pane. Next, a label is created and added to the content pane.

The tree selection is displayed in this label. To receive selection events from the tree, a **TreeSelectionListener** is registered for the tree. Inside the **valueChanged( )** method, the current selection is obtained and displayed. Although this example displays only a few of Java's keywords, you might enjoy expanding it to include additional keywords.

```java
// Demonstrate JTree.
import java.awt.*;
import javax.swing.event.*;
import javax.swing.*;
import javax.swing.tree.*;

public class JTreeDemo {
  JTree tree;
  JLabel jlab;

  JTreeDemo() {

    // Create a new JFrame container.
    JFrame jfrm = new JFrame("JTree Example");

    // Give the frame an initial size.
    jfrm.setSize(300, 240);

    // Terminate the program when the user closes the application.
    jfrm.setDefaultCloseOperation(JFrame.EXIT_ON_CLOSE);

    // Create root node of tree.
    DefaultMutableTreeNode root =                        ◄——————— Create the root node.
          new DefaultMutableTreeNode("Java Keywords");

    // Create subtree for types.
    DefaultMutableTreeNode types = new DefaultMutableTreeNode("Types");
    root.add(types);

    // Create subtree for floating point types.
    DefaultMutableTreeNode fpTypes =
          new DefaultMutableTreeNode("Floating Point");
    types.add(fpTypes);
    fpTypes.add(new DefaultMutableTreeNode("float"));
    fpTypes.add(new DefaultMutableTreeNode("double"));

    // Create subtree for integer types.
    DefaultMutableTreeNode intTypes =
          new DefaultMutableTreeNode("Integer");
    types.add(intTypes);
    intTypes.add(new DefaultMutableTreeNode("byte"));
    intTypes.add(new DefaultMutableTreeNode("short"));
    intTypes.add(new DefaultMutableTreeNode("int"));
    intTypes.add(new DefaultMutableTreeNode("long"));
```

Create subtree for types and add it to the root.

Create the floating-point types subtree.

Create the integer types subtree.

```
    // Create nodes for char and boolean.
    types.add(new DefaultMutableTreeNode("char"));
    types.add(new DefaultMutableTreeNode("boolean"));
```
——— Add nodes for **char** and **boolean**.

```
    // Create subtree for loops.
    DefaultMutableTreeNode loops = new DefaultMutableTreeNode("Loops");
    root.add(loops);
    loops.add(new DefaultMutableTreeNode("for"));
    loops.add(new DefaultMutableTreeNode("while"));
    loops.add(new DefaultMutableTreeNode("do"));
```
Create subtree for loops.

```
    // Create the tree.
    tree = new JTree(root);
```
◄——— Construct a **JTree** from the tree just created.

```
    // Add the tree to a scroll pane.
    JScrollPane jsp = new JScrollPane(tree);
```
◄——— Wrap the tree in a scroll pane.

```
    // Add the scroll pane to the center of the default BorderLayout.
    jfrm.add(jsp);

    // Add the label to the south region of the default BorderLayout.
    jlab = new JLabel("Select from the tree.");
    jfrm.add(jlab, BorderLayout.SOUTH);

    // Handle tree selection events.
    tree.addTreeSelectionListener(new TreeSelectionListener() {
      public void valueChanged(TreeSelectionEvent tse) {
        jlab.setText("Selection is " +
            tse.getPath().getLastPathComponent());
      }
    });

    // Display the frame.
    jfrm.setVisible(true);
  }

  public static void main(String[] args) {
    // Create the GUI on the event dispatching thread.
    SwingUtilities.invokeLater(new Runnable() {
      public void run() {
        new JTreeDemo();
      }
    });
  }
}
```

Output from the tree example is shown here:

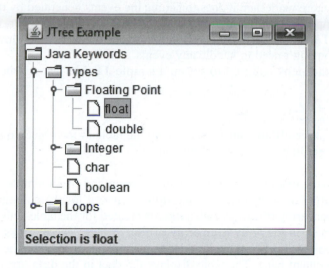

JTable

JTable is a component that displays rows and columns of data. You can drag the cursor on column boundaries to resize columns. You can also drag a column to a new position. Depending on its configuration, it is also possible to select a row, column, or cell within the table, and to change the data within a cell. **JTable** is a sophisticated component that offers many more options and features than are discussed here. (It is perhaps Swing's most complicated component.) However, in its default configuration, **JTable** still offers substantial functionality that is easy to use—especially if you simply want to use the table to present data in a tabular format. The overview presented here will give you a general understanding of this powerful component.

Like **JTree**, **JTable** has many classes and interfaces associated with it. These are packaged in **javax.swing.table**.

At its core, **JTable** is conceptually simple. It is a component that consists of one or more columns of information. At the top of each column is a heading. In addition to describing the data in a column, the heading also provides the mechanism by which the user can change the size of a column or change the location of a column within the table. **JTable** does not provide any scrolling capabilities of its own. Instead, you will normally wrap a **JTable** inside a **JScrollPane**.

JTable supplies several constructors. The one used here is

    JTable(Object[ ] [ ] *data*, Object[ ] *colHeads*)

Here, *data* is a two-dimensional array of the information to be presented, and *colHeads* is a one-dimensional array with the column headings.

A **JTable** can generate several different events. However, handling these events requires a bit more work than it does to handle the events generated by the previously described components and is beyond the scope of this book. However, if you simply want to use **JTable** to display data and allow it to be edited (as the following example does), then you don't need to handle any events.

Here are the steps required to set up a simple **JTable** that can be used to display data:

1. Create an instance of **JTable**.
2. Create a **JScrollPane** object, specifying the table as the object to scroll.
3. Add the scroll pane to the content pane.

The following example illustrates how to create and use a simple table. A one-dimensional array of strings called **Headings** is created for the column headings. A two-dimensional array of strings called **data** is created for the table cells. You can see that each element in the array is an array of four strings. These arrays are passed to the **JTable** constructor. The table is added to a scroll pane, and then the scroll pane is added to the content pane. The table displays the data in the **data** array. The default table configuration also allows the contents of a cell to be edited. Changes affect the underlying array, which is **data** in this case.

```java
// Demonstrate JTable.
import java.awt.*;
import javax.swing.*;

public class JTableDemo {

  JTableDemo() {

    // Create a new JFrame container.
    JFrame jfrm = new JFrame("JTable Example");

    // Give the frame an initial size.
    jfrm.setSize(400, 300);

    // Terminate the program when the user closes the application.
    jfrm.setDefaultCloseOperation(JFrame.EXIT_ON_CLOSE);

    // Initialize column headings.
    String[] Headings = { "Name", "Student ID", "Midterm", "Final" };

    // Initialize data.
    String[][] data = {
        { "Tom",    " 4-616",  " 97",  " 87" },
        { "Ken",    " 3-786",  " 88",  " 95" },
        { "Rachel", " 4-674",  " 92",  " 83" },
        { "Sherry", " 3-235",  " 91",  " 99" },
        { "Adam",   " 2-923",  " 76",  " 96" },
        { "Jon",    " 3-561",  " 84",  " 80" },
        { "Stuart", " 1-337",  " 62",  " 74" },
        { "Mary",   " 4-731",  " 68",  " 58" },
```

```
       { "Todd",   " 2-924", " 82", " 72" },
       { "Shane",  " 2-434", " 93", " 91" },
       { "Robert", " 3-769", " 99", " 92" },
    };

    // Create the table.
    JTable table = new JTable(data, Headings);  ◄──────  Create a JTable using the specified
                                                         data and headings.
    // Add the table to a scroll pane.
    JScrollPane jsp = new JScrollPane(table);  ◄──────  Wrap the table in a scroll pane.

    // Add the scroll pane to the content pane.
    jfrm.add(jsp);

    // Display the frame.
    jfrm.setVisible(true);
  }

  public static void main(String[] args) {

    // Create the GUI on the event dispatching thread.
    SwingUtilities.invokeLater(new Runnable() {
      public void run() {
        new JTableDemo();
      }
    });
  }
}
```

Output from this example is shown here:

Name	Student ID	Midterm	Final
Tom	4-616	97	87
Ken	3-786	88	95
Rachel	4-674	92	83
Sherry	3-235	91	99
Adam	2-923	76	96
Jon	3-561	84	80
Stuart	1-337	62	74
Mary	4-731	68	58
Todd	2-924	82	72
Shane	2-434	93	91
Robert	3-769	99	92

Progress Check

1. A tree control is created by use of what class?
2. When an item in a **JTree** is selected, what event is generated?
3. What control creates a table?

A BRIEF WORD ABOUT MODELS

To support the Model-Delegate architecture described in the preceding chapter, most Swing controls utilize a model that determines how the data associated with a control is handled. For example, the model for a button is defined by the **ButtonModel** interface. The examples in this chapter have not made explicit use of any of the models associated with a control. The reason is that often your code won't need to use a model directly because (as a general rule) the component exposes the functionality of the model. Also, for many (perhaps most) uses, the default model provided by the controls is precisely what you want. Thus, there is often no reason to change it. However, Swing does let you work with the model directly, if necessary. This can be helpful in more advanced GUIs. The ability to access the model is another reason why Swing is so powerful.

Ask the Expert

Q In addition to the controls you discussed, what other types of controls does Swing offer?

A Swing offers a rich assortment of controls that make it easy to create both pleasing and sophisticated GUIs. First, and most importantly, Swing supports a powerful menu system, which is described in Chapter 19. Second, it supports several built-in dialog controls; these are described in Chapter 20. Finally, Swing supports several other user-interface controls. For example, here are a few more that you will find interesting. Their names indicate their function.

JFormattedTextField	JPasswordField	JProgressBar
JScrollBar	JSlider	JSpinner
JTabbedPane	JTextArea	JToolBar

You will want to explore these, and other, Swing controls as you advance in your GUI programming skills.

Answers:

1. **JTree**
2. **TreeSelectionEvent**
3. **JTable**

EXERCISES

1. Does **JLabel** generate an **ActionEvent**?
2. What event is generated when a push button is pressed?
3. Can **JButton** include an icon?
4. What control toggles between two states: selected and cleared?
5. When using **JTextField**, cut and paste is supported by what methods?
6. Show how to create a text field that has 32 columns.
7. Can a **JTextField** have its action command set? If so, how?
8. What Swing component creates a check box? What event is generated when a check box is selected or deselected?
9. **JRadioButton** creates a list of buttons shaped like radios. True or False?
10. **JList** displays a list of items from which the user can select. True or False?
11. What event is generated when the user selects or deselects an item in a **JList**?
12. What does **JScrollPane** do?
13. What method sets the selection mode of a **JList**? What method obtains the index of the first selected item?
14. To display information in a tabular format, you can use _____.
15. To display information in a tree format, you can use _____.
16. What is **JComboBox**?
17. Enhance the **JCheckBoxDemo** program discussed in this chapter so that the text for each check box is red if the check box is selected and black if it is unselected. To set the text color to red, use HTML for the text and surround the text with the tags **<font color="red">** and **</font>**.
18. Change the **JCheckBoxDemo** program discussed in this chapter by adding a new **JButton** with text "Count". When the button is clicked, the **jlabSupported** label displays the number of checked check boxes instead of a list of the supported operating systems.
19. Modify the program in Try This 18-2 so that the label **jlabOptions** is not part of the scroll pane and is centered over the top of all the check boxes regardless of the size of the window. To do so, add **jlabOptions** to the north side of the content pane of the window. To the center of the content pane, add the scrolling pane with the check boxes.
20. Two constructors for the **JTree** class were mentioned in this chapter, but only the second one was used. The first constructor has an array of **Object**s as its parameter. How is that array converted into a tree? That is, what is the root of the tree, and what are the other nodes? To find out, write a small test program.
21. In the section describing the **JTree** class, we used the term "root" for the node that is passed as an argument to the **JTree** constructor. Why use the word "root?"

22. In the section describing the **JTree** class, we used the terms "parent node," "child node," "subtree," and "terminal node." Define these terms in your own words.

23. Write a program that creates a **JFrame**. The **JFrame** displays a **JTree** showing the inheritance hierarchy for the Java Swing classes we discussed in this chapter. The root of the tree is the **JComponent** class. It has nine children: **AbstractButton, JComboBox, JLabel, JList, JScrollPane, JTable, JTextComponent, JTree,** and **JPanel**. The **AbstractButton** class has two children: **JButton** and **JToggleButton**. The **JToggleButton** class has two children: **JCheckBox** and **JRadioButton**. The **JTextComponent** class has one child: **JTextField**. Put the tree in a scrolling pane. No events need to be dealt with.

24. Rework the Help demo in Try This 4-1 in Chapter 4 so that it uses a **JList** to display the help topics in a window. Use the **JList** constructor that takes an array as its parameter. The array should contain the topics (as strings). When the user clicks on an item in the list, the help information on that topic is displayed in a label at the bottom of the window.

25. Get any three pictures you want. Then write a program that creates a window containing one **JToggleButton** only. The button displays the first picture. When you hover the mouse over the button, it displays the second picture. When you click the button to select it, it displays the third picture. The **JToggleButton** class has a **setSelectedIcon( )** method that sets the icon to be displayed when the button is selected. It looks like this:

    void setSelectedIcon(Icon *selectedIcon*)

26. Modify the **JComboBoxDemo** example in the text so that, if an item in the **JComboBox** is selected, that item is deleted from the **JComboBox**.

27. Write a program that creates a window with the following contents:

    A. a label centered across the top saying "Choose a color and style".

    B. a label centered across the bottom saying "Sample text".

    C. a column on the left consisting of a label saying "Style" and two check boxes labeled "Bold" and "Italics".

    D. a column on the right consisting of a label saying "Color" and three radio buttons saying "Red", "Green", "Black".

    The black radio button is initially selected. If the user clicks on a different radio button, the sample text at the bottom is changed to the new color. If the user checks one or more check boxes on the left, the styles selected are applied to the sample text on the bottom. To change the style and color of the text, use HTML. For example, for red text, set the text of the bottom label to "<html><font color=\"red\">Sample text.</font>". For bold and italics and red text, set the text of the label to "<html><font color = \"red\"><b><i>Sample text</i></b></font>". The tag <b> indicates bold text, and <i> indicates italicized text.

28. Both **JComboBox**es and **JList**s display a list of items from which you can select one item. Why have two controls that do the same thing?

29. Write a program that creates a window. In the window put a **JTable** with two rows and two columns, with column headers "First name" and "Last name". Put arbitrary names in the two rows. Include a "Sort" button under the table. When the button is clicked, the program checks whether the two rows are sorted alphabetically by last name. If not, it swaps the data in the two rows. Use the **getValueAt( )** and **setValueAt( )** methods of the **JTable** class to do the checking and swapping. Here are the details of these methods:

> Object getValueAt(int *row*, int *column*)
>
> void setValueAt(Object *newValue*, int *row*, int *column*)

The first method returns the value at the given row and column. Note that its return type is **Object,** so you will have to cast the value it returns to a string. Also, note that rows and columns start with index 0. The second method sets the value at the given row and column to the new value.

30. What is the difference between a check box and a radio button that is not part of any group of radio buttons?

31. There are two ways to handle events in **JToggleButton**s: You can create an **ItemListener** for handling **ItemEvent**s in the button, or you can use an **ActionListener** for handling **ActionEvent**s in the button. Is there any advantage to using one instead of the other?

32. What is the main difference between a **JButton** and a **JToggleButton**?

33. Write a program that creates a window. In the window add a **JList** of strings. The **JList** should use multiple selection mode. (To select more than one item, hold down the command or control key on your keyboard when you click on an item.) Every time an item is selected in the list, your program should compare that item against all other selected items. If the selected items all are equal, a label at the bottom of the window should display the message "All *x* selections are equal" where *x* is the number of selected items. If not, it should display the message "They are not all equal". To get all the selected items, use the **getSelectedIndices( )** method of the **JList** class. Here are the details:

> int[ ] getSelectedIndices( )

It returns an array of the indices of the selected items. If there are no selected items, it returns an array of length 0.

CHAPTER 19

Working with Menus

KEY SKILLS & CONCEPTS

- Know menu basics
- **JMenuBar**
- **JMenu**
- **JMenuItem**
- Create a main menu
- Add mnemonics and accelerators to menu items
- Add images and tooltips to menu items
- **JRadioButtonMenuItem**
- **JCheckBoxMenuItem**

The modern GUI is comprised of two principal features. The first are controls, which were introduced in the previous chapter. The second are menus, which are introduced here. Menus form an integral part of all but the simplest applications because they display a program's functionality to the user. Because of their importance, Swing provides extensive support for menus. Although we can't look at all of their features here, this chapter describes their fundamentals along with several commonly used options.

MENU BASICS

The Swing menu system is supported by several classes. The ones discussed in this chapter are shown here:

Menu Classes	Description
JMenuBar	An object that holds the top-level menu for the application.
JMenu	A standard menu. A menu consists of one or more **JMenuItem**s.
JMenuItem	An object that populates menus.
JCheckBoxMenuItem	A check box menu item.
JRadioButtonMenuItem	A radio button menu item.

Although menus may seem a bit intimidating at first, Swing menus are very easy to use. Swing allows a high degree of customization, if desired, but you will often use the menu classes as-is because they support all of the most needed options. For example, you can easily add images and keyboard shortcuts to a menu.

Here is brief overview of how the classes fit together. To create a main menu for an application, you will first create a **JMenuBar** object. This class is, loosely speaking, a container for menus. To the **JMenuBar** instance, you will add instances of **JMenu**. Each **JMenu** object defines a menu. That is, each **JMenu** object contains one or more selectable items. The items displayed by a **JMenu** are objects of **JMenuItem**. Thus, a **JMenuItem** defines a selection that can be chosen by the user.

In addition to "standard" menu items, you can also include check boxes and radio buttons in a menu. A check box menu item is created by **JCheckBoxMenuItem**. A radio button menu item is created by **JRadioButtonMenuItem**. Both of these classes extend **JMenuItem**. They can be used in both standard menus and popup menus.

One key aspect of Swing menus is that each menu item extends **AbstractButton**. Recall that **AbstractButton** is also the superclass of all of Swing's button components, such as **JButton**. Thus, all menu items are, essentially, buttons. Obviously, they won't actually look like buttons when used in a menu, but they will, in many ways, act like buttons. For example, selecting a menu item generates an action event in the same way that pressing a button does.

Another important point is that **JMenuItem** is a superclass of **JMenu**. This allows the creation of submenus, which are, essentially, menus within menus. To create a submenu, you first create and populate a **JMenu** object and then add it to another **JMenu** object. You will see this process in action in the following section.

As mentioned previously, when a menu item is selected, an action event is generated. The action command string associated with that action event will, by default, be the name of the selection. Thus, you can determine which item was selected by examining the action command. Of course, there are other approaches. For example, you can also use a separate anonymous inner class to handle each menu item's action events. Be aware, however, that menu systems tend to get quite large. Using a separate class to handle events for each menu item can cause a large number of classes to be created.

Progress Check

1. What class creates a top-level menu bar?
2. What class creates a menu item?
3. Can a menu item be a check box or a radio button?

Answers:

1. **JMenuBar**
2. **JMenuItem**
3. Yes.

AN OVERVIEW OF JMenuBar, JMenu, AND JMenuItem

Before you can create a menu, it's necessary to know something about the three core menu classes: **JMenuBar**, **JMenu**, and **JMenuItem**. These form the minimum set of classes needed to construct a main menu for an application. Thus, these classes form the foundation of Swing's menu system.

JMenuBar

As mentioned, **JMenuBar** is essentially a container for menus. Like all components, it inherits **JComponent** (which inherits **Container** and **Component**). It has only one constructor, which is the default constructor. Therefore, the menu bar will initially be empty, and you will need to populate it with menus prior to use. Each application has one and only one menu bar.

   JMenuBar defines several methods, but often you will only need to use one: **add( )**. The **add( )** method adds a **JMenu** to the menu bar. It is shown here:

   JMenu add(JMenu *menu*)

Here, *menu* is a **JMenu** instance that is added to the menu bar. A reference to the menu is returned. Menus are positioned in the bar from left to right, in the order in which they are added. If you want to add a menu at a specific location, then use this version of **add( )**, which is inherited from **Container**:

   Component add(Component *menu*, int *idx*)

Here, *menu* is added at the index specified by *idx*. Indexing begins at 0, with 0 being the leftmost menu.

   In some cases you might want to remove a menu that is no longer needed. You can do this by calling **remove( )**, which is inherited from **Container**. It has these two forms:

   void remove(Component *menu*)

   void remove(int *idx*)

Here, *menu* is a reference to the menu to remove, and *idx* is the index of the menu to be removed. Indexing begins at 0.

   Another method that is sometimes useful is **getMenuCount( )**, shown here:

   int getMenuCount( )

It returns the number of elements contained within the menu bar.

   Once a menu bar has been created and populated, it is added to a **JFrame** by calling **setJMenuBar( )** on the **JFrame** instance. The **setJMenuBar( )** method is shown here:

   void setJMenuBar(JMenuBar *mbar*)

Here, *mbar* is a reference to the menu bar. The menu bar will be displayed in a position determined by the look and feel. Usually, this is at the top of the window.

JMenu

JMenu encapsulates a menu, which is populated with **JMenuItem**s. As mentioned, it is derived from **JMenuItem**. This means that one **JMenu** can be a selection in another **JMenu**. This enables one menu to be a submenu of another. **JMenu** defines several constructors. The one we will use in this chapter is shown here:

> JMenu(String *name*)

It creates a menu that has the title specified by *name*. The menu is empty until menu items are added to it.

JMenu defines many methods. Here are brief descriptions of some of the more commonly used ones. To add an item to the menu, use the **add( )** method, which has a number of forms, including the two shown here:

> JMenuItem add(JMenuItem *item*)
> JMenuItem add(Component *item*, int *idx*)

Here, *item* is the menu item to add. The first form adds the item to the end of the menu. The second form adds the item at the index specified by *idx*. As expected, indexing starts at 0. (The second version is inherited from **Container**. Typically, you will pass a **JMenuItem** reference to *item*.) Both return a reference to the item added. As a point of interest, you can also use **insert( )** to add menu items to a menu.

You can add a visual separator to a menu by calling **addSeparator( )**, shown here:

> void addSeparator( )

The separator is added onto the end of the menu. You can insert a separator at a specified index by calling **insertSeparator( )**, shown next:

> void insertSeparator(int *idx*)

Here, *idx* specifies the zero-based index at which the separator will be added.

You can remove an item from a menu by calling **remove( )**. Here are two of its forms:

> void remove(JMenuItem *menu*)
> void remove(int *idx*)

Here, *menu* is a reference to the item to remove, and *idx* is the index of the item to remove.

You can obtain the number of items in the menu by calling **getMenuComponent-Count( )**, shown here:

> int getMenuComponentCount( )

You can get an array of the items in the menu by calling **getMenuComponents( )**, shown next:

> Component[ ] getMenuComponents( )

An array containing the components is returned.

JMenuItem

JMenuItem encapsulates an element in a menu. This element can be either a selection linked to some program action, such as Save or Close, or it can cause a submenu to be displayed. As mentioned, **JMenuItem** is derived from **AbstractButton**, and every item in a menu can be thought of as a special kind of button. Therefore, when a menu item is selected, an action event is generated. (This is similar to the way a **JButton** fires an action event when it is pressed.) **JMenuItem** defines several constructors. Here is the one we will use first:

> JMenuItem(String *name*)

This creates a menu item with the name specified by *name*.

Because menu items inherit **AbstractButton**, you have access to the functionality provided by **AbstractButton**. For example, you can enable/disable a menu item by calling **setEnabled( )**, shown here:

> void setEnabled(boolean *enable*)

If *enable* is **true**, the menu item is enabled. If *enable* is **false**, the item is disabled and cannot be selected.

Progress Check

1. What method adds an item to a menu?
2. What does **addSeparator( )** do?
3. A menu item cannot be disabled. True or False?

CREATE A MAIN MENU

Perhaps the most commonly used menu is the *main menu*. This is the menu defined by the menu bar, and it is the menu that defines the main functionality of an application. Fortunately, Swing makes it very easy to create and manage the main menu. This section shows how to construct a basic main menu. Subsequent sections will show how to add options to it.

Constructing the main menu requires several steps. First, create the **JMenuBar** object that will hold the menus. Next, construct each menu that will be in the menu bar. In general, a menu is constructed by first creating a **JMenu** object and then adding **JMenuItem**s to it. After the menus have been created, add them to the menu bar. The menu bar, itself, must then be added to the frame by calling **setJMenuBar( )**. Finally, for each menu item, you must add an action listener that handles the action event fired when the menu item is selected.

Answers:

1. **add( )**
2. It adds a separator (which visually separates menu items) to a menu.
3. False.

The best way to understand the process of creating and managing menus is to work through an example. Here is a program that creates a simple menu bar that contains three menus. The first is a standard File menu that contains Open, Close, Save, and Exit selections. The second menu is called Options, and it contains two submenus called Colors and Priority. The third menu is called Help, and it has one item called About. When a menu item is selected, the name of the selection is displayed in a label in the content pane. Sample output is shown here:

```java
// Demonstrate a simple main menu.

import java.awt.*;
import java.awt.event.*;
import javax.swing.*;

class MenuDemo implements ActionListener {

  JLabel jlab;

  MenuDemo() {
    // Create a new JFrame container.
    JFrame jfrm = new JFrame("Menu Demo");

    // Specify FlowLayout for the layout manager.
    jfrm.setLayout(new FlowLayout());

    // Give the frame an initial size.
    jfrm.setSize(220, 200);

    // Terminate the program when the user closes the application.
    jfrm.setDefaultCloseOperation(JFrame.EXIT_ON_CLOSE);

    // Create a label that will display the menu selection.
    jlab = new JLabel();
```

```
// Create the menu bar.
JMenuBar jmb = new JMenuBar();
```
────── Create a menu bar.

```
// Create the File menu.
JMenu jmFile = new JMenu("File");
JMenuItem jmiOpen = new JMenuItem("Open");
JMenuItem jmiClose = new JMenuItem("Close");
JMenuItem jmiSave = new JMenuItem("Save");
JMenuItem jmiExit = new JMenuItem("Exit");
```
────Create the File menu items.

```
jmFile.add(jmiOpen);
jmFile.add(jmiClose);
jmFile.add(jmiSave);
jmFile.addSeparator();
jmFile.add(jmiExit);
```
────Add the File menu items to the File menu.

```
jmb.add(jmFile);
```
──────Add the File menu to the menu bar.

```
// Create the Options menu.
JMenu jmOptions = new JMenu("Options");
```
──────Create the Options menu.

```
// Create the Colors submenu.
JMenu jmColors = new JMenu("Colors");
JMenuItem jmiRed = new JMenuItem("Red");
JMenuItem jmiGreen = new JMenuItem("Green");
JMenuItem jmiBlue = new JMenuItem("Blue");
jmColors.add(jmiRed);
jmColors.add(jmiGreen);
jmColors.add(jmiBlue);
```
──── Create the Colors submenu.

```
jmOptions.add(jmColors);
```
────── Add Colors submenu to the Options menu.

```
// Create the Priority submenu.
JMenu jmPriority = new JMenu("Priority");
JMenuItem jmiHigh = new JMenuItem("High");
JMenuItem jmiLow = new JMenuItem("Low");
jmPriority.add(jmiHigh);
jmPriority.add(jmiLow);
```
──── Create the Priority submenu.

```
jmOptions.add(jmPriority);
```
────── Add Priority submenu to
the Options menu.

```
// Create the Reset menu item.
JMenuItem jmiReset = new JMenuItem("Reset");
jmOptions.addSeparator();
jmOptions.add(jmiReset);
```
──── Create the Reset item and
add it to the Options menu.

```
// Finally, add the entire Options menu to the menu bar
jmb.add(jmOptions);
```
────────── Add the Options menu to the menu bar.

```
// Create the Help menu.
JMenu jmHelp = new JMenu("Help");
JMenuItem jmiAbout = new JMenuItem("About");
jmHelp.add(jmiAbout);
jmb.add(jmHelp);
```
──── Create the Help menu
and add it to the menu bar.

```
                   // Add action listeners for the menu items.
                   jmiOpen.addActionListener(this);
                   jmiClose.addActionListener(this);
                   jmiSave.addActionListener(this);
                   jmiExit.addActionListener(this);
                   jmiRed.addActionListener(this);
                   jmiGreen.addActionListener(this);          Add the action listeners for the menu items.
                   jmiBlue.addActionListener(this);
                   jmiHigh.addActionListener(this);
                   jmiLow.addActionListener(this);
                   jmiReset.addActionListener(this);
                   jmiAbout.addActionListener(this);


                   // Add the label to the content pane.
                   jfrm.add(jlab);


                   // Add the menu bar to the frame.
                   jfrm.setJMenuBar(jmb);   ◄─────────────  Add the menu bar to the frame.


                   // Display the frame.
                   jfrm.setVisible(true);
               }

               // Handle menu item action events.
               public void actionPerformed(ActionEvent ae) {
                   // Get the action command from the menu selection.
                   String comStr = ae.getActionCommand();

                   // If user chooses Exit, then exit the program.
                   if(comStr.equals("Exit")) System.exit(0);   ◄──  Exit the program when the user
                                                                    chooses Exit from the File menu.
                   // Otherwise, display the selection.
                   jlab.setText(comStr + " Selected");
               }

               public static void main(String[] args) {
                   // Create the GUI on the event dispatching thread.
                   SwingUtilities.invokeLater(new Runnable() {
                       public void run() {
                           new MenuDemo();
                       }
                   });
               }
           }
```

Let's examine in detail how the menus are created, beginning with the **MenuDemo** constructor. It begins with the usual statements. Then, the menu bar is constructed, and a reference to it is assigned to **jmb** by this statement:

```
// Create the menu bar.
JMenuBar jmb = new JMenuBar();
```

Next, the File menu **jmFile** and its menu entries are created by this sequence:

```
// Create the File menu.
JMenu jmFile = new JMenu("File");
JMenuItem jmiOpen = new JMenuItem("Open");
JMenuItem jmiClose = new JMenuItem("Close");
JMenuItem jmiSave = new JMenuItem("Save");
JMenuItem jmiExit = new JMenuItem("Exit");
```

The names Open, Close, Save, and Exit will be shown as selections in the menu. Next, the menu entries are added to the File menu by this sequence:

```
jmFile.add(jmiOpen);
jmFile.add(jmiClose);
jmFile.add(jmiSave);
jmFile.addSeparator();
jmFile.add(jmiExit);
```

Finally, the file menu is added to the menu bar by this line:

```
jmb.add(jmFile);
```

Once the preceding code sequence completes, the menu bar will contain one entry: File. The File menu will contain four selections in this order: Open, Close, Save, and Exit. However, notice that a separator has been added before Exit. This visually separates the Exit menu item from the preceding three selections.

The Options menu is constructed using the same basic process as the File menu. However, the Options menu consists of two submenus, Colors and Priority, and a Reset entry. The submenus are first constructed individually and then added to the Options menu. The Reset item is added last. Then, the Options menu is added to the menu bar. The Help menu is constructed using the same process.

Notice that **MenuDemo** implements the **ActionListener** interface, and action events generated by a menu selection are handled by the **actionPerformed( )** method defined by **MenuDemo**. Therefore, the program adds **this** as the action listener for the menu items. Notice that no listeners are added to the Colors or Priority items because they are not actually selections. They simply activate submenus.

Finally, the menu bar is added to the frame by the following line:

```
jfrm.setJMenuBar(jmb);
```

Menu bars are not added to the content pane. They are added directly to the **JFrame**.

The **actionPerformed( )** method handles the action events generated by the menu. It obtains the action command string associated with the selection by calling **getAction-Command( )** on the event. It stores a reference to this string in **comStr**. Then it tests the action command against "Exit", as shown here:

```
if(comStr.equals("Exit")) System.exit(0);
```

If the action command is "Exit", then the program terminates by calling **System.exit( )**. This method causes the immediate termination of a program and passes its argument as a status code to the calling process, which is usually the operating system or the browser.

By convention, a status code of 0 means normal termination. Anything else indicates that the program terminated abnormally.

At this point, you might want to experiment a bit with the **MenuDemo** program. Try adding another menu or adding more items to an existing menu. It is important that you understand the basic menu concepts before moving on because you will be evolving the program throughout the remainder of this chapter.

ADD MNEMONICS AND ACCELERATORS TO MENU ITEMS

The menu created in the preceding example is functional, but it is possible to make it better. In real applications, a menu usually includes support for keyboard shortcuts. These come in two forms: mnemonics and accelerators. As it applies to menus, a mnemonic defines a key that lets you select an item from an active menu by typing a key. Thus, a mnemonic allows you to use the keyboard to select an item from a menu that is already being displayed. An accelerator is a key that lets you select a menu item without having to activate the menu first. For example, you might use CTRL-S to activate the "save" function.

A mnemonic can be specified for both **JMenuItem** and **JMenu** objects. There are two ways to set the mnemonic for **JMenuItem**. First, it can be specified when an object is constructed by use of this constructor:

JMenuItem(String *name*, int *mnem*)

Here, the mnemonic is specified by *mnem*. Second, you can set the mnemonic by calling **setMnemonic( )**. To specify a mnemonic for **JMenu**, you must call **setMnemonic( )**. This method is inherited by both classes from **AbstractButton** and is shown here:

void setMnemonic(int *mnem*)

Here, *mnem* specifies the mnemonic. It should be one of the constants defined in **java.awt.event.KeyEvent**, which defines named constants for the keys on the keyboard, such as **KeyEvent.VK_A**, **KeyEvent.VK_B**, **KeyEvent.VK_C**, and so on. The nonalphabetical keys are also defined. Mnemonics are not case sensitive, so in the example of **VK_A**, typing either *a* or *A* will work.

By default, the first matching letter in the menu item will be underscored. In instances in which you want to underscore a letter other than the first match, specify the index of the letter as an argument to **setDisplayedMnemonicIndex( )**, which is inherited by both **JMenu** and **JMenuItem** from **AbstractButton**. It is shown here:

void setDisplayedMnemonicIndex(int *idx*)

The index of the letter to underscore is specified by *idx*.

An accelerator can be associated with a **JMenuItem** object. It is specified by calling **setAccelerator( )**, shown next:

    void setAccelerator(KeyStroke *ks*)

Here, *ks* is the key combination that is pressed to select the menu item. **KeyStroke** is a class that contains several factory methods that construct various types of keystroke accelerators. The one used here is

    static KeyStroke getKeyStroke(int *ch*, int *modifier*)

Here, *ch* specifies the accelerator character, which is a value of type **KeyEvent**, previously described. The value of *modifier* must be one or more of the following constants, defined in the **java.awt.event.InputEvent** class:

InputEvent.ALT_DOWN_MASK	InputEvent.ALT_GRAPH_DOWN_MASK
InputEvent.CTRL_DOWN_MASK	InputEvent.META_DOWN_MASK
InputEvent.SHIFT_DOWN_MASK	

Therefore, if you pass **VK_A** for the key character and **InputEvent.CTRL_DOWN_-MASK** for the modifier, the accelerator key combination is CTRL-A.

The following sequence adds both mnemonics and accelerators to the File menu created by the **MenuDemo** program in the previous section. Here is how this menu looks when activated:

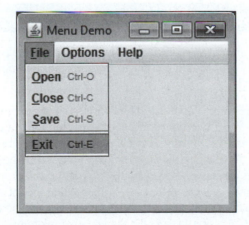

```
// Create the File menu with mnemonics and accelerators.
JMenu jmFile = new JMenu("File");
jmFile.setMnemonic(KeyEvent.VK_F);
```
←————————————The File menu has *F* as its mnemonic.

```
JMenuItem jmiOpen = new JMenuItem("Open",
                             KeyEvent.VK_O);
jmiOpen.setAccelerator(
      KeyStroke.getKeyStroke(KeyEvent.VK_O,
                       InputEvent.CTRL_DOWN_MASK));

JMenuItem jmiClose = new JMenuItem("Close",
                           KeyEvent.VK_C);
jmiClose.setAccelerator(
      KeyStroke.getKeyStroke(KeyEvent.VK_C,
                       InputEvent.CTRL_DOWN_MASK));

JMenuItem jmiSave = new JMenuItem("Save",
                          KeyEvent.VK_S);
jmiSave.setAccelerator(
      KeyStroke.getKeyStroke(KeyEvent.VK_S,
                       InputEvent.CTRL_DOWN_MASK));

JMenuItem jmiExit = new JMenuItem("Exit",
                          KeyEvent.VK_E);
jmiExit.setAccelerator(
      KeyStroke.getKeyStroke(KeyEvent.VK_E,
                       InputEvent.CTRL_DOWN_MASK));
```

In each case, the mnemonic is the first letter of the item's name. The accelerator is the same letter in combination with the CTRL key.

After making this change, you can select the File menu by typing ALT-F. Then, you can use the mnemonics O, C, S, or E to select an option. Alternatively, you can select a File menu option directly by pressing CTRL-O, CTRL-C, CTRL-S, or CTRL-E.

Ask the Expert

Q Given that accelerators work both when a menu is displayed and when it is not displayed, why would I want to bother with also defining mnemonics for menu selections?

A Although accelerators can be used by themselves, for the reason stated in your question, they have one downside: they must be used in conjunction with a modifier key, such as CTRL or ALT. However, by specifying a mnemonic, you give the user the option of selecting an item by simply typing its key (without a modifier) when a menu is displayed. For example, if you make the mnemonic for a Save option the letter *S* and its accelerator CTRL-S, then when the menu is displayed, the user can select Save by simply typing S, without needing to also press the CTRL key. While it may seem like a small issue, it's the way that many real applications work. Therefore, to give your programs a professional look and feel, both mnemonics and accelerators are needed.

ADD IMAGES AND TOOLTIPS TO MENU ITEMS

Menu items are not limited to only text. You can use images instead of text, or use both images and text. The easiest way to add an image is to specify it when the menu item is being constructed. For example, here are the **JMenuItem** constructors that allow you to add an icon to the menu item:

> JMenuItem(Icon *image*)
>
> JMenuItem(String *name*, Icon *image*)

The first creates a menu item that displays the image specified by *image*. The second creates a menu item with the name specified by *name* and the image specified by *image*. For example, here an image is added to the About menu item when it is created:

```
ImageIcon icon = new ImageIcon("AboutIcon.gif");
JMenuItem jmiAbout = new JMenuItem("About", icon);
```

After this addition, the icon specified by **icon** will be displayed next to the text "About" when the Help menu is displayed, as shown here:

You can also add an icon to a menu item after the item has been created by calling **setIcon( )** (which is inherited from **AbstractButton**).

As a point of interest, you can specify a disabled icon, which is shown when the menu item is disabled, by calling **setDisabledIcon( )**. Normally, when a menu item is disabled, the default icon is shown in gray. If a disabled icon is specified, then that icon is displayed when the menu item is disabled.

A *tooltip* is a short piece of text that is automatically displayed when the mouse hovers over a component. It is typically used to give the user additional information about the component. In Swing, you can easily add a tooltip to any lightweight component. The reason is that **JComponent** (which is, of course, the base class for all Swing lightweight components) supplies a method called **setToolTipText( )**. It is shown here:

> void setToolTipText(String *tipStr*)

This method adds the tooltip specified by *tipStr* to the component. Because all menu items inherit **JComponent**, you can add a tooltip to a menu item. For example, this creates a tooltip for the About item:

```
jmiAbout.setToolTipText("Info about the MenuDemo program.");
```

Progress Check

1. Both **setMnemonic( )** and **setAccelerator( )** take objects of type **KeyEvent** as an argument. True or False?
2. What is the mask for the CTRL key?
3. What method sets a menu item's tooltip text?

Ask the Expert

Q You mention that a tooltip can be added to any lightweight component. Does this mean that I can add tooltips to controls such as buttons, lists, and trees, for example?

A Yes. You might want to experiment with adding tooltips to some of the examples shown in the previous chapter. Just use the same approach as that shown for menu items: call **setToolTipText( )** on the control.

TRY THIS 19-1   DYNAMICALLY ADD AND REMOVE MENU ITEMS

```
DynMenuDemo.java
```

It is possible to change the contents of a menu during the execution of your program. For example, you can add an item when it is needed and remove it when it is no longer needed. You can also change the name of an item at run time. These capabilities make it possible to create dynamic menus that change as necessary to meet the needs of the user. This project demonstrates the process by walking through the steps needed to add and remove additional colors to the Colors menu of the **MenuDemo** program shown at the start of this chapter.

The project adds a menu item to the Colors menu called More Colors. When More Colors is selected, it causes the colors Yellow, Purple, and Orange to be

Answers:

1. False, **setAccelerator( )** requires a **KeyStroke** object.
2. **InputEvent.CTRL_DOWN_MASK**
3. **setToolTipText( )**

added to the menu, and the More Colors menu item is changed to Fewer Colors. When Fewer Colors is selected, the colors are removed and Fewer Colors is changed back to More Colors. Sample output is shown here:

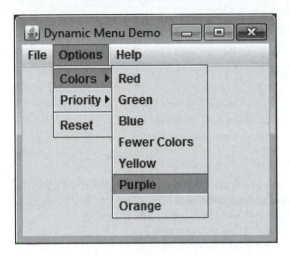

STEP-BY-STEP

1. Copy the **MenuDemo** program shown at the start of this chapter into a file called **DynMenuDemo.java**. (If you have been following along, you can use the version of **MenuDemo** that includes the accelerators, mnemonics, and icon. However, for brevity, the code shown here simply uses the original **MenuDemo** program as the starting point.)

2. Change the name of the class from **MenuDemo** to **DynMenuDemo**. Then, add three **JMenuItem**s called **jmiYellow**, **jmiPurple**, and **jmiOrange** as instance variables. Also, make the local variable **jmColors** into an instance variable. After these changes, the beginning of the program will look like this:

```
// Try This 19-1: Add and remove menu items dynamically.

import java.awt.*;
import java.awt.event.*;
import javax.swing.*;

class DynMenuDemo implements ActionListener {

    JLabel jlab;

    JMenuItem jmiYellow;
    JMenuItem jmiPurple;
    JMenuItem jmiOrange;

    JMenu jmColors;
```

3. Create a menu item called **jmiMoreLess** with the name More Colors and add it to the **jmColors** menu, as shown here:

```
// Create the More/Fewer Colors Menu item.
JMenuItem jmiMoreLess = new JMenuItem("More Colors");
jmColors.add(jmiMoreLess);
```

4. Create the Yellow, Purple, and Orange color selections like this:

```
// Create the additional colors. These will be
// added or removed on demand.
jmiYellow = new JMenuItem("Yellow");
jmiPurple = new JMenuItem("Purple");
jmiOrange = new JMenuItem("Orange");
```

5. Add listeners for the new menu items as shown next:

```
// Add listeners for the additional colors option.
jmiMoreLess.addActionListener(this);
jmiYellow.addActionListener(this);
jmiPurple.addActionListener(this);
jmiOrange.addActionListener(this);
```

6. Change the **actionPerformed( )** method to handle the new selections, as shown here:

```
// Handle menu item action events.
public void actionPerformed(ActionEvent ae) {
  // Get the action command from the menu selection.
  String comStr = ae.getActionCommand();

  // If user chooses Exit, then exit the program.
  if(comStr.equals("Exit"))
    System.exit(0);
  else if(comStr.equals("More Colors")) {
    jmColors.add(jmiYellow);
    jmColors.add(jmiPurple);
    jmColors.add(jmiOrange);
    JMenuItem mi = (JMenuItem) ae.getSource();
    mi.setText("Fewer Colors");
  } else if(comStr.equals("Fewer Colors")) {
    jmColors.remove(jmiYellow);
    jmColors.remove(jmiPurple);
    jmColors.remove(jmiOrange);
    JMenuItem mi = (JMenuItem) ae.getSource();
    mi.setText("More Colors");
  }

  // Otherwise, display the selection.
  jlab.setText(comStr + " Selected");
}
```

Notice that when More Colors is selected, the three new colors are added to the Colors menu and the name of the **jmiMoreLess** menu item is changed to Fewer Colors. When Fewer Colors is chosen, the new colors are removed from the menu and the name of **jmiMoreLess** is returned to More Colors. Recall that a menu item can be removed from a menu by calling **remove( )**.

7. After making all of the changes, the program will look like that shown here:

```java
// Try This 19-1: Add and remove menu items dynamically.

import java.awt.*;
import java.awt.event.*;
import javax.swing.*;

class DynMenuDemo implements ActionListener {

  JLabel jlab;

  JMenuItem jmiYellow;
  JMenuItem jmiPurple;
  JMenuItem jmiOrange;

  JMenu jmColors;

  DynMenuDemo() {
    // Create a new JFrame container.
    JFrame jfrm = new JFrame("Dynamic Menu Demo");

    // Specify FlowLayout for the layout manager.
    jfrm.setLayout(new FlowLayout());

    // Give the frame an initial size.
    jfrm.setSize(220, 200);

    // Terminate the program when the user closes the application.
    jfrm.setDefaultCloseOperation(JFrame.EXIT_ON_CLOSE);

    // Create a label that will display the menu selection.
    jlab = new JLabel();

    // Create the menu bar.
    JMenuBar jmb = new JMenuBar();

    // Create the File menu.
    JMenu jmFile = new JMenu("File");
    JMenuItem jmiOpen = new JMenuItem("Open");
    JMenuItem jmiClose = new JMenuItem("Close");
    JMenuItem jmiSave = new JMenuItem("Save");
    JMenuItem jmiExit = new JMenuItem("Exit");
```

```
jmFile.add(jmiOpen);
jmFile.add(jmiClose);
jmFile.add(jmiSave);
jmFile.addSeparator();
jmFile.add(jmiExit);
jmb.add(jmFile);

// Create the Options menu.
JMenu jmOptions = new JMenu("Options");

// Create the Colors submenu.
jmColors = new JMenu("Colors");
JMenuItem jmiRed = new JMenuItem("Red");
JMenuItem jmiGreen = new JMenuItem("Green");
JMenuItem jmiBlue = new JMenuItem("Blue");
jmColors.add(jmiRed);
jmColors.add(jmiGreen);
jmColors.add(jmiBlue);

// Create the More/Fewer Colors Menu item.
JMenuItem jmiMoreLess = new JMenuItem("More Colors");
jmColors.add(jmiMoreLess);

// Add Colors menu to the Options menu.
jmOptions.add(jmColors);

// Create the additional colors. These will be
// added or removed on demand.
jmiYellow = new JMenuItem("Yellow");
jmiPurple = new JMenuItem("Purple");
jmiOrange = new JMenuItem("Orange");

// Create the Priority submenu.
JMenu jmPriority = new JMenu("Priority");
JMenuItem jmiHigh = new JMenuItem("High");
JMenuItem jmiLow = new JMenuItem("Low");
jmPriority.add(jmiHigh);
jmPriority.add(jmiLow);

// Add the Priority menu to the Options menu.
jmOptions.add(jmPriority);

// Create the Reset menu item.
JMenuItem jmiReset = new JMenuItem("Reset");
jmOptions.addSeparator();
jmOptions.add(jmiReset);

// Finally, add the entire Options menu to the menu bar
jmb.add(jmOptions);
```

```java
    // Create the Help menu.
    JMenu jmHelp = new JMenu("Help");
    JMenuItem jmiAbout = new JMenuItem("About");
    jmHelp.add(jmiAbout);
    jmb.add(jmHelp);

    // Add action listeners for the menu items.
    jmiOpen.addActionListener(this);
    jmiClose.addActionListener(this);
    jmiSave.addActionListener(this);
    jmiExit.addActionListener(this);
    jmiRed.addActionListener(this);
    jmiGreen.addActionListener(this);
    jmiBlue.addActionListener(this);
    jmiHigh.addActionListener(this);
    jmiLow.addActionListener(this);
    jmiReset.addActionListener(this);
    jmiAbout.addActionListener(this);

    // Add listeners for the additional colors option.
    jmiMoreLess.addActionListener(this);
    jmiYellow.addActionListener(this);
    jmiPurple.addActionListener(this);
    jmiOrange.addActionListener(this);

    // Add the label to the content pane.
    jfrm.add(jlab);

    // Add the menu bar to the frame.
    jfrm.setJMenuBar(jmb);

    // Display the frame.
    jfrm.setVisible(true);
  }

  // Handle menu item action events.
  public void actionPerformed(ActionEvent ae) {
    // Get the action command from the menu selection.
    String comStr = ae.getActionCommand();

    // If user chooses Exit, then exit the program.
    if(comStr.equals("Exit"))
      System.exit(0);
    else if(comStr.equals("More Colors")) {
      jmColors.add(jmiYellow);
      jmColors.add(jmiPurple);
      jmColors.add(jmiOrange);
      JMenuItem mi = (JMenuItem) ae.getSource();
      mi.setText("Fewer Colors");
```

```
        } else if(comStr.equals("Fewer Colors")) {
          jmColors.remove(jmiYellow);
          jmColors.remove(jmiPurple);
          jmColors.remove(jmiOrange);
          JMenuItem mi = (JMenuItem) ae.getSource();
          mi.setText("More Colors");
        }

        // Otherwise, display the selection.
        jlab.setText(comStr + " Selected");
      }

      public static void main(String[] args) {
        // Create the GUI on the event dispatching thread.
        SwingUtilities.invokeLater(new Runnable() {
          public void run() {
            new DynMenuDemo();
          }
        });
      }
    }
```

USE JRadioButtonMenuItem AND JCheckBoxMenuItem

Although the types of menu items described by the preceding examples are frequently used, Swing defines two others you will find helpful: check boxes and radio buttons. These items can streamline a GUI by allowing a menu to provide functionality that would otherwise require additional, stand-alone components. Also, sometimes including check boxes or radio buttons in a menu simply seems the most natural place for a specific set of features.

To add a check box to a menu, create a **JCheckBoxMenuItem**. It inherits **JMenuItem**. **JCheckBoxMenuItem** works like a stand-alone check box. For example, it generates action events and an item event when its state changes. Check boxes are especially useful in menus when you have options that can be selected and you want to display their selected/deselected status.

JCheckBoxMenuItem has several constructors. The two used here are

JCheckBoxMenuItem(String *name*)

JCheckBoxMenuItem(String *name*, boolean *state*)

The first creates a check box menu item with the name specified by *name*. It is not selected. The second creates a check box menu item with the specified name and selection state. If *state* is **true**, the box is initially checked; otherwise, it is cleared.

A radio button can be added to a menu by creating an object of type **JRadioButtonMenuItem**. It also inherits **JMenuItem**. **JRadioButtonMenuItem** works like a stand-alone radio button, generating item and action events. Like stand-alone radio buttons, menu-based radio buttons must be put into a button group in order for them to exhibit mutually exclusive selection behavior.

JRadioButtonMenuItem also has several constructors. These are the two used here:

> JRadioButtonMenuItem(String *name*)
>
> JRadioButtonMenuItem(String *name*, boolean *state*)

The first creates a radio button menu item that is associated with the name passed in *name*. It is not selected. The second creates a radio button menu item with the specified name and selection state. If *state* is **true**, the button is initially selected; otherwise, it is deselected.

To try check box and radio button menu items, first remove the code that creates the Options menu in the **MenuDemo** example program. Then substitute the following code sequence, which uses check boxes for the Colors submenu and radio buttons for the Priority submenu. After making the substitution, the Options menu will look like that shown here:

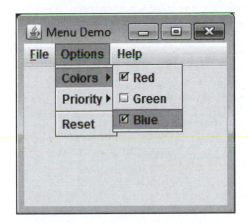

```
// Create the Options menu.
JMenu jmOptions = new JMenu("Options");

// Create the Colors submenu.
JMenu jmColors = new JMenu("Colors");

// Use check boxes for colors. This allows
// the user to select more than one color.
// Notice that Red is initially selected.
JCheckBoxMenuItem jmiRed = new JCheckBoxMenuItem("Red", true);
JCheckBoxMenuItem jmiGreen = new JCheckBoxMenuItem("Green");
JCheckBoxMenuItem jmiBlue = new JCheckBoxMenuItem("Blue");
```

Use check boxes for the colors.

```
jmColors.add(jmiRed);
jmColors.add(jmiGreen);
jmColors.add(jmiBlue);
jmOptions.add(jmColors);

// Create the Priority submenu.
JMenu jmPriority = new JMenu("Priority");

// Use radio buttons for the priority setting.
// This lets the menu show which priority is used
// but also ensures that one and only one priority
// can be selected at any one time. Notice that
// the High radio button is initially selected.
JRadioButtonMenuItem jmiHigh =
  new JRadioButtonMenuItem("High", true);
JRadioButtonMenuItem jmiLow =
  new JRadioButtonMenuItem("Low");
```

Use radio buttons for the priorities.

```
jmPriority.add(jmiHigh);
jmPriority.add(jmiLow);
jmOptions.add(jmPriority);

// Create button group for the radio button menu items.
ButtonGroup bg = new ButtonGroup();
bg.add(jmiHigh);
bg.add(jmiLow);
```

Put the Priority radio buttons into a button group.

```
// Create the Reset menu item.
JMenuItem jmiReset = new JMenuItem("Reset");
jmOptions.addSeparator();
jmOptions.add(jmiReset);

// Finally, add the entire Options menu to
// the menu bar
jmb.add(jmOptions);
```

Ask the Expert

Q   Can I use icons with check box and/or radio button menu items?

A   Yes. For example, you can specify an icon for a radio button item using this constructor:

   JRadioButtonMenuItem(Icon *icon*)

You can specify an icon for a check box using this constructor:

   JCheckBoxMenuItem(Icon *icon*)

Other constructors are available that let you include text and/or set the selected state.

You can also set a mnemonic and/or an accelerator key for radio button and check box menu items. To do so, use **setMnemonic( )** and **setAccelerator( )**, which were described earlier.

Progress Check

1. What class creates a check box menu item?
2. When **JRadioButtonMenuItem**s are added to a menu, they are automatically part of a button group. True or False?

Ask the Expert

Q Can I create popup menus that are activated by right-clicking the mouse?

A Yes. To create a popup menu, use **JPopupMenu**. As you mention in your question, a popup menu is normally activated by clicking the right mouse button when the mouse is over a component for which a popup menu has been defined. To create a popup menu, first create an object of type **JPopupMenu**. Then, add **JMenuItem**s to it. You will also need to watch for mouse events (which are events of type **MouseEvent**) by implementing the **MouseListener** interface, which is declared in **java.awt.event**. Although the process is not overly difficult, a complete description is beyond the scope of this book.

EXERCISES

1. What are the core Swing menu classes?
2. What class creates a menu? To create a main menu bar, what class is used?
3. What event is generated when a menu item is selected?
4. Images are not allowed in menus. True or False?
5. What method adds a menu bar to a window?

Answers:

1. **JCheckBoxMenuItem**
2. False. You must explicitly put radio button menu items in a button group.

6. What method adds a mnemonic to a menu item?

7. Can an icon be used as a menu item? If so, does it prevent the use of a name?

8. What class creates a radio button menu item?

9. Although check box menu items are permitted, their use is discouraged because they make a menu look strange. True or False?

10. In the course of this chapter, several changes were suggested to the **MenuDemo** program that demonstrate additional menu features. Except for the dynamic menu items in Try This 19-1, integrate the other changes into the original **MenuDemo** program. In the process, reorganize the program for clarity by using separate methods to construct the various menus.

11. True or False?

   A. You can disable a menu item without disabling the whole menu.

   B. You can disable a menu without disabling all the menu items in the menu.

12. As mentioned in the chapter, the **JMenu** class has a **getMenuComponents( )** method that returns an array containing the components of the menu. Suppose a menu has one or more separators in it. Are those separators included in the array returned by **getMenuComponents( )**?

13. Suppose you have a menu **m** with only three parts: an Open menu item, a separator, and a Close menu item. If you then execute **m.remove(1)**, will the separator or the Close menu item be removed?

14. Write a program that creates a window with a menu bar and a File menu. The File menu has three menu items: Open, Recent, and Exit. The Recent menu item is a submenu that initially has no menu items. Each time Open is selected, a new menu item is added to the Recent submenu. The new menu item's name is "Open" followed by an integer that is incremented for each new menu item. For example, the first menu item in the Recent submenu should be Open1, then the next menu item should be Open2, and so on. When the Exit menu item is selected, the program quits. No action listeners are necessary for the Recent menu items.

15. Enhance the preceding exercise so that the Recent submenu displays only the five most recent menu items added.

16. Suppose you have a menu with two menu items.

   A. If both menu items have the same mnemonic key, what happens when you press that key when the menu is displayed?

   B. If both menu items have the same accelerator, what happens when you type in that accelerator key?

   C. What happens if you try to use, for the mnemonic key for a menu item, a character that isn't part of the text of the menu item? For example, what if you try to use **VK_A** as the mnemonic key for the Open menu item?

17. Write a program with a Help menu containing a FAQ menu item that brings up a new **JFrame** with a question and answer in it. Closing the new **JFrame** should not cause the application to quit.

18. Write a program that displays a window with four menus: File, Edit, Text, and Show. Add one menu item to each of the first three menus and add three menu items to the Show menu: File, Edit, and Text. The menu items in the Show menu should all be check box menu items, and all should be initially checked. If any of the menu items in the Show menu are unchecked by the user, then the menu with the same name should be disabled. If the menu item is later checked, the menu with the same name should be enabled.

19. Write a program that displays a window with one menu containing one menu item and containing a label in the center. Add appropriate tooltips to the menu bar, the menu, the menu item, and the label.

20. In the section of the chapter on mnemonics and accelerators, it was mentioned that one or more modifier keys can be specified as part of the accelerator. However, the examples in the chapter used only one modifier key. If you want the accelerator to use more than one modifier key, you need to combine the constants in the **InputEvent** class corresponding to the desired modifier keys. Suppose you have a menu item **m** and you want an accelerator for **m** that consists of the letter 'A' in combination with both the CTRL key and the SHIFT key. What Java statement will set the accelerator for **m**?

CHAPTER 20

Dialogs

KEY SKILLS & CONCEPTS

- **JOptionPane**
- **showMessageDialog( )**
- **showConfirmDialog( )**
- **showInputDialog( )**
- **showOptionDialog( )**
- **JDialog**
- Create a modeless dialog
- **JFileChooser**

Although the individual controls provided by Swing, such as text fields, buttons, and lists, form the foundation of any GUI, there will be times when you need to link two or more of these controls together as a unit in order to handle more sophisticated input operations. For example, if your program needs to display an error message and then offer options (such as Retry and Cancel), you will usually want to link these in a single logical and visual unit. This is accomplished by creating a *dialog*.

A dialog is a separate window that requests some form of response from the user. It will contain at least a message and a button, but much more sophisticated dialogs are both possible and commonplace. Dialogs are also commonly referred to as *dialog boxes* or *dialog windows*.

A dialog provides a means by which your program can achieve two important goals. First, a dialog gives you a way to organize the components necessary for complex input situations that go beyond what the basic components can handle individually. For example, a word processor would use a dialog to allow the user to select a type font, point size, and style. Such a dialog would be a composite of several individual components that, when combined, define a typeface. Second, a dialog gives your program a way to request input from the user that is necessary before the program proceeds. For example, you might use a dialog to prompt the user for a password and then wait until the password is entered. Whatever the use, dialogs are an important part of many Swing applications.

Swing provides extensive support for dialogs. The ones we will examine here are **JDialog**, **JOptionPane**, and **JFileChooser**. The main dialog class is **JDialog**, but somewhat surprisingly, you won't often use it directly. Instead, many dialog situations can be handled by using **JOptionPane**, which provides a wide variety of built-in dialog styles. **JFileChooser** is a built-in dialog that lets a user choose a file.

JOptionPane

In the modern GUI programming environment, dialogs are used in two basic ways. First, there are the larger, more complicated dialogs that link several input components. An example is a dialog that enables a user to configure a modem connection. Such a dialog might contain components that allow the user to specify the modem speed and protocol, enable hardware flow control, specify an initialization command, and so on. To create such a sophisticated dialog requires the use of **JDialog**, which is discussed later in this chapter.

The second type of dialog is much simpler. This is a dialog that prompts the user and then waits for a response. Perhaps the most common example is the "Exit? Yes/No" dialog that simply confirms if you really want to exit a program. Because these relatively simple dialogs form such an important part of Java programming, Swing provides extensive built-in support for them through the **JOptionPane** class.

JOptionPane is an easy-to-use dialog class that offers solutions to many common dialog-based problems. **JOptionPane** supports the four basic types of dialogs listed here:

- Message
- Confirmation
- Input
- Option

A message dialog displays a message and then waits until the user presses the OK button. This dialog provides an easy and effective way to ensure that the user is aware of some pieces of information. For example, you could use a message dialog to tell the user that a network connection has been lost by displaying "Connection Lost" inside the dialog.

A confirmation dialog asks the user a question that typically has a Yes/No answer, and then waits for a response. This dialog is used in cases in which a course of action needs to be confirmed. For example, a confirmation dialog that displays the message "Exit without saving changes?" could be used to ensure that the user *does* actually want to exit a program without saving the changes.

An input dialog allows the user to enter a string or select an item from a list. The advantage of this dialog is that it allows users to respond by entering a string of their own choosing. Thus, it goes beyond a simple Yes/No/OK/Cancel response. You might use this type of dialog to obtain the URL of some resource, for example.

An option dialog lets you specify a list of options from which the user will choose. Thus, it enables you to create a dialog that supplies options that are not available with the other dialogs.

Interestingly, **JOptionPane** is not derived from **JDialog**. Instead, **JOptionPane** is a container for the components that will be used by the dialog. However, it does *use* **JDialog**. **JOptionPane** constructs a **JDialog** object automatically and adds itself to that object. It then handles the details of displaying the dialog, obtaining the response, and closing the dialog. In essence, **JOptionPane** provides a streamlined way to create and manage simple dialogs.

All dialogs created by **JOptionPane** are *modal*. A modal dialog demands a response before the program will continue. As a result, you cannot refocus input to another part of the application without first closing the dialog. Thus, a modal dialog stops the program until the user responds. Although modal dialogs are quite common, you can also create *modeless* (also called *nonmodal*) dialogs. A modeless dialog *does not* prevent other parts of the program from being used. Thus, the rest of the program remains active, and input can be refocused to other windows. However, you cannot create a modeless dialog using **JOptionPane**. (Modeless dialogs are easily created by **JDialog**, however, as described later in this chapter.)

Although you can create a **JOptionPane** by using one of its constructors, you normally won't do so. Instead, you will usually use one of its **show** factory methods. These methods automatically construct a dialog in one of the four styles and then return the user's response. For example, to create a simple message dialog, you can use the **showMessageDialog( )** method. It creates a dialog that displays a message and then waits until the user clicks the OK button. As you will see, the factory methods make **JOptionPane** extraordinarily easy to use.

JOptionPane supports two basic categories of **show** methods. The first creates a dialog that uses **JDialog** to hold the dialog. This is the type of **JOptionPane** that you will normally create, and it is the only type described in this book. The second category uses a **JInternalFrame** to hold the dialog. This type of dialog is much less common, and the topic of internal frames is beyond the scope of this book.

JOptionPane defines the following four factory methods that create standard, **JDialog**-based dialogs: **showConfirmDialog( )**, **showInputDialog( )**, **showMessageDialog( )**, and **showOptionDialog( )**. Each creates the type of dialog implied by its name. All are static methods. The first three have several overloaded forms. The remainder of this discussion examines each style of dialog separately.

Progress Check

1. What are the four types of dialogs that can be created by **JOptionPane**?
2. What is the difference between modal and modeless dialogs?
3. Is **JOptionPane** derived from **JDialog**?

Answers:

1. Message, confirmation, input, and option.
2. A modal dialog demands a response before other parts of the program can be used. A modeless dialog allows the rest of the program to remain active.
3. No.

showMessageDialog( )

The **showMessageDialog( )** method creates the simplest dialog that can be constructed. It displays a message and then waits until the user presses the OK button. Despite this simplicity, **showMessageDialog( )** still has three forms. Its shortest version is shown here:

static void showMessageDialog(Component *parent*, Object *msg*)
throws HeadlessException

Here, *parent* specifies the component relative to which the dialog is displayed. If you pass **null** for this argument, the dialog is usually displayed in the center of the screen. The message to display is passed in *msg*. Technically, this does not have to be a string. For example, you could pass a **JLabel**. However, for simple dialogs, a string is typically used. When the dialog is displayed, an OK button is included. The dialog waits until the user presses OK. Therefore, the call to **showMessageDialog( )** will not return until the user either presses OK or closes the dialog by clicking the close box. (As mentioned, all dialogs created by the **show** methods are modal.) This means that the calling thread waits until the call returns. Because there is only one option for the user (the OK button), there is no need to return a response and the return type is **void**.

Notice that **showMessageDialog( )** can throw a **HeadlessException**. This exception is thrown if you attempt to show a dialog in a noninteractive environment, such as one in which no screen, mouse, or keyboard is attached. In general, a **show** method will throw a **HeadlessException** if an attempt is made to show a dialog in a noninteractive environment.

The following program shows **showMessageDialog( )** in action. It displays a dialog that tells the user that disk space is low.

```java
// A very simple JOptionPane demonstration.

import java.awt.*;
import java.awt.event.*;
import javax.swing.*;

class MsgDialogDemo {

  JLabel jlab;
  JButton jbtnShow;
  JFrame jfrm;

  MsgDialogDemo() {
    // Create a new JFrame container.
    jfrm = new JFrame("Simple Message Dialog");
```

```
    // Specify FlowLayout for the layout manager.
    jfrm.setLayout(new FlowLayout());

    // Give the frame an initial size.
    jfrm.setSize(400, 250);

    // Terminate the program when the user closes the application.
    jfrm.setDefaultCloseOperation(JFrame.EXIT_ON_CLOSE);

    // Create a label that will show when the dialog returns.
    jlab = new JLabel();

    // Create a button that will display the dialog.
    jbtnShow = new JButton("Show Dialog");

    // Add action listener for the button.
    jbtnShow.addActionListener(new ActionListener() {
      public void actionPerformed(ActionEvent le) {
        jlab.setText("Dialog Opened");

        // Create a dialog that shows a message.
        JOptionPane.showMessageDialog(jfrm,
                          "Disk space is low.");

        // This statement won't execute until the
        // call to showMessageDialog() returns.
        jlab.setText("Dialog Closed");
      }
    });

    // Add the button and label to the content pane.
    jfrm.add(jbtnShow);
    jfrm.add(jlab);

    // Display the frame.
    jfrm.setVisible(true);
  }

  public static void main(String[] args) {
    // Create the GUI on the event dispatching thread.
    SwingUtilities.invokeLater(new Runnable() {
      public void run() {
        new MsgDialogDemo();
      }
    });
  }
}
```

—Create a message dialog.

The dialog produced is shown here:

Here is how the program works. The main window contains a button called Show Dialog. When this button is pressed, the action listener linked to the button displays the dialog by calling **showMessageDialog( )**. The parent of the dialog is the **jfrm**, which is the main window of the program. The message to display is "Disk space is low." When the call to **showMessageDialog( )** executes, the dialog is displayed. At that point, the dialog has input focus and, because the dialog is modal, focus cannot be redirected to the main window. Therefore, the main window is inactive until the dialog is closed, by the user clicking either the OK button or the close box in the dialog window. When the dialog is closed, the call to **showMessageDialog( )** returns and the text in **jlab** is set to indicate this fact.

There are two other forms of **showMessageDialog( )** that let you more precisely configure various aspects of the dialog. The first is shown here:

static void showMessageDialog(Component *parent*, Object *msg*,

String *title*, int *msgT*)

throws HeadlessException

The first two parameters are the same as the version of the method shown earlier. The *title* parameter lets you specify a title for the dialog. By default, the title is Message, but it is usually better to specify a title that fits the message that you are displaying precisely. The *msgT* parameter indicates the nature of the message. It must be one of the following values defined by **JOptionPane**:

ERROR_MESSAGE	Indicates that an error message is displayed. The standard error icon is used.
INFORMATION_MESSAGE	Indicates that an informational message is displayed. The standard information icon is used. This is the default message type.
PLAIN_MESSAGE	Indicates a "plain" message, which is one in which no icon is displayed.
QUESTION_MESSAGE	Indicates that a question message is displayed. The question mark icon is used.
WARNING_MESSAGE	Indicates that a warning message is displayed. The standard warning icon is used.

Like many other aspects of Swing, the precise effect of the *msgT* parameter is determined by the look and feel.

To see the benefits of specifying a title and a message type, substitute the following call to **showMessageDialog( )** in the preceding example:

```
JOptionPane.showMessageDialog(jfrm,
                        "Disk Space is Low.",
                        "Warning",
                        JOptionPane.WARNING_MESSAGE);
```

The message dialog will now look like this:

By default, a message dialog displays a standard system icon. You can specify one of your own by using this version of **showMessageDialog( )**:

static void showMessageDialog(Component *parent*, Object *msg*,
String *title*, int *msgT*, Icon *image*)
throws HeadlessException

Here, the icon to display is passed in *image*. Keep in mind, however, that if your message falls into one of the predefined categories, then it is probably best to use the standard icon rather than a custom one because the standard icon will be the most easily recognized.

Progress Check

1. What type of response does **showMessageDialog( )** request?
2. What is the constant that indicates a warning message?
3. Must the message displayed by **showMessageDialog( )** be a string?

Answers:

1. OK
2. **WARNING_MESSAGE**
3. No, it can be any type of object.

showConfirmDialog( )

Another very common dialog type is one that requests a basic Yes/No response from the user. In Swing, this is called a confirmation dialog, and it is created by calling **showConfirmDialog( )**. There are several versions of this method. The simplest one is shown here:

static int showConfirmDialog(Component *parent*, Object *msg*)
throws HeadlessException

Here, *parent* specifies the component relative to which the dialog is displayed. If you pass **null** for this argument, then the dialog is usually displayed in the center of the screen. The message to display is passed in *msg*. This can be any type of object, but normally a string is used. The dialog automatically contains three buttons called Yes, No, and Cancel. The title of the dialog is Select an Option.

The method returns an integer value that indicates the user's choice (that is, which button was pressed). The return value will be one of these constants defined by **JOptionPane**:

CANCEL_OPTION	Returned if the user clicks Cancel
CLOSED_OPTION	Returned if the user closes the dialog without making a choice
NO_OPTION	Returned if the user clicks No
YES_OPTION	Returned if the user clicks Yes

Notice **CLOSED_OPTION**. This value is returned when the user closes the dialog (by clicking on the close box) instead of pressing one of the buttons. Typically, you should handle a **CLOSED_OPTION** response as if it represented "No" or "Cancel", depending on the context. A **CLOSED_OPTION** should never be interpreted as a **YES_OPTION**.

The following program creates a simple confirmation dialog and shows how to handle the responses.

```java
// Use a simple confirmation dialog.

import java.awt.*;
import java.awt.event.*;
import javax.swing.*;

class ConfirmDialogDemo {

  JLabel jlab;
  JButton jbtnShow;
  JFrame jfrm;
```

```
ConfirmDialogDemo() {
    // Create a new JFrame container.
    jfrm = new JFrame("A Confirmation Dialog");

    // Specify FlowLayout for the layout manager.
    jfrm.setLayout(new FlowLayout());

    // Give the frame an initial size.
    jfrm.setSize(400, 250);

    // Terminate the program when the user closes the application.
    jfrm.setDefaultCloseOperation(JFrame.EXIT_ON_CLOSE);

    // Create a label that will show the user's response.
    jlab = new JLabel();

    // Create button that will display the dialog.
    jbtnShow = new JButton("Show Dialog");

    // Add action listener for the button.
    jbtnShow.addActionListener(new ActionListener() {
        public void actionPerformed(ActionEvent le) {
            // Create a confirmation dialog.
            int response = JOptionPane.showConfirmDialog(
                        jfrm,
                        "Remove unused files?");
```
       ← Create a confirmation dialog.

```
            // Show the response.
            switch(response) {
```
       ← Check the user's response and respond appropriately.

```
              case JOptionPane.YES_OPTION:
                jlab.setText("You answered Yes.");
                break;
              case JOptionPane.NO_OPTION:
                jlab.setText("You answered No.");
                break;
              case JOptionPane.CANCEL_OPTION:
                jlab.setText("Cancel pressed.");
                break;
              case JOptionPane.CLOSED_OPTION:
                jlab.setText("Dialog closed without response.");
                break;
            }
        }
    });

    // Add the button and label to the content pane.
    jfrm.add(jbtnShow);
    jfrm.add(jlab);
```

```
    // Display the frame.
    jfrm.setVisible(true);
  }

  public static void main(String[] args) {
    // Create the GUI on the event dispatching thread.
    SwingUtilities.invokeLater(new Runnable() {
      public void run() {
        new ConfirmDialogDemo();
      }
    });
  }
}
```

The dialog produced is shown here:

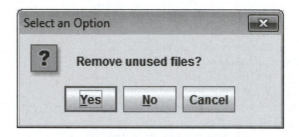

As you can see, the code for handling the response from the user is straightforward. Because all dialogs created with **JOptionPane**'s **show** methods are modal, the call to **showConfirmDialog( )** will not return until the user either chooses an option or closes the dialog window by clicking on its close box. The response is returned by **showConfirmDialog( )** and is assigned to a variable called **response**. This variable controls a **switch** statement that displays the user's choice.

Although the preceding form of **showConfirmDialog( )** is quite easy to use, it may not be suitable for some applications because it always uses the title Select an Option. In certain cases, a more descriptive title for the dialog, such as "Disk Space Is Low", would be better. Fortunately, it is easy to change the title and other aspects of the dialog by using one of the following overloaded versions of **showConfirmDialog( )**:

static int showConfirmDialog(Component *parent*, Object *msg*,
String *title*, int *optT*)
throws HeadlessException

static int showConfirmDialog(Component *parent*, Object *msg*,
String *title*, int *optT*, int *msgT*)
throws HeadlessException

static int showConfirmDialog(Component *parent*, Object *msg*,

String *title*, int *optT*, int *msgT*,

Icon *image*)

throws HeadlessException

Here, *parent* and *msg* are the same as described earlier. The title of the dialog is specified by *title*. The options (i.e., the buttons) from which the user can choose are specified by *optT*. It must be one of the following constants defined by **JOptionPane**:

OK_CANCEL_OPTION	The dialog includes buttons for OK and Cancel.
YES_NO_OPTION	The dialog includes buttons for Yes and No.
YES_NO_CANCEL_OPTION	The dialog includes buttons for Yes, No, and Cancel.

By default, Yes, No, and Cancel are supplied. However, Cancel is not appropriate in all cases. In situations in which only a Yes or No response is meaningful, pass **YES_NO_OPTION** to the *optT* parameter. If the **OK_CANCEL_OPTION** is used, then the dialog might also return the value **OK_OPTION**.

The general type of dialog displayed is passed in *msgT*. It must be one of the following constants described earlier:

ERROR_MESSAGE	INFORMATION_MESSAGE	PLAIN_MESSAGE
QUESTION_MESSAGE	WARNING_MESSAGE	

The default message type is **QUESTION_MESSAGE**.

The icon displayed within the dialog is specified by *image*. By default, a question mark is used.

The dialog displayed by the preceding example can be easily improved by adding a title and removing the Cancel button, as shown in this version of the **ActionListener** from the previous example:

```
jbtnShow.addActionListener(new ActionListener() {
  public void actionPerformed(ActionEvent le) {
    // Create a dialog that shows a message.
    int response = JOptionPane.showConfirmDialog(
                     jfrm,
                     "Remove unused files?", ◄——————— This is the prompt.
                     "Disk Space Is Low", ◄——————— This is the title.
                     JOptionPane.YES_NO_OPTION); ◄——————— Display only a Yes and No option.

    switch(response) {
      case JOptionPane.YES_OPTION:
        jlab.setText("You answered Yes.");
        break;
      case JOptionPane.NO_OPTION:
        jlab.setText("You answered No.");
        break;
```

```
        case JOptionPane.CLOSED_OPTION:
          jlab.setText("Dialog closed without response.");
          break;
      }
    }
  });
```

After substituting the code, the dialog will look like this:

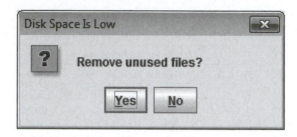

Notice that the title is now "Disk Space Is Low" and that the Cancel button has been removed.

Progress Check

1. By default, **showConfirmDialog( )** requests a Yes/No/Cancel response. True or False?
2. What effect does passing **YES_NO_OPTION** to the *optT* parameter of **showConfirmDialog( )** have?

showInputDialog( )

Although a Yes/No response is adequate for some simple dialogs, often other, more flexible input is required. To handle these cases, **JOptionPane** provides two other types of dialogs. One is created by **showOptionDialog( )**, which is described in the next section. The other is **showInputDialog( )**, and it is described here.

showInputDialog( ) supports several different forms. The simplest displays a text field into which the user can enter a string. This version is shown here:

    static String showInputDialog(Object *msg*) throws HeadlessException

Here, the message to display is passed in *msg*. As a general rule, the dialog is centered on the screen because no parent window is specified. The method returns the string entered by the user. The dialog displays buttons labeled OK and Cancel.

Answers:

1. True.
2. It causes just the Yes and No options to be displayed.

Pressing OK causes the string to be returned. Pressing Cancel (or clicking the close button on the window) causes the dialog to discard any string entered by the user and return **null**. Pressing OK when no string has been entered causes a zero-length string to be returned.

Here is an example that demonstrates the simplest form of **showInputDialog( )**. It simply prompts for a name.

```java
// A simple input dialog.

import java.awt.*;
import java.awt.event.*;
import javax.swing.*;

class InputDialogDemo {

  JLabel jlab;

  JButton jbtnShow;

  JFrame jfrm;

  InputDialogDemo() {
    // Create a new JFrame container.
    jfrm = new JFrame("A Simple Input Dialog");

    // Specify FlowLayout for the layout manager.
    jfrm.setLayout(new FlowLayout());

    // Give the frame an initial size.
    jfrm.setSize(400, 250);

    // Terminate the program when the user closes the application.
    jfrm.setDefaultCloseOperation(JFrame.EXIT_ON_CLOSE);

    // Create a label that shows the response.
    jlab = new JLabel();

    // Create button that will display the dialog.
    jbtnShow = new JButton("Show Dialog");

    // Add action listener for the button.
    jbtnShow.addActionListener(new ActionListener() {
      public void actionPerformed(ActionEvent le) {
        // Create a dialog that inputs a string.
        String response = JOptionPane.showInputDialog(
                    "Enter Name");

        // If the response is null, then the dialog
        // was cancelled or closed. If response is a
```

Create an input dialog that reads a string.

```
            // zero-length string, then no input was entered.
            // Otherwise, response contains a string entered
            // by the user.
            if (response == null)                              A null response means that the
               jlab.setText("Dialog cancelled or closed");     dialog was cancelled or closed.
            else if (response.length() == 0)
               jlab.setText("No string entered");
            else
               jlab.setText("Hi there " + response);
         }
      });

      // Add the button and label to the content pane.
      jfrm.add(jbtnShow);
      jfrm.add(jlab);

      // Display the frame.
      jfrm.setVisible(true);
   }

   public static void main(String[] args) {
      // Create the GUI on the event dispatching thread.
      SwingUtilities.invokeLater(new Runnable() {
         public void run() {
            new InputDialogDemo();
         }
      });
   }
}
```

The dialog produced is shown here:

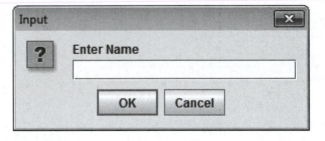

Although the input dialog created by the preceding program is fully functional, it is quite limited. For example, it always uses the title "Input", it positions the dialog in the center of the screen rather than within the application window, and it does not let you give an initial value to the text field. Fortunately, all of these deficiencies are easy to rectify by using one of the overloaded forms of **showInputDialog( )**, shown here:

static String showInputDialog(Object *msg*, Object *initVal*)
                                                   throws HeadlessException

static String showInputDialog(Component *parent*, Object *msg*)

throws HeadlessException

static String showInputDialog(Component *parent*, Object *msg*, Object *initVal*)

throws HeadlessException

static String showInputDialog(Component *parent*, Object *msg*, String *title*,

int *msgT*) throws HeadlessException

Here, *parent* specifies the component relative to which the dialog is displayed. The initial value to put into the text field is passed via *initVal*. The value passed in *title* specifies the title. The type of dialog is passed in *msgT*. It must be one of the following constants described earlier:

ERROR_MESSAGE	INFORMATION_MESSAGE	PLAIN_MESSAGE
QUESTION_MESSAGE	WARNING_MESSAGE	

The default message type is **QUESTION_MESSAGE**.

For example, the following call to **showInputDialog( )** creates a dialog that will be positioned relative to the main window and initialized to the name "Bob Smith".

```
String response = JOptionPane.showInputDialog(
                     jfrm, "Enter Name", "Bob Smith");
```

To see the effect of this change, substitute this call to **showInputDialog( )** into the preceding program. After making this change, the dialog window will look like this:

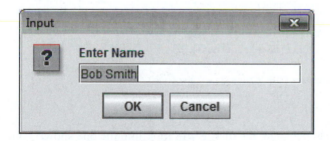

There is one more form of **showInputDialog( )** that lets you specify a list of possible selections from which the user can choose and the icon that is displayed. This form is shown here:

static Object showInputDialog(Component *parent*, Object *msg*,

String *title*, int *msgT*, Icon *image*,

Object[ ] *vals*, Object *initVal*)

throws HeadlessException

Here, *parent, title,* and *msgT* are as just described. The icon to be displayed is passed in *image*. If *image* is **null**, then the standard icon associated with the specified message type is displayed. A list of selections is passed in *vals*. These selections are displayed in a list. However, if *vals* is **null**, then a text field is displayed into which the user can enter a value. The initial value displayed is passed in *initVal*.

The dialog created by this version of **showInputDialog( )** is especially useful when you want to limit the user to a range of choices. To see this type of input dialog in action, substitute the following action listener for the one shown in the example program.

```
jbtnShow.addActionListener(new ActionListener() {
  public void actionPerformed(ActionEvent le) {
    String[] names = { "Tom Jones", "Bob Smith",
                       "Mary Doe", "Nancy Oliver" };

    // Create a dialog that lets the user
    // choose from a list of names.
    String response =
              (String) JOptionPane.showInputDialog(   ← This creates an input dialog
                         jfrm,                           that displays a list of strings.
                         "Choose User",
                         "Select User Name",
                         JOptionPane.QUESTION_MESSAGE,
                         null,
                         names,
                         "Bob Smith");

    if(response == null)
      jlab.setText("Dialog cancelled or closed");
    else if(response.length() == 0)
      jlab.setText("No string entered");
    else
      jlab.setText("Hi there " + response);
  }
});
```

After making this change, the dialog will look like the one shown here:

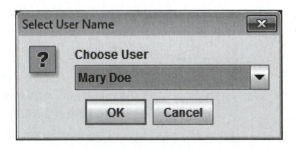

Progress Check

1. What two types of input are supported by **showInputDialog( )**?
2. When using **showInputDialog( )**, can you initialize the response?

showOptionDialog( )

Although the dialogs created by **showMessageDialog( )**, **showConfirmDialog( )**, and **showInputDialog( )** satisfy many common dialog needs, there are situations for which they are not appropriate. For this reason **JOptionPane** supplies one more **show** method: **showOptionDialog( )**. This method creates a dialog that contains the elements that you specify. Thus, using **showOptionDialog( )** you can create a dialog tailored more precisely to your needs.

The **showOptionDialog( )** method is shown here:

static int showOptionDialog(Component *parent*, Object *msg*, String *title*,

int *optT*, int *msgT*, Icon *image*,

Object[ ] *options*, Object *initVal*)

throws HeadlessException

You are already familiar with most of the parameters. The *parent, msg,* and *title* specify the parent of the dialog (which can be **null** if the default frame is used), the prompt displayed, and the title of the dialog. The options (i.e., the buttons) from which the user can choose are specified by *optT*. It must be one of the following constants defined by **JOptionPane**:

DEFAULT_OPTION

OK_CANCEL_OPTION

YES_NO_OPTION

YES_NO_CANCEL_OPTION

Understand, however, that the *optT* parameter is used only if the *options* parameter is **null**. Otherwise, it is ignored. In this case, you can use the constant **DEFAULT_OPTION** as a placeholder. The general type of dialog displayed is passed in *msgT*. It must be one of the following constants, also described earlier:

ERROR_MESSAGE	INFORMATION_MESSAGE	PLAIN_MESSAGE
QUESTION_MESSAGE	WARNING_MESSAGE	

The icon displayed within the dialog is specified by *image*. To use the standard icon, simply pass **null** to this parameter. The initial selection is passed through *initVal*.

Answers:

1. Depending on what you request, **showInputDialog( )** can have the user enter a string or select an item from a list.
2. Yes.

The one new parameter is *options*. It is an array of **Object** that contains the options that will be displayed in the dialog. Typically, you will pass an array of strings. In this case, each string becomes the label of a button. When you press a button, the dialog ends and the index of the string is returned. You can also pass an array of icons or an array that contains a mix of strings or icons. When an icon is passed, it is automatically embedded in an icon-based button. Other types of objects can be passed. (See "Ask the Expert" at the end of this section.)

Here is an example that uses **showOptionDialog( )** to let the user choose how to connect to the network.

```java
// Demonstrate an option dialog.

import java.awt.*;
import java.awt.event.*;
import javax.swing.*;

class OptionDialogDemo {

  JLabel jlab;
  JButton jbtnShow;
  JFrame jfrm;

  OptionDialogDemo() {
    // Create a new JFrame container.
    jfrm = new JFrame("A Simple Option Dialog");

    // Specify FlowLayout for the layout manager.
    jfrm.setLayout(new FlowLayout());

    // Give the frame an initial size.
    jfrm.setSize(400, 250);

    // Terminate the program when the user closes the application.
    jfrm.setDefaultCloseOperation(JFrame.EXIT_ON_CLOSE);

    // Create a label that will show the selection.
    jlab = new JLabel();

    // Create button that will display the dialog.
    jbtnShow = new JButton("Show Dialog");

    // Add action listener for the button.
    jbtnShow.addActionListener(new ActionListener() {
      public void actionPerformed(ActionEvent le) {

        // Define the connection options.
        String[] connectOpts = { "Modem", "Wireless",
                                 "Satellite", "Cable" };
```

These are the options that will be displayed.

```
        // Create a dialog that lets the user
        // choose how to connect to the network.
        int response = JOptionPane.showOptionDialog(
                          jfrm,
                          "Choose Network Connection",
                          "Connection Type",
                          JOptionPane.DEFAULT_OPTION,
                          JOptionPane.QUESTION_MESSAGE,
                          null,
                          connectOpts,
                          "Wireless");
```

Create an option dialog that displays a list of connection options. Each option is displayed in its own button.

```
        // Display the choice.
        switch(response) {
          case 0:
            jlab.setText("Connect via modem.");
            break;
          case 1:
            jlab.setText("Connect via wireless.");
            break;
          case 2:
            jlab.setText("Connect via satellite.");
            break;
          case 3:
            jlab.setText("Connect via cable.");
            break;
          case JOptionPane.CLOSED_OPTION:
            jlab.setText("Dialog cancelled.");
            break;
        }
      }
    });
```

The response contains the index of the option that was clicked.

```
    // Add the button and label to the content pane.
    jfrm.add(jbtnShow);
    jfrm.add(jlab);

    // Display the frame.
    jfrm.setVisible(true);
  }

  public static void main(String[] args) {
    // Create the GUI on the event dispatching thread.
    SwingUtilities.invokeLater(new Runnable() {
      public void run() {
        new OptionDialogDemo();
      }
    });
  }
}
```

The dialog produced is shown here:

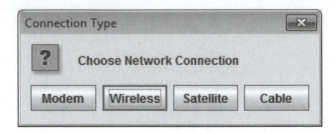

Looking closely at how the **actionPerfomed( )** handler activates the dialog, first notice the **String** array **names**, which specifies the names of the various connection methods. This name, along with the other information, is passed to **showOptionDialog( )**. When the dialog is created, the names are used as the labels for buttons. When one of these buttons is pressed, an integer corresponding to the index of the name within the array is returned. Therefore, pressing Modem returns 0, pressing Wireless returns 1, and so on.

When specifying options, it is important to remember one point: they override the standard options. Therefore, if you specify a "Cancel" option, the value returned when it is selected will be its index in the array, not **CANCEL_OPTION**. The only standard option that you will be able to check for is **CLOSED_OPTION** because it is generated when the user clicks the window's close box.

Although **showOptionDialog( )** does offer a significant amount of flexibility in determining what a dialog contains, its use is a bit more limited than you might at first think. The reason is that you don't have any real control over the layout of the dialog. In general, all **show** dialogs, including the ones created by **showOptionDialog( )**, use the same pattern. They all have a title, a single-line message, an icon to the left of the message, and a single line of choices. Input dialogs add a text field or list. There is no way to change this layout.

Ask the Expert

Q When using **showOptionDialog( )**, can I pass something other than strings or icons to the *options* parameter?

A Yes. You can pass any type of object, including other Swing components. If you pass an array of components, the components are added to the dialog. Thus, it is possible to construct a dialog that contains a text field, two check boxes, and an OK button by passing references to these components. If you pass another type of object, a button is created that contains the results of calling **toString( )** on the object.

Unfortunately, because of the layout limitations inherent in **showOption-Dialog( )**, you will usually pass either strings or icons. Other components often produce unsatisfying results. For example, if you use the following sequence to construct a dialog:

```
Object[] ops = { new JLabel("Name"),
                 new JTextField(10),
                 new JLabel("Phone Number"),
                 new JTextField(10),
                 "OK", "Cancel" };

int response = JOptionPane.showOptionDialog(
                 jfrm,
                 "Enter Info",
                 "Get Name and Telephone",
                 JOptionPane.OK_CANCEL_OPTION,
                 JOptionPane.QUESTION_MESSAGE,
                 null,
                 ops,
                 "Cancel");
```

it will produce the following output:

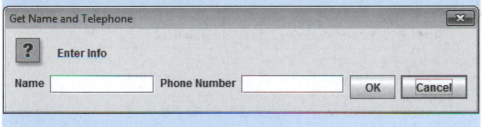

As you can see, the layout is less than optimal.

Progress Check

1. **showOptionDialog( )** is very limited because its options cannot be changed. True or False?
2. Why is **showOptionDialog( )** not as useful as one might hope?

Answers:

1. False.
2. **showOptionDialog( )** is not as useful as one might hope because its basic format is fixed and you have limited control over the layout of the options.

JDialog

Although **JOptionPane** offers the easiest way to display a dialog, it is not applicable to all situations. When you need a dialog that contains more fields or requires special handling, then you will need to use **JDialog** instead. **JDialog** is the Swing class that creates a dialog. **JDialog** is a top-level container that is *not* derived from **JComponent**. Thus, it is a heavyweight component. As explained earlier, **JDialog** is the class that **JOptionPane** uses to construct dialogs.

In general, you create and manage a **JDialog** much like you create a **JFrame**. For example, you add components to the content pane of the **JDialog** just like you add them to a **JFrame**. You can set the layout manager and specify its size. You use **setVisible( )** to show or hide its window. You can also give it a menu bar. **JDialog** inherits several AWT classes: **Container**, **Component**, **Window**, and **Dialog**. Thus, it has all of the functionality offered by the AWT.

JDialog allows you to construct either a modal or modeless dialog. As explained previously, a modal dialog causes the application to pause until the dialog is closed. A modeless dialog allows other parts of the application to remain active. The ability to create a modeless dialog is one of the reasons you might need to create a **JDialog** rather than using one of the **JOptionPane show** methods. As you will see, it is easy to construct either style of dialog.

JDialog defines many constructors. The one we will begin with is shown here:

JDialog(Frame *parent*, String *title*, boolean *isModal*)

It creates a dialog whose owner is specified by *parent*. If *isModal* is **true**, the dialog is modal. If *isModal* is **false**, the dialog is modeless. The dialog has the title specified by *title*.

Here are the steps that you will follow to create and display a dialog created by **JDialog**:

1. Create a **JDialog** object.
2. Specify the dialog's layout manager, size, and default close policy.
3. Add components to the dialog's content pane.
4. Show the dialog by calling **setVisible(true)** on it.

To remove a dialog from the screen use either **setVisible(false)** or **dispose( )**, which is inherited from **Window**. Use **setVisible(false)** when you will be reusing the dialog frequently within the same application. Use **dispose( )** when the dialog is unlikely to be displayed again. Calling **dispose( )** frees all resources associated with the dialog. Calling **setVisible(false)** simply removes the dialog from view.

The following program shows how to create a simple modal dialog by using **JDialog**. The dialog, which has the title Direction, allows the user to choose a direction. It displays two buttons. One is called Up and the other is called Down. When a button is pressed, the dialog is closed. The main application window contains two buttons and a label. The label displays the current direction. The button called Show Dialog displays the Direction dialog. The button called Reset Direction resets the direction displayed in the label.

```java
// Demonstrate a simple JDialog.

import java.awt.*;
import java.awt.event.*;
import javax.swing.*;

class JDialogDemo {

  JLabel jlab;

  JButton jbtnShow;
  JButton jbtnReset;

  // These buttons are contained within the dialog.
  JButton jbtnUp;
  JButton jbtnDown;

  JDialog jdlg;

  JDialogDemo() {
    // Create a new JFrame container.
    JFrame jfrm = new JFrame("JDialog Demo");

    // Specify FlowLayout for the layout manager.
    jfrm.setLayout(new FlowLayout());

    // Give the frame an initial size.
    jfrm.setSize(400, 200);

    // Terminate the program when the user closes the application.
    jfrm.setDefaultCloseOperation(JFrame.EXIT_ON_CLOSE);

    // Create a label that shows the direction.
    jlab = new JLabel("Direction is pending.");

    // Create a button that will show the dialog.
    jbtnShow = new JButton("Show Dialog");

    // Create button that will reset the direction.
    jbtnReset = new JButton("Reset Direction");

    // Create a simple modal dialog.
    jdlg = new JDialog(jfrm, "Direction", true);
    jdlg.setSize(200, 100);
    jdlg.setLayout(new FlowLayout());
```

Create and set up a modal dialog.

```
// Create buttons used by the dialog.
jbtnUp = new JButton("Up");
jbtnDown = new JButton("Down");

// Add buttons to the dialog.
jdlg.add(jbtnUp);
jdlg.add(jbtnDown);

// Add a label to the dialog.
jdlg.add(new JLabel("Press a button."));
```

Add buttons and a label to the dialog.

```
// Show the dialog when the Show Dialog button is pressed.
jbtnShow.addActionListener(new ActionListener() {
  public void actionPerformed(ActionEvent le) {
    jdlg.setVisible(true);
  }
});
```

Show the dialog when the user requests it.

```
// Reset the direction when the Reset Direction
// button is pressed.
jbtnReset.addActionListener(new ActionListener() {
  public void actionPerformed(ActionEvent le) {
    jlab.setText("Direction is pending.");
  }
});

// Respond to the Up button in the dialog.
jbtnUp.addActionListener(new ActionListener() {
  public void actionPerformed(ActionEvent le) {
    jlab.setText("Direction is Up");

    // Hide the dialog after the user selects
    // a direction.
    jdlg.setVisible(false);
  }
});

// Respond to the Down button in the dialog.
jbtnDown.addActionListener(new ActionListener() {
  public void actionPerformed(ActionEvent le) {
    jlab.setText("Direction is Down");

    // Hide the dialog after the user selects
    // a direction.
    jdlg.setVisible(false);
  }
});
```

Hide the dialog after the user selects a direction.

```
      // Add the Show Dialog button and label to the content pane.
      jfrm.add(jbtnShow);
      jfrm.add(jbtnReset);
      jfrm.add(jlab);

      // Display the frame.
      jfrm.setVisible(true);
  }

  public static void main(String[] args) {
    // Create the GUI on the event dispatching thread.
    SwingUtilities.invokeLater(new Runnable() {
      public void run() {
        new JDialogDemo();
      }
    });
  }
}
```

The dialog produced by the program is shown here:

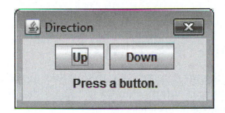

There are several important things in this program. To begin, notice how the following sequence constructs a modal **JDialog**:

```
// Create a simple modal dialog.
jdlg = new JDialog(jfrm, "Direction", true);
jdlg.setSize(200, 100);
jdlg.setLayout(new FlowLayout());
```

First, a modal dialog called **jdlg** is created that has Direction as its title, that is owned by the main window of the application, **jfrm**, and that is modal because **true** is passed as the third parameter to the **JDialog** constructor. Then, its size is set, and it is given a flow layout manager. At this point, the dialog is fully constructed but does not contain any components and is not visible.

Next, two buttons and one label are created and added to **jdlg**:

```
// Create buttons used by the dialog.
jbtnUp = new JButton("Up");
jbtnDown = new JButton("Down");

// Add buttons to the dialog.
jdlg.add(jbtnUp);
jdlg.add(jbtnDown);

// Add a label to the dialog.
jdlg.add(new JLabel("Press a button."));
```

As you can see, components are added to the dialog in the same way as they are added to the main window. After this sequence executes, the dialog is fully formed, but is not visible. It won't be made visible until the Show Dialog button (displayed in the main window) is pressed. To display the dialog, the Show Dialog button handler simply calls **setVisible(true)** on **jdlg**.

Next, notice the handlers for the Up and Down buttons that are contained within **jdlg**. Each simply sets the text in **jlab** and then calls **setVisible(false)**, which causes the dialog to be removed from the screen. Using **setVisible(false)** is the most efficient way to hide a dialog that will be needed later.

CREATE A MODELESS DIALOG

Using **JDialog**, you will find it quite easy to create a modeless (that is, nonmodal) dialog because, by default, **JDialog** creates a modeless dialog. For example, you can use this constructor to create a modeless dialog:

JDialog(Frame *parent*, String *title*)

Here, the owner is specified by *parent*. The dialog has the title specified by *title*. Alternatively, you can explicitly pass **false** to the third parameter of the constructor shown earlier. Furthermore, several other **JDialog** constructor variations are available that let you supply other options.

The advantage of a modeless dialog is that the rest of the application remains active. Of course, this is useful only when the rest of the application is not dependent on the user input requested by the dialog. For example, a photo touch-up application might have a dialog that allows you to select various touch-up filters. In this case, a modeless dialog would be the best choice because it would let the user change filters interactively without having to constantly close and then reopen the dialog. In general, most dialogs will be modal, but in cases in which a modeless dialog can be used, they tend to be *very useful*.

To see the effects of a modeless dialog, we will rework the preceding program so that the Direction dialog is modeless. Before we begin, run the **JDialogDemo** program and activate the Direction dialog. Then, try to click the Reset Direction button in the main window. As you will see, because the Direction dialog is modal, you cannot access the Reset Direction button while the dialog is active. By making the Direction dialog modeless, both windows will be active and you will be able to reset the direction at any time.

To make the Direction dialog modeless requires very few changes. First, change the call to the **JDialog** constructor by removing the third argument, as shown here:

```
jdlg = new JDialog(jfrm, "Direction");
```

This form of the constructor automatically creates a modeless dialog.

Next, remove the calls to **setVisible(false)** that are inside the event handlers for the Up and Down buttons. In other words, these two handlers should now look like this:

```
// Respond to the Up button in the dialog.
jbtnUp.addActionListener(new ActionListener() {
  public void actionPerformed(ActionEvent le) {
    jlab.setText("Direction is Up");
  }
});

// Respond to the Down button in the dialog.
jbtnDown.addActionListener(new ActionListener() {
  public void actionPerformed(ActionEvent le) {
    jlab.setText("Direction is Down");
  }
});
```

After making these changes, the Direction dialog will remain on the screen until you click its close box. Thus, you will be able to make repeated direction changes. You will also be able to press the Reset Direction button in the main window without closing the Direction dialog.

Progress Check

1. Is **JDialog** derived from **JComponent**?
2. Components in a **JDialog** must be added to the content pane. True or False?
3. What does **dispose( )** do?

SELECT FILES WITH JFileChooser

One of the most common uses for a dialog is also one of the more complicated and tedious to implement: allowing the user to select a file. Thankfully, Swing provides a built-in dialog that handles this somewhat difficult task for you. This dialog is called a *file chooser* and is an instance of **JFileChooser**.

Answers:

1. No.
2. True.
3. The **dispose( )** method removes a window from the screen, releasing all of its resources in the process.

JFileChooser offers two important benefits. The first is consistency. Choosing a file is a common activity. **JFileChooser** ensures that all file selection dialogs will look and feel the same. Thus, once users know how to use one file chooser, they can use them all. This is true even between programs written by different programmers. **JFileChooser** provides a standard mechanism that users understand.

The second **JFileChooser** benefit is efficiency. Although conceptually simple, implementing a file selection dialog requires a significant programming effort. By providing a built-in, standard implementation, Swing prevents programmers from having to duplicate this effort over and over again. Therefore, except for some specialized applications, if you need a dialog that lets the user choose a file, you should use **JFileChooser**. It prevents wasted effort.

JFileChooser is derived from **JComponent**. It specifies several constructors. Here are three:

JFileChooser( )

JFileChooser(File *dir*)

JFileChooser(String *dir*)

The first creates a file chooser that initially displays the default directory. The second and third create a file chooser that initially displays the directory specified by *dir*. If *dir* is **null**, the default directory is used.

After you have created a **JFileChooser**, it is displayed by calling one of the following methods:

int showOpenDialog(Component *parent*) throws HeadlessException

int showSaveDialog(Component *parent*) throws HeadlessException

int showDialog(Component *parent*, String *name*) throws HeadlessException

In each, *parent* is the component relative to which the file chooser is positioned. If *parent* is **null**, then the file chooser is typically centered on the desktop. The **showOpenDialog( )** method displays the standard Open dialog. The **showSaveDialog( )** displays the standard Save dialog. The only difference between the two is their title and the name on the button that signifies that a file has been chosen. For **showOpenDialog( )**, this button is called Open. For **showSaveDialog( )**, this button is called Save. To specify your own title and button name, call **showDialog( )** with the desired name. This still creates a standard file chooser; only the title and button name are different. For example, if you want a file chooser that selects a file for deletion, then you would pass "Delete" to *name*.

Each of the methods returns an integer that indicates the outcome of the file selection process. It will be one of these values defined by **JFileChooser**:

APPROVE_OPTION	The user selected a file.
CANCEL_OPTION	The user cancelled the selection process by clicking the Cancel button or by clicking the close box.
ERROR_OPTION	An error was encountered.

Keep in mind that the user can enter any file name. It does not have to exist or even be a valid file name. Therefore, just because one of the **show** methods returns **APPROVE_OPTION** does not mean that the file will be valid.

Once a file has been chosen, you can obtain that file by calling **getSelectedFile( )** on the **JFileChooser** instance. It is shown here:

        File getSelectedFile( )

It returns a **File** object that represents the selected file. (Remember, this file is not opened by **FileChooser**.)

Recall from Chapter 11 that the **File** class encapsulates information about a file. **File** is packaged in **java.io**, and it contains several useful methods. For example, to obtain the name of the file, call **getName( )** on the **File** object. It is shown here:

        String getName( )

The name is returned as a string. Depending on what options you specify, it is possible for the file chooser to allow you to select both files and directories. (Directories are really just special types of files.) You can determine if the **File** object returned by **getSelectedFile( )** is actually a file by calling **isFile( )** or whether it is a directory by calling **isDirectory( )**. These methods are shown here:

        boolean isFile( )
        boolean isDirectory( )

Each returns **true** if the object is of the indicated type and returns **false** otherwise.

The following program demonstrates **JFileChooser**. It displays an Open dialog initialized to the default directory. The file chooser dialog is shown here:

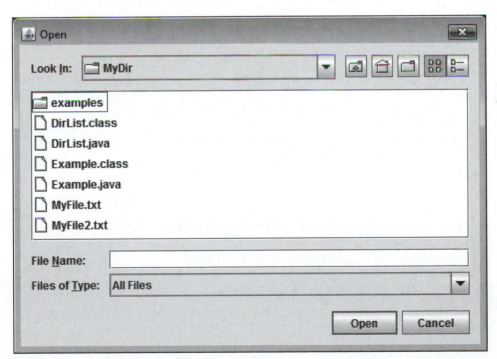

```
// Demonstrate JFileChooser.

import java.awt.*;
import java.awt.event.*;
import javax.swing.*;

class FileChooserDemo {

  JLabel jlab;
  JButton jbtnShow;
  JFileChooser jfc;

  FileChooserDemo() {
    // Create a new JFrame container.
    JFrame jfrm = new JFrame("JFileChooser Demo");

    // Specify FlowLayout for the layout manager.
    jfrm.setLayout(new FlowLayout());

    // Give the frame an initial size.
    jfrm.setSize(400, 200);

    // Terminate the program when the user closes the application.
    jfrm.setDefaultCloseOperation(JFrame.EXIT_ON_CLOSE);

    // Create a label that will show the selected file.
    jlab = new JLabel();

    // Create button that will show the dialog.
    jbtnShow = new JButton("Show File Chooser");

    // Create the file chooser.
    jfc = new JFileChooser();                        // Create a file chooser that starts
                                                     // at the default directory.
    // Show the file chooser when the Show File Chooser button
    // is pressed.
    jbtnShow.addActionListener(new ActionListener() {
      public void actionPerformed(ActionEvent le) {
        // Pass null for the parent. This centers the dialog
        // on the screen.
        int result = jfc.showOpenDialog(null);       // Display the file chooser.

        if(result == JFileChooser.APPROVE_OPTION)    // If a file has been selected,
          jlab.setText("Selected file is: " +        // display its name.
                        jfc.getSelectedFile().getName());
        else
          jlab.setText("No file selected.");
```

```
      }
   });

   // Add the Show File Chooser button and label to the
   // content pane.
   jfrm.add(jbtnShow);
   jfrm.add(jlab);

   // Display the frame.
   jfrm.setVisible(true);
}

public static void main(String[] args) {
   // Create the GUI on the event dispatching thread.
   SwingUtilities.invokeLater(new Runnable() {
      public void run() {
         new FileChooserDemo();
      }
   });
}
}
```

The operation of the program is straightforward. When the program begins, a **JFileChooser** called **jfc** is created. Notice that no initial directory is specified, so the file chooser uses the default directory. When the Show File Chooser button is pressed, the **actionPerformed( )** handler displays the file chooser dialog by calling **showOpenDialog( )**. When the method returns, if the return value is **APPROVE_OPTION**, then the name of the selected file is displayed in **jlab**. Otherwise, a message indicating that no file was selected is displayed. One other point: By constructing the file chooser outside of the **actionPerformed( )** handler, it can be used repeatedly without having to be reconstructed each time.

Before moving on, try calling **showSaveDialog( )** instead of **showOpenDialog( )**. As you will see, the only difference is the name.

TRY THIS 20-1   USE A FILE FILTER WITH JFileChooser

FileFilterDemo.java

By default, **JFileChooser** displays all files in the selected directory. When using a **JFileChooser**, you can change this behavior by specifying a file name that includes wildcard characters. You can also change this behavior under program control by using a custom file filter. This project shows how. It creates a filter that displays Java source files. These are files that end in **.java**. It also displays directories, which enable the user to navigate the file system. When you run the program, you will see something similar to the following:

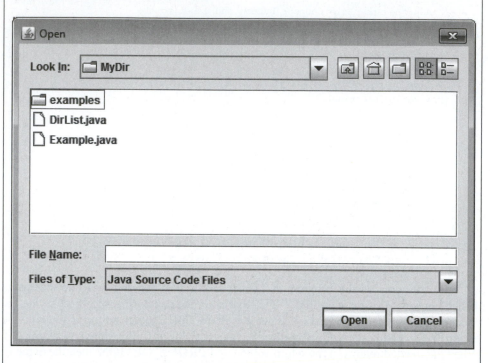

Notice that only Java source files are displayed.

A file filter for a **FileChooser** is an object that extends the **FileFilter** abstract class defined in the **javax.swing.filechooser** package. The **FileFilter** class defines the two methods shown here:

abstract boolean accept(File *file*)

abstract String getDescription( )

Both must be implemented by your custom file filter. The **accept( )** method must return **true** to accept the file passed via *file*. In other words, if you want the file to be displayed in the file list, return **true**. To prevent the file from being displayed, return **false**. The **getDescription( )** method must return a string that describes the filter. It is displayed in the Files of Type list in the file chooser.

One important point: When you create a custom file filter, directories are not automatically displayed. If you want directories to be displayed, you must explicitly accept them within the **accept( )** method.

To enable a file chooser to use your file filter, you can call **setFileFilter( )** on the **JFileChooser** instance. This method is shown here:

void setFileFilter(FileFilter *ff*)

Here, *ff* is the file filter that you want the file chooser to use.

STEP-BY-STEP

1. Begin by creating a file called **FileFilterDemo.java** and then enter the following comment and **import** statements:

```
// Try This 20-1: Demonstrate a custom file filter.

import java.io.*;
import java.awt.*;
import java.awt.event.*;
import javax.swing.*;
import javax.swing.filechooser.FileFilter;
```

Notice how **javax.swing.filechooser.FileFilter** is imported. Its name is fully qualified. Here is why. As you learned in Chapter 11, Java also includes an interface called **FileFilter** that is packaged in **java.io**. When creating a **FileChooser** file filter, you often need to import both packages (**java.io** and **javax.swing.filechooser**). One way to avoid a name conflict is to import the file chooser version of **FileFilter** using its fully qualified name, as shown above. This approach avoids the name conflict between the two packages.

2. Define the **JavaFileFilter** class, as shown next. It accepts only files with the **.java** extension and directories.

```
// A custom file filter that displays Java source files
// and directories.
class JavaFileFilter extends FileFilter {
  public boolean accept(File file) {
    // Return true if the file is a Java source file
    // or if it is a directory.
    if(file.getName().endsWith(".java")) return true;
    if(file.isDirectory()) return true;

    // Otherwise, return false.
    return false;
  }

  public String getDescription() {
    return "Java Source Code Files";
  }
}
```

Notice how the **accept( )** method works. If a file name uses the ".java" extension or is a directory, then it returns **true**. In all other cases, **accept( )** returns **false**. This means that only **.java** files and directories are displayed. Notice the use of the **endsWith( )** method. This method is defined by the **String** class, and it returns **true** if and only if the invoking string ends with the specified character sequence.

3. Begin the **FileFilterDemo** class, as shown next.

```
public class FileFilterDemo {

    JLabel jlab;
    JButton jbtnShow;
    JFileChooser jfc;

    FileFilterDemo() {
        // Create a new JFrame container.
        JFrame jfrm = new JFrame("File Filter Demo");

        // Specify FlowLayout for the layout manager.
        jfrm.setLayout(new FlowLayout());

        // Give the frame an initial size.
        jfrm.setSize(400, 200);

        // Terminate the program when the user closes the application.
        jfrm.setDefaultCloseOperation(JFrame.EXIT_ON_CLOSE);

        // Create a label that will show the selected file.
        jlab = new JLabel();

        // Create a button that will show the dialog.
        jbtnShow = new JButton("Show File Chooser");

        // Create the file chooser.
        jfc = new JFileChooser();

        // Set the file filter.
        jfc.setFileFilter(new JavaFileFilter());
```

Pay special attention to the last line. In order for the file filter to be in effect, it must be set. This is done by calling **setFileFilter( )** on **jfc** immediately after it is created.

4. Add the **ActionListener** shown here:

```
        // Show the file chooser when the Show File Chooser button
        // is pressed.
        jbtnShow.addActionListener(new ActionListener() {
            public void actionPerformed(ActionEvent le) {
                // Pass null for the parent. This typically centers
                // the dialog on the screen.
                int result = jfc.showOpenDialog(null);

                if(result == JFileChooser.APPROVE_OPTION)
                    jlab.setText("Selected file is: " +
                             jfc.getSelectedFile().getName());
```

```
                else
                    jlab.setText("No file selected.");
            }
        });
```

5. Finish the **FileFilterDemo** constructor as shown next:

```
        // Add the Show File Chooser button and label to the
        // content pane.
        jfrm.add(jbtnShow);
        jfrm.add(jlab);

        // Display the frame.
        jfrm.setVisible(true);
    }
```

6. Finish **FileFilterDemo** by adding the following **main( )** method:

```
    public static void main(String[] args) {
        // Create the GUI on the event dispatching thread.
        SwingUtilities.invokeLater(new Runnable() {
            public void run() {
                new FileFilterDemo();
            }
        });
    }
}
```

7. The entire program is shown here. Before moving on, you might want to experiment a bit by creating some file filters of your own design.

```
// Try This 20-1: Demonstrate a custom file filter.

import java.io.*;
import java.awt.*;
import java.awt.event.*;
import javax.swing.*;
import javax.swing.filechooser.FileFilter;

// A custom file filter that displays
// Java source files and directories.
class JavaFileFilter extends FileFilter {
    public boolean accept(File file) {
        // Return true if the file is a Java source file
        // or if it is a directory.
        if(file.getName().endsWith(".java")) return true;
        if(file.isDirectory()) return true;

        // Otherwise, return false.
        return false;
    }
```

```java
    public String getDescription() {
      return "Java Source Code Files";
    }
}

public class FileFilterDemo {

  JLabel jlab;
  JButton jbtnShow;
  JFileChooser jfc;

  FileFilterDemo() {
    // Create a new JFrame container.
    JFrame jfrm = new JFrame("File Filter Demo");

    // Specify FlowLayout for the layout manager.
    jfrm.setLayout(new FlowLayout());

    // Give the frame an initial size.
    jfrm.setSize(400, 200);

    // Terminate the program when the user closes the application.
    jfrm.setDefaultCloseOperation(JFrame.EXIT_ON_CLOSE);

    // Create a label that will show the selected file.
    jlab = new JLabel();

    // Create a button that will show the dialog.
    jbtnShow = new JButton("Show File Chooser");

    // Create the file chooser.
    jfc = new JFileChooser();

    // Set the file filter.
    jfc.setFileFilter(new JavaFileFilter());

    // Show the file chooser when the Show File Chooser button
    // is pressed.
    jbtnShow.addActionListener(new ActionListener() {
      public void actionPerformed(ActionEvent le) {
        // Pass null for the parent. This typically centers
        // the dialog on the screen.
        int result = jfc.showOpenDialog(null);

        if(result == JFileChooser.APPROVE_OPTION)
          jlab.setText("Selected file is: " +
                        jfc.getSelectedFile().getName());
```

```
              else
                jlab.setText("No file selected.");
            }
        });

        // Add the Show File Chooser button and label to the
        // content pane.
        jfrm.add(jbtnShow);
        jfrm.add(jlab);

        // Display the frame.
        jfrm.setVisible(true);
    }

    public static void main(String[] args) {
        // Create the GUI on the event dispatching thread.
        SwingUtilities.invokeLater(new Runnable() {
            public void run() {
                new FileFilterDemo();
            }
        });
    }
}
```

Ask the Expert

Q Are there other options supported by **JFileChooser**?

A Yes, **JFileChooser** supports several options. Here are three you might find interesting. By default, **JFileChooser** allows the user to select only files. To allow a directory to be selected, call **setFileSelectionMode( )**, shown here:

    void setFileSelectionMode(int *fsm*)

Here, *fsm* specifies the selection mode, which must be one of these constants defined by **JFileChooser**:

FILES_ONLY

DIRECTORIES_ONLY

FILES_AND_DIRECTORIES

Each specifies the mode indicated by its name. Therefore, to enable the selection of both files and directories, use **FILES_AND_DIRECTORIES**.

You can allow the user to select more than one file by calling **setMultiSelectionEnabled( )**, shown here:

    void setMultiSelectionEnabled(boolean *on*)

Ask the Expert (Continued)

If *on* is **true**, then multiple file selection is allowed. If *on* is **false**, then only single files can be selected. By default, only single file selection is allowed. When using multiple selection mode, you can obtain a list of the selected files by calling **getSelectedFiles( )**, shown here:

File[ ] getSelectedFiles( )

It returns an array of **File** objects that contains the selected files (or directories).

By default, hidden files are not displayed by the file chooser. To change this, call **setFileHidingEnabled( )**, shown here:

void setFileHidingEnabled(boolean *on*)

If *on* is **true**, then hidden files are not displayed. If *on* is **false**, then hidden files are shown in the file window.

Progress Check

1. What method displays the Open file chooser?
2. As it relates to **JFileChooser**, what class do you extend to create a file filter?
3. What **FileFilter** method is used to filter files?

EXERCISES

1. A dialog is a composite of two or more components that prompts the user and waits for a response. True or False?
2. What **JOptionPane** method creates an input dialog? Which one creates a message dialog?
3. What **JOptionPane** method would you normally use to create a dialog that confirms that the user wants to save changes to a document? Show what the call would look like.
4. When using a confirmation dialog, what return type indicates that the user clicked the Yes button?
5. What option type is used to show only the Yes and No buttons in a confirmation dialog?

Answers:

1. **showOpenDialog( )**
2. **FileFilter**
3. **accept( )**

6. If you want to request a string response from the user, what **JOptionPane** method do you call?

7. Must the message parameter to any of **JOptionPane**'s **show** methods be a string? Explain.

8. **JDialog** is a top-level container. True or False?

9. What are the four steps needed to create and display a **JDialog**-based dialog?

10. Can **JDialog** create a modeless dialog?

11. Explain the difference between **setVisible(false)** and **dispose( )** as it relates to dialogs.

12. What **JFileChooser** method creates a Save file chooser? Which one creates a file chooser that uses your own title?

13. What two methods must be overridden when implementing a **FileFilter** for **JFileChooser**?

14. Chapter 19 described menus. In that chapter, the examples included a File menu that had an Exit entry. The action event handler that processed menu selections handled the Exit entry, as shown here:

```
// Handle menu item action events.
public void actionPerformed(ActionEvent ae) {
  // Get the action command from the menu selection.
  String comStr = ae.getActionCommand();

  // If user chooses Exit, then exit the program.
  if(comStr.equals("Exit")) System.exit(0);
  .
  .
  .
```

Change this code so that it activates a dialog that confirms the user really wants to exit before terminating the program.

15. Why would you want a modal dialog, and why would you want a nonmodal dialog? Give examples where each of them is useful other than the examples given in this chapter.

16. Write a program that creates a window with a button labeled "Show message". When the button is clicked, a dialog appears asking "Do you really want to see the message?" and, if you click Yes, a second dialog appears with the message.

17. Give examples of situations in which it would be meaningful to create a message dialog of each of the following types:

   A. ERROR_MESSAGE

   B. INFORMATION_MESSAGE

   C. PLAIN_MESSAGE

   D. QUESTION_MESSAGE

   E. WARNING_MESSAGE

18. Give examples of situations in which it would be meaningful to create a confirmation dialog with each of the following button options:

   A. OK_CANCEL_OPTION

   B. YES_NO_OPTION

   C. YES_NO_CANCEL_OPTION

19. When calling **JOptionPane**'s **showOptionDialog( )** method, you are asked to provide an array of options and an initial value as the last two arguments. What happens if, for the initial value, you provide **null** or a value that is not in the array of options?

20. What should you use as arguments to the **showOptionDialog( )** method so that the dialog looks and acts as much as possible like the dialog you get when you call **JOptionPane.showMessageDialog(null, "Hello", "Message", JOptionPane.PLAIN_MESSAGE)**?

21. Write a program that creates and displays a **JDialog** that looks and acts as much as possible like the dialog you get when you call **JOptionPane.showMessageDialog(null, "Hello", "Hello message", JOptionPane.PLAIN_MESSAGE)**.

22. As the two preceding exercises show, to display a message in a dialog box, you can use the **showMessageDialog( )** or the **showOptionDialog( )**, or you can create a **JDialog**. Why does Java give you so many ways to do the same thing? In particular, you can use **JDialog** which can do everything the **show** methods do, so why bother with them?

23. Write a program that creates a window entitled "File Copier". It contains one button saying "Choose a file to copy". When the button is clicked, an open file chooser dialog appears. If a file is selected, a save file chooser dialog appears that allows the user to specify the name to use for the copy and the directory to contain the copy. Then the file is copied. If an **IOException** occurs, it does not print an error message to the console. Instead, it displays the error message in a dialog.

24. If you create a **JFileChooser** dialog using the constructor that takes no arguments and then show the dialog, it will initially display the default directory. What is meant by the "default" directory?

25. Modify the **FileChooserDemo** class discussed in the chapter so that the **JFileChooser** dialog allows multiple selections (as described in the Ask the Expert section at the end of the chapter) of both files and directories. The program should then display all the files and directories selected.

26. If you call **showMessageDialog(null, obj)** where **obj** is an object other than a string, the dialog will display the string returned by a call to **obj.toString( )**. To see this in action, create a class **Data** that has only a **public String toString( )** method that returns the string "A Data Object was here." Then write a program that creates an object **obj** of the **Data** class and calls **showMessageDialog(null, obj)**.

27. Write a program that displays a window with one button. When the user clicks the button, an input dialog appears asking the user for an integer number of inches. If the input is a valid integer, the program displays an information message dialog telling how many miles are equal to the given number of inches. If the input is not a valid integer, an error message dialog appears. Use the **parseInt( )** method discussed in Chapter 11.

28. Create a custom class that extends **javax.swing.jfilechooser.FileFilter** that filters out all files except directories and hidden files. Use the **isHidden( )** method of the **File** class mentioned in Chapter 11. Then write a program that tests your new filter.

Threading, Applets, and Painting

KEY SKILLS & CONCEPTS

- Use threads with Swing
- Use the **Timer** class
- Know Swing applet basics
- Understand the Swing applet skeleton
- Construct an applet GUI
- Know painting fundamentals
- Use the graphics context
- Compute the paintable area

As the preceding chapters have shown, when you think about Swing, you usually think about its visual controls. However, there are other aspects and techniques related to Swing that do not directly involve its controls. This chapter examines three important ones: threading, applets, and painting. As you will see, each of these requires special handling when used with a Swing GUI.

MULTITHREADING IN SWING

As you know from Chapter 12, multithreading is that aspect of Java that enables different parts of a program to execute concurrently. It gives you the ability to write very efficient programs that make maximum use of the CPU by using otherwise idle time, or in the case of multiple CPUs, it lets portions of your program run with true concurrency, thus optimizing throughput. Multithreading also prevents the entire application from pausing when some part of it is performing a time-consuming task. It is this second reason that makes multithreading especially important to a Swing application. In Swing, time-consuming operations must be executed in their own thread to prevent the application (including its user interface) from becoming sluggish or unresponsive. Therefore, multithreading is part of many Swing programs.

In general, you will use additional threads within a Swing program in the same way that you use them in any other type of Java program. Thus, what you already know about creating and managing threads also applies to Swing. However, there is a very important, additional threading issue that relates specifically to Swing, and it is the subject of this section.

In Chapter 17, you learned that any code that interacts with a visual component must be executed on the event-dispatching thread. Observing this important rule avoids problems, such as two different threads trying to update the same component at the same time. This rule is why **invokeLater( )** is called within **main( )** by all of the Swing programs shown previously to construct and display the GUI at program startup. It causes the GUI to be created on the event-dispatching thread.

It is important to emphasize that this same rule applies *any time* you need to update, change, interrogate, or alter any component. If a piece of code affects a component, it *must be executed* from the event-dispatching thread. Because event handlers are automatically executed on the event-dispatching thread, the code within an event handler can freely affect the GUI. However, code that is executing on another thread cannot. This brings up a potential problem: often, code in another thread needs to update a component. For example, consider a program that uses a **JLabel** to display the outside temperature, updated once every minute. To do this, a separate thread must be used to monitor the temperature. However, this thread cannot be used to update the label because it is not the event-dispatching thread. So, how does the thread that monitors the temperature update the label? Or, more generally, how does any other thread update a component in the GUI?

One solution is to use either the **invokeLater( )** or the **invokeAndWait( )** methods defined by **SwingUtilities** in much the same way as you have been using **invokeLater( )** to construct and display the GUI. Let's review them now. They are shown again here, for your convenience:

static void invokeLater(Runnable *obj*)

static void invokeAndWait(Runnable *obj*)
       throws InterruptedException, InvocationTargetException

Here, *obj* is a **Runnable** object that will have its **run( )** method called by the event-dispatching thread. Inside **run( )** put the code that interacts with a Swing component. Thus, when you need to update a component, put the code inside a **Runnable** object and pass that object to either **invokeLater( )** or **invokeAndWait( )**. This causes the code to execute on the event-dispatching thread, which means that the component can be safely changed.

The difference between the two methods is that **invokeLater( )** returns immediately, but **invokeAndWait( )** waits until **obj.run( )** returns. You will normally want to use **invokeLater( )**. However, as you will soon see, when constructing the initial GUI for an applet, you will want to use **invokeAndWait( )**. For simplicity, the rest of this discussion refers to **invokeLater( )**, but the general principles also apply to **invokeAndWait( )**.

Here is an example that illustrates one way to handle a separate thread that continuously updates the GUI. It is an improved version of the **StopWatch** class first created in Try This 17-1. This version displays the elapsed time while the stopwatch is running. It does this by creating a separate thread that updates the elapsed time label 10 times a second. Notice its use of **invokeLater( )** inside the second thread. Sample output is shown here:

```java
// An improved version of the StopWatch class from Try This 17-1.
// This version uses a separate thread to display the elapsed
// time when the stopwatch is running.

import java.awt.*;
import java.awt.event.*;
import javax.swing.*;
import java.util.Calendar;

class ThreadStopWatch {

  JLabel jlab; // display the elapsed time

  JButton jbtnStart; // start the stopwatch
  JButton jbtnStop;  // stop the stopwatch

  long start; // holds the start time in milliseconds

  boolean running=false; // true when stopwatch is running

  Thread thrd; // reference to the timing thread
```

This will refer to the thread that updates the time display as the stopwatch runs.

```java
  ThreadStopWatch() {

    // Create a new JFrame container.
    JFrame jfrm = new JFrame("Thread-based Stopwatch");

    // Specify FlowLayout for the layout manager.
    jfrm.setLayout(new FlowLayout());

    // Give the frame an initial size.
    jfrm.setSize(230, 90);
```

```
// Terminate the program when the user closes the application.
jfrm.setDefaultCloseOperation(JFrame.EXIT_ON_CLOSE);

// Create the elapsed-time label.
jlab = new JLabel("Press Start to begin timing.");

// Make the Start and Stop buttons.
jbtnStart = new JButton("Start");
jbtnStop = new JButton("Stop");

// Initially disable the Stop button.
jbtnStop.setEnabled(false);

// Create the Runnable instance that will become the second thread.
Runnable myThread = new Runnable() {
  // This method will run in a separate thread.
  public void run() {
    try {
      // Report elapsed time every tenth of a second.
      for(; ; ) {
        // Pause for a tenth of a second.
        Thread.sleep(100);

        // Invoke updateTime() on the event dispatching thread.
        SwingUtilities.invokeLater(new Runnable() {
          public void run() {
            updateTime();
          }
        });
      }
    } catch(InterruptedException exc) {
      System.out.println("Call to sleep was interrupted.");
      System.exit(1);
    }
  }
};

// Create a new thread.
thrd = new Thread(myThread);

// Start the thread.
thrd.start();

// Add the action listeners for the Start and
// Stop buttons.
jbtnStart.addActionListener(new ActionListener() {
  public void actionPerformed(ActionEvent ae) {
```

Create a **Runnable** object that will execute in its own thread.

Pause for a tenth of a second.

Update the time displayed. This invokes **updateTime( )** on the event-dispatching thread.

Create the thread.

Start the thread.

```
      // Store start time.
      start = Calendar.getInstance().getTimeInMillis();

      // Reverse the state of the buttons.
      jbtnStop.setEnabled(true);
      jbtnStart.setEnabled(false);

      // Start the stopwatch.
      running = true;
    }
  });

  jbtnStop.addActionListener(new ActionListener() {
    public void actionPerformed(ActionEvent ae) {
      long stop = Calendar.getInstance().getTimeInMillis();

      // Compute the elapsed time.
      jlab.setText("Elapsed time is "
            + (double) (stop - start)/1000);

      // Reverse the state of the buttons.
      jbtnStart.setEnabled(true);
      jbtnStop.setEnabled(false);

      // Stop the stopwatch.
      running = false;
    }
  });

  // Add the buttons and label to the content pane.
  jfrm.add(jbtnStart);
  jfrm.add(jbtnStop);
  jfrm.add(jlab);

  // Display the frame.
  jfrm.setVisible(true);
}

// Update the elapsed time display.
void updateTime() {                    This method gets executed
  if(!running) return;                 on the event-dispatching
                                       thread.
  long temp = Calendar.getInstance().getTimeInMillis();
  jlab.setText("Elapsed time is " +
            (double) (temp - start)/1000);
}
```

```
public static void main(String[] args) {
  // Create the frame on the event-dispatching thread.
  SwingUtilities.invokeLater(new Runnable() {
    public void run() {
      new ThreadStopWatch();
    }
  });
}
}
```

Let's look closely at how this program works. First, notice the fields **running** and **thrd**. The **running** variable is initially set to **false**. When the stopwatch is running, it is set to **true**. When **running** is **true**, the elapsed time is displayed. The **thrd** field will hold a reference to the thread that updates the time.

Next, notice how the second thread of execution is created. First, a **Runnable** object called **myThread** is created by the following code:

```
// Create the Runnable instance that will become the second thread.
Runnable myThread = new Runnable() {
  // This method will run in a separate thread.
  public void run() {
    try {
      // Report elapsed time every tenth of a second.
      for(; ; ) {
        // Pause for a tenth of a second.
        Thread.sleep(100);

        // Invoke updateTime() on the event dispatching thread.
        SwingUtilities.invokeLater(new Runnable() {
          public void run() {
            updateTime();
          }
        });
      }
    } catch(InterruptedException exc) {
      System.out.println("Call to sleep was interrupted.");
      System.exit(1);
    }
  }
};
```

The **Runnable** interface defines only one method: **run( )**. This method is executed in a separate thread of execution. In essence, when the thread starts running, it calls **run( )**. Inside **run( )**, an infinite loop is established that simply sleeps for a tenth of a second and then calls **invokeLater( )**. Remember, the code within the loop is executing in its own thread, not the event-dispatching thread. (If it were executing in the event-dispatching thread, the window could become sluggish or unresponsive because the loop could prevent the other parts of the program from executing.)

Now, notice the argument to **invokeLater( )**. It is called with **Runnable** whose **run( )** method calls the **updateTime( )** method. The **updateTime( )** method is shown here:

```
// Update the elapsed time display.
void updateTime() {
  if(!running) return;

  long temp = Calendar.getInstance().getTimeInMillis();
  jlab.setText("Elapsed time is " +
              (double) (temp - start)/1000);
}
```

The code first tests the value of **running**. If it is false, then the method returns immediately because the stopwatch is not currently being used. Otherwise, **updateTime( )** obtains the current time, subtracts the start time from it, and then updates **jlab** with the current elapsed time. Because **updateTime( )** changes the contents of the label, it must be executed on the event-dispatching thread. This is accomplished by calling **invokeLater( )** with a **Runnable** argument that calls **updateTime( )**. Thus, **updateTime( )** executes on the event-dispatching thread, and it can safely update the time shown in **jlab**. When the program is terminated (by clicking on the close box), this thread is also automatically terminated.

After the declaration of **myThread**, a new thread is created that uses **myThread** and is then started by the following code:

```
// Create a new thread.
thrd = new Thread(myThread);

// Start the thread.
thrd.start();
```

At this point, the new thread is executing. However, it isn't being used for anything because the stopwatch has not yet been started.

When the user clicks the Start button, the current system time is obtained and stored in the **start** variable. The Start button is disabled, the Stop button is enabled, and **running** is set to **true**. When the Stop button is pressed, the current system time is obtained. The difference between the current time and the start time is displayed in **jlab**. Then, the enabled state of the buttons is reversed and **running** is set to **false**.

As this program shows, the key to using threads safely in Swing is to make sure that any code that interacts with a Swing component is executed on the event-dispatching thread. If you are not sure which thread is executing a piece of code, you can call **isEventDispatchThread( )** defined by **SwingUtilities**.

Progress Check

1. Why must your code interact with Swing components through the event-dispatching thread?
2. What does **invokeLater( )** do?

USE Timer

The preceding stopwatch example showed how a separate thread of execution can be used in conjunction with **invokeLater( )** to interact with a Swing component. As you will see, it is actually a bit more complicated than it needs to be. In some cases, you don't really need to create a separate thread explicitly. Instead, what you need is a *timer* that generates an event at periodic intervals. For example, to scroll a banner, you can use a timer to redraw the banner repeatedly in order to achieve an animated appearance. (See Try This 21-1.)

The timer class defined by Swing is called **Timer**. It is packaged in **javax.swing**. It must not be confused with another class called **Timer** that is packaged in **java.util**. You will need to specify explicitly which timer you are using when importing both packages into the same program.

Swing's **Timer** automatically fires an action event that will be received by the specified listener. Because this is an event, it will automatically be executed on the event-dispatching thread. Therefore, the **actionPerformed( )** method defined by the **ActionListener** registered with the timer will be executed on the event-dispatching thread as normal. There is no need to use **invokeLater( )** or **invokeAndWait( )**. Thus, to use **Timer**, you will simply create a **Timer** instance, specifying the action listener that will receive the event.

Timer defines only one constructor, shown here:

Timer(int *period*, ActionListener *al*)

Here, *period* specifies the length of time between events in milliseconds. In other words, *period* specifies the timing interval. The action listener that will receive the events is specified by *al*. You can specify additional action listeners that will be notified when the timer goes off by calling **addActionListener( )** on the timer.

To start the timer, call **start( )**. To stop the timer, call **stop( )**. These methods are shown here:

void start( )

void stop( )

Answers:

1. It avoids conflicts between threads, such as two different threads trying to update the same component at the same time.
2. It causes a **Runnable** object to be executed on the event-dispatching thread. It returns immediately rather than waiting for the thread to end.

By default, the timer continues to fire events at the specified interval. You can cause the timer to fire only one event by calling **setRepeats( )**, shown here:

    void setRepeats(boolean *repeats*)

Here, if *repeats* is **true**, the time repeats. If it is **false**, the time stops after one interval.

As mentioned, the thread-based stopwatch program shown in the previous section is more complicated than it needs to be. Instead of explicitly creating a separate thread, a timer can be used. This approach is shown by the following version of the program.

```java
// This version of the stopwatch uses the Timer class.

import java.awt.*;
import java.awt.event.*;
import javax.swing.*;
import java.util.Calendar;

class TimerStopWatch {

  JLabel jlab; // display the elapsed time

  JButton jbtnStart; // start the stopwatch
  JButton jbtnStop;  // stop the stopwatch

  long start; // holds the start time in milliseconds

  Timer swTimer; // the timer for the stopwatch          Use a Timer to update
                                                          the time display.

  TimerStopWatch() {

    // Create a new JFrame container.
    JFrame jfrm = new JFrame("Timer-based Stopwatch");

    // Specify FlowLayout for the layout manager.
    jfrm.setLayout(new FlowLayout());

    // Give the frame an initial size.
    jfrm.setSize(230, 90);

    // Terminate the program when the user closes the application.
    jfrm.setDefaultCloseOperation(JFrame.EXIT_ON_CLOSE);

    // Create the elapsed-time label.
    jlab = new JLabel("Press Start to begin timing.");
```

```
// Make the Start and Stop buttons.
jbtnStart = new JButton("Start");
jbtnStop = new JButton("Stop");
jbtnStop.setEnabled(false);

// This action listener is called when the timer
// goes off.
ActionListener timerAL = new ActionListener() {
  public void actionPerformed(ActionEvent ae) {
    updateTime();
  }
};

// Create a timer that goes off every tenth of a second.
swTimer = new Timer(100, timerAL);

// Add the action listeners for the start and
// stop buttons.
jbtnStart.addActionListener(new ActionListener() {
  public void actionPerformed(ActionEvent ae) {

    // Store start time.
    start = Calendar.getInstance().getTimeInMillis();

    // Reverse the state of the buttons.
    jbtnStop.setEnabled(true);
    jbtnStart.setEnabled(false);

    // Start the stopwatch.
    swTimer.start();
  }
});

jbtnStop.addActionListener(new ActionListener() {
  public void actionPerformed(ActionEvent ae) {
    long stop = Calendar.getInstance().getTimeInMillis();

    // Compute the elapsed time.
    jlab.setText("Elapsed time is "
          + (double) (stop - start)/1000);

    // Reverse the state of the buttons.
    jbtnStart.setEnabled(true);
    jbtnStop.setEnabled(false);

    // Stop the stopwatch.
    swTimer.stop();
  }
});
```

This listener is notified when the timer goes off.

Create the timer. Notice that **timerAL** is specified to handle the action events generated by the timer.

```
    // Add the buttons and label to the content pane.
    jfrm.add(jbtnStart);
    jfrm.add(jbtnStop);
    jfrm.add(jlab);

    // Display the frame.
    jfrm.setVisible(true);
  }

  // Update the elapsed time display. Notice
  // that the running variable is no longer needed.
  void updateTime() {
    long temp = Calendar.getInstance().getTimeInMillis();
    jlab.setText("Elapsed time is " +
                 (double) (temp - start)/1000);
  }

  public static void main(String[] args) {
    // Create the frame on the event-dispatching thread.
    SwingUtilities.invokeLater(new Runnable() {
      public void run() {
        new TimerStopWatch();
      }
    });
  }
}
```

As you can see, the program is substantially shorter because it does not contain the code that creates a thread. It also does not need to use the **running** variable. The use of **Timer** greatly simplifies the task. Notice how little code is required to use the timer. First, it is created by this single line:

```
swTimer = new Timer(100, timerAL);
```

This constructs a timer that goes off once every tenth of a second. Here, **timerAL** specifies the action listener that will receive the action events generated by the timer. It is shown next:

```
ActionListener timerAL = new ActionListener() {
  public void actionPerformed(ActionEvent ae) {
    updateTime();
  }
};
```

The **actionPerformed( )** method simply calls **updateTime( )**. Because this code is already executing on the event-dispatching thread, there is no need for **invokeLater( )**.

The timer is started when the user clicks the Start button. It is stopped when Stop is clicked. As you will see when you try the program, the timer can be repeatedly started and stopped. There is no restriction in this regard.

In general, when you need to use a separate thread whose sole purpose is to keep the GUI updated, using **javax.swing.Timer** is a better choice than manually creating your own thread. However, if you will be using a separate thread to perform other duties, then you have no choice but to create one explicitly.

Progress Check

1. What method starts a **Timer**?
2. What event does a **Timer** generate?

Ask the Expert

Q What is the **SwingWorker** class?

A Beginning with JDK 6, Swing has provided a class called **SwingWorker** that can be used to simplify the solution to some types of multithreading tasks. Here are two of **SwingWorker**'s principal advantages. First, it provides a built-in means of executing code on the event-dispatching thread. This means that you can avoid the use of **invokeLater( )** and **invokeAndWait( )**. Second, it streamlines the creation and management of background threads.

SwingWorker is an abstract generic class that is declared like this:

SwingWorker<T, V>

Here, **T** specifies the result type of its **doInBackground( )** method (discussed shortly), and **V** represents the type of any interim results. When either (or both) is not needed by a worker thread, **Void** can be used.

To create a **SwingWorker**, you must extend it, providing at minimum an implementation for **doInBackground( )**. Inside this method you will put the code that you want executed in a background thread. It is shown here:

protected T doInBackground() throws Exception

It should throw an exception if, for any reason, the background task fails.

Once you create a **SwingWorker**, you can start the thread by calling **execute( )**, shown here:

final void execute( )

The task is executed on a worker thread that is automatically provided.

Answers:

1. **start( )**
2. **Timer** generates an action event.

To obtain the value returned by **doInBackground( )**, called **get( )**. Here is one version:

final T get( ) throws InterruptedException, ExecutionException

This method will wait until a value is available; it should not be called from the event-dispatching thread until that value has been returned by **doInBackground( )**.

When **doInBackground( )** has finished, the **done( )** method is called on the event-dispatching thread. It is shown here:

protected void done( )

You can override this method to obtain the result returned by **doInBackground( )**.

You can "publish" interim results by calling **publish( )**, shown here:

protected final void publish(V ... *data*)

Here, *data* is a variable-length argument that contains the data that you want to make other parts of your application aware of. It does this by working with another **SwingWorker** method called **process( )**. Importantly, **process( )** is called on the event-dispatching thread. This means that you can use the information that it receives to update the GUI. The data is passed to **process( )** in a **List**, which is part of Java's Collections Framework. (**List** is described in Chapter 25.) The **process( )** method is shown here:

protected void process(List<V> *list*)

Since **process( )** is called on the event-dispatching thread, it is possible that two or more calls to **publish( )** will occur before **process( )** is actually executed. Therefore, you must cycle through *list* to ensure that you have retrieved all of the data. You can use a for-each style **for** loop for this purpose, as shown in the example that follows.

To see **SwingWorker** in action, you can substitute the **SwingWorker** shown here for the **Runnable** code in the first stopwatch example, **ThreadStopWatch**.

```java
// Create a new Swingworker thread to update the time.
final SwingWorker<Void, Long> sw = new SwingWorker<Void, Long>() {
  public Void doInBackground() {
    try {
      // Report elapsed time every tenth of a second.
      for(;;) {
        // Pause for a tenth of a second.
        Thread.sleep(100);
        publish(Calendar.getInstance().getTimeInMillis());
      }
    } catch(InterruptedException exc) {
      System.out.println("Call to sleep was interrupted.");
      System.exit(1);
    }
    return null; // placeholder return value
  }
```

Ask the Expert (Continued)

```
// Update the elapsed time display. This is called on
// the event-dispatching thread
protected void process(List<Long> times) {
  if(!running) return;

  for(long curTime : times)
    jlab.setText("Elapsed time is " +
           (double) (curTime - start)/1000);
  }
};

sw.execute();
```

You will also need to add this **import** statement:

```
import java.util.List;
```

After making these changes, the program will function the same, only now **SwingWorker** is being used to provide the background thread.

CREATE SWING APPLETS

All of the preceding Swing examples are stand-alone Java applications that run on the desktop, but you can also use Swing to create the GUI for an applet. Applets were introduced in Chapter 15, where the general form of an AWT-based applet was described. As you will see, although Swing-based applets are similar to AWT-based applets shown in Chapter 15, some special rules apply.

As you know from Chapter 15, all applets are based on the **Applet** class. However, to create a Swing-based applet, you will use **JApplet**, which inherits **Applet**. **JApplet** is a top-level container and is *not* derived from **JComponent**. Because **JApplet** is a top-level Swing container, it includes the various panes described in Chapter 17. This means that all components are added to its content pane, in the same way that you have been adding components to **JFrame**'s content pane. Furthermore, all interaction with Swing components must take place on the event-dispatching thread, as described by the previous section.

Recall that applets are not executed directly on the desktop. Instead, they are executed within a Java-enabled browser or by an applet viewer, such as **appletviewer** supplied by the JDK. During development, it is easier to test applets by using an applet viewer than it is to load them into a browser. However, for final testing, a browser should be used.

All applets (whether or not they use Swing) have the same lifecycle methods. Recall that these are **init( )**, **start( )**, **stop( )**, and **destroy( )**. They are defined by **Applet** and are inherited by **JApplet**. Default empty implementations for all of these methods are provided. Therefore, applets do not need to override those methods they do not use.

Like a Swing application, an applet must interact with its components using the event-dispatching thread. This means that you cannot use the **init( )** method itself to build the initial GUI. Instead, inside **init( )** you will call **invokeAndWait( )** to specify a **Runnable** object whose **run( )** method will be executed on the event-dispatching thread. Using this approach, a skeletal form of the **init( )** method is shown here:

```
public void init() {
  try {
    SwingUtilities.invokeAndWait(new Runnable () {
      public void run() {                                              A Swing-based applet
        guiInit(); // a method that initializes the Swing components   must create its GUI on the
      }                                                                event-dispatching thread.
    });
  } catch(Exception exc) {
    System.out.println("Can't create because of " + exc);
  }
}
```

Inside **run( )**, a method called **guiInit( )** is called. This is a method that you provide that sets up and initializes the Swing components. Of course, the name of the method is arbitrary.

Ask the Expert

Q The applications throughout this book call **invokeLater( )** to construct the GUI. Why does an applet use **invokeAndWait( )**?

A Applets must use **invokeAndWait( )** because the **init( )** method must not return until the entire initialization process has been completed. In essence, the **start( )** method cannot be called until after initialization, which means that the GUI must be fully constructed.

A Simple Swing Applet

Here is a simple Swing-based applet that displays two buttons. Each time a button is clicked, a message is displayed that states which button was clicked. Sample output of the applet being executed by **appletviewer** is shown here:

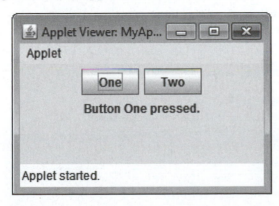

```java
// A simple Swing-based applet

import javax.swing.*;
import java.awt.*;
import java.awt.event.*;

/*
This HTML can be used to launch the applet:

<object code="MyApplet" width=240 height=100>
</object>

*/

public class MyApplet extends JApplet {
  JButton jbtnOne;
  JButton jbtnTwo;

  JLabel jlab;

  // Called first.
  public void init() {
    try {
      SwingUtilities.invokeAndWait(new Runnable () {
        public void run() {
          guiInit(); // initialize the GUI
        }
      });
    } catch(Exception exc) {
      System.out.println("Can't create because of " + exc);
    }
  }

  // Set up and initialize the GUI.
  private void guiInit() {
    // Set the applet to use flow layout.
    setLayout(new FlowLayout());

    // Create two buttons and a label.
    jbtnOne = new JButton("One");
    jbtnTwo = new JButton("Two");

    jlab = new JLabel("Press a button.");

    // Add action listeners for the buttons.
    jbtnOne.addActionListener(new ActionListener() {
      public void actionPerformed(ActionEvent le) {
        jlab.setText("Button One pressed.");
      }
    });
```

```
    jbtnTwo.addActionListener(new ActionListener() {
      public void actionPerformed(ActionEvent le) {
        jlab.setText("Button Two pressed.");
      }
    });

    // Add the components to the applet's content pane.
    add(jbtnOne);
    add(jbtnTwo);
    add(jlab);
  }
}
```

There are two important things about this applet. First, the **init( )** method initializes the Swing GUI by setting up a call to **guiInit( )**. This is accomplished through the use of **invokeAndWait( )**. Inside **guiInit( )**, two buttons and a label are created. Then, an action listener is added to each button. They simply set the text in the label to indicate which button was pressed. Although this example is quite simple, this same general approach must be used when building any Swing GUI that will be used by an applet.

The second point of interest in the applet is the fact that neither **start( )**, **stop( )**, nor **destroy( )** is used by the applet. This is not uncommon for simple applets. In such cases, there is actually no reason to specify empty implementations because **Applet** provides default implementations for you. Therefore, if you don't need to use one of the applet lifecycle methods, you don't need to override it.

Progress Check

1. What class is used to create a Swing-based applet?
2. What method do you call to construct the GUI on the event-dispatching thread when a Swing-based applet initializes?

TRY THIS 21-1 SCROLL TEXT IN AN APPLET

`ScrollText.java`

This project demonstrates both Swing-based applets and Swing timers. It uses a timer to scroll a text message within a **JLabel**. As you will see, the code to accomplish this is surprisingly short and concise because Swing's **Timer** class makes the process extremely easy to code.

There is one other point of interest in this program. Recall that Try This 15-1 created an AWT-based applet that displayed a moving banner. It was mentioned

Answers:

1. **JApplet**
2. **invokeAndWait( )**

there that some flicker would be experienced and that the way to avoid the flicker was to use double-buffering. Fortunately, Swing uses double-buffering by default. Therefore, when you run this example, the scrolling banner will appear smooth and no flicker will be seen. The use of double-buffering is another important advantage that Swing brings to GUI design.

Sample output from the applet is shown here:

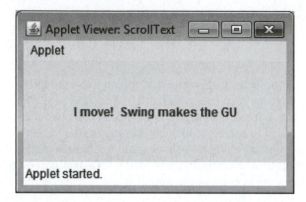

STEP-BY-STEP

1. Create a file called **ScrollText.java** and add the following comments and **import** statements:

```
// Try This 21-1: A Swing-based applet that scrolls
// text through a label.

import javax.swing.*;
import java.awt.*;
import java.awt.event.*;


/*
This HTML can be used to launch the applet:

<object code="ScrollText" width=240 height=100>
</object>

*/
```

2. Begin creating the **ScrollText** class as shown here:

```
public class ScrollText extends JApplet {

    JLabel jlab;

    String msg = " Swing makes the GUI move! ";

    ActionListener scroller;

    Timer stTimer; // this timer controls the scroll rate
```

Because **ScrollText** is a Swing-based applet, it extends **JApplet**. It then declares a label that will be used to display the scrolling message, the message that will be scrolled, an action listener that will perform the scrolling, and a timer that controls the rate of scroll.

3. Add the **init( )** method shown next:

```
// Initialize the applet.
public void init() {
  try {
    SwingUtilities.invokeAndWait(new Runnable () {
      public void run() {
        guiInit();
      }
    });
  } catch(Exception exc) {
    System.out.println("Can't create because of " + exc);
  }
}
```

This method simply invokes **guiInit( )** on the event-dispatching thread as described earlier.

4. Add the **start( )**, **stop( )**, and **destroy( )** methods, shown here:

```
// Start the timer when the applet is started.
public void start() {
  stTimer.start();
}

// Stop the timer when the applet is stopped.
public void stop() {
  stTimer.stop();
}

// Stop the timer when the applet is destroyed.
public void destroy() {
  stTimer.stop();
}
```

Although very short, these methods perform important functions. Each time the applet is displayed in a page, the timer is started. Each time the browser stops the applet, the timer is stopped. The timer is also stopped when the applet is destroyed.

5. Finish the applet with the **guiInit( )** method shown here:

```
// Initialize the timer GUI.
private void guiInit() {

  // Create the label that will scroll the message.
  jlab = new JLabel(msg);
  jlab.setHorizontalAlignment(SwingConstants.CENTER);
```

```
      // Create the action listener for the timer.
      scroller = new ActionListener() {
        public void actionPerformed(ActionEvent ae) {
          // Left-scroll the message one character.
          char ch = msg.charAt(0);
          msg = msg.substring(1, msg.length());
          msg += ch;
          jlab.setText(msg);
        }
      };

      // Create the timer.
      stTimer = new Timer(200, scroller);

      // Add the label to the applet content pane.
      add(jlab);
    }
  }
```

This method creates the label in which the text is scrolled. The text is aligned in the center. This is done to make the scrolling text more visually appealing. It is not technically necessary. Next, an action listener is created that scrolls the text left one character each time it is called. This listener is then passed to the **Timer** constructor when the timer is created. The timing period is one-fifth of a second, but you might want to experiment with the delay period. Obviously, the shorter the period, the faster the scroll. Finally, the label is added to the content pane.

6. The entire **ScrollText** applet is shown here:

```
// Try This 21-1: A Swing-based applet that scrolls
// text through a label.

import javax.swing.*;
import java.awt.*;
import java.awt.event.*;

/*
This HTML can be used to launch the applet:

<object code="ScrollText" width=240 height=100>
</object>

*/

public class ScrollText extends JApplet {

  JLabel jlab;

  String msg = " Swing makes the GUI move! ";
```

```java
ActionListener scroller;

Timer stTimer; // this timer controls the scroll rate

// Initialize the applet.
public void init() {
  try {
    SwingUtilities.invokeAndWait(new Runnable () {
      public void run() {
        guiInit();
      }
    });
  } catch(Exception exc) {
    System.out.println("Can't create because of " + exc);
  }
}

// Start the timer when the applet is started.
public void start() {
  stTimer.start();
}

// Stop the timer when the applet is stopped.
public void stop() {
  stTimer.stop();
}

// Stop the timer when the applet is destroyed.
public void destroy() {
  stTimer.stop();
}

// Initialize the timer GUI.
private void guiInit() {

  // Create the label that will scroll the message.
  jlab = new JLabel(msg);
  jlab.setHorizontalAlignment(SwingConstants.CENTER);

  // Create the action listener for the timer.
  scroller = new ActionListener() {
    public void actionPerformed(ActionEvent ae) {
      // Left-scroll the message one character.
      char ch = msg.charAt(0);
      msg = msg.substring(1, msg.length());
      msg += ch;
      jlab.setText(msg);
    }
  };
```

```
            // Create the timer.
            stTimer = new Timer(200, scroller);

            // Add the label to the applet content pane.
            add(jlab);
        }
    }
```

PAINTING

The primary focus of the preceding chapters has been on elements of the Swing component set and the techniques required to use them. However, there is another part of Swing that lets you create your own visual output by writing directly into the display area of a frame, panel, or one of Swing's other components, such as **JLabel**. Although many (perhaps most) uses of Swing will *not* involve drawing directly to the surface of a component, it is available for those applications that need this capability. To write output directly to the surface of a component involves one or more drawing methods, such as **drawLine( )** or **drawRect( )**, and requires that you take some manual control over the painting process. Although a detailed discussion of painting is beyond the scope of this book, this section covers the basic techniques.

Painting Fundamentals

The first thing to understand about painting in Swing is that it is a somewhat complicated process. In fact, Swing has an entire subsystem dedicated to managing painting, which is built on the original AWT-based approach. Before examining the specifics of Swing-based painting, it is useful to review the AWT mechanism that underlies it.

To begin, recall that **JComponent** inherits the AWT class **Component**. This class defines a method called **paint( )**. This method is called when the component needs to be displayed on the screen. As a general rule, **paint( )** is not called by your program. Rather, **paint( )** is called by the run-time system whenever a component must be rendered. This situation can occur for several reasons. For example, the window in which the component is displayed can be overwritten by another window and then uncovered. Or the window might be minimized and then restored. The **paint( )** method is also called when a program begins running. When writing AWT-based code, an application will override **paint( )** when it needs to write output directly to the surface of the component.

Although Swing's lightweight components do inherit the **paint( )** method from **Component**, you will not override it to paint directly to the surface of a component. The reason is that Swing uses a bit more sophisticated approach to painting that involves three distinct methods: **paintComponent( )**, **paintBorder( )**, and **paintChildren( )**. These methods paint the indicated portion of a component and divide the painting process into its three distinct, logical actions. In a lightweight component, the original AWT method **paint( )** simply executes calls to these methods, in the order just shown.

To paint to the surface of a Swing component, you will create a subclass of the component and then override its **paintComponent( )** method. This is the method that paints the interior of the component. You will not normally override the other two painting methods. As a general rule, when overriding **paintComponent( )**, the first thing you must do is call **super.paintComponent( )**, so that the superclass portion of the painting process takes place. After that, write the output that you want to display.

The **paintComponent( )** method is shown here:

protected void paintComponent(Graphics g)

Notice that the method is protected. Thus, it can be called by a subclass. The parameter g is the graphics context to which output is written.

The Graphics Context

In Java, each component has a *graphics context* associated with it. This context is encapsulated by the **java.awt.Graphics** class, and it maintains various pieces of information about the display environment, such as the drawing color and font. As just described, this context is passed to the various paint methods, such as **paintComponent( )**. When you paint to a component, you will do so through this context, using methods that it provides.

Graphics defines many methods that write output to the component. One, **drawString( )**, was used in Chapter 15. Here are five more examples:

void drawLine(int *startX*, int *startY*, int *endX*, int *endY*)

void drawRect(int *left*, int *top*, int *width*, int *height*)

void fillRect(int *left*, int *top*, int *width*, int *height*)

void drawOval(int *left*, int *top*, int *width*, int *height*)

void fillOval(int *left*, int *top*, int *width*, int *height*)

The **drawLine( )** method draws a line in the current drawing color that begins at *startX,startY* and ends at *endX,endY*. **drawRect( )** draws a rectangle in the current drawing color that begins at *left,top* and is *width* wide and *height* tall. **fillRect( )** is the same as **drawRect( )** except that the rectangle is filled with the current drawing color. **drawOval( )** draws an oval in the current drawing color that begins at *left,top* and is *width* wide and *height* tall. **fillOval( )** is the same as **drawOval( )** except that the oval is filled with the current drawing color. On your own, you should explore the **Graphics** class in Java's documentation to learn about its other capabilities.

For all components, the origin of the display area is located at the upper-left corner and has the coordinates 0,0. Furthermore, all display locations are relative to this origin. All coordinates are specified in terms of pixels. Therefore, if you write output at location 12,14, the output is written 12 pixels right and 14 pixels down from the upper-left corner.

Compute the Paintable Area

When drawing to the surface of a component, you may need to restrict your output to the area that is inside a border. Although Swing automatically clips any output that will exceed the boundaries of a component, it is still possible to paint into the border region, which will then get overwritten when the border is drawn. To avoid this, you can compute the *paintable area* of the component. This is the area defined by the current size of the component minus the space used by the border. Therefore, before you paint to a component, you must obtain the width of the border and then adjust your drawing accordingly.

To obtain the border width, call **getInsets( )**, shown here:

Insets getInsets( )

This method is defined by **Container** and overridden by **JComponent**. It returns an **Insets** object that contains the dimensions of the border. The inset values can be obtained by using these fields:

int top;

int bottom;

int left;

int right;

These values are then used to compute the drawing area given the width and the height of the component. You can obtain the width and height of the component by calling **getWidth( )** and **getHeight( )** on the component. They are shown here:

int getWidth( )

int getHeight( )

By subtracting the value of the insets, you can compute the overall width and height of the drawable area within a component.

Request Painting

As just explained, normally a component is painted only when its **paint( )** method is called, which in the case of a Swing component causes calls to **paintComponent( )**, **paintBorder( )**, and **paintChildren( )**. To request painting, you will use the **repaint( )** method, in the same way as described in Chapter 15. Calling it causes the system to call **paint( )** as soon as it is possible to do so. As explained, this causes a call to **paintComponent( )**. Therefore, to output to the surface of a component, your program will store the output until **paintComponent( )** is called. Inside the overridden **paintComponent( )**, you will draw the stored output.

A Paint Example

Here is a program that puts into action the preceding discussion. It creates a class called **PaintPanel** that extends **JPanel**. We will use the surface of a **PaintPanel** to draw output. **PaintPanel** specifies a border. This way, you can easily see its paintable area. The program then uses an object of that class to display a bar graph that plots randomly generated data. In addition to the bar graph, the program includes two buttons. One allows you to display a different set of values. The other lets you change the size of the border around the graph. Sample output is shown here:

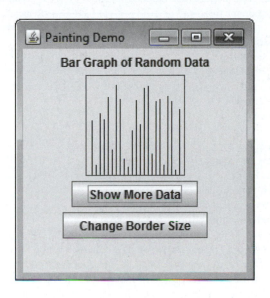

```
// Paint lines to a panel.

import java.awt.*;
import java.awt.event.*;
import javax.swing.*;
import java.util.*;

// This class extends JPanel. It overrides
// the paintComponent() method so that random
// data is plotted in the panel.
class PaintPanel extends JPanel {              ←——————————— PaintPanel extends JPanel.
  Insets ins; // holds the panel's insets

  Random rand; // used to generate random numbers

  PaintPanel(int w, int h) {

    // Use a red line border.
    setBorder(BorderFactory.createLineBorder(Color.RED, 1));

    // Set the preferred dimension as specified.
    setPreferredSize(new Dimension(w, h));
```

```
    rand = new Random();
  }

  // Override the paintComponent() method.
  protected void paintComponent(Graphics g) {
    // Always call the superclass method first.
    super.paintComponent(g);

    // Get the height and width of the component.
    int height = getHeight();
    int width = getHeight();

      // Get the insets.
    ins = getInsets();

    // Fill the panel by plotting random data
    // in the form of a bar graph.
    for(int i=ins.left+5; i <= width-ins.right-5; i += 4) {
      // Obtain a random number between 0 and
      // the maximum height of the drawing area.
      int h = rand.nextInt(height-ins.bottom);

      // If a generated value is in or too close to the
      // border, change it to just inside the border.
      if(h <= ins.top) h = ins.top+1;

      // Draw a line that represents the data.
      g.drawLine(i, height-ins.bottom, i, h);
    }
  }

  // Change the border size.
  public void changeBorderSize(int size) {
    setBorder(
      BorderFactory.createLineBorder(Color.RED, size));
  }
}

// Demonstrate painting directly onto a panel.
class PaintDemo {

  JButton jbtnMore;
  JButton jbtnSize;
  JLabel jlab;
  PaintPanel pp;

  boolean big; // use to toggle size of panel

  PaintDemo() {
```

Override **paintComponent( )** to paint to the surface of the component.

Remember to call the superclass implementation.

Draw the graph of random data.

```java
// Create a new JFrame container.
JFrame jfrm = new JFrame("Painting Demo");

// Specify FlowLayout for the layout manager.
jfrm.setLayout(new FlowLayout());

// Give the frame an initial size.
jfrm.setSize(240, 260);

// Terminate the program when the user closes the application.
jfrm.setDefaultCloseOperation(JFrame.EXIT_ON_CLOSE);

// Create the panel that will be painted.
pp = new PaintPanel(100, 100);

// Make the buttons.
jbtnMore = new JButton("Show More Data");
jbtnSize = new JButton("Change Border Size");

// Describe the graph.
jlab = new JLabel("Bar Graph of Random Data");

// Repaint the panel when the Show More Data button
// is clicked.
jbtnMore.addActionListener(new ActionListener() {
  public void actionPerformed(ActionEvent ae) {
    pp.repaint();   ←————————————————— Request that the panel be painted.
  }
});

// Set the border size of the panel when the
// Change Border Size button is clicked.
// Changing the border size automatically
// results in a repaint.
jbtnSize.addActionListener(new ActionListener() {
  public void actionPerformed(ActionEvent ae) {   ←——— Change the border
    if(!big) pp.changeBorderSize(5);                    size of the graph.
    else pp.changeBorderSize(1);
    big = !big;
  }
});

// Add the buttons, label, and panel to the content pane.
jfrm.add(jlab);
jfrm.add(pp);
jfrm.add(jbtnMore);
jfrm.add(jbtnSize);
```

```
      big = false;

      // Display the frame.
      jfrm.setVisible(true);
    }

    public static void main(String[] args) {
      // Create the frame on the event-dispatching thread.
      SwingUtilities.invokeLater(new Runnable() {
        public void run() {
          new PaintDemo();
        }
      });
    }
  }
}
```

This program is a bit more complicated than many other programs in this chapter. It also introduces a few new elements. Therefore, it warrants a close examination. The **PaintPanel** class extends **JPanel** and overrides the **paintComponent( )** method. This enables **PaintPanel** to write directly to the surface of the component when painting takes place. The **PaintPanel** constructor takes two parameters that specify the preferred width and height of the panel. The constructor also specifies a 1-pixel-wide red border. It does this by use of the following call to **setBorder( )**:

```
setBorder(BorderFactory.createLineBorder(Color.RED, 1));
```

The **setBorder( )** method is defined by **JComponent**. It attaches a border to the component. A border is an object of type **Border**, which is defined in **javax.swing.border**. Swing provides several different built-in borders, which can be obtained by use of the static methods in **BorderFactory**, which is in **javax.swing**. The one used here is a simple line border. It is created by this method:

static Border createLineBorder(Color *color*, int *width*)

The color of the border is specified by *color*. You can design your own colors, but often you will use one of the constants defined by the **Color** class, such as **Color.RED**, **Color.BLUE**, or **Color.GREEN**. The **Color** class is packaged in **java.awt**. The width of the border is passed in *width*.

Inside the override of **paintComponent( )**, notice that it first calls **super.paintComponent( )**. As explained, this is necessary to ensure that the component is properly drawn. Next the width and height of the panel are obtained along with the insets. These values are used to restrict the height and position of the graph bars to within the drawing area of the panel. The drawing area is the overall width and height of a component less the border widths. The computations are designed to work with differently sized **PaintPanel**s and borders.

Next, **paintComponent( )** uses the **Random** class to obtain pseudorandom numbers. (Pseudorandom numbers approximate a sequence of random values.) This class is described in Chapter 24, when Java's utilities classes are examined. Since it is used here, a brief description is warranted. **Random** is Java's random number generator. You can obtain the values generated by **Random** in a variety of ways. Here, its

nextInt( ) method is called. It has two forms. The one used in the program is shown here:

> int nextInt(int *max*)

Here, *max* specifies an upper bound for the value. The method will return a pseudo-random integer that will be within the range zero to *max*-1. The bound used by the program is

```
height-ins.bottom
```

This bound ensures that the pseudorandom value is within the lower bound of the panel. The upper bound is handled by this line:

```
if(h <= ins.top) h = ins.top+1;
```

This ensures that the line is not drawn into the top border.

The line is actually drawn, using this statement:

```
g.drawLine(i, height-ins.bottom, i, h);
```

Remember, the coordinate system begins in the upper-left corner. So the coordinates might seem reversed until you think about it a bit.

The **changeBorderSize( )** method changes the border size of the panel. Because **paintComponent( )** automatically displays data that fills the current size of the drawing area of the panel, the border width can be changed without any problems.

The **PaintDemo** class demonstrates **PaintPanel**. It creates a **PaintPanel** called **pp** with the dimensions 100 by 100. It also creates two buttons called **jbtnMore** and **jbtnSize**. When **jbtnMore** is clicked, **repaint( )** is called on **pp**. This results in **PaintPanel**'s **paintComponent( )** being called. Thus, each time **jbtnMore** is pressed, new randomly generated data is displayed. When **jbtnSize** is clicked, the width of the border is toggled between 1 and 5. Because **paintComponent( )** computes the boundaries of the drawing area dynamically, the border can be set to any valid arbitrary value.

Progress Check

1. To write output directly into the drawing area of a Swing component, what method must you override?
2. What method obtains the width of the current border?
3. How do you cause the **paintComponent( )** method to be called?

Answers:

1. **paintComponent( )**
2. **getInsets( )**
3. To cause **paintComponent( )** to be called, call **repaint( )**.

EXERCISES

1. Any code that affects a Swing component must be executed on the _____ _____ thread.

2. When using **javax.swing.Timer**, what event is generated when the timer goes off?

3. What methods start and stop **javax.swing.Timer**?

4. What is **SwingWorker**?

5. What method must an applet use to create its GUI?

6. Can your program paint directly onto the surface of a component?

7. What three paint methods are called when a Swing component must display itself?

8. What methods obtain the current width and height of a component?

9. Rework the applet in Try This 21-1 so that the direction of scroll reverses at periodic intervals. For example, have the text scroll left for a while, and then right for a while, and so on. The precise timing is up to you, but the answer shown in Appendix C reverses scroll direction every 20 seconds.

10. Write a program that displays a window containing a picture of a traffic light, similar to those shown in Chapter 18, except the traffic light should show all three colors at once. Use a rectangle 30 pixels wide by 100 pixels high and use a circle of diameter 20 pixels for each of the three colors. You will need to use another method defined in the **Graphics** class:

    void setColor(Color *color*)

    This method sets the color that will be used by the graphics context for future drawing. For this exercise, use the color constants **Color.BLACK**, **Color.RED**, **Color.YELLOW**, and **Color.GREEN**.

11. Extend the preceding exercise so that it uses a **Timer** to run the traffic light. The traffic light should display only green for 10 seconds (during which the other two circles are filled with white), then only yellow for 5 seconds, and then only red for 15 seconds. It should repeat this pattern forever.

12. If **g** refers to a **Graphics** object, what is the difference, if any, between the call to **g.drawLine(10, 20, 50, 60)** and the call to **g.drawLine(50, 60, 10, 20)**?

13. If **g** refers to a **Graphics** object, what is the difference, if any, between the call to **g.drawRect(10, 20, 50, 60)** and the call to **g.drawRect(60, 80, –50, –60)**?

14. Write a program that creates a window with a tall, narrow rectangle displayed in it and with a ball inside the rectangle. The ball moves at a constant speed down the rectangle until it reaches the bottom and then reverses direction and heads up at a constant speed. It keeps bouncing forever back and forth between the top and bottom edges of the rectangle. Use a **Timer** to move the ball.

15. Redo exercise 10 of the exercises in Chapter 15 using a **JApplet** instead of an **Applet**. That is, create a **JApplet** that draws a house. Note that with a **JApplet**, you shouldn't override its **paint( )** method to draw in the applet. Instead, you should subclass **JPanel** (or some other **JComponent**), override the **paintComponent( )** method in the subclass so that it draws a house, and then add an instance of the subclass to the applet's content pane.

16. The **TimerStopWatch** example in the chapter creates a **JFrame** to contain the stopwatch. Modify the example so that the stopwatch is in a **JApplet** instead.

17. Write a program that creates a window containing a **JTextArea** inside a **JScrollPane**. A **JTextArea** is a Swing component that can display several lines of text. Here is one of the constructors:

    public JTextArea(int *rows*, int *cols*)

    This constructor creates an empty **JTextArea** with the given number of rows and columns. Use this constructor to create a **JTextArea** with 20 rows and 30 columns. To add lines of text to it, use its **append( )** method, shown here:

    void append(String *text*)

    This method appends the given text to the text being displayed. Create a separate thread that repeatedly (forever) sorts longer and longer integer arrays using bubble sort. It first creates and sorts an array of length 1,000, then creates and sorts an array of length 1,200, and so on. Each array should have length 200 more than the preceding array and should initially be in reverse order (largest to smallest). Bubble sort will sort it from smallest to largest. The thread also should keep track of how long it takes to sort the array each time. Whenever it finishes a sort, it inserts a new line at the end of the **JTextArea** indicating the length of the array and how long it took to sort it.

18. True or False?

    A. Only two threads are used in the **ThreadStopWatch** program at the beginning of this chapter, namely, the event-dispatching thread and the thread that calls **updateTime( )** every tenth of a second.

    B. Whenever you create a **JApplet**, you need to implement **start( )**, **stop( )**, **init( )**, and **destroy( )** methods for it.

    C. When specifying the position of a figure for painting in a **JComponent**, the position (0,0) corresponds to the center of the component.

PART THREE

Exploring the Java API Library

Part Three examines key portions of the Java Application Programming Interface (API) library. The API library contains the standard classes and interfaces supplied with the JDK. As you might expect, it is very large, and a full examination of its contents is far beyond the scope of this book. Instead, we will focus on several core elements of the library that are frequently used when writing Java programs and that were not described elsewhere in this book. Chapter 22 examines string handling via the **String** class. Chapter 23 describes key portions of **java.lang**. Chapter 24 examines several parts of **java.util**. Chapter 25 discusses the Collections Framework. Chapter 26 looks at networking fundamentals. Chapter 27 concludes the book by examining the concurrency API, including the Fork/Join Framework.

In addition to the packages described here, another key part of the Java API is contained in **java.io**. It was covered in Chapter 11, and that discussion is not repeated here.

Note: The material presented here and elsewhere in this book offers overviews and summaries of portions of the Java API. A complete description of the Java API library is found in the Java documentation, which is available online from Oracle. Furthermore, Java's history is one of innovation and evolution. Therefore, it is possible that additions or changes have been made to the API library since this book was written.

CHAPTER 22

String Handling

KEY SKILLS & CONCEPTS

- The **String** constructors
- Three string-related language features
- Override **toString( )**
- Use **length( )**
- Obtain characters from a string
- Compare strings
- Use **indexOf( )** and **lastIndexOf( )**
- Obtain a modified string
- Change the case of characters within a string
- Understand how **StringBuffer** and **StringBuilder** relate to **String**

One of the most commonly used Java classes is **String**. This is because string handling is an integral part of many Java programs. A brief overview of **String** was presented in Chapter 5. In this chapter, we will explore it in greater detail. It is important to state at the outset that **String** supports a wide range of functionality and it is not possible to examine all of its aspects here. Rather, our purpose is to give you a general understanding and a solid working knowledge of its core features. **String** is a class that you will want to reexamine from time to time as you advance in your study of Java.

The **String** class is packaged in **java.lang**. Thus, it is automatically available to all programs. Although the next chapter examines other aspects of **java.lang**, because of **String**'s widespread use and importance, it merits an entire chapter of its own. We will begin by reviewing **String**'s fundamentals.

STRING FUNDAMENTALS

As you already know from Chapter 5, in Java a string is a sequence of characters. But unlike some other languages that implement strings as character arrays, Java implements strings as objects of type **String**. Implementing strings as objects allows Java to provide a full complement of features that make string handling convenient. For example, Java has methods to compare two strings, search for a substring, concatenate two strings, and change the case of letters within a string. Also, **String** objects can be constructed a number of ways, making it easy to obtain a string when needed.

The **String** class implements the following interfaces: **Comparable<String>**, **CharSequence**, and **Serializable**. The **Comparable** interface specifies how objects are compared. **CharSequence** defines a set of methods that are applicable to a character sequence. **Serializable** simply indicates that the state of a **String** can be saved and restored using Java's serialization mechanism.

When you create a **String** object, you are creating a string that cannot be changed. That is, once a **String** object has been constructed, you cannot change the characters that comprise that string. This may seem to be a serious restriction, but as explained in Chapter 5, such is not the case. You can still perform all types of string operations. The difference is that each time you need an altered version of an existing string, a new **String** object is created that contains the modifications. The original string is left unchanged. This approach is used because fixed, immutable strings can be implemented more efficiently than changeable ones.

It is important to emphasize that when we say that the strings within objects of type **String** are immutable, we mean that the contents of a **String** instance cannot be altered after it has been created. However, a variable declared as a **String** reference can be changed to refer to a different **String** object.

*Note: For those cases in which a modifiable string is desired, Java provides two options: **StringBuffer** and **StringBuilder**. They are briefly mentioned at the end of this chapter. Both hold strings that can be modified after they are created.*

The **String** class is declared **final**, which means that it can't be subclassed. This allows certain optimizations that increase performance to take place on common string operations.

THE STRING CONSTRUCTORS

The **String** class supports a large number of constructors. We will look at several examples. To create an empty **String**, call the default constructor. For example,

```
String str = new String();
```

will create an instance of **String** with no characters in it.

Frequently, you will want to create strings that have initial values. The **String** class provides a variety of constructors to handle this task. For example, to create a **String** initialized by an array of characters, use the constructor shown here:

String(char[ ] *chrs*)

You can specify a subrange of a character array as an initializer using the following constructor:

String(char[ ] *chrs*, int *startIndex*, int *numChrs*)

Here, *startIndex* specifies the index at which the subrange begins, and *numChrs* specifies the number of characters to use.

When constructing a **String** from an array, the contents of the array are copied into the **String**. In other words, the array does not underlie the **String** instance. This means that the two are separate. Therefore, after the **String** has been constructed, altering the array does not change the contents of the string.

You can construct a **String** object that contains the same character sequence as another **String** object using this constructor:

> String(String *strObj*)

Here, *strObj* is a **String** object.

Here is a program that puts the preceding constructors into action. In each case, notice how a **String** instance is constructed.

```java
// Demonstrate several String constructors.

class StringConsDemo {

  public static void main(String[] args) {

    char[] digits = new char[16];

    // Create an array that contains the digits 0 through 9
    // plus the hexadecimal values A through F.
     for(int i=0; i < 16; i++) {
       if(i < 10) digits[i] = (char) ('0'+i);
       else digits[i] = (char) ('A' + i - 10);
     }

    // Create a string that contains all of the array.
    String digitsStr = new String(digits);
    System.out.println(digitsStr);

    // Create a string the contains a portion of the array.
    String nineToTwelve = new String(digits, 9, 4);
    System.out.println(nineToTwelve);

    // Construct a string from a string.
    String digitsStr2 = new String(digitsStr);
    System.out.println(digitsStr2);

    // Now, create an empty string.
    String empty = new String();

    // This will display nothing:
    System.out.println("Empty string: " + empty);
  }
}
```

Construct strings in a variety of ways.

The output is shown here:

```
0123456789ABCDEF
9ABC
0123456789ABCDEF
Empty string:
```

String also provides several constructors that initialize a string when given a **byte** array. Here are two examples:

String(byte[ ] *chrs*)
String(byte[ ] *chrs*, int *startIndex*, int *numChrs*)

Here, *chrs* specifies the array of bytes. The second form allows you to specify a subrange. In each of these constructors, the byte-to-character conversion is done by using the default character mapping. (A character mapping defines the relationship between bytes and characters.) Extended versions of the byte-to-string constructors are also defined in which you can specify the character mapping. As you know from the discussion of I/O in Chapter 11, at the lowest level I/O is byte oriented. Thus, the **byte**-array constructors can be especially useful when building a string from input provided by a byte stream.

In addition to the constructors just described, you can construct a **String** from a **StringBuilder** or a **StringBuffer** object. You can also construct a **String** from an array of Unicode code points.

Progress Check

1. What are three ways of passing characters as arguments to **String** constructors?
2. A Java string is mutable. True or False?
3. You need to explicitly import a package to use strings in Java. True or False?

THREE STRING-RELATED LANGUAGE FEATURES

Because strings are a common and important part of programming, Java supports three especially useful string features directly within the syntax of the language. These are the automatic creation of new **String** instances from string literals, concatenation of multiple **String** objects by use of the + operator, and the conversion of other data types to a string representation. There are explicit methods available to perform all of these functions, but Java's built-in support makes them more convenient.

_____

Answers:

1. In character arrays, byte arrays, and other strings.
2. False.
3. False. The **java.lang** package, which contains the **String** class, is automatically imported.

String Literals

As you know, a string literal is created by specifying a quoted string. For each string literal in your program, Java automatically constructs a **String** object. Thus, you can use a string literal to initialize a **String** object. For example, the following code creates a **String** that contains the string "this is an example string literal".

```
String str = "this is an example string literal"; // use string literal
```

In this case, **str** is assigned a reference to the object that represents the quoted string.

Because a **String** object is created for every string literal, you can use a string literal any place you can use a **String** instance. For example, you can pass a string literal as an argument to a method that is expecting a **String**. Therefore, given a method called **myMethod( )** that is declared like this:

```
void myMethod(String arg) { ...
```

the following call is legal:

```
myMethod("a string literal");
```

String Concatenation

In general, Java does not allow operations on **String** objects through operators. One exception to this rule is the + operator, which concatenates two strings, producing a **String** object as the result. This allows you to chain together a series of + operations. For example, the following fragment concatenates three strings:

```
String age = "19";
String str = "He is " + age + " years old.";
System.out.println(str);
```

This displays the string "He is 19 years old."

One practical use of string concatenation is found when you are creating very long strings. Instead of letting long strings wrap around within your source code, you can break them into smaller pieces, using the + to concatenate them. Here is an example:

```
// Using concatenation to prevent long lines.
class ConCat {
  public static void main(String[] args) {
    String longStr = "This could have been " +
      "a very long line that would have " +
      "wrapped around.  But string concatenation " +
      "prevents this.";

    System.out.println(longStr);
  }
}
```

String Concatenation with Other Data Types

You can concatenate strings with other types of data. For example, consider this slightly different version of the earlier example:

```
int age = 19;
String str = "He is " + age + " years old.";
System.out.println(str);
```

In this case, **age** is an **int** rather than another **String**, but the output produced is the same as before. This is because the **int** value in **age** is automatically converted into its string representation as a **String** object. This string is then concatenated as before. The compiler will convert an operand to its string equivalent whenever the other operand of the + is an instance of **String**.

Be careful when you mix other types of operations with string concatenation expressions, however. You might get surprising results. Consider the following:

```
String str = "four: " + 2 + 2;
System.out.println(str);
```

This fragment displays

```
four: 22
```

rather than the

```
four: 4
```

that you probably expected. Here's why. The concatenation of "four:" with the string equivalent of 2 takes place first. This result is then concatenated with the string equivalent of 2 a second time. To complete the integer addition first, you must use parentheses, like this:

```
String str = "four: " + (2 + 2);
```

Now **str** contains the string "four: 4".

Overriding toString( )

When Java converts an object into its string representation during concatenation, it does so by calling the object's **toString( )** method. As you know, every class implements **toString( )** because it is defined by **Object**. It has this general form:

```
String toString( )
```

It returns a string that describes the object. Although the **Object** class provides a default implementation of **toString( )**, it may not be adequate for some uses. Frankly, for most important classes that you create, you will want to override **toString( )** and provide your own string representation for objects of your class. Fortunately, this is easy to do. When overriding **toString( )** for your class, simply return a **String** object that contains a human-readable string that appropriately describes an object of your class. By overriding **toString( )** for classes that you create, you allow them to be fully integrated into Java's programming environment. For example, they can be meaningfully used in **print( )** and **println( )** statements and in concatenation expressions. The following program demonstrates this by overriding **toString( )** for the **Box** class:

```
// Override toString() for Box class.
class Box {
  double width;
```

```
   double height;
   double depth;

   Box(double w, double h, double d) {
      width = w;
      height = h;
      depth = d;
   }

   // Provide string representation of Box.
   public String toString() {          ◄──────────Override toString() for Box.
      return "Dimensions are " + width + " by " +
             depth + " by " + height + ".";
   }
}

class OverrideToString {
   public static void main(String[] args) {
      Box b = new Box(10, 12, 14);
      String str = "Box b: " + b; // toString() called here

      System.out.println(b); // toString() called here.

      System.out.println(str);
   }
}
```

The output of this program is shown here:

```
Dimensions are 10.0 by 14.0 by 12.0
Box b: Dimensions are 10.0 by 14.0 by 12.0
```

As you can see, **Box's toString( )** method is automatically invoked when a **Box** object is used in a concatenation expression or in a call to **println( )**.

Ask the Expert

Q Why would anyone want to create an empty string? Since strings are immutable, you can't add new characters to them. This means that an empty string will always be empty. Can you give me an example that uses an empty string?

A Yes. An empty string is useful in a loop in which strings are concatenated. In such a case, the empty string is often the appropriate starting string. Here is an example:

```
String[] data = {"abc, "def", "ghi"};
String result = "";

for(String s : data)
   result += s;
```

Ask the Expert (Continued)

Note that the string variable **result** is initialized to an empty string. Thus, after the first concatenation, **result** will contain only the string "abc" since "abc" was concatenated with the empty string. Thus, the empty string provides the proper starting condition.

TRY THIS 22-1   ADD A toString( ) METHOD TO THE GenSimpleStack CLASS

GenStackToStringDemo.java
GenSimpleStack.java

As mentioned earlier, for many classes you create, you will want to override the **toString( )** method inherited from **Object** so that it returns a meaningful string representation for an object of your class. In this project you will apply this principle to the **GenSimpleStack** class created in Try This 14-1 in Chapter 14. You will first see what the version of **toString( )** inherited from **Object** returns for **GenSimpleStack**. You will then create an override of **toString( )** for **GenSimpleStack** that returns a more useful result.

STEP-BY-STEP

1. The first step is to write a program that displays the result of calling **toString( )** on a **GenSimpleStack** object. Put the following code into a file called **GenStackToStringDemo.java** and save the file in the same directory as the Java files for the **StackFullException**, **StackEmptyException**, and **GenSimpleStack** classes and the **IGenSimpleStack** interface from Try This 14-1.

```
class GenStackToStringDemo {
  public static void main(String[] args)
      throws StackFullException, StackEmptyException {
    Integer iStore[] = new Integer[10];
    GenSimpleStack<Integer> stack =
            new GenSimpleStack<Integer>(iStore);

    System.out.println("Empty stack: " + stack);

    stack.push(1);
    stack.push(2);
    stack.push(3);
    stack.push(4);
    stack.pop();

    System.out.println("Non-empty stack: " + stack);
  }
}
```

2. Before overriding **toString( )** for the **GenSimpleStack** class, compile the program from Step 1 and run it. You will see output similar to the following, although you will likely see different characters after the '@' character.

```
Empty stack: GenSimpleStack@7369ca65
Non-empty stack: GenSimpleStack@7369ca65
```

These strings are generated by the **Object** class's **toString( )** method. Notice that the first part of the string is the name of the class, the last part is a sequence of hexadecimal characters and there is an '@' character separating them. This string is useful in that it tells us the class of the object, but in most applications, you would like a more meaningful string representation.

3. Add the following method to **GenSimpleStack** from Try This 14-1. This method overrides **toString( )** so that it returns a more meaningful result. Compile the class.

```
// Override toString() for GenSimpleStack.
public String toString() {
  String result = "(";

  // Add the string representations of all the
  // items in the stack, separated by commas.
  for(int i = 0; i < tos; i++) {
    result += data[i];
    if(i < tos-1) // if not the last item,
      // add a comma and space
      result += ", ";
  }

  // Add the right parenthesis and return it.
  result += ")";
  return result;
}
```

4. Compile and run the **GenStackToStringDemo** program again. You will see the following output:

```
Empty stack: ()
Non-empty stack: (1, 2, 3)
```

The elements of the stack are listed inside parentheses and separated by commas, with the top of the stack on the right end. These strings are more meaningful than the ones generated by **Object**'s version of **toString( )**.

Notice that, in the **for** loop, the **toString( )** method that you created implicitly calls the **toString( )** methods of all the items in the stack. In this way, if all classes provide helpful **toString( )** methods, then even complex objects like stacks that contain objects of other classes can generate useful string representations.

5. For your convenience, here is the complete **GenSimpleStack** class that includes the override of **toString( )**:

```java
class GenSimpleStack<T> implements IGenSimpleStack<T> {
  private T[] data; // this array holds the stack
  private int tos; // index of top of stack

  // Construct an empty stack with the given array as storage.
  GenSimpleStack(T[] arrayRef) {
    data = arrayRef;
    tos = 0;
  }

  // Push an item onto the stack.
  public void push(T obj) throws StackFullException {
    if (isFull())
      throw new StackFullException(data.length);

    data[tos] = obj;
    tos++;
  }

  // Pop an item from the stack.
  public T pop() throws StackEmptyException {
    if (isEmpty())
      throw new StackEmptyException();

    tos--;
    return data[tos];

  }

  // Override toString() for GenSimpleStack.
  public String toString() {
    String result = "(";

    // Add the string representations of all the
    // items in the stack, separated by commas.
    for (int i = 0; i < tos; i++) {
      result += data[i];
      if (i < tos - 1) // if not the last item,
        // add a comma and space
        result += ", ";
    }

    // Add the right parenthesis and return it.
    result += ")";
    return result;
  }
```

```
      // Return true if the stack is empty.
      public boolean isEmpty() {
         return tos == 0;
      }

      // Return true if the stack is full.
      public boolean isFull() {
         return tos == data.length;
      }
   }
```

THE length() METHOD

Since strings aren't arrays, they don't have a **length** field. However, **String** does have a method called **length( )** that returns the length of a string. A string's length is the number of characters that it contains. The **length( )** method is shown here:

> int length( )

For example,

```
String str = "Theta";
System.out.println(str.length());
```

displays 5, because there are five characters in **str**. As demonstrated in the next section, **length( )** makes it easy to perform operations over the individual characters of a string.

Progress Check

1. To obtain the number of characters in a string, you use the string's **length** field, like you do for an array. True or False?
2. Most classes should override the _____ method to create meaningful string representations of its instances.
3. What does the + operator do if its operands are strings?

Answers:

1. False. You use the **length( )** method in the **String** class.
2. **toString( )**
3. It concatenates the strings.

OBTAINING THE CHARACTERS WITHIN A STRING

The **String** class provides three ways in which characters (that is, values of type **char**) can be obtained from a **String** object. Each is examined here. Although the characters that comprise a string cannot be indexed as if they were a character array, a number of **String** methods employ an index (in other words, an offset) into the string for their operation. Like arrays, string indices begin at zero.

charAt( )

To obtain a single character from a **String**, you can use the **charAt( )** method. It has this general form:

        char charAt(int *where*)

Here, *where* is the index of the character that you want to obtain. The value of *where* must be nonnegative and specify a location within the string. The **charAt( )** method returns the character at the specified location.

   The following program shows **charAt( )** in action. It is used to display a string using double-spacing. In the process, it also demonstrates the **length( )** method.

```
// Demonstrate charAt() and length().

class CharAtAndLength {
  public static void main(String[] args) {
    String str = "Programming is both art and science.";

    // Cycle through all characters in the string.
    for(int i=0; i < str.length(); i++)
      System.out.print(str.charAt(i) + " ");

    System.out.println();
  }
}
```

The output is shown here:

```
P r o g r a m m i n g   i s   b o t h   a r t   a n d   s c i e n c e .
```

In the program, notice how **length( )** is used to control the number of iterations and **charAt( )** is used to obtain each character in sequence.

getChars( )

If you need to obtain more than one character at a time, you can use the **getChars( )** method. It has this general form:

        void getChars(int *sourceStart*, int *sourceEnd*, char[ ] *target*, int *targetStart*)

Here, *sourceStart* specifies the index of the beginning of the substring to obtain, and *sourceEnd* specifies an index that is one past the end of the desired substring. Thus, the substring contains the characters from *sourceStart* through *sourceEnd*–1. The array that will receive the characters is specified by *target*. The index within *target* at which the substring will be copied is passed in *targetStart*. Care must be taken to ensure that the *target* array is large enough to hold the number of characters in the specified substring.

The following program demonstrates **getChars( )**:

```java
class GetCharsDemo {
  public static void main(String[] args) {
    String str = "Programming is both art and science.";
    int start = 15;
    int end = 23;
    char[] buf = new char[end - start];

    str.getChars(start, end, buf, 0);
    System.out.println(buf);
  }
}
```

Here is the output of this program:

```
both art
```

toCharArray( )

If you want to convert all the characters in a **String** object into a character array, the easiest way is to call **toCharArray( )**. It returns an array of characters for the entire string. It has this general form:

    char[ ] toCharArray( )

For example, here is how to obtain an array that contains the entire contents of **str**:

```java
String str = "Programming is both art and science.";
char[] chrs = str.toCharArray();
System.out.println(chrs);
```

After this sequence executes, **chrs** will contain the characters that were in **str**, and the **println( )** statement will display

```
Programming is both art and science.
```

One other point: The **toCharArray( )** method is essentially a convenience, since it is possible to use **getChars( )** to achieve the same result.

Ask the Expert

Q Earlier, you mentioned that a string literal can be used any place that a **String** instance can. Does this mean that I can call a **String** method directly on a string literal?

A Yes, you can call methods directly on a quoted string. For example, the following statement calls **length( )** on the string literal "mystring".

```java
System.out.println("mystring".length());
```

As you might expect, it displays 8. Here is another example,

```java
System.out.println("Code and Data".charAt(9));
```

This displays the character D.

Progress Check

1. To get the sixth character of a string **s**, what method call should you make?
2. The **getChars( )** method returns a new array of characters. True or False?
3. Any modification to the **char** array returned by **s.toCharArray( )** causes a corresponding modification to the string **s**. True or False?

STRING COMPARISON

The **String** class includes a number of methods that compare strings or substrings within strings. Several examples are described here.

equals( ) and equalsIgnoreCase( )

To compare two strings for equality, use **equals( )**. It has this general form:

> boolean equals(Object *str*)

Here, *str* is the object being compared with the invoking **String** object. This method is specified by **Object** and overridden by **String**. The **equals( )** method returns **true** if the strings contain the same characters in the same order. It returns **false** if the strings differ, or if *str* is not a **String**. The comparison is case sensitive.

To perform a case-insensitive comparison (that is, a comparison that ignores differences in the case of the characters), call **equalsIgnoreCase( )**. When it compares two strings, it considers **A-Z** to be the same as **a-z**, for example. It has this general form:

> boolean equalsIgnoreCase(String *str*)

Here, *str* is the **String** object being compared with the invoking **String** object. It returns **true** if, independent of case differences, the strings contain the same characters in the same order, and **false** otherwise.

Here is an example that demonstrates **equals( )** and **equalsIgnoreCase( )**:

```
// Demonstrate equals() and equalsIgnoreCase().

class EqualityDemo {
  public static void main(String[] args) {
    String str1 = "table";
    String str2 = "table";
    String str3 = "chair";
    String str4 = "TABLE";
```

Answers:

1. **s.charAt(5)**
2. False. It puts characters in an array that you provide as one of the method's arguments.
3. False.

```
   if(str1.equals(str2))
      System.out.println(str1 + " equals " + str2);
   else
      System.out.println(str1 + " does not equal " + str2);

   if(str1.equals(str3))
      System.out.println(str1 + " equals " + str3);
   else
      System.out.println(str1 + " does not equal " + str3);

   if(str1.equals(str4))
      System.out.println(str1 + " equals " + str4);
   else
      System.out.println(str1 + " does not equal " + str4);

   if(str1.equalsIgnoreCase(str4))
      System.out.println("Ignoring case differences, " + str1 +
                          " equals " + str4);
   else
      System.out.println(str1 + " does not equal " + str4);
   }
}
```

These two comparisons produce different results.

The output from the program is shown here:

```
table equals table
table does not equal chair
table does not equal TABLE
Ignoring case differences, table equals TABLE
```

equals( ) Versus ==

Before moving on, it is important to emphasize that the **equals( )** method and the **==** operator perform two different operations. As just explained, the **equals( )** method compares the characters inside a **String** object. The **==** operator compares two object references to see whether they refer to the same instance. Thus, they perform two fundamentally different operations. The following program shows how two different **String** objects can contain the same characters, but references to these objects will not compare as equal:

```
// equals() vs ==
class EqualsNotEqualTo {
   public static void main(String[] args) {
      String str1 = "Alpha";
      String str2 = new String(str1);

      System.out.println(str1 + " equals " + str2 + " is " +
                         str1.equals(str2));
      System.out.println(str1 + " == " + str2 + " is " + (str1 == str2));
   }
}
```

The variable **str1** refers to the **String** instance created by the literal **"Alpha"**. The object referred to by **str2** is created with **str1** as an initializer. Thus, the contents of the two **String** objects are identical, but they are distinct objects. This means that **str1** and **str2** do not refer to the same objects and are, therefore, not ==, as is shown here by the program's output:

```
Alpha equals Alpha is true
Alpha == Alpha is false
```

regionMatches( )

The **regionMatches( )** method compares a subset (that is, a region) of a string with a subset of another string. There is an overloaded form that allows you to ignore case in such comparisons. Here are the general forms for these two methods:

> boolean regionMatches(int *startIndex*, String *str2*,
>   int *str2StartIndex*, int *numChrs*)
>
> boolean regionMatches(boolean *ignoreCase*,
>   int *startIndex*, String *str2*,
>   int *str2StartIndex*, int *numChrs*)

For both versions, *startIndex* specifies the index at which the region to compare begins within the invoking **String** object. The **String** being compared is specified by *str2*. The index at which the comparison will start within *str2* is specified by *str2StartIndex*. The length of the region being compared is passed in *numChrs*. The first version is case sensitive. In the second version, if *ignoreCase* is **true**, the case of the characters is ignored. Otherwise, case is significant.

Here is an example:

```java
// Demonstrate RegionMatches.

class CompareRegions {
  public static void main(String[] args) {
    String str1 = "Standing at river's edge.";
    String str2 = "Running at river's edge.";

    if(str1.regionMatches(9, str2, 8, 12))
      System.out.println("Regions match.");

    if(!str1.regionMatches(0, str2, 0, 12))
      System.out.println("Regions do not match.");
  }
}
```

The output is

```
Regions match.
Regions do not match.
```

startsWith( ) and endsWith( )

String defines two methods that are, more or less, specialized forms of **regionMatches( )**. The **startsWith( )** method determines whether a given **String** begins with a specified string. Conversely, **endsWith( )** determines whether the **String** in question ends with a specified string. They have the following general forms:

> boolean startsWith(String *str*)
> boolean endsWith(String *str*)

Here, *str* is the string being tested. In the case of **startsWith( )**, if *str* matches the beginning of the invoking string, **true** is returned. In the case of **endsWith( )**, if *str* matches the end of the invoking string, **true** is returned. Otherwise, both methods return **false** on a mismatch. The comparisons are case sensitive.

For example, given

```
String str = "Status: Complete";
```

Then the following two expressions are true:

```
str.startsWith("Status:")
```

and

```
str.endsWith("Complete")
```

There is a second form of **startsWith( )** that lets you specify a starting point. It is shown here:

> boolean startsWith(String *str*, int *startIndex*)

Here, *startIndex* specifies the index into the invoking string at which point the search will begin.

compareTo( ) and compareToIgnoreCase( )

Often, it is not enough to simply know whether two strings, or portions of two strings, are identical. For sorting applications, you need to know which is *less than, equal to,* or *greater than* the next. A string is less than another if it comes before the other in dictionary order. A string is greater than another if it comes after the other in dictionary order. The method **compareTo( )** serves this purpose. It is specified by the **Comparable<T>** interface, which **String** implements. The **compareTo( )** method has this general form:

> int compareTo(String *str*)

Here, *str* is the **String** being compared with the invoking **String**. The comparison is case sensitive. The result of the comparison is returned and is interpreted, as shown here:

Value	Meaning
Less than zero	The invoking string is less than *str*.
Greater than zero	The invoking string is greater than *str*.
Zero	The two strings are equal.

If you want to perform a case-insensitive comparison, use **compareToIgnoreCase( )**, as shown here:

> int compareToIgnoreCase(String *str*)

This method returns the same results as **compareTo( )**, except that case differences are ignored.

The following example shows the difference between **compareTo( )** and **compareToIgnoreCase( )**.

```
// Demonstrate compareTo() and compareToIgnoreCase().

class CompareStrings {
  public static void main(String[] args) {
    String str1 = "alpha";
    String str2 = "ALPHA";
    String str3 = "Beta";

    int result;

    // Demonstrate the differences between compareTo()
    // and compareToIgnoreCase().
    result = str1.compareTo(str2);
    if(result != 0)
      System.out.println("Using compareTo(): " +
                         str1 + " and " + str2 + " differ");

    result = str1.compareToIgnoreCase(str2);
    if(result == 0)
      System.out.println("Using compareToIgnoreCase(): " +
                         str1 + " and " + str2 + " are the same\n");

    // Now, compare alpha to Beta using compareTo().
    System.out.println("Using compareTo() to compare " + str1 +
                       " with " + str3);
    result = str1.compareTo(str3);
    if(result < 0)
      System.out.println(str1 + " is less than " + str3);
    else if(result == 0)
      System.out.println(str1 + " is equal to " + str3);
    else if(result > 0)
      System.out.println(str1 + " is greater than " + str3);

    System.out.println();

    // Next, compare alpha to Beta using compareToIgnoreCase().
    System.out.println("Using compareToIgnoreCase() to compare " +
                       str1 + " with " + str3);
    result = str1.compareToIgnoreCase(str3);
    if(result < 0)
      System.out.println(str1 + " is less than " + str3);
    else if(result == 0)
      System.out.println(str1 + " is equal to " + str3);
    else if(result > 0)
      System.out.println(str1 + " is greater than " + str3);
```

These two comparisons produce a different ordering.

```
     }
  }
```

The output is shown here.

```
Using compareTo(): alpha and ALPHA differ
Using compareToIgnoreCase(): alpha and ALPHA are the same

Using compareTo() to compare alpha with Beta
alpha is greater than Beta

Using compareToIgnoreCase() to compare alpha with Beta
alpha is less than Beta
```

Do you see something unusual in the output? Notice that when "alpha" is compared to "Beta" using **compareTo( )**, alpha is greater than Beta. However, when the comparison is done using **compareToIgnoreCase( )**, alpha is less than Beta. Here's why. Even though Beta comes after alpha in alphabetical order, if you use a case sensitive comparison on the strings, alpha will be greater than Beta because Beta begins with an uppercase letter. In ASCII/Unicode, uppercase letters have a *lower value* than do the lowercase letters. However, when case is ignored, as is the case in the second comparison, the expected order is obtained. This is why **compareToIgnoreCase( )** is often a useful alternative when sorting strings.

USING indexOf( ) AND lastIndexOf( )

The **String** class provides two methods that allow you to search a string for a specified character or substring, and obtain an index to that item if it is found. They are

- **indexOf( )** Searches for the first occurrence of a character or substring.
- **lastIndexOf( )** Searches for the last occurrence of a character or substring.

These two methods are overloaded in several different ways. In all cases, the methods return the index at which the character or substring was found, or –1 on failure.

To search for the first occurrence of a character, use

  int indexOf(int *ch*)

To search for the last occurrence of a character, use

  int lastIndexOf(int *ch*)

Here, *ch* is the character being sought.

To search for the first or last occurrence of a substring, use

  int indexOf(String *str*)
  int lastIndexOf(String *str*)

Here, *str* specifies the substring.

You can specify a starting point for the search using these forms:

  int indexOf(int *ch*, int *startIndex*)
  int lastIndexOf(int *ch*, int *startIndex*)
  int indexOf(String *str*, int *startIndex*)
  int lastIndexOf(String *str*, int *startIndex*)

Here, *startIndex* specifies the index at which point the search begins. For **indexOf( )**, the search runs from *startIndex* to the end of the string. For **lastIndexOf( )**, the search runs from *startIndex* to zero.

The following example shows how to use several of the various index methods to search the contents of **Strings**:

```java
// Demonstrate indexOf() and lastIndexOf().

class IndexOfDemo {
  public static void main(String[] args) {
    String str = "alpha beta gamma theta zeta";

    System.out.println("The string is: " + str);
    System.out.println("The first index of t is " + str.indexOf('t'));

    System.out.println("The last index of t is " + str.lastIndexOf('t'));

    System.out.println("The first index of eta is " + str.indexOf("eta"));

    System.out.println("The last index of eta is " + str.lastIndexOf("eta"));

    System.out.println("The first index of eta after position 10 is " +
                       str.indexOf("eta", 10));
  }
}
```

Here is the output of this program:

```
The string is: alpha beta gamma theta zeta
The first index of t is 8
The last index of t is 25
The first index of eta is 7
The last index of eta is 24
The first index of eta after position 10 is 19
```

Progress Check

1. To compare two strings for equality without regard to upper or lower case, use the method _____.
2. To compare two strings to see which one comes first alphabetically, use the method _____.
3. The expression **s.equals(t)** is the same as **s == t**. True or False?
4. To determine if a string **t** is a substring of a string **s** call _____.
   The result is −1 if and only if **t** is not a substring of **s**.

_____

Answers:

1. **equalsIgnoreCase( )**
2. **compareTo( )**
3. False.
4. **s.indexOf(t)**

OBTAINING A MODIFIED STRING

As explained, **String** objects are immutable. It is, however, still easy to obtain a modified version of a **String** through the use of one or more methods defined by **String**. These methods return a modified copy of the original string. Because the original string is never modified, the rule of immutability is not violated. Here we will look at **substring( )**, **replace( )**, and **trim( )**, all of which return modified versions of the string on which they are invoked.

substring( )

You can obtain a portion of a string by use of **substring( )**. It has two forms. The first is

String substring(int *startIndex*)

Here, *startIndex* specifies the index at which the desired substring will begin. This form returns a copy of the substring that begins at *startIndex* and includes the remainder of the invoking string.

The second form of **substring( )** allows you to specify both the beginning and ending index of the substring. This form was introduced in Chapter 5, but is shown again here for completeness:

String substring(int *startIndex*, int *endIndex*)

Here, *startIndex* specifies the beginning index, and *endIndex* specifies an index one beyond the stopping point. The string returned contains all the characters from *startIndex*, up to, but not including, *endIndex*.

The following program demonstrates both forms of **substring( )**. In the process, it also shows another example of **indexOf( )** in action. The program defines a string that contains the following two sentences:

This is a test. This is, too.

The program then uses **indexOf( )** to find the beginning of the second sentence. It then obtains the second sentence by using the single-argument form of **substring( )**. The program then uses a combination of **indexOf( )**, **substring( )**, and string concatenation to progressively replace one substring with another within the string.

```
// This program demonstrates both forms of substring().

class UseSubStrings {
  public static void main(String[] args) {
    String orgStr = "This is a test. This is, too.";
    String searchStr = "is";
    String subStr = "was";
    String resultStr = "";
    int i;

    System.out.println("Original string: " + orgStr);

    // Obtain the second sentence in orgStr. This is
    // done by first finding the end of the first sentence
    // and then obtaining the remainder of the string.
    i = orgStr.indexOf(".") + 2;  ◄─────────────Find the end of the first sentence.
```

```
String str = orgStr.substring(i);                          Use substring( ) to obtain the
System.out.println("Second sentence: " + str + "\n");      second sentence.

// Replace all occurrences of searchStr with subStr.
System.out.println ("Progressively replacing " +
                   searchStr + " with " + subStr);
do {
  System.out.println(orgStr);

  // find next occurrences of searchStr.
  i = orgStr.indexOf(searchStr);                            Find the index of the next
  if(i != -1) {                                             replacement..
    // obtain the first part of the string
    resultStr = orgStr.substring(0, i);                     Obtain the first part of the string,
                                                            up to the point of replacement.

    // add the replacement sequence
    resultStr = resultStr + subStr;                         Add in the substitute string.

    // add the remainder of the string, skipping searchStr
    resultStr = resultStr + orgStr.substring(i + searchStr.length());

    // make the resulting string, the new orgstr
    orgStr = resultStr;
  }
} while(i != -1);                                           Now, use substring( ) to
}                                                           obtain the remainder of
}                                                           the string.
```

The output from this program is shown here:

```
Original string: This is a test. This is, too.
Second sentence: This is, too.

Progressively replacing is with was
This is a test. This is, too.
Thwas is a test. This is, too.
Thwas was a test. This is, too.
Thwas was a test. Thwas is, too.
Thwas was a test. Thwas was, too.
```

In the program, pay special attention to how the progressive modification of **orgStr** takes place. Each time through the **do** loop, an attempt is made to find **searchStr**. If it succeeds, the first part of **orgStr** is assigned to **resultStr**. Then, **subStr** is appended to **resultStr**. Finally, the remainder of **orgStr**, less the characters that match **searchStr**, are appended to **resultStr**. Finally, **resultStr** is assigned to **orgStr**, and the process repeats until no more matches are found.

replace( )

The **replace( )** method has two forms. The first replaces one character with another throughout a string. It has the following general form:

String replace(char *original*, char *replacement*)

Here, *original* specifies the character to be replaced by the character specified by *replacement*. The modified copy of the invoking string is returned.

The second form of **replace( )** replaces one character sequence with another throughout a string. It has this general form:

String replace(CharSequence *original*, CharSequence *replacement*)

The sequences can be objects of type **String**, because **String** implements the **CharSequence** interface. The modified copy of the invoking string is returned.

The following program demonstrates both forms of **replace( )**. Notice that each replaces all occurrences of the original item with the replacement.

```java
// This program demonstrates both forms of replace().

class Replace {
  public static void main(String[] args) {
    String orgStr = "alpha beta gamma alpha beta gamma";
    String resultStr;

    System.out.println("Original string: " + orgStr);

    // First, replace g with X.
    resultStr = orgStr.replace('g', 'X');
    System.out.println(resultStr);

    // Now, replace beta with zeta.
    resultStr = resultStr.replace("beta", "zeta");
    System.out.println(resultStr);
  }
}
```

The output from the program is shown here:

```
Original string: alpha beta gamma alpha beta gamma
alpha beta Xamma alpha beta Xamma
alpha zeta Xamma alpha zeta Xamma
```

trim( )

The **trim( )** method deletes leading and trailing whitespace (typically, spaces, tabs, and newline characters) from a string. It has this general form:

String trim( )

If the invoking string has leading and/or trailing whitespace, then **trim( )** removes the whitespace and returns a new string that contains the result. Otherwise, the resulting string is simply equivalent to the invoking string.

Here is an example. Given the string:

```java
String str = "   Gamma   ";
```

After

```java
str = str.trim();
```

str will contain only the string "Gamma". The leading or trailing whitespace has been deleted.

The **trim( )** method is quite useful when you process user commands. For example, the following program prompts the user for the name of a state and then displays that state's capital. It uses **trim( )** to remove any leading or trailing whitespace that may have inadvertently been entered by the user.

```java
// Using trim() to process commands.
import java.io.*;

class UseTrim {
  public static void main(String[] args)
    throws IOException
  {
    // create a BufferedReader using System.in
    BufferedReader br = new
      BufferedReader(new InputStreamReader(System.in));
    String str;

    System.out.println("Enter 'stop' to quit.");
    System.out.println("Enter State: ");
    do {
      str = br.readLine();
      str = str.trim(); // remove whitespace

      if(str.equals("Illinois"))
        System.out.println("Capital is Springfield.");
      else if(str.equals("Missouri"))
        System.out.println("Capital is Jefferson City.");
      else if(str.equals("California"))
        System.out.println("Capital is Sacramento.");
      else if(str.equals("Washington"))
        System.out.println("Capital is Olympia.");
      // ...
    } while(!str.equals("stop"));
  }
}
```

Use **trim( )** to remove leading and trailing whitespace from the string entered by the user.

When this program is run, if the user enters something like " Illinois ", the call to **trim( )** will remove the leading and trailing whitespace, enabling the input to match "Illinois".

*Note: If you are using JDK 7 or later, you can use a **String** to control a **switch**. You might want to try changing the preceding example to take advantage of this new feature.*

CHANGING THE CASE OF CHARACTERS WITHIN A STRING

It is sometimes helpful to change the case of the letters within a string. For example, you might want to normalize the string for use by some other process. The method **toLowerCase( )** converts all the characters in a string from upper case to lower case. The **toUpperCase( )** method converts all the characters in a string from lower case to upper case. Nonalphabetical characters, such as digits, are unaffected. Here are the simplest forms of these methods:

```
String toLowerCase( )
String toUpperCase( )
```

Both methods return a **String** that contains the uppercase or lowercase equivalent of the invoking **String**.

Here is an example that uses **toLowerCase( )** and **toUpperCase( )**:

```
// Demonstrate toUpperCase() and toLowerCase().

class ChangeCase {
  public static void main(String[] args)
  {
    String str = "This is a test.";

    System.out.println("Original: " + str);

    String upper = str.toUpperCase();
    String lower = str.toLowerCase();

    System.out.println("Uppercase: " + upper);
    System.out.println("Lowercase: " + lower);
  }
}
```

The output produced by the program is shown here:

```
Original: This is a test.
Uppercase: THIS IS A TEST.
Lowercase: this is a test.
```

String also supplies overloaded versions of **toLowerCase( )** and **toUpperCase( )** that let you specify a **Locale** object to govern the case conversion. (See Chapter 24 for a description of **Locale**.) Specifying the locale can be quite useful in some situations and can help internationalize your application.

Progress Check

1. The **trim( )** method eliminates _____.
2. To convert a string **s** to all capital letters, use _____.
3. The call **s.substring(0, 3)** returns a string of length _____.

Answers:

1. whitespace at the beginning and end of the string
2. **s.toUpperCase( )**
3. 3 (assuming **s** has at least three characters in it)

Ask the Expert

Q In addition to the methods that you have discussed, can you tell me about other methods that **String** provides?

A Because of its importance **String** is a powerful, full-featured class. As such, it offers the programmer a rich assortment of methods. Here are a few more that you will find both interesting and useful.

Method	Description
String concat(String *str*)	Returns the result of appending *str* to the end of the invoking string. Thus, it performs the same function as +.
boolean contains(CharSequence *str*)	Returns **true** if the invoking object contains the string specified by *str*. Otherwise, returns **false**.
boolean contentEquals(CharSequence *str*)	Returns **true** if the invoking string contains the same string as *str*. Otherwise, returns **false**.
static String format(String *fmtstr*, Object ... *args*)	Returns a string formatted as specified by *fmtstr*. (See Chapter 24 for details on formatting.)
boolean isEmpty( )	Returns **true** if the invoking string contains no characters. Otherwise, returns **false**.
boolean matches(string *regExp*)	Returns **true** if the invoking string matches the regular expression specified by *regExp*. Otherwise, returns **false**.
String replaceAll(String *regExp*, String *newStr*)	Returns a string in which all substrings that match the regular expression specified by *regExp* are replaced by *newStr*.
String replaceFirst(String *regExp*, String *newStr*)	Returns a string in which the first substring that matches the regular expression specified by *regExp* is replaced by *newStr*.
String[ ] split(String *regExp*)	Decomposes the invoking string into parts and returns an array that contains the result. Each part is delimited by the regular expression passed in *regExp*.

Notice that several of these methods work with regular expressions. An introduction to regular expressions is found in Appendix B. Also notice that two of the methods take a **CharSequence** as an argument. Recall that **String** implements **CharSequence**. Thus, strings can be passed to those methods. Furthermore, any object that implements **CharSequence** can be passed to these methods.

   String also provides several overloaded versions of the **static** method **valueOf( )**, which is used to produce a string representation of an object, character array, or primitive type. **String** also supports methods that handle Unicode code points.

StringBuffer AND StringBuilder

Before leaving the topic of string handling, it is important to mention two alternatives to **String**. These are **StringBuffer** and **StringBuilder**. Both offer capabilities similar to **String** with one important addition: they contain strings that can be modified. For example, you can insert characters and substrings in the middle or append to the end. Both **StringBuffer** and **StringBuilder** will automatically grow to make room for such additions. You can also delete characters. To support these types of operations, both classes include methods such as **setCharAt( )**, **append( )**, **insert( )**, and **delete( )**.

   StringBuffer has been part of Java since version 1.0. **StringBuilder** is a more recent addition, being added by JDK 5. **StringBuilder** is similar to **StringBuffer** except for one important difference: it is not synchronized, which means that it is not thread-safe. The advantage of **StringBuilder** is faster performance. However, in cases in which a mutable string will be accessed by multiple threads, and no external synchronization is employed, you must use **StringBuffer** rather than **StringBuilder**.

EXERCISES

1. Write a statement that displays the substring of a string **s** consisting of all but the last character of **s**.

2. Assume **s** is a string and consider the following statement:

   ```
   boolean b = s.isEmpty();
   ```

   Find an equivalent statement or set of statements using **length( )** instead of **isEmpty( )**.

3. What happens if you call **charAt( )** and the value you pass in for the index is out of range?

4. Suppose you want to create one string that consists of two lines of text, each on a separate line. You cannot use a statement such as

   ```
   String s = "This is the first line.
              This is the second line";
   ```

   because this statement will generate a compiler error. How can you do it?

5. What is the value of the expression 2+2+"ME"? Is it "22ME" or "4ME"?

6. Suppose you want to test whether a string variable **s** contains the string "abcdef". Is it sufficient to call **s.startsWith("abc")** and **s.endsWith("def")** and then see whether both method calls return true?

7. In the **UseTrim** example in the chapter that demonstrated how to use the **trim( )** method, the **if-else-if** ladder repeatedly tested the equality of two strings using the **equals( )** method. Why didn't the ladder repeatedly test the equality using ==?

8. Explain the difference between **startsWith(substring, index)** and **indexOf(substring, index)**.

9. Suppose you have a string **s** containing some English text that always uses male gender pronouns (e.g., he, his, him) and you want to change it to use female pronouns. The following program reads a string that is input by the user and uses the **replace( )** method to attempt such a conversion. It will correctly convert sentences such as "He went to his house." into "She went to her house." Unfortunately, this program doesn't work correctly for other English sentences. Find a sentence that the program doesn't correctly convert.

```java
import java.io.*;

public class ReplaceGender {
  public static void main(String[] args)
    throws IOException
  {
    // create a BufferedReader using System.in
    BufferedReader br = new
      BufferedReader(new InputStreamReader(System.in));
    String str;

    str = br.readLine();
    str = str.replace(" he ", " she ");
    str = str.replace("His ", "Her ");
    str = str.replace("He ", "She ");
    str = str.replace(" his ", " her ");
    str = str.replace(" him ", " her ");

    System.out.println(str);
  }
}
```

10. Write a method that takes a string as its parameter and returns **true** if all the characters in the string are the same character.

11. Assume **s** is a string and consider the following statement:

```java
boolean b = s.isEmpty();
```

Find three different equivalent statements or sets of statements. Do not use the **String**'s **length( )** method as was done in exercise 2 above.

12. Even though a **String** instance is immutable, there are a variety of ways to create an arbitrary new string from an existing string. One way is to use a **StringBuilder** or **StringBuffer**. Another way is to convert the string into a **char** array using **toCharArray( )**, manipulate the characters in the array, and then create the new string using the **String** constructor that takes a **char** array as its argument. Follow this last approach to implement a **replaceChar( )** method that takes three parameters: a string, an integer index, and a **char**. It returns a new string identical to the first argument except that the character at the given index is replaced by the character that is the third argument to the method. For example, **replaceChar("abc", 0, 'd')** returns the string "dbc".

13. Implement a **reverse( )** method that takes a string as its parameter and returns a new string in which the order of the characters is reversed. Use the same approach as described in the preceding problem. That is, convert the string to a **char** array, manipulate the array, and then convert it back into a string.

14. A common idiom seen in Java programming is to take a variable of any type and add the empty string to it, as in **x + ""**. What does that addition accomplish?

15. If **s** and **t** are strings and you want to know whether **s** starts with the string **t**, you can execute **s.startsWith(t)**. As mentioned in the text, you can also use **regionMatches( )** instead of **startsWith( )**. Give an expression using **regionMatches( )** that is equivalent to **s.startsWith(t)**.

16. Assume **s** is a string and consider the following statement:

```
char[] cArray = s.toCharArray( );
```

Find an equivalent statement or set of statements using **getChars( )** instead of **toCharArray( )**.

17. Implement a method **isSubstring( )** that takes two strings **s** and **t** as its parameters and returns **true** if **t** is a substring of **s**. Use the second form of **startsWith( )** (that has two parameters). Do not use the overloaded **indexOf( )** methods.

18. Assume **s** and **t** are strings, and consider the following statement.

```
boolean b = s.equalsIgnoreCase(t);
```

Create an equivalent statement or set of statements using **equals( )** and **toLowerCase( )** instead of **equalsIgnoreCase( )**.

19. Which string comes first in alphabetical order: "$*%" or "&;@"? Why?

20. Implement a method **myTrim( )** that takes a string as its parameter and returns a new string with all the whitespace characters removed from the beginning and end of the string. Do not use the **String** class's **trim( )** method. Instead, repeatedly call **substring( )** to get shorter and shorter strings. Assume that whitespace characters are the space ' ', tab '\t', newline '\n', and return '\r' characters.

21. Implement a method **isEmailAddress( )** that takes a string **s** as its parameter. It returns **true** if **s** is of the form "x@y.com" where x and y can be any mixture of one or more alphabetical letters (lower or upper case) or digits.

22. Assume **s** and **t** are strings, and consider the following statement.

```
String v = s.concat(t);
```

Create an equivalent statement or set of statements without using the **concat( )** method and without using the + operator on strings.

CHAPTER 23

Exploring java.lang

KEY SKILLS & CONCEPTS

- The primitive type wrappers
- The **Math** class
- The **Process** class
- The **ProcessBuilder** class
- The **Runtime** class
- The **System** class
- The **Object** class
- The **Class** class
- The **Enum** class
- The **Comparable** interface
- The **Appendable** interface
- The **Iterable** interface
- The **Readable** interface
- The **CharSequence** interface
- The **AutoCloseable** interface

This chapter explores **java.lang**. As you know, **java.lang** is automatically imported into all programs. It contains classes and interfaces that are fundamental to virtually all of Java programming. It is Java's most widely used package, and all Java programmers must have a general understanding of what it provides.

The **java.lang** package includes the following top-level classes:

Boolean	Byte	Character
Class	ClassLoader	ClassValue
Compiler	Double	Enum
Float	InheritableThreadLocal	Integer
Long	Math	Number

843

Object	Package	Process
ProcessBuilder	Runtime	RuntimePermission
SecurityManager	Short	StackTraceElement
StrictMath	String	StringBuffer
StringBuilder	System	Thread
ThreadGroup	ThreadLocal	Throwable
Void		

The top-level interfaces defined by **java.lang** include those shown next:

Appendable	Cloneable	Readable
AutoCloseable	Comparable	Runnable
CharSequence	Iterable	

As you can imagine, **java.lang**'s classes and interfaces define a very large amount of functionality. Some parts of **java.lang**, such as **String**, **StringBuilder**, **StringBuffer**, **Throwable**, **Thread**, and **Runnable**, have been described elsewhere in this book. Furthermore, not every part of **java.lang** is commonly used, or used by all programmers. For example, some classes, such as **StrictMath** and **Compiler**, apply mostly to specialized situations. For these reasons, we will focus on several classes that are applicable to a wide range of situations and not described elsewhere in this book. The chapter concludes with an overview of **java.lang**'s interfaces. We begin by revisiting the primitive type wrappers.

PRIMITIVE TYPE WRAPPERS

As explained in Part One, Java uses primitive types, such as **int** and **char**, for performance reasons. These data types are not part of the object hierarchy. They are passed by value to methods and cannot be directly passed by reference. Also, there is no way for two methods to refer to the *same instance* of a primitive type. At times, you will need to create an object representation for one of these primitive types. For example, there are collection classes discussed in Chapter 25 that deal only with objects; to store a primitive type in one of these classes, you need to encapsulate the primitive type in a class. To address this need, Java provides classes that correspond to each of the primitive types. In essence, these classes encapsulate, or *wrap*, the primitive types within a class. Thus, they are commonly referred to as *type wrappers*. Although several aspects of the type wrappers were covered in Part One, here we will look at some of their other features and capabilities. We will begin by reviewing the superclass of the numeric type wrappers: **Number**.

Number

Recall from Part One that the abstract class **Number** defines a superclass that is extended by (among others) the classes that wrap the numeric types **byte**, **short**, **int**, **long**, **float**, and **double**. **Number** declares methods that return the value of the object in each of the different number formats. For example, **doubleValue( )** returns the value as a **double**, **floatValue( )** returns the value as a **float**, and so on. The need for these methods has been greatly reduced because of auto-unboxing. However, they are still available if you want to use them. **Number** implements the **java.io.Serializable** interface.

In **java.lang**, **Number** has concrete subclasses that hold explicit values of each numeric type: **Double**, **Float**, **Byte**, **Short**, **Integer**, and **Long**.

Double and Float

Double and **Float** are wrappers for floating-point values of type **double** and **float**, respectively. Both extend **Number** and implement the **Comparable<T>** interface. The constructors for **Float** are shown here:

> Float(double *num*)
> Float(float *num*)
> Float(String *str*) throws NumberFormatException

As you can see, **Float** objects can be constructed with values of type **float** or **double**. They can also be constructed from the string representation of a floating-point number.

The constructors for **Double** are shown here:

> Double(double *num*)
> Double(String *str*) throws NumberFormatException

Double objects can be constructed with a **double** value or a string containing a floating-point value.

The following example creates two **Double** objects—one by using a **double** value and the other by passing a string that can be parsed as a **double**:

```
class DoubleDemo {
  public static void main(String[] args) {
    Double d1 = new Double(3.14159);
    Double d2 = new Double("314159E-5");

    System.out.println(d1 + " " + d2);
  }
}
```

As you can see from the following output, both constructors created identical **Double** instances.

```
3.14159 3.14159
```

Both **Float** and **Double** define several constants that are useful when working with numbers. Among them are

MAX_VALUE	Maximum positive value
MIN_VALUE	Minimum positive value
NaN	A value the represents something that is not a number
POSITIVE_INFINITY	Positive infinity
NEGATIVE_INFINITY	Negative infinity

For **Float**, these values are type **float**. For **Double**, they are of type **double**.

In addition to the methods inherited from **Number**, both **Float** and **Double** define several other methods. For example, you can compare two numbers for equality by use of **equals( )** and for an ordering relationship by use of **compareTo( )**, which is specified by **Comparable<T>**. As explained in Chapter 11, **Float** defines the method **parseFloat( )** and **Double** defines the method **parseDouble( )**. These methods can be used to convert numeric strings into **float** or **double** values.

Two of the more interesting methods are **isInfinite( )** and **isNaN( )**. These methods are defined by both **Float** and **Double**. Their **Double** versions are shown here, but the **Float** versions are similar.

```
boolean isInfinite( )
boolean isNaN( )
```

The **isInfinite( )** method returns **true** if the invoking object contains an infinite value, which can be either positive or negative. The **isNaN( )** method returns **true** if the invoking object contains a value that is not a number.

The following example creates two **Double** objects; one is infinite, and the other is not a number:

```
// Demonstrate isInfinite() and isNaN()
class InfNaN {
  public static void main(String[] args) {
    Double d1 = new Double(1/0.0);
    Double d2 = new Double(0/0.0);

    System.out.println(d1 + ": " + d1.isInfinite() + ", " + d1.isNaN());
    System.out.println(d2 + ": " + d2.isInfinite() + ", " + d2.isNaN());
  }
}
```

This program generates the following output:

```
Infinity: true, false
NaN: false, true
```

Note: As a point of interest, if the division in the program had used an integer for the divisor, a divide-by-zero exception would have been thrown rather than generating an infinite or NaN value.

Both **Float** and **Double** also provide **static** versions of **isInfinite( )** and **isNaN( )**. The **Double** versions are shown here:

```
static boolean isInfinite(double num)
static boolean isNaN(double num)
```

In both cases, the number is passed in *num* and the result is returned.

Byte, Short, Integer, and Long

The **Byte**, **Short**, **Integer**, and **Long** classes are wrappers for **byte**, **short**, **int**, and **long** integer types, respectively. They all extend **Number** and implement the **Comparable<T>** interface. Their constructors are shown here:

```
Byte(byte num)
Byte(String str) throws NumberFormatException
```

Short(short *num*)
Short(String *str*) throws NumberFormatException

Integer(int *num*)
Integer(String *str*) throws NumberFormatException

Long(long *num*)
Long(String *str*) throws NumberFormatException

As you can see, these objects can be constructed from numeric values or from strings that contain valid whole number values.

Among other fields, all of the integer numeric wrappers define the following constants:

MIN_VALUE	Minimum value
MAX_VALUE	Maximum value

The type of these values is that of the wrapped type.

In addition to the methods inherited from **Number**, all of the integer wrappers define several other methods. For example, you can compare two numbers for equality by use of **equals( )** and for an ordering relationship by use of **compareTo( )**, which is specified by **Comparable<T>**.

All of the integer numeric wrappers define several methods for parsing integers from strings and converting strings back into integers. As you already know, the **Byte**, **Short**, **Integer**, and **Long** classes provide the **parseByte( )**, **parseShort( )**, **parseInt( )**, and **parseLong( )** methods, respectively. These methods return the **byte**, **short**, **int**, or **long** equivalent of the numeric string with which they are called. However, variants of these methods allow you to specify the *radix*, or numeric base, for conversion. Common radixes are 2 for binary, 8 for octal, 10 for decimal, and 16 for hexadecimal. Here are the radix versions of the parse methods:

static byte parseByte(String *str*, int *radix*) throws NumberFormatException
static short parseShort(String *str*, int *radix*) throws NumberFormatException
static int parseInt(String *str*, int *radix*) throws NumberFormatException
static long parseLong(String *str*, int *radix*) throws NumberFormatException

In all cases, *str* specifies the numeric string to be converted and *radix* specifies the radix. The result of the conversion is returned. A **NumberFormatException** is thrown if *str* does not contain a valid number. Here is an example that parses a binary value:

```java
// Demonstrate parseInt().

class ParseBinary {
  public static void main(String[] args) {
    int num;
    String str = "10011101";

    num = Integer.parseInt(str, 2);

    System.out.println("Here is " + str + " in decimal: " + num);
  }
}
```

The output is shown here:

```
Here is 10011101 in decimal: 157
```

To convert a number into a decimal string, use the versions of **toString( )** defined in the **Byte**, **Short**, **Integer**, or **Long** classes. The **Integer** and **Long** classes also provide the methods **toBinaryString( )**, **toHexString( )**, and **toOctalString( )**, which convert a value into a binary, hexadecimal, or octal string, respectively. Here are the versions for **Integer**:

> static String toBinaryString(int *num*)
> static String toHexString(int *num*)
> static String toOctalString(int *num*)

In all cases, *num* specifies the value to convert into its string representation.

*Note: Both **Float** and **Double** also provide the method **toHexString( )**, which converts a floating-point value into its hexadecimal floating point format.*

The following program demonstrates binary, hexadecimal, and octal conversion:

```
// Convert an integer into binary, hexadecimal,
// and octal.

class StringConversions {
  public static void main(String[] args) {
    int num = 19648;

    System.out.println(num + " in binary: " +
                       Integer.toBinaryString(num));

    System.out.println(num + " in octal: " +
                       Integer.toOctalString(num));

    System.out.println(num + " in hexadecimal: " +
                       Integer.toHexString(num));
  }
}
```

The output of this program is shown here:

```
19648 in binary: 100110011000000
19648 in octal: 46300
19648 in hexadecimal: 4cc0
```

Both **Integer** and **Long** contain two methods that rotate the bits within an integer value. These are called **rotateLeft( )** and **rotateRight( )**. Their **Integer** forms are shown here:

> static int rotateLeft(int *num*, int *n*)
> static int rotateRight(int *num*, int *n*)

Here, *num* is the number being rotated, and *n* specifies the number of positions to rotate. A rotate is similar to a shift, except that a bit shifted off one end is brought back in on the other end. Here is an example:

```
// Demonstrate rotateLeft() and rotateRight()

class Rotations {
  public static void main(String[] args) {
    int num = -3356756;

    System.out.println(Integer.toBinaryString(num));

    num = Integer.rotateLeft(num, 2);
    System.out.println(Integer.toBinaryString(num));


    num = Integer.rotateRight(num, 2);
    System.out.println(Integer.toBinaryString(num));
  }
}
```

The output is shown here:

```
11111111110011001100011110101100
11111111001100110001111010110011
11111111110011001100011110101100
```

Character

Character is a simple wrapper around a **char**. It implements **java.io.Serializable** and **Comparable<T>**. It has only one constructor:

> Character(char *ch*)

Here, *ch* specifies the character that will be wrapped by the **Character** object being created. To obtain the **char** value contained in a **Character** object, call **charValue( )**, shown here:

> char charValue( )

It returns the character.

    Character includes several **static** methods that categorize characters. Others alter the case of characters. A sampling is shown in Table 23-1. These methods can be quite helpful when working with characters. For example, if a file separates fields with a space, you might use **isSpaceChar( )** to find the end of one field and the start of the next. If you are parsing a line of text, you might use **isDigit( )** to find the start of a number, or **isLetterOrDigit( )** to read an employee ID, such as HR534R, that contains both letters and digits. The following example demonstrates several of these methods:

```
// Demonstrate several is... methods.

class IsDemo {
  public static void main(String[] args) {
    char[] a = {'a', 'b', '5', '?', 'A', ' ', '\t', '\n'};

    for(int i=0; i<a.length; i++) {
```

```
      if(Character.isDigit(a[i]))
        System.out.println(a[i] + " is a digit.");

      if(Character.isLetter(a[i]))
        System.out.println(a[i] + " is a letter.");

      if(Character.isLetterOrDigit(a[i]))
        System.out.println(a[i] + " is a letter or digit.");

      if(Character.isWhitespace(a[i])) {
        String chStr = "";
        if(a[i] == ' ') chStr = "<space>";
        else if(a[i] == '\t') chStr = "<tab>";
        else if(a[i] == '\n') chStr = "<newline>";
        System.out.println(chStr + " is whitespace.");
      }

      if(Character.isSpaceChar(a[i])) {
        String chStr = "";
        if(a[i] == ' ') chStr = "<space>";
        else if(a[i] == '\t') chStr = "<tab>";
        else if(a[i] == '\n') chStr = "<newline>";
        System.out.println(chStr + " is space.");
      }

      if(Character.isUpperCase(a[i]))
        System.out.println(a[i] + " is uppercase.");

      if(Character.isLowerCase(a[i]))
        System.out.println(a[i] + " is lowercase.");

      System.out.println();
    }
  }
}
```

In the output, notice that these match different sets of characters.

The output from this program is shown here:

```
a is a letter.
a is a letter or digit.
a is lowercase.

b is a letter.
b is a letter or digit.
b is lowercase.

5 is a digit.
5 is a letter or digit.


A is a letter.
A is a letter or digit.
```

```
A is uppercase.

<space> is whitespace.
<space> is space.

<tab> is whitespace.

<newline> is whitespace.
```

In the output, notice that there is a difference between **isSpaceChar( )** and **isWhitespace( )**. The **isSpaceChar( )** method matches spaces, which can also include line separators and paragraph separators. The **isWhitespace( )** method matches all whitespace, such as tabs and newlines.

Two other methods you may find interesting are **forDigit( )** and **digit( )**. They enable you to convert between integer values and the digits they represent. They are shown here:

> static char forDigit(int *num*, int *radix*)
> static int digit(char *digit*, int *radix*)

TABLE 23-1: A Sampling of Character Methods

Method	Description
static boolean isDigit(char *ch*)	Returns **true** if *ch* is a digit. Returns **false** for all other characters.
static boolean isJavaIdentifierPart(char *ch*)	Returns **true** if *ch* is allowed in a Java identifier, except that it can't be first. Returns **false** for all other characters.
static boolean isJavaIdentifierStart(char *ch*)	Returns **true** if *ch* is allowed as the first character of a Java identifier. Returns **false** for all other characters.
static boolean isletter(char *ch*)	Returns **true** if *ch* is a letter. Returns **false** for all other characters.
static boolean isLetterOrDigit(char *ch*)	Returns **true** if *ch* is a letter or a digit. Returns **false** for all other characters.
static boolean isLowerCase(char *ch*)	Returns **true** if *ch* is a lowercase letter. Returns **false** for all other characters.
static boolean isSpaceChar(char *ch*)	Returns **true** if *ch* is a space character, including paragraph and line separators. Returns **false** for all other characters.
static boolean isUpperCase(char *ch*)	Returns **true** if *ch* is an uppercase letter. Returns **false** for all other characters.
static boolean isWhitespace(char *ch*)	Returns **true** if *ch* is whitespace, such as spaces, tabs, and newlines. Returns **false** for all other characters.
static char toLowerCase(char *ch*)	Returns the lowercase representation of *ch*.
static char toUpperCase(char *ch*)	Returns the uppercase representation of *ch*.

forDigit( ) returns the digit character associated with the value of *num*. The radix of the conversion is specified by *radix*. **digit( )** returns the integer value associated with *digit* (which is presumably a digit) according to the radix specified by *radix*.

Character defines several constants and includes several other methods beyond those discussed here. It is a class that you will want to explore more fully as you advance in your study of Java.

Before leaving the topic of **Character**, it is necessary to mention a change that took place a few years ago. Beginning with JDK 5, the **Character** class has included support for 32-bit Unicode characters. In the past, all Unicode characters could be held by 16 bits, which is the size of a **char** (the value wrapped by **Character**). However, the Unicode character set was subsequently expanded, and more than 16 bits were required. The additional characters are called *supplementary characters*. Additions were made to **Character** to support the expanded Unicode set, including several overloaded methods that take an **int** instead of a **char** parameter. Also, in an array or string, when a character whose value is outside the range of **char** is needed, it is divided into two pieces, called a *low surrogate* and a *high surrogate*. Java uses UTF-16 (Unicode Transformation Format) to encode these characters. At this point in your study of Java, you won't typically need to use supplemental characters. However, they may be important in applications that you develop in your professional career.

Boolean

Boolean is a very thin wrapper around **boolean** values, which is useful mostly when you want to pass a **boolean** variable by reference. It implements **java.io.Serializable** and **Comparable<T>**. **Boolean** defines these constructors:

Boolean(boolean *boolValue*)
Boolean(String *boolString*)

In the first version, *boolValue* must be either **true** or **false**. In the second version, if *boolString* contains the string "true" (in upper case or lower case), then the new **Boolean** object will be **true**. Otherwise, it will be **false**.

Two of the constants specified by **Boolean** are **TRUE** and **FALSE**, which define true and false **Boolean** objects.

Boolean supplies a few methods of its own. One of particular interest is **parseBoolean( )** which converts a string into its **boolean** equivalent. It is shown here:

static boolean parseBoolean(String *str*)

If, independent of case differences, *str* contains the string "true", then **true** is returned. Any other value for *str* causes **parseBoolean( )** to return **false**.

Boolean's **toString( )** method returns "true" if the invoking value is **true**, and "false" if it is **false**.

Autoboxing and the Type Wrappers

As explained in Part One, because of autoboxing, you do not need to construct a type wrapper instance by explicitly invoking a constructor. For example, the variable **hypot** can be constructed using this line:

```
Double hypot = 170.54;
```

rather than

```
| Double hypot = new Double(170.54);
```

Autoboxing can be used with any of the type wrappers.

Progress Check

1. The **Byte**, **Short**, **Integer**, **Long**, **Float**, and **Double** wrapper classes are all subclasses of _____.
2. Because of the feature called _____, you rarely need to explicitly construct a wrapper for primitive values.
3. The primitive wrapper classes have two main benefits. The first is that they allow you to create an object representation of a primitive value. What is the second benefit?

THE Math CLASS

For some types of applications, one of the most important classes in **java.lang** will be **Math**. The **Math** class contains a large number of **static** methods that perform common mathematical functions, such as computing the sine of an angle or obtaining a logarithm. Therefore, if you will be "number crunching," you will likely be using methods defined by **Math**. Although **Math** defines too many methods for us to examine each one, a sampling is described here to give you a sense of what **Math** has to offer.

Note: If numerical analysis is a part of your future, then you will want to examine the **Math** *class in detail.*

Math defines a number of trigonometric methods. Here are the ones for sine, cosine, and tangent:

```
static double sin(double arg)
static double cos(double arg)
static double tan(double arg)
```

For each, *arg* specifies the angle in radians.

The arc sine, arc cosine, and arc tangent functions are supported by these methods:

```
static double asin(double arg)
static double acos(double arg)
static double atan(double arg)
```

These methods return the indicated result.

_____

Answers:

1. **Number**
2. autoboxing
3. They provide a useful set of methods and constants for working with the primitive values.

You can obtain the natural logarithm of a value by use of **log( )**. To obtain the base 10 logarithm, use **log10( )**. They are shown here:

    static double log(double *arg*)
    static double log10(double *arg*)

Here, *arg* specifies the value whose logarithm is being obtained.

To compute the result of raising a value to a specified power, use **pow( )**:

    static double pow(double *v*, double *x*)

It returns *v* raised to the *x*; for example, **pow(2.0, 3.0)** returns 8.0.

As you have already seen earlier in this book, you can obtain the square root of a value by calling **sqrt( )**. What might surprise you is that **Math** also supplies the method **cbrt( )**, which returns the cube root. Both methods are shown here:

    static double sqrt(double *arg*)
    static double cbrt(double *arg*)

The value for which the square or cube root is being obtained is passed in *arg*. The root is returned.

It is sometimes useful to obtain the *floor* or *ceiling* of a value. The floor is the largest whole number less than or equal to the value. The ceiling is the smallest whole number greater than or equal to the value. To perform these functions, **Math** includes **floor( )** and **ceil( )**, shown here:

    static double floor(double *arg*)
    static double ceil(double *arg*)

The floor or ceiling of *arg* is returned.

Math defines several overloaded versions of absolute value methods. They are shown here:

    static int abs(int *arg*)
    static long abs(long *arg*)
    static float abs(float *arg*)
    static double abs(double *arg*)

In each case, the absolute value of *arg* is returned.

It is often helpful to convert from radians to degrees, and vice versa. To handle these tasks, **Math** supplies **toDegree( )** and **toRadians( )**, shown next:

    static double toDegrees(double *angle*)
    static double toRadians(double *angle*)

For **toDegrees( )**, the angle passed to *angle* must be specified in radians. The result in degrees is returned. For **toRadians( )**, the angle passed to *angle* must be specified in degrees. The result in radians is returned.

Another interesting method is **hypot( )**:

    static double hypot(double *side1*, double *side2*)

Given the length of the two opposing sides, **hypot( )** returns the length of the hypotenuse of a right triangle. In other words, it returns the square root of the sum of the squares of *side1* and *side2*.

One way to obtain a pseudorandom number is to use **Math**'s **random( )** method shown here:

> static double random( )

It returns a pseudorandom number between 0 and 1.

In addition to the methods defined by **Math**, it also declares two **static final** constants. The first is **E**, which is approximately 2.72. The second is **PI**, which is approximately 3.14. You can use these constants instead of entering the values by hand.

The following program demonstrates several of the **Math** functions.

```java
// Demonstrate several Math functions.

class MathDemo {
  public static void main(String[] args) {

    // convert between radians and degrees
    double theta = 120.0;

    System.out.println(theta + " degrees is " +
                       Math.toRadians(theta) + " radians.");

    theta = 1.312;
    System.out.println(theta + " radians is " +
                       Math.toDegrees(theta) + " degrees\n");

    // demonstrate sin() and asin()
    theta = 1.0;
    double sine = Math.sin(theta);
    double asine = Math.asin(sine);
    System.out.println("Sine of " + theta + " is " + sine);
    System.out.println("Arc sine of " + sine + " is " + asine + "\n");

    // find the hypotenuse of a right triangle
    double h = Math.hypot(3.0, 4.0);
    System.out.println("Hypotenuse is " + h + "\n");

    // compute a power
    double p = Math.pow(3.0, 3.0);
    System.out.println("pow(3.0, 3.0) is " + p + "\n");

    // use log10()
    double lg = Math.log10(100.0);
    System.out.println("log10(100.0) is " + lg + "\n");

    // display E and PI
    System.out.println("PI: " + Math.PI + "\n E: " + Math.E);
  }
}
```

The output is shown here:

```
120.0 degrees is 2.0943951023931953 radians.
1.312 radians is 75.17206272116401 degrees

Sine of 1.0 is 0.8414709848078965
Arc sine of 0.8414709848078965 is 1.0

Hypotenuse is 5.0

pow(3.0, 3.0) is 27.0

log10(100.0) is 2.0

PI: 3.141592653589793
 E: 2.718281828459045
```

Ask the Expert

Q What are some of the other methods in the **Math** class?

A One interesting method is **copySign( )** with the following form:

static double copySign(double *value*, double *signValue*)

This method changes the sign of the first argument so that it matches the sign of the second argument and returns the result. For example, **copySign(3.14, −4)** returns −3.14 and **copySign(−3.14, 5.3)** returns 3.14.

Another interesting method is **exp( )** with the following form:

static double exp(double *arg*)

This method computes e^{arg} where e is the mathematical constant that is represented in Java by the value **Math.E**. In other words, **exp(arg)** is just a convenience method that does the same thing as **pow(Math.E, arg)**.

Progress Check

1. To raise a number to a power, use the **Math.**_____ method.
2. To convert radians to degrees, use the **Math.**_____ method.

_____

Answers:

1. **pow( )**
2. **toDegrees( )**

THE Process CLASS

The abstract **Process** class encapsulates a *process*—that is, an executing program. It is used primarily as a superclass for the type of objects created by **start( )** in the **ProcessBuilder** class, or by **exec( )** in the **Runtime** class. **Process** contains the abstract methods shown here.

Method	Description
void destroy( )	Terminates the process.
int exitValue( )	Returns an exit code obtained from the process.
InputStream getErrorStream( )	Returns an input stream that reads input from the process's **err** output stream.
InputStream getInputStream( )	Returns an input stream that reads input from the process's **out** output stream.
OutputStream getOutputStream( )	Returns an output stream that writes output to the process's **in** input stream.
int waitFor( ) throws InterruptedException	Returns the exit code obtained from the process. This method does not return until the process on which it is called terminates.

Pay special attention to **exitValue( )**, **destroy( )**, and **waitFor( )**. We will be using these methods in the examples in the following section.

THE ProcessBuilder CLASS

Subject to security restrictions, Java allows you to start the execution of another heavyweight process (that is, another program) through the use of the **ProcessBuilder** class. As just explained, all processes are represented by the **Process** class. **ProcessBuilder** creates a new process and gives you access to it through a **Process** instance. As you will see, creating a new process is an easy job. The following examples demonstrate the procedure. Keep in mind, however, that unsigned (untrusted) applets cannot start a new process because of security restrictions.

ProcessBuilder defines two constructors. The one used here is:

    ProccessBuilder(String ... *args*)

Here, *args* is a list of arguments that specify the name of the program to be executed along with any required command-line arguments. Notice that *args* is a varargs parameter. This means that you can pass it a list of arguments, or an array of arguments.

Creating an instance of **ProcessBuilder** does not start execution of the process. Instead, the process must be started by use of the **start( )** method, shown here:

    Process start( ) throws IOException

The **start( )** method begins the process specified by the invoking object. In other words, it runs the specified program. It returns a **Process** object that encapsulates the process. Thus, the new process can be managed through the **Process** instance.

Here is an example that executes the Windows text editor **notepad**. Notice that it specifies the name of the file to edit as an argument. (If you are not using Windows, then substitute an appropriate program supplied by your operating system.)

```
// Demonstrate ProcessBuilder.

import java.io.IOException;

class PBDemo {
  public static void main(String[] args) {

    try {
      ProcessBuilder procBldr =
        new ProcessBuilder("notepad", "testfile");
      procBldr.start();  ←──────────────────────  Start the process.
    } catch (IOException exc) {
      System.out.println("Error executing notepad.\n" + exc);
    }
  }
}
```

The **Process** object returned by **ProcessBuilder** can be managed by **Process**'s methods after the new program starts running. For example, the **waitFor( )** method causes your program to wait until the child process finishes. It then returns the value returned by the child process. This is typically 0 if no problems occur. Here is the preceding example modified to wait for the running process to exit:

```
// Wait until the process is terminated.

import java.io.IOException;

class PBDemo2 {
  public static void main(String[] args) {
    try {
      ProcessBuilder procBldr =
        new ProcessBuilder("notepad", "testfile");

      Process p = procBldr.start();
      p.waitFor();  ←──────────────────────  Wait for the process to end.
      System.out.println("Notepad returned " + p.exitValue());
    } catch (IOException exc) {
      System.out.println("Error executing notepad.\n" + exc);
    } catch (InterruptedException exc) {
      System.out.println("Wait interrupted\n" + exc);
    }

  }
}
```

You can terminate the child process with the **destroy( )** method. The following program illustrates this by starting **notepad**, waiting two seconds, and then terminating it via **destroy( )**.

```java
// Demonstrate destroy().

import java.io.IOException;

class PBDemo3 {
  public static void main(String[] args) {
    try {
      ProcessBuilder procBldr =
        new ProcessBuilder("notepad", "testfile");

      Process p = procBldr.start();

      try {
        Thread.sleep(2000);
      } catch (InterruptedException exc) {
        System.out.println("Sleep interrupted\n" + exc);
      }

      // terminate the process.
      p.destroy();  ◀─────────────────── Terminate the process.

    } catch (IOException exc) {
      System.out.println("Error executing notepad.\n" + exc);
    }
  }
}
```

ProcessBuilder provides several other features, such as the ability to access the run-time environment, set the directory, and redirect a process's standard input, output, and error streams. You might want to explore these on your own.

THE Runtime CLASS

The **Runtime** class encapsulates the run-time environment. Using **Runtime**, you can call several methods related to the state and behavior of the Java Virtual Machine. For example, you can execute other processes (although **ProcessBuilder** is often a better choice), obtain the number of available processors, check memory levels, request garbage collection, and exit the program, among other uses.

Runtime does not define any constructors. Instead, you acquire a reference to the run-time environment by calling the **static** method **Runtime.getRuntime( )**, shown here:

    static Runtime getRuntime( )

You can access the run-time environment through the returned reference.

Here we will look at one example that uses **Runtime**. Although Java provides automatic garbage collection, sometimes you will want to know how much memory is available for your program to use and how much of it is left. You can use this information, for example, to check your code for efficiency or to approximate how many more objects of a certain type can be instantiated. To obtain these values, use the **totalMemory( )** and **freeMemory( )** methods, shown here:

> long totalMemory( )
> long freeMemory( )

The **totalMemory( )** method returns the total number of bytes of memory available to the JVM. The **freeMemory( )** method returns the approximate number of bytes of memory that is currently unused.

As mentioned in Part One, Java's garbage collector runs periodically to recycle unused objects. However, you can also request garbage collection. One way to do this is by calling **Runtime**'s **gc( )** method shown next:

> void gc( )

Understand that, normally, there is no need for your program to call **gc( )**, because the JVM will automatically initiate garbage collection when it deems it appropriate. The **gc( )** method simply lets you request garbage collection at a time of your choosing.

Through the use of **gc( )** and **freeMemory( )**, you can obtain information about how your program uses memory. For example, to check the memory usage of a portion of your program, first call **gc( )** followed by a call to **freeMemory( )**. This will give you a baseline memory usage. Next, execute that portion of your code in which you are interested, followed by another call to **freeMemory( )**. The difference between the two calls to **freeMemory( )** indicates (approximately) how much memory was allocated by the objects being created. The following program illustrates this procedure. It also demonstrates **totalMemory( )**.

```
// Demonstrate totalMemory(), freeMemory() and gc().

class MemoryDemo {
  public static void main(String[] args) {
    Runtime r = Runtime.getRuntime();
    long mem1, mem2;
    Integer[] someints = new Integer[1000];

    System.out.println("Total memory is: " +
                       r.totalMemory());
    mem1 = r.freeMemory();
    System.out.println("Initial free memory: " + mem1);
    r.gc();
    mem1 = r.freeMemory();
    System.out.println("Free memory after garbage collection: "
                       + mem1);

    for(int i=0; i<1000; i++)
      someints[i] = new Integer(i); // allocate integers
```

```
    mem2 = r.freeMemory();
    System.out.println("Free memory after allocation: "
                        + mem2);
    System.out.println("Memory used by allocation: "
                        + (mem1-mem2));

    // discard Integers
    for(int i=0; i<1000; i++) someints[i] = null;

    r.gc(); // request garbage collection

    mem2 = r.freeMemory();
    System.out.println("Free memory after collecting" +
                        " discarded Integers: " + mem2);
  }
}
```

Sample output from this program is shown here (of course, your actual results may vary):

```
Total memory is: 16252928
Initial free memory: 15956816
Free memory after garbage collection: 16173656
Free memory after allocation: 15989984
Memory used by allocation: 183672
Free memory after collecting discarded Integers: 16173216
```

Progress Check

1. What class do you use to start up an external process?
2. What abilities does the **Runtime** class have?

THE System CLASS

The **System** class holds a collection of static methods and variables. As you already know, the standard input, output, and error output of the Java run time are stored in **System**'s **in**, **out**, and **err** variables. A sampling of the methods defined by **System** is shown in Table 23-2. Several of these methods can throw a **SecurityException** if the requested operation is not allowed because of security restrictions. Notice that **System** also provides a **gc( )** method, which is a **static** member. Thus it can be called directly without creating a **System** object. The following sections look at four common uses of **System**.

Answers:

1. **ProcessBuilder**
2. The ability to modify and give you information about the run-time environment.

TABLE 23-2: A Sampling of the Methods Defined by System	
Method	**Description**
static void arraycopy(Object *source*, int *sourceStart*, Object *target*, int *targetStart*, int *size*)	Copies an array. The array to be copied is passed in *source*, and the index at which point the copy will begin within *source* is passed in *sourceStart*. The array that will receive the copy is passed in *target*, and the index at which point the copy will begin within *target* is passed in *targetStart*. *size* is the number of elements that are copied.
static long currentTimeMillis( )	Returns the current time in terms of milliseconds since midnight, January 1, 1970.
static void exit(int *exitCode*)	Halts execution and returns the value of *exitCode* to the parent process. By convention, 0 indicates normal termination. All other values indicate some form of error.
static void gc( )	Requests garbage collection.
static String getProperty(String *which*)	Returns the property associated with *which*. A **null** object is returned if the desired property is not found.
static long nanoTime( )	Returns a value in terms of nanoseconds since some unspecified starting point.
static void setErr(PrintStream *eStream*)	Sets the standard **err** stream to *eStream*.
static void setIn(InputStream *iStream*)	Sets the standard **in** stream to *iStream*.
static void setOut(PrintStream *oStream*)	Sets the standard **out** stream to *oStream*.

Using currentTimeMillis( ) to Time Program Execution

One use of the **System** class that you might find particularly interesting is to use the **currentTimeMillis( )** method to time how long various parts of your program take to execute. The **currentTimeMillis( )** method returns the current time in terms of milliseconds since midnight, January 1, 1970. To time a section of your program, store this value just before beginning the section in question. Immediately upon completion, call **currentTimeMillis( )** again. The elapsed time will be the ending time minus the starting time (plus the overhead of the statements that call **currentTimeMillis( )**). The following program demonstrates this:

```
// Timing program execution.

class Elapsed {
  public static void main(String[] args) {
    long start, end;

    System.out.println("Timing a for loop from 0 to 100,000,000");

    // time a for loop from 0 to 100,000,000
```

```
    start = System.currentTimeMillis(); // get starting time
    for(long i=0; i < 100000000L; i++) ;
    end = System.currentTimeMillis(); // get ending time

    System.out.println("Elapsed time: " + (end-start));
  }
}
```

Here is a sample run (remember that your results probably will differ):

```
Timing a for loop from 0 to 100,000,000
Elapsed time: 62
```

If your system has a timer that offers nanosecond precision, then you could rewrite the preceding program to use **nanoTime( )** rather than **currentTimeMillis( )**. For example, here is the key portion of the program rewritten to use **nanoTime( )**:

```
start = System.nanoTime(); // get starting time
for(long i=0; i < 100000000L; i++) ;
end = System.nanoTime(); // get ending time
```

Using arraycopy( )

The **arraycopy( )** method can be used to quickly copy an array of any type from one place to another. This is much faster than the equivalent loop written out longhand in Java. Here is an example of two arrays being copied by the **arraycopy( )** method. First, **a** is copied to **b**. Next, all of **a**'s elements are shifted *down* by one. Then, **b** is shifted *up* by one.

```
// Using arraycopy().

class ACDemo {
  static byte[] a = { 65, 66, 67, 68, 69, 70, 71, 72, 73, 74 };
  static byte[] b = { 77, 77, 77, 77, 77, 77, 77, 77, 77, 77 };

  public static void main(String[] args) {
    System.out.println("a = " + new String(a));
    System.out.println("b = " + new String(b));
    System.arraycopy(a, 0, b, 0, a.length);
    System.out.println("a = " + new String(a));
    System.out.println("b = " + new String(b));
    System.arraycopy(a, 0, a, 1, a.length - 1);
    System.arraycopy(b, 1, b, 0, b.length - 1);
    System.out.println("a = " + new String(a));
    System.out.println("b = " + new String(b));
  }
}
```

As you can see from the following output, you can copy using the same source and destination in either direction:

```
a = ABCDEFGHIJ
b = MMMMMMMMMM
```

```
a = ABCDEFGHIJ
b = ABCDEFGHIJ
a = AABCDEFGHI
b = BCDEFGHIJJ
```

Obtaining Property Values

Java defines a number of properties, called *system properties*, which contain useful information about the Java execution environment. The names of the properties include those shown here.

file.separator	java.specification.version	java.vm.version
java.class.path	java.vendor	line.separator
java.class.version	java.vendor.url	os.arch
java.compiler	java.version	os.name
java.ext.dirs	java.vm.name	os.version
java.home	java.vm.specification.name	path.separator
java.io.tmpdir	java.vm.specification.vendor	user.dir
java.library.path	java.vm.specification.version	user.home
java.specification.name	java.vm.vendor	user.name
java.specification.vendor		

You can obtain the values of these properties by calling the **System.getProperty( )** method. For example, the following program displays the path to the current user directory, the version of Java, the name of the operating system, and the character used as a file separator.

```java
class ShowProperties {
  public static void main(String[] args) {
    System.out.println(System.getProperty("user.dir"));
    System.out.println(System.getProperty("java.version"));
    System.out.println(System.getProperty("os.name"));
    System.out.println(System.getProperty("file.separator"));
  }
}
```

Redirecting Standard I/O Streams

The **System** class defines the methods **setIn( )**, **setErr( )**, and **setOut( )** that let you redirect a standard stream. For example, instead of writing to console, **System.out** could write to a file. The following program shows an example. It redirects **System.out** to the file whose name is specified as a command-line argument.

```java
// Redirect System.out to a file.

import java.io.*;
```

```
class RedirectOut {
  public static void main(String[] args) throws IOException
  {

    // First, confirm that a file has been specified.
    if(args.length != 1) {
      System.out.println("RedirectOut: to");
      return;
    }

    // Create a Printstream linked to the specified file.
    try (PrintStream fout = new PrintStream(args[0]))
    {
      // save original System.out
      PrintStream orgOut = System.out;

      // redirect System.out to the file.
      System.setOut(fout);                          Redirect System.out to fout.

      // notice that System.out is used here
      System.out.println("This goes in the file.");

      // restore original System.out
      System.setOut(orgOut);

      System.out.println("This is shown on the screen.");

    } catch(IOException exc) {
      System.out.println("I/O Error: " + exc);
    }
  }
}
```

There are several interesting points in this program. First, notice how a new **PrintStream** is created. **PrintStream** defines several constructors. The one used by the program is shown here:

PrintStream(String *filename*) throws FileNotFoundException

It opens (or creates if necessary) the files specified by *filename* for output. If the file can't be opened, a **FileNotFoundException** will be thrown. Recall that **FileNotFoundException** is a subclass of **IOException**. Because it is opened in a **try**-with-resources statement, the file is automatically closed when the **try** block is exited.

Next, the program saves the reference to the current **System.out** stream. Then, using **setOut( )**, it redirects **System.out** to the file and outputs a line of text. That output will be written to the file. Next, the original **System.out** is restored, and a line of text is written to the console.

Progress Check

1. In a Java program, you can determine whether the program is being run on a Windows computer or a Mac. True or False?
2. The method in the **System** class for copying an array is named _____.
3. What does the method **currentTimeMillis( )** in the **System** class return?

THE Object CLASS

Object is a superclass of all other classes. It was introduced in Chapter 7. For convenience, the methods defined by **Object** are shown in Table 23-3. Most of **Object**'s methods have already been described elsewhere in this book. However, two merit a brief discussion. The first is **clone( )**. This method returns a copy of the object on which it is called. The invoking object's class must implement the **Cloneable** interface. If it doesn't, a **CloneNotSupportedException** is thrown. This interface has no members; it simply indicates that the class allows instances to be cloned. Cloning is potentially risky because it can cause unintended side effects. For example, the **Object** version of **clone( )** creates an object whose members are the same as those as the original object. Thus, if a member is a reference to some other object, then both the original and the clone will refer to the same object, and either can change the state of that object. Therefore, as a general rule, **clone( )** will need to be overridden to prevent such problems. Because cloning is a specialized technique, it is not discussed further in this book.

The second method is **hashCode( )**. This method returns a *hash code* for the invoking object. In somewhat simplified terms, a hash code is a value that is derived from some aspect of the object. Hash codes are especially useful when storing objects in some types of collections. (See Chapter 25.)

THE Class CLASS

Class encapsulates information about a class or interface. Objects of type **Class** are created automatically when classes are loaded. You cannot explicitly declare a **Class** object. Generally, you obtain a **Class** object by calling the **getClass( )** method defined by **Object**. **Class** is a generic type that is declared as shown here:

    class Class<T>

Here, **T** is the type of the class or interface represented.

The methods defined by **Class** are often useful in situations where run-time type information about an object is required. Methods are provided that allow you to determine additional information about a particular class, such as its public constructors,

---

Answers:

1. True. You can do so by calling **System.getProperty("os.name")**.
2. **arraycopy**
3. A **long** value giving the number of milliseconds since midnight, January 1, 1970.

TABLE 23-3: The Methods Defined by Object

Method	Description
Object clone( ) throws CloneNotSupportedException	Creates a new object that is the same as the invoking object.
boolean equals(Object *object*)	Returns **true** if the invoking object is equivalent to *object*.
void finalize( ) throws Throwable	Default **finalize( )** method. It is called before an unused object is recycled.
final Class<?> getClass( )	Obtains a **Class** object that describes the invoking object.
int hashCode( )	Returns the hash code associated with the invoking object.
final void notify( )	Resumes execution of a thread waiting on the invoking object.
final void notifyAll( )	Resumes execution of all threads waiting on the invoking object.
String toString( )	Returns a string that describes the object.
final void wait( ) throws InterruptedException	Waits on another thread of execution.
final void wait(long *milliseconds*) throws InterruptedException	Waits up to the specified number of *milliseconds* on another thread of execution.
final void wait(long *milliseconds*, int *nanoseconds*) throws InterruptedException	Waits up to the specified number of *milliseconds* plus *nanoseconds* on another thread of execution.

fields, and methods. You can also obtain information about interfaces. Among other things, this is important for Java's reflection features.

Although a more sophisticated use of **Class** is beyond the scope of this book, the following program will demonstrate two of its capabilities. It uses **getClass( )** (inherited from **Object**) to obtain a **Class** reference. It then demonstrates the **getName( )** and **getSuperclass( )** methods, defined by **Class**. These methods are shown here:

        String getName( )
        Class<? super T> getSuperclass( )

The **getName( )** method returns the name of the class represented by the invoking **Class** instance. The **getSuperclass( )** method returns a reference to a **Class** object that represents the superclass of the invoking **Class** object.

```
// Demonstrate Run Time Type Information.

class X {
  int a;
  float b;
}

class Y extends X {
  double c;
}
```

```
class RTTI {
  public static void main(String[] args) {
    X x = new X();
    Y y = new Y();
    Class<?> clObj;

    clObj = x.getClass(); // get Class reference
    System.out.println("x is object of type: " +
                        clObj.getName());

    clObj = y.getClass(); // get Class reference
    System.out.println("y is object of type: " +
                        clObj.getName());
    clObj = clObj.getSuperclass();          ◄─────────────── Notice how the superclass
    System.out.println("y's superclass is " +                is obtained.
                        clObj.getName());
  }
}
```

The output from this program is shown here:

```
x is object of type: X
y is object of type: Y
y's superclass is X
```

THE Enum CLASS

As described in Chapter 13, enumerations are integrated into the Java language via the **enum** keyword. All such enumerations automatically inherit **Enum**. **Enum** is a generic class that is declared as shown here:

>   abstract class Enum<E extends Enum<E>>

Here, **E** stands for the enumeration type. **Enum** has no public constructors. It was first discussed in Chapter 13.

In addition to the methods described in Chapter 13, here is one more that you might find interesting:

>   static <T extends Enum<T>> T valueOf(Class<T> *e-type*, String *name*)

The **valueOf( )** method returns the constant associated with *name* in the enumeration type specified by *e-type*.

THREAD-RELATED CLASSES
AND THE Runnable INTERFACE

Java's key thread-related classes are packaged in **java.lang**. These are

>   **Runnable**
>   **Thread**

ThreadGroup

ThreadLocal

InheritableThreadLocal

Two of these, the **Runnable** interface and the **Thread** class, were already extensively described in Chapter 12. A **ThreadGroup** creates a group of threads. Thread groups offer a convenient way to manage groups of threads as a unit. **ThreadLocal** is used to create thread local variables. Each thread will have its own copy of a thread local variable. **InheritableThreadLocal** creates thread local variables that may be inherited.

OTHER CLASSES

In addition to the classes just described and those described elsewhere in this book, **java.lang** includes several others. They are summarized here:

ClassLoader	An abstract class that determines how classes are loaded.
ClassValue<T>	This is a special-use class added by JDK 7 that associates a value with a type.
Compiler	Supports environments in which Java bytecode is compiled into executable code rather than interpreted. It is not for normal programming use.
Package	Encapsulates information about a package. Among other things, this information includes such things as its name, version, title, vendor, and annotations.
RuntimePermission	Relates to Java's security mechanism. It encapsulates a permission available at run time.
SecurityManager	Defines a security manager.
StackTraceElement	Describes a stack frame, which is an individual element of a stack trace when an exception occurs.
StrictMath	Defines a complete set of mathematical methods that parallel those in **Math**. The difference is that the **StrictMath** version is guaranteed to generate precisely identical results across all implementations, whereas the methods in **Math** are given more latitude in order to improve performance.
Void	Represents the **void** type.

THE java.lang INTERFACES

The **java.lang** package defines eight top-level interfaces. The **Runnable** interface was described earlier in this book, in Chapter 12, when multithreading was described. The **Cloneable** interface was mentioned when **Object** was described. The others are examined here.

The Comparable Interface

Objects of classes that implement **Comparable** can be ordered. In other words, classes that implement **Comparable** contain objects that can be compared in some meaningful manner. **Comparable** is generic and is declared like this:

    interface Comparable<T>

Here, **T** represents the type of objects being compared.

The **Comparable** interface declares one method that is used to determine what Java calls the *natural ordering* of instances of a class. The general form of the method is shown here:

    int compareTo(T *obj*)

This method compares the invoking object with *obj*. It returns 0 if the values are equal. A negative value is returned if the invoking object has a lower value. Otherwise, a positive value is returned.

As a general rule, the outcome of comparing two objects with **compareTo( )** should be compatible with the outcome of comparing those two objects with **equals( )**. Therefore, if the two objects are equal according to **equals( )**, then **compareTo( )** should return zero, and vice versa.

This interface is implemented by several of the classes already discussed in this book, such as **Byte**, **Character**, **Double**, **Float**, **Long**, **Short**, **String**, and **Integer**.

TRY THIS 23-1   CREATE A GENERIC METHOD FOR FINDING THE MINIMUM IN AN ARRAY

Finder.java
MinElementDemo.java

Suppose you have an array and you want to find the minimum element. This is easy if the elements are integers. (See the **MinMax** example in Chapter 5.) It is also easy if the elements are strings for which the "minimum" string is the string that comes first alphabetically. For example, here is one way to write a method that finds the minimum element in a non-empty array of strings:

```
String minStr(String[] data) {
   String currMin = data[0];

   for(String s : data)
     if(s.compareTo(currMin) < 0) currMin = s;

   return currMin;
}
```

This method works by looping through the array comparing the values and keeping track of the smallest one found. After the loop ends, the value in **currMin** will be the smallest value, which is returned. Notice that strings are compared by use of the **compareTo( )** method, which is specified by the **Comparable** interface and implemented by **String**. (See Chapter 22.)

Can we use the same basic approach for other types of arrays, such as **Integer** arrays or arrays of user-defined types? More precisely, can we adapt the logic in **minStr( )** to create a generic method that finds the minimum value in different types of arrays? The answer is Yes if the array's element type implements the **Comparable** interface. If a class implements this interface, then we can use the **compareTo( )** method to compare objects of that class.

In this project, we create a generic method called **minElement( )** that finds the minimum element of any type of array, as long as the element type implements the **Comparable** interface.

STEP-BY-STEP

1. Create a new file called **Finder.java**. The generic **minElement( )** method will be contained in a class called **Finder**. Furthermore, **minElement( )** will be **static**, so that no object of type **Finder** need be instantiated. This makes it more convenient to use. Enter the following code into **Finder.java**:

    ```java
    class Finder {

      public static <T extends Comparable<T>> T minElement(T[] data) {
        T currMin = data[0];

        for(T x : data) {
          if (x.compareTo(currMin) < 0)
            currMin = x;
        }
        return currMin;
      }
    }
    ```

2. Let's examine the **minElement( )** method in detail. It looks very much like the **minStr( )** method above except that it is a generic method with type parameter **T**. The type **T** can be any type as long as it implements the **Comparable<T>** interface. This means that elements of type **T** can be compared to each other using the **compareTo( )** method.

    Because the **String** class implements **Comparable**, the **minElement( )** method can replace the **minStr( )** method shown above. The type wrappers, such as **Integer** and **Double**, also implement **Comparable**. This means that you can use **minElement( )** to find the minimum in arrays of **Integers**, for example. In general, **minElement( )** can be used to find the minimum element of any non-empty array, including those of user-defined types, as long as the element type implements **Comparable**.

3. To see how **minElement( )** works with arrays of integers, arrays of strings, and arrays of **Double**s, create a file called **MinElementDemo.java** that contains the following code:

```
class MinElementDemo {
  public static void main(String[] args) {
    Integer[] intArray = { 3, 1, 4, 3, 6, 5};
    int intMin = Finder.minElement(intArray);
    System.out.println(intMin);

    String[] strArray = {"every", "good", "boy", "does", "fine"};
    String strMin = Finder.minElement(strArray);
    System.out.println(strMin);

    Double[] doubleArray = {3.14, 2.8, 6.023, 1.414};
    Double doubleMin = Finder.minElement(doubleArray);
    System.out.println(doubleMin);
  }
}
```

Notice that the **minElement( )** method is called three times, each time with an array of a different type. When you run the **main( )** method in the **MinDemo** class, you will get the following output:

```
1
boy
1.414
```

4. You can use the same basic approach used by **minElement( )** whenever you create a generic method that needs to compare objects. Simply specify that the type parameter extends **Comparable**. Then, use **compareTo( )** to compare objects.

The Appendable Interface

Objects of a class that implements **Appendable** can have a character or character sequences appended to it. **Appendable** defines these three methods:

Appendable append(char *ch*) throws IOException

Appendable append(CharSequence *chars*) throws IOException

Appendable append(CharSequence *chars*, int *begin*, int *end*)
                               throwsIOException

In the first form, the character *ch* is appended to the invoking object. In the second form, the character sequence *chars* is appended to the invoking object. The third form allows you to indicate a portion (the characters running from *begin* through *end*–1) of the sequence specified by *chars*. In all cases, a reference to the invoking object is returned.

The Iterable Interface

Iterable must be implemented by any class whose objects will be used by the for-each version of the **for** loop. In other words, in order for an object to be used within a for-each style **for** loop, its class must implement **Iterable**. **Iterable** is a generic interface that has this declaration:

> interface Iterable<T>

Here, **T** is the type of the elements being iterated. It defines one method, **iterator( )**, which is shown here:

> Iterator<T> iterator( )

It returns an iterator to the elements contained in the invoking object.

Note: Iterators are described in detail in Chapter 25.

The Readable Interface

The **Readable** interface indicates that an object can be used as a source for characters. It defines one method called **read( )**, which is shown here:

> int read(CharBuffer *buf*) throws IOException

This method reads characters into *buf*. It returns the number of characters read, or −1 if the invoking object is empty.

The CharSequence Interface

The **CharSequence** interface defines methods that read from a sequence of characters. These methods are shown here:

> char charAt(int *idx*)
> int length( )
> CharSequence subSequence(int *startIdx*, int *stopIdx*)
> String toString( )

The **charAt( )** method returns the character at the index specified by *idx*. The number of characters in the invoking sequence is returned by **length( )**. A subset of the invoking sequence beginning at *startIdx* and ending at *stopIdx*–1 is returned by **subSequence( )**. Finally, **toString( )** returns the **String** equivalent of the invoking sequence.

Ask the Expert

Q The **CharSequence** interface was mentioned in the last chapter, in conjunction with the **String** class. What other classes implement this interface, and why is it important?

A It is implemented by the **CharBuffer**, **Segment**, **String**, **StringBuffer**, and **StringBuilder** classes and is used in several packages in the JDK. The value of this interface, as in all interfaces, is that it helps minimize coupling, as described in Chapter 16. That is, classes that use this interface are less tightly bound, so they offer more flexibility and reusability.

Ask the Expert (Continued)

For example, one of the **replace( )** methods in the **String** class mentioned in the preceding chapter has the general form

String replace(CharSequence *original*, CharSequence *replacement*)

This method will take not only objects of class **String** as its parameters, but also objects of any class implementing the interface, such as **StringBuffer** and **StringBuilder**. Therefore, the method is much more useful than it would be if it had not used the **CharSequence** interface.

One other point: the **subSequence( )** method in the **CharSequence** interface returns a **CharSequence** instead of a **String** or another class. The advantage of doing so is, again, the flexibility it provides. In this case, the flexibility is of benefit to the implementer of the method, who can choose to create and return any kind of object he or she wants, as long as it implements the interface.

The AutoCloseable Interface

AutoCloseable was added by JDK 7, and it provides support for the **try**-with-resources statement, which implements what is sometimes referred to as *automatic resource management* (ARM). The **try**-with-resources statement automates the process of releasing a resource (such as a stream) when it is no longer needed. (See Chapter 11 for details.) Only objects of classes that implement **AutoCloseable** can be used with **try**-with-resources. The **AutoCloseable** interface defines only the **close( )** method, which is shown here:

void close( ) throws Exception

This method closes the invoking object, releasing any resources that it may hold. It is automatically called at the end of a **try**-with-resources statement, thus eliminating the need to explicitly invoke **close( )**. **AutoCloseable** is implemented by several classes, including all of the I/O classes that open a stream that can be closed.

Progress Check

1. What methods do you call to obtain the class and superclass of an object?
2. What interface declares a method that is used to determine the "natural" ordering of objects of a class?
3. What interface must a class implement if it is to allow the use of for-each loops for accessing the data of objects of the class?

Answers:

1. **getClass( )** and **getSuperclass( )**
2. **Comparable<T>**
3. **Iterable<T>**

EXERCISES

1. The classes that are used to encapsulate primitive values so that they can be used where only objects are allowed are called _____ classes.

2. Infinity is not a number. More precisely, for a **double d**, if **isInfinite(d)** is **true**, then **isNaN(d)** is **true**. True or False?

3. The **Double.MIN_VALUE** is the smallest positive **double** value, and **Integer.MIN_VALUE** is the smallest positive integer value (namely, 1). True or False?

4. Determine the values of the following expressions. The constants are all defined in the **Double** class:

   A. MAX_VALUE / MIN_VALUE
   B. MAX_VALUE * MAX_VALUE
   C. POSITIVE_INFINITY / POSITIVE_INFINITY
   D. POSITIVE_INFINITY / NEGATIVE_INFINITY
   E. POSITIVE_INFINITY − POSITIVE_INFINITY
   F. POSITIVE_INFINITY − NEGATIVE_INFINITY
   G. NaN − NaN

5. For every character **ch**, the expression

   ```
   Character.isUpperCase(Character.toUpperCase(ch))
   ```

   evaluates to **true**. True or False?

6. For every **double d**, the expression **Math.ceil(Math.floor(d))** is equal to the expression **Math.floor(Math.ceil(d))**. True or False?

7. To start another program (another heavyweight process) in a Java program, you call the constructor for the **Process** class. True or False?

8. The **nanoTime( )** method in the **System** class returns the number of nanoseconds since midnight, January 1, 1970. True or False?

9. The **getName( )** method in **Class** returns just the name of the class without the package it is in. True or False?

10. Write a method **numWords( )** that takes a string as its parameter. It computes and returns the number of words in the string. For our purposes, a *word* is a substring consisting of one or more non-whitespace characters separated from other words by one or more whitespace characters. Loop through the characters in the string and use the **isWhitespace( )** method in the **Character** class.

11. Write a method **toAllUpperCase( )** that takes a string as its parameter. It returns a copy of the string in which all letters are now in upper case. Use the **toUpperCase( )** method in the **Character** class, not the **toUpperCase( )** method in the **String** class.

12. Will the following expression compile? If not, why not? If so, what is the value of the expression?

```
new Boolean(Boolean.parseBoolean(new
          Boolean("false").toString())).equals(Boolean.FALSE);
```

13. Modify the **PBDemo2** class so that its **main( )** method starts up a web browser on your computer and opens your favorite web page.

14. Write a program similar to **RedirectOut** that, instead of redirecting **System.out**, redirects **System.in** to get data from a file whose name is specified as a command-line argument.

15. Write a method **getLineage( )** that takes any object as its parameter. It returns an array of strings that contains the name of the object's class, the name of its superclass, the name of the superclass's superclass, and so on, all the way up to and including the **Object** class.

16. Write a program that creates two integer arrays of length 10 million or larger (assuming your system can handle arrays that large). Then it measures how long (in milliseconds) it takes to copy the data from the first array to the second array using two different approaches: using a **for** loop and using the **arraycopy( )** method in the **System** class. It then displays the time each approach takes.

17. Add a **maxElement( )** method to the **Finder** class defined in Try This 23-1. It is identical to the **minElement( )** method in the **Finder** class except that it returns the largest element in the array instead of the smallest element.

18. The **MemoryDemo** program showed that an array of 1,000 **Integer**s took about 183,672 bytes of memory. However, an **int** variable takes only 4 bytes. Therefore, shouldn't the array have taken only 4,000 bytes? Why did it take more?

19. Use the **Math** class to write a program that demonstrates the following equalities. More precisely, the program should calculate and display the values on the left side of each equality. For comparison purposes, it should also display the values on the right side of each equality. Recall that the mathematical constant e is represented by **Math.E** and π is represented by **Math.PI** in Java.

A. $e^{\log(2.0)} = 2.0$

B. $\log(e^{2.0}) = 2.0$

C. $\sin^2(\pi/3) + \cos^2(\pi/3) = 1.0$

D. $\tan(\arctan(\pi/3)) = \pi/3$

20. Implement a function **roundDownTenth( )** that takes a **double** value as its parameter. It rounds the value down to the nearest tenth and returns it. For example, **roundDownTenth(3.16)** returns 3.1 and **roundDownTenth(−3.51)** returns −3.6.

21. As noted in this chapter, the **Math** class declares two **static final** constants: **E** and **PI**. If you need to calculate the area of a circle given its radius **r**, which of the following expressions is better and why?

    A. **Math.PI * r * r**

    B. **3.141592653589793238462643 * r * r**

CHAPTER 24

Exploring java.util

KEY SKILLS & CONCEPTS

- Work with locales using the **Locale** class
- Work with date and time with the **Date**, **Calendar**, and **GregorianCalendar** classes
- Format output with the **Formatter** class
- Use the **printf( )** method for formatting
- Read formatted input with the **Scanner** class
- Generate pseudorandom numbers with the **Random** class
- Use the **Observable** class and the **Observer** interface
- Schedule tasks using the **Timer** and **TimerTask** classes

The **java.util** package defines classes and interfaces that handle a wide range of tasks that are commonly encountered when programming. For example, **java.util** contains the *Collections Framework*. The Collections Framework is one of Java's most powerful subsystems. It supports a sophisticated hierarchy of interfaces and classes that manage groups of objects. **java.util** also provides various utility classes, including those that format data for output, read formatted data, and work with date and time.

Because **java.util** supports such a wide range of functionality, it is quite large. It includes the following top-level classes:

AbstractCollection	EventObject	PropertyResourceBundle
AbstractList	FormattableFlags	Random
AbstractMap	Formatter	ResourceBundle
AbstractQueue	GregorianCalendar	Scanner
AbstractSequentialList	HashMap	ServiceLoader
AbstractSet	HashSet	SimpleTimeZone
ArrayDeque	Hashtable	Stack
ArrayList	IdentityHashMap	StringTokenizer

Arrays	LinkedHashMap	Timer
BitSet	LinkedHashSet	TimerTask
Calendar	LinkedList	TimeZone
Collections	ListResourceBundle	TreeMap
Currency	Locale	TreeSet
Date	Objects	UUID
Dictionary	Observable	Vector
EnumMap	PriorityQueue	WeakHashMap
EnumSet	Properties	
EventListenerProxy	PropertyPermission	

The top-level interfaces defined by **java.util** include those shown next:

Collection	Comparator	Deque
Enumeration	EventListener	Formattable
Iterator	List	ListIterator
Map	NavigableMap	NavigableSet
Observer	Queue	RandomAccess
Set	SortedMap	SortedSet

Although **java.util** is quite large, its size is made manageable by the fact that the classes and interfaces that comprise the Collections Framework can be examined separately, as a group. For this reason, the description of **java.util** is broken into two chapters. This chapter covers those parts of **java.util** that are not part of the Collections Framework. The Collections Framework is covered in the next chapter.

The primary focus of this chapter is on the next classes:

- **Locale**
- **Date**, **Calendar**, and **GregorianCalendar**
- **Formatter** and **Scanner**

The **Locale** class encapsulates information related to a geographic, political, or cultural region. It aids in internationalization. **Date**, **Calendar**, and **GregorianCalendar** manage date and time. The **Formatter** class formats data, and the **Scanner** class reads formatted data. Also covered are

- **Random**
- **Observer** and **Observable**
- **Timer** and **TimerTask**

Random is used to produce a sequence of pseudorandom numbers. **Observer** and **Observable** support the Observer pattern described in Chapter 16. **Timer** and **TimerTask** let you execute a thread at some future time. The remaining classes and interfaces that are not part of the Collections Framework are summarized at the end of this chapter.

THE Locale CLASS

The **Locale** class encapsulates information related to geopolitical or cultural conventions. It is one of several classes that help you write programs that can be internationalized. Internationalization is important to many commercial programs because they often have aspects that are locale-dependent. One locale-dependency is, of course, the language used for messages. However, other aspects of a program also depend on the locale. For example, the formats used to display dates, times, and numbers sometimes differ between countries or languages. The **Locale** class helps manage the differences between locales. Although internationalization is a very large topic that is beyond the scope of this book, the **Locale** class provides a starting point.

The **Locale** class implements the **Serializable** and **Cloneable** interfaces. Here are two of the constructors for **Locale**:

> Locale(String *language*)
>
> Locale(String *language*, String *country*)

These constructors build a **Locale** object to represent a specific language. The *language* parameter receives a *language code*, which must comply with ISO 639 (Codes for the Representation of Names of Languages). Examples are en, de, and fr, which correspond to English, German, and French, respectively. The *country* parameter specifies a country code, which can be one of the codes defined by ISO 3166 (Codes for the Representation of Names of Countries and Their Subdivisions). Examples are US, DE, and FR, for the United States, Germany, and France, respectively.

Note: ISO stands for International Organization for Standardization.

For example, the following constructs a **Locale** object that represents the conventions for English in the United States.

```
Locale usLocale = new Locale("en", "US");
```

Although the **Locale** constructor is not hard to use, **Locale** provides a convenient alternative for many common locales. It defines the following constants, which are **static final Locale** objects. You can use one when a locale corresponding to the name is needed.

CANADA	GERMAN	KOREAN
CANADA_FRENCH	GERMANY	PRC
CHINA	ITALIAN	SIMPLIFIED_CHINESE
CHINESE	ITALY	TAIWAN
ENGLISH	JAPAN	TRADITIONAL_CHINESE
FRANCE	JAPANESE	UK
FRENCH	KOREA	US

For example, the constant **Locale.CANADA** represents the **Locale** for Canada, the constant **Locale.GERMAN** represents the **Locale** for the German language, and **Locale.GERMANY** represents the **Locale** for Germany.

You can obtain the default **Locale** used by the JVM by calling **Locale.getDefault( )** shown here.

    static Locale getDefault( )

The default locale reflects the settings used by the system in which the JVM is running. It is the locale used when no other locale is explicitly specified.

Locale defines several methods that obtain information about a **Locale** instance. Here are three examples:

    final String getDisplayCountry( )

    final String getDisplayLanguage( )

    final String getDisplayName( )

These return localized strings that can be used to display the name of the country, the name of the language, and the complete name of the locale.

Here is an example that demonstrates **Locale**. First, it obtains the current locale, which in this case is the United States. It then displays the country, language, and name. Next, the program manually creates a locale for Germany and displays the country, language, and name. Finally, it displays the country, language, and name associated with the standard locale, **Locale.FRANCE**.

```
// Demonstrate Locale.
import java.util.*;

class LocaleDemo {
  public static void main(String[] args) {

    // get the default locale.
    Locale defLocale = Locale.getDefault();          Obtain the default locale.

    // display name, country, and language
    System.out.println("Default locale: ");
    System.out.println("Name: " + defLocale.getDisplayName());
    System.out.println("Country: " + defLocale.getDisplayCountry());
    System.out.println("Language: " + defLocale.getDisplayLanguage());

    System.out.println();

    // manually, create a locale for Germany
    Locale germanLocale = new Locale("de", "DE");          Create a locale for Germany.
    System.out.println("German locale: ");
    System.out.println("Name: " + germanLocale.getDisplayName());
    System.out.println("Country: " +
                      germanLocale.getDisplayCountry());
    System.out.println("Language: " +
                      germanLocale.getDisplayLanguage());

    System.out.println();
```

```
    // now, use standard locale for France.
    System.out.println("Locale.FRANCE: ");
    System.out.println("Name: " +
                    Locale.FRANCE.getDisplayName());    ◄──────── Use the locale for France.
    System.out.println("Country: " +
                    Locale.FRANCE.getDisplayCountry());
    System.out.println("Language: " +
                    Locale.FRANCE.getDisplayLanguage());
  }
}
```

Sample output is shown here:

```
Default locale:
Name: English (United States)
Country: United States
Language: English

German locale:
Name: German (Germany)
Country: Germany
Language: German

Locale.FRANCE:
Name: French (France)
Country: France
Language: French
```

Several classes in the Java API library operate in a locale-sensitive manner. These include **Calendar** and **GregorianCalendar** described in the next section, and **Formatter**, described a bit later.

Ask the Expert

Q I was looking through Java's online documentation for **Locale** and noticed that it mentions BCP 47 and UTS 35. What are these?

A JDK 7 added significant upgrades to the **Locale** class. Among them are support for Internet Engineering Task Force (IETF) BCP 47, which defines tags for identifying languages, and Unicode Technical Standard (UTS) 35, which defines the Locale Data Markup Language (LDML). As a consequence, several new methods were added to **Locale**. Also added was the **Locale.Builder** class, which constructs **Locale** instances. It ensures that a locale specification is well-formed as defined by BCP 47. (The **Locale** constructors do not provide such a check.)

Progress Check

1. The **Locale** constant that represents the United States is **Locale.**____.
2. To obtain the default locale used by the JVM on a system, use the **Locale static** method _____.

WORKING WITH DATE AND TIME

It is not uncommon for a program to need to use the date and time. Here are some examples. An order entry application might want to provide a time stamp that indicates when an order was placed. An inventory program might include a field that indicates when a new shipment of items is expected. You might want to display the current date and time as a user amenity. Whatever the reason, Java provides significant support for date and time through several classes. The ones discussed here are **Date**, **Calendar**, and **GregorianCalendar**.

Date

The **Date** class encapsulates date and time, and it was part of the original 1.0 release of Java. However, **Date** is less widely used than you might at first guess. The reason is that when Java 1.1 was released, many of the functions carried out by the original **Date** class were integrated into **Calendar** and **DateFormat** (which is part of **java.text**). As a result, many of the original 1.0 **Date** methods were *deprecated*. In the language of Java, deprecated means still supported, but obsolete. Since the deprecated 1.0 methods should not be used for new code, they are not described here.

Date supports the following nondeprecated constructors:

Date( )

Date(long *millisec*)

The first constructor initializes the object with the current date and time provided by the machine. The second constructor accepts one argument that equals the number of milliseconds that have elapsed since midnight, January 1, 1970. **Date** implements the **Comparable**, **Serializable**, and **Cloneable** interfaces.

Date supports a few nondeprecated methods. For example, you can obtain the date and time in terms of milliseconds from January 1, 1970 by calling the **getTime( )** method. You can set the date and time by calling **setTime( )** and passing in the number of milliseconds since January 1, 1970. You can compare **Date**s by use of **equals( )**, **compareTo( )**, **after( )**, and **before( )**. The **toString( )** method has been overridden to display a simple form of the date and time.

As explained, many of the methods defined by **Date** have been deprecated. These methods provided access to the individual components of the date and time, such as the hour, day, or year. However, because these methods are now deprecated,

Answers:

1. **US**
2. **getDefault( )**

they should not be used. Instead, to obtain this type of information, you will use the **Calendar** class, described next.

Calendar and GregorianCalendar

The modern way to work with date and time in Java is to use the abstract **Calendar** class and its concrete subclass **GregorianCalendar**. **Calendar** provides a set of methods that allow you to convert a date and time represented in terms of milliseconds to a number of useful components. For example, you can obtain the year, month, day, hour, minute, and second. **GregorianCalendar** is a subclass of **Calendar** that supports the familiar Gregorian Calendar.

    Calendar implements the **Serializable**, **Comparable**, and **Cloneable** interfaces. **Calendar** provides no public constructors. **Calendar** defines the following **static int** constants:

ALL_STYLES	FRIDAY	PM
AM	HOUR	SATURDAY
AM_PM	HOUR_OF_DAY	SECOND
APRIL	JANUARY	SEPTEMBER
AUGUST	JULY	SHORT
DATE	JUNE	SUNDAY
DAY_OF_MONTH	LONG	THURSDAY
DAY_OF_WEEK	MARCH	TUESDAY
DAY_OF_WEEK_IN_MONTH	MAY	UNDECIMBER
DAY_OF_YEAR	MILLISECOND	WEDNESDAY
DECEMBER	MINUTE	WEEK_OF_MONTH
DST_OFFSET	MONDAY	WEEK_OF_YEAR
ERA	MONTH	YEAR
FEBRUARY	NOVEMBER	ZONE_OFFSET
FIELD_COUNT	OCTOBER	

As you will see, several of these are useful when setting or getting a date or time component, such as the hour, the minute, or the year.

    Although **Calendar** is abstract, you can obtain a reference to a **Calendar** object by calling **getInstance( )**. It has several forms. Its simplest is shown here:

    static Calendar getInstance( )

It returns a reference to a **Calendar** object that contains the current system date and time. The default locale and time zone are used. Other forms let you specify a locale and a time zone. A key point to understand is that a **Calendar** object represents one specific instance in time.

    Calendar defines many methods. One of particular interest is **get( )**, which obtains the value of a time or date component, such as the hour, year, month, or day of week. It is shown here:

    int get(int *what*)

It returns the value of the time or date component indicated by *what*. The value passed to *what* must be one of the integer constants, just shown. For example, to obtain the year, pass **Calendar.YEAR**, to obtain the minute, pass **Calendar.MINUTE**, and so forth.

Another method that can be quite useful is **getDisplayName( )**, shown next:

String getDisplayName(int *what*, int *style*, Locale *loc*)

Here, *what* specifies the date or time component to obtain. It must be one of the previously shown values defined by **Calendar**. The *style* must be either **Calendar.SHORT** or **Calendar.LONG**. Some names, such as the month or the day of the week, have both a long and short form. This parameter lets you choose which you obtain. The locale that determines the specific representation of the name is passed in *loc*. Not all date and time components have string representations. If no string representation is available, **null** is returned.

GregorianCalendar is an implementation of **Calendar** that supports the standard Gregorian calendar which is in widespread use. **GregorianCalendar** adds two **static int** fields: **AD** and **BC**. These represent the two eras defined by the Gregorian calendar.

There are several constructors for **GregorianCalendar**. The default constructor initializes the object with the current date and time in the default locale and time zone. Other constructors let you construct a **GregorianCalendar** for a specific date and time. Here are three examples:

GregorianCalendar(int *year*, int *month*, int *day*)

GregorianCalendar(int *year*, int *month*, int *day*, int *hours*,
                  int *minutes*)

GregorianCalendar(int *year*, int *month*, int *day*, int *hours*,
                  int *minutes*, int *seconds*)

All three versions set the day, month, and year. Here, *year* specifies the year. The month is specified by *month*, with zero indicating January. The day of the month is specified by *day*. The first day of the month is 1. The first constructor sets the time to midnight. The second version sets the hours and the minutes. The third version adds seconds.

To obtain the individual date and time components of a **GregorianCalendar** you can use the **get( )** method, inherited from **Calendar**. Obtaining most of the date and time components is straightforward. However, when obtaining the hour, you can use either a 12-hour or a 24-hour clock format. If you specify the **Calendar.HOUR** constant, a 12-hour clock is used. Specifying **Calendar.HOUR_OF_DAY** uses a 24-hour clock. For a 12-hour clock, you can determine if it is AM or PM by getting the value **Calendar.AM_PM**. If the value equals **Calendar.AM**, then the time is AM; otherwise it is PM.

The following program demonstrates **GregorianCalendar**. Notice that it manually formats the date and time itself. Later in this chapter, when **Formatter** is described, you will see an easier, better way to format date and time.

```
// Demonstrate GregorianCalendar
import java.util.*;

class CalendarDemo {
  public static void main(String[] args) {

    // Create a calendar initialized with the
    // current date and time.
    GregorianCalendar calendar = new GregorianCalendar();    ◄──── Get the current date and time.

    // Display current date and time information.
    System.out.print("Date: ");
    System.out.print(calendar.getDisplayName(Calendar.DAY_OF_WEEK, ─┐
                                      Calendar.LONG,
                                      Locale.getDefault()));
    System.out.print(" " + calendar.getDisplayName(Calendar.MONTH,  ├──── Display the date.
                                      Calendar.LONG,
                                      Locale.getDefault()));
    System.out.print(" " + calendar.get(Calendar.DATE) + ", ");
    System.out.println(calendar.get(Calendar.YEAR));  ─────────────┘

    System.out.print("Time: ");
    System.out.print(calendar.get(Calendar.HOUR) + ":");    ─┐
    System.out.print(calendar.get(Calendar.MINUTE) + ":");   ├──── Display the time.
    System.out.print(calendar.get(Calendar.SECOND));         ┘

    // determine AM or PM
    int am = calendar.get(Calendar.AM_PM);    ─┐
    if(am == Calendar.AM)                       ├──── Display either AM or PM.
      System.out.println(" AM");
    else                                        │
      System.out.println(" PM");    ─────────────┘

    // Set the time information and display it.
    calendar.set(Calendar.HOUR, 10);    ─┐
    calendar.set(Calendar.AM_PM, Calendar.PM);   ├──── Set the time.
    calendar.set(Calendar.MINUTE, 29);           │
    calendar.set(Calendar.SECOND, 22);    ────────┘
    System.out.print("Updated time: ");
    System.out.print(calendar.get(Calendar.HOUR) + ":");
    System.out.print(calendar.get(Calendar.MINUTE) + ":");
    System.out.print(calendar.get(Calendar.SECOND));

    am = calendar.get(Calendar.AM_PM);
    if(am == Calendar.AM)
      System.out.println(" AM");
    else
      System.out.println(" PM");
  }
}
```

Sample output is shown here:

```
Date: Monday July 11, 2011
Time: 10:53:53 AM
Updated time: 10:29:22 PM
```

In addition to the methods **GregorianCalendar** inherits from **Calendar**, it also provides some of its own. Perhaps the most interesting is **isLeapYear( )**, which tests if the year is a leap year. Its form is

boolean isLeapYear(int *year*)

This method returns **true** if *year* is a leap year and **false** otherwise. The following program shows **isLeapYear( )** in action. It determines if the current year is a leap year.

```
// Demonstrate isLeapYear().

import java.util.*;

class LeapYearDemo {
  public static void main(String[] args) {

    // get the current system date and time
    GregorianCalendar calendar = new GregorianCalendar();

    // get the current year
    int year = calendar.get(Calendar.YEAR);

    System.out.print(year);

    // test if the current year is a leap year
    if(calendar.isLeapYear(year)) {        ◄————————— Check for leap year.
      System.out.println(" is a leap year");
    }
    else {
      System.out.println(" is not a leap year");
    }
  }
}
```

Sample output is shown here:

```
2011 is not a leap year
```

Calendar (and, therefore, **GregorianCalendar**) support many other capabilities. Before leaving the topic of date and time, it is useful to mention a few. You can set a time or date component by use of this version of **set( )**.

void set(int *what*, int *newValue*)

The constant indicating the time or date component to set is passed in *what*. The new value is passed in *newValue*. For example, given a **Calendar** object called **myCalendar**, the following sets the year to 2025:

```
myCalendar.set(Calendar.YEAR, 2025);
```

To determine if the date and time in one **Calendar** object are before those in another, use **before( )**. To determine if the date and time in one **Calendar** object are after those in another, use **after( )**. They are shown here:

boolean after(Object *calendarObj*)

boolean before(Object *calendarObj*)

For example, given

```
GregorianCalendar myCalendarA = new GregorianCalendar(2025, 0, 1);
GregorianCalendar myCalendarB = new GregorianCalendar(2025, 0, 2);
```

then

```
myCalendarA.before(myCalendarB)
```

is true, but

```
myCalendarA.after(myCalendarB)
```

is false.

You can add a value to a time or date component by use of **add( )**. It is shown here:

void add(int *what*, int *value*)

It adds *value* to the time or date component specified by *what*. To subtract, add a negative value. The **add( )** method is very useful in cases in which adding a value might cause another time or date component to "roll over." For example, the following creates a **Calendar** object with the date January 29, 2025.

```
GregorianCalendar myCalendar = new GregorianCalendar(2025, 0, 29);
```

After this call to **add( )**:

```
myCalendar.add(Calendar.DAY_OF_MONTH, 3);
```

myCalendar will contain the date February 1, 2025. This is because adding three days to January 29 causes the month to roll over to February.

Ask the Expert

Q In the preceding discussion, you mentioned time zone. Are there classes that encapsulate time zones?

A Yes. Two other time-related classes provided by **java.util** are **TimeZone** and **SimpleTimeZone**. These classes enable you to work with time zone offsets from Coordinated Universal Time (UTC), also commonly referred to as Greenwich Mean Time (GMT). **TimeZone** is an abstract class that defines the basic functionality. **SimpleTimeZone** is a concrete subclass of **TimeZone**.

Progress Check

1. To instantiate a **Calendar** object, you use _____ .
2. To instantiate a **GregorianCalendar** object, you use _____ .
3. A **Calendar** object is immutable. True or False?

FORMATTING OUTPUT WITH Formatter

As several of the examples in previous chapters have shown, the default format used by Java to display numeric values is not always ideal. For example, this statement:

```
System.out.println(10.0/3.0);
```

displays the following output:

```
3.3333333333333335
```

Although there may be cases in which you want that level of precision, often you don't. Perhaps you simply want to display two decimal places, for example. More generally, often you want to precisely specify the format in which data is displayed rather than using the default provided by Java.

One way to obtain formatted output is through the **Formatter** class. It lets you display numbers, strings, dates, and times in virtually any format you like. Although **Formatter** supports a rich set of features, it is actually quite easy to use. Although **Formatter** is important in its own right, mastering it offers a second advantage. The same formatting mechanism used by **Formatter** is also used by certain other parts of the Java library, including the **printf( )** method provided by **PrintStream**, which is also described in this chapter.

The Formatter Constructors

Before you can use **Formatter** to format output, you must create an instance of **Formatter**. In general, **Formatter** works by converting the binary form of data used by a program into formatted, human-readable text. It then outputs that formatted text to a destination, which can be a buffer in memory, a file, or some other type of stream. When using a buffer for output, it is possible to let **Formatter** supply this buffer automatically.

The **Formatter** class defines many constructors. Here is the form that we will be using:

Formatter( )

Answers:

1. the static **getInstance( )** method of the **Calendar** class
2. one of the constructors of the **GregorianCalendar** class
3. False. The **set( )** and **add( )** methods can be used to change the instant in time that it represents.

This is the default constructor. It uses a **StringBuilder** to hold the formatted output and uses the default locale. Recall that **StringBuilder** is similar to **String**, except that its contents can be modified.

Other constructors give you control over the destination for formatted output and over which locale is used. For example:

> Formatter(Locale *loc*)

This constructor uses a **StringBuilder** for output, but lets you specify the locale. As explained earlier in this chapter, the locale determines the precise form of several items, such as the decimal point or currency symbol. The next constructor directs formatted output to a file:

> Formatter(String *filename*)
>   throws FileNotFoundException

Here, *filename* specifies the name of a file that will receive the formatted output. You can direct output to any output stream by using this constructor:

> Formatter(OutputStream *outStream*)

The stream that will receive the formatted text is specified by *outStream*.

The next two constructors let you send output to any object that implements the **Appendable** interface. The **Appendable** interface is packaged in **java.lang** and is implemented by several classes, including **StringBuilder**, **java.io.PrintStream**, and **java.io.Writer**.

> Formatter(Appendable *buffer*)
>
> Formatter(Appendable *buffer*, Locale *loc*)

Here, *buffer* specifies the target for output, and *loc* specifies the locale. In addition to the constructors just shown, **Formatter** supplies many more. You will want to explore them on your own.

Formatter implements the **Closeable** and **Flushable** interfaces defined in **java.io** and the **Autocloseable** interface defined in **java.lang**. The methods defined by **Formatter** are summarized in Table 24-1. The sections that follow describe the use of **Formatter**.

Formatting Basics

After you have created a **Formatter**, you can use it to create a formatted output. To do so, use the **format( )** method. The version we will use is shown here:

> Formatter format(String *fmtString*, Object ... *args*)

The *fmtSring* consists of two types of items. The first type is composed of characters that are simply copied to the output buffer. The second type contains *format specifiers* that define the way the subsequent arguments are displayed.

TABLE 24-1: The Methods Defined by Formatter	
Method	**Description**
void close( )	Closes the invoking **Formatter**. This causes any resources used by the object to be released. After a **Formatter** has been closed, it cannot be reused.
void flush( )	This applies mostly to a **Formatter** tied to a stream. It causes any buffered output to be written to the stream.
Formatter format(String *fmtString*, Object ... *args*)	Formats the arguments passed via *args* according to the format specifiers contained in *fmtString*. Returns the invoking object.
Formatter format(Locale *loc*, String *fmtString*, Object ... *args*)	Formats the arguments passed via *args* according to the format specifiers contained in *fmtString*. The locale specified by *loc* is used for this format. Returns the invoking object.
IOException ioException( )	If the underlying object that is the destination for output throws an **IOException**, then this exception is returned. Otherwise, **null** is returned.
Locale locale( )	Returns the invoking object's locale.
Appendable out( )	Returns a reference to the underlying object that is the destination for output.
String toString( )	For buffers based on **StringBuilder**, this method returns a **String** containing the formatted output. For buffers of other types, the formatted output may or may not be returned.

In its simplest form, a format specifier begins with a percent sign followed by a *format conversion specifier,* or *format specifier* for short. All format specifiers consist of a single character. For example, the format specifier for floating-point data is **%f**. In general, there must be the same number of arguments as there are format specifiers, and the format specifiers and the arguments are matched in order from left to right. For example, consider this fragment:

```
Formatter fmt = new Formatter();
fmt.format("Formatting %s is easy %d %f", "with Java", 10, 98.6);
```

This sequence creates a **Formatter** that contains the following string:

```
Formatting with Java is easy 10 98.600000
```

In this example, the format specifiers, **%s**, **%d**, and **%f**, are replaced with the arguments that follow the format string. Thus, **%s** is replaced by "with Java", **%d** is replaced by 10, and **%f** is replaced by 98.6. All other characters are simply used as-is. As you might guess, the format specifier **%s** specifies a string, and **%d** specifies an integer value. As mentioned earlier, the **%f** specifies a floating-point value.

The **format( )** method accepts a wide variety of format specifiers, which are shown in Table 24-2. Notice that many specifiers have both upper- and lowercase forms. When an uppercase specifier is used, then letters are shown in uppercase.

TABLE 24-2: The Format Specifiers	
Format Specifier	**Format**
%a %A	Floating-point hexadecimal
%b %B	Boolean
%c %C	Character
%d	Decimal integer
%h %H	Hash code of the argument
%e %E	Scientific notation
%f	Decimal floating-point
%g %G	Uses decimal or scientific notation
%o	Octal integer
%n	Inserts a newline character
%s %S	String
%t %T	Date and time
%x %X	Integer hexadecimal
%%	Inserts a **%** sign

Otherwise, the upper- and lowercase specifiers produce the same format. It is important to understand that Java type-checks each format specifier against its corresponding argument. If the argument doesn't match, an **IllegalFormatException** is thrown.

For **Formatter**s that use a **StringBuilder** as a buffer, once you have generated the formatted output, you can obtain it by calling **toString( )**. For example, continuing with the preceding example, the following statement obtains the formatted string contained in **fmt**:

```
String str = fmt.toString();
```

Of course, if you simply want to display the formatted string, there is no reason to first assign it to a **String** object. When a **Formatter** object is passed to **println( )**, for example, its **toString( )** method is automatically called.

When you are done with a **Formatter**, you should close it by calling **close( )**. This is especially important for **Formatter**s linked to files. Closing the **Formatter** also closes the file, thus releasing the resources used by that file.

Here is a short program that puts together all of the pieces, showing how to create and display a formatted string:

```
// A very simple example that uses Formatter.
import java.util.*;

class FormatDemo {
  public static void main(String[] args) {
    Formatter fmt = new Formatter();                          Create formatted output.

    fmt.format("Formatting %s is easy %d %f", "with Java", 10, 98.6);

    System.out.println(fmt);  ◄──── Display the formatted output.
    fmt.close();
  }
}
```

One other point: You can obtain a reference to the object to which formatted output is written by calling **out( )**. It returns a reference to an **Appendable** object. As explained, by default, this is a **StringBuilder**. However, you can use any **Appendable** as an output target. Understand, however, that some targets will not preserve the output in a buffer. For example, if you use a file, then the output is written to that file. You cannot obtain it by using **toString( )**, for example.

Now that you know the general mechanism used to format output, the remainder of this section discusses several of the formats and shows a number of examples. It also describes various options, such as justification, minimum field width, and precision.

Formatting Strings and Characters

To format an individual character, use **%c**. This causes the matching character argument to be output, unmodified. To format a string, use **%s**.

Formatting Numbers

To format an integer in decimal format, use **%d**. To format a floating-point value in decimal format, use **%f**. To format a floating-point value in scientific notation, use **%e**.

The **%g** format specifier causes **Formatter** to use either decimal or scientific notation based on whether the number of significant digits exceeds the precision, which is 6 by default. The following program demonstrates the effect of the **%g** format specifier:

```
// Demonstrate the %g format specifier.
import java.util.*;

class GFormatDemo {
  public static void main(String[] args) {
    Formatter fmt = new Formatter();

    for(double i=1000; i < 1.0e+10; i *= 100) {
      fmt.format("%g ", i);
      System.out.println(fmt);
    }
    fmt.close();

  }
}
```

It produces the following output:

```
1000.00
1000.00 100000
1000.00 100000 1.00000e+07
1000.00 100000 1.00000e+07 1.00000e+09
```

You can display integers in octal or hexadecimal format by using **%o** and **%x**, respectively. For example, this fragment:

```
fmt.format("Hex: %x, Octal: %o", 196, 196);
```

produces this output:

```
Hex: c4, Octal: 304
```

Formatting Date and Time

One of the more powerful conversion specifiers is **%t**. It lets you format date and time information. The **%t** specifier works a bit differently than the others because it requires the use of a suffix to describe the component and precise format of the time or date desired. The suffixes are shown in Table 24-3. For example, to display minutes, you would use **%tM**, where **M** indicates minutes in a two-character field. The argument corresponding to the **%t** specifier must be of type **Calendar**, **GregorianCalendar**, **Date**, **Long**, or **long**.

Here is a program that demonstrates several of the date and time formats. Notice that it uses the **GregorianCalendar** class to obtain the current date and time. Also notice how much easier it is to format date and time using a **Formatter** than it was to format it manually as the example for **GregorianCalendar**, shown earlier, did.

```java
// Formatting date and time.

import java.util.*;

class TimeDateFormat {
  public static void main(String[] args) {
    Formatter fmt = new Formatter();
    GregorianCalendar calendar = new GregorianCalendar();

    // standard 12-hour time format
    fmt.format("%tr\n", calendar);

    // complete date and time information
    fmt.format("%tc\n", calendar);

    // just hour and minute
    fmt.format("%tl:%tM\n", calendar, calendar);

    // month by name and number
    fmt.format("%tB %tb %tm", calendar, calendar, calendar);
```

TABLE 24-3: The Date and Time Format Suffixes	
Suffix	**Replaced by**
a	Abbreviated weekday name
A	Full weekday name
b	Abbreviated month name
B	Full month name
c	Date and time string formatted as *day month date hh::mm:ss timezone year*
C	First two digits of year
d	Day of month as a decimal (01–31)
D	Month/day/year
e	Day of month as a decimal (1–31)
F	Year-month-day
h	Abbreviated month name
H	Hour (00 to 23)
I	Hour (01 to 12)
j	Day of year as a decimal (001 to 366)
k	Hour (0 to 23)
l	Hour (1 to 12)
L	Millisecond
m	Month as decimal (01 to 13)
M	Minute as decimal (00 to 59)
N	Nanosecond
p	Locale's equivalent of AM or PM in lowercase
Q	Milliseconds from 1/1/1970
r	*hh:mm:ss* (12-hour format)
R	*hh:mm* (24-hour format)
S	Seconds
s	Seconds from 1/1/1970 UTC
T	*hh:mm:ss* (24-hour format)
y	Year in decimal without century (00 to 99)
Y	Year in decimal including century (0001 to 9999)
z	Offset from UTC
Z	Time zone name

```
    // display the formats
    System.out.println(fmt);
    fmt.close();
  }
}
```

Sample output is shown here:

```
11:11:27 AM
Mon Jul 11 11:11:27 CDT 2011
11:11
July Jul 07
```

Before moving on, you might want to experiment with various time and date formats. For example, try displaying the long forms of the month and day, or showing milliseconds.

The %n and %% Specifiers

The **%n** and **%%** format specifiers differ from the others in that they do not match an argument. Instead, they are simply escape sequences that insert a character into the output sequence. The **%n** inserts a newline. The **%%** inserts a percent sign. Of course, you can also use the standard escape sequence **\n** to embed a newline character, as the previous example did.

Specifying a Minimum Field Width

An integer placed between the **%** sign and the format specifier acts as a *minimum field-width specifier*. This pads the output to ensure that it reaches a certain minimum length. For example, **%5f** formats a floating-point value in a field that is at least five characters wide. If a string or number is longer than the minimum, it will still be printed in full. The default padding is done with spaces.

The following program demonstrates the minimum field-width specifier by applying it to the **%s** and **%f** conversions:

```
// Demonstrate a field-width specifier.
import java.util.*;

class FieldWidthDemo {
  public static void main(String[] args) {
    Formatter fmt = new Formatter();

    fmt.format("|%f|\n|%12f|\n",
               10.12345, 10.12345);

    fmt.format("|%s|\n|%10s|",
               "Java", "Java");

    System.out.println(fmt);
    fmt.close();
  }
}
```

This program produces the following output:

```
|10.123450|
|    10.123450|
|Java|
|       Java|
```

The first line displays the number 10.12345 in its default width. The second line displays that value in a width of 12 characters. The third and fourth lines display the string "Java" in its default width and then in a 10-character-wide field.

The minimum field-width modifier is often used to produce tables in which the columns line up. For example, the next program produces a table of squares and cubes for the numbers between 1 and 10:

```java
// Create a table of squares and cubes.
import java.util.*;

class TableFormatDemo {
  public static void main(String[] args) {
    Formatter fmt = new Formatter();

    for(int i=1; i <= 10; i++) {
      fmt.format("%4d %4d %4d\n", i, i*i, i*i*i);
    }

    System.out.println(fmt);
    fmt.close();
  }
}
```

Its output is shown here:

```
 1    1     1
 2    4     8
 3    9    27
 4   16    64
 5   25   125
 6   36   216
 7   49   343
 8   64   512
 9   81   729
10  100  1000
```

Specifying Precision

A *precision specifier* can be used with several format specifiers. It follows the minimum field-width specifier (if there is one) and consists of a period followed by an integer. Its exact meaning depends on the format specifier to which it is applied. Let's look at some examples.

When you apply the precision specifier to the **%f** or **%e** specifiers, it determines the number of decimal places displayed. For example, **%10.4f** displays a number at least ten characters wide with four decimal places. When using **%g**, the precision determines the number of significant digits displayed. (Rounding may occur.) The default precision is 6.

Applied to strings, the precision specifier specifies the maximum field length. For example, **%5.7s** displays a string at least five and not exceeding seven characters long. If the string is longer than the maximum field width, the end characters will be truncated.

The following program illustrates the precision specifier:

```java
// Demonstrate the precision modifier.
import java.util.*;

class PrecisionDemo {
  public static void main(String[] args) {
    Formatter fmt = new Formatter();

    // Format 4 decimal places.
    fmt.format("%.4f\n", 123.1234567);

    // Format to 2 decimal places in a 16 character field
    fmt.format("%16.2e\n", 123.1234567);

    // Display at most 15 characters in a string.
    fmt.format("%.15s\n", "Formatting with Java is now easy.");

    System.out.println(fmt);
    fmt.close();
  }
}
```

It produces the following output:

```
123.1235
        1.23e+02
Formatting with
```

The precision specifier can also be applied to the **%h** and **%b** formats. In these cases, it specifies a maximum field width.

Using the Format Flags

Formatter recognizes a set of format *flags* that lets you control various aspects of a conversion. All format flags are single characters, and a format flag follows the **%** in a format specification. The flags are shown here:

Flag	Effect
–	Left justification
#	Alternate conversion format
0	Output is padded with zeros rather than spaces
space	Positive numeric output is preceded by a space
+	Positive numeric output is preceded by a + sign
,	Numeric values include grouping separators
(	Negative numeric values are enclosed within parentheses

Not all flags apply in all cases. For example, the + flag cannot be used with the **%s** specifier. The following sections show several examples of these flags in use.

JUSTIFYING OUTPUT

By default, all output is right-justified. That is, if the field width is larger than the data printed, the data will be placed on the right edge of the field. You can force output to be left-justified by placing a minus sign directly after the %. For instance, **%–10.2f** left-justifies a floating-point number with two decimal places in a 10-character field. For example, consider this program:

```
// Demonstrate left justification.
import java.util.*;

class LeftJustify {
  public static void main(String[] args) {
    Formatter fmt = new Formatter();

    // Right justify by default
    fmt.format("|%10.2f|\n", 123.123);

    // Now, left justify.
    fmt.format("|%-10.2f|", 123.123);

    System.out.println(fmt);
    fmt.close();
  }
}
```

It produces the following output:

```
|    123.12 |
|123.12     |
```

As you can see, the first line uses the default, right-justification. The second line is left-justified within a 10-character field.

THE +, SPACE, 0, AND (FLAGS

To cause a + sign to be shown before positive numeric values, add the + flag. For example,

```
fmt.format("%+.2f", 100.25);
```

creates this output:

```
+100.25
```

You can add a space instead of a + sign before positive numeric values by using the space flag. For example,

```
fmt.format("%.2f\n", -100.25);
fmt.format("% .2f", 100.25);
```

creates the following output:

```
-100.25
 100.25
```

Notice that the positive value has a leading space.

To show negative numeric output inside parentheses, rather than with a leading –, use the **(** flag. For example,

```
fmt.format("%(.2f", -100.25);
```

creates this string:

```
(100.25)
```

The 0 flag causes output to be padded with zeros rather than spaces. It can be applied to numeric values. For example,

```
fmt.format("%07.2f\n", 1.23);
```

produces the following output:

```
0001.23
```

In general, the space, **+**, 0, and **(** format flags can be used with the **%d**, **%f**, **%e**, and **%g** specifiers. The 0 flag can also be used with the **%x** and **%o** specifiers.

Note: The space, +, and (flags can also be used with %x and %o when formatting a ***BigInteger**, which is a special integer class that supports very large integers. It is in* ***java.math**.*

THE COMMA FLAG

When displaying large decimal numbers, it can be useful to add grouping separators, which in English are commas. For example, the value 1234567 is more easily read when formatted as 1,234,567. To add grouping specifiers, use the comma (,) flag. For example,

```
fmt.format("%,.2f", 4356783497.34);
```

creates this string:

```
4,356,783,497.34
```

THE # FLAG

The # specifies an alternate format. Here are some examples. For **%f**, the # ensures that there will be a decimal point even if there are no decimal digits. If you use the **%x** format specifier with a #, the hexadecimal number will be printed with a **0x** prefix. Using the **%o** specifier with # causes the number to be printed with a leading zero.

The Uppercase Option

As mentioned earlier, several of the format specifiers have uppercase versions that cause the formatted output to use upper case where appropriate. Here are some examples. **%C** upper cases the corresponding character. **%S** upper cases the corresponding string. **%E** and **%G** upper case the *e* symbol. **%X** causes the hexadecimal digits *a* through *f* to be displayed in upper case as *A* through *F*. Also, the optional prefix **0x** is displayed as **0X**. **%T** causes all alphabetical date and time items to be uppercased.

The following sequence shows the effects of **%X** and **%E**:

```
fmt.format("%#x\n", 250);
fmt.format("%#X\n", 250);
fmt.format("%e\n", 123.1234);
fmt.format("%E", 123.1234);
```

The output is shown here:

```
0xfa
0XFA
1.231234e+02
1.231234E+02
```

Using an Argument Index

Formatter includes a very useful feature that lets you specify the argument to which a format specifier applies. As you have seen, format specifiers and arguments are normally matched in order, from left to right. That is, the first format specifier matches the first argument, the second format specifier matches the second argument, and so on. However, by using an *argument index,* you can explicitly control which argument a format specifier matches. This enables arguments and format specifiers to be matched out of strict left-to-right order.

An argument index immediately follows the **%** in a format specifier. It has the following format:

n$

where *n* is the index of the desired argument, beginning with 1. For example, consider this example:

```
fmt.format("%3$d %1$d %2$d", 10, 20, 30);
```

It produces this string:

```
30 10 20
```

In this example, the first format specifier matches 30, the second matches 10, and the third matches 20. Thus, the arguments are used in an order other than strictly left to right.

One advantage of argument indices is that they enable you to reuse an argument without having to specify it twice. For example, consider this line:

```
fmt.format("%d in hex is %1$x", 255);
```

It produces the following string:

```
255 in hex is ff
```

As you can see, the argument 255 is used by both format specifiers.

There is a convenient shorthand called a *relative index* that enables you to reuse the argument matched by the preceding format specifier. Simply specify < for the argument index. For example, the following call to **format( )** produces the same results as the previous example:

```
fmt.format("%d in hex is %<x", 255);
```

Relative indices are especially useful when creating custom date and time formats. Consider the following example:

```
// Use relative indexes to simplify the
// creation of a custom date and time format.
import java.util.*;

class RelativeIndexDemo {
  public static void main(String[] args) {
    Formatter fmt = new Formatter();
    GregorianCalendar calendar = new GregorianCalendar();

    fmt.format("Today is day %te of %<tB, %<tY", calendar);
    System.out.println(fmt);
    fmt.close();
  }
}
```

Here is sample output:

```
Today is day 11 of July, 2011
```

Because of relative indexing, the argument **calendar** need only be passed once, rather than three times.

Formatting for a Different Locale

So far, all of the examples have formatted output for the default locale. This is often what you will want. However, if you specify a **Locale** argument when creating a **Formatter**, then output will be formatted relative to that locale. For example, the following program shows the difference in the use of the comma and decimal point between formatting conventions in US English, and German.

```
// Demonstrate a formatting difference based on locale.
import java.util.*;

class LocaleFormat {
  public static void main(String[] args) {
    Formatter usFmt = new Formatter(Locale.US);
    Formatter germanFmt = new Formatter(Locale.GERMAN);
    double n = 1234567.24;
```

```
        usFmt.format("English: %,.2f", n);
        System.out.println(usFmt);
        usFmt.close();

        germanFmt.format("German:   %,.2f", n);
        System.out.println(germanFmt);
        germanFmt.close();
    }
}
```

The output is shown here:

```
English: 1,234,567.24
German:   1.234.567,24
```

Notice that in English, the decimal point is a period and the grouping separator is a comma. This is reversed in the German version.

Closing a Formatter

In general, you should close a **Formatter** when you are done using it. Doing so frees any resources that it was using. This is especially important when formatting to a file, but it can be important in other cases, too. For the sake of illustration, all of the preceding examples have explicitly closed the formatter, even when the program was ending. As these examples have shown, one way to close a **Formatter** is to explicitly call **close( )**. However, beginning with JDK 7, **Formatter** implements the **AutoCloseable** interface. This means that it supports the new **try**-with-resources statement. Using this approach, the **Formatter** is automatically closed when it is no longer needed.

For example, here is the first **Formatter** example reworked to use **try**-with-resources:

```
// Use automatic resource management with Formatter.
import java.util.*;

class FormatDemo {
  public static void main(String[] args) {

    try (Formatter fmt = new Formatter())
    {
      fmt.format("Formatting %s is easy %d %f", "with Java",
                 10, 98.6);
      System.out.println(fmt);
    }
  }
}
```

The output is the same as before.

Progress Check

1. If there are two calls to **format( )** using the same **Formatter**, then the string that is generated by the second call to **format( )** replaces the string that was generated by the first call to **format( )**. True or False?
2. The string "%z" is a legal format specifier in a **format( )** method call. True or False?
3. A **Formatter** should be _____ when it is done formatting all the text.

TRY THIS 24-1   FORMATTING A TABLE OF CITIES AND POPULATIONS

`CitiesDemo.java`

In this project, you will display an array of data related to a city in a formatted table. The data will consist of two pieces of information about each city: the name of the city and its current population.

The formatting will be done by a method that uses **Formatter** to generate a string containing a table, each row of which displays the data for one city. The first column will show the city name, and the second column will show the population. Columns will be separated by vertical bars, and the vertical bars will be aligned and have spaces on both sides of them. Also, there will be a column of vertical bars along the left and right edges of the table. The column of names will be left-justified and be just wide enough for the longest city name. The column of populations will be right-justified and just wide enough for the largest value. We will assume that a monospaced font is used to make the alignment easier.

STEP-BY-STEP

1. The city information will be stored in an array of **City** objects. To define the **City** class, create a new file called **CitiesDemo.java** and enter the following code:

```
import java.util.*;

class City {
   String name;
   int pop; // current population
```

Answers:

1. False. The two strings are appended.
2. False.
3. closed

```
    City(String n, int p) {
      name = n;
      pop = p;
    }
  }
```

2. Next, begin entering the **CitiesDemo** class as shown here. This is the class that we will use to demonstrate the formatting:

```java
public class CitiesDemo {

  public static void main(String[] args) {
    City[] cities = {
        new City("Dallas", 1197816),
        new City("Portland", 583776),
        new City("Frostbite Falls", 6424),
        new City("New York", 8175133)
    };

    String result = formatCities(cities);

    System.out.println(result);
  }
```

3. Finally, finish the **CitiesDemo** class by adding the **static** method **formatCities( )** to the **CitiesDemo** class. It is shown here:

```java
  static String formatCities(City[] cities) {
    Formatter formatter = new Formatter();
    String result;
    int col1 = 0, col2 = 0;

    // find width of the columns
    for(City city : cities) {
      if(city.name.length() > col1)
        col1 = city.name.length();
      if(Integer.toString(city.pop).length() > col2)
        col2 = Integer.toString(city.pop).length();
    }

    // construct the format string
    String frmt = "| %-" + col1 + "s | %" + col2 + "d |\n";
    for(City city : cities) {
      formatter.format(frmt, city.name, city.pop);
    }

    result = formatter.toString();
    formatter.close();
    return result;
  }
}
```

Notice that **formatCities( )** takes an array of **City** objects and returns a string containing the formatted table. To do so, the method first needs to find the width for each column. It does this by iterating through the names and populations, keeping track of the width of the largest values. Then it uses a **Formatter** to format each row of the table.

Pay particular attention to the **frmt** string that is used to format each row. It is a little complicated because it needs to include the column widths, which are specified by **col1** and **col2**. For the sake of discussion, let's assume the first column has a width of 15 and the second column a width of 10. With these values, the string assigned to **frmt** becomes:

    "| %-15s | %10d |\n"

The first column is left-justified, needs 15 spaces, and specifies a string. The second column is right-justified, needs 10 spaces, and specifies an integer. Notice the vertical bars at the beginning, end, and between the two columns, separated by spaces from the data in the columns. They delineate the columns in the table.

4. Run the **main( )** method in the **CitiesDemo** class. You will see the following output:

```
|| Dallas          | 1197816 |
|| Portland        |  583776 |
|| Frostbite Falls |    6424 |
|| New York        | 8175133 |
```

5. Although the table is now properly formatted, two improvements can be made. The first is to add commas to the population numbers. The second is to complete the box around the table. These are left to you as exercises.

FORMATTING AND THE printf( ) METHOD

Although there is nothing technically wrong with using **Formatter** directly (as the preceding examples have done) when creating output that will be written to **System.out**, there is a more convenient alternative: the **printf( )** method. This method is defined by both **PrintStream** and **PrintWriter**. It uses the same format specifiers and mechanism as **Formatter**, just described. Here are its two forms for **PrintStream**:

PrintStream printf(String *fmtString*, Object ... *args*)

PrintStream printf(Locale *locale*, String *fmtString*, Object ... *args*)

The first version writes *args* to standard output in the format specified by *fmtString* using the default locale. The second form uses the locale specified by *locale*. Both return a reference to the invoking **PrintStream**. The **PrintWriter** versions of **printf( )** are similar except that a **PrintWriter** is returned.

Because **System.out** is a **PrintStream**, you can use **printf( )** to output formatted values to the console. This makes is easier to display formatted output because you don't need to construct a **Formatter**, closing it when you are done. You can simply call **printf( )**. For example, the following program uses **printf( )** to output numeric values in various formats.

```
// Demonstrate printf().

class PrintfDemo {
  public static void main(String[] args) {
    System.out.println("Here are some numeric values " +
                      "in different formats.\n");

    System.out.printf("Various integer formats: ");
    System.out.printf("%d %(d %+d %05d\n", 3, -3, 3, 3);

    System.out.println();
    System.out.printf("Default floating-point format: %f\n",
                      1234567.123);
    System.out.printf("Floating-point with commas: %,f\n",
                      1234567.123);
    System.out.printf("Negative floating-point default: %,f\n",
                      -1234567.123);
    System.out.printf("Negative floating-point option: %,(f\n",
                      -1234567.123);

    System.out.println();

    System.out.printf("Line up positive and negative values:\n");
    System.out.printf("% ,.2f\n% ,.2f\n",
                      1234567.123, -1234567.123);
  }
}
```

The output is shown here:

```
Here are some numeric values in different formats.

Various integer formats: 3 (3) +3 00003

Default floating-point format: 1234567.123000
Floating-point with commas: 1,234,567.123000
Negative floating-point default: -1,234,567.123000
Negative floating-point option: (1,234,567.123000)

Line up positive and negative values:
 1,234,567.12
-1,234,567.12
```

Because of the convenience that **printf( )** offers, you will normally want to use it when outputting to **System.out**.

*Note: **PrintStream** and **PrintWriter** also define a method called **format( )**, which works just like **printf( )**. Either may be used to output formatted data.*

THE Scanner CLASS

Scanner is the complement of **Formatter**. It reads formatted input and converts it into its binary form. **Scanner** can be used to read input from standard input (normally the keyboard), a file, or a string, among others. For example, you can use **Scanner** to read a number from the keyboard and assign its value to a variable. As you will see, given its power, **Scanner** is surprisingly easy to use. The **Scanner** class was briefly introduced in Chapter 11. Here we will examine it in greater detail.

The Scanner Constructors

Scanner defines several constructors that let you create instances in a variety of ways. For example, you can construct a **Scanner** that reads from a **String**, an **InputStream**, a **File**, or any object that implements the **Readable** interface (packaged in **java.lang**), among others. Here are the constructors used in this chapter:

Scanner(InputStream *from*)

Scanner(String *from*)

Scanner(Readable *from*)

The first constructor creates a **Scanner** that uses the stream specified by *from* as the source for input. The second reads input from the specified **String**. The third obtains its input from a source that implements **Readable**.

Here are some examples. The following sequence creates a **Scanner** that reads the file **Test.txt**:

```
FileReader fin = new FileReader("Test.txt");
Scanner src = new Scanner(fin);
```

This works because **FileReader** implements the **Readable** interface. Thus, the call to the constructor resolves to **Scanner(Readable)**.

This next line creates a **Scanner** that reads from standard input, which is the keyboard by default:

```
Scanner conin = new Scanner(System.in);
```

This works because **System.in** is an object of type **InputStream**. Thus, the call to the constructor maps to **Scanner(InputStream)**.

The next sequence creates a **Scanner** that reads from a string.

```
String instr = "10 99.88 scanning is easy.";
Scanner conin = new Scanner(instr);
```

Scanning Basics

Once you have created a **Scanner**, it is a simple matter to use it to read formatted input. In general, a **Scanner** reads *tokens* from the underlying source that you specified when the **Scanner** was created. As it relates to **Scanner**, a token is a portion of input that is delineated by a set of delimiters, which is whitespace by default. A token is read by matching it with a particular *regular expression,* which defines the format of the data. (An introduction to regular expressions is found in Appendix B.) Although **Scanner** allows you to define the specific type of expression that its next input operation will match, it includes many predefined patterns, several of which match the primitive types, such as **int** and **double**, and arbitrary strings. Thus, often you won't need to specify a pattern to match. Since regular expressions are introduced in Appendix B, we will only be using predefined patterns in this chapter.

In general, to use **Scanner**, follow this procedure:

1. Determine if a specific type of input is available by calling one of **Scanner**'s **hasNext**X methods, where X is the type of data desired.
2. If input is available, read it by calling one of **Scanner**'s **next**X methods.
3. Repeat the process until input is exhausted.
4. Close the **Scanner** when you are done with it.

As the preceding indicates, **Scanner** defines two sets of methods that enable you to read input. The first are the **hasNext**X methods, a sampling of which are shown in Table 24-4. These methods determine if the specified type of input is available. For example, calling **hasNextInt( )** returns **true** only if the next token to be read is an integer. Notice that **hasNext( )** returns **true** if any type of token is available. If the desired data is available, then you can read it by calling one of **Scanner**'s **next**X methods. A sampling is shown in Table 24-5. For example, to read the next integer, call **nextInt( )**. Notice that **next( )** can read any type of token, returning it as a **String**.

The following sequence shows how to read a list of integers from the keyboard.

```
Scanner conin = new Scanner(System.in);
int i;

// Read a list of integers.
while(conin.hasNextInt()) {
  i = conin.nextInt();
  // ...
}
```

The **while** loop stops as soon as the next token is not an integer. Thus, the loop stops reading integers as soon as a non-integer is encountered in the input stream (or there are no more tokens available).

If a **next** method cannot find the type of data it is looking for, it throws an **InputMismatchException**. A **NoSuchElementException** is thrown if no more input is available. For this reason, it is best to first confirm that the desired type of data is available by calling a **hasNext** method before calling its corresponding **next** method.

As mentioned, when you are done with a **Scanner**, it should be closed. However, when a **Scanner** is linked to **System.in**, closing the **Scanner** will also close **System.in**! This means that you can't use **System.in** again. As a result, it is not uncommon to see a **Scanner** linked to **System.in** not closed, or not closed until the end of the program. For the sake of illustration, the following examples explicitly close the **Scanner** at the end of the program.

TABLE 24-4: A Sampling of the Scanner hasNext Methods

Method	Description
boolean hasNext( )	Returns **true** if another token of any type is available to be read. Returns **false** otherwise.
boolean hasNextBoolean( )	Returns **true** if a **boolean** value is available to be read. Returns **false** otherwise.
boolean hasNextByte( )	Returns **true** if a **byte** value is available to be read. Returns **false** otherwise.
boolean hasNextDouble( )	Returns **true** if a **double** value is available to be read. Returns **false** otherwise.
boolean hasNextFloat( )	Returns **true** if a **float** value is available to be read. Returns **false** otherwise.
boolean hasNextInt( )	Returns **true** if an **int** value is available to be read. Returns **false** otherwise.
boolean hasNextLong( )	Returns **true** if a **long** value is available to be read. Returns **false** otherwise.
boolean hasNextShort( )	Returns **true** if a **short** value is available to be read. Returns **false** otherwise.

TABLE 24-5: A Sampling of the Scanner next Methods

Method	Description
String next( )	Returns the next token of any type from the input source.
boolean nextBoolean( )	Returns the next token as a **boolean** value.
byte nextByte( )	Returns the next token as a **byte** value. The default radix is used.
double nextDouble( )	Returns the next token as a **double** value.
float nextFloat( )	Returns the next token as a **float** value.
int nextInt( )	Returns the next token as an **int** value. The default radix is used.
long nextLong( )	Returns the next token as a **long** value. The default radix is used.
short nextShort( )	Returns the next token as a **short** value. The default radix is used.

Some Scanner Examples

Scanner makes what could be a tedious task into an easy one. To understand why, let's look at some examples. The following program averages a list of numbers entered at the keyboard. It first creates a **Scanner** linked to **System.in**. It then reads numbers, summing them in the process, until the user enters the string "done". It then stops reading input and displays the average of the numbers.

```
// Use Scanner to compute an average of the values.
import java.util.*;

class AvgNums {
  public static void main(String[] args) {
    Scanner conin = new Scanner(System.in);  ◄── Create a Scanner that reads from
                                                   System.in.
    int count = 0;
    double sum = 0.0;

    System.out.println("Enter numbers to average.");

    // Read and sum numbers.
    while(conin.hasNext()) {  ◄── Loop while there are tokens to read.
      if(conin.hasNextDouble()) {  ──┐
        sum += conin.nextDouble();  ─┴── Check if the next token can be read
        count++;                          as a double. If so, read it.
      }
      else {
        String str = conin.next();
        if(str.equals("done")) break;  ◄── Otherwise, check for the string "done".
        else {
          System.out.println("Data format error.");
          return;
        }
      }
    }

    System.out.println("Average is " + sum / count);
    conin.close();
  }
}
```

Here is a sample run:

```
Enter numbers to average.
1.2
2
3.4
4
done
Average is 2.65
```

Let's look closely at how this program works. First, notice that it uses **hasNext( )** to determine if there are any more tokens of any type in the input stream. If there are, the program then checks if the next token represents a **double**. If it does, that number is read. If the next token is not a **double**, then the next token is read by calling **next( )**, which can read any type of token. When this occurs, the program checks if the token is the string "done". If it is, the program terminates normally. Otherwise, it displays an error.

Notice that the numbers are read by calling **nextDouble( )**. This method reads any number that can be converted into a **double** value, including an integer value, such as 2, and a floating-point value like 3.4. Thus, a number read by **nextDouble( )** need not specify a decimal point. This same general principle applies to all **next** methods. They will match and read any data format that can represent the type of value being requested.

One thing that is especially nice about **Scanner** is that the same technique used to read from one source can be used to read from another. For example, here is the preceding program reworked to average a list of numbers contained in a text file:

```java
// Use Scanner to compute an average of the values in a file.
import java.util.*;
import java.io.*;

class AvgFile {
  public static void main(String[] args)
    throws IOException {

    int count = 0;
    double sum = 0.0;

    // Write output to a file.
    FileWriter fout = new FileWriter("test.txt");
    fout.write("2 3.4 5 6 7.4 9.1 10.5 done");
    fout.close();

    FileReader fin = new FileReader("Test.txt");

    Scanner src = new Scanner(fin); // ◄─── Create a Scanner that reads from a file.

    // Read and sum numbers.
    while(src.hasNext()) {
      if(src.hasNextDouble()) {
        sum += src.nextDouble();
        count++;
      }
      else {
        String str = src.next();
        if(str.equals("done")) break;
        else {
          System.out.println("File format error.");
          return;
        }
      }
    }

    src.close();

    System.out.println("Average is " + sum / count);
  }
}
```

Here is the output:

```
Average is 6.2
```

The preceding program illustrates another important feature of **Scanner**. Notice that the file reader referred to by **fin** is not closed directly. Rather, it is closed automatically when **src** calls **close( )**. When you close a **Scanner**, the **Readable** associated with it is also closed (if that **Readable** implements the **Closeable** interface). Therefore, in this case, the file referred to by **fin** is automatically closed when **src** is closed.

One other point: To keep this and the next example compact, I/O exceptions are simply thrown out of **main( )**. However, your real-world code will normally handle I/O exceptions itself.

You can use **Scanner** to read input that contains several different types of data—even if the order of that data is unknown in advance. You must simply check what type of data is available before reading it. For example, consider this program:

```java
// Use Scanner to read various types of data from a file.
import java.util.*;
import java.io.*;

class ScanMixed {
  public static void main(String[] args)
    throws IOException {

    int i;
    double d;
    boolean b;
    String str;

    // Write output to a file.
    FileWriter fout = new FileWriter("test.txt");
    fout.write("Testing Scanner 10 12.2 one true two false");
    fout.close();

    FileReader fin = new FileReader("Test.txt");

    Scanner src = new Scanner(fin);

    // Read to end.
    while(src.hasNext()) {
      if(src.hasNextInt()) {                          ←┐
        i = src.nextInt();
        System.out.println("int: " + i);
      }
      else if(src.hasNextDouble()) {                  ←── Check for different types of data.
        d = src.nextDouble();
        System.out.println("double: " + d);
      }
      else if(src.hasNextBoolean()) {                 ←┘
        b = src.nextBoolean();
        System.out.println("boolean: " + b);
      }
```

```
      else {
        str = src.next();
        System.out.println("String: " + str);
      }
    }

    src.close();
  }
}
```

Here is the output:

```
String: Testing
String: Scanner
int: 10
double: 12.2
String: one
boolean: true
String: two
boolean: false
```

When reading mixed data types, as the preceding program does, you need to be a bit careful about the order in which you call the **next** methods. For example, if the loop reversed the order of the calls to **nextInt( )** and **nextDouble( )**, both numeric values would have been read as **doubles**, because **nextDouble( )** matches any numeric string that can be represented as a **double**.

Beginning with JDK 7, **Scanner** also implements the **AutoCloseable** interface. This means that it can be managed by a **try**-with-resources block. When **try**-with-resources is used, the scanner is automatically closed when the block ends. For example, **src** in the preceding program could have been managed like this:

```
try (Scanner src = new Scanner(fin))
{
  // Read to end.
  while(src.hasNext()) {
    if(src.hasNextInt()) {
      i = src.nextInt();
      System.out.println("int: " + i);
    }
    else if(src.hasNextDouble()) {
      d = src.nextDouble();
      System.out.println("double: " + d);
    }
    else if(src.hasNextBoolean()) {
      b = src.nextBoolean();
      System.out.println("boolean: " + b);
    }
    else {
      str = src.next();
      System.out.println("String: " + str);
    }
  }
}
```

To clearly demonstrate the closing of a **Scanner**, the previous examples did not use **try**-with-resources. Explicitly calling **close( )** also allows them to be compiled by versions of Java prior to JDK 7. However, the **try**-with-resources approach is more streamlined and can help prevent errors. Its use is recommended for new code.

Some Other Scanner Features

Scanner has several other capabilities in addition to those already discussed. A few are mentioned here to give you an idea of its capabilities. As stated earlier, you can use a **Scanner** to input any sequence that matches a regular expression. After you learn about regular expressions, you should try using the versions of **hasNext( )** and **next( )** that take a regular expression as an argument.

You can set the *delimiters* that **Scanner** uses to determine where a token starts and ends. The default delimiters are the whitespace characters, and this is the delimiter set that the preceding examples have used. However, it is possible to change the delimiters by calling the **useDelimiter( )** method. You can pass it any regular expression, but you can also pass something as simple as a comma, if you want to use a comma as the delimiter.

Another method that is particularly useful in some circumstances is **findInLine( )**. This method searches for the specified regular expression within a line of text. If a match is found, the token (and any preceding, nonmatching characters) is consumed and the token is returned. This method is useful if you want to locate a specific pattern within a larger input sequence.

Related to **findInLine( )** is **findWithinHorizon( )**. This method attempts to find an occurrence of the specified pattern within a specified number of characters. If successful, it returns the matching token.

You can bypass a pattern using **skip( )**. It searches for a sequence that matches a regular expression. If a match is found, **skip( )** simply advances beyond it.

Progress Check

1. For a **Scanner** whose input is "1234", **next( )** returns "1". True or False?
2. To test whether the input source has any more tokens, call the **Scanner** method _____.
3. To get the next integer, call the **Scanner** method _____.

Answers:

1. False. **next( )** returns "1234".
2. **hasNext( )**
3. **nextInt( )**

THE Random CLASS

The **Random** class is a generator of pseudorandom numbers. These are called *pseudorandom* numbers because they are uniformly distributed sequences rather than truly random values. **Random** defines the following constructors:

Random( )

Random(long *seed*)

The first version creates a number generator that uses an arbitrary, but generally unique value, called a *seed*, to set its initial state. The second form allows you to specify a seed value manually. Initializing a **Random** object with a seed effectively defines the sequence that it will produce. If you use the same seed to initialize another **Random** object, you will extract the same random sequence. If you want to generate different sequences, specify different seed values. The public methods defined by **Random** are summarized in Table 24-6.

As you can see, there are seven types of pseudorandom numbers that you can extract from a **Random** object. True/false values are available from **nextBoolean( )**. Bytes can be obtained by calling **nextBytes( )**. Integers can be extracted via the **nextInt( )** method. Long integers can be obtained with **nextLong( )**. For integer types, the range of values is the range of the specified type. The **nextFloat( )** and **nextDouble( )** methods return values of types **float** and **double**, respectively, between 0.0 and less than 1.0. Finally, **nextGaussian( )** returns a **double** value centered at 0.0 with a standard deviation of 1.0. This is the distribution that produces what is commonly known as a *bell curve*.

Here is an example that demonstrates the sequence produced by **nextGaussian( )**. It obtains 100 random Gaussian values and averages these values. The program also counts the number of values that fall within two standard deviations, plus or minus, using increments of 0.5 for each category. The result is graphically displayed sideways on the screen.

TABLE 24-6: The Public Methods Defined by Random	
Method	**Description**
boolean nextBoolean( )	Returns either **true** or **false**.
void nextBytes(byte[ ] *vals*)	Fills *vals* with generated **byte** values.
double nextDouble( )	Returns the next value as a **double**.
float nextFloat( )	Returns the next value as a **float**.
double nextGaussian( )	Returns the next value as a **double**, using the Gaussian distribution.
int nextInt( )	Returns the next value as an **int**.
int nextInt(int *n*)	Returns the next value as an **int** within the range zero to *n*−1.
long nextLong( )	Returns the next value as a **long**.
void setSeed(long *newSeed*)	Sets the seed value to that specified by *newSeed*.

```
// Demonstrate random Gaussian values.
import java.util.Random;

class RandomDemo {
  public static void main(String[] args) {
    Random r = new Random();
    double val;
    double sum = 0;
    int[] bell = new int[9];

    for(int i=0; i<100; i++) {
      val = r.nextGaussian();   ←——— Generate pseudorandom values.
      sum += val;
      double t = -2;

      for(int x=0; x < bell.length; x++, t += 0.5)
        if(val < t) {
          bell[x]++;
          break;
        }
    }
    System.out.println("Average of values: " + (sum/100));

    // display bell curve, sideways
    for(int i=0; i < bell.length; i++) {
      for(int x=bell[i]; x>0; x--)
        System.out.print("*");
      System.out.println();
    }
  }
}
```

Here is a sample program run.

```
Average of values: 0.02569021377810979
*
*****
*******
**************
*************************
******************
*************
**********
******
```

USE Observable AND Observer

The **Observable** class is used to create subclasses that other parts of your program can observe. Thus, it provides a framework that supports the Observer pattern described in Chapter 16. When an object of such a subclass undergoes a change, observing classes are notified. Observing classes must implement the **Observer** interface, which defines the **update( )** method. The **update( )** method is called when an observer is notified of a change in an observed object.

Observable defines the methods shown in Table 24-7. An object that is being observed must follow three simple rules. First, it must add any observers to its list of observers so that they can be notified of a change. This is done by calling **addObserver( )**. Second, if the object has changed, it must call **setChanged( )**. Third, when it is ready to notify observers of this change, it must call **notifyObservers( )**. This causes the **update( )** method in the observing object(s) to be called. Be careful—if the object calls **notifyObservers( )** without having previously called **setChanged( )**, no action will take place. The observed object must call both **setChanged( )** and **notifyObservers( )** before **update( )** will be called.

Notice that **notifyObservers( )** has two forms: one that takes an argument and one that does not. If you call **notifyObservers( )** with an argument, this object is passed to the observer's **update( )** method as its second parameter. Otherwise, **null** is passed to **update( )**. You can use the second parameter for passing any type of object that is appropriate for your application.

TABLE 24-7: The Methods Defined by Observable	
Method	**Description**
void addObserver(Observer *obj*)	Adds *obj* to the list of objects observing the invoking object.
protected void clearChanged( )	Calling this method returns the status of the invoking object to "unchanged."
int countObservers( )	Returns the number of objects observing the invoking object.
void deleteObserver(Observer *obj*)	Removes *obj* from the list of objects observing the invoking object.
void deleteObservers( )	Removes all observers for the invoking object.
boolean hasChanged( )	Returns **true** if the state of the invoking object has been set to "changed." This occurs only when **setChanged( )** has been called on the invoking object and no subsequent call to **notifyObservers( )** or **clearChanged( )** has occurred. Otherwise, it returns **false**.
void notifyObservers( )	If the state of the invoking object indicates that it has changed, then this method notifies all observers of the invoking object by calling their **update( )** method (defined by **Observer**). It then calls **clearChanged( )** to return the object to an "unchanged" state. A **null** is passed as the second argument to **update( )**.
void notifyObservers(Object *obj*)	If the state of the invoking object indicates that it has changed, then this method notifies all observers of the invoking object by calling their **update( )** method (defined by **Observer**). It then calls **clearChanged( )** to return the object to an "unchanged" state. The argument passed to **update( )** is specified by *obj*.
protected void setChanged( )	Called when the invoking object has changed.

To observe an observable object, you must implement the **Observer** interface. This interface defines only the one method shown here:

void update(Observable *observedOb*, Object *arg*)

Here, *observedOb* is the object being observed, and *arg* is the value passed by **notifyObservers( )**. The **update( )** method is automatically called by **notifyObservers( )** when a change in the observed object takes place.

Here is an example that demonstrates **Observable** and **Observer**. It creates two observer classes, called **Watcher1** and **Watcher2**. Both implement the **Observer** interface. Each displays the value of the argument that is passed via **update( )**. **Watcher2** also beeps when the count reaches zero. (This is done by outputting the value 7, which is the ASCII/Unicode value for the computer's "bell".) The class being monitored is called **BeingWatched**. It extends **Observable**.

Inside **BeingWatched** is the method **counter( )**, which simply counts down from a specified value. It uses **sleep( )** to wait a fifth of a second between counts. Each time the count changes, **notifyObservers( )** is called with the current count passed as its argument. This causes the **update( )** method inside any observing object to be called.

Inside **main( )**, instances of **Watcher1** and **Watcher2**, named **observing1** and **observing2**, are created. Next, a **BeingWatched** object is constructed. It is named **observed**. Then, **observing1** and **observing2** are added to the list of observers for **observed**. This means that their **update( )** methods will be called each time **counter( )** calls **notifyObservers( )**.

```java
// Demonstrate Observable and Observer.

import java.util.*;

// This is the first observing class.
class Watcher1 implements Observer {              // Implement Observer.
  public void update(Observable obj, Object arg) {
    System.out.println("update() in Watcher1 called, count is " +
                        ((Integer)arg).intValue());
  }
}

// This is the second observing class.
class Watcher2 implements Observer {
  public void update(Observable obj, Object arg) {

    System.out.println("update() in Watcher2 called, count is " +
                        ((Integer)arg).intValue());

    // Ring bell when done
    if(((Integer)arg).intValue() == 0)
      System.out.print('\7');
  }
}
```

```java
// This is the class being observed.
class BeingWatched extends Observable {  ◄──── Extend Observable.

  // Just count down to zero. Each count
  // represents a change about which the
  // observers are notified.
  void counter(int count) {
    for( ; count >= 0; count--) {

      setChanged(); // set state to changed. ◄──── Indicate that the state has changed.

      notifyObservers(count); // notify observers ◄──── Notify all observers.

      try {
        Thread.sleep(200);
      } catch(InterruptedException e) {
        System.out.println("Sleep interrupted");
      }
    }
  }
}

class TwoObservers {
  public static void main(String[] args) {

    BeingWatched observed = new BeingWatched(); ◄──── Create an object that is observed.

    Watcher1 observing1 = new Watcher1();
    Watcher2 observing2 = new Watcher2(); ◄──── Create two observers.

    // add both observers to the observed object
    observed.addObserver(observing1);
    observed.addObserver(observing2); ◄──── Add the observing objects so they can
                                             receive change notifications.

    observed.counter(5);
  }
}
```

The output from this program is shown here:

```
update() in Watcher2 called, count is 5
update() in Watcher1 called, count is 5
update() in Watcher2 called, count is 4
update() in Watcher1 called, count is 4
update() in Watcher2 called, count is 3
update() in Watcher1 called, count is 3
update() in Watcher2 called, count is 2
update() in Watcher1 called, count is 2
update() in Watcher2 called, count is 1
update() in Watcher1 called, count is 1
update() in Watcher2 called, count is 0
update() in Watcher1 called, count is 0
```

THE Timer AND TimerTask CLASSES

An interesting and useful feature offered by **java.util** is the ability to schedule a task for execution at some future time. The classes that support this are **Timer** and **TimerTask**. Using these classes, you can create a thread that runs in the background, waiting for a specific time. When the time arrives, the task linked to that thread is executed. Various options allow you to schedule a task for repeated execution, and to schedule a task to run on a specific date. Although it is always possible to manually create a task that would be executed at a specific time using the **Thread** class, **Timer** and **TimerTask** greatly simplify this process.

Timer and **TimerTask** work together. **Timer** is the class that you will use to schedule a task for execution. The task being scheduled must be an instance of **TimerTask**. Thus, to schedule a task, you will first create a **TimerTask** object and then schedule it for execution using an instance of **Timer**.

TimerTask implements the **Runnable** interface; thus, it can be used to create a thread of execution. Its constructor is shown here:

protected TimerTask( )

Notice that the constructor is **protected**.

TimerTask defines the three methods shown here:

abstract void run( )

boolean cancel( )

long scheduledExecutionTime( )

The **run( )** method, defined by the **Runnable** interface, contains the code that will be executed. Notice that **run( )** is abstract, which means that it must be overridden. Thus, the easiest way to create a timer task is to extend **TimerTask** and override **run( )**. The **cancel( )** method terminates the task. It returns **true** only if an execution of the task was prevented. The time at which the last execution of the task was scheduled to have occurred is returned by **scheduledExecutionTime( )**. This value is in terms of milliseconds from January 1, 1970.

Once a task has been created, it is scheduled for execution by an object of type **Timer**. The constructors for **Timer** are shown here:

Timer( )

Timer(boolean *DThread*)

Timer(String *tName*)

Timer(String *tName*, boolean *DThread*)

The first version creates a **Timer** object that runs as a normal thread. The second uses a daemon thread if *DThread* is **true**. A daemon thread will execute only as long as the rest of the program continues to execute. The third and fourth constructors allow you to specify a name for the **Timer** thread.

To schedule a task for execution, you can use one of **Timer**'s **schedule( )** methods. There are several forms. Two of them are shown here:

> void schedule(TimerTask *tTask*, long *wait*)
>
> void schedule(TimerTask *tTask*, long *wait*, long *repeat*)

Here, *tTask* is scheduled for execution after the period passed in *wait* has elapsed. When the second constructor is used, the task is then executed repeatedly at the interval specified by *repeat*. Both *wait* and *repeat* are specified in milliseconds. Other forms of **schedule( )** let you specify a date at which the task will execute.

You can stop the timer by calling **cancel( )**:

> void cancel( )

All tasks are also terminated.

If you create a non-daemon task, then you will want to call **cancel( )** to end the task when your program ends. If you don't do this, then the timer task will continue to execute even though the **main( )** method has ended.

The following program demonstrates **Timer** and **TimerTask**. It defines a timer task whose **run( )** method displays the message "Timer task executed." This task is scheduled to run once every half second after an initial delay of one second.

```java
// Demonstrate Timer and TimerTask.

import java.util.*;

class MyTimerTask extends TimerTask {
  public void run() {
    System.out.println("Timer task executed.");
  }
}

class TimerTest {
  public static void main(String[] args) {
    MyTimerTask myTask = new MyTimerTask();
    Timer myTimer = new Timer();

    // Set an initial delay of 1 second,
    // then repeat every half second.
    myTimer.schedule(myTask, 1000, 500);

    try {
      Thread.sleep(5000);
    } catch (InterruptedException exc) {}

    myTimer.cancel();
  }
}
```

Another method provided by **Timer** that you might find interesting is **scheduleAtFixedRate( )**. It lets you schedule a task for repeated executions that more faithfully approximate a fixed rate of execution. The time of each repetition is relative to the first execution, not the preceding execution. Thus, any "drift" in the timing will be limited.

Progress Check

1. The **Observer** interface and **Observable** class provide a framework for using the _____ pattern.
2. If you have a **Random** object and you want a **double** value from a uniform distribution in the interval from 0 to 1, use the method _____ and if you want a **double** value from a Gaussian distribution, use the method _____.
3. If you want to execute a task at regular intervals, create an object of class _____ to execute the task and then schedule it for execution at regular intervals using an object of class _____.

MISCELLANEOUS UTILITY CLASSES AND INTERFACES

Here is a brief description of other top-level classes in **java.util** that are not discussed elsewhere in this book.

BitSet	Defines a collection of bits.
EventListenerProxy	Extends the **EventListener** class to allow additional parameters.
Currency	Encapsulates information about currency.
EventObject	The superclass for all event classes.
FormattableFlags	Defines formatting flags that are used with the **Formattable** interface.
ListResourceBundle	Manages resources as an array.
Objects	Various methods that operate on objects.
PropertyPermission	Manages property permissions.
PropertyResourceBundle	Manages resources by use of property files.
ResourceBundle	Encapsulates a collection of locale-sensitive resources as key/value pairs.
ServiceLoader	Provides a means of finding service providers.
StringTokenizer	Breaks a string into individual parts called tokens.
UUID	Encapsulates and manages Universally Unique Identifiers (UUIDs).

Answers:

1. Observer
2. **nextDouble( )**, **nextGaussian( )**
3. **TimerTask**, **Timer**

With the exception of **Formattable** and **EventListener**, all of the interfaces in **java.util** are discussed here or in the following chapter. The **Formattable** interface is implemented by a class that provides custom formatting. **EventListener** is inherited by all event listeners.

Ask the Expert

Q What do the methods in the **Objects** class do?

A All the methods defined in that class are **static** methods. Some of them perform actions similar to the non-**static** methods in the **Object** class. For example, **Objects** contains a **toString( )** method shown here:

static String toString(Object *obj*)

This method calls **obj.toString( )** and returns the result if **obj** is not **null**, and it returns "null" if **obj** is **null**. Therefore, **obj.toString( )** and **Objects.toString(obj)** are almost identical. The only difference occurs when **obj** is **null**. In that case, **obj.toString( )** throws a **NullPointerException**, whereas **Objects.toString(obj)** returns "null".

The **Objects** class also has convenient methods for comparing two objects or for testing whether an object is **null**. For example, there is a **requireNonNull( )** method that has this general form:

public static <T> T requireNonNull(T *obj*)

This method returns **obj** if **obj** is not **null**. Otherwise, it throws a **NullPointerException**. Therefore the code segment:

```
Object obj = Objects.requireNonNull(x);
```

performs basically the same function as the code segment:

```
Object obj;
if(x != null) obj = x;
else throw new NullPointerException();
```

EXERCISES

1. What are the main differences between the **javax.swing.Timer** class discussed in Chapter 21 and the **java.util.Timer** class?

2. What is the difference between the value returned by a call to **System.currentTimeMillis( )** mentioned in the last chapter and the value returned by a call to **Calendar.getInstance( ).getTimeInMillis( )** used in earlier chapters?

3. When a **Formatter** sees a '%' character in the format string, how does it know whether that character is part of a format specifier or just a regular character that should be inserted in the output string?

4. Assume you have a **GregorianCalendar** object **cal** and you want to display, using **System.out.printf( )**, the date it represents in the form *year:month:day: hour:minute:second* using the long form of the year, month, and day, and using the 24-hour format. For example, if **cal** represents noon on March 11, 1984, then the output should be "1984:March:11:12:00:00". What should the arguments be for the call to **printf( )**? Use relative indices where possible.

5. Assume that **x** is a **long** variable and it is to be displayed using **System.out.printf( )** with a minimum field width of 20, a leading '+' if it is positive, commas after each three digits from the right, and left-justified. What should the arguments be for the call to **printf( )**?

6. Assume you have a **double** variable **x** and you use a **Formatter** to create a string containing the value of **x** and then you use a **Scanner** to get back the value of **x** from the string. Are you guaranteed to end up with the same value for **x** as you started with? Why or why not?

7. What is the output of the following instruction?

```
System.out.printf("%%%(-11.2E%%", -1.23456789);
```

8. What happens if you create a **GregorianCalendar** object that represents an illegal date such as January 32, 1970? More precisely, what happens if you execute the following code segment:

```
GregorianCalendar cal = new GregorianCalendar(1970, 0, 32);
```

and then you output the month, day, and year stored in **cal** using calls to **getDisplayName( )**?

9. Write a program that prints out the names of all the months in German.

10. Write a program that determines whether the date that is 70 days before April 1, 2000 is before or after the date that is 500 days after September 1, 1998. The program should display the two dates and tell which comes first.

11. Create a **static** method **numDaysLeftInYear( )** that takes a **GregorianCalendar** variable **cal** as its parameter and returns the number of days left in the year represented by **cal**. For example, if **cal** represents December 28, 2000, then **numDaysLeftInYear(cal)** returns 3 (it does not include December 28 as one of the days left in the year). Also write a program to test your method.

12. Assume that **x** is an integer variable previously initialized. Does **System.out.printf("%d", x)** output the same string as **System.out.print(new java.util.Formatter( ).format("%d", x))**?

13. Improve the **formatCities( )** method in Try This 24-1 so that it displays the numbers with commas separating every three digits from the right.

14. Improve the **formatCities( )** method in Try This 24-1 so that it displays a row of hyphens across the top and bottom of the table. The row starts at the left vertical bar and ends at the right vertical bar.

15. Write a program similar to the **TableFormatDemo** class discussed in the chapter but, instead of listing the squares and cubes of the numbers from 1 to 10, it lists the decimal, octal, hexadecimal, and scientific notation forms of the numbers from 1 to 20. Use relative indexing where possible.

16. Create a method **weekDay( )** that takes a **Calendar** as its parameter. It returns the full name of the day of the week represented by the **Calendar**.

17. Create a method **convertToRows( )** that takes two parameters: the name of a text file for input and the name of a text file for output. The input file should contain a list of integers separated by whitespace. The **convertToRows( )** method reads the integers from the input file and writes them to the output file, four integers per line. In the output file, the integers should be right-justified in four columns whose width is 15 characters. The last row might have fewer than four integers. Write a program to test your new method. Use a **Scanner** for reading the input and a **Formatter** for writing the output.

18. When sampling from a standard normal (Gaussian) distribution, approximately 68% of the samples should be between −1 and +1, approximately 95% of the samples should be between −2 and +2, and approximately 99.7% should be between −3 and +3. Write a program that generates 1,000 random values from a Gaussian distribution and keeps track of how many of them fall into each of those ranges. It then displays the results.

19. Redo the **SavingsAccountDemo** program in Chapter 16 so that it uses **Observer/Observable** instead of creating your own classes and interfaces from scratch. The **SavingsAccount** class should inherit from **Observable** and the **FeeHandler** and **FraudHandler** classes should implement **Observer** instead of implementing **BalanceChangeHandler**.

20. Write a program that uses a **Timer** that starts immediately counting up from 1 to 10 in half-second intervals and then, after another half second, rings a bell.

CHAPTER 25

Using the Data Structures in the Collections Framework

This chapter continues our examination of **java.util** by describing one of Java's most powerful subsystems: the *Collections Framework*. The Collections Framework is a sophisticated hierarchy of interfaces and classes that provide state-of-the-art technology for managing groups of objects (collections). A basic understanding of the Collections Framework is important for all Java programmers because it is widely used in Java applications and within other parts of the Java API library.

The Collections Framework provides a number of ways to store a collection of objects. It does so by providing generic implementations of several common data structures. Although you will study data structures in depth in a later course, a general understanding is needed to effectively use the Collections Framework. Thus, we begin with a brief overview of data structures.

*Note: This chapter discusses only those portions of the Collections Framework defined in **java.util**. Java also defines concurrent collections, which are designed for use in highly parallel execution environments. They are packaged in **java.util.concurrent**.*

AN OVERVIEW OF DATA STRUCTURES

Before discussing any specific data structure, it will be helpful to define the term *data structure*. Here is one definition: a data structure defines a way to arrange data and specifies the rules by which that data can be accessed. Thus, a data structure determines the basic shape, form, and characteristics of a conceptual framework used to manage groups of data.

There are many different types of data structures. The simplest one is the array, which you have already learned about in Part One. The arrays built into the Java language are implemented as fixed-length, linear lists. Individual elements are accessed via an index, by use of the array subscript notation. As a result, arrays support fast, random access to elements. As you will see, the Collections Framework also provides support for dynamic arrays, which can grow as needed.

Here are some other common data structures:

- stack
- queue
- linked list
- tree
- hash table

Each of these is supported by the Collections Framework. Each has different properties, capabilities, and performance characteristics. Thus, not every data structure is suitable for every task. Rather, the choice of data structure depends on the application.

Stacks and Queues

You have already seen examples of a stack and a queue because both have been used as examples earlier in this book. To review, both a stack and a queue strictly define the order in which elements can be added and removed. In the case of a stack, the order is last-in, first-out (LIFO). Thus, the first element put on the stack is the last element to be used. To visualize a stack, imagine a stack of plates. The first plate on the table is the last to be used, and the last plate put on the stack is the first to be used. Stacks do not support random access to their elements. Instead, they support two basic operations: *push* and *pop*. An item is put onto the stack by use of a push operation. The top item is taken off the stack by a pop operation.

In its standard form, a queue is, essentially, the opposite of a stack. Its order is first-in, first-out (FIFO). This means that the first item put in the queue is the first item retrieved, the second item put in is the second item retrieved, and so on. A checkout line at a store is a real-world example of a queue. The queue's FIFO ordering is enforced by the fact that items are added only to the end of a queue and items are taken off only by removing them from the front. Thus, queues do not support random access to their elements. Often, the front of a queue is referred to as the *head*, and the end of a queue is called the *tail*. It must be pointed out, however, that other types of queues exist in which the order of the elements is determined by some factor other than insertion order, such as priority. However, in all cases, the general mechanism of putting an element into a queue and removing an element from a queue remains the same.

Linked Lists

Stacks and queues share a common trait: They both have strict rules that define the order in which data can be accessed. A linked list is different because its elements can be accessed in a more flexible fashion. In a linked list, each piece of information carries with it a link to the next element in the list. New elements can be inserted into the list at any point by simply rearranging the links. Likewise, an element can be removed from the list by rearranging the links. As a result, linked lists are dynamic data structures that grow or shrink automatically as new elements are added or removed.

Linked lists can be either singly linked or doubly linked. Each element in a singly linked list contains a link to the next element. In a doubly linked list, each element contains links to both the next and the previous element. (See Figure 25-1.) The main difference between the two is that a singly linked list can be followed in only one direction. A doubly linked list can be followed in either direction. The linked list implementation in the Collections Framework uses a doubly linked list.

Although linked lists offer a convenient way to store variable-length lists, finding an element can be slow because a sequential search must be used. In other words, to search for an item in a linked list, you must start with the first item. If it is not the one you are looking for, you must follow the link to the next item and check it. This process repeats until the item is found. This makes linked lists very good for situations in which an operation will be applied to an entire list, but inefficient when random access to a specific element is needed.

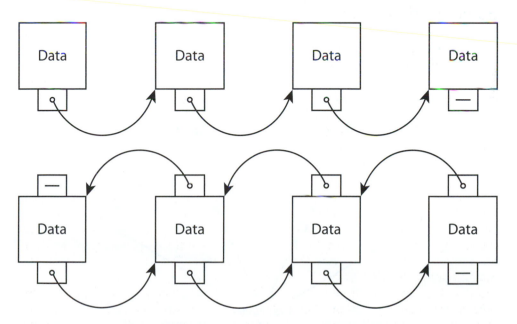

Figure 25-1. Singly linked and doubly linked lists

Trees

One of the most powerful data structures is the tree. As the name implies, a tree organizes data as a hierarchy. When depicted visually, this organization has a tree structure. However, in computer science, trees are often drawn upside down. This makes for some interesting terminology. The *root* is the first item in the tree. Each item is called a *node* of the tree. Any part of the tree that descends from a node is called a *subtree*, with that node forming the root of the subtree. A node that has no subtrees is called a *terminal node* or *leaf.* The *height* of the tree is equal to the number of layers *deep* that its nodes descend from the root. When working with trees, you can think of them existing in memory looking the way they do on paper. But remember: a tree is only a way to logically organize data in memory, and memory is linear.

One common type of tree is the *sorted binary tree,* also called a *binary search tree.* In a sorted binary tree, each node contains a link to a left member and a right member. For each node in the tree, items with smaller keys are stored on one side and items with greater keys are stored on the other. For the sake of this discussion, assume that the smaller keys are on the left of the root node and larger keys are on the right. Given this arrangement, to find a node in a sorted binary tree, simply follow the links, going left or right based on whether the current node's key is greater than or less than the search key. This approach makes for fast searches because the number of nodes that need to be checked will not exceed the height of the tree. Figure 25-2 shows a small sorted binary tree.

It is important to point out that the fast search times of a sorted binary tree only apply if the tree is in reasonably good *balance.* In other words, no subtree is more than

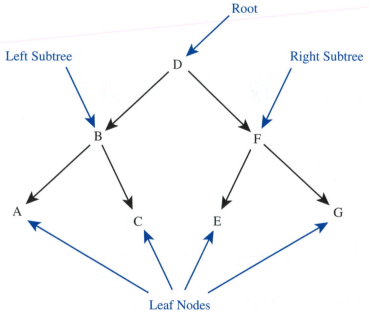

Figure 25-2. A sorted binary tree

one level deeper than another. In a worst-case, an unbalanced tree can degenerate into a linear list, which would result in much degraded performance.

Hash Tables

A hash table is a data structure that stores information in some form of table (such as an array) in which the location at which data is stored is determined by the *hash code* associated with that data. In general, the hash code is computed based on some identifying aspect of the data, which acts as the *key*. In Java's hash tables, the hash code is computed from a key that you explicitly specify. The computation of the hash code must work in such a way that each key produces a (reasonably) unique value. The principal advantage of a hash table is that very fast access times can be achieved because the hash code acts like an index to the data. For this reason, insertions, deletions, and searches in a hash table can be performed very quickly. However, as a general rule, hash tables do not store data in sorted order.

Choosing a Data Structure

You can use the characteristics of the basic data structures to help you choose the one right for the job. Here are some guidelines. When you need a last-in, first-out list, use a stack. When you need a first-in, first-out list, use a queue. For constant access time, a hash table is a good choice if sorted order is not needed. A sorted binary tree is an excellent choice when a sorted list is required and fast search times are a priority. A linked list is appropriate when a list will be accessed mostly in sequential order and sorting is not required (or only occasionally required). A dynamic array offers very fast random access to its elements. However, insertions and deletions can be expensive in terms of time.

Now that you have a basic understanding of the fundamental data structures, it is time to examine the Collections Framework.

Progress Check

1. A *data structure* is _____.
2. In what order does a queue store its elements?
3. Name two types of linked lists.
4. Is a sorted binary tree a good choice when fast access to elements is needed?

_____

Answers:

1. a way of arranging data and a specification of the rules by which the data can be accessed
2. First-in, first-out.
3. Singly linked and doubly linked.
4. Yes.

Ask the Expert

Q You mentioned that linked lists are less efficient than arrays when access to a specific element is needed. The reason is because you can access the element directly in an array but you need to traverse the linked list starting at one of the endpoints to access the element. Given the speed of modern computers, does it really matter?

A Yes, it does, especially for programs handling large amounts of data. Consider the following example. Assume that a program needs to store 100 million items in a list and assume that random access to the items is needed 4 million times a day. Furthermore, assume that the computer is so fast that it can perform 1 billion array accesses or traverse 1 billion list links a second. In other words, assume that each of these operations takes only one nanosecond (one billionth of a second). If you store the 100 million items in an array, then accessing 4 million items each day will take 4 million nanoseconds or only about four thousandths of a second. In other words, accessing the 4 million items will take a very insignificant amount of computer time each day. But consider what happens if you store the 100 million items in a linked list. In that case, to get to any given element in the list from the nearest end, you'll need to traverse a quarter of the list on average. That means that 25 million links will need to be traversed on average to access the element. Since 4 million items need to be accessed each day, there will be 4 million list traversals, each of them traversing an average of 25 million links. This amounts to 100 trillion link traversals, which will take 100 trillion nanoseconds, or over 27 hours. In other words, there are not enough hours in the day for the computer to perform all the 4 million accesses, let along do any other work!

As the preceding discussion shows, the subject of the efficiency of algorithms and data structures is an important one that you will study in detail in your data structures course.

COLLECTIONS OVERVIEW

The Collections Framework standardizes the way in which a Java program handles groups of objects. It does this by providing implementations for several of the most commonly used data structures, such as the dynamic array, stack, queue, doubly linked list, tree, and hash table just described. You will seldom need to code one of these data structures yourself. In short, the Collections Framework offers "off-the-shelf" solutions to many common programming tasks.

The Collections Framework is built on a set of well-defined interfaces. Several implementations of these interfaces are provided. The advantage to this approach is that once you understand the functionality described by an interface, you can use any specific implementation. Also, you can easily substitute a different implementation if the requirements of your program change.

In addition to collections, the framework also defines several map interfaces and classes. *Maps* store key/value pairs. Although maps are part of the Collections Framework, they are not "collections" in the strict use of the term. You can, however, obtain a *collection-view* of a map. Such a view contains the elements from the map stored in a collection. Thus, you can process the contents of a map as a collection, if you choose.

Algorithms are another important part of the Collections Framework. They operate on collections and are defined as **static** methods within the **Collections** class. Algorithms provide a standard means of manipulating collections.

Another item closely associated with the Collections Framework is the iterator. An *iterator* offers a general-purpose, standardized way of accessing the elements within a collection, one after another. Thus, an iterator provides a means of *enumerating the contents of a collection*. Because each collection provides an iterator, the elements of any collection class can be accessed through one.

THE COLLECTION INTERFACES

The Collections Framework defines several interfaces. These interfaces determine the fundamental nature of the collection classes because they specify most of the functionality provided by those classes. The collections classes simply provide different implementations of the standard interfaces. Therefore, to understand the Collections Framework, you must begin by understanding its interfaces.

The collection interfaces packaged in **java.util** are summarized in the following table:

Interface	Description
Collection	Enables you to work with groups of objects; it is at the top of the collections hierarchy.
Deque	Extends **Queue** to handle a double-ended queue. This can be used to implement a stack or a queue.
List	Extends **Collection** to handle lists of objects.
NavigableSet	Extends **SortedSet** to handle the retrieval of an element based on how close its value is to another value.
Queue	Extends **Collection** to handle queues.
Set	Extends **Collection** to handle sets, which must contain unique elements.
SortedSet	Extends **Set** to handle sorted sets.

In addition to these interfaces, collections also use the **Comparator**, **Iterator**, and **ListIterator** interfaces, which are described in depth later in this chapter. Briefly, **Comparator** determines how two objects are compared; **Iterator** and **ListIterator** support iterators. Another interface used by some collections is **RandomAccess**. By implementing **RandomAccess**, a collection indicates that it supports efficient, random access to its elements.

To provide the greatest flexibility in their use, the collection interfaces allow some methods to be optional. The optional methods enable you to modify the contents of a collection. Collections that support these methods are called *modifiable*. Collections that do not allow their contents to be changed are called *unmodifiable*. All the built-in collections are modifiable.

The following sections examine the collection interfaces.

The Collection Interface

The **Collection** interface is the foundation on which the Collections Framework is built because it must be implemented by any class that defines a collection. **Collection** is a generic interface that has this declaration:

interface Collection<E>

Here, **E** specifies the type of objects that the collection will hold. **Collection** extends the **Iterable** interface. This is important because only classes that implement **Iterable** can be used with a for-each **for** loop. **Iterable** also enables a collection to be iterated over using an iterator.

Collection declares the core methods that all collections will have. These methods are summarized in Table 25-1. Because all collections implement **Collection**, familiarity with its methods is necessary for a clear understanding of the framework. Let's look at each.

At its foundation, a data structure supports two fundamental operations: the insertion of an item into a collection and the removal of an item from a collection. In the **Collection** interface, these operations are supported by the **add( )** and **remove( )** methods. Notice that **add( )** takes an argument of type **E**, which is the type parameter for **Collection**. This means that objects added to a collection must be compatible with the type of data expected by the collection.

Now, notice the **size( )** and **isEmpty( )** methods. These are two more fundamental operations commonly implemented by a data structure. The number of elements currently stored in the collection can be obtained by calling **size( )**. You might use this value, for example, as the stopping point when cycling through a collection using a loop. Be aware that the value returned by **size( )** will change if the number of elements stored in the collection changes. When a collection contains no elements, **isEmtpy( )** returns **true**. You can use this method to avoid accessing an empty collection, for example. A collection can be emptied by calling **clear( )**.

Although the operations just described are sufficient to handle many types of collection operations, **Collection** specifies three methods that add convenience when working with groups of elements. These are **addAll( )**, **removeAll( )**, and **retainAll( )**. You can add the entire contents of one collection to another by calling **addAll( )**. To remove a group of objects, call **removeAll( )**. You can remove all elements except those of a specified group by calling **retainAll( )**.

Two collections can be compared for equality by calling **equals( )**. The precise meaning of "equality" is allowed to differ from collection to collection. For collections that implement **List** or **Set** interfaces, the contents of the collections are compared. You can determine if a collection holds an element by calling **contains( )**. To determine if all elements of one collection are part of another, call **containsAll( )**.

The **iterator( )** method returns an iterator to a collection. Iterators are frequently used when working with collections because, as explained earlier, they provide a means by which elements of the collection can be enumerated. The for-each **for** loop, which also cycles through a collection, offers a convenient alternative in some cases.

Finally, the **toArray( )** methods return an array that contains the elements stored in the collection. One version returns an array of **Object**. The other version returns an array of elements that have the same type as the array specified as a parameter. The second form is convenient because it returns the desired array type. These methods

TABLE 25-1: The Methods Declared by Collection	
Method	**Description**
boolean add(E *obj*)	Adds *obj* to the invoking collection. Returns **true** if *obj* was added to the collection. Otherwise, returns **false**.
boolean addAll(Collection<? extends E> *col*)	Adds the elements in *col* to the invoking collection. Returns **true** if at least one element was added. Otherwise, returns **false**.
void clear( )	Empties the invoking collection.
boolean contains(Object *obj*)	Returns **true** if *obj* is in the invoking collection. Otherwise, returns **false**.
boolean containsAll(Collection<?> *col*)	Returns **true** if all elements of *col* are also in the invoking collection. Otherwise, returns **false**.
boolean equals(Object *obj*)	Returns **true** if the invoking collection and *obj* are equal. Otherwise, returns **false**.
int hashCode( )	Returns the invoking collection's hash code.
boolean isEmpty( )	Returns **true** if the invoking collection is empty. Otherwise, returns **false**.
Iterator<E> iterator( )	Returns an iterator for the invoking collection.
boolean remove(Object *obj*)	Removes one item equal to *obj* from the invoking collection. Returns **true** if successful. Returns **false** if *obj* was not in the collection.
boolean removeAll(Collection<?> *col*)	Removes all elements in *col* from the invoking collection. Returns **true** if at least one item was removed. Otherwise, returns **false**.
boolean retainAll(Collection<?> *col*)	Removes all elements from the invoking collection except those in *col*. Returns **true** if at least one element was removed. Otherwise, returns **false**.
int size( )	Returns the number of elements currently stored in the invoking collection.
Object[ ] toArray( )	Returns the elements stored in the invoking collection in the form of an array. The array is independent from the invoking collection.
<T> T[ ] toArray(T[ ] *array*)	Returns the elements stored in the invoking collection in the form of an array. The array is independent from the invoking collection. If the size of *array* equals or exceeds the number of elements, these are returned in *array*. If the size of *array* is less than the number of elements, a new array of the necessary size is allocated and returned.

are more important than it might at first seem because there can be times when you need to process the contents of a collection as an array. For example, you might want to pass a collection to a method that expects an array. The array obtained from **toArray( )** is independent of the collection, except, of course, that both refer to the same elements.

The List Interface

The **List** interface extends **Collection** and declares the behavior of a collection that stores a sequence of elements. Elements can be inserted or accessed by their position in the list, using a zero-based index. It is legal for a **List** implementation to contain duplicates. **List** is a generic interface that has this declaration:

interface List<E>

Here, **E** specifies the type of objects that the list will hold.

In addition to the methods defined by **Collection**, **List** adds some of its own, which are summarized in Table 25-2.

Notice that most of the methods added by **List** either take an index as an argument or return an index. These methods provide support for index-based random access to a **List**. For example, to obtain the object stored at a specific location, call **get( )**, specifying the index of the object. To set the value at a specific location, call **set( )**, passing in the index and the value. To find the index of an object, use **indexOf( )** or **lastIndexOf( )**.

Another method to notice is **subList( )**. It lets you obtain a sublist of a list by specifying its beginning and ending indices. As you can imagine, **subList( )** makes list processing quite convenient. Be careful, though, because the list returned uses the original list. Thus, changing one changes the other. This arrangement is referred to as a *view* of the collection. In the Java API documentation, such a view is said to be "backed" by the collection on which it is called. One other point: if you make a change to the structure of the underlying collection (except through the view), for example, by changing its size, then the sublist will become invalid. The key point is to use sublists with care.

One other point: **List** changes the semantics of **add(E)** and **addAll(Collection)** defined by **Collection** so that they add elements to the end of the list. To add an element in a specific location, use the index forms of **add( )** or **addAll( )** specified by **List**.

The Set Interface

The **Set** interface defines a set. It extends **Collection** and declares the behavior of a collection that does not allow duplicate elements. Therefore, the **add( )** method returns **false** if an attempt is made to add duplicate elements to a set. It does not declare any additional methods of its own. **Set** is a generic interface that has this declaration:

interface Set<E>

Here, **E** specifies the type of objects that the set will hold.

The SortedSet Interface

The **SortedSet** interface extends **Set** and declares the behavior of a set sorted in ascending order. **SortedSet** is a generic interface that has this declaration:

interface SortedSet<E>

Here, **E** specifies the type of objects that the set will hold. In addition to those methods provided by **Set**, the **SortedSet** interface adds the methods summarized in Table 25-3.

TABLE 25-2: The Methods Declared by List

Method	Description
void add(int *index*, E *obj*)	Adds *obj* to the invoking list at the index passed in *index*.
boolean addAll(int *index*, Collection<? extends E> *col*)	Adds the elements of *col* to the invoking list at the index passed in *index*. Returns **true** if at least one element was added and **false** otherwise.
E get(int *index*)	Returns the object stored at the index passed in *index* within the invoking collection.
int indexOf(Object *obj*)	Searches for the first instance of *obj* in the invoking list. If found, its index is returned. Otherwise, –1 is returned.
int lastIndexOf(Object *obj*)	Searches for the last instance of *obj* in the invoking list. If found, its index is returned. Otherwise, –1 is returned.
ListIterator<E> listIterator( )	Returns an iterator to the start of the invoking list.
ListIterator<E> listIterator(int *index*)	Returns an iterator to the invoking list that begins at the index passed in *index*.
E remove(int *index*)	Removes the element at the index passed in *index* from the invoking list and returns the deleted element.
E set(int *index*, E *obj*)	Assigns *obj* to the location specified by *index* within the invoking list. Returns the old value.
List<E> subList(int *start*, int *end*)	Returns a list that includes elements from *start* to *end*–1 in the invoking list. The resulting list is a view of the invoking list.

TABLE 25-3: The Methods Declared by SortedSet

Method	Description
Comparator<? super E> comparator( )	Returns the invoking set's comparator. If no comparator is used, **null** is returned.
E first( )	Returns the element with the smallest value. Because the set is sorted, this will be the first element in the invoking set.
SortedSet<E> headSet(E *end*)	Returns a **SortedSet** that includes those elements in the invoking set that are less than *end*. The resulting set is a view of the invoking set.
E last( )	Returns the element with the largest value. Because the set is sorted, this will be the last element in the invoking set.
SortedSet<E> subSet(E *start*, E *end*)	Returns a **SortedSet** that includes those elements in the invoking set that are between *start* and *end*–1. The resulting set is a view of the invoking set.
SortedSet<E> tailSet(E *start*)	Returns a **SortedSet** that includes those elements in the invoking set that are greater than or equal to *start*. The resulting set is a view of the invoking set.

Notice that **SortedSet** defines three methods that obtain subsets. These can make set processing more convenient. You can obtain a subset of a sorted set by calling **subSet( )**, specifying the first and last object in the desired set. If you need the subset that starts with the first element in the set, use **headSet( )**. If you want the subset that ends the set, use **tailSet( )**. These methods make it easy to obtain a range of the elements in a set. In all three cases, the returned set is a "view," meaning that it refers to the original set. Changing one affects the other. Unlike the views obtained from a **List**, these views allow changes to the structure of the underlying collection without invalidating the view. One other point: you can't add an element to one of these views that is outside the range of the view. Attempting to do so will cause an exception.

The NavigableSet Interface

The **NavigableSet** interface extends **SortedSet** and declares the behavior of a collection that supports the retrieval of an element based on how close its value is to another value. **NavigableSet** is a generic interface that has this declaration:

interface NavigableSet<E>

Here, **E** specifies the type of objects that the set will hold. In addition to the methods that it inherits from **SortedSet**, **NavigableSet** adds those summarized in Table 25-4.

Pay special attention to the **ceiling( )** and **floor( )** methods. They find the next element in the set that is closest to or equal to another element. To find an element that is closest to but not equal to another element, use **higher( )** and **lower( )**. Notice also that additional forms of **subSet( )**, **tailSet( )**, and **headSet( )** have been added that work with near matches.

The Queue Interface

The **Queue** interface extends **Collection** and declares the behavior of a queue. Typically, this is a first-in, first-out list. However, there are types of queues in which the ordering is based on other criteria. **Queue** is a generic interface that has this declaration:

interface Queue<E>

Here, **E** specifies the type of objects that the queue will hold. The methods added by **Queue** are shown in Table 25-5.

Despite its simplicity, **Queue** offers several points of interest. First, elements can only be removed from the head (front) of the queue. Second, the point of element insertion is not specified. For a FIFO queue, elements would be added to the tail of the queue, but other implementations are allowed. Third, there are two methods that obtain and remove elements: **remove( )** and **poll( )**. The difference between them is what occurs when called on an empty queue. In this case, the **remove( )** method throws a **NoSuchElementException** exception. The **poll( )** method returns **null**. Fourth, there are two methods, **element( )** and **peek( )**, that obtain but don't remove the element at the head of the queue. They also differ in their behavior when called on an empty queue, the first throwing a **NoSuchElementException** exception; the other returning **null**.

TABLE 25-4: The Methods Declared by NavigableSet	
Method	**Description**
E ceiling(E *obj*)	Searches the set for the smallest element *e* such that *e* >= *obj*. If such an element is found, it is returned. Otherwise, **null** is returned.
Iterator<E> descendingIterator( )	Returns an iterator that moves from the greatest to least. In other words, it returns a reverse iterator.
NavigableSet<E> descendingSet( )	Returns a **NavigableSet** that contains the entries in the invoking set in reverse order. The resulting set is a view of the invoking set.
E floor(E *obj*)	Searches the set for the largest element *e* such that *e* <= *obj*. If such an element is found, it is returned. Otherwise, **null** is returned.
NavigableSet<E> headSet(E *upperBound*, boolean *incl*)	Returns a **NavigableSet** that includes all elements from the invoking set that are less than *upperBound*. If *incl* is **true**, then an element equal to *upperBound* is included. The resulting set is a view of the invoking set.
E higher(E *obj*)	Searches the set for the smallest element *e* such that *e* > *obj*. If such an element is found, it is returned. Otherwise, **null** is returned.
E lower(E *obj*)	Searches the set for the largest element *e* such that *e* < *obj*. If such an element is found, it is returned. Otherwise, **null** is returned.
E pollFirst( )	Returns the first element in the invoking set, removing the element in the process. Because the set is sorted, this is the element with the smallest value. Returns **null** if called on an empty set.
E pollLast( )	Returns the last element in the invoking set, removing the element in the process. Because the set is sorted, this is the element with the largest value. Returns **null** if called on an empty set.

NavigableSet<E>
    subSet(E *lowerBound*,
        boolean *lowIncl*,
        E *upperBound*,
        boolean *highIncl*)
	Returns a **NavigableSet** that includes all elements from the invoking set that are greater than *lowerBound* and less than *upperBound*. If *lowIncl* is **true**, then an element equal to *lowerBound* is included. If *highIncl* is **true**, then an element equal to *upperBound* is included. The resulting set is a view of the invoking set.

NavigableSet<E> tailSet(E *lowerBound*, boolean *incl*)	Returns a **NavigableSet** that includes all elements from the invoking set that are greater than *lowerBound*. If *incl* is **true**, then an element equal to *lowerBound* is included. The resulting set is a view of the invoking set.

TABLE 25-5: The Methods Declared by Queue

Method	Description
E element( )	Returns the element at the head of the queue. The element is not removed. If called on an empty queue, a **NoSuchElementException** is thrown.
boolean offer (E *obj*)	Attempts to add *obj* to the queue. Returns **true** if *obj* was added and **false** otherwise. This method will fail if an attempt is made to add an element to a full capacity-restricted queue.
E peek( )	Returns the element at the head of the queue. The element is not removed. Returns **null** if called on an empty queue.
E poll( )	Returns the element at the head of the queue, removing the element in the process. Returns **null** if called on an empty queue.
E remove( )	Removes the element at the head of the queue, returning the element in the process. If called on an empty queue, a **NoSuchElementException** is thrown.

Finally, notice that **offer( )** only attempts to add an element to a queue. Although the queue implementations in **java.util** are dynamic, a capacity-restricted queue implementation is permissible. For example, a queue might be of fixed length. In a capacity-restricted queue, **offer( )** can fail when the queue is full. In this case, it returns **false**. The **add( )** method, which is inherited from **Collection**, can also be used to add an element to a queue. If the queue is fixed length, it will throw an **IllegalStateException** when called on a full queue.

The Deque Interface

The **Deque** interface extends **Queue** and declares the behavior of a double-ended queue. Double-ended queues can function as standard, first-in, first-out queues or as last-in, first-out stacks. **Deque** is a generic interface that has this declaration:

    interface Deque<E>

Here, **E** specifies the type of objects that the deque will hold. In addition to the methods that it inherits from **Queue**, **Deque** adds those methods shown in Table 25-6.

Notice that **Deque** includes the methods **push( )** and **pop( )**. These methods enable a **Deque** to function as a stack. Of course, you can also use a **Deque** as a queue. There are various ways to do this. Here is one way: use **offerLast( )** to put an item on the tail of the queue and **pollFirst( )** to remove an item from the head of the queue.

Although the implementations of **Deque** in **java.util** are dynamic, a **Deque** implementation can also be capacity-restricted. When this is the case, an attempt to add an element to the deque can fail. **Deque** allows you to handle such a failure in two ways. First, methods such as **addFirst( )** and **addLast( )** throw an **IllegalStateException** if a capacity-restricted deque is full. Second, methods such as **offerFirst( )** and **offerLast( )** return **false** if the element cannot be added. You also have two ways to handle

TABLE 25-6: The Methods Declared by Deque

Method	Description
void addFirst(E *obj*)	Attempts to add *obj* to the head of the deque. It throws an **IllegalStateException** if a capacity-restricted deque is out of space.
void addLast(E *obj*)	Attempts to add *obj* to the tail of the deque. It throws an **IllegalStateException** if a capacity-restricted deque is out of space.
Iterator<E> descendingIterator( )	Returns an iterator that moves from the tail to the head of the deque. In other words, it returns a reverse iterator.
E getFirst( )	Returns the element at the head of the deque. The object is not removed. If called on an empty deque, a **NoSuchElementException** is thrown.
E getLast( )	Returns the element at the tail of the deque. The object is not removed. If called on an empty deque, a **NoSuchElementException** is thrown.
boolean offerFirst(E *obj*)	Attempts to add *obj* to the head of the deque. Returns **true** if *obj* was added and **false** otherwise. Therefore, this method returns **false** when an attempt is made to add *obj* to a full, capacity-restricted deque.
boolean offerLast(E *obj*)	Attempts to add *obj* to the tail of the deque. Returns **true** if *obj* was added and **false** otherwise. Therefore, this method returns **false** when an attempt is made to add *obj* to a full, capacity-restricted deque.
E peekFirst( )	Returns the element at the head of the deque. The object is not removed. Returns **null** if called on an empty deque.
E peekLast( )	Returns the element at the tail of the deque. The object is not removed. Returns **null** if called on an empty deque.
E pollFirst( )	Returns the element at the head of the deque, removing the element in the process. Returns **null** if called on an empty deque.
E pollLast( )	Returns the element at the tail of the deque, removing the element in the process. It returns **null** if called on an emtpy deque.
E pop( )	Returns the element at the head of the deque, removing it in the process. If called on an empty deque, a **NoSuchElementException** is thrown.
void push(E *obj*)	Adds *obj* to the head of the deque. It throws an **IllegalStateException** if a capacity-restricted deque is out of space.
E removeFirst( )	Returns the element at the head of the deque, removing the element in the process. If called on an empty deque, a **NoSuchElementException** is thrown.

Table 25-6: The Methods Declared by Deque (Continued)	
Method	**Description**
boolean removeFirstOccurrence(Object *obj*)	Searches for the first instance of *obj*. If found, the element is removed. Returns **true** if successful and **false** if the deque did not contain *obj*.
E removeLast( )	Returns the element at the tail of the deque, removing the element in the process. If called on an empty deque, a **NoSuchElementException** is thrown.
boolean removeLastOccurrence(Object *obj*)	Searches for the last instance of *obj*. If found, the element is removed. Returns **true** if successful and **false** if the deque did not contain *obj*.

an attempt to remove an element from an empty deque. Methods such as **removeFirst( )** and **removeLast( )** throw a **NoSuchElementException**. Methods such as **pollFirst( )** and **pollLast( )** return **null**.

One other point: Notice the **descendingIterator( )** method. It returns an iterator that returns elements in reverse order. In other words, it returns an iterator that moves from the end of the deque to the start.

Progress Check

1. The Collections Framework provides implementations of the standard data structures. True or False?
2. The **Collections** interface defines all the following methods: **add( )**, **remove( )**, **clear( )**, **contains( )**, **isEmpty( )**, **iterator( )**, **size( )**, **toArray( )**. True or False?
3. A **List** can store duplicates. True or False?
4. A **Set** can store duplicates. True or False?

THE COLLECTION CLASSES

The collection interfaces are implemented by several classes. Some of the classes provide full implementations that can be used as-is. Others are abstract, providing partial implementations that are used as starting points for creating concrete collections. As a general rule, the collection classes are not synchronized.

Answers:

1. True.
2. True. It also defines several other methods.
3. True.
4. False.

The standard collection classes packaged in **java.util** are summarized in the following table:

Class	Description
AbstractCollection	Implements parts of the **Collection** interface.
AbstractList	Extends **AbstractCollection** and implements parts of the **List** interface.
AbstractQueue	Extends **AbstractCollection** and implements parts of the **Queue** interface.
AbstractSequentialList	Extends **AbstractList** for use by a collection designed for sequential rather than random access of its elements.
AbstractSet	Extends **AbstractCollection** and implements parts of the **Set** interface.
ArrayList	Implements a dynamic array by extending **AbstractList**.
ArrayDeque	Implements a dynamic double-ended queue by extending **AbstractCollection**. It also implements the **Deque** interface.
EnumSet	Extends **AbstractSet** for use with **enum** elements.
HashSet	Implements a set stored in a hash table by extending **AbstractSet**.
LinkedHashSet	Extends **HashSet** to allow insertion-order iterations.
LinkedList	Implements a linked list by extending **AbstractSequentialList**. Also implements **Deque**.
PriorityQueue	Implements a priority-based queue by extending **AbstractQueue**.
TreeSet	Implements a set stored in a tree by extending **AbstractSet**. Also implements **SortedSet**.

The abstract classes, such as **AbstractCollection**, supply partial implementations that are completed by the concrete classes. **EnumSet** is a specialized collection that is used to store **enum** elements and is not examined here. The other concrete collection classes are described in the sections that follow.

*Note: In addition to the collection classes just shown, **java.util** includes several legacy classes that also work with groups of data. These include **Vector**, **Stack**, and **Hashtable**. The legacy classes have been part of Java since the beginning. They are briefly described at the end of this chapter.*

The ArrayList Class

The **ArrayList** class extends **AbstractList** and implements the **List** interface. **ArrayList** is a generic class that has this declaration:

```
class ArrayList<E>
```

Here, **E** specifies the type of objects that the list will hold.

ArrayList supports dynamic arrays that can grow as needed. In Java, standard arrays are of a fixed length. After an array has been created, it cannot grow or shrink, which means that you must know in advance how many elements an array will hold. But sometimes you may not know until run time precisely how large an array you need. To handle this situation, the Collections Framework defines **ArrayList**. In essence, an **ArrayList**

is a variable-length array of object references. That is, an **ArrayList** can dynamically increase or decrease in size. Array lists are created with an initial size. When this size is exceeded, the collection is automatically enlarged. When objects are removed, the array can be shrunk. The elements in an **ArrayList** are accessed through an index.

ArrayList has the constructors shown here:

ArrayList( )

ArrayList(Collection<? extends E> *col*)

ArrayList(int *initCapacity*)

The first constructor creates an empty array list. The second constructor builds an array list that is initialized with the elements of the collection *col*. The third constructor creates an array list that has the initial capacity passed to *initCapacity*. The capacity is the size of the underlying array that is used to store the elements. In all cases, the capacity grows automatically as elements are added to an array list. The default initial capacity is 10.

The following program demonstrates **ArrayList**. An array list is created for objects of type **Character**, and then several characters are added to it. Then, various operations are performed on the list. Although a collection can store only references, we can still add **char** literals to it because autoboxing automatically boxes them as **Character** objects.

```
// Demonstrate ArrayList.

import java.util.*;

class ArrayListDemo {
  public static void main(String[] args) {
    // Create an array list.
    ArrayList<Character> al = new ArrayList<Character>();   // ← Construct an
                                                            //   ArrayList for
    System.out.println("Initial size: " + al.size());       //   characters.

    // Add elements to the end of the list one at a time.
    al.add('A');   ┐
    al.add('B');   │
    al.add('C');   ├── Add elements to
    al.add('D');   │   the list.
    al.add('E');   ┘

    System.out.println("\nSize after additions: " + al.size());

    // Display the array list using its toString() representation.
    System.out.println("Contents: " + al);

    // Now, add elements to middle of the list.
    // This will cause the array to expand.
    for(int i = 0; i < 3; i++)
      al.add(2, (char) ('x' + i));

    System.out.println("\nSize after additions: " + al.size());
    System.out.println("Contents: " + al);
```

```
// Now, delete the elements just added.
// This will cause the array to contract.
for(int i = 0; i < 3; i++)
   al.remove(2);  ◄─────────────────────── Remove an element.

System.out.println("\nSize after deletions: " + al.size());
System.out.println("Contents: " + al);

// Use set() to set the value at an index.
for(int i=0; i < al.size(); i++)
   al.set(i, Character.toLowerCase(al.get(i)));  ◄───── Change an element.

System.out.println("\nAfter changing to lowercase.");
System.out.println("Contents: " + al);

// Find and remove a value
int idx = al.indexOf('d');  ◄─────────────────────── Find the index of a value.
if(idx >= 0) al.remove(idx);

System.out.println("\nAfter finding and removing d.");
System.out.println("Contents: " + al);

// Empty the list.
al.clear();  ◄─────────────────────── Remove all elements in the list.
System.out.println("\nAfter clearing the list.");
System.out.println("Contents: " + al);

// Add the digits 0 through 9
for(int i=0; i < 10; i++)
   al.add((char) ('0' + i));

// Display every other element.
System.out.print("\nHere is every other digit: ");
for(int i=0; i < al.size(); i+=2)
   System.out.print(al.get(i) + " ");
  }
}
```

The output from this program is shown here:

```
Initial size: 0

Size after additions: 5
Contents: [A, B, C, D, E]

Size after additions: 8
Contents: [A, B, z, y, x, C, D, E]

Size after deletions: 5
Contents: [A, B, C, D, E]

After changing to lowercase.
Contents: [a, b, c, d, e]
```

```
After finding and removing d.
Contents: [a, b, c, e]

After clearing the list.
Contents: []

Here is every other digit: 0 2 4 6 8
```

Notice that **al** starts out empty and its size increases as elements are added to it. When elements are removed, its size is reduced. Because **ArrayList** implements a dynamic array, its elements can be accessed through an index. This is demonstrated by the use of the index forms of **add( )**, **remove( )**, **get( )**, and **set( )**. For example, consider this line from the program:

```
al.set(i, Character.toLowerCase(al.get(i)));
```

It uses **get( )** to obtain the character at the specified index and then uses **set( )** to store the lowercase version of that character back into the same location. Also notice that the non-index form of **add( )** simply puts new elements on the end of the array.

In the example, notice that the contents of a collection are displayed using the default conversion provided by **toString( )**, which was inherited from **AbstractCollection**. The **toString( )** conversion is very convenient when experimenting with the collections because it gives you an easy way to see their contents. Of course, you can also display the elements of a collection individually, using a loop, as the last line of output does.

Although the capacity of an **ArrayList** object increases automatically as objects are stored in it, you can increase the capacity of an **ArrayList** object manually by calling **ensureCapacity( )**. You might want to do this if you know in advance that you will be storing many more items in the collection than it can currently hold. By increasing its capacity once, at the start, you can prevent several reallocations later. Because reallocations are costly in terms of time, preventing unnecessary ones improves performance. The **ensureCapacity( )** method is shown here:

> void ensureCapacity(int *cap*)

Here, *cap* specifies the new minimum capacity of the collection.

Conversely, if you want to reduce the capacity of an **ArrayList** object so that it fits the number of items that it is currently holding, call **trimToSize( )**, shown here:

> void trimToSize( )

The LinkedList Class

The **LinkedList** class extends **AbstractSequentialList** and implements the **List** and **Deque** interfaces. It provides a doubly linked list data structure. **LinkedList** is a generic class that has this declaration:

> class LinkedList<E>

Here, **E** specifies the type of objects that the list will hold. **LinkedList** has the two constructors shown here:

> LinkedList( )
>
> LinkedList(Collection<? extends E> *col*)

The first constructor creates an empty linked list. The second constructor builds a linked list that is initialized with the elements of the collection *col*.

Because **LinkedList** implements the **Deque** interface, you have access to the methods defined by **Deque**. For example, to add elements to the start of a list, you can use **addFirst( )** or **offerFirst( )**. To add elements to the end of the list, use **addLast( )** or **offerLast( )**. To obtain the first element, you can use **getFirst( )** or **peekFirst( )**. To obtain the last element, use **getLast( )** or **peekLast( )**. To remove the first element, use **removeFirst( )** or **pollFirst( )**. To remove the last element, use **removeLast( )** or **pollLast( )**. Of course, you also have access to all of the functionality provided by **List**, such as the ability to access the list via an index or to obtain a sublist.

The following program demonstrates several features of **LinkedList**:

```java
// Demonstrate LinkedList.

import java.util.*;

class LinkedListDemo {
  public static void main(String[] args) {
    // Create a linked list.
    LinkedList<Character> ll = new LinkedList<Character>();

    // Add elements to the linked list.
    ll.add('B');
    ll.add('E');
    ll.add('F');
    System.out.println("Original contents: " + ll);

    // Demonstrate addLast() and addFirst().
    ll.addLast('G');              ← Add elements to the end and beginning of the list.
    ll.addFirst('A');
    System.out.println("\nAfter calls to addFirst() and addLast().");
    System.out.println("Contents: " + ll);

    // Add elements at an index.
    ll.add(2, 'D');               ← Add elements at a specific index.
    ll.add(2, 'C');
    System.out.println("\nAfter insertions.");
    System.out.println("Contents: " + ll);

    // Display first and last elements.
    System.out.println("\nHere are the first and last elements: " +
                   ll.getFirst() + " " + ll.getLast());  ← Obtain the elements at the
                                                             beginning and end of the list.
```

```
    // Create a sublist view.
    List<Character> sub = ll.subList(2, 5);              Obtain a view of a sublist.
    System.out.println("\nContents of sublist view: " + sub);

    // Create a new list that contains the sublist
    LinkedList<Character> ll2 = new LinkedList<Character>(sub);

    // Remove the elements in ll2 from ll.
    ll.removeAll(ll2);                      Remove all elements in ll2 from ll.

    System.out.println("\nAfter removing ll2 from ll.");
    System.out.println("Contents: " + ll);

    // Remove first and last elements.
    ll.removeFirst();
    ll.removeLast();                    Remove the first and last elements.

    System.out.println("\nAfter deleting first and last element: ");
    System.out.println("Contents: " + ll);

    // Get and set a value through an index.
    ll.set(0, Character.toLowerCase(ll.get(0)));        Change a value.

    System.out.println("\nAfter change: " + ll);
  }
}
```

The output from this program is shown here:

```
Original contents: [B, E, F]

After calls to addFirst() and addLast().
Contents: [A, B, E, F, G]

After insertions.
Contents: [A, B, C, D, E, F, G]

Here are the first and last elements: A G

Contents of sublist view: [C, D, E]

After removing ll2 from ll.
Contents: [A, B, F, G]

After deleting first and last element:
Contents: [B, F]

After change: [b, F]
```

As the program shows, because **LinkedList** implements the **List** interface, calls to **add( )** append items to the end of the list, as do calls to **addLast( )**. To insert items at a specific location, use the **add(int, E)** form of **add( )**, as illustrated by the call to **add(2, 'D')** in the example. The **removeFirst( )** and **removeLast( )** methods give you an easy way to remove the first or last element without having to specify an index.

Notice how a portion of **ll** is obtained by calling **sublist( )**. Recall that **sublist( )** returns a "view" that uses the list upon which it is called. However, in a **List**, this view is invalidated if any changes in the size of the underlying collection occur. This is why a new **LinkedList** must be created that contains the elements in **sub** before **removeAll( )** can be used to delete those elements from **ll**. If you were to try to call **removeAll( )**, using **sub** directly, as shown here:

```
ll.removeAll(sub); // Wrong!
```

it would throw an exception because the size of **ll** would change during the removal process, thus invalidating the view.

TRY THIS 25-1   COLLECTION VIEWS VERSUS ARRAYS OBTAINED FROM A COLLECTION

`ViewAndArrayDemo.java`

As you have seen, several of the interfaces in the Collections Framework have methods that return a collection that uses the same underlying data structure as the original collection. As explained, this is called a *view* of the collection. The **subList( )** method in the **List** interface is an example of such a method. Because a view is not independent of the underlying collection, changing one will change the other. It was also explained that the array returned by the **toArray( )** method in the **Collection** interface is independent of the collection. This means that it provides its own storage for the collection elements, rather than using a view of the collection. Thus, changes to it do *not* affect the collection. In this project, you will write a small program that verifies this key difference between a view of a collection and an array generated from a collection.

STEP-BY-STEP

1. Create a new file called **ViewAndArrayDemo.java** and enter the following code:

```java
import java.util.*;

public class ViewAndArrayDemo {
  public static void main(String[] args) {
    LinkedList<String> list = new LinkedList<String>();

    list.add("A");
    list.add("B");
```

```
list.add("C");
list.add("D");

String[] array = list.toArray(new String[4]);
List<String> sublist = list.subList(0,4);
```

Initially we construct a simple **LinkedList** of strings containing "A", "B", "C", and "D". Then we call **toArray( )**, which returns an array containing the same strings as the list. Next we call **subList( )**, which returns a list also containing the same strings as the original list. Now we are ready to verify the difference between **array** and **sublist** as they relate to the original list.

2. Add the following code to complete the **ViewAndArrayDemo.java** file:

```
array[1] = "F";
sublist.set(2,"O");
System.out.println(list);
    }
}
```

The first line changes the second string in **array** to "F", and the second line changes the third string in **sublist** to "O". The last line displays the original list, so that we can see whether the changes to **array** or to **sublist** affect the original list.

3. Compile and run the **ViewAndArrayDemo** program. You will see the following output:

```
[A, B, O, D]
```

This output shows that changing the array did not change the original list, verifying the fact that the array is independent of the list. However, changing **sublist** (the view) caused a corresponding change to the original list. This verifies the fact that the view uses the same underlying data structure as the original list. In other words, that **sublist** is just a different "view" of the original list. In summary, it is important to understand the difference between a view of a collection and an array obtained from a collection. Different effects occur when one is changed.

The HashSet Class

HashSet extends **AbstractSet** and implements the **Set** interface. It creates a collection that uses a hash table for storage. **HashSet** is a generic class that has this declaration:

```
class HashSet<E>
```

Here, **E** specifies the type of objects that the set will hold.

As explained earlier in this chapter, a hash table stores information by using a mechanism called *hashing*. In hashing, the informational content of a key is used to determine a unique value, called its *hash code*. The hash code is then used as a form of index that is used to locate the data associated with the key. When using **HashSet**, the transformation of the key into its hash code is performed automatically—you don't need to compute the hash code yourself. The advantage of hashing is that it allows the execution time of **add( )**, **contains( )**, **remove( )**, and **size( )** to remain constant even for large sets.

HashSet has the following constructors:

HashSet( )

HashSet(Collection<? extends E> *col*)

HashSet(int *initCapacity*)

HashSet(int *initCapacity*, float *fillRatio*)

The first constructor creates an empty hash set. The second form initializes the hash set by using the elements of *col*. The third form initializes the initial capacity of the hash set to *initCapacity*. The default initial capacity is 16. The fourth form initializes both the initial capacity and the fill ratio (also called the *load factor*) of the hash set from its arguments. The fill ratio should be between 0.0 and 1.0, and it determines how full the hash set can be before it is resized upward. Specifically, when the number of elements is greater than the capacity of the hash set multiplied by its fill ratio, the hash set is expanded. For constructors that do not take a fill ratio, 0.75 is used.

It is important to note that **HashSet** does not store its elements in any specific order, because the process of hashing doesn't lend itself to the creation of sorted sets. If you need sorted storage, then another collection, such as **TreeSet**, is a better choice.

Here is an example that demonstrates **HashSet**:

```java
// Demonstrate HashSet.

import java.util.*;

class HashSetDemo {
  public static void main(String[] args) {
    // Create a hash set.
    HashSet<Character> hs = new HashSet<Character>();

    // Add elements to the hash set.
    hs.add('A');
    hs.add('B');
    hs.add('C');
    hs.add('D');
    System.out.println("Original contents: " + hs);

    // Add more elements.
    hs.add('E');
    hs.add('F');
    hs.add('G');
    hs.add('H');
    System.out.println("\nContents after additions: " + hs);

    // Delete E and H.
    hs.remove('E');
```

```
        hs.remove('H');
        System.out.println("\nContents after deleting E and H: " + hs);

        // Add E back in.
        hs.add('E');
        System.out.println("\nContents after adding E: " + hs);

        // Add a collection of elements to hash set.
        ArrayList<Character> al = new ArrayList<Character>();
        al.add('X');
        al.add('Y');
        al.add('Z');
        hs.addAll(al);

        System.out.println("\nContents after adding collection: " + hs);
    }
}
```

The following is the output from this program:

```
Original contents: [D, A, B, C]

Contents after additions: [D, E, F, G, A, B, C, H]

Contents after deleting E and H: [D, F, G, A, B, C]

Contents after adding E: [D, E, F, G, A, B, C]

Contents after adding collection: [D, E, F, G, A, B, C, Y, X, Z]
```

Pay special attention to the ordering of the elements. As explained, **HashSet** does not store its elements in any particular order. Instead, the order is related to the hash code of each element. Even when the contents of **al** (an **ArrayList**) are added to **hs**, the elements are not ordered in the same sequence.

Before leaving this example, an important point needs to be emphasized. **HashSet** (and any collection that implements the **Set** interface) cannot contain duplicate elements. Therefore, if you added these lines to the end of the program:

```
hs.add('Q');
hs.add('Q');
```

only one Q would be added to the set. The second call would fail and return **false**.

The TreeSet Class

TreeSet extends **AbstractSet** and implements the **NavigableSet** interface. It creates a collection that uses a form of balanced, sorted binary tree for storage. Objects are stored in sorted, ascending order. Access and retrieval times are quite fast, which makes **TreeSet** an excellent choice when storing large amounts of sorted information that must be found quickly. **TreeSet** is a generic class that has this declaration:

    class TreeSet<E>

Here, **E** specifies the type of objects that the set will hold.

TreeSet has the following constructors:

> TreeSet( )
>
> TreeSet(Collection<? extends E> *col*)
>
> TreeSet(Comparator<? super E> *comp*)
>
> TreeSet(SortedSet<E> *ss*)

The first form creates an empty tree set that will be sorted in ascending order. The second form builds a tree set that contains the elements of *col*. The third form creates an empty tree set that will be sorted according to the comparator specified by *comp*. (Comparators are described later in this chapter.) The fourth form builds a tree set that contains the elements of *ss*.

Here is an example that demonstrates a **TreeSet**, comparing it to **HashSet**. It creates an array that holds characters in unsorted order. These elements are then added to a **HashSet** and then to a **TreeSet**. In the hash set, the order of the elements will be indeterminate. However, the **TreeSet** will sort them as it builds the tree.

```java
// A TreeSet creates a sorted tree.

import java.util.*;

class TreeSetDemo {
  public static void main(String[] args) {
    char[] chrs = { 'V', 'J', 'L', 'E', 'T', 'Q', 'C', 'P' };

    // Create a tree set and a hash set.
    TreeSet<Character> ts = new TreeSet<Character>();
    HashSet<Character> hs = new HashSet<Character>();

    System.out.print("Contents of chrs:      ");
    for(char ch : chrs)
      System.out.print(ch + "   ");

    System.out.println();

    // First, add the characters to the hash set.
    for(char ch : chrs)
      hs.add(ch);

    System.out.println("Contents of hash set: " + hs);

    // Next, add the characters to the tree set.
    for(char ch : chrs)
      ts.add(ch);

    System.out.println("Contents of tree set: " + ts);
  }
}
```

The output from this program is shown here:

```
Contents of chrs:     V  J  L  E  T  Q  C  P
Contents of hash set: [T, E, V, Q, P, C, L, J]
Contents of tree set: [C, E, J, L, P, Q, T, V]
```

As you can see, the elements in the tree set are stored in sorted order.

Because **TreeSet** implements the **NavigableSet** interface, you can use the methods defined by **NavigableSet** to retrieve elements of a **TreeSet**. For example, assuming the preceding program, the following statement uses **subSet( )** to obtain a subset of **ts** that contains the elements between **C** (inclusive) and **P** (exclusive). It then displays the resulting set.

```
System.out.println(ts.subSet('C', 'P'));
```

The output from this statement is shown here:

```
[C, E, J, L]
```

You might want to experiment with the other methods defined by **NavigableSet**.

The LinkedHashSet Class

The **LinkedHashSet** class extends **HashSet** and adds no members of its own. It is a generic class that has this declaration:

    class LinkedHashSet<E>

Here, **E** specifies the type of objects that the set will hold. Its constructors parallel those in **HashSet**.

Like **HashSet**, **LinkedHashSet** uses a hash table to store elements. However, it also overlays a doubly linked list of the entries in the set, linking in the order in which they were inserted. This allows insertion-order iteration over the set. That is, when cycling through a **LinkedHashSet** using an iterator or a for-each **for**, the elements will be returned in the order in which they were inserted. This is also the order in which they are contained in the string returned by **toString( )** when called on a **LinkedHashSet** object.

The following demonstrates the differences between **Set** implementations by adding **LinkedHashSet** to the preceding example.

```
// LinkedHashSet compared with HashSet and TreeSet.

import java.util.*;

class SetsDemo {
  public static void main(String[] args) {
    char[] chrs = { 'V', 'J', 'L', 'E', 'T', 'Q', 'C', 'P' };

    // Create all three sets.
    TreeSet<Character> ts = new TreeSet<Character>();
    HashSet<Character> hs = new HashSet<Character>();
    LinkedHashSet<Character> lhs = new LinkedHashSet<Character>();
```

```
   System.out.print("Contents of chrs:                ");
   for(char ch : chrs)
     System.out.print(ch + "   ");

   System.out.println();

   // First, add the characters to the hash set.
   for(char ch : chrs)
     hs.add(ch);

   System.out.println("Contents of hash set:          " + hs);

   // Next, add the characters to the tree set.
   for(char ch : chrs)
     ts.add(ch);

   System.out.println("Contents of tree set:          " + ts);

   // Finally, add the characters to the linked hash set.
   for(char ch : chrs)
     lhs.add(ch);

   System.out.println("Contents of linked hash set: " + lhs);
  }
}
```

The output is shown here:

```
Contents of chrs:              V  J  L  E  T  Q  C  P
Contents of hash set:          [T, E, V, Q, P, C, L, J]
Contents of tree set:          [C, E, J, L, P, Q, T, V]
Contents of linked hash set:   [V, J, L, E, T, Q, C, P]
```

Notice that in the linked hash set, the order reflects the order in which elements were added.

The ArrayDeque Class

The **ArrayDeque** class extends **AbstractCollection** and implements the **Deque** interface. **ArrayDeque** creates a dynamic array that will grow as needed. Because **ArrayDeque** implements **Deque**, it can be used to support both queues and stacks. **ArrayDeque** is a generic class that has this declaration:

> class ArrayDeque<E>

Here, **E** specifies the type of objects stored in the collection.
   ArrayDeque defines the following constructors:

> ArrayDeque( )
>
> ArrayDeque(int *initCapacity*)
>
> ArrayDeque(Collection<? extends E> *col*)

The first form creates an empty deque. Its starting capacity is 16. The second constructor builds a deque that has the initial capacity passed in *initCapacity*. The third constructor creates a deque that is initialized with the elements of the collection passed in *col*. In all cases, the capacity grows as needed to handle the elements added to the deque.

Because **ArrayDeque** implements **Deque**, it can be used as either a queue or a stack. Recall that **Deque** specifies the traditional stack methods called **push( )** and **pop( )**. By using these methods, you can make an **ArrayDeque** work in a stack-like manner. By using methods such as **offerLast( )** and **pollFirst( )**, an **ArrayDeque** will work like a FIFO queue. The following program demonstrates the use of an **ArrayDeque** both as a stack and as a queue.

```java
// Demonstrate ArrayDeque.
// First the use the deque as as a stack.
// Then, use it as a FIFO queue.

import java.util.*;

class ArrayDequeDemo {
  public static void main(String[] args) {
    // Create an array deque.
    ArrayDeque<Character> adq = new ArrayDeque<Character>();

    System.out.println("Using adq as a stack.");
    // Use adq like a stack.
    System.out.print("Pushing: ");

    // push items on the stack
    for(char ch = 'A'; ch <= 'Z'; ch++) {
      adq.push(ch);
      System.out.print(ch);
    }

    System.out.println();

    // now, pop them off
    System.out.print("Popping: ");
    while(adq.peek() != null)
      System.out.print(adq.pop());

    System.out.println("\n");

    System.out.println("Using adq as a FIFO queue.");
    // Now, use adq as a FIFO queue.
    System.out.print("Queueing: ");
    for(char ch = 'A'; ch <= 'Z'; ch++) {
      adq.offerLast(ch);
      System.out.print(ch);
    }

    System.out.println();
```

Use **adq** as a stack.

Now, use **adq** as a queue.

```
    // now, remove them
    System.out.print("Removing: ");
    while(adq.peek() != null)
      System.out.print(adq.pollFirst());
  }
}
```

The output is shown here:

```
Using adq as a stack.
Pushing: ABCDEFGHIJKLMNOPQRSTUVWXYZ
Popping: ZYXWVUTSRQPONMLKJIHGFEDCBA

Using adq as a FIFO queue.
Queueing: ABCDEFGHIJKLMNOPQRSTUVWXYZ
Removing: ABCDEFGHIJKLMNOPQRSTUVWXYZ
```

As the output shows, through the use of **push( )** and **pop( )**, stack-like behavior is achieved. When **offerLast( )** and **pollFirst( )** is used, a first-in, first-out queue is implemented.

The PriorityQueue Class

PriorityQueue extends **AbstractQueue** and implements the **Queue** interface. It creates what is, essentially, a sorted queue, with the sort order indicating the priority. The head of the queue contains the highest priority element, and the tail contains the lowest priority element. **PriorityQueue** is a generic class that has this declaration:

    class PriorityQueue<E>

Here, **E** specifies the type of objects stored in the queue. **PriorityQueue**s are dynamic, growing as necessary.

PriorityQueue defines the several constructors. Here are three of them:

    PriorityQueue( )

    PriorityQueue(int *initCapacity*)

    PriorityQueue(int *initCapacity*, Comparator<? super E> *comp*)

The first form creates an empty queue. Its starting capacity is 11. The second constructor builds a queue that has the initial capacity passed to *initCapacity*. The third constructor creates a queue with the specified initial capacity and comparator. Other constructors create queues that are initialized with the elements of another collection.

If no comparator is specified when a **PriorityQueue** is constructed, then the queue is sorted according to its natural ordering. Thus, by default the head of the queue will be the smallest value. However, by providing a comparator, you can specify a different ordering scheme. For example, when storing items that include a time stamp, you could prioritize the queue such that the oldest items are first in the queue.

One word of caution: although you can iterate through a **PriorityQueue** using an iterator or a for-each **for** loop, the order of that iteration is undefined. To properly use a **PriorityQueue**, you must call methods such as **offer( )** and **poll( )**, which are defined by the **Queue** interface.

Progress Check

1. An **ArrayList** differs from an array in that _____.
2. A **PriorityQueue** is a queue in which _____.
3. The **LinkedList** class can be used as a stack. True or False?
4. **HashSet** uses a _____ _____ to store its elements.

ACCESSING A COLLECTION VIA AN ITERATOR

Often, you will want to cycle through the elements in a collection. For example, you might want to display each element. One way to do this is to employ an *iterator*, which is an object that implements either the **Iterator** or the **ListIterator** interface. **Iterator** enables you to cycle through a collection, obtaining or removing elements. **ListIterator** extends **Iterator** to allow bidirectional traversal of a list and the modification of elements. **Iterator** and **ListIterator** are generic interfaces that are declared as shown here:

interface Iterator<E>

interface ListIterator<E>

Here, **E** specifies the type of objects being iterated.

The **Iterator** interface specifies the methods shown in Table 25-7. The methods specified by **ListIterator** are shown in Table 25-8. (The ones inherited from **Iterator** are also shown to clarify their behavior relative to a **ListIterator**.) Notice that both **Iterator** and **ListIterator** let you remove an element from the collection being iterated by calling **remove( )**. In **ListIterator**, the methods **add( )** and **set( )** let you change the collection that is being iterated. Understand, however, that operations that modify the underlying collection are optional. For example, **remove( )** will throw an **UnsupportedOperationException** when used with a read-only collection.

When using an **Iterator**, you need to be careful about the order in which you call **remove( )**. A call to **remove( )** that is not preceded by a call to **next( )** will result in an **IllegalStateException** being thrown. The same thing applies to **ListIterator**. If **remove( )** is not preceded by a call to either **next( )** or **previous( )**, or if the collection being iterated was changed by an intervening call to **add( )** or **remove( )**, then an **IllegalStateException** is thrown.

Using an Iterator

Before you can access a collection through an iterator, you must obtain one. Each of the collection classes provides an **iterator( )** method that returns an iterator to the start of the collection. By using this iterator, you can access each element in the collection,

---

Answers:

1. it uses **get( )** and **set( )** methods, among others, to access the array instead of using bracket notation, and it is dynamically resizeable.
2. elements have priorities, and the element of highest priority is at the head of the queue. Thus, it is the next one removed.
3. True. It has **push( )** and **pop( )** methods that make it easy to use as a stack.
4. hash table

TABLE 25-7: The Methods Declared by Iterator

Method	Description
boolean hasNext( )	Returns **true** if there is a next element. Otherwise, returns **false**.
E next( )	Returns the next element. If there are no more elements, **NoSuchElementException** is thrown.
void remove( )	Removes the element returned by **next( )** from the collection being iterated.

TABLE 25-8: The Methods Declared by ListIterator

Method	Description
void add(E *obj*)	Adds *obj* to the collection in front of the element that will be returned by the next call to **next( )**.
boolean hasNext( )	Returns **true** if there is a next element. Otherwise, returns **false**. This method is used when moving forward.
boolean hasPrevious( )	Returns **true** if there is a previous element. Otherwise, returns **false**. This method is used when moving backwards.
E next( )	Returns the next element in the forward direction. If there are no more elements in that direction, **NoSuchElementException** is thrown.
int nextIndex( )	Returns the index of the next element in the forward direction. If there is not a next element, the size of the collection being iterated is returned.
E previous( )	Returns the previous element, which is the next element in the backwards direction. If there are no more elements in that direction, **NoSuchElementException** is thrown.
int previousIndex( )	Returns the index of the next element in the backward direction. If there is not a previous element, −1 is returned.
void remove( )	Removes the element returned by **next( )** or **previous( )** from the collection being iterated.
void set(E *obj*)	Assigns *obj* to the currently iterated element. This is the element last returned by a call to either **next( )** or **previous( )**. This change affects the collection being iterated.

one element at a time. In general, to use an iterator to cycle through the contents of a collection, follow these steps:

1. Obtain an iterator to the start of the collection by calling the collection's **iterator( )** method.
2. Set up a loop that makes a call to **hasNext( )**. Have the loop iterate as long as **hasNext( )** returns **true**.
3. Within the loop, obtain each element by calling **next( )**.

For collections that implement **List**, you can also obtain an iterator by calling **listIterator( )**. As explained, a list iterator gives you the ability to access the collection in either the forward or backward direction and lets you change or add an element to the collection being iterated. Otherwise, **ListIterator** is used like **Iterator**.

The following example implements these steps, demonstrating both the **Iterator** and **ListIterator** interfaces. It uses an **ArrayList** of strings, but the general principles apply to any type of collection that supports iterators. Notice how the underlying collection is modified by the use of **remove( )**, **add( )**, and **set( )**.

```
// Demonstrate both Iterator and ListIterator.

import java.util.*;

class IteratorDemo {
  public static void main(String[] args) {
    // Create a list of strings.
    ArrayList<String> al = new ArrayList<String>();

    // Add entries to the array list.
    al.add("Alpha");
    al.add("Beta");
    al.add("Gamma");
    al.add("Delta");
    al.add("Epsilon");
    al.add("Zeta");
    al.add("Eta");

    // First, use Iterator.

    // Use Iterator to display the contents of the list.
    System.out.print("Original contents:        ");
    Iterator<String> itr = al.iterator();                    ──────── Obtain an iterator.
    while(itr.hasNext())                                     ──────── Check for a next element.
      System.out.print(itr.next() + " ");                   ──────── Obtain the next element.
    System.out.println();

    // Use Iterator to remove Gamma from the list.
    itr = al.iterator();
    while(itr.hasNext()) {
      if(itr.next().equals("Gamma"))
        itr.remove();                          ──────── Use an iterator to remove an element.
    }

    System.out.print("Contents after deletion: ");
    itr = al.iterator();
    while(itr.hasNext())
      System.out.print(itr.next() + " ");
    System.out.println();


    // Now, use ListIterator.

    // Use ListIterator to add Gamma back to the list.
    ListIterator<String> litr = al.listIterator();          ──────── Obtain a list iterator.
    while(litr.hasNext()) {
      if(litr.next().equals("Beta"))
        litr.add("Gamma");                     ──────── Add an element using the list iterator.
    }
```

```
System.out.print("Contents after addition: ");
litr = al.listIterator();
while(litr.hasNext())
  System.out.print(litr.next() + " ");
System.out.println();

// Use ListIterator to modify the objects being iterated.
String str;
litr = al.listIterator();
while(litr.hasNext()) {
  str = litr.next();

  if(str.equals("Eta"))
    litr.set("Omega");             Use a list iterator to change an element.
  else if(str.equals("Zeta"))
    litr.set("Psi");
  else if(str.equals("Epsilon"))
    litr.set("Chi");
  else if(str.equals("Delta"))
    litr.set("...");
}

System.out.print("Contents after changes:  ");
litr = al.listIterator();
while(litr.hasNext())
  System.out.print(litr.next() + " ");
System.out.println();

// Use ListIterator to display the list backwards.
System.out.print("Modified list backwards: ");
while(litr.hasPrevious()) {
  System.out.print(litr.previous() + " ");       Display the list in reverse order.
}
System.out.println();
  }
}
```

The output is shown here:

```
Original contents:       Alpha Beta Gamma Delta Epsilon Zeta Eta
Contents after deletion: Alpha Beta Delta Epsilon Zeta Eta
Contents after addition: Alpha Beta Gamma Delta Epsilon Zeta Eta
Contents after changes:  Alpha Beta Gamma ... Chi Psi Omega
Modified list backwards: Omega Psi Chi ... Gamma Beta Alpha
```

At the end of the program, pay special attention to how the list is displayed in reverse. After the list is displayed in the forward direction, **litr** points to the end of the list. (Remember, **litr.hasNext( )** returns **false** when the end of the list has been reached.) To traverse the list in reverse, the program continues to use **litr**, but this time it checks to see whether it has a previous element. As long as it does, that element is obtained and displayed.

The For-Each Alternative to Iterators

If you won't be modifying the contents of a collection or obtaining elements in reverse order, then the for-each version of the **for** loop is often a more convenient alternative to cycling through a collection than is using an iterator. Recall that the for-each **for** can cycle through any collection of objects that implement the **Iterable** interface. Because all of the collection classes implement this interface, they can all be operated upon by the for-each **for**.

For example, assuming the **ArrayList** called **al** in the previous example, the following **for** loop displays its contents:

```
for(String s : al)
  System.out.println(s);
```

As you can see, the **for** loop is substantially shorter and simpler to use than the iterator-based approach. However, it can only be used to cycle through a collection in the forward direction, and you can't modify the contents of the collection.

Progress Check

1. The two methods in the **Iterator** interface that are used for stepping through the elements of a **Collection** are _____ and _____.
2. For collections that implement **List**, a **ListIterator** is an **Iterator** that allows you to step forward and backward through the collection and change the values in the collection. True or False?

WORKING WITH MAPS

As it relates to the Collections Framework, a *map* stores associations between keys and values, or *key/value pairs*. Given a key, you can find its value. There is one aspect to maps that is important to mention at the outset: they don't implement the **Iterable** interface. This means that you *cannot* cycle through a map using a for-each style **for** loop. Furthermore, you can't obtain an iterator to a map. However, as you will soon see, you can obtain a collection-view of a map, which does allow the use of either the **for** loop or an iterator.

The Map Interfaces

Because the map interfaces define the character and nature of maps, this discussion of maps begins with them. The following interfaces in **java.util** support maps:

Answers:

1. **hasNext( )** and **next( )**
2. True.

Interface	Description
Map	Maps unique keys to values.
Map.Entry	Encapsulates an element (a key/value pair) in a map.
NavigableMap	Extends **SortedMap** to handle the retrieval of entries based on how close one key is to another.
SortedMap	Extends **Map** so that the keys are maintained in ascending order.

Each interface is examined in turn.

THE Map INTERFACE

The **Map** interface maps unique keys to values. A key is an object that you use to retrieve a value. Given a key and a value, you can store the value in a **Map**. After the value is stored, you can retrieve it by using its key. **Map** is generic and is declared as shown here:

> interface Map<K, V>

Here, **K** specifies the type of keys, and **V** specifies the type of values. The methods declared by **Map** are summarized in Table 25-9.

At the foundation of **Map** are two basic operations: **get( )** and **put( )**. To put a value into a map, use **put( )**, specifying the key and the value. To obtain a value, call **get( )**, passing the key as an argument. The value is returned. These two methods satisfy the essences of the map contract: storing a key/value pair and returning the value when given the key.

As mentioned earlier, although maps are part of the Collections Framework, they do not implement the **Collection** interface. However, you can obtain a collection-view of a map. To do this, you can use the **entrySet( )** method. It returns a **Set** that contains the elements in the map. To obtain a collection-view of the keys, use **keySet( )**. To get a collection-view of the values, use **values( )**. For all three collection-views, the collection-views refer to the elements in the original map. Changing one affects the other. You cannot, however, add an entry to the map through the view. Collection-views are the means by which maps are integrated into the larger Collections Framework.

Finally, notice the methods **containsKey( )** and **containsValue( )**. These let you search a map for a specific key or value, respectively.

THE SortedMap INTERFACE

The **SortedMap** interface extends **Map**. It stores entries in ascending order based on the keys. **SortedMap** is generic and is declared as shown here:

> interface SortedMap<K, V>

Here, **K** specifies the type of keys, and **V** specifies the type of values. The methods added by **SortedMap** are summarized in Table 25-10.

Notice that **SortedMap** provides methods that enable you to work with *submaps*, (in other words, subsets of a map). To obtain a submap, use **headMap( )**, **tailMap( )**, or **subMap( )**. Because the map is sorted, these methods let you specify a range of

TABLE 25-9: The Methods Declared by Map	
Method	**Description**
void clear( )	Empties the invoking map by deleting all key/value pairs.
boolean containsKey(Object *k*)	Returns **true** if the invoking map contains *k* as a key. Otherwise, returns **false**.
boolean containsValue(Object *v*)	Returns **true** if the invoking map contains *v* as a value. Otherwise, returns **false**.
Set<Map.Entry<K, V>> entrySet( )	Returns a **Set** that includes all of the entries in the invoking map as objects of type **Map.Entry**. The resulting collection is a view of the invoking map.
boolean equals(Object *obj*)	Returns **true** if *obj* is a **Map** and contains the same entries as the invoking **Map**. Otherwise, returns **false**.
V get(Object *k*)	Returns the value associated with the key *k* in the invoking map. Returns **null** if the key is not found.
int hashCode( )	Returns the invoking map's hash code.
boolean isEmpty( )	Returns **true** if the invoking map is empty. Otherwise, returns **false**.
Set<K> keySet( )	Returns a **Set** that includes all of the keys in the invoking map. The resulting collection is a view of the invoking map.
V put(K *k*, V *v*)	Puts an entry in the invoking map, overwriting any previous value associated with the key. The key and value are *k* and *v*, respectively. Returns **null** if the key did not already exist. Otherwise, the previous value is returned.
void putAll(Map<? extends K, ? extends V> *map*)	Puts all the entries from *map* into the invoking map.
V remove(Object *k*)	Removes the entry whose key equals *k* in the invoking map. The value of the removed element is returned, or if *k* is not in the map, **null** is returned.
int size( )	Returns the number of entries in the invoking map.
Collection<V> values( )	Returns a collection that includes all of the values in the map. The resulting collection is a view of the invoking map.

entries to obtain based on the values of the keys they are passed. Be aware that the submaps returned by these methods are "views" and various restrictions apply.

Also notice that you can get the first key in the map by calling **firstKey( )**. To get the last key, call **lastKey( )**. Because the map is sorted, these are the smallest and largest keys in the map, respectively.

THE NavigableMap INTERFACE

The **NavigableMap** interface extends **SortedMap**. It declares the behavior of a map that supports the retrieval of an entry based on how close one key is to another. In other

TABLE 25-10: The Methods Declared by SortedMap

Method	Description
Comparator<? super K> comparator( )	Returns the invoking sorted map's comparator. If no comparator is used, **null** is returned.
K firstKey( )	Returns the key with the smallest value. Since the map is sorted, this will be the first key in the invoking map. If called on an empty map, **NoSuchElementException** is thrown.
SortedMap<K, V> headMap(K *end*)	Returns a **SortedMap** that includes those elements in the invoking map with keys that are less than *end*. The resulting map is a view of the invoking map.
K lastKey( )	Returns the key with the largest value. Since the map is sorted, this will be the last key in the invoking map. If called on an empty map, **NoSuchElementException** is thrown.
SortedMap<K, V> subMap(K *start*, K *end*)	Returns a **SortedMap** that includes those elements in the invoking map that are between *start* and *end*–1. The resulting map is a view of the invoking map.
SortedMap<K, V> tailMap(K *start*)	Returns a **SortedMap** that includes those elements in the invoking map that are greater than or equal to *start*. The resulting map is a view of the invoking map.

words, a **NavigableMap** lets you find an entry based on near matches. **NavigableMap** is a generic interface that has this declaration:

interface NavigableMap<K,V>

Here, **K** specifies the type of the keys, and **V** specifies the type of values associated with the keys. In addition to the methods that it inherits from **SortedMap**, **NavigableMap** adds those summarized in Table 25-11.

Pay special attention to the **ceiling***X* and **floor***X* methods. These methods search the map for a key that is close to another. For example, the **ceilingEntry( )** and **floorEntry( )** methods find an entry whose key is close to or equal to another key. Also notice the **higher***X* and **lower***X* methods. These methods search the map for a key that is close, but not equal to another key. You can also obtain various submaps that are based on near matches.

THE Map.Entry INTERFACE

The **Map.Entry** interface enables you to work with a map entry. Recall that the **entrySet( )** method declared by the **Map** interface returns a **Set** containing the map entries. Each of these set elements is a **Map.Entry** object. **Map.Entry** is generic and is declared like this:

interface Map.Entry<K, V>

Here, **K** specifies the type of keys, and **V** specifies the type of values.

TABLE 25-11: The Methods Declared by NavigableMap

Method	Description
Map.Entry<K,V> ceilingEntry(K *obj*)	Searches the map for the smallest key k such that $k >= obj$. If such a key is found, its entry is returned. Otherwise, **null** is returned.
K ceilingKey(K *obj*)	Searches the map for the smallest key k such that $k >= obj$. If such a key is found, it is returned. Otherwise, **null** is returned.
NavigableSet<K> descendingKeySet( )	Returns a **NavigableSet** that includes all of the keys in the invoking map in reverse order. The resulting collection is a view of the invoking map.
NavigableMap<K,V> descendingMap( )	Returns a **NavigableMap** that contains the entries in the invoking map in reverse order. The resulting map is a view of the invoking map.
Map.Entry<K,V> firstEntry( )	Returns the first entry. Since the map is sorted, this will be the entry with the smallest key.
Map.Entry<K,V> floorEntry(K *obj*)	Searches the map for the largest key k such that $k <= obj$. If such a key is found, its entry is returned. Otherwise, **null** is returned.
K floorKey(K *obj*)	Searches the map for the largest key k such that $k <= obj$. If such a key is found, it is returned. Otherwise, **null** is returned.
NavigableMap<K,V> headMap(K *upperBound*, boolean *incl*)	Returns a **NavigableMap** that includes those elements in the invoking map with keys that are less than *upperBound*. If *incl* is **true**, then an element equal to *upperBound* is included. The resulting map is a view of the invoking map.
Map.Entry<K,V> higherEntry(K *obj*)	Searches the map for the smallest key k such that $k > obj$. If such a key is found, its entry is returned. Otherwise, **null** is returned.
K higherKey(K *obj*)	Searches the set for the smallest key k such that $k > obj$. If such a key is found, it is returned. Otherwise, **null** is returned.
Map.Entry<K,V> lastEntry( )	Returns the last entry. Since the map is sorted, this will be the entry with the largest key.
Map.Entry<K,V> lowerEntry(K *obj*)	Searches the set for the largest key k such that $k < obj$. If such a key is found, its entry is returned. Otherwise, **null** is returned.
K lowerKey(K *obj*)	Searches the set for the largest key k such that $k < obj$. If such a key is found, it is returned. Otherwise, **null** is returned.
NavigableSet<K> navigableKeySet( )	Returns a **NavigableSet** that includes all of the keys in the invoking map. The resulting set is a view of the invoking map.

TABLE 25-11: The Methods Declared by NavigableMap (Continued)

Method	Description
Map.Entry<K,V> pollFirstEntry( )	Returns the first entry, removing the entry in the process. Because the map is sorted, this is the entry with the smallest key value. If the map is empty, **null** is returned.
Map.Entry<K,V> pollLastEntry( )	Returns the last entry, removing the entry in the process. Because the map is sorted, this is the entry with the largest key value. If the map is empty, **null** is returned.
NavigableMap<K,V> subMap(K *lowerBound*, boolean *lowIncl*, K *upperBound*, boolean *highIncl*)	Returns a **NavigableMap** that includes all entries from the invoking map that have keys that are greater than *lowerBound* and less than *upperBound*. If *lowIncl* is **true**, then a key equal to *lowerBound* is included. If *highIncl* is **true**, then an element equal to *upperBound* is included. The resulting map is a view of the invoking map.
NavigableMap<K,V> tailMap(K *lowerBound*, boolean *incl*)	Returns a **NavigableMap** that includes all entries from the invoking map that have keys that are greater than *lowerBound*. If *incl* is **true**, then a key equal to *lowerBound* is included. The resulting map is a view of the invoking map.

In addition to overrides of **equals( )** and **hashCode( )**, **Map.Entry** specifies three methods that give you access to a map entry. They are shown here:

    K getKey( )

    V getValue( )

    V setValue(V *v*)

As the names imply, for any given **Map.Entry** instance, **getKey( )** returns its key and **getValue( )** returns its value. You can set the value by calling **setValue( )**, passing in the new value.

The Map Classes

Several classes provide implementations of the map interfaces. The abstract class **AbstractMap** implements most of the **Map** interface. It is extended by several concrete map classes. We will examine the following three:

Class	Description
HashMap	Extends **AbstractMap** to use a hash table.
TreeMap	Extends **AbstractMap** to use a tree.
LinkedHashMap	Extends **HashMap** to allow insertion-order iterations.

*Note: Other map classes include **WeakHashMap**, **IdentifyHashMap**, and **EnumMap**. Their use is specialized, and they are not examined here.*

THE HashMap CLASS

The **HashMap** class extends **AbstractMap** and implements the **Map** interface. It uses a hash table to store the map. This allows the execution time of **get( )** and **put( )** to remain constant even for large data sets. **HashMap** is a generic class that has this declaration:

> class HashMap<K, V>

Here, **K** specifies the type of keys, and **V** specifies the type of values.

The following constructors are defined:

> HashMap( )
>
> HashMap(Map<? extends K, ? extends V> *map*)
>
> HashMap(int *initCapacity*)
>
> HashMap(int *iniCapacity*, float *fillRatio*)

The first constructor creates an empty hash map. The second constructor initializes the hash map by using the elements of *map*. The third constructor initializes the initial capacity of the hash map to *initCapacity*. The fourth constructor initializes both the initial capacity and fill ratio (load factor) of the hash map by using its arguments. The meaning of capacity and fill ratio is the same as for **HashSet**, described earlier. The default initial capacity is 16. The default fill ratio is 0.75.

You should note that a hash map does *not* store elements in a specific order. Furthermore, the order may change over the lifetime of the map. Therefore, the order in which elements are added to a hash map is not necessarily the order in which they will be obtained when iterating over a collection-view of the map.

The following program illustrates **HashMap**. It maps names to account balances. Notice how a collection-view is obtained and used.

```
import java.util.*;

class HashMapDemo {
  public static void main(String[] args) {

    // Create a hash map.
    HashMap<String, Double> hm = new HashMap<String, Double>();

    // Put elements to the map
    hm.put("John Doe", 3434.34);
    hm.put("Tom Smith", 123.22);
    hm.put("Jane Baker", 1378.00);       Use put( ) to insert entries.
    hm.put("Todd Hall", 99.22);
    hm.put("Ralph Smith", -19.08);

    // Get a set of the entries.
    Set<Map.Entry<String, Double>> set = hm.entrySet();       Obtain a set view
                                                              of the entries.

    // Display the set.
    for(Map.Entry<String, Double> me : set) {
```

```
        System.out.print(me.getKey() + ": ");  ◄───────────Display the keys
        System.out.println(me.getValue());  ◄───────── and values.
    }

    System.out.println();

    // Deposit 1000 into John Doe's account.
    double balance = hm.get("John Doe");
    hm.put("John Doe", balance + 1000);

    System.out.println("John Doe's new balance: " +
        hm.get("John Doe"));
    }
}
```

Output from this program is shown here (the precise order may vary):

```
Ralph Smith: -19.08
Tom Smith: 123.22
John Doe: 3434.34
Todd Hall: 99.22
Jane Baker: 1378.0

John Doe's new balance: 4434.34
```

The program begins by creating a hash map and then adds the mapping of names to balances by calling **put( )**. Next, the contents of the map are displayed by using a collection-view, obtained by calling **entrySet( )**. The keys and values are displayed by calling the **getKey( )** and **getValue( )** methods that are defined by **Map.Entry**. Pay close attention to how the deposit is made into John Doe's account. First, the current balance is obtained by calling **get( )**. Then, **put( )** is called with the new balance. This automatically replaces any preexisting value that is associated with the specified key with the new value. Thus, after John Doe's account is updated, the hash map will still contain just one "John Doe" account.

THE TreeMap CLASS

The **TreeMap** class extends **AbstractMap** and implements the **NavigableMap** interface. It creates maps stored in a tree structure. A **TreeMap** provides an effective means of storing key/value pairs in sorted order and allows rapid retrieval. You should note that, unlike a hash map, a tree map guarantees that its elements will be sorted in ascending key order. **TreeMap** is a generic class that has this declaration:

    class TreeMap<K, V>

Here, **K** specifies the type of keys, and **V** specifies the type of values.

The following **TreeMap** constructors are defined:

    TreeMap( )

    TreeMap(Comparator<? super K> *comp*)

    TreeMap(Map<? extends K, ? extends V> *map*)

    TreeMap(SortedMap<K, ? extends V> *map*)

The first constructor creates an empty tree map. The second constructor builds a tree map that will be sorted by using the **Comparator** specified by *comp*. The third constructor initializes a tree map with the entries from *map*, in sorted order. The fourth constructor initializes a tree map with the entries from *map,* which will be sorted in the same order as *map.*

The following program reworks the preceding example so that it uses **TreeMap**:

```java
import java.util.*;

class TreeMapDemo {
  public static void main(String[] args) {

    // Create a tree map.
    TreeMap<String, Double> tm = new TreeMap<String, Double>();

    // Put elements to the map.
    tm.put("John Doe", 3434.34);
    tm.put("Tom Smith", 123.22);
    tm.put("Jane Baker", 1378.00);
    tm.put("Todd Hall", 99.22);
    tm.put("Ralph Smith", -19.08);

    // Get a set of the entries.
    Set<Map.Entry<String, Double>> set = tm.entrySet();

    // Display the elements.
    for(Map.Entry<String, Double> me : set) {
      System.out.print(me.getKey() + ": ");
      System.out.println(me.getValue());
    }
    System.out.println();

    // Deposit 1000 into John Doe's account.
    double balance = tm.get("John Doe");
    tm.put("John Doe", balance + 1000);

    System.out.println("John Doe's new balance: " +
      tm.get("John Doe"));
  }
}
```

The following is the output from this program:

```
Jane Baker: 1378.0
John Doe: 3434.34
Ralph Smith: -19.08
Todd Hall: 99.22
Tom Smith: 123.22

John Doe's current balance: 4434.34
```

Notice that **TreeMap** sorts the entries based on the keys. However, in this case, they are sorted beginning with the first name instead of the last name. You can alter this behavior by specifying a comparator when the map is created, as described shortly.

THE LinkedHashMap CLASS

LinkedHashMap extends **HashMap**. It is similar to **HashMap** in that its entries are stored in a hash table. However, it also overlays a doubly linked list onto the entries. Unless specified otherwise, the order of the entries in the list is the same as the order in which they were inserted. This allows insertion-order iteration over the map. That is, when iterating through a collection-view of a **LinkedHashMap**, the elements will be returned in the order in which they were inserted. You can also create a **LinkedHashMap** that returns its elements in the order in which they were last accessed.

LinkedHashMap is a generic class that has this declaration:

    class LinkedHashMap<K, V>

Here, **K** specifies the type of keys, and **V** specifies the type of values.

LinkedHashMap defines the following constructors:

    LinkedHashMap( )
    LinkedHashMap(Map<? extends K, ? extends V> map)
    LinkedHashMap(int initCapacity)
    LinkedHashMap(int initCapacity, float fillRatio)
    LinkedHashMap(int initCapacity, float fillRatio, boolean orderByAccess)

The first constructor creates an empty map. The second constructor builds a map that is initialized with the elements from *map*. The third constructor initializes the initial capacity. The fourth constructor initializes both initial capacity and fill ratio (load factor). The meaning of capacity and fill ratio are the same as for **HashMap**. The default initial capacity is 16. The default fill ratio is 0.75. The last constructor allows you to specify whether the elements will be stored in the linked list by insertion order, or by order of last access. If *orderByAccess* is **true**, then access order is used. If *orderByAccess* is **false**, then insertion order is used. When access order is used, the last element in the list is the most recently used.

LinkedHashMap adds only one method to those defined by **HashMap**. This method is **removeEldestEntry( )** and it is shown here:

    protected boolean removeEldestEntry(Map.Entry<K, V> entry)

This method is called by **put( )** and **putAll( )**. The oldest entry is passed in *entry*. By default, this method returns **false** and does nothing. However, if you override this method, then you can have the **LinkedHashMap** remove the oldest entry in the map. To do this, your override must return **true**. To keep the oldest entry, return **false**.

Progress Check

1. A **Map** always maps unique keys to unique values. True or False?
2. What method do you use in a **Map** to retrieve the value associated with a given key? What method do you use to add a new key/value pair to a **Map**?
3. To get a **Collection** of the keys in a **Map**, use the method _____ and to get a **Collection** of the values in a **Map**, use the method _____.
4. What makes a **LinkedHashMap** unique?

COMPARATORS

Both **TreeSet** and **TreeMap** store elements in sorted order. However, it is how the elements are compared that defines precisely what "sorted order" means. By default, these classes store their elements by using what Java refers to as "natural ordering." This is the order defined by the way a class implements the **compareTo( )** method specified by **Comparable**. Often, this is the ordering that you want and would expect (A before B, 1 before 2, and so forth). If you want to order elements a different way, then specify a **Comparator** when you construct the set or map. Doing so gives you the ability to govern precisely how elements are stored within sorted collections and maps. It also lets you store an object in a collection that does not implement the **Comparable** interface.

Comparator is a generic interface that has this declaration:

    interface Comparator<T>

Here, **T** specifies the type of objects being compared.

The **Comparator** interface defines two methods: **compare( )** and **equals( )**. The **compare( )** method, shown here, compares two elements for order:

    int compare(T obj1, T obj2)

Here, *obj1* and *obj2* are the objects to be compared. This method returns zero if the objects are equal. It returns a positive value if *obj1* is greater than *obj2*. Otherwise, a negative value is returned. By implementing **compare( )**, you can alter the way that objects are ordered. For example, to sort in reverse order, you can create a comparator that reverses the outcome of a comparison.

The **equals( )** method, shown here, tests whether an object equals the invoking comparator:

    boolean equals(Object obj)

_____

Answers:

1. False. All the keys must be unique, but not the values. In fact, all the keys could map to the same value.
2. **get( )** and **put( )**
3. **keySet( )** and **values( )**
4. **LinkedHashMap** overlays a doubly linked list on the entries, enabling them to be accessed in a known order.

Here, *obj* is the object to be tested for equality. The method returns **true** if *obj* and the invoking object are both **Comparator** objects and use the same ordering. Otherwise, it returns **false**. In many cases, you can simply use the default version of **equals( )** provided by **Object**. This is what the following examples do.

Before looking at an example that uses a **Comparator**, an important point needs to be made. As a general rule, the outcome of comparing two objects with **compare( )** should be compatible with the outcome of comparing those two objects with **equals( )**. Therefore, if the two objects are equal according to **equals( )**, then **compareTo( )** must return zero, and vice versa. Failure to follow this rule could result in a corrupted collection, for example.

Note: In cases in which a collection will be serialized, a class that implements Comparator should also implement the Serializable interface. Since the following examples do not involve serialization, the comparator does not implement Serializable. The details concerning the implementation of Serializable are beyond the scope of this book.

The following program demonstrates the use of a comparator. It is an updated version of the **TreeMap** program shown earlier that stores account balances. In the previous version, the accounts were sorted by name, but the sorting began with the first name. The following program sorts the accounts by last name. To do so, it uses a comparator that compares the last name of each account. This results in the map being sorted by last name rather than first name.

```java
// Use a comparator to sort accounts by last name.
import java.util.*;

// Compare last whole words in two strings.
class NameComp implements Comparator<String> {          Implement a comparator.
  public int compare(String aStr, String bStr) {
    int i, j, k;

    // Find index of beginning of last name.
    i = aStr.lastIndexOf(' ');
    j = bStr.lastIndexOf(' ');

    k = aStr.substring(i).compareTo(bStr.substring(j));
    if(k==0) // last names match, check entire name
      return aStr.compareTo(bStr);
    else
      return k;
  }

  // No need to override equals.
}                                             Specify a comparator when constructing
                                              a TreeMap.
class TreeMapDemo2 {
  public static void main(String[] args) {
    // Create a tree map that uses the specified comparator.
    TreeMap<String, Double> tm = new TreeMap<String,
                                   Double>(new NameComp());
```

```
    // Put elements to the map.
    tm.put("John Doe", 3434.34);
    tm.put("Tom Smith", 123.22);
    tm.put("Jane Baker", 1378.00);
    tm.put("Todd Hall", 99.22);
    tm.put("Ralph Smith", -19.08);

    // Get a set of the entries.
    Set<Map.Entry<String, Double>> set = tm.entrySet();

    // Display the elements.
    for(Map.Entry<String, Double> me : set) {
      System.out.print(me.getKey() + ": ");
      System.out.println(me.getValue());
    }
    System.out.println();

    // Deposit 1000 into John Doe's account.
    double balance =  tm.get("John Doe");
    tm.put("John Doe", balance + 1000);

    System.out.println("John Doe's new balance: " +
      tm.get("John Doe"));
  }
}
```

Here is the output; notice that the accounts are now sorted by last name:

```
Jane Baker: 1378.0
John Doe: 3434.34
Todd Hall: 99.22
Ralph Smith: -19.08
Tom Smith: 123.22

John Doe's new balance: 4434.34
```

The comparator class **TComp** compares two strings that hold first and last names. It does so by first comparing last names. To do this, it finds the index of the last space in each string and then compares the substrings of each element that begin at that point. In cases where last names are equivalent, the entire string is compared. This yields a tree map that is sorted by last name and within last name by first name. You can see this because Ralph Smith comes before Tom Smith in the output.

THE COLLECTION ALGORITHMS

The Collections Framework defines many algorithms that can be applied to collections and maps. These algorithms are defined as **static** methods within the **Collections** class. While it's not practical to look at them all, we will show five examples that will give you an idea of what is available. These are **sort( )**, **binarySearch( )**, **replaceAll( )**, **reverse( )**, and **rotate( )**.

Perhaps the two most important algorithms in **Collections** are **sort( )** and **binarySearch( )**. The **sort( )** algorithm can sort any collection that implements the **List** interface. Here is one of its forms:

> static <T extends Comparable<? super T>> void sort(List<T> *list*)

It sorts the elements of *list* as determined by their natural ordering. Recall that this is the order determined by the **compareTo( )** method of **Comparable**, which **T** must implement. A second form lets you specify a comparator that can be used for types that don't implement **Comparable**. A primary benefit of **sort( )** is that it enables you to use an unsorted collection, such as **LinkedList** and **ArrayList**, but still obtain a sorted list when you want one.

Once you have a sorted **List**, the **binarySearch( )** method can be used to perform very fast look-ups. It uses a binary search to find a specified value. (For a description of a binary search, see the following Ask the Expert.) Here is one form of **binarySearch( )**:

> static <T> int binarySearch(List<? extends Comparable<? super T>> *list*,
> T *value*)

It searches for *value* in *list*. It returns the index of *value*, or a negative result if *value* is not found. As with **sort( )**, the type of objects stored in the list must implement **Comparable**. A second form of **binarySearch( )** lets you to specify a comparator that can be used for types that don't implement **Comparable**.

Another very handy algorithm is **replaceAll( )**. It replaces one item with another throughout an entire list. It is shown here:

> static <T> boolean replaceAll(List<T> *list*, T *old*, T *new*)

On return, all instances of *old* will have been replaced by *new*. It returns **true** if at least one replacement occurred. Otherwise, it returns **false**.

To reverse a list, call **reverse( )**, shown next:

> static void reverse(List<T> *list*)

This method can be useful when you have a sorted list and you simply want it in reverse order.

A list can be rotated by use of the **rotate( )** method. A rotate shifts the contents of a collection either left or right. The element shifted off one end is inserted on the other end. It is shown here:

> static void rotate(List<T> *list*, int *n*)

The elements in *list* are rotated *n* places to the right. To rotate left, use a negative value for *n*.

The following program demonstrates the algorithms just described.

```
// Demonstrate several algorithms.

import java.util.*;

class AlgorithmsDemo {
  public static void main(String[] args) {
```

```java
// Create a linked list.
LinkedList<Character> ll = new LinkedList<Character>();

// Put items in the list.
for(int i = 0; i < 26; i+=2) {
  ll.add((char) ('A' + i));
  ll.add((char) ('Z' - i));
}

// Display original list.
System.out.print("Original list: ");
for(char ch : ll)
  System.out.print(ch);

System.out.println();

// Sort the list.
Collections.sort(ll);                  ←─────────────── Sort the list.
System.out.print("List sorted:    ");
for(char ch : ll)
  System.out.print(ch);

System.out.println("\n");

// Search the list.
System.out.println("Using binarySearch() to find X.");
int i = Collections.binarySearch(ll, 'X');  ←──────────Search the list.
if(i >= 0)
  System.out.println("X found. Index is " + i);

System.out.println();

// Reverse the list.
Collections.reverse(ll);  ←─────────────────────────── Reverse the list.
System.out.print("List reversed: ");
for(char ch : ll)
  System.out.print(ch);

System.out.println("\n");

// Rotate the List.
Collections.rotate(ll, 5);  ←─────────────────────────Rotate the list.
System.out.print("List rotated:    ");
for(char ch : ll)
  System.out.print(ch);

System.out.println("\n");

// Create a new list.
ll = new LinkedList<Character>();
```

```
    // Add a string to it.
    String str = "this is a test";
    for(char ch : str.toCharArray())
      ll.add(ch);

    System.out.print("Here is the new list: ");
    for(char ch : ll)
      System.out.print(ch);

    System.out.println();

    // Replace all t's with *
    Collections.replaceAll(ll, 't', '*');                         Replace elements in the list.
    System.out.print("After replacements:   ");
    for(char ch : ll)
      System.out.print(ch);
  }
}
```

Output from this program is shown here:

```
Original list: AZCXEVGTIRKPMNOLQJSHUFWDYB
List sorted:   ABCDEFGHIJKLMNOPQRSTUVWXYZ

Using binarySearch() to find X.
X found. Index is 23

List reversed: ZYXWVUTSRQPONMLKJIHGFEDCBA

List rotated:  EDCBAZYXWVUTSRQPONMLKJIHGF

Here is the new list: this is a test
After replacements:   *his is a *es*
```

In addition to the methods just described, **Collections** provides many more, including some that layer on additional functionality. For example, if you want a synchronized version of a nonsynchronized collection, you can obtain one by using one of the **synchronized***X* methods, such as **synchronizedSet( )** or **synchronizedMap( )**. You can obtain read-only versions of a collection by using one of the **unmodifiable***X* methods, such as **unmodifiableSet( )** or **unmodifiableSortedMap( )**. You will want to explore the capabilities of the **Collections** class on your own. It offers a wide range of ready-to-use functionality that helps you manage collections.

Ask the Expert

Q In the discussion of the collection algorithms, you described the **binarySearch( )** method. What is a binary search, and why is it valuable?

A In general, there are two ways to search a collection for a value. The first is a *sequential search*. A sequential search starts at the beginning of a collection,

Ask the Expert (Continued)

checking each element in sequence until either the item is found, or the end of the collection is reached. Although this approach works, it implies that many elements may need to be tested until the one being sought is found. This can result in long search times. However, for unsorted data, it is essentially the only approach that will work.

If the data is sorted, then a much faster approach, called a *binary search*, can be used. A binary search uses what can be characterized as a "divide and conquer" strategy to find an element in a sorted collection. It works like this. The middle element in the collection is checked. If it is larger than the item being sought, then the middle element of the lower half of the collection is tested. Otherwise, the middle element of the higher half is tested. This process of dividing the collection continues until either the element is found or the search fails. For large data sets, this process makes a binary search much faster than a sequential search, on average. This is because, on average, fewer elements need to be tested. (Of course, if the element being sought is near the front of the list, then a sequential search might beat the binary search in that case!) Also, remember that the binary search applies only to sorted collections.

THE Arrays CLASS

Before moving on to the legacy classes, there is one more class that is part of the Collections Framework that requires a brief mention. The class is **Arrays**. It provides several **static** methods that are useful when working with Java's built-in, fixed-length arrays. For example, it provides methods that copy an array, fill an array with a value, sort an array, and search an array. It also provides a method called **asList( )** that returns a **List** that refers to a specified array. This lets you operate on an array as if it were a collection.

Progress Check

1. The method in the **Comparator** interface is _____.
2. The **Collections** class is a class that implements the **Collection** interface. True or False?
3. What algorithm in **Collections** searches a sorted list?
4. What algorithm in **Collections** rotates a list?

Answers:

1. **compare( )**
2. False. The **Collections** class is a class with **static** methods for manipulating **Collection**s
3. **binarySearch( )**
4. **rotate( )**

THE LEGACY CLASSES AND INTERFACES

Early versions of **java.util** did not include the Collections Framework. Instead, they defined several classes and an interface that provided an ad hoc method of storing objects. When collections were added (by J2SE 1.2), two of the original classes were reengineered to support the collection interfaces and are now technically part of the Collections Framework. However, where a modern collection duplicates the functionality of a legacy class, you will usually want to use the newer collection class.

The legacy classes defined by **java.util** are shown here:

Dictionary	Hashtable	Properties	Stack	Vector

There is one legacy interface called **Enumeration**. The following sections briefly examine **Enumeration** and each of the legacy classes.

The Enumeration Interface

The **Enumeration** interface defines the methods by which you can *enumerate* (obtain one at a time) the elements in a collection of objects. Although not deprecated, this legacy interface has been superseded by **Iterator**.

Vector

Vector implements a dynamic array. It is similar to **ArrayList**, but with two main differences. First, **Vector** is synchronized. Second, it contains many legacy methods that duplicate the functionality of methods defined by the Collections Framework. With the advent of collections, **Vector** was reengineered to extend **AbstractList** and to implement the **List** interface. This means that **Vector** has been integrated into the Collections Framework. Because **Vector** implements **List**, you can use a **Vector** just like you use an **ArrayList** instance. You can also manipulate one using its legacy methods. Generally, however, if you don't need a synchronized dynamic array, **ArrayList** is a better choice.

Stack

Stack is a subclass of **Vector** that implements a standard last-in, first-out stack. **Stack** includes all the methods defined by **Vector** and adds methods such as **push( )** and **pop( )** which support stack operations. For new code, **ArrayDeque** or **LinkedList** is recommended. Each supports the modern **Deque** interface.

Dictionary

Dictionary is an abstract class that represents a key/value storage repository and operates much like **Map**. Although not currently deprecated, **Dictionary** is classified as obsolete because it is fully superseded by **Map**.

Hashtable

Hashtable is a concrete implementation of a **Dictionary**. However, with the advent of collections, **Hashtable** was reengineered to also implement the **Map** interface. Thus,

Hashtable is integrated into the Collections Framework. It is similar to **HashMap**, but is synchronized. Generally, however, if you don't need a synchronized hash table, **HashMap** is a better choice.

Properties

Properties is a subclass of **Hashtable**. It is used to maintain lists of values in which the key is a **String** and the value is also a **String**. The **Properties** class is used by methods such as **System.getProperties( )** when obtaining environmental values.

EXERCISES

1. What is the purpose of the following collection classes: **AbstractCollection**, **AbstractList**, **AbstractQueue**, **AbstractSequentialList**, **AbstractSet**? That is, why are these classes included in the Collections Framework?

2. Both the **poll( )** and **remove( )** methods in the **Queue** interface remove and return the element at the head of the queue. What is the difference between them?

3. A **Collection** represents an arbitrary group of data. In contrast, a **Set** represents a group of data in which _____.

4. What happens if you use the **add( )** method to try to add an element to a **Set** that is already in the **Set**?

5. If **m** is a **Map**, then **m.keySet( ).size( )** = **m.values( ).size( )**. True or False?

6. Suppose you have three collections of strings **c1, c2, c3**, and you want to find out which, if any, strings appear in all three collections. Write a code segment that creates a collection **c4** that contains only those strings that appear in all three collections. It should not modify any of the three original collections.

7. Suppose you have three collections of strings **c1, c2, c3**, and you want to find out which, if any, strings appear in **c1**, but do not appear in either **c2** or **c3**. Create a code segment that creates a collection **c4** that contains only the desired strings. It should not modify any of the three original collections.

8. What will be displayed by the following code segment? Explain.

```
Collection<Object> c = new ArrayList<Object>();
c.add(new Object());
c.add(new Object());
System.out.println(c.contains(new Object()));
```

9. Suppose you have an **ArrayList<String>** named **list** and an array of type **String[ ]** named **data**, both of the same length. If you want to copy the data from either data structure to the other, you could do so using a loop. But there are easier ways. Create a code segment that assigns the strings in

list to **data** and a code segment that assigns the strings in **data** to **list** without using any loops.

10. Write a program that converts an **ArrayList** to a **HashSet** to a **Priority-Queue** to an **ArrayDeque** to a **TreeSet** using the version of their constructors that takes a **Collection** as its argument. Start by creating a small **ArrayList** of strings and displaying the list using its **toString( )** method. Then similarly construct and display the other **Collection**s, using each of them as the argument to the constructor for next one. Even though the **Collection**s all contain the same strings, you are likely to see those strings displayed in different orders for some of the **Collection**s. Why?

11. Write a program that displays the elements of a non-empty **ArrayList** of strings using each of the following approaches. For example, if the list contains "A", "B", "C", and "D", then, in every case, the output should be "A, B, C, D".

    A.   a **for** loop using calls to **get( )**
    B.   a loop using the iterator returned by **iterator( )**
    C.   a for-each **for** loop
    D.   the **toString( )** method of the **LinkedList** class

12. Write a program that creates a **LinkedList** containing the strings "A", "B", "C", and "D". It then uses a **ListIterator** to step through the list to display the following output: "ABCBCD". The iterator should not modify the list.

13. Write a program that creates a **LinkedList** containing four strings. It then uses a **ListIterator** to swap the two middle values of the list, using the iterator's **set( )** method (not the list's **set( )** method). The program should display the list before and after the swap.

14. Implement a **sort( )** method that takes an array of integers as its parameter. The method should first create a **PriorityQueue<Integer>**. Then it should add all the integers from the array to the queue. Finally, it should extract the elements from the queue one at a time using **poll( )** and put them back to the array. Write a program to test your method.

15. To add an element **x** at the end of an **ArrayList** named **data**, you could invoke **data.add(x)**. Give another method call that will do the same thing.

16. To add an element **x** at the front of a **LinkedList** named **data**, there are four methods in the **LinkedList** class that you could invoke on **data**. Give the four method calls.

17. To get the element at the front of a non-empty **LinkedList** named **data**, there are at least six methods, other than the **toArray( )** methods, in the **LinkedList** class that you could invoke on **data**. Give the six method calls. These method calls should not remove the element from **data**.

18. Suppose you have a non-empty **LinkedList<String>** named **data**. Suppose you want to assign to a string variable **s** the first string in **data** using either of the two **toArray( )** methods. Show how to do so. That is, give assignment statements that use each of the **toArray( )** methods to assign to **s** the first string in **data**.

19. The following code segment compiles without errors or warnings, but throws an exception when you run it. Explain why.

```
TreeSet<Object> t = new TreeSet<Object>();
t.add(new Object());
```

20. If a **TreeSet** is created with a **Comparator** and the elements implement **Comparable**, how is the sorted order of the set determined? Are the elements compared using the **Comparator**, or are they compared using their **compareTo( )** method?

21. Write a program that creates a **PriorityQueue** of strings that gives highest priority to the longest string. That is, the **poll( )** method always returns the longest string in the collection. The program should then test the **PriorityQueue**.

22. Modify the **HashMapDemo** program so that it displays the same output as it did before, but it does it without calling **entrySet( )**. Instead it calls **keySet( )** and then iterates through the keys, displaying them and their associated values.

23. Suppose you have an **ArrayList<Integer>** named **list** that you want sorted from largest to smallest. Unfortunately, the **sort( )** method in the **Collections** class will sort **list** from smallest to largest. What is the easiest way to sort **list** from largest to smallest?

24. Pretend that there is no **get( )** method in the **LinkedList** class and implement such a method yourself. More precisely, implement a generic **get( )** method that takes an integer **i** and a **LinkedList<E>** as its two parameters and returns the **i**th value in the list. It should throw an **IndexOutOfBoundsException** if **i** is negative or greater than or equal to the length of the list. Use the **rotate( )** method in the **Collections** class to move the desired element to the front of the list and then use the **getFirst( )** method in the **LinkedList** class to get the element to be returned. When the method returns, the list should be back in its original form.

25. The **Map**'s **get( )** method takes a key and finds the associated value. Write a method that does the opposite, namely, given a value, it finds an associated key. More precisely, write a generic method **getReverse( )** that takes an object of type **V** and a **Map<K,V>** as its parameters and determines whether the object appears as one of the values in the map. If so, it returns the key (or any one of the keys if there are more than one) associated with the value. If not, it returns **null**. Use the object's **equals( )** method to compare the object to other values. Write a program to test your method.

CHAPTER 26

Networking with java.net

KEY SKILLS & CONCEPTS

- Know networking fundamentals
- The **InetAddress** class
- The **Socket** class
- The **URL** class
- The **URLConnection** class
- The **HttpURLConnection** class
- The **DatagramSocket** class
- The **DatagramPacket** class

As you learned in Chapter 1, Java was designed to address the needs of the Internet programming environment. Therefore, it should come as no surprise that it provides extensive support for networking in its API library. The primary Java networking package is **java.net**. It provides classes that enable an application to access network resources in a convenient, efficient manner.

Before we begin, it is necessary to emphasize that networking is an advanced subject. Moreover, it is a very large and, at times, complicated subject. A discussion of networking can easily involve several other topics, such as details relating to protocols and the general architecture of the Internet, which are beyond the scope of this book. Our purpose here is to introduce key elements of **java.net** and demonstrate their use. This will give you a general understanding of the networking capabilities provided by Java and enable you to write simple networked applications.

NETWORKING FUNDAMENTALS

At the core of Java's networking support is the concept of a *socket*. A socket identifies an endpoint in a network. Sockets are at the foundation of modern networking because a socket allows a single computer to serve many different clients at once, as well as to serve many different types of information. This is accomplished through the use of a *port*, which is a numbered socket on a particular machine. A server process is said to "listen" to a port until a client connects to it. A server is allowed to accept multiple clients connected to the same port number, although each session is unique.

Socket communication takes place via a protocol. *Internet Protocol* (*IP*) is a low-level routing protocol that breaks data into small packets and sends them to an address across a network. It does not, however, guarantee to deliver these packets to the destination, or deliver them in the order in which they were sent. *Transmission Control Protocol* (*TCP*) is a higher-level protocol that manages the transmission of packets, sorting and retransmitting them as necessary to reliably transmit data. To accomplish this, TCP establishes a *connection*, which is a link between two sockets. A third protocol, *User Datagram Protocol* (*UDP*), can be used directly to support fast, connectionless, but unguaranteed transmission of packets.

Once a connection has been established, a higher-level protocol ensues, which is dependent on which port you are using. TCP/IP reserves the lower 1,024 ports for specific protocols. Here are some examples: port number 21 is for FTP, 25 is for e-mail, 43 is for whois, and 80 is for HTTP. It is up to each protocol to determine how a client should interact with the port. The one with which you are probably the most familiar is HTTP (Hypertext Transfer Protocol). HTTP is the protocol that web browsers and servers use to transfer resources, such as web pages and images. Here's how it works. When a client requests a file from an HTTP server, it simply sends the name of the file to a predefined port. The server sends back the contents of the file. The server also responds with a status code to tell the client whether the request can be fulfilled and, if not, why not.

A key component of the Internet is the *address*. Every computer on the Internet has one. An Internet address is a number that uniquely identifies each computer on the Net. Originally, all Internet addresses consisted of 32-bit values, organized as four 8-bit values. This address type was specified by IPv4 (Internet Protocol, version 4). However, a new addressing scheme, called IPv6 (Internet Protocol, version 6) has come into play. IPv6 uses a 128-bit value to represent an address, organized into eight 16-bit units. The principal advantage of IPv6 is that it supports a much larger address space than does IPv4. Fortunately, when using Java, you won't normally need to worry about whether IPv4 or IPv6 addresses are used because Java handles the details for you.

Usually, you won't work directly with numerical addresses. Rather, you will use a human-readable *domain name*. For example, **www.mcgraw-hill.com** is in the *COM* top-level domain. Its name is *mcgraw-hill*. An Internet domain name is mapped to an IP address by the *Domain Name System* (*DNS*). This enables users to work with domain names, but the Internet operates on IP addresses. An address like **www.mcgraw-hill.com** is also called a *host name*.

THE NETWORKING CLASSES AND INTERFACES

Java provides extensive support for both the TCP and UDP protocol families. As such, **java.net** provides many classes and several interfaces. To give you an idea of its wide range of capabilities, here are the classes defined by **java.net** at the time of this writing:

Authenticator	Inet6Address	ServerSocket
CacheRequest	InetAddress	Socket
CacheResponse	InetSocketAddress	SocketAddress
ContentHandler	InterfaceAddress	SocketImpl
CookieHandler	JarURLConnection	SocketPermission
CookieManager	MulticastSocket	StandardSocketOptions
DatagramPacket	NetPermission	URI
DatagramSocket	NetworkInterface	URL
DatagramSocketImpl	PasswordAuthentication	URLClassLoader
HttpCookie	Proxy	URLConnection
HttpURLConnection	ProxySelector	URLDecoder
IDN	ResponseCache	URLEncoder
Inet4Address	SecureCacheResponse	URLStreamHandler

The interfaces in **java.net** include:

ContentHandlerFactory	CookiePolicy	CookieStore
DatagramSocketImplFactory	FileNameMap	ProtocolFamily
SocketImplFactory	SocketOption	SocketOptions
URLStreamHandlerFactory		

As these tables suggest, **java.net** provides a rich array of functionality that offers detailed control over network communications.

In the sections that follow, we will examine several core classes provided by **java.net** and show examples that illustrate their use. The classes described here are

InetAddress	Socket	URL
URLConnection	HttpURLConnection	DatagramPacket
DatagramSocket		

These represent several fundamental aspects of Java-based networking, including how to create an address, how to make a connection, and how to send and receive data. A general understanding of these basic operations provides a foundation on which other aspects of Java's networking can be integrated.

THE InetAddress CLASS

The **InetAddress** class is used to encapsulate both the numerical IP address and the domain name for that address. You interact with this class by using the name of an IP host, which is more convenient and understandable than its IP address. **InetAddress** can handle both IPv4 and IPv6 addresses.

The **InetAddress** class has no visible constructors. To create an **InetAddress** object, you will use one of its **static** methods. Two are shown here:

static InetAddress getLocalHost( )
   throws UnknownHostException

static InetAddress getByName(String *hostName*)
   throws UnknownHostException

The **getLocalHost( )** method returns the **InetAddress** object that represents the local host (which is the local computer). The **getByName( )** method returns an **InetAddress** for a host name passed to it. If these methods are unable to resolve the host name, they throw an **UnknownHostException**. There is also a **getAllByName( )** method that returns an array of **InetAddress**es that represent all of the addresses that a particular name resolves to. This method is useful in cases in which a single name is used to represent several machines. It will also throw an **UnknownHostException** if it can't resolve the name to at least one address.

There are several methods that can be called on an instance of **InetAddress**. We will use two of them:

String getHostAddress( )

String getHostName( )

The **getHostAddress( )** method returns a string that lists the host IP address using its numeric form. The **getHostName( )** address returns the name that represents the host address. For convenience, **InetAddress** also overrides **toString( )**. It returns both the host name and its address.

The following example demonstrates **InetAddress** by displaying the addresses and names of several web sites.

```java
// Demonstrate InetAddress.

import java.net.*;

class InetAddressDemo {
  public static void main(String[] args) {

    try {
      InetAddress address = InetAddress.getByName("www.mcgraw-hill.com");
      System.out.println("Host name: " + address.getHostName());
      System.out.println("Address: " + address.getHostAddress());

      System.out.println();

      address = InetAddress.getByName("www.mhhe.com");
      System.out.println("Host name: " + address.getHostName());
      System.out.println("Address: " + address.getHostAddress());

      System.out.println();
```

```
            address = InetAddress.getByName("www.mheducation.com");
            System.out.println("Host name: " + address.getHostName());
            System.out.println("Address: " + address.getHostAddress());
        } catch (UnknownHostException exc) {
            System.out.println(exc);
        }
    }
}
```

Here is the output produced by this program. (Of course, the output you see may be slightly different.)

```
Host name: www.mcgraw-hill.com
Address: 204.8.135.3

Host name: www.mhhe.com
Address: 12.26.55.139

Host name: www.mheducation.com
Address: 12.163.148.101
```

Ask the Expert

Q How does **InetAddress** handle the differences between IPv4 and IPv6?

A To handle the differences between IPv4 and IPv6, JDK 1.4 added two sub-classes of **InetAddress**: **Inet4Address** and **Inet6Address**. **Inet4Address** represents a traditional-style IPv4 address. **Inet6Address** encapsulates a new-style IPv6 address. Because they are subclasses of **InetAddress**, an **InetAddress** reference can refer to either. This is one way that Java was able to add IPv6 functionality without breaking existing code or adding many more classes. For the most part, you can simply use **InetAddress** when working with IP addresses because it can accommodate both styles.

THE Socket CLASS

TCP/IP sockets are used to implement reliable, bidirectional, persistent, point-to-point, stream-based connections between hosts on the Internet. Through a socket, you can use Java's stream-based I/O to communicate with other programs that may reside either on the local machine or on any other machine on the Internet. Of course, such connections are subject to restrictions imposed by the security manager. For example, as a general rule, applets may only establish socket connections back to the host from which the applet was downloaded. This restriction exists because it would be dangerous for applets loaded through a firewall to have access to any arbitrary machine.

There are two kinds of TCP sockets in Java. One is for servers, and the other is for clients. The **ServerSocket** class is designed to be a "listener," which waits for clients to connect before doing anything. Thus, **ServerSocket** is for servers. The **Socket** class is for clients. It is designed to connect to server sockets and initiate protocol exchanges. Here we will examine **Socket**.

Socket defines several constructors. Here is the one we will use:

> Socket(String *hostName*, int *port*)
>
>   throws UnknownHostException, IOException

It creates a socket connected to the named host and port. It implicitly establishes a connection between the client and server. It will throw an **UnknownHostException** if the host cannot be found and an **IOException** if an I/O error occurs.

Socket defines several instance methods. For example, a **Socket** can be examined at any time for the address and port information associated with it, by use of the following methods:

> InetAddress getInetAddress( )
>
> int getPort( )
>
> int getLocalPort( )

If the socket is connected to a server, then the **getInetAddress( )** method returns its address in the form of an **InetAddress** instance. Otherwise, it returns **null**. Likewise, if the socket is connected to a server, then the **getPort( )** method returns the port number on the server. Otherwise, it returns 0. You can obtain the local port number by calling **getLocalPort( )**. It returns –1 if the socket is not bound to a port.

You can gain access to the input and output streams associated with a **Socket** by use of the **getInputStream( )** and **getOutputStream( )** methods, as shown here. Each can throw an **IOException** if an I/O error occurs. These streams are used exactly like the I/O streams described in Chapter 11 to send and receive data.

> InputStream getInputStream( ) throws IOException
>
> OutputStream getOutputStream( ) throws IOException

The **getInputStream( )** method returns the input stream associated with the invoking socket. The socket's output stream is returned by **getOutputStream( )**.

Socket supplies several other methods. For example, you can determine if a socket is connected to a server by calling **isConnected( )**. To check if a socket is bound to an address, call **isBound( )**. If a socket has been closed, then **isClosed( )** will return **true**. To close a socket, call **close( )**. Closing a socket also closes the I/O streams associated with the socket. Beginning with JDK 7, socket also implements **AutoCloseable**, which means that you can use a **try**-with-resources block to manage a socket.

The following program provides a simple **Socket** example. It uses "whois" to determine a domain name. It works by opening a connection to a whois port (port 43) on the **Whois.InterNIC.net** server. It then sends a domain name to the server. Finally, it displays the data that is returned. The whois server will look up the argument as a registered Internet domain name. If the name is found, it then sends back the IP address and contact information for that site.

```
// Demonstrate Sockets.

import java.net.*;
import java.io.*;

class SocketDemo {
  public static void main(String[] args) {
    int ch;
    Socket socket = null;

    try {
      // Create a socket connected to whois.internic.net, port 43.
      socket = new Socket("whois.internic.net", 43);      Construct a Socket.

      // Obtain input and output streams.                Obtain the input and
      InputStream in = socket.getInputStream();            output streams for the
      OutputStream out = socket.getOutputStream();         socket.

      // Construct a request string.
      String str = (args.length == 0 ? "mcgraw-hill.com" :
                                   args[0]) + "\n";
      // Convert to bytes.
      byte[] buf = str.getBytes();

      // Send request.
      out.write(buf);      Send a request.

      // Read and display response.
      while ((ch = in.read()) != -1) {      Obtain the response.
        System.out.print((char) ch);
      }
    } catch(IOException exc) {
      System.out.println(exc);
    } finally {
      try {
        if(socket != null) socket.close();
      } catch(IOException exc) {
        System.out.println("Error closing socket: " + exc);
      }
    }
  }
}
```

To use the program, specify the name of the web site in which you are interested on the command line. If you don't specify a command-line argument, then the site **mcgraw-hill.com** is used by default. If you use the default, you will see something similar to the following:

```
Whois Server Version 2.0

Domain names in the .com and .net domains can now be registered
with many different competing registrars. Go to http://www.internic.net
for detailed information.
```

```
Domain Name: MCGRAW-HILL.COM
Registrar: MELBOURNE IT, LTD. D/B/A INTERNET NAMES WORLDWIDE
Whois Server: whois.melbourneit.com
Referral URL: http://www.melbourneit.com
Name Server: CORP-55W-NS1.MCGRAW-HILL.COM
Name Server: CORP-HTS-NS1.MCGRAW-HILL.COM
Name Server: CORP-UKC-NS1.MCGRAW-HILL.COM
Status: clientTransferProhibited
Updated Date: 07-mar-2011
Creation Date: 07-may-1994
Expiration Date: 08-may-2012
  .
  .
  .
```

Here is how the program works. First, a **Socket** is constructed that specifies the host name "whois.internic.net" and the port number 43. **Internic.net** is the InterNIC web site that handles whois requests. Port 43 is the whois port. Next, both input and output streams are opened on the socket. Then, a string is constructed that contains the name of the web site you want to obtain information about. As mentioned, if no web site is specified on the command line, then "mcgraw-hill.com" is used. The string is converted into a **byte** array by use of the **String** method **getBytes( )** and then sent out the socket. The response is obtained by reading from the socket, and the results are displayed. Finally, the socket is closed, which also closes the I/O streams.

In the preceding example, the socket was closed manually by calling **close( )**. If you are using JDK 7 or later, then you can use a **try**-with-resources block to automatically close the socket. For example, here is another way to write the **main( )** method of the previous program:

```
// Use automatic resource management to close a socket.
public static void main(String[] args) {
  int ch;

  // Create a socket connected to internic.net, port 43. Manage this
  // socket with a try-with-resources block.
  try ( Socket socket = new Socket("whois.internic.net", 43) ) {

    // Obtain input and output streams.
    InputStream in = socket.getInputStream();
    OutputStream out = socket.getOutputStream();

    // Construct a request string.
    String str = (args.length == 0 ? "mcgraw-hill.com" :
                                      args[0]) + "\n";
    // Convert to bytes.
    byte[] buf = str.getBytes();

    // Send request.
    out.write(buf);
```

```
    // Read and display response.
    while ((ch = in.read()) != -1) {
      System.out.print((char) ch);
    }
  } catch(IOException exc) {
    System.out.println(exc);
  }
  // The socket is now closed.
}
```

In this version, the socket is automatically closed when the **try** block ends.

So the examples will work with versions of Java prior to JDK 7, and to clearly illustrate when a network resource can be closed, subsequent examples will continue to call **close( )** explicitly. However, in your own code, you should consider using automatic resource management since it offers a more streamlined approach.

Ask the Expert

Q In the discussion above, you mentioned **ServerSocket**. Can you tell me something about it?

A The **ServerSocket** class is used to create server applications. When you create a **ServerSocket**, it will register itself with the system as having an interest in client connections on a specified port. **ServerSocket** has a method called **accept( )**, which waits for a client to initiate communications. When this occurs, **accept( )** returns a **Socket** that is then used for communication with the client.

Progress Check

1. What does an **InetAddress** object encapsulate?
2. What is a "socket"?
3. **Socket**s send data back and forth to **ServerSocket**s using _____.

THE URL CLASS

URL stands for Uniform Resource Locator, and you are, no doubt, familiar with it because URLs provide a way to identify or address resources on the Internet. When you enter a web site into a browser, you are specifying that web site's URL. Java provides support for URLs with the **URL** class. After you have created a **URL** instance, you can use it to access the Internet.

Answers:

1. Both the numerical IP address and the domain name for that address.
2. It is one end of a connection between a client and a server over a network.
3. **InputStream**s and **OutputStream**s

All URLs share the same basic format, although some variation is allowed. Here are two examples: **http://www.mhhe.com/** and **http://www.mhhe.com:80/index.html**. A URL specification is based on four main components. The first is the protocol to use, separated from the rest of the locator by a colon (:). Common protocols include HTTP and FTP. The second component is the host name or IP address of the host to use; this is delimited on the left by double slashes (//) and on the right by a slash (/) or optionally a colon (:). The third component, the port number, is an optional parameter, delimited on the left from the host name by a colon (:) and on the right by a slash (/). (For HTTP, the port number defaults to 80, the predefined HTTP port; thus for HTTP, the ":80" is redundant. Other defaults are used for other protocols.) The fourth part is the resource path, such as to a file.

URL has several constructors. We will look at three, beginning with its simplest one, shown here:

URL(String *urlSpecifier*) throws MalformedURLException

Here, *urlSpecifier* is a string that specifies a complete URL, similar to what you would enter into a browser. The next two constructors allow you to break up the URL into its component parts:

URL(String *protocolName*, String *hostName*, int *port*, String *path*)

    throws MalformedURLException

URL(String *protocolName*, String *hostName*, String *path*)

    throws MalformedURLException

Here, each portion of the URL is specified by an individual string. For all three, a **MalformedURLException** is thrown if the protocol is invalid or if an argument is **null**.

There are methods defined by **URL** that let you obtain the individual components of a URL. Here are some examples. To obtain the protocol, called **getProtocol( )**. To obtain the host name, called **getHost( )**. To obtain the file name, call **getFile( )**. They are shown here:

String getProtocol( )

String getHost( )

String getFile( )

All return a string containing the desired information. You can retrieve the port number by calling **getPort( )**. It is shown here:

int getPort( )

It returns the port associated with the URL, or −1 if the port is not specified.

The following example creates a URL to **www.mhhe.com:80/index.html** and displays its components:

```
// Demonstrate URL.

import java.net.*;

class URLDemo {
  public static void main(String[] args) {
```

```
    try {
      URL url = new URL("http://www.mhhe.com:80/index.html");

      System.out.println("Protocol: " + url.getProtocol());
      System.out.println("Port: " + url.getPort());

      System.out.println("Host: " + url.getHost());
      System.out.println("File: " + url.getFile());
    } catch (MalformedURLException exc) {
      System.out.println("Invalid URL: " + exc);
    }
  }
}
```

When you run this, you will get the following output:

```
Protocol: http
Port: 80
Host: www.mhhe.com
File: /index.html
```

In addition to the methods just demonstrated, **URL** defines several others. One of particular interest is **openConnection( )**. It returns a **URLConnection** instance. **URLConnection** encapsulates information about a connection. The **openConnection( )** method shown here:

> URLConnection openConnection( ) throws IOException

Notice that it may throw an **IOException**. You will see this method in action in the following section.

THE URLConnection CLASS

URLConnection is an abstract class that encapsulates a URL-based connection. As a general rule, you obtain a **URLConnection** by using the **openConnection( )** method of **URL**, as just described in the previous section. Once you make a connection to a remote server, you can use **URLConnection** to inspect the properties of the resource. You can also open an input stream that lets you download the resource. **URLConnection** defines several methods. A sampling is shown in Table 26-1.

Notice that **URLConnection** defines several methods that handle header information. A header consists of pairs of keys and values represented as strings. By using **getHeaderField( )**, you can obtain the value associated with a header key. By calling **getHeaderFields( )**, you can obtain a map that contains all of the headers. Several standard header fields are available directly through methods such as **getDate( )** and **getContentType( )**.

The following example creates a **URLConnection** using the **openConnection( )** method of a **URL** object and then uses it to examine the document's properties and content:

```
// Demonstrate URLConnection.
import java.net.*;
import java.io.*;
import java.util.*;
```

TABLE 26-1: A Sampling of Methods Defined by URLConnection

Method	Description
int getContentLength( )	Returns the size in bytes of the content associated with the resource. If the length is unavailable, –1 is returned.
long getContentLengthLong( )	Returns the size in bytes of the content associated with the resource. If the length is unavailable, –1 is returned. (Added by JDK 7.)
String getContentType( )	Returns the type of content found in the resource. Returns **null** if the content type is not available.
long getDate( )	Returns the time and date of the response represented in terms of milliseconds since January 1, 1970 GMT. Zero is returned if the time and date are not available.
long getExpiration( )	Returns the expiration time and date of the resource represented in terms of milliseconds since January 1, 1970 GMT. Zero is returned if the expiration date is unavailable.
String getHeaderField(int *idx*)	Returns the value of the header field at index *idx*. (Header field indices begin at 0.) Returns **null** if the value of *idx* exceeds the number of fields.
String getHeaderField(String *fieldName*)	Returns the value of the header field whose name is specified by *fieldName*. Returns **null** if the specified name is not found.
String getHeaderFieldKey(int *idx*)	Returns the header field key at index *idx*. (Header field indices begin at 0.) Returns **null** if the value of *idx* exceeds the number of fields.
Map<String, List<String>> getHeaderFields( )	Returns a map that contains all of the header fields and values.
long getLastModified( )	Returns the time and date, represented in terms of milliseconds since January 1, 1970 GMT, of the last modification of the resource. Zero is returned if the last-modified date is unavailable.
InputStream getInputStream( ) throws IOException	Returns an **InputStream** that is linked to the connection.
OutputStream getOutputStream( ) throws IOException	Returns an **OutputStream** that is linked to the connection.

```
class UCDemo
{
  public static void main(String[] args) {

    InputStream in = null;
    URLConnection connection = null;

    try {
      URL url = new URL("http://www.mcgraw-hill.com");
```

```
connection = url.openConnection();  ◄────────────Open a connection.

// get date
long d = connection.getDate();  ◄──────┐
if(d==0)                                │
  System.out.println("No date information.");
else                                    │
  System.out.println("Date: " + new Date(d));
                                        │
// get content type                     │
System.out.println("Content-Type: " +   │
                   connection.getContentType());
                                        │
// get expiration date                  │
d = connection.getExpiration();  ◄──────┤
if(d==0)                                │
  System.out.println("No expiration information.");         ├──Obtain various values.
else                                    │
  System.out.println("Expires: " + new Date(d));
                                        │
// get last-modified date               │
d = connection.getLastModified();  ◄────┤
if(d==0)                                │
  System.out.println("No last-modified information.");
else                                    │
  System.out.println("Last-Modified: " + new Date(d));
                                        │
// get content length                   │
long len = connection.getContentLengthLong();  ◄──┘
if(len == -1)
  System.out.println("Content length unavailable.");
else
  System.out.println("Content-Length: " + len);

if(len != 0) {
  System.out.println("=== Content ===");
  in = connection.getInputStream();  ◄────────Obtain the input stream.

  int ch;
  while (((ch = in.read()) != -1)) {  ◄────────Read and display the content.
    System.out.print((char) ch);
  }
} else {
  System.out.println("No content available.");
}
} catch(IOException exc) {
  System.out.println("Connection Error: " + exc);
} finally {
  try {
    if(in != null) in.close();
```

```
      } catch(IOException exc) {
        System.out.println("Error closing connection: " + exc);
      }
    }
  }
}
```

The program establishes an HTTP connection to **www.mcgraw-hill.com**. It then displays several header values and retrieves the content. Here are the first lines of the output (the precise output will vary over time).

```
Date: Mon Jul 18 10:59:42 CDT 2011
Content-Type: text/html;charset=ISO-8859-1
No expiration information.
No last-modified information.
Content-Length: 50631
=== Content ===
<!DOCTYPE html PUBLIC "-//W3C//DTD XHTML 1.0 Strict//EN"
  .
  .
  .
```

TRY THIS 26-1 DOWNLOAD A FILE FROM THE INTERNET

GetFileFromSite.java

In this project, you will write a program that downloads a file from the Internet and saves it on your computer. The program is called **GetFileFromSite**. It takes as input the URL of a file and the name to be given to the file on your computer. For example, to use the program to download the home page of **www.mhhe.com** and store it in a file named "mhhehomepage.html", you would use the command

```
java GetFileFromSite http://www.mhhe.com mhhehomepage.html
```

The program uses a **URLConnection** to download the contents of the file.

STEP-BY-STEP

1. Create a new file called **GetFileFromSite.java** and enter in the following code:

```
import java.net.*;
import java.io.*;

class GetFileFromSite {
  public static void main(String[] args) {
    if(args.length != 2) {
```

```
          System.out.println("Usage: java GetFileFromSite url file");
          return;
        }

        InputStream in = null;
        URLConnection connection = null;
        FileOutputStream fout = null;

        try {
          URL url = new URL(args[0]);
          connection = url.openConnection();
          in = connection.getInputStream();
          fout = new FileOutputStream(args[1]);

          // Download and save the file.
          int b;
          while (((b = in.read()) != -1)) {
            fout.write(b);
          }
        } catch (IOException exc) {
          System.out.println("Connection Error: " + exc);
        } finally {
          try {
            if(in != null) in.close();
            if(fout != null) fout.close();
          } catch (IOException exc) {
            System.out.println("Error closing stream: " + exc);
          }
        }
      }
    }
```

2. Let's look closely at how this program works. The program first tests for the correct number of command-line arguments. It then creates three references. The first is an **InputStream** called **in**. The second is a **URLConnection** called **connection**. The third is a **FileOutputStream** called **fout**. The main action of the program occurs inside the **try** block.

The **try** block begins by creating a **URL** object called **url** for the URL specified on the command line. Next, a connection to the URL is opened by calling **openConnection( )** on **url**. This connection is assigned to **connection**. Then, an **InputStream** is obtained by calling **getInputStream** on **connection** and assigned to **in**. Thus, **in** refers to the file that will be downloaded. A **FileOutputStream** associated with the file name specified as the target file on the command line is assigned to **fout**. Finally, the program copies the bytes received from the network input stream to the file output stream. This results in the file being downloaded and stored on the computer.

3. Now compile the program and, to test it, run it with the following command (all on one line):

```
java GetFileFromSite http://highered.mcgraw-hill.com/sites/dl/
free/0072974168/584690/SourceCode.zip Projects.zip
```

The URL in the command corresponds to a zip file created by one of the authors for use with an object-oriented design textbook. When the program finishes running, you will see a new file named "Projects.zip" in the same directory as your program. If you unzip that file, you will see folders containing Java source code.

THE HttpURLConnection CLASS

Java provides a subclass of **URLConnection** that provides additional support for HTTP connections. This class is called **HttpURLConnection**. You obtain an **HttpURLConnection** in the same way just shown, by calling **openConnection( )** on a **URL** object, but you must cast the result to **HttpURLConnection**. Of course, you must make sure that you are actually opening an HTTP connection.

Once you have obtained a reference to an **HttpURLConnection** object, you can use any of the methods inherited from **URLConnection**. You can also use any of the several methods defined by **HttpURLConnection**. The example that follows will use three of them. The first is **getRequestMethod** shown here:

String getRequestMethod( )

It returns a string representing how HTTP requests are made. The default is GET. Other options, such as POST, are available.

The next method is **getResponseCode( )**, shown next:

int getResponseCode( ) throws IOException

It returns the HTTP response code. −1 is returned if no response code can be obtained. An **IOException** is thrown if the connection fails. A response code in the 200 range indicates success. A response code in the 300 range indicates a redirection. A response in the 400 range indicates a request error of some sort, such as bad syntax. Responses in the 500 range indicate a server error. Typically, if all goes well, 200 is returned to indicate success.

The third method we will use is **getResponseMessage( )**:

String getResponseMessage( ) throws IOException

It returns the response message associated with the response code. It returns **null** if no message is available. An **IOException** is thrown if the connection fails.

The following program demonstrates **HttpURLConnection**. It first establishes a connection to **www.mcgraw-hill.com**. Then it displays the request method, the response code, and the response message. Finally, it displays the keys and values in the response header.

```
// Demonstrate HttpURLConnection.

import java.net.*;
import java.io.*;
import java.util.*;

class HttpURLConnectionDemo
{
  public static void main(String[] args) {

    try {
      URL url = new URL("http://www.mcgraw-hill.com");
        HttpURLConnection connection =
            (HttpURLConnection) url.openConnection();

      // Display request method.
      System.out.println("Request method is " +
                      connection.getRequestMethod());

      // Display response code.
      System.out.println("Response code is " +
                      connection.getResponseCode());

      // Display response message.
      System.out.println("Response Message is " +
                      connection.getResponseMessage());

      // Get a list of the header fields and a set
      // of the header keys.
      Map<String, List<String>> hdrMap = connection.getHeaderFields();
      Set<String> hdrKeys = hdrMap.keySet();

      System.out.println("\nHere is the header:");

      // Display all header keys and values.
      for(String k : hdrKeys) {
        System.out.println("Key: " + k +
                      "  Value: " + hdrMap.get(k));
      }
    } catch(IOException exc) {
      System.out.println(exc);
    }
  }
}
```

Notice how a set of the keys is obtained. (annotation pointing to `Map<String, List<String>> hdrMap = connection.getHeaderFields();` and `Set<String> hdrKeys = hdrMap.keySet();`)

Now, display the keys and the values. (annotation pointing to `System.out.println("Key: " + k +`)

The output produced by the program is shown here. (Of course, the exact response returned by **www.mhhe.com** will vary over time.)

```
Request method is GET
Response code is 200
Response Message is OK
```

```
Here is the header:
Key: null   Value: [HTTP/1.1 200 OK]
Key: Date   Value: [Mon, 18 Jul 2011 16:15:47 GMT]
Key: Content-Length   Value: [50631]
Key: Keep-Alive   Value: [timeout=5, max=100]
Key: Content-Type   Value: [text/html;charset=ISO-8859-1]
Key: Connection   Value: [Keep-Alive]
Key: X-Powered-By   Value: [Servlet/2.5 JSP/2.1]
```

Notice how the header keys and values are displayed. First, a map of the header keys and values is obtained by calling **getHeaderFields( )** (which is inherited from **URLConnection**). Next, a set of the header keys is retrieved by calling **keySet( )** on the map. Then the key set is cycled through by using a for-each style **for** loop. The value associated with each key is obtained by calling **get( )** on the map.

Ask the Expert

Q In the table of classes in **java.net** shown earlier, I noticed the **URI** class. What is it?

A The **URI** class encapsulates a *Uniform Resource Identifier (URI)*. URIs are similar to URLs. In fact, URLs constitute a subset of URIs. A URI represents a standard way to identify a resource. A URL also describes how to access the resource. You can convert from a **URI** instance to a **URL** instance by using the **toURL( )** method. To convert from a **URL** to a **URI**, use **toURI( )**.

Progress Check

1. The four components of a URL are _____.
2. You create a **URLConnection** by invoking _____.
3. What are two methods added by the **HttpURLConnection** class?

DATAGRAMS

Datagrams provide an alternative to the TCP/IP-style networking just discussed. *Datagrams* are bundles of information passed between machines. Datagrams differ from TCP/IP networking in a very important way: a datagram is not guaranteed to reach its destination. Once the datagram has been sent to its intended target, there is no assurance that it will arrive or even that the target will be there to receive it.

_____

Answers:

1. protocol, host name, port, and file path
2. the **openConnection( )** method of the **URL** class
3. **getRequestMethod( )** and **getResponseCode( )**

Furthermore, when the datagram is received, there is no assurance that it hasn't been damaged in transit or that whoever sent it is still there to receive a response. Also, datagrams might reach their destination in an order that differs from the order in which they are sent.

Two primary classes support datagrams. The first is **DatagramPacket**, which contains the data. The second is **DatagramSocket**, which is the socket class that is used to send or receive the **DatagramPacket**s. Each is examined here.

Note: *Another class that supports datagrams is **MulticastSocket**. It is used for multicasting datagrams. Muliticasting enables a server to send a datagram to multiple clients.*

DatagramSocket

DatagramSocket defines several constructors. The one we will use is shown here:

DatagramSocket(int *port*) throws SocketException

It creates a **DatagramSocket** for the local host that uses the port specified by *port*. Notice that it can throw a **SocketException** if an error occurs while creating the socket.

DatagramSocket defines many methods, but we only need three for the example in this chapter. The first two are **send( )** and **receive( )** and are shown here:

void send(DatagramPacket *packet*) throws IOException

void receive(DatagramPacket *packet*) throws IOException

The **send( )** method sends a packet to the port and address specified by *packet*. The **receive( )** method waits for a packet to be received from the port specified by *packet*. It then puts the received packet into *packet*. The third method we will use is **close( )**, which closes the socket. Beginning with JDK 7, **DatagramSocket** implements **AutoCloseable**, which means that a **DatagramSocket** can be managed by a **try**-with-resources block.

DatagramPacket

DatagramPacket defines several constructors. The two we will use are shown here:

DatagramPacket(byte[ ] *data*, int *size*)

DatagramPacket(byte[ ] *data*, int *size*, InetAddress *ipAddress*, int *port*)

The first constructor is used for receiving packets. Here, *data* specifies a buffer that will receive the data, and *size* specifies the length of the data, which must not exceed the size of the buffer. The second constructor is used for sending packets. In this version, *data* specifies a buffer that contains the data to be sent, and *size* indicates the number of bytes to send. It also specifies a target address and port, which are used by a **DatagramSocket** to determine where the data in the packet will be sent.

DatagramPacket defines several methods that give access to the address and port number of a packet, as well as the raw data and its length. In general, the **get** methods are used on packets that are received, and the **set** methods are used on packets that will be sent. Here is a sampling of the methods defined by **DatagramPacket**:

InetAddress getAddress( )	Returns the address of the source (for datagrams being received) or destination (for datagrams being sent).
byte[ ] getData( )	Returns the **byte** array that contains the data buffer. Mostly used to retrieve data from the datagram after it has been received.
int getLength( )	Returns the number of bytes of data contained in the buffer. This may be less than the size of the underlying **byte** array.
int getOffset( )	Returns the starting index of the data in the buffer.
int getPort( )	Returns the port number used by the host on the other side of the connection.
void setData(byte[ ] *data*)	Sets the packet data to *data*, the offset to zero, and the length to the number of bytes in *data*.
void setData(byte[ ] *data*, int *idx*, int *size*)	Sets the packet data to *data,* the offset to *idx,* and the length to *size*.
void setLength(int *size*)	Sets the length of the packet to *size*. This value plus the offset must not exceed the length of the underlying **byte** array.

A Datagram Example

The following example demonstrates datagrams by implementing a very simple client and server. In this example, the server reads strings entered at the keyboard and sends them to the client. The client simply waits until it receives a packet and then displays the string. This process continues until "stop" is entered. In that case, both the client and server terminate. In the program, the port numbers were chosen somewhat arbitrarily because they were unused ports in the author's system. Therefore, you may have to choose different ports. If a port is already bound to a socket, then the attempt to create a datagram socket will fail. One other point: the use of datagrams may be prohibited by your system, such as by a firewall. If this is the case, the following example will not work.

This example consists of two classes. The first is **DGServer**, which is the class that serves data. It is shown here:

```
// Demonstrate datagrams -- server side.

import java.net.*;
import java.io.*;

class DGServer {
```

```java
// These ports were chosen arbitrarily. You must use
// unused ports on your machine.
public static int clientPort = 50000;
public static int serverPort = 50001;

public static DatagramSocket ds;

public static void dgServer() throws IOException {
  byte[] buffer;
  String str;

  BufferedReader conin = new BufferedReader(
                         new InputStreamReader(System.in));

  System.out.println("Enter characters. Enter 'stop' to quit.");
  for(;;) {
    // read a string from the keyboard
    str = conin.readLine();

    // convert string to byte array for transmission
    buffer = str.getBytes();

    // send a new packet that contains the string
    ds.send(new DatagramPacket(buffer, buffer.length,      ─────── Send a packet.
            InetAddress.getLocalHost(), clientPort));

    // quit when "stop" is entered
    if(str.equals("stop")) {
      System.out.println("Server Quits.");
      return;
    }
  }
}

public static void main(String[] args) {
  ds = null;

  try {
    ds = new DatagramSocket(serverPort);
    dgServer();
  } catch(IOException exc) {
    System.out.println("Communication error: " + exc);
  } finally {
    if(ds != null) ds.close();
  }
}
}
```

Each time a new string is entered, a **DatagramPacket** is created that contains the string as an array of **bytes**. This packet is then sent to the client via a call to **send( )**. The process repeats until "stop" is entered.

The second file, called **DGClient**, receives the data sent by the server. It is shown here:

```
// Demonstrate datagrams -- client side.

import java.net.*;
import java.io.*;

class DGClient {
  // This port was choosen arbitrarily. You must use
  // an unused port on your machine.
  public static int clientPort = 50000;
  public static int buffer_size = 1024;

  public static DatagramSocket ds;

  public static void dgClient() throws IOException {
    String str;
    byte[] buffer = new byte[buffer_size];

    System.out.println("Receiving Data");
    for(;;) {
      // create a new packet to receive the data
      DatagramPacket p = new DatagramPacket(buffer, buffer.length);

      // wait for a packet
      ds.receive(p); ◄————————Receive a packet.

      // convert buffer into String
      str = new String(p.getData(), 0, p.getLength());

      // display the string on the client
      System.out.println(str);

      // quit when "stop" is received.
      if(str.equals("stop")) {
        System.out.println("Client Stopping.");
        break;
      }
    }
  }

  public static void main(String[] args) {
    ds = null;

    try {
      ds = new DatagramSocket(clientPort);
      dgClient();
    } catch(IOException exc) {
      System.out.println("Communication error: " + exc);
```

```
    } finally {
        if(ds != null) ds.close();
    }
  }
}
```

Here, a new **DatagramPacket** is created to receive the data. Then, **receive( )** is called. It waits until a packet has been received. Next, the buffer is converted into a string and then displayed. The process repeats until "stop" is received.

This example is restricted by the **DatagramSocket** constructor to running between two ports on the local machine. To use the program, first run

```
java DGClient
```

in one window; this will be the client. Then run

```
java DGServer
```

This will be the server. Anything that is typed in the server window will be sent to the client window after a newline is received. To stop the programs, enter "stop".

Progress Check

1. The **DatagramSocket** class's **receive( )** method takes a **DatagramPacket** as its parameter. What does that method use its parameter for?
2. The **DatagramPacket** and **DatagramSocket** classes use the protocol TCP. True or False?

EXERCISES

1. **Socket**s are designed to send and receive data using the protocol HTTP. True or False?
2. **URLConnection**s are designed to send and receive data using the protocol HTTP. True or False?
3. What two pieces of information does a **Socket** need to have in order to connect to another computer on the network?
4. When you enter a URL using HTTP in your web browser, why aren't you required to enter a port number?
5. How does sending data using datagrams differ, with respect to guarantees of arrival, from sending data using a method that uses the protocol TCP?

Answers:

1. The data that is received is loaded into the **DatagramPacket**. It can be extracted by the **getData( )** method.
2. False. They use UDP.

6. Modify the **SocketDemo** program so that it takes any number of domain names as arguments on the command line and sends them to the "whois" port of the **whois.internic.net** server. For each domain name argument, it outputs the data received from the socket. If there are no arguments, it doesn't output anything. Note that you will need to close the socket and create a new one after receiving each response from the socket.

7. Write a method **getIPSegments( )** that takes a host name as its parameter and returns an array of strings, one string containing each segment (separated by periods) of a numerical IP address. For example, if the host name's IP address is 111.222.333.444, then the method should return the array {"111", "222", "333", "444"}. Your method should work for both IPv4 and IPv6 addresses. Your method should throw an **UnknownHostException** if it can't find the host. Write a test program for your method.

8. Write a program that outputs the host name and numerical IP address for your local host machine.

9. If you invoke a **URL** constructor with the argument "http://www.mhhe.com/index.html?a=Jonathon#start" and then invoke the **URL**'s **getFile( )** method, what is returned, if anything?

10. Modify the **HttpURLConnectionDemo** program so that it only outputs a number indicating how many header fields there are in the response header.

11. Modify the **DGClient** example at the end of the chapter so that **buffer_size** = 6 instead of 1024. What difference, if any, does this make?

12. In the **dgClient( )** method of the **DGClient** example, there is a loop in which a new **DatagramPacket** is constructed for receiving each new packet of information from the sender. Would it also work to reuse the same **DatagramPacket**? That is, suppose we rewrite the code so that one **DatagramPacket** is created outside the loop and that packet is repeatedly passed as the argument to the **receive( )** method. Will the program still work correctly?

CHAPTER 27

The Concurrency Utilities

KEY SKILLS & CONCEPTS

- The **Semaphore** class
- The **CountDownLatch** class
- The **CyclicBarrier** class
- The **Exchanger** class
- The **Phaser** class
- Use an **Executor**
- Use **Callable** and **Future**
- Use locks
- The Fork/Join Framework

From the start, Java has provided built-in support for multithreading and synchronization. For example, new threads can be created by implementing **Runnable** or by extending **Thread**; synchronization is available by use of the **synchronized** keyword; and interthread communication is supported by the **wait( )** and **notify( )** methods that are defined by **Object**. In general, this built-in support for multithreading was one of Java's most important innovations and is still one of its major strengths.

As conceptually pure as Java's original support for multithreading is, it is not ideal for all applications—especially those that make extensive use of multiple threads. For example, the original multithreading support does not provide several high-level features, such as semaphores, thread pools, and execution managers, that facilitate the creation of intensively concurrent programs.

It is important to explain at the outset that many Java programs make use of multithreading and are, therefore, "concurrent." For example, many applets use multithreading. However, as it is used in this chapter, the term *concurrent program* refers to a program that makes *extensive, integral* use of concurrently executing threads. An example of such a program is one that uses separate threads to simultaneously compute the partial results of a larger computation. Another example is a program that coordinates the activities of several threads, each of which seeks access to information in a database. In this case, read-only accesses might be handled differently from those that require read/write capabilities.

To begin to handle the needs of a concurrent program, JDK 5 added the *concurrency utilities*, also commonly referred to as the *concurrent API*. The original set of concurrency utilities supplied many features that had long been wanted by programmers who develop concurrent applications. For example, it offered synchronizers (such as the semaphore), thread pools, execution managers, locks, several concurrent collections, and a streamlined way to use threads to obtain computational results.

Although the original concurrent API was impressive in its own right, it was significantly expanded by JDK 7. One of these additions is the *Fork/Join Framework*. The Fork/Join Framework facilitates the creation of certain types of programs that make use of multiple processors (such as those found in multicore systems). Thus, it streamlines the development of programs in which two or more pieces execute with true simultaneity (that is, true parallel execution). As you can easily imagine, parallel execution can dramatically increase the speed of certain operations.

The original concurrent API was quite large, and the Fork/Join Framework increases its size substantially. As you might expect, many of the issues surrounding the concurrency utilities are quite complex. It is beyond the scope of this book to discuss all of its facets. The preceding notwithstanding, it is important for all programmers to have a general, working knowledge of the concurrent API. Even in programs that are not intensively parallel, features such as synchronizers, callable threads, and executors are applicable to a wide variety of situations. Perhaps most importantly, because of the rise of multicore computers, solutions involving the Fork/Join Framework will become more common. For these reasons, this chapter presents an overview of the concurrency utilities and shows several examples of their use. It concludes with an in-depth examination of the Fork/Join Framework.

THE CONCURRENT API PACKAGES

The concurrency utilities are contained in the **java.util.concurrent** package and in its two subpackages: **java.util.concurrent.atomic** and **java.util.concurrent.locks**. A brief overview of their contents is given here.

java.util.concurrent

java.util.concurrent defines the core features that support alternatives to the built-in approaches to synchronization and interthread communication. It defines the following key features:

- Synchronizers
- Executors
- Concurrent collections
- The Fork/Join Framework

Synchronizers offer high-level ways of synchronizing the interactions between multiple threads. The synchronizer classes defined by **java.util.concurrent** are

Semaphore	Implements the classic semaphore.
CountDownLatch	Waits until a specified number of events have occurred.
CyclicBarrier	Enables a group of threads to wait at a predefined execution point.
Exchanger	Exchanges data between two threads.
Phaser	Synchronizes threads that advance through multiple phases of an operation.

Notice that each synchronizer provides a solution to a specific type of synchronization problem. This enables each synchronizer to be optimized for its intended use. In the past, these types of synchronization objects had to be crafted by hand. The concurrent API standardizes them and makes them available to all Java programmers.

Executors manage thread execution. At the top of the executor hierarchy is the **Executor** interface, which is used to initiate a thread. **ExecutorService** extends **Executor** and provides methods that manage execution. There are three implementations of **ExecutorService**: **ThreadPoolExecutor**, **ScheduledThreadPoolExecutor**, and **ForkJoinPool**. **java.util.concurrent** also defines the **Executors** utility class, which includes a number of **static** methods that simplify the creation of various executors.

Related to executors are the **Future** and **Callable** interfaces. A **Future** contains a value that is returned by a thread after it executes. Thus, its value becomes defined "in the future," when the thread terminates. **Callable** defines a thread that returns a value.

java.util.concurrent defines several concurrent collection classes, including **ConcurrentHashMap**, **ConcurrentLinkedQueue**, and **CopyOnWriteArraylist**. These offer concurrent alternatives to their related classes defined by the Collections Framework in **java.util**.

The *Fork/Join Framework* supports parallel programming. Its main classes are **ForkJoinTask**, **ForkJoinPool**, **RecursiveTask**, and **RecursiveAction**. As mentioned, the Fork/Join Framework was added by JDK 7.

Finally, to better handle thread timing, **java.util.concurrent** defines the **TimeUnit** enumeration.

java.util.concurrent.atomic

java.util.concurrent.atomic facilitates the use of variables in a concurrent environment. It provides a means of efficiently updating the value of a variable without the use of locks. This is accomplished through the use of classes, such as **AtomicInteger** and **AtomicLong**, and methods, such as **compareAndSet( )**, **decrementAndGet( )**, and **getAndSet( )**. These methods execute as a single, noninterruptible operation.

java.util.concurrent.locks

java.util.concurrent.locks provides an alternative to the use of synchronized methods. At the core of this alternative is the **Lock** interface, which defines the basic mechanism used to acquire and relinquish access to an object. The key methods are lock( ), **tryLock( )**, and **unlock( )**. The advantage of using these methods is greater control over synchronization.

The remainder of this chapter takes a closer look at the constituents of the concurrent API.

USING SYNCHRONIZATION OBJECTS

A key part of the concurrent API are its synchronization objects. These are supported by the **Semaphore**, **CountDownLatch**, **CyclicBarrier**, **Exchanger**, and **Phaser** classes. Collectively, they enable you to handle otherwise difficult synchronization situations with ease. They are also applicable to a wide range of programs—even those that contain only limited concurrency. Because the synchronization objects will be of interest to nearly all Java programmers, each is examined here in some detail.

Semaphore

The **Semaphore** class implements a classic semaphore. A semaphore controls access to a shared resource through the use of a counter. If the counter is greater than zero, then access is allowed. If it is zero, then access is denied. What the counter is counting are *permits* that allow access to the shared resource. Thus, to access the resource, a thread must be granted a permit from the semaphore.

In general, to use a semaphore, the thread that wants access to the shared resource tries to acquire a permit. If the semaphore's count is greater than zero, then the thread acquires a permit, which causes the semaphore's count to be decremented. Otherwise, the thread will be blocked until a permit can be acquired. When the thread no longer needs access to the shared resource, it releases the permit, which causes the semaphore's count to be incremented. If there is another thread waiting for a permit, then that thread will acquire a permit at that time. Java's **Semaphore** class implements this mechanism.

Semaphore has the two constructors shown here:

Semaphore(int *num*)

Semaphore(int *num*, boolean *how*)

Here, *num* specifies the initial permit count. Thus, *num* specifies the number of threads that can access a shared resource at any one time. If *num* is one, then only one thread can access the resource at any one time. By default, waiting threads are granted a permit in an undefined order. By setting *how* to **true**, you can ensure that waiting threads are granted a permit in the order in which they requested access.

To acquire a permit, call the **acquire( )** method, which has these two forms:

void acquire( ) throws InterruptedException

void acquire(int *num*) throws InterruptedException

The first form acquires one permit. The second form acquires *num* permits. If the permit cannot be granted at the time of the call, then the invoking thread suspends until the permit is available.

To release a permit, call **release( )**, which has these two forms:

> void release( )
>
> void release(int *num*)

The first form releases one permit. The second form releases the number of permits specified by *num*.

To use a semaphore to control access to a resource, each thread that wants to use that resource must first call **acquire( )** before accessing the resource. When the thread is done with the resource, it must call **release( )**. Here is an example that illustrates the use of a semaphore:

```java
// A simple semaphore example.

import java.util.concurrent.*;

class SemDemo {

  public static void main(String[] args) {
    Semaphore sem = new Semaphore(1);         // Create a semaphore that
                                               // has only 1 permit.

    new IncThread(sem, "A");
    new DecThread(sem, "B");

  }
}

// A shared resource.
class Shared {
  static int count = 0;
}

// A thread of execution that increments count.
class IncThread implements Runnable {
  String name;
  Semaphore sem;

  IncThread(Semaphore s, String n) {
    sem = s;
    name = n;
    new Thread(this).start();
  }

  public void run() {

    System.out.println("Starting " + name);

    try {
      // First, get a permit.
      System.out.println(name + " is waiting for a permit.");
      sem.acquire();          // Wait until a permit can be
                              // acquired.
      System.out.println(name + " gets a permit.");
```

```
      // Now, access shared resource.
      for(int i=0; i < 5; i++) {
        Shared.count++;
        System.out.println(name + ": " + Shared.count);

        // Now, allow a context switch -- if possible.
        Thread.sleep(10);
      }
    } catch (InterruptedException exc) {
      System.out.println(exc);
    }

    // Release the permit.
    System.out.println(name + " releases the permit.");
    sem.release();
  }
}

// A thread of execution that decrements count.
class DecThread implements Runnable {
  String name;
  Semaphore sem;

  DecThread(Semaphore s, String n) {
    sem = s;
    name = n;
    new Thread(this).start();
  }

  public void run() {

    System.out.println("Starting " + name);

    try {
      // First, get a permit.
      System.out.println(name + " is waiting for a permit.");
      sem.acquire();
      System.out.println(name + " gets a permit.");

      // Now, access shared resource.
      for(int i=0; i < 5; i++) {
        Shared.count--;
        System.out.println(name + ": " + Shared.count);

        // Now, allow a context switch -- if possible.
        Thread.sleep(10);
      }
    } catch (InterruptedException exc) {
      System.out.println(exc);
    }

    // Release the permit.
    System.out.println(name + " releases the permit.");
```

Access the
shared resource.

Release the permit.

Wait until a permit
can be acquired.

Access the shared
resource.

```
      sem.release();  ◄──────────────────Release the permit.
   }
}
```

The output from the program is shown here. (The precise order in which the threads execute may vary.)

```
Starting A
A is waiting for a permit.
A gets a permit.
A: 1
Starting B
B is waiting for a permit.
A: 2
A: 3
A: 4
A: 5
A releases the permit.
B gets a permit.
B: 4
B: 3
B: 2
B: 1
B: 0
B releases the permit.
```

The program uses a semaphore to control access to the **count** variable, which is a static variable within the **Shared** class. **Shared.count** is incremented five times by the **run( )** method of **IncThread** and decremented five times by **DecThread**. To prevent these two threads from accessing **Shared.count** at the same time, access is allowed only after a permit is acquired from the controlling semaphore. After access is complete, the permit is released. In this way, only one thread at a time will access **Shared.count**, as the output shows.

In both **IncThread** and **DecThread**, notice the call to **sleep( )** within **run( )**. It is used to "prove" that accesses to **Shared.count** are synchronized by the semaphore. In **run( )**, the call to **sleep( )** causes the invoking thread to pause between each access to **Shared.count**. This would normally enable the second thread to run. However, because of the semaphore, the second thread must wait until the first has released the permit, which happens only after all accesses by the first thread are complete. Thus, **Shared.count** is first incremented five times by **IncThread** and then decremented five times by **DecThread**. The increments and decrements are *not* intermixed.

Without the use of the semaphore, accesses to **Shared.count** by both threads would have occurred simultaneously, and the increments and decrements would be intermixed. To confirm this, try commenting out the calls to **acquire( )** and **release( )**. When you run the program, you will see that access to **Shared.count** is no longer synchronized, and each thread accesses it as soon as it gets a timeslice.

CountDownLatch

Sometimes you will want a thread to wait until one or more events have occurred. (Here, we are using the term *event* to mean some program action, such as the completion of a task by a separate thread.) To handle such a situation, the concurrent API supplies **CountDownLatch**. A **CountDownLatch** is initially created with a count of the number of events that must occur before the latch is released. Each time an event happens, the count is decremented. When the count reaches zero, the latch opens.

CountDownLatch has the following constructor:

CountDownLatch(int *num*)

Here, *num* specifies the number of events that must occur in order for the latch to open.

To wait on the latch, a thread calls **await( )**, which has the forms shown here:

void await( ) throws InterruptedException

boolean await(long *wait*, TimeUnit *tu*) throws InterruptedException

The first form waits until the count associated with the invoking **CountDownLatch** reaches zero. The second form waits only for the period of time specified by *wait*. The units represented by *wait* are specified by *tu*, which is an object of the **TimeUnit** enumeration. (**TimeUnit** is described later in this chapter.) It returns **false** if the time limit is reached and **true** if the countdown reaches zero.

To signal an event, call the **countDown( )** method, shown next:

void countDown( )

Each call to **countDown( )** decrements the count associated with the invoking object.

The following program demonstrates **CountDownLatch**. It creates a latch that requires five events to occur before it opens.

```
// An example of CountDownLatch.

import java.util.concurrent.CountDownLatch;

class CDLDemo {
  public static void main(String[] args) {
    CountDownLatch cdl = new CountDownLatch(5);    Create a CountDownLatch
                                                   that waits for 5 events.
    System.out.println("Starting");

    new MyThread(cdl);

    try {
      cdl.await();                                 Wait until the count
    } catch (InterruptedException exc) {           down finishes.
      System.out.println(exc);
    }

    System.out.println("Done");
  }
}

class MyThread implements Runnable {
  CountDownLatch latch;

  MyThread(CountDownLatch c) {
    latch = c;
```

```
      new Thread(this).start();
   }

   public void run() {
      for(int i = 0; i<5; i++) {
         System.out.println(i);
         latch.countDown(); // decrement count
      }
   }
}
```

Decrement the count each time through the loop.

The output produced by the program is shown here:

```
Starting
0
1
2
3
4
Done
```

Inside **main( )**, a **CountDownLatch** called **cdl** is created with an initial count of five. Next, an instance of **MyThread** is created, which begins execution of a new thread. Notice that **cdl** is passed as a parameter to **MyThread**'s constructor and stored in the **latch** instance variable. Then, the main thread calls **await( )** on **cdl**, which causes execution of the main thread to pause until **cdl**'s count has been decremented five times.

Inside the **run( )** method of **MyThread**, a loop is created that iterates five times. With each iteration, the **countDown( )** method is called on **latch**, which refers to **cdl** in **main( )**. After the fifth iteration, the latch opens, which allows the main thread to resume.

CountDownLatch is a powerful yet easy-to-use synchronization object that is appropriate whenever a thread must wait for one or more actions to occur.

Progress Check

1. To get a permit from a **Semaphore**, call its _____ method and to return a permit, call its _____ method.
2. A thread can get at most one permit at a time from a **Semaphore**. True or False?
3. A **CountDownLatch** is useful when you want a thread to wait until _____.
4. To force a thread to wait until a **CountDownLatch**'s count reaches 0, the thread should call the **CountDownLatch**'s _____ method.

Answers:

1. **acquire( )** and **release( )**
2. False. A thread can acquire any number of permits (assuming they are available) from a semaphore by calling **acquire(n)**, where n is the number of permits desired.
3. a certain number of events have occurred
4. **await( )**

CyclicBarrier

A situation not uncommon in concurrent programming occurs when a set of two or more threads must wait at a predetermined execution point, called a *barrier*, until all threads in the set have reached that point. To handle such a situation, the concurrent API supplies the **CyclicBarrier** class. It enables you to define a synchronization object that suspends until the specified number of threads has reached the barrier.

CyclicBarrier has the following two constructors:

> CyclicBarrier(int *numThreads*)
>
> CyclicBarrier(int *numThreads*, Runnable *action*)

Here, *numThreads* specifies the number of threads that must reach the barrier before execution continues. In the second form, *action* specifies a thread that will be executed when the barrier has been reached by all threads.

Here is the general procedure that you will follow to use **CyclicBarrier**. First, create a **CyclicBarrier** object, specifying the number of threads that you will be waiting for. Next, when each thread reaches the barrier, have it call **await( )** on that object. This will pause execution of the thread until all of the other threads also call **await( )**. Once the specified number of threads has reached the barrier, **await( )** will return, and execution will resume. Also, if you have specified an action, then that thread is executed.

The **await( )** method has the following two forms:

> int await( ) throws InterruptedException, BrokenBarrierException
>
> int await(long *wait*, TimeUnit *tu*)
>
>   throws InterruptedException, BrokenBarrierException, TimeoutException

The first form waits until the all threads have reached the barrier point. The second form waits only for the period of time specified by *wait*. The units represented by *wait* are specified by *tu*. It will throw a **TimeoutException** if the wait period expires. Both forms return a value that indicates the order in which the threads arrive at the barrier point. The first thread returns a value equal to the number of threads waited upon minus one. The last thread returns zero.

Here is an example that illustrates **CyclicBarrier**. It waits until a set of three threads has reached the barrier. When that occurs, the thread specified by **BarAction** executes.

```
// An example of CyclicBarrier.

import java.util.concurrent.*;

class BarDemo {
  public static void main(String[] args) {
    CyclicBarrier cb = new CyclicBarrier(3, new BarAction() );

    System.out.println("Starting");
```

Create a **CyclicBarrier** for 3 threads.

```
    new MyThread(cb, "A");
    new MyThread(cb, "B");
    new MyThread(cb, "C");


  }
}

// A thread of execution that uses a CyclicBarrier.

class MyThread implements Runnable {
  CyclicBarrier cbar;
  String name;

  MyThread(CyclicBarrier c, String n) {
    cbar = c;
    name = n;
    new Thread(this).start();
  }

  public void run() {

    System.out.println(name);

    try {
      cbar.await();  ◄──────────────────────  Wait for all threads to call await( ).
    } catch (BrokenBarrierException exc) {
      System.out.println(exc);
    } catch (InterruptedException exc) {
      System.out.println(exc);
    }
  }
}

// An object of this class is called when the
// CyclicBarrier ends.
class BarAction implements Runnable {
  public void run() {
    System.out.println("Barrier Reached!");
  }
}
```

The output is shown here. (The precise order in which the threads execute may vary.)

```
Starting
A
B
C
Barrier Reached!
```

A **CyclicBarrier** can be reused because it will release waiting threads each time the specified number of threads calls **await( )**. For example, if you change **main( )** in the preceding program so that it looks like this:

```
public static void main(String[] args) {
CyclicBarrier cb = new CyclicBarrier(3, new BarAction() );

  System.out.println("Starting");

  new MyThread(cb, "A");
  new MyThread(cb, "B");
  new MyThread(cb, "C");
  new MyThread(cb, "X");
  new MyThread(cb, "Y");
  new MyThread(cb, "Z");


}
```

the following output will be produced. (The precise order in which the threads execute may vary.)

```
Starting
A
B
C
Barrier Reached!
X
Y
Z
Barrier Reached!
```

As the preceding example shows, the **CyclicBarrier** offers a streamlined solution to what would otherwise be a complicated problem.

Exchanger

Perhaps the most interesting of the synchronization classes is **Exchanger**. It is designed to simplify the exchange of data between two threads. The operation of an **Exchanger** is astoundingly simple: it simply waits until two separate threads call its **exchange( )** method. When that occurs, it exchanges the data supplied by the threads. This mechanism is both elegant and easy to use. Uses for **Exchanger** are easy to imagine. For example, one thread might prepare a buffer for receiving information over a network connection. Another thread might fill that buffer with the information from the connection. The two threads work together so that each time a new buffer is needed, an exchange is made.

Exchanger is a generic class that is declared as shown here:

    Exchanger<V>

Here, **V** specifies the type of the data being exchanged.

The only method defined by **Exchanger** is **exchange( )**, which has the two forms shown here:

> V exchange(V *exchgObj*) throws InterruptedException
>
> V exchange(V *exchgObj*, long *wait*, TimeUnit *tu*)
>> throws InterruptedException, TimeoutException

Here, *exchgObj* is a reference to the data to exchange. The data received from the other thread is returned. The second form of **exchange( )** allows a time-out period to be specified. The key point about **exchange( )** is that it won't succeed until it has been called on the same **Exchanger** object by two separate threads. Thus, **exchange( )** synchronizes the exchange of the data.

Here is an example that demonstrates **Exchanger**. It creates two threads that exchange strings with each other. One thread creates a reference to an empty string. The second thread creates an initialized string. These string references are then exchanged. The net result is that the first thread exchanges an empty string for a full one.

```
// An example of Exchanger.

import java.util.concurrent.Exchanger;

class ExgrDemo {
  public static void main(String[] args) {
    Exchanger<String> exgr = new Exchanger<String>();   ◄——————— Create an Exchanger for strings.

    new UseString(exgr);
    new MakeString(exgr);
  }
}

// A Thread that constructs an initialized string.
class MakeString implements Runnable {
  Exchanger<String> ex;
  String str;

  MakeString(Exchanger<String> c) {
    ex = c;
    str = new String();

    new Thread(this).start();
  }

  public void run() {
    char ch = 'A';

    for(int i = 0; i < 3; i++) {
```

```
      // Make a string.
      for(int j = 0; j < 5; j++)
        str += ch++;

      try {
        // Exchange an initialized string for an empty one.
        str = ex.exchange(str);                    Exchange an initialized
      } catch(InterruptedException exc) {           string for an empty string.
        System.out.println(exc);
      }
    }
  }
}


// A Thread that uses a string.
class UseString implements Runnable {
  Exchanger<String> ex;
  String str;
  UseString(Exchanger<String> c) {
    ex = c;
    new Thread(this).start();
  }

  public void run() {

    for(int i=0; i < 3; i++) {
      try {
        // Exchange an empty string for an initialized one.
        str = ex.exchange(new String());          Exchange an empty
        System.out.println("Got: " + str);         string for an initialized
      } catch(InterruptedException exc) {           string.
        System.out.println(exc);
      }
    }
  }
}
```

Here is the output produced by the program:

```
Got: ABCDE
Got: FGHIJ
Got: KLMNO
```

In the program, the **main( )** method creates an **Exchanger** for strings. This object
is then used to synchronize the exchange of strings between the **MakeString** and
UseString classes. The **MakeString** class initializes a string. **UseString** exchanges
an empty string for a full one. It then displays the contents of the newly constructed
string. The exchange of strings is synchronized by the **exchange( )** method, which is
called by both class's **run( )** method.

Progress Check

1. A **CyclicBarrier** is useful in a situation where _____.
2. An **Exchanger** provides an easy way to _____.

Phaser

JDK 7 adds a new synchronization class called **Phaser**. Its primary purpose is to enable the synchronization of threads that represent one or more phases of activity. For example, you might have a set of threads that implement three phases of an order-processing application. In the first phase, separate threads are used to validate customer information, check inventory, and confirm pricing. When that phase is complete, the second phase has two threads that compute shipping costs and all applicable tax. After that, a final phase confirms payment and determines estimated shipping time. In the past, to synchronize the multiple threads that comprise this scenario would require a bit of work on your part. With the inclusion of **Phaser**, the process is now much easier.

To begin, it helps to know that a **Phaser** works somewhat like a **CyclicBarrier**, described earlier, except that it supports multiple phases. As a result, **Phaser** lets you define a synchronization object that waits until a specific phase has completed. It then advances to the next phase, again waiting until that phase concludes. It is important to understand that **Phaser** can also be used to synchronize only a single phase. In this regard, it acts much like a **CyclicBarrier**. However, its primary use is to synchronize multiple phases.

Phaser defines four constructors. Here are the two used in this section:

Phaser( )

Phaser(int *numParties*)

The first creates a phaser that has a registration count of zero. The second sets the registration count to *numParties*. The term *party* refers to the objects that register with a phaser. Although often there is a one-to-one correspondence between the number of registrants and the number of threads being synchronized, this is not required. In both cases, the current phase is zero. That is, when a **Phaser** is created, it is initially at phase zero.

In general, here is how you use **Phaser**. First, create a new instance of **Phaser**. Next, register one or more parties with the phaser, either by calling **register( )** or by specifying the number of parties in the constructor. For each registered party, have the phaser wait until all registered parties complete a phase. A party signals this by

---

Answers:

1. You want every thread in a set of threads to reach a certain point before any of them continues beyond it.
2. Exchange data between two threads.

calling one of a variety of methods supplied by **Phaser**, such as **arrive( )** or **arrive-AndAwaitAdvance( )**. After all parties have arrived, the phase is complete, and the phaser can move on to the next phase (if there is one), or terminate. The following sections explain the process in detail.

To register parties after a **Phaser** has been constructed, call **register( )**. It is shown here:

    int register( )

It returns the phase number of the phase to which it is registered.

To signal that a party has completed a phase, you must call **arrive( )** or some variation of **arrive( )**. When the number of arrivals equals the number of registered parties, the phase is completed and the **Phaser** moves on the next phase (if there is one). The **arrive( )** method has this general form:

    int arrive( )

This method signals that a party (normally a thread of execution) has completed some task (or portion of a task). It returns the current phase number. If the phaser has been terminated, then it returns a negative value. The **arrive( )** method does not suspend execution of the calling thread. This means that it does not wait for the phase to be completed. This method should be called only by a registered party.

If you want to indicate the completion of a phase and then wait until all other registrants have also completed that phase, use **arriveAndAwaitAdvance( )**. It is shown here:

    int arriveAndAwaitAdvance( )

It waits until all parties have arrived. It returns the next phase number or a negative value if the phaser has been terminated. This method should be called only by a registered party.

A thread can arrive and then deregister itself by calling **arriveAndDeregister( )**. It is shown here:

    int arriveAndDeregister( )

It returns the current phase number or a negative value if the phaser has been terminated. It does not wait until the phase is complete. This method should be called only by a registered party.

To obtain the current phase number, call **getPhase( )**, which is shown here:

    final int getPhase( )

When a **Phaser** is created, the first phase will be 0, the second phase 1, the third phase 2, and so on. A negative value is returned if the invoking **Phaser** has been terminated. To determine if a **Phaser** is terminated, use the **isTerminated( )** method. It returns **true** if the phaser is terminated and **false** otherwise.

Here is an example that shows **Phaser** in action. It creates three threads, each of which has three phases. It uses a **Phaser** to synchronize each phase.

```
// An example of Phaser.

import java.util.concurrent.*;

class PhaserDemo {
  public static void main(String[] args) {
    Phaser phsr = new Phaser(1);          Create a Phaser with one initial
    int curPhase;                          party, which is for the main
                                           thread.
    System.out.println("Starting");

    new MyThread(phsr, "A");
    new MyThread(phsr, "B");
    new MyThread(phsr, "C");

    // Wait for all threads to complete phase one.
    curPhase = phsr.getPhase();
    phsr.arriveAndAwaitAdvance();
    System.out.println("Phase " + curPhase + " Complete");

    // Wait for all threads to complete phase two.
    curPhase =  phsr.getPhase();                       The main thread arrives
    phsr.arriveAndAwaitAdvance();                      and then waits until each
    System.out.println("Phase " + curPhase + " Complete");   phase completes.

    curPhase =  phsr.getPhase();
    phsr.arriveAndAwaitAdvance();
    System.out.println("Phase " + curPhase + " Complete");

    // Deregister the main thread.
    phsr.arriveAndDeregister();

    if(phsr.isTerminated())
       System.out.println("The Phaser is terminated");
  }
}

// A thread of execution that uses a Phaser.
class MyThread implements Runnable {
  Phaser phsr;
  String name;

  MyThread(Phaser p, String n) {
    phsr = p;
    name = n;
    phsr.register();                        Register this thread.
    new Thread(this).start();
  }

  public void run() {
```

```
        System.out.println("Thread " + name + " Beginning Phase One");
        phsr.arriveAndAwaitAdvance(); // Signal arrival.

        // Pause a bit to prevent jumbled output. This is for illustration
        // only. It is not required for the proper operation of the phaser.
        try {
            Thread.sleep(10);
        } catch(InterruptedException e) {
            System.out.println(e);
        }

        System.out.println("Thread " + name + " Beginning Phase Two");
        phsr.arriveAndAwaitAdvance(); // Signal arrival.

        // Pause a bit to prevent jumbled output. This is for illustration
        // only. It is not required for the proper operation of the phaser.
        try {
            Thread.sleep(10);
        } catch(InterruptedException e) {
            System.out.println(e);
        }

        System.out.println("Thread " + name + " Beginning Phase Three");
        phsr.arriveAndDeregister(); // Signal arrival and deregister.
    }
}
```

Arrive and then wait until all threads arrive.

Deregister when done.

The output is shown here:

```
Starting
Thread A Beginning Phase One
Thread C Beginning Phase One
Thread B Beginning Phase One
Phase 0 Complete
Thread B Beginning Phase Two
Thread C Beginning Phase Two
Thread A Beginning Phase Two
Phase 1 Complete
Thread C Beginning Phase Three
Thread B Beginning Phase Three
Thread A Beginning Phase Three
Phase 2 Complete
The Phaser is terminated
```

Let's look closely at the key sections of the program. First, in **main( )**, a **Phaser** called **phsr** is created with an initial party count of 1 (which corresponds to the main thread). Then three threads are started by creating three **MyThread** objects. Notice that **MyThread** is passed a reference to **phsr** (the phaser). The **MyThread** objects use this phaser to synchronize their activities. Next, **main( )** calls **get-Phase( )** to obtain the current phase number (which is initially zero) and then calls **arriveAndAwaitAdvance( )**. This causes **main( )** to suspend until phase zero has completed. This won't happen until all **MyThread**s also arrive. When this occurs, **main( )** will resume execution, at which point, it displays that phase zero has completed, and it moves on to phase two. This process repeats until all three phases have finished. Then, **main( )** calls **arriveAndDeregister( )**. At that point, all three **MyThread**s have also deregistered. Since this results in there being no registered parties when the phaser advances to the next phase, the phaser is terminated.

Now look at **MyThread**. First, notice that the constructor is passed a reference to the phaser that it will use and then registers the new thread as a party on that phaser. Thus, each new **MyThread** becomes a party registered with the passed-in phaser. Also notice that each thread has three phases. In this example, each phase consists of a placeholder that simply displays the name of the thread and what it is doing. Obviously, in real-world code, the thread would be performing more meaningful actions. Between the first two phases, the thread calls **arriveAndAwaitAdvance( )**. Thus, each thread waits until all threads have completed the phase (and the main thread is ready). After all threads have arrived (including the main thread), the phaser moves on to the next phase. After the third phase, each thread deregisters itself with a call to **arriveAndDeregister( )**. As the comments in **MyThread** explain, the calls to **sleep( )** are used for the purposes of illustration to ensure that the output is not jumbled because of the multithreading. They are not needed to make the phaser work properly. If you remove them, the output may look a bit jumbled, but the phases will still be synchronized correctly.

One other point: Although the preceding example used three threads that were all of the same type, this is not a requirement. Each party that uses a phaser can be unique, with each performing some separate task.

It is possible to take control of precisely what happens when a phase advance occurs. To do this, you must override the **onAdvance( )** method. This method is called by the run time when a **Phaser** advances from one phase to the next. It is shown here:

> protected boolean onAdvance(int *phase*, int *numParties*)

Here, *phase* will contain the current phase number prior to being incremented, and *numParties* will contain the number of registered parties. To terminate the phaser, **onAdvance( )** must return **true**. To keep the phaser alive, **onAdvance( )** must return **false**. The default version of **onAdvance( )** returns **true** (thus terminating the phaser) when there are no registered parties. As a general rule, your override should also follow this practice. One reason to override **onAdvance( )** is to enable a phaser to execute a specific number of phases and then stop. You will see an example of this in Try This 27-1.

TRY THIS 27-1   DEMONSTRATE PHASER'S onAdvance( ) METHOD

`StarPhaserDemo.java`

This project demonstrates the use of the **onAdvance( )** method defined by **Phaser**. It develops a program that uses multiple threads and a **Phaser** to draw a 4-by-3 rectangle of stars (asterisks) on the console. To draw the rectangle, four threads are used, and their actions are coordinated by the phaser. In each phase, each thread will draw one star and then await the next phase. It uses **Phaser**'s **onAdvance( )** method to output a newline after each phase completes, and to terminate the phaser after the rectangle has been drawn. Thus, the phaser will be responsible for moving to the next line and then initiating the next phase.

STEP-BY-STEP

1. Create a new file called **StarPhaserDemo.java** and enter the following code:

```java
import java.util.concurrent.Phaser;

public class StarPhaserDemo {
  public static void main(String args[]) {
    Phaser phsr = new NewlinePhaser(4,3);

    new StarThread(phsr);
    new StarThread(phsr);
    new StarThread(phsr);
    new StarThread(phsr);
  }
}
```

Notice that all the **main( )** method needs to do is create the **NewlinePhaser** and the four threads. The threads will handle the drawing of the rectangle.

2. Now add the code for the **NewlinePhaser** class:

```java
class NewlinePhaser extends Phaser {
  int numPhases;

  public NewlinePhaser(int numParties, int phases) {
    super(numParties);
    numPhases = phases;
  }

  public boolean onAdvance(int phase, int numParties) {
    System.out.println(); // print a newline
    return phase == numPhases-1; // stop after numPhases
  }
}
```

As you can see, **NewlinePhaser** does two things. First, it keeps track of the number of phases it will allow to occur. Second, it overrides the **onAdvance( )** method. This override outputs a newline after each phase and stops the phaser after the given number of phases have occurred. (Recall that a **Phaser** terminates when **onAdvance( )** returns **true**.)

3. Finally, add the code for the **StarThread** class:

```java
class StarThread implements Runnable {
  Phaser phsr;

  StarThread(Phaser p) {
    phsr = p;
    new Thread(this).start();
  }

  public void run() {
    while (!phsr.isTerminated()) {
      System.out.print('*');
      phsr.arriveAndAwaitAdvance();
    }
  }
}
```

As you can see, the thread repeatedly displays one star and then awaits the end of that phase. It keeps performing this activity until the phaser has terminated.

4. Here is the entire program:

```java
import java.util.concurrent.Phaser;

public class StarPhaserDemo {
  public static void main(String args[]) {
    Phaser phsr = new NewlinePhaser(4,3);

    new StarThread(phsr);
    new StarThread(phsr);
    new StarThread(phsr);
    new StarThread(phsr);
  }
}

class NewlinePhaser extends Phaser {
  int numPhases;

  public NewlinePhaser(int numParties, int phases) {
    super(numParties);
    numPhases = phases;
  }

  public boolean onAdvance(int phase, int numParties) {
    System.out.println(); // print a newline
    return phase == numPhases-1; // stop after numPhases
  }
}
```

```
class StarThread implements Runnable {
  Phaser phsr;

  StarThread(Phaser p) {
    phsr = p;
    new Thread(this).start();
  }

  public void run() {
    while (!phsr.isTerminated()) {
      System.out.print('*');
      phsr.arriveAndAwaitAdvance();
    }
  }
}
```

5. When you run the program, you will see the following output.

```
****
****
****
```

As the output confirms, three lines of four stars have been drawn, with each star in a row displayed by a separate thread. The actions of the threads have been coordinated by the phaser.

Progress Check

1. A **Phaser** that is used to synchronize only one phase is very much like a _____.

2. To signal a **Phaser** that a thread has completed a phase and needs to wait until the other threads complete the phase, the thread should call the **Phaser**'s _____ method.

3. If you want a **Phaser** to execute some code at the completion of a phase before the next phase begins, you should _____.

USING AN EXECUTOR

The concurrent API supplies a feature called an *executor* that initiates and controls the execution of threads. As such, an executor offers an alternative to managing threads through the **Thread** class.

Answers:

1. **CyclicBarrier**
2. **arriveAndAwaitAdvance( )**
3. subclass **Phaser** and override the **onAdvance( )** method inherited by your subclass so that it contains the code you want to be executed

At the core of an executor is the **Executor** interface. It defines the following method:

> void execute(Runnable *task*)

The code specified by *task* is executed.

The **ExecutorService** interface extends **Executor** by adding methods that help manage and control the execution of threads. For example, **ExecutorService** defines **shutdown( )**, shown here, which stops the invoking **ExecutorService**.

> void shutdown( )

ExecutorService also defines methods that execute threads that return results, that execute a set of threads, and that determine the shutdown status.

Also defined is the interface **ScheduledExecutorService**, which extends **ExecutorService** to support the scheduling of threads.

The concurrent API defines three predefined executor classes: **ThreadPoolExecutor**, **ScheduledThreadPoolExecutor**, and **ForkJoinPool**. **ThreadPoolExecutor** implements the **Executor** and **ExecutorService** interfaces and provides support for a managed pool of threads. **ScheduledThreadPoolExecutor** also implements the **ScheduledExecutorService** interface to allow a pool of threads to be scheduled. **ForkJoinPool** implements the **Executor** and **ExecutorService** interfaces and is used by the Fork/Join Framework. It is described later in this chapter.

A thread pool provides a set of threads that is used to execute various tasks. Instead of each task using its own thread, the threads in the pool are used. This reduces the overhead associated with creating many separate threads. Although you can use **ThreadPoolExecutor** and **ScheduledThreadPoolExecutor** directly, most often you probably will want to obtain an executor by calling one of the following **static** factory methods defined by the **Executors** utility class. Here are some examples:

> static ExecutorService newCachedThreadPool( )
>
> static ExecutorService newFixedThreadPool(int *numThreads*)
>
> static ScheduledExecutorService newScheduledThreadPool(int *numThreads*)

newCachedThreadPool( ) creates a thread pool that adds threads as needed but reuses threads if possible. **newFixedThreadPool( )** creates a thread pool that consists of a specified number of threads. **newScheduledThreadPool( )** creates a thread pool that supports thread scheduling. Each returns a reference to an **ExecutorService** that can be used to manage the pool.

A Simple Executor Example

Before going any further, a simple example that uses an executor will be of value. The following program creates a fixed thread pool that contains two threads. It then uses that pool to execute four tasks. Thus, four tasks share the two threads that are in the pool. After the tasks are completed, the pool is shut down and the program ends.

```
// A simple example that uses an Executor.

import java.util.concurrent.*;

class SimpExec {
  public static void main(String[] args) {
    CountDownLatch cdl = new CountDownLatch(5);
    CountDownLatch cdl2 = new CountDownLatch(5);
    CountDownLatch cdl3 = new CountDownLatch(5);
    CountDownLatch cdl4 = new CountDownLatch(5);
    ExecutorService es = Executors.newFixedThreadPool(2);
```
← Create an executor that has two threads.
```

    System.out.println("Starting");

    // Start the threads.
    es.execute(new MyThread(cdl, "A"));
    es.execute(new MyThread(cdl2, "B"));
    es.execute(new MyThread(cdl3, "C"));
    es.execute(new MyThread(cdl4, "D"));
```
Execute four threads using the thread pool.
```

    try {
      cdl.await();
      cdl2.await();
      cdl3.await();
      cdl4.await();
    } catch (InterruptedException exc) {
      System.out.println(exc);
    }

    es.shutdown();
```
← Shut down the executor.
```
    System.out.println("Done");
  }
}

class MyThread implements Runnable {
  String name;
  CountDownLatch latch;

  MyThread(CountDownLatch c, String n) {
    latch = c;
    name = n;
  }

  public void run() {

    for(int i = 0; i < 5; i++) {
      System.out.println(name + ": " + i);
      latch.countDown();
    }
  }
}
```

The output from the program is shown here. (The precise order in which the threads execute may vary.)

```
Starting
B: 0
A: 0
B: 1
A: 1
A: 2
B: 2
B: 3
B: 4
A: 3
C: 0
C: 1
A: 4
C: 2
D: 0
D: 1
C: 3
D: 2
D: 3
C: 4
D: 4
Done
```

As the output shows, even though the thread pool contains only two threads, all four tasks are still executed. However, only two can run at the same time. The others must wait until one of the pooled threads is available for use.

The call to **shutdown( )** is important. If it were not present in the program, then the program would not terminate because the executor would remain active. To try this for yourself, simply comment out the call to **shutdown( )** and observe the result.

USING Callable AND Future

One quite interesting feature of the concurrent API is the **Callable** interface. This interface represents a thread that returns a value. An application can use **Callable** objects to compute results that are then returned to the invoking thread. This is a powerful mechanism because it facilitates the coding of many types of numerical computations in which partial results are computed simultaneously. It can also be used to run a thread that returns a status code that indicates the successful completion of the thread.

Callable is a generic interface that is defined like this:

    interface Callable<V>

Here, **V** indicates the type of data returned by the task. **Callable** defines only one method, **call( )**, which is shown here:

    V call( ) throws Exception

Inside **call( )**, you define the task that you want performed. After that task completes, you return the result. If the result cannot be computed, **call( )** must throw an exception.

A **Callable** task is executed by an **ExecutorService**, by calling its **submit( )** method. There are three forms of **submit( )**, but only one is used to execute a **Callable**. It is shown here:

$\qquad$ <T> Future<T> submit(Callable<T> *task*)

Here, *task* is the **Callable** object that will be executed. The result is returned through an object of type **Future**.

Future is a generic interface that represents the value that will be returned by a **Callable** object. Because this value is obtained at some future time, the name **Future** is appropriate. **Future** is defined like this:

$\qquad$ interface Future<V>

Here, **V** specifies the type of the result.

To obtain the returned value, you will call **Future**'s **get( )** method, which has these two forms:

$\qquad$ V get( )
$\qquad\qquad$ throws InterruptedException, ExecutionException
$\qquad$ V get(long *wait*, TimeUnit *tu*)
$\qquad\qquad$ throws InterruptedException, ExecutionException, TimeoutException

The first form waits for the result indefinitely. The second form allows you to specify a time-out period in *wait*. The units of *wait* are passed in *tu*, which is an object of the **TimeUnit** enumeration, described later in this chapter.

The following program illustrates **Callable** and **Future** by creating three tasks that perform three different computations. The first returns the summation of a value, the second computes the length of the hypotenuse of a right triangle given the length of its sides, and the third computes the factorial of a value. All three computations can occur simultaneously.

```java
// An example that uses a Callable.

import java.util.concurrent.*;

class CallableDemo {
  public static void main(String[] args) {
    ExecutorService es = Executors.newFixedThreadPool(3);
    Future<Integer> f;
    Future<Double> f2;
    Future<Integer> f3;

    System.out.println("Starting");

    f = es.submit(new Sum(10));
    f2 = es.submit(new Hypot(3, 4));
    f3 = es.submit(new Factorial(5));
```

Submit tasks for execution.

```
    try {
      System.out.println(f.get());
      System.out.println(f2.get());
      System.out.println(f3.get());
    } catch (InterruptedException exc) {
      System.out.println(exc);
    }
    catch (ExecutionException exc) {
      System.out.println(exc);
    }

    es.shutdown();
    System.out.println("Done");
  }
}

// Following are three computational threads.

class Sum implements Callable<Integer> {
  int stop;

  Sum(int v) { stop = v; }

  public Integer call() {
    int sum = 0;
    for(int i = 1; i <= stop; i++) {
      sum += i;
    }
    return sum;
  }
}

class Hypot implements Callable<Double> {
  double side1, side2;

  Hypot(double s1, double s2) {
    side1 = s1;
    side2 = s2;
  }

  public Double call() {
    return Math.sqrt((side1*side1) + (side2*side2));
  }
}

class Factorial implements Callable<Integer> {
  int stop;

  Factorial(int v) { stop = v; }
```

Obtain and display the results.

```
      public Integer call() {
        int fact = 1;
        for(int i = 2; i <= stop; i++) {
          fact *= i;
        }
        return fact;
      }
  }
}
```

The output is shown here:

```
Starting
55
5.0
120
Done
```

Progress Check

1. To create an **ExecutorService** that manages a thread pool of a fixed size, invoke the factory method _____.
2. If you create an **Executor** and then call its **execute( )** method four times in succession, each time passing in a different **Runnable**, then each **Runnable** will not execute until the preceding **Runnable** has completed. True or False?
3. To execute a **Callable** object, you invoke the _____ method of an **ExecutorService**.
4. Why is "Future" an appropriate name for the **Future** interface?

THE TimeUnit ENUMERATION

The concurrent API defines several methods that take an argument of type **TimeUnit**, which indicates a time-out period. **TimeUnit** is an enumeration that is used to specify the *granularity* (or resolution) of the timing. **TimeUnit** is defined within **java.util.concurrent**. It can be one of the following values:

> DAYS
> HOURS
> MINUTES
> SECONDS
> MILLISECONDS
> MICROSECONDS
> NANOSECONDS

Answers:

1. **Executors.newFixedThreadPool( )**
2. False, unless the **Executor** manages a fixed thread pool of size 1.
3. **submit( )**
4. Because it represents a value that will be available sometime in the future.

Although **TimeUnit** lets you specify any of these values in calls to methods that take a timing argument, there is no guarantee that the system is capable of the specified resolution.

Here is an example that uses **TimeUnit**. The **CallableDemo** class, shown in the previous section, is modified as shown next to use the second form of **get( )** that takes a **TimeUnit** argument.

```
try {
    System.out.println(f.get(10, TimeUnit.MILLISECONDS));
    System.out.println(f2.get(10, TimeUnit.MILLISECONDS));
    System.out.println(f3.get(10, TimeUnit.MILLISECONDS));
} catch (InterruptedException exc) {
    System.out.println(exc);
}
catch (ExecutionException exc) {
    System.out.println(exc);
} catch (TimeoutException exc) {
    System.out.println(exc);
}
```

In this version, no call to **get( )** will wait more than 10 milliseconds.

The **TimeUnit** enumeration defines various methods that convert between units. These are shown here:

long convert(long *tval*, TimeUnit *tu*)

long toMicros(long *tval*)

long toMillis(long *tval*)

long toNanos(long *tval*)

long toSeconds(long *tval*)

long toDays(long *tval*)

long toHours(long *tval*)

long toMinutes(long *tval*)

The **convert( )** method converts *tval* into the specified unit and returns the result. The **to** methods perform the indicated conversion and return the result.

Three more methods defined by **TimeUnit** are shown here:

void sleep(long *delay*) throws InterruptedExecution

void timedJoin(Thread *thrd*, long *delay*) throws InterruptedExecution

void timedWait(Object *obj*, long *delay*) throws InterruptedExecution

Here, **sleep( )** pauses execution for the specified delay period, which is specified in terms of the invoking enumeration constant. It translates into a call to **Thread.sleep( )**. The **timedJoin( )** method is a specialized version of **Thread.join( )** in which *thrd* pauses for the time period specified by *delay*, which is described in terms of the invoking time unit. The **timedWait( )** method is a specialized version of **Object.wait( )** in which *obj* is waited on for the period of time specified by *delay*, which is described in terms of the invoking time unit.

THE CONCURRENT COLLECTIONS

As explained, the concurrent API defines several collection classes that have been engineered for concurrent operation. They include:

ArrayBlockingQueue	ConcurrentHashMap	ConcurrentLinkedDeque
ConcurrentLinkedQueue	ConcurrentSkipListMap	ConcurrentSkipListSet
CopyOnWriteArraylist	CopyOnWriteArraySet	DelayQueue
LinkedBlockingDeque	LinkedBlockingQueue	LinkedTransferQueue
PriorityBlockingQueue	SynchronousQueue	

These offer concurrent alternatives to their related classes defined by the Collections Framework. These collections work much like the other collections except that they provide concurrency support.

LOCKS

The **java.util.concurrent.locks** package provides support for *locks*, which are objects that offer an alternative to using **synchronized** to control access to a shared resource. In general, here is how a lock works. Before accessing a shared resource, the lock that protects that resource is acquired. When access to the resource is complete, the lock is released. If a second thread attempts to acquire the lock when it is in use by another thread, the second thread will suspend until the lock is released. In this way, conflicting access to a shared resource is prevented.

Locks are particularly useful when multiple threads need to access the value of shared data. For example, an inventory application might have a thread that first confirms that an item is in stock and then decreases the number of items on hand as each sale occurs. If two or more of these threads are running, then without some form of synchronization, it would be possible for one thread to be in the middle of a transaction when the second thread begins its transaction. The result could be that both threads would assume that adequate inventory exists, even if there is only sufficient inventory on hand to satisfy one sale. In this type of situation, a lock offers a convenient means of handling the needed synchronization.

All locks implement the **Lock** interface. The methods defined by **Lock** are shown in Table 27-1. In general, to acquire a lock, call **lock( )**. If the lock is unavailable, **lock( )** will wait. To free a lock, call **unlock( )**. To see if a lock is available, and to acquire it if it is, call **tryLock( )**. This method will not wait for the lock if it is unavailable. Instead, it returns **true** if the lock is acquired and **false** otherwise. The **newCondition( )** method returns a **Condition** object associated with the lock. Using a **Condition**, you gain detailed control of the lock through methods such as **await( )** and **signal( )**, which provide functionality similar to **Object.wait( )** and **Object.notify( )**.

java.util.concurrent.locks supplies an implementation of **Lock** called **ReentrantLock**. **ReentrantLock** implements a *reentrant lock*, which is a lock that can be repeatedly entered by the thread that currently holds the lock. In the case of a

TABLE 27-1: The Lock Methods

Method	Description
void lock( )	Waits until the invoking lock can be acquired.
void lockInterruptibly( ) throws InterruptedException	Waits until the invoking lock can be acquired, unless interrupted.
Condition newCondition( )	Returns a **Condition** object that is associated with the invoking lock.
boolean tryLock( )	Attempts to acquire the lock. This method will not wait if the lock is unavailable. Instead, it returns **true** if the lock has been acquired and **false** if the lock is currently in use by another thread.
boolean tryLock(long *wait*, TimeUnit *tu*) throws InterruptedException	Attempts to acquire the lock. If the lock is unavailable, this method will wait no longer than the period specified by *wait*, which is in *tu* units. It returns **true** if the lock has been acquired and **false** if the lock cannot be acquired within the specified period.
void unlock( )	Frees the lock, allowing it to be used by another thread.

thread reentering a lock, all calls to **lock( )** must be offset by an equal number of calls to **unlock( )**. Otherwise, the lock will not be released.

The following program demonstrates the use of a lock. It creates two threads that access a shared resource called **Shared.count**. Before a thread can access **Shared.count**, it must obtain a lock. After obtaining the lock, **Shared.count** is incremented, and then, before releasing the lock, the thread sleeps. This causes the second thread to attempt to obtain the lock. However, because the lock is still held by the first thread, the second thread must wait until the first thread stops sleeping and releases the lock. The output shows that access to **Shared.count** is, indeed, synchronized by the lock.

```java
// A simple lock example.

import java.util.concurrent.locks.*;

class LockDemo {

  public static void main(String[] args) {
    ReentrantLock lock = new ReentrantLock();  // Create a reentrant lock.

    new LockThread(lock, "A");
    new LockThread(lock, "B");
  }
}

// A shared resource.
class Shared {
  static int count = 0;
}
```

```
// A thread of execution that increments count.
class LockThread implements Runnable {
  String name;
  ReentrantLock lock;

  LockThread(ReentrantLock lk, String n) {
    lock = lk;
    name = n;
    new Thread(this).start();
  }

  public void run() {

    System.out.println("Starting " + name);

    try {
      // First, lock count.
      System.out.println(name + " is waiting to lock count.");
      lock.lock();                                                  ←———————— Acquire the lock.
      System.out.println(name + " is locking count.");

      Shared.count++;                                              ←———————— Access the resource.
      System.out.println(name + ": " + Shared.count);

      // Now, allow a context switch -- if possible.
      System.out.println(name + " is sleeping.");
      Thread.sleep(1000);
    } catch (InterruptedException exc) {
      System.out.println(exc);
    } finally {
      // Unlock
      System.out.println(name + " is unlocking count.");
      lock.unlock();                                               ←———————— Release the lock.
    }
  }
}
```

The output is shown here. (The precise order in which the threads execute may vary.)

```
Starting A
A is waiting to lock count.
A is locking count.
A: 1
A is sleeping.
Starting B
B is waiting to lock count.
A is unlocking count.
B is locking count.
B: 2
B is sleeping.
B is unlocking count.
```

java.util.concurrent.locks also defines the **ReadWriteLock** interface. This interface specifies a lock that maintains separate locks for read and write access. This enables multiple locks to be granted for reading a resource as long as the resource is not being written. **ReentrantReadWriteLock** provides an implementation of **ReadWriteLock**.

Ask the Expert

Q What are the main differences between a **Semaphore**, a **Lock**, and the implicit monitor lock used in **synchronized** blocks as discussed in Chapter 12?

A All three objects provide a way of limiting the number of threads that can access a shared resource at a given time, but they have different properties. Monitor locks are acquired and released implicitly at the beginning and end of a **synchronized** block. **Lock**s have more flexibility. For example, in addition to the **lock( )** method, **Lock**s have a nonblocking version called **tryLock( )** and a temporarily blocking version **tryLock(*wait, tu*)**. A **ReentrantLock** (a class implementing the **Lock** interface) is a lock that becomes "owned" by a thread when the thread calls **lock( )** and must be released by the same thread by calling **unlock( )**. For that reason, it is recommended that the call to **unlock( )** be in a **finally** block to ensure that the lock is released even in the case when an exception is thrown. A second call to **lock( )** by the same thread that owns the lock does not block, but there eventually needs to be a corresponding call to **unlock( )** for every call to **lock( )**. A **RentrantLock** can also be queried concerning its current owner and the queue of threads waiting to acquire the lock.

A **Semaphore** manages a set of "permits" that it issues to requesting threads. If there is more than one permit, then multiple threads can receive permits at the same time and can access the shared resource at the same time. This behavior is useful, for example, when the shared resource is a pool of objects that two or more threads want to use. If the pool has N objects, then a semaphore with N permits is one way to manage access to the pool. A semaphore essentially keeps track only of how many permits are still available, not who received a permit. Thus, it is possible for one thread to acquire a permit, which decreases the number still available, and a second thread to release a permit, which increases the number of available permits, even if it didn't first acquire a permit. If a thread has acquired a permit and then tries to acquire another, it will block if there are no more permits available (this behavior is different from the behavior of a reentrant lock, as mentioned above, in that the thread owning the lock can call **lock( )** as often as it wants without blocking). A semaphore that manages only one permit is called a *binary* semaphore and is most similar to a lock.

ATOMIC OPERATIONS

java.util.concurrent.atomic offers an alternative to the other synchronization features when reading or writing the value of some types of variables. This package offers methods that get, set, or compare the value of a variable in one uninterruptible (that is, atomic) operation. This means that no lock or other synchronization mechanism is required. Atomic operations are accomplished through the use of classes, such as **AtomicInteger** and **AtomicLong**, and methods such as **get( )**, **set( )**, **compareAndSet( )**, **decrementAndGet( )**, and **getAndSet( )**, which perform the action indicated by their names. In general, the atomic operations offer a convenient (and possibly more efficient) alternative to the other synchronization mechanisms when only a single variable is involved.

Progress Check

1. What are the seven values in the **TimeUnit** enumeration?
2. How do **AtomicInteger**s differ from **Integer**s?
3. To get access to a shared resource that is protected by a **Lock**, a thread should call the **Lock**'s _____ method and when it is finished with the resource it should call the **Lock**'s _____ method.

PARALLEL PROGRAMMING VIA THE FORK/JOIN FRAMEWORK

Parallel programming is the name commonly given to the techniques that take advantage of computers that contain two or more processors (or cores). In recent years, multicore computers have become commonplace. The advantage that multiprocessor environments offer is the ability to significantly increase program performance. As a result, there has been a growing need for a mechanism that gives Java programmers a simple, yet effective, way to make use of multiple processors in a clean, scalable manner. To answer this need, JDK 7 added several new classes and interfaces that support parallel programming. They are commonly referred to as the *Fork/Join Framework*. The Fork/Join Framework is defined in the **java.util.concurrent** package.

The Fork/Join Framework enhances multithreaded programming in two important ways. First, it simplifies the creation and use of multiple threads. Second, it automatically makes use of multiple processors. In other words, by using the Fork/Join Framework, you enable your applications to automatically scale to make use of the number of available processors. These two features make the Fork/Join Framework the recommended approach to multithreading when certain types of parallel processing is desired.

Before continuing, it is important to point out the distinction between traditional multithreading and parallel programming. In the past, most computers had a single

---

Answers:

1. DAY, HOUR, MINUTE, SECOND, MILLISECOND, MICROSECOND, NANOSECOND
2. An **AtomicInteger** is a mutable object that stores an integer value and that has several uninterruptible operations, which allow you to read, compare, and modify the value without having to worry about synchronization.
3. **lock( )** and **unlock( )**

CPU, and multithreading was primarily used to take advantage of idle time, such as when a program is waiting for user input. Using this approach, one thread can execute while another is waiting. In other words, on a single-CPU system, multithreading is used to allow two or more tasks to share the CPU. This type of multithreading is typically supported by an object of type **Thread** (as described in Chapter 12). Although this type of multithreading will always remain quite useful, it was not optimized for situations in which two or more CPUs are available (as in multicore computers).

When multiple CPUs are present, a second type of multithreading capability that supports true parallel execution is required. With two or more CPUs, it is possible to execute portions of a program simultaneously, with each part executing on its own CPU. This can be used to significantly speed up the execution of some types of operations, such as sorting, transforming, or searching a large array. In many cases, these types of operations can be broken down into smaller pieces (each acting on a portion of the array), and each piece can be run on its own CPU. As you can imagine, the gain in efficiency can be quite significant. Simply put: Parallel programming offers a way to dramatically improve program performance.

THE MAIN FORK/JOIN CLASSES

The Fork/Join Framework is packaged in **java.util.concurrent**. At the core of the Fork/Join Framework are the following four classes:

ForkJoinTask<V>	An abstract class that defines a task
ForkJoinPool	Manages the execution of **ForkJoinTasks**
RecursiveAction	A subclass of **ForkJoinTask<V>** for tasks that do not return values
RecursiveTask<V>	A subclass of **ForkJoinTask<V>** for tasks that return values

Here is how they relate. A **ForkJoinPool** manages the execution of **ForkJoinTasks**. **ForkJoinTask** is an abstract class that is extended by two other abstract classes: **RecursiveAction** and **RecursiveTask**. Typically, your code will extend these classes to create a task. Before looking at the process in detail, an overview of the key aspects of each class will be helpful.

ForkJoinTask<V>

ForkJoinTask<V> is an abstract class that defines a task that can be managed by a **ForkJoinPool**. The type parameter **V** specifies the result type of the task. **ForkJoinTask** differs from **Thread** in that **ForkJoinTask** represents a lightweight abstraction of a task, rather than a thread of execution. **ForkJoinTasks** are executed by threads managed by a thread pool of type **ForkJoinPool**. This mechanism allows a large number of tasks to be managed by a small number of actual threads. Thus, **ForkJoinTasks** are very efficient when compared to threads.

ForkJoinTask defines many methods. At the core are **fork( )** and **join( )**, shown here:

```
final ForkJoinTask<V> fork( )
final V join( )
```

The **fork( )** method submits the invoking task for asynchronous execution. This means that the thread that calls **fork( )** continues to run. The **fork( )** method returns **this** after the task is scheduled for execution. It can be executed only from within the computational portion of another **ForkJoinTask**, which is running within a **ForkJoinPool**. (You will see how to do this, shortly.) The **join( )** method waits until the task on which it is called terminates. The result of the task is returned. Thus, through the use of **fork( )** and **join( )**, you can start one or more new tasks and then wait for them to finish.

Another important **ForkJoinTask** method is **invoke( )**. It combines the fork and join operations into a single call because it begins a task and then waits for it to end. It is shown here:

    final V invoke( )

The result of the invoking task is returned.

You can invoke more than one task at a time by using **invokeAll( )**. Two of its forms are shown here:

    static void invokeAll(ForkJoinTask<?> *taskA*, ForkJoinTask<?> *taskB*)

    static void invokeAll(ForkJoinTask<?> ... *taskList*)

In the first case, *taskA* and *taskB* are executed. In the second case, all specified tasks are executed. In both cases, the calling thread waits until all of the specified tasks have terminated. The **invokeAll( )** method can be executed only from within the computational portion of another **ForkJoinTask**, which is running within a **ForkJoinPool**.

RecursiveAction

A subclass of **ForkJoinTask** is **RecursiveAction**. This class encapsulates a task that does not return a result. Typically, your code will extend **RecursiveAction** to create a task that has a **void** return type. **RecursiveAction** specifies four methods, but only one is of interest here: the abstract method called **compute( )**. When you extend **RecursiveAction** to create a concrete class, you will put the code that defines the task inside **compute( )**. The **compute( )** method represents the *computational* portion of the task.

The **compute( )** method is defined by **RecursiveAction** like this:

    protected abstract void compute( )

Notice that **compute( )** is abstract. This means that it must be implemented by a subclass (unless that subclass is also abstract). There is no default implementation.

In general, **RecursiveAction** is used to implement a recursive, divide-and-conquer strategy for tasks that don't return results. (See "The Divide-and-Conquer Strategy" later in this chapter.)

RecursiveTask<V>

Another subclass of **ForkJoinTask** is **RecursiveTask<V>**. This class encapsulates a task that returns a result. The result type is specified by **V**. Typically, your code will extend **RecursiveTask<V>** to create a task that returns a value. Like

RecursiveAction, it too specifies four methods, but we will use only the abstract **compute( )** method, which represents the computational portion of the task. When you extend **RecursiveTask<V>** to create a concrete class, put the code that represents the task inside **compute( )**. This code must also return the result of the task.

The **compute( )** method is defined by **RecursiveTask<V>** as follows:

protected abstract V compute( )

Notice that **compute( )** is also abstract, which means that it must be implemented by a subclass. When implemented, it must return the result of the task.

In general, **RecursiveTask** is used to implement a recursive, divide-and-conquer strategy for tasks that return results. (See "The Divide-and-Conquer Strategy" later in this chapter.)

ForkJoinPool

The execution of **ForkJoinTask**s takes place within a **ForkJoinPool**, which also manages the execution of the tasks. Therefore, in order to execute a **ForkJoinTask**, you must first have a **ForkJoinPool**.

ForkJoinPool defines several constructors. Here are two commonly used ones:

ForkJoinPool( )
ForkJoinPool(int *pLevel*)

The first creates a default pool that supports a level of parallelism equal to the number of processors available in the system. The second lets you specify the level of parallelism. Its value must be greater than zero and not more than the limits of the implementation. The level of parallelism determines the number of threads that can execute concurrently. As a result, the level of parallelism effectively determines the number of tasks that can be executed simultaneously. (Of course, the number of tasks that can execute simultaneously cannot exceed the number of processors.) It is important to understand that the level of parallelism *does not*, however, limit the number of tasks that can be managed by the pool. A **ForkJoinPool** can manage many more tasks than its level of parallelism. Also, the level of parallelism is only a target. It is not a guarantee.

After you have created an instance of **ForkJoinPool**, you can start a task in a number of different ways. The first task started is often thought of as the main task. Frequently, the main task begins subtasks that are also managed by the pool. One common way to begin a main task is to call **invoke( )** on the **ForkJoinPool**. It is shown here:

<T> T invoke(ForkJoinTask<T> *task*)

This method begins the task specified by *task*, and it returns the result of the task. This means that the calling code waits until **invoke( )** returns.

To start a task without waiting for its completion, you can use **execute( )**. Here is one of its forms:

void execute(ForkJoinTask<?> *task*)

In this case, *task* is started, but the calling code does not wait for its completion. Rather, the calling code continues execution asynchronously.

ForkJoinPool manages the execution of its threads using an approach called *work-stealing*. Each worker thread maintains a queue of tasks. If one worker thread's queue is empty, it will take a task from another worker thread. This adds to overall efficiency and helps maintain a balanced load.

One other point: **ForkJoinPool** uses daemon threads. As explained in Chapter 12, a daemon thread is automatically terminated when all user threads have terminated. Thus, there is no need to explicitly shut down a **ForkJoinPool**. However, it is possible to do so by calling **shutdown( )**.

THE DIVIDE-AND-CONQUER STRATEGY

Many uses of the Fork/Join Framework will employ a *divide-and-conquer* strategy that is based on recursion. This is why the two subclasses of **ForkJoinTask** are called **RecursiveAction** and **RecursiveTask**. It is anticipated that you will extend one of these classes when creating your own fork/join task.

The divide-and-conquer strategy is based on recursively dividing a task into smaller subtasks until the subtask is small enough to be handled sequentially. For example, a task that applies a transform to each element in an array of N integers can be broken down into two subtasks in which each transforms half the elements in the array. That is, one subtask transforms the elements 0 to $N/2$, and the other transforms the elements $N/2+1$ to $N-1$. In turn, each subtask can be reduced to another set of subtasks, each transforming half of the remaining elements. This process of dividing the array will continue until a threshold is reached in which a sequential solution is faster than creating another division.

The advantage of the divide-and-conquer strategy is that the processing can occur in parallel. Therefore, instead of cycling through an entire array using a single thread, pieces of the array can be processed simultaneously. Of course, the divide-and-conquer approach works in many cases in which an array (or collection) is not present, but many uses will involve some type of array, collection, or grouping of data.

One of the keys to best employing the divide-and-conquer strategy is correctly selecting the threshold at which sequential processing (rather than further division) is used. Typically, an optimal threshold is obtained through profiling the execution characteristics. However, very significant speed-ups will still occur even when a less than optimal threshold is used. It is, however, best to avoid overly large or overly small thresholds. At the time of this writing, the Java API documentation for **ForkJoinTask<T>** states that, as a rule of thumb, a sequential task should perform somewhere between 100 and 10,000 computational steps.

For applications that are to be run on a known system, with a known number of processors, you can use the number of processors to make informed decisions about the threshold value. However, for applications that will be running on a variety of systems, the capabilities of which are not known in advance, you can make no assumptions about the execution environment.

One other point: Although multiple processors may be available on a system, other processes (and the operating system, itself) will be competing with your application for

CPU time. Thus, it is important not to assume that your program will have unrestricted access to all CPUs. Furthermore, different runs of the same program may display different run-time characteristics because of varying task loads.

A Simple First Fork/Join Example

At this point, a simple example that demonstrates the Fork/Join Framework and the divide-and-conquer strategy will be helpful. Following is a program that transforms the elements in an array of **double** into their square roots. It does so via a subclass of **RecursiveAction**.

```java
// A simple example of the basic divide-and-conquer strategy.
// In this case, RecursiveAction is used.
import java.util.concurrent.*;
import java.util.*;

// A ForkJoinTask (via RecursiveAction) that transforms
// the elements in an array of doubles into their square roots.
class SqrtTransform extends RecursiveAction {                          A task based on
                                                                      RecursiveAction.
  // The threshold value is arbitrarily set at 1,000 in this example.
  // In real-world code, its optimal value can be determined by
  // profiling and experimentation.
  final int seqThreshold = 1000;

  // Array to be accessed.
  double[] data;

  // Determines what part of data to process.
  int start, end;

  SqrtTransform(double[] vals, int s, int e ) {
    data = vals;
    start = s;
    end = e;
  }

  // This is the method in which parallel computation will occur.
  protected void compute() {                               This is where computation occurs.

    // If number of elements is below the sequential threshold,
    // then process sequentially.
    if((end - start) < seqThreshold) {
      // Transform each element into its square root.
      for(int i = start; i < end; i++) {                   Process sequentially.
        data[i] = Math.sqrt(data[i]);
      }
    }
    else {
      // Otherwise, continue to break the data into smaller pieces.
```

```
        // Find the midpoint.
        int middle = (start + end) / 2;

        // Invoke new tasks, using the subdivided data.
        invokeAll(new SqrtTransform(data, start, middle),          Break the task in
                  new SqrtTransform(data, middle, end));           two.
      }
    }
  }

// Demonstrate parallel execution.
class ForkJoinDemo {
  public static void main(String[] args) {
    // Create a task pool.
    ForkJoinPool fjp = new ForkJoinPool();

    double[] nums = new double[100000];

    // Give nums some values.
    for(int i = 0; i < nums.length; i++)
      nums[i] = (double) i;

    System.out.println("A portion of the original sequence:");

    for(int i=0; i < 10; i++)
      System.out.print(nums[i] + " ");
    System.out.println("\n");
                                                                  Create a task.

    SqrtTransform task = new SqrtTransform(nums, 0, nums.length);

    // Start the main ForkJoinTask.
    fjp.invoke(task);                                             Run the task.

    System.out.println("A portion of the transformed sequence" +
                       " (to four decimal places):");
    for(int i=0; i < 10; i++)
      System.out.format("%.4f ", nums[i]);
    System.out.println();
  }
}
```

The output from the program is shown here:

```
A portion of the original sequence:
0.0 1.0 2.0 3.0 4.0 5.0 6.0 7.0 8.0 9.0

A portion of the transformed sequence (to four decimal places):
0.0000 1.0000 1.4142 1.7321 2.0000 2.2361 2.4495 2.6458 2.8284 3.0000
```

As you can see, the values of the array elements have been transformed into their square roots.

Let's look closely at how this program works. First, notice that **SqrtTransform** is a class that extends **RecursiveAction**. As explained, **RecursiveAction** extends **ForkJoinTask** for tasks that do not return results. Next, notice the **final** variable **seqThreshold**. This is the value that determines when sequential processing will take place. This value is set (somewhat arbitrarily) to 1,000. Next, notice that a reference to the array to be processed is stored in **data** and that the fields **start** and **end** are used to indicate the boundaries of the elements to be accessed.

The main action of the program takes place in **compute( )**. It begins by checking if the number of elements to be processed is below the sequential processing threshold. If it is, then those elements are processed (by computing their square root in this example), and then returning. If the sequential processing threshold has not been reached, then two new tasks are started by calling **invokeAll( )**. In this case, each subtask processes half the elements. As explained earlier, **invokeAll( )** waits until both tasks return. After all of the recursive calls unwind, each element in the array will have been modified, with much of the action taking place in parallel (if multiple processors are available).

Understanding the Impact of the Level of Parallelism

Before moving on, it is important to understand the impact that the level of parallelism has on the performance of a fork/join task and how the parallelism and the threshold interact. The program shown in this section lets you experiment with different degrees of parallelism and threshold values. Assuming that you are using a multicore computer, then you can interactively observe the effect of these values.

In the preceding example, because the default **ForkJoinPool** constructor was used, the default level of parallelism was used, which is equal to the number of processors in the system. However, you can specify the level of parallelism that you want. One way shown earlier is to specify it when you create a **ForkJoinPool** using this constructor:

```
ForkJoinPool(int pLevel)
```

Here, *pLevel* specifies the level of parallelism, which must be greater than zero and less than the implementation-defined limit.

The following program creates a fork/join task that transforms an array of **double**s. The transformation is arbitrary, but it is designed to consume several CPU cycles. This was done to ensure that the effects of changing the threshold or the level of parallelism would be more clearly displayed. To use the program, specify the threshold value and the level of parallelism on the command line. The program then runs the tasks. It also displays the amount of time it takes the tasks to run. To do this, it uses **System.nanoTime( )**, which returns the value of the JVM's high-resolution timer.

```
// A simple program that lets you experiment with the effects of
// changing the threshold and parallelism of a ForkJoinTask.
import java.util.concurrent.*;

// A ForkJoinTask (via RecursiveAction) that performs a
// a transform on the elements of an array of doubles.
class Transform extends RecursiveAction {
```

```java
    // Sequential threshold, which is set by the constructor.
    int seqThreshold;

    // Array to be accessed.
    double[] data;

    // Determines what part of data to process.
    int start, end;

    Transform(double[] vals, int s, int e, int t ) {
      data = vals;
      start = s;
      end = e;
      seqThreshold = t;
    }

    // This is the method in which parallel computation will occur.
    protected void compute() {

      // If number of elements is below the sequential threshold,
      // then process sequentially.
      if((end - start) < seqThreshold) {
        // The following code assigns an element at an even index the
        // square root of its original value. An element at an odd
        // index is assigned its cube root. This code is designed
        // to simply consume CPU time so that the effects of concurrent
        // execution are more readily observable.
        for(int i = start; i < end; i++) {
          if((data[i] % 2) == 0)
            data[i] = Math.sqrt(data[i]);
          else
            data[i] = Math.cbrt(data[i]);
        }
      }
      else {
        // Otherwise, continue to break the data into smaller pieces.

        // Find the midpoint.
        int middle = (start + end) / 2;

        // Invoke new tasks, using the subdivided data.
        invokeAll(new Transform(data, start, middle, seqThreshold),
                  new Transform(data, middle, end, seqThreshold));
      }
    }
}

// Demonstrate parallel execution.
class FJExperiment {
```

```
public static void main(String[] args) {
    int pLevel;
    int threshold;

    if(args.length != 2) {
        System.out.println("Usage: FJExperiment parallelism threshold ");
        return;
    }

    pLevel = Integer.parseInt(args[0]);
    threshold = Integer.parseInt(args[1]);

    // These variables are used to time the task.
    long beginT, endT;

    // Create a task pool. Notice that the parallelism level is set.
    ForkJoinPool fjp = new ForkJoinPool(pLevel);

    double[] nums = new double[1000000];

    for(int i = 0; i < nums.length; i++)
        nums[i] = (double) i;

    Transform task = new Transform(nums, 0, nums.length, threshold);

    // Starting timing.
    beginT = System.nanoTime();

    // Start the main ForkJoinTask.
    fjp.invoke(task);

    // End timing.
    endT = System.nanoTime();

    System.out.println("Level of parallelism: " + pLevel);
    System.out.println("Sequential threshold: " + threshold);
    System.out.println("Elapsed time: " + (endT - beginT) + " ns");
    System.out.println();
    }
}
```

Set the level of parallelism and the sequential threshold limit as specified on the command line.

To use the program, specify the level of parallelism followed by the threshold limit. You should try experimenting with different values for each, observing the results. Remember, to be effective, you must run the code on a computer with at least two processors. Also, understand that two different runs may (almost certainly will) produce different results because of the effect of other processes in the system consuming CPU time.

To give you an idea of the difference that parallelism makes, try this experiment. First, execute the program like this:

```
java FJExperiment 1 1000
```

This requests one level of parallelism (essentially sequential execution) with a threshold of 1,000. Here is a sample run produced on a dual-core computer:

```
Level of parallelism: 1
Sequential threshold: 1000
Elapsed time: 259677487 ns
```

Now, specify two levels of parallelism like this:

```
java FJExperiment 2 1000
```

Here is sample output from this run produced by the same dual-core computer:

```
Level of parallelism: 2
Sequential threshold: 1000
Elapsed time: 169254472 ns
```

As is evident, adding parallelism substantially decreases execution time, thus increasing the speed of the program. You should experiment with varying the threshold and parallelism on your own computer. The results may surprise you.

You might find two other methods useful when experimenting with the execution characteristics of a fork/join program. First, you can obtain the level of parallelism by calling **getParallelism( )**, which is defined by **ForkJoinPool**. It is shown here:

    int getParallelism( )

It returns the parallelism level currently in effect. Recall that, by default, this will equal the number of available processors. Second, you can obtain the number of processors available for use by the JVM by calling **availableProcessors( )**, which is defined by the **Runtime** class. It is shown here:

    int availableProcessors( )

An Example That Uses RecursiveTask\<V>

The two preceding examples are based on **RecursiveAction**, which means that they concurrently execute tasks that do not return results. To create a task that returns a result, use **RecursiveTask**. In general, solutions are designed in the same manner as just shown. The key difference is that the **compute( )** method returns a result. Thus, you must aggregate the results, so that when the first invocation finishes, it returns the overall result. Another difference is that you will typically start a subtask by calling **fork( )** and **join( )** explicitly (rather than implicitly by calling **invokeAll( )**, for example).

The following program demonstrates **RecursiveTask**. It creates a task called **Sum** that returns the summation of the value in an array of **double**. In this example, the array consists of 5,000 elements, which contain the values 0 through 5,000. However, every other value is negative. Thus, the first values in the array are 0, –1, 2, –3, 4, and so on.

```
// A simple example that uses RecursiveTask<V>.
import java.util.concurrent.*;

// A RecursiveTask that computes the summation of an array of doubles.
class Sum extends RecursiveTask<Double> {
```
◄——————— A task based on **RecursiveTask**.

```java
    // The sequential threshold value.
    final int seqThresHold = 500;

    // Array to be accessed.
    double[] data;

    // Determines what part of data to process.
    int start, end;

    Sum(double[] vals, int s, int e ) {
      data = vals;
      start = s;
      end = e;
    }

    // Find the summation of an array of doubles.
    protected Double compute() {
      double sum = 0;

      // If number of elements is below the sequential threshold,
      // then process sequentially.
      if((end - start) < seqThresHold) {
        // Sum the elements.
        for(int i = start; i < end; i++) sum += data[i];
      }
      else {
        // Otherwise, continue to break the data into smaller pieces.

        // Find the midpoint.
        int middle = (start + end) / 2;

        // Invoke new tasks, using the subdivided data.
        Sum subTaskA = new Sum(data, start, middle);
        Sum subTaskB = new Sum(data, middle, end);

        // Start each subtask by forking.
        subTaskA.fork();                    ◄─────────────── Use fork( ) to start the tasks.
        subTaskB.fork();

        // Wait for the subtasks to return, and aggregate the results.
        sum = subTaskA.join() + subTaskB.join();  ◄──────── Aggregate the partial results.
      }
      // Return the final sum.
      return sum;
    }
  }
}

// Demonstrate parallel execution.
class RecurTaskDemo {
  public static void main(String[] args) {
    // Create a task pool.
    ForkJoinPool fjp = new ForkJoinPool();
```

```
      double[] nums = new double[5000];

      // Initialize nums with values that alternate between
      // positive and negative.
      for(int i=0; i < nums.length; i++)
        nums[i] = (double) (((i%2) == 0) ? i : -i) ;

      Sum task = new Sum(nums, 0, nums.length);

      // Start the ForkJoinTasks.  Notice that, in this case,
      // invoke() returns a result.
      double summation = fjp.invoke(task);

      System.out.println("Summation " + summation);
  }
}
```

Here's the output from the program:

```
Summation -2500.0
```

There are a couple of interesting items in this program. First, notice that the two subtasks are executed by calling **fork( )**, as shown here:

```
subTaskA.fork();
subTaskB.fork();
```

In this case, **fork( )** is used because it starts a task but does not wait for it to finish. (Thus, it asynchronously runs the task.) The result of each task is obtained by calling **join( )**, as shown here:

```
sum = subTaskA.join() + subTaskB.join();
```

This statement waits until each task ends. It then adds the results of each and assigns the total to **sum**. Thus, the summation of each subtask is added to the running total. Finally, **compute( )** ends by returning **sum**, which will be the final total when the first invocation returns.

There are other ways to approach the handling of the asynchronous execution of the subtasks. For example, the following sequence uses **fork( )** to start **subTaskA( )** and uses **invoke( )** to start and wait for **subTaskB( )**:

```
subTaskA.fork();
sum = subTaskB.invoke() + subTaskA.join();
```

Another alternative is to have **subTaskB( )** call **compute( )** directly, as shown here:

```
subTaskA.fork();
sum = subTaskB.compute() + subTaskA.join();
```

Executing a Task Asynchronously

The preceding programs have called **invoke( )** on a **ForkJoinPool** to initiate a task. This approach is commonly used when the calling thread must wait until the task has completed (which is often the case) because **invoke( )** does not return until the task has terminated. However, you can start a task asynchronously. In this approach, the calling thread continues to execute. Thus, both the calling thread and the task execute simultaneously. To start a task asynchronously, use **execute( )**, which is also defined by **ForkJoinPool**. It has the two forms shown here:

> void execute(ForkJoinTask<?> *task*)
>
> void execute(Runnable *task*)

In both forms, *task* specifies the task to run. Notice that the second form lets you specify a **Runnable** rather than a **ForkJoinTask** task. Thus, it forms a bridge between Java's traditional approach to multithreading and the new Fork/Join Framework. It is important to remember that the threads used by a **ForkJoinPool** are daemon. Thus, they will end when the main thread ends. As a result, you may need to keep the main thread alive until the tasks have finished.

THE CONCURRENCY UTILITIES VERSUS JAVA'S TRADITIONAL APPROACH

Given the power and flexibility found in the concurrency utilities, it is natural to ask the following question: Do they replace Java's traditional approach to multithreading and synchronization? The answer is no! The original support for multithreading and the built-in synchronization features are still the mechanism that should be employed for many Java programs. For example, **synchronized, wait( )**, and **notify( )** offer elegant solutions to a wide range of problems. However, when extra control is needed, the concurrency utilities are available to handle the chore. Furthermore, the Fork/Join Framework offers a powerful way to integrate parallel programming techniques into your more sophisticated applications.

Progress Check

1. How does a **RecursiveAction** differ from a **RecursiveTask**?
2. In a **ForkJoinTask**, the _____ method schedules the task for execution, and the _____ method waits until the task is completed and returns the result.
3. The _____ method in the **ForkJoinTask** class is a method that combines calls to **fork( )** and **join( )**.

Answers:

1. A **RecursiveTask** returns a result but a **RecursiveAction** does not.
2. **fork( )** and **join( )**
3. **invoke( )**

EXERCISES

1. How does a semaphore work?

2. In the **SemDemo** program in this chapter, what happens if you add a call to **sem.release( )** immediately before both of the calls to **sem.acquire( )**? Explain.

3. In the **SemDemo** program in this chapter, what happens if you replace each of the two calls to **sem.acquire( )** with **sem.acquire(2)**? Explain.

4. Consider a horse race where the horses and riders need to line up at the gate and wait there until all the horses and riders are ready before the gate opens and the horses can start racing. What Java synchronization tool does this situation remind you of?

5. Suppose you add the statement **System.out.println(name);** as the last statement of the **run( )** method of the **MyThread** class in the **BarDemo** program. In that case, "Barrier reached!" would be displayed before the names "A", "B", and "C" are displayed a second time. True or False? Explain.

6. Using an **Exchanger**, it is possible that a **String** can be exchanged for an **Integer**. True or False?

7. If a thread attempts to get the value of a **Future** object before its value has been computed, then an exception is thrown. True or False?

8. A **Callable** object is like a **Runnable** object except that it represents a thread that _____.

9. A **ForkJoinPool** uses an approach called "work-stealing" to execute waiting tasks. What does "work-stealing" mean?

10. A very appropriate strategy to use with the Fork/Join Framework is "divide and conquer." How does that strategy work?

11. In the **RecurTaskDemo** program, the **compute( )** method of the **Sum** class includes the following three lines:

```
subTaskA.fork();
subTaskB.fork();
sum = subTaskA.join() + subTaskB.join();
```

Since the **invoke( )** method is a combined fork and join, why not just call **invoke( )** for each subtask? That is, why not replace those three lines with the following line?

```
sum = subtaskA.invoke() + subtaskB.invoke();
```

12. Modify the **CDLDemo** program in this chapter so that it creates two **MyThread** objects instead of just one. Then run the program and explain the output you get.

13. Suppose you were to modify the **SemDemo** program in this chapter so that it creates two **Semaphore**s with permit counts of 1 and each of the two threads needs to acquire both semaphores before it can access the shared resource.

What can go wrong if the two threads try to acquire the two semaphores but in the opposite order?

14. Here is a simple program that creates and starts two threads of the same class. In the **run( )** method of the threads, there are two print statements, the first of which outputs "before" and the second outputs "after". There are two possible outputs: "before after before after" and "before before after after". Modify the program using a **CountDownLatch** to ensure that the first possible output, namely, "before after before after", never occurs.

```java
class Exercise {
  public static void main(String[] args) {
    new MyThread();
    new MyThread();
  }
}


class MyThread implements Runnable {
  MyThread() {
    new Thread(this).start();
  }
  public void run() {
    System.out.print("before ");
    System.out.print("after ");
  }
}
```

15. Redo the preceding exercise using a **CyclicBarrier** instead of a **CountDownLatch**.

16. In the **BarDemo** program in this chapter, what would happen if you replaced the value 3 with the value 4 as the first argument to the **CyclicBarrier** constructor? Explain.

17. In the **ExgrDemo** program, the **UseString** class's **run( )** method contains the line:

```java
str = ex.exchange(new String());
```

What would happen if you replaced that line with the line:

```java
str = ex.exchange(str);
```

that appears in the **run( )** method of the **MakeString** class? Explain.

18. An **Exchanger** is very useful if two threads need to exchange values, but what if three threads need to exchange values? More precisely, suppose you have three threads A, B, and C and you want to exchange values among them so that A's value is passed to B, B's value is passed to C, and C's value is passed to A. Explain how you could do it.

19. Suppose you have three threads A, B, and C with time-consuming jobs, such as downloading large files. Suppose you want to start the threads all at the same time, but you want them to do their jobs sequentially in the order A, B, C instead of concurrently. Tell how you can use a **Phaser** to accomplish your goal.

20. Modify the program in Try This 27-1 so that, instead of a rectangle, it displays a triangle of stars like this:

```
****
***
**
*
```

It should use four threads as before, each responsible for drawing at most one star per phase.

21. Modify the **SimpExec** program in this chapter so that **MyThread**'s **run( )** method sleeps for 10 milliseconds between each call to **countDown( )**. Then run the program four times, each time using a different value (1, 2, 3, or 4) as the argument to the **newFixedThreadPool( )** method. Explain the results you see.

22. In the **CallableDemo** program in this chapter, add a fourth **Callable** whose constructor takes an integer array as its parameter and whose **call( )** method returns the largest value in the array. It throws an **Exception** if the array is null or empty.

23. Look up the documentation for the **get( )** and **set( )** methods in the **AtomicInteger** class. Assume that **ai** is an **AtomicInteger**. Does the atomic nature of **ai**'s operations guarantee that, by executing **ai.set(ai.get( ) – ai.get( ))**, **ai** will have the value 0?

24. Modify the **RecurTaskDemo** program so that instead of finding and displaying the sum of the elements of an array of **double**s, it finds and displays the largest value in the array.

A P P E N D I X   A

Using Java's Documentation Comments

As explained in Part I, Java supports three types of comments. The first two are the // and the /* */. The third type is called a *documentation comment*. It begins with the character sequence /**. It ends with */. Documentation comments allow you to embed information about your program into the program itself. You can then use the **javadoc** utility program (supplied with the JDK) to extract the information and put it into an HTML file. Documentation comments make it convenient to document your programs. You have almost certainly seen documentation generated with **javadoc** because that is the way the Java API library was documented.

THE javadoc TAGS

The **javadoc** utility recognizes the following tags:

Tag	Meaning
@author	Identifies the author.
{@code}	Displays information as-is, without processing HTML styles, in code font.
@deprecated	Specifies that a program element is deprecated.
{@docRoot}	Specifies the path to the root directory of the current documentation.
@exception	Identifies an exception thrown by a method or constructor.
{@inheritDoc}	Inherits a comment from the immediate superclass.
{@link}	Inserts an in-line link to another topic.
{@linkplain}	Inserts an in-line link to another topic, but the link is displayed in a plain-text font.
{@literal}	Displays information as-is, without processing HTML styles.
@param	Documents a parameter.
@return	Documents a method's return value.

@see	Specifies a link to another topic.
@serial	Documents a default serializable field.
@serialData	Documents the data written by the **writeObject( )** or **writeExternal( )** methods.
@serialField	Documents an **ObjectStreamField** component.
@since	States the release when a specific change was introduced.
@throws	Same as **@exception**.
{@value}	Displays the value of a constant, which must be a **static** field.
@version	Specifies the version of a class.

Document tags that begin with an "at" sign (@) are called *stand-alone* tags, and they must be used on their own line. Tags that begin with a brace, such as **{@code}**, are called *in-line* tags, and they can be used within a larger description. You may also use other, standard HTML tags in a documentation comment. However, some tags, such as headings, should not be used because they disrupt the look of the HTML file produced by **javadoc**.

As it relates to documenting source code, you can use documentation comments to document classes, interfaces, fields, constructors, and methods. In all cases, the documentation comment must immediately precede the item being documented. Some tags, such as **@see**, **@since**, and **@deprecated**, can be used to document any element. Other tags apply only to the relevant elements. Each tag is examined next.

*Note: Documentation comments can also be used for documenting a package and preparing an overview, but the procedures differ from those used to document source code. See the JDK **javadoc** documentation for details on these uses. This appendix refers only to documentation comments in a Java program.*

@author

The **@author** tag documents the author of a class or interface. It has the following syntax:

> @author *description*

Here, *description* will usually be the name of the author. You will need to specify the **-author** option when executing **javadoc** in order for the **@author** field to be included in the HTML documentation.

{@code}

The **{@code}** tag enables you to embed text, such as a snippet of code, into a comment. That text is then displayed as-is in code font, without any further processing, such as HTML rendering. It has the following syntax:

> {@code *code-snippet*}

@deprecated

The **@deprecated** tag specifies that a program element is deprecated. It is recommended that you include **@see** or **{@link}** tags to inform the programmer about available alternatives. The syntax is the following:

@deprecated *description*

Here, *description* is the message that describes the deprecation. The **@deprecated** tag can be used in documentation for fields, methods, constructors, classes, and interfaces.

{@docRoot}

{@docRoot} specifies the path to the root directory of the current documentation.

@exception

The **@exception** tag describes an exception to a method. It has the following syntax:

@exception *exception-name explanation*

Here, the name of the exception is specified by *exception-name*, and *explanation* is a string that describes how the exception can occur. The **@exception** tag can be used only in documentation for a method or constructor.

{@inheritDoc}

This tag inherits a comment from the immediate superclass.

{@link}

The **{@link}** tag provides an in-line link to additional information. It has the following syntax:

{@link *pkg.class#member text*}

Here, *pkg.class#member* specifies the name of a class or method to which a link is added, and *text* is the string that is displayed.

{@linkplain}

Inserts an in-line link to another topic. The link is displayed in plain-text font. Otherwise, it is similar to **{@link}**.

{@literal}

The **{@literal}** tag enables you to embed text into a comment. That text is then displayed as-is, without any further processing, such as HTML rendering. It has the following syntax:

{@literal *description*}

Here, *description* is the text that is embedded.

@param

The **@param** tag documents a parameter. It has the following syntax:

@param *parameter-name explanation*

Here, *parameter-name* specifies the name of a parameter. The meaning of that parameter is described by *explanation*. The **@param** tag can be used only in documentation for a method or constructor, or a generic class or interface.

@return

The **@return** tag describes the return value of a method. It has the following syntax:

@return *explanation*

Here, *explanation* describes the type and meaning of the value returned by a method. The **@return** tag can be used only in documentation for a method.

@see

The **@see** tag provides a reference to additional information. Two commonly used forms are shown here:

@see *anchor*
@see *pkg.class#member text*

In the first form, *anchor* is a link to an absolute or relative URL. In the second form, *pkg.class#member* specifies the name of the item, and *text* is the text displayed for that item. The text parameter is optional, and if not used, then the item specified by *pkg.class#member* is displayed. The member name, too, is optional. Thus, you can specify a reference to a package, class, or interface in addition to a reference to a specific method or field. The name can be fully qualified or partially qualified. However, the dot that precedes the member name (if it exists) must be replaced by a hash character.

@serial

The **@serial** tag defines the comment for a default serializable field. It has the following syntax:

@serial *description*

Here, *description* is the comment for that field.

@serialData

The **@serialData** tag documents the data written by the **writeObject( )** and **writeExternal( )** methods. It has the following syntax:

@serialData *description*

Here, *description* is the comment for that data.

@serialField

For a class that implements **Serializable**, the **@serialField** tag provides comments for an **ObjectStreamField** component. It has the following syntax:

> @serialField *name type description*

Here, *name* is the name of the field, *type* is its type, and *description* is the comment for that field.

@since

The **@since** tag states that an element was introduced in a specific release. It has the following syntax:

> @since *release*

Here, *release* is a string that designates the release or version in which this feature became available.

@throws

The **@throws** tag has the same meaning as the **@exception** tag.

{@value}

{**@value**} has two forms. The first displays the value of the constant that it precedes, which must be a **static** field. It has this form:

> {@value}

The second form displays the value of a specified **static** field. It has this form:

> {@value *pkg.class#field*}

Here, *pkg.class#field* specifies the name of the **static** field.

@version

The **@version** tag specifies the version of a class or interface. It has the following syntax:

> @version *info*

Here, *info* is a string that contains version information, typically a version number, such as 2.2. You will need to specify the **-version** option when executing **javadoc** in order for the **@version** field to be included in the HTML documentation.

THE GENERAL FORM OF A DOCUMENTATION COMMENT

After the beginning /**, the first line or lines become the main description of your class, interface, field, constructor, or method. After that, you can include one or more of the various @ tags. Each @ tag must start at the beginning of a new line or follow one or more asterisks (*) that are at the start of a line. Multiple tags of the same type should be grouped together. For example, if you have three **@see** tags, put them one after the other. In-line tags (those that begin with a brace) can be used within any description.

Here is an example of a documentation comment for a class:

```
/**
 * This class draws a bar chart.
 * @author Herbert Schildt
 * @version 3.2
 */
```

WHAT javadoc OUTPUTS

The **javadoc** program takes as input your Java program's source file and outputs several HTML files that contain the program's documentation. Information about each class will be in its own HTML file. **javadoc** will also output an index and a hierarchy tree. Other HTML files can be generated.

AN EXAMPLE THAT USES DOCUMENTATION COMMENTS

Following is a sample program that uses documentation comments. Notice the way each comment immediately precedes the item that it describes. After being processed by **javadoc**, the documentation about the **SquareNum** class will be found in **SquareNum.html**.

```
import java.io.*;
/**
 * This class demonstrates documentation comments.
 * @author Herbert Schildt
 * @version 1.2
 */
public class SquareNum {
  /**
   * This method returns the square of num.
   * This is a multiline description. You can use
   * as many lines as you like.
   * @param num The value to be squared.
   * @return num squared as a double.
   */
  public double square(double num) {
    return num * num;
  }

  /**
   * This method inputs a number from the user.
   * @return The value input as a double.
   * @exception IOException On input error.
```

```
  * @see IOException
 */
public double getNumber() throws IOException {
    // create a BufferedReader using System.in
    InputStreamReader isr = new InputStreamReader(System.in);
    BufferedReader inData = new BufferedReader(isr);
    String str;

    str = inData.readLine();
    return (new Double(str)).doubleValue();
}

/**
  * This method demonstrates square().
  * @param args Unused.
  * @exception IOException On input error.
  * @see IOException
 */
public static void main(String[] args)
    throws IOException
{
    SquareNum ob = new SquareNum();
    double val;

    System.out.println("Enter value to be squared: ");
    val = ob.getNumber();
    val = ob.square(val);

    System.out.println("Squared value is " + val);
}
}
```

APPENDIX B

An Introduction to Regular Expressions

This appendix presents a brief introduction to what is both a powerful and sometimes complicated feature: the regular expression. As the term is used here, a *regular expression* is a string of characters that describes a general form, called a *pattern*. This pattern can then be used to find matches in other character sequences. Through the use of regular expressions you can perform sophisticated pattern matching operations. For example, regular expressions can specify a wildcard character, sets of characters, and various quantifiers. These and other elements let a regular expression match many different sequences with great flexibility.

Java provides extensive support for regular expressions in the **java.util.regex** package. It defines two classes that support regular expression processing: **Pattern** and **Matcher**. These classes work together. **Pattern** defines a regular expression. The pattern is matched against another sequence using **Matcher**.

THE Pattern CLASS

The **Pattern** class defines no constructors. Instead, a pattern is created by calling its **compile( )** method. One of its forms is shown here:

    static Pattern compile(String *pattern*)

Here, *pattern* is the regular expression that you want to use. The **compile( )** method transforms the string in *pattern* into a pattern that can be used for pattern matching by the **Matcher** class. It returns a **Pattern** object that contains the pattern. If *pattern* does not represent a legal expression, a **PatternSyntaxException** will be thrown.

Once you have created a **Pattern** object, you will use it to create a **Matcher**. This is done by calling the **matcher( )** method defined by **Pattern**. It is shown here:

    Matcher matcher(CharSequence *str*)

Here *str* is the character sequence that the pattern will be matched against. This is called the *input sequence*. As mentioned in Chapter 23, a **CharSequence** is an interface that defines a read-only set of characters. It is implemented by the **String** class, among others. Thus, you can pass a string to **matcher( )**.

THE Matcher CLASS

The **Matcher** class has no constructors. Instead, you create a **Matcher** by calling the **matcher( )** method defined by **Pattern**, as just explained. Once you have created a **Matcher**, you will use its methods to perform various pattern matching operations.

The simplest pattern matching method is **matches( )**, which simply determines whether the character sequence matches the pattern. It is shown here:

    boolean matches( )

It returns **true** if the sequence and the pattern match, and **false** otherwise. Understand that the entire sequence must match the pattern, not just a subsequence of it.

To determine if a subsequence of the input sequence matches the pattern, use **find( )**. One version is shown here:

    boolean find( )

It returns **true** if there is a matching subsequence and **false** otherwise. This method can be called repeatedly, allowing it to find all matching subsequences. Each call to **find( )** begins where the previous one left off.

You can obtain a string containing the currently matching sequence by calling **group( )**. One of its forms is shown here:

    String group( )

The matching string is returned. If no match exists, then an **IllegalStateException** is thrown.

You can obtain the index within the input sequence of the current match by calling **start( )**. The index that is one past the end of the current match is obtained by calling **end( )**. One form of each of these methods is shown here:

    int start( )
    int end( )

Both throw **IllegalStateException** if no match exists.

You can replace all occurrences of a matching sequence with another sequence by calling **replaceAll( )**, shown here:

    String replaceAll(String *newStr*)

Here, *newStr* specifies the new character sequence that will replace the ones that match the pattern. The updated input sequence is returned as a string.

REGULAR EXPRESSION SYNTAX BASICS

Before demonstrating **Pattern** and **Matcher**, it is necessary to explain how to construct a regular expression. Although no rule is complicated by itself, there are a large number of them, and a complete discussion is beyond the scope of this book. However, a few of the fundamental constructs are described here.

In general, a regular expression is comprised of normal characters, character classes (sets of characters), the wildcard character, and quantifiers. A normal character is matched as-is. Thus, if a pattern consists of "xy", then the only input sequence that will match it is "xy". Characters such as newline and tab are specified using the standard escape sequences, which begin with a \. For example, a newline is specified by \n. In the language of regular expressions, a normal character is also called a *literal*.

A character class is a set of characters. A character class is specified by putting the characters in the class between brackets. For example, the class [wxyz] matches w, x, y, or z. To specify an inverted set, precede the characters with a ^. For example, [^wxyz] matches any character except w, x, y, or z. You can specify a range of characters using a hyphen. For example, to specify a character class that will match the digits 1 through 9, use [1-9]. Java also provides several predefined classes. Here are two examples: the class \d matches the digits 0 through 9 and the class \w matches characters that can be part of a word.

Another predefined class is the **.** (dot). It is, essentially, a *wildcard character* because it matches any character except a line terminator. (It is possible to alter the behavior of the dot to also catch line terminators, but we won't do so here.) Thus, a pattern that consists of "." will match these (and other) input sequences: "A", "a", "x", and so on.

A quantifier determines how many times an expression is matched. Here are the basic quantifiers:

+	Match one or more.
*	Match zero or more.
?	Match zero or one.

For example, the pattern "x+" will match "x", "xx", and "xxx", among others. As you will see shortly, these quantifiers are called *greedy* because of their behavior.

DEMONSTRATING PATTERN MATCHING

The best way to understand how regular expression pattern matching operates is to work through some examples. The first, shown here, looks for a match with a literal pattern:

```java
// A simple pattern matching demo.
import java.util.regex.*;

class RegExpr {
  public static void main(String[] args) {
    Pattern pat;
    Matcher mat;
    boolean found;

    pat = Pattern.compile("Alpha");
    mat = pat.matcher("Alpha");
    found = mat.matches(); // check for a match
```

```
     System.out.println("Testing Alpha against Alpha.");
     if(found) System.out.println("Matches");
     else System.out.println("No Match");

     System.out.println();

     System.out.println("Testing Alpha against Alpha Beta Gamma.");
     mat = pat.matcher("Alpha Beta Gamma"); // create a new matcher

     found = mat.matches(); // check for a match

     if(found) System.out.println("Matches");
     else System.out.println("No Match");
   }
}
```

The output from the program is shown here:

```
Testing Alpha against Alpha.
Matches

Testing Alpha against Alpha Beta Gamma.
No Match
```

Let's look closely at this program. The program begins by creating the pattern that contains the sequence "Alpha". Next, a **Matcher** is created for that pattern that has the input sequence "Alpha". Then, the **matches( )** method is called to determine if the input sequence matches the pattern. Because the sequence and the pattern are the same, **matches( )** returns **true**. Next, a new **Matcher** is created with the input sequence "Alpha Beta Gamma", and **matches( )** is called again. In this case, the pattern and the input sequence differ, and no match is found. Remember, the **matches( )** function returns **true** only when the input sequence precisely matches the pattern. It will not return **true** just because a subsequence matches.

You can use **find( )** to determine if the input sequence contains a subsequence that matches the pattern. Consider the following program:

```
// Use find() to find a subsequence.
import java.util.regex.*;

class RegExpr2 {
  public static void main(String[] args) {
    Pattern pat = Pattern.compile("Alpha");
    Matcher mat = pat.matcher("Alpha Beta Gamma");

    System.out.println("Looking for Alpha in Alpha Beta Gamma.");

    if(mat.find()) System.out.println("subsequence found");
    else System.out.println("No Match");
  }
}
```

The output is shown here:

```
Looking for Alpha in Alpha Beta Gamma.
subsequence found
```

In this case, **find( )** finds the subsequence "Alpha".

The **find( )** method can be used to search the input sequence for repeated occurrences of the pattern because each call to **find( )** picks up where the previous one left off. For example, the following program finds two occurrences of the pattern "Beta":

```java
// Use find() to find multiple subsequences.
import java.util.regex.*;

class RegExpr3 {
  public static void main(String[] args) {
    Pattern pat = Pattern.compile("Beta");
    Matcher mat = pat.matcher("Alpha Beta Gamma Beta Theta");

    while(mat.find()) {
      System.out.println("Beta found at index " + mat.start());
    }
  }
}
```

The output is shown here:

```
Beta found at index 6
Beta found at index 17
```

As the output shows, two matches were found. The program uses the **start( )** method to obtain the index of each match.

USING THE WILDCARD CHARACTER AND QUANTIFIERS

Although the preceding programs show the general technique for using **Pattern** and **Matcher**, they don't show their power. The real benefit of regular expression processing is not seen until the wildcard and quantifiers are used. To begin, consider the following example that uses the + quantifier to match any arbitrarily long sequence of Ws. Recall that + matches an expression one or more times.

```java
// Use a quantifier.
import java.util.regex.*;

class RegExpr4 {
  public static void main(String[] args) {
    Pattern pat = Pattern.compile("W+");
    Matcher mat = pat.matcher("W WW WWW");

    while(mat.find())
      System.out.println("Match: " + mat.group());
  }
}
```

The output from the program is shown here:

```
Match: W
Match: WW
Match: WWW
```

As the output shows, the regular expression pattern "W+" matches any arbitrarily long sequence of Ws.

The next program uses a wildcard to create a pattern that will match any sequence of length 3 or more that begins with *e* and ends with *d*. To do this, it uses the dot character along with the + quantifier.

```
// Use wildcard and quantifier.
import java.util.regex.*;

class RegExpr5 {
  public static void main(String[] args) {
    Pattern pat = Pattern.compile("e.+d");
    Matcher mat = pat.matcher("extend cup end table");

    while(mat.find())
      System.out.println("Match: " + mat.group());
  }
}
```

You might be surprised by the output produced by the program, which is shown here:

```
Match: extend cup end
```

Only one match is found, and it is the longest sequence that begins with *e* and ends with *d*. You might have expected two matches: "extend" and "end". The reason that the longer sequence is found is that by default, **find( )** matches the longest sequence that fits the pattern. This is called *greedy behavior*. All three of the basic quantifiers exhibit greedy behavior. Thus, they are called the *greedy quantifiers*.

You can use two other types of quantifier behavior. They are *reluctant* and *possessive*. You can specify reluctant behavior by adding a **?** to the quantifier. Therefore, the reluctant quantifiers are **+?**, ***?**, and **??**. The reluctant quantifiers cause the shortest matching pattern to be obtained. For example, if you substitute "e.+?d" for the regular expression in the previous program you will see the following output:

```
Match: extend
Match: end
```

As the output shows, the pattern "e.+?d" matches the shortest sequence of length 3 or more that begins with *e* and ends with *d*. Thus, two matches are found.

A possessive quantifier will match the longest sequence it can, even if matching a shorter sequence would enable the entire regular expression match to succeed. A possessive quantifier is created by appending a **+**. Thus, the possessive quantifiers are **++**, ***+**, and **?+**. For example, if you substitute "e.++d" into the preceding program as the pattern, it will report no matches because the **.++** consumes all the characters to the end of the string. Thus, there is no match for the **d**.

One other point: there are forms of the quantifiers that let you specify how many times you want to match a pattern. This is done by enclosing a count after the quantifier, between braces. Other variations let you specify the minimum number of times to match, or a range of times to match.

WORKING WITH CLASSES OF CHARACTERS

Sometimes you will want to match any sequence that contains one or more characters, in any order, that are part of a set of characters. For example, to match whole words, you want to match any sequence of the letters of the alphabet. One of the easiest ways to do this is to use a character class, which defines a set of characters. Recall that a character class is created by putting the characters you want to match between brackets. For example, to match the lowercase characters a through z, use **[a-z]**. The following program demonstrates this technique:

```java
// Use a character class.
import java.util.regex.*;

class RegExpr6 {
  public static void main(String[] args) {
    // Match lowercase words.
    Pattern pat = Pattern.compile("[a-z]+");
    Matcher mat = pat.matcher("this is a test.");

    while(mat.find())
      System.out.println("Match: " + mat.group());
  }
}
```

The output is shown here:

```
Match: this
Match: is
Match: a
Match: test
```

USING replaceAll( )

The **replaceAll( )** method supplied by **Matcher** lets you perform powerful search and replace operations that use regular expressions. For example, the following program replaces all occurrences of sequences that begin with "Jon" with "Eric":

```java
// Use replaceAll().
import java.util.regex.*;

class RegExpr7 {
  public static void main(String[] args) {
    String str = "Jon Jonathan Frank Ken Todd";
```

```
        Pattern pat = Pattern.compile("Jon.*? ");
        Matcher mat = pat.matcher(str);

        System.out.println("Original sequence: " + str);

        str = mat.replaceAll("Eric ");

        System.out.println("Modified sequence: " + str);
    }
}
```

The output is shown here:

```
Original sequence: Jon Jonathan Frank Ken Todd
Modified sequence: Eric Eric Frank Ken Todd
```

Because the regular expression "Jon.*?" reluctantly matches any string that begins with Jon followed by zero or more characters, ending in a space, it can be used to match and replace both Jon and Jonathan with the name Eric. Such a substitution would be more difficult without pattern matching capabilities.

THE String CLASS CONNECTION

When working with **String**s, you can perform a pattern match without creating a **Matcher** or a **Pattern** directly. To do so, use the **matches( )** method provided by **String**. It is shown here:

boolean matches(String *pattern*)

If the invoking string matches the regular expression in *pattern*, then **matches( )** returns **true**. Otherwise, it returns **false**. If *pattern* does not represent a legal expression, a **PatternSyntaxException** will be thrown. The **matches( )** method of **String** is very convenient when only an occasional match is required.

THINGS TO EXPLORE

This brief introduction to regular expressions presented several key features. However, there is much more to regular expressions. Here are some areas to explore: working with groups, the OR operator, using boundary matchers, and the use of various flags. Also, both **Pattern** and **Matcher** define additional methods beyond those mentioned here that you will find helpful in some cases. Here are two examples. **Pattern** defines the **split( )** method that lets you reduce a string to its individual parts. The **replaceFirst( )** method of **Matcher** replaces the first match of a regular expression with a specified string.

A P P E N D I X   C

Answers to Selected Exercises

CHAPTER 1 ANSWERS TO SELECTED EXERCISES

1. Name the three necessary pieces of a computer.

   The CPU, memory, and input/output device.

2. What is source code? What is object code?

   Source code is the human-readable form of a program. Object code is the program's executable form.

3. What is the value 14 in binary? What is decimal equivalent of this binary number 1010 0110?

   14 in binary is 1110. The value 1010 0110 in decimal is 166.

4. As a general rule, a byte is comprised of _____ bits.

   8

5. What is bytecode, and why is it important to Java's use for Internet programming?

   Bytecode is a highly optimized set of instructions that is executed by the Java Virtual Machine.

   Bytecode helps Java achieve both portability and security.

6. What are the three main principles of object-oriented programming?

   Encapsulation, polymorphism, and inheritance.

7. Where do Java programs begin execution?

   Java programs begin execution at **main( )**.

8. What is a variable?

   A variable is a named memory location. The contents of a variable can be changed during the execution of a program.

9. Which of the following variable names is invalid?

   The invalid variable is **D**. Variable names cannot begin with a digit.

10. How do you create a single-line comment? How do you create a multiline comment?

A single-line comment begins with // and ends at the end of the line. A multiline comment begins with /* and ends with */.

11. Show the general form of the **if** statement. Show the general form of the **for** loop.

The general form of the **if**:

if(*condition*) *statement*;

The general form of the **for**:

for(*initialization*; *condition*; *iteration*) *statement*;

12. How do you create a block of code?

A block of code is started with a { and ended with a }.

13. The moon's gravity is about 17 percent that of the earth's. Write a program that computes your effective weight on the moon.

```
/*
   Compute your weight on the moon.

   Call this file Moon.java.
*/
class Moon {
  public static void main(String[] args) {
    double earthWeight; // weight on earth
    double moonWeight; // weight on moon

    earthWeight = 165;

    moonWeight = earthWeight * 0.17;

    System.out.println(earthWeight +
                       " earth-pounds is equivalent to " +
                       moonWeight + " moon-pounds.");
  }
}
```

14. Adapt Try This 1-2 so that it prints a conversion table of inches to meters. Display 12 feet of conversions, inch by inch. Output a blank line every 12 inches. (One meter equals approximately 39.37 inches.)

```
/*
   This program displays a conversion
   table of inches to meters.

   Call this program InchToMeterTable.java.
*/
class InchToMeterTable {
  public static void main(String[] args) {
```

```
        double inches, meters;
        int counter;

        counter = 0;
        for(inches = 1; inches <= 144; inches++) {
          meters = inches / 39.37; // convert to meters
          System.out.println(inches + " inches is " +
                             meters + " meters.");

          counter++;
          // every 12th line, print a blank line
          if(counter == 12) {
            System.out.println();
            counter = 0; // reset the line counter
          }
        }
      }
    }
```

15. If you make a typing mistake when entering your program, what sort of error will result?

A syntax error.

16. Does it matter where on a line you put a statement?

No, Java is a free-form language.

CHAPTER 2: ANSWERS TO SELECTED EXERCISES

1. Why does Java strictly specify the range and behavior of its primitive types?

Java strictly specifies the range and behavior of its primitive types to ensure portability across platforms.

2. What is Java's character type, and how does it differ from the character type used by some other programming languages?

Java's character type is **char**. Java characters are Unicode rather than ASCII, which is used by some other computer languages.

3. A **boolean** value can have any value you like because any non-zero value is true. True or False?

False. A **boolean** value must be either **true** or **false**.

4. Given this output,

```
One
Two
Three
```

use a single string to show the **println( )** statement that produced it.

```
System.out.println("One\nTwo\nThree");
```

5. What is wrong with this fragment?

```
for(i = 0; i < 10; i++) {
  int sum;

  sum = sum + i;
}
System.out.println("Sum is: " + sum);
```

There are three fundamental flaws in the fragment. First, **sum** is created each time the block created by the **for** loop is entered and destroyed on exit. Thus, it will not hold its value between iterations. Attempting to use **sum** to hold a running sum of the iterations is pointless. Second, **sum** will not be known outside of the block in which it is declared. Thus, the reference to it in the **println( )** statement is invalid. Finally, **sum** is not initialized.

6. Explain the difference between the prefix and postfix forms of the increment operator.

When the increment operator precedes its operand, Java will perform the corresponding operation prior to obtaining the operand's value for use by the rest of the expression. If the operator follows its operand, then Java will obtain the operand's value before incrementing.

7. Show how a short-circuit AND can be used to prevent a divide-by-zero error.

```
if((b != 0) && (val / b == 1)) ...
```

8. In an expression, what type are **byte** and **short** promoted to?

In an expression, **byte** and **short** are promoted to **int**.

9. In general, when is a cast needed?

A cast is needed when a narrowing conversion is occurring.

10. Write a program that finds all of the prime numbers between 2 and 100.

```
// Find prime numbers between 2 and 100.
class Prime {
  public static void main(String[] args) {
    int i, j;
    boolean isprime;

    for(i=2; i < 100; i++) {
      isprime = true;

      // see if the number is evenly divisible
      for(j=2; j <= i/j; j++)
        // if it is, then it's not prime
        if((i%j) == 0) isprime = false;

      if(isprime)
        System.out.println(i + " is prime.");
    }
  }
}
```

11. Does the use of redundant parentheses affect program performance?

No.

12. Does a block define a scope?

Yes.

CHAPTER 3: ANSWERS TO SELECTED EXERCISES

1. Write a program that reads characters from the keyboard until a period is received. Have the program count the number of spaces. Report the total at the end of the program.

```java
// Count spaces.
class Spaces {
  public static void main(String[] args)
    throws java.io.IOException {

    char ch;
    int spaces = 0;


    System.out.println("Enter a period to stop.");

    do {
      ch = (char) System.in.read();
      if(ch == ' ') spaces++;
    } while(ch != '.');

    System.out.println("Spaces: " + spaces);
  }
}
```

2. Show the general form of the **if-else-if** ladder.

if(*condition*)
   statement;
else if(*condition*)
   statement;
else if(*condition*)
   statement;
.
.
.
else
   statement;

3. Given

```
if(x < 10)
   if(y > 100) {
      if(!done) x = z;
      else y = z;
   }
else System.out.println("error"); // what if?
```

to what **if** does the last **else** associate?

The last **else** associates with **if(y > 100)**.

4. Show the **for** statement for a loop that counts from 1000 to 0 by –2.

```
for(int i = 1000; i >= 0; i -= 2) // ...
```

5. Is the following fragment valid?

```
for(int i = 0; i < num; i++)
   sum += i;

count = i;
```

No; **i** is not known outside of the **for** loop in which it is declared.

6. Explain what **break** does. Be sure to explain both of its forms.

A **break** without a label causes termination of its immediately enclosing loop or **switch** statement.

A **break** with a label causes control to transfer to the end of the labeled statement or block.

7. In the following fragment, after the **break** statement executes, what is displayed?

```
for(i = 0; i < 10; i++) {
   while(running) {
      if(x<y) break;
      // ...
   }
   System.out.println("after while");
}
System.out.println("After for");
```

After **break** executes, "after while" is displayed.

8. What does the following fragment print?

```
for(int i = 0; i<10; i++) {
   System.out.print(i + " ");
   if((i%2) == 0) continue;
   System.out.println();
}
```

Here is the answer:

```
0 1
2 3
4 5
6 7
8 9
```

9. The iteration expression in a **for** loop need not always alter the loop control variable by adding or subtracting a fixed amount. Instead, the loop control variable can change in any arbitrary way. Using this concept, write a program that uses a **for** loop to generate and display the progression 1, 2, 4, 8, 16, 32, and so on.

```java
/* Use a for loop to generate the progression

   1 2 4 8 16 32 64
*/
class Progress {
  public static void main(String[] args) {

    for(int i = 1; i < 100; i += i)
      System.out.print(i + " ");
  }
}
```

10. The ASCII lowercase letters are separated from the uppercase letters by 32. Thus, to convert a lowercase letter to uppercase, subtract 32 from it. Use this information to write a program that reads characters from the keyboard. Have it convert all lowercase letters to uppercase and all uppercase letters to lowercase, displaying the result. Make no changes to any other character. Have the program stop when the user presses period. At the end, have the program display the number of case changes that have taken place.

```java
// Change case.
class CaseChg {
  public static void main(String[] args)
      throws java.io.IOException {

    char ch;
    int changes = 0;

    System.out.println("Enter period to stop.");

    do {
      ch = (char) System.in.read();
      if(ch >= 'a' & ch <= 'z') {
        ch -= 32;
        changes++;
        System.out.println(ch);
      }
```

```
        else if(ch >= 'A' & ch <= 'Z') {
          ch += 32;
          changes++;
          System.out.println(ch);
        }
      } while(ch != '.');
      System.out.println("Case changes: " + changes);
    }
  }
```

11. What is an infinite loop?

    An infinite loop is a loop that runs indefinitely.

12. When using **break** with a label, must the label be on a statement or block that contains the **break**?

    Yes.

CHAPTER 4: ANSWERS TO SELECTED EXERCISES

1. What is the difference between a class and an object?

   A class is a logical abstraction that describes the form and behavior of an object. An object is a physical instance of the class.

2. How is a class defined?

   A class is defined by using the keyword **class**. Inside the **class** statement, you specify the code and data that comprise the class.

3. What does each object have its own copy of?

   Each object of a class has its own copy of the class's instance variables.

4. Using two separate statements, show how to declare a variable called **counter** of a class called **MyCounter** and assign it a new object of that class.

```
MyCounter counter;
counter = new MyCounter();
```

5. Show how a method called **myMeth( )** is declared if it has a return type of **double** and has two **int** parameters called **a** and **b**.

```
double myMeth(int a, int b) { // ...
```

6. How must a method return if it returns a value?

   A method that returns a value must return via the **return** statement, passing back the return value in the process.

7. What name does a constructor have?

   A constructor has the same name as its class.

8. What does **new** do?

   The **new** operator allocates memory for an object and initializes it using the object's constructor.

9. What is garbage collection and how does it work? What is **finalize( )**?

   Garbage collection is the mechanism that recycles unused objects so that their memory can be reused. An object's **finalize( )** method is called just prior to an object being recycled. It is not used by most Java programs.

10. What is **this**?

    The **this** keyword is a reference to the object on which a method is invoked. It is automatically passed to a method.

11. Can a constructor have one or more parameters?

    Yes.

12. If a method returns no value, what must its return type be?

    void

CHAPTER 5: ANSWERS TO SELECTED EXERCISES

1. Show two ways to declare a one-dimensional array of 12 **double**s.

```
double x[] = new double[12];
double[] x = new double[12];
```

2. Show how to initialize a one-dimensional array of integers to the values 1 through 5.

```
int[] x = { 1, 2, 3, 4, 5 };
```

3. Write a program that uses an array to find the average of 10 **double** values. Use any 10 values you like.

```
// Average 10 double values.
class Avg {
  public static void main(String[] args) {
    double[] nums = { 1.1, 2.2, 3.3, 4.4, 5.5,
                      6.6, 7.7, 8.8, 9.9, 10.1 };

    double sum = 0;

    for(int i=0; i < nums.length; i++)
      sum += nums[i];

    System.out.println("Average: " + sum / nums.length);
  }
}
```

4. Change the sort in Try This 5-1 so that it sorts an array of strings. Demonstrate that it works.

```
// Demonstrate the Bubble sort with strings.
class StrBubble {
  public static void main(String[] args) {
    String[] strs = {
                      "this", "is", "a", "test",
                      "of", "a", "string", "sort"
                    };
    int a, b;
    String t;
    int size;

    size = strs.length; // number of elements to sort

    // display original array
    System.out.print("Original array is:");
    for(int i=0; i < size; i++)
      System.out.print(" " + strs[i]);
    System.out.println();

    // This is the bubble sort for strings.
    for(a=1; a < size; a++)
      for(b=size-1; b >= a; b--) {
        if(strs[b-1].compareTo(strs[b]) > 0) { // if out of order
          // exchange elements
          t = strs[b-1];
          strs[b-1] = strs[b];
          strs[b] = t;
        }
      }

    // display sorted array
    System.out.print("Sorted array is:");
    for(int i=0; i < size; i++)
      System.out.print(" " + strs[i]);
    System.out.println();
  }
}
```

5. What is the difference between the **String** methods **indexOf( )** and **lastIndexOf( )**?

The **indexOf( )** method finds the first occurrence of the specified substring. **lastIndexOf( )** finds the last occurrence.

6. Since all strings are objects of type **String**, show how you can call the **length( )** and **charAt( )** methods on this string literal: "I like Java".

As strange as it may look, this is a valid call to **length( )**:

```
System.out.println("I like Java".length());
```

The output displayed is 11. **charAt( )** is called in a similar fashion.

7. Expanding on the **SimpleCipher** class, modify it so that it uses an eight-character string as the key.

```java
// An improved XOR cipher.
class SimpleCipher2 {
  public static void main(String[] args) {
    String msg = "This is a test";
    String encMsg = "";
    String decMsg = "";
    String key = "abcdefgi";
    int j;

    System.out.print("Original message: ");
    System.out.println(msg);

    // encode the message
    j = 0;
    for(int i=0; i < msg.length(); i++) {
      encMsg = encMsg + (char) (msg.charAt(i) ^ key.charAt(j));
      j++;
      if(j==8) j = 0;
    }

    System.out.print("Encoded message: ");
    System.out.println(encMsg);

    // decode the message
    j = 0;
    for(int i=0; i < msg.length(); i++) {
      decMsg = decMsg + (char) (encMsg.charAt(i) ^ key.charAt(j));
      j++;
      if(j==8) j = 0;
    }

    System.out.print("Decoded message: ");
    System.out.println(decMsg);
  }
}
```

8. Can the bitwise operators be applied to the **double** type?

No.

9. Show how this sequence can be rewritten using the **?** operator.

```java
if(x < 0) y = 10;
else y = 20;
```

Here is the answer:

```java
y = x < 0 ? 10 : 20;
```

10. In the following fragment, is the **&** a bitwise or logical operator? Why?

```
boolean a, b;
// ...
if(a & b) ...
```

It is a logical operator because the operands are of type **boolean**.

11. Is it an error to overrun the end of an array?

Yes.

Is it an error to index an array with a negative value?

Yes. All array indexes start at zero.

12. What is the symbol used for the unsigned right-shift operator?

>>>

13. Rewrite the **MinMax** class shown earlier in this chapter so that it uses a for-each style **for** loop.

```java
// Find the minimum and maximum values in an array.
class MinMax {
  public static void main(String[] args) {
    int[] nums = new int[10];
    int min, max;

    nums[0] = 99;
    nums[1] = -10;
    nums[2] = 100123;
    nums[3] = 18;
    nums[4] = -978;
    nums[5] = 5623;
    nums[6] = 463;
    nums[7] = -9;
    nums[8] = 287;
    nums[9] = 49;

    min = max = nums[0];
    for(int v : nums) {
      if(v < min) min = v;
      if(v > max) max = v;
    }
    System.out.println("min and max: " + min + " " + max);
  }
}
```

14. Can the **for** loops that perform sorting in the **Bubble** class shown in Try This 5-1 be converted into for-each style loops? If not, why not?

No, the **for** loops in the **Bubble** class that perform the sort cannot be converted into for-each style loops. In the case of the outer loop, the current value of its loop counter is needed by the inner loop. In the case of the inner loop, out-of-order values must be exchanged, which implies assignments. Assignments to the underlying array cannot take place when using a for-each style loop.

15. Can a **String** control a **switch** statement?

Beginning with JDK 7, the answer is Yes.

CHAPTER 6: ANSWERS TO SELECTED EXERCISES

1. Given this fragment,

```
class X {
  private int count;
```

is the following fragment correct?

```
class Y {
  public static void main(String[] args) {
    X ob = new X();

    ob.count = 10;
```

No; a **private** member cannot be accessed outside of its class.

2. An access modifier must _____ a member's declaration.

precede

3. Given this class,

```
class Test {
  int a;
  Test(int i) { a = i; }
}
```

write a method called **swap( )** that exchanges the contents of the objects referred to by two **Test** object references.

```
void swap(Test ob1, Test ob2) {
  int t;

  t = ob1.a;
  ob1.a = ob2.a;
  ob2.a = t;
}
```

4. Is the following fragment correct?

```
class X {
  int meth(int a, int b) { ... }
  String meth(int a, int b) { ... }
```

No. Overloaded methods can have different return types, but they do not play a role in overload resolution. Overloaded methods *must* have different parameter lists.

5. Write a recursive method that displays the contents of a string backwards.

```
// Display a string backwards using recursion.
class Backwards {
  String str;
```

```
Backwards(String s) {
    str = s;
}

void backward(int idx) {
    if(idx != str.length()-1) backward(idx+1);

    System.out.print(str.charAt(idx));
}
}

class BWDemo {
    public static void main(String[] args) {
        Backwards s = new Backwards("This is a test");

        s.backward(0);
    }
}
```

6. If all objects of a class need to share the same variable, how must you declare that variable?

Shared variables are declared as **static**.

7. Why might you need to use a **static** block?

A **static** block is used to perform any initializations related to the class, before any objects are created.

8. What is an inner class?

An inner class is a nonstatic nested class.

9. To make a member accessible by only other members of its class, what access modifier must be used?

private

10. The name of a method plus its parameter list constitutes the method's _____.

signature

11. An **int** argument is passed to a method by using call-by-_____.

value

12. Create a varargs method called **sum( )** that sums the **int** values passed to it. Have it return the result. Demonstrate its use.

There are many ways to craft the solution. Here is one:

```
class SumIt {
    int sum(int ... n) {
        int result = 0;

        for(int i = 0; i < n.length; i++)
            result += n[i];
```

```
      return result;
    }
}

class SumDemo {
  public static void main(String[] args) {

    SumIt siObj = new SumIt();

    int total = siObj.sum(1, 2, 3);
    System.out.println("Sum is " + total);

    total = siObj.sum(1, 2, 3, 4, 5);
    System.out.println("Sum is " + total);
  }
}
```

13. Can a varargs method be overloaded?

Yes.

14. Show an example of an overloaded varargs method that is ambiguous.

Here is one example of an overloaded varargs method that is ambiguous:

```
double myMeth(double ... v ) { // ...
double myMeth(double d, double ... v) { // ...
```

If you try to call **myMeth( )** with one argument, like this,

```
myMeth(1.1);
```

the compiler can't determine which version of the method to invoke.

CHAPTER 7 ANSWERS TO SELECTED EXERCISES

1. Does a superclass have access to the members of a subclass? Does a subclass have access to the members of a superclass?

No, a superclass has no knowledge of its subclasses. Yes, a subclass has access to all nonprivate members of its superclass.

2. Create a subclass of **TwoDShape** called **Circle**. Include an **area( )** method that computes the area of the circle and a constructor that uses **super** to initialize the **TwoDShape** portion.

```
// A subclass of TwoDShape for circles.
class Circle extends TwoDShape {
  // A default constructor.
  Circle() {
    super();
}
```

```
// Construct Circle
Circle(double x) {
    super(x, "circle"); // call superclass constructor
}

// Construct an object from an object.
Circle(Circle ob) {
    super(ob); // pass object to TwoDShape constructor
}

double area() {
    return (getWidth() / 2) * (getWidth() / 2) * 3.1416;
}
}
```

3. How do you prevent a subclass from having access to a member of a superclass?

To prevent a subclass from having access to a superclass member, declare that member as **private**.

4. Describe the purpose and use of both versions of **super**.

The **super** keyword has two forms. The first is used to call a superclass constructor. The general form of this usage is

super (*param-list*);

The second form of **super** is used to access a superclass member. It has this general form:

super.*member*

5. Given the following hierarchy, in what order are the constructors for these classes executed when a **Gamma** object is instantiated?

```
class Alpha { ...

class Beta extends Alpha { ...

Class Gamma extends Beta { ...
```

Constructors are always executed in order of derivation. Thus, when a **Gamma** object is created, the order is **Alpha**, **Beta**, **Gamma**.

6. A superclass reference can refer to a subclass object. Explain why this is important as it is related to method overriding.

When an overridden method is called through a superclass reference, it is the type of the object being referred to that determines which version of the method is called.

7. What is an abstract class?

A class with at least one abstract method is abstract.

8. How do you prevent a method from being overridden? How do you prevent a class from being inherited?

To prevent a method from being overridden, declare it as **final**. To prevent a class from being inherited, declare it as **final**.

9. Explain how inheritance, method overriding, and abstract classes are used to support polymorphism.

Inheritance, method overriding, and abstract classes support polymorphism by enabling you to create a generalized class structure that can be extended by a variety of classes. Thus, the abstract class defines a consistent interface that is shared by all implementing classes. This embodies the concept of "one interface, multiple methods."

10. What class is a superclass of every other class?

The **Object** class.

11. A class that contains at least one abstract method must itself be declared abstract. True or False?

True.

12. What keyword is used to create a named constant?

final

CHAPTER 8 ANSWERS TO SELECTED EXERCISES

1. "One interface, multiple methods" is a key tenet of Java. What feature best exemplifies it?

The interface best exemplifies the one interface, multiple methods principle of OOP.

2. How many classes can implement an interface?

An interface can be implemented by an unlimited number of classes.

3. How many interfaces can a class implement?

A class can implement as many interfaces as it chooses.

4. A class declares that it implements an interface by use of a/an _____ _____.

implements clause

5. Can interfaces be extended?

Yes, interfaces can be extended by other interfaces.

6. Create an interface for the **Vehicle** class from Chapter 7. Call the interface **IVehicle**.

```
interface IVehicle {

  // Return the range.
  int range();
```

```
    // Compute fuel needed for a given distance.
    double fuelNeeded(int miles);

    // Accessor methods.
    int getPassengers();
    void setPassengers(int p);
    int getFuelCap();
    void setFuelCap(int f);
    int getMpg();
    void setMpg(int m);
}
```

7. Variables declared in an interface are implicitly **static** and **final**. What good are they?

   Interface variables create named constants that can be shared by all classes in a program. They can be brought into view by implementing their interface.

8. Can one interface be a member of another?

   Yes.

9. Given two interfaces called **Alpha** and **Beta**, show how a class called **MyClass** specifies that it implements each.

   ```
   class MyClass implements Alpha, Beta { // ...
   ```

CHAPTER 9: ANSWERS TO SELECTED EXERCISES

1. Using the code from Try This 8-1, put the **ISimpleStack** interface and its two implementations into a package called **stackpack**. Keeping the stack demonstration class **ISimpleStackDemo** in the default package, show how to import and use the classes in **stackpack**.

   To put **ISimpleStack** and its implementations into the **stackpack** package, make each implementation class **public**, and add this statement to the top of each file.

   ```
   package stackpack;
   ```

   Once this has been done, you can use **stackpack** by adding this **import** statement to **ISimpleStackDemo**.

   ```
   import stackpack.*;
   ```

2. What is a namespace? Why is it important that Java allows you to partition the namespace?

   A namespace is a declarative region. By partitioning the namespace, you can prevent name collisions.

3. Packages are stored in _____.

   directories

4. Explain the difference between **protected** and default access.

A member with **protected** access can be used within its package and by a subclass in any package.

A member with default access can be used only within its package.

5. Explain the two ways that the members of a package can be accessed by other packages.

To use a member of a package, either you can fully qualify its name, or you can import it using **import**.

6. A package is, in essence, a container for classes. True or False?

True.

7. What standard Java package is automatically imported into a program?

java.lang

8. In your own words, what does static import do?

Static import brings into the global namespace the static members of a class or interface. This means that static members can be used without having to be qualified by their class or interface name.

9. What does this statement do?

```
import static somepack.SomeClass.myMethod;
```

The statement brings into the global namespace **SomeClass.myMethod( )**, which is part of the **somepack** package.

10. Is static import designed for special-case situations, or is it good practice to bring all static members of all classes into view?

Static import is designed for special cases. Bringing many static members into view will lead to namespace collisions and destructure your code.

CHAPTER 10: ANSWERS TO SELECTED EXERCISES

1. What class is at the top of the exception hierarchy?

Throwable is at the top of the exception hierarchy.

2. Briefly explain how to use **try** and **catch**.

The **try** and **catch** work together. Program statements that you want to monitor for exceptions are contained within a **try** block. An exception is caught using **catch**.

3. What is wrong with this fragment?

```
// ...
vals[18] = 10;
catch (ArrayIndexOutOfBoundsException exc) {
  // handle error
}
```

There is no **try** block preceding the **catch**.

4. What happens if an exception is not caught?

If an exception is not caught, abnormal program termination results.

5. What is wrong with this fragment?

```
class A extends Exception { ...

class B extends A { ...

// ...

try {
   // ...
}
catch (A exc) { ... }
catch (B exc) { ... }
```

In the fragment, a superclass **catch** precedes a subclass **catch**. Since the superclass **catch** will catch all subclasses too, unreachable code is created.

6. Can an inner **catch** rethrow an exception to an outer **catch**?

Yes, an exception can be rethrown.

7. The **finally** block is the last bit of code executed before your program ends. True or False? Explain your answer.

False. The **finally** block is the code executed when a **try** block ends.

8. What type of exceptions must be explicitly declared in a **throws** clause of a method?

All exceptions except those of type **RuntimeException** and **Error** must be declared in a **throws** clause.

9. What is wrong with this fragment?

```
class MyClass { // ... }
// ...
throw new MyClass();
```

MyClass does not extend **Throwable**. Only subclasses of **Throwable** can be thrown by **throw**.

10. What are the three ways that an exception can be generated?

An exception can be generated by an error in the JVM, by an error in your program, or explicitly by a **throw** statement.

11. What are the two direct subclasses of **Throwable**?

Error and **Exception**

12. What is the multi-catch feature?

The multi-catch feature allows one **catch** clause to catch two or more exceptions.

13. Should your code typically catch exceptions of type **Error**?

No.

CHAPTER 11: ANSWERS TO SELECTED EXERCISES

1. Why does Java define both byte and character streams?

The byte streams are the original streams defined by Java. They are especially useful for binary I/O, and they support random-access files. The character streams are optimized for Unicode characters.

2. Even though console input and output is text-based, why does Java still use byte streams for this purpose?

The predefined streams, **System.in**, **System.out**, and **System.err**, were defined before Java added the character streams.

3. Show how to open a file for reading bytes.

Here is one way to open a file for byte input:

```
FileInputStream fin = new FileInputStream("test");
```

4. Show how to open a file for reading characters.

Here is one way to open a file for reading characters:

```
FileReader fr = new FileReader("test");
```

5. Show how to open a file for random-access I/O.

Here is one way to open a file for random access:

```
RandomAccessFile randfile = new RandomAccessFile("test", "rw");
```

6. How do you convert a numeric string such as "123.23" into its binary equivalent?

One way to convert numeric strings into their binary equivalents is to use the parsing methods defined by the type wrappers, such as **Integer** or **Double**.

7. Write a program that copies a text file. In the process, have it convert all spaces into hyphens. Use the byte stream file classes. Use the traditional approach to closing a file by explicitly calling **close( )**.

```
/* Copy a text file, substituting hyphens for spaces.

   This version uses byte streams.

   To use this program, specify the name
   of the source file and the destination file.
   For example,

   java Hyphen source target
*/

import java.io.*;
```

```
class Hyphen {
  public static void main(String[] args)
  {
    int i;
    FileInputStream fin = null;
    FileOutputStream fout = null;

    // First make sure that both files have been specified.
    if(args.length !=2 ) {
      System.out.println("Usage: Hyphen From To");
      return;
    }

    // Copy file and substitute hyphens.
    try {
      fin = new FileInputStream(args[0]);
      fout = new FileOutputStream(args[1]);

      do {
        i = fin.read();

        // convert space to a hyphen
        if((char)i == ' ') i = '-';

        if(i != -1) fout.write(i);
      } while(i != -1);
    } catch(IOException exc) {
      System.out.println("I/O Error: " + exc);
    } finally {
      try {
        if(fin != null) fin.close();
      } catch(IOException exc) {
        System.out.println("Error closing input file.");
      }

      try {
        if(fin != null) fout.close();
      } catch(IOException exc) {
        System.out.println("Error closing output file.");
      }
    }
  }
}
```

8. Rewrite the program in exercise 7 so that it uses the character stream classes. This time, use the **try**-with-resources statement to automatically close the file.

```
/* Copy a text file, substituting hyphens for spaces.

   This version uses character streams.
```

```
      To use this program, specify the name
      of the source file and the destination file.
      For example,

      java Hyphen2 source target

      This code requires JDK 7 or later.
*/

import java.io.*;

class Hyphen2 {
  public static void main(String[] args)
  {
    int i;

    // First make sure that both files have been specified.
    if(args.length !=2 ) {
      System.out.println("Usage: CopyFile From To");
      return;
    }

    // Copy file and substitute hyphens.
    // Use the try-with-resources statement.
    try (FileReader fin = new FileReader(args[0]);
         FileWriter fout = new FileWriter(args[1]))
    {
      do {
        i = fin.read();

        // convert space to a hyphen
        if((char)i == ' ') i = '-';

        if(i != -1) fout.write(i);
      } while(i != -1);
    } catch(IOException exc) {
      System.out.println("I/O Error: " + exc);
    }
  }
}
```

9. What type of stream is **System.in**?

   InputStream

10. What does the **read( )** method of **InputStream** return when the end of the
    stream is reached?

    –1

11. What type of stream is used to read binary data?

    DataInputStream

12. **Reader** and **Writer** are at the top of the _____ class hierarchies.

    character-based I/O

13. The **try**-with-resources statement is used for _____ _____

    _____.

    automatic resource management

14. If you are using the traditional method of closing a file, then closing a file within a **finally** block is generally a good approach. True or False?

    True.

15. What class gives you access to the attributes of a file?

    File

16. Can you use the **File** class to delete a file?

    Yes.

CHAPTER 12: ANSWERS TO SELECTED EXERCISES

1. How does Java's multithreading capability enable you to write more efficient programs?

    Multithreading allows you to take advantage of the idle time that is present in nearly all programs. When one thread can't run, another can. In multicore systems, two or more threads can execute simultaneously.

2. Multithreading is supported by the _____ class and the _____ interface.

    Multithreading is supported by the **Thread** class and the **Runnable** interface.

3. When creating a runnable object, why might you want to extend **Thread** rather than implement **Runnable**?

    You will extend **Thread** when you want to override one or more of **Thread**'s methods other than **run( )**.

4. Show how to use **join( )** to wait for a thread object called **myThrd** to end.

    ```
    myThrd.join();
    ```

5. Show how to set a thread called **myThrd** to three levels above normal priority.

    ```
    myThrd.setPriority(Thread.NORM_PRIORITY+3);
    ```

6. What is the effect of adding the **synchronized** keyword to a method?

    Adding **synchronized** to a method allows only one thread at a time to use the method for any given object of its class.

7. The **wait( )** and **notify( )** methods are used to perform

    _____.

    interthread communication

8. Change the **TickTock** class so that it actually keeps time. That is, have each tick take one half second and each tock take one half second. Thus, each tick-tock will take one second. (Don't worry about the time it takes to switch tasks, etc.)

To make the **TickTock** class actually keep time, simply add calls to **sleep( )**, as shown here.

```java
// Make the TickTock class actually keep time.

class TickTock {

  String state; // contains the state of the clock

  synchronized void tick(boolean running) {
    if(!running) { // stop the clock
      state = "ticked";
      notify(); // notify any waiting threads
      return;
    }

    System.out.print("Tick ");

    // wait 1/2 second
    try {
      Thread.sleep(500);
    } catch(InterruptedException exc) {
      System.out.println("Thread interrupted.");
    }

    state = "ticked"; // set the current state to ticked

    notify(); // let tock() run
    try {
      while(!state.equals("tocked"))
        wait(); // wait for tock() to complete
    }
    catch(InterruptedException exc) {
      System.out.println("Thread interrupted.");
    }
  }

  synchronized void tock(boolean running) {
    if(!running) { // stop the clock
      state = "tocked";
      notify(); // notify any waiting threads
      return;
    }

    System.out.println("Tock");
```

```
          // wait 1/2 second
          try {
            Thread.sleep(500);
          } catch(InterruptedException exc) {
            System.out.println("Thread interrupted.");
          }

          state = "tocked"; // set the current state to tocked

          notify(); // let tick() run
          try {
            while(!state.equals("ticked"))
              wait(); // wait for tick to complete
          }
          catch(InterruptedException exc) {
            System.out.println("Thread interrupted.");
          }
        }
      }
    }
```

9. Why can't you use **suspend( )**, **resume( )**, and **stop( )** for new programs?

   The **suspend( )**, **resume( )**, and **stop( )** methods have been deprecated because they can cause serious run-time problems.

10. What method defined by **Thread** obtains the name of a thread?

    getName( )

11. What does **isAlive( )** return?

    It returns **true** if the invoking thread is still running, and **false** if it has been terminated.

CHAPTER 13 ANSWERS TO SELECTED EXERCISES

1. Enumeration constants are said to be *self-typed*. What does this mean?

   In the term *self-typed*, the "self" refers to the type of the enumeration in which the constant is defined. Thus, an enumeration constant is an object of the enumeration of which it is a part.

2. What class do all enumerations automatically inherit?

   The **Enum** class is automatically inherited by all enumerations.

3. Given the following enumeration, write a program that uses **values( )** to show a list of the constants and their ordinal values.

```
enum Tools {
  SCREWDRIVER, WRENCH, HAMMER, PLIERS
}
```

The solution is:

```
enum Tools {
   SCREWDRIVER, WRENCH, HAMMER, PLIERS
}

class ShowEnum {
   public static void main(String[] args) {
     for(Tools d : Tools.values())
       System.out.print(d + " has ordinal value of " +
                        d.ordinal() + '\n');
   }
}
```

4. The traffic light simulation developed in Try This 13-1 can be improved with a few simple changes that take advantage of an enumeration's class features. In the version shown, the duration of each color was controlled by the **TrafficLightSimulator** class by hard-coding these values into the **run( )** method. Change this so that the duration of each color is stored by the constants in the **TrafficLightColor** enumeration. To do this, you will need to add a constructor, a private instance variable, and a method called **getDelay( )**.

The improved version of the traffic light simulation is shown here. There are two major improvements. First, a light's delay is now linked with its enumeration value, which gives more structure to the code. Second, the **run( )** method no longer needs to use a **switch** statement to determine the length of the delay. Instead, **sleep( )** is passed **tlc.getDelay( )**, which causes the delay associated with the current color to be used automatically.

```
// An improved version of the traffic light simulation that
// stores the light delay in TrafficLightColor.

// An enumeration of the colors of a traffic light.
enum TrafficLightColor {
   RED(12000), GREEN(10000), YELLOW(2000);

   private int delay;

   TrafficLightColor(int d) {
     delay = d;
   }

   int getDelay() { return delay; }
}

// A computerized traffic light.
class TrafficLightSimulator implements Runnable {
   private Thread thrd; // holds the thread that runs the simulation
   private TrafficLightColor tlc; // holds the current traffic light color
   boolean stop = false; // set to true to stop the simulation
   boolean changed = false; // true when the light has changed
```

```
TrafficLightSimulator(TrafficLightColor init) {
  tlc = init;

  thrd = new Thread(this);
  thrd.start();
}

TrafficLightSimulator() {
  tlc = TrafficLightColor.RED;

  thrd = new Thread(this);
  thrd.start();
}

// Start up the light.
public void run() {
  while(!stop) {
    // Notice how this code has been simplified!
    try {
      Thread.sleep(tlc.getDelay());
    } catch(InterruptedException exc) {
      System.out.println(exc);
    }

    changeColor();
  }
}

// Change color.
synchronized void changeColor() {
  switch(tlc) {
    case RED:
      tlc = TrafficLightColor.GREEN;
      break;
    case YELLOW:
      tlc = TrafficLightColor.RED;
      break;
    case GREEN:
      tlc = TrafficLightColor.YELLOW;
  }

  changed = true;
  notify(); // signal that the light has changed
}

// Wait until a light change occurs.
synchronized void waitForChange() {
  try {
    while(!changed)
      wait(); // wait for light to change
```

```
        changed = false;
      } catch(InterruptedException exc) {
        System.out.println(exc);
      }
    }

    // Return current color.
    synchronized TrafficLightColor getColor() {
      return tlc;
    }

    // Stop the traffic light.
    synchronized void cancel() {
      stop = true;
    }
  }

class TrafficLightDemo {
  public static void main(String[] args) {
    TrafficLightSimulator tl =
      new TrafficLightSimulator(TrafficLightColor.GREEN);

    for(int i=0; i < 9; i++) {
      System.out.println(tl.getColor());
      tl.waitForChange();
    }

    tl.cancel();
  }
}
```

5. Define boxing and unboxing. How does autoboxing/unboxing affect these actions?

Boxing is the process of storing a primitive value in a type wrapper object. Unboxing is the process of retrieving the primitive value from the type wrapper. Autoboxing automatically boxes a primitive value without having to explicitly construct an object. Auto-unboxing automatically retrieves the primitive value from a type wrapper without having to explicitly call a method, such as **intValue( )**.

6. Change the following fragment so that it uses autoboxing.

```
Short val = new Short(123);
```

The solution is:

```
Short val = 123;
```

7. An annotation is syntactically based on a/an _____.

interface

8. What is a marker annotation?

A marker annotation is one that does not take arguments.

9. An annotation can be applied only to methods. True or False?

False. Any type of declaration can have an annotation.

CHAPTER 14 ANSWERS TO SELECTED EXERCISES

1. Generics are an important addition to Java because they enable the creation of code that is

A. Type-safe

B. Reusable

C. Reliable

D. All of the above

D all of the above

2. Can a primitive type be used as a type argument?

No, type arguments must be reference types.

3. Show how to declare a class called **FlightSched** that takes two generic parameters.

The solution is

```
class FlightSched<T, V> {
```

4. Beginning with your answer to question 3, change **FlightSched**'s second type parameter so that it must extend **Thread**.

The solution is

```
class FlightSched<T, V extends Thread> {
```

5. Now, change **FlightSched** so that its second type parameter must be a subclass of its first type parameter.

The solution is

```
class FlightSched<T, V extends T> {
```

6. As it relates to generics, what is the **?** and what does it do?

The **?** is the wildcard argument. It matches any valid type.

7. Can the wildcard argument be bounded?

Yes, a wildcard can have either an upper or a lower bound.

8. A generic method called **MyGen( )** has one type parameter. Furthermore, **MyGen( )** has one parameter whose type is that of the type parameter. It also returns an object of that type parameter. Show how to declare **MyGen( )**.

The solution is

```
<T> T MyGen(T o) { // ...
```

9. Given this generic interface

```
interface IGenIF<T, V extends T> { // ...
```

show the declaration of a class called **MyClass** that implements **IGenIF**.

The solution is

```
class MyClass<T, V extends T> implements IGenIF<T, V> { // ...
```

10. Given a generic class called **Counter\<T>**, show how to create an object of its raw type.

To obtain **Counter\<T>**'s raw type, simply use its name without any type specification, as shown here:

```
Counter x = new Counter();
```

11. Do type parameters exist at run time?

No. All type parameters are erased during compilation, and appropriate casts are substituted. This process is called erasure.

12. When a generic class is inherited, its type parameters must also be specified by the subclass. True or False?

True.

13. What is < >?

The diamond operator.

14. When using JDK 7, how can the following be simplified?

```
MyClass<Double,String> obj = new MyClass<Double,String>(1.1,"Hi");
```

It can be simplified by use of the diamond operator as shown here:

```
MyClass<Double,String> obj = new MyClass<>(1.1,"Hi");
```

CHAPTER 15: ANSWERS TO SELECTED EXERCISES

1. What method is called when an applet first begins running? What method is called when an applet is removed from the system?

When an applet begins, the first method called is **init( )**. When an applet is removed, **destroy( )** is called.

2. Explain why an applet must use multithreading if it needs to run continually.

An applet must use multithreading if it needs to run continually because applets must not enter a "mode" of operation. For example, if **start( )** never returns, then **paint( )** will never be called.

3. Enhance Try This 15-1 so that it displays the string passed to it as a parameter. Add a second parameter that specifies the time delay (in milliseconds) between each rotation.

```
/* A simple banner applet that uses parameters.
```

```
*/
import java.awt.*;
import java.applet.*;

/*
<applet code="ParamBanner" width=300 height=50>
<param name=message value=" I like Java! ">
<param name=delay value=500>
</applet>
*/

public class ParamBanner extends Applet implements Runnable {
  String msg;
  int delay;
  Thread t;

  boolean stopFlag;

  // Initialize t to null.
  public void init() {
    String temp;

    msg = getParameter("message");
    if(msg == null) msg = " Java Rules the Web ";

    temp = getParameter("delay");

    try {
      if(temp != null)
        delay = Integer.parseInt(temp);
      else
        delay = 250; // default if not specified
    } catch(NumberFormatException exc) {
        delay = 250 ; // default on error
    }

    t = null;
  }

  // Start thread when the applet is needed.
  public void start() {
    t = new Thread(this);
    stopFlag = false;
    t.start();
  }

  // Entry point for the thread that runs the banner.
  public void run() {
    // Request a repaint at the specified interval.
    for( ; ; ) {
      try {
        repaint();
```

```
        Thread.sleep(delay);
        if(stopFlag) break;
      } catch(InterruptedException exc) {}
    }
  }

  // Pause the banner.
  public void stop() {
    stopFlag = true;
    t = null;
  }

  // Display the banner.
  public void paint(Graphics g) {
    char ch;

    ch = msg.charAt(0);
    msg = msg.substring(1, msg.length());
    msg += ch;

    g.drawString(msg, 50, 30);
  }
}
```

4. **Extra challenge:** Create an applet that displays the current time, updated once per second.

```
// A simple clock applet.

import java.util.*;
import java.awt.*;
import java.applet.*;
/*
<object code="Clock" width=200 height=50>
</object>
*/

public class Clock extends Applet implements Runnable {
  String msg;
  Thread t;
  Calendar clock;

  boolean stopFlag;

  // Initialize
  public void init() {
    t = null;
    msg = "";
  }
```

```
// Start thread when the applet is needed.
public void start() {
  t = new Thread(this);
  stopFlag = false;
  t.start();
}

// Entry point for the clock.
public void run() {
  // Request a repaint every second.
  for( ; ; ) {
    try {
      repaint();
      Thread.sleep(1000);
      if(stopFlag) break;
    } catch(InterruptedException exc) {}
  }
}

// Pause the clock.
public void stop() {
  stopFlag = true;
  t = null;
}

// Display the clock.
public void paint(Graphics g) {
  clock = Calendar.getInstance();

  msg = "Current time is " +
        Integer.toString(clock.get(Calendar.HOUR));
  msg = msg + ":" +
        Integer.toString(clock.get(Calendar.MINUTE));
  msg = msg + ":" +
        Integer.toString(clock.get(Calendar.SECOND));

  g.drawString(msg, 30, 30);
}
}
```

5. To request that an applet's window be redisplayed, what method do you call?

repaint( )

6. Briefly describe the **assert** keyword.

The **assert** keyword creates an assertion, which is a condition that should be true during program execution. If the assertion is false, an **AssertionError** is thrown.

7. Give one reason why a native method might be useful to some types of programs.

A native method is useful when interfacing to routines written in languages other than Java, or when optimizing code for a specific run-time environment.

8. What operator can you use to determine the type of an object at run time?

instanceof

CHAPTER 16: ANSWERS TO SELECTED EXERCISES

1. For methods, classes, and variables, you should use _____ names.

intention-revealing

2. All the principles discussed in this chapter are iron-clad rules that must be followed in order to have elegant software. True or False?

False.

3. A good programmer writes self-documenting code and so never needs to add internal comments. True or False?

False. Internal documentation provides information not readily available from the code itself.

4. It is generally better to put all the important methods in one class and make most of the other classes simple servant classes. True or False?

False.

5. Out-of-date documentation is better than no documentation at all. True or False?

False.

6. A method with method chaining of the form **a.getB( ).getC( ).getD( ).doSomething( )** does not obey _____.

Demeter's Law

7. Suppose you have a **Person** class with instance variables containing the person's name, birth date, address, spouse, children, and occupation. According to the Expert pattern, this class should have methods that handle any manipulations of this data that are needed by other classes. However, an unlimited number of manipulations of a **Person** object can be performed. What is the correct number of methods that the **Person** class should have?

It should include all the essential methods and an appropriate set of convenience methods.

8. A class typically has both instance variables and methods. Consider the two extreme cases: a class **A** that has several instance variables but no methods and a class **B** that has several methods but no instance variables. Which one of the principles discussed in this chapter is most likely violated by such classes?

The Expert pattern.

9. When you are trying to reach an executive in a company, you have at least three choices:

   A. Call and be put on hold until the executive is free.

   B. Keep calling back every few minutes until the executive is free.

   C. Leave a message asking the executive to call you back when she is free.

   Which one of these choices corresponds most closely to the Observer pattern?

   C. The executive is the subject/publisher, and you are the observer/subscriber.

10. What is one flaw in the following class that makes it inelegant?

```
class NamedObject {
  private String name;
  NamedObject(String n) { name = n; }
  void setName(String n) { name = n; }
}
```

There is no **getName( )** method, and so there is no way to find out what the name is. Therefore the name is worthless. The problem is that the class has an incomplete interface.

CHAPTER 17: ANSWERS TO SELECTED EXERCISES

1. Most AWT components translate into native peers. Why is this a problem, and how does Swing fix it?

   Native peers are problematic because their use may cause a component to look or act differently on different platforms. Because they use native resources, the appearance of a native peer is not easily changed. They also have limitations, such as being opaque. Swing addresses these issues by using lightweight components and a pluggable look and feel.

2. Most Swing components are written in 100 percent Java code. True or False?

   True.

3. What are the four top-level, heavyweight containers?

   JFrame, **JApplet**, **JDialog**, and **JWindow**

4. What is the most commonly used top-level container for an application?

   JFrame

5. **JFrame** contains several panes. To what pane are components added?

   Components are added to the content pane.

6. An event listener must _____ with a source in order to receive event notifications.

   register

7. To receive an action event, a class must implement what interface?

   ActionListener

8. When using a **JButton** or a **JTextField**, what method must be called to set the action command?

   setActionCommand( )

9. Name three layout managers.

Here are a few of the layout managers: **FlowLayout**, **BorderLayout**, **GridLayout**, **GridBagLayout**, **BoxLayout**, and **SpringLayout**.

10. The stopwatch example in Try This 17-1 uses two buttons, one to start the stopwatch and the other to stop it. However, it is possible to use only one button, which alternates between starting and stopping the stopwatch. One way to do this is to reset the text within the button after each press, alternating between Start and Stop. Because, by default, this text is also the action command associated with the button, you can use the same button for two different purposes. Your job is to rewrite Try This 17-1 so that it implements this approach.

```java
// A version of the stopwatch for Try This 17-1 that
// uses a single push button.

import java.awt.*;
import java.awt.event.*;
import javax.swing.*;
import java.util.*;

class StopWatch implements ActionListener {

  JLabel jlab;
  long start; // holds the start time in milliseconds
  JButton jbtnStartStop; // a start or stop button

  StopWatch() {

    // Create a new JFrame container.
    JFrame jfrm = new JFrame("A Simple Stopwatch");

    // Specify FlowLayout for the layout manager.
    jfrm.setLayout(new FlowLayout());

    // Give the frame an initial size.
    jfrm.setSize(250, 90);

    // Terminate the program when the user closes the application.
    jfrm.setDefaultCloseOperation(JFrame.EXIT_ON_CLOSE);

    // Make one button.
    jbtnStartStop = new JButton("Start");

    // Add action listeners.
    jbtnStartStop.addActionListener(this);

    // Add the buttons to the content pane.
    jfrm.add(jbtnStartStop);
```

```
      // Create a text-based label.
      jlab = new JLabel("Press Start to begin timing.");

      // Add the label to the frame.
      jfrm.add(jlab);

      // Display the frame.
      jfrm.setVisible(true);
    }

  // Handle button events.
  public void actionPerformed(ActionEvent ae) {
    // get the current system time
    Calendar cal = Calendar.getInstance();

    if(ae.getActionCommand().equals("Start")) {
      // Store start time.
      start = cal.getTimeInMillis();
      jlab.setText("Stopwatch is Running...");
      jbtnStartStop.setText("Stop");
    }
    else {
      // Compute the elapsed time.
      jlab.setText("Elapsed time is "
          + (double) (cal.getTimeInMillis() - start)/1000);
      jbtnStartStop.setText("Start");
    }
  }

  public static void main(String[] args) {

    // Create the frame on the event dispatching thread.
    SwingUtilities.invokeLater(new Runnable() {
      public void run() {
        new StopWatch();
      }
    });
  }
}
```

CHAPTER 18: ANSWERS TO SELECTED EXERCISES

1. Does **JLabel** generate an **ActionEvent**?

   No.

2. What event is generated when a push button is pressed?

   ActionEvent

3. Can **JButton** include an icon?

   Yes.

4. What control toggles between two states: selected and cleared?

   JToggleButton and its subclasses.

5. When using **JTextField**, cut and paste is supported by what methods?

   cut( ) and **paste( )**

6. Show how to create a text field that has 32 columns.

   ```
   new JTextField(32)
   ```

7. Can a **JTextField** have its action command set? If so, how?

   Yes, by calling **setActionCommand( )**.

8. What Swing component creates a check box? What event is generated when a check box is selected or deselected?

   JCheckBox creates a check box. An **ItemEvent** is generated when a check box is selected or deselected.

9. **JRadioButton** creates a list of buttons shaped like radios. True or False?

   False.

10. **JList** displays a list of items from which the user can select. True or False?

    True.

11. What event is generated when the user selects or deselects an item in a **JList**?

    ListSelectionEvent

12. What does **JScrollPane** do?

    It scrolls the contents of another component.

13. What method sets the selection mode of a **JList**? What method obtains the index of the first selected item?

    setSelectionMode( ) sets the selection mode. **getSelectedIndex( )** obtains the index of the first selected item.

14. To display information in a tabular format, you can use _____.

    JTable

15. To display information in a tree format, you can use _____.

    JTree

16. What is **JComboBox**?

    JComboBox is a combination of a text field and a drop-down list.

CHAPTER 19: ANSWERS TO SELECTED EXERCISES

1. What are the core Swing menu classes?

The core Swing menu classes are **JMenu**, **JMenuItem**, and **JMenuBar**.

2. What class creates a menu? To create a main menu bar, what class is used?

JMenu creates a menu. **JMenuBar** creates a menu bar.

3. What event is generated when a menu item is selected?

An action event is generated when a menu item is selected.

4. Images are not allowed in menus. True or False?

False; images are allowed in menus.

5. What method adds a menu bar to a window?

To add a menu bar to a window, call **setJMenuBar( )**.

6. What method adds a mnemonic to a menu item?

The **setMnemonic( )** method adds a mnemonic to a menu item.

7. Can an icon be used as a menu item? If so, does it prevent the use of a name?

Yes, an icon can be used as a menu item. No, it does not prevent the use of a name.

8. What class creates a radio button menu item?

JRadioButtonMenuItem creates a radio button menu item.

9. Although check box menu items are permitted, their use is discouraged because they make a menu look strange. True or False?

False, check box menu items are popular, standard menu options.

10. In the course of this chapter, several changes were suggested to the **MenuDemo** program that demonstrate additional menu features. Except for the dynamic menu items in Try This 19-1, integrate those changes into the original **MenuDemo** program. In the process, reorganize the program for clarity by using separate methods to construct the various menus.

```java
// Menu demo program, final version.

import java.awt.*;
import java.awt.event.*;
import javax.swing.*;

class MenuDemo implements ActionListener {

  JLabel jlab;
  JMenuBar jmb;

  MenuDemo() {
    // Create a new JFrame container.
    JFrame jfrm = new JFrame("Menu Demo");
```

```java
    // Specify FlowLayout for the layout manager.
    jfrm.setLayout(new FlowLayout());

    // Give the frame an initial size.
    jfrm.setSize(220, 200);

    // Terminate the program when the user closes the application.
    jfrm.setDefaultCloseOperation(JFrame.EXIT_ON_CLOSE);

    // Create a label that will display the menu selection.
    jlab = new JLabel();

    // Create the menu bar.
    jmb = new JMenuBar();

    // Create the File menu.
    makeFileMenu();

    // Create the Options menu.
    makeOptionsMenu();

    // Create the Help menu.
    makeHelpMenu();

    // Add the label to the content pane.
    jfrm.add(jlab);

    // Add the menu bar to the frame.
    jfrm.setJMenuBar(jmb);

    // Display the frame.
    jfrm.setVisible(true);
  }

  // Create the File menu with mnemonics and accelerators.
  void makeFileMenu() {

    JMenu jmFile = new JMenu("File");
    jmFile.setMnemonic(KeyEvent.VK_F);

    JMenuItem jmiOpen = new JMenuItem("Open",
                              KeyEvent.VK_O);
    jmiOpen.setAccelerator(
          KeyStroke.getKeyStroke(KeyEvent.VK_O,
                            InputEvent.CTRL_DOWN_MASK));

    JMenuItem jmiClose = new JMenuItem("Close",
                              KeyEvent.VK_C);
    jmiClose.setAccelerator(
          KeyStroke.getKeyStroke(KeyEvent.VK_C,
                            InputEvent.CTRL_DOWN_MASK));
```

```
      JMenuItem jmiSave = new JMenuItem("Save",
                                KeyEvent.VK_S);
      jmiSave.setAccelerator(
            KeyStroke.getKeyStroke(KeyEvent.VK_S,
                              InputEvent.CTRL_DOWN_MASK));

      JMenuItem jmiExit = new JMenuItem("Exit",
                                KeyEvent.VK_E);
      jmiExit.setAccelerator(
            KeyStroke.getKeyStroke(KeyEvent.VK_E,
                              InputEvent.CTRL_DOWN_MASK));

      jmFile.add(jmiOpen);
      jmFile.add(jmiClose);
      jmFile.add(jmiSave);
      jmFile.addSeparator();
      jmFile.add(jmiExit);
      jmb.add(jmFile);

      jmiOpen.addActionListener(this);
      jmiClose.addActionListener(this);
      jmiSave.addActionListener(this);
      jmiExit.addActionListener(this);

   }

   // Create the Options menu.
   void makeOptionsMenu() {

      // Create the Options menu.
      JMenu jmOptions = new JMenu("Options");

      // Create the Colors submenu.
      JMenu jmColors = new JMenu("Colors");

      // Use check boxes for colors. This allows
      // the user to select more than one color.
      // Notice that Red is initially selected.
      JCheckBoxMenuItem jmiRed = new JCheckBoxMenuItem("Red", true);
      JCheckBoxMenuItem jmiGreen = new JCheckBoxMenuItem("Green");
      JCheckBoxMenuItem jmiBlue = new JCheckBoxMenuItem("Blue");

      jmColors.add(jmiRed);
      jmColors.add(jmiGreen);
      jmColors.add(jmiBlue);
      jmOptions.add(jmColors);

      // Create the Priority submenu.
      JMenu jmPriority = new JMenu("Priority");

      // Use radio buttons for the priority setting.
      // This lets the menu show which priority is used
```

```
      // but also ensures that one and only one priority
      // can be selected at any one time. Notice that
      // the High radio button is initially selected.
      JRadioButtonMenuItem jmiHigh =
        new JRadioButtonMenuItem("High", true);
      JRadioButtonMenuItem jmiLow =
        new JRadioButtonMenuItem("Low");

      jmPriority.add(jmiHigh);
      jmPriority.add(jmiLow);
      jmOptions.add(jmPriority);

      // Create button group for the radio button menu items.
      ButtonGroup bg = new ButtonGroup();
      bg.add(jmiHigh);
      bg.add(jmiLow);

      // Create the Reset menu item.
      JMenuItem jmiReset = new JMenuItem("Reset");
      jmOptions.addSeparator();
      jmOptions.add(jmiReset);

      jmiRed.addActionListener(this);
      jmiGreen.addActionListener(this);
      jmiBlue.addActionListener(this);
      jmiHigh.addActionListener(this);
      jmiLow.addActionListener(this);
      jmiReset.addActionListener(this);

      // Finally, add the entire Options menu to
      // the menu bar
      jmb.add(jmOptions);
    }

  // Create the Help menu.
  void makeHelpMenu() {

      // Create the Help menu.
      JMenu jmHelp = new JMenu("Help");
      ImageIcon iconAbout = new ImageIcon("AboutIcon.gif");
      JMenuItem jmiAbout = new JMenuItem("About", iconAbout);
      jmiAbout.setToolTipText("Info about the MenuDemo program.");
      jmHelp.add(jmiAbout);
      jmb.add(jmHelp);

      jmiAbout.addActionListener(this);
    }

  // Handle menu item action events.
  public void actionPerformed(ActionEvent ae) {
```

```
        // Get the action command from the menu selection.
        String comStr = ae.getActionCommand();

        // If user chooses Exit, then exit the program.
        if(comStr.equals("Exit")) System.exit(0);

        // Otherwise, display the selection.
        jlab.setText(comStr + " Selected");
    }

    public static void main(String[] args) {
        // Create the GUI on the event dispatching thread.
        SwingUtilities.invokeLater(new Runnable() {
            public void run() {
                new MenuDemo();
            }
        });
    }
}
```

CHAPTER 20: ANSWERS TO SELECTED EXERCISES

1. A dialog is a composite of two or more components that prompts the user and waits for a response. True or False?

    True.

2. What **JOptionPane** method creates an input dialog? Which one creates a message dialog?

    The **showInputDialog( )** method creates an input dialog. The **showMessageDialog( )** method creates a message dialog.

3. What **JOptionPane** method would you normally use to create a dialog that confirms that the user wants to save changes to a document? Show what the call would look like.

    The method is **showConfirmDialog( )**. Here is an example of how to call it:

    ```
    showConfirmDialog(null, "Save Changes?");
    ```

4. When using a confirmation dialog, what return type indicates that the user clicked the Yes button?

    The return type **YES_OPTION** indicates that the user clicked the Yes button.

5. What option type is used to show only the Yes and No buttons in a confirmation dialog?

    YES_NO_OPTION

6. If you want to request a string response from the user, what **JOptionPane** method do you call?

   To request a string response from the user, call the **showInputDialog( )** method.

7. Must the message parameter to any of **JOptionPane**'s **show** methods be a string? Explain.

   No. The message parameter to any of **JOptionPane**'s show methods can be, but does not have to be, a string.

8. **JDialog** is a top-level container. True or False?

   True.

9. What are the four steps needed to create and display a **JDialog**-based dialog?

   Here are the four steps needed to create and display a **JDialog**-based dialog.

   A. Create a **JDialog** object.
   B. Specify the dialog's layout manager, size, and default close policy.
   C. Add components to the dialog's content pane.
   D. Show the dialog by calling **setVisible(true)** on it.

10. Can **JDialog** create a modeless dialog?

    Yes.

11. Explain the difference between **setVisible(false)** and **dispose( )** as it relates to dialogs.

    setVisible(false) removes a dialog from the screen. **dispose( )** removes the dialog and also frees its resources.

12. What **JFileChooser** method creates a Save file chooser? Which one creates a file chooser that uses your own title?

    The **showSaveDialog( )** method creates a Save file chooser. The **showDialog( )** method lets you specify your own title.

13. What two methods must be overridden when implementing a **FileFilter** for **JFileChooser**?

    The **accept( )** and **getDescription( )** methods must be overridden when implementing a **FileFilter** for **JFileChooser**.

14. Chapter 19 described menus. In that chapter, the examples included a File menu that had an Exit entry. Change that code so that it has the user confirm that terminating the program is actually desired.

    Here is the code that uses a dialog to confirm that the user actually wants to exit the program:

```
// If user chooses Exit, then exit the program.
if(comStr.equals("Exit")) {
  int response = JOptionPane.showConfirmDialog(
                            null,
                            "Exit Now?",
                            "Terminate Program",
                            JOptionPane.YES_NO_OPTION);
```

```
        if(response == JOptionPane.YES_OPTION) {
            System.exit(0);
        }
    }
}
```

CHAPTER 21: ANSWERS TO SELECTED EXERCISES

1. Any code that affects a Swing component must be executed on the _____ _____ thread.

event-dispatching

2. When using **javax.swing.Timer**, what event is generated when the timer goes off?

An **ActionEvent** is fired when a **javax.swing.Timer** goes off.

3. What methods start and stop **javax.swing.Timer**?

The methods that start and stop **javax.swing.Timer** are **start( )** and **stop( )**.

4. What is **SwingWorker**?

SwingWorker creates and manages background threads.

5. What method must an applet use to create its GUI?

An applet must use **invokeAndWait( )** to create its GUI.

6. Can your program paint directly onto the surface of a component?

Yes, your program can paint directly onto the surface of a component.

7. What three paint methods are called when a Swing component must display itself?

The following three paint methods are called when a Swing component must display itself: **paintComponent( )**, **paintBorder( )**, and **paintChildren( )**.

8. What methods obtain the current width and height of a component?

To obtain the current width and height of a component, call **getWidth( )** and **getHeight( )**.

9. Rework the applet in Try This 21-1 so that the direction of scroll reverses at periodic intervals. For example, have the text scroll left for a while, and then right for a while, and so on. The precise timing is up to you, but the answer shown here reverses scroll direction every 20 seconds.

```
// Answer to question 9.

import javax.swing.*;
import java.awt.*;
import java.awt.event.*;

/*
This HTML can be used to launch the applet:
```

```java
<object code="ScrollText" width=240 height=100>
</object>
*/

public class ScrollText extends JApplet {

  JLabel jlab;

  String msg = " Swing makes the GUI move! ";

  ActionListener scroller;

  Timer stTimer; // This timer controls the scroll rate.
  int counter; // use to reverse the scroll.

  // This value controls when the scroll direction changes.
  int scrollLimit;

  // Initialize the applet.
  public void init() {
    counter = 0;
    scrollLimit = 100;

    try {
      SwingUtilities.invokeAndWait(new Runnable () {
        public void run() {
          guiInit();
        }
      });
    } catch(Exception exc) {
      System.out.println("Can't create because of " + exc);
    }
  }

  // Start the timer when the applet is started.
  public void start() {
    stTimer.start();
  }

  // Stop the timer when the applet is stopped.
  public void stop() {
    stTimer.stop();
  }

  // Stop the timer when the applet is destroyed.
  public void destroy() {
    stTimer.stop();
  }
```

```java
// Initialize the timer GUI.
private void guiInit() {

  // Create the label that will scroll the message.
  jlab = new JLabel(msg);
  jlab.setHorizontalAlignment(SwingConstants.CENTER);

  // Create the action listener for the timer.
  // This version reverse the direction of scroll
  // every 20 seconds.
  scroller = new ActionListener() {
    public void actionPerformed(ActionEvent ae) {
      if(counter < scrollLimit) {
        // Left-scroll the message one character.
        char ch = msg.charAt(0);
        msg = msg.substring(1, msg.length());
        msg += ch;
      } else {
        // Right-scroll the message one character.
        char ch = msg.charAt(msg.length()-1);
        msg = msg.substring(0, msg.length()-1);
        msg = ch + msg;
        if(counter == scrollLimit*2) counter = 0;
      }
      counter++;
      jlab.setText(msg);
    }
  };

  // Create the timer.
  stTimer = new Timer(200, scroller);

  // Add the label to the applet content pane.
  getContentPane().add(jlab);
}
}
```

CHAPTER 22 ANSWERS TO SELECTED EXERCISES

1. Write a statement that displays the substring of a string **s** consisting of all but the last character of **s**.

```java
System.out.println(s.substring(0, s.length( )-1));
```

2. Assume **s** is a string and consider the following statement:

```java
boolean b = s.isEmpty();
```

Find an equivalent statement or set of statements using **length( )** instead of **isEmpty( )**.

```java
boolean b = (s.length() == 0);
```

3. What happens if you call **charAt( )** and the value you pass in for the index is out of range?

   An **IndexOutOfBoundsException** is thrown.

4. Suppose you want to create one string that consists of two lines of text, each on a separate line. You cannot use a statement such as

   ```
   String s = "This is the first line.
                This is the second line";
   ```

   because this statement will generate a compiler error. How can you do it?

   ```
   String s = "This is the first line.\nThis is the second line";
   ```

5. What is the value of the expression 2+2+"ME"? Is it "22ME" or "4ME"?

   "4ME"

6. Suppose you want to test whether a string variable **s** contains the string "abcdef". Is it sufficient to call **s.startsWith("abc")** and **s.endsWith("def")** and then see whether both method calls return true?

   No. Strings other than "abcdef" can start with "abc" and end with "def". For example, the string "abczdef" has those properties.

7. In the **UseTrim** example in the chapter that demonstrated how to use the **trim( )** method, the **if-else-if** ladder repeatedly tested the equality of two strings using the **equals( )** method. Why didn't the ladder repeatedly test the equality using ==?

   The **==** operator tests object identity, whereas **equals( )** tests whether the contents of the strings are identical. In the **UseTrim** example, we wanted to know whether the string **str** contained the same sequence of characters as another string, not whether **str** was the same object as another string.

8. Explain the difference between **startsWith(substring, index)** and **indexOf(substring, index)**.

   Both methods test whether a string is a substring of another string. However, the **startsWith( )** method only tests whether the substring starts at the given index and returns **true** or **false**. The **indexOf( )** method tests whether the substring starts at or after the given index. It returns the index where the substring starts, or -1 if the substring does not appear in the string.

CHAPTER 23 ANSWERS TO SELECTED EXERCISES

1. The classes that are used to encapsulate primitive values so that they can be used where only objects are allowed are called _____ classes.

   type wrapper

2. Infinity is not a number. More precisely, for a **double d**, if **isInfinite(d)** is **true**, then **isNaN(d)** is **true**. True or False?

   False.

3. The **Double.MIN_VALUE** is the smallest positive **double** value, and **Integer.MIN_VALUE** is the smallest positive integer value (namely, 1). True or False?

The statement is true regarding the **Double.MIN_VALUE** but not regarding the **Integer.MIN_VALUE**. **Integer.MIN_VALUE** is the negative integer value with largest absolute value.

4. Determine the values of the following expressions. The constants are all defined in the **Double** class:

A. MAX_VALUE / MIN_VALUE

B. MAX_VALUE * MAX_VALUE

C. POSITIVE_INFINITY / POSITIVE_INFINITY

D. POSITIVE_INFINITY / NEGATIVE_INFINITY

E. POSITIVE_INFINITY – POSITIVE_INFINITY

F. POSITIVE_INFINITY – NEGATIVE_INFINITY

G. NaN – NaN

A. Infinity

B. Infinity

C. NaN

D. NaN

E. NaN

F. Infinity

G. NaN

5. For every character **ch**, the expression

```
Character.isUpperCase(Character.toUpperCase(ch))
```

evaluates to **true**. True or False?

False. The expression is **true** only if **ch** is a letter.

6. For every **double d**, the expression **Math.ceil(Math.floor(d))** is equal to the expression **Math.floor(Math.ceil(d))**. True or False?

False. For most values of **d**, they are not equal. For example, for **d** = 1.5, the first expression has value 2.0, and the second expression has value 1.0.

7. To start another program (another heavyweight process) in a Java program, you call the constructor for the **Process** class. True or False?

False. You create a **ProcessBuilder** and call its **start( )** method, which returns a **Process**.

8. The **nanoTime( )** method in the **System** class returns the number of nanoseconds since midnight, January 1, 1970. True or False.

False. It returns the number of nanoseconds since some unspecified starting point.

9. The **getName( )** method in **Class** returns just the name of the class without the package it is in. True or False.

False. It returns the full name, which includes the package prefix.

CHAPTER 24: ANSWERS TO SELECTED EXERCISES

1. What are the main differences between the **javax.swing.Timer** class discussed in Chapter 21 and the **java.util.Timer** class?

   They both provide the same basic functionality of causing code to execute at regular intervals. The **javax.swing.Timer** class fires off **ActionEvent**s at a regular interval, and the listeners that receive the events execute in the event-dispatching thread, making this timer useful in Swing applications. The **java.util.Timer** class is more general in that it executes an arbitrary **TimerTask** at regular intervals.

2. What is the difference between the value returned by a call to **System.currentTimeMillis( )** mentioned in the last chapter and the value returned by a call to **Calendar.getInstance( ).getTimeInMillis( )** used in earlier chapters?

   There is no difference. They both return the number of milliseconds that have elapsed since midnight, January 1, 1970.

3. When a **Formatter** sees a '%' character in the format string, how does it know whether that character is part of a format specifier or just a regular character that should be inserted in the output string?

   A '%' character is always part of a format specifier in a format string. To insert the '%' character in the output string, use the format specifier "%%".

4. Assume you have a **GregorianCalendar** object **cal** and you want to display, using **System.out.printf( )**, the date it represents in the form *year:month:day: hour:minute:second* using the long form of the year, month, and day, and using the 24-hour format. For example, if **cal** represents noon on March 11, 1984, then the output should be "1984:March:11:12:00:00". What should the arguments be for the call to **printf( )**? Use relative indices where possible.

   ```
   "%tY:%<tB:%<te:%<tT", cal
   ```

5. Assume that **x** is a **long** variable and it is to be displayed using **System.out.printf( )** with a minimum field width of 20, a leading '+' if it is positive, commas after each three digits from the right, and left justified. What should the arguments be for the call to **printf( )**?

   ```
   "%+,-20d", x
   ```

6. Assume you have a **double** variable **x** and you use a **Formatter** to create a string containing the value of **x** and then you use a **Scanner** to get back the value of **x** from the string. Are you guaranteed to end up with the same value for **x** as you started with? Why or why not?

   No, the value of **x** you end up with may be different. For example, if initially **x** = 1.2345 and if you tell the **Formatter** to format **x** with only two decimal places of precision, then you will end up with **x** = 1.23.

7. What is the output of the following instruction?

   ```
   System.out.printf("%%%(-11.2E%%", -1.23456789);
   ```

   ```
   %(1.23E+00) %
   ```

8. What happens if you create a **GregorianCalendar** object that represents an illegal date such as January 32, 1970? More precisely, what happens if you execute the following code segment:

```
GregorianCalendar cal = new GregorianCalendar(1970, 0, 32);
```

and then you output the month, day, and year stored in **cal** using calls to **getDisplayName( )**?

It converts the date to February 1, 1970 and outputs that date.

CHAPTER 25: ANSWERS TO SELECTED EXERCISES

1. What is the purpose of the following collection classes: **AbstractCollection**, **AbstractList**, **AbstractQueue**, **AbstractSequentialList**, **AbstractSet**? That is, why are these classes included in the Collections Framework?

They provide partial implementations that are used as starting points for creating concrete implementations of various collection classes. In fact, they can also be used for creating your own collection classes.

2. Both the **poll( )** and **remove( )** methods in the **Queue** interface remove and return the element at the head of the queue. What is the difference between them?

The first returns **null** if the **Queue** is empty, whereas the second throws a **NoSuchElementException** if the **Queue** is empty.

3. A **Collection** represents an arbitrary group of data. In contrast, a **Set** represents a group of data in which _____.

every element is distinct (that is, you cannot include the same element twice)

4. What happens if you use the **add( )** method to try to add an element to a **Set** that is already in the **Set**?

The **add( )** method will not add the element and will return **false**.

5. If **m** is a **Map**, then **m.keySet( ).size( ) = m.values( ).size( )**. True or False?

True.

6. Suppose you have three collections of strings **c1**, **c2**, **c3**, and you want to find out which, if any, strings appear in all three collections. Write a code segment that creates a collection **c4** that contains only those strings that appear in all three collections. It should not modify any of the three original collections.

```
Collection c4 = new ArrayList(c1);
c4.retainAll(c2);
c4.retainAll(c3);
```

7. Suppose you have three collections of strings **c1**, **c2**, **c3**, and you want to find out which, if any, strings appear in **c1**, but do not appear in either **c2** or **c3**.

Create a code segment that creates a collection **c4** that contains only the desired strings. It should not modify any of the three original collections.

```
Collection<String> c4 = new ArrayList<String>(c1);
c4.removeAll(c2);
c4.removeAll(c3);
```

8. What will be displayed by the following code segment? Explain.

```
Collection<Object> c = new ArrayList<Object>();
c.add(new Object());
c.add(new Object());
System.out.println(c.contains(new Object()));
```

The code will display "false". The **ArrayList** will contain two objects, but neither of them is the object being tested for containment.

CHAPTER 26: ANSWERS TO SELECTED EXERCISE

1. **Sockets** are designed to send and receive data using the protocol HTTP. True or False?

   False. They send and receive data using the TCP protocol.

2. **URLConnection**s are designed to send and receive data using the protocol HTTP. True or False?

   False. They can also be used with other protocols such as FTP to communicate with another computer on the web.

3. What two pieces of information does a **Socket** need to have in order to connect to another computer on the network?

   A host name and a port number.

4. When you enter a URL using HTTP in your web browser, why aren't you required to enter a port number?

   There is a default port number (80) that is used when you don't specify one.

5. How does sending data using datagrams differ, with respect to guarantees of arrival, from sending data using a method that uses the protocol TCP?

   Datagrams are not guaranteed to arrive at their destination at all. If they do arrive, there is no guarantee they are undamaged or in any special order. Data packets sent using TCP are expected to arrive undamaged and in order.

CHAPTER 27: ANSWERS TO SELECTED EXERCISES

1. How does a semaphore work?

   It issues permits to threads to access a shared resource. A thread calls **acquire( )** when it wants a permit and calls **release( )** when it is finished with the permit.

2. In the **SemDemo** example in this chapter, what happens if you add a call to **sem.release( )** immediately before both of the calls to **sem.acquire( )**? Explain.

The program still runs but there is no longer controlled access to the shared resource.

3. In the **SemDemo** example in this chapter, what happens if you replace each of the two calls **sem.acquire( )** with **sem.acquire(2)**? Explain.

Both threads will be trying to acquire two permits, but **sem** has only one permit, so they will both wait forever.

4. Consider a horse race where the horses and riders need to line up at the gate and wait there until all the horses and riders are ready before the gate opens and the horses can start racing. What Java synchronization tool does this situation remind you of?

A **CyclicBarrier**.

5. Suppose you add the statement **System.out.println(name);** as the last statement of the **run( )** method of the **MyThread** class in the **BarDemo** program. In that case, "Barrier reached" would be displayed before the names "A", "B", and "C" are displayed a second time. True or False? Explain.

True. The **BarAction** thread runs before any of the other threads are allowed to resume.

6. Using an **Exchanger**, it is possible that a **String** can be exchanged for an **Integer**. True or False?

True. In this case, the **Exchanger**'s type parameter would have to be **Object**, and, after the exchange, the results exchanged would likely need to be cast to the correct type.

7. If a thread attempts to get the value of a **Future** object before its value has been computed, then an exception is thrown. True or False?

False. The thread requesting the **Future**'s value waits until the value is available.

8. A **Callable** object is like a **Runnable** object except that it represents a thread that _____.

returns a value

9. A **ForkJoinPool** uses an approach called "work-stealing" to execute waiting tasks. What does "work-stealing" mean?

Each thread maintains a queue of waiting tasks. If one thread empties its queue, it steals one or more tasks from another queue.

10. A very appropriate strategy to use with the Fork/Join Framework is "divide and conquer." How does that strategy work?

A task is recursively broken into two or more subtasks until each subtask is small enough to be executed sequentially by one thread.

INDEX

SYMBOLS

& (ampersand)
  bitwise AND operator, 189, 190, 191
  logical AND operator, 60, 68
&& (short-circuit AND) operator, 60, 62, 68
&= (logical AND with assignment) operator, 65
< > (angle brackets)
  << (bitwise left shift) operator, 194
  >> (bitwise right shift) operator, 194
  >>> (bitwise unsigned right shift) operator, 194
  > (greater than) operator, 29, 60, 61, 68
  >= (greater than or equal to) operator, 29, 60, 61, 68
  < (less than) operator, 29, 60, 61, 68
  <= (less than or equal to) operator, 29, 60, 61, 68
  diamond operator, 539
  type parameters within, 508
* (asterisk)
  *= (multiplication and assignment) operator, 65
  multiplication operator, 24, 58, 68
@ (at sign), in annotation names, 497
\ (backslash), in escape sequences, 52
^ (caret)
  bitwise XOR operator, 189, 190, 192

logical XOR operator, 60, 68
^= (XOR with assignment) operator, 65, 196
, (comma), in comma-separated lists, 30
{ } (curly braces)
  enclosing class definitions, 20
  enclosing code blocks, 32, 33
enclosing method body, 21
= (equal sign)
  == (equal to) operator, 29, 60, 61, 184, 827
  assignment operator, 64, 68
! (exclamation mark)
  ! (logical NOT) operator, 60, 68
  != (not equal to) operator, 29, 60, 61, 68
/ (forward slash)
  /* */ enclosing multiline comments, 20
  /** */ enclosing documentation comments, 1059
  // in single-line comments, 20
  /= (division and assignment) operator, 65
  division operator, 24, 58, 68
– (minus sign)
  – – (decrement) operator, 32, 58, 59, 68
  –= (subtraction and assignment) operator, 65
  subtraction operator, 24, 58, 68
  unary minus, 68
( ) (parentheses)

in expressions, 72
following method names, 126
. (period)
  separating package names, 329
. . . (three periods), specifying varargs, 245
| (pipe symbol)
  bitwise OR operator, 189, 190, 191
  logical OR operator, 60, 68
  |= (logical OR with assignment) operator, 65
  || (short-circuit OR) operator, 60, 62, 68
% (percent sign)
  %= (modulus and assignment) operator, 65
  %n and %% specifiers, 897
  modulus operator, 58, 68
+ (plus sign)
  += (addition and assignment) operator, 65
  ++ (increment) operator, 58, 59
  addition operator, 24, 58
  string concatenation operator, 184, 816
  unary plus, 68
? (question mark)
  wildcard argument, 517
  ?: (ternary) operator, 68, 200
  " (quotation marks, double), escaping, 52
  ' (quotation marks, single), escaping, 52